Wolves

To Martha.

[signature]

May 16/2012.

ISABEL
LEVESQUE

Ecology and Conservation of

Wolves

in a Changing World

Ludwig N. Carbyn
Canadian Wildlife Service
and
Canadian Circumpolar Institute
University of Alberta
Edmonton, Alberta, Canada
and
Department of Renewable Resources
University of Alberta

Steven H. Fritts
U.S. Fish and Wildlife Service
Helena, Montana, USA

Dale R. Seip
British Columbia Forest Service
Prince George, B.C., Canada

Editors

Published by:
Canadian Circumpolar Institute
University of Alberta
Edmonton, Alberta, Canada

This monograph is a compilation of selected papers presented at the Second North American Symposium on Wolves, held in Edmonton in August 1992.

Cite as: Carbyn, L.N., S.H. Fritts and D.R. Seip, 1995. Ecology and Conservation of Wolves in a Changing World. Canadian Circumpolar Institute, Occasional Publication No. 35, 642 pp.

Canadian Cataloguing in Publication Data

Main entry under title:

Ecology and conservation of wolves in a changing world

(Occasional publication series, ISSN 0068-0303; 35)
Includes bibliographical references and index.
"Proceedings of the Second North American Symposium on Wolves held in Edmonton, Alberta, Canada, 25-27 August 1992"

ISBN 0-919058-92-2 (bound) 0-919058-93-0 (softcover)

1. Wolves — Congresses. I. Carbyn, Ludwig N. II. Fritts, Steven H. III. Seip, Dale R. IV. North American Symposium on Wolves (2nd: 1992: Edmonton, Alberta) V. Canadian Circumpolar Institute. VI. Series: Occasional publication series (Canadian Circumpolar Institute); no. 35.

QL 737.C22E32 1995 599.74'442 C95-910275-2

Keywords: Wolf - abundance, behavior, computer modelling, conservation, control, dispersal, ecology, historical evidence, genetics, management, movements, pathology, predator-prey dynamics, recovery, reintroduction, reproduction, status, survival, taxonomy, wolf-human relationships

Cover photo: J. Dutcher

Copyright 1995 Canadian Circumpolar Institute
Cover design by Art Design Printing Inc.
Printed by Art Design Printing Inc., Edmonton, Alberta, Canada

Proceedings of the Second North American Symposium
on Wolves held in Edmonton, Alberta, Canada
25-27 August 1992

Organizer
Ludwig N. Carbyn

Editorial Committee
Ludwig Carbyn
Steven Fritts
Dale Seip

Planning Committee
Ludwig Carbyn
Dean Cluff
Janice James
Helen Milne
Helgard Proft-Mather

Sponsored by
U.S. Fish and Wildlife Service
The Canadian Wildlife Service
U.S. Forest Service
Canadian Circumpolar Institute
Wolf Haven International
Canadian Nature Federation
Ontario Ministry of Natural Resources
World Wildlife Fund Canada
Alberta Fish and Wildlife Division
Alberta Environmental Protection
Alaska Department of Fish and Game
Wyoming Game and Fish Department
Arizona Game and Fish Department
Québec Ministre du Loisir
Canadian Parks Service
U.S. National Park Service
Grasslands Art Gallery

Table of Contents

Acknowledgements xi

Preface xiii

List of Contributors xvii

Part One: Setting the Stage

Boitani, L.
  *Ecological and cultural diversities in the evolution of
  wolf-human relationships.* 3

Gilbert, F.F.
  *Historical perspectives on wolf management in North America
  with special reference to humane treatments in capture methods.* 13

Part Two: A Review of the Status of Wolves

Hayes, R.D., and J.R. Gunson.
  Status and management of wolves in Canada. 21

Miller, F.L.
  Status of wolves on the Canadian Arctic Islands. 35

Stephenson, R.O., W.B. Ballard, C.A. Smith, and K. Richardson.
  Wolf biology and management in Alaska, 1981-1992 43

Marquard-Petersen, U.
  Status of wolves in Greenland. 55

Thiel, R.P., and R.R. Ream.
  Status of the gray wolf in the lower 48 United States to 1992. 59

Schullery, P., and L. Whittlesey.
  *Summary of the documentary record of wolves and other
  wildlife species in the Yellowstone National Park area prior to 1882* 63

Kay, C.E.
  *An alternative interpretation of the historical evidence relating
  to the abundance of wolves in the Yellowstone ecosystem.* 77

Dekker, D., W. Bradford, and J.R. Gunson.
  *Elk and wolves in Jasper National Park, Alberta, from
  historical times to 1992* 85

Fox, J.L., and R.S. Chundawat.
  Wolves in the transhimalayan region of India: the continued
  survival of a low-density population. 95

Part Three: Recovery Programs

Fritts, S.H., E.E. Bangs, J.A. Fontaine, W.G. Brewster, and J.F. Gore.
  Restoring wolves to the northern Rocky Mountains of the United States. 107

Bangs, E.E., S.H. Fritts, D.R. Harms, J.A. Fontaine, M.D. Jimenez,
  W.G. Brewster, and C.C. Niemeyer.
  Control of endangered gray wolves in Montana. 127

Boyd, D.K., P.C. Paquet, S. Donelon, R.R. Ream, D.H. Pletscher, and C.C. White.
  Transboundary movements of a recolonizing wolf population
  in the Rocky Mountains. 135

Parsons, D.R., and J.E. Nicholopoulos.
  Status of the Mexican wolf recovery program in the United States. 141

Wydeven, A.P., R.N. Schultz, and R.P. Thiel.
  Monitoring of a recovering gray wolf population in
  Wisconsin, 1979-1991. 147

Phillips, M.K., R. Smith, V.G. Henry, and C. Lucash.
  Red wolf reintroduction program. 157

Thiel, R.P., and T. Valen.
  Developing a state timber wolf recovery plan with public input:
  the Wisconsin experience. 169

Part Four: Wolf-Prey Interactions

Seip, D.R.
  Introduction to wolf-prey interactions. 179

Messier, F.
  On the functional and numerical responses of wolves to
  changing prey density. 187

Boyce, M.S.
  Anticipating consequences of wolves in Yellowstone: model validation. 199

Vales, D.J., and J.M. Peek.
  Projecting the potential effects of wolf predation on elk and mule deer
  in the east front portion of the northwest Montana wolf recovery area. 211

Dale, B.W., L.G. Adams, and R.T. Bowyer.
  Winter wolf predation in a multiple ungulate prey system,
  Gates of the Arctic National Park, Alaska. 223

Mech, L.D., T.J. Meier, J.W. Burch, and L.G. Adams.
  Patterns of prey selection by wolves in Denali National Park, Alaska. 231

Adams, L.G., B.W. Dale, and L.D. Mech.
  Wolf predation on caribou calves in Denali National Park, Alaska. 245

Thomas, D.C.
  A review of wolf-caribou relationships and conservation
  implications in Canada. 261

Klein, D.R.
  The introduction, increase, and demise of wolves on
  Coronation Island, Alaska. 275

Part Five: Behavior and Social Interactions

Asa, C.S.
*Physiological and social aspects of reproduction of the wolf
and their implications for contraception.* 283

Asa, C.S., and L.D. Mech.
*A review of the sensory organs in wolves and their
importance to life history.* 287

Meier, T.J., J.W. Burch, L.D. Mech, and L.G. Adams.
*Pack structure and genetic relatedness among wolf packs in a
naturally-regulated population.* 293

Forbes, G.J., and J.B. Theberge.
*Influences of a migratory deer herd on wolf movements and
mortality in and near Algonquin Park, Ontario.* 303

Peterson, R.O.
Wolves as interspecific competitors in canid ecology. 315

Fuller, T.K.
*Comparative population dynamics of North American wolves
and African wild dogs.* 325

Fancy, S.G., and W.B. Ballard.
Monitoring wolf activity by satellite. 329

Vila, C., V. Urios, and J. Castroviejo.
Observations on the daily activity patterns in the Iberian wolf. 335

Anderson, R.E., B.L.C. Hill, J. Ryon, and J.C. Fentress.
*Attitudes and the perception of wolf social interactions:
implications for public information programs.* 341

Part Six: Taxonomy

Brewster, W.G., and S.H. Fritts.
*Taxonomy and genetics of the gray wolf in western
North America: a review.* 353

Nowak, R.M.
Another look at wolf taxonomy. 375

Wayne, R.K., N. Lehman, and T.K. Fuller.
Conservation genetics of the gray wolf. 399

Nowak, R.M., M.K. Phillips, V.G. Henry, W.C. Hunter, and R. Smith.
The origin and fate of the red wolf. 409

Part Seven: Diseases and Physiology

Brand, C.J., M.J. Pybus, W.B. Ballard, and R.O. Peterson.
*Infectious and parasitic diseases of the gray wolf and their
potential effects on wolf populations in North America.* 419

Johnson, M.R.
Rabies in wolves and its potential role in a Yellowstone wolf population. 431

Bailey, T.N., E.E. Bangs, and R.O. Peterson.
*Exposure of wolves to canine parvovirus and distemper on the
Kenai National Wildlife Refuge, Kenai Peninsula, Alaska, 1976-1988.* 441

Drag, M.D.
Serum chemistry values for captive Mexican wolves. 447

Part Eight: Research Techniques

Ballard, W.B., G.M. Matson, and P.R. Krausman.
Comparison of two methods to age gray wolf teeth............................ 455

Ballard, W.B., D.J. Reed, S.G. Fancy, and P.R. Krausman.
Accuracy, precision and performance of satellite telemetry for
monitoring wolf movements. 461

Ballard, W.B., M.E. McNay, C.L. Gardner, and D.J. Reed.
Use of line-intercept track sampling for estimating wolf densities. 469

Haggstrom, D.A., A.K. Ruggles, C.M. Harms, and R.O. Stephenson.
Citizen participation in developing a wolf management plan for Alaska:
an attempt to resolve conflicting human values and perceptions............. 481

Part Nine: Management Techniques

Cluff, H.D., and D.L. Murray.
Review of wolf control methods in North America. 491

Boertje, R.D., David G. Kelleyhouse, and R.D. Hayes.
Methods for reducing natural predation on moose in Alaska
and Yukon: an evaluation... 505

Reid, R., and D. Janz.
Economic evaluation of Vancouver Island wolf control...................... 515

Coppinger, R., and L. Coppinger.
Interactions between livestock guarding dogs and wolves................... 523

Clarkson, P.L.
Recommendations for more effective wolf management..................... 527

Part Ten: Looking Ahead Into the 21st Century

Mech, L.D.
What do we know about wolves and what more do we need to learn? 537

Epilogue

Hummel, M.
A personal view on wolf conservation and threatened carnivores
in North America. 549

Literature Cited 555

Index.. 609

Acknowledgements

For help in running the symposium, we acknowledge, with a deep sense of gratitude, the efforts of the following: Mauraide Baynton, Corey Bradshaw, Dean Cluff, Dick Dekker, Paul Joslin, Leon Levesque, Helen Milne, Axel Moehrenschlager, Dennis Murray, John Nishi, Cathy Shanks, Paul Sir, and Carol Smith. Janice James was charged with the major responsibility of coordination, planning and execution of administrative details. Isabel Levesque and Andrew Raszewski were the official artists and provided sketches for all promotional material. Jim Dutcher freely gave us access to his extensive photo collection.

Editorial assistance was provided by Anne le Rougetel, Elaine Maloney, Cindy Mason, Cathy Shanks, and Elaine Street. Thanks to Elaine Maloney and Maryhelen Vicars who took on the major responsibility of coordinating publication of the book and text formatting; to Elaine Street for her extensive review of the Literature Cited; and to Cindy Reekie for publication marketing efforts.

Special thanks go to Clifford Hickey (Director, Canadian Circumpolar Institute, University of Alberta), Gerald McKeating (Regional Director, Canadian Wildlife Service, Prairie and Northern Region) and Gordon Kerr (former Regional Director, C.W.S.) for encouragement and support for the project from beginning to end.

We are grateful for the assistance of all reviewers. Each paper was reviewed by two or more referees.

Interest in the wolf is high in the public image worldwide. Wolves currently are one of the most common subjects of wildlife art. T-shirts adorned with wolves are commonly seen around the world, as are wolf calendars and various novelties featuring wolf images. The commercial impact of all this public attention is considerable. (Photo: Idaho Department of Fish and Game)

Preface

In 1981, a symposium called *Status and Management of Wolves in North America* was held in Edmonton, Alberta. The symposium was well attended and received wide recognition as a significant event that consolidated information on a controversial species. The published volume (*Wolves in Canada and Alaska: their status, biology and management*, Canadian Wildlife Service Report 45) was a landmark publication on wolves for the 1980's.

The *Second North American Symposium on Wolves* was held in Edmonton from 25-27 August, 1992. Since the first symposium, major efforts had been underway for the reintroduction of gray wolves and red wolves to portions of the United States, where they had been eliminated. Hence, the 1992 meetings extended the scope to the southern half of the continent.

Collected in this book are contributions from a large number of scientists, many of whom have dedicated their careers to the study of one of the world's most enigmatic and controversial carnivores. Without exception, no other species has had the same impact on the collective consciousness of mankind. The wolf simply has no equal.

Why, for example, does an environmental impact statement to return wolves to Yellowstone National Park and central Idaho prompt comments and questions from people in every state and from over 40 countries outside the United States? Why is it that undercover police officers have shadowed field biologists in northern Canada when the killing of 40-60 wolves, out of a Yukon population estimated at 4,000 is being carried out and, why is it that threats of boycotts to the Alaskan tourist trade are made when the proposed killing of fewer than 1% of Alaska's wolves is being planned? In contrast, the widespread killing of coyotes has been accepted with much less opposition. The answers to these questions are varied and complex.

As the 20th century draws to a close, we are reminded that shortly after the turn of this century, man's relationship with wolves in North America had reached its darkest hours. Like a hurricane sweeping across the continent, humanities' energies to kill the last wolf were unleashed. In the United States, the "gale" eliminated the last vestiges of wolf populations in the west. Canada followed suit, and so did Mexico. Five decades later, the late Douglas Pimlott would ask the probing question, "Will the species still exist when the 20th century passes into history? The wolf presents one of the most important conservation questions of our time". At the *First North American Wolf Symposium*, answers were emerging. Society was not to allow wolves to vanish from the face of the continent—the tides of change were real. Ten years later, those trends had become firmly established.

New issues emerged. Cross-currents of different environmental value systems competed in the public arena. The wolf commonly made headlines around the world. One newly emerging paradigm stated that nature is good, and that all human impact on nature is bad. Where there once was "pro-wolf" and "anti-wolf" sentiment, new debates pitted wildlife management against a "hands off" approach to nature. Voices are now being raised that, as we enter the 21st century, push some traditional conservation initiatives into new directions. One such issue is man's potential, if not real, impact on the very nature of manipulated wolf populations. For example, can partial reductions of wolf packs impair the stability and social bonding, and the stabilities of territory boundaries? How is the social organization of a hunting unit affected by the loss of adults? Without extensive experimentation, answers to these questions are hard to obtain.

Central to the wolf debate have been proposals to temporarily reduce the number of wolves in some areas in order to increase game populations. People living north of 60° latitude argue that, for example, in one region of Alaska, temporary wolf control (efforts sustained over several years) can increase moose production by 2,000 animals, thereby considerably increasing the availability of meat for human consumption. By contrast, modern food production requires enormous sources of fossil fuels. Many Alaskans, Yukoners, and to a lesser extent, hunting societies elsewhere, have argued that in managed wildlife systems (an oxymoron to some), the completeness of the system remains intact (i.e., portions are still together, even though man influences the proportions). Wilderness systems that are manipulated provide resources for man, yet remain pristine in their functional constituents. Moose and caribou can be utilized by man without significant consumption of fossil fuel energy, and without the additives, fertilizers, herbicides, pesticides, or growth hormones that characterize food production in conventional agriculturally driven industries.

One emerging conservation ethic in the north emphasizes the connections between reliance on local resources, attitudes toward the environment, and energy conservation. The controversy over predator management brings these issues into sharp focus. The values and concerns of an increasingly urban public often conflict with the needs of local communities seeking to maintain local economies and cultures based on renewable resources including wild game, fish, and plants. Individuals with this viewpoint argue that relying on intact natural systems with a more direct conversion of solar energy into food and material, has advantages over the prevailing system, and fosters a sense of stewardship that has diminished as people become more and more removed from the production and harvesting of basic necessities.

The opposing point of view is that man should not tamper with natural processes in areas north of 60° latitude or elsewhere. It is only human arrogance and shortsighted thinking that drives mankind to kill wolves in order to kill more game, according to this view. The very act of hunting, be it for food or recreation, has come under close scrutiny. At best, it is suggested that natural systems containing wolf populations should be left completely alone. At worst, man should only kill surplus game and leave predators alone.

In the epilogue to this book, Monte Hummel points out a rapidly evolving modern perception of the value of nature, unimpacted by man. Yet, as long as man continues to derive food from domestic and wild animals, his urge to control predators will continue by those who live closest to the resources. People not close to the resources in that sense will likely continue to have a different view. Debate surrounding the wolf reintroduction program in Yellowstone is a case in point. The livestock owners oppose attempts at wolf introductions. Conservation groups promote the program. Not uncommonly, the media benefits most from such disagreements.

An important development during the past decade was the use of public involvement in building consensus and developing wildlife management plans. While early efforts have not always been easy or successful, they show that improved communication and trust between institutions and various public interests, combined with respect for others' values and willingness to compromise, can increase the effectiveness of those with conservation interests.

While the debates described above have transpired, it is heartening to report that the number and distribution of wolves has increased in several areas of the continent over the past decade. Wolves are being reintroduced to parts of their former range, a feat that would have been unthinkable three decades ago. Will restoration programs eventually lead to more controversy from having more wolves in more places, with increased public scrutiny of how they are managed? Time will tell. For now, the species continues to increase in popularity. Approximately 75 organizations exist (a total of at least 120,000 members), for the sole purpose of promoting wolf conservation. Wolves are currently one of the most common subjects in wildlife art. T-shirts adorned with wolves are commonly seen all across the continent, as are wolf calendars and various novelties featuring wolf images. Interest in the species in the USA for the present time is focused on plans to reintroduce wolves to Yellowstone National Park, the world's first national park, where over three million people visit each year. Three agencies of the American federal government joined to conduct an environmental impact statement (EIS) on the reintroduction of wolves into Yellowstone and central Idaho. The EIS process involved over 120 public meetings and generated more public comments (170,000) than any other EIS ever conducted by the United States government. Planning for the recovery of wolves in Yellowstone and the northern Rocky Mountains of the United States has extended over two decades with some $6 million spent leading up to the formal transfer of the species from Canada to its former United States range, a distance of about 1,000 kilometers.

Taxonomy of wolves has become a major issue during the past several years. Debate over the taxonomic standing of the red wolf, the number of gray wolf subspecies, and the use of molecular genetics *versus* more traditional approaches to wolf systematics has ensued. Not all questions of wolf taxonomy can be answered at this time, yet at least one thing is clear: all lines of evidence suggest fewer wolf subspecies should be recognized.

Prominent at this symposium was the fact that much knowledge on a broad range of subjects has been accumulated over the last decade. From the beginnings of observational work on the ground to sophisticated instrumentation, the wolf has been the subject of much research. Uniquely typical of science is to arrive at ever more complete explanations for events in the natural world. For wolf biologists, that meant uncovering secrets about the "way of the wolf", and often we have been forced to admit that discoveries in one area might not apply to another part of the continent. Not uncommonly, we look back, then forge new pathways, only to be reminded with humility that we still know so very little about a subject with enormous complexity. Once in a while, we all come together to evaluate what is known. So, it was fitting that continuity be maintained by reconvening in Edmonton in order to look ahead to what may be in store for wolf conservation in the 21st century.

About 500 people from 12 countries attended the three-day event. A number of themes crossed the sessions. The ones that held most of the energies focused on taxonomy and genetics, wolves and prey in northern systems, and the reintroduction of wolves to the Yellowstone ecosystem. While our intellectual pursuits provided reasons to interact, they also reinforced friendships and comraderie that centered on common goals and the need for information exchange. The event was uniquely successful because it brought so many like-minded people together. Debates on different views were lively and informative. Our task would not have been complete, however, until the results of these deliberations were made available to the community at large; hence our responsibility in coming full circle and producing this document. We hope it will serve as a useful reference to the scientific community and to the interested public.

L.N. Carbyn, S.H. Fritts, D.R. Seip

Contributors

ADAMS, Layne G. United States National Biological Service, 1011 East Tudor Road, Anchorage, Alaska 99503 USA

ANDERSON, Rita E. Department of Psychology, Memorial University of Newfoundland, St. John's, Newfoundland, A1B 3X9 Canada

ASA, Cheryl S. St. Louis Zoological Park, Forest Park, St. Louis, Missouri 63110 USA

BAILEY, Theodore N. Kenai National Wildlife Refuge, P.O. Box 2139, Soldotna, Alaska 99669 USA

BALLARD, Warren B. Cooperative Wildlife Research Unit, Faculty of Forestry, P.O. Box 44555, University of New Brunswick, Fredericton, N.B. E3B 6C2 Canada

BANGS, Edward E. United States Fish and Wildlife Service, 100 N. Park, Suite 320, Helena, Montana 59601 USA

BOERTJE, Rodney D. Alaska Department of Fish and Game, 1300 College Road, Fairbanks, Alaska 99701 USA

BOITANI, Luigi. Department of Animal and Human Biology, University of Rome, "La Sapienza", Viale Universita 32, 00185 Rome, Italy

BOWYER, R. Terry. Institute of Arctic Biology, University of Alaska Fairbanks, Fairbanks, Alaska 99701 USA

BOYCE, Mark S. College of Natural Resources, University of Wisconsin, Stevens Point, Wisconsin 54481 USA

BOYD, Diane K. School of Forestry, University of Montana, Missoula, Montana 59812 USA

BRADFORD, Wesley. Jasper National Park, Warden Office, P.O. Box 10, Jasper, Alberta, T0E 1E0 Canada

BRAND, Christopher J. United States National Biological Survey, National Wildlife Health Center, 6006 Schroeder Road, Madison, Wisconsin 53711-6223 USA

BREWSTER, Wayne G. National Park Service, Yellowstone National Park, Yellowstone Center for Resources, P.O. Box 168, Yellowstone National Park, Wyoming 82190 USA

BURCH, John W. United States National Park Service, Bryce Canyon National Park, Bryce Canyon, Utah 84717 USA

CARBYN, Ludwig N. Canadian Wildlife Service, 4999-98 Avenue, Room 200, Edmonton, Alberta, T6B 2X3 Canada *and* Canadian Circumpolar Institute, University of Alberta, Old St. Stephen's College (8820-112 Street), Edmonton, Alberta, T6E 2E2 Canada

CASTROVIEJO, Javier. Estación Biológica de Donana - CSIC, Apdo. 1056, 41080, Sevilla, Spain.

CHUNDAWAT, Raghunandan S. Wildlife Institute of India, P.O. Box 18, Chandrabani, Dehra Dun -248006 U.P., India

CLARKSON, Peter L. Department of Renewable Resources, Government of the Northwest Territories, Inuvik, N.W.T. X0E 0T0 Canada

CLUFF, H. Dean. Wildlife Management Division, Department of Renewable Resources, Government of the Northwest Territories, Yellowknife, N.W.T. X1A 3S8 Canada

COPPINGER, Lorna. Hampshire College, School of Natural Science, Amherst, Massachussetts 01002 USA

COPPINGER, Raymond. Hampshire College, School of Natural Science, Amherst, Massachusetts 01002 USA

DALE, Bruce W. United States National Park Service, Alaska Region, 2525 Gambell Street, Room 107, Anchorage, Alaska 99503 USA

DEKKER, Dick. 3819 -112 A Street, Edmonton, Alberta, T6J 1K4 Canada

DONELON, Steve. Peter Lougheed Provincial Park, Kananaskis Village, Alberta, T0L 2H0, Canada

DRAG, Marlene D. Animal Science Research Field Operations, Merck Research Laboratories, Merck and Co., Inc., 6498 Jade Road, Fulton, Missouri 65251 USA

FANCY, Steven G. National Biological Service, Pacific Islands Science Centre, P.O. Box 44, Hawaii National Park, Hawaii 96718 USA

FENTRESS, John C. Department of Psychology, Dalhousie University, Halifax, Nova Scotia, B3H 4J1 Canada

FONTAINE, Joseph A. United States Fish and Wildlife Service, 100 N. Park, Suite 320, Helena, Montana 59601 USA

FORBES, Graham J. Cooperative Wildlife Research Unit, University of New Brunswick, Fredericton, New Brunswick, E3B 6C2 Canada

FOX, Joseph L. Department of Ecology/Zoology, IBG, University of Troms, N-9037 Troms, Norway

FRITTS, Steven H. United States Fish and Wildlife Service, 100 N. Park, Suite 320, Helena, Montana 59601 USA

FULLER, Todd K. Department of Forestry and Wildlife Management, University of Massachusetts, Amherst, Massachusetts 01003 USA

GARDNER, Craig L. Alaska Department of Fish and Game, P.O. Box 355, Tok, Alaska 99780 USA

GILBERT, Frank University of Northern British Columbia, 3333 University Way, Prince George, British Columbia, V2N 4Z9 Canada

GORE, James F. United States Forest Service, 324-25th Street, Ogden, Utah 84401 USA

GUNSON, John R. Alberta Fish and Wildlife Division, 6909 - 116 Street, Edmonton, Alberta, T6H 4P2 Canada

HAGGSTROM, Dale A. Department of Fish and Game, 1300 College Road, Fairbanks, Alaska 99701 USA

HARMS, Catherine M. Department of Fish and Game, 1300 College Road, Fairbanks, Alaska 99701 USA

HARMS, Dale R. United States Fish and Wildlife Service, 100 N. Park, Suite 320, Helena, Montana 59601 USA

HAYES, Robert D. Yukon Fish and Wildlife Branch, P.O. Box 2703, Whitehorse, Yukon Territory, Y1A 2C6 Canada

HENRY, V. Gary. United States Fish and Wildlife Service, 330 Ridgefield Court, Asheville, North Carolina 28801 USA

HILL, Bonny L.C. 4043 Mars St., Port Coquitlam, British Columbia, V3B 6B9 Canada

HUMMELL, Monte World Wildlife Canada, 90 Eglinton Ave. E., Suite 504, Toronto, Ontario, M4P 2Z7 Canada

HUNTER, William C. United States Fish and Wildlife Service, Federal Building, 75 Spring Street, Atlanta, Georgia 30303 USA

JANZ, Doug. Regional Operations (Wildlife Branch), British Columbia Ministry of Environment, Lands and Parks, 2569 Kenworth Road, Nanaimo, British Columbia, V9T 4P7 Canada

JIMENEZ, Michael D. School of Forestry, University of Montana, Missoula, Montana 59812 USA

JOHNSON, Mark R. United States National Park Service, Division of Research, P.O. Box 168, Yellowstone National Park, Wyoming 82190 USA

KAY, Charles E. Institute of Political Economy, Utah State University, Logan, Utah 84322-0725 USA

KELLEYHOUSE, David G. Alaska Department of Fish and Game, 1300 College Road, Fairbanks, Alaska 99701 USA

KLEIN, David R. United States National Biological Service, Alaska Cooperative Fish and Wildlife Research Unit, University of Alaska Fairbanks, Fairbanks, Alaska 99775 USA

KRAUSMAN, Paul R. School of Renewable Natural Resources, 325 Biological Sciences East Building, University of Arizona, Tucson, Arizona 85721 USA

LEHMAN, Niles. Department of Molecular Biology MB4M, The Scripts Research Institute, 10666 N. Torrey Pines Road, La Jolla, California 92037 USA

LUCASH, Chris. United States Fish and Wildlife Service, Cades Cove Ranger Station, Townsend, Tennessee 37882 USA

MARQUARD-PETERSEN, Ulf. P.O. Box 80183, Fairbanks, Alaska, 99708 USA

MATSON, Gary M. Matson's Laboratory, P.O. Box 308, Milltown, Montana 59851 USA

McNAY, Mark E. Alaska Department of Fish and Game, 1300 College Road, Fairbanks, Alaska 99701 USA

MECH, L. David. United States National Biological Service, North Central Forest Experiment Station, 1992 Folwell Avenue, St. Paul, Minnesota 55108 USA

MEIER, Thomas J. Department of Fisheries and Wildlife, University of Minnesota, 1980 Folwell Avenue, St. Paul, Minnesota 55108 USA

MESSIER, François. Department of Biology, University of Saskatchewan, 112 Science Place, Saskatoon, Saskatchewan, S7N 5E2 Canada

MILLER, Frank L. Canadian Willdife Service, 4999-98 Avenue, Room 200, Edmonton, Alberta, T6B 2X3 Canada

MURRAY, Dennis L. Department of Wildlife Ecology, University of Wisconsin, Madison, Wisconsin 53706 USA

NICHOLOPOULOS, Joy E. Department of Biology, New Mexico State University, Las Cruces, New Mexico 88003 USA

NIEMEYER, Carter C. USDA/APHIS/Animal Damage Control, P.O. Box 982, East Helena, Montana 59635 USA

NOWAK, Ronald M. United States Fish and Wildlife Service (OSA), Mail Stop 725, Arlington Square, Washington, D.C. 20240 USA

PAQUET, Paul C. Box 150, Meacham, Saskatchewan, S0K 2V0 Canada

PARSONS, David R. United States Fish and Wildlife Service, P.O. Box 1306, Albuquerque, New Mexico 87103 USA

PEEK, James M. Department of Fish and Wildlife Resources, University of Idaho, Moscow, Idaho 83844-1136 USA

PETERSON, Rolf O. School of Forestry and Wood Products, 1400 Townsend Drive, Michigan Technological University, Houghton, Michigan 49931-1295 USA

PHILLIPS, Michael K. United States Fish and Wildlife Service, P.O. Box 1969, Manteo, North Carolina 27954 USA

PLETSCHER, Daniel H. School of Forestry, University of Montana, Missoula, Montana 59812 USA

PYBUS, Margo J. Alberta Fish and Wildlife Division, 6909 - 116 Street, Edmonton, Alberta, T6H 4P2 Canada

REAM, Robert R. School of Forestry, Montana Cooperative Wildlife Research Unit, University of Montana, Missoula, Montana 59812 USA

REED, Daniel J. Alaska Department of Fish and Game, 1300 College Road, Fairbanks, Alaska 99701 USA

REID, Roger Wildlife Branch, B.C. Ministry of the Environment, Lands and Parks, 780 Blanshard Street, 3rd Floor, Victoria, British Columbia, V8V 1X4 Canada

RICHARDSON, Katharine. P.O. Box 80766, Fairbanks, Alaska 99708 USA

RUGGLES, Anne K. Alaska Board of Game, P.O. Box 25526 Juneau, Alaska 99802 USA

RYON, Jenny. Department of Psychology, Dalhousie University, Halifax, Nova Scotia, B3H 4J1 Canada

SCHULLERY, Paul. United States National Park Service, Yellowstone Center for Resources, P.O. Box 168, Yellowstone National Park, Wyoming 82190 USA

SCHULTZ, Ronald N. P.O. Box 325, Minocqua, Wisconsin 54548 USA

SEIP, Dale R. British Columbia Forest Service, 1011-4th Avenue, Prince George, British Columbia, V2L 3H9 Canada

SMITH, Christian A. Alaska Department of Fish and Game, 1300 College Rd., Fairbanks, Alaska 99708 USA

SMITH, Roland. Point Defiance Zoo and Aquarium, 5400 North Pearl Street, Tacoma, Washington 98407 USA

STEPHENSON, Robert O. Alaska Department of Fish and Game, 1300 College Road, Fairbanks, Alaska 99701 USA

THEBERGE, John B. Faculty of Environmental Studies, University of Waterloo, Waterloo, Ontario, N2L 3G1 Canada

THIEL, Richard P. Wisconsin Department of Natural Resources, Sandhill Wildlife Area, P.O. Box 156, Babcock, Wisconsin 54413 USA

THOMAS, Donald C. Canadian Wildlife Service, 4999-98 Avenue, Room 200, Edmonton, Alberta, T6B 2X3 Canada

URIOS, Vicente. Estación Biológica de Donana -CSIC, Apdo. 1056, 41080 - Sevilla, Spain

VALEN, Terry. Department of Natural Resources, 1300 Clairmont Avenue, P.O. Box 4001 Eau Claire, Wisconsin 54702 USA

VALES, David J. Department of Fish and Wildlife Resources, University of Idaho, Moscow, Idaho 83844-1136 USA

VILÀ, Carles. Department of Biology, University of California at Los Angeles, 621 Circle Drive South, Los Angeles, California 90024 USA

WAYNE, Robert K. Biology Dept., University of California, 621 Circle Drive South, Los Angeles, California 90024 USA

WHITE, Cliff C. Canadian Parks Service, Banff National Park, Alberta, T0L 0C0 Canada

WHITTLESEY, Lee. United States National Park Service, Yellowstone Center for Resources, P.O. Box 168, Yellowstone National Park, Wyoming 82190 USA

WYDEVEN, Adrian P. Wisconsin Department of Natural Resources, P.O. Box 220, Park Falls, Wisconsin 54552 USA

Wolf recovery and management issues quickly become highly politicized as evidenced in Alaska, Yukon, and more recently in the northwestern United States. This photograph shows a display booth set up by recovery advocates in collecting names for a petition. (Photo: E. Bangs)

This photo shows a demonstration organized by those objecting to wolf recovery in Yellowstone and central Idaho. (Photo: Courtesy of Defenders of Wildlife)

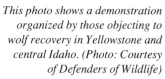

Part One:
Setting the Stage

Ecological and Cultural Diversities in the Evolution of Wolf-human Relationships

■ Luigi Boitani

The history of wolf persecution and extermination in Europe and North America followed a pattern that did not match the availability of suitable habitat for the wolf or any ecological factor linked to human density. An explanation of past and present attitudes toward wolves may be found in the early ecologies of human cultures in various regions of Eurasia. Nomadic shepherds seemed to have the most negative attitudes toward wolves, whereas sedentary crop and livestock growers appeared to be more ambivalent. Hunters and warriors had positive images of the wolf. When Europeans colonized North America, they brought with them their cultures, religions, and traditions. As most immigrants were from north and central Europe, they carried with them the worst attitudes toward wolves, that is, the negative attitudes of the Anglo-Saxon and the German world. Past attitudes have deeply influenced the relationships between humans and wolves throughout history; knowledge and management of the deep motivations for today's attitudes deserve highest priority in any wolf recovery or management program.

Introduction

The wolf (*Canis lupus*) was exterminated by humans from most of Europe (Delibes 1990), as well as from much of North America (Harrington and Paquet 1982). In Europe, wolf populations survive in the Iberian Peninsula, Italy, Greece, Sweden, and Norway. Larger populations can be found in Finland and in some eastern European countries (Poland, Czechoslovakia, Romania, Bulgaria, and former Yugoslavia) (Zimen and Boitani 1979, Delibes 1990) (Fig. 1). In North America, wolves are found in significant numbers in Alaska, Canada, and Minnesota, and are increasing in other parts of the continent (Harrington and Paquet 1982, cf. this volume).

The present distribution of wolves in Europe does not relate to human density, or activities, or availability of suitable habitat; yet the impact of humans on wolves is clear. Wolves survive only in the three Mediterranean "peninsulas," having been long exterminated from the rest of Europe, in some cases, for centuries. Why is this so? Explaining these distribution patterns might give insight into the extermination process, which in turn may affect conservation efforts not only in Europe, but worldwide. Determining the psychological and historical reasons for such major attitude differences among European countries might result in more sophisticated conservation plans and successful reintroduc-

tion and management of wolf-human conflicts. Why, in our contemporary culture, is the wolf considered "bad" to a much greater extent than its behavior and ecological role would justify? The answer to this question might be linked to the history of human cultures, and could provide hints for species management.

The hypothesis: I argue that wolf extermination follows a pattern closely linked to different early human ecology types and to the interactions among cultures. For example, I believe the ambiguous attitudes of contemporary Italians can be traced back to the ecology of the first important cultures of Roman times (Boitani 1982, 1986, 1992). Likewise, the negative attitudes of central-European cultures can be traced back to the ecological settings of those human populations.

As evidence for my hypothesis I will briefly review the extermination patterns of the wolf in Europe and North America, and compare those patterns to the role of the wolf in the most important human cultures throughout the last two millennia. Finally, I will briefly scan basic human ecology types behind those cultures, and merge them with some considerations of the way wolves reacted in those ecological relationships. Emphasis on the European context is necessary to explain North American patterns, as colonization is carried out mostly by Europeans. The implication of my conclusions for contemporary conservation and management of wolves are then presented.

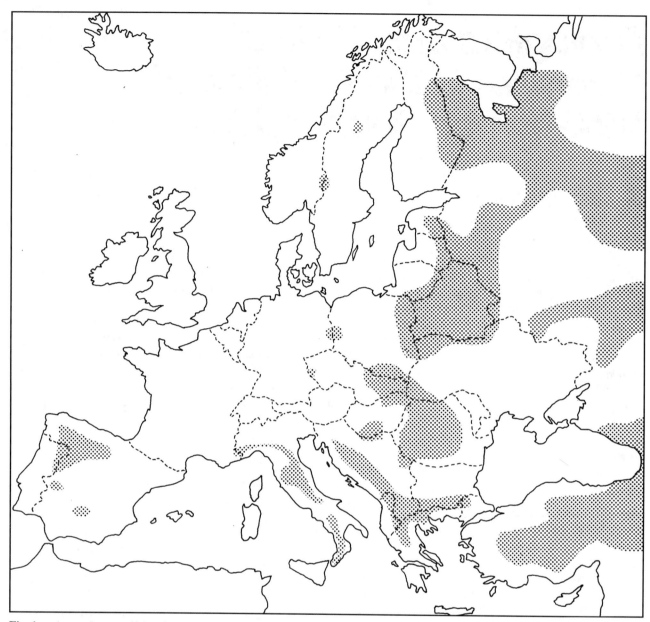

Fig. 1. *Approximate wolf distribution in Europe, 1993.*

Wolf Extermination in Europe and North America

The extermination of wolves in northern and central Europe started early. It became well-organized and consistent between the Early Middle Ages and the early part of this century (Mallinson 1978, Zimen 1978).

Great Britain and Central Europe

Great Britain's history of wolf extermination exemplifies an organized elimination campaign (Fiennes 1976). Livestock were the most important economic asset, and the wolf was a constant threat. The Celts hunted wolves in the third and fourth centuries B.C. with the help of specially trained Irish wolf hounds. Later, Edward the Peaceful created amnesty laws related to the wolf; lawbreakers could pay their dues in wolf heads. The first kings of England asked for wolf scalps as payment. England's last wolf was killed in early 1500 under Henry VII (Harmer and Shipley 1902).

During the Middle Ages, especially under King James I in Scotland, the wolf population was at a high density. As a result, the king organized hunts that occurred just after birth of the wolf pups. Despite the carnage that occurred, many wolves found refuge in the immense Scottish forests. During the reign of King James IV (1488–1513) the wolf population increased dramatically. In 1560, King James VI declared that all men — no matter how old or young — participate in the hunt. Scotland rid itself of wolves by destroying its forests. A few animals were seen in the forests of Braemar and Sutherland until 1684, the probable date of the animal's extinction. In Ireland, the wolf was extinct by approximately 1770 (Harmer and Shipley 1902).

In central Europe, the battle against the wolf took on a less frantic pace and its results appeared at a slower rate. In France, between 800 AD and 813 AD, Charlemagne founded a special wolf hunting corps, called the "Louveterie" (Hainard 1961). When a member of the corps killed a wolf, they had the right to exact payment from those living within a radius of two leagues from where the animal was caught. Consequently, the Louvetier rarely hunted wolves in unpopulated areas. Therefore, the wolf population in the more remote areas of France was left undisturbed.

The French Revolution in 1789 saw the end of the Louveterie, but in 1814 the corps was revived. The Louvetier was paid by the central government, and had to report their activity annually to the prefect. In 1883, about 1,386 wolves were killed and the next year another 1,035; but when poison was introduced, many more wolves were killed (Victor and Larivière 1980). The last wolves were killed in 1927 in Deux-Sevres and in Haute-Vienne (Beaufort 1987).

The last wolves were reported in central Europe at the beginning of the 19th century, when many large herbivores were seen for the last time. Deer and wild boar were exterminated by organized and effective hunts. Persecuted and deprived of its prey, the wolf eventually disappeared. In Denmark the last wolf was killed in 1772, and in Switzerland before the end of 19th century. In 1847, the last wolf in Bavaria was killed, and by 1899 they had completely disappeared in the regions of the Rhine from Coblenz to the Saar (Zimen 1978, Boitani 1986).

Northern Europe

Wolf extermination was not fully accomplished in Northern Europe until the beginning of this century. In Scandinavia, the wolf's main prey was the moose, which became extinct because it was killed for its meat and to reduce its competition with domestic beasts. Once again, the wolf was without prey and had to resort to domestic animals. Bloody persecution gradually confined wolves to the northern regions of the country. Here, the Laps hunted them to the last individual by organizing drives with hundreds of people participating (Turi 1931). By 1960, there were only a few wolves left; in the meantime, the moose population recovered to a peak of 70,000 (Curry-Lindahl 1965). Today only five to 10 wolves remain along the Norway-Sweden border, whereas Finland has a higher population supported by dispersal from the adjacent Russian regions.

Eastern and Southern Europe

Human densities in the Eastern Alps never reached the levels they did in central Europe, and there was never any grand-scale campaign to destroy wolves. In the 19th century,

wolves were said to be abundant and widespread in Poland, Hungary, and Transylvania. Their extermination was only possible at the beginning of this century by means of firearms and poison. The wolf was exterminated in nearly all of central-eastern Europe except in Czechoslovakia, Poland, Romania, Bulgaria, the former Yugoslavia, Albania, and Russia. Wolf populations in the Balkans were favored by their connections with those living in the vast lands of what was to be the Soviet Union (Zimen and Boitani 1979).

In southern countries around the Mediterranean basin, organized killing did not follow the consistent patterns of central European regions. The only organized extermination campaigns similar to those in France were conducted by Carlo VI in 1404 and then by Francisco I. Today, in the Iberian peninsula, the wolf is mostly confined to the mountainous regions and to the area across Spain and Portugal in the northern part of the peninsula (Grande del Brio 1984, Blanco et al. 1990).

Efforts to eradicate the wolf in Italy were more consistent between the Early Middle Ages and the last century. Bounties were regularly paid in the 12th and 13th centuries, and as recently as 1950 (Cagnolaro et al. 1974). The professional wolf-hunting corps lacked the organization and persistence of its counterpart in France and the mountain regions in the interior were not as easily patrolled. Therefore, in the Iberian peninsula and Italy, campaigns against the wolf were not as rigorous or well-organized as in Central and Northern Europe.

North America

The history of wolf extermination in North America is reported previously (cf. Young and Goldman 1944, Matthiessen 1959, Mech 1970, Lopez 1978, Brown 1983, Dunlap 1988). Prior to European colonization, the wolf enjoyed a congenial relationship with the American Indians; wolves were respected and also hunted (cf. Lopez 1978).

When the first domestic animals arrived in 1609 at Jamestown, Virginia, the war against the wolf was official. More than effective weapons, the American pioneer had a sense of solidarity and social cohesion, which in part was the effect of having common enemies, including the wolf. The battle against wolves was not an individual's affair, but a challenge to all. The wolf was the essence of wildness and cruel predation, the ally of barbaric Indians, a creature of twilight. Its elimination was depicted as more than just practical; it tested the resolve and spiritual fortitude of the pioneer. Its destruction could enable the spirit and unite a community. Massachusetts established the first bounty (one cent) in 1630. Pioneers, having fresh in mind the final victory over wolves back in England, were determined in their efforts to eliminate the predators from their homeland.

In the second half of the 19th century the battle against the wolf became more intense. Hunters had more effective killing methods including Newhouse traps (1843), and poison, mostly strychnine (Cluff and Murray this volume).

When the frontier moved west, another reason to kill wolves became more important: their fur. In 1870, the new livestock industry expanded into the vast rangelands beyond the prairies; the extermination of wolves, and many other game and predator species, reached its highest intensity (Rutter and Pimlott 1968). In the first decade of the 20th century, most of the 48 states were already cleared of wolves. Finally in 1915, wolf control became the responsibility of the federal government, and official full-time hunters were paid to eradicate the last animals. Only a small population in Minnesota survived; the recent comeback of the wolf in many northern United States is today's history (this volume).

The Wolf in Human Cultures

Examination of myths and legends surrounding the wolf is useful in understanding the history of the animal's extermination, as are the reasons why the persecution of the animal was so fervent in some regions and not in others.

Hunters and Warriors

Human cultures whose main subsistence was hunting and war shared a positive image of the wolf in all historical periods and geographical areas. In Palaeolithic times, humans were seminomadic hunters. Because they depended on animals for food and clothing, they developed an intimate relationship with the animals they pursued. Primitive hunters thought that certain animals were supernatural and believed it possible for the hunter and the prey to switch places, that is, to be mutually transformed. They believed in "guardian spirits" that would protect both humans and animals. The "Lord of the beasts" was a spirit with the power to provide prey and protection for the hunters (Hultkrantz 1965). Hunters would propitiate the gods for success by using special sacrifices and rituals. Examples can be found from most subarctic cultures (Ainu, Gilyak, Ciukci, Laps), and in all Eurasian cultures of hunters and warriors from Mongolia to the Caucasus and the Balkans (Paulson 1970).

The Inuit practiced a religion that was centered around a ceremony tied to the hunt. Inuit honored the wolf above all other animals. While ecology would have appeared to place these two hunters at odds, the wolf's role as hunter placed it, instead, in a seat of honor within human culture. Inuit and American Indians even tried to copy the wolf's hunting behavior. Because the wolf was such a significant role model, these peoples often associated the animal with the sun and its power with light and life (Paulson 1970). The Mongolians' myth of origins says Genghis Khan's first ancestors were a gray wolf sent from heaven and a white fawn. Myths of origin in most hunting communities have the wolf among the first ancestors, confirming the strong positive bond between humans and wolves.

When hunters settled down and became farmers, bands of people protected small villages from wild animals and from potential human invaders. These people were the first

"military bodies," the Indo-German "Mannerbunde" that behaved much like a group of wolves. The link between hunter and warrior is evident here. Evidence of this role in early hunter cultures can be found in "contemporary" similar cultures, such as the American Indians (e.g., Cheyenne, Sioux, Pawnee) (Mails 1972, Bird 1972, Hultkrantz 1965).

Nomadic Shepherds

Shepherds had a negative image of wolves because wolves were the main threat to shepherds' economic survival. When the cultures of the northern Asiatic peoples mixed with those of nomadic herders in south-central Asia, attitudes towards the wolf became more ambiguous. The myth of the wolf as the first ancestor is recurrent (as for the T'u Kiue or for the Hsiung-u Chinese), but the image of the wolf as a dangerous beast also emerges. Among the Kara-Kirghisi, seven large wolves were identified by the seven stars of the Bear, and stalked horses in the steppes. These people also had a myth of a wolf ancestor similar to that of the Hsiung-u Chinese (Puech 1970).

Life for the Germanic people, who were basically nomadic shepherds and then warriors, meant a constant struggle with the environment. The wolf played a large role in this struggle and its image was among the most negative (in the German apocalypse, the wolf Fenrir murders Odin, father of the gods). The Germans were also warriors (though their culture maintained its strong pastoral roots) and often had the wolf as a totem. Warriors were called alfhednar or "humans with wolf skins." They could only be called by this name after an initiation ritual in which they would kill the wolf. Germanic people were mostly responsible for exporting this link between wolf and warrior into western cultures; their invasions of southern European countries were referred to as wolves' descents.

Farmers and Sedentary Shepherds

These cultures often had a positive view of the wolf, or at least an ambiguous attitude, mixing fear, respect, hate, and love. In central Europe, between 1300 and 700 B.C., the Celts developed a basically sedentary farming society and in their mythology the wolf was viewed positively. It was connected with the cult of light and sun (the name of the Celtic god of light comes from that of the wolf "bleiz").

The Mediterranean cultures of southern Europe where most people were sedentary and farmers, also showed a consistently positive image of the wolf. Apollo, the master of light and order, an important god in Greek mythology, was associated with the wolf. The Greek word for wolf (lukos or luke) also means the light of dawn. The figure of Apollo was said to have arrived from the Nordic regions (the Celts?) (Curotto 1958). The Greek myths included Apollo's returning once a year to a "northern region" to rest. Wolves were also killed in Greece, and bounties were paid in Athens Solone in the sixth century BC. While this went on for many years, there were no more documented cases of prizes given for killing the animal in the Greek or Roman worlds.

The wolf was a major figure in the lives of the Romans. The well-known legend of the founding of Rome by the twins Romulus and Remus comes from a Greek legend. However, the truth behind the legend is tied to the wolf cult present in the neighboring Sabine culture. The Sabines had two words for the wolf: lupus (the animal), and hirpus (the animal in its religious sense). The latin word "lupus" comes from the Sabine language. Whereas the Romans were farmers, the Sabines were both shepherds and hunter-warriors and had religious practices (similar to those of Germanic peoples) that centered around the wolf with rituals, temples, and priests (Boitani 1986). Like the Indo-European Mannerbunde, the Sabine warriors fought under the sign of the wolf, which was their guide and totem. Romans never defeated the Sabines in battle, but won by merging with them. Romulus and Remus were the symbol of the Romans and the Sabines, unified and "twinned" in Roma (the she-wolf). Thus, the wolf became the symbol of the pax romana, its legions, its central power, and Rome's tradition of tolerance (Boitani 1986). The Roman feast of the Lupercali celebrated the peace between the Romans and the Sabines, and was established both to propitiate the gods for the fecundity of the herd (and of woman) and to defend humans from risks and dangers.

The Church Domination

The advent of Christianity imposed radically new ways of thinking on Western people. People's attitudes towards the environment and the wolf changed considerably (Ortalli 1973).

The Bible presents the perspective of people that lived in a hostile environment within a pastoralist economy; hence they had a negative attitude toward wolves. While the figure of Jesus Christ replaced that of Apollo — the god of light and order — these figures were rarely associated with the positive image of the wolf. In Christian symbolism, the wolf became more a symbol of human rapacity and deceit, of wantonness and sexual excess, the animal ready to attack sheep, symbols of mildness, moderation, and goodness (Ortalli 1973). The sheep-wolf counterposition was often used symbolically. As an example, Isaiah says that during the Second Coming the lamb will sit with the wolf, as a triumph of peace. In the New Testament, Christ calls false prophets "wolves" and warns the disciples they will be like sheep in the land of predators when they go out to preach his word.

Humanity passed from a world of tolerant pagan polytheism to the black and white duality of Christianity. Something was either on the side of God, salvation, and goodness or on the side of the devil, evil, and perdition. The tolerance, logic, rationality, and knowledge of natural phenomena that were an integral part of the Classical world were manipulated by the Church in favor of the supernatural, the mysterious, and faith in providence.

Politically the Church was ruthless and succeeded in completely subjugating contemporary culture (Lopez 1962, 1971). The Church was obsessed with the fear of heresy and therefore discouraged both oral and written traditions in order to eliminate any liberal interpretations of the Bible. The apostolic and papal traditions were the only points of reference for the Church, and the attitudes that were expressed in the Gospels and the Acts of the Apostles reflected the original relationship between people and the environment in the Middle East. Symbols and metaphors were taken from everyday life. The invasion of German culture, and its belief that the wolf was a dangerous predator, was used for all its worth by the Church. The wolf as heretic was a widely spread symbol after the fifth century.

The 10th century became known as the "Peace of God" era. After centuries of economic depression, farmers were trying to cultivate vast areas of unsettled land. In this "new frontier" climate, the wolf was seen as the enemy, symbol of the difficulties to the conquest of new land (Duby 1974, Fumagalli 1992). The Italians' more ambiguous attitude toward the wolf partially derived from the geography of central Italy, which did not lend itself to major settlement. Unlike the plains of central Europe, wolves were able to find refuge where people would not pursue them.

The Early Middle Ages saw the animal as a major obstacle to expansion and gave us our image of the "evil wolf." The wolf was seen as the most dangerous animal humans had to face and the codification of this role, in the legends of the saints (like St. Francis) reinforced the image of the wolf as predator (Ortalli 1973).

The Renaissance and the Wolf in Literature

The Early Middle Ages laid the groundwork for attitudes toward the wolf. The 15th to the 17th centuries saw the most fervent campaign against the animal. It was also during this period that the most shocking stories of wolves devouring humans appeared (Zimen 1978, Bradier 1985).

The Church increased its control over the people by providing "scientific proof" of its doctrine. Scientific information was found in the famous "Physiologus" books. They were written to perpetuate the popular image of the natural world; authors added little moral lessons and often changed biological facts into religious metaphors. For many centuries these manuscripts were the only sources of knowledge of natural history (Brezzi 1978). Texts that preceded them were scarce. Aristotle in *Historia Animalium,* Pliny in *Naturalis Historia,* and many classical authors wrote in depth about wolves, drawing a rather accurate picture in light of their knowledge of the animal. Classical authors thought the wolf was more of a threat to herds than to people. Horace, as an example, gave an impartial observation of the behavior of the animal. He reported once meeting a wolf by chance, but when the animal saw him, it fled immediately. Even by the late Middle Ages, a few Christian writers such as Albertus Magnus and Bartholomew Angelico wrote about wolves in an objective and accurate manner (Ortalli 1973). Unfortunately, their most scholarly writings rarely became part of popular culture. The Physiologus, on the other hand, inspired more popular works on natural history: the bestiaries. These books were filled with terrifying natural and fantastical animals, with many tales of the wolf being portrayed as a deceitful and lascivious beast. The roots of most beliefs could be traced back to the bestiaries of the Middle Ages (Ortalli 1973).

Fables, too, are a fundamental means of understanding the traditional cultural image of the wolf. The body of literature is immense, ranging from Aesop to Jack London, and its analysis becomes an itinerary of different epochs, environments, and moral attitudes. In Aesop's stories, typical of Mediterranean cultures, the wolf is a predator and a potential danger for herds, but is not "evil." Aesop frequently depicted the wolf in difficulty — while it was powerful, it was not attentive or quick-witted. It could be easily fooled or tricked, often by clever use of language. There were more fables that describe the wolf as a loser than as a winner, even if it seemed a terrifying predator.

The first written version of Little Red Riding Hood appeared in 1600, a dark time for the wolf. This fable is a perfect example of a culture detaching itself from the biological reality of an animal in order to construct an image for its own use. This fable represents the ultimate "other" wolf — that of the imagination as compared to the biological animal.

Ecological Roots of Human Attitudes Toward the Wolf

There are three distinct relationships that humans have had with the environment: hunting, shepherding (both sedentary and nomadic), and agricultural. Agriculture refers to producing crops and farm animals.

Hunters were almost completely dependent on herbivores. Predators were their greatest competitors, but they never presented a serious threat. Hunters developed a sense of respect for the predator. They tended to identify with the wolf and emulated its behavior, because the animal's social and territorial behavior resembled that of humans (Hultkrantz 1965). Because humans have been hunters for a longer period than they have been shepherds or farmers, their relationship with the wolf is deeply rooted in their collective consciousness. Remnants of that relationship can be found in our beliefs, languages, and attitudes.

Hunters were also frequently warriors and their identification with the wolf during the hunt was transferred to their identification with the wolf when they were in battle. It worked the other way too. When warriors wore wolf skins

in battle, their victims immediately made the connection between wolf and conqueror (Brezzi 1978).

When the hunter became the nomadic shepherd, his relationship with the environment changed drastically. Nomadic herders had a good ecological reason to fear the wolf. Always on the move, with just a few animals and few means of defending themselves, they were economically vulnerable. Their main concern was protecting and maintaining their herds. The wolf was no longer a predator worthy of emulation, but a threat to defenceless livestock — an animal to fear and hate.

A clear shift in attitude is evident for those cultures that were first hunters, and then shepherds. The Laps in Scandinavia originally had an immense respect for the wolf. Their attitude changed when they started reindeer domestication; they began to refer to the animal as one of their worst enemies (Turi 1931).

Sedentary herders, to the contrary, had housing to protect their herds. Over the centuries, they were able to develop somewhat of an ecological compromise, where the loss of a few domestic animals was accepted as any other natural accident, like lightning or drought (Ortalli 1973). Where people were sedentary shepherds, the attitude toward the wolf was more tolerant. With the help of dogs that protected their herds, they learned the wolf's behavior patterns, and in turn, the wolf learned theirs. This relationship led to a tense, but relatively peaceful coexistence. Given enough time, the wolf learned to cope with human activities and avoid dangerous situations (Boitani 1982, 1986). Ecology and behavior of the wolf in Italy is among the best evidence of this capacity for "cultural" adaptation. Wolves and humans coexist in an overcrowded land with little conflict (Boitani 1986).

The different relationships the nomadic and sedentary shepherds had with wolves is reflected in the type of dogs they used. Nomadic shepherds selected strong and powerful hounds for pursuing and attacking wolves, e.g., the Irish wolfhound and the asiatic Borzoi, or Russian wolfhound. The sedentary shepherds selected a mastiff type and bred for a calm and strong guard dog, e.g., the ancient Maremma dog in Italy. The former is clear evidence of an attitude of actively destroying wolves; the latter is evidence of a passive, defensive attitude, an acceptance of the wolf's presence as long as it does not harm human property.

The next stage — the farmer, producing mostly crops, and only to a limited extent, livestock — lent itself to an even easier relationship with the wolf. Agriculture is perforce more sedentary. The farmer usually thought of the wolf as one of many environmental menaces — one that had to be accepted because it was inevitable (Capogrossi 1982).

A Synthesis, A Look at North America, and a Conclusion

In northern and central Europe, the wolf had three major factors working against it: 1) the initial attitude of the nomadic shepherd; 2) the political and social structure that helped plan organized hunts; and 3) geographical and ecological homogeneity that encouraged systematic expansion and societal organization.

In southern Europe all of these existed, but on a much smaller scale. Expansion was limited, and there was little large-scale social and political organization. Roman civilization had agriculture at the root of its power, but Roman society was based in the city (Capogrossi 1982). The dominant agricultural class resided in the city and rarely had to suffer the day-to-day problems of country living. Their flocks of sheep were small, and agriculture in mountainous areas was confined to small terraces. This left huge, wooded areas to the wolf where it hunted its natural prey. The myth of the Roman wolf and its ties with the Sabines and warriors sanctioned the positive hunter-wolf relationship. The nomadic shepherd period was completely skipped.

Rome, therefore, had no reason to hate the wolf, that is until the time of the barbaric invasions. The Lombards invaded in the name of the wolf, and their devastations were closely associated with wolf raids. These began to change the generally positive view of the wolf in the Classical world (Lopez 1962, Ortalli 1973).

Barbarians dedicated most of their time to hunting and raising livestock, mostly cows and pigs. Crop production dropped to its lowest level in history. Many Romans left the city for their villas in the country — the nuclei of the later aristocrats' castles. Nature became an enemy, and the relaxed relationship the Romans had with the natural world gave way to a dark and negative representation of the external (to the village-castle) world (Fumagalli 1992).

Herein lies a fundamental difference between the Mediterranean regions and central Europe. Farms in the Mediterranean were small and dispersed, while those in Central Europe were nearer to one another in the plains. The latter situation lent itself to greater unification and cooperation among people. In Italy, this happened to a lesser extent. Lack of centralized powers translated into a less organized, less effective campaign for wolf eradication. Only in the seventh century did the fusion of the Roman and Germanic lifestyles result in a more pastoral society. Thus, organization for killing wolves assumed a larger importance (Duby 1974).

However, Roman and Greek cultures developed a positive image of the wolf that persisted for centuries, despite subsequent north-European negative influences. The positive image of the wolf started to abate by the end of the Roman Empire, but the heritage of the previous millennia was too deeply ingrained to disappear. This was the real origin of the ambiguity toward the wolf found in several contemporary cultures. This original positive attitude survived, in spite of the negative attitude later imported. Hundreds of examples can still be found in several legends, myths, and in our current languages (Hoffman-Krayer 1942). This ambivalence prevented a full-scale extermination effort and allowed the wolf to survive in those countries.

When Europeans colonized North America they brought with them their culture, religion, and traditions. As most immigrants were from north and central Europe, they carried with them the most negative attitudes toward the wolf, those of the Anglo-Saxon and Germanic world (Oakley 1986). In addition to a negative attitude toward wolves, already imbedded in the pioneer's cultural background, the conflict between wolves and American pioneers combined several of the worst conditions that occurred in the Old World. When American pioneers moved westward, their relationship with the wolf was equivalent to that of the nomadic shepherd, with all its negative components. At first, the prevailing form of animal husbandry was to allow large herds to range over vast areas, a most difficult challenge in the presence of wolves. Pioneers identified wolves and Indians as their worst enemies, a threat to personal safety and livestock, and an impediment in the march of progress and civilization. Wolves and Indians became symbols of the hostile environment they were trying to conquer (Nash 1967). The geography of the new land (vast and inaccessible areas) helped, and the pioneers were socially organized. Integration with the Indians did not occur (Lopez 1978), which may explain why the Indians' positive attitudes about wolves did not influence the pioneers' negative attitudes. The results were inevitable, as the history of wolf extermination in most of North America shows (Lopez 1978, Brown 1983).

Since European settlement in North America, the wolf has been largely perceived in negativistic, utilitarian, and dominative terms (*sensu* Kellert 1980b), and only during the second half of the 20th century is the basic attitude shifting. The wolf became a symbol of human persecution of animals. It was among the first species to be officially listed as endangered under the Endangered Species Act of 1973.

Contemporary American attitudes toward the wolf are ambivalent and stem from recent changes in perceptions of wildlife, not from the deeply embedded cultural ambiguity as suggested for the Mediterranean countries. Several studies of American views of predators in different contexts find a consistently hostile perception of the wolf, especially among the non-educated, farmers, lower income peoples, hunters, and livestock producers (Arthur et al. 1977, Buys 1975, Llewellyn 1978, Hook and Robinson 1982, Kellert 1985a, 1986). Studies by Johnson (1974) and More (1978) suggest that negative attitudes toward the wolf may be strongly related to generally hostile depictions of this animal in various myths, children's stories, and literature.

However, Kellert (1986) in Minnesota, and Briggs (1988) in New Mexico, found a trend toward positive appreciation of the wolf by more educated persons, urban dwellers, young males, and those having a lifestyle with closer contact with nature. These results fit the above suggestion for a "recent" cultural shift in attitudes toward wolves and wilderness, especially when considering the substantial effort of the American culture to reevaluate its appreciation of Indian cultures (Nee and Oakley 1986). Several recent attitude surveys in the northwestern States suggest ambivalence toward wolves (McNaught 1987, Lenihan 1987, Tucker and Pletscher 1989, Bath and Buchanan 1989, Bath 1991a), although they also show different attitudes being strongly related to special interest groups. These results are affected by the "hot" issue of wolf reintroduction in the Yellowstone area.

Today's ambiguity in North American attitudes toward wolves is related to recent cultural changes, not to historical background. Unfortunately, we do not have a survey on the different attitudes of Americans immigrating from different European regions, as this might help test my hypothesis.

The red wolf reintroduction program faces little opposition in the southeastern States, where the prevailing rural economy is based on crop production (W. Parker, U.S. Fish and Wildlife Service, pers. commun.). However, the Yellowstone reintroduction program is facing its strongest opposition from well-organized livestock organizations (Bath 1991a).

The effects of the irrational and deep-rooted negative attitudes towards the wolf are seen clearly in three recent events in Europe: 1) the escape of a few wolves from an enclosure in Bavaria (Germany) in 1976 (Zimen 1978); 2) the return of a small group of wolves to Norway-Sweden since 1977 (Bjarvall 1983); and 3) the hunt of a wolf near Basel, Switzerland in 1990. In all cases, the reactions were disproportionate (not to say ridiculous) to the potential dangers. Such reactions are only partly explainable in terms of real dangers or of rational appraisal of the biological dimensions of the events. The ultimate explanation lies in the deep, irrational, and emotional attitude that is embedded in the cultures of those countries.

Lessons for Wolf Conservation and Management

The most obvious lesson from this analysis is that the most important issue in wolf conservation is public opinion. This factor is more difficult to handle than any biological problem posed by the wolf itself. Almost any wolf "problem" is first a human problem, and as such it should be addressed (Boitani and Zimen 1979). Wolf conservation is accomplished mostly by psychology and education. In many cases of conflict, the solution should be worked out by management through ad hoc programs, and through carefully selected groups of people representing different views of the wolf (livestock producers, hunters, wolf advocates, antiwolf groups). When planning for reintroduction, a number of human variables should be considered if the biological possibilities of reintroduction are to be consistent with socio-economic reality.

Wolf control and extermination in the past were often possible only by a powerful organization of antiwolf groups. Such groups should receive careful attention in any wolf management program. Wolf advocate groups, on the other hand, are dispersed and disorganized. Their motivation extends beyond a love for wolves. It will be important to evaluate all possible reasons for their establishment and growth, e.g., reevaluation of nature *per se*, appreciation of the Indian and Inuit cultures, identification with the positive symbolism of the wolf (wildness, war, strength, social life, loyalty, predation, the balance of nature, etc.), and distance from ecological conflicts. We probably can expect their effectiveness to be related to their different motivations. Dealing with these groups should start from an understanding of their primary motivations.

Fig. 2 *One of the greatest riddles in the ecology of wolves is the question why wolves have not attacked and killed humans more frequently than it appears from the historical record. Wolves in Canada's High Arctic (as seen in this photograph) are particularly accepting of man within close quarters. (Photo H.J. Russel)*

The second lesson is that wolf-human conflicts are best contained through long-lasting associations between the two species, to allow them to learn about each other and find a compromise. The recent (1980-1985) recolonization by wolves of areas in the Italian northern Appenines (Tuscany and Liguria) where they were exterminated several decades ago, raised opposition by local people, yet conflicts with livestock are minimal. Conversely, opposition is lower in central Italy where wolves were never exterminated (Boitani 1992). The same patterns can be found when comparing areas of long-term wolf presence in Alaska or Minnesota with areas where reintroduction is proposed (Kellert 1985a). The difference in attitudes is likely the level of direct and personal knowledge of the wolf (cf. Kellert 1985a, 1990a). Prolonged coexistence with the wolf allows development of understanding and appreciation of the species as it is, whereas lack of close contact fosters the deeply irrational image of the wolf and the potential exacerbation of this image by the mass media.

Wolf-human conflicts are best resolved when both species "agree" on a certain amount of tolerance for the other's rights. Wolves can find the "agreement" through a process of natural/artificial selection and learning (cf. Fritts 1982, for the USFWS' approach in Minnesota); humans must be educated to increase their tolerance of the wolf (and their rationality!). When planning for a reintroduction, perhaps the best approach is to provide the legislative and technical means to halt the program if necessary. The proposed "experimental population" status for the Yellowstone wolves will partly provide for this flexibility.

The third lesson is that humans should learn to view the depredations by the wolf as one more cause of natural mortality. Even though all reasonable means should be used to prevent depredations, we must accept the fact that not all are preventable. Consequently, compensation for damage done by wolves should be provided by society as a whole, and should not be left on the shoulders of stock producers (Boitani and Fabbri 1983).

Acknowledgments
Stephen R. Kellert has given useful comments on the manuscript and added material on contemporary North American attitudes toward the wolves. I am grateful for the input by L.N. Carbyn, S.H. Fritts and D.R. Seip. Their review and collaboration is most gratefully appreciated.

Historical Perspectives on Wolf Management in North America with Special Reference to Humane Treatments in Capture Methods

■ Frederick F. Gilbert

*Ethical and moral value systems are subject to change and the relationship of **Homo sapiens** to **Canis lupus** exemplifies a major attitudinal change by the public. The attitude has evolved and is still evolving from the perception of the wolf as a symbol of evil and savagery to one of environmental quality. The philosophy and methods of wolf control raise a number of ethical questions that have a bearing on its management. These management practices are discussed in light of their acceptability to the public. The ethical positions taken related to wolf control can be summarized as: 1) utilitarian — wolves can be controlled because they compete with humans, or affect their prey too drastically; 2) naturalistic — wolf control is unacceptable because natural systems are superior to managed systems; 3) humane — control methods that cause injury or do not kill quickly are inhumane and thus unacceptable; and, 4) animal rightist — killing wolves is unacceptable because of their inherent right to life.*

Introduction

As a component of human folklore, the wolf (*Canis lupus*) has garnered an unenviable reputation as a symbol of evil and savagery. Part of this image probably was based on fact, as for example, in the Middle Ages when human populations in Europe decimated the prey base of wolves, and the wolves for a time had sufficiently high populations to threaten human life in remote or forested areas. The many human conflicts at the time may have provided human carcasses for wolves to scavenge. Also, rabies may have been a factor. Even if the events were built out of proportion to reality, the one reality was that wolves were, and continue to be (or at least intuitively appear to be), in direct competition with man for the prey species both utilize. This has resulted in almost continuous efforts through recorded history to kill wolves. Extermination of predators was an obligation of all the inhabitants of Sweden from about 1350, and after 1442 Swedish law required farmers to maintain wolf nets. Bounties were in place in England in the 1500's, in Sweden in 1647, and in Norway in 1730. As a result of all this pressure, wolves were exterminated from England in the 1500's, from Ireland in the 1600's from Scotland in the 1700's and from Denmark in 1813 (Myrberget 1990).

Although many of the control methods used have raised legitimate ethical concerns, the question of whether or not to control wolves by any means has only recently generated much controversy. Not only is there considerable variability in the positions held on wolf control by individuals in modern society, but there also is rapid evolution of the societal consensus position as it relates to wildlife in general. Kellert and Westervelt (1981) reported that urban United States (U.S.) citizens were moving away from wildlife consumerism to anthropomorphic attitudes toward wildlife. The rise of animal rights groups to increasing positions of influence is part of this overall phenomenon.

The viewpoint that welfare of individual animals is paramount is strongly adhered to by humane society members and animal rightists and now represents the attitude of an increasing proportion of the general public. This attitudinal shift has been facilitated by recent events in human society. The movement in North America from a rural agrarian-based society to an urban service-oriented society has severed many of the natural ties *Homo sapiens* had to nature and moved discussion of issues of concern to wildlife managers from a pragmatic arena to one that is based more on emotion and rhetoric. Emotions range from those of the rural "wolf hater" to the unconditional support shown by "wolf lovers" in urban areas. What this has done though, is cause managers to view more seriously the reasons and the methods used for wolf control. In this paper, I discuss the ethics of wolf management and the systems that have been used in that process. But to do so requires some preliminary assessment of how society establishes ethical positions or makes value judgments relative to issues like predator control.

Ethics, Public Attitudes, and Effects on Wolf Management

While at any time a dominant societal attitude prevails that influences the type of management programs that are considered acceptable, we are in an era of significant attitudinal change. Until quite recently, the historical viewpoint was that wolves were "vermin" and thus there was little opposition to any form of control or exploitation of the species.

Aldo Leopold and Farley Mowat, by their writing, influenced people's thinking and perspectives. Both authors held that wolves are essential components of natural ecosystems and society would be advised to protect the species' interests. While Leopold's (1949) position developed from a land ethic perspective that represented a personal attitudinal evolution, Mowat's (1963) conviction was presented in a fictional context that engendered negative reaction from a number of wildlife managers who questioned the use of fiction presented as fact, and plagiarism in the text. Managers often failed to concentrate on the public support for the ideas in the book. Douglas Pimlott (1967a) took a different approach. He questioned the long-term viability of the species and what types of wilderness, if any, future generations would have. By being exposed to the options, the reader was left to draw his/her own conclusions and indirectly public opinion was influenced and the wolf raised as an issue in the public arena. Thus, the motives and the methods used for presenting personal ethical positions vary considerably among individuals as contrasted by these three personalities. However, it is apparent that writings, and more recently the mass media, are effective means to sway public opinion on an issue. Public opinion then becomes a factor in the development of wildlife policy. But it is important to be aware that ethics ultimately reflect a set of societal consensus points.

Public opinion can influence the management of wolves, but ethical considerations are only one variable in Kellert's (1991) description of the forces affecting wildlife policy discussions. For example, Kellert (1986) found that the majority of U.S. citizens liked wolves, yet within rural communities, earlier research on why a wolf reintroduction to Michigan in 1974 had failed, found a strong negative public attitude (Hook and Robinson 1982). These rural populations had a strong anti-predator attitude and showed significant hostility to government authority as well as distrust of government. Kellert (1985a, 1990b, 1991) and others (cf. Bath and Buchanan 1989, Bath 1991b, McNaught 1987; and Tucker and Pletscher 1989, Vest 1988) have consistently shown the importance of social, economic, and human valuation factors related to wolf reintroduction proposals. To

illustrate this point, a state-wide survey in Wyoming of general public attitude toward wolf restoration in Yellowstone National Park, showed 48.5% favored reintroduction and 34.5% were opposed. When the predominantly rural Wyoming counties around Yellowstone were surveyed, 51.7% of the respondents opposed reintroductions (Bath and Buchanan 1989).

Public support for wolf control programs is high among interior residents in places like Yukon, Alaska, and northern British Columbia, but low in urban centers and with external publics (cf. Hoffos 1987). Support for wolf control is likely to hinder successful establishment of wolves in areas of limited prey base and/or suitable habitat, as is the situation in Europe (cf. Boitani and Zimen 1979, Boitani 1982, Bjarvall 1983). Opposition to wolf control, by contrast, can stymie predator control programs, as Alaskan wildlife managers have repeatedly discovered. Such opposition is now so large that Theberge (1989) commented, "Quite possibly the majority of Canadians see it (wolf killing to increase prey) as unacceptable, now, on the same ethical grounds that govern attitudes towards the killing of harp seals, the trade in endangered species, and commercial whaling."

It is important to recognize that wolves are viewed very differently by different segments of the public. Most North Americans, having had little exposure to wolves, or the environmental conditions that support wolves, will associate them with real or perceived endangered or threatened wildlife predator species such as the black-footed ferret (*Mustela nigripes*) or the leopard (*Panthera pardus*). It matters not that northern Canada and Alaska support viable, self-sustaining wolf populations. Attitudes are based on the southern Canadian and lower 48 United States' realities that wolves have disappeared or are endangered where people live in substantial numbers. In such circumstances, the wolf can assume a high profile status, as does the spotted owl (*Strix occidentalis*) and the African elephant (*Loxodonta africana*) as a symbol of threatened value systems or environments. Whether it be old-growth forests or wilderness, these wildlife species carry significance far beyond their ecological status. Resource managers who fail to recognize this reality are doomed to be damned by the general public when they propose actions that may affect these symbols, be it cutting of old-growth Douglas-fir stands or deciding in favor of hunters over wolves. Species like the elephant and spotted owl actually represent paradoxes because there are other important ethical questions involved, such as the destruction of national parks, and of food crops in Africa by elephants, and the economic impact of lost jobs and the destruction of forest resource-based communities in the Pacific Northwest, if the spotted owl is fully protected. And in the case of the wolf, control may be necessary when the combined mortality pressures on an ungulate population drive it to very low numbers or toward extirpation.

Ethics and the Means of Killing Wolves

In North America, wolf control activities have taken many forms, from hunting, trapping, and poisoning, to shooting from aircraft. Ethical concerns vary somewhat with each type of control. Animal rightists reject the exploitation of any other species and consider it morally wrong. By contrast, the newly-formed United Conservation Alliance supports ethical, responsible, reasonable uses of animals, including lawful hunting and trapping (Anonymous 1991). This position has also been recently adopted by the prestigious international organization of IUCN (World Conservation Union) of the United Nations' Environmental Program. Thus, one person's ethics is another's anathema. Because of this wide ethical response, it can be questioned whether it is possible to clinically and objectively analyze a single "ethical perspective" on wolf management in North America. Perhaps it is not possible, but it becomes easier if it is recognized that much of the basis for wolf management has been economic, although a non-economic case has been made to control and protect threatened populations of woodland caribou (*Rangifer tarandus*). Wolves prey on livestock as well as on commercially important big game species. Furthermore, their pelts have commercial value and they often are managed as furbearers (Novak 1987).

Techniques primarily used to trap wolves up to the mid 1800's included snares, steel traps, and deadfalls. The use of snares and steel traps was destined to arouse controversy over humaneness. Canids have well-muscled necks and reinforced trachea, so no neck snare system is likely to result in a quick death. Current deliberations on the development of international humane trap standards would be quick to condemn conventional snares for wolves as unethical on this basis alone. Leg-hold steel traps in the past were designed simply to hold the animal and thus usually had teeth on the jaws. While arguments have been made that toothed jaws actually reduce injury and prevent oedema (Kuehn et al. 1986), they have been banned from North America because of their perceived cruel and inhumane action. Humane arguments aside, there is little evidence that early trapping techniques were very selective or that there was much control of the trapping effort. Indeed, some furbearing species, including wolves, were exterminated from large areas of their range by 1900 as a result of overexploitation. Wolves became extinct in Newfoundland in 1911 (Tuck 1952), from the maritime provinces of Canada and New England by 1900, and declined in numbers even in western Canada until about 1930 (Carbyn 1987). Concerns over the humaneness of trapping were voiced during the latter half of the 19th century and yet, despite some modest improvements in trapping technology, traps even today continue to maim target wolves and nontarget species alike (e.g., Van Ballenberghe 1984). This becomes a basic question of animal welfare and one that has prompted governments to respond by seeking alternatives to trapping or establishing standards

of humaneness for traps (Gilbert 1991). Because of the size and behavior of wolves, the species is most likely to be captured by restraining devices like leg-hold traps, so there is little likelihood that humane killing traps could ever be used for the species. Because the act of trapping a wild animal, for whatever reason, is a willfully directed human event, it carries with it certain responsibilities regarding the welfare of the animal. Although wildlife managers tend to concentrate on the effect on the population of such willful activities, society demands that individual animals not be allowed to "suffer" pain or undue injury in a trapping device or as a result of any other management practice, such as hunting, where substantive crippling losses and thus "suffering" can occur. This suggests a conflict between management goals to harvest populations and the welfare interests for individual animals. As these animals are sentient beings that we (mankind) have consciously decided to kill, we also have the obligation to assure as humane treatment as possible. That is the emerging international position related to humane standards for restraining devices (Gilbert 1991). Therefore, using restraining traps that consistently cause moderate to severe injury to a captured wolf is unacceptable. Whatever the ultimate disposition of the individual, it will be an ethical responsibility to assure, with a reasonable degree of reliability, minimal injury to the animal upon its capture and while it is being restrained.

Pragmatists may argue that, as they are to be killed, wolves captured for the purpose of harvest or damage control need not be afforded such humane treatment. To apply double standards, depending on whether the animals are to be released or to be killed, is indefensible. Wright (1990) develops the arguments, both logical and pragmatic, relative to the rights of animals in a more equitable fashion than found in the hard-core animal rights literature (Singer 1975). The article by Wright, which ultimately supports limited rights and full welfare, probably reflects the general public's attitude fairly well. Trapping then becomes acceptable if done in a humane way and not for frivolous purposes (Singer would consider fur coats to be frivolous).

Probably the least socially acceptable form of wolf control was the broadcast poisoning, conducted in Alaska and the Canadian north during 1950–70. (i.e., mid-50's in Alaska: Gasaway et al. 1983; and in the Northwest Territories in the 50's and 60's: Kelsall 1968). Considerable debate over predator control and the advisability of selective *versus* indiscriminate control prompted a critical examination by a U.S. government committee (Leopold et al. 1964). In 1972, the use of toxicants for predator control was banned in the United States by presidential decree following the advice of a committee (the Cain Commission: Cain et al. 1972). Poison baits, including sodium monofluoroacetate (compound 1080) laced meat and strychnine tallow pellets had been dropped from aircraft or placed in caribou wintering areas from the ground, but broadcast so widely that most predator species were affected. Secondary poisoning of scavengers and nontarget poisoning of other predators were real consequences of strychnine (e.g., Anonymous 1990, Bjorge and Gunson 1985). Additionally, the clinical action of some of the toxicants was questioned on the basis of their effects. Poisoning by strychnine, for example, causes excitability of the central nervous system. The animal becomes excessively reactive to external stimulation and undergoes violent convulsions that are associated with painful contraction of the skeletal muscles (Franz 1975). Death thus occurs so inhumanely that the American Veterinary Medicine Association's Panel on Euthanasia absolutely condemned this chemical or any of its salts for euthanasia purposes (Anonymous 1986). Because use of compound 1080 was not banned by the Canadian government, it continues to be used for predator control in some provinces, as does strychnine.

Wolves also have been shot from aircraft and snow machines, both for predator control and for sport hunting. The debatable point here is the technological advantages of humans. Someone on a snow machine can easily wear down a wolf, especially if it is caught in the open, as on a frozen lake or a large cut-over area. The animal becomes exhausted and can be dispatched at close range. Shooting a wolf from helicopters or fixed-wing aircraft was considered sport until recently, when many jurisdictions required the aircraft to land before the wolf could be shot. While this is an improvement, problems with enforcement suggest that it may be more of a paper regulation than a real one. The basic issue in such approaches is the argument presented by Leopold (1949), that when we advance so far technologically that we are perceived as having an unfair advantage over the hunter's quarry, the "sporting" activity will no longer be acceptable to the general public.

Ecosystem Considerations in Wolf Control

Individual wolf populations have been considerably reduced within the 20th century, but the species is not endangered on a continent-wide basis. Where control is intended to benefit

ungulate populations, hunters will benefit as well. If man were a direct substitute for the wolf, as a predator, then we could remove the wolf and replace it with human hunters. No one could then argue that ecosystem function had been significantly affected by the substitution of predators, even though nutrient cycling would have been changed somewhat. But, when man replaces the wolf as a harvester of big game, there are important differences in what segments of the prey populations are killed. Where the wolf tends to harvest the vulnerable segments of prey populations, and this vulnerability changes considerably dependent on environmental conditions and population densities (c.f. Pimlott 1967a, Fuller and Keith 1980, Nelson and Mech 1986b, Theberge and Gauthier 1985, Carbyn 1983b, Carbyn et al. 1993), man tends to select the prime animals, males with large antler racks and reproductive-age females, rather than the young or the debilitated. Not only does this cause social

Fig. 1 *New innovative methods of wolf capture for research purposes have been developed by biologists in Poland. The technique involves age-old methods of driving wolves into "traplike nets" by using red flagging called "fladre." Photo above shows how the flags are strung onto a pole, photo below shows how lines are set out. (Photos: L.N. Carbyn)*

disruption in the prey species (Bubenik 1972), but it also countervails the issue of sustainable ecosystems. In a sustainable ecosystem, the predator-prey relationship serves an important role in elongating the normal cyclical fluctuations in prey populations. This allows vegetation sufficient time to recover from population highs of the prey species, thereby increasing long-term habitat variability and helping to maintain the complex of form, structure, and diversity inherent in the system. By substituting man for wolves, we artificially maintain prey populations at higher levels and induce an ecosystem trajectory that results in vegetative simplification, and thus reduced biodiversity.

Wildlife managers have stated that maximizing recreation days of hunting is often the main objective of big game management. Participation rates increase when harvest rates are higher. Therefore, such a focus can run counter to ecosystem management and wolves may become an obstacle to meeting the objective. Nonetheless, in such a scenario, wolf control still can be justified (see Theberge and Gauthier 1985). However, it is likely that single species management, outside the context of the broader reality of community structure and ecosystem function (Theberge 1992), will become history in the 21st century as everyone recognizes the futility of such myopic approaches to the environment and its overall management (Theberge 1992).

Wildlife managers are on shaky ground unless they adopt the premise that man is an integral part of ecosystems and thus should be considered a natural perturbation. Many consider man to be an environmental aberration that drains the vitality from natural systems and may doom the planet in the process. The ultimate hypocrisy, however, is to afford the same single-minded focus to wolf management that often is given to the wolf's prey species. The current endangered species programs and game species management programs both may be viewed by future generations as unethical responses when we should have been striving for sustainable ecosystems with our wildlife management actions, not the protection of individual species.

Ethics and Scientific Evidence

Use of animals in research has raised ethical issues of increasing public concern. Although much of that concern relates to the use of captive animals, the principles involved apply as well to wild ones. For example, the Canadian Committee on Animal Care requires permits for all researchers handling either captive or wild animals.

Pertinent to the wolf is the issue of experimental killing and whether or not that activity, like other issues discussed in this paper, goes beyond the bounds of public acceptability. This killing normally takes place as part of deductive experimental design to determine if wolves are limiting prey numbers. The possibility that wolves may be killed unnecessarily is a concern and the practice has raised the ire of some members of the public. Theberge (1989) referred to

such an experimental approach as "according no worth whatsoever to the wolf. It works on the premise that no harm, no injustice, no malpractice is done if a bunch of wolves is killed unnecessarily." The possibility for conflict between the government agency and its managers and other segments of the scientific community is real when such outcomes occur. This suggests that experimental killing of wolves should be approached with extreme caution and adequate justification.

Conclusions

The public attitude toward wolves now is symbolic of the larger relationship between man and nature, and ultimately how wolves fare may predict the outcome of our overall relationship with the planet. What makes the wolf issue important is the recognition that our options are fast disappearing. Unless we deal with the real problems of human population growth, the staggering rapidity of land use change, and more pressing global environmental concerns, the wolf question will be viewed as a momentary diversion as we sealed the planet's fate. Pragmatically, it makes little difference that wolf populations may be capable of sustaining control efforts without damaging the long-term viability of those populations. Nor can wildlife managers be bolstered by the argument that if it is good management to harvest prey species on a sustainable basis, it should be equally good management to harvest wolves and other predators in a similar fashion. It may not even be a question of ethics, but rather one of killing members of a species to which the majority of the public has ascribed a special value. Under such circumstances, the transition of the wolf from a symbol of evil and savagery to one of environmental integrity becomes complete and puts current management objectives in direct conflict with the new emotional perspective. If ecologically sound wolf management activities are to continue, managers must confront this reality with morally-defensible arguments. This is not impossible, but it does translate into a new way of doing business for wildlife management agencies. In the process, the wolf may attain "medicine" status for humankind in general and wildlife managers in particular, as it always has had for some native Americans (Vest 1988). And, if we prove successful in coping with the larger crisis affecting the earth, some credit may ultimately devolve on how we were able to deal with the issue of wolf management.

Acknowledgments

I would like to thank J. Theberge and J. Gunson, who reviewed this paper and provided useful comments. Thanks is also extended to L. Carbyn and the co-editors for their input. The paper proved to be more controversial than I expected, which helped to emphasize the degree of polarization that has developed with regard to the ethics of wolf management.

Frederick F. Gilbert

Wolves in a Changing World

Part Two:
A Review of the Status of Wolves

Status and Management of Wolves in Canada

■ Robert D. Hayes and John R. Gunson

Wolf population status and management in Canada is summarized to 1992. Wildlife biologists reported wolves as stable or increasing in their current range in Canada, except for part of northern Alberta and on some of the Arctic islands of the Northwest Territories. During the 1980's, wolves rapidly expanded southward through the Rocky Mountain of British Columbia and western Alberta. The current Canadian wolf population is estimated at between 52,000 and 60,000. Recreational hunting of wolves, including licensing, reporting, and annual bag limits and seasons varied across Canada. In most areas, wolf trapping was better managed through coordinated reporting and restricted seasons. Wolf fur harvest declined by 40% since 1982. Human-caused wolf mortality varied from 4–11% regionally, and was not considered a primary limitation to wolves in Canada, except along the southern edge of their distribution. During the 1980's, research into wolf ecology and prey relations was carried out in 19 study areas in Canada. Wolf predation was believed to be an important limiting factor to ungulate populations recorded in both eastern and western Canada. Large-scale wolf control programs were conducted in four areas to increase low-density ungulate populations. The impact of wolf predation on caribou is a concern of managers in most of western and northern Canada.

Introduction

Pimlott (1961a), Theberge (1973a), and Carbyn (1983a) summarized the status and management of wolves (*Canis lupus*) in Canada from the 1950's through the 1970's. The most recent, comprehensive regional status reports were in the early 1980's (for Alberta, see Gunson 1983a; British Columbia, Tompa 1983a; Quebec, Banville 1983; Manitoba, Stardom 1983; Northwest Territories, Heard 1983; Ontario, Kolenosky 1983; Yukon, Smith 1983). Carbyn (1987) updated management status to 1984, showing population estimates, management, and research programs on wolves in each province and territory. Theberge (1991) further updated the status of wolves in Canada to 1990, including regional population estimates and harvest regulations. To provide an assessment of the status and management of wolves in Canada to 1992, a questionnaire was given to wildlife biologists responsible for managing wolves in the provinces and territories. This paper summarizes the regional population status and trends, hunter and trapper harvest trends, recent wolf research projects, wolf control programs, and current management problems. We recommend ways to improve wolf management in Canada.

Wolf Population Status and Trends

Carbyn (1987) summarized the history of the wolf in Canada. The species originally occupied all regions of Canada, except Prince Edward Island and the Queen Charlotte Is-

lands. The chronology of wolf extirpation in the southern parts of provinces closely followed the pattern of agricultural and industrial settlement. Wolves were extirpated in New Brunswick, Nova Scotia, and southern parts of Quebec and Ontario between 1870 and 1900, and from insular Newfoundland by the early 1930's (J.E. Maunder, Newfoundland Museum, pers. commun.). Wolf numbers fell to their lowest levels in the western provinces by the 1930's, following widespread persecution and declines in prey related to severe weather, overhunting, and habitat loss. Wolves increased rapidly during the 1930's (Nowak 1983), reoccupying substantial portions of their former range. In the west, the increase was depressed during the 1950's when government wolf control was widespread in Alberta, British Columbia, Yukon, and Northwest Territories (Pimlott 1961a, Theberge 1973a). Wolves remain extirpated from New Brunswick, Nova Scotia, insular Newfoundland, the southern prairie provinces, and the lower mainland of British Columbia (Fig. 1).

Wolves in Canada number between 52,000 and 60,000, similar to the estimate of 58,000 by Theberge (1991). Numbers are stable in most parts of the country (Fig. 1). Wolf density is increasing in most regions of Ontario and Quebec, where recent mild winters have allowed for white-tailed deer and moose populations to grow. Numbers are declining in northern Alberta in response to declining natural prey populations, and on some of the arctic islands in the Northwest Territories.

Recent range expansions indicate that wolves are continuing to increase in parts of southwestern Canada. During the 1980's, wolves colonized southward through the Rocky Mountain of British Columbia and western Alberta. They have colonized portions of Montana. They have also appeared in northern portions of Idaho and Washington (Ream et al. 1991).

Assessing wolf population size and trends on a national scale is difficult because there is no consistent methodology used to estimate density and monitor population change in various habitat types. Wolf density and population trends are evaluated using various methods. Ontario wolf density is estimated from past wolf studies there, prey ungulate trends, and trapper questionnaires. In Manitoba, wolf density is estimated from public information and field observations of biologists, and long-term telemetry and ground studies in Riding Mountain National Park. In Saskatchewan, density is extrapolated from studies in nearby provinces. Alberta density is extrapolated from six wolf studies conducted there. In British Columbia, aerial censuses have been conducted in the northeastern part of the province. Wolves are censused by ground counts on Vancouver Island. Province-wide population trend is monitored by trapper questionnaire, public information, and range expansions. In Yukon, wolf density and trends are monitored by snow-tracking techniques, trapper questionnaire, and radiotelemetry studies. Correlation between caribou density and wolf numbers is used in Labrador and the Northwest Territories. In the western Northwest Territories, wolf numbers are monitored by radiotelemetry studies. Quebec has not estimated wolf density in recent years.

None of the census methods provide a measure of statistical variation, relying on total population counts or gross estimation of population change. Except for Yukon, there are no systematic wolf inventory programs. About 30% of Yukon (160,000 km^2) has been censused for wolves since 1983.

Human-Related Causes of Wolf Mortality

1. Trapping and Hunting

The legal status of wolves, and hunting and trapping regulations vary by province and territory. Throughout Canada, wolves can be hunted without restriction by any native person. Other resident hunters take wolves under big game licences in Yukon, Northwest Territories, British Columbia and Manitoba; and under small game licences in Ontario and Quebec. Wolves can be hunted only by trappers in Labrador, but any resident can be issued a trapper's licence. Alberta residents do not require a licence to hunt wolves, but nonresidents do. Wolves cannot be hunted in Saskatchewan, or in the Okanagan region of British Columbia.

Except for nonresident hunters in Alberta and British Columbia, Canadian jurisdictions do not charge special licence fees for wolves, or require special hunting tags or seals for wolves. Most provinces do not require or collect hunting statistics for wolves. Quebec required compulsory reporting of wolves to 1984, but discontinued collection due to a small

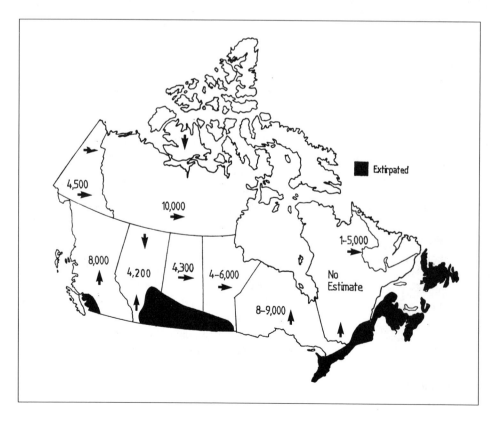

Fig. 1 *Wolf population estimates and trends, by Canadian province and territory, 1992. (Methods for estimating wolf abundance are summarized under the heading* **Wolf Population Status and Trends.**)

Table 1. Average number of wolves killed by hunting, trapping, and control for livestock depredation and ungulate population recovery in Canadian provinces and territories, 1986-1991.

Province or Territory	Average Number of Wolves Killed Annually				Estimated Percent of Population Taken Annually
	Hunted	*Trapped*	*Controlled*[1]	*Total*	
Yukon	30	100	44	174	4
Northwest Territories	25	768[2]	0	793	7-8
British Columbia	606[2]	105	234	945	11
Alberta	100	351	40	491	11
Saskatchewan	0[3]	223	61	283	7
Manitoba	50	204	41	295	7-10
Ontario	no record	565	na	565+	6-7
Quebec	no record	439	na	450+	na
Labrador	0	57	0	57+	na
Total				**4,053+**	

1 Most provinces controlled wolves for livestock depredation only. The exceptions were Yukon and British Columbia. In Yukon, an annual average of 40 wolves were killed for ungulate depredation and four for livestock depredation. In British Columbia, 125 were killed annually for ungulate depredation and 109 for livestock depredation.

2 Most wolves killed by trappers in the Northwest Territories are shot by hunters using snowmachines. In British Columbia, the data require additional analyses.

3 Wolves cannot be hunted in Saskatchewan.

reported harvest. In British Columbia, compulsory reporting is required in the Kootenay and Vancouver Island regions. Noncompulsory, questionnaire reporting occurs in Yukon and the Northwest Territories. Trappers and hunters in some communities in the Northwest Territories are paid a small fee to submit wolf carcasses or heads for biological study (P. Clarkson, N.W.T. Renewable Resources, Inuvik, pers. commun.). The number of wolves killed by hunters is not accurately reported in most areas of Canada, and the average annual take in the last five years is a minimum (Table 1).

In most regions, wolf harvest by hunting is lower than by trapping. The exception is the Northwest Territories, where most wolves that are reported as trapped are actually shot from snowmobiles (Table 1). In the open tundra areas of the arctic, wolf harvest can be high especially around communities. During the winter of 1978–1979, at least 850 wolves were killed near Coppermine, N.W.T. when a large part of the Bathurst caribou herd wintered near that community (D. Heard, N.W.T. Renewable Resources, unpubl. data). Other communities in the western Arctic also had increased numbers of wolves killed during years when migratory caribou wintered nearby (P. Clarkson, N.W.T. Ren. Res., Inuvik, pers. commun.). Forest cover and terrain limits hunting success in most of Canada.

The hunting season for wolves is year-round in Ontario, Northwest Territories and in parts of British Columbia. Elsewhere, hunting closes between March and June, and re-opens between August and October (Fig. 2). Only British Columbia, Northwest Territories, Manitoba and Yukon limit the number of wolves that can be taken by a hunter (Fig. 2). Wolves are classified as furbearers in all Canadian areas except Yukon, where they are legally classified as big game, but can still be trapped.

Throughout Canada, wolves can be taken by leg-hold traps, snares, or shot by trappers. Most areas do not set bag limits for wolves. By 1995, the European Economic Community will ban the import of furs from those countries that still use steel leg-hold traps, or have not met internationally agreed-upon standards for humane trapping. Research into alternative capture devices for wolves is a priority of Canada (Fur Institute of Canada, 1991 Annual Report).

Compared to hunting, trapping harvest is better recorded and monitored throughout Canada. Mandatory wolf pelt sealing is required for commercial sale in Ontario (M. Buss, Ont. Min. Nat. Res., pers. commun.) and Yukon. In other parts of Canada, trapping harvest is closely monitored from fur auction sale records, or reported by trapper questionnaires. Year-round trapping is legal in the Northwest Territories and Ontario. In other areas, the season is limited to periods when pelts are relatively prime. Seasons open in October and close by April in most areas (Fig. 3). In the Okanagan region of British Columbia, trapping is closed because of low wolf density.

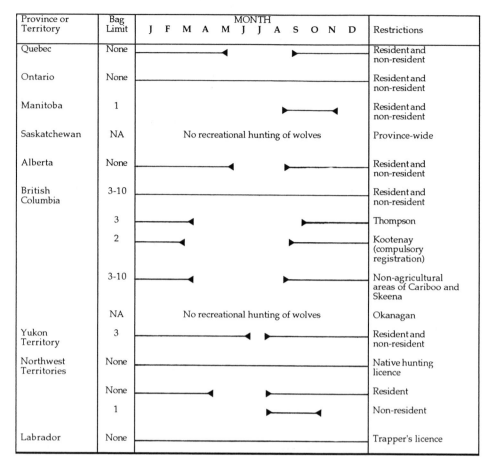

Fig. 2 *Wolf hunting seasons in Canada, by province and territory.*

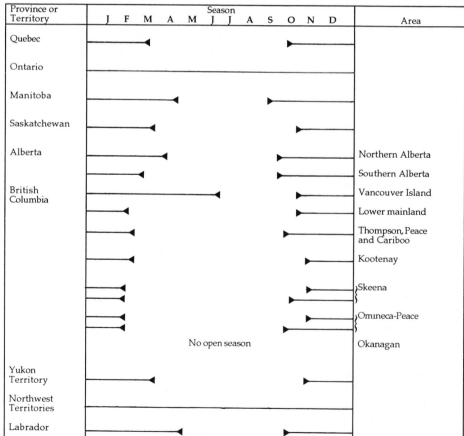

Fig. 3 *Wolf trapping seasons in Canada, by province and territory.*

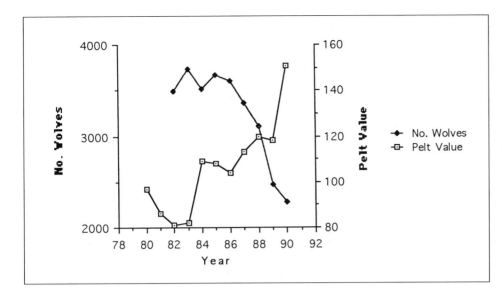

Fig. 4 *The decline in annual wolf trapping and the increase in average wolf pelt value in Canadian dollars from 1980-1990 in Canada. (Data from Statistics Canada annual reports: fur production).*

The number of wolves trapped in Canada has declined by 40%, from a high of 3,738 in 1983 to 2,285 in 1990. At the same time, average pelt values increased from $80.91 to $151.40 (Fig. 4). This drop follows a corresponding decline for all wild-caught fur in Canada during the 1980's (Statistics Canada, annual reports).

A breakdown of harvest by province shows that most of the decline in wolf trapping happened in five jurisdictions: Ontario, Manitoba, Saskatchewan, Alberta, and British Columbia (Fig. 5). Ontario showed the largest decline (70%), falling from 1,311 wolves in 1983 to a low of 353 in 1990. In the other four provinces, declines ranged from 56–59%. Harvest has remained stable in Quebec, Yukon, Labrador, and Northwest Territories (Fig. 5).

While researching wolf harvest statistics, we discovered that harvest increased sharply from 2,500 in 1970–71 to 7,000 by 1982-83 (Statistics Canada, annual reports). We

found this to be incorrect because coyotes (*Canis latrans*) were not separated from wolves in Quebec harvest records until 1983 (R. Lafond, Ministère de Loisir, de la Chasse et de la Pêche, pers. commun.). This was mainly because it was difficult to separate the two species by pelt size and colour. This error represented up to 50% of the reported wolf harvest in Canada during that period. Quebec wolf harvest was actually about 12% (360 wolves) of the total (R. Lafond, Ministère de Loisir, de la Chasse et de la Pêche, pers. commun.).

The decline in the Canadian wolf harvest is clearly a result of fewer active trappers, especially in the last five years. Because many wolves are taken incidentally to other trapping activities, wolf harvest will likely remain low in Canada unless the trapping industry recovers. The declines in wolf trapping in some provinces will probably result in increased survival of wolves, which could lead to

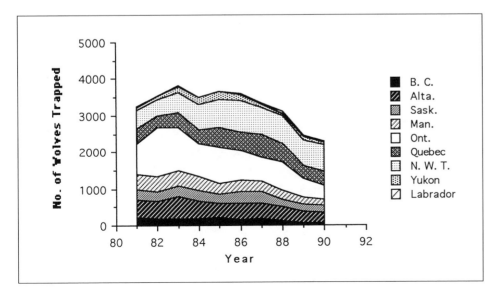

Fig. 5 *The declining trend in wolf trapping, by province and territory in Canada, 1981-1990.*

Table 2. Average number of annual wolf-livestock conflicts and wolves killed, by Canadian province and territory, 1987-1991.

Province or Territory	Annual Number of complaints	Wolf control		
		Method of Kill	Average Number Removed	Compensation
Yukon	< 10	trapping, helicopter rare	6	no
N.W.T.	few (dogs only)	helicopter (rare)	N/A	no
British Columbia	74	1080, trapping	109	no
Alberta	108	strychnine, trapping	40	yes[1]
Saskatchewan	24	strychnine, trapping helicopter (rare) bounties[2]	60	no
Manitoba	83	strychnine, cyanide	41	no
Ontario	> 100[3]	contract trapping	unknown	yes
Quebec	few	licenced trappers	unknown	no
Labrador	rare	trapping	unknown	no

1   See Alberta Fish and Wildlife (1991) and Gunson (1992).
2   By rural municipalities.
3   Complaints about wolves and coyotes increased dramatically in 1990/1991; includes livestock and other complaints.

Table 3. Annual number of wolves removed from four wolf control programs in Canada, 1982 - 1989.

AREA (km^2)	YEAR							
	82-83	83-84	84-85	85-86	86-87	87-88	88-89	TOTAL
Muskwa, B.C. 3,000 - 18,000		182	198	0	125	11		516
Vancouver Is., B.C. 10,000					108	64	83	255
Finlayson, Yukon Territory 24,000	105	106	49	54	45	42	59	460
Coast Mnts., Yukon Territory 13,000	62	56	133					251
							Total	1,482

Wolves in a Changing World

Fig. 6 *Areas in Canada where wolves were killed to allow ungulate populations to recover during the 1980's and 1990's: 1. Coast Mountains, Yukon; 2. Finlayson, Yukon; 3. Muskwa, northeastern British Columbia; 4. Vancouver Island, British Columbia; 5. Quesnel Highlands, British Columbia; 6. Papineau-Labelle Reserve, Quebec; * Aishihik, Yukon Territory (wolf control began February 1993).*

more livestock depredations, especially in the southern portions of wolf range. This situation happened in central Ontario during 1991–1992, when conflicts with wolves, coyotes, and hybrids increased markedly (R. Rosatte, Ont. Min. Nat. Res., pers. commun.).

2. *Control of Wolves for Depredation on Livestock and Wildlife*

Wherever Canadian wolves and domestic animals coexist, depredation occurs (Tompa 1983b, Bjorge and Gunson 1983, Gunson 1983b). The control of wolf predation on livestock is a concern for provinces with important agricultural areas. The average annual number of wolves killed in response to livestock losses during the last five years is shown in Table 2. Most wolves removed in the western provinces were poisoned (strychnine, 1080 and cyanide) or trapped.

Toxicants are not used in Quebec or Ontario, but there is little data on livestock-related control of wolves in the eastern provinces (H. Smith, Ontario Ministry of Natural Resources, pers. commun.; H. Jolicoeur, Qubec Ministère de Loisir, de la Chasse et de la Pêche, pers. commun.). Ontario and Alberta have livestock compensation programs. Payment is made to owners if there is evidence that wolves killed livestock.

The systematic control of wolves to recover low density ungulate populations has been a controversial management problem during the 1980's. Large-scale wolf control programs were carried out in four areas of British Columbia and Yukon (Table 3, Fig. 6), removing a reported total of 1,482

wolves from 1982 through 1989. Most wolves were shot from helicopters, except on Vancouver Island, where trapping was used (Archibald et al. 1991). Control programs lasted from two to seven years, with up to 85% annual reduction of the original population size in the Finlayson area, Yukon. Small-scale experimental manipulations of wolves were carried out in western Quebec (Potvin et al. 1992a, 1992b) to increase white-tailed deer numbers, and in the Quesnel Highlands of British Columbia (Seip 1992a) to recover woodland caribou (*Rangifer tarandus tarandus*) (Fig. 6). Other smaller-scale reduction programs (10-20 wolves/year) were conducted in Ontario (Theberge 1991), Manitoba and Saskatchewan.

Wolf recovery studies, including both numerical and functional responses, were conducted in two areas in Yukon after wolf reductions ended (Hayes et al. 1991, Farnell et al., unpubl. ms.). Wolf recovery was studied in the Muskwa (Bergerud and Elliott, unpubl. data) and Vancouver Island, B.C. (D. Janz, B.C. Min. Env., pers. commun.). Public controversy in Alberta indefinitely delayed a wolf control proposal to restore a threatened woodland caribou herd (Edmonds 1986 and 1988, Gunson 1992).

In February 1993, the Yukon Fish and Wildlife Branch combined hunting closures and wolf control in an attempt to recover a declining woodland caribou herd in the Aishihik area. Sixty-one wolves were killed during the first winter. Control will continue at least through the winter of 1993–1994. Wolf control is also under consideration in three previously-controlled areas of British Columbia: the

Table 4. Locations and particulars of wolf-prey population research in Canada during the 1980's and 1990's.

Area	Period	Prey	Principal Researcher	Institution or Agency	Published References
1. La Vérendrye Reserve, Quebec	1980 1984	moose	F. Messier	Univ. B.C.	Messier 1984 Messier 1985a&b Messier & Crete 1985
2. Papineau-Labelle Reserve, Quebec	1980-1984	white-tailed deer	F. Potvin H. Jolicoeur	Ministère de Loisir, de la Chasse et de la Pêche, Que.	Potvin et al. 1988 Potvin et al. 1992a Potvin et al. 1992b
3. Algonquin Park, Ontario	1989*	white-tailed deer and moose	J. Theberge	Univ. of Waterloo, World Wildlife Fund	
4. Riding Mountain National Park, Manitoba	1978*	elk, deer and moose	L. Carbyn P. Paquet	Canadian Wildlife	Carbyn 1983b Paquet 1991a & 1992
5. Flathead, B.C.	1984*	elk, deer	R. Ream	Univ. of Montana	
6. Banff National Park, Alberta	1988*	elk, sheep, moose, deer	P. Paquet	Parks Canada	
7. Jasper National Park, Alberta	1989-1992	elk, sheep, moose, deer	J. Weaver	University of Montana	
8. Nordegg, Alberta	1983-1986	elk, sheep moose, deer, wild horse	J. Gunson P. Clarkson K. Schmidt	Alberta Fish and Wildlife	
9. Simonette River, Alberta	1975-1981	moose, deer, elk	R. Bjorge J. Gunson	Alberta Fish and Wildlife	Bjorge & Gunson 1989
10. Spatsizi Provincial Park, B.C.	1990*	elk, sheep, caribou, moose deer	D. Hatler	Spatsizi Wilderness Association	
11. Bathurst Inlet, Northwest Territories	1990*	migratory caribou	D. Heard	N.W.T. Renewable Res.	
12. Bluenose, Northwest Territories	1987*	migratory caribou	P. Clarkson	N.W.T. Renewable Res.	
13. Finlayson, Yukon Territory	1982*	woodland caribou, moose	R. Hayes A. Baer	Yukon Fish and Wildlife	Farnell & Hayes in preparation
14. Coast Mountains, Yukon	1983-1988	moose, sheep	R. Hayes A. Baer	Yukon Fish and Wildlife	Hayes et al. 1991
15. Kluane Game Sanctuary, Yukon	1984-1988	sheep, moose	R. Sumanik	Yukon Fish and Wildlife	Sumanik 1987
16. Northern Yukon Territory and Northwest Territories	1987*	migratory caribou, moose, sheep	R. Hayes A. Baer P. Clarkson D. Cooley	Yukon Fish and Wildlife and N.W.T. Renewable Res.	
17. Wood Buffalo National Park, Alberta	1978*	bison	L. Carbyn S. Oosenbrug	Univ. of Alta and Canadian Wildlife Serv.	Oosenbrug&Carbyn 1982 Carbyn&Trottier1987&88 Carbyn et al. 1993
18. Vancouver Island, B.C.	1980-1982	black-tailed deer	I. Hatter	B.C. Ministry of Environment	Hatter 1988 Jones & Mason 1983 Janz & Hatter 1986
19. Quesnel Highlands, B.C.	1984-1989	woodland caribou, moose	D. Seip D. Hebert	B.C. Ministry of Environment	Seip 1992a

* denotes study is continuing (as of 1992)

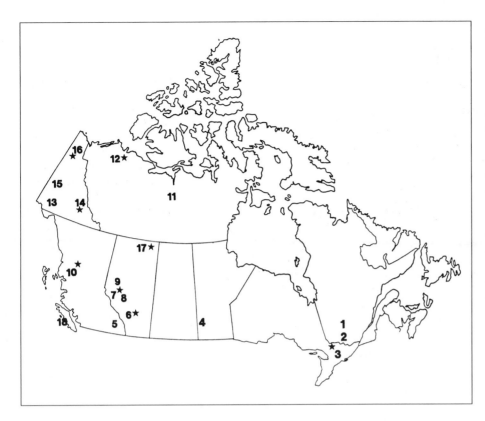

Fig. 7 *Areas in Canada where wolf radiotelemetry research was conducted during the 1980's and 1990's (see Table 4 for more information): 1) La Vérendrye Reserve, Quebec; 2) Papineau-Labelle Reserve, Quebec; 3) Algonquin Provincial Park, Ontario; 4) Riding Mountain National Park, Manitoba; 5) Flathead, B.C.; 6) Banff National Park, Alberta; 7) Jasper National Park, Alberta; 8) Nordegg, Alberta; 9) Simonette River, Alberta; 10) Spatsizi Provincial Park, B.C.; 11) Bathurst Inlet area, N.W.T.; 12) Bluenose, N.W.T.; 13) Coast Mountains, Yukon; 14) Finlayson, Yukon; 15) Kluane Game Sanctuary, Yukon; 16) Northern Yukon; 17) Wood Buffalo National Park, Alberta; 18) Vancouver Island, B.C.; 19) Quesnel Highlands, B.C. * ongoing study (as of 1992)*

Muskwa drainage, Quesnel Highlands, and Vancouver Island.

3. Trends in Human-Caused Mortality

Since 1986, a reported annual average of 4,025 wolves were either trapped, hunted, or taken because of depredation on livestock or wild ungulates. Human-caused mortality accounted for between 4–11% of provincial and territorial wolf numbers (Table 1). It was not possible to determine if there were areas where wolves were being overharvested because most management agencies do not collect area-specific harvest data. Some local populations at the edge of wolf ranges are expected to experience the highest harvest rates (Theberge 1991). Minimum mortality rates of about 30–40% of early winter populations (Keith 1983, Fuller 1989) are required to cause wolf numbers to decline the following year.

Wolf Research Programs

Nineteen wolf research projects using radiotelemetry were conducted in Canada during the 1980's and 1990's (Fig. 7, Table 4). Nine projects were conducted in the western mountain ranges of British Columbia, Alberta, and Yukon. Five of these were conducted in the eastern slopes of the Rocky Mountain, along the Alberta-British Columbia border. All studies examined aspects of wolf ecology in relation to natural prey populations (Table 4).

There have been recent, positive changes in park management that encourage the study of park wildlife systems.

During the 1980's and 1990's, wolf/prey research was initiated in Spatsizi Provincial Park, British Columbia; Jasper and Banff National Parks, Alberta; Wood Buffalo National Park, Alberta and Northwest Territories; Ivvavik National Park and Kluane National Park Reserve, Yukon; and Algonquin Provincial Park, Ontario.

Research in Quebec included the study of wolf predation rates on moose in La Vérendrye Reserve (Messier 1985a, Messier and Crete 1985) and wolf predation on deer in Papineau-Labelle Reserve (Potvin 1988, Potvin et al. 1988, 1992a,b, Potvin et al. 1988, 1992a,b). Canadian research in the 1980's also expanded to include ecological studies of migratory arctic wolves. The relationship of wolf denning ecology and availability of the Bathurst caribou herd is under study in the Northwest Territories. Studies of the life history and population dynamics of migratory arctic wolves are continuing in the range of Bluenose caribou herd (P. Clarkson, N.W.T. Renewable Resources, unpubl. data) and the Porcupine caribou herd in Yukon. The Yukon Fish and Wildlife Branch has been studying functional and numerical responses of wolves to rapidly increasing moose and caribou density in the Finlayson area.

There are currently nine active wolf research projects in Canada involving radiotelemetry (Fig. 7). In addition to telemetry studies, wolves are being monitored on Vancouver Island to measure recovery rates following control and to determine impacts of wolf predation on black-tailed deer (*Odocoileus hemionus*). In the Northwest Territories, wolf carcass studies have been carried out on the ranges of the

Fig. 8 *Percentage of area in each province and territory where wolves are protected by law. (Includes these national parks where natives are allowed to hunt wolves for subsistence purposes: Wood Buffalo, Baffin, Nahanni, Kluane, and Ivvavik). * includes Cold Lake Air Weapons Range*

Bathurst and Kaminuriak caribou herds to determine physical characteristics, reproductive ecology, and food habits. Similar studies were reported by Parker and Luttich (1986) for wolves in the George River caribou herd range in Labrador. Williams (1990) examined denning behavior and ecology of arctic wolves in the western arctic. Wolf-wood bison (*Bison bison athabascae*) relations in Wood Buffalo National Park, Alberta were studied during the 1980's and 1990's (Oosenbrug and Carbyn 1982, Carbyn and Trottier 1987, 1988, Carbyn et al. 1993).

Wolf Management Planning

Alberta (Alberta Fish and Wildlife 1991), Saskatchewan (Seguin 1991), and Yukon (Yukon Wolf Mgmt. Planning Team 1992) recently completed wolf management plans or strategies. British Columbia and Manitoba are in the planning process. Ontario, Quebec, and N.W.T. do not have recent policies for wolf management.

Public groups have recently participated in wolf management planning in Alaska (Alaska Dept. Fish and Game 1991), Yukon (Yukon Wolf Mgmt. Planning Team 1992) and British Columbia. The B.C. Wolf Working Group was initiated in 1988 but has yet to develop a management plan for wolves.

Protected Areas

Wolves are protected from human exploitation in 218,000 km² of Canada; about 2.7% of the land area. The percentage of protected areas varies regionally (Fig. 8), ranging from 0–9%. Protected areas include five national parks where natives are allowed to hunt and trap for subsistence purposes. Some protected wolves are hunted, trapped, or killed in defence of livestock near boundaries of parks and reserves because pack territories and seasonal migratory movements are not limited to core protected areas. The World Wildlife Fund (Hummel 1990) proposed the development of "Large Carnivore Conservation Areas" to protect wolves, brown bears (*Ursus arctos*), cougars (*Felis concolor*), and wolverine (*Gulo gulo*) in Canada. Theberge (1991) proposed increasing wolf protection areas in Canada, based on wolf ecological classifications.

Important Management Problems

The impact of wolf predation on caribou was the most common problem of wolf/ungulate management in Canada. The implications of prey switching from a primary predator (moose, white-tailed deer) to low density caribou herds is a conservation concern in Labrador, Manitoba, Saskatchewan, Alberta, British Columbia, and Yukon. In the Northwest Territories, there is growing concern for wolf predation on declining Peary caribou on Banks Island (P. Clarkson, N.W.T. Ren. Res., Inuvik, pers. commun.). In other parts of the arctic islands, Miller (this volume) speculated that wolf density is below the theoretical maximum carrying capacity. Arctic wolves are the least researched wolves in Canada. Recent general declines in Peary caribou (*Rangifer tarandus*

Table 5. Response of management agencies to questions regarding communication of wolf management problems in Canada.

QUESTION	B.C.	ALTA	YUKON	N.W.T.	SASK.	MAN.	ONT.	QUEBEC	LABR.
Are wolf managers communicating?	NO	YES	YES	YES	NO	NO	NO	NO	NO
Do you know about the I.U.C.N. Wolf Specialist Group?	YES	YES	YES	YES	YES	YES	YES	NO	NO
Do you know Canadian membership?	NO	YES	YES	YES	NO	NO	N/A	NO	NO

pearyi) throughout the area have prompted interest in wolf control in some arctic communities (A. Gunn, N.W.T. Ren. Resourc., pers. commun.). Research on arctic wolf populations and their relations with prey should be increased to better manage these highly vulnerable wolves.

Other management concerns include: 1) developing ways to maintain corridors in expanding wolf range in Alberta to assist the recovery of wolves in the northwestern United States; 2) determining the numerical response of wolves to changing density of large barren-ground caribou herds in the Northwest Territories, Yukon, and northern Quebec and Labrador; 3) assessing the impact of uncontrolled forest roads on wolf movements and wolf predation rates on ungulates in British Columbia; and 4) determining whether wolves will regulate ungulate prey to a single stable state in Yukon.

Communication among Biologists Responsible for Wolf Management

Communication among biologists responsible for wolf management is divided geographically (Table 5). Only Alberta, Yukon, and N.W.T. felt that wolf management problems were being communicated adequately. The western provinces and territories have formed a carnivore technical committee to inform and seek inter-agency advice on common problems of wolf and other carnivore management. Biologists in the eastern provinces knew the least about the International Union of Conservation of Nature (IUCN) Wolf Specialist Group or the Canadian membership. Canadian members (L.N. Carbyn, Can. Wildl. Serv., J. Theberge, Univ. of Waterloo, and R. Hayes, Yukon Fish and Wildl. Br.) annually meet with other Wolf Specialist Group experts to discuss global wolf issues. Regular meetings of all Canadian wolf managers and researchers should be considered.

Wolf Value Enhancement

There is growing public interest in managing wildlife populations for their intrinsic value and for viewing (Strickland 1983). Within Canada, there are few programs that encourage wolf viewing. Wolf howling programs are located in some national and provincial parks and reserves. Little effort is spent on the interpretation of wolves in wildlife viewing programs.

Wolves pose one of the most difficult wildlife management problems in Canada because they often fall within a negative economic sphere (Carbyn 1987). Our review showed a low value placed on the knowledge of wolf population trends throughout Canada, and widely different wolf hunting practices and seasons. The wolf is currently the only big game animal in Canada that is hunted year-round, has no bag limits in most areas, and does not require special seals or licences to hunt. Management agencies should reconsider harvest management regulations to reflect changes in public ethics and growing understanding of wolf biology. In areas where wolves are not being actively controlled or regulated, bag limits should be set by reasonable public expectation and ability, and seasons should be restricted to encourage the survival of pups and reflect the maximum fur or trophy value. Public interest in conserving wolves is growing in Canada, as indeed it is throughout North America and the world. By recognizing these trends, Canada will be better positioned to develop strategies that can both facilitate wolf conservation and wolf population control.

The Future of Wolves in Canada

The future of wolves in Canada appears bright. Limited control programs for livestock, and the reluctance of management agencies to engage in wolf control for ungulate recovery, has allowed wolf populations to increase and continue to reoccupy former ranges in Canada. No management agency reported wolves were threatened with extirpation by hunting, trapping, industrial development,

Two historical photographs depicting predator control activities in northwestern Canada during the 1950's. Similar programs were carried out in Alaska at the time. These control activities followed the intensive wolf extermination efforts carried out in the first half of the 20th century in the western United States. (Photos: W.A. Fuller).

inbreeding, hybridization (dog or coyotes), or the absence of prey. Wolf range is not expected to shrink significantly in any area of Canada.

Wolves are thought to be a factor presently limiting the size of certain caribou herds in all provinces and territories. Ontario, Quebec, Manitoba, and the Northwest Territories indicated there were no empirical data to show wolves were limiting moose, but the other provinces and Yukon indicated wolves were important. Deer are presently thought to be limited by wolf predation on Vancouver Island, and in regions of Quebec. In Alberta, wolves are limiting the recovery of various ungulates including: woodland caribou in west-central area (Edmonds 1988), moose in

the northeast (Fuller and Keith 1980), elk on the eastern slopes (Gunson 1992), and wood bison in Wood Buffalo National Park (Carbyn et al. 1993). All agencies indicated that hunting or weather events may be more important than wolves in initiating population declines. In five areas (Alberta, Yukon, Manitoba, Quebec, and Labrador), research data suggest that wolf predation is a primary factor presently limiting the recovery of some low density ungulate populations.

All provinces and territories indicated that there is currently inadequate data to manage wolf/prey relations. Priority for wolf research should be increased in parts of Canada to improve our knowledge of wolf/prey dynamics and develop adaptive management strategies for wolves. We also believe that additional experimental reductions of wolf populations will be necessary to restore threatened woodland caribou herds.

The abundance of natural prey and their habitat is what currently limits the distribution of wolves in Canada. At the southern edges of wolf range, the alienation of natural habitat

will continue to restrict where wolves can range. There are many wilderness areas that have low density ungulates for natural and human-caused reasons. The management of healthy and viable wolf populations in Canada will depend on how wildlife agencies protect these populations and their habitats.

The continued success of the wolf as a natural carnivore in Canada will require that adequate prey populations remain available. This will require careful attention to sustainable use of wolves and their prey, and to classical preservation (park) models. The application of these conservation models must be sensitive to the regional differences in human interest in wolves and their prey, as well as to the national view of the wolf as a carnivore and a symbol of Canada's wilderness.

Cooperators

The authors thank the following cooperators for promptly completing questionnaires:

British Columbia: V. Banci, Acting Fur/Carnivore Specialist. Wildlife Branch, B.C. Environment, Land and Parks, 780 Blanshard St., Victoria, B.C., V8V 1X5

Northwest Territories: M. Williams. N.W.T. Renewable Resources. Box 1320 Yellowknife, N.W.T. X1A 2L9. Peter Clarkson, N.W.T. Renewable Resources, Inuvik, N.W.T., X0E 1E0

Saskatchewan: R. Sequin. Saskatchewan Parks and Renewable Resources, Box 5890, Meadow Lake, Saskatchewan, S0M 1V0

Manitoba: D. Pastuck. Manitoba Department of Natural Resources, Wildlife Branch, Box 24, 1495 St. James St., Winnipeg, Manitoba, P3H 0W9

Ontario: R. Rosatte. Ontario Ministry of Natural Resources, Wildlife Research Section. Box 5000, Maple, Ontario. L6A 1S9 and H. Smith, Ontario Ministry of Natural Resources, Wildlife Policy Branch, 90 Sheppard Ave. East, North York, Ontario.

Quebec: H. Jolicoeur. Gouvernement du Quebec, Ministère de Loisir, de la Chasse et de la Pêche. 150 Est. Boul. Saint-Cyrille, Quebec, G1R 4Y1

New Brunswick: G. Redmond. New Brunswick Fish and Wildlife Branch. Department of Natural Resources and Energy. Box 600, Fredericton, New Brunswick.

Labrador/Newfoundland: S. Luttich, Newfoundland Wildlife Branch, Box 488 Stn. C., Goose Bay, Labrador.

Acknowledgments

H. Slamma summarized wild fur and wolf harvest statistics. T. Rodger drafted the maps and figures.

Status of Wolves on the Canadian Arctic Islands

■ Frank L. Miller

*Three subspecific forms of the gray wolf (**Canis lupus** spp.) have been recognized in the Canadian Arctic Archipelago: **C. l. arctos** (Pocock 1935), **C. l. bernardi** (Anderson 1943), and **C. l. manningi** (Anderson 1943). Wolf numbers and densities are low throughout the archipelago, although there are more wolves on Baffin Island and the southern Arctic Islands than on the Queen Elizabeth Islands. Caribou (**rangifer tarandus** spp.) and muskoxen (**Ovibos moschatus**) are the only large prey available to wolves. The potential number of wolves was estimated, based on the number of ungulate prey at a rate of one wolf per 100 prey. Estimates are currently about 200 **C. l. arctos** on the Queen Elizabeth Islands; 1,100 on the southern tier of Arctic Islands; and 2,100 **C. l. manningi** on Baffin Island. Only tentative conclusions can be drawn about the status of wolves within these three major regions of the Canadian Arctic Archipelago: 1) wolves classified as **C. l. bernardi** appear to have become extinct on Banks Island between 1918 and 1952; 2) supposition about **C. l. bernardi** having also occurred on at least northwestern Victoria Island remains unsubstantiated by fact, as **bernardi** is known only from its type locality on southwest Banks Island; 3) the validity of **bernardi** as a distinct subspecies of **Canis lupus** remains debatable; that is, did those eight wolves used to describe the subspecies represent a valid subspecies or were they merely immigrants from the mainland; 4) wolves (**C. l. manningi**) are common, but at low densities on Baffin Island and their overall number does not appear to approach their extrapolated current "theoretical maximum carrying capacity" of approximately 2,100; 5) wolves (**C. l. arctos**) generally occur at low densities and are often rare or absent in large areas throughout the southern tier of Arctic Islands; thus, those wolves do not appear to even closely approach their currently extrapolated "theoretical maximum carrying capacity" of approximately 1,100; and 6) wolves (**C. l. arctos**), with a few local exceptions, generally occur at low densities and are rare or absent over large areas throughout the Queen Elizabeth Islands; however, they currently may be near or at their extrapolated low "theoretical maximum carrying capacity" of 200.*

Introduction

The Canadian Arctic Archipelago (approximately 1.3 million km^2) is the northern apex of the North American continent and its most remote and isolated region. Known primarily for its extremes in harsh, prolonged, wintry weather and the long "polar night," the Arctic Archipelago is locked in sea ice and thus fastened to the Canadian mainland for most of each year. In stark contrast to the long winter, during the brief, cool polar summer, the Arctic Archipelago comes alive in a flush of plant and animal life. In this setting, a meagre array of terrestrial mammals have adapted to the severities of the polar winter to live on the Arctic Archipelago year-round. The gray wolf is the only large land carnivore found throughout the Canadian Arctic Islands, although the ice-bound waters of the Arctic Archipelago are the domain of the polar bear (*Ursus maritimus*). Only two ungulate species serve as major prey for those wolves: the caribou and the muskox.

Systematic information on numbers and distributions of wolves on the Canadian Arctic Archipelago is lacking.

Therefore, I approached the status of the wolves through an examination of numbers of ungulate prey available to support wolves.

Materials and Methods

Three subspecies of the North American gray wolf have been described for the Canadian Arctic Islands: 1) *C. l. arctos*, Pocock (1935), first called the "American arctic wolf" by Pocock, but renamed the "Canadian polar wolf" by Anderson (1946). It was described for the Queen Elizabeth Islands, but was likely found throughout the entire archipelago, except in the Baffin Island region; 2) *C. l. bernardi*, Anderson (1943), the "Banks Island tundra wolf," known only for southwest Banks Island (although originally suggested for, but not found on, northwest Victoria Island), and currently considered to have become extinct some time between 1918 and 1952 and of doubtful subspecific position (Manning and Macpherson 1958); and 3) *C. l. manningi*, Anderson (1943), the "Baffin Island tundra wolf," known only for Baffin Island, but most recently placed by Nowak (this volume) in the mainland race (*C. l. nubilus*. Nowak also includes the adjacent mainland race *C. l. hudsonicus* in *C. l. nubilus*). *C. l. arctos* is described as a medium-sized wolf, but smaller than coastal mainland arctic races and with a narrower brain case (Pocock 1935, Young and Goldman 1944). *C. l. bernardi* is considered to be a relatively large but rangy wolf, with a long narrow skull (Anderson 1943, Young and Goldman 1944). *C. l. manningi* is smaller than other arctic races and with a much smaller and less massive skull than *arctos* (Anderson 1943, Young and Goldman 1944).

Wolves on the Arctic Islands are typically white or whitish in appearance (Fig. 1A and 2). The white wolves of Ellesmere Island have received detailed photographic coverage in two popular books (Mech 1988b, Brandenburg 1991). The prevailing white coloration of some individuals is altered by a greater prevalence of black-tipped hairs on the dorsum and especially along the median dorsal line and across the upper side of the tail near the base. Even otherwise completely white wolves tend to have a small blackish area across the upper side of the tail associated with a clump of

stiff black-tipped hairs that surround the precaudal gland located on the back approximately 7 cm above the base of the tail (e.g., Mech 1970). I have seen some wolves (possibly immature animals) on the Arctic Islands, however, that could best be described as reddish-buff, greyish, dusky, or, on one occasion, even black.

Many arctic-island wolves, at least among those on the Queen Elizabeth Islands, are bold, readily investigate humans or their camps, and often behave like shy dogs when coaxed by humans (Fig. 1B). Wolves on the Queen Elizabeth Islands have been bold enough to visit occupied weather stations, exploration camps, and field camps; to come within touching distance of humans; to take food from the extended hand of a person; to carry off novel objects; and even to lick the face of a person (Miller 1978). Bold investigative behavior has, however, on occasion led to the demise of wolves (e.g., Grace 1976, Miller 1978).

In the absence of essentially any systematically collected quantitative data on past or present numbers of wolves on the Canadian Arctic Archipelago, I have estimated an index to the numbers of wolves based on the "theoretical maximum carrying capacities" for wolves on the Canadian Arctic Islands in terms of their available ungulate prey. I have approximated the possible trends in wolf numbers (trend directions and magnitudes) over the last three decades (1961–90) from changes in the reported estimated numbers of caribou and muskoxen and hearsay evidence. When survey estimates do not extend back to 1960, related literature about generalized trends and relative numbers of caribou and muskoxen in those areas was used to support generalizations about likely changes in wolf numbers over the entire period. Those extrapolations allow only approximations of the potential status of wolves on the Canadian Arctic Islands. They do, however, permit some insight into the status or possible status of those wolves when considering the need for their

A

B

Fig. 1 *Wolves on western Melville Island, Northwest Territories: (A) white wolf in short summer pelage; and (B) three wolves closely investigating the author. Note variation in early August pelage condition among individual wolves. (Photo: H.J. Russell)*

Fig. 2 *The flexibility of wolf behavior allowed the species a wide range of distribution from the High Arctic of Canada to the arid zones in northern Mexico. The winter pelage of these arctic wolves gives the animal a different appearance from that in the summer (see Fig. 1A). (Photo L.D. Mech)*

Wolves in a Changing World

conservation. The approach is simplistic but is a biologically sound starting point for an otherwise undocumented subject.

I calculated a mean rate of kill from Keith (1983:76, Table 10) of 32.3 days' time lapse per wolf per ungulate and assumed that it applied roughly to the entire year. Thus, I obtained an average of 11.3 ungulates killed per year per wolf. The body weights of caribou and muskoxen mostly fall intermediate to those ungulate species reported by Keith (white-tailed deer (*Odocoileus virginianus*), elk (*Cervus elaphus*), and moose (*Alces alces*)). Most importantly, no data exist for evaluating the probable ratios of ungulate prey used by arctic-island wolves by species (caribou *versus* muskoxen) or by sex/age classes of either species. Therefore, I did not calculate an "ungulate biomass index," as I had no way of assigning any level of confidence to such a refinement of this exercise. Based on existing data, any rate of annual kill by wolves in excess of 10% (excluding newborn calves) together with other additional natural mortality (even in the absence of human hunting) would likely tax ungulate populations on the Arctic Islands beyond their sustainable capacities. Thus, I chose an annual mean rate of kill of 10% at an overall mean density of 100 ungulates per wolf as a reasonable measure to use in my calculation of the "theoretical maximum carrying capacities" for wolves on the Cana-

dian Arctic Islands. The ratio of one wolf per 100 ungulates agrees with the equilibrium value of one wolf per 100 deer suggested by Pimlott (1967a:276). The extrapolations of past and present populations of ungulate prey available to wolves on the Arctic Islands are drawn from a wide array of sources: Queen Elizabeth Islands, 22 references; southern Arctic Islands, 22 references; and Baffin Island, seven references (see Miller 1993 for complete references to those data sources).

Results and Discussion

Queen Elizabeth Islands

All of the islands lying north of the Parry Channel water passage in the Canadian Arctic Archipelago (Fig. 3: north of 74° N latitude) are collectively known as the Queen Elizabeth Islands. Peary caribou (*R. t. pearyi*) and muskoxen are the two major prey available to wolves on those islands. There is indirect evidence that at least some wolves have learned to hunt seals (*Phoca hispida* or *Erignathus barbatus*) at breathing holes in the sea ice (Stirling and Archibald 1977). Some wolves also are known to scavenge on seal carcasses left on the sea ice from polar bear kills (Stirling and Archibald 1977). Arctic hares (*Lepus arcticus*) could be

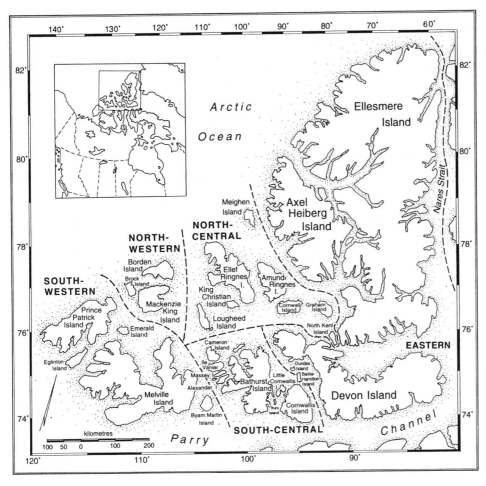

Fig. 3 *Current northern range of the Canadian High Arctic form of gray wolf (**Canis lupus arctos**): Queen Elizabeth Islands divided into five areas of relative importance based on estimated size of potential ungulate prey base (after Miller, 1993).*

locally and seasonally important in the diets of wolves, at least in years of hare population highs, especially on the eastern islands. Arctic foxes (*Alopex lagopus*), lemmings (*Dicrostonyx torquatus*), and a wide variety of birds and their eggs in summer could also contribute to the wolves' sustenance on these islands.

Most of the collective landmass of the Queen Elizabeth Islands has no value in terms of forage production for caribou, and particularly for muskoxen. Permanent snow and ice, unsuitable substrata (calcareous bedrock), and areas too wet or too dry prevent or limit forage growth. Most importantly, periods of widespread, unfavorable snow and ice restrict forage availability and have in the past (e.g., Parker et al. 1975, Miller et al. 1977), and will in the future, lead to major or catastrophic winter die-offs of both caribou and muskoxen. The fluctuations of potential prey may prevent the wolves on the Queen Elizabeth Islands from ever normally exceeding 500 > 1-year-old wolves for many consecutive years, based on my empirical assumption that a maximum sustainable carrying capacity for ungulates would approximate 40,000 > 1-year-old animals at three caribou for every two muskoxen. The potential "theoretical maximum carrying capacity" for wolves on the Queen Elizabeth Islands has declined by one-third over three decades (1961-

90), based on an extrapolation of aerial survey results for caribou and muskoxen from 1961 to 1990.

The recent loss of the caribou and fixed stringent limitations on the maximum population size of *C. l. arctos* on the Queen Elizabeth Islands makes the welfare of those wolves a pressing concern. Providing some form of protection for *C. l. arctos* on the Queen Elizabeth Islands is problematic because one of its principal prey items, the Peary caribou, is recognized as an "endangered" form of wildlife in Canada (Miller 1990). Most Inuit hunters view wolves mainly as competitors for caribou (and occasionally for muskoxen), because caribou are generally the preferred source of fresh red meat in the diets of high arctic Inuit. Additionally, a prime wolf pelt has considerable cash value in a cash-hungry economy, and wolf fur is also sought for domestic use.

Only 6% of the extrapolated size of the entire ungulate prey base on the Canadian Arctic Archipelago currently occurs on the Queen Elizabeth Islands which currently could then support only one-sixteenth (n = 205) of the "theoretical maximum carrying capacity" for wolves on all the Arctic Islands (Table 1). These wolves are most likely the purest stock of *C. l. arctos* on the archipelago. The Queen Elizabeth Islands represent a discrete and unique high arctic "ecoregion" in Canada. Phenotypically and, apparently, genetically

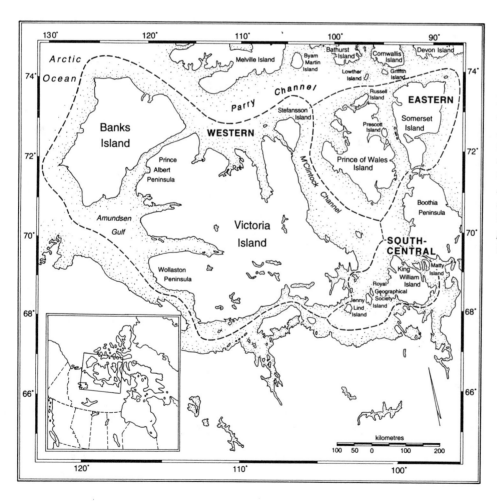

Fig. 4 *Current southern range of the Canadian Arctic form of gray wolf (**Canis lupus arctos**) and past range of the Banks Island tundra wolf (**Canis lupus bernardi**): Southern tier of Arctic Islands divided into three areas of relative importance based on estimated size of potential ungulate prey base (after Miller, 1993).*

Table 1. Theoretical maximum carrying capacities and related statistics for wolves in the three major regions of the Canadian Arctic Archipelago, based on a ratio of one wolf per 100 ungulates.

| Region[1] | Size (km²) | % of Canadian Arctic Archipelago | Ungulate prey base | | Theoretical maximum carrying capacity for wolves | km²/wolf |
			Size of prey base	Mean density (/100km²)		
QEI	415 310	31.6	20 500	4.9	205	2026
STI	365 880	27.8	111 300	30.4	1113	329
BIR	534 893	40.6	210 000	39.3	2100	255
(CAA)[2]	1 316 083	100.0	341 800	26.0	3418	385

1 Regions: QEI, Queen Elizabeth Islands; STI, Southern tier of Arctic Islands; and BIR, Baffin Island Region.

2 CAA equals entire Canadian Arctic Archipelago

C. l. arctos is a clearly recognizable subspecies. However, their current overall number is low and future numbers are not likely to exceed several hundred wolves even under the most favorable of sustainable prey densities. There is also a strong likelihood of future, large-scale nonrenewable resource exploitation on the Queen Elizabeth Islands. Therefore, *Canis lupus arctos* on the Queen Elizabeth Islands warrants recognition as a potentially "threatened," if not "endangered," form of North American gray wolf in Canada.

Southern Tier of Arctic Islands

The southern Arctic Islands are all the islands lying south of the Parry Channel water passage: (Fig. 4: south of 74° N latitude), but excluding the Baffin Island region. Muskoxen and arctic-island caribou (*R. t. groenlandicus* x *pearyi*) are the available large prey. Seals, at least as carrion, could be important in winter. Periodically, high numbers of arctic foxes could contribute notably to the diets of wolves. Arctic hares may be of secondary importance; lemmings and a wide array of birds and their eggs could also be seasonally well-represented in the diets of wolves.

The productivity of plants is higher than on the Queen Elizabeth Islands. There is, however, evidence that large areas of the southern Arctic Islands can suffer significant losses of the ungulate prey base from winter die-off (caused by extreme undernutrition) due to widespread forage unavailability brought on by prolonged periods of unfavorable snow/ice conditions (e.g., McEwan 1955, Manning and Macpherson 1958, Morrison 1978).

The potential "theoretical maximum carrying capacity" for wolves on the southern Arctic Islands has apparently increased by 3.3 times during the past two or three decades, mostly from significant increases in muskoxen on the south-

western islands. Wolf numbers were apparently slow to increase in response to increases in ungulate prey. Hunters from Holman on Victoria Island have only recently observed greater numbers of wolves, suggesting that wolf numbers have been increasing since mid 1980's after being low for decades (A. Gunn, Dep. Renew. Res., Gov. N.W.T., Yellowknife, pers. commun.). Until the late 1980's and early 1990's, hunters from Sachs Harbour on Banks Island reported few wolves. Gunn et al. (1991) speculated that the high numbers of arctic foxes maintained epidemics of canine distemper and rabies which held the wolves down. In any event, by the late 1980's and early 1990's, hunters reported more wolves: in autumn 1992, 36 wolves were killed. However, Sachs Harbour hunters had previously reported killing only 19 wolves, or six wolves annually between 1989 and 1991 (P. Clarkson, Dep. Renew. Res., Gov. N.W.T., Inuvik, pers. commun.).

The genome of wolves on the southern Arctic Islands almost certainly has been influenced by breeding with mainland wolves and may, in turn, have influenced the coastal mainland wolves. Prior to the 1940's, tens, if not hundreds, of thousands of barren-ground and intergrade caribou crossed the sea ice annually in spring from mainland winter ranges to calve and summer on the southern tier of islands, usually returning in autumn to the mainland (e.g., Hoare 1927, Manning 1960). Those migrations of caribou were undoubtedly accompanied by wolves. Some wolves might have remained on southern islands and, over time, some could have mixed with the original resident island wolves (most likely *C. l. arctos*). Likewise, some island wolves may have bred with mainland wolves. Seasonal remnant migrations of caribou from the mainland to summer ranges on the southern Arctic Islands began again in the 1980's and now involve thousands of caribou (A. Gunn, Dep. Renew. Res., Gov. N.W.T., Coppermine, pers. commun.) and those migrations are accompanied by wolves: tracks indicate wolves crossing the straits in both directions. Therefore, the taxonomic position(s) of wolves on the southern tier of Arctic Islands is unclear and needs further investigation, including examination of DNA to shed light on current and, if possible, past occurrences.

The possibility of contagious canid disease (rabies or canine distemper) sporadically or periodically markedly reducing wolf numbers on the southern Arctic Islands (or all the Arctic Islands) cannot be ruled out, especially if arctic foxes are the source carriers for such disease. Disease alternatingly or in combination with widespread loss of ungulate prey likely are the long-term limitations or regulation of wolves within this region.

Currently, about one-third of the ungulate prey base available to wolves on the Canadian Arctic Archipelago is found on the southern Arctic Islands. Therefore, the current "theoretical maximum carrying capacity" for wolves on the southern tier of Arctic Islands (n = 1113) is 33% of the wolves on all Arctic Islands (Table 1). The literature suggests that value represents a 70% increase in ungulates within this region in the last two or three decades. The southern Arctic Islands will likely remain an important region for wolves on the Canadian Arctic Archipelago, but the taxonomic status and genetic uniqueness of those wolves is essentially unknown.

Baffin Island Region

The Baffin Island region forms the southeastern flank of the Canadian Arctic Archipelago and includes Baffin Island, its principal satellite island of Bylot, 10 other major satellite islands, and many lesser satellite islands (Fig. 5). The only major prey for wolves within this region is barren-ground caribou (*R. t. groenlandicus*). Seals, arctic hares, arctic foxes, red foxes (*Vulpes vulpes*), lemmings, and a wide array

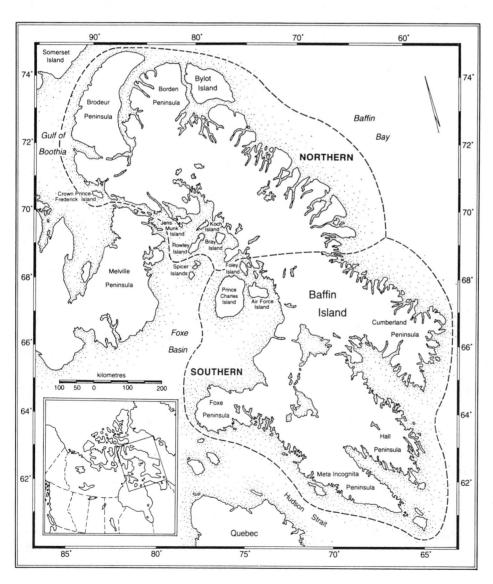

Fig. 5 *Current range of the Baffin Island tundra wolf (**Canis lupus manningi**): Baffin Island region divided into two areas of relative importance, based on estimated size of potential ungulate prey base (after Miller, 1993).*

of birds and their eggs could also contribute, at least seasonally, to the diets of those wolves. Wolverines (*Gulo gulo*) would be a rare dietary item at most.

Although much of the range in the Baffin Island region is unsuitable for year-round caribou use, the vastness of the remaining usable range apparently allows relatively high-density populations of caribou to build up. Mean density of caribou on Baffin Island is probably 24–59 caribou/100 km^2. Thus, the actual current "theoretical maximum carrying capacity" for wolves should fall somewhere between at least 1,200 and 3,000 wolves within the entire Baffin Island region.

The best informed guess for the current number of caribou on Baffin Island is 120,000–300,000 (M.A.D. Ferguson, Dep. Renew. Res., Gov. N.W.T., Pond Inlet, pers. commun.). I have chosen the mid-point value (210,000) of Ferguson's wide-range approximation and thus assumed that currently about three-fifths of the ungulate prey base on the Canadian Arctic Archipelago is found in the Baffin Island region. Therefore, the current "theoretical maximum carrying capacity" for wolves in the Baffin Island region (n = 2,100) is 61% of the wolves on all Arctic Islands (Table 1). It is unknown how much more the caribou population can or will grow, or how accurate the recent and current impressions are about the size and distribution of the caribou population on Baffin Island. If the current size is close to 300,000 caribou, a decline is probable as the population has a history of fluctuations. Currently, and barring cataclysmic loss of the caribou or contagious endemic canine disease, wolves should continue to populate the Baffin Island region. As there are no alternate ungulate prey on Baffin Island, the wolves will sharply fluctuate with the caribou.

Whether *C. l. arctos* from the Queen Elizabeth Islands or southern Arctic Islands, *C. l. orion* from Greenland, or some mainland race (possibly, *C. l. hudsonicus* or *C. l. labradorius*) has in the recent past or will in the near future invade the Baffin Island region is problematic in the absence of any genetic study of the wolves. The need for additional evaluations of the taxonomic standing and the genetics of wolves on Baffin Island has become more apparent with Nowak's conclusion that *C. l. manningi* should be considered as belonging to the *C. l. nubilus* mainland race (Nowak this volume). Therefore, examination of old and new wolf specimens from Baffin Island, including the use of new DNA procedures, could be fruitful in clarifying the taxonomic position(s) of Baffin Island wolves.

Conservation and Management Implications

Like all other interrelationships in the natural world, the importance of wolf predation on caribou and muskoxen on the Arctic Islands is interwoven in a maze of ecological intricacies. Thus, we are unlikely to understand fully the importance of wolf predation on these ungulates, both of

which fluctuate widely in numbers but not necessarily in synchrony.

The high arctic wolf is an important component in the biodiversity of the Canadian Arctic Archipelago and, as a distinct subspecies of the North American gray wolf, it warrants protection as a valuable part of Canada's natural heritage. This issue now becomes complicated, however, because caribou on the Queen Elizabeth Islands and on Banks Island are classified as "endangered," and caribou on the other southern Arctic Islands (excluding the Baffin Island region) are classified as "threatened."

If caribou were the only ungulate on the Arctic Islands, the problem of wolf predation on caribou would seemingly be simple, as wolves would have declined as caribou declined. Muskoxen do occur throughout most of the archipelago (except the Baffin Island region), however, and currently are more numerous than caribou. On Banks Island there are 50 muskoxen estimated for every one caribou and there are on average more than three muskoxen for every one caribou throughout the entire southern tier of Arctic Islands. Muskoxen on the Queen Elizabeth Islands are four times more common than caribou. Wolves probably prey preferentially on caribou which are smaller than adult muskoxen (of either sex), as wolves supposedly prefer medium-sized over larger prey when both are available (e.g., Pimlott et al. 1969, Potvin et al. 1988). High numbers of muskoxen, especially with an abundance of calves and yearlings present, could support wolves which preferentially kill caribou whenever possible. Thus, alternative preferential predation could become a key factor in accelerating a decline or impeding a recovery of caribou in areas with high densities of muskoxen.

In this situation the biologist is faced with the dilemma of needing to do everything possible to preserve and promote the growth of caribou populations as rapidly as possible to meet demands for subsistence utilization by Inuit living on the Arctic Islands, while at the same time recognizing the wolf's place in this ecosystem and its eminence as a symbol of Canada's wilderness.

Caribou on the Queen Elizabeth Islands and Banks Island have declined to dangerously low numbers, where the localized and judicious reduction of wolf numbers as a valid conservation tool in areas chosen for prime importance to caribou is being discussed. Any such removal of wolves would have to be localized so as not to threaten regional populations. My estimates suggest that there are likely only a couple of hundred wolves on the High Arctic Islands and they are assuredly the most developed form of a unique subspecies. The long-term goal should be maintenance of healthy, balanced populations of wolves, caribou, and muskoxen, wherever they occur in common, throughout the entire Canadian Arctic Archipelago.

Wolf numbers on the Canadian Arctic Archipelago probably have always been regulated by ongoing fluctuations in the numbers of ungulate prey. The history of caribou and muskox populations on the Arctic Islands is highly dynamic due largely to sporadic widespread forage scarcity brought on by unfavorable snow/ice conditions in winter or spring-time. Thus, both caribou and muskoxen are subject to major winter die-offs, sometimes at cataclysmic levels (such as in the winter of 1973–74 on the Queen Elizabeth Islands). Such large-scale winter die-offs apparently occur at various levels of severity every several years on major portions of the Canadian Arctic Archipelago. Thus, changes in the sizes of wolf populations could be rather volatile within a period of only a few years due to the relative scarcity of their ungulate prey. This is especially true for wolves on the Queen Elizabeth Islands, where mean ungulate densities are relatively low at the best of times.

The only other limiting factor that likely could have impacted significantly on wolves, either sporadically or periodically on local, extended, or essentially range-wide bases, is contagious endemic canid diseases (hunting could be important locally, at least on occasion). A canine distemper outbreak was detected in dogs and arctic foxes throughout the Canadian Arctic and Greenland in the late 1980's (Leighton et al. 1988). No data exist, however, for the frequency or intensity (importance) of such diseases among arctic-island wolves.

My review of the caribou-muskox prey base suggests that, simplistically, the highest number of wolves older than one year that currently could be supported on the Arctic Islands would be approximately 200 for *C. l. arctos* on the Queen Elizabeth Islands, approximately 1,100 wolves on the southern tier of Arctic Islands (some *C. l. arctos* but also some of unclear taxonomy), and approximately 2,100 wolves in the Baffin Island region, currently classified as *C. l. manningi*. There is no way to do more than guess at the present numbers but there is no known reason to believe that wolves are currently even approaching, let alone exceeding, those maximums, except on the Queen Elizabeth Islands where about 200 wolves may currently live. There is also no reason to doubt that the fortunes of the arctic wolf tracks the fate of its ungulate prey populations. Ultimately, the fate of arctic-island wolves will be determined by the long-term success of their major ungulate prey — the caribou and the muskox. At least this will be true in the absence of unforeseen catastrophic environmental events, either natural or human-induced.

Acknowledgments

I thank Department of Renewable Resources, Government of the Northwest Territories biologists P. Clarkson, M.A.D. Ferguson, A. Gunn, and B.D. McLean for providing unpublished data. I am grateful to Polar Continental Shelf Project (PCSP), Natural Resources Canada, for significant support of many of the caribou and muskox studies used in this paper and I thank B. Hrycyk, Director PCSP, for her continuing support of my Peary caribou studies. Dr. A. Gunn, Department of Renewable Resources, Government of the Northwest Territories, and F. D. Reintjes, Canadian Wildlife Service, critically read the manuscript and provided many helpful suggestions.

Wolf Biology and Management in Alaska 1981-92

■ **Robert O. Stephenson, Warren B. Ballard, Christian A. Smith,and Katharine Richardson**

Wolves remain widely distributed throughout their historic range in Alaska; the population is estimated at 5,900–7,200 and numbers have generally increased in recent years. Numerous long-range movements of dispersing wolves between regions in Alaska and Canada have been documented, emphasizing the mobility of wolves and potential for genetic exchange. Research during the decade continued to demonstrate the important role predation by wolves and bears often plays in ungulate population dynamics, sometimes contributing to chronically low densities. Predation by both black and brown bears is a major source of ungulate mortality in much of Alaska, particularly for moose calves. The effects of bear predation continued to confound the issue of wolf management. Although the past decade was marked by significant advances in understanding the ecology of wolves and their prey, controversy and litigation continued to characterize the management of wolves. Legal and political controversies focused on proposals for wolf reduction and the use of aircraft in hunting and trapping wolves. A process that sought to involve all segments of the public in the development of a statewide plan helped move wolf management in a more constructive direction.

Introduction

Harbo and Dean (1983) reviewed the history of wolf (*Canis lupus*) population status and management in Alaska through 1980. They described five major phases during this century: a period of indiscriminate and largely unsuccessful wolf control efforts prior to World War II; a period of intense federally sponsored control during the 1950's that significantly lowered wolf numbers in several areas of the state; a transitional phase between federal and state management during which biologists in the emerging Alaska Department of Fish and Game (ADF&G) increasingly challenged the need for federal wolf control in view of high (often excessive) ungulate numbers; a period following full state assumption of management authority in 1960 when wolves were reclassified from vermin to fur and game animals and all control efforts were halted; and finally a period of turmoil beginning in the early 1970's when ADF&G proposed limited control efforts in a few small areas following recovery of the wolf population and declines in prey numbers.

Rausch and Hinman (1977) also discussed changes in government policy and public perception of wolves and suggested that the future of wolf management in Alaska was uncertain because of strongly polarized views in the public. Harbo and Dean (1983) were more optimistic, concluding that professional and public attitudes had moderated in the face of improved knowledge of the impacts of wolf predation, and that litigation during the late 1970's had largely settled the issue of agency authority to implement wolf control programs. They also predicted that, "Wolf control will continue to become more of an operational process for ADF&G..." and expressed the hope that "...the future will be characterized by substantially increased knowledge of basic ecology and significantly more effective and mutually sympathetic communication between the many interested segments of society."

Harbo and Dean's (1983) predictions have not been borne out during the ensuing decade and their hope for better communication appears to have been premature. Although research did expand scientific awareness of the effects of wolf predation on ungulate population dynamics, opposition to wolf control strengthened in some segments of society. While some biologists and members of the public began the decade viewing wolf control as a routine part of management programs, opponents of control rallied forces and developed new legal and political strategies. The 1980's were marked by continued litigation and acrimonious debate, often characterized by misinformation or selective use of information about wolf-prey relationships. Late in the decade, as the demands for broader public involvement in decision making increased, ADF&G launched an initiative to develop public consensus on wolf management. This planning effort was designed to bring together people with diverse views who share a common interest in the long-term conservation of wolves and their prey.

Robert O. Stephenson, Warren B. Ballard, Christian A. Smith, and Katharine Richardson

This paper reviews wolf research and management during the 1980's and discusses their relationship to public debate. It begins with a discussion of the status and trends of populations followed by a review of recently completed and on-going research into wolf ecology. Finally, it chronicles major developments in the evolution of wolf management policies during the 1980's and offers a prognosis for the future.

Wolf Population Status in Alaska, 1981-1991

During the 1980's the distribution and abundance of wolves remained fairly stable in Alaska, although some increases in distribution and numbers have occurred. Wolves continued to be regularly distributed over most of their original range, occupying at least 85% of the state's 1,517,740 km². Autumn population density in closely studied populations ranged

from about two to 20 wolves/1,000 km² (Gasaway et al. 1983, 1992; Peterson et al. 1984; Ballard et al. 1987; Adams et al. 1989b; Mech et al. 1991). Wolves continue to be absent from areas which were not colonized after the last glacial recession, including the Aleutian, Kodiak, Admiralty, Baranof, and Chichagof Islands.

Radiotelemetry studies in Alaska and Yukon revealed that extensive movements of individuals and packs occur regularly (Fig. 1). Consequently, localized reductions due to human harvest of wolves are usually soon offset by immigration when harvest is reduced, and genetic exchange between regions appears to be common.

Although estimates of wolf numbers in Alaska were available prior to 1984, the methods and assumptions upon which they were based are unknown. In a review of wolf management in Alaska, Harper (1970) stated that, "A con-

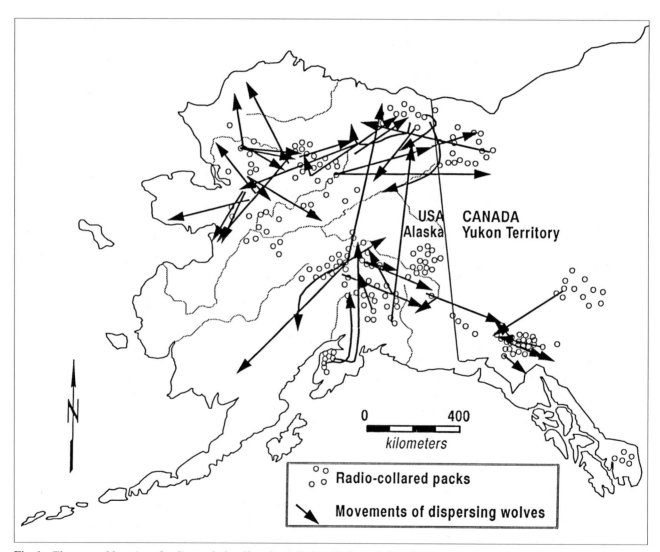

Fig. 1 *The general location of radio-marked wolf packs studied in Alaska and the adjacent Yukon from 1975 to 1991, and also the known long-range movements of dispersing wolves. Packs were monitored for periods of two to eight years. Principal sources of data include: Stephenson and James (1982), Ballard et al. (1983, 1987, 1990), Peterson et al. (1984), Weiler et al. (1986), Adams et al. (1989b), Mech et al. (1989, 1991), and Hayes et al. (1991).*

servative figure for the present statewide population is approximately 5,000 wolves." Mech and Rausch (1975) concluded:

> No accurate estimate of total numbers of wolves in Alaska is available. In the past, a qualified estimate of 5,000 wolves was made; it has crept into the literature and has been arbitrarily lowered or raised to suit the individual viewpoints being expressed. The estimate of 5,000 probably is extremely conservative. Whatever the case, wolves continue to exist throughout their historic range at very high population levels in most areas.

Skoog (1983) estimated Alaska's wolf population to be in excess of 10,000 animals. In addition to these published estimates, similar figures ranging from 6,000 to 10,000 appeared in ADF&G informational leaflets during the early 1980's, and figures of 15,000 or higher were cited in popular literature during the late 1970's and early 1980's.

Unfortunately, wolf protection groups have compared the highest estimates with ADF&G's current estimates, suggesting that wolf numbers have declined by as much as 50% since the 1970's. While this alarmed some people who are not well informed about wolves, there is no validity in comparing these numbers in view of the unknown and highly subjective basis for estimates prior to 1984.

In 1984, ADF&G began assembling systematic annual estimates of wolf numbers (expressed as a minimum and maximum for most areas) on a Game Management Unit (GMU) basis (Fig. 2), which also yielded a statewide total. These estimates are derived from aerial wolf surveys, telemetry studies in limited areas, and sightings of wolves and wolf tracks provided by pilots, trappers, and other members of the public. In a few areas in coastal and southeastern Alaska, where terrain or weather limit the usefulness of conventional survey techniques, estimates are based on extrapolations from adjacent areas with similar habitat and prey availability. While the accuracy and precision of the estimates vary depending on the basis for the estimate, these figures are generally accepted as the most reasonable available.

In winter 1989-90 the ADF&G estimated the statewide wolf population to be 5,900–7,200 wolves in 700–900 packs. Aerial surveys and telemetry studies suggest that numbers are stable or slightly increasing in most areas, with higher numbers being recorded in GMU's 6, 13, 19, 20, 21, and 24 (Morgan 1990a). These increases correspond with those in several caribou (*Rangifer tarandus*) herds (Davis and Valkenburg 1991) and some moose (*Alces alces*) (Ballard et al. 1991a) and Sitka black-tailed deer (*Odocoileus hemionus sitkensis*) (Morgan 1990b) populations, combined with increased restrictions on wolf hunting and trapping. In other areas, such as GMU 24, an increase in estimated numbers is primarily the result of better data from intensive surveys or telemetry studies (Morgan 1990a).

While the total number of wolves in the state is of interest, annual changes in the statewide population estimate are of limited value in assessing the status of wolves. Increases in one region can be offset by decreases in another, and the varying quality and unknown direction of bias in some estimates limit the usefulness of the statewide total.

The status of wolves is best evaluated on a regional or local basis relative to prey density and availability and land use and resource management policies and objectives. With respect to prey availability, the status of wolves in Alaska can be viewed as falling into three general categories: 1) prey are abundant and wolf density is as high as can be sustained in view of ungulate density and productivity (e.g., the eastern and central Brooks Range where moose, caribou, and Dall sheep (*Ovis dalli*) are numerous and wolf harvest is generally low); 2) prey abundance is high and could support higher wolf populations, but total wolf mortality or other factors are preventing an increase in wolf numbers (e.g., parts of GMU's 7, 13, 14, 15, 16, 22, 23, and 26); and 3) areas where moose, caribou, or deer remain at chronically low densities due in part to wolf predation, and wolf densities remain low, despite little harvest (e.g., parts of eastern interior and southeastern Alaska).

Evaluating the status of wolves relative to land use and management objectives is difficult because these are, in many cases, in the process of being developed or revised. There has been virtually no reduction in habitat availability during the past decade. There is, however, a concern that wolf populations may decline in portions of southeastern Alaska as a result of an expanding road system, reduced habitat for Sitka black-tailed deer resulting from logging of old-growth forest, and reduced genetic variability and fitness as insular subpopulations decline (M. D. Kirchhoff, Alaska Dept. Fish and Game, Juneau, pers. commun.).

Wolf Research in Alaska, 1981–92

During the 1970's, ADF&G initiated studies to better evaluate the role of wolf predation in ungulate population dynamics. During this period, biologists were reevaluating the role of wolf predation in limiting ungulate populations. Several of these studies were mentioned by Harbo and Dean (1983), but conclusions were not available at the time. During the 1980's, biologists from federal agencies including the National Park Service (NPS), U.S. Fish and Wildlife Service (USFWS), U.S. Forest Service, and Bureau of Land Management also took part in important studies of wolf ecology, often in cooperation with ADF&G. By the end of the decade, telemetry had been used to study approximately 140 packs for periods of two to eight years in various parts of Alaska, and about 60 packs in the adjacent Yukon (Fig. 1).

In this section we chronologically review scientific research concerning wolf-prey relationships and wolf management conducted in Alaska during 1981–91. Also included are brief descriptions of ongoing research. Other studies that indirectly addressed wolf-prey relationships or management are briefly mentioned.

Advances in ecological knowledge did not diminish the controversy over Alaskan wolf management. As will be discussed later, however, better ecological insight fostered a change in the nature of the debate.

1981

Moose calf mortality studies in the Nelchina Basin indicated that grizzly bears (*Ursus arctos*) were the primary cause of neonatal moose calf mortality (Ballard et al. 1981a), accounting for 79% of the deaths of radio-collared moose calves. Ninety-four percent of the calf mortalities occurred before 19 July each year. Wolves accounted for 3% of the calf mortalities. Although wolves were not an important source of neonatal moose mortality, they were a major cause of winter calf and year-round adult moose mortality (Ballard et al. 1981b).

Holleman and Stephenson (1981) showed that the level of Cesium-137 in wolf skeletal muscle could be useful in assessing prey selection and consumption by wolves. The highest radiocesium concentrations in wolves occurred where caribou or black-tailed deer were available. Prey species that select nonlichen vegetation had lower radiocesium concentrations in skeletal muscle, which were reflected in low levels in wolves preying on them. Radiocesium concentration in wolves has since been widely used in Alaska and northern Canada as an economical way to provide insight into prey selection, especially in areas where both caribou and moose are available.

James (1983) found that two radio-marked wolf packs in northwestern Alaska migrated between summer and winter

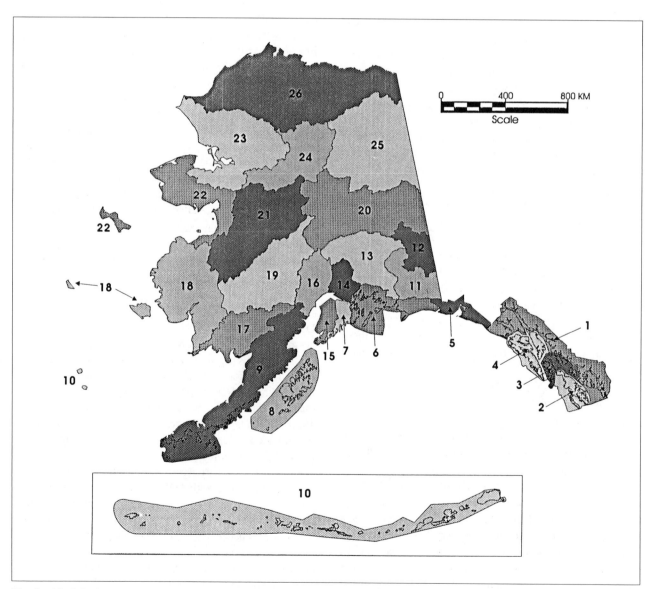

Fig. 2 *Alaska's Game Management Units.*

range in response to migrations of caribou. He found no evidence of selective predation on caribou calves and estimated that during summer wolves preyed on caribou at the rate of 23–38 caribou/wolf/year.

Van Ballenberghe (1981) proposed a revision of all but one of several wolf population estimates made by various investigators in the Nelchina Basin from 1952 through 1978. These estimates later became a focal point in a debate about the effects of wolf predation on caribou (Van Ballenberghe 1985).

1982

Based on the results of an experimental wolf reduction, Ballard and Stephenson (1982) suggested that wolf control measures would be more effective if one to three pack members were radio-collared and left in each pack territory. Advantages of this approach were more reliable information on wolf populations during and after control, continued occupation and defense of territories by radio-collared pack members, and greater efficiency in locating wolves in subsequent population control efforts. Typically, wolf control measures without the above procedures cost $770 to $873 per wolf, and annual removal was necessary to maintain low densities. This study also demonstrated that wolves could quickly repopulate a control area through immigration and reproduction.

Concerns about the taxonomic status of Alaska's wolves led Pedersen (1982) to review the morphological basis for Goldman's (1944) determination that there were four Alaska subspecies. Goldman (1944) based his assessment on 15 skull measurements and recognized the following subspecies: *C. lupus ligoni*, Alexander Archipelago wolf; *C. lupus alces*, Kenai Peninsula wolf; *C. lupus pambasileus*, Interior Alaskan wolf; and *C. lupus tundrarum*, Alaska tundra wolf. Pedersen (1982) reanalyzed Goldman's (1944) data and examined additional skulls using multi-variate statistical tools which had not been available to Goldman. Pedersen concluded that only two subspecies warranted continued recognition; *C. l. pambasileus* and *C. l. ligoni*, the latter occurring in southeast Alaska.

Peterson and Woolington (1982) reviewed the history of wolves on the Kenai Peninsula. Wolves were exterminated by about 1915, largely through the use of poison. They recolonized the area during the 1960's and by 1975 occupied most of the suitable habitat on the peninsula.

Stephenson et al. (1982) evaluated blood sera from 57 wolves for evidence of previous exposure to infectious canine hepatitis virus (ICHV) and canine distemper virus (CDV). Ninety-five percent of the sera were positive for ICHV exposure and 7% were positive for exposure to CDV. The greater incidence of ICHV exposure may have been related to the greater ease of transmission of ICHV or to a higher mortality rate among wolves exposed to CDV. However, the wolf populations studied were generally productive and healthy despite evidence of exposure to these viruses.

1983

Gasaway et al. (1983) studied the interrelationships among wolves, moose, caribou, and man in interior Alaska and reviewed several studies of northern predator-prey systems. They concluded that wolf predation could sustain declines in ungulate populations that were initiated by other factors. Mortality from severe winters, hunting, and wolf predation was largely additive. A 61% reduction in the Tanana Flats wolf population resulted in a two- to four-fold increase in calf and yearling moose survival, respectively. Caribou calf survival also increased significantly, and both moose and caribou populations increased as a result of the wolf reduction program. The study found no evidence of a sensitive, fast-acting feedback mechanism between ungulate and wolf populations. Once ungulate populations reached low levels and were limited by predation, predator reduction appeared to be necessary to allow ungulate populations to escape the effects of predation. The authors showed that prey:wolf ratios can assist in interpreting ecological relationships, but cautioned that predation on young animals often caused survival of young ungulates to be an unreliable indicator of the vegetation-ungulate relationship.

1984

Peterson et al. (1984) studied the ecology of three to seven wolf packs on the Kenai Peninsula during 1976–81. Wolves recolonized the Peninsula in the 1960's after an absence of nearly 50 years. Population density ranged from 11–20 wolves/1,000 km^2. Wolves fed primarily on moose and winter predation rates averaged one moose/pack/4.7 days. Calf moose composed 20% of the early winter moose population but 47% of the wolf-killed moose. Adult moose killed by wolves were relatively old and debilitated. Wolf mortality was largely human caused, averaging 33% annually. Harvests of 30–40% of the early winter population caused declines, and the wolf population was regulated by harvest at the close of the study.

1985

Kellert (1985a) explored American attitudes toward and knowledge of predators, particularly the wolf and coyote (*Canis latrans*), through a national survey. The study showed that Alaskan respondents had the most positive perceptions of the wolf and the greatest knowledge of predatory animals among the various demographic groups studied.

Van Ballenberghe (1985) reviewed the history and dynamics of the Nelchina caribou herd during 1950–81. Based on revised estimates of wolf numbers (Van Ballenberghe 1981), he concluded that severe winters and hunting were the major causes of the herd's decline and that predation by wolves had a minor effect. This manuscript set the stage for further debate on caribou-wolf relationships (Bergerud and Ballard 1988, 1989).

1986

Franzmann and Schwartz (1986) described the importance of black bear predation on moose calves, and compared predation levels in productive and marginal habitats. The level of bear predation was similar (33% vs. 34%) in both habitats. Adams et al. (1989b) initiated a study of wolf ecology in Gates of the Arctic National Park and Preserve in the central Brooks Range. This five-year study focused on population size and distribution, productivity, mortality, seasonal food habits, predation rates, prey selection relative to prey availability, and the effect of annual harvests by man. Eleven to 19 radio-marked packs were monitored annually, more than 2,000 scats were collected from den sites, and more than 100 carcasses of wolves taken by hunters and trappers were necropsied.

The central Brooks Range wolf population was found to be relatively dense (approximately 6.5 wolves/1,000 km^2) and productive, with an average of 47% pups in autumn populations. Yearlings dispersed more frequently than adults, with movements as far as 700 km being documented. Harvest by man and intraspecific strife were major causes of mortality, with harvest being composed of 62% pups and removing about 17% of the park population annually. Caribou, Dall sheep, and moose were common prey for wolves. Intensive monitoring during three seasons showed that the predation rate of packs preying mainly on caribou was nearly stable over a wide range of caribou densities.

Mech et al. (1989) initiated a long-term study of wolf ecology in Denali National Park and Preserve. Preliminary estimates indicated that average wolf density approached 10 wolves/1,000 km^2. Intraspecific strife and trapping along park boundaries appeared to be the major causes of mortality. Wolf numbers more than doubled during the study.

1987

Ballard et al. (1990) initiated a wolf study in northwestern Alaska. Principal objectives included determining the number of wolves within the range of the Western Arctic caribou herd, developing and testing new census methods, and evaluating satellite telemetry for determining movements and territories of wolves. Wolf densities during the first two years of study ranged from 2.7 wolves/1,000 km^2 in spring 1987 to 6.3/1,000 km^2 in autumn 1988. The average life span of seven satellite transmitters was 10 months.

Ballard and Larsen (1987) reviewed knowledge of predator-prey relationships, particularly wolf predation, in relation to moose management. It had become well established that predation by wolves was capable of limiting moose population growth. Moose populations limited by wolves had initially suffered declines due to the combination of severe winters, excessive hunting, and predation. Predation, however, was not a principal cause of most ungulate declines. When moose populations were limited by wolf predation, mortality from predation was additive to other mortality. Moose populations limited by predation appar-

ently could remain at low levels for decades if wolf numbers were not reduced. The possibility of reducing bear density was also discussed. The authors concluded that managers attempting to provide a sustained yield of ungulates would sometimes find predator management necessary where predator populations were naturally regulated.

Ballard et al. (1987) described the ecology of a heavily exploited wolf population in south-central Alaska. Pack territories averaged 1,645 km^2 and did not overlap. Moose were the principal prey and wolves were not migratory. Twenty-eight percent of the dispersing wolves left during April–June and October–November, and 22% of those were accepted into existing packs. Average annual litter sizes ranged from 3.7 to 7.3 pups. Seven to 10% of the packs had two litters per season. When total mortality exceeded 30–40% of autumn numbers, the wolf population declined. Annual finite rates of increase ranged from 0.88 during years of heavy exploitation to 2.4 following termination of population control. Wolf densities during 1975 through spring 1982 ranged from 2.6 to 10.3/1,000 km^2. Seventy percent of observed wolf kills were moose. Wolves preyed on moose calves in proportion to their presence in the moose population during May-October, but killed a disproportionately high number of calves during winter. Kill rates for packs during winter averaged one adult moose/9.3 days, and summer predation rates were similar. Spring wolf densities were negatively correlated with autumn moose calf:cow ratios.

Van Ballenberghe (1987) reviewed the effects of wolf predation on moose numbers and concluded that it was no longer a question of whether controlling effects by predators occurred, but rather under what conditions and how long control lasted. He described two conceptual models (low density equilibria and recurrent fluctuations), which held promise as general theories of predation on moose in naturally regulated ecosystems. Moose were capable of escaping the constraints of predation in the latter, but remained at low densities for long periods in the former model.

Zarnke and Ballard (1987) analyzed blood serum samples from 116 wolves captured in the Nelchina Basin during 1975 through 1982. Rabies, brucellosis, and leptospirosis were rare and had little effect on the wolf population. Exposure to ICHV, canine parvovirus, CDV, tularemia, and Q-fever was relatively common, and these diseases may have negatively affected some individuals in the population.

1988

Boertje et al. (1988) described the extent of predation on moose and caribou by radio-collared grizzly bears in east central Alaska. Adult bears regularly killed adult female moose, especially during spring. Male bears killed moose at a higher rate than did females. The impact of bear predation was estimated to be greatest for low density moose populations. Grizzly bears killed about 4 times more animal biomass than they scavenged. Bergerud and Ballard (1988) compared historical caribou and wolf population fluctuations in the Nelchina Basin and concluded that hunting and wolf predation played an important role in shaping the dynamics of the herd. During years that wolf numbers were low, caribou calf recruitment was high and the population increased. When wolf numbers were high, caribou recruitment was low. Recruitment of 2.5-year-olds from 1952 to 1967 was correlated with wolf numbers. Low recruitment of 3 cohorts during 1964 through 1965, when deep snow caused caribou to calve closer to predators, was a key element in the population decline. There was no evidence of winter starvation. When wolf populations were reduced during the mid-1970's, caribou populations again increased.

1989

Schwartz and Franzmann (1989) explored relationships between bears, wolves, moose, and forest succession on the Kenai Peninsula, concluding that the impact of predation varied with changes in habitat carrying capacity. They concluded that clearly defined management objectives would determine when habitat enhancement or predator control was appropriate.

In an effort to evaluate alternatives to lethal predator control, Boertje of wolves and bears could reduce predation on calf caribou and moose during summer. Results suggested that artificial feeding did not improve caribou calf survival, but may have improved moose calf survival (Boertje et al. 1988).

Gasaway et al. (1990) also investigated alternatives to lethal predator control by determining whether increases in alternate prey, particularly caribou, would reduce wolf predation on moose. Radiocesium concentration was used to assess consumption of caribou by wolves under conditions of high and low caribou numbers (Holleman and Stephenson 1981). As caribou increased in the Delta, Nelchina, and Fortymile herds, consumption of caribou by wolves increased, decreased, and remained constant, respectively. The effect of increased caribou numbers in a wolf-bear-moose-caribou system appeared to be variable and unpredictable (Boertje et al. 1988).

Van Ballenberghe (1989) challenged Bergerud and Ballard's (1988) interpretation of the Nelchina Basin caribou-wolf data, arguing that data on wolf and caribou numbers and caribou recruitment did not warrant statistical analysis because they lacked accuracy and precision. He suggested that when multispecies prey biomass exceeded 200 ungulates per wolf, caribou populations increased. Because multispecies prey biomass consistently exceeded 200 in the Nelchina Basin, he concluded that wolf predation played a minor role in the population dynamics of the Nelchina caribou herd.

Bergerud and Ballard (1989) argued that Van Ballenberghe's (1985) principal reason for discounting the importance of wolf predation was that wolf numbers were low and stable from 1962 to 1974. They pointed out that Van Ballenberghe (1981) had revised nine of 10 wolf population estimates.

Original estimates indicated that wolf numbers increased at an annual finite rate of 1.30, which was close to the average of other wolf populations in North America, and were negatively correlated with caribou recruitment. Historically, caribou recruitment improved three times following reductions in wolf numbers. Bergerud and Ballard (1989) concluded that the decline of the herd from 1962 through 1972 could be explained by excessive human harvest combined with poor recruitment.

1990

Based on a study of predator-prey relationships in east-central Alaska, Gasaway et al. (1992) concluded that high-density moose populations in Alaska were generally the result of predator management. Where both wolves and grizzly bears were exploited by humans at moderate to high levels, moose appeared to stabilize at moderate densities. In areas where two to three large predator species were naturally regulated, moose populations existed at low-density equilibria (Gasaway et al. 1992). The authors concluded that in northern systems moose will not escape low levels without predator management.

1991

The history of the Nelchina Basin moose population was reviewed, and the effects of wolf predation on moose were intensively studied from 1976 through 1986 by Ballard et al. (1991a). Wolf predation did not cause a moose population decline in the late 1960's and early 1970's, but did appear to accelerate it. Population modeling indicated that if wolf populations had not been reduced during the 1970's, moose recruitment would have remained low and the moose population might have continued to decline. A combination of mild winters, reduced predator numbers, and restricted harvests allowed the moose population to increase 3–6% annually from 1976 through 1985 (Ballard et al. 1986, 1991a).

In addition to research pertaining directly to wolf-prey relationships and wolf management, numerous other studies were published during the decade. The range of topics included various aspects of life history (Ballard 1982, Eide and Ballard 1982, Stephenson and James 1982, Ballard et al. 1983, Ballard and Dau 1983), capture techniques (Ballard et al. 1982, 1991b, Tobey and Ballard 1985), cementum aging techniques (Goodwin and Ballard 1985), wolf census techniques (Becker and Gardner 1990), and a comparison of the knowledge of wolves possessed by Nunamiut Eskimos and western scientists and the methods used in developing it (Stephenson 1982).

1992

The research completed in 1990 and first presented in an ADF&G final report (Gasaway et al. 1990a) was published in 1992 as a wildlife monograph (Gasaway et al. 1992). The Wildlife Society recognized the work as the best wildlife monograph of 1992. A study of wolf productivity in Interior

Alaska concluded that productivity of wolf populations declined after prey availablity reached extremely low levels (Boertje and Stephenson 1992), with high reproductive potential occurring at ungulate densities found in most parts of North America.

The conclusions of other important studies became available in 1992 and are represented in this volume. These include the results of a major study of wolf-prey relationships in Denali National park addressing prey selection (Mech et al. this volume), predation on caribou calves (Adams et al. this volume), and pack structure and genetic relatedness (Meier et al. this volume). Winter predation by wolves was studied in Gates National park (Dale et al. this volume). Boertje et al. (this volume) concluded an evaluation of several lethal and nonlethal methods of reducing predation on moose. A study of the effectiveness of satellite radiocollars in tracking wolf movements was completed, as were studies of techniques for surveying and aging wolves (Ballard et al. this volume). Klein (this volume) reviewed the results of the experimental introduction of wolves to Coronation Island in Southeast Alaska.

Research Needs

The results of some wolf control programs indicate that wolf predation on moose neonates can be a major mortality factor (Gasaway et al. 1983). However, results of moose calf mortality studies in other areas suggest that wolves only account for about 17% of early summer moose calf mortality (Ballard 1992), with bear predation being the major source of mortality. Accurately assessing the effects of bear and wolf predation, both separately and combined, in northern systems continues to be a challenge, with bear predation the most difficult to assess. Improving our ability to estimate bear populations and the effects of bear predation on moose and caribou would allow better assessments of the cost, benefits, and advisability of predation control in specific situations.

The nature of the functional responses through which wolves persist at low prey densities are poorly understood and deserve more study. Long-term studies of wolves are necessary to help predict functional and numerical responses of wolves to changes in prey.

Although some investigators (James 1983, Ballard et al. 1987) have found that summer and winter food habits and predation rates are similar, a number of questions remain. Relatively little is known about nutritional condition or sex and age composition of prey killed by wolves during summer. Whether scats collected at dens and rendezvous sites accurately represent food habits is unknown, as is the accuracy of scat analyses. The conditions in which wolves cause significant neonate mortality are unknown These and many other questions concerning wolf life history during summer constitute a knowledge deficiency about northern wolves.

Wolf Management in Alaska, 1981–91

Although research helped resolve a number of biological and management questions, in some cases contradictory findings or attempts to reevaluate historical data seemed to fuel both scientific and public debate. Wildlife managers acknowledged that human values and ethical judgments about the treatment of wildlife populations or individual animals were at the heart of the controversy.

Harbo and Dean (1983) indicated that all the major legal issues surrounding state-conducted wolf control programs had been settled by the 5 February 1980 ruling of the U.S. Court of Appeals for the DC Circuit. In a case brought by Defenders of Wildlife and other plaintiffs, the court ruled that state aerial wolf control could proceed in Alaska on federal land without an environmental impact statement (EIS). In addition, it affirmed the state's authority over resident non-endangered wildlife and thereby lifted all legal prohibitions against wolf control conducted by ADF&G. Legal challenges during the 1980's also had only temporary effects. However, wolf management continued to be dominated by political obstacles and debate which maintained the costly stalemate through the end of the decade.

In February 1980 the Alaska Board of Game (Board) had approved five of seven areas recommended for aerial wolf hunts to reduce predation on moose. GMU's 19A, 19B, 20A, and 21 had been reapproved; GMU's 20B, 20C, and 20D were added; and GMU 20E was not approved because of pending federal land withdrawals in the vicinity of the Yukon and Charley rivers. Permits were issued to private hunters to hunt wolves from fixed-wing aircraft. Because of poor hunting conditions during spring 1980, only 53 wolves were killed, half of them by ADF&G personnel.

Later that spring, ADF&G presented a draft revision of its 1973 wolf management policy to the Board for review. This policy detailed ADF&G's basic philosophy and approach to wolf management, including the application of wolf control. After limited public and agency review, these policies were finalized and published in December 1980.

The following is a chronological review of major events, issues, and decisions affecting wolf management since 1980.

1981

During winter 1980-81, wolf control continued in six GMU's and a total of 113 wolves were taken by ADF&G and private aerial hunters. In April 1981, the Board adopted Policy #81-28-GB, "Letter of Intent Regarding Wolf Reduction in Alaska," that stated that the primary purpose of wolf reduction was to rehabilitate and restore depressed ungulate populations.

In September, ADF&G recommended continued aerial shooting of wolves in the five previously-approved GMU's, as well as in GMU's 20E and northern GMU 12. To achieve a 60–80% reduction of wolves in specific parts of these GMU's, ADF&G recommended that fixed-wing and helicopter aircraft be used. These proposals were reviewed by the Board in November 1981.

1982

In February the director of the Division of Wildlife Conservation and the commissioner of ADF&G approved the new programs in GMU's 12 and 20E. The total number of wolves killed in control programs during 1981–82 was 85. At their December 1982 meeting, the Board again reviewed ADF&G's wolf management policies and plans for wolf control programs. Although a public hearing on the policies and plans was held, public comment was limited because the plan was distributed on the afternoon of the hearing and only written comments were accepted.

The following day the Board adopted ADF&G's "Wolf Management Policy" with a "Supplement on Wolf Population Control" as Board policy. This action set the stage for the next legal challenge to implementation of wolf control in Alaska.

Following the December Board meeting, the Alaska Wildlife Alliance (Alliance) filed complaints with the State Ombudsman Office (Ombudsman) claiming that ADF&G did not allow sufficient public input into its wolf control program and was unresponsive to requests for information. The Alliance also questioned ADF&G's authority to issue an aerial wolf hunting permit to the Reindeer Herders Association in GMU 22 on the Seward Peninsula without public notice or input.

1983

At the March Board meeting, the Ombudsman reported that, in its opinion, the wolf management policy adopted by the Board was a regulation and the Board should not bypass the regulatory process by calling it a policy. The Ombudsman further stated that wolf control policies adopted by the Board to date were invalid because they were intended to have the effect of regulations, but were not adopted according to rules established by the Administrative Procedures Act (APA). The APA, among other things, requires public notice and provision for public comments on any proposed regulations. The Ombudsman indicated that ADF&G could not legally conduct a wolf control program in the absence of regulations promulgated by the Board.

As a result of the Ombudsman's opinion, the Board recommended a full public review of wolf management and control programs at its December 1983 meeting. The Alliance asked the Board and ADF&G to suspend wolf control until the public review was completed and new regulations were adopted. ADF&G declined this request and resumed control efforts in late October 1983.

On 2 November 1983, the Alliance filed a complaint against the state in Alaska Superior Court challenging the authority of ADF&G to conduct any predator control programs in the absence of regulations developed by the Board through the public process required by the Alaska APA. A

temporary restraining order was issued on 4 November 1983 prohibiting ADF&G from aerial shooting after nine wolves had been killed. On 14 December 1983, Alaska Superior Court Judge Shortell granted the preliminary injunction sought by the Alliance. However, ADF&G was allowed to proceed with preparatory efforts, such as the radio-collaring of wolves.

ADF&G and the Board requested the Alliance postpone any further legal proceedings until after the March 1984 meeting to allow the state to meet APA requirements. The Alliance agreed to this because the preliminary injunction prevented any resumption of aerial wolf hunting until March.

1984

At the March meeting, the Board considered hunting and trapping regulations and policy proposals in addition to aerial wolf hunting and predator control issues. Many state Fish and Game Advisory Committees favored maintaining wolf control as a management tool. Most opposing testimony came from private individuals, organizations such as the Alliance and Defenders of Wildlife, and non-Alaskans. The Alliance submitted a proposal to replace the "Wolf Management Policy" with a regulation that defined predator control as an emergency measure, which should be limited to specific situations, rather than being considered as a standard management tool.

On the advice of the Alaska Department of Law, the Board adopted a proposal placing wolf control under regulatory requirements for public review before authorization. This new regulation required all control programs to be based on scientific evidence and consider both consumptive and nonconsumptive users of wildlife. Regulations were required to identify population objectives for both wolves and prey. This caused wolf control to be viewed primarily in relation to long-term management objectives, instead of as isolated programs. In addition, programs had to be reviewed and reauthorized after three years, and both denning and poisoning continued to be prohibited. Wolf control on federal lands required the consent of the appropriate federal land managers. As a result of the Board's adoption of this regulation, the Alliance lawsuit was dismissed by joint agreement and the injunction against wolf control was lifted.

In August, the Board held public hearings in Delta Junction and Fairbanks as ADF&G proposed renewing wolf control in GMU's 12, 20A, 20B, 20D, 20E, and possibly adding 25D. The Board also received four wolf control proposals from local Fish and Game Advisory Committees.

In September, acting under the new regulations, the Board voted to reauthorize aerial shooting of wolves, now called wolf predation control, in GMU's 20A and 20B beginning 1 November. No public aerial hunting permits were to be issued. All control was to be done by ADF&G, and the Board authorized the use of radiotelemetry and helicopters to locate wolves to increase efficiency of control.

The Board postponed a decision on GMU's 20D, 20E, and part of 12 until the December meeting.

In December, the Board held a public meeting in Anchorage at which the majority of the testimony was opposed to aerial wolf control. Nevertheless, the Board voted to authorize aerial wolf hunting in adjacent parts of GMU's 12 and 20E. ADF&G's plan called for killing 100 of the 125 wolves in a 13,000-km^2 area. The Board rejected a proposal for an aerial wolf hunt in the McGrath area.

Although ADF&G moved to implement these programs, on 27 December 1984 the Federal Communications Commission (FCC) sent a letter to the State of Alaska ordering ADF&G to stop using radiotelemetry to locate wolves during authorized control programs. The FCC claimed that such use violated the license granted to ADF&G for the use of radio transmitters in research. However, a review of the license stipulations found that some frequencies could legally be used for this purpose.

1985

The controversy over wolf control spread beyond ADF&G and the Board and entered the legislative arena in January. At that time, five "bills" or "resolutions" regarding wolf management were introduced into the Alaska Legislature: SB 62 to prohibit aerial wolf hunting, HCR 15 regarding the harmful effects of wolves, SB 241 calling for a $250 bounty on wolves, and companion bills HB 397 and SB 298 that would take the authority to make decisions on wolf control programs away from the Board and the statewide public process and transfer it to ADF&G and the local Fish and Game Advisory Committees with no requirement for public review. Although none of these initiatives reached a final vote in the legislature, heated debate occurred in committee sessions.

In early 1985, Board chairwoman Johnson wrote to the Commissioner of Fish and Game requesting that ADF&G not implement the aerial wolf hunts approved by the Board in September and December 1984. She also requested that all previously authorized aerial wolf hunts be proposed again for reconsideration by the Board at their March–April meeting, and that ADF&G be prepared to discuss alternatives to current wolf control programs at that time. In February, ADF&G initiated a review of their approach to wolf management. It had become apparent that the public should be more deeply involved in the decision-making process regarding both policies and regulations. These ideas were considered in light of contemporary approaches to conflict resolution, consensus building, and citizen participation (Haggstrom et al., this volume).

During the spring meeting, the Board considered five new proposals for aerial wolf hunts in addition to three programs authorized in 1984. The Board voted not to approve new control programs and repealed the previously authorized programs in GMU's 12, 20A, and 20E, leaving only the GMU 20B program in effect.

The Board also requested that ADF&G prepare an analysis and report for the autumn Board meeting to reassess the existing program in GMU 20B and to further develop possible alternatives to aerial hunting. A report, entitled *An Assessment of Wolf Predation Control Alternatives for Portions of Interior Alaska*, was presented to the Board in November 1985. At this meeting the Board reauthorized the previous regulations regarding wolf control programs, including continuation of wolf control in GMU 20B. Following the Board's authorization, employees of ADF&G used fixed-wing aircraft, helicopters, and radiotelemetry to reduce the wolf population in the Minto Flats area near Fairbanks. By late winter, 34 wolves had been killed, 29 of them by aerial shooters. Although the GMU 20B wolf control program was authorized through 1990, no aerial shooting occurred after March 1986. Population monitoring indicated that wolf numbers had been reduced sufficiently to achieve the desired increase in moose numbers.

One alternative to aerial wolf control that ADF&G identified was trapper education and assistance. After debating whether these were a form of wolf control, the Board authorized trapper education programs for GMU's 19D and 25D. Neither program resulted in any increase in wolf harvest. However, because the Board had authorized control in a large part of the Yukon Flats National Wildlife Refuge, Defenders of Wildlife threatened a lawsuit if an EIS was not prepared. The USFWS considered preparing an EIS, but in December 1985 the USFWS wrote ADF&G reaffirming their policy, based on prior court rulings that neither was necessary, and they concurred with the proposed trapper education program. No litigation was initiated.

While the Board's adoption of regulations governing wolf control seemed to resolve the legal obstacles to officially sanctioned programs, a related controversy developed over state trapping regulations that allowed a person to fly in an airplane to locate wolves, then land and attempt to shoot them. This practice came to be known as land-and-shoot taking. The official term, same-day-airborne, is sometimes used interchangeably.

Two concerns were expressed. First, many people believed that aircraft were being used to drive wolves into the open and that in some cases people shot from the air before landing. Either action would be a violation of both the Federal Airborne Hunting Act and state regulations. Second, because land-and-shoot taking was an effective method for killing wolves in open areas, it was believed that this practice was, in fact, wolf control. This view eventually led to legal action.

1986

In July the Alliance, Greenpeace USA, and four individuals filed a lawsuit against the state in Alaska Superior Court in Anchorage. The plaintiffs claimed that land-and-shoot trapping was a method of wolf control and should therefore be subject to the procedures and standards set forth in the

Alaska Administrative Code. The suit further alleged that ADF&G was using land-and-shoot trapping as a means to evade the wolf predation control regulations, and it requested the Board to hold public hearings to develop an implementation plan for the land-and-shoot method for each GMU. It also asked that this method be prohibited statewide except in areas where wolf predation had caused moose and caribou populations to be severely depressed.

1987

After hearing oral arguments in January, Alaska Superior Court Judge Ripley signed a Summary Judgment in favor of the state which read in part: "This court finds that the Board of Game's regulations that allow a trapper to take wolves the same day the trapper has been airborne...is reasonably necessary to carry out the board's authorities to regulate methods and means of harvest..., that the regulations are not arbitrary and capricious, and that they do not constitute an authorized program for wolf control."

The Alliance and other plaintiffs filed an appeal to the Alaska Supreme Court in February maintaining their allegation that the Board's regulations allowing aerial trapping constituted an unauthorized program for wolf control. In December, the Alaska Supreme Court decided against the plaintiffs and affirmed the Superior Court decision that land-and-shoot trapping was not a form of wolf control and was therefore not subject to the administrative regulations governing wolf control programs.

While litigation over land-and-shoot trapping proceeded, the Board met again in November 1987 to discuss wolf hunting and trapping regulations. After public hearings in Fairbanks and Anchorage, the Board voted to place further restrictions on land-and-shoot taking. This was accomplished by classifying this method as hunting rather than trapping and authorizing it only in GMU's 9, 17, 19, 21, 23, 24, and most of 25 with a bag limit of 10 wolves. Although these changes reduced wolf harvests to some degree, they did little to resolve the controversy between supporters and opponents of the method. Placing land-and-shoot in hunting regulations also led to a confrontation between the state and the NPS regarding wolf hunting in national preserves.

The NPS held that land-and-shoot hunting was not a fair chase method of taking wolves. As such, it was in conflict with NPS policies governing hunting in preserves. NPS had previously prohibited land-and-shoot trapping by refusing to recognize firearms as a legal method of trapping. As a result of the Board's actions, NPS initiated development of federal and state regulations to close preserves to land-and-shoot hunting.

1988

In September, the NPS submitted a regulation proposal to the Board requesting the closure of eight national preserves to land-and-shoot hunting of wolves. The Board returned the proposal because their schedule did not provide for the

discussion of wolf regulations until the following year. Because there was no biological problem caused by the hunting, the Board also refused to consider the ban on an emergency basis.

The NPS held hearings in October on their proposed regulation and public opinion was strongly in favor of the ban; in November they enacted a temporary one-year ban on land-and-shoot hunting of wolves in eight preserves. The state objected to the NPS regulation, claiming it was not necessary and usurped state management authority. Wolf regulations were not on the agenda for the autumn 1988 Board meeting, so the NPS asked the Board to agree to consider a proposal at its March 1989 meeting to permanently ban land-and-shoot hunting in the preserves. Because there was no biological justification for the temporary ban the NPS already had in place and was working to make permanent, the Board decided not to discuss the issue at this meeting.

1989

The NPS published a proposal in the 9 June *Federal Register* to adopt a permanent ban on land-and-shoot hunting of wolves on the national preserves in Alaska. In August, the NPS resubmitted their proposal to the Board to close national preserves to land-and-shoot hunting. Informal discussions between NPS and ADF&G indicated that if the Board adopted the proposal, NPS would halt development of the federal regulation.

At their November meeting, the Board discussed wolf regulation proposals. ADF&G recommended that land-and-shoot hunting be authorized only where it provided some management benefit and supported the NPS proposal to close the preserves. Despite ADF&G recommendations, the Board expanded land-and-shoot hunting by adding four GMU's to the seven in which it was already legal, and deleting one. However, the Board imposed additional conditions requiring all hunters to obtain a permit from ADF&G before hunting, limiting hunters to no more than three GMU's at any given time, and requiring hunters to immediately tag wolves they killed. The Board also voted to adopt the NPS proposal resulting in NPS postponement of its move to establish a permanent ban.

At this Board meeting, ADF&G proposed the development of a strategic wolf management plan for Alaska, emphasizing public involvement. ADF&G recommended appointing 10 or 12 citizens, representing a diversity of interests, to a Wolf Management Planning Team. Public forums and other means to involve the public in guiding wolf management were also suggested. The Board endorsed this proposal, and, as a result, took no action on seven proposals for wolf control programs nor on proposals to revise the state's guidelines for wolf management programs.

Robert O. Stephenson, Warren B. Ballard, Christian A. Smith, and Katharine Richardson

The Future of Wolves in Alaska

Until recently, ADF&G was solely responsible for wolf management in Alaska. However, in December 1989, the Alaska Supreme Court ruled that elements of the state's subsistence law, which gave preference to rural Alaskans in the allocation of wildlife, violated the State Constitution. Under provisions of the Alaska National Interest Lands Conservation Act of 1980, the federal government was therefore required to take over management of subsistence hunting and trapping on federal lands and provide the rural preference mandated by the U.S. Congress. This resulted in a dual management system on federal land, which comprises about two-thirds of the state. The implications for management of wolves are not clear at this time.

The outlook for the continued existence of a large wolf population in Alaska is good, and it is ADF&G's policy to maintain viable wolf populations in all parts of the wolf's historic range. There is broad public support in Alaska and elsewhere for maintaining an extensive population of wolves in the state. However, to many Alaskans, maintaining or enhancing game populations through regulation or periodic reduction of wolf populations is valid and necessary. To others, and to many people outside Alaska, such management is viewed as extreme and unethical and a continuation of the pattern of events that exterminated the wolf in parts of its historic range.

Predation by wolves and bears often plays an important role in maintaining ungulates at low densities. Consequently, local residents, to whom the quantity of wildlife is important, and ADF&G, operating under its constitutional and statutory mandates, will periodically find it necessary to propose regulating or temporarily reducing a local wolf population in order to maintain ungulate numbers near levels that habitat can support. Although recent control programs have involved a maximum of three percent of Alaska's land area, they continue to place Alaska's wildlife management at odds with the convictions of a large number of people who currently view the manipulation of wolf populations as undesirable and as a threat to wolf conservation.

The effects of bear predation on ungulate populations will continue to confound the issue of wolf management (Hayes et al. 1991) in areas such as Alaska and the Yukon, where bears and wolves often coexist at high densities. Research has shown that predation by bears can slow the recovery of ungulate populations even when wolf numbers are dramatically reduced. The management of bear populations and predation poses special problems in addition to those inherent in wolf management due to differences in public perception and population biology. The risk of long-term effects resulting from high harvests is greater for bears because of their lower productivity.

Despite the conflicts inherent in the relationship of people to large predators and prey, we should not lose sight of the fact that wolf and bear populations are extensive in Alaska and adjacent regions and have generally expanded in recent years. Both official policy and public opinion are clearly supportive of maintaining these populations, and the outlook for their continued coexistence with people is good.

The recent history of wolf-human relationships suggests that some level of controversy inevitably accompanies success in wolf conservation. In many respects the management of large predators, such as wolves, is a lightning rod for attitudes toward the environment. The fact that people with different values care deeply enough about wolves and wild country to express their concerns should be cause for optimism.

Acknowledgments

The preparation of this paper, and much of the material cited, was in large part supported by Alaska Federal Aid in Wildlife Restoration and by the Alaska Department of Fish and Game. We also thank the many National Park Service and U.S. Fish and Wildlife Service biologists for their generous sharing of data and important contributions in wolf biology and management.

Status of Wolves in Greenland

■ Ulf Marquard-Petersen

Until 1978 the arctic wolf was considered extinct in Greenland, but since then an influx has taken place from Ellesmere Island, Canada. Wolves are now commonly observed throughout northeast Greenland, where wolf range extends from about 70° N to Cape Morris Jesup at 83° 39' N. This is the northernmost wolf population in the world. Observations indicate that population size is less than 75 animals. Availability of wolf habitat capable of sustaining reproduction is likely to be limited to areas where muskoxen are common. Three core habitats are presently known.

Introduction

The wolf (*Canis lupus arctos*) in east Greenland was exterminated during the 1930's. Hunting and trapping pressures were considered important in the decline. Dawes (1978) reported that the arctic wolf was apparently in the process of reclaiming its previous habitat. Since then, many expeditions have reported seeing wolf tracks or wolves. These animals are believed to be immigrants from nearby Ellesmere Island crossing the frozen Robeson Channel (Dawes et al. 1986).

Literature dealing with the arctic wolf in Greenland consists primarily of reports of observations, as data on the population are virtually nonexistent. Dawes (1978) reported the renewed influx of wolves into the area. Dawes et al. (1986) published an excellent review of the history and status of the wolf in Greenland. Muskox investigations from 1984–1985 prompted Aastrup et al. (1986) to include notes on wolves in North Greenland. Bennike et al. (1989) described observations of wolves. Mågård (1988) gave an account of wolf observations at Danmarkshavn, and Turner and Dennis (1989), Higgins (1990) and Burton (1990) published notes on observations of breeding.

This paper summarizes what is presently known about population size, current distribution, and reproduction of the Greenland wolf. The paper is based on field work in northeast Greenland in 1991 and 1992, a literature survey, and observations by a number of people who have visited the region during the past five years.

Results and Discussion

Study of the overall observations made during the last 12 years suggests a pattern of key wolf habitat in some of the areas most frequently visited by expeditions. Based on these observations, I suggest that there are at least three important wolf habitats. I define "important" as an area where reproduction has been documented and where a number of wolf sightings have been made. One of these areas is located in northern Greenland; the other two areas are in eastern Greenland (Fig. 1). It should be noted, however, that wolves are commonly observed throughout northeast Greenland. All observations refer to white wolves. No grey or black variations have been reported.

Wolves currently inhabit the ice-free area along the northeastern coast of Greenland (Fig. 1). The terrain is mountainous with numerous fjords, islands, and peninsulas as well as broad valleys and lowlands, and the climate is diverse. The northern Greenland climate is classified as "arctic desert," characterized by low yearly precipitation, low temperature, and a short summer. Eastern Greenland has a more unstable climate, which is primarily determined by the extent of winter drift ice along the coast. Most of the wolf range falls within the boundaries of the North East Greenland National Park, the largest in the world (972,000 km^2) and about 100 times the size of Yellowstone National Park in the United States.

Arctic wolves inhabit the island as far north as Cape Morris Jesup (83°39' N 33°52' W) located only 800 km from the North Pole. This is the northernmost wolf population in the world. As recently as 1985, wolves have been observed as far west as Nyboe Land (82°43' N 57°00' W), the western distribution border of the muskox in northern Greenland (Bennike et al. 1989), and as far south as Scoresbysund (70°15' N 23°15' W) (Dawes et al. 1986).

Abundance

The arctic wolf was apparently never abundant in Greenland. Systematic surveys have never been carried out and population density is largely unknown. There is no accurate estimate of total wolf numbers. Based on my review of recent observations, I estimate the total population at less than 75 animals.

Important Known Wolf Habitat In Greenland

Some of the largest packs observed in Greenland since the immigration began in 1978 have occurred in northern Greenland from Nansen Land (82°56' N 41°40' W) to the Cape Morris Jesup region. A pack of eight animals was observed in Peary Land, on 3 March 1984 (Dawes et al. 1986), and a pack numbering seven visibly emaciated animals came near a cabin in Nansen Land on 9 July 1984 (Bennike et al. 1989). More recently, packs of five, six, and seven wolves have been observed in the Cape Morris Jesup region in 1990, 1991, and 1992 respectively. These observations likely refer to the same pack.

In eastern Greenland, two areas are believed important to wolves. Mågård (1988) provided the first evidence that Germania Land (77°N 20' W) may be an important wolf habitat.

Germania Land contains a weather station, Danmarkshavn, where continuous human presence provides a more stable record of wolf occurrence than elsewhere in Greenland.

Since 1979, wolves have been observed at Danmarkshavn each year except 1981, 1982, and 1983 (Mågård, 1988). Wolves often follow sled tracks to the station — apparently attracted by the possibilities of interacting with sled dogs, scavenging on human refuse, or picking up pieces of dried fish left by sled dogs. During summer, wolves sometimes walk between buildings to raid the nests of common eiders (*Somateria mollissima*).

Wolf pups were observed at Danmarkshavn in 1988, when a pack of four adult wolves and two pups visited the station and scavenged at the dump (Mågård 1988). During the summer of 1990, four different wolves were observed here. In April 1991, a female wolf approached the chained sled dogs, and succeeded in copulating with a male sled dog. In early June, this wolf joined a pack of three wolves.

The second important wolf habitat in East Greenland is Hold with Hope (74°N 22°W) in the southern part of the

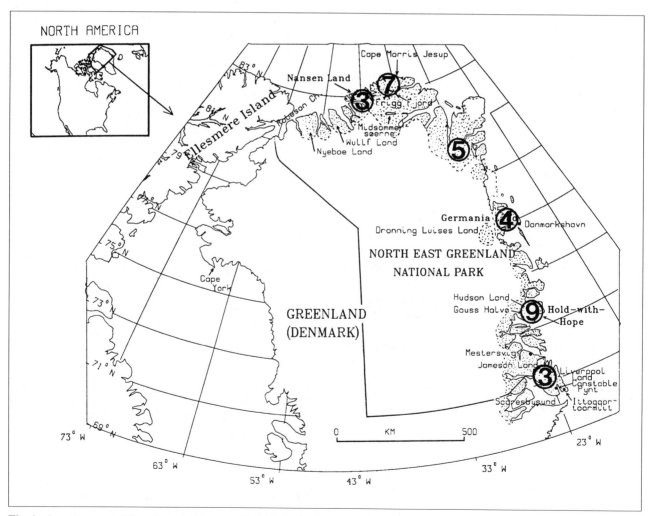

Fig. 1 *Location map of Greenland. Arctic wolves inhabit the ice-free area along the northeastern coast of the island (dotted area). Circles indicate known pack sizes, 1991–1992.*

National park. Wolves have been observed there regularly since 1980. This area has become the most important known breeding area for wolves in eastern Greenland.

Wolf pups were observed there in 1988, 1990 and 1992. Indirect evidence suggests that reproduction also took place in 1991 (Marquard-Petersen 1994). Four different den sites, with a total of six dens, have been located in the area.

Availability of Wolf Habitat

The Greenland wolf lives at the northern edge of wolf range with large areas characterized by low prey density or classified as arctic desert. Therefore, possibilities for successful dispersal of yearling wolves may be limited. Habitat capable of sustaining wolf packs in northern Greenland may be limited to areas surrounding the four most richly vegetated areas: Nansen Land, Nares Land, Frigg Fjord, and the area around the Midsommersøerne. Wolf observations in eastern Greenland are concentrated around Hold with Hope and Germania Land, both traditionally areas with seasonally high prey densities (Bay and Boertmann 1988).

Full legal protection has been accorded to the wolf in Greenland, except in Jameson Land and Liverpool Land in the southern part of its range. Wolves venturing into these areas are likely to be killed by Inuit hunters from Ittoqqortoormiit.

Acknowledgments

I am indebted to R.O. Stephenson, Alaska Department of Fish and Game, for his valued comments on earlier drafts of the manuscript.

Status of The Gray Wolf in the Lower 48 United States to 1992

■ Richard P. Thiel and Robert R. Ream

Gray wolves were extirpated in the conterminous United States (U.S.) outside Minnesota by 1960, but have since reappeared in several areas. Some 1,650 wolves exist in Minnesota and 100–120 wolves exist in small breeding populations in Michigan, Montana, Wisconsin, and possibly Washington. Lone wolves occur in Idaho and dispersers have reached the Dakotas and Wyoming. The wolf was classified as endangered in 1967 and was protected in 1974 under the Endangered Species Act of 1973. Federal recovery plans outline steps for restoring populations of the eastern timber wolf, northern Rocky Mountain wolf and the Mexican wolf and guide the respective recovery programs. Under state statutes, wolves are classified as extirpated, endangered, threatened, game animal, predator, and furbearer in 17 states where their presence is known or possible. State management plans exist or are being written in four states; five states indicate a willingness to cooperate with federal recovery efforts. Problems aggravating recovery efforts include public resistance to declassification and management of recovered populations, debate between state and federal governments over take (legal killing), and antagonism from the livestock industry.

Introduction

Biological Status Before 1970

As recently as 150 years ago wolves roamed throughout most of North America, including much of the lower 48 states exclusive of the Gulf Coast states east of Texas, where the red wolf (*Canis rufus*) lived (Young and Goldman 1944, Nowak 1983). Conflict with agrarian interests resulted in government-sponsored annihilation campaigns beginning in colonial Massachusetts in 1630 (Young and Goldman 1944). Wolves disappeared from the northeastern states and the Ohio River Valley by 1900 (Young and Goldman 1944). They lingered on in the southwest and intermountain west and occurred sporadically in the northern Great Plains until 1940 (Young and Goldman 1944, Young 1970, Brown 1983). The species persisted in the forested region of the upper Great Lakes states for another two decades. By 1960 the last population within the lower 48 states was restricted to northeastern Minnesota and Isle Royale National Park in Lake Superior (Stenlund 1955, Mech 1966a, Thiel 1993).

Biological Status, 1970–1990

Wolves were found only in northeastern Minnesota early in the period but breeding activity was noted in five states by 1990 (Fig. 1). Minnesota's wolf population ranged from an estimated low of 350–700 in 1963 to approximately 850 in 1971–72, but expanded gradually throughout the 1970's and 1980's to an estimated 1,500–1,750 wolves in 1989 (Fuller et al. 1992a).

By the mid 1970's wolves reappeared in Wisconsin (Mech and Nowak 1981, Thiel and Welch 1981, Fuller et al. 1992a) and slowly increased to about 45 individuals in 12 packs by 1990 (Wydeven et al. this volume). Wolves began colonizing upper Michigan in the 1980's and as many as 20 animals in three breeding packs were identified in 1991–92 (Thiel and Hammill 1988; Hammill 1992; J. Hammill, Michigan Dept. of Natural Resources, pers. commun.). Recently dispersers from Manitoba and Minnesota have been killed in the Dakotas (Licht and Fritts 1994).

Control programs in western Canadian provinces, active until the 1960's, eliminated wolf stocks in the Canada-U.S. border area (Gunson 1983a, Tompa 1983a, Gunson 1992). Wolves began recolonizing mountainous terrain near the international boundary during the late 1970's (Gunson 1983a, Ream and Mattson 1982). A lone wolf was collared in 1979 along the international boundary near Glacier-Waterton Lakes National Parks and breeding in the U.S. Rockies was documented for the first time in 50 years in 1986 (Ream et al. 1985, Ream et al. 1989). By 1992, wolves had increased to approximately 50 individuals in at least four packs scattered along the continental divide of Montana (Pletscher et al. 1991, Ream et al. 1991, Fritts et al. this volume). A few wolves have been verified in Idaho since the early 1980's and pack activity was discovered in the North Cascades of Washington in the early 1990's. In 1992, a single wolf was also documented in northwestern Wyoming (Fritts et al. this volume).

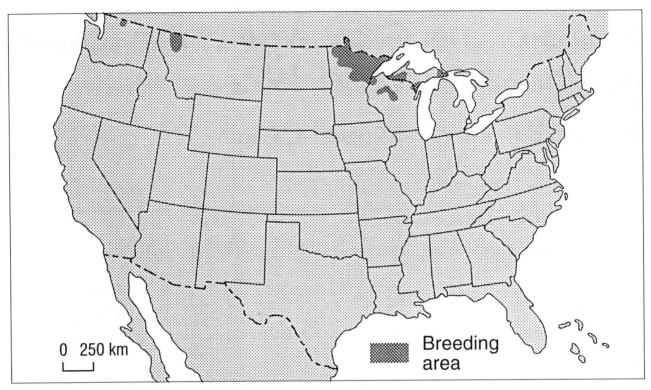

Fig. 1 *Distribution of gray wolves in the lower 48 states.*

The Mexican wolf is believed to be extirpated within the U.S. (Brown 1983). Unconfirmed sightings of wolves have been reported from southern Arizona and southwestern New Mexico in recent years, and survey work is under way in Mexico (Parsons and Nicholopoulos this volume; D. Parsons, U.S. Fish and Wildlife Service, pers. commun.).

Federal Legal Classification

Under provisions of the Endangered Species Act (ESA) of 1973, the gray wolf (*Canis lupus*) is protected as an endangered species in the contiguous U.S., except in Minnesota where wolves were downlisted to threatened in 1978. The U.S. Fish and Wildlife Service, a lead agency in recovery of wolves, began development of wolf recovery plans in three geographic regions in the 1970's. These plans delineate restoration activities for the eastern timber wolf (*C.l. lycaon*) in the upper Great Lakes (plan completed in 1978 and revised in 1992), gray wolves in the northern Rockies (plan completed in 1980 and revised in 1987) and the Mexican wolf (*C.l. baileyi*) in the southwest (plan completed in 1982, revisions pending). Federal recovery goals call for re-establishing wolf populations in each of these areas. These plans serve as guides for recovery activities for federal agencies to follow. The Service has no overall plan or recovery goal for the lower 48 states as a whole.

Each recovery plan addresses specific needs for restoring regional wolf populations; hence goals and management activities differ between areas. Goals for the eastern timber wolf

in the upper Great Lakes region are: 1) assuring the survival of the Minnesota population and, 2) establishing an additional viable population outside of Minnesota. Five management zones are established in Minnesota, linked to varying types of habitat and the relative amount of human conflicts experienced therein. Natural colonization of wolves presently occurring in northern Wisconsin and upper Michigan lessens the likelihood that restocking will be attempted and reduces the need for a reintroduction program in the northeastern U.S. (U.S. Fish and Wildlife Service 1992b).

For gray wolves in the northern Rockies region, the Yellowstone, central Idaho, and northwestern Montana recovery areas have been established. Recovery will be achieved when at least 10 breeding pairs are present in each of these areas for three consecutive years. Wolves may be downlisted to "threatened" in any of the three areas when these criteria are met. Reintroductions to establish a non-essential experimental population (Section 10(j) ESA) are recommended in the Yellowstone zone[1], and natural recolo-

---

1 Under a 1982 amendment to the ESA, introduced populations can be designated as "experimental". This designation allows greater flexibility in their management in order to address local concerns, and presumably, reduce local opposition to reintroduction. Individuals of such populations can be taken (i.e., removed from the population or killed) in certain circumstances (cf. Parker and Phillips 1991, Fritts 1993a). Conversely, where the species is classified as "endangered" (i.e., nonexperimental), it may be taken only in extremely limited circumstances (e.g., in defence of human life) and when specifically authorized by a permit (e.g. for research purposes).

Table 1. State legal classification and take status of the gray wolf among states within or adjacent to recovery regions. On the federal level, the gray wolf is classified as endangered in every state except Minnesota, where it is classified as threatened.

STATE	LEGAL CLASSIFICATION						"TAKE" STATUS		
	Endan-gered	Threat-ened	Predator	Game Animal	Fur-bearer	Extir-pated	Protected	Predator[1]	Unprotected
AZ				√			√		
CA						√			√
CO-nr[2]									
CN-nr									
IO					√		√		
ID	√						√		
MA	√						√		
ME						√	√		
MI	√						√		
MN		√						√	
MT	√						√		
ND					√			√	
NE						√			√
NH-nr									
NM	√							√	
NY	√						√		
OR-nr									
SD-nr									
TX-nr									
UT-nr									
VT						√			√
WA	√							√	
WI	√						√		
WY			√						√

1   Protected, but can be controlled if causing damage
2   nr = no response

nization is the preferred avenue in the latter zones. National public interest in reintroducing wolves to Yellowstone is driving wolf recovery in the intermountain west and a congressionally mandated Environmental Impact Statement (EIS) examines how wolves could be restored to the Yellowstone and central Idaho recovery zones (U.S. Fish and Wildlife Service 1987, Fritts et al. this volume, Bangs and Fritts, U.S. Fish and Wildlife Service, pers. commun.).

The current Mexican wolf goal in the southwest region is to maintain a captive breeding program and to establish a viable wild population somewhere within the subspecies' historic range (U.S. Fish and Wildlife Service 1982), but this goal will likely be modified following plan revision. Presently potential release areas are being evaluated in New Mexico and Arizona and an EIS is being prepared for proposed reintroductions to one or more of these areas (U.S.

Fish and Wildlife Service 1982, Parsons and Nicholopoulos this volume).

Recently wolves have appeared in states not considered within these recovery regions. Wolves presently occurring in the state of Washington and sporadically in the Dakotas present somewhat of a management dilemma because these areas lie outside the regions covered by existing recovery plans. The U.S. Fish and Wildlife Service is developing management plans to guide response to any wolf depredation problems that might occur in the Dakotas and Washington, and consideration is being given to including the state of Washington within the scope of the northern Rockies regional plan (S. Fritts, U.S. Fish and Wildlife Service, pers. commun.).

Individual State Legal Classifications

Inquiries were sent to state agencies within or adjacent to the three wolf recovery regions to ascertain individual state legal classification for the wolf, whether it is protected or unprotected under state law, whether a state recovery plan exists to manage the species if it should return, and whether the state would cooperate with federal recovery objectives. States were selected based on these criteria: 1) wolves presently occur within the state, but are not necessarily breeding, or 2) the state lies adjacent to a state where wolves presently occur or may occur in the future. For the upper Great Lakes region, states surveyed were: Connecticut, Iowa, Maine, Massachusetts, Michigan, Minnesota, Nebraska, New Hampshire, New York, North Dakota, South Dakota, Vermont, and Wisconsin. For the northern Rockies region: California, Colorado, Idaho, Montana, Oregon, Utah, Washington, and Wyoming. For the southwest region: Arizona, New Mexico, and Texas.

Responses were received from 17 states (Table 1). The wolf is listed under six different legal classifications and is protected in all but four of the states from which responses were received.

Arizona and Michigan are presently preparing, and Wisconsin has implemented a state-oriented recovery plan (Thiel and Valen this volume). Minnesota has a population management plan. No other state plans exist. The states of California, Idaho, Michigan, Minnesota, New Mexico, New York, Washington, Wisconsin, and Wyoming would cooperate or are already cooperating with federal recovery objectives. Iowa, Montana, and Nebraska indicated they would not cooperate under current provisions of ESA, and Arizona, Maine, Massachusetts, North Dakota, and Vermont would not speculate whether cooperation would occur.

The Future?

The past 15 years have witnessed an expansion in the distribution and number of gray wolves along the international border from the Great Lakes through the intermountain west. Decreased value and interest in pursuing furbearers (Gunson 1992), more favorable attitudes towards the wolf (cf. Tucker and Pletscher 1989, Kellert 1990), and an increased emphasis in implementing federal recovery programs have perhaps facilitated the return of the wolf to areas where it had been absent for, in some cases, 50 years.

Natural proliferation trends are likely to continue and therefore should result in re-establishing wolf populations in areas of the mountainous northwest, including the Yellowstone region, and in the forested habitats within Wisconsin and Michigan. Reintroduction is probably the only option for restoring the Mexican wolf.

Controversy may accompany the wolves and complicate recovery efforts of state and federal agencies. We perceive principal difficulties to be focused in three areas: 1) public opposition to delisting recovered populations and turning management over to states that would likely entail management of wolf populations either through government programs or through regulated sport harvests; 2) legal controversy over "take" in relation to experimental populations *versus* populations subjected to full protection under ESA and implications for dealing with livestock depredations; and 3) public perceptions that wolves will suppress coveted game species populations and adversely affect hunting and the hunting guide industry.

Our survey indicates that certain states are not willing to cooperate with federal recovery efforts. Several states have expressed frustration over various ESA restrictions, especially rules prohibiting take and this may be cause for a gridlock in recovery efforts.

Threats of court action from pro-ESA and pro-wolf organizations in response to petitions for delisting, or state appeals for more flexible management options may escalate the hostility between state and federal agencies. Those states that make honest attempts to ameliorate controversy through an open dialogue with the public may spend less of their precious fiscal resources in mitigation. In states where cooperation is withheld, conservation efforts on behalf of the species will be unwieldy and less effective, as the relentless bickering of various interests intensifies. Despite these problems, wolves will likely reclaim areas within the lower 48 states from which the species had been exterminated in an earlier era.

Summary of the Documentary Record of Wolves and Other Wildlife Species in the Yellowstone National Park Area Prior to 1882

■ Paul Schullery and Lee Whittlesey

Since the early 1900's, numerous investigators have examined the late Holocene (paleontological and archaeological) and early historical record of faunal conditions in the Yellowstone National Park area, and have disagreed over whether or not wolves and their prey species were abundant or rare. It is widely assumed that if prey species were abundant, then wolves were also present. Previous investigators of the early historical literature have all relied on 25 or fewer accounts prior to about 1880 for their information base, and this topic has not previously been examined by historians. The present paper makes use of 168 sources in the period between 1806 and 1881, and provides summaries of the evidence found in these sources. This much larger documentary resource establishes the presence and wide distribution of wolves and numerous other predators and scavengers. It likewise establishes the abundance and wide distribution of elk, bison, mule deer, bighorn sheep, and pronghorn, and to a lesser extent moose, in the present park area and the Greater Yellowstone Ecosystem. However, the faunal record as provided even by this much larger informational resource is not of sufficient resolution to allow precise comparisons with modern animal populations in the area. The historiographical utility and opportunities of this informational resource are also discussed.

Introduction

This analysis will concentrate on the documentary record of wolves (*Canis lupus*), other predators, and large mammal prey species, especially elk (*Cervus elaphus*), in the period between the first recorded Euro-American visits to the Greater Yellowstone Ecosystem (GYE), and 1882, the year before hunting became illegal in Yellowstone National Park. The record for wolves is provided to clarify the history of this predator in the GYE. The record for prey species is provided because it is generally believed in the scientific community that if prey were abundant, so were predators, including the wolf (Keith 1983).

We recognize that other methods, including paleoecological and paleolimnological studies, and comparative photography have been used to attempt to understand Yellowstone's prehistoric and early historical faunal conditions, and we review those studies here. Our own analysis, however, will be focused primarily on the written documentary record — how it has been used in the past, and how it may be used by applying the full resources of the historical discipline. In short, we are not attempting to address every aspect of the ongoing debate and controversy over Yellowstone's ungulates and their effects on vegetation. Instead, we provide here a thorough examination of one aspect of that debate that has not previously been analyzed by historians, in the hope that other elements of the Yellowstone dialogues might be advanced in the process.

Previous Analyses of the Historical Record

The early historical record of fauna in what is now Yellowstone National Park has only been lightly examined prior to this paper. Several views of that faunal community — its most common species and their relative abundance — have prevailed since the first Euro-American travellers came to the GYE. As will be shown, practically all travellers prior to 1882 who commented on the matter assumed wildlife to be abundant at the time of their visits, or to have been abundant prior to the establishment of the park.

Around the turn of the present century, however, a different viewpoint came into dominance: that the park area was only sparsely inhabited by large mammals prior to the settlement of the surrounding country by Euro-Americans. This new viewpoint grew out of a broader, apparently national perception among many wildlife authorities that in the western United States, large mammals had been plains animals and had been "crowded farther back into the mountains" (Graves and Nelson 1919:5) by loss of more desirable habitats to human settlement.

This viewpoint became common in Yellowstone National Park. Skinner (1927:170–176) reviewed several exploration accounts from the period 1870 to 1875 and concluded that large mammals were abundant in the lower country, such as the plains and valleys, but were rare in mountainous regions. However, Skinner also suggested, in the same publication and another (Skinner 1924:102), that elk did use the park as summer range, but settlement around the park forced them to winter in the park instead of leaving as they had done prehistorically. Rush (1932:11–16) apparently agreed completely that elk had been rare in the park area prior to 1872, quoting Skinner verbatim at great length. Bailey (1930:45) and Grimm (1939:295) agreed that elk were forced to stay in the park longer due to loss of winter range outside the park, but did not take clear positions on the prehistoric abundance of elk in the park area.

The view that elk were rare in the park area prehistorically was challenged very quickly. Murie (1940:2-8) reviewed more accounts than any previous investigator. Murie's observations on the abundance of large mammals in the park area form the foundation for later debates, and so must be quoted (in unedited form) at some length, to establish context for later discussions.

> In analyzing the statements made by early explorers some points must be kept in mind. First, negative evidence must yield to positive evidence because failure to report game does not disprove its abundance. Difficulty in finding game where it is known to be abundant is a common experience.... It is not at all surprising to me to read of early hunting parties failing to shoot game in good mountain game country. Some other factors operating to varying degrees to give the impression that game was originally scarce in the mountains are: 1) game in summer was largely at high elevations away from travelled routes; 2) game was often much hunted along the routes and may have been locally scarce; 3) large parties were noisy, resulting in game being scared away; 4) large parties needed a big supply of game and at regular intervals, so it was not unexpected that they should run out of food; 5) although game was no doubt more plentiful in the plains country than in the mountains the contrast was accentuated by wider visibility and easier hunting on the plains; 6) as in present-day journals, game was often referred to only casually, so all game was not necessarily listed; and 7) some habitats in the mountains, such as the dense lodgepole pine, are poor in game today, and the naturalists of the 1872 Hayden party travelled through Yellowstone largely in this habitat and not through the best summer game country. So much for explaining the impression sometimes obtained that game was scarce in the mountains.

Several later investigators (Cole 1969a, Lovaas 1970, Gruell 1973, Meagher 1973, Houston 1982, Barmore 1987) generally reinforced or elaborated on Murie's interpretation. Weaver (1978:7) concluded, based on his review of the

historical record in good part compiled by Meagher (NPS, unpubl. data), that "Wolves were members of Yellowstone's native fauna. Although few observations were recorded during the 1800's..., this could reflect either an actual low density of wolves or simply a lack of records."

Houston (1982:23–24) analyzed about 20 pre-1883 accounts, which he found cumulatively persuasive that "the Yellowstone area was historical summer range for large numbers of elk," that "it seems likely to me that elk have inhabited these areas in winter for as long as postglacial climates and plant communities would support them," and that, "historical accounts also do not support the interpretation that large numbers of elk were compressed into a smaller area in the park" by hunting or settlement.

Houston also expressed his doubt that useful winter ranges would have remained unoccupied: "Complete occupancy of all available winter range, the most limited seasonal energy source, probably evolved early on. The alternative interpretation of Skinner…and others is not supported by the records and also requires postulating an unlikely biological vacuum if elk moved from the area."

Kay (1990:288) on the other hand, conducted an extended analysis of 20 "first-person historical accounts of exploration in the Yellowstone area from 1835 to 1876." Compiling references to large mammals in three categories (game seen, game sign encountered or referenced, and game shot), Kay concluded that bison (*Bison bison*) were rare; moose (*Alces alces*) were "extremely rare" and are therefore now unnaturally abundant; mule deer and bighorn sheep were, in relation to elk, proportionately more common than they are today; no sightings were made of either wolves or mountain lions (*Felis concolor*); and elk and other ungulates were not abundant throughout the "Greater Yellowstone Area."

As will be seen, our analysis of a much more complete set of sources allows us to correct or modify the erroneous conclusions of previous investigators. For example, Kay (1990) missed many reports of ungulates, as well as a number of wolf and mountain lion sightings, by not reviewing enough sources. We cannot stress too strongly the need in this sort of project to employ as many sources as can possibly be gathered. Using only a few easily accessible sources leads to the same kinds of misunderstandings and errors that would occur from relying on a grossly inadequate data base in a scientific study.

At the same time, we cannot stress too strongly the inherent weaknesses of historical material of this sort. Sightings of wildlife, even from 168 sources, gathered over a period of more than 80 years, are at best indicative of general patterns. As well, ecological effects of native Americans — whose activities in Yellowstone prior to 1872 are only now undergoing serious scholarly attention — were no doubt complex, varying, and perhaps even significant, but until further study is done remain nearly impossible to quantify. In the present study, we have taken a period in the human occupation of Yellowstone — not at the beginning but in an

Wolves in a Changing World

important transitional stage, from native use through a combination of native use and Euro-American use to almost completely Euro-American use — and examined it through the eyes of firsthand observers.

The present examination of the historical record has proven useful, and heightens our understanding of how animals used the park area prior to 1882, but it should not be seen as an attempt to establish what is in any sense "right" for the park's wildlife today. Variables abound, not only in human use, but in fire history, climate, and other environmental factors.

Study Area

Our study area included all of present Yellowstone National Park, as well as commonly used travel routes to and from the park in the larger area known as the Greater Yellowstone Ecosystem (Glick et al. 1991). Most accounts were from the park or within a few kilometres of its boundaries, but some of special significance are cited from as much as 80–100 kilometres distant. Our use of accounts from outside of Yellowstone National Park was not as exhaustive as our use of park accounts; frequently, travellers who left accounts of the park also left accounts of surrounding country through which they travelled on their way to and from the park.

We must emphasize that accounts of early travellers do not provide systematic coverage of an area. Most visitors approaching the park area prior to 1882 (like most visitors today) used a few easy valley routes, just as most visitors within the park area did. Thus, we would expect wildlife observations, as well as comments on the lack of wildlife, to be concentrated in those areas.

Methods

For this analysis we reviewed 168 accounts of GYE wildlife prior to 1882. We defined an account as a report of a visit to the park, or a report of conditions in the park. Most of our 168 were firsthand accounts of the park by visitors, but some regional and local newspaper accounts were extremely important as well.

The accounts considered here varied enormously in length and detail, from entire books to single paragraphs in local newspapers (Schullery and Whittlesey 1992). If an account was serialized in a periodical, it was still defined as one account in our total. For example, H.B. Leckler's (1884) long and informative 18-part magazine series on his 1881 visit, or C.C. Clawson's (1871) 11-part magazine series on his 1871 visit, were considered one account each. On the other hand, if a single work, such as an extended diary, contained material on more than one visit to the park, each visit reported in that work was considered to be a separate account. This was rare, but one important example was the unpublished diary of A.B. Henderson (1894), who visited the park area at least six times between 1866 and 1873; this one work, then, contained six accounts. The goal was not to

report as large a number of publications as possible; the goal was to reflect the number of distinct sources of information.

The year 1882 provided a convenient stopping place for this paper for several reasons. Events set in motion in 1882, including the prohibition of hunting in the park in January 1883 (Avant Courier 1883b) and the creation of the first park police force, seem to have resulted in a decrease in the destruction of park animals. In 1886, when the U.S. Cavalry began its 32-year stay in the park, mass killing of park wildlife by hide-hunters became nearly impossible, though persistent poaching continued (Haines 1977).

For the purposes of this paper, we adopted a simple tabulation system, by which we were able to identify the types information provided by the reports (Table 1). There are, for most species, seven categories of reports, as follow.

1. *Sighting of an individual animal.* In this category we included any sighting or killing of an individual animal. If two or more members of the same party saw the same animal, we counted it only as one sighting. In all cases, we sought to use the most conservative number; if we suspected, but were not sure, that two different accounts were discussing the same animal, we counted the two reports as one sighting.

2. *Sighting of a small group.* In this category we included all reports of 10 or fewer of an animal. This category became a convenient catch-all for the common reports that made such vague statements as, "We saw three moose during the day," or, "during our march yesterday we shot five antelope." It is not possible in these contexts to determine if the animals were seen or shot singly or all at once, and so to simplify the tabulation (and, again, because it is the most conservative course in totalling number of sightings), we treated these small groups as single sightings.

3. *Sighting of a herd.* Many writers used terms such as "band," "group," "herd," and other words. It was often difficult to know how large a group they meant. Through careful review of the context, including other reports by the same writers in which they were more specific, we attempted to sort out small groups from large. Most of the time, it was obvious whether they meant more, or less, than 10. As in other categories, we sought not to count duplicate sightings (i.e., sightings of the same herd by different observers) of the same herd as more than one sighting.

4. *Sounds.* Several animals besides wolves made noises readily identifiable by these early travellers. Elk bugles and mountain lion screams may have been the most noteworthy.

5. *Reports of meat, skin, bones, antlers, or other parts.* Sometimes in these historical accounts, the first mention of an animal occurred after its death, as when a writer reported that a member of the party brought in a load of elk meat, or that camp dinner consisted of venison. These are legitimate reports of animal pres-

Table 1. Reports of wildlife in documentary records prior to 1882.

	Sightings of individuals	Sightings of small groups	Sightings of herds	Reports of sounds	Reports of meat, skin or other parts	Reports of tracks, trails scat, or other sign	General statements of presence
Wolf	2	2	—	10	1	2	17
Mountain lion	3	—	—	9	2	3	17
Coyote	1	—	—	1	—	—	8
Grizzly bear	14	7	—	—	—	3	9
Black bear	5	3	—	—	—	1	7
Bear, unspec.	24	20	—	—	5	16	47
Wolverine	8	—	—	—	1	—	7
Fox	4	1	—	—	—	—	6
Lynx	1	—	—	—	—	—	2
Bobcat	1	—	—	—	—	—	—
Elk	43	53	35	9	25	31	84
Bison	6	8	17	—	8	9	26
Moose	4	2	—	2	—	2	23
Mule deer	38	29	3	1	10	18	70
White-tailed deer	1	—	—	—	—	—	10
Bighorn sheep	1	9	15	—	8	9	34
Pronghorn	18	24	24	—	7	1	45
Mountain goat	1	—	—	—	—	—	1
Beaver	—	—	—	1	4	5	21

ence. In some cases, as in the reports of great numbers of cast antlers on the Northern Range or of wolf hides, they are especially significant evidence.

6. *Reports of tracks, trails, scat, or other signs of animals.* Tracks and trails were frequently mentioned in the early accounts, and though we sometimes must question the skills of the writers at identifying different kinds of tracks, these are important evidence. For example, when Leckler (1884) described the area near Mount Washburn in 1881 as "completely covered with deer and elk tracks, in many places cut up like a barnyard," the extent of the tracks is in itself significant, regardless of which species or set of species made them. However, these broad statements of track abundance are treated as one report. It may be an indication of the changes in public tastes and tolerances that observations of feces (and its numerous euphemisms) go more or less unmentioned by these early travellers.

7. *General statements of the presence of a species.* These statements include such things as listings of animals believed to be in the park. They also include some of the most important reports of animals that were seen. For example, when Raynolds reported that in the Madison River Valley, "antelopes have been visible in large numbers upon all sides" (Raynolds 1868:100), or when Drummond reported that along the Madison River in 1879, there was "abundant game, antelope, everywhere for twelve miles" (Smith 1901:186), there is no category that will fully portray that abundance of antelope. If such statements described the great number of animals as a herd, specifically, or referred to "herds," then one or two sightings of herds were added to the tabulation. If the statement was less specific, as are these by Raynolds and Drummond, it was tabulated as a general statement of presence. If an official report of the park, such as a superintendent's report or a government survey report, made repeated general statements of animal abundance in the same document, only one of those was counted as a general statement. If, on the other hand, such a report mentioned animals present in one part of the park, and then elsewhere in the report mentioned their presence in another part of the park, those two mentions would be tabulated separately.

In short, these categories and their tabulations as given below must be seen as absolute minimum representations. They are not presented here to suggest precisely how often early visitors saw animals, but only to allow some simple generalizations.

Fig. 1 *Hide-hunting was practised in the Yellowstone area even before the park was created. William Henry Jackson photograph No. 203, taken during the 1871 Hayden Survey, shows the Bottler Ranch, near present Emigrant, Montana, about 50 km north of the present Yellowstone National Park boundary. Great numbers of hides are stacked and hung around and in the shed. A young pronghorn stands next to the third man from the left.*

Results and Discussion

We cannot overstate our agreement with Murie (1940) on the point that negative evidence must yield to positive evidence. Some previous commentators have dealt with animal sightings as if they were tallying up a vote, that is as if a majority of negative reports somehow wins the "evidence election" over a minority of positive reports, even if that minority includes reliable reports of great numbers of animals. It quickly became evident that the larger the number of sources employed, the fuller the reporting of observed wildlife became; merely because an early observer did not mention seeing wildlife or evidence of wildlife (such as tracks or scat) is no proof that wildlife was not seen.

The traditional view of the game having been "pushed back into the mountains" continues to intrigue us. Though the evidence here, which is persuasive that in the earliest historical period large animals were present and often abundant in the park, renders the question moot in the case of Yellowstone, we think it worth consideration, if only because it is so pervasive and will no doubt endure as part of the body of public "common knowledge" for a long time.

We find important things lacking in the theory that the park's wildlife were forced into the park area by settlements. The theory implies that when settlement occurred, animals formerly occupying the settled areas abandoned their native range and moved to an entirely new one that had been unoccupied or only lightly occupied prior to that point. This suggests that usable vacant habitat existed for some indefinite period prior to the migration, and brings up the question raised by Houston (1982) of why that habitat was not occupied all along.

Viewing the theory as sympathetically as possible, however, we might propose that these mountain habitats were of much poorer quality, and therefore only of marginal interest to the animals until they were compelled to abandon better habitats. But recent studies of Yellowstone's Northern Range (for example, Merrill et al. 1988, Frank 1990) do not support the idea that the park is poor habitat. Long-term and short-term climatic changes (Haines 1977, 1:18–20, Hadly 1990, Whitlock et al. 1991) probably made it quite variable both as summer and as winter range.

What we find least acceptable about the theory, however, is the supposed cause of the migrations. Where were the settlements or other anthropogenic influences (a fairly small but well organized hunting effort could possibly have effects as great as a large settlement) that forced the animals into the park? The historical accounts suggest that large numbers of ungulates inhabited the park area through the earliest historical period. Settlement in the GYE was slight until the 1880's. Fort Ellis, and later Bozeman, existed as a small outpost on the northwest corner of the GYE prior to the time of the park's creation. Livingston, Montana, and Jackson, Wyoming, did not exist before about 1883, and Cody, Wyoming, was founded in 1895; West Yellowstone, Montana, was not established until 1907. Before 1883, scattered ranching and mining operations were under way in some areas near the park, but no settlements or large-scale agricultural enterprises. We do not doubt, in fact we assume, that some hide-hunting was going on, for example, down the Yellowstone River Valley to the north of the park as early as 1871, when William Henry Jackson photographed the Bottler ranch, near present Emigrant, Montana, including a large shed containing many hanging hides (Fig. 1). We do not see

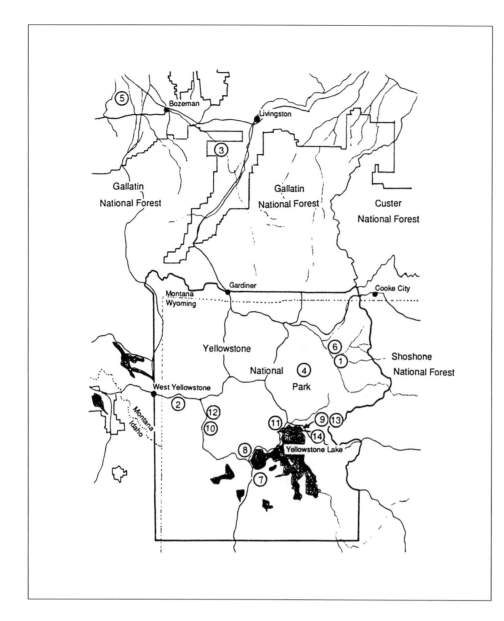

Fig. 2 *Locations of wolf sightings, howls and tracks of known location, 1836–1881. NOTE: This figure only includes reports for which a specific location was given by the observer. Other reports of sightings with no specified location, of collected skins, and general statements about the presence or distribution of wolves, are reviewed in the text: 1) sighting, group of wolves, 1870 (Henderson 1894:57); 2) sighting, pair of wolves, 1872 (Norton 1873:8); 3) sighting, single wolf, 1881 (Leckler 1884b); 4) howl, 1836 (Russell 1955:46); 5) howl, 1863 (Stuart 1876:159); 6) howl, 1869 (Haines 1965:27); 7) howl, 1870 (Everts 1871:3); 8) howl, 1871 (Clawson 1872a, Raymond 1873:274); 9) howl, 1873 (Comstock 1875:92); 10) howl, 1875 (Norris n.d.); 11) howl, 1876 (Doane 1970:480); 12) howl, 1879 (Geikie 1882:228; Smith 1901:183); 13) bedding site, 1873 (Comstock 1875:92); 14) track, 1872 (Norton 1873:37).*

evidence, at least in the sources we have so far located, that there were sufficient human pressures on the ungulate herds of the Yellowstone area to force wholesale withdrawal into the present park area.

As far as animals being forced one way or another by settlement or human activities, the opposite pressures existed in Yellowstone. As numerous accounts reveal, human inhabitants of and travellers in the region did their game killing in the heart of the supposed "safe" habitat, taking large numbers of animals from the Lamar Valley, where the theory proposes that the animals were driven for refuge.

Our study only included wildlife reports up to 1882. Among the many unresolved aspects of Yellowstone ecological history is what effect settlements and other activities (including continued hunting) may have had on ungulates after the region became more densely inhabited by Euro-Americans. There remains the issue of whether later settle-

ment, that is settlement of the Yellowstone region after 1882, somehow affected animal densities in the park, especially after 1886, when the U.S. Cavalry arrived to protect the park itself from poaching, thus turning it into a more genuine refuge.

Historical Evidence of Wolves

Though many of the references to wolves were not specific as to a particular location in the park, others provided reports of sightings, howls, or other evidence of wolves in named locations (Fig. 2). The historical record provides several sightings of wolves in the GYE, including in the present park area. Although William Clark stated that in 1806 he saw wolves in the Gallatin Valley (Thwaites 1905, 5:260), that sighting was probably outside most definitions of the GYE (Glick et al. 1991). As well, Russell (1955:35) reported that in 1835, at Ray's Lake, in the Snake River Valley southwest of the present park area, he "was awakened by the howling of wolves who had formed a complete circle within thirty paces of me and my horse at the flashing of my pistol however they soon dispersed." These sightings provide some background for the additional evidence from the GYE.

The first reported sighting in the present park area in the historical record is from Henderson (1894:57), who said that on 3 August 1870, somewhere in the upper Lamar Valley, probably near the mouth of Cache Creek or Miller Creek, his camp was "attacked by wolves," leaving us to wonder exactly what form the attack took. We assume that this meant he or his party actually saw the wolves near camp. Norton (1873:8) said that in the Madison River Canyon, his party saw "two sour-looking timber wolves, who scampered affrightedly away at our approach." Grinnell (1876:90) reported that during his 1875 visit he saw a wolf in the park, but he did not give a location. This is an exceptionally important sighting, coming from a trained professional naturalist, but we are unable to determine if this was a living wolf or some proof of a wolf, such as a skin. Leckler (1884) reported seeing an "immense wolf" near the head of Trail Creek, north of the park, in 1881.

Superintendent Norris (1881:6) in several accounts asserted that wolves were common in the park until the mid-1870's. He left a report of at least one specimen in his possession, saying that in the early winter of 1880, while gathering a supply of meat for his assistants, he and they were able to collect "fine hides of the bear, wolf, and wolverine." We cannot determine if this means one hide of a wolf, or more than one. Most important of Norris's mentions of wolves is his official report of their destruction:

> The large, ferocious gray or buffalo wolf, the sneaking, snarling coyote, and a species apparently between the two, of a dark-brown or black color, were once exceedingly numerous in all portions of the Park, but the value of their hides and their easy slaughter with strychnine-poisoned carcasses of animals have nearly led to their extermination (Norris 1881:42).

This is an especially important statement. It indicates that wolves were quite common when the park was established (Norris first visited the park area in 1870, and toured it extensively in 1875, becoming superintendent in 1877). Unfortunately, Norris did not leave us any tally of how many wolves he saw, or how many he estimated to have been killed by the poisons.

Excluding the Clark and Russell sightings, we thus have a minimum of four sightings of wolves in these accounts. That this is a minimum must be emphasized; the context of Norris's remarks suggests that he saw wolves more than once, presumably on numerous occasions (as a consequence of the poisoning work), and considered them to be a common resident of the park. Even without the numerous other historical accounts, we regard the Norris reports, alone, as

reasonable proof that wolves inhabited and were relatively common in the park area at the time of its establishment.

A second category of historical accounts of wolves includes howls and other noises heard and attributed to wolves. Some of the descriptions of wolf howls are almost as compelling as evidence as are the actual sightings. We counted 12 reports of at least 10 different episodes of wolf howling.

Russell (1955:46), on the night of 19 August 1836, on the Mirror Plateau reported that "all is silent except for the occasional howling of the solitary wolf on the neighbouring mountain whose senses are attracted by the flavours of roasted meat but fearing to approach nearer he sits on a rock and bewails his calamities in piteous moans which are re-echoed among the Mountains." Stuart (1876:159), on 19 April 1863, in the Gallatin Valley near the present site of Bozeman, reported that he "was serenaded by a full band of wolves last night." Folsom, on 16 September 1869, while camped near the mouth of Calfee Creek, reported that "the wolf scents us from afar and the mournful cadence of his howl adds to our sense of solitude" (Haines 1965:27).

During his 37 days of wandering alone in the present park area in the fall of 1870, Everts (1871:3) mentioned that he heard the "dismal howl of the gray wolf," probably south of Yellowstone Lake. Later, after he had moved north to some unknown location between the lake and the Tower Fall area, he reported that "the prolonged howl of the wolf" was one of the things that made him "insensible to all other forms of suffering" Everts (1871:3). Clawson (1872), late in the summer of 1871, reported that one night, apparently near West Thumb, "a band of hungry wolves sat upon a point some distance away and howled and yelled a most heart-rending war song, that seemed to terrify even our dog, who was a wolf-hunter by profession." Clawson's account was generally corroborated by Raymond (1873:274), a traveller in the same party, who said that "the prairie wolf, or coyote, and his larger cousin, the mountain wolf, howl plaintively o'nights."

Comstock (1875:92) heard the howling of a wolf near Steamboat Point (on Yellowstone Lake on 6 August 1873, and then saw sign of it the next day: "Being much fatigued, I turned in early, but, when fairly in a doze I was aroused by the frightened movements of my mule picketed near by, and I presently heard the doleful howl of a large wolf, which was slowly approaching along the trail. In anticipation of a trifling adventure, I lay down again with my carbine close at hand. It was late in the morning when I woke, and all was quiet; but a little investigation showed that the animal had been lying in the grass at the edge of the bluff, just above my head."

In 1875, Philetus Norris, on his second visit to the GYE but prior to his superintendency, reported the "prolonged howl of the mountain wolf" at the Lower Geyser Basin (Norris n.d.). On the night of 26 October 1876, Doane (1970:480) reported "a pack of wolves howling far down the lake shore" of Yellowstone Lake, near present Bridge Bay.

In 1879, probably along or near the Firehole River, Geikie (1882:228) reported "the mingled bark and howl of the wolves" at night. Drummond (in Smith 1901:183) left a diary of the same trip, in which he seemed to corroborate Geikie by mentioning "the wolf barking" while the party was near the Firehole River on 10 September.

It may be difficult for most listeners to know a wolf howl from a coyote (*Canis latrans*) howl. We also recognize that prior to 1900, there was some overlap in the naming of the two animals; coyotes were at least occasionally known as prairie wolves. We do have, however, some credible observers. Grinnell was a professional naturalist, Doane was a seasoned and respected western traveller whose other writings do not lead us to doubt his reliability, and Geikie and Comstock were both professional scientists. We see no reason to doubt that some, if not most, of these writers were seeing, or hearing the howls of, actual wolves.

Besides Comstock's report of the bedding site of a wolf, Norton (1873:37) reported tracks of a wolf on Stevenson Island. We also counted 17 general statements about the presence of wolves in the GYE, almost all of which applied to the park area. These assertions that wolves were present started as early as the 1849 account by Gunnison (1852:151). We consider this combination of sightings, reports of howls, and general statements to be compelling proof that wolves were widely distributed through the park and surrounding areas prior to 1882.

The slaughter of wolves in the 1870's requires additional comment. The destruction of wolves during that period may be the most significant single event to date in the history of wolf-human interactions in Yellowstone National Park. Norris (1881:42) said that "their easy slaughter with strychnine-poisoned carcasses of animals [has] nearly led to their extermination." The slaughter of Yellowstone wildlife was in fact no more or less intense than in many other areas of the west at the time, and wolves were being destroyed, especially by poison, in extraordinary numbers. Curnow (1969:31) reported that in Montana a "conservative estimate" of the number of wolves killed between 1870 and 1877 would be 100,000 per year. This number, however, suggests a density of wolves in Montana that is literally incredible; perhaps the number included coyotes and other predators. In any event, estimates of the number of wolves that would inhabit the park area once fully restored are around 150 (Koth et al. 1990), and if even comparable levels existed in 1870, all historical evidence suggests that Norris was right to presume their "easy slaughter." Curnow (1969:28), reporting on wolfing techniques in Montana, said that "up to one hundred wolves were found dead at one bait."

Weaver (1978:7) reported that few sightings were made of wolves between 1881 and 1908; though much more remains to be done with historical sources from this period, we suspect that these relatively few sightings may reflect a dramatic decrease in the number of wolves present due to the poisoning campaign of the 1870's. Weaver also reported

that the population, at least in northern Yellowstone, apparently began to increase after that, and that in the 1914–1926 period "a minimum of 136 wolves — including about 80 pups (59%) — were removed from dens, trapped, shot, and probably poisoned in the park" (Weaver 1978:7–8). After this period, the wolf was essentially, though not totally, gone from the park area.

It seems most likely to us that Yellowstone Park's notorious wolf-killing era of 1914 to 1926 may have been little more than a mopping-up operation of a job almost finished by 1880. Additional study, as well as the restoration of wolves to Yellowstone National Park and the subsequent study of their fortunes, would shed more light on these early times.

Wildlife Abundance

Elk and mule deer were far more frequently reported than any other large animals, but bears, bighorn sheep, bison, and pronghorn were also frequently observed (Table 1). This accumulation of information, despite the very real limitations of its sources, reveals the utility of analyzing anecdotal material if enough sources are available and are carefully used.

For example, so many sources mentioned elk, and reported their presence in herds or in evidence of great numbers (such as tracks) that it became overwhelmingly obvious to us that elk were in fact widely distributed in large numbers. The second most frequently sighted ungulate was the mule deer, individuals of which were reported almost as frequently as were individual elk.

We believe that some earlier investigators placed more confidence in their much smaller information bases than we would place in our large one, and though there is some truth to the idea that anecdote multiplied often enough eventually becomes data, we take a very conservative approach to interpreting our findings. That said, we do think it worth subjecting the information in Table 1 to a simple review, as follows. An analysis of these numbers serves to show both the strengths and weaknesses of the information.

Singer (1990) estimated average ungulate ratios on Yellowstone's Northern Range in the 1980's as follows: 100 elk:10 mule deer:two bison:two pronghorn:one bighorn sheep:one moose. Our tabulation of reports of these six ungulate species was for the entire GYE rather than on the Northern Range, but a comparison of the relative abundance of the six species in the 1980's with the total reports of the six species in the period prior to 1882 is an interesting and possibly illuminating exercise.

If we add all sightings and reports of each species, excluding general statements of presence, we have this ratio: 196 elk:99 mule deer:74 pronghorn:48 bison:42 bighorn sheep:10 moose. Converting these proportions to the same scale as Singer's proportions, above, with a base of 100 elk, we get 100 elk:51 mule deer:38 pronghorn:25 bison:21

bighorn sheep:five moose. Several aspects of this sequence are of interest here.

- The only difference in the order of relative abundance between the 1980's and the period before 1882 is that bison and pronghorn have traded places in the middle of the sequence.
- Though mule deer were reported about half as often as elk, they were also reported only about half as often in small groups, and less than 10% as often in herds, leading us to assume that they were much less numerous than elk during this period. Taking advantage of as many sources as we did helps shed light on such intriguing observations as that of Osborne Russell, who in 1839 reported seeing "vast numbers" of mule deer in the geyser basins. Even keeping in mind that Russell was an intelligent and often very careful observer, his single comment becomes something of an "outlier" in the larger context of the many other reports of deer. We cannot completely rule out that he saw a huge number of deer, but with the added background of so many other sightings, his becomes an oddity rather than the compelling evidence it might seem to someone who had used fewer sources.
- Though bighorn sheep reports total more than 20% of elk reports (42:196), many of the reports of herds of sheep did not come from the Northern Range. Again, this suggests one of the limitations of relying too heavily on a tabulation created at such a simplistic level as this one; it is very difficult to represent precisely the real meaning of the anecdotal evidence. However, our interpretation of the accounts of bighorn sheep is that the numbers of sheep were indeed higher prior to the establishment of the park (1872) than now, perhaps substantially higher, especially in the Absaroka Range along the east boundary of the present park.
- The high number of pronghorn reports, including two-thirds as many herds as elk (24:35), seems to reflect a real difference between park pronghorn numbers prior to 1882 and pronghorn numbers today. Even considering the more consistent visibility of pronghorn as an open-country dweller, pronghorn appear to have been much more numerous throughout the GYE then than they are now. Large herds were apparently common down the Madison and Yellowstone River valleys to the west and north of the present park. Houston (1982) documented the history of the pronghorn decline on the Northern Range; the accounts we reviewed also suggested significant declines, and the declines appear to have been even more spectacular outside the park.
- We documented only two possible references to moose on the Northern Range, and another just to the south of it; moose reports were generally from the southern third of the park.
- We arbitrarily established a definition of a herd as more than 10 animals. This definition does not reflect differences in herding behavior (timing, locations, or size of herds) among the six ungulate species; nor does it reflect the great range of sizes of herds that occur in the historical record. Elk, and to a lesser extent pronghorn and bighorn sheep were more often reported in large herds (hundreds or thousands of animals) than were other ungulates.

Besides tabulating reports of individual species of wildlife, we counted 77 general statements about "game" in which it was not possible to determine what species were intended. Of these, 21 were specific references to some particular feature or area, such as a comment on a "game trail" being followed. The other 56 were broader statements about game being abundant or scarce. Of these 56 general statements about game abundance, five reflected the belief that game was rare in the park and 51 supported the belief that game was abundant. The writers of the five did not give reasons for their belief; that is, they did not say that game was scarce because it had always been scarce, or because of overhunting, or for some other reason. We consider this an especially important exercise. It shows the extent to which the early travellers and authorities who should have known the park best differed with the viewpoint that arose around the turn of the century, a viewpoint that held that game was scarce in the mountainous regions of the west. The early writers who described the park area as a "hunter's paradise" might have been surprised at how quickly their firsthand observations would be forgotten (Figs. 3 and 4). Even recognizing the probability of boosterism among some travellers who wanted to make their region look as good as possible, or portray their travels as romantically as possible, we are persuaded by a 90% majority that many animals were present, in part because enough accounts gave us specific, credible descriptions of them. Again, this is not a conclusion based on use of a few accounts, but an impression based on repeated support. For example, in the case of elk, we find Russell, in 1837, describing the country around Yellowstone Lake "swarming with elk," and William Henry Jackson (1875:32) in his catalog of photographs taken in the park area in 1871, saying that elk were "very abundant about the lake." We have the prospector A.B. Henderson (1894:49–57) describing great numbers of elk in various parts of the Northern Range in 1870, and being corroborated by the diary of one of his travelling companions (Gourley 1929:2), who said that in the Lamar Valley they came upon "hundreds of elk so tame that they only moved a little distance to the side of us," and by members of the Folsom-Cook-Peterson expedition (Haines 1965:28) who, the year before, while camped on Flint Creek (a tributary of the upper Lamar River), reported that they saw "a great many deer today, and judging from their tracks, elk are also abundant."

Historical Evidence for Wintering Elk

Historical accounts from the mid-to-late 1880's (just after our study period) suggest that the present park area was used

Fig. 3 *Many early travellers in the park found elk and other large mammals abundant. William Henry Jackson photograph No. 302, taken during the 1871 Hayden Survey in Yellowstone National Park, and described by Jackson as showing, "Our hunters, Jose and Joe Clark, returning from a successful hunt, with pack animals laden with elk-meat" (Jackson 1875:31).*

as winter range by substantial numbers of animals, 4,500 or 5,000, in the period 1883–1887 (Avant Courier 1883a, Hofer 1887:319, Harris 1887:12,13). Houston (1982) reviewed the numerous reports of wildlife numbers in the period after the United States Cavalry assumed protection of the park in 1886; in this period, elk especially were reported as very abundant. Prior to the mid 1880's, however, there is little quantitative information available on the size of elk and other herds.

Houston (1982:206) considered Blackmore's observation of an "abundance" of cast elk antlers on the Blacktail Plateau (Blackmore 1872, 6:71–72) as evidence of wintering elk. A similar, but even more comprehensive, observation was made by Doane (1970:473), who reported "thousands" of elk antlers in 1874 near Mount Washburn, and reported that "there are many such places in the park."

Perhaps the most important evidence of wintering elk may be the details of the slaughter as provided by Strong

Fig. 4 *William Henry Jackson photograph No. 500, taken during the Hayden Survey of 1872, and described by Jackson as showing, "The successful hunter. Fred Boteler [sic.], who accompanied the survey as hunter, killed, within an area of fifty feet diametre, five large elk, before breakfast. The view shows them as they fell, with the hunter in the center of the group. The locality is on the Yellowstone River, about three miles above the Great Falls" (Jackson 1875:46). The "Great Falls" are the Lower Falls of the Yellowstone River, at the head of the Grand Canyon of the Yellowstone in east-central Yellowstone National Park.*

(1968), Grinnell (1876), Norris (n.d.), Ludlow (1876:66), and Baronett (in Strong 1968:106), who made it clear the animals were being killed in the winter when they were defenceless in the deep snow. Though these accounts leave no doubt that thousands of elk were being killed in the park, and were sometimes killed in winter conditions, they do not usually contain the detail in dates, numbers, or location that the later reports (after 1883) do. For example, Norris (n.d.), discussing his 1875 visit in an unpublished memoir, said that the Bottlers (local hide-hunters living north of the park) told him that they took more than 2,000 elk skins from the "forks of the Yellowstone" (the mouth of the Lamar River), but he said they did so "in the spring of 1875," so we cannot know if this was proof of wintering elk or elk on their spring migrations into higher parts of the park. Strong (1968), who visited in 1875, at one point suggested that elk were killed in the park in late fall and early winter as they moved to lower country, but at another point describes animals being killed in deep snow while in a weakened state (we presume he means weakened from exposure and hunger, which would suggest animals wintering in the snow, but he could have meant weakened by attempting to flee from hunters).

Park gamekeeper Harry Yount (1881:62) gave us some of the first useful winter wildlife observations, reporting that some animals did winter in the park despite an apparently severe winter in 1880-1881. Yount said that "about 400" elk wintered on the Lamar River and Soda Butte Creek. Houston (1982:11) commented on Yount's report, saying that "only 400 animals remaining in this upper portion of the range during a severe winter is not unusual." Houston (1982:210) interpreted Yount's reports of winter conditions that year as follows: "Apparently a very severe winter as Yount's own weather records show snow falling on 66 of 90 days from December 1880 to February 1881."

In short, the accounts of the park prior to 1882 indicate that elk and other animals wintered in the park but only rarely provide meaningful information on their numbers. Houston (1982:23-25) reviewed interpretations of wintering elk numbers from this earlier period into recent times, suggesting, in contrast to earlier investigators (Cahalane 1941, Craighead et al. 1972), that prehistoric elk populations down the Yellowstone River valley to the north of the park may have actually constituted a "biological barrier" to the migratory movements of elk that wintered in the park. Houston (1982:24) also acknowledged the "possibility that densities [of wintering elk in the park today] are somewhat different now (either higher or lower) for other reasons, e.g., climatic changes, plant succession, [or] levels of predation."

We can only concur that the many variables that affect animal distribution were in effect throughout the early historical period. Though not yet analyzed in print, the potential influences of the Little Ice Age, which ended in the mid 1800's, on reducing winter use of the park area by ungulates prior to the creation of the park in 1872, have been under discussion by several investigators (M. Meagher, NPS, pers.

commun.; D. Frank, Idaho St. Univ., pers. commun.; C. Whitlock, Univ. Oregon, pers. commun.).

We offer two sets of conclusions. The first concern the historiography of this material, that is, what the historical accounts have taught us about their nature as evidence.

1. As a general rule, the more accounts that are evaluated from a particular party's experience in the park, the more the story of their experiences with park wildlife is fleshed out. One observer in a group frequently noted animals or evidence of animals not noted, or even observed, by another member of the same group.

2. There were sometimes large differences in the success of different parties in the same year at observing wildlife.

3. Large, noisy parties were likely to frighten wildlife and decrease their chances of observing it; members of those parties often saw more wildlife when travelling alone. Kay (1990) disagreed with Murie's (1940) contention that large parties did not see wildlife because they frightened it. Kay cited the example of General Marcy, a member of the Strong party (on an 1875) visit, who hunted alone (away from his large party) for three to four days without success. Marcy left little mention of where he hunted — how far from his party, or how far from regular travel routes where tourists routinely shot at wildlife and made them wary. The precise causes of an individual hunter's failure are extremely hard to quantify from the information given in these accounts. We did, however, record several accounts where small parties leaving their main party did encounter more wildlife. On the Strong trip itself, four men travelling alone for a few days shot "a grizzly, an elk, and six deer, and they saw a great many more, while on this side of the river we have seen very few" (Strong 1968:92). Comstock (1875:93), leaving the large Jones survey party of 1873, and travelling with one companion from Yellowstone Lake to the Lamar River, reported "plentiful tracks of game were noticed, but we saw very little until near the summit, when we met a large drove of elk and some deer." He then reported that he was able to move through the fallen timber for some distance "by following the very numerous game-trails high above the stream." Kelly (1926:217–227), visiting the southern part of the park in 1878, described several encounters with wildlife, including the shooting of a bull elk that he then shared with a party of soldiers who were unable to get any game because of "the bell mare that led the train and scared all game within sound of its brazen appendage."

4. The behavior of animals when encountered by early travel parties was widely variable. Sometimes animals fled, sometimes they didn't.

5. Most writers of accounts of the park prior to 1882, with a few notable exceptions among sportsmen, were far more likely to discuss the park's famous nonwildlife

features (geysers, waterfalls, canyons, and the lake) than they were to report on animal observations. Multiple accounts from single parties suggest that animal observations were often incidental. This leads us to a general conclusion that reports of wildlife observations (whether of tracks, actual animals, or other evidence) in these early accounts will tend to understate the number of animals observed.

6. The historical record as used by previous investigators, and limited to no more than two dozen accounts, is perilously slight for the purposes of more than anything but the most general of comments about animal presence and abundance.

7. Even the much larger historical record we employed in the present study lacks the depth or resolution to allow accurate estimates of animal numbers. The record is not sufficiently detailed, for example, to allow us to say with any confidence that elk numbers on the Northern Range during any given year in that period equalled, exceeded, or were less than, at present.

8. The historical record will, however, allow for meaningful general impressions of the relative abundance of various species of animals over the course of the period 1830 to 1881, and in the case of some species, may permit arguable hypotheses regarding their comparative abundance then and now.

Here, then, are our conclusions about the abundance and distribution of wolves and other species in the period 1830 through 1881.

1. Wolves were present and distributed throughout the present GYE.

2. Other predators and scavengers, including mountain lions, grizzly bears (*Ursus arctos*), black bear (*Ursus americanus*), wolverine (*Gulo gulo*), coyote, red fox (*Vulpes vulpes*), and smaller mammals were present. In the case of mountain lions, their numbers or willingness to encounter humans (or some combination of the two) made them more evident to travellers than they are today. Wolverine and fox may have been more abundant, and coyotes less abundant, then than now.

3. Almost all (more than 90%) of the observers who commented on the abundance of wildlife in the park area expressed the belief that it was very abundant. This included almost all of the observers who did not actually see many animals. For a combination of reasons, including the observation of tracks and other signs, communication with other travellers and residents of the area, and some received knowledge or standing presumptions, even those who did not personally see animals in numbers assumed them to be present.

4. Elk were widely distributed throughout the park area, and were observed, often in groups and occasionally in large herds, in every portion of the park where such observations would be expected today. Bighorn sheep may have been more abundant then than now, especially

in the earlier part of the period. Mule deer were common. Bison were present in several parts of the park, and still survived in the hundreds in 1880. Moose were common in the southern part of the park, and were even rarely reported near or on the Northern Range. White-tailed deer (*Odocoileus virginianus*) were never common, and mountain goats (*Oreamnos americanus*) apparently did not occur in the park. Elk and other ungulates were heavily harvested by hide-hunters in the 1870's.

5. The historical record suggests that the park was winter range prior to 1882, and at times this winter range was occupied by large numbers of animals. After 1882 the historical record is clearer, and even more convincing that thousands of animals wintered in the park.

6. The combination of hide-hunting, recreational hunting, subsistence hunting by residents, carcass-poisoning, and commercial trapping dramatically affected the wildlife regime in Yellowstone National Park in the 1870's. The apparent effects included a great reduction, perhaps even the near-extermination, of wolves, and a great reduction in beaver. Other effects that might be inferred but which are not supported as clearly by the historical record include reduction of some smaller carnivores, especially wolverine and fox. Effects on ungulate populations are difficult to assess, but by the early 1880's elk remained quite abundant in the park.

One recent investigator has proposed that the many contemporary reports of the slaughter of thousands of elk and other large animals in the park were not true. Kay (1990), based on his review of 20 accounts, decided that reports of large numbers of animals, as well as reports of large numbers of animals being killed by hide hunters in the 1870's, were exaggerated or fabricated by observers for political reasons. Kay proposed that Ludlow (1876), Strong (1968), Norris (1880, 1881), Hayden (1872), and Henderson (1894) all dishonestly reported, for various reasons, the number of animals seen.

The examples of reported elk numbers given above should dispel doubts about their presence in large numbers, but the hide-hunting episode is also far better documented than Kay could determine from using only 20 sources. Besides the reports of various legitimate government officials, such as Ludlow, Grinnell, Strong, Norris, and Hayden, private-citizen reports (Horr 1873, 1874; Norris n.d.) exist, and were further corroborated by two regional petitions. In 1873, 71 Montana citizens petitioned the Secretary of the Interior to better protect the park, mentioning among other things the vandalism that was "driving off and killing its game" (H.R. Exec. Doc. 241:6). In 1878, a group of 148 Montana citizens petitioned the Secretary again, objecting to the "destruction" of "valuable animals" in the park (Montana citizens 1878). The extensive hide-hunting of elk and other animals in Yellowstone National Park in the 1870's did without question occur, and made national news (Fig. 5).

Fig. 5 *The slaughter of large mammals in Yellowstone in the 1870's received national media attention. On 11 July 1878, the New York Daily Graphic ran this series of illustrations of the slaughter of wildlife then occurring in Yellowstone National Park. The caption read as follows: "The splendid game in the so-called National Park, on the Yellowstone, is being recklessly destroyed by hunters, simply for the pleasure of killing, notwithstanding the laws of Congress and of Wyoming and Montana, intended to protect the region from the spoiler. Elk, of which the park contains thousands, are shot down, and the carcasses left upon the plain, not even the skin being removed. One hunter has slaughtered as many as seventy-five elk in one day. It is the duty of the prosecuting authorities of the Territories in which the Park is situated to see that such criminal and wanton waste be punished and repressed." Notice that the antlers on the dead elk in the large picture are palmate; the illustrator almost certainly was unfamiliar with the details of Yellowstone wildlife, though apparently aware of the Lower Falls of the Yellowstone River. The smaller pictures show the editor's sarcasm, proposing more efficient ways to continue the slaughter by the use of explosives and cannon.*

The abundance of wildlife in the GYE prehistorically and in the 19th century has been analyzed in other disciplines than documentary history. For example, Hadly (1990) provided persuasive paleontological evidence suggesting that elk used habitats in the Lamar Valley prehistorically (during the past 2,000 years) much as they do now; Hadly also reported wolf bones in the same excavation. Cannon (1992) was one of several investigators to review paleontological and archaeological sites in the northern Rockies of the U.S.; he concluded that wolves were resident of the park area prehistorically, and that elk and bison were as well, though he was not able to resolve questions of their abundance. Engstrom et al. (1991) determined that sediments in eight Northern Range ponds indicated no sudden changes in ungulate densities or use of the pond basins during the 19th century, thus indicating that animal numbers did not increase abruptly in the park, as numerous writers cited above have

proposed. Houston (1982) and Kay (1990) examined early photographs of vegetation on the Northern Range, and reached opposite conclusions: Houston concluded that changes in vegetation (such as apparent declines in willow and aspen) were not the result of great increases in elk, while Kay concluded the opposite. Our findings regarding wildlife numbers and distribution prior to 1882 should be of interest to investigators attempting to understand park ecosystem processes after that date. For example, the extensive hide-hunting of elk in the 1870's, and the destruction of beaver in the same period (Norris 1881:43–44), should be of interest to investigators concerned with the status of aspen in the park. Aspen are known to have declined significantly, in their adult (tree-sized) form since early in this century (Houston 1982). This decline is a source of great controversy, with many observers proposing that an increase in elk numbers is responsible (Kay 1990). Among the little-appreciated aspects of the aspen story in Yellowstone is the sudden surge in aspen growth through the 1880's and early 1890's (William Romme, pers. commun.). Most trees now growing old and dying on the park's northern range date from that one short period of successful aspen establishment. It seems improbable to us that there is no connection between the abrupt reduction of two of the park's premier aspen predators, elk and beaver, and this sudden aspen "birth storm," though we assume that there were other factors involved, especially climate.

For another example, notably few of the early travellers in the park made mention of coyotes. This could be in part because coyotes were too routinely seen in western landscapes to be mentioned by diarists, but it could also be because of the greater presence of wolves prior to the 1870's. Coyote numbers are sometimes known to be lower in the presence of wolves (Fuller and Keith 1981a, Carbyn 1982a, Paquet 1991a), and these changes in predator numbers will be of interest to those involved in today's dialogues over the restoration of wolves to the park.

The science and management of Yellowstone National Park's predator-prey systems are extraordinarily complex. We recognize that our findings in the present study tend to corroborate some previous studies while they confound others. We conclude that functionings of this unique ecological community remain at least partly a puzzle, and that no single discipline will alone resolve the issues involved. Only an interdisciplinary approach, of as much breadth as can be achieved, stands a chance of yielding meaningful results.

Acknowledgments

This summary is based on a much larger work — a full documentary history — that provided all the original accounts summarized in Table 1. We thank N. Bishop, W. Brewster, M. Johnson, J. Mack, M. Meagher, T. Tankersley, and J. Varley of the National Park Service in Yellowstone National Park for help with specific questions. As usual in our historical research, B. Whitman and B. Zafft, of the Yellowstone Park Research Library, helped in many ways. The manuscript of the documentary history was read and commented on by W. Brewster, National Park Service, Yellowstone; D. Houston, National Park Service, Olympic National Park; K. Cannon, National Park Service Midwest Archaeological Center; D. Flores, Texas Tech University; and S.R. Neel, Montana State University. Their many comments and suggestions significantly improved not only this paper, but our sense of direction for the greater work that we hope will grow from this one. Sarah Broadbent, National Park Service, Yellowstone, materially improved the presentation of this paper with her attention to countless editorial details. We are grateful to the many helpful suggestions made by the scientists who reviewed the manuscript as part of the peer-review process, and to C. Shanks and L. Carbyn for many editorial suggestions. Last, we are always grateful to Aubrey Haines, former National Park Service historian, whose exhaustive scholarship pioneered the use of countless important sources in early Yellowstone history.

An Alternative Interpretation of the Historical Evidence Relating to the Abundance of Wolves in the Yellowstone Ecosystem

■ Charles E. Kay

The plan to reintroduce wolves in Yellowstone is predicated, in part, on the premise that large numbers of wolves inhabited that ecosystem before the National Park Service eliminated them from the park. According to some, wolves were a relatively common sight in Yellowstone when it was declared the United States' first national park in 1872. To test this assertion, I conducted a continuous-time analysis of first-person journals written by people who explored Yellowstone between 1835 and 1876. During that period, 20 different parties spent a total of 765 days travelling through the Yellowstone Ecosystem, yet no reliable observer reported seeing or killing even a single wolf, and on only three occasions did explorers report hearing wolves howl. The available historical journals do not suggest that wolves were common in Yellowstone during the 1835–1876 period. Those same journals indicate that ungulates were also rarely encountered in the park. Bison were reportedly seen only three times (none of which were in the park) and elk were seen on only 42 occasions, or an average of one elk observation per party in 18 days. The fact that a number of parties broke into small groups and spread out to hunt makes these observation rates all the more meager. Moreover, while the explorers were in Yellowstone, their journals contain 45 references to a lack of game or a shortage of food. Historically, Yellowstone contained few ungulates, and accordingly, wolves were rare. An Aboriginal Overkill hypothesis is presented to account for the observed rarity of ungulates and wolves.

Introduction

During the 1920's, the U.S. National Park Service exterminated wolves from Yellowstone National Park, while other federal and state agencies eliminated wolves (*Canis lupus*) from the remainder of the Greater Yellowstone Ecosystem (Weaver 1978). In 1978, the wolf was listed as an endangered species throughout the United States except for Minnesota, where wolves are classified as a threatened species, and Alaska where they are managed as a game animal under state regulations (U.S. Fish and Wildlife Service 1987).

Under provisions of the Endangered Species Act of 1973, the U.S. Fish and Wildlife Service (1987) formulated a recovery plan for wolves in the northern Rocky Mountain including Yellowstone. The plan calls for reintroducing wolves into the Yellowstone Ecosystem, and is supported by the Fish and Wildlife Service, the Park Service, and various environmental organizations. Wolf recovery, however, is opposed by the states of Montana, Wyoming, and Idaho as well as by livestock producers and some sportsmen.

The plan to reintroduce wolves in Yellowstone is predicated, in part, on the premise that large numbers of wolves inhabited the ecosystem before they were eliminated by predator control efforts. According to some, "[wolves] were a relatively common sight in Yellowstone when it was declared the nation's first national park in 1872" (Anonymous 1987a:B1). Randall (1980:188) claimed that "when trappers and explorers reported on the Yellowstone region in the mid-1800's, they sang [of] a land teeming with bison, elk, mule deer, bighorn sheep, and antelope. The great carnivores — grey wolf, grizzly bear, and mountain lion — flourished." Federal agencies contend that Yellowstone Park could support at least 10 wolf packs totalling 100–150 animals and imply that number of wolves has always inhabited the park (National Park Service and Fish and Wildlife Service 1990a, 1990b). Based on wolf habitat requirements and prey densities, the remainder of the ecosystem could support another 600 or so wolves, discounting political considerations (Bennett 1994).

To test the assertion that wolves were common in the Greater Yellowstone Ecosystem prior to predator control, I conducted a continuous-time analysis of first-person journals written by people who explored the area between 1835 and 1876.

Study Area

The Greater Yellowstone Ecosystem encompasses 7.3 million hectares in northwest Wyoming, south-central Montana, and northeastern Idaho (Clark and Zaunbrecker 1987) and contains the headwaters for three of the major river systems in the western United States; the Yellowstone-Missouri, the Snake-Columbia, and the Green-Colorado. The Yellowstone Ecosystem is now home to over 200,000 ungulates including, in order of occurrence, elk (*Cervus elaphus*), mule deer (*Odocoileus hemionus*), moose (*Alces alces*), white-tailed deer (*O. virginianus*), bighorn sheep (*Ovis canadensis*), pronghorn antelope (*Antilocapra americana*), bison (*Bison bison*), and mountain goats (*Oreamnos americanus*) (Glick et al. 1991). A description of Yellowstone's climate, physiography, vegetation, and wildlife management history are provided in Houston (1982), Despain et al. (1986), Boyce (1989), Despain (1990), Kay (1990), and Glick et al. (1991).

Methods

As part of my research on the historical distribution and abundance of wildlife throughout the West, I conducted a continuous-time analysis of accounts left by early Yellowstone explorers. This included the following journals. 1) Osborne Russell (1965) five separate trips between 1835 and 1839; 2) William Raynolds (1868) 1860; 3) Walter Delacy (1876) 1863; 4) Bart Henderson (1867) 1867; 5) Cook-Folsom-Peterson Expedition (Cook et al. 1965) 1869; 6) Bart Henderson (1870) 1870; 7) Washburn Expedition, three accounts by Gillette (1870), Doane (1875), and Langford (1972) 1870; 8) Barlow-Heap Expedition (Barlow and Heap 1872) 1871; 9) Hayden survey (1872) 1871; 10) Frank Bradley (Bradley 1873) 1872; 11) Sidford Hamp (Brayer 1942) 1872; 12) William Blackmore (1872) 1872; 13) Jones Expedition (Jones 1875) 1873; 14) Earl of Dunraven (Dunraven 1967) 1874; 15) William Ludlow (Ludlow 1876) 1875; 16) General Strong (Strong 1968) 1875; and 17) Doane Expedition, two accounts by Doane (1876), and Server (1876–77) 1876.

This list includes the earliest first-person accounts for the Yellowstone Ecosystem (Haines 1977) including all such journals cited by Houston (1982: 204–208). Other published first-person journal accounts of comparable quality are not known to exist (Haines 1977). There are other narrative accounts of Yellowstone exploration, but these are not included in my analysis because historians have determined that narrative accounts are not as accurate as first-person journals written at the time of the event (White 1991:613–

632). Even "the humblest narrative is always more than a chronological series of events" (McCullagh 1987:30). The ideological implications of most narrative historical accounts are "no different from those of the narrative form in fiction" (Galloway 1991:454), because narrative accounts are always influenced by prevailing cultural myths (White 1991:618).

Standard techniques, developed and employed by historians to judge the validity of historical accounts (Forman and Russell 1983), were used to gauge the accuracy of all the Yellowstone journals cited above (Kay 1990: Chapter 9). To overcome problems of selection bias, I systematically recorded all observations of wolves, ungulates, and other large mammals found in these historical accounts. Data were tabulated in three ways.

First, game seen. I listed the observer, the date of his trip, the length of his trip within the Greater Yellowstone Ecosystem, the size of the party, and the number of occasions on which the explorers actually saw wolves and other game animals. Seeing one animal was recorded as a single observation, and if they reported two or more animals together at a time, that was also recorded as a single observation for that species. When an explorer reported killing one or more animals of a particular species at a time, that was recorded as one sighting of that animal. The number of references to abundant game where the species were not identified was also included.

Second, game sign encountered or referenced. I listed the number of occasions when specific animal sign, usually tracks, was seen or referenced. For instance, if explorers said they were going deer hunting, that was recorded as a single reference to deer. Included in these counts are any references to hearing specific animals, such as wolves howling or mountain lions (*Felis concolor*) screaming, as well as references to Native American artifacts. For example, Osborne Russell (1965), who met Native Americans on Yellowstone's northern range, noted that they had various animal skins. Each of those observations was recorded as a single reference to that species. I also listed the number of occasions on which Native Americans were seen or their sign, trails, and the like were referenced. In addition, I included the number of references made by each party to a lack of food or lack of game. Acts such as shooting a horse for food were considered a single reference to a food shortage.

Third, game shot. I listed the number of wolves and other large animals that each explorer reportedly killed within the Greater Yellowstone Ecosystem. In nearly every instance, those people recorded the exact number of animals killed. At the time, explorers were free to kill any animals they saw. There were no state game laws and even after Yellowstone Park was established, shooting animals for camp food was permitted for a number of years.

Yellowstone was not "officially" discovered by Europeans until 1869 and was one of the last regions to be explored in the western United States (Haines 1977). Fur trappers,

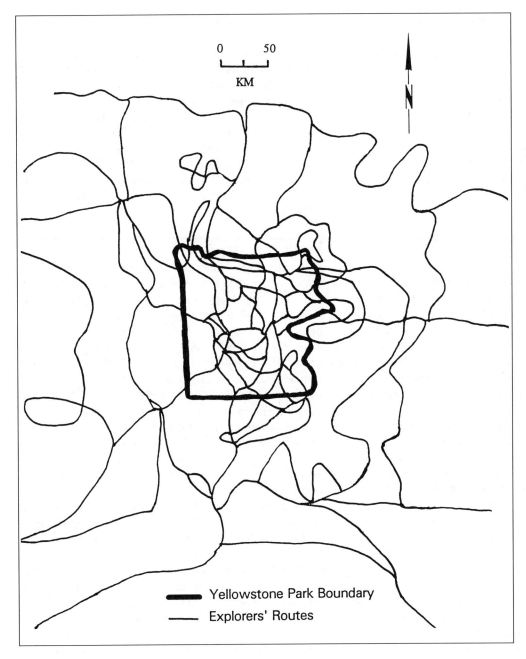

Fig. 1 *Approximate routes travelled by people who explored the Greater Yellowstone Ecosystem between 1835 and 1876. Some routes were used by more than one expedition.*

0   50

KM

N

——— Yellowstone Park Boundary

——— Explorers' Routes

such as John Colter, probably visited the area as early as 1807–1808 but only Osborne Russell (1835–1839) left a written account known to have survived (Haines 1977). Russell's journal, however, was not published until 1914, well after the official "discovery" of Yellowstone. Unlike other regions of the West, Yellowstone was not on established travel routes, and therefore was subject to less direct European disturbance than other areas (Haines 1977).

Results

Early explorers visited most parts of the Greater Yellowstone Ecosystem, though their travels were concentrated along routes to major scenic attractions such as thermal

areas, Yellowstone Lake, and Yellowstone Falls (Fig. 1). Between 1835 and 1876, 20 different expeditions spent a total of 765 days travelling through the Greater Yellowstone Ecosystem, yet no one reported killing a single wolf. There was only one account of a wolf sighting. In 1870, Henderson (1870:57) reported that "soon after camping [in Yellowstone's Lamar Valley] our camp was attacked by wolves." During the 765 days, wolf sign was reported on only three occasions (Table 1). In 1836, Osborne Russell (1965:46) reported that he heard "the occasional howling of the solitary wolf" east of Yellowstone Park. While camped in Lamar Valley in 1864, Cook et al. (1965:27) observed that "the wolf scents us afar and the mournful cadre of his howl adds to our sense of solitude." In 1876, Doane (1876:13) reported that he heard "a pack of wolves howling far down the…shore" of Yellowstone Lake.

Given their lack of scientific training, Yellowstone's early explorers may have mistaken coyote (Canis latrans) howls or other animal calls for those of wolves. During this era, coyotes were frequently called wolves or prairie wolves even by trained observers. Moreover, Native Americans often imitated wolf howls for communication, especially while on raiding parties or when near Europeans (Trenholm and Carley 1964). Reports of animal sign are always less reliable than reports of sighting or kills (Kay 1990).

Discussion

Historical Abundance

Although Henderson (1870) recorded seeing wolves in Yellowstone, that may not have been a valid sighting because evidence shows he was not a reliable observer. Henderson reported seeing and killing more game in Yellowstone than any other early explorer. In fact, he reported seeing and killing more elk, bison, deer, and bears than nearly all the explorers before or after him (Kay 1990). He reported having "27 bearskins" in camp, most of which, judging from the text, were grizzlies (Ursus arctos). He also reported seeing moose on Yellowstone's Northern Range and implied that they were common. If he, in fact, killed 20 or more grizzlies, that would represent over 10% of the current grizzly bear population in the entire Greater Yellowstone Ecosystem (Knight and Eberhardt 1985). In addition, Houston (1982:131) stated that there were no verified observations of moose on the Northern Range until 1913. Finally, there is no evidence that wolves ever "attacked" a camp similar to Henderson's anywhere in North America (U.S. Fish and Wildlife Service 1987).

This suggests that Henderson exaggerated or invented some of his diary entries. His entry of July 24 sheds some light on his observational abilities. On that day, he travelled through Yellowstone's Upper Lamar Valley and reported it contained "thousands of hot or boiling springs." Today, there are fewer than 50 hot springs in the Lamar Valley including lower Cache Creek (Bryan 1979). This small thermal area never contained "thousands" of hot springs and certainly did not when Henderson visited that area in 1870 (Bryan 1979). There is little doubt Henderson's diary entry on this point represents a gross exaggeration. Thus, it is unwise to rely on any of the wildlife observations in Henderson's journal.

When only one of the early explorers reported seeing a wolf, and he is at best unreliable, the most that can be said is that wolves were rare in the Greater Yellowstone Ecosystem during the 1835 and 1876 period of written record. Given the detail in many of these journals, it is doubtful that explorers simply failed to record observations of wolves. Moreover, given the length of time explorers spent in the ecosystem, and the fact that they travelled by horseback or

on foot, it is also doubtful that wolves were simply too shy to be seen.

Other records indicate that wolves were not particularly common even after Yellowstone Park was established. From 1880 to the early 1900's, few observations of wolves were recorded in the park (Weaver 1978), and from 1914 to 1926 when the Park Service was actively working to eradicate wolves, only 136 wolves were killed. This may seem like a lot, but it included only 56 adults over a 13-year interval (U.S. Fish and Wildlife Service 1987:1). Park Service records suggest that during this time there were, at most, only four wolf packs in the park and possibly only two (Weaver 1978:11).

Why Were Wolves Rare?

Evidence suggests that there were few wolves in Yellowstone between 1835 and 1876 because there were few ungulate prey. Despite spending 765 days in the Yellowstone Ecosystem, early explorers reported seeing bison only three times, none of which were in the park, and they reported seeing elk on only 42 occasions, or an average of one elk observation per party in 18 days. The fact that a number of parties broke into small groups to hunt makes these observation rates all the more meagre. Despite travelling through areas where hundreds or thousands of ungulates are now commonly seen, early explorers consistently saw little game. For instance, Hayden (1872:131) noted that "our hunters returned, after a diligent search for two and a half days with only a black-tailed [mule] deer, which, though poor was an important addition to our larder."

These same journals also contain 45 references to a lack of game or a shortage of food while the explorers were in Yellowstone (Table 1). While travelling through part of the Yellowstone Ecosystem in 1863 where today large numbers of elk and moose are common, DeLacy (1876:107) noted, "as usual, some men went out to hunt, and others to prospect, but brought in neither gold or game. Up to this time, and for a long time after, we saw nothing larger than rabbits." Colonel Gibbon (1874:136) described how his 1871 Yellowstone exploration party "fell short of provisions, and had to kill squirrels, blue-jays, and a pelican, and finally to grub for wild roots for subsistence." Other parties that ran short of supplies sent for additional food, a round trip of nearly 300 km. Still others shot their horses to survive. Historically, Yellowstone was not a land teeming with game.

A few of these journals, however, do contain narrative references to an abundance of game or that the whole country was swarming with game. Those accounts, though, may have been inspired by political motives or cultural myths rather than fact (see Kay 1990: Chapter 9 for a detailed accounting of observer reliability). During the late 1870's, the U.S. military was lobbying Congress to have Yellowstone Park transferred to its jurisdiction. So Captain Ludlow (1876), General Strong (1968), and others had reason to exaggerate the early abundance of game in the park and the

Table 1. Historical observations on wolves, Native Americans, and a lack of game in the Greater Yellowstone Ecosystem.

Observer	Date[1]	Length of trip (days)	Size of party	Number of occasions wolves were reported			Number of references to a lack of game or food	Number of references to Native Americans
				Seen	*Killed*	*Sign*		
1. Osborne Russell								
a.	1835	61	Varied, usually	-	-	-	-	3
b.	1836	34	3-4, but some	-	-	1	-	1
c.	1837	56	groups contained	-	-	-	-	3
d.	1838	15	up to 60 people	-	-	-	1	-
e.	1839	68		-	-	-	1	2
Subtotal	1835-3	634		-	-	1	2	9
2. William Raynolds	1860	26	32+	-	-	1	3	9
3. Walter DeLacy	1863	27	13-40	-	-	-	2	5
4. Bart Henderson	1867	13	4	-	-	-	-	2
5. Cook-Folsom-Peterson Expedition	1869	22	3	-	-	1	2	5
6. Bart Henderson	1870	68	5	1	-	-	-	4
7. Washburn expedition								
a. Langford	1870	29	19	-	-	-	8	8
b. Doane	1870	29	19	-	-	-	1	7
c. Gillette	1870	35	19	-	-	-	-	2
8. Barlow & Heap Exped.	1871	41	17	-	-	-	1	4
9. Hayden survey	1871	39	40	-	-	-	1	-
10. Frank Bradley	1872	55	12	-	-	-	1	-
11. Sidford Hamp	1872	17	8-35	-	-	-	-	-
12. Willian Blackmore	1872	21	20-30	-	-	-	-	6
13. Jones Expedition	1873	44	45	-	-	-	8	2
14. Earl of Dunraven	1874	30	7	-	-	-	7	3
15. William Ludlow	1875	15	22	-	-	-	-	-
16. William Strong	1875	14	35	-	-	-	6	-
17. Doane Expedition	1876	64	6-8					
a. Doane				-	-	1	6	-
b. Server				-	-	-	3	-
Total[2]	1835-76	765	Varied	1	-	3	45	53

1   For exact dates and trip routes, see Kay (1990: Chapter 9).
2   Does not include duplicate sightings or references to the same event.

Fig. 2 *Yellowstone National Park's Mammoth Hot Springs as it appeared in 1872. According to the Park Service, 12,000 to 15,000 elk have wintered on Yellowstone's northern range for the last several thousand years and those elk have always had a dramatic impact on the park's woody vegetation. The agency contends that aspen, willows, and conifers were as heavily browsed or high-lined by ungulates in the early years of the park's existence as they are today. The Park Service believes that high-lined conifers are natural and not a sign of overgrazing. Yet, in this 1872 photograph, as well as in all other historical photographs, conifers show no sign of ungulate browsing or high-lining. Instead, the trees have branches that extend to ground level, except where light ground fires killed the lower branches. Today, all trees around Mammoth Hot Springs have had their lower branches consumed as high as the starving elk can reach. Historical photographs of the more palatable aspen and willows also do not show evidence of ungulate browsing. Despite what certain narrative historical accounts may appear to suggest, the available physical evidence indicates that large numbers of resource-limited elk and other ungulates did not winter in Yellowstone until after the national park was established (see Kay 1990, Chadde and Kay 1991, Kay and Wagner 1994 for additional early photographs). William H. Jackson photograph (F-28,835) courtesy of the Colorado Historical Society, Denver, Colorado.*

amount of poaching which supposedly occurred. By discrediting the early civilian administrators and showing that they were incapable of protecting Yellowstone, the military hoped to sway Congress (Haines 1977). In that they were successful, for the military was given control over Yellowstone in 1886 and ran the park until the National Park Service was created in 1916 (Hampton 1971).

Narrative and secondhand accounts of an abundance of game may also have been inspired by cultural myths of the day. White (1991:618) noted that daily journals kept by early western travellers often differ from their latter narrative accounts because the narratives were written to conform with accepted social myths. Unlike journals, which were usually written for personal use, narratives were written for publication and had to conform to accepted social traditions if they were to be widely read and financially successful.

During the 1800's, the myth that the Intermountain West was a "Garden of Eden" teeming with wildlife colored many narrative accounts (White 1991:613–632).

Others, however, have cited those passages to support their belief that tens of thousands of ungulates have always inhabited Yellowstone (Murie 1940, Gruell 1973), and that wintering ungulates have always had a dramatic impact on the park's plant communities (Houston 1982). They believe that Yellowstone is not now nor has ever been overgrazed by native ungulates (Despain et al. 1986). They contend that high-lining of conifers and of other woody vegetation is "natural" and not a sign of overgrazing (Houston 1982).

Photographs taken in the park between 1871 and 1890, though, do not show any evidence of ungulate browsing or high-lining (Kay and Wagner 1994). Repeat photosets (n = 125) show that since Yellowstone Park was established aspen (*Populus tremuloides*) and tall willows (*Salix* spp.) have declined 95% as a result of repeated ungulate browsing, not other factors (Kay 1990, Chadde and Kay 1991). Since conifers and other woody vegetation in the earliest images were 70 to 100 years old or older when they were first photographed and since they showed no evidence of ungulate browsing, this would indicate that few, if any, ungulates wintered in Yellowstone from the late 1700's through the 1870's (Fig. 2). These photographs do not support the contention that Yellowstone was always home to thousands of ungulates (Kay and Wagner 1994). Instead, they support the conclusion that few ungulates inhabited the ecosystem prior to European arrival, thus explaining why wolves were rare.

Why Were Ungulates Rare?

In addition to their historical rarity, ungulates, and especially elk, were also rare prehistorically (Kay 1990). Although a complete discussion of this subject is beyond the scope of this paper and has been presented elsewhere (Kay 1994), I offer the following observations and hypothesis.

Studies of contemporary ungulate populations typically focus on whether they are limited by resources (food), severe winter weather, carnivorous predation, disease, or some combination thereof. In pondering what factors limited ungulate numbers in pre-Columbian times, most authors invoke these same influences. The role of Native Americans is generally not considered, dismissed out of hand, or glossed over with a few cursory statements (Jobes 1991:388). Although not often explicitly stated, the idea that prehistoric humans lived a brutish existence where they spent every waking moment in the quest for food underlies most biologists' dismissal of Native Americans as important ecological factors (Simms 1992). Anthropologists, however, abandoned this stereotype of "primitive" people more than 20 years ago (Lee and DeVore 1968). Anthropologists have shown that hunter-gatherers had more leisure time than the average person living in today's "most advanced" western civilizations (Hawkes and O'Connell 1981). Sahlins (1972) even went so far as to call hunter-gatherers "the original affluent society."

Based on my research and analysis, I believe that prior to European contact, predation by Native Americans was the major factor limiting the numbers and distribution of ungulates in Yellowstone and throughout the Intermountain West (Kay 1994). My Aboriginal Overkill hypothesis arises from analyses of: 1) the efficiency of Native American predation, including cooperative hunting, use of dogs, food storage, use of non-ungulate foods, and hunting methods; 2) optimal-foraging studies; 3) tribal territory boundary zones as prey reservoirs; 4) ungulate species ratios in archaeological contexts compared with those of present ungulate communities; 5) sex and age of ungulates killed by native peoples; 6) impact of European diseases on aboriginal populations; 7) lack of effective aboriginal conservation practices; and 8) the apparent synergism between aboriginal and carnivore

predation. Accordingly, none of the North American ungulate-predator systems studied to date represents the conditions that existed prior to European arrival.

Contrary to common perception, not only did Native Americans have no effective practices to conserve ungulates, but the manner in which those peoples harvested ungulates was the exact opposite of any predicted conservation strategy (Simms 1992). There is also no evidence that Native American's system of religious beliefs prevented aboriginal peoples from overutilizing ungulate populations (Kay 1985a, 1985b). Little correlation exists between how a people say they manage their resources and what they actually do; the difference between emic and etic behavior (Tuan 1970, Kay and Brown 1985). Instead of being "noble savages" who were too wise to overexploit their resources, Native Americans acted in ways that maximized their individual fitness regardless of their impact on the environment (Simms 1992). Because native peoples in Yellowstone and throughout the Intermountain West could subsist on vegetal foods, small mammals, and fish (Wright 1984), they could take their preferred ungulate prey to low levels or extinction without adversely impacting human populations (Simms 1984). Although diminishing returns acts as a homeostatic mechanism to control populations of most predators, like wolves, little such control has operated in the case of man (Cohen 1977:187).

Mech (1977a) reported that wolf packs used the edges of their territories less frequently than the central part of their ranges in order to avoid encounters with neighboring wolves. This reduced predation pressure along the territorial edges, thus permitting more white-tailed deer to survive in those areas and to live to older ages (Hoskinson and Mech 1976). Mech (1977a) could find only one other instance of this buffer zone phenomena in the literature, a paper by Hickerson (1965) entitled "The Virginia deer and intertribal buffer zones in the upper Mississippi Valley." Hickerson (1965:45) noted that, "Warfare between members of the two tribes had the effect of preventing hunters from occupying the best game region intensively enough to deplete the (deer) supply….In the one instance in which a lengthy truce was maintained between certain Chippewa and Sioux, the buffer, in effect a protective zone for the deer, was destroyed and famine ensued."

While Mech could find only a single reference to tribal buffer zones, my research has uncovered at least 100 similar references in historical journals and studies of modern hunter-gatherers. For instance, Lewis and Clark (1893:1197), who made the first recorded exploration of the northern Rockies in the United States, noted that, "With regard to game in general, we observe that the greatest quantities of wild animals are usually found in the country lying between [Indian] nations at war." There is a direct correlation between where Lewis and Clark saw game and where they saw native peoples. Where there were no Native Americans, there was abundant game — primarily on the plains of eastern Montana — and where Native Americans were common, there was no game. Lewis and Clark would have starved in the mountains if they had not obtained food, primarily fish and roots, from native peoples.

In some instances, tribal territory buffer zones were up to 200 km wide. The presence of tribal territory buffer zones demonstrates that aboriginal hunting limited ungulate numbers and that Native Americans had no effective conservation practices, as predicted by central place optimal-foraging theory. The presence of tribal territory buffer zones can not be explained by wolf predation and suggests that carnivores played a secondary role in limiting ungulate populations during prehistoric times (Kay 1994).

I believe that Native Americans were keystone predators who structured entire ecosystems. It is now commonly recognized that systems with native peoples are entirely different from those without aboriginal populations (Simms 1992). Thus, the modern western concept of wilderness as areas without human influence is a myth (Gomez-Pompa and Kaus 1992). Prior to European arrival, most of North America was owned, used, and modified by native peoples. North America was not a "wilderness" waiting to be discovered but home to tens of millions of aboriginal peoples before European-introduced diseases decimated their numbers (Dobyns 1983, Ramenofsky 1987). While early Yellowstone explorers made, at most, four references to wolves, they made 53 references to native people who once called that ecosystem home (Table 1).

Conclusion

The information available does not support the belief that wolves were common in Yellowstone at any point in recorded history. There is no historical support for the belief that restoring 10 wolf packs to the park would reestablish the conditions that existed prior to European influences, commonly referred to as "natural" or "pristine" conditions. The data, in fact, suggest that wolves were always rare in Yellowstone.

Acknowledgments

I thank R. Taylor and R. Simmons for helpful comments on the manuscript. This research was funded by the Rob and Bessie Welder Wildlife Foundation, Sinton, Texas (Contribution No. 398) and the Quest For Truth Foundation, Seattle, Washington. Publication of this paper was supported by the Foundation for North American Wild Sheep, Cody, Wyoming; the Wyoming Farm Bureau, Laramie, Wyoming; the Meeteetse Multiple Use Association, Meeteetse, Wyoming; and Utah State University's Political Science Department.

Elk and Wolves in Jasper National Park, Alberta, from Historical Times to 1992

■ **Dick Dekker, Wesley Bradford, and John R. Gunson**

Hunting and severe winters reduced elk populations in western Alberta during the 1800's. Reintroduced to Jasper National Park (JNP) in 1920, elk multiplied to 3,000 by 1945 when herds were culled yearly until 1970. During 1973–1975, elk in JNP declined from 2,000–2,500 to 850–1,000 and remained near that level until 1992. Causes of the decline include winter starvation, hunting near park boundaries, and predation. Wolves were numerous in western Alberta in 1754–1859, but became scarce in the late 1800's when prey populations were low. Wolves in the park numbered 35–55 in 1945, increased to 80–100 by 1974, and declined to 27–50 during 1983–1992. Elk cow:calf ratios were 100:18–19 in districts where wolf denning sites were associated with elk calving grounds, and 100:48 where elk occur throughout the year along roadways and near human habitation. Elk in the backcountry use river islands for calving, and escape into rivers and on cliffs to avoid wolves. The effect of wolf predation on elk calf survival in JNP's backcountry is severe because elk have a clumped and restricted distribution.

Introduction

The sympatric distribution of elk (*Cervus elaphus*) and wolves (*Canis lupus*) in North America is at present more limited than before European settlement. Observations of elk/wolf demographics in mountainous habitats such as JNP are of particular interest in view of the proposed reintroduction of wolves into Yellowstone National Park, United States, where wolves are absent and elk numerous (Singer 1990).

The literature on historical populations of elk and wolves in the JNP region was reviewed. After the park's establishment, periodic estimates of elk and wolf numbers have been recorded by the Canadian Parks Service and the Canadian Wildlife Service. This study reports elk calf survival rates for three areas in JNP with different wolf densities during 1983–1992. The interaction of elk and wolves and the causes of population declines are discussed.

Study Area

The mountainous terrain of JNP's 10,880 km^2 extends north to a latitude of 52°29' and south to 52°08'. Elevations decrease west to east from a maximum of 3,747 m in the main ranges to a minimum of 990 m along the lower Athabasca River. A major highway and railroad parallel the river. Secondary roads connect the town of Jasper with various tourist facilities and scenic attractions. A network of horse trails ascends most of the major valleys.

Three main ecoregions exist: the alpine, subalpine, and montane. Within each of these regions there is a wide variety of landforms and vegetative zones, as well as lakes, ponds, and streams. Timberline extends to the upper limit of the subalpine, which is covered with coniferous forests, interspersed with bogs of alpine fir (*Abies lasiocarpa*), spruce (*Picea* spp.), and lodgepole pine (*Pinus contorta*). The most productive life-zone is the lower montane, which is restricted to the lower valleys and characterized by rough meadows and mixed woods of white spruce (*Picea glauca*), lodgepole pine, balsam poplar (*Populus balsamifera*), trembling aspen (*Populus tremoloides*), and willow (*Salix* spp.).

The climate of the JNP region is subarctic with short summers and long, cold winters that are modified by frequent "chinook" winds in the front ranges. Snow cover in the montane is intermittent, making this habitat of critical importance as winter range for grazing ungulates. A diversity of large mammals includes seven different species of ungulates, as well as wolves, cougars (*Felis concolor*), grizzly bears (*Ursus arctos*), black bears (*Ursus americanus*), and a number of smaller predators. For more detailed information on JNP's fauna and flora, see Soper (1970) and Holroyd and Van Tighem (1983).

Methods

Historical information was gathered from narratives of early explorers and diaries of fur company post-masters. Elk population estimates for 1926–1975 are based on periodic

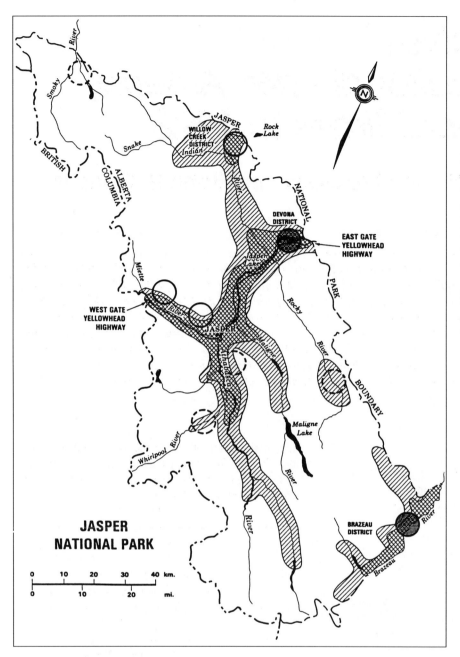

Fig. 1 *Map of Jasper National Park, Alberta, showing elk range and wolf denning areas. Hatching represents pre-1975 year-round elk range; cross hatching represents post-1975 year-round range. (During summer, some elk expand into adjacent regions.) Solid circles indicate traditional wolf denning areas in current use; open circles indicate intermittent use; dotted-line circles indicate areas used in the 1970's when wolf populations were highest.*

surveys by the Canadian Wildlife Service during autumn and spring when elk are on traditional winter ranges. During November 1986–1991, JNP staff conducted yearly roadside counts of elk, classified as to age and sex, in the Athabasca and Miette valleys (Fig. 1).

Estimates of wolf numbers are based on sightings by park wardens, observations by the senior author, and studies by the Canadian Wildlife Service and the Alberta Fish and Wildlife Division. Factors that support the reliability of wolf population estimates include: 1) year-round wolf habitat in JNP is limited to the major valley systems that are frequently visited by wardens; 2) wolf habitat includes much semi-open terrain where the chance of seeing wolves is greater, especially during winter; 3) wolves in JNP are often seen to travel during the daytime; and 4) variation in pelage color of JNP's wolves is a help in distinguishing packs (Dekker 1986). Since 1974, the Jasper Warden Service has recorded all sightings of wolves on Wildlife Survey Data Forms that were entered into a computerized Cansis Data Recording System.

In 1983-1985, the Alberta Fish and Wildlife Division studied a wolf pack that denned near the Brazeau River in JNP, but ranged widely on adjacent provincial lands. Three wolves in this pack were captured and fitted with radio collars. The wolves were monitored every two weeks from a fixed-wing aircraft for the duration of the project and on a daily basis from a helicopter during two months of each winter. Eleven survey flights were flown to classify elk nursery herds on alpine summer range east of the Brazeau River.

The senior author conducted wildlife observations in JNP with a special focus on wolves in 1965–1992. Until 1982, the major study area was the Willow Creek district in the Snake Indian drainage. After wolves stopped denning at Willow Creek, field observations were centred in the Devona district near the confluence of the Snake Indian and Athabasca rivers (Fig. 1). The study areas were visited 10–20 times a year at irregular intervals. Each visit lasted two to five days. Both study areas included denning and rendezvous sites of wolf packs in association with elk calving grounds. At Devona, if weather conditions were calm, simulated howling was used in early morning and evening to get a response from wolves on semi-open meadows where they could be observed, through binoculars or telescope, from a lookout hill (Dekker 1985a). Prey species were counted and classified as to age and sex. To avoid duplication, cow:calf ratios of elk at Devona reported here were restricted to one observation per autumn on the date when the largest herd was seen. No attempt was made to distinguish between adult and yearling females of over one year of age.

Weather data for the town of Jasper were obtained from Environment Canada. Chi-square statistics were used to compare some results.

Results and Discussion

Historical Elk Populations

Elk were apparently part of the post-Pleistocene fauna in present-day JNP, although archeological excavations are few and paleo-faunal information is scarce. Near Pocahontas some antler fragments were classified as elk with an estimated age of 1900 B.P. (Pickard 1987).

Journals of the first European fur scouts indicate that elk were common on the plains and in the foothills of western Alberta during the mid 1700's and early 1800's (Burpee 1907, Glover 1962). However, it is not possible to obtain a reliable, pre-European perspective on large mammal populations in the mountainous region that is now JNP. In 1811, David Thompson, ostensibly the first European to travel through the Athabasca valley, sighted no elk and few other ungulates (Glover 1962). Prior to Thompson's journey, the valley was a travel corridor for bands of Indians dispersing from eastern Canada, where they had obtained rifles from white traders (MacGregor 1974). Living off the land, these nomadic aboriginals probably had a great impact on mountain elk that winter at lower elevations and are vulnerable to hunters due to their herding habits and preference for semi-open terrain. In 1814, a fur company post in the lower Athabasca valley was supplied with wild meat by Metis hunters who ranged as far as 100 km away to find game (MacGregor 1974).

Unpublished diary notes of the fur company post (Jasper House) for the period 1827-1831 frequently refer to the scarcity of game and to starving Indians. During the winter of 1830-1831, post hunters saw only three "red deer" of which two were killed (Dekker 1987). In 1845, a visitor to Jasper House reported that, during his 20-day stay, hunters brought in 12 moose (*Alces alces*) and 30 bighorn sheep (*Ovis canadensis*), but no elk or deer (MacGregor 1974). During an extensive foraging trip in 1855, post hunters killed 70 moose, as well as sheep, caribou (*Rangifer tarandus*), and mountain goats (*Oreamnos americanus*), but no elk (Moberly and Cameron 1929). By the turn of the century, all indigenous ungulates in the Alberta mountains and foothills declined to low numbers through the combined impact of hunting and severe winters (Stelfox 1971).

Contemporary Elk Populations

By 1907, when JNP was established, elk were believed to be absent in the park, and in 1920, 88 elk from Yellowstone National Park were reintroduced. They multiplied to 1,000–1,200 by 1926 (Lloyd 1927) and to about 3,000 in the early 1940's (Table 1). Overgrazing and destruction of browse on winter range were noted by Cowan (1947) and Flook (1963). Stelfox (1971) stated that elk herds were destroying forage on a large scale with negative consequences for wintering bighorn sheep. During the 1960's, there was added concern that elk were invading alpine summer range where caribou were declining (Stelfox et al. 1974). To alleviate grazing pressure in the Athabasca valley, wardens culled elk herds each winter from 1945 to 1970. A total of 2,100 elk, mostly females, were slaughtered (Holroyd and Van Tighem 1983).

Estimated at 2,000–2,500 in 1971–1973 (Stelfox et al. 1974), elk numbers dropped to 850–1,000 by 1975, a 57–66% decline that was paralleled by 53–94% declines in all districts with discrete elk populations, such as the Athabasca valley, upper Snake Indian, and Brazeau (Table 2). Declines in elk were also recorded in the valleys of the Whirlpool, Maligne, and Rocky rivers, and few or no elk were observed in alpine regions at Cavell or Watchtower Basin where 150–200 elk were summering in 1968 (Stelfox et al. 1974). After 1975, year-round elk range in JNP was reduced to core areas of superior habitat (Fig. 1). Estimates of JNP's total elk population remained near 1,000 from 1980 to 1992.

During 1986–1991, roadside surveys of elk in the Athabasca and Miette valleys yielded a mean cow:calf ratio of 100:48 in mid November (Table 3). December counts at Devona in 1983–1992 found a mean ratio of 100:19 (Table 4), and aerial surveys of elk herds at Brazeau had a mean ratio of 100:18 in July, 1983–1986 (Table 5).

Because both were obtained during late autumn, the Devona data can be compared to the roadside data; the difference is highly significant ($P \leq 0.01$). The July data from Brazeau are particularly low in view of the possibility of further calf losses during summer and autumn.

Historical Wolf Populations

Anthony Henday, the first European scout to reach Alberta in 1754, noted that wolves were common around bison (*Bison bison*) on the plains: "I cannot say whether them or the

Table 1. Chronology of elk and wolf populations in Jasper National Park, Alberta.

Year	Remarks	Elk estimates	Elk/ 1.000 km²	Wolves	Wolves/ 1,000 km²
1907	JNP established	1		1	
1920	Elk reintroduced	88		-	
1926	Elk multiply	1,000-1,200	9-11	-	
1943	Wolf control	-		35-55²	3-5
1945	Start of elk cull	3,000²	28	-	
1959	End of wolf control	-		-	
1966	End of wolf control on provincial lands	-		-	
1970	End of elk cull	2,000-2,500⁵	18-23	48-50³	4
1974	Wolves increase	-		80-100⁴	7-9
1975	Elk decline	850-1,000⁵	8-9	-	
1983	Wolves decline	-		27-50⁵	2-4
1992	Populations stabilized	1,000⁵	9	40-50⁵	4

1 Believed absent or very scarce
2 Source: Cowan (1947).
3 Source: Carbyn (1975).
4 Source: Kaye and Roulet (1983).
5 Source: Warden Files, unpubl. data
- = no estimate

buffalo are most numerous" (Burpee 1907:336). In 1787–1811, explorer David Thompson saw wolves on the plains as well as in the foothills and mountains of west-central Alberta (Glover 1962). In 1829–1831, wolves were killing horses that were wintering in the Athabasca valley of JNP (Michel Klyne, Hudson's Bay Company Archives, unpubl. data). Paul Kane made frequent references to the abundance of wolves during his 1848 journey across the plains of Alberta to Jasper (Harper 1971). The narratives of mid-1800 hunters and trappers, such as the Earl of Southesk, John Palliser, James Hector, and Moberly, contain many anecdotes pertaining to wolves in the Jasper region (Stelfox 1969). To protect their horses, Hudson's Bay Company post-masters were poisoning wolves in the Athabasca valley in 1859 (Spry 1963). As a result of poisoning, coupled with the near-total destruction of ungulate prey species, wolves practically disappeared from the JNP region by the end of the 1800's (Stelfox 1971). Wolves remained scarce throughout Alberta, south of the Peace River, from the late 1800's until the mid–1930's (Stelfox 1969). The status of wolves in JNP from 1900 to 1930 is not well documented, but the absence of data probably indicates their scarcity (Carbyn 1974).

Contemporary Wolf Populations

During the late 1930's, after ungulate populations rebuilt, wolves returned to JNP and increased to a level that "was

arousing concern" among park staff (Cowan 1947:139). Cowan (1947) conducted the first wolf research in JNP in 1943-1946 to study the effect of predation on elk and other ungulates. Based on warden reports, he estimated the park's wolf population at 35–55. Wolves and other large carnivores were shot and trapped in JNP until 1959 to protect ungulates. In 1952, to halt the spread of rabies, the province of Alberta began an intensive poisoning program to reduce wild canids near settled areas (Ballantyne 1956). From 1952 to 1954, poison baits were also set out in JNP. Use of poison was continued on provincial lands near JNP until 1966. Carbyn (1974) believed that wolf numbers in JNP reached their lowest point around 1957. Based on his field studies in the Snake Indian drainage and on warden reports from other districts, Carbyn (1975) placed the number of wolves in JNP at 48–50 in 1969–1972 (Table 1).

During the early 1970's, JNP's wolf population increased further as evidenced by large pack sizes and an increase in known denning sites. Packs of 18–25 wolves were seen in the valleys of the Smoky, Moosehorn, Snake Indian, and Miette rivers (Warden reports). In 1973, wolves were again denning in the lower Athabasca valley, where none had been known to den after the control programs of the 1950's. A different wolf pack ranged the upper Athabasca valley during winter. During the 1970's, wolves with pups were re-

Table 2. Population estimates for elk in various districts of Jasper National Park.

Area	Years	Season	No. of elk	% decline
All of JNP	1971-1973	Year-round	2,000-2,500[1]	
	1975	Year-round	850	57-66
	1990	Year-round	1,000	50-60
Athabasca valley	1969	Winter	1,650*	
	1990	Winter	500-600	64-69
Lower Athabasca	1970	Winter	300	
	1990	Winter	100-120	60-67
Snake Indian drainage	1971-1973	Summer	180-350*	
	1990	Summer	20-40	78-94
Brazeau district	1971-1973	Summer	225-290*	
	1990	Summer	80-100	53-72

1   Source: Stelfox and Warden Service (1974). Unpubl. Canadian Wildlife Service report.

corded in the following districts: Smoky River, Willow Creek, Devona, Brazeau, Rocky Forks, Whirlpool River, and Miette-Decoigne. In the Snake Indian drainage, where there was only one wide-ranging wolf pack in 1971 (Carbyn 1975), there were three packs with pups in 1981 (Dekker 1986).

In 1974, JNP's wolf population was estimated at 80–100 (Kaye and Roulet 1983) and remained near that level until 1981. The lack of consistent year-to-year data does not allow for the precise determination of a peak or turning point in the population trend. Declines and/or absences of wolves in some districts began in 1982 when there was no sign of winter pack activity in the upper Athabasca valley. After 1983, no packs with more than two members were reported in the Snake Indian drainage and wolves did not den at Devona and Willow Creek in 1983 (Dekker 1986). In the autumn of 1984, and each subsequent year until 1992, wolves with pups were observed at Devona. The only other wolf denning area known to have been in continuous use after 1984 was the Brazeau district. Estimates of JNP's total wolf population dropped to 40–50 in 1983 and reached a low of 27–40 in 1990. The 1992 population is estimated at 40–50 including six to eight breeding packs.

No more than one or two packs that den inside JNP are believed to have territories contained entirely within JNP boundaries. Radio-collared wolves that denned in the Brazeau district were found to travel in winter as far as 50 km away onto provincial lands (Schmidt and Gunson, 1985). Wolves denning at Willow Creek routinely travelled across park boundaries (Carbyn 1975, Dekker 1985b).

Six known wolf denning locations in JNP were on valley bottom lands characterized by montane meadows, mixed woods, and water bodies. These semi-open habitats were also favored by prey species, particularly deer and elk. Five known wolf denning sites are associated with elk calving grounds. In their choice of denning locations, wolves in JNP appear to be highly traditional. Ungulate bones scattered around main dens at each site indicate that they had been used long before they were first found by researchers. Wolf activity during 1969–1992 was concentrated in the same districts as reported by Cowan (1947).

Wolf-Elk Interaction and Antipredator Strategies of Elk

During June–August of each year, elk with calves were seen on heavily wooded islands in a 5 km stretch of the Athabasca River in the Devona district. The islands appeared to be used as a traditional elk calving ground. Carbyn (1975) hypothesized that elk at Willow Creek selected calving grounds near water as an anti-predator strategy. In Riding Mountain National Park, Manitoba, a traditional elk calving ground was located on an island in a lake (Carbyn 1980). As noted by the Palliser Expedition of 1857–1860, aboriginal people visited islands in Kananaskis Lakes, Alberta, to hunt elk and their calves in early summer (Spry 1963).

Elk use a number of strategies to avoid predators. As reported by Cowan (1947) and Carbyn (1975), elk chased by wolves ran into rivers. During this study, the authors and park wardens saw elk enter or stand in water to avoid wolves on 10 or more occasions. On 3 October 1987, the senior author observed five wolves chase a herd of 16 elk cows and

Table 3. Elk cow:calf ratios along roadsides in Jasper National Park.

Year	Survey date	Total number of cows and calves	Calves/100 cows
1986	14-16 Nov.	369	50
1987	14-16 Nov.	226	40
1988	14-16 Nov.	323	61
1990	14-16 Nov.	328	48
1991	12-16 Nov.	475	43
Subtotal		**1,721**	**48**

Table 4. Elk cow:calf ratios at Devona, Jasper National Park.

Year	Survey date	Cows and calves Herd size	Calves/100 cows
1983	13 December	30	76[1]
1984	8 December	39	30
1986	1 December	61	5[2]
1987	12 December	42	11[2]
1988	3 December	28	12[2]
1989	1 December	33	27[3]
1990	14 December	34	21
1991	10 December	55	17
1992	8 November	52	15
Subtotal		**374**	**19**

1 No wolf pack in area from spring 1983 to summer 1984.
2 Pack of 8-10 wolves denning near elk calving grounds.
3 Pack of 4-5 wolves absent for much of summer.

Table 5. Elk cow:calf ratios near Brazeau, Jasper National Park.

Year	Survey date	Total number of cows and calves	Calves/100 cows
1983	20 July	152	33
1984	24 July	152	25
1985	24 July	72	7[1]
1986	24 July	49	4[1]
Subtotal		**425**	**18**

1 Wolf pack observed with elk herd.
Source: Schmidt and Gunson (1985). Alberta F. & W. Unpubl. Report.

Table 6. Comparison of elk cow:calf ratios from three localities in Jasper National Park.

Locality	Month	Years	Cows and calves	Calves/100 cows
Roadsides	November	1986-1990	1,721	48
Devona wolf range	December	1983-1992	374	19
Brazeau wolf range	July	1983-1986	425	18

three calves across the Snake Indian River at Devona. They disappeared into woods on the opposite shore. A mature bull elk that was with the herd was ignored by the wolves and did not flee. Presently, one cow came back and re-entered the river, followed by the wolves, lunging at her rear. The cow vainly tried to make a stand in shallows. She crossed and recrossed the main channel, harassed by the wolves, until she found a spot by a cliff where the water was swift and about one metre deep. At this point the river was 15–20 m wide. Three times one or two wolves swam towards the elk, but she waded upstream and remained out of reach, up to her belly in turbulent water. About 25 m downstream from the cow, one wolf managed to hold on to a shallow spot or submerged rock for about 10 minutes, only its head visible, while the other wolves waited on either side of the river. After about 20 minutes, the wolves left. The elk stayed in the water for another 30 minutes until she slowly walked to the bank.

The above observation illustrates that rivers offer refuge from wolf attack only if the depth and speed of the current are sufficient. Schmidt and Gunson (1985) reported elk killed by wolves in the Brazeau River. At Devona, the senior author found the fresh remains of two elk cows and one calf that had been killed in backwaters of the Athabasca River. Wolves at Devona were often seen to wade or swim across rivers. Three wolves swimming a wide stretch of the Athabasca River in pursuit of three elk appeared to gain on them and continued the pursuit on the other shore, disappearing in woods (Brian Genereux, Edmonton, pers. commun.).

During winter, elk chased by wolves may enter water even when rivers are mostly frozen. On two occasions, the senior author found evidence that elk (one mature bull and one calf) had been unable to get out of water holes in the Snake Indian River and had frozen into the ice. There was no evidence that the wolves had fed on the carcasses. Half a dozen similar incidents were seen by JNP wardens and reported to Cowan (1947).

At the approach of wolves, some elk run to and make a stand on the edge of a precipice that protects their rear from attack. Evidence (tracks) for such behavior was seen at Devona on 14 occasions, particularly during winter when the Snake Indian River was frozen. Cowan (1947) reported one similar incident observed by park wardens. Schmidt and

Gunson (1985) photographed a cow elk standing on a steep cliff while wolves were nearby, unable to reach the elk. Similar use of cliffs by elk to avoid wolves was seen in JNP by Van Tighem et al (1980) and Kansas (1981).[1]

A third anti-predator strategy of elk in JNP is their concentration along roads, near the townsite and in campgrounds.[2] During summer, 50–60% of JNP's elk population occurs near human habitation, up to 80% during winter. Similar wolf-avoidance strategies were noted of moose at Isle Royale by Stephens and Peterson (1984). In Manitoba, elk herds with calves left wolf-inhabited Riding Mountain National Park and frequented the edges of farmland (Carbyn 1980).

In the southern portion of JNP, including the Brazeau district, and in adjacent Banff National Park, elk with young calves isolate themselves on summer range in the sub-alpine and alpine. At these elevations elk may escape detection by wolves that den in the lower valleys. In addition, the open terrain of the alpine allows early discovery of approaching predators (Schmidt and Gunson 1985).

Causes of the Elk Decline

The 1975 elk decline in JNP occurred simultaneously with the wolf increase (Fig. 2), however the extent to which predation by wolves was implicated in the elk decline could not be accurately assessed during this study. The role of wolf predation in JNP's elk population dynamics was examined by several researchers. Thirty-four of 67 winter kills by the Brazeau wolf pack, during 1983–1986, were elk (J. Gunson, Alberta Fish and Wildlife, unpubl. data). Cowan (1947) and Carbyn (1975) reported that elk in JNP were preyed upon by wolves on a year-round basis and that elk

---

1. On 14 February, 1994 the senior author observed a pack of 11 wolves keep a yearling bull elk at bay on a steep-sided bluff for at least four hours.
2. During June 1993 a pack of three wolves was known to have killed at least five elk calves inside the Whistlers campground and along the highway near Jasper town. These wolves, often observed at close range by the public and by park wardens, appeared to be less shy than usual and may have become habitutated to the presence of people after frequently feeding at sites where park personnel had been dumping traffic-killed ungulates during the winter of 1992-1993.

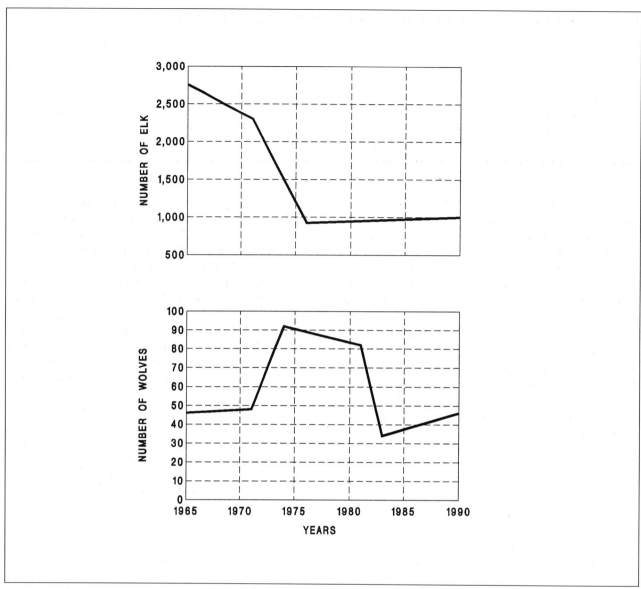

Fig. 2 *Population fluctuations of elk and wolves in Jasper National Park, Alberta, 1965–1992.*

contributed 42–46% of the summer diet. Mule deer (*Odocoileus hemionus*) represented the preferred prey of the Willow Creek wolf pack, but it shifted to elk calves as soon as they became available and "only 27% of elk cows had calves at their heels after three months of life" (Carbyn 1975:145). However, both Cowan (1947) and Carbyn (1975) concluded that wolves were not controlling or limiting JNP's elk population because of the low wolf density, particularly on the major winter ranges in the Athabasca valley. According to population estimates given by Carbyn (1975), the maximum wolf:elk ratio in 1969–1972 was 1:50. That ratio changed to 1:10 during 1975–1980 after elk declined and wolves increased. Wolf numbers in JNP remained at the raised level of 80–100 for another

five to seven years after the elk decline. During this period, the role of wolf predation may well have prevented the elk from regaining pre-1975 numbers. Such an antiregulatory effect of predation was described for wolves and moose in Alaska and Quebec (Gasaway et al. 1983; Messier and Crete 1985).

The impact of wolf predation in JNP's elk dynamics is further suggested by a comparison of the cow:calf ratios obtained during this study in districts with and without wolves (Table 6). At Devona, in 1986-1988, when the local pack of eight to ten wolves was denning about 3 km from elk calving grounds, the cow:calf ratios were 100:8 (n = 131) (Table 4). An even lower ratio of 100:6 (n = 121) (Table 5) was obtained at Brazeau in late July, 1985-1986,

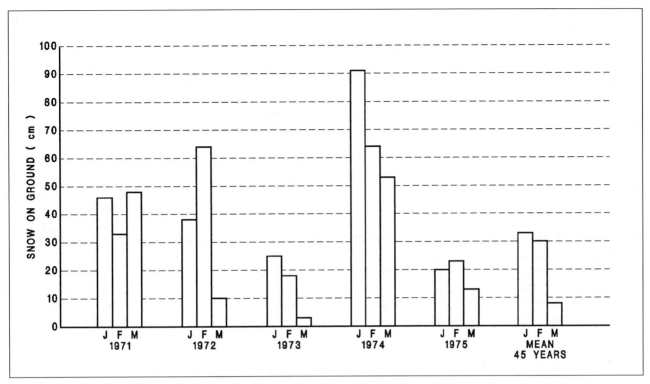

Fig. 3 *Snow on ground at end of month (January, February, March) at Jasper, Alberta 1971-1975, compared to the mean for 1941–1985.*

when the local wolf pack had left their denning site in the valley and was seen with its pups near the elk herd on the alpine slopes. By contrast, cow-calf ratios were 100:48 along roadsides where wolves were not known to den.

Following years of high wolf presence at Devona (1986-1988), elk herd sizes (cows and calves) declined. By contrast, herd sizes increased following years of low wolf presence (1983 and 1989) (Table 4).

The decline of JNP's elk population in 1973–1975 was the result of a combination of factors. Starvation was evident in the severe winter of 1973–1974 when wardens shot elk in poor condition. Snow depth at Jasper was the highest on record (1941–1985) in January and March 1974, and second highest in February 1974 (Fig. 3).

Extreme winter conditions are especially hard on ungulates in combination with poor food supplies. During the 1960's and 1970's, elk winter range in JNP was severely overgrazed (Flook 1963, Stelfox 1971). Scarcity of browse and destruction of poplar regeneration caused by elk was noted by Cowan (1947) in the Athabasca valley and by Dekker (1985b) in the Snake Indian drainage. After fire suppression became JNP policy, elk winter range on open grasslands has been shrinking due to forest succession and the encroachment of bog birch (*Betula glandulosa*) and willows on montane meadows.

The above limiting factors, which may have resulted in adult elk mortality as well as in a drop in calf survival, were superimposed on other causes of direct mortality — accidents, hunting and predation. Holroyd and Van Tighem (1983:417) stated that "the major factor implicated in the (1975) decline of elk in the Athabasca valley was excessive mortality on roads and railways." This view is not supported by available data; known traffic fatalities in 1971–1975 included 151 elk, representing a mean of 30 per year, roughly 2% of the estimated population in the Athabasca valley. However, from 1986 to 1990, rail and road kills in the lower Athabasca valley totalled 41, representing a mean of eight per year or 6–7% of the estimated winter population in the lower valley. Thus, traffic accidents could contribute to local population declines if elk calf survival is low.

Although a few incidents of poaching have been recorded, elk that remain all year within the park are protected from hunting. By contrast, herds migrating out onto provincial lands, particularly at Brazeau and Willow Creek, were exposed to long hunting seasons that lasted from September to December 1960–1975, and included the legal harvest of antlerless animals. Along the park's boundary east of the Brazeau River, the yearly elk kill by sports hunters was estimated at 13% of the 1963–1966 population (W. Wishart, Alberta Fish and Wildlife, unpubl. data). In addition, the elk harvest by Treaty Indians was unrestricted and unrecorded. Hunting pressure was probably greatest where road access was good, particularly at Rock Lake where all or part of the Willow Creek elk herd wintered. No data are available for the number of elk killed by hunters east of Willow Creek, but it is in this district that the greatest elk declines (78–94%) were recorded (Table 2). Estimated at 120–150 in 1969–1972 (Carbyn 1975), the Willow Creek elk herd declined to 10–20 in the 1980's.

Causes of the Wolf Decline

Known wolf mortality during 1980–1990 includes 23 road and railway fatalities and two disease-related deaths, of which one was diagnosed as canine distemper. Hair loss in wolves, probably due to sarcoptic mange, was reported in three animals in 1983 (JNP Warden Office, unpubl. data). An unspecified number of wolves were taken by trappers along JNP boundaries. During the 1970's, when wolf numbers were high, there were unsubstantiated reports of hunters "shooting up" wolf packs in semi-open montane and subalpine regions along the north boundary. The disappearance of the Willow Creek pack in 1983 coincided with a rumor that five wolves had been shot by a sheep hunter on the park boundary at Moosehorn (K. Campbell, Grande Cache, pers. commun.). Perhaps indicative of the high mortality rate of wolves in western Alberta, six wolves in two radio-collared packs were known to have died within two years; four of the six had been shot (Schmidt and Gunson 1985). However, it remains to be seen whether human-caused mortality in the JNP wolf population exceeded the natural capacity of the species to compensate for yearly losses of 30% (Keith 1983).

Food stress resulting in high intraspecific strife and low pup survival has been implicated in wolf population declines in Minnesota and on Isle Royale (Mech 1977b, Peterson and Page 1988). We believe that food stress was the major cause of the post-1981 wolf decline in JNP in view of the substantial drop in the elk prey base after 1975. Elk calves are particularly important as wolf prey during summer. Wolves stopped denning at Willow Creek and Rocky Forks after the local elk nursery herds had all but disappeared. According to warden reports, other wolf prey have also declined in JNP. Sightings of mule deer and moose at Willow Creek declined by a factor of three to one between 1970 and 1984 (Dekker 1985b).

Conclusions

Before drawing a conclusion on wolf/elk dynamics in JNP, the following points need to be considered: 1) The low cow:calf ratios (100:18–19) observed at Brazeau and Devona may in part be due to poor habitat quality. This possibility is believed to exist at Brazeau where inferior forage conditions may play a role in depressing elk fecundity. However, at Devona elk habitat appeared to be similar or superior to roadsides. 2) The cow:calf ratios of 100:48 observed along JNP roadsides may be biased if elk cows with calves are more likely to seek out roadsides than cows

without calves. This possibility remains to be investigated. 3) The cow:calf ratios observed at Brazeau may be biased if elk cows with calves react to harassment from predators by leaving the open alpine summer range and by isolating themselves in forest cover. At Devona, the senior author observed on two occasions that elk cows accompanied by calves were the first to flee when wolves approached the herd. The classified count of such herds could present a false impression of the overall cow:calf ratio in the area if antipredator behavior results in the formation of elk herds that are made up mainly of barren cows, yearlings, and cows that have already lost their calves. Yet, such segregation of herds with and without calves was not noted at Devona where observations were carried out throughout the year. 4) Predation by other large carnivores, particularly bears, may be responsible for losses of calves at Brazeau and at Devona, although no incidents of bear predation were noted in either area. Bears are present in all habitats, also along roadsides in JNP where incidents of bear predation on elk calves are occasionally observed. In 1992, four elk calves were killed by a grizzly and one by a black bear near the Jasper townsite (JNP Warden files, unpubl. data).

Wolves may occur in all valley bottom habitats of JNP at any time of year. However, during spring and summer, pack activity is concentrated near denning sites in the back country. The study of wolf/prey relationships confined to one pack and one localized elk summer range, such as Brazeau or Devona, might overestimate the impact of wolf predation if the results of the study are extrapolated over a larger area. In JNP, away from traditional elk calving grounds and wolf denning sites, single or small groups of elk may raise their calves in isolation, escaping detection by predators during most or all of summer and fall. However, the impact of wolf predation on elk productivity in JNP's backcountry is particularly direct and profound because packs appear to establish denning sites near elk calving grounds and elk in JNP have a clumped and restricted distribution.

Acknowledgments

Since 1987, field observations by the senior author were conducted under a volunteer contract and with logistic support from the Jasper Wardens' Office. Partial and intermittent financial support was received from the Alberta Recreation, Parks and Wildlife Foundation, the Canadian Wolf Defenders, and World Wildlife Fund Canada. P. De-Mulder and B. Genereux assisted in the field. G. Langemann of Archaeology Services Unit, Canadian Parks Service, provided information on archeological digs in JNP. W. Prusak of the Edmonton Weather Office supplied data on winter snow accumulations at Jasper. We thank I. McTaggart-Cowan and three anonymous referees for critical comments on an earlier version of this paper.

Wolves in The Transhimalayan Region of India: The Continued Survival of a Low-Density Population

■ Joseph L. Fox and Raghunandan S. Chundawat

The Tibetan wolf is still widely distributed, although in decreased numbers because of hunting over the past 30 years, in the high elevation, dry mountains and plains of India's Transhimalayan region. During foot surveys of 945 km along valleys in this region several wolves were seen and sign was most common in the relatively open terrain of large valleys. Wolves prey primarily on wild ungulates in mountainous areas, but on the high plains and in more inhabited regions where wild ungulates are less common, domestic animals constitute a substantial component of their diet (including scavenging). Recent estimates of about 300 wolves within the Transhimalayan region of Jammu and Kashmir (60,000 km^2) and another 50 individuals in the 10,000 km^2 of similar habitat in Himachal Pradesh appear reasonable, given the populations of wild ungulate prey and conservative estimates of livestock losses to predators. However, this number should also include the central Asian dhole whose sign can easily be confused with wolf, thus making accurate assessment of their relative status difficult. The occurrence of such a low density (1/200 km^2) wolf/(dhole) population is the result of relatively low wild prey densities coupled with the presence of competitors such as the snow leopard and lynx.

Although the persistence of large predator populations is in part a function of relatively limited persecution by the sparse human populations, the wolf is still much disparaged as a major predator on livestock, therefore hunting and trapping continue. With the increasing use of modern predator control techniques, hunting weapons, and vehicle access throughout this open treeless region, survival of the wolf is clearly threatened except perhaps in the more rugged and inaccessible regions, where it must compete with the snow leopard.

Introduction

Although the Tibetan wolf (*Canis lupus chanco*) is present throughout the mountains and plains of central Asia, little is known of its current status and ecology in much of this region. Other than in the former Soviet republics where wolf status has been monitored, recent information on its distribution, abundance, or other ecological parameters is limited to anecdotal and some food habits information from western China and parts of northern Pakistan and Nepal (Schaller 1977, Schaller et al. 1987, 1988a, 1988b, Achuff and Petocz 1988). A small portion of northernmost India (approximately 70,000 km^2; Fig. 1) lies in the northern rainshadow of the Himalaya Mountains within typical central Asian steppe and mountain habitats of the Palearctic faunal region. Recent wildlife surveys that concentrated on determining snow leopard status in India's northwest Himalaya (Fox et

al. 1991b) and additional follow-up work have produced some basic information on current status and ecology of wolves in the region, and are reviewed here along with other recent information from the area. The persistence of wolves and other large predators in this region has resulted from the continued existence of sufficient wild prey coupled with available domestic livestock and a history of relatively limited persecution by man. However, recent increases in economic development and military activity in this previously remote Transhimalayan region have brought about dramatic reductions in wildlife populations (Fox et al. 1991a). They mirror or presage similar changes in other parts of the highlands of central Asia, and perhaps are comparable with the effects on wildlife of similar incursions of modern man into North America more than a century ago.

Study Area and Methods

The Transhimalayan region of India is the country's northernmost area (33–35° N, 76–79° E). It is a high elevation, dry land of rugged mountains and open plains north of the main Himalaya and south of the Karakoram mountains within the states of Jammu and Kashmir (Ladakh 60,000 km^2) and Himachal Pradesh (10,000 km^2 in parts of Lahul, Spiti and Kinnaur). Some of India's border regions with China and Pakistan are still in dispute and our study area map

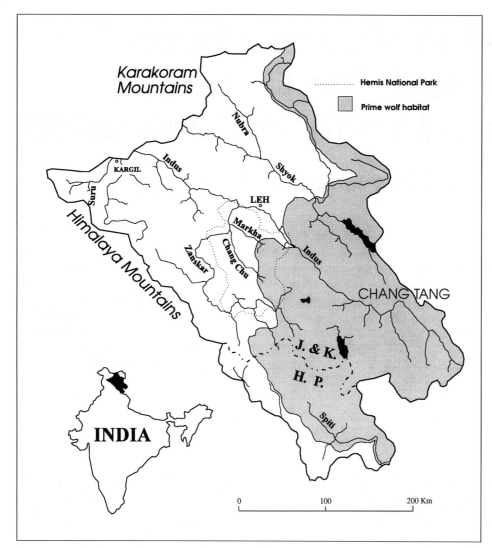

Fig. 1 *The Transhimalayan region of India, primarily within the state of Jammu and Kashmir (J.&K.) and with a small portion in the state of Himachal Pradesh (H.P.). Although the shaded area indicates prime wolf habitat in the open rolling mountains and plains of the Tibetan Plateau, extensive hunting there of both predator and prey has today brought about low wolf densities comparable to that in the unshaded extremely rugged terrain less favored by wolves and less hunted by people.*

(Fig. 1) reflects Transhimalayan areas currently under Indian control.

Elevations vary from about 2,800 m where the major rivers (e.g., Indus) leave the region to over 7,000 m peaks in the Himalaya and Karakoram mountains and over 6,000 m peaks in the intervening Transhimalayan ranges. India's Transhimalayan region is its least densely human-populated area. In Ladakh, for example, some 150,000 inhabitants (2.5/km²) live primarily in irrigated farming villages along the outwashes of tributary streams in most major valleys of the region. The people are traditionally pastoralists and farmers, predominantly Tibetan Buddhist in the east and Muslim in the west.

Annual precipitation ranges from 500–1,000 mm in valleys just north of the high Himalayan ranges to approximately 100 mm in the central Transhimalayan valleys, such as the upper Indus near Leh (Hartmann 1983). Vegetation in Ladakh varies from alpine meadow (*Kobresia, Carex, Potentilla, Nepeta*) on the north side of the Himalayan crest and grades north and east into steppe vegetation (*Tanacetum,*

Artemisia, Stachys, Caragana, Ephedra, Stipa) with shrubland (*Hippophae, Salix, Myricaria*) along the lower river courses (Kachroo et al. 1977, Hartmann 1983, 1990). The region is virtually treeless, save for isolated patches of juniper (*Juniperus macropoda, J. indica*) and birch (*Betula utilis*) on some valley slopes and mostly cultivated varieties of poplar (*Populus* spp.) and willow (*Salix* spp.) along the major water courses.

Within Ladakh and the dry Transhimalayan parts of Lahul, Spiti and Kinnaur eight species of wild ungulates are present and provide the main source of wild prey for wolves. Blue sheep (*Pseudois nayaur*) and Asiatic ibex (*Capra ibex sibirica*) are the most common wild ungulates; small viable populations of Ladakh urial (*Ovis vignei vignei*), Tibetan argali (*Ovis ammon hodgsoni*), and kiang, or Tibetan wild ass, (*Equus hemionus kiang*) are still present; and small numbers of Tibetan gazelle (*Procapra picticaudata*), Tibetan antelope (*Pantholops hodgsoni*) and wild yak (*Bos grunniens*) remain (Fox et al. 1991a, Fox and Johnsingh, in press). Smaller mammals and birds known to comprise prey

Fig. 2 *Typical wolf habitat in the open steppelands of eastern Ladakh, here near the Tso Kar (lake) at about 4,500 m elevation. Domestic yak-cow hybrids are present in the foreground. (Photo: Chering Nurbu).*

of wolves include marmot (*Marmota bobak* and *M. caudata*), hare (*Lepus ostioleous*), mouse hare (*Ochotona* spp.), snowcock (*Tetraogallus himalayensis*, *T. tibetanus*) and chukar (*Alectoris chukar*). Besides the wolf other large predators in the Transhimalayan region include the snow leopard (*Uncia uncia*), lynx (*Lynx lynx isabellina*), dhole (*Cuan alpinus laniger*) and brown bear (*Ursus arctos*), with the lynx and brown bear relatively rare and patchily distributed.

In 1985–1986 during wildlife surveys in India's northwest Himalaya designed to document the status of snow leopard (Fox et al. 1991b), information on wolf presence was also obtained. One side of a valley bottom was searched for sign, and although search efforts were concentrated on typi-

cal snow leopard travel routes along valley bottom edges, likely wolf travel routes along major trails were also monitored (for more detail regarding survey methods see Fox et al. 1991b). A total of 745 km of the original snow leopard surveys were located in Transhimalayan regions and 200 km of similar surveys were conducted in Ladakh during 1988, 1989, and 1991, with 150 km of these in small catchments tributary to the upper Indus valley and along the edge of the Indus valley itself, and 50 km within the Khurnak region (Chang Chu drainage) in the eastern portion of Hemis National Park (Fig. 1). Finding wolf tracks in areas other than on trails is difficult because of the stony ground, but is productive when there is snow cover. This provided limited information on relative abundance of wolf and snow leopard

Fig. 3 *The upper Suru valley (4,300 m) of western Ladakh, where evidence of wolves was most common along the main valley, and that of snow leopards and brown bears in the tributary valleys (Photo: J.L. Fox).*

Table 1. Average habitat characteristics over 5 km survey sections associated with the occurrence of wolf (including dhole, see text) and snow leopard tracks in Transhimalayan India. In all categories means were different between the canids and snow leopard (p<0.01, Tukey multiple comparison test, Zar 1984:186).

CATEGORY	WOLF (DHOLE) TRACKS	SNOW LEOPARD TRACKS	SURVEY HABITAT
	n = 37	n = 45	n = 189
Elevation of valley bottom (m)	4240*	3915	3940
Valley side slope angle (degrees)	31*	41*	35
Percent of valley bottom with cliffs	19*	51*	30
Percent of valley slopes with cliffs	30*	48*	35
Valley width (m)	662*	70*	260

Means marked with * are different from that for the overall survey habitat (p < 0.01, Tukey multiple comparison test).

in one area during winter. Because of the wolf's propensity to use well-travelled roads and trails, daily herding of livestock quickly obliterates their sign. Therefore, reliable year-round measure of relative abundance based on tracks was not feasible, and the total evidence of sign we provide should be taken as indication of presence. Nevertheless, predator tracks found throughout the year provide an indication of habitat use. We compare average habitat characteristics (Tukey multiple comparison test) of the locations in which wolf and snow leopard sign were found. Other than the sign surveys, information presented here is based on opportunistic sightings, discovery of characteristic sign and travel routes, and information from local people.

Results and Discussion

Comprehensive winter surveys were limited to November and December 1985 in the upper Suru valley (Fig. 3) of western Ladakh and during January and March 1986 in the Markha valley (Fig. 4) and vicinity of central Ladakh. Before heavy winter snowfalls set in along the wide valley of the upper Suru (4,300 m elevation) during 14 days (approximately 30 km) of repeated early morning searching prior to livestock herding activities on the valley bottom road and trails, wolf tracks were found on six occasions (five lone, one pair). It was clear that at least two wolves were active on the upper valley floor during our visit. No wolves were seen during this time and no wolf tracks or other sign were found during the much more extensive surveys of adjacent tributary valleys and ridges in this area. Nath (1982) described incidences of wolves hunting ibex in the main upper Suru valley during late winter.

During 32 days (approximately 265 km) of long-distance winter survey (predominantly snow-covered ground) in the narrow Markha and adjacent valleys of central Ladakh, wolf

tracks were found on eight occasions (five lone, three pairs). In these same surveys snow leopard tracks were found on 19 occasions (12 lone, five pairs, two threesomes), with 70% of the wolf tracks and 40% of the snow leopard tracks occurring in the upper, open parts of the Markha watershed (Fig. 4). Single wolves were observed on three occasions during these winter surveys in the Markha area, one in the vicinity of a blue sheep carcass, freshly killed, probably by snow leopard.

Surveys during summer produced no consistent reliable compilations of positively identified wolf tracks, because of livestock obliterating tracks. Other than along the valley bottoms, wolf tracks were occasionally found near high mountain passes and in the summers of 1988 and 1989 well-used (low human use) wolf travel routes were found along the edge of the Indus valley (Fig. 5). In August of 1991, two adult wolves were observed hunting marmots (unsuccessfully) in meadows at about 4,800 m elevation during a short (10 km) survey high above the Zanskar-Markha river confluence, and in the upper Chang Chu drainage wolf tracks were observed near the Yar La and Zalung Karpo La (mountain passes).

Over the entire 945 km of valley-route surveys in Transhimalayan regions a total of 37 wolf tracks were found (17 lone, eight pairs, one foursome). Wolf tracks (including dhole) were associated more with open valleys and gentle terrain than was sign of snow leopard in the same surveys (Table 1; see also Fox et al. 1991b). Wolf sign was found at higher elevations than that of snow leopard (Table 1). This reflected the fact that the open valleys of gentle terrain occurred at the higher elevations (i.e., in eastern Ladakh). Within a particular valley section where both predators were present, wolves were usually more active around the valley bottom, with snow leopard activity concentrated in the higher and more rugged tributary valleys (Fig. 6). Still, a

Fig. 4 *Tracks of two wolves in snow in the upper Markha valley (4,200 m) where both wolves and snow leopards are frequently present. (Photo: J.L. Fox).*

significant portion of wolf sign was present in the rugged regions, indicating that an important portion of their range is located in these areas.

Other than sightings and tracks, the primary evidence of wolf presence available for survey is their scats, but confusion with droppings of the other large predators made estimation of relative abundance difficult in areas of overlap. Lynx are rare in the areas of our survey and did not pose a problem, whereas wolf and snow leopard are sympatric and relatively common throughout much of mountainous Ladakh, and in many areas their travel routes overlap. Separation of sign can be made on the basis of the snow leopard's propensity to travel along the edge of cliff bases and other

terrain junctures where they leave very distinctive scrape and spray markings (often leaving scats on or near such markings). Snow leopards also deposit scats in open terrain and on mountain cols, which are also typical sites for wolves. Positive identification of such scats must involve association with other sign such as fresh tracks. Wolves, however, also have characteristic "signpost" sites, which they mark with urine and scats and there were some areas surveyed (with low snow leopard presence) that indicated well-used wolf travel routes providing definite tracks and scats even in summer.

Wolf scats were abundant, for example, around a 35 cm diameter lone rock on open terrain at the junction of two

Fig. 5 *A view south across the Indus valley from Leh (3,500 m) with Stok Kangri (6,121 m) in the background on the border of Hemis National Park. Well-used wolf trails are present along the edge of the foothills within Ladakh urial habitat. Blue sheep are common higher in the mountains, where they are hunted by snow leopards as well as wolves and dholes. (Photo: J.L. Fox).*

branches of the upper Markha valley (4,100 m), farther up the northern branch of this valley (4,700 m) around a small stone prayer wall on the open slopes, and around rock cairns on passes at the head of both valley branches (5,000 m). Wolf scats were also positively identified on the pass at the head of the Suru valley as well as in the upper portions of this and adjacent valleys. Surveys in summer 1988 and 1989 identified wolf travel routes along little-used (by humans) trails along the Indus valley at the base of the Zanskar range foothills (3,500–3,600 m) (Fig. 5), which revealed abundant wolf scats and occasional tracks. Scats were present around small rock cairns at passes (4,900 m) between adjacent catchments in the nearby mountains.

Preliminary indications of wolf food habits based on analysis of over 100 scats from central Ladakh suggest a reliance on wild prey in remote regions (primarily blue sheep in our collection area), significant use of domestic animals in all areas and substantial use of domestic animals near the most heavily inhabited areas (Chundawat and Fox, unpubl. data). Smaller prey items were dominated by marmot (Chundawat and Fox, unpubl. data). Scavenging appears to be an important component of wolf feeding behavior in the region (Fig. 7), as is also indicated by Achuff and Petocz (1988) in western China. Wolves in India's rugged western Transhimalaya follow their prey's seasonal altitudinal migrations of up to 1,000 m, which usually take place within short horizontal distances. In the high eastern plains and open mountains wolves have had to contend with more mobile prey (i.e., migratory gazelle, antelope, yak, and domestic livestock of nomadic herders). Annual home ranges may be larger and more variable than those associated with the more sedentary prey in rugged areas.

In central Ladakh people reported approximately equal losses of livestock to wolves and snow leopards, but in more open (and inhabited) regions livestock losses were primarily attributed to wolves. Besides snow leopard predation and occasional predation by lynx, in isolated locations of western Ladakh the few remaining brown bear were reported to cause more damage to livestock than either wolves or snow leopards. On the whole in Ladakh the wolf is considered the most destructive predator on livestock (Chering Nurbu, J.&K. Dept. Wildlife Protection, pers. commun.). In the southern Hemis National Park during the year ending March 1986, livestock owners reported losses of 130 sheep and goats and 10 larger livestock out of a total of about 2,600 sheep and goats and 450 yaks, cows, horses, and donkeys, with approximately equal portions attributed to wolf (wild canids) and to snow leopards. These losses were somewhat greater (i.e., 5% *versus* 2% sheep and goats; 2% *versus* 1% larger livestock) but comparable to predator (wolf and snow leopard) related losses reported in the Mount Everest region of southern Tibet (Jackson 1991).

Up to now we have referred to all nonfelid sign as that of wolf, but this impression must be corrected to indicate that a significant and unknown portion of wild canid sign in our survey areas is that of the dhole or central Asian wild dog. Somewhat smaller than the local wolf, the dhole (15–20 kg *versus* 20–30 kg; 90–100 cm *versus* 95–150 cm body length) has long been known to occur in Ladakh (Kinloch 1885, Burton 1940, Heptner et al. 1974). At the start of our surveys its continued presence was questionable. Thus, sightings during the past few years in the upper Indus valley call into question some of the sign and predation attributed solely to wolves. The locals do have a name for the dhole ("phara"), but many people are familiar with neither the name nor the animal and large wild canid sign is usually referred to the "chanku" or wolf. According to locals who are familiar with both species, the dhole is much rarer and prone to greater

Fig. 6 *Sand dunes along the Nubra valley (3,200 m) of north central Ladakh, habitat of feral camels with Ladakh urial present along the valley foothills and blue sheep and ibex in the mountains. Wolves and dholes are known to frequent the main valley, snow leopards are present in the mountains, and lynx occur within the valley floor thickets of* **Hippophae** *spp. (Photo: R.S. Chundawat).*

Fig. 7 *A wolf feeding at night on a horse carcass in the vicinity of Rumbak village in the Hemis National Park of central Ladakh. (Photo: R.S. Chundawat).*

movement than the wolves in the area. The largest canid tracks and scats found were undoubtedly of wolf, but spoor of smaller (and female) wolves can easily be confused with dholes (A.J.T. Johnsingh, Wildlife Institute of India, pers. commun.).

The senior author observed a group of three dholes at 4,500 m elevation in a minor tributary of the upper Indus valley during August 1989, a day after they had unsuccessfully attacked a herd of well-tended domestic sheep and goats. Several dholes were photographed nearby in February 1989 where, contrary to Ganhar's (1979) contention that "the wild dog is a ferocious beast whom even the snow leopard considers it prudent to leave alone," a domestic goat kill made by a pack of four dholes was appropriated by a snow leopard (J. Van Gruisen, Survival Anglia, pers. commun.). Also during the summer of 1989, dholes were photographed at an active den in eastern Ladakh (Chering Nurbu, J.&K. Dept. Wildlife Protection, pers. commun.). We must conclude that although wolves appear to be substantially more common than dholes (based on interviews with knowledgable locals) a small but significant portion of the surveyed tracks, scats, and reported kills were probably made by dholes.

Predator Control and Conservation

The most common means of capturing and killing wolves in retaliation for livestock raiding was through the use of either stone pits or deadfall traps, constructed near villages or seasonal grazing areas. The deadfall trap is set with a bait of meat, which when disturbed causes a boulder to fall on the wolf (Nath 1982). Pit traps are more common and distinctive, often producing conspicuous structures on the valley landscape (Fig. 8). They are commonly constructed either from a shallow hole dug into the ground, or are begun on the

ground surface, with a cylindrical stone wall (3–4 m diameter) built up to enclose the pit to a height of about 2–3 m. The walls slant slightly inward and large flat stones are placed near the top layer to form an inner lip, both of these features making it difficult for the wolf to exit the pit. Bait in the form of dead or live livestock is placed in the bottom of the pit. A wolf when caught is stoned to death. Wolves are also killed when they get into livestock pens, and when active dens are found the pups are taken. When a wolf is killed the persons responsible display it to livestock owners around the village to receive small rewards for their efforts.

Several of the wolf's wild ungulate prey (e.g., Ladakh urial, Tibetan argali, Tibetan antelope, Tibetan gazelle) have been greatly reduced through hunting (especially by army personnel) over the past 30 years in eastern Ladakh and along the Indus valley (Fox et al. 1991a). This reduction in prey abundance, coupled with hunting of wolves with modern vehicles and weapons, has led to some reduction in the wolf population. Furthermore, the practice of poisoning carcasses to kill wolves appears to be increasing. In the past, wolf populations were relatively more abundant in the eastern plains and rolling mountains because they had little competition from other large predators, but with recent persecution of wolves (and wild prey losses) occurring in these areas, densities are likely to be now similar to the lower figures characteristic of the rugged western mountains (Fig. 1), where snow leopards are relatively common.

In the early 1980's some 300 wolves (average approx. 1/200 km^2) were estimated to occur in Ladakh (Dar and Gaur, no date), although Nath (1982) believed there were considerably more. Similar habitats probably support a comparable density in the Transhimalayan parts of Himachal Pradesh and we expect another 50 wolves in this area. Using wolf consumption rates based on studies in North America (e.g., Fuller 1989), estimates of wild ungulate numbers (converted to biomass) in Ladakh (Fox et al. 1991a), domestic livestock numbers and depredation loss rates (e.g., Jackson 1991 and the present study), and the proportion of ungulates in wolf diet, 350 wild canids in India's Transhimalayan region appears to be a reasonable figure, especially if we are to include the dhole in this total (Chundawat and Fox, unpubl. data). If accurate, this low density of wolf and dhole indicates that concern for their continued survival is warranted.

Both India's Wildlife (Protection) Act of 1972, in force within Himachal Pradesh, and the Jammu and Kashmir Wildlife Protection Act of 1978 have listed the wolf as a big game species (the dhole is listed in the slightly more restrictive special game category) for which hunting licences may be obtained (Anonymous 1972, Ganhar 1979). Nevertheless, few licenses have been issued and most hunting is either illegal or in protection of livestock. Comprehensive records of numbers killed are not kept. Although use of firearms is the most common hunting method today, the poisoning of carcasses on which wolves feed is increasing as substances such as zinc phosphate become available. Such persecution of wolves will probably continue and increase in the more accessible areas of Ladakh. The Wildlife (Protection) Act of 1972 has been revised (October 1991) to institute strict exploitation bans on wildlife, including complete protection for the wolf and other large predators except in cases of protection of life and property or for research and education (A.J.T. Johnsingh, Wildlife Institute of India, pers. commun.). However, enforcement will be difficult in the case of Transhimalayan wolves. Interviews with local residents indicate that the greatest reduction in wolf numbers has been in eastern Ladakh where people with motor vehicles and firearms are able to chase down wolves on the open step-pelands and flat plains. Low human-population density and the large expanses of suitable habitat may allow the continued survival of wolves in Ladakh, but efforts to modernize and expand the livestock industry will increasingly threaten wolves within their preferred habitats of eastern Ladakh. Concerted efforts to maintain viable populations of wild ungulate prey in eastern Ladakh will be essential to the survival of wolves in this region (Fox et al. 1991a).

Wolves in India's Transhimalayan region do not constitute an isolated population. Similar low density populations occur across the borders within China and Pakistan, and different (but interbreeding) subspecies occur on the southern side of the Himalaya. Widespread decimation of both ungulate and predator populations in western China (Rowell 1983, Schaller 1990) are similar to those in eastern Ladakh, and are reminiscent of the wildlife decimation accompanying the introduction of firearms, military presence, wagon roads, and railroads in western North America during the 1800's. The elimination of wildlife has been especially dramatic in the vicinity of major roads such as the one skirting China's border with Transhimalayan India. The prospects for maintenance of viable wildlife populations in the face of a large military presence are uncertain. Along the rugged Pakistan border, wolf populations are relatively undisturbed by modern developments, but they are sparse in these regions anyway. The concentrated military presence has probably kept a high hunting pressure on the wolves that do occur as well as on their wild prey. India's central Transhimalayan region represents something akin to an island of relatively little disturbed natural habitat, and the efforts to conserve habitats and wildlife species in this area (e.g., Hemis National Park) will be important to wildlife conservation in the entire region (Fox and Nurbu 1990, Fox et al. 1994).

Fig. 8 *A pit trap for wolf near the village of Hankar at 4,100 m in the Markha valley of central Ladakh. (Photo: J.L. Fox).*

Efforts are being made to protect endangered species such as the snow leopard (Fox and Nurbu 1990, Fox et al. 1991b), but to date the wolf is still considered a menace and initiatives for its conservation are lacking. About 9% of Ladakh is designated as national park or wildlife sanctuaries and an additional 10–30% has been proposed (see Fox et al. 1991a), which if effectively managed would protect a proportional segment of the wolf population. The largest protected area (4,800 km^2 Hemis National Park) may support some 25–50 wolves (Fox and Nurbu 1990). Thus, the protected areas by themselves cannot ensure the survival of viable populations of large predators such as wolf and dhole. Corridors both within Ladakh, and to protected areas south of the Himalaya and internationally, must be viewed as part of the conservation picture.

In Ladakh's eastern plains wildlife protection action is less advanced than in the central region, and unless conservation measures are soon taken, many areas of eastern Ladakh could soon become devoid of large, wild ungulates and their mammalian predators. With concerted government efforts to increase productivity of the livestock industry (Darokhan 1986) there will be increasing pressure for predator control throughout the region, especially in the pastoral high plains of eastern Ladakh. Thus, unless strong efforts are made to ensure protection of endangered plains ungulates in eastern Ladakh, the most secure areas for wolves in the future may be the more rugged regions, where they will be in direct competition with snow leopard.

Acknowledgments

Several organizations and numerous individuals made possible the various studies during which information on wolves was gathered. We especially want to thank the Wildlife Institute of India, United States Fish and Wildlife Service (Office of International Affairs), International Snow Leopard Trust, Jammu and Kashmir Department of Wildlife Protection and The School for Field Studies. Special thanks goes to the late Chering Nurbu, Wildlife Range Officer in Ladakh, for his inspiring dedication to wildlife conservation and much appreciated companionship in the field, and to A.J.T. Johnsingh for informative discussions on canids in India.

Part Three:
Recovery Programs

Restoring Wolves to the Northern Rocky Mountains of the United States

■ **Steven H. Fritts, Edward E. Bangs, Joseph A. Fontaine, Wayne G. Brewster, and James F. Gore**

Wolves were eliminated from the northern Rocky Mountain area of the United States by the 1930's, which led to their being listed as an endangered species and protected under the federal Endangered Species Act of 1973, as amended. A revised Wolf Recovery Plan for the northern Rockies, approved in 1987, recommended natural recovery be promoted in portions of northwestern Montana and central Idaho and wolves be reintroduced into the greater Yellowstone area. The U.S. Fish and Wildlife Service leads a complex recovery program, based on the plan, which emphasizes interagency coordination, monitoring, public information, research, and control of problem wolves. Five federal agencies, three state wildlife departments, at least seven Native American tribes, and land management agencies in at least four levels of government are involved. The executive, legislative, and judicial branches of the U.S. government have been involved. Many recovery issues are perceptional, having more to do with deeply held personal values about government, outside influences, people's relationship to "nature" and the political role of special interest groups than to wolves themselves. An increasing population (22% per year) estimated at 50–70 wolves lives in Montana and immediately adjacent in Canada; a few lone wolves inhabit Idaho and possibly Yellowstone, but reproduction has not been documented; reintroduction to Yellowstone National Park has been extensively studied and debated. Congress required an Environmental Impact Statement (EIS) on reintroduction of wolves to Yellowstone and central Idaho be completed by 1994. Key future wolf recovery issues include: 1) implementation of the EIS decision; 2) removal from the threatened and endangered species list and assumption of management responsibility by the states and tribes; 3) public reaction to wolf control; and 4) appeals to restore wolves to additional areas.

Introduction

Restoration of wolves (*Canis lupus*) to the northern Rocky Mountain (NRM) area of the United States (U.S.) is extremely complex, controversial, symbolic, and as much a socio-political as a biological challenge. Our objectives are to: 1) chronicle major events in the return of wolves to the region; 2) describe the federal program for restoring wolves and its underlying philosophy; and 3) report overall progress. Our discussion pertains to the gray wolf in the NRM, rather than to any particular subspecies (Nowak 1983 this volume; Brewster and Fritts this volume). Geographically, we refer to Montana, Idaho, and Wyoming, although adjacent British Columbia (B.C.) and Alberta are closely involved in wolf recovery in those states (Fig. 1).

Wolves were present throughout the NRM prior to colonization by Europeans (Young 1944:48-49). The fervor with which Americans went about eradication of the wolf has been addressed by many authors (cf. Lopez 1978). As elsewhere, the species was vilified and killed by settlers in the American West (cf. Fogleman 1989), and was eliminated

from all the northwestern states, south-central B.C. and southern Alberta by 1930. Contributing factors in the U.S. included drastic reduction of native ungulate populations by settlers and market hunters, introduction of domestic livestock, trapping and poisoning by "wolfers," and finally, the Congressionally mandated predator control programs by the federal Bureau of Biological Survey which began in 1915 to eliminate wolves from all federal lands (Young 1944, Curnow 1969, Lopez 1978, Weaver 1978). By 1925, no viable wolf population remained anywhere in the NRM area.

Wolves were reported and occasionally killed from the 1940's through the 1970's in Montana, Idaho, and the greater Yellowstone area (Cole 1969b, 1971; Weaver 1978; Day 1981; Ream and Mattson 1982; Kaminski and Hansen 1984; Hansen 1986; Meagher 1986; U.S. Fish and Wildlife Service [USFWS] 1987; Brewster and Fritts this volume); yet, no breeding activity was confirmed. Conditions for the potential return of wolves to the region steadily improved as ungulate populations rebounded from their lows near the turn of the century. By the late 1960's, even before passage

Steven H. Fritts, Edward E. Bangs, Joseph A. Fontaine, Wayne G. Brewster, and James F. Gore

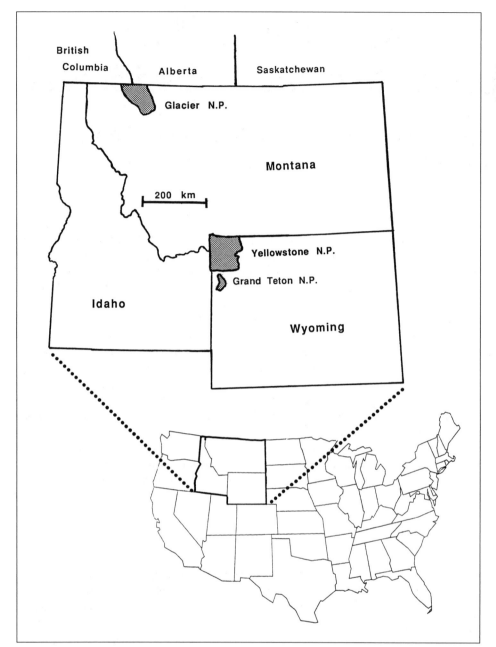

Fig. 1 *The Northern Rocky Mountains of the United States, as defined in this paper.*

of the Endangered Species Act of 1973 (ESA), calls were being made to restore wolves to Yellowstone National Park (YNP) (see references in Mech 1991a).

The Wolf Ecology Project was initiated in 1973 by the University of Montana (Table 1) when a network for collecting wolf reports and selective field-checking of areas with persistent reports was established (Day 1981). A similar investigative effort was established in Idaho in 1982 (Kaminski and Hansen 1984). In addition, surveys of hunters, outfitters, and guides for wolf observations were conducted in 1978 in Idaho (Siddall 1989, Johnston and Erickson 1990). These records indicated that wolf activity increased in the NRM area during the 1970's (Ream and Mattson 1982). Single wolves were killed in Montana in

1964, 1968, 1972, 1974, 1977, 1979, and 1980. A wolf was killed in Idaho in 1978 and a lone individual was photographed there in 1978, 1982, and 1983 (Table 1) (Ream and Mattson 1982, Kaminski and Hansen 1984). Others were killed in the Dakotas and Washington (Nowak 1983). These wolves were thought to be dispersing animals from B.C. and Alberta (Ream and Mattson 1982, Nowak 1983).

As wolves began to reappear in areas of their former range, human interest in restoring the species also increased. Various state and federal agencies and conservation groups in the U.S. became interested in offsetting the decades of wolf eradication. An improving public attitude toward the wolf reflected changes in attitudes about wildlife, the environment, and use of public lands — changes rooted in

Table 1. Major events in the restoration of wolves to the Northern Rocky Mountains of the United States.

YEAR	EVENT
1971	First Interagency meeting in YNP to discuss wolf recovery. Based only on reports, 5-10 wolves were thought to live in Glacier National Park and 10-15 in YNP.
1973	Second Endangered Species Act passed by U.S. Congress.
	Wolf Ecology Project organized to investigate sightings.
1974	USFWS appoints NRM Wolf Recovery Team.
1977	Drafting of first recovery plan.
1978	Wolf killed in Boise National Forest, Idaho; confirmed wolf sighting in Clearwater National Forest, Idaho.
1979	Lone female wolf radio-collared near Glacier National Park, 11 km north of international boundary.
1980	First livestock depredation by a wolf in recent history, lone wolf, Big Sandy, Montana.
	Original NRM Wolf Recovery Plan approved.
1981	First known wolf denning in 50 years, 10 km north of U.S. border
1982	Wolf photographed in Clearwater National Forest, Idaho.
	First litter of pups born in Flathead drainage in decades, 8 km north of Glacier National Park.
1983	NRM Wolf Recovery Plan revision begins.
	Wolf photographed in Clearwater National Forest, Idaho.
1985	Radio-collared pack moves south into Glacier National Park from Canada.
1986	First known denning of wolves in western U.S. in over 50 years.
1987	Revised NRM Wolf Recovery Plan approved.
	First livestock depredation by wolf pack in Northern Rockies, Babb area.
	USNPS Director Mott suggests beginning EIS for reintroduction to Yellowstone.
	Rep. Owens (Utah) introduces bill (H.R. 3387) to Congress requiring initiation of EIS for reintroduction to Yellowstone.
1988	USFWS appoints a Montana Wolf Project Leader and an assistant.
	Interagency Wolf Working Group formed in Montana.
	Congress mandates and funds studies to answer four questions about reintroduction to YNP.
	Interim Wolf Control Plan approved.
1989	Idaho Wolf Recovery Steering Committee organized.
	USFWS appoints Wolf Recovery Coordinator for Northern Rockies.
	First management translocation in Western U.S.
	Rep. Owens (Utah) introduces bill (H.R. 2687) that would have required preparation of Environmental EIS for reintroduction to Yellowstone.
1990	Farm Bureaus of Wyoming, Montana, and Idaho file petition to remove gray wolf from endangered and threatened lists (USFWS 1990b).
	USNPS and USFWS release first *Wolves for Yellowstone?* document.
	Senator McClure (Idaho) introduces bill (S.2674) to Congress that would have required three breeding pairs of wolves to be introduced to both YNP and central Idaho.
	Population in Glacier National Park area (including adjacent B.C.) increases to 34 wolves (September).
1991	Wolf Management Committee develops and submits report to Congress on wolf reintroduction and management in Central Idaho and YNP.
	ADC established Wolf Management Specialist position for Northern Rockies.
	Small group of wolves (≥2) discovered in Idaho; same wolf/wolves illegally poisoned.
	Defenders of Wildlife files suit to force USFWS to implement 1987 recovery plan.
	Two radio-collared wolves move independently into northern Idaho.
	Congress mandates EIS to begin with draft completed by May 1993.
1992	EIS begins on reintroduction to YNP and central Idaho.
	National Park Service and USFWS release second *Wolves for Yellowstone?* report.
	Possible wild wolf photographed in YNP.
	Wolf shot just south of YNP.

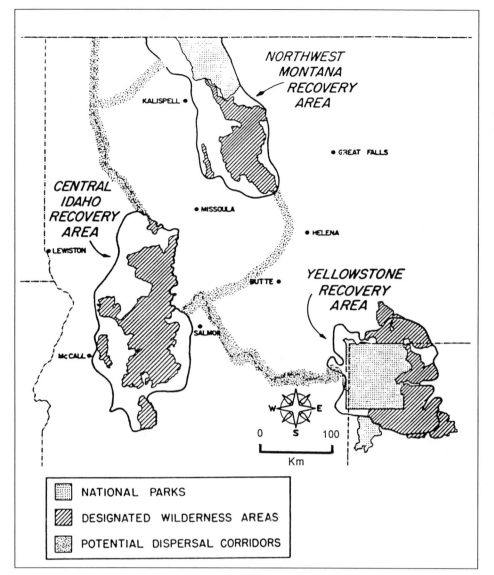

Fig. 2 *Recovery areas for the wolf in the Northern Rocky Mountains, according to the Northern Rocky Mountain Wolf Recovery Plan (USFWS 1987:23).*

fundamental social, cultural, and economic trends eventually reflected in federal legislation (cf. Dunlap 1988, Keiter and Holscher 1990). Policies of the National Park Service (USNPS) similarly evolved to emphasize "natural" regulation of animal populations (Dunlop 1983).

Attitudes also changed in Canada. Bounties were removed from wolves in B.C. in 1955 and they were classified as a game animal in 1966, protecting them from indiscriminate killing (Pletscher et al. 1991). Wolf hunting and trapping seasons in southeastern B.C. were closed from 1968 until population goals were reached in 1987. The season has been intermittently closed since then in specific management units when wolf numbers were below population goals. The bounty was also removed in Alberta in 1955; recreational hunting was restricted to September to March in 1964. Wolves increased in Alberta during the 1960's and 1970's when protection was the primary management goal (Gunson

1992). An increase in wolves in southeastern B.C. and southwestern Alberta ultimately allowed wolves to colonize northwestern Montana, with the first pack becoming established in Montana in 1986 (Ream et al. 1989).

The wolf had no legal protection in the NRM until passage of the ESA. Originally the subspecies *C. l. irremotus* was listed by the USFWS as endangered (38 Federal Register 14678, 4 June 1973). Its former range was thought to have included Idaho, the southwestern two-thirds of Montana, northwestern two-thirds of Wyoming, and eastern Washington and Oregon (Hall and Kelson 1959). Because of the trend among taxonomists to recognize fewer subspecies and the likelihood of enforcement problems stemming from inability to routinely recognize subspecies, the entire species (*Canis lupus*) was listed in 1978 as endangered throughout the lower 48 states, except in Minnesota where it was reclassified as "threatened" (43 Federal Register 9612, 9 March

1978). Wolves were protected by state law in Montana in 1973 and Idaho in 1977. Wolves in Wyoming still have no protection under state statutes.

The Recovery Plan

The Secretary of the Interior was required by the ESA to develop and implement plans for the conservation and survival of endangered and threatened species. One year after passage of the ESA, the USFWS appointed an NRM Wolf Recovery Team. Membership included federal and state agencies, conservation groups, and (later) a livestock organization representative. The team completed a Recovery Plan in 1980 (USFWS 1980), which was revised, after considerable review, and approved in 1987 (USFWS 1987:112). Thirteen years were required for the development, review, and final approval of the current Recovery Plan.

The Recovery Team evaluated Montana, Idaho, and Wyoming for areas that could support at least 10 breeding pairs of wolves. Criteria included: 1) a substantial population of large ungulates as a prey base; 2) at least 7,770 km^2 of designated wilderness (or similar) area that could support wolves; 3) maximum 10% private land ownership; 4) absence, if possible, of livestock grazing; and 5) isolation from populated or heavy-use recreational areas. The recovery areas identified were northwestern Montana, central Idaho, and the greater Yellowstone area (USFWS 1987:23) (Fig. 2). Historically, these areas harbored fewer wolves because of their higher elevation and lower carrying capacity for prey. Plains and large river valleys in Montana, Idaho, and Wyoming probably supported the highest densities of large ungulate prey and wolves, but now are mostly in residential, municipal, or agricultural use.

The 1987 Recovery Plan defined recovery as 10 breeding pairs (about 100 individuals) of wolves in each of the three separate areas for a minimum of three consecutive years (USFWS 1987:12). After achieving this goal and transfer to state management, removal from federal ESA protection would occur. Natural recovery was to be promoted in northwestern Montana and central Idaho; reintroduction was recommended to YNP and reintroduction to Idaho was to be considered if two breeding pairs had not established there within five years. The recommendation to reintroduce wolves to Yellowstone (based on a one-vote margin) was made on the assumption that natural recovery was not likely in the near future (USFWS 1987:25). Opposition within the team to reintroduction was based on the desire to avoid intrusive management and an expected political opposition.

The Recovery Plan recommended that wolves reintroduced to Yellowstone be designated as a nonessential experimental population, as has since been done with the red wolf (*Canis rufus*) (Parker and Phillips 1991), providing management flexibility to accommodate local concerns. The experimental population approach has since received considerable promotion (cf. Tilt et al. 1987, Mech 1991a, Peek

et al. 1991), and appears to be a viable option (Fritts 1990). However, some are sceptical of its use, preferring special legislation or other Congressional action to guarantee provisions such as delisting after recovery, state control, and ability of ranchers to kill wolves seen near livestock (Wolf Management Committee 1991). The National Environmental Policy Act requires that an Environmental Impact Statement (EIS) be prepared for federal actions that significantly affect the quality of the human environment. Following approval of the Recovery Plan, preparation of an EIS was the next logical step toward a Yellowstone reintroduction and was recommended in the Recovery Plan. Discussion of that EIS follows discussion of events leading to its onset.

Roles and Perspectives of Government Agencies in Wolf Recovery

Federal Agencies' Perspectives and Concerns
Listing the wolf as endangered under the ESA had at least three major effects: 1) individuals, businesses, and government entities are prohibited from conduct that will "take" (attempt to kill, harm, or harass) a wolf; 2) all federal agencies are to "insure" that actions they undertake, fund, or permit do not "jeopardize the continued existence" of a wolf; and 3) each federal agency is directed to carry out conservation programs to enhance wolf recovery.

Ironically, the Bureau of Biological Survey was the agency most responsible for the demise of the wolf, and the agency that evolved from it, the USFWS, became responsible for restoring it. While seemingly contradictory, this fact merely reflects public and Congressional attitudes of the times. Enactment of ESA vested the USFWS with responsibility to list threatened and endangered species, prepare and approve recovery plans, coordinate recovery programs, consult with other federal agencies on the effects of those agencies' actions on endangered species, and enforce laws against various prohibited acts (take). Whether the USFWS is legally responsible for fully implementing its recovery plans is less clear (Bader 1989, Keiter and Holscher 1990).

In addition to its ESA responsibility, the USNPS has an interest in wolf restoration to some national parks, especially YNP, because parks seek to maintain or restore original fauna and flora. The USNPS manages animal and plant populations within parks to maintain natural diversity and perpetuate natural processes (USNPS 1988). Since the recovery areas in the NRM region include three national parks (Fig. 1) the USNPS has a major role in wolf recovery in that region.

The U.S. Forest Service (USFS) (Department of Agriculture) and Bureau of Land Management (BLM) (Department of Interior) are multiple use agencies that manage most of the habitat (millions of hectares) where wolves are expected to occur. Congress has mandated that those lands be managed for recreation, wildlife and fisheries, grazing, mining, oil and gas, watershed, timber, and wilderness. Section 7 of the ESA requires that those activities be managed in such a way that they do not jeopardize the continued existence of endangered species and specifies that all federal agencies are obligated to take action to enhance recovery of endangered species. The Animal Damage Control Section (ADC) of the U.S. Department of Agriculture is responsible for controlling wildlife that cause damage, including listed species, and has taken an active role in wolf control and wolf recovery as well.

State Agencies' Perspectives and Concerns

State agencies most affected by wolf recovery in the NRM are the Idaho, Montana, and Wyoming Departments of Fish and Wildlife, State Lands, and Agriculture. Under ESA, federal agencies have ultimate responsibility for managing listed species, with state authority under this umbrella. Concerns of state governments are that 1) wolves cannot be managed freely during recovery while under federal protection; 2) wolves may not be quickly delisted after recovery is achieved; and 3) local interests may not be sufficiently considered (Keiter and Holscher 1990). State concerns often seem to be driven in large part by livestock interests. Wolf recovery involves primarily federal lands, but the prey base (ungulates) is state-managed, and recovered wolf populations on federal lands would certainly move to repopulate state lands. In general, the states doubt that ESA is flexible enough to accommodate livestock and wildlife management interests (particularly as they apply to wolf control), and fear that federally protected wolves may ultimately limit land use options on federal lands due to Section 7 provisions of the ESA (Keiter and Holscher 1990). Other issues are costs of wolf management and imposition of the will of "outsiders" on state residents. In 1991, the state legislatures of Idaho and Wyoming each passed joint resolutions opposing reintroduction, protection, and recovery of wolves.

Although generally opposing a federal wolf recovery effort, Montana, Idaho, and Wyoming each have different management concerns and preferences (Keiter and Holscher 1990, Strauch 1992). Montana proposes that the wolf be removed from the protection of ESA and recovered by the state under its own Nongame and Endangered Species Act, contending that recovery can occur faster and less expensively than under ESA. The Idaho Department of Fish and Game supports wolf recovery within the designated recovery area. The goal of the department is for the wolf to be removed from the list of endangered and threatened species when it is no longer threatened in the recovery area. Idaho statutes severely restrict participation of Department of Fish and Game personnel in federal wolf recovery efforts. Wyoming, while listing the wolf statutorily as a predator with no protection, supports federally funded research and monitoring to manage the wolf as a state-regulated species and to ensure state ungulate objectives are not compromised. The Wyoming Game and Fish Commission decided in summer 1992 to support the ongoing EIS regarding reintroduction of

wolves to Yellowstone and central Idaho (J. Talbott, Wyoming Game and Fish Dept., pers. commun.). Despite major concerns of state legislatures about wolf recovery under federal terms, state biologists and managers work cooperatively on federal field recovery activities.

Tribal Perspectives and Concerns

Six Native American tribes are located on five reservations in or adjacent to NRM wolf recovery areas: the Blackfeet and Confederated Salish and Kootenai Tribes in Montana, Shoshone and Arapaho Tribes in Wyoming, and the Nez Perce and Shoshone/Bannock Tribes in Idaho. Many Native Americans in the region would like to see the wolf return to its former range because of the cultural significance of the animal. They view the wolf as a powerful religious symbol and as being placed on earth to fill a niche in the scheme of life (Vest 1988). Other tribal members who raise livestock believe the wolf may affect their livelihood. Degree of support for wolf recovery by a tribe depends on the current make-up of the tribal council. The tribes are generally taking a wait-and-see approach to wolf recovery, but some participate in monitoring efforts. The Shoshone even investigated the possibility of reintroducing wolves onto the Wind River Reservation in northwestern Wyoming.

Major tribal concerns are: recognition of tribal sovereignty, culture, and authority; involvement in the recovery process; and management responsibility for the wolf. Currently, the Blackfeet, and Confederated Salish and Kootenai tribes are cooperators in the Montana Wolf Working Group and the Nez Perce are members of the Idaho Information and Education Working Group. No working groups have been formed in Wyoming pending the outcome of the EIS, but the Arapaho/Shoshone are active participants in development of the EIS.

With tribal permission, the USFWS would assist or actually radio-collar wolves on tribal lands in Montana for tribal monitoring of wolves, if the opportunity arises. Problem wolves are currently controlled by ADC as directed by the USFWS. All control and monitoring of problem wolves is done cooperatively with the tribes, with respect for their sovereignty on their land.

The Public's Perspectives and Concerns

An understanding of the public's perception of wolves is vital to developing an effective restoration program. Wolves are symbolic on a range of issues, with the perception of the importance of the species varying among various demographic and socioeconomic groups (Kellert 1985a; Lenihan 1987, McNaught 1987, Bath and Buchanan 1989; Bath and Phillips 1990; Bath 1991a,b). Few wildlife issues are so driven by misperceptions that have no basis, rather than by biological fact, as wolf recovery and management. Wolf recovery appears to be an amalgam of issues in the minds of many people, both within and outside the NRM.

In 1978, approximately 50% of the public within the Rocky Mountain region were found to like, and 30% to dislike, the wolf (Kellert 1985a). Younger, more educated, and urban-dwelling respondents tended to hold the most positive view of wolves. Most livestock producers expressed negative attitudes that may be historically ingrained and sociologically maintained.

In Montana, Idaho, and Wyoming a mixed but overall positive attitude exists toward wolves (Lenihan 1987; Tucker and Pletscher 1989; Bath and Buchanan 1989; Bath and Phillips 1990; Bath 1991b, 1992; Thompson and Gasson 1991, Freemuth 1992). A strong majority of visitors to YNP support wolf reintroduction to the park (McNaught 1987, Bath 1992). Although residents of states bordering YNP have mixed attitudes about reintroduction, a majority in each state favors it, with support being strongest in Idaho and weakest in Montana (Bath 1991b, 1992, Thompson and Gasson 1991). Idahoans (72%) favor having wolves in the wilderness and roadless areas of central Idaho (Freemuth 1992).

In a 1987 survey, a majority of Montanans indicated approval (52% *versus* 38% who disapproved) of wolf reintroduction into areas in Montana, Idaho, and YNP where wolves are now extinct (Lenihan 1987). However, 56% of those from rural areas did not approve, versus 39% who did. Similarly, support for reintroduction to YNP among Wyoming residents diminished with increasing proximity to the park (Bath and Buchanan 1989, Thompson and Gasson 1991, Bath 1992). Wyoming stockgrowers were strongly opposed to wolf reintroduction to YNP (Bath and Buchanan 1989). Most of the Wyoming residents opposed were adamant in their opposition and generally unwilling to change their minds (Bath and Buchanan 1989, Bath 1991a, 1992, Thompson and Gasson 1991). Primary reasons for opposition to reintroduction included cost, fear of wolves spreading outside the intended area, and expectations of livestock losses, big game declines, and land-use restrictions (Bath 1991a,b, 1992, Bath and Phillips 1990, Thompson and Gasson 1991). Opposition may also relate to wolf recovery being symbolic of the larger issue of government or outside control of the great western frontier (cf. Cohn 1990, Kirwan 1992). Primary reasons for support of reintroduction were the belief that wolves are important members of the ecological community and were historically present (Thompson and Gasson 1991).

Most respondents living near wolves in northwestern Montana were supportive of having wolves, but indicated their support would erode if restrictions on recreational and commercial land uses were imposed to promote recovery (Tucker and Pletscher 1989). Wyoming residents likewise indicated little support for additional restrictions on public use of public land for wolves (Thompson and Gasson 1991). Those conducting public opinion surveys concluded that knowledge about wolves in the region is deficient and called for more public education (Tucker and Pletscher 1989, Bath

1992). We also conclude that misinformation about wolves is pervasive. Wolf recovery was an important issue to three-quarters of Wyoming, Montana, and Idaho residents surveyed (Bath 1987, Bath and Phillips 1990). Hunters, nonconsumptive outdoor users, members of environmental or industry groups, residents of counties near YNP, and males all felt more strongly about the issue than other respondents. Newspapers, magazines, and television were the main information sources; scientific literature was rarely read (Tucker and Pletscher 1989, Thompson and Gasson 1991).

Numerous groups are involved in wolf recovery at local, regional, and national levels, and from a variety of perspectives; their interest generally focuses on Yellowstone. The Defenders of Wildlife, National Wildlife Federation, The Wolf Fund, Wolf Haven International, Wolf Education and Research Center (formerly Wolf Recovery Foundation), and others actively promote wolf recovery in the NRM. Several organizations of agricultural interests, some sportsmen, and others who advocate substantial economic use of natural resources and public lands actively oppose wolf reintroduction to Yellowstone.

Perhaps the most pertinent finding for a wolf recovery program is that members of the public most likely to encounter wolves or to perceive being affected by them have the least favorable attitude toward them. Because of their disproportionate potential impact on wolf survival, those individuals warrant special attention in conducting a recovery program.

Philosophy of the Recovery Program

Related to the public's perspectives and concerns, certain basic philosophies underlie the recovery program. One is that success depends on local support. Humans are the prime factor that can prevent wolf recovery. Because of the potential for illegal killing of wolves, the USFWS (the lead agency) believes that heavy emphasis on public information and education, with a well-conceived information and education program, is vital (Pomerantz and Blanchard 1992). Human reactions to wolves are critical when wolves attempt to settle in human-inhabited areas, as at least four packs have done in western Montana (Fritts et al. 1994). Therefore, emphasis is on building the trust of local citizens through one-on-one contact and presenting balanced accurate information. This approach is labor intensive, and the payoff is usually not immediately seen; nevertheless, long-term change in public attitudes and acceptance of wolves is vital. A related basic tenet of the program is the importance of gaining the interest and involvement of the maximum number of citizens and agency personnel.

Another philosophy is to avoid unnecessary use of restrictions upon human activities to accomplish wolf recovery. Misunderstanding exists about the need for land-use restrictions to accomplish recovery in the NRM area. Some members of the public fail to recognize that habitat is excellent for wolves and that the greatest potential threat to recovery is direct killing by humans. This misunderstanding is derived largely from erroneously assuming that the wolf has the same habitat and security needs as the grizzly bear (*Ursus arctos*), which has been the subject of an intensive conservation effort, including some land-use restrictions, in the same general area. Potentially, recovery opponents argue, the provisions of Section 7 of the ESA might be used to close off large areas of public lands from grazing, mining, logging, and other uses if a possible "adverse affect" or "take" situation is identified; many environmentalists would welcome that action. USFWS believes that few restrictions are necessary for wolves, owing to their flexible habitat requirements, ability to live near people so long as they are not killed, and high reproductive potential. Moreover, a backlash effect from local people affected by land-use restrictions could easily result in more illegal killing which would quickly offset any advantage gained through restrictions (Tucker and Pletscher 1989, Tucker et al. 1990). There are only two restrictions associated with wolf recovery: 1) a 1.6 km area around active dens and rendezvous sites *may* be protected from intensive human use between 15 March and 1 July; and 2) ADC personnel may not use nonselective controls, i.e., poison, to control predators in areas occupied by wolves, primarily because toxicant registration restricts their use around endangered species (Bangs 1991). The former is intended to protect wolf dens and rendezvous areas from disturbances that could jeopardize pup survival by causing them to be moved prematurely. For public lands, no other restrictions are planned by the USFWS unless illegal killing makes them necessary.

Critics have charged or inferred that the wolf recovery program goes too far to appease local interests, particularly the livestock industry (cf. Keiter and Holscher 1990, Goble 1992). Another view is that the program is a rare example of local concerns being addressed within the confines of the ESA (Keiter and Holscher 1990). The extent of the USFWS's authority to control wolves in Montana has been an issue of legal discussion (R. B. Keiter, Univ. of Wyoming, pers. commun.), but no litigation has occurred. The USFWS remains convinced, as was the Recovery Team, that wolf recovery will not succeed without local support, and the recovery program will continue to reflect this pragmatic view. Various studies have shown that illegal killing of wolves can be an important mortality cause, despite ESA protection (Weise et al. 1979, Mech 1977b, Fritts and Mech 1981, Fuller 1989, Wydeven et al. this volume). Archibald et al. (1991) concluded that if wildlife managers do not address the concerns of those being affected by wolf predation, those affected will take matters into their own hands. Even if the general public, including the public in the affected states, is sympathetic to wolves, a disgruntled minority can easily jeopardize wolf recovery through illegal killing. Therefore, a vital element in recovery (as vital as adequate prey) is an atmosphere where it is socially unac-

ceptable within local communities to indiscriminately and illegally kill wolves.

The Current USFWS-led Multiagency Recovery Program

In 1988, two biologists were hired by the USFWS with responsibility for effecting wolf recovery in Montana, using the Recovery Plan as a general guide. In 1992, the Montana program employed two full-time and one part-time biologists. The USFWS offices in Boise, Idaho, and Cheyenne, Wyoming, have one permanent employee working part time on wolf recovery. In 1989, a Wolf Recovery Coordinator was appointed and stationed with the Montana personnel as the result of Congressional interest in wolf restoration to Yellowstone. The coordinator led agency response to questions asked by Congress about wolf recovery in Yellowstone and coordinates and facilitates interagency and interregional wolf recovery efforts in Montana, Idaho, Yellowstone (Wyoming), Washington, and other northwestern states. Roles of endangered species coordinators are discussed by Clark et al. (1989).

In 1988 and 1989, the USFWS coordinated development of interagency organizations to implement and coordinate wolf recovery in Montana (Bangs 1991) and Idaho (Central Idaho Wolf Recovery Steering Committee 1990). The Montana Wolf Working Group consists of representatives of the USFWS, USFS, USNPS, BLM, and ADC, with cooperation from the Confederated Salish and Kootenai Tribes, the Blackfeet Nation, University of Montana, and Montana Departments of Fish, Wildlife, and Parks, State Lands, and Livestock. The Idaho Wolf Recovery organization is similarly organized and consists of two sub-committees (Fig. 3). Both organizations address the challenging but critical functions of communication and cooperation among agencies in recovery efforts (Salwasser et al. 1987, Clark et al. 1989).

No comparable multiagency recovery organization has been established for the Yellowstone recovery area. This is due in part to the controversy about recovery there, uncertainty about whether a reintroduction will occur, and lack of clear direction to the affected agencies. An interagency group there may be more unwieldy than in the other recovery areas because of involvement of three states, two national parks, and six national forests in three separate USFS regions.

The recovery program in each of the three recovery areas came to consist of four intertwined major elements: monitoring, wolf and ungulate research, public information, and control of problem wolves (USFWS 1989, Bangs 1991). Actual implementation of all four elements has occurred only in Montana, as it is the only area with a wolf population. All four elements involve and emphasize public education. The importance attributed to public education is reflected in the expenditure of an estimated 60% of USFWS personnel's

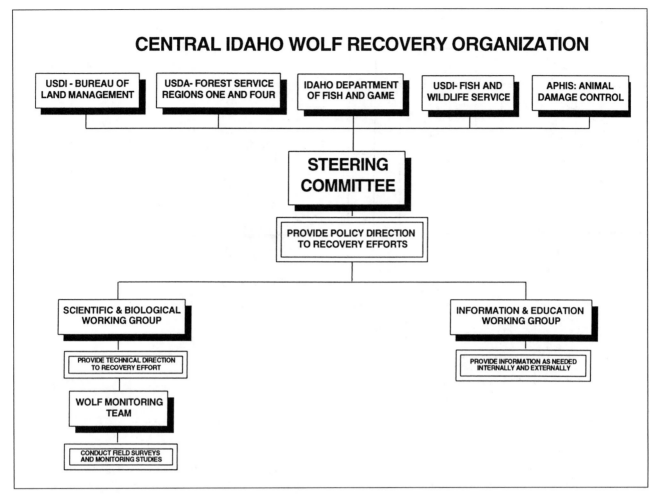

Fig. 3 *Organizational chart of the Central Idaho Wolf Recovery Organization, illustrating the involvement of multiple government agencies.*

time as opposed to 25% for monitoring, 5% for research, 5% for control, and 5% other activities.

Monitoring

Although efforts to locate and document the presence of wolves predates interagency organization activities (Weaver 1978, Flath 1979, Day 1981, Kaminski and Boss 1981, Ream and Mattson 1982, Kaminski and Hansen 1984, Hansen 1986, Central Idaho Wolf Recovery Steering Committee 1990), determining the distribution and number of wolves quickly became a priority task for them. Knowledge of wolf numbers and distribution defines progress toward recovery and allows agencies to better coordinate their activities with an expanding wolf population. An enhanced three-phase monitoring system was implemented in Montana in 1989 and in Idaho and Wyoming in 1991. It involves: 1) detection (public reports) to identify areas where wolves may occur; 2) confirmation (agency surveys) to confirm presence of breeding pairs or packs through survey techniques; and 3)

monitoring (radiotelemetry), which is used to systematically document and monitor established packs or pairs. A secondary objective of the monitoring is to involve the public and personnel of the agencies on the assumption that the wolf will benefit from the sense of program "ownership" and local interest that such involvement creates. Description of the three stages of the monitoring program follows.

Detection (Phase 1)

A wolf observation reporting card to be used by all cooperators was distributed in 1989 to record wolf observations and sign. The cards are pre-addressed and postage prepaid. Completed cards are mailed to the USFWS in Helena, Montana, Boise, Idaho, and Cheyenne, Wyoming where data are compiled on computer files and included in periodic reports to cooperators and contributors. The Idaho program has a toll-free phone number for reporting sightings. Earlier, reports were ranked by authenticity (cf. Weaver 1978, Central Idaho Wolf Steering Committee 1990); this practice was discontinued in Montana because accurate assessment of

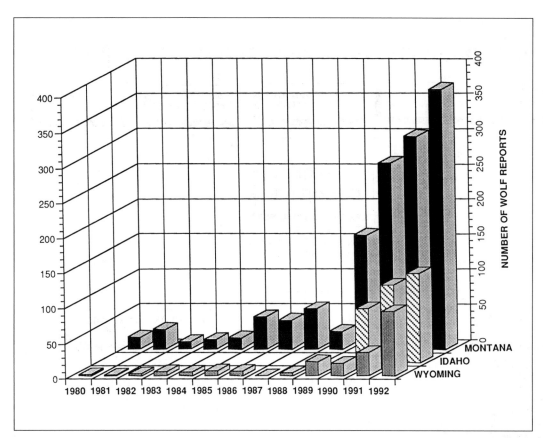

Fig. 4 *Reports of wolves in Montana, Idaho, and Wyoming, 1980-1992. Many reports were received prior to 1980 in all three states. Several reports were received from 1980-1989 in Idaho, but have not been compiled by calendar year.*

validity is impossible, and single observations are of limited importance compared to clusters of multiple observations. The number of Montana observations reported to the USFWS has drastically increased since development and implementation of the system in 1989 (Fig. 4). Similarly, over 600 reports of sightings have been made in Idaho in the last 15 years from a broad area of the state, some of which were received in response to questionnaires about sightings (Kaminski and Hansen 1984, Siddall 1989, Johnston and Erickson 1990). The number of wolf reports in Idaho totalled 76 in 1990, 110 in 1991, and 127 in 1992 (compared to 367 in Montana) (Fig. 4). Wyoming wolf reports increased substantially to 91 in 1992 (Fig. 4). The reporting system in Wyoming was last to be organized, so records prior to the past two years are not necessarily complete. Reporters of wolves are highly sensitive to publicity about the species and our solicitations for reports and thus numbers of reports must be interpreted with caution.

Confirmation (Phase 2)
Reports of single wolves rarely result in field investigation because lone wolves are highly mobile, can be almost anywhere, and are of little immediate consequence to recovery. However, when clusters of reports indicating more than one animal are received from an area, USFWS personnel, or trained biologists from cooperating agencies, conduct field surveys to confirm wolf presence. Various conservation

groups have assisted in these surveys. The detection/confirmation approach has led to discovery of three pairs or packs of wolves during the past three years in Montana (all were subsequently radio-collared) and one in Idaho (did not survive).

Monitoring — Radiotelemetry (Phase 3)
After confirmation of a probable pack or breeding pair, the wolves may be captured and radio-collared for quality information about numbers and range. Capture and handling also gives an opportunity to sample blood and examine animals for genetics (Lehman et al. 1991), disease (Brand et al. this volume), or evidence of captive rearing. Wolf packs had already been under study in the Glacier National Park area by the University of Montana before the Working Groups' monitoring programs (Pletscher et al. 1991, Ream et al. 1991) (Table 1). By the end of 1992, four radio-collared wolf packs were being monitored in northwestern Montana (Fig. 5). Also being monitored was a pack living along the international border and another living in adjacent B.C. Forty-one wolves have been radio-collared in Montana and adjacent B.C., including 31 by the Wolf Ecology Project and 10 by the interagency team. No wolves have been radio-collared in Idaho, but two wolves radio-collared in Montana and B.C. are known to have entered Idaho (one travelled back to Canada), and other confirmation of wolf presence has occurred.

Wolf and Ungulate Research in Northwestern Montana and Idaho

The USFWS and other federal agencies funded wolf research in Idaho and Montana from the early 1970's through the mid-1980's. Early research in Idaho examined the historical and current status of wolves and evaluated elk habitat (Kaminski and Hansen 1984, Hansen 1986). A modeling study of the effects of wolf predation on elk (*Cervus elaphus*) and deer (*Odocoileus hemionus*) along the eastern Rocky Mountain Front was sponsored (Peek and Vales this volume), and a study of wolf-mountain lion (*Felis concolor*) interactions began in 1992. Research in the North Fork of the Flathead River in Montana has been funded cooperatively by the USFWS, USNPS, USFS, and University of Montana with logistical support provided by USFS, Glacier National Park, Montana Department of Fish, Wildlife and Parks, and B.C. Wildlife Branch from the mid-1980's until 1992. This research has determined numbers, distribution, movements, immigration, dispersal, natality, mortality, and feeding ecology of wolves in the area (Ream 1984, Ream et al. 1985, Ream et al. 1989, Pletscher et al. 1991, Ream et al. 1991, Boyd et al. this volume). Studies of white-tailed deer (*O. virginianus*) (Rachael 1992), moose (*Alces alces*) (M. Langley, Univ. of Montana, pers. commun.), and elk (Bureau 1992) in that area have been completed. A five-year study of wolf-ungulate landscape ecology in the North Fork of the Flathead River began in 1991 (D. H. Pletscher, Univ. of Montana, pers. commun.).

Information and Education

Public information efforts are the highest priority because accurate knowledge of wolves is a primary factor affecting public attitudes toward the species (Kellert 1985a). All phases of the wolf recovery program are designed to maximize their informational value to the public.

Examples of public information tasks include presentations to local businesses, stockgrower, sportsmen, educator, and conservationist groups; a wolf education booth at state and county fairs; talking about wolves in local classrooms; and films and pamphlets on correctly identifying wolves, dogs, and coyotes. In Montana alone, from 1989 through 1992, more than 260 presentations were made to approximately 13,000 people about wolf natural history and recovery. These presentations are in addition to numerous other informal meetings with the Wolf Working Group, other agencies, conservation organizations, reporters, journalists, television and radio talk shows, and telephone and personal interviews, and does not include presentations made by the Wolf Recovery Coordinator, cooperating agencies, and conservation organizations. Information has been provided for hundreds of newspaper and magazine articles, books, and other public media about wolves and wolf recovery in the NRM. Program personnel strive to present a factual and balanced view of the wolf, describe the legal and biological rationale for recovery, point out that some wolf control must accompany recovery, stress that few restrictions on use of

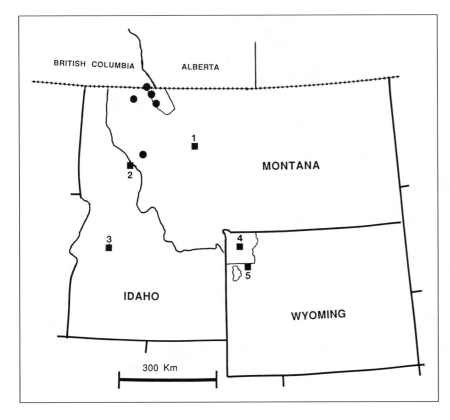

Fig. 5 *Locations of wolf packs monitored by telemetry in 1992 (dots) and other noteworthy recent wolf activity (squares) in the Northern Rockies of the U.S. One additional radio-collared pack (not shown) lived just north of the international border in British Columbia. Reports of wolf observations have been received from much of western Montana, the northern two-thirds of Idaho and northwestern Wyoming. "1" = site of formation of a new pack in early 1993 (not discussed in this paper). "2" = area used by radio-collared lone adult male that dispersed from Glacier National Park. "3" = location where ≥ 2 wolves were discovered in Boise National Forest in summer 1991. At least one was illegally poisoned in July, and no subsequent wolf activity in the area has been documented. "4" = site where an apparent single wolf was filmed in August 1992. "5" = site of illegal shooting of an adult male wolf in the Teton Wilderness in September 1992.*

public lands need accompany wolf recovery, and stress the differences between wolves and other canids.

Twenty wolf education trunks were prepared by the National Wildlife Federation, with support from the USFWS, the Central Idaho Wolf Recovery Steering Committee, and the USFS. The trunks are popular with teachers and are booked for months in advance. Each contains hides and skulls from wolves and coyotes; scats from wolves, coyotes, dogs, and elk; an elk skull; plaster casts of wolf, coyote, lion and elk tracks; pieces of hide from common wolf prey, an audio tape of wolves howling, four wolf education videotapes, a three-ring binder containing lesson plans for kindergarten though twelfth grade, and other materials. Wolf posters requesting individuals to report wolf sightings were distributed to agencies, sporting goods stores, schools, and other establishments willing to display them.

A variety of public education programs are conducted by conservation groups and volunteers, including the Wolf Educational Research Center in Idaho, the National Wildlife Federation, Defenders of Wildlife in Montana, the Wolf Fund, Wolf Haven International, Mission Wolf, and others. A full range of opinions about wolves is expressed by the great diversity of organizations interested in the species, with appeal to the emotion not uncommon. Programs that stress accurate information are a strong asset to wolf recovery and management; the value and impact of others is difficult to assess. Some organizations that most oppose wolf recovery distribute materials that include clearly distorted information or are selected to depict only the negative side of wolves. These materials perpetuate the same myths and misperceptions that have existed for decades and that legitimate educators have labored to dispel. In view of the pro-wolf and anti-wolf campaigns in progress, getting accurate information and the USFWS' position on recovery out to the public has been a major challenge.

Control

The Recovery Plan stresses that livestock-depredating wolves should not be the founders of the population in the NRM. The USFWS developed Interim Wolf Control Plans to guide control of wolves that attack livestock in Montana and Wyoming (USFWS 1988a) and Idaho (USFWS 1990a). Control of problem wolves is the most controversial aspect of the program, and is seen by some as a contradiction in terms for a recovery program and illegal under the ESA (Goble 1992). The USFWS, however, contends that controlling a few depredating wolves will enhance the survival of the species by reducing indiscriminate illegal killing of wolves that can result from unresolved wolf-livestock conflicts, and thus is consistent with the ESA conservation mandate. Investigation of depredation reports and capture of problem wolves is conducted by ADC with guidance and cooperation from the USFWS. ADC has a Wolf Management Specialist to conduct wolf control and related functions (including public information) in the NRM.

Since 1980, 17 cattle (seven calves, six steers, four cows) and 12 sheep have been confirmed lost to wolves in the entire NRM, all on private land (Bangs et al. this volume). Seventeen wolves have been controlled (one twice): two were released on site, six killed, three placed in captivity, and seven translocated. The translocations have been especially controversial (Bangs et al. this volume), although one resulted in the formation of the southern-most known pack in the northern Rockies (Ninemile Valley, about 56 km northwest of Missoula, Montana) (Fig. 5). Control has been directly or indirectly responsible for 13 wolves being removed from the Montana population since 1985, about 52% (13 of 25) of all known losses in the state.

Defenders of Wildlife implemented a compensation fund for wolf-related losses (Fischer 1989, Bangs et al. this volume). Although this program covers the entire NRM, no losses have occurred outside Montana. In 1992, Defenders initiated a $5,000 reward program for landowners on whose property wolf pups are successfully raised; no payment was made that year (H. Fischer, Defenders of Wildlife, pers. commun.)

Recovery Progress

Independent of the continuing sociopolitical side to wolf recovery, wolves are recolonizing the region (Table 1, Fig. 5). The wolf population in northwestern Montana and adjacent southeastern B.C. has grown from at least one wolf in 1979 (Ream et al. 1985, Ream et al. 1989) to at least 46 in 1990 (Pletscher et al. 1991) to about 59 in August 1992 (Fig. 6). The average annual rate of increase of the population is therefore 37% since 1979 when the first lone wolf was radio-collared and 22.8% since 1985 when the first pack appeared in Montana. The minimum average population for Montana has been 25.3 wolves since 1985. The core population continues to live in and near Glacier National Park along the North Fork of the Flathead River, but an increasing number of wolves are surviving outside that area in Montana. The population in Montana is nearly half way to recovery level (10 breeding pairs) only 10 years after colonization. Nonetheless, it is far too small to be considered viable in the usual sense (Soulé 1987), and is dependent on its tenuous connection to the Canadian population through southeastern B.C. and southwestern Alberta to the Banff and Jasper National Parks areas in Alberta.

Minimum recent reproduction in Montana was at least four litters (21 pups) in 1990; two litters (10 pups) in 1991; and four litters (15 pups) in 1992. Two more packs, living partly or totally within Canada, produced pups — seven and six, respectively, in 1992. With Canadian packs adjacent to the border included, a total of 127 pups are known to have been produced in 27 litters from 1985–1992.

Losses to the Montana *and* adjacent Canadian population have been documented from 1985-92 (Pletscher et al. 1991, D. Pletscher, Univ. of Montana, pers. commun., USFWS

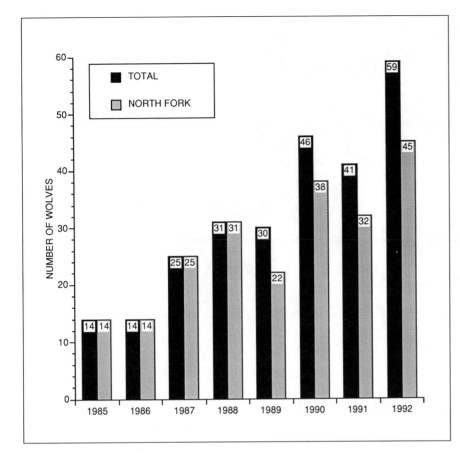

Fig. 6 *Estimated wolf population in and immediately adjacent to northwestern Montana, 1985–1992. Pack activity was first documented in Montana in 1985. "North Fork" indicates known wolves in North Fork of the Flathead River Ecosystem including those just north of the border in British Columbia (Pletscher et al. 1991, in prep.; Ream et al. 1991). "Total" indicates all known wolves throughout western Montana including those in the North Fork of the Flathead ecosystem. August population levels are presented; wolf numbers in each subsequent winter would be 20-40% smaller. (Authors' note: On 1 October 1993, there were at least 87 "total" wolves in the area, including 63 in the North Fork).*

unpubl. data). In Montana, these ($\overline{x} = 3.1$/year) consisted of: illegal killing (five), legal wolf control (13), suspected disease (at least five pups), road kill (one), and one found frozen in lake ice. Our control program was directly or indirectly responsible for 52% of known mortalities and affected six percent of the population annually in Montana. Humans were responsible for 72% of all known wolf mortality in Montana and removed about 9% of the population each year. On the Canadian side of the border known mortality causes were: legal hunting (nine), illegal killing (six), and other causes (four), including one dying in an avalanche.

Known losses to the *entire* population (U.S. and Canadian side of border) from all causes averaged nearly five wolves per year. Humans were responsible for approximately 85% of mortality for the entire population, four wolves per year, and removed about 13% of the wolf population annually. These mortalities have slowed but not greatly hindered population growth. Roughly 15 radio-collared or ear-tagged wolves are known to have dispersed (Boyd et al. this volume), and some 40 wolves (mostly unmarked) could not be accounted for, and may have dispersed. No significant factor seems present to prevent the population from continuing to increase — with the possible exception of direct killing by humans. Even so, it is clear that humans are frequently foregoing opportunities to kill wolves in the region as evidenced by observations that have been reported, especially when the wolves were viewed through a rifle scope.

Several Montana wolves have settled outside the recovery areas described in the Recovery Plan (Figs. 2 and 5). A pack occupied the Blackfeet Indian Reservation just east of Glacier National Park in 1987 before being removed for depredations (Bangs et al. this volume). Another pack, northwest of Kalispell, was removed in 1989 because of depredations. The Ninemile pack near Missoula is far from a recovery area and has depredated twice. The Murphy Lake Pack in the Eureka area is also outside the recovery area, but has not yet depredated. Preferred habitat seems to be large river valley systems in lower elevations with abundant white-tailed deer (Fritts et al. 1994). More people and domestic animals generally occupy those sites. The recovery area concept has led some to expect that wolves will be confined to designated recovery areas, yet no legal mechanism exists to do so, even if it was desired. If wolves continue to colonize human-inhabited areas, conflicts could be fairly common and overall population growth further slowed by wolf control.

There has been less known about recovery progress in Idaho than Montana, with no proof of reproduction. Kaminski and Hansen (1984) estimated that no more than 15 wolves occupied Idaho, and that appears to still be true. Although wolves have been confirmed there, and at least one

Steven H. Fritts, Edward E. Bangs, Joseph A. Fontaine, Wayne G. Brewster, and James F. Gore

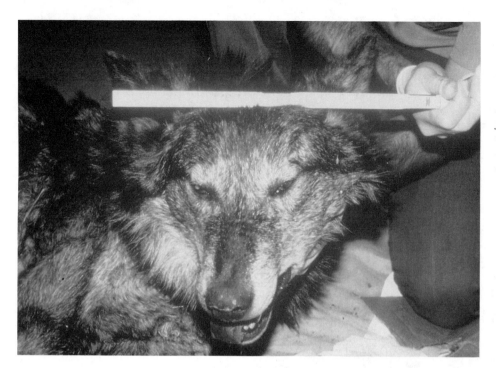

Fig. 7 *Wolf illegally shot near Yellowstone National Park in September 1992, possibly the first wild wolf killed in the Greater Yellowstone Ecosystem in several decades. (Photo: W.G. Brewster)*

wolf (radio-collared) is currently (August 1993) known to be in Idaho (Fig. 5), the situation is less promising than in summer 1991 when a small group (≥2 wolves) was discovered in the Boise National Forest, 470 km south of the Glacier National Park population (Fig. 5). However, at least one of these was found poisoned in July 1991 by illegal application of Furadan (carbofuran), and no further wolf activity in the area has been documented. Presence of singles and a large number of reports date back to the 1970's in Idaho, so progress is hard to document. However, the state contains large roadless areas where wolves may be less likely to be detected by the monitoring system. The number of reports from the Idaho-Montana border area may suggest an increase in wolf activity there. Idaho appears biologically capable of easily supporting a recovery level population.

Reports from the Yellowstone area continue to be made, as they have been since 1971, and interest in possible wolf presence there is high. An apparent wolf was filmed in YNP in August 1992 (Fig. 5). A wolf judged from its DNA to be closely related to Montana wolves (S. R. Fain, U. S. Fish and Wildlife Serv., pers. commun.) was shot just south of YNP in September 1992 (Figs. 5 and 7), leading some to conclude that a small wolf population is already present — a conclusion we consider doubtful. However, one change has definitely occurred in the past 10 years to increase the probability of single wolves dispersing to Idaho and Yellowstone — the production of dozens of young wolves in Montana. Establishment of packs by dispersers in previously unoccupied areas in and near Banff National Park, Alberta, and Glacier National Park, Montana has been demonstrated (Boyd et al. this volume).

Recent Events Regarding Wolf Restoration to Yellowstone

Yellowstone has become the most recognized and controversial of the three recovery areas because of national and international interest in the park and the potential use of a reintroduction. The American and international public, the news media, and the Congress are intensely interested in the possibility of wolf reintroduction to YNP, and as a result, the final decision on reintroduction will probably be made in Washington, D.C. Because of this intense interest, events affecting this recovery area have the potential to promote or inhibit recovery in the other two areas.

Following approval of the Recovery Plan by the USFWS in 1987, the USNPS authorized wolf research, sponsored public opinion polls on reintroduction, and implemented an aggressive public education program in the Yellowstone area. Stockgrower associations, outfitters, some hunters, land developers, and others began voicing strong concern about wolf recovery. The objections included expected depredation on livestock, decline of big game hunting, potential land-use restrictions, danger to humans, negative effects on grizzly bears, concern that reintroduced wolves would be a different subspecies, and the claim that wolves were not original members of the Yellowstone fauna. Many discussions of wolf recovery in the West were held in Congress, especially about initiating an EIS for a Yellowstone reintroduction. Congress twice opted for further study instead of the EIS that reintroduction proponents were urging.

In 1987, Utah Representative Wayne Owens introduced a bill in Congress that would have directed the USNPS to restore wolves to Yellowstone within three years; it was not enacted (Table 1). Mr. Owens introduced another bill in 1989 that would have required an EIS be conducted with cooperation of the states and address local concerns. Congress did not enact this proposed legislation either. The USNPS Director, in testimony to the House Subcommittee conducting the hearing on this proposed legislation, indicated that the political reality was that the USNPS would likely need Congressional direction to initiate an EIS on wolf reintroductions.

In the meantime the USFWS was noncommittal on reintroduction. Its director repeatedly stated that his agency would not propose or support reintroduction into the Yellowstone area until the research was completed in northwestern Montana and that population was well on its way to recovery (Keiter and Holscher 1990, Kirwan 1992, Strauch 1992). With the recommended Yellowstone reintroduction in mind, the USFWS has been accused of not implementing its Recovery Plan because of political pressures and the positions of the States (cf. Bader 1989, Keiter and Holscher 1990). Implementation of the Plan in the less prominent northwestern Montana and Idaho recovery areas is undeniable, however. The question of whether the USFWS could or should be forced by the courts into fully implementing its Recovery Plan (i.e., including reintroduction to YNP) has been debated (Bader 1989, Keiter and Holscher 1990, Kirwan 1992).

In the Department of Interior (DOI) Appropriations Bill for fiscal year 1989, Congress noted that return of the wolf to Yellowstone was desirable and provided $200,000 for the USNPS and USFWS to conduct studies to address four questions: 1) would wolves be controlled either inside or outside the park? 2) how might a reintroduced population of wolves affect the prey base? 3) would a reintroduced population of wolves harm or benefit grizzly bears in and near the park? and 4) how would wolf management zones be delineated? The results of the initial investigations were issued in May 1990 in the document *Wolves for Yellowstone? A report to the United States Congress, Volumes I and II* (Yellowstone National Park et al. 1990). The studies indicated no major negative effects to prey, big game hunting, or grizzly bears. Elk, mule deer, and bison (*Bison bison*) were expected to be the main prey. The highest concentration of wolves was expected to be in the northern winter range of Yellowstone. About 150 or fewer wolves were anticipated to eventually live in and near the park, with seven to nine packs within north-central YNP. Size and distribution of the wolf population would be strongly affected by type of management outside YNP. The studies highlighted a fact that Congress and the public was becoming increasingly aware of: the management options for wolves in the greater Yellowstone area are highly dependent on wolves' means of arrival (Fritts 1993a). If wolves were to colonize the area on their own they would be protected and managed under all protections of the ESA. If they were reintroduced as a nonessential experimental population under Section 10(j) of ESA, more manage-

ment options would be available. Reintroduced wolves could not be designated "experimental" if a population of wolves was already present, but existence of a few lone wolves would not preclude that designation. The report concluded that reintroduction of an experimental population was a viable option, and discussed the management flexibility of an experimental population. The possibility of natural recolonization, with Yellowstone area wolves being protected by all protections of the ESA, has been increasingly publicized in recent deliberations.

Shortly after release of the first two volumes of *Wolves for Yellowstone?* Idaho Senator James McClure proposed a bill that provided for reintroduction of three mated pairs of wolves into YNP and certain designated wilderness portions of central Idaho. Wolves would be delisted and managed by the states outside those areas and outside a northwest Montana core area (S. 2674-Northern Rocky Mountain Wolf Restoration Act of 1990). This "legislative solution" to the impasse was not enacted by Congress. During hearings on this proposed legislation, representatives of federal agencies testified that YNP wolf reintroduction should be accomplished as an experimental population under ESA rather than by special legislation. Opponents of the bill feared it would weaken the ESA by making an exception for wolves and objected to the limited area in which wolf recovery would be allowed (Committee on Energy and Natural Resources 1990). Surprisingly, the bill garnered little support even among interests most opposed to wolf recovery, even though it would have eliminated their concerns about land-use restrictions and delisting.

In the DOI appropriations bill for fiscal year 1990, Congress provided an additional $175,000 to continue studies on the effects of wolf restoration to Yellowstone, specifying that none of the funds could go toward reintroduction or preparation of an EIS. The reports were issued in 1992 (see below).

In October 1990, in the DOI appropriations bill for fiscal year 1991, Congress directed the Secretary of Interior to appoint a 10-member Wolf Management Committee (WMC) to develop a wolf reintroduction and management plan for central Idaho and YNP and authorized $375,000 for the task (Table 1). The WMC was required to consist of representatives of the USNPS; USFWS; USFS; Game and Fish Departments of Idaho, Montana, and Wyoming; two conservation groups; and the livestock and hunting communities. The WMC's report recommended that Congress designate wolves in Idaho, Wyoming, and Montana (with the exception of the Glacier National Park area) as an experimental population, effective until 1 July 1993 (WMC 1991). During this interval, wolves in the experimental population area would be managed by the USFWS with ample control for depredations on livestock, including taking of wolves seen killing or harassing livestock, by livestock producers. By 1 July 1993, the states would prepare and adopt wolf management plans agreeable to the Secretaries of Interior

Steven H. Fritts, Edward E. Bangs, Joseph A. Fontaine, Wayne G. Brewster, and James F. Gore

and Agriculture and governors of the three states. An EIS and rulemaking process would be conducted during the same period. Following completion of the necessary processes, states would assume primary management authority throughout the experimental population area except in national parks and national wildlife refuges. The WMC recommended that states follow guidelines in its report in developing management plans. The report called for reintroduction to YNP. If a breeding population had not been confirmed in central Idaho after five years, a reintroduction would likely be initiated there.

Thus, the WMC proposal was an attempt to deal with concerns about perceived wolf impacts on livestock and big game and still accomplish wolf recovery. Some of the specific provisions were: 1) allowing livestock operators to kill wolves on private or public land when depredations occurred *or* when wolves were "harassing" livestock (subject to reporting provisions and other conditions); 2) compensating for livestock depredations from a publicly administered trust fund; 3) having a regulated public harvest managed by the states after wolves reached specified recovery levels; and 4) controlling wolves where they were conflicting with a state's ungulate management objectives.

Critics of the WMC proposal believed that broad interpretation of point one above would jeopardize wolf recovery in the northern Rockies (cf. Fischer 1991). They also objected that the proposal exceeded ESA authority and intent for use of experimental populations (Kirwan 1992). A major point of contention throughout was whether a compromise could be reached under the experimental population provision of ESA or whether special legislation, or at least Congressional sanction, was needed. Although the WMC's proposal was a compromise and had the approval of at least two of the three federal agencies and three states (previous opponents to YNP reintroduction), Congress took no action on it. The deliberations for crafting of the WMC's final proposal illustrated the great difficulty in reaching a compromise suitable to all interests and still consistent with current law (Thieszen 1992).

In August 1991, Defenders of Wildlife filed suit against the Secretary of the Interior and directors of the USFWS and USNPS, in part for their failure to implement recovery strategies for the wolf as required by the ESA. The suit sought to force a reintroduction to YNP, as was recommended in the Recovery Plan. The suit was dismissed as moot, primarily because the USFWS was operating under Congressional direction that required that the funds being used to conduct an EIS not be used for a reintroduction. A second suit was filed by a group called "In Defense of Endangered Species" for similar reasons. These cases relate to the larger question referred to earlier of whether the Secretary has a nondiscretionary duty to implement recovery plans, and whether this duty is enforceable by the courts.

Instead of acting on the WMC's proposal, Congress in November 1991 directed the USFWS, in consultation with the USNPS and USFS, to prepare an EIS concerning reintroduction of wolves in the Yellowstone area and central Idaho. This marked the end of a four-year period of rejection of EIS funding by the Senate and began the process that wolf reintroduction advocates had long awaited. In November 1991, a suit was filed to prevent the USFWS from reintroducing wolves into the Yellowstone area and to compel enhanced conservation efforts for the wolves asserted by the plaintiffs to already be present (Urbigkit *versus* Lujan 1991). This suit was dismissed, as no specific plan existed for a reintroduction.

In July 1992, the studies funded by Congress in 1989 were completed and results published (Varley and Brewster 1992). The report, *Wolves for Yellowstone? A report to the United States Congress, Volumes III and IV*, provided confirmation that wolves and their prey had inhabited the park for at least 1,000 years, concluded that wolf taxonomic issues should not stand in the way of a reintroduction, projected the number and distribution of packs that might live in the area after 10-20 years, provided additional information on ungulate and small mammal abundance, projected the effect of wolves on prey numbers and hunter harvest for different species in different areas of the ecosystem, determined the number of livestock grazed on public land allotments during summer and predicted that losses would be low, summarized data on wolf depredation on livestock in other areas, provided additional data on public attitudes about wolves and wolf reintroduction, summarized previous wolf reintroductions and management translocations, and predicted wolves would not be a significant disease vector or threat to humans or grizzlies. Perhaps the most socially significant of the studies was the economic analysis which projected economic benefits at about $42 million per year through increased tourism (Duffield 1992).

The studies in the first and second versions of *Wolves for Yellowstone?* concluded that YNP alone probably could support a recovery level wolf population (Boyce 1990; Fritts 1990; Garten et al. 1990; Koth et al. 1990; Singer 1990, 1991a; Boyce and Gaillard 1992); however, protection in some areas outside the park would increase the wolf population size and carrying capacity, increasing the probability of long term survival of the population (Boyce 1990, Fritts 1990). The reports highlighted the large numbers of ungulates in the Yellowstone ecosystem (Mack et al. 1990). Ungulates in YNP alone (8,992 km^2) average over 36,000 in summer and over 24,000 in winter (Singer 1990, 1991a). Taken together, these studies have addressed just about every aspect of wolf recovery in Yellowstone that can be covered without wolves actually being present.

Additional papers have applied research findings from other parts of North America to Yellowstone. These have concluded that reintroduction is biologically feasible (Mech 1991a, Mech et al. 1991a, Peek et al. 1991) and no additional research is necessary (Mech 1991a). Others have drawn conclusions for Yellowstone wolf biology based on research

Fig. 8 *Member of Environmental Impact Statement (EIS) team explains EIS process to local citizens at EIS alternative scoping meeting in Hamilton, Montana, August 1992. (Photo: S.H. Fritts)*

in similar situations (cf. Ream et al. 1991, Boyd et al. this volume, Dekker et al. this volume). The historical evidence of wolves in YNP has been examined and different conclusions drawn about their original abundance (Kay this volume, Schullery and Whittlesey this volume). Numerous popular articles have been written on wolf reintroduction to YNP and its possible effects.

The Environmental Impact Statement

In November 1991, Congress directed the USFWS, in consultation with the USNPS and the USFS, to prepare a draft EIS concerning recovery of wolves in Yellowstone and central Idaho. In developing an EIS, the agency identifies the problem, defines what information is required to make an informed decision, lists the significant issues that need to be resolved, provides a reasonable range of alternatives, and recommends an action that will best solve the problem. The EIS process requires full public review and participation. Program direction from Congress on wolf reintroduction to YNP has come through Appropriations Committee language, rather than through the Interior Committee, agency policy, or specific legislation. Ironically, the same was true in 1915-16 in funding and implementing predator elimination programs on federal lands that resulted in the eradication of the wolf. Appropriations of $344,000 to the USFWS and $150,000 to the USNPS were included for the wolf EIS, with the stipulation that none of the funds could be used to reintroduce wolves. Congress directed that the draft EIS consider a broad range of alternatives and be completed by May 1993. In 1992, Congress again put in specific language with appropriations funding to complete the EIS by January

1994 and expected the preferred alternative to be consistent with existing law.

The EIS has become a focal point for public interest in wolves. During the issue scoping stage, nearly 4,000 comments on EIS issues were received, representing every state in the U.S. and several foreign countries. Issues most often mentioned by the public were the wolf as a missing component of the ecosystem, livestock depredation, compensation for depredations, private property rights, cost in taxpayers' dollars, effects on big game species, not weakening the ESA, need for public education, wolves' rights, illegal killing of wolves, and control strategies. In the alternative scoping stages, the public was asked to identify alternatives and comment on five preliminary alternatives already identified (Fig. 8). More than 5,000 comments were received on the five EIS alternatives, the majority supporting some form of wolf recovery. Nearly 40,000 people, representing all 50 states and 40 foreign countries requested to be placed on the EIS mailing list. The USFWS released the draft EIS on 1 July 1993. It recommended reintroduction of Canadian wolves into Yellowstone National Park and central Idaho in late 1994 under the experimental population provision of the ESA unless at least two packs are located in either area by then. After extensive public comment on the draft, a final EIS will be prepared and should be completed by early 1994.

Conclusions and Future Issues

Elimination of wolves from the NRM of the U.S. occurred a short time ago by historical and ecological standards; therefore, some disagreement over whether and how to restore them should be expected. Wolf recovery appears to

Steven H. Fritts, Edward E. Bangs, Joseph A. Fontaine, Wayne G. Brewster, and James F. Gore

have more to do with other issues than with the wolf itself, examples being deeply held personal values about the wolf, about government, outside influences, people's relationship to "nature", and the political role of special interest groups. Restoring wolves to areas where they were intentionally eradicated involves biological, social, and political challenges, and relies heavily on public support. Nonetheless, public opinion is in favor of the wolf in the NRM, and we expect this condition to continue. Opposition, however, will persist indefinitely.

Any decision of the current EIS is likely to be challenged by every legal means possible. Therefore, implementation of the decision may take additional years, and wolf reintroduction to YNP and central Idaho remains uncertain. Continued natural recovery in Montana is likely in the meantime, regardless of the outcome of the EIS. The eventual natural recolonization of Yellowstone and Idaho is an increasing possibility as wolf numbers increase in Montana.

Some wolf advocates will resist removal of the wolf from the endangered species list in the NRM after recovery goals are met, preferring that the animal remain under federal protection indefinitely. Nonetheless, delisting and state management are the ultimate goals of the program and the ESA, and these accomplishments will signal successful completion of the recovery process.

Another concern for the future is being able to manage wolves in light of strong national sympathy for the species and ethical concerns about wolf management methods (Fritts 1993a, Gilbert this volume, Mech 1995). The American public has received little exposure to wolf control in recent decades and may not be prepared for it. Killing of wolves is a highly emotional issue (Stephenson et al. this volume), and the lack of agreement among Wyoming, Montana, and Idaho residents on killing wolves for controlling livestock depredations (Thompson and Gasson 1991) might foretell conflict on this issue. However in this case, particularly near YNP, the conflict could be center stage for the entire nation. Education on the necessity of wolf control must be a part of wolf recovery, whether occurring naturally or by reintroduction.

Less public support exists for controlling wolves for ungulate management than for livestock depredations, especially if the method of taking is considered unfair (Kellert 1986, Cluff and Murray this volume, Stephenson et al. this volume). Eventually, state wildlife departments may choose to reduce wolf populations as part of their overall wildlife management program, and the public needs to be informed and, hopefully, accept their decision to do so. However the growing animal rights movement causes concern for the future management of wolves in the northern Rockies, as elsewhere (Schmidt 1989, Seip 1992b, Gilbert this volume). In addition, direct involvement of high level government officials makes the application of wildlife management even more difficult.

Wolves could return to Idaho and Yellowstone by natural recolonization or by reintroduction. The probability of recolonizing both areas is increasing, yet could be several years or decades away, especially in Yellowstone. The confirmation of lone wolves may precede breeding by several years (cf. Ream and Mattson 1982), and confirmation of pack activity may precede attainment of a recovery-level population by a decade or more (cf. Ream and Mattson 1982, Wydeven et al. this volume). Reintroduction would hasten the process of recovery and delisting in Yellowstone and central Idaho. Illegal killing could slow or temporarily halt recovery. If this were to occur, public outrage would further complicate an already polarized and controversial issue (L. N. Carbyn, Canadian Wildlife Serv., pers. commun.). How wolves return to Idaho and Yellowstone will determine how they are managed there, at least until they are delisted.

The next revision of the NRM Wolf Recovery Plan will await EIS finalization. Many contentious issues will have to be addressed, e.g., whether to promote recovery in additional areas, recovery area size, population viability, compensation for livestock losses, and whether to consider packs occupying both sides of the international border as counting toward the recovery goal. Whether in association with plan revision or not, we expect the USFWS to be besieged with requests, demands, petitions, and legal actions to compel it and cooperating agencies to restore wolves to additional areas in the western U.S., such as Rocky Mountain National Park, Colorado, and Olympia National Park, Washington. Wolf advocates in Utah, Oregon, and California are already asking about recovery in those areas, too. Wolves are dispersing into the Dakotas creating a management dilemma, as a recovery program in those states does not currently seem practical (Licht and Fritts 1994). The USFWS must decide and clearly define the extent of its responsibilities for wolf restoration, addressing such issues as viable populations, suitable areas, public interest, and the biological need to focus on recovery of other long neglected endangered species.

Continued progress towards wolf recovery depends on continued interagency cooperation, particularly the international cooperation of the B.C. and Alberta Wildlife Branches. It is becoming increasingly obvious that in a shrinking world with a mobile human population, instantaneous communication, and better access to information, complex conservation programs such as wolf recovery and conservation will need to be addressed on a continent-wide basis. Local public cooperation will continue to be extremely important, too. Continued emphasis on public education is essential, but the need for wolf control coincident with recovery must always be stressed. Maintenance of funding and emphasis will be the primary determinants of the program's success.

The authors expect public interest in wolves to remain high. The only prediction that we consider absolutely safe is that extreme controversy will continue to characterize wolves and wolf recovery in the NRM for years to come.

Acknowledgments

The authors thank C. Davis, D.R. Harms, M.D. Jimenez, C. Lobdell, K.M. McMaster, J. Roybal, L. Shanks, and B.W. Zoellick for their roles in program development, implementation, and for information. Some of the biological information was provided by D.H. Pletscher and R.R. Ream of the University of Montana's Wolf Ecology Project. We greatly appreciate the manuscript reviews by D.K. Boyd, L.N. Carbyn, R. Demarchi, J.R. Gunson, D.R. Harms, R.B. Keiter, L.D. Mech, D.R. Parsons, D.H. Pletscher, R.R. Ream, and J. Till.

Addendum

The EIS was completed in April 1994. Over a 32-month period, some 130 public meetings had been held, 750,000 documents distributed, and 170,000 comments received from the public. The final EIS recommended that wolves designated as members of non-essential experimental populations [under Sec. 10(j) of the Endangered Species Act] be reintroduced into both YNP and central Idaho. In June 1994, the Secretary of the Interior directed that the recommendation be implemented. In November 1994 the USFWS published final rules that described how the reintroduction would be conducted, how reintroduced wolves would be managed, and the exact areas where they would be managed as "non-essential experimental" (*Federal Register* Vol. 59, No. 224, pages 60252-60281). The USFWS developed a reintroduction plan that involved capture of wolves in southwestern Canada and *hard* release of dispersal age wolves into Idaho and *soft* release of family groups into YNP after about 8 weeks of on-site acclimation in pens.

The first 29 wolves were reintroduced in January 1995 (14 to YNP; 15 to central Idaho) amid intense media coverage and despite legal attempts to halt the project. Wolves were taken from near Hinton, Alberta, about 1,000 km from their release sites. In January 1996, 20 additional wolves were released into central Idaho and 17 into acclimation pens in YNP, these being taken from north of Fort St. John, B.C., some 1500 km to the north. Progress of the reintroduction effort to date has far exceeded expectations. By February 1, 1996, only two of the original reintroduced wolves were known to have died; both were illegally shot. At least three male-female pairs have formed in Idaho, and three packs and one pair exist in or near YNP (exclusive of 4 social units brought to YNP in 1996 and currently being held in pens). Two Yellowstone groups produced a total of nine pups in 1995. The only livestock killed by reintroduced wolves are 2-4 sheep by a dispersing subadult male outside YNP in December 1995. The animal was translocated back to the park, but later returned to the same area, and was killed by government agents in February 1996 after it wounded another sheep.

The naturally colonizing population in northwestern Montana has continued to increase with a minimum of depredation problems. Effective February 1, 1996, at least 7 packs are known to exist there, and the total population is >70 wolves. The Yellowstone area contains a known 37 wolves (including 17 in pens awaiting release), and the Idaho and adjacent southwestern Montana area has 33. Therefore, the known wolf population in the northern Rockies of the U.S. is about 140 wolves. The population appears well on the way to reaching the recovery goals in the NRM Wolf Recovery Plan. As expected, the amount of controversy associated with wolf restoration remains high; far out of proportion to any actual problems caused by the wolves.

Steven H. Fritts, Edward E. Bangs, Joseph A. Fontaine, Wayne G. Brewster, and James F. Gore

Control of Endangered Gray Wolves in Montana

■ Edward E. Bangs, Steven H. Fritts, Dale R. Harms, Joseph A. Fontaine, Michael D. Jimenez, Wayne G. Brewster, and Carter C. Niemeyer

Wolves were deliberately eliminated from the western United States by 1930, largely because of depredations on livestock. In 1974, wolves became protected under the federal Endangered Species Act. By 1980 they began to recolonize northwestern Montana, and by 1993 had been involved in seven depredation events. Wolf-caused livestock losses (12 sheep and 17 cattle) have been rare compared to other reported predator-caused losses, but have invoked disproportionate attention and controversy. Seventeen problem wolves were controlled as part of a program to further tolerance of non-depredating wolves and promote recovery. In Montana, control was responsible for 52% of all known wolf losses since 1985 and annually affected 6% of the expanding wolf population. Professional animal damage control apparently has reduced controversy by efficiently controlling problem wolves and improving communications with rural residents, thus contributing to wolf recovery in Montana.

Introduction

Depredation on livestock was the primary factor responsible for the deliberate extirpation of wolves (*Canis lupus*) from Montana by 1930 (Young and Goldman 1944, Curnow 1969, Lopez 1978). In 1974, wolves were protected under the federal Endangered Species Act of 1973 (ESA). The Northern Rocky Mountain Wolf Recovery Plan (Recovery Plan) [U.S. Fish and Wildlife Service (USFWS) 1987] anticipated attacks on livestock and management of problem wolves if recovery was to be tolerated by rural residents, many of whom are concerned about potential depredations (Lenihan 1987, Tucker and Pletscher 1989, Bath and Phillips 1990). In 1988, a Control Plan (USFWS 1988a) was developed by the USFWS and implemented jointly by USFWS and U.S. Department of Agriculture, Animal and Plant Health Inspection Service, Animal Damage Control (ADC).

Wolf depredations on livestock are controversial and a challenge to successful wolf recovery in a variety of areas (cf. Fritts 1993a). We report the only information on management of wolf-livestock conflicts in a listed population of wolves in the contiguous United States (U.S.) outside Minnesota. We examined livestock losses, wolf depredations, and control, to give a perspective of their magnitude in Montana. We also examined the current wolf control policy to assess its effectiveness at resolving livestock depredations, improving communications with livestock producers, increasing tolerance of wolves, and enhancing wolf recovery. Our findings may foretell the nature and extent of wolf-livestock conflicts in other northern Rocky Mountain states and the feasibility of managing depredations there under the ESA.

Background

Wolves recolonized the North Fork of the Flathead River (North Fork), in and near Glacier National Park, Montana in the early 1980's (Ream et al. 1991). By August 1992, an estimated 59 wolves were in or immediately adjacent to northwestern Montana, most still in the North Fork (Fritts et al. this volume).

The Recovery Plan recommended a zone management system to encourage wolves to naturally recolonize areas with few livestock and a responsive wolf control program when livestock were attacked. Three wolf recovery areas, composed primarily of Forest Service and National Park Service lands, were recommended because they were large remote areas of public land, had adequate wild prey, and potential for conflicts with livestock was low (USFWS 1987). The Montana recovery area is centered around Glacier National Park and Forest Service Wilderness to the south (Fig. 1).

The Control Plan established guidelines identifying when and how wolves would be controlled. Wolves would not be controlled for killing pets (one dog was killed in 1990) or reducing big game populations. Outside recovery areas,

E.E. Bangs, S.H. Fritts, D.R. Harms, J.A. Fontaine, M.D. Jimenez, W.G. Brewster, and C.C. Niemeyer

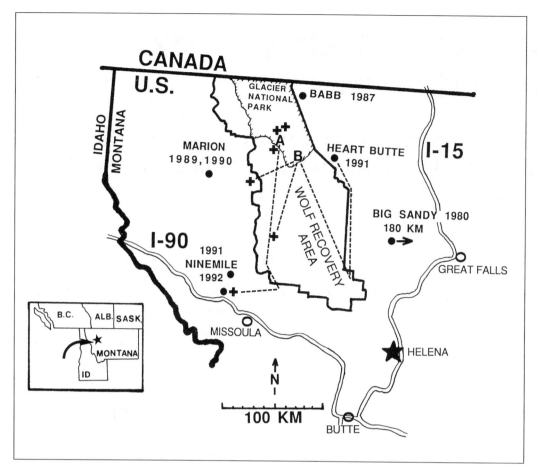

Fig. 1
Northwestern Montana and the Montana Wolf Recovery Area around and to the south of Glacier National Park. The locations of depredations by wolves are represented by black dots. The movements of wolves translocated into Glacier National Park in 1989(A) (three died near the release site and one adult female dispersed) and 1990(B) (three yearling wolves dispersed) are displayed by small dashed lines. The crosses indicate sites where dispersing translocated wolves were killed.

wolves could be controlled if livestock depredations appeared likely. Within recovery areas, livestock must have been attacked, wolves must not have been artificially fed or attracted, livestock allotment management plans on public lands must have been followed, and in areas and times critical to wolves, other options for resolving conflicts must have been exhausted before wolves would be controlled. Before 1 August, females and their young would be radio-collared and released on site. All other wolves and females and their young after 1 August would be translocated after their first depredation event (multiple depredations by the same wolves in an area within a growing season are considered one event). Wolves that depredate after being translocated would be placed in captivity or killed.

The policy of controlling problem wolves in an "endangered" population is based on three assumptions: 1) wolf populations can sustain annual human-caused mortality of around 30% and still increase (Keith 1983, Fuller 1989); 2) intolerance and illegal killing of wolves by local residents is the greatest challenge to successful recovery (Archibald et al. 1991, Fritts et al. this volume); and 3) control of depredating wolves, as part of a comprehensive conservation program, will enhance the survival of the majority of wolves, which do not depredate (Gunson 1983b, Tompa 1983b, USFWS 1988a, Fritts et al. 1992). The legal basis for con-

trolling "endangered" wolves is found in Section 10(a) of the ESA, which allows the Secretary of Interior to permit acts otherwise prohibited by Section 9 (taking of an endangered species) to enhance survival of the species.

Study Area

Montana is the fourth largest state in the U.S. and has the third lowest human density (2.04 people/km²). Eastern Montana (273,000 km²) is an open plain and river breaks habitat with a predominantly agricultural (livestock and wheat) economy and culture. Western Montana (108,500 km²) is mountainous forest and meadow with extensive public land. The economy and culture are more diverse in the west, with logging, mining, tourism, agriculture, and other activities interspersed throughout the area (Montana Agriculture Statistics 1991). Western Montana contains 453,500 cattle and 58,420 sheep or 19% and 8.5% of state totals. Most suitable wolf habitat is in western Montana because of larger blocks of remote public land, more forest cover, lower numbers of livestock, higher societal tolerance of wolves, and abundant wild ungulates. It also has the highest concentration of wolf activity (Fritts et al. this volume), and is more likely to experience further wolf recolonization in the near future.

Table 1. Summary of average annual sheep and cattle losses reported by Animal Damage Control (ADC) in Montana, 1986-1991; average annual number of predators controlled by ADC in Montana, 1986-1991; and estimated sheep and cattle losses reported to Montana Agricultural Statistics Service (MAS) by livestock producers in 1991.

| | | *Reported by ADC* | | | *# Predator* | *Reported to MAS* | | |
		$	*Number*	*% Adult*	*Controlled*	*$*	*Number*	*% Adult*
Mountain Lion	Sheep	3,825	47	18	2.0	20,000	600	—
	Cattle	650	1.5	0		<99,000	<300	33
Coyote	Sheep	145,408	2,106	12	4,880	1,186,800	33,700	—
	Cattle	53,712	127	1		<429,000	<1,300	1
Fox	Sheep	3,561	64	4	1,075	140,400	4,900	—
	Cattle	71	0.3	0		—	—	—
Black Bear	Sheep	8,893	102	60	25	26,400	600	—
	Cattle	1,733	3.4	23		—	—	—
Brown Bear	Sheep	777	13.5	68	1.5	—	—	—
	Cattle	854	1.8	28		—	—	—
Wolf	Sheep	263	2.3	65	2.5	—	—	—
	Cattle	1,336	3.8	39		<66,000	<200	—
Dog	Sheep	5,880	60	48	1.8	162,000	3,500	—
	Cattle	71	0.5	40		<66,000	<200	<50
Total Predator Losses	Sheep	168,607	2,394	15	5,988	1,587,200	44,900	24
	Cattle	58,427	138	3		825,000	2,112	15
Total Annual	Sheep	—	—	—	—	5,320,000	142,000	30
	Cattle	—	—	—	—	39,700,000	86,000	30

Agriculture is Montana's top income-producing industry ($1,899,000,000/year) (Montana Agriculture Statistics 1991). Cattle and calves comprise 48% and sheep and wool, hogs, and other livestock about 2% each of total agricultural income. About 65% of Montana is in farms or ranches (24,600 farms and ranches, covering over 242,812 km^2) with about 66% used for rangeland and pasture. The farm and ranch population is estimated to be 67,500 people, 8.6% of Montana's population. Ranchers are the most likely people to utilize the same habitats as wolves and are most likely to oppose wolf recovery (Kellert 1985a, Bath and Buchanan 1989, Bath and Phillips 1990).

ADC, which investigates and controls livestock damage, employs 25 people and has a $1,200,000 annual budget in Montana. Nearly $40,000,000 in cattle (34.6/1000 head) and $5,300,000 in sheep (172/1000 head) are reportedly lost in Montana annually, 2.4% (0.8/1000) and 30% (54/1000), respectively, allegedly caused by predators (Montana Agriculture Statistics 1992). Only 6.5% of cattle and 5.3% of sheep losses allegedly caused by predators result in requests for assistance from ADC. Coyotes (*Canis latrans*) cause most of the damage and are the primary species controlled (Table 1).

Methods

Standard procedures (Roy and Dorrance 1976, Fritts 1982, Paul and Gipson 1994) were used to document losses allegedly caused by predators. The only compensation for livestock killed by wolves is provided by a private group, the Defenders of Wildlife (Fischer 1989), and is based upon rancher-estimated market value. Standard capture, control, and radiotelemetry techniques were used to remove and monitor depredating wolves (USFWS 1988a, Bangs 1991, Fritts et al. 1992).

Results

Wolves depredated on livestock seven times since 1980, killing 12 sheep (three lambs and nine ewes) and 17 cattle (seven calves, six steers and four cows) (Table 2, Fig. 1).

E.E. Bangs, S.H. Fritts, D.R. Harms, J.A. Fontaine, M.D. Jimenez, W.G. Brewster, and C.C. Niemeyer

Cattle production is Montana's top income-producing industry. The ranching community has strenuously opposed wolf reintroduction efforts. (Photo: S.H. Fritts)

ADC suspected wolves might have been involved in the loss of another 29 sheep and 34 cattle, but evidence was not convincing. All depredations occurred on private land. Five of seven depredations occurred between March and May, when young livestock were available, but neonate wild ungulates were not. Several depredations occurred after extenuating circumstances. Wolves in Marion depredated after the suspected alpha male was illegally shot and a severe winter caused the loss of many sheep and calves that were left in the field. Few natural prey were available in the Big Sandy, Babb, and Heart Butte areas.

In Montana from 1985–1992 (eight years), the average estimated wolf population was 25.3 wolves and wolf deaths from all known causes (n = 25) averaged 3.1 wolves per year (Fritts et al. this volume). Humans caused 72% of wolf mortality and removed about 9% of the wolf population annually despite legal protection and a control program that emphasized translocation. Control was directly or indirectly responsible for 13 (52%) wolf losses and annually affected 6% of the population in Montana.

From 1987–1992 (six years) an annual average of $18,930 was spent controlling wolves. Administration by the USFWS cost an additional $4,500/year. In 1991, Congress provided USFWS and ADC an additional $291,000 to fund ≤ 5 years of future wolf control activities. From 1987–1992, wolves may have caused an average annual loss (confirmed and possible) of livestock valued at ≤ $1,839 (cattle $1,635 and sheep $204). This comprises a small fraction of the annual predator-caused losses reported to ADC of cattle $58,427 (2.3% wolf-caused) and sheep $168,607 (0.16% wolf-caused) and ≤ 0.004% of reported cattle and sheep losses from all causes (Table 2).

Cattle producers in the 18 mountain and western states reported losing 1,400 head ($480,000) of cattle to wolves in 1991 (National Agriculture Statistics 1992). However, less than 200 head of those losses occurred in Montana, where the only known wolf packs exist. In 1990 (September-December), 1991, and 1992 ADC investigated four, 28, and 16 reports of wolf depredations in Montana; zero, four, and one were confirmed, respectively. Of those 48 reports, seven (15%) involved dogs and five (10%) coyotes.

Wolf packs have continuously occupied the North Fork where there are ≤400 cattle and ≤50 horses, since 1980 without conflict (D. Pletscher, Univ. of Montana, pers. commun.). While these wolves have been located near livestock on several occasions, they spend > 90% of their time inside Glacier National Park or areas in Canada where there are virtually no livestock (D. Pletscher, Univ. of Montana, pers. commun.).

Four wolf packs have denned in Montana outside the North Fork and were regularly exposed to livestock. While these packs lived a year or more in areas with abundant livestock without conflict, three eventually depredated. Since 1980, 17 wolves have been controlled 18 times (Table 2). Six were killed, three were placed in permanent captivity, seven were translocated, and two were released on site. Of the translocated wolves, two pups died of starvation, one adult was euthanized, one yearling was placed in captivity, and one adult and two yearlings were illegally killed.

Summary of Wolf Translocations

The first wolf translocation in the western U.S. involved one adult female, one two-year-old male with damaged teeth, and two five-month-old pups that depredated near Marion in 1989 (Fig. 1). Two pups were held 20 days and the two adults

Table 2. Summary of wolf depredation and control in Montana, 1980–1992.

	1980 Big Sandy	1987 Babb	1989 Marion	1990 Marion	1991 Ninemile	1991 Heart Butte	1992 Ninemile
Date first Depredation	12/22/80	5/8/87	8/31/89	3/20/90	3/29/91	5/23/91	5/16/92
Wolves involved	1	7	5	2	4	1	7
Wolves controlled	1	6	4	1	3	1	2
Control method	aerial gun	4 trap 2 aerial gun	3 trap 1 aerial dart	aerial gun	aerial dart	aerial dart	trapped
Fate of wolves	killed	4 killed 2 captivity	trans- located	killed	trans- located	captivity	released on site
Possible livestock losses	27 sheep 27 cattle	9 ewe 1 lamb 2 cows 1 calf 3 steers	0 sheep 2 cows 8 calves	0 sheep 5 calves	0 sheep 2 steers	4 lambs 0 cattle	0 sheep 1 steer
Confirmed losses	0 sheep 0 cattle	9 ewe 1 lamb 2 cows 1 calf 3 steers	0 sheep 2 cows 1 calf	0 sheep 5 calves	0 sheep 2 steers	2 lambs 0 cattle	0 sheep 1 steer
Control Cost[1]	$4,578	$41,000	$15,500	$5,000	$9,000	$1,500	$1,200
Value losses[2]	$27,750	$3,049	$3,910	$2,500	$1,000	$200	$375
Amount Compensated[3]	0	$3,049	$2,920	$2,500	$1,000	$150	$375
Control days	373	125	18	17	9	1	2
Other losses within 6 months after control[4]	none	1 calf	none	1 calf	none	none	none

1 includes all salary, travel, specific equipment purchases, services
2 includes confirmed losses, possible losses, and losses after control
3 Defenders of Wildlife Program — 100% compensation for confirmed and 50% for possible losses
4 There were no wolf depredations in 1993; 4 calves were killed at 2 ranches in 1994. Near Helena, MT, 2 wolves were translocated

seven days at a veterinary clinic before being immobilized, separately translocated into Glacier National Park (85 km northeast of the Marion depredation site) and released near one another (hard release) on 14 September 1989. Carrion was not left at the release site.

The wolves immediately separated. The pups travelled less than 8 km to higher elevations where wild prey was scarce and starved by 26 September and 2 October. The adult male had two toes injured by trapping and was released with a bandaged foot that became infected. He moved 16 km to private land and stayed near livestock before being euthanized on 1 October. The female rapidly traveled southwest, an azimuth of 205 degrees (generally toward Marion). She swam a 1.6-km-wide reservoir before travelling back and forth along the east shore of Flathead Lake and the Flathead Valley, a heavily-developed ranch and farming area with several towns and numerous rural residences, apparently trying to find her way across this area. In December 1989, she followed a forested corridor around the southern end of the Flathead Valley into the Ninemile Valley where she began to travel with a male wolf of unknown origin. She denned in late April 1990 and was illegally killed in June 1990. The male tended the six pups until 3 September 1990, when he was killed by a vehicle on highway Interstate 90 (Boyd and Jimenez 1994). White-tailed deer (*Odocoileus virginianus*) carcasses were left for the orphaned pups until November, when they began feeding on remains of deer killed by hunters. They killed a white-tailed deer in late December. The young wolves gradually expanded their movements and began utilizing most of their parents' old home range (260 km²). The Ninemile Valley is about 160 km southwest on an azimuth of 205 degrees from the release site in Glacier National Park and has many livestock (Fig. 1). The second translocation occurred in 1991 after four yearling survivors from the orphaned litter described above left the Ninemile valley for the first known time and killed two steers. Three were captured, held in a veterinarian's clinic for seven days, immobilized, placed in a large culvert trap, transported to Glacier National Park, allowed to recover from the anesthesia, and hard-released together on 13 April 1991 (Fig. 1). Several deer carcasses were left at the release site, but the wolves were never located near them. The wolves moved together throughout the area for seven days, then separated and began traveling more widely. One female traveled over 120 km south along the eastern edge of mountains and then north again. She was placed in captivity on 23 May, after killing lambs, 42 km southeast (105 degrees) of the release site (Fig. 1). One male was found illegally shot near Kalispell on 17 June, 40 km southwest (240 degrees) from the release site. The remaining female was shot by a livestock producer who reportedly thought it was a dog chasing his cattle 74 km southwest (190 degrees) of the release site on 17 June 1991. All three wolves were in excellent condition when recovered.

Discussion

Control is part of every wolf management program in North America where the ranges of wolves and livestock overlap, including those involving recovering populations (Dorrance 1982, Bjorge and Gunson 1983, 1985; Gunson 1983b, 1992; Tompa 1983b; Fritts et al. 1992). Control of wolves in Minnesota was tested in court and found acceptable, under certain guidelines (Fritts 1982, O'Neill 1988, Fritts et al. 1992), for wolves classified as "endangered" (translocation) and "threatened" (lethal). The legality of wolf control in Montana has not been tested in court, but is modeled after the Minnesota program.

The pattern of wolf-livestock interactions in Montana appears, at this early date, to be similar to those found in more intensively studied areas of North America where annual wolf depredations ranged from 0.23 to 3.0 per 1000 cattle and 0.54 to 2.66 per 1000 sheep (Gunson 1983b, Tompa 1983b, Fritts et al. 1992, Mack et al. 1992). Wolves in Montana inhabited areas where they were regularly ex-

posed to livestock, but few depredations occurred. Livestock husbandry practices (carcass disposal) and the lack of natural prey seemed to be associated with several depredations, as has been suggested elsewhere (Fritts 1982, Bjorge and Gunson 1983, Gunson 1983b, Tompa 1983b, Fritts et al. 1992). Several additional years of data will be necessary to see if these patterns continue.

As in other studies, hard release resulted in pack breakup and long distance movements (Fritts et al. 1984, 1985; Fritts 1993b). Wolves in Montana were translocated more than 80 km from their home ranges and none found their way back. Older wolves apparently had greater motivation to home than yearlings; pups had little such inclination or ability. The survival of translocated wolves ≥ 1 year-old was high, unless killed by people. In Minnesota, translocated pups older than four months had survival rates similar to non-translocated pups (Fritts et al. 1985). Two five-month old pups did not survive translocation in Montana, while a lone littermate that was not captured survived in its original home range. Translocated wolves did not readily cross open terrain or areas with high levels of human activity. They travelled widely, were generally located in drainages, and appeared particularly vulnerable to humans. These findings are consistent with translocated wolves in Minnesota (Fritts 1993b), except for the effect of terrain in Montana and low survival of translocated pups.

Our information suggests that wolf depredations have a minor impact on the livestock industry of Montana compared to other factors. Producers already absorb, tolerate, and personally address 70% of sheep and 97% of cattle losses, which are not related to predation and 89% of sheep and 93% of cattle losses they believed were caused by predators without requesting ADC assistance or receiving compensation. The addition of wolves to the array of Montana's predators will have a minor effect on livestock losses, although a few individual producers may be seriously affected.

The large number of alleged wolf depredations throughout the western states (National Agriculture Statistics 1992), where there are no wolves, suggests the livestock community is more sensitized to wolves than other predators or other causes of livestock loss. This may be due to local cultural values, traditions, and legends regarding depredating wolves in the early 1900's and to the ESA (representing government intervention and outside influences), which prohibits producers from initiating private control. The few depredations that have occurred, particularly in 1987 and 1989, attracted almost daily reporting by news media. This has perhaps resulted in an exaggerated perception of the magnitude of the problem by the public and politicians. In Minnesota, up to 50% of reported wolf depredations were caused by coyotes (W. Paul, ADC, pers. commun.). The reputation and novelty of wolves and attributing coyote damage (the most common predator damage) to wolves will continue to result in a high level of reported, compared to

Wilderness areas with potential wolf habitat frequently also serve as important areas for raising livestock. This combination of suitable wolf range, distribution of ungulates interspersed with cattle herds creates a potential for major human/wolf conflict. Successful management of wolf/livestock conflicts will be a major challenge for wolf conservation in the 21st century. (Photo: M.D. Jimenez)

actual, wolf depredations and an overestimation of the threat that wolves actually pose.

Success in the Montana wolf control program is difficult to measure. The concept of minimizing wolf-livestock conflict by "encouraging" wolf population growth into specific recovery areas via natural dispersal has been largely unsuccessful (Fritts et al. 1994). While wolves in the recovery area (North Fork) have not depredated, those that recolonized outside the recovery area have been involved in several depredations. However, there have been no reliable criteria to predict depredations or which wolves could be removed to prevent depredations. While three of the four packs that established outside the recovery area eventually depredated on livestock, they previously lived around livestock for extended periods of time without problems. Even when livestock were lost, depredations stopped when wolves remained in the area, as often happens in Minnesota (Fritts et al. 1992). For these reasons, the concept of confining naturally dispersing wolves to a specific recovery area, especially when natural dispersal into other nearby recovery areas is encouraged, has been largely abandoned in favor of a program that addresses conflicts as they occur.

Since 1989, ADC has quickly captured offending wolves, defusing a once commonly heard argument (probably originating from stories about the famous last "lobo" wolves around 1900) (cf. Young and Goldman 1944) that wolves were too crafty to be controlled. While there will certainly be exceptions, recent control actions were completed within a few days or weeks, which greatly reduced media coverage and local concerns about additional losses. Helicopter darting combined with radiotelemetry has been particularly effective in capturing wolves. However, control of wolf packs never resulted in the capture of all pack members as also was

the case in Minnesota (Fritts et al. 1992). Wolf activity is still reported at all locations where control occurred, except Big Sandy.

The fact that livestock producers readily contact ADC when they suspect livestock were attacked by wolves is the most apparent indicator of success of the control program. In addition, USFWS and ADC biologists are often asked to speak to livestock groups about wolves and wolf recovery. Personnel involved in wolf recovery believe that, although still controversial, communications with most livestock producers seem less polarized and discussions more focused on substantial issues than at any time in the past several years.

Whether illegal killing of wolves has actually been reduced because of the control program is unknown. The deaths of three translocated wolves indicate wolves are still being illegally killed. However, the Ninemile and Murphy Lake packs (Fritts et al. this volume) are associated with livestock on almost a daily basis, and are regularly seen and reported by local residents who appear tolerant of them if livestock are not attacked. We believe more local residents would attempt to kill wolves if agencies did not have an effective control program.

Whether and to what extent the control program has actually enhanced wolf recovery is speculative. Two of four packs that formed outside the recovery area were eliminated by agency control. Of the 17 wolves controlled, only one contributed to population growth in Montana. However, that translocated female established the southern-most pack in the western U.S., where eight wolves live at the time of this writing. The information gained so far should improve success of future translocations. Data indicated that survival of pups translocated prior to mid-September will be low, so pups ≤ 6 months old should be released on site. In addition,

E.E. Bangs, S.H. Fritts, D.R. Harms, J.A. Fontaine, M.D. Jimenez, W.G. Brewster, and C.C. Niemeyer

the control program has evolved from strictly a removal program in 1980 and 1987, to a translocation program in 1989 and 1991, to being able to release wolves on site, with landowner approval, in 1992. The program will continue to evolve as more information and experience is obtained.

Wolf control is but one component of a conservation program that emphasizes education and information to improve local tolerance of wolves (Bangs 1991, Pomerantz and Blanchard 1992, Fritts et al. this volume). The importance of quickly reporting wolf activity as well as possible wolf depredations was emphasized to livestock producers as the most effective way to identify problems, initiate control to minimize additional losses, and receive compensation (Gunson 1983b, Tompa 1983b, Fritts et al. 1992). In several instances, livestock producers voluntarily initiated improved livestock carcass disposal after being made aware of the suspected relationship between wolf depredations and livestock carrion (Fritts 1982).

Most importantly, the wolf population in northwestern Montana continues to increase, indicating that a recovering wolf population can overcome human-caused mortality of $\leq 9\%$. Our observations support those of Gunson (1983b) and Fritts et al. (1992) that damage prevention, control, and compensation programs improved communications with agriculturists, improved tolerance of predators, and reduced animosity between the rural public and resource agencies. We believe that these achievements reduce attempts to illegally kill wolves and thus are consistent with wolf recovery and long-term conservation of wolf populations.

Acknowledgments

We thank J. Mack, N. Bishop, D. Pletscher, and four anonymous reviewers, whose comments greatly improved this manuscript. We also thank the many livestock producers in western Montana who cooperated with us to help resolve and minimize wolf-livestock conflicts.

Transboundary Movements of a Recolonizing Wolf Population in the Rocky Mountains

■ Diane K. Boyd, Paul C. Paquet, Steve Donelon, Robert R. Ream, Daniel H. Pletscher, and Cliff C. White

The concurrent recolonization of Glacier and Banff National parks by wolves (**Canis lupus**) was monitored from 1984 to 1991. Seventeen (40%) of 42 marked wolves either dispersed > 40 km or were long distance travellers (> 40 km) and generally moved north or southeast along the Rocky Mountain corridor that links the parks. Six females and five males dispersed, whereby all six long-distance travellers were females. Mean dispersal age was 23 months for females and 33 months for males, and mean distance was 264 km for females and 152 km for males. Seven of 10 dispersals occurred between December and February. Four dispersers became founding members of new packs. Interpack exchange occurred within and between the two parks without apparent hostilities. During different time periods, two individuals were accepted members of two distinct packs, freely associating with adults and pups of both packs. Three factors may allow such interpack tolerance: the high density of prey; the low density of wolves; and the close relatedness of recolonizing wolves.

Introduction

Most wolves were eliminated from the Rocky Mountain south of Jasper National Park (JNP), Alberta, before 1914 (Hornaday 1906, Millar 1915), and by 1930 a viable population ceased to exist in the area between JNP and Glacier National Park (GNP), Montana (Cowan 1947, Brittan 1953, Singer 1979, Day 1981, Ream and Mattson 1982). In the late 1930's wolves reestablished in most areas of the Canadian Rockies from which they had been eliminated (Cowan 1947; I. M. Cowan, Univ. of B.C., pers. commun.). Wolves were eliminated again in the 1950's by a carnivore reduction program for rabies control (Gunson 1983a).

In the mid- to late-1970's observations of solitary wolves were reported in Banff National Park (BNP) and adjacent Kananaskis Country, Alberta, and GNP (Ream and Mattson 1982). Pack activity was documented in the Bow Valley of BNP (M. Gibeau, BNP, pers. commun.) and near GNP in 1982 (Ream et al. 1991). However, the 226-km Southern Rocky Mountain Cordillera between BNP and GNP remained devoid of packs. During the 1980's, BNP and GNP served as sanctuaries where wolves increased steadily and produced dispersers that colonized adjacent unoccupied range in British Columbia (B.C.), Alberta, Montana, and Idaho (Pletscher et al. 1991, Ream et al. 1991).

Characteristics of dispersers (including age, sex, distance, and recruitment into packs) are documented for established, high density wolf populations (Kuyt 1962, Van Camp and Gluckie 1979, Ballard et al. 1983, Messier 1985b, Mech 1987, Gese and Mech 1991). Fritts and Mech (1981) and Peterson et al. (1984) documented the role of dispersers in the dynamics of colonizing, low-density wolf populations through their period of establishment in northwestern Minnesota and the Kenai Peninsula, Alaska, respectively. Our objective was to determine the role of wolf dispersal in the dynamics of a low-density recolonizing population in the Rocky Mountain of Canada and the U.S.

Study Area and Methods

The study was conducted in the Rocky Mountains of southeastern B.C., southwestern Alberta and northwestern Montana (Fig. 1) from 1984 to 1991. The area is characterized by long, narrow valley bottoms surrounded by rugged mountains. Elevations range from 1,020 m in the valleys to 3,600 m along the Continental Divide. Dense coniferous forests dominate the area, with meadows and riparian areas less common (Habeck 1970, Koterba and Habeck 1971). Prey species include white-tailed deer (*Odocoileus virginianus*), mule deer (*O. hemionus*), elk (*Cervus elaphus*), moose (*Al-*

Diane K. Boyd, Paul C. Paquet, Steve Donelon, Robert R. Ream, Daniel H. Pletscher, and Cliff C. White

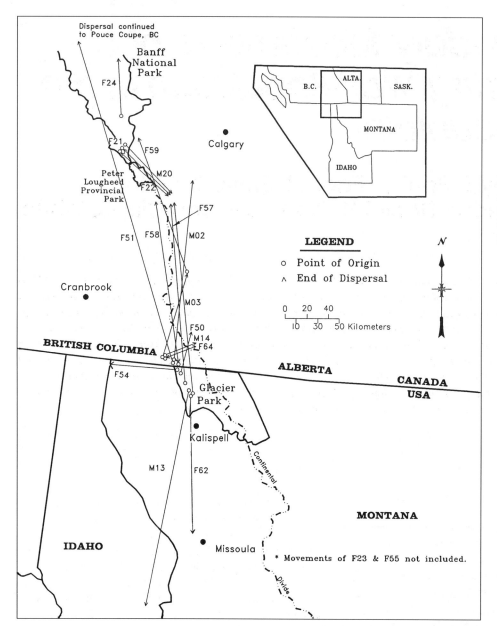

Fig. 1 *Dispersal and extraterritorial movements of wolves in and near Glacier National Park and Banff National Park, 1984-1991.*

ces alces), bighorn sheep (*Ovis canadensis*), mountain goat (*Oreamnos americanus*), mountain caribou (*Rangifer tarandus*), beaver (*Castor canadensis*), and various small mammals. The study area is a mosaic of numerous land management classifications, including two countries, two states, two provinces, B.C. Forestry lands, Elk Lakes Provincial Park, BNP, Peter Lougheed Provincial Park (PLPP), Kananaskis Country, GNP, Flathead National Forest, Kootenai National Forest, Montana and Idaho state-owned lands, and private land.

We captured and radio-collared wolves as described by Mech (1974a) and Kuehn et al. (1986) and tracked them via ground triangulation, aircraft, and satellite (ARGOS). Resident wolves were located two to 12 times per week in the study area. Radio contact with some dispersing wolves was

lost for periods of one month to two years, but upon relocation regular monitoring resumed. Wolves were classified as "dispersers" if they permanently remained more than 40 km from the periphery of their natal home range. We measured dispersal distance from the point of capture to the center of the disperser's new home range or point of death. Wolves that made extraterritorial movements (40 km or more) and appeared to associate temporarily with members of more than one pack were classified as "long distance travellers" (LDTs) after Messier (1985b). A pack has been defined as a mated pair and their offspring (Mech 1970, 1991c). For purposes of this paper, we defined a pack as three or more wolves that travelled together in a territory, because the sex and familial status of newly formed groups was often unknown in our colonizing population. Wolves located tempo-

Table 1. Characteristics of dispersers and long distance travellers (LDTs) captured in Glacier National Park (GNP), Montana, Banff National Park (BNP), Alberta, and Peter Lougheed Provincial Park (PLPP), Alberta, from 1984-1991.

ID	Capture age	Sex	Capture Location	Status	Dispersal Age (mos)[1]	# Packs Associated With	Maximum Dispersal Distance
F51	pup	F	Near GNP	Disp	21	1	840
M02	pup	M	Near GNP	Disp	17	1	200
F54	pup	F	GNP	Disp	23	3[2]	120
M03	yearling	M	GNP	Disp	34	2	205
F57	yearling	F	Near GNP	Disp	22	3	230
F58	yearling	F	Near GNP	LDT	33	3	155
F59	yearling	F	Near GNP	Disp	18	3+pair+single	180
F62	yearling	F	GNP	Disp	33	2	100
M13	adult	M	GNP	Disp	$\geq 45^3$	1	170
M14	yearling	M	Near GNP	Disp	22	1	52
F64	yearling	F	Near GNP	LDT	22	1	40
M20	adult	M	BNP	Disp	$\geq 46^3$	2	134
F21	adult	F	BNP	LDT	$\geq 93^3$	1	115
F22	adult	F	BNP	LDT	$\geq 43^3$	2	115
F23	adult	F	PLPP	LDT	$\geq 63^3$	1	290
F55	yearling	F	GNP	LDT	25	2	45
F24	yearling	F	BNP	Disp	20	2	111

1   age at first dispersal or extraterritorial foray (LDT).
2   the original pack eventually divided into two separate but adjacent packs and this wolf was a member of all three packs.
3   based on minimum estimated age upon capture.

---

rarily with other wolves were considered an association (as opposed to a pack), whether it be for one or several locations. Tests of spatial and temporal interaction (Minta 1992) were used to analyze avoidance or attraction of dispersers to wolf groups of various sizes.

Results and Discussion

We marked 31 wolves in GNP from August 1984 through July 1991; five pups were only ear-tagged and 26 wolves older than four months were radio-collared and ear-tagged. The GNP wolves were located more than 6,000 times. We radio-collared and ear-tagged 11 wolves older than five months in BNP and PLPP from February 1987 through July 1991 and located them more than 2,200 times. Seventeen males and 25 females (68 M:100 F) were captured in the combined GNP/BNP study area. Nine marked wolves from GNP and two marked wolves from BNP dispersed (Table 1, Fig. 1). In addition, six tagged wolves engaged in long-dis-

tance extraterritorial forays and were referred to as LDTs (Table 1, Fig. 1). Altogether, 40% of marked wolves either dispersed or were LDTs. Six additional wolves (two adult males, one yearling male, two adult females, one female pup) left their natal packs, but travelled < 40 km from their natal home range. These wolves were not included in our analysis, because much visitation between adjacent packs precluded clear analyses of pack membership and such forays were common. They must, nonetheless, be considered when characterizing the overall spatial and social dynamics of this population relative to others.

Pre-Dispersal Behavior

Before dispersal, most wolves remained with their pack and made few solo exploratory forays. Wolves that left their pack usually left the pack's home range abruptly and moved long distances rapidly. Seven wolves (three adults and four yearlings) permanently left their pack's home range one week or less after they were first known to separate from the pack. A

Diane K. Boyd, Paul C. Paquet, Steve Donelon, Robert R. Ream, Daniel H. Pletscher, and Cliff C. White

yearling travelled alone within her pack's home range for one month before dispersing. Two additional yearlings remained within their pack's home range for three months after separating from their natal pack, before permanently dispersing. Messier (1985b) found that dispersal was a more gradual dissociation process extending over a few months to a few years. The difference between his findings and ours may be due to the abundant prey base and low density wolf population in our study area, which minimized stress and enhanced survival of dispersers.

Age and Sex of Dispersers

Dispersal age of six females ranged from 18 to 33 months and averaged 23 months. Additionally, F50 (not included in Table 1) dispersed at approximately age 7.5 years, after cessation of radio transmission. After January 1990, she was often seen by local residents 45 km north of her natal home range in the area of West Castle, Alberta, and was legally harvested there in December 1992 and her radio-collar returned. She was not included in this analysis because of the late confirmation of her presence, but is mentioned because her dispersal at such an advanced age is noteworthy. Age of dispersal for five males ranged from 17 to 46 months, and averaged 33 months. The combined mean age of dispersal for both sexes was 27 months. In south-central Alaska, Ballard et al. (1987) reported mean dispersal age as 30 and 33 months for males and females. In northeastern Minnesota, Mech (1987) reported mean dispersal ages of 21 months for males and 14 months for females.

We observed no pup dispersals; seven of 11 dispersers were yearlings, and four of 11 were adults. Subadult and young adult wolves were the most likely to disperse in other areas (Mech 1970, Fritts and Mech 1981, Peterson et al. 1984, Messier 1985b, Ballard et al. 1987, Mech 1987, Gese and Mech 1991, Mech 1991c). Our findings were most similar to those of Fritts and Mech (1981) and Peterson et al. (1984), with little or no pup dispersal, high dispersal rates of yearlings and a low number of adult dispersers. Fritts and Mech (1981) reported no incidents of radio-collared juveniles staying with their natal pack past breeding age (22 months) unless they became breeders after the alpha wolves died. The wolf population we studied and those of Fritts and Mech (1981) and Peterson et al. (1984) were low density and/or increasing, with relatively high prey densities, and low incidence of intraspecific strife. This is in contrast to data reported in the high density, saturated wolf populations with low prey densities and an increased incidence of intraspecific strife studied by Gese and Mech (1991) and Messier (1985b). The opportunity for dispersing wolves to successfully establish their own pack in unoccupied territory may have been a factor in our high rate of yearling dispersals.

The dispersers and LDTs included five males and 12 females (42 M:100 F) which was not significantly different from the population we sampled ($\chi^2 = 0.634$, 1 df, P > 0.5). We documented nearly equal numbers of males (n = 5) and

females (n = 6) dispersing, but all six LDTs were females. No overall trend regarding sex bias of dispersers is apparent in the literature (Fritts and Mech 1981, Peterson et al. 1984, Messier 1985b, Ballard et al. 1987, Fuller 1989, Gese and Mech 1991).

Month of Dispersal

Month of dispersal was determined for 10 of the 12 marked dispersers: seven of 10 occurred in December-February, and one each during March, May, and October. Previous studies have revealed that dispersal generally peaks during the January–April period with a lesser peak in October-November, although some variation on this general theme occurs (Fritts and Mech 1981, Peterson et al. 1984, Messier 1985b, Ballard et al. 1987, Mech 1987, Fuller 1989, Gese and Mech 1991). Most dispersals reported in the literature occurred in January and February, the period when pair-bonding, courtship, mating, and howling activities peak (Mech 1970, Harrington and Mech 1978, Rothman and Mech 1979) as well as increased aggression (Zimen 1976).

Direction Dispersed

There was a strong tendency for GNP wolves to travel northerly and the BNP wolves to travel southeastwardly along the Rocky Mountain corridor that links GNP, PLPP, and BNP (Fig. 1). Three dispersers and one LDT from GNP travelled to the BNP/Kananaskis area (F57, F59, M03, and F58), and one BNP wolf (F23) visited northwestern Montana. The movements of F23 were erratic up to the cessation of radio-collar transmission, with no obvious end point, therefore she was omitted from Figure 1. We located dispersers and LDTs in the Elk Valley of B.C., in various drainages along the east side of the Great Divide, in the Oldman River drainage, in the Sheep River area of Alberta, near Missoula, Montana, near Yahk, B.C., and near Kelly Creek, Idaho. The Rocky Mountain landscape provides a natural north-south travel and dispersal route for wolf movement between Jasper and Yellowstone national parks. The area is sparsely inhabited by humans, contains a series of refugia in a matrix of private lands, harbors abundant ungulates, and includes areas not yet recolonized by wolves. Most dispersers and LDTs that we monitored used this major corridor. Several factors appeared to influence the movements of wolves including physiographic barriers, natural topographic funnels, integrated patches of prey, and concentrations of human habitations.

Distance Dispersed

Females and males dispersed mean distances of 264 km and 152 km respectively (Table 1, Fig. 1). If the 840-km dispersal of F51 is omitted, the mean dispersal distance of females, 148 km, was virtually identical to that for males. Dispersals ranging up to 886 km have been reported in the literature (Van Camp and Gluckie 1979, Ballard et al. 1983, Fritts 1983, Van Ballenberghe 1983a). The 840-km dispersal of

F51 from GNP to northeastern B.C. is the longest distance reported for a female wolf (Pletscher et al. 1991, Ream et al. 1991). In the older literature males reportedly dispersed longer distances than females, but more recent studies have disputed that conclusion (Ballard et al. 1987, Mech 1987, Fuller 1989). Gese and Mech (1991) found no strong indication that one sex dispersed farther than the other.

Short distance extraterritorial forays (5–40 km) by LDTs as individuals or in groups were common in our study area and too numerous to detail here. LDT wolves of the GNP/BNP ecosystem appeared to exhibit more frequent and longer distance extraterritorial movements than those reported elsewhere. Dispersal distances we recorded were comparable to those reported elsewhere (Van Camp and Gluckie 1979, Ballard et al. 1983, Fritts 1983, Gese and Mech 1991). Long-distance movements facilitate genetic exchange and may reduce the probability of inbreeding depression and, therefore, may be critical to the health of low-density, recolonizing populations such as ours. The documentation of long-distance dispersals in our study area and elsewhere suggests that genes may be exchanged in widely separate populations, and supports a reduction in number of wolf subspecies (Brewster and Fritts this volume, Nowak this volume). Various agencies often debate the subspeciation issue to decide the proper management of select wolf populations. We suggest this may now be a moot point in light of recent field investigations and population level genetic studies (Lehman et al. 1992, Wayne et al. 1992b, Brewster and Fritts this volume).

Post-Dispersal Behavior

Dispersing wolves and LDTs were members of one to three packs plus additional liaisons of one to two wolves during the course of the study. The mean number of packs visited by dispersing and LDT females was 2.0 packs, 1.4 packs for males, and 1.8 packs for combined females and males (Table 1). Two individuals travelled freely between two packs and were observed caring for pups in two packs during one denning season (M20 and F55). The movements of F55 were not included in Figure 1 because they were in the area of the most concentrated endpoints and would have made the other data points unreadable. Mech and Nelson (1989) documented one incident of successful polygyny and pup rearing in northeastern Minnesota, but that liaison involved only the three individuals and did not involve shared parenting duties within and between packs as did our observation. In areas of established populations it is generally accepted that trespassing wolves are often harassed or killed by resident wolves (Mech 1970 and 1991c, Van Ballenberghe 1983a). Intraspecific pack tolerance has been reported infrequently in the literature (cf. Fritts and Mech 1981) but may be common in the GNP/BNP wolves and other colonizing populations. In contrast to saturated wolf populations, colonizing wolves in areas of high prey density and low wolf density may not need to vigorously defend their territories against trespassers be-

cause food and space are adequate. Colonizing wolves may enhance their chances of inclusive fitness by cooperating with closely related wolves in nearby packs. This strategy may also increase their probability of breeding by developing familiarity with more than one pack.

The mechanism by which wolves locate other disjunct wolf populations or solitary individuals is not understood. Siblings M03 and F57 (one year younger than M03) dispersed from their natal pack nine months apart and ended up together in a new pack 150 km north of their natal home range three years later. F62 dispersed 140 km south to the Ninemile area where an isolated pack of wolves had established its home range one year before. F62 arrived in the same area approximately two weeks after most members of the Ninemile pack had been removed for livestock depredations (Bangs et al. this volume).

The length of time before a dispersed wolf was recruited into an established pack or became a founding member of a new pack was often difficult to determine because of irregular monitoring during dispersal, but regular monitoring resumed upon dispersal cessation. Dispersed wolves often were associating with other wolves by the time we located them in their new home ranges. This time period (in months) was four (F59), five (F62), six (F57), seven (F51), and 38 (M03) for five dispersing wolves that became members of other packs. Two wolves, F54 and M13, remained alone for at least one year following dispersal. Litter mates F64 and M14 died within two months after dispersing and did not join other wolves before dying (Boyd et al. 1992).

Four dispersers (F57, F62, M03, M20) became founding members of new packs in areas packs had not occupied since the 1950's. Before establishment of the new territories, these same areas had been visited by nondispersing wolves from at least two established packs (Spray River Pack, Camas Pack). These visits appeared to be exploratory forays and included entire packs, subunits of packs, and individuals. We regularly monitored 12 of these exploratory moves by wolves from the Spray River Pack, BNP, and the reaction of two solitary wolves that had dispersed from GNP and were using the area. The dispersers avoided large packs (≥ 5 wolves, n = 3), reacted neutrally to small subgroups (≤ 3 wolves, n = 2) and single wolves (n = 2), or were attracted to small subgroups (n = 4) and single wolves (n = 1). On four occasions, at least two wolves from the Spray River Pack and the dispersers from GNP were observed resting together. In all instances they remained together less than 24 hours. The same wolves were always involved in these liaisons (M20, F22, F57), and the dispersers avoided the Spray River Pack when the pack was accompanied by the alpha female (F21).

In addition to our reported dispersals, several LDTs made extraterritorial forays ranging from 40–290 km from their home range. Most dispersers and LDTs journeyed alone, but on occasion travelled with another wolf. Yearling siblings

Diane K. Boyd, Paul C. Paquet, Steve Donelon, Robert R. Ream, Daniel H. Pletscher, and Cliff C. White

F64 and M14 dispersed together 40 km east of their natal territory. After M14 was killed in an avalanche (Boyd et al. 1992), F64 immediately returned to her natal territory. Pack-mates F62 and M13 disappeared from GNP the same day. Two months later, two different radio-collared wolves matching descriptions of F62 and M13 were observed in the Ninemile area (R. Thisted, rancher, pers. commun.). It appeared that F62 and M13 probably dispersed together from GNP and eventually established separate territories near Ninemile and Kelly Creek, Idaho. Wolf F58 left GNP on 18 January 1990. We located her on 26 January 1990, 200 km north of the 18 January location, and she remained in that area accompanied by another wolf through February 1990. She and the companion returned to GNP and her natal Camas Pack on 24 March 1990 and remained with this pack throughout the summer.

Intraspecific Strife

We documented 60 wolf mortalities in the GNP/BNP area during this study; no mortality of dispersing wolves or any others was caused by wolves killing their conspecifics. Ninety-five percent of the GNP/BNP mortalities were caused by humans. Researchers studying low density or colonizing populations report relatively low rates of intraspecific strife (Fritts and Mech 1981, Peterson et al. 1984). In contrast, mortalities caused by wolves killing wolves in saturated populations accounted for a higher percentage of the mortalities (Meier et al. this volume, Mech 1970 and 1977b). The apparent intraspecific tolerance of our population may be a factor in increased interpack exchanges and, therefore, enhance dispersal success.

Conclusions and Management Implications

The variability of wolf dispersal schemes (i.e., age, sex, distance, direction, season) documented here and in other studies likely increased survival of dispersers. This flexibility may be particularly important for recolonizing populations. The low density of wolves, abundance of prey, and close relatedness of wolves in the GNP/BNP ecosystem apparently allowed for increased intraspecific tolerance and aided the natural recovery process.

During dispersals and extraterritorial forays the wolves we studied crossed numerous physiographic and political boundaries, including provincial, state, federal, or international, where management objectives varied from no protection to total protection. Clearly, interagency and international cooperation are required to successfully manage and enhance wolf recovery. The area we studied is of extreme importance to wolf conservation in the Northern Rocky Mountains of the U.S. (Fritts et al. this volume) because it apparently is a corridor allowing natural repopulation of Montana from Canada and, in the future, may be the most effective corridor between the Canadian and U.S. populations in the western part of the continent. The long-distance movements reported here and elsewhere emphasize the need for coordination between management jurisdictions to ensure the preservation of wolves and other large carnivores. Biologists and managers must maintain refugia and habitat connectivity for wolf recovery to occur.

Acknowledgments

We gratefully acknowledge funding from the U.S. Fish and Wildlife Service, U.S. National Park Service, U.S. Forest Service, the School of Forestry and Montana Cooperative Wildlife Research Unit, University of Montana, Missoula, Canadian Park Service, Kananaskis Country, Alberta Fish and Wildlife Division, World Wildlife Fund Canada, World Wildlife Fund U.S., Rocky Mountain Elk Foundation, and anonymous private contributors. Logistical support was provided by R. Demarchi, B.C. Wildlife Branch, J. Gunson and J. Jorgenson, Alberta Fish and Wildlife Division, U.S. Customs and Immigration, Revenue Canada, and the Moose City Corporation. Many individuals contributed greatly to the success of the project including M. Fairchild, M. Jimenez, R. and B. Thisted, M. Gibeau, R. Kunelius, G. Peers, I. Ross, M. Jalkotzy, G. Neale, and numerous volunteers. S. Fritts made many helpful suggestions in revision of this manuscript.

Status of The Mexican Wolf Recovery Program in the United States

■ David R. Parsons and Joy E. Nicholopoulos

The Mexican wolf is the southernmost and smallest subspecies of the North American gray wolf, historically occupying montane woodlands in the southwestern United States (U.S.) and central and northern Mexico. It was extirpated from the wild in the U.S. by private and government control and was listed as an endangered species in 1976. In 1977, the U.S. Fish and Wildlife Service (USFWS) initiated captive propagation with the capture of five wild wolves in Mexico. By January 1995, 170 Mexican wolves had been born in captivity, and 88 living wolves were in the captive population. Two uncertified populations of putative Mexican wolves exist and are being evaluated for genetic purity. The Mexican Wolf Recovery Plan, approved by the USFWS and Dirección General de la Fauna Silvestre (Mexico) in 1982, recommended reintroduction to the wild and maintenance of a captive population. The USFWS has proposed a reintroduction of Mexican wolves. An Environmental Impact Statement that will address relevant issues and concerns associated with the proposal has been initiated. Public support for the recovery and preservation of the Mexican wolf is strong.

Introduction

The Mexican wolf (*Canis lupus baileyi*) is the smallest subspecies of gray wolf in North America. Goldman (1937:45) recognized five subspecies in the southwestern U.S. and Mexico: southern Rocky Mountain wolf (*Canis lupus youngi*), Texas gray wolf (*Canis lupus monstrabilis*), Mogollon Mountain wolf (*Canis lupus mogollonensis*), buffalo wolf (*Canis lupus nubilis*), and Mexican wolf.

Bogan and Mehlhop (1983) assessed the systematic affinities of the five southwestern subspecies recognized by Goldman (1937:45) utilizing univariate and multivariate statistical procedures. They confirmed *C. l. baileyi* and *C. l. youngi* to be taxonomically distinct subspecies and further determined that *C. l. monstrabilis* and *C. l. mogollonensis* were intermediate between *C. l. baileyi* and *C. l. youngi*. Bogan and Mehlhop referred *C. l. monstrabilis* and *C. l. mogollonensis* to *C. l. baileyi*, thus, recognizing only three southwestern subspecies: *C. l. youngi*, *C. l. nubilus*, and *C. l. baileyi*.

Nowak (1983, this volume) suggests only five subspecies of *C. lupus* were present in North America: arctos (in the arctic); occidentalis (in Alaska and western Canada); nubilus (from Oregon to Newfoundland and Hudson Bay to Texas); lycaon (in southeastern Canada); and baileyi (in the south-

western U.S.). Wayne et al. (1992b) reported that the Mexican wolf has a unique mitochondrial DNA genotype. Confusion and disagreement over North American wolf taxonomy persists (Brewster and Fritts this volume). However, most data lead to the conclusion that the Mexican wolf is a distinct subspecies. The USFWS (1982) concurred with the conclusions of Bogan and Mehlhop (1983); however, Nowak (this volume) refers the former *C. l. mogollonensis* and *C. l. monstrabilis* to *C.l. nubilus*.

The Mexican wolf once ranged over portions of central and northern Mexico, western Texas, southern New Mexico, and southeastern and central Arizona (Fig. 1). The wolf used natural corridors or "runways" such as stream beds (arroyos) and topographic breaks to travel within and between areas of suitable habitat. Later, roads and trails were often utilized for ease of travel (Brown 1983).

The Mexican wolf showed affinity for montane woodlands, presumably because of the favorable combination of cover, water, and prey availability. Most wolf collections came from pine, oak, and piñon-juniper woodlands, and intervening or adjacent grasslands above 1,363 m in elevation. Wolves avoided desert scrub and semidesert grasslands, which provided little cover or water (Brown 1983).

The Mexican wolf is believed to have preyed on white-tailed deer (*Odocoileus virginianus*), mule deer (*O.*

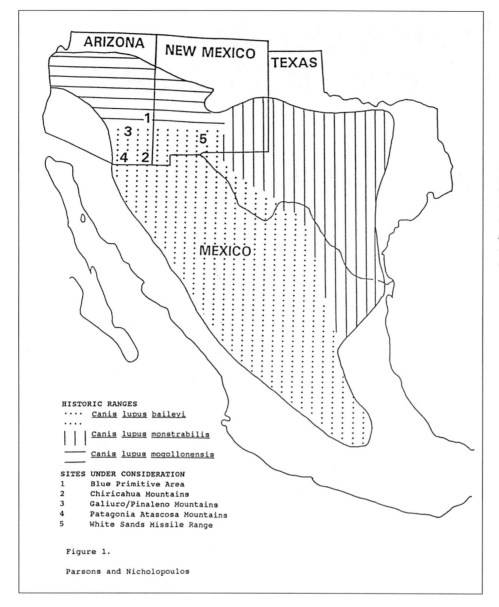

Fig. 1 *Historic ranges of* **Canis lupus baileyi, Canis lupus monstrabilis**, *and* **Canis lupus mogollonensis**; *and proposed sites for the initial reintroduction of* **Canis lupus baileyi**.

HISTORIC RANGES
···· Canis lupus baileyi
····
||| Canis lupus monstrabilis
——— Canis lupus mogollonensis

SITES UNDER CONSIDERATION
1   Blue Primitive Area
2   Chiricahua Mountains
3   Galiuro/Pinaleno Mountains
4   Patagonia Atascosa Mountains
5   White Sands Missile Range

Figure 1.

Parsons and Nicholopoulos

hemionus), javelina (*Tayassu tajacu*), small mammals, and rabbits (*Sylvilagus* sp., *Lepus* sp.). With the introduction of livestock, the encroachment of humans, and the subsequent reduction of native ungulates in the southwestern U.S., the Mexican wolf began to prey on livestock. Wild ungulate populations have since been restored in areas being considered for Mexican wolf reintroduction.

Little is known of the natural history of the Mexican wolf. Most data were obtained by trappers employed by the Predatory Animal and Rodent Control Service (PARC). Numbers, weights, and details were often embellished (Brown 1983). The average weights of wild Mexican wolves are known only from carcasses. Males averaged 25–34 kg, while females averaged 22–25 kg. Adult Mexican wolves ranged from 1.4 m to 1.7 m in total length (nose to tail), and averaged 0.72 m to 0.80 m in shoulder height. The Mexican wolf, like most other North American wolves, has a broad range of pelage colors and patterns (Brown 1983).

Mexican wolves are believed to form small packs, but data supporting this belief are lacking. Most information obtained regarding free-ranging Mexican wolves was provided by trappers who most often targeted lone wolves. Occasionally, groups of wolves were taken together, but the ongoing harassment and molestation in areas where this was observed affected the structure of the wolf social unit, and eliminated any basis for scientific determination of pack size and social structure. Likewise, the only data obtained on the reproductive behavior of wild Mexican wolves was provided by trappers who were "denning" for young wolves (Brown 1983).

McBride (1980) reported a mean litter size of 4.5 from eight dens in Mexico. Mean litter size before parturition for eight females was 6.8, indicating a degree of mortality during or after birth (McBride 1980). Captive Mexican wolves have produced 39 litters ranging from 1–9 ($\bar{x}$ = 4.4). Captive females usually come into estrous between mid-February and mid-March. Gestation averages 63 days, with parturition occurring in April and May.

Population Status in the Wild

Wolves have inhabited the Southwest since the Pleistocene. Fossil remains have been reported from Arizona (Lindsay and Tessman 1974) and New Mexico (Findley et al. 1975). Bednarz (1988) estimated 16.1 wolves per 1,000 km^2 or about 1,500 animals for the suitable habitat in New Mexico prior to control measures initiated by PARC in 1915.

Many methods of extermination were utilized on Mexican wolves, including trapping with snares and steel leg-hold traps, shooting, and poisoning with strychnine, arsenic, and sodium cyanide (used in the M-44 or "coyote getter"). Public and private bounties were paid for each wolf turned in. PARC reported over 900 Mexican wolves killed in New Mexico and Arizona by PARC trappers or cooperators from 1915 to 1925. However, it is believed that a greater number of wolves were killed for bounties from 1890 to 1915 (Brown 1983).

The Mexican wolf is believed to be extirpated from the wild in the U.S. Bednarz (1988), utilizing a regression model, proposed 1942 as the estimated year of extirpation in New Mexico. McBride (1980) estimated that fewer than 50 Mexican wolves existed in the states of Chihuahua and Durango, Mexico, and speculated that no more than 50 adult breeding pairs existed within the Republic of Mexico in 1978. The present status of wild populations in Mexico is unknown but thought to be lower than McBride's estimates for 1978. The USFWS continues to receive unconfirmed reports of wolf sightings primarily from U.S./Mexico border areas of Arizona and New Mexico. These "wolves" could be dispersers from Mexico, coyotes, pet wolves, or wolf-dog hybrids that escaped or were set free.

The Mexican wolf was listed as an endangered species in May 1976 under the Endangered Species Act (ESA) of 1973 as amended. Under provisions of the ESA, it is illegal to "take" any wolf without a permit unless a human life is in danger.

Recovery Efforts

Under an agreement reached between the U.S. and Mexico, Roy McBride (Alpine, Texas) captured five Mexican wolves between 1977 and 1980 in Durango and Chihuahua. These wolves (four males and one pregnant female) were transferred to the Arizona-Sonora Desert Museum in Tucson, Arizona, to establish a captive breeding program.

The Mexican Wolf Recovery Team (Team) was formed by the USFWS in August 1979. The Team prepared the Mexican Wolf Recovery Plan (Plan), which was approved and signed by the director of the USFWS and the director general of the Dirección General de la Fauna Silvestre (Mexico) on 15 September 1982. Citing human demands for space and resources present in historic wolf habitat, the Team concluded that there was "no possibility for complete delisting of the Mexican wolf" (USFWS 1982:23). The unstated implication is that down-listing to a threatened status is the best that could be hoped for. The Plan contains the following objective: "To conserve and ensure the survival of *C. l. baileyi* by maintaining a captive breeding program and reestablishing a viable, self-sustaining population of at least 100 Mexican wolves in the middle to high elevations of a 8,000 km^2 area within the Mexican wolf's historic range" (USFWS 1982:23). The two key components of this objective are maintenance of a captive breeding program and reestablishment of a viable wild population.

The Captive Breeding Specialist Group (CBSG) of the Species Survival Commission of the International Union for the Conservation of Nature and Natural Resources conducted a Population Viability Analysis Workshop for the Mexican wolf in October 1990. The CBSG is expected to issue the results from the workshop soon.

The Plan is being revised by a newly appointed recovery team. Based on advances in conservation biology and findings presented in the population viability assessment, the current recovery objective for the Mexican wolf will be reviewed, and revised if necessary.

Given the fragmentation of remaining habitat for the Mexican wolf, a number of isolated reintroductions likely will be required to ensure long-term conservation of the subspecies. Reestablishment efforts will most likely result in a metapopulation, which will require active management to ensure adequate gene flow among reestablished subpopulations (Lande and Barrowclough 1987).

Captive Breeding Program

A certified Mexican wolf is defined by the USFWS as a wolf of known wild origin, within the historical range of *C. l. baileyi*, or their offspring. In addition, certified Mexican wolves have no known or identifiable hybridization (USFWS 1982). Only certified Mexican wolves are protected by the ESA.

A captive breeding program for certified Mexican wolves was initiated at the Arizona-Sonora Desert Museum with the delivery of the five wild-caught wolves beginning in 1977 and the birth of a litter of five pups by the captured pregnant female (studbook number 5) in 1978. The only female of this litter died at the age of four days. Two of the wild-caught males and the lone female were later bred and produced offspring in captivity. Including the unknown mate of the pregnant female, the founding stock of the captive population comprises four wild Mexican wolves. In 1981, at the Wild Canid Survival and Research Center in Eureka, Missouri, female number 5 produced her second litter in captiv-

Table 1. U.S. Facilities cooperating in the management of the captive population of Mexican wolves.

Alameda Park Zoo, Alamogordo, New Mexico
Arizona-Sonora Desert Museum, Tucson, Arizona
Belle Isle Zoo, Royal Oak, Michigan
Binder Park Zoo, Battle Creek, Michigan
Bronx Zoo, Bronx, New York
Cheyenne Mountain Zoo, Colorado Springs, Colorado
Columbus Zoological Gardens, Powell, Ohio
El Paso Zoo, El Paso, Texas
Fort Worth Zoological Park, Fort Worth, Texas
Fossil Rim Wildlife Center, Glen Rose, Texas
Freeport McMoran — Audubon Species
Survival Center, New Orleans, Louisiana
Living Desert State Park, Carlsbad, New Mexico
Minnesota Zoo, Apple Valley, Minnesota
Phoenix Zoo, Phoenix, Arizona
Rio Grande Zoo, Albuquerque, New Mexico
Sedgewick County Zoo, Wichita, Kansas
The Living Desert, Palm Desert, California
Wild Canid Survival and Research Center, Eureka, Missouri
Wolf Haven International, Tenino, Washington

ity (one male and three female pups). All four of these pups survived and reproduced, producing a total of 11 litters to date. By 1983, the captive breeding program was firmly established with the birth of three litters totalling 15 pups (Siminski 1990).

To date, 170 Mexican wolves have been born in captivity. This includes 146 pups from 30 litters born in U.S. facilities and 24 pups from nine litters born in Mexican facilities. Eight captive born wolves were transferred to Mexico (three pairs in 1987 and one pair in 1988) and used to establish a captive breeding program.

As of January 1995, the captive population consisted of 88 wolves: 75 at 19 cooperating facilities in the U.S. (Table 1) and 13 at five facilities in Mexico (P. Siminski, Mexican Wolf Studbook Keeper, unpubl. data). Demographics of the U.S. population of certified Mexican wolves are depicted in Figure 2.

From 1985 to 1994, management of captive certified Mexican wolves was conducted by the Mexican Wolf Captive Management Committee (MWCMC). The MWCMC comprised nine elected representatives of facilities authorized by the USFWS to hold or breed Mexican wolves, and was recognized by the USFWS as an expert authority for the propagation and management of captive Mexican wolves. The MWCMC made recommendations to the USFWS on all aspects of the management of the captive population and

implemented those recommendations approved by the USFWS. The captive population is now managed under a Species Survival Plan, approved by the American Association of Zoos and Aquariums.

Two uncertified lineages of putative Mexican wolves are known to exist, one each in the U.S. and Mexico. The U.S. population is referred to as the Arizona-Sonora Desert Museum/Ghost Ranch (ASDM/GR) lineage and the Mexican population is referred to as the Parque Zoológico de San Juan de Aragón (Aragón) lineage. The ASDM/GR lineage consists of 18 known animals (descended from two founders) kept by five institutions or individuals in the U.S. The original sire was live trapped in 1959 near Tumacacori, Arizona. The founding female was purchased as a pup in 1961 by a Canadian tourist in Yecora, Sonora, Mexico. A question remains as to whether it was born in the wild or in captivity (N. Ames, *Mexican wolves in captivity: A review of the lineage originating in the 1960's at the Arizona-Sonora Desert Museum*, Mexican Wolf Recovery Team, Santa Fe, NM, 1980). The Aragón lineage consists of 10 animals held at the Parque Zoológico de San Juan de Aragón in Mexico City. The origin of this population cannot be traced to the wild or to known founding animals (G. Lopez Islas and C.B. Vasquez Gonzales, *Linaje de lobos Mexicanos "San Juan de Aragon": Historia, evidencias de su authen-*

AGE	MALES	FEMALES	YEAR OF BIRTH	NO. OF WOLVES
13	1		1981	1
12			1982	0
11	1	2	1983	3
10	1	2	1984	3
09	1	0	1985	1
08	1		1986	1
07		2	1987	2
06	2		1988	2
05	3	2	1989	5
04	2	1	1990	3
03	2	4	1991	6
02	4	7	1992	11
01	14	9	1993	23
<1	5	9	1994	14
Totals	**37**	**38**		**75**

Fig. 2 *Demographics of certified Mexican wolves (all captive) in the United States as of January 1995.*

ticidad y posibilidad de certificacion, Parque Zoológico de San Juan de Aragón, Mexico City, 1991).

Genetics Analyses

Blood and other tissue samples have been obtained from living and dead wolves representing all three lineages. DNA analyses are being conducted by Dr. Steven R. Fain at the USFWS's National Fish and Wildlife Forensics Laboratory in Ashland, Oregon and by Dr. Robert K. Wayne at the University of California at Los Angeles. Answers to the following questions are being sought: are wolves in the certified lineage "pure" *C. l. baileyi*; are wolves in the ASDM/GR and Aragón lineages pure *C. l. baileyi*; what levels of genetic variation exist in each of the three lineages; has introgression of other canid genes into any of the three lineages occurred; is *C. l. baileyi* genetically distinct from other subspecies of *Canis lupus*; and what is the degree of relatedness between certified founders number 2 and number 5?

Reestablishment of Wild Populations

Reestablishment of Mexican wolves into historically occupied habitat in the U.S. will follow a phased approach. As currently planned, the initial reintroduction will be conducted on one area. Future releases to other areas will await the outcome of the initial release and the revision of the Mexican Wolf Recovery Plan. Releases will likely be conducted one area at a time until recovery objectives are met.

The USFWS has proposed the release and subsequent monitoring and management of Mexican wolves on one of five areas under consideration in Arizona and New Mexico (Fig. 1). In accordance with Section 10(j) of the ESA, the reintroduced population would be designated experimental and not essential to the continued existence of the species. Objectives of the proposed release are to: establish and maintain a wild population of Mexican wolves in the release area, develop proven reestablishment techniques, and enhance understanding of the biology and ecology of free-ranging Mexican wolves. Data, information, and experience obtained will be used to formulate plans for future releases.

Compliance with applicable laws and regulations is required before wolves can be released. The most notable and rigorous of these is the National Environmental Policy Act (NEPA), which requires full evaluation and disclosure of anticipated environmental effects of the proposed action and alternative courses of action prior to any agency decision to implement a proposal. In order to comply with the provisions of NEPA, the USFWS began an Environmental Impact Statement (EIS) on the proposed reintroduction in April 1992; completion of the final EIS is expected in early 1996. Public participation will be integrated throughout the NEPA process.

Sociopolitical Aspects

Public support for Mexican wolf recovery is strong. Public opinion surveys revealed that 64% of rural dwellers in

The Mexican wolf is the smallest subspecies of the North American gray wolf complex. This population was designated as an endangered species in 1976. A captive breeding program has formed the nucleus for a reintroduction program. (Photo: J.E. Nicholopoulus)

Arizona and 79% of those living outside of Albuquerque in New Mexico favored the reintroduction of Mexican wolves to the southwestern U.S., as did 75% of urban dwellers in Arizona and 88% of Albuquerque residents (Biggs 1988, Arizona Game and Fish Department 1990). The USFWS has received thousands of letters and petitions regarding Mexican wolf recovery; over 90% support continued recovery efforts and the remainder oppose such efforts. Arizona, New Mexico, and Texas have well-organized "grass roots" organizations dedicated to recovery of the Mexican wolf. Several national conservation organizations also support Mexican wolf recovery. The Defenders of Wildlife has established a Mexican Wolf Compensation Fund to reimburse livestock owners for any verified livestock depredation caused by Mexican wolves.

Four public meetings have been held to identify issues and concerns regarding the USFWS proposal to conduct an experimental release. While a majority of comments favored the return of Mexican wolves to the wild, many concerns were raised. Identified issues and concerns are grouped into eight general categories: livestock depredation, economic effects, ecological/biological considerations, population viability concerns, wildlife management considerations, land use effects, Mexican wolf recovery program-related issues, and philosophical/ethical viewpoints (USFWS, unpubl. data). Relevant issues and concerns will be addressed in the EIS.

Public opinion seems to indicate strong, broad-based support for reintroduction of the Mexican wolf. Previous authors and accounts have doomed the Mexican wolf to extinction or permanent life in captivity (Brown 1983, Burbank 1990). It is our hope that the unique ecological role of the Mexican wolf will be restored in the southwestern U.S.

The Blue Range Primitive Area, eastern Arizona, close to New Mexico, is a potential release site for the Mexican wolf. Several other sites have been examined. (Photo: D. Parsons)

Monitoring of a Recovering Gray Wolf Population in Wisconsin, 1979-1991

■ Adrian P. Wydeven, Ronald N. Schultz, and Richard P. Thiel

The gray wolf was extirpated in Wisconsin in the late 1950's; a breeding population became reestablished in the 1970's. Wolf numbers have been monitored since 1979 by radio tracking, howling surveys, winter track surveys, and wolf observations from the public. Between 1979 and 1991, 64 wolves were radio-collared in Wisconsin and adjacent areas of Minnesota. The wolf population ranged from a low of 15 in 1985 to a high of 40 in winter 1991. The mean annual rate of increase (λ) was 1.21 from 1986 to 1991. Winter territory size averaged 137 km² (range = 47-287 km²) and year-round territory size averaged 179 km² (range = 49-323 km²). The mean dispersal distance of 16 wolves was 114 km; the longest being 480 km into Ontario. Humans caused 72% of mortality during 1979-1985, but only 22% in 1986-1992. Mean pack size has ranged annually from 2.6 to 6.2 ($\bar{x}$ = 3.9) and mean wolf density per occupied territory was 18.9/1,000 km², (range = 12.2 to 24.6 wolves/1,000 km²). Deer densities in wolf range have varied from 2,300 to 12,000 deer/1,000 km²; winter territory size of wolf packs was negatively related to deer density (p < 0.01). Circumstantial evidence indicated that canine parvovirus was prevalent in the mid-1980's and may have caused high mortality of wolves.

Introduction

Gray wolves (*Canis lupus*) originally ranged across most of North America, including the present State of Wisconsin (Jackson 1961, Hall 1981). Wisconsin was within the western portion of the range of the eastern timber wolf (*Canis lupus lycaon*) as described by Young and Goldman (1944), but Nowak (1983) suggested that Wisconsin's wolves may have been more closely related to those in the central and western United States.

Jackson (1961) estimated Wisconsin's wolf population in 1835 prior to European settlement at 20,000–25,000, but the estimate was probably too high based on recent research. A more realistic estimate for an area the size of Wisconsin (145,000 km²) would be about 3,000–5,000 wolves (Wydeven 1993). The demise of this wolf population to zero wolves occurred over about 130 years. Human persecution, loss of habitat, and reduction of ungulates eliminated wolves from most of southern and central Wisconsin by 1900 (Jackson 1961). The bounty system that lasted from 1865 to 1957, was a major factor in reducing wolves. The population was 100 animals or fewer by the early 1940's, and by 1950 was reduced to less than 50 wolves (Thiel 1993).

Despite the designation of a protected status in 1957, breeding populations disappeared from the state by the late 1950's (Thiel 1978). Between 1960 and 1975 the wolf was considered extirpated, although scattered observations of singles and pairs persisted (Thiel 1978). By the mid 1970's wolves were recolonizing Wisconsin (Mech and Nowak 1981, Thiel and Welch 1981). The U.S. Fish and Wildlife Service (USFWS) granted protection for the eastern timber wolf as an endangered species in 1974 and the Wisconsin Department of Natural Resources (WDNR) reclassified the wolf as endangered in 1975.

Since 1979 the WDNR has monitored the status of the wolf population in the state. Study objectives were to determine: population status, pack sizes and distributions, mortality factors and rates, productivity, rates of recolonization, dispersal behaviour, and disease/health status. This paper summarizes the result of that monitoring through 1991.

Study Area

Wolf population monitoring was done in the mixed conifer-hardwood forest region of northern Wisconsin (Curtis 1959). About 70% of the area is forested, consisting of 31% maple-birch (*Acer-Betula*), 33% aspen-birch (*Populus-Betula*), 8% pine and pine barrens (*Pinus* spp.), 5% boreal forest, 8% lowland conifers, 7% lowland hardwoods, and 6% oak (*Quercus*) (Spencer et al. 1988). Nonforested areas generally include bogs, forest openings, old fields, pasture, farmland, roads and residential/commercial areas. Numerous lakes dot the landscape, with several areas of extensive lake concentrations. Topography is flat to rolling and elevations range from 183 m at Lake Superior to 593 m; much of northern Wisconsin is part of a plateau with elevation generally from 420 m to 500 m (Black 1964). The area has an extensive network of road systems, and wolves generally occupied areas with low road densities (Thiel 1985). White-tailed deer (*Odocoileus virginianus*) were the only ungulates inhabiting the area in significant numbers (Creed et al. 1984). A small number of moose (*Alces alces*) were present (Krefting 1974), and beaver (*Castor canadensis*) were abundant.

Methods

Monitoring of wolves was conducted via radio-tracking marked individuals, winter track surveys, and summer howling surveys. Additional wolf distribution data were obtained by reports from government workers and the general public.

Wolves monitored by radiotelemetry were initially caught with number 4 or number 14 offset foothold traps (Kuehn et al. 1986) and tranquillized either with ketamine hydrochloride and promazine hydrochloride (Fuller and Kuehn 1983) or telatemine hydrochloride and zolazepam hydrochloride (Kreeger et al. 1990). Wolves were weighed, ear-tagged, and measured, then examined for parasites and injuries, treated with antibiotics, and fitted with radio collars (217-218 MHz; Telonics Inc., Mesa, Arizona) (Mech 1974a). We used tooth eruption, tooth wear, and reproductive status to age wolves as pups (< 12 months starting 1 April), yearlings (12–24 months) or adults (> 24 months). Blood samples for assessing metabolic conditions, and testing for diseases were collected from most individuals (Seal et al. 1975, Goyal et al. 1986). Trapping was conducted throughout northern Wisconsin and in adjacent Pine County, Minnesota.

Radio-collared wolves were located from the air or ground once or twice per week throughout the year, and locations were plotted on topographic maps (1:24,000 or 1:100,000). Home range sizes were determined using the minimum area polygon (Mohr 1947). Locations 5 km or more from other locations or inside other pack territories were excluded from calculation of home range area or territory size (Fuller 1989). We used the seasonal territorial periods of Fuller (1989) for "summer" (15 April–14 September) and "winter" (15 September–14 April). Because 30–35 locations are needed to describe winter territories (Fuller and Snow 1988), only wolves with 30 or more locations per winter were used to determine home range or winter territory size. The summer period is shorter and therefore a minimum of 25 locations were used to calculate home range for that season. Year-round home range or territories were calcu-

lated for wolves from which at least 50 locations were obtained, including at least 20 locations for each period.

Dispersal distances were calculated from the initial capture site to the last location of a wolf. Dispersals were movements of 5 km or more from the natal or established territory. Calculations were made only for wolves whose final fate was known, or for wolves having ≥ 10 locations within 5 km of each other in an area outside the original territory (indicating a new territory was established).

Summer pup production by packs and locations of non radio-collared packs was determined by howling surveys (Harrington and Mech 1982b). Although pup production was documented, data on litter production and size were considered too sparse to describe overall recruitment into the population and therefore that subject is not included in this paper. Winter track surveys were conducted within a few days after fresh snow by following forest roads and trails by vehicle and on foot (Thiel 1978, Thiel and Welch 1981). By locating urination markings and examining urine for presence of blood, terrotoriality and breeding status of wolves were determined (Peters and Mech 1975, Rothman and Mech 1979). Public sightings were verified by examining locations and interviewing observers. Only verified observations were included in wolf population estimates.

Radio-collared wolves found dead in the field were necropsied by the USFWS National Wildlife Health Lab [now called National Biological Service, National Wildlife Health Center] in Madison, Wisconsin, unless decomposition was too extensive. Survival and mortality were determined on radio-collared wolves actively monitored from October 1979 to April 1992; annual survival rates of radio-collared wolves were determined by Micromort Computer analysis (Heisey and Fuller 1985).

Data on deer populations in areas occupied by wolves were obtained by using the sex-age-kill method (Creed et al. 1984). Annual deer densities for management units averaging 930 km^2 were compared to wolf populations to determine prey abundance.

Results

Between 1979 and 1991, 64 wolves (31 adults, 25 yearlings, and eight pups) were caught 72 times in Wisconsin (Table 1). Sex ratio of adults (58% males), pups (38% males), and yearlings (28% males) varied (P = 0.07). Mean weight of adult males (34.8 kg) was 24% heavier than females; yearling males were 11% heavier than yearling females (Table 1).

A total of 3,945 radio locations were obtained on the wolves. The mean home range size between various sex-age groups of wolves did not differ (P > 0.10, Table 2). Mean home range of all adults was 136 km^2 in summer, 137 km^2 in winter, and 179 km^2 year-round. Although no obvious shifts occurred between winter and summer home ranges,

Table 1. Numbers and weights of wolves captured and radio-collared in Wisconsin and Pine County, Minnesota, 1979–1991.

Age/Sex	N		Weights (kg) $\bar{x}$	Range
Adult Males	21[1]	(18)	34.8	26-46
Adult Females	16	(13)	28.1	21-34
Yearling Males	7	(7)	28.4	23-35
Yearling Females	18	(18)	25.7	18-31
Pup Males	5	(3)	12.8	6-20
Pup Females	5	(5)	10.8	8-15

1 Number of captures; number in parentheses are the total number of wolves.

Table 2. Home range of wolves radio-tracked in Wisconsin and adjacent areas of Minnesota, 1980-1990.

Age/Sex	Season[1]	N	Home range (km^2) $\bar{x}$	Range
Adult Males	Summer	14	122	(50-310)
	Winter	9	130	(47-258)
	Year-round	8	169	(84-323)
Adult Females	Summer	10	155	(38-312)
	Winter	12	142	(48-287)
	Year-round	7	191	(49-296)
Yearling Males	Summer	3	141	(103-200)
	Winter	1	108	
	Year-round	1	139	
Yearling Females	Summer	9	126	(30-264)
	Winter	5	180	(78-227)
	Year-round	5	235	(145-312)
Pup Females	Winter	3	129	(116-146)

1 Season: Summer = 15 April — 14 September; Winter = 15 September — 14 April.

the increased size of year-round home range suggests a slightly different use pattern of the pack territory seasonally.

Because pup home ranges generally were smaller than the extent of pack territories, and yearlings often had home ranges that extended outside areas occupied by dominant adults in packs, the radio locations of adults seemed to be the best indicator of pack territory size. Therefore, we used data on adults when available to describe territory size and location.

Sixteen radio-collared wolves dispersed a mean distance of 114 km, with distance seeming to be shorter for older wolves (Table 3). The longest dispersal involved a yearling female that moved 480 km from north-central Wisconsin to the Rainy Lake area of Ontario between November 1988 and November 1989. Seven (44%) of the dispersers moved into territories or vacated areas adjacent to their original territory (≤ 23 km). Of 14 dispersing wolves originally caught in Wisconsin, six moved into Minnesota, one into Michigan,

Table 3. Dispersal distances of wolves caught in Wisconsin and Pine County, Minnesota.

Sex/Age	N	Dispersal distances (km)	
		$\bar{x}$	range
Adult Males	2	14	11- 18
Adult Females	5	67	14-270
Yearling Males	4	90	23-249
Yearling Females	4	218	99-480
Pup Female	1	234	-
All Dispersers	**16**	**114**	**11-480**

Table 4. Mean annual survival and mean annual mortality for radio-collared wolves ≥ 1 year old in Wisconsin and adjacent areas of Minnesota during two periods. (October 1979–December 1985, January 1986–April 1992).

Period	Mean annual survival rate	Mean annual mortality rate	Mortality factors
1979-1985 (33 Wolves)[1]		0.28	Human caused[2]
		0.08	Natural
		0.02	Unknown mortality
	0.61	0.39	Total mortality
1986-1992 (28 Wolves)[1]		0.04	Human caused[2]
		0.11	Natural mortality
		0.02	Unknown mortality
	0.82	0.18	Total mortality

1   Total wolves monitored were 57, and four wolves were monitored during both periods.
2   Human caused mortality included seven shootings and one trapping; 17 total mortalities were recorded on actively monitored wolves.

one into Ontario, and six to other locations in Wisconsin. One of the two dispersing wolves originally caught in Minnesota moved into Wisconsin and the other moved to another location in Minnesota. Six of eight wolves dispersing as yearlings left their packs in fall or early winter, and four of seven adults dispersed in the fall. Only one pup dispersed, and it apparently left its natal territory in late winter. The oldest dispersing wolf was an adult female who had been the alpha female of a pack in east Minnesota before she dispersed at age $\geq$ 4, and joined a dispersing yearling male to

form a new pack in Wisconsin. At least one other dispersing wolf was known to establish a new pack.

A mean of 9% of adults and 23% of yearlings being monitored dispersed per year. These rates were probably minimum, because loss of some radio signals were probably due to undetected dispersal.

Annual survival and cause-specific mortality rates (Heisey and Fuller 1985) were determined from telemetry data on 57 wolves and 17 wolf deaths. Mean annual survival rate of actively monitored wolves one year old or more increased

Table 5. Midwinter wolf population estimates and areas occupied by wolf packs in Wisconsin, 1979–1991.

Year	Minimum Wolf Mid-Winter Population	No. lone wolves	No. of packs	Mean Pack size	Area of Occupied territories (km^2)	Wolf Density per $1000km^2$ of occupied territories
1979-1980	25	-	5	5.0	1,076	24.6
1980-1981	21	-	5	4.2	1,279	17.2
1981-1982	27	2	4	6.2	956	24.4
1982-1983	19	2	5	3.4	1,279	13.6
1983-1984	17	1-2	4	4.2	987	17.4
1984-1985	15	1	3	4.0	703	17.5
1985-1986	16	3	5	2.6	1,098	12.2
1986-1987	18	?	5	3.4	867	20.0
1987-1988	27	2-3	6	3.8	907	24.2
1988-1989	31	2	7	4.0	1,282	22.2
1989-1990	34	2	11	3.0	2,043	15.6
1990-1991	40	2	12	3.2	2,098	18.3

from 0.61 during 1979–1985, to 0.82 in 1986–1992 (P < 0.10, Table 4). Overall average annual survival rates of adult males (0.66) did not differ from adult females (0.74, P > 0.10). Adult females did not differ from yearling females (0.74, P > 0.10). Data on male yearlings and pups were too sparse to compare to adults.

Mortality shifted from mainly human-caused deaths (72%) in 1979–1985 to higher rates of natural mortality (61%) during 1986–1992. Natural mortality was nearly equally divided between disease and death caused by other wolves (Table 4).

Among all 29 radio-collared wolves found dead in 1979–1991 (including 12 wolves not used in the micromort analysis), 15 died from human-caused mortality (including 12 shootings), three were killed by other wolves, four died of disease, three died from unknown natural causes, and four died from undetermined causes. Mortality was recorded for all months except April, and 20 (69%) occurred from August to December. The major disease that seemed to impact wolves during the study period was canine parvovirus. Between 1982 and 1986, 24 (75%) of 32 wolves tested positive for parvovirus (hemagglutination inhibition test). During the period 1988 through 1991, four (29%) of 14 wolves tested positive for parvovirus (immunoflurencence test). Although some of the difference in positive reaction between 1982–1986 and 1988–1991 may have been due to the type of tests

used, it appeared that the incidence of parvovirus declined (Thiel, unpubl. data).

Overall midwinter population estimates ranged from 15 to 40 wolves (Table 5). These estimates represented minimum counts as they probably did not include all lone wolves. Wolves and wolf packs that occurred near the Minnesota border and spent a large part of their time in Wisconsin were included as part of the Wisconsin population.

The wolf population declined in the early 1980's, possibly because of the spread of canine parvovirus and low adult survival from human-caused mortality. Between 1986 to 1991 the wolf population increased annually at a mean λ of 1.21 (range = 1.10 — 1.50).

Total area occupied by wolf packs doubled between 1979 and 1991, but the mean wolf density in occupied territories (intrapack density) varied, and averaged 18.9 per 1,000 km^2. Highest wolf density occurred in 1979–1980, 1981–1982, and 1987–1988 when the density exceeded 24 wolves/1,000 km^2 of territory and the lowest was in 1985–1986 when the overall population was only 16. Mean pack size has remained relatively low in Wisconsin, ranging from 2.6 to 6.3 (overall $\bar{x}$ = 3.9).

In the 1970's breeding packs became established in Douglas County in northwest Wisconsin (Fig. 1). Wolves appeared approximately the same time in Lincoln County in north-central Wisconsin. Activity of one or two loners was detected in northeast Wisconsin, but no packs were found.

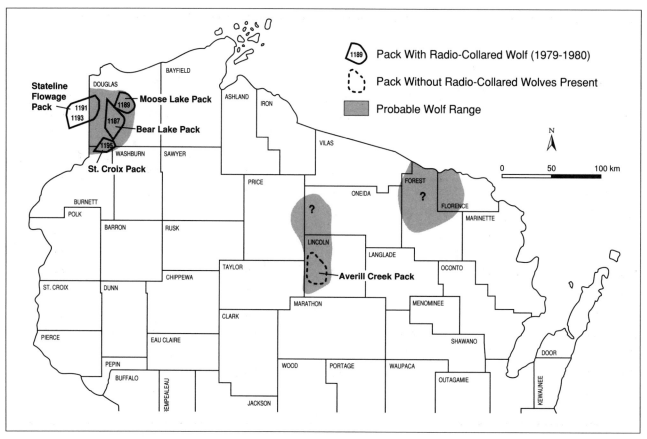

Fig. 1 *Gray wolf distribution in northern Wisconsin: Winter 1979–1980.*

Although the statewide population had declined to about 16 by 1986, wolves had spread into Bayfield county and between Price and Oneida Counties (Fig. 2). The Wisconsin wolf population reached its highest level since the early 1950's in 1990-1991, with about 40 wolves counted in 12 packs, and observations of wolves were reported from throughout the northern part of the state (Fig. 3).

Because white-tailed deer are the most important food of wolves in Wisconsin (Thompson 1952, Mandernack 1983), comparisons were made of wolf and deer population density in five deer management units (Table 6). The average density of units 30 and 31 were used because the Bootjack Lake Pack straddled both. The overall wolf:deer ratios were very high and averaged 18 wolves and 7,200 deer per 1,000 km^2 of wolf territory.

A significant inverse relationship (P < 0.01) existed for winter territory size and deer density (Fig. 4). The largest winter territories of 250-300 km^2 occurred at low deer densities ($\approx$2/km^2), while small territories of 50 km^2 occurred at high deer densities (7-11/km^2).

Discussion

Mean winter wolf pack territory size of 137 km^2 found for northern Wisconsin was within the range of sizes (110- >

190 km^2) found in Minnesota studies (Mech 1973, Van Ballenberghe et al. 1975, Fritts and Mech 1981, Berg and Kuehn 1982, Fuller 1989). In Minnesota, Ontario, and Quebec wolf territory size in winter is influenced by deer density (Fuller 1989), as was found in this study. Fluctuation in deer density and variability in deer habitat quality contribute to the wide range of winter territory size in Wisconsin.

Except in Douglas County, most wolf territories in Wisconsin do not abut other territories, but rather exist as "islands," similar to the situation found at the southern edge of the wolf range in Minnesota (Berg and Kuehn 1982). Areas occupied by wolf packs were usually wildland areas with low road densities (Thiel 1985).

Dispersing wolves most frequently moved northwest into Minnesota, but movement northeast to Michigan also occurred (Thiel 1988). Mean dispersal distance for Wisconsin wolves of 114 km was higher than mean dispersal of 77 km for northeast Minnesota (Gese and Mech 1991) but lower than the mean of 130 km for northwest and north-central Minnesota (S.H. Fritts, U.S. Fish and Wildlife Service, pers. commun.). The 480 km dispersal record for a wolf from northcentral Wisconsin to western Ontario is exceeded in the Great Lakes region only by the 886 km dispersal of a Minnesota wolf into Saskatchewan (Fritts 1983).

Table 6. Density of wolves and deer per 1,000 km2 of occupied wolf territory in Wisconsin, 1980-1991.

Deer mgt. unit	County	Mean Area of wolf territories (km^2)	Species	Mean Density	Range
4	Douglas	660	Wolf	15	7-22
			Deer	5,600	2,300-9,300
5[1]	Bayfield	111	Wolf	22	9-45
			Deer	9,100	5,400-12,000
30 & 31	Price and Oneida	284	Wolf	10	4-18
			Deer	7,000	4,200-10,800
32	Lincoln	237	Wolf	26	9-37
			Deer	8,100	5,000-11,600

1   Data for Unit 5 covers only the period 1985-1991.

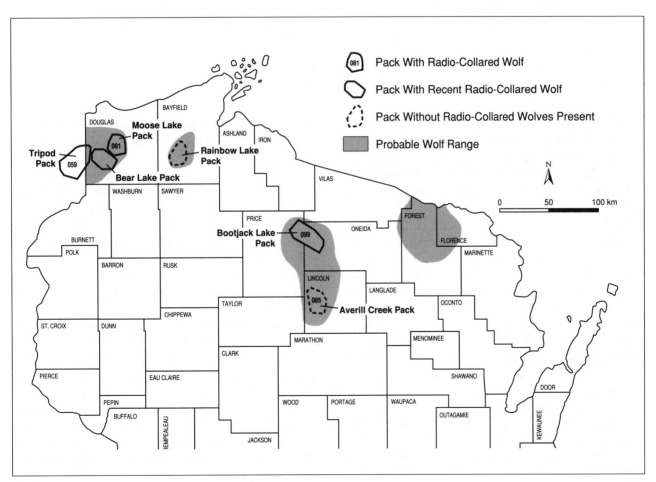

Fig. 2   *Gray wolf distribution in northern Wisconsin: Winter 1985-1986.*

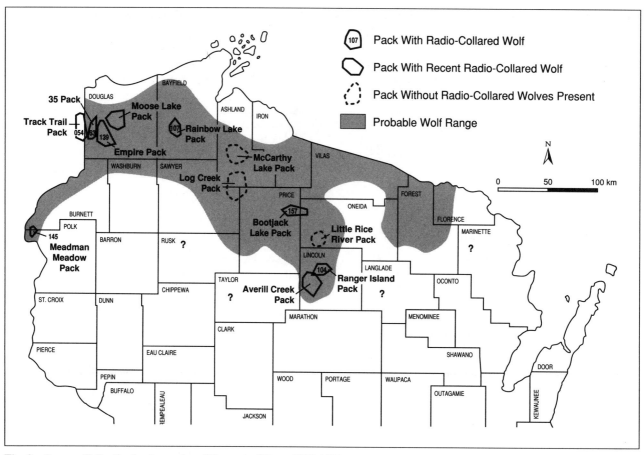

Fig. 3 *Gray wolf distribution in northern Wisconsin: Winter 1990-1991.*

Only one of eight monitored pups was thought to have dispersed from a Wisconsin wolf pack. Pup dispersal was also rare ($\leq 10\%$) in other wolf populations (Fritts and Mech 1981, Ballard et al. 1987, Fuller 1989, Gese and Mech 1991, Boyd et al. this volume). Often 50% or more of dispersers are yearlings (Fritts and Mech 1981, Ballard et al. 1987, Fuller 1989, Gese and Mech 1991, Boyd et al. this volume), but Messier (1985b) found only one of seven dispersing wolves to be a yearling. Peterson et al. (1984) indicated that no dispersal apparently occurred among alpha wolves on the Kenai Peninsula, Alaska. An adult female in this study had been the breeding female in a pack in eastern Minnesota before she dispersed and established a new pack in north-western Wisconsin. Gese and Mech (1991) reported that dispersing adults had a high degree of success at settling, pairing, and denning, whereas yearlings had moderate success and pups low success.

Obviously the Wisconsin population would have increased at a higher rate if more dispersers had remained in the state, paired, and denned there. The incidence of wolves successfully settling, pairing, and denning (three of 16) appeared lower than in Minnesota (Berg and Kuehn 1982, Fuller 1989, Gese and Mech 1991), especially northwestern

Minnesota where dispersers (primarily yearlings) played a major role in rapid population recovery (Fritts and Mech 1981).

The importance of humans as a mortality factor (72%) among radio-collared Wisconsin wolves in 1979-1985 was similar to that reported in north-central Minnesota (77%-80%, Berg and Kuehn 1982, Fuller 1989). Human-caused mortality of wolves accounted for only 42% of the losses in northeast Minnesota (Mech 1977c). The decline of human-caused deaths to 22% of total mortality in Wisconsin probably was a major factor in the increase of the wolf population during 1986-1991.

Mean annual survival for yearling and adult wolves was 0.61 during 1979-1985 when wolves declined in Wisconsin. Between 1986-1991 when wolf populations increased at an average annual rate of $\lambda = 1.21$, mean annual survival was 0.82. Mean annual survival was 0.67 for wolves on the Kenai Peninsula in Alaska (Peterson et al. 1984), 0.64 for wolves in north-central Minnesota (Fuller 1989), and 0.62 for wolves in northwestern Minnesota (S.H. Fritts, U.S. Fish and Wildlife Service, pers. commun.). Peterson et al. (1984) estimated that survival rates of 0.67 or less could prevent wolf increases, although both the Minnesota and Alaska populations

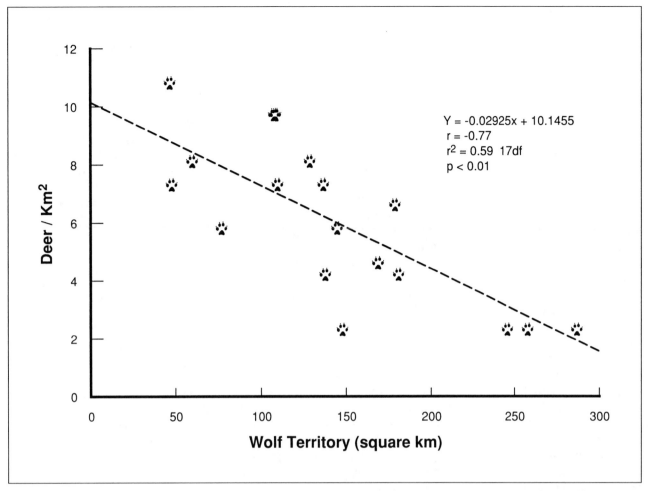

Fig. 4 *Wolf winter territory size compared to deer density in five deer management units of northern Wisconsin: 1980-1990.*

were stable or slightly increasing. The survival rates do seem to correspond well to population changes in Wisconsin.

Between 1979 and 1985 when Wisconsin's wolves declined, the majority of captured wolves tested positive for exposure to canine parvovirus, but during the period of increase, less than one third tested positive. Mech and Goyal (1993) found that annual population changes of wolves was inversely related to the percentage of wolves testing serologically positive for parvovirus, with increases in the population generally occurring when the percentage of wolves testing positive was less than 51%.

Mean pack size of 3.9 in Wisconsin is among the smallest reported. Elsewhere in the Great Lakes region mean pack sizes have ranged from 4.3–8.0 (Pimlott et al. 1969, Mech 1977c, Fritts and Mech 1981, Fuller 1989). Low pack size has been related to low density prey populations (Mech 1977c, Messier 1985a) and high human exploitation rates (Peterson et al. 1984) A newly established population in northwest Minnesota also had small packs ($\bar{x} = 4.3$); however, this was in part the result of averaging in newly formed

pairs, which were common in that increasing population (Fritts and Mech 1981).

Wolf densities in Wisconsin have fluctuated from 12 to 25 wolves per 1,000 km^2. Although densities as high as 91 wolves/1,000 km^2 occurred on Isle Royale (Peterson and Page 1988), wolf densities generally do not average more than 40 wolves/1,000 km^2 over large geographic areas for long periods of time (Pimlott et al. 1969, Mech 1973, Van Ballenberghe et al. 1975, Nelson and Mech 1986a, Fuller 1989).

The ungulate density in Wisconsin 2,300–12,000/1,000 km^2 appears to vary similarly to those found elsewhere in North America (Fuller 1989). Densities of wolves and deer in deer management units give a general impression of high prey abundance. Using the index developed by Fuller (1989), the ungulate biomass ratio per wolf in Wisconsin deer management units ranged from 311 to 700. Ungulate biomass index ratios per wolf for other areas of North American ranged from 112 to 659 (Fuller 1989). These ratios suggest an abundant food supply for wolves in Wisconsin.

Adrian P. Wydeven, Ronald N. Schultz, and Richard P. Thiel

Wisconsin's wolf population increased over the 12-year period of monitoring. The population of 40 wolves present in 1991 is one-half of the state recovery goal of 80 wolves (Thiel 1989). If this rate is maintained the population goal could be achieved by 1995.

Conclusion

Despite favorable wolf population performance in Wisconsin in recent years, the species may continue to face some major problems. Canine parvovirus has been apparently prevalent in Wisconsin and Minnesota (Mech et al. 1986) wolves. Although there is some evidence that parvovirus may be declining in Wisconsin, because of high potential losses due to the disease (Goyal et al. 1986), it will continue to pose a threat to wild wolves even at moderate levels. Other diseases may also pose specific threats to small isolated populations such as Wisconsin's wolves.

There are several indications that exploitation and/or high losses of pups are still occurring in Wisconsin's wolf population. Wolves in Wisconsin occur at densities below those found in saturated populations in Minnesota and Ontario, despite the high prey base. Packs are smaller than in other populations in the Great Lakes Region, and the finite rate of increase (λ) is below the potential maximum that would be expected with such high deer populations available.

Successful reestablishment of the wolf in Wisconsin depends on implementation of the State Recovery Program (Thiel 1989). Educational efforts need to continue to improve public perception of wolves. Enforcement of legal protection and prosecution of illegal killing should continue. The integrity of suitable wolf habitat must be protected by maintaining wildland with low road densities and low human populations (Fuller et al. 1992a). Monitoring of populations and disease status should continue to provide surveillance of new diseases entering the population, to determine potential environmental threats to wolf habitat, and to assess the general well-being of this recovering population.

Acknowledgments

Funding for this study has come from U.S. Fish and Wildlife Service, Endangered Species Grants Programs Section 6 (Job 101) and Section 15 (Job 104 and 105); Wisconsin Federal Aid in Wildlife Restoration Project W-154-R; Wisconsin Endangered Resources Fund; Chequamegon National Forest; Nicolet National Forest; Timber Wolf Alliance; and contributions from the general public. Many people assisted and provided guidance on the project over the last 12 years including some of the following: L.J. Prenn, T.J. Meier, F.A. Iwen, S.H. Fritts, N.J. Thomas, R.G. Grant, D.P. Shelley, T. Kaminski, P. Freeman, C. Schultz, L.D. Mech, T. Amundson, J.R. Archer, S.J. Taft, M.M. Maula, R.L. Jurewicz, W.S. Meier, J.W. Burch, J. Zuba, B.A. Mandernack, D. J. Groebner, W.L. Robinson, J.W. Scheier, R.J. Welch, as well as many WDNR wildlife managers, wildlife technicians, conservation wardens, and other field personnel. Aerial radio locations of radio-collared wolves have been obtained from WDNR pilots under the direction of F.E. Kruger, Jr., D.A. Doberstein, J. Dienstl, J. Weiss, D. Kroll, and R. Mickelson. Many useful comments were provided by reviewers including T.K. Fuller, L.E. Gregg, W.B. Ballard, G.C. Haber, S.H. Fritts, C.A. Shanks, K.A. Bauer, S.A. Walker, and P. Smith.

Red Wolf Reintroduction Program

■ Michael K. Phillips, Roland Smith, V. Gary Henry, and Chris Lucash

Following an education program, 36 captive-born red wolves were released at the Alligator River National Wildlife Refuge in northeastern North Carolina from September 1987 through March 1992. In several instances wide-ranging movements within two months after release created management situations or led to an animal's death. As a result, intensive management of the wolves was required throughout the reintroduction. Twenty-one released wolves died, mainly from automobile strikes, intraspecific aggression, or drowning. Seven wolves were removed for management reasons, six were free-ranging through March 1992, and the fate of two is unknown. A minimum of 17 wolves have been born in the wild, of which 14 were free-ranging through March 1992. Survival of wild-born pups was significantly greater than released captive-born pups. Successfully established wolves utilized home ranges of 50–100 km^2 and preyed primarily on white-tailed deer, raccoons, and marsh rabbits. As of March 1992, 26 zoological institutions were involved in the captive breeding program, propagation projects involving free-ranging wolves had been established on three islands, and four red wolves had been released in the Great Smoky Mountains National Park, Tennessee.

Introduction

Red wolves (*Canis rufus*) ranged throughout the southeastern United States (U.S.) before European settlement of that region, but by 1980 were considered extinct in the wild [McCarley and Carley 1979, U.S. Fish and Wildlife Service (USFWS) 1990c]. Demise of the species was due to many factors. Man's persecution of wild canids and destruction of habitat forced the last few red wolves to use marginal habitat in Louisiana and Texas where they bred with coyotes (*Canis latrans*) and suffered heavy parasite infestation (Goldman 1944; Carley 1975; Nowak 1972, 1979). The plight of the species was recognized in the early 1960's (McCarley 1962); the red wolf was listed as endangered in 1967, and a recovery program was initiated after passage of the Endangered Species Act of 1973 (ESA) (Public Law No. 93-205). During the early 1970's, the USFWS realized that recovery could only be achieved through captive breeding and reintroductions.

Captive Breeding

By 1976, a captive breeding program was established utilizing 17 red wolves captured in Texas and Louisiana (Carley 1975, USFWS 1990c). In 1977, the first pups were born in the captive program. By 1985, six zoological facilities held red wolves and the captive population had grown to 65 individuals.

With the species reasonably secure in captivity the USFWS initiated a reintroduction project in 1987. Because the reintroduction represented the first attempt in history to restore a carnivore species that was determined to be extinct in its former range, the project generated tremendous public interest. From September 1987 through April 1991, 19 more zoological facilities committed themselves to maintaining red wolves, and the annual federal budget for captive breeding increased from about $30,000 to $191,000. As of 31 March 1992, 129 red wolves existed in captivity.

Red Wolf Recovery/Special Survival Plan

In 1984, the red wolf was selected for inclusion in the American Association of Zoological Parks and Aquaria Species Survival Plan (Plan) program. Inclusion in this program provided the impetus and expertise needed to intensify management of the species in captivity.

The Plan delineates and schedules actions necessary to ensure genetic stability and reintroduction of the species to the wild (USFWS 1990c). Specifically, the goal of the plan is to maintain 80-85% of the genetic diversity found in original founder stock for at least 150 years. This goal is equivalent to preserving 90% of the heterozygosity present in the existing captive population. A population viability analysis indicated that to meet the above objective, the USFWS would have to establish and maintain 330 red wolves in captivity and 220 red wolves in the wild (USFWS 1990c).

Michael K. Phillips, Roland Smith, V. Gary Henry, and Chris Lucash

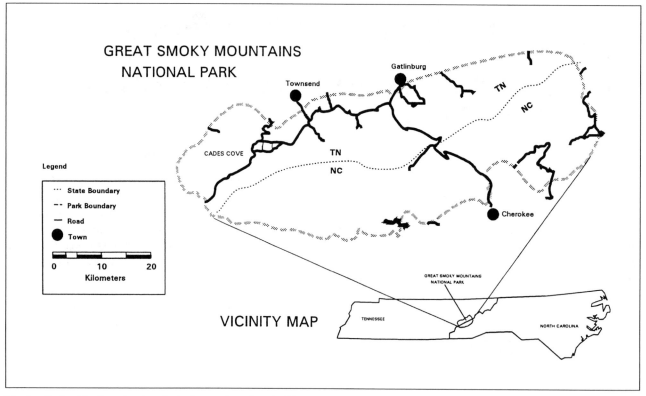

Fig. 1 *Red wolf reintroduction site in the southern Appalachian mountains.*

Reintroduction to Alligator River National Wildlife Refuge

Study Area

In 1987 a reintroduction project was initiated in northeastern North Carolina in the 63,636 ha Alligator River National Wildlife Refuge (ARNWR) and adjacent Department of Defense land, which covers 20,454 ha (Fig. 2). The reintroduction area consists of marshes, nonriverine swamp forests, and agricultural fields (Noffsinger et al. 1984). Climate of the area is characterized by hot summers, mild winters, and high humidity. The area is bisected by numerous logging roads; many are only seasonally passable with a four-wheel drive vehicle or on foot. The area supports abundant prey including white-tailed deer (*Odocoileus virginianus*), raccoons (*Procyon lotor*), and marsh rabbits (*Sylvilagus palustris*); but there are no coyotes, feral dogs, or livestock present. Additionally, the area is sparsely settled and surrounded on three sides by large bodies of water that wolves are not likely to cross.

Public Planning and Experimental/ Nonessential Designation

The decision to conduct the reintroduction was dependent upon public acceptance of the proposal (Parker 1986). The USFWS briefed representatives of environmental organiza-

tions in Washington, D.C., the North Carolina Congressional Delegation, the North Carolina Department of Agriculture, the Governor's office, local officials, and local landowners. The U.S. Air Force and Navy were briefed because they conduct training missions on 20,454 ha adjacent to the refuge. Numerous personal contacts were made with local citizens, especially hunters and trappers, in preparation for four public meetings held during February 1986. At the briefings and meetings considerable effort was made to explain the significance of the decision to consider reintroduced wolves as members of an "experimental/nonessential" population.

The experimental/nonessential designation was promulgated under the 1982 amendments to the ESA and provided the USFWS the opportunity to relax restrictions of the ESA to encourage cooperation from those likely to be affected by the reintroduction (Parker et al. 1986, Parker and Phillips 1991). The flexibility of the designation was important in soliciting support for the reintroduction. Not surprisingly, recovery plans calling for reintroduction of other endangered carnivores including the Northern Rocky Mountain wolf (*Canis lupus irremotus*) (USFWS 1987), Mexican wolf (*Canis lupus baileyi*) (USFWS 1982), and black-footed ferret (*Mustela nigripes*) (USFWS 1988b) indicate that reintroduced animals will probably be designated as members of experimental/nonessential populations.

The regulation developed for the reintroduction project prohibited taking of red wolves by the public to prevent the loss of livestock or property damage. In the event of depredations, citizens were required to contact USFWS or state conservation officers authorized to initiate control measures. Such control could include lethal means only if attempts to capture the animal(s) failed, or if there was clear danger to human life. No compensation program to offset depredations was developed because virtually no livestock existed in the area.

Human activities in the refuge included public trapping and hunting, which could accidentally kill a red wolf despite reasonable care by sportsmen. The USFWS proposed that prosecution not be pursued when the accident was unavoidable, unintentional, did not result from negligent conduct, and was immediately reported to authorized personnel. The regulation also stated that wolves could be taken in defense of human life, though such circumstances were considered extremely unlikely.

Acclimation

Wolves selected for release were taken from the USFWS's certified captive-breeding stock. Age, health, genetics, reproductive history, behavior, and physical traits representative of the species were considered in the selection process.

Before release, each wolf was acclimated in 225 m^2 pens at the refuge for periods lasting from two weeks to over two years. During acclimation we minimized human contact, hoping to reduce the wolves' tolerance of humans, varied the feeding regime to expose the animals to feast or famine, weaned the wolves from dog food and fed them an all meat diet, and provided the opportunity to hone predatory skills by giving them live prey.

During pre-release health checks we administered a standard series of canine vaccines, vitamin supplements, and a parasiticide; took blood samples; determined weights; and fitted wolves with motion-sensitive radio collars. The first nine adults were also implanted with abdominal transmitters as back-ups to radio collars. Nine of the first 10 adults were also implanted with radioactive tags that allowed us to assign collected scats to individual wolves (Crabtree et al. 1989). All pups were outfitted with abdominal transmitters at about 10 weeks of age.

Releases

From September 1987 through March 1992, 36 captive-born wolves (nine adult males, nine male pups, eight adult females, two yearling females, and eight female pups) were initially released on 14 occasions (Table 1). Most releases were carried out between August and October when pups were four to six months old. Unforseen circumstances resulted in most wolves being re-released on numerous occasions at various times of the year.

Animals were initially released either as members of nine adult pairs, four families, or one sibling group. Adults are defined as animals > 24 months of age, yearlings between 12–24 months, and pups ≤ 12 months.

White-tailed deer carcasses were placed at initial release sites with the intent of decreasing the chances of wolves immediately ranging widely in search of food. Supplemental feeding continued for one to two months after release to provide the wolves the opportunity to learn to successfully forage in unfamiliar terrain. Supplemental food was sometimes provided to wolves being re-released.

Results of Releases

Of the 36 animals released, 21 died, seven were removed from the wild for management reasons, the fate of two is unknown, and six are still free-ranging (Table 1). Total length of time in the wild was 16 to 1,254 days. Of the 21 wolves that died, 10 were pups, nine were released as adults, and one was released as a pup and died as a yearling. All animals removed for management reasons were initially released as adults. The two wolves with unknown fates were released as an adult and a pup. Of the six animals still free-ranging, all are now adults: one was released as an adult, one as a yearling, and four as pups.

Sixteen (59%) of 27 releases of adults or the yearling and 10 (55%) of 18 releases of pups, were considered failures: within two months we either had to return the wolf to captivity or it had died.

With the exception of three releases, acclimation periods for adults were purposefully lengthy ($\bar{x}$ = 13.7 months, SD = 9.1 months). The three releases of adults following short acclimation periods ($\bar{x}$ = 2.3 months, SD = 0.3 months) resulted in failure.

Intraspecific strife between recently released adults and established wolves was responsible for seven (44%) of the failures, whereas five failures (31%) were probably due to releasing wolves at biologically inappropriate sites. One failure (6%) resulted from a medical problem, and one failure (6%) resulted from the wolf wandering widely and eventually being struck and killed by an automobile. We do not know what prompted this animal to wander widely.

Although adult males were involved in 10 (71%) of 14 failures and adult females were only involved in six (46%) of 13 failures, the difference was not significant (Z = 1.32, 0.10 < P < 0.20). Adults released as members of a family were involved in five of eight failures, whereas adults released with just another wolf were involved in 12 (60%) of 20 failures; the difference was not significant (Z = 0.125, 0.10 < P < 0.20).

Of the 11 releases that resulted in the adults remaining in a free-ranging condition for more than two months, nine (82%) resulted in eight different adults (four males and four females) eventually producing pups in the wild.

For the 10 releases of pups that failed, five were due to intraspecific strife with established wolves, three were prob-

Table 1. Captive-born red wolves reintroduced in the Alligator River National Wildlife Refuge, eastern North Carolina, from September 1987 through March 1992.

Wolf # & sex	Release age (mos)	Period in Wild	#Days in wild[1]	Fate
140M	88	09/14/87-06/15/88	177	captured twice because frequenting a community and once because left reintroduction area, died after collision with automobile
184M	77	10/01/87-05/29/88	235	captured once to replace radio-collar, died after collision with automobile
194F	77	10/01/87-12/11/87	65	captured twice because left reintroduction area, not re-released after last capture
196F	77	10/01/87-06/25/88	267	captured once to replace radio-collar, died of uterine infection
205F	65	10/01/87-11/03/91	1,254	captured three times to replace radio collars, and twice for breeding purposes, remaining in captivity after last capture
208M	86	07/03/89-07/31/89	29	died after collision with automobile
211M	65	10/01/87-12/27/88	451	captured twice to replace radio-collar, died of suffocation
227M	53	10/01/87-09/05/89	108	captured once to replace radio-collar and once because frequenting a community, died of intraspecific aggression
231F	52	09/14/87-12/18/87	85	captured once for translocation, died of pleural effusion and internal bleeding
300F	23	04/12/88-present[2]	1,252	captured once for breeding purposes, once to replace radio-collar and once for management purposes, still free-ranging
304F	52	09/17/90-11/19/90	56	accidentally captured once, captured a second time and returned to captivity for breeding purposes
313F	28	08/22/89-09/18/91	407	captured once because left reintroduction area and twice because frequenting a community, returned to captivity after last capture
316F	28	09/04/89-12/27/89	115	radio-collar malfunctioned, fate unknown
319M	28	09/04/89-present	551	captured twice to replace radio collars, still free-ranging
322F	11	04/14/88-06/06/88	54	returned to captivity because frequenting a community
327M	40	09/17/90-10/04/90	18	drowned
328M	27	08/22/89-07/01/91	324	returned to captivity once because left reintroduction area, re-released and returned to captivity second time after being injured by automobile
331M	9	01/25/89-present	1,210	still free-ranging
332M	9	01/25/89-11/21/89	301	died after collision with automobile
337F	39	08/13/91-10/26/91	75	returned to captivity for breeding purposes
352M	28	08/13/91-09/15/91	34	died after collision with automobile
392M	3	08/01/89-present	943	captured once to replace radio-collar, still free-ranging
393F	3	08/01/89-01/24/90	177	died after collision with automobile
394F	3	08/01/89-present	971	captured once to replace radio-collar, still free-ranging
395F	3	08/01/89-01/11/90	164	drowned after being captured in a leghold traps set by a trapper
397M	5	09/17/90-10/12/90	18	accidentally captured once, drowned
398F	5	09/17/90-10/15/90	19	accidentally captured once, drowned
399F	5	09/17/90-10/12/90	16	accidentally captured once, last recorded location on 10/12/90, fate unknown, probably drowned
426M	5	10/03/90-07/15/91	286	died after collision with automobile
427M	5	10/03/90-10/20/90	18	shot
430F	5	10/03/90-present	592	still free-ranging
459M	5	08/13/91-09/09/91	28	died of intraspecific aggression
460M	5	08/13/91-09/09/91	28	died due of intraspecific aggression
461M	5	08/13/91-09/10/91	29	died of intraspecific aggression
462F	5	08/13/91-09/09/91	28	died due of intraspecific aggression
466F	5	08/13/91-09/12/91	31	died after collision with automobile

1 Not continuous due to varying periods of time in captivity between captures and releases.
2 Present continues through 31 March 1992.

Table 2. Red wolves born in the wild in the Alligator River National Wildlife Refuge, eastern North Carolina from May 1988 through March 1992.

Wolf # & sex	Litter #	Birth date[1]	Collar date[2]	Death date[3]	# Mos. alive[4]	Cause of death
344F	1	05/05/88	04/16/89	—	47	—
351F	2	04/28/88	11/10/88	01/24/91	33	intra-specific aggression
442M	3	05/07/90	09/11/90	—	23	—
443F	3	05/07/90	09/11/90	—	23	—
444F	3	05/07/90	01/23/91	—	23	—
496F	4	04/15/91	09/18/91	—	12	—
497M	4	04/15/91	09/30/91	—	12	—
498F	4	04/15/91	09/30/91	12/15/91	08	vehicle collision
499?	4	04/15/91	—	?	?	—
500F	5	05/01/91	08/15/91	—	11	—
501F	5	05/01/91	08/15/91	—	11	—
502F	5	05/01/91	08/23/91	—	11	—
503F	5	05/01/91	10/18/91	—	11	—
504M	5	05/01/91	10/18/91	—	11	—
505F	6	04/28/91	10/31/91	—	11	—
506M	6	04/28/91	11/14/91	—	11	—
507M	6	04/28/91	11/14/91	—	11	—
508?	6	04/28/91	—	?	?	—
509?	7	05/01/91	—	?	?	—
510?	8	05/01/90	—	?	?	—

1 Birth date was estimated based on movements of the adult pair.
2 All wolves, except 442M and 501F, wore functional radio collars since the date listed. The first radio collars worn by 442M and 501F malfunctioned which resulted in them being "off the air" from 11/23/90 -02/05/91 and 09/18/91 -10/17/91, respectively.
3 No date listed indicates that the wolf is still alive, except for 499, 508, 509, and 510 who were never captured.
4 Calculated by rounding to the nearest month.

---

ably due to social attachments to adults that were disrupted after the adults left the release area, one occurred because a pup was released at a biologically inappropriate site, and one was shot after wandering widely. The cause of this animal's wide movements was unknown.

Of the eight releases that resulted in pups remaining in a free-ranging condition for more than two months, two (25%) resulted in male pups attaining sexual maturity and producing pups. From the six pups that were free-ranging for more than two months but failed to breed in the wild, four died before reaching sexual maturity and two failed because they probably were subordinate females in the pack. Nonetheless, these six animals survived in the wild for an average of 13.8 months (SD = 10.6 months).

Reintroduced wolves were killed by one of at least seven mortality factors (Table 1). Automobile strikes (n = 8), in-

traspecific aggression (n = 5), and drownings (n = 4) were the predominant causes.

Three animals that drowned were members of a family that was released on Durant Island, which lies about 2 km north of ARNWR. Between two and 11 days after release these animals drowned while trying to swim across a 25-km expanse of water. Their wanderings were probably a result of a short acclimation period (2.2 months). The fourth animal that drowned did so after being captured in a leg-hold trap set for bobcats (*Felis rufus*).

The size of home ranges for reintroduced wolves that established themselves in the wild and wild-born wolves varied according to habitat. In a forested area consisting of pine/hardwood swamps in various stages of succession, the home range of one pack that included 11 different wolves was about 100 km². In agricultural areas consisting of

Table 3. Information about dispersal by red wolves born in the wild at the Alligator River National Wildlife Refuge, eastern North Carolina from May 1988 through March 1992.

Wolf # & sex	Dispersal date	age (mos)	Minimum distance and direction ravelled to new home range	Comments
344F	03/05/90	22	22 km southwest	established herself as breeding female in area
442M	01/10/92	20	21 km southwest	lone wolf
443F	10/21/91	17	21 km southwest	lone wolf
496F	12/25/91	8	35 km southwest	lone wolf
497M	11/25/91	7	79 km west	lone wolf
498F	11/15/91	7	13 km south	killed by automobile before she established home range
505F	02/09/91	10	85 km west	lone wolf

planted fields interspersed among early to mid-successional fallow fields and pine/hardwood stands, the home ranges of eight lone wolves and four packs involving 30 different wolves measured about 50 km^2. The relative abundance of prey in agricultural areas (Lee et al. 1982, Noffsinger et al. 1984) may account for the differences in home range size exhibited by red wolves.

A minimum of 20 wolves (five males, 12 females, and three unknown sex) were born in the wild (Table 2). The modal birth date was 1 May (n = 7). The proportion of females produced was not significantly greater than the proportion of males produced (x^2 = 2.88, 0.05 <P <0.10). Wild-born pups were members of eight litters produced by 11 adults (six males and five females). Two litters were produced in 1988, two in 1990, and four in 1991. No pups were born in the wild during 1989 because there were no adult pairs together during the breeding season. Only two (12%) of the 16 wild-born wolves whose fates are known died (Table 2), and these two survived for 1,006 and 244 days. In contrast 12 (75%) of 16 captive-born pups that we released survived an average of only 94 days (SD = 109 days). Survival of wild-born pups was significantly greater than captive-born pups that were released (x^2 = 12.69, P<0.001). As of 31 March 1992, wild-born wolves accounted for at least 74% of the free-ranging population (14 of 20).

Of the 16 wild-born wolves studied, seven dispersed from their natal home ranges between seven and 22 months of age (Table 3). These wolves traveled 13–85 km before establishing new home ranges. Only one disperser died; she was killed by an automobile. Two of the animals that dispersed left their natal home range while their parents were still present in the area. A parent or both parents of the other five dispersers had either died or been removed from the wild before the pup(s) dispersed. It seems possible that some of the pups that dispersed would not have done so if their parents had been present.

Scat analysis indicated that white-tailed deer, raccoon, and marsh rabbits accounted for 88.7% of the biomass consumed by wolves (Table 4). The percent biomass values presented for each food item are based on the model by Weaver (1993).

Management

Twenty-four of the 36 released wolves were recaptured 61 times, and 16 of the wild-born wolves were recaptured 33 times. Most captures were necessary in order to meet program objectives (replace radio collars, pair with a mate, translocate to a suitable site, etc.), although some wolves were accidentally captured in traps set for other wolves.

We used leg-hold traps (usually a modified number 3 Victor "soft-catch") for 76 captures, modified acclimation pens for 12 captures, dart rifles for five captures, and a box trap for one capture.

Involvement of Private Citizens and the Media

As expected, the reintroduction project attracted considerable interest from citizens and the media (Phillips 1990a). Thirty-five citizens (mostly college students) donated approximately 10,000 hours of volunteer time to the project. Local civic groups initiated fund-raising activities. Since the fall of 1986, a minimum of 22 magazines and 24 newspapers

Table 4. Prey contained in red wolf scats (n = 1,708) collected in the Alligator River National Wildlife Refuge, eastern North Carolina from September 1987 through March 1992.

Species[1]	No. of Occurences	% Scats[2]	% Biomass[3]
MAMMALIAN FOOD ITEMS			
Odocoileus virginianus (adult) (35.0)	706	59.4	39.2
Procyon lotor (8.0)	883	74.3	38.5
Sylvilagus palustris (1.1)	339	28.5	11.0
Mus musculus (0.025)	169	14.2	3.9
Odocoileus virginianus (juvenile) (15.0)	29	2.4	1.7
Sigmodon hispidus (0.08)	67	5.6	1.2
Ondatra zibethica (1.2)	25	2.1	0.8
Unid. rodent (0.025)	54	4.5	0.7
Myocaster coypu (6.5)	19	1.6	0.7
Sciuris carolinensis (0.4)	20	1.7	0.5
Capra hircus (35.0)	6	0.5	0.4
Oryzomysy palustris (0.035)	32	2.7	0.3
Microtus pennsylvanicus (0.04)	20	1.7	0.3
Mephitis (3.0)	7	0.6	0.3
Urocyon cinereoargenteus (8.0)	6	0.5	0.3
Didelphis marsupialis (4.0)	5	0.4	0.2
Peromyscus maniculatus (0.025)	20	1.7	0.1
Reithrodontomys humulis (0.025)	8	0.7	0.1
Lynx rufus (10.0)	1	0.1	tr[4]
NON-MAMMALIAN FOOD ITEMS			
Insects (n/a)[5]	300	17.6	n/a[5]
Seeds (n/a)	177	10.4	n/a
Birds (n/a)	158	9.2	n/a
Grass (n/a)	80	4.7	n/a
Reptile (n/a)	27	1.6	n/a
Amphibian Eggs (n/a)	23	1.3	n/a
Crustacean (n/a)	11	0.6	n/a
Turtle (n/a)	8	0.5	n/a
Fish (n/a)	2	0.1	n/a

1 The numeric value that follows the specific epithet is the assumed mean weight of the species in kgs for use in the biomass model.
2 Percent of scat does not indicate the relative amount of a food item consumed. It indicates the percent of the scats analyzed in which the item occurred.
3 Based on the model of Weaver (1993). See text for details.
4 trace is used to indicate less than 0.1%.
5 Biomass model does not apply to non-mammalian prey.

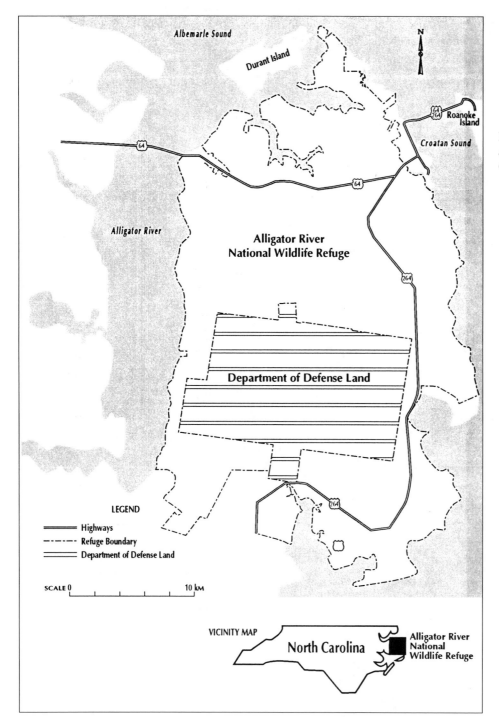

Fig. 2 *Red wolf reintroduction site in northeastern North Carolina.*

had published stories about the project (cf. Banks 1988). Additionally, the project was discussed during the nightly newscasts of five national and four regional television networks, and was the focus of four television documentaries including one produced by the Australian Broadcasting Company.

Private landowners also cooperated with the reintroduction. Their involvement came after prompting by the USFWS, which believed that wolves would disperse onto private land.

During April 1989, the USFWS negotiated leases with the two owners of Durant Island, a tract of land covering about 1,538 ha north of the refuge. Lease number 1 is renewed annually at a cost of $1. Lease number 2 is renewed every fourth year at a cost of $1. The leases provide the USFWS the legal right to release red wolves on the island.

In addition to the leases, the refuge negotiated a Memorandum of Understanding (MOU) with John Hancock Life Insurance (Philadelphia, Pa.). The MOU was signed on 15 February 1990, and designates approximately 18,218 ha of

John Hancock property as a conservation easement of the refuge. Due to the MOU, wolves can now inhabit the 18,218 ha owned by John Hancock in northeastern North Carolina. Seven red wolves were using this area in March 1992.

The 18,218 ha tract not only provides badly needed habitat, but acts as a corridor connecting ARNWR with the 44,534 ha Pocosin Lakes NWR (PLNWR). A proposal to expand the release area westward to include PLNWR is under consideration.

Reintroduction to Southern Appalachians

Study Area

The second reintroduction was initiated in the Southern Appalachian Mountains in 1991 at a site 960 km west of ARNWR. Climate in the area is characterized by warm, humid summers, and relatively mild winters. Precipitation averages 1,625 mm annually, with most in the form of snow at higher elevations.

Cades Cove, which is located in the Tennessee portion of the Great Smoky Mountains National Park (GSMNP), was chosen as the release site (Fig. 1). The Cove covers 10 km^2 of cleared pasture land interspersed with woodlots and surrounded by low mountains (1,200 m). A private livestock owner leases the Cove from the U.S. National Park Service (USNPS) to breed, calve, and maintain 300–500 Black Angus cattle. It is hoped that the abundance of natural prey and the protectiveness of cows will deter the wolves from taking calves.

Public Planning and Experimental/Nonessential Designation

USFWS and USNPS personnel spent a year developing strategy (Parker 1990) and assessing local interests and concerns. North Carolina and Tennessee congressional representatives, state wildlife agencies, state agricultural agencies, farm bureaus, local agricultural interests, and a variety of local organizations were apprised of the proposal. Details were presented to approximately 25 civic groups and organizations in the local communities. Articles concerning the proposal appeared in local and regional newspapers, and local radio and television stations featured the proposed reintroduction at various times. The two federal agencies developed and distributed educational materials concerning the proposal. A public education package was produced by a local television station in cooperation with the Southern Appalachian Man and the Biosphere Cooperative and the two federal agencies. The package includes a 30-minute video, a poster, and a teachers' packet; this material was distributed free to 400 schools in the area (Henry 1991b).

An experimental/nonessential designation was also used in the southern Appalachians reintroduction, with three differences from the rule developed for the ARNWR reintroduction. Livestock owners were permitted to harass red wolves that were pursuing or killing livestock on private

property, utilizing methods that are not lethal or physically injurious to the red wolf, provided that such incidents are reported to project personnel. In addition, after reporting attempted depredations and if efforts to capture depredating animals proved unsuccessful, the livestock owner was allowed to kill red wolves observed in the act of pursuing or killing livestock (Henry 1991a). And finally, a compensation program to offset depredations was developed and administered by the GSMNP Association.

Acclimation

Two pairs of adult red wolves were placed in 225 m^2 acclimation pens near the Cove during January 1991. Both pairs were allowed to breed to ensure that a family was available for release. Only one pair produced a litter, which consisted of five pups.

During acclimation, human contact was minimized; the wolves were provided dry dog food from automatic feeders and carcasses of white-tailed deer and pigs. A standard series of canine vaccines, heartworm preventative, and parasiticide were administered to all wolves.

Prior to release, the wolves were implanted with abdominal transmitters as backups to radio collars. Only two pups were readied for release in order to minimize stress to the adults and decrease the number of animals monitored. A vasectomy was performed on the adult male to prevent reproduction, while allowing reproductive behaviour, during the experimental phase. The wolves were allowed to recuperate for seven weeks, given final health checks, and released after 10 months of acclimation.

Release

On 12 November 1991, the family was released from the acclimation pen, with the gate left open so that the wolves could continue to use the pen. A deer carcass was placed at the release site in hopes of discouraging the wolves from immediately ranging widely in search of food. Supplemental feeding continued for several weeks to provide the wolves with an opportunity to learn to successfully forage in unfamiliar terrain.

During the first few months of the experiment the wolves wandered throughout the Cove. Analysis of 50 scats indicated that the wolves ate deer, rabbit (*Sylvilagus floridanus*), raccoon, grouse (*Bonasa umbellus*), and pigs.

Wolf-Human Interactions

Not only does the GSMNP have the highest visitor-use of any national park, but Cades Cove is particularly attractive to visitors because of an abundance of observable wildlife. During the first few weeks of the experiment the adult pair was frequently observed as they travelled and hunted in open pastures. By late December the adult male began exhibiting tolerance for humans and inhabited areas. He was captured on 21 January 1992 and returned to captivity. Since the male's return to captivity the other three wolves became more wary and were observed less frequently.

Wolf-Coyote Interactions

Coyotes were first reported in the Cove during the mid 1980's. Prior to 1992 there were approximately two to eight coyotes in the area. However, by March 1992 the coyote population had increased to 10–12 animals.

On 30 December 1991, project personnel heard the sounds of a "canid fight." Shortly thereafter, they saw the adult wolves chasing an uncollared coyote, while another coyote left the vicinity of the fight and moved into backcountry away from the Cove. The adult female wolf was later captured and examined; she had many healed wounds that could have been sustained during fights with coyotes.

One of the wolf pups was observed being chased by two coyotes in late February. In early March, sign indicated that the adult female wolf was displaced from an area by two coyotes. On 1 May, the adult female wolf and a pup were observed chasing a coyote through a pasture into a woodlot. After several minutes of barking and growling, the wolves pursued the coyote through another pasture and into another woodlot. More barking and growling ensued.

Wolf-Livestock Interactions

On five occasions, project personnel observed adult wolves within 100 m of only adult cattle. These interactions resulted in the wolves being chased from the area by the cattle. Calving season began in early March, and the wolves were located adjacent to the calving pasture during several evenings. Calving apparently attracted the wolves and coyotes to the area. Coyotes attacked at least three calves (one killed and two injured) and three calves disappeared. Wolves were implicated in one of the disappearances.

On two occasions, the adult male wolf killed domestic fowl. In late December 1991, he took a chicken from a barn at a residence in Cades Cove and in January 1992, he killed several domestic turkeys from a residence outside the GSMNP boundary.

Management

The adult male and one pup were recaptured because they exhibited movements or behavior that created management problems. The adult female was recaptured three times because of technical problems with the dart collar. The dart-collar was used to capture wolves on two occasions, and a dart gun, a leg-hold trap, and a modified acclimation pen were used to capture wolves on one occasion each.

Island Propagation Projects

In an attempt to reduce the reintroduction projects' dependence on captive-reared wolves, a strategy was developed to gradually infuse into reintroductions wolves experienced with life in the wild. This was accomplished by releasing adult red wolves and their 10- to 14-week-old pups

onto protected islands off the southeastern coast of the U.S. (Parker 1987). The islands utilized were Bulls Island, a 2,000 ha component of the Cape Romain National Wildlife Refuge off the coast of South Carolina; St. Vincent Island, a 5,003 ha National Wildlife Refuge off the coast of Florida; and Horn Island, a 1,477 ha component of the Gulf Island National Seashore.

From July 1988 through April 1991, seven adults produced 16 pups on the islands. The families were released on the islands on four separate occasions over a three-year period. All wolves were outfitted with radio transmitters before release. Animals were recaptured when the pups were nine months of age or older. By this time the pups and adults had gained experience in the wild and were available for permanent release at ARNWR or Cades Cove.

Of the 23 animals involved in island projects, two adults and one pup were transported to GSMNP, one adult and nine pups were transported to ARNWR, two pups were transported to other islands, and three pups were left on their natal islands and provided mates in hopes that they would breed. The remaining six wolves died before being removed from the islands: one pup and three adult females killed by alligators (*Alligator mississippiensis*), one adult female from pancreatic cancer, and one male of unknown causes.

Red wolf, born in captivity and reintroduced at Alligator River National Wildlife Refuge, North Carolina, feeding on antlered white-tailed deer, which it apparently killed. (Photo: B. Lea)

Conclusions

Two island-reared wolves were released at ARNWR. Although these animals quickly adjusted to life in the refuge, neither evinced unusual survival skills compared to captive-reared wolves released under similar circumstances. Indeed, one was killed by an automobile nine months after being released. Two "island" adults were transported to Cades Cove and released during November 1991. Within a few weeks the male was returned to captivity because of a high degree of tolerance for people. The female was still free-ranging on 31 March 1992. The reintroduction at ARNWR progressed well during the first four-and-a-half years (Phillips 1990b). As of 31 March 1992, a minimum of 19 wolves were free-ranging, including 14 wild-born animals. We feel that by every measure the reintroduction was successful and generated benefits that extended beyond the immediate preservation of red wolves, to positively affect local citizens and communities, larger conservation efforts and other imperiled species. During the ARNWR reintroduction two important points surfaced:

1. Wide-ranging movements that required management intervention (e.g. a wolf wandered outside the reintroduction area) or led to an animal's death soon after release were common. As a result, intensive monitoring and management of the wolves was required throughout

Red wolf, born in captivity and reintroduced at Alligator River National Wildlife Refuge, North Carolina, feeding on antlered white-tailed deer, which it apparently killed. (Photo: B. Lea)

the reintroduction. However, since every management issue that arose was resolved without inflicting long-term damage to the wolves and with little inconvenience to residents of the area, we know that wolves can be restored to at least northeastern North Carolina in a controlled manner.

2. Significant land-use restrictions were not necessary in order for wolves to survive. Indeed, the rather lenient hunting and trapping regulations for the refuge remained unchanged or were further relaxed during the experiment.

Red wolves can now inhabit approximately 95,951 ha of federal and private land in eastern North Carolina. The precedent established by the owners of Durant Island and John Hancock will hopefully prompt other landowners to cooperate with the recovery program. If this happens and if PLNWR is incorporated into the reintroduction, red wolves would have access to approximately 243,000 ha of suitable habitat. With adequate funding, it is reasonable to expect that 50–100 wolves could be restored to such an area within five to10 years.

Initial assessment of the Cades Cove release is positive. Currently there is acceptance of the program. Management objectives have been met by quickly recapturing wide-ranging and depredating wolves. Expedient compensation by the GSMNP Historical Association was made for wolf-related

Michael K. Phillips, Roland Smith, V. Gary Henry, and Chris Lucash

Captive breeding of red wolves has been an important element in this ecosystem restoration program. The Swift fox project in Canada and the red wolf project in the United States are both projects where captive breeding were used to return canid populations to areas of former abundance. (Photo: M. Phillips)

depredations. The adult pair of wolves was intolerant of and aggressive toward coyotes. Plans for an extended experimental phase are being considered that would include the release of a second family in Cades Cove and possibly the release of a third family at another site in the GSMNP.

Because of the ability of a satisfactory percentage of captive-reared wolves to adjust to life in the wild, wolves from the island propagation projects may not be necessary to recover the species. However, small sample size precludes conclusions concerning the comparative value of island wolves. Thus, the island propagation strategy will continue until sufficient data are available to determine its value. If the value is positive, the strategy will become a permanent component of the red wolf recovery program.

Red wolves can flourish in a wide variety of habitats. Hence, insufficient habitat and habitat destruction per se are not limiting red wolf recovery; there is sufficient habitat available to meet the population objectives outlined in the Recovery Plan (USFWS 1990c). However, much of that habitat is privately owned. Landowner support is therefore required for successful reintroduction initiatives. Thus, unlike most endangered species, recovery of the red wolf is not

so much dependent on the setting aside of undisturbed habitat as it is on overcoming the political and logistical obstacles to human coexistence with wild wolves. This may also be true for reintroductions of gray wolves in some areas.

Acknowledgments

Many people and organizations contributed to the red wolf project. Biologists M. Morse, A. Beyer, J. Dagen, J. Windley, and other field personnel contributed mightily. W. Parker, J. Taylor, and J. Johnson all provided guidance and support. B. Strawser helped with educational programs, volunteers, and procurement. B. Midgett and J. Lane provided secretarial and moral support. Other staff members at ARNWR also contributed. W. Waddell and S. Behrns from the Point Defiance Zoo and Aquarium and recovery team members D. Wood, and Drs. D. Mech, U. Seal, M. Pelton, and V. Nettles provided technical and moral support. S. Jackson, J. Walker, the North Banks Rotary Club, the Wake County Wildlife Club, the Coastal Wildlife Refuge Society, and the National Fish and Wildlife Foundation assisted with fund-raising.

Developing a State Timber Wolf Recovery Plan with Public Input: The Wisconsin Experience

■ Richard P. Thiel and Terry Valen

A 12-member wolf recovery team appointed by the Wisconsin Department of Natural Resources (DNR) developed a state recovery plan for the endangered eastern timber wolf between 1986 and 1989 using a conflict-resolution oriented Citizen Participation (CP) process. The recovery team used mass-produced and personal correspondence, presentations and media releases to inform the public of the team's responsibility, invite public input, keep the public apprised of progress, and to respond to requests for information on wolf ecology and management. Special meetings with affected interest groups were used to resolve conflicting views. A plan took form as work progressed through four public contact phases. This process enabled the team to address concerns, respond to requests for more information, and to mesh the ideas and concerns of Wisconsin citizens with the management needs for recovering this species. The CP process culminated in department approval of a state recovery plan in spring 1989. The plan to restore a population of 80 wolves in 10 packs by the year 2000 was devised with public input and thus reflects activities most acceptable to Wisconsin's citizens.

Introduction

The eastern timber wolf (*Canis lupus lycaon*) was native to Wisconsin but settlement, habitat changes, and government bounties eliminated them from the state by the late 1950's (Thiel 1993). The wolf was listed as a United States (U.S.) endangered species in Wisconsin in 1973 and was listed as an endangered species by the state of Wisconsin in 1975 (Thiel 1978).

Wolf populations in neighboring Minnesota expanded between the late 1960's and 1980's, and wolves returned to Wisconsin in the mid-1970's, apparently by emigrating from Minnesota (Fuller et al. 1992a, Mech and Nowak 1981, Thiel 1978, Thiel and Welch 1981). The DNR initiated wolf studies in cooperation with the U.S. Fish and Wildlife Service in 1979. Those studies identified impediments to natural recolonization by wolves (Wydeven et al. this volume) and provided information on habitat needs for the species in the state (Thiel 1985).

The ultimate objective of the federal Endangered Species Act (ESA) of 1973, as amended, is to restore species, remove them from the list of threatened and endangered, and return management authority to the states. Recovering wolf populations in the continental U. S. currently present enormous challenges to resource management agencies primarily because of divergent public opinion over the value of the wolf and legal interpretations of management options allowed under the ESA (Llewellyn 1978, Henshaw 1982, Holmes et al. 1991, Paseneaux and Tucker 1991). Public opinions about wolves range from intense antipathy to complete sympathy among various demographic and regional cross-sections of the American public (cf. Kellert 1980a, Hook and Robinson 1982, Kellert 1985a, McNaught 1987, Kellert 1990).

Surveys conducted by Hook and Robinson (1982) and Kellert (1990) in neighboring Michigan and Minnesota (1986) revealed highly antagonistic views by some segments of the public, especially within or near wolf populations. In Wisconsin, 15–20% of firearm hunters of deer (*Odocoileus viginianus*) surveyed in 1982, who purchased licenses within the two counties known to harbor wolves, indicated they would shoot a wolf despite its protected status (J. Knight and R. Thiel, Wisconsin DNR, unpubl. data), thus affirming the potential for conflict that confronts the DNR in managing the natural recovery of wolves.

The pace of natural wolf recovery in several states may prompt those states to develop recovery management strategies. The purpose of this paper is to share Wisconsin's experiences in developing a state-oriented wolf recovery plan that emphasized public acceptance of the final product.

Methods

The Wisconsin endangered species statute (NR29.415) directs the DNR to develop and implement programs to restore "selected endangered species...to the maximum extent possible." Unlike federal plans which address only pertinent biological issues, Wisconsin's plans also consider budgetary, sociological, and other relevant information. In the case of the wolf, the federal recovery plan is an overall guide to regional recovery work. The state plan was needed to guide state-oriented activities.

The director of DNR's Bureau of Endangered Resources established a 12-member wolf recovery team in 1986. The team consisted of 10 DNR employees; six in wildlife management, two in endangered resources, and one each in forestry and public information and education. In addition, one team member represented the U.S. Forest Service and another represented the County Forest Association of Wisconsin. The two non-DNR members provided outside perspective; their agencies managed a majority of the land with the greatest recovery potential for wolves.

Citizen Participation Framework

Based on published public opinion surveys (Llewellyn 1978, Hook and Robinson 1982, Kellert 1986) and on the team's empirical knowledge of Wisconsin citizen opinions regarding wolves, public involvement in creating a plan was deemed essential to the success of a plan once implemented. The recovery team formed two committees to develop its plan using public input; a CP committee and a wolf biology committee. Several members of the CP committee were previously trained at the University of Wyoming, by Hans and Annemarie Bleiker.[1] The objective of the committee was to manage public participation in an orderly fashion and to reconcile public input with the recommendations of the team's technical wolf biology committee. The wolf biology committee provided technical advice and suggested management alternatives based on data from field investigations and input supplied by wolf biologists elsewhere.

Team integrity was considered essential to the program's ultimate success. Belief that the DNR and its team members were the appropriate agency and experts to develop a plan, belief that public comments were really being considered, and belief that having a reasonable plan was better than having no plan at all were critical to its acceptance.

The CP effort was designed to meet the following five criteria:

1) Understanding why a wolf recovery plan was being developed and agreeing that this was a serious matter worthy of attention.
2) Knowledge of who the recovery team represented, and agreeing it was the appropriate group to take on this task.
3) Understanding the problem-solving/decision-making process and considering it reasonable and fair.

---

1 Presently located at the Institute for Participatory Management and Planning, 969 Pacific St. Suite 10, Monterey, Calif. 93940.

4) The various interest groups that made up the public had to feel that they were being listened to during plan development.
5) Belief that supporting or accepting the recovery plan was better than having no recovery plan at all.

Records were kept of all media and personal communications. Persons/groups who neither acknowledged nor participated in the process were pared from mailing lists, thus saving some costs. Records prevented late-comers from undermining team integrity by claiming team bias because their group had been "overlooked."

Effective communication functioned to:
1) Inform the public of the team's task.
2) Provide instructions on how the public could participate and how the information would be used.
3) Respond to citizen comments and recurring questions; and
4) Quell any misinformation (campaigns) likely to surface given the controversial subject.

Statewide DNR news releases were the chief mechanisms used to communicate with the public. Informational mailings, both mass-produced and personal correspondence, were also used. Team members made themselves available to be interviewed by the media upon request and to discuss wolves and recovery issues with interest groups.

The CP program targeted the Wisconsin public but also focused on several prominent national organizations and non-DNR agencies involved in wildlife habitat management such as the U.S. Forest Service, County Forest Association, Indian tribes, and individual county forestry boards. DNR employees were included because their views towards wolves varied. Also, nonteam employees frequently answered questions from the public, and it was necessary that they were informed about wolf recovery planning.

A four-phase interactive CP management system was devised to obtain constructive public input (Table 1) as the plan coalesced. They were: Phase I, announce team, its intention and invite participation; Phase II, summarize public input and combine it with facts on wolf biology to identify management issues that may be mutually beneficial to wolves and people; Phase III, based on input, prepare a draft plan; and Phase IV, using further input, prepare a final plan. Participants were usually given 45 days in each phase to provide input.

At the conclusion of each phase, citizen input was segregated into four categories: comments, suggestions, concerns, and questions. Petitions were not included in any analysis because these documents carry a stigma of swaying public policy and are used to that end. They were accepted, but the public was informed they would not be utilized by the team. No attempt was made to statistically quantify input during the process; the objective was to identify problems and reach acceptable solutions.

Various issues were expressed in each of the four categories. For instance, 10 people may have the concern, "I fear

Table 1. The four-phased Citizens Participation appropriately develop Wisconsin's wolf recovery plan.

Phase	Communications	CP Effort	Product
I.	* Announce purpose and solicit input * Explain wolf's needs and management options	* 9 public forums * Mail 3,000 invitations * 25-day comment period	* ID public concerns * ID affected groups * Draft Issues Report
II.	* Announce purpose and solicit input * Mail Issues Rpt. * Correspond to answer questions	* 60-day comment period on Issues Report * Meet with affected groups	* Open dialogue with affected groups * Gather citizen input * Prepare Draft Plan
III.	* Announce purpose and solicit input * Mail Draft Plan * Correspond to resolve problems	* 60-day comment period on Draft * Meet with affected groups	* Resolve conflicts between groups/Team * Prepare Final Plan * Prepare Environmental Assessment (EA)
IV.	* EA available * Final Plan mailed	* 25-day comment period on EA * Conclude dialogue	* Plan and EA approved

that closing roads will affect my bear hunting," four may have issued a suggestion, "I wouldn't mind some road closures provided the areas aren't closed to hunters," 15 may have commented, "I think closing roads will create an undue burden on hunters and loggers who have a right to use them," and five may have asked, "How will closing roads affect hunters' ability to harvest bears?" The recurring theme in this example was access, and the team interpreted the input as follows:

1) Access is an issue that should be treated as potentially controversial.
2) Hunters are an affected group.
3) Not all hunters categorically disapprove of access limitations; and
4) More information (via media and personal correspondence) on the topic was warranted in response to questions and confusion over the issue.

Results and Discussion

The four-phased CP process
The goal in Phase I was to introduce the team, inform the public of its purpose and authority, acquaint team members

with prospective participants and learn of their views on recovering wolves in Wisconsin. The team and the public interacted through a series of nine public forums.

Two advance news releases identified the team, its purpose and authority, announced the forums, and gave information on how the public could participate. Sixty-eight newspapers, and radio and television stations throughout the state initiated this effort, making the wolf recovery program highly visible. In addition, more than 3,000 groups and individuals representing various views of wolves received personal invitations to participate, informing them of the entire process.

In an effort to identify regional perspectives, five of the nine forums were held in northern Wisconsin where wolves were most likely to occur and two in central and southern parts of the state. The forums were concentrated in a four-day period to minimize opportunities for repeat testimony by especially vociferous groups.

At each forum a slide presentation outlined the wolf's basic needs, its history of extermination in the state, and the intent of the DNR to develop a recovery program. Citizens were each given five minutes to express any concerns, opinions, and suggestions. Team members recorded these

Table 2. Public input during the four phases of Citizen Participation.

Event	Total Responses	Public Responses / Comments
Forums	225	* Concerns affecting multiple use management (especially hunting, logging, trapping & access) * Concerns regarding impact on deer herd * Concerns on government handling of livestock depredations * Public education necessary * Better enforcement needed * Concerns that DNR will force other agencies to comply rather than working cooperatively
Issues Report	37 letters 1 petition (292 signatures) 7 meetings	* Education ranked highest priority * Do & do not practice multiple use * Concerns about impact on deer continue * Concerns regarding cost (sportspeople are paying for recovery) * Concerns regarding wolf reintroductions * Stress cooperation with landowners
Draft Plan	169 letters 6 petitions 6 meetings	* Deer herd concerns narrowed to ensuring an availability for recreational hunting * Concerns that access management needs may impede transportation of timber products; motorized recreation (snowmobile trails and ATV users) * Question government's ability to control depredating wolves (public understands implications of ESA take restrictions) * Opponents fault Team for weak/aggressive stance on wolf stocking issue, disease abatement & protective measures * Opponents fault the Team for spending too little/much on wolves * Sport hunting fraternity complains that recovery program will be funded from license and PR revenues
Environmental Assessment	24	* Oppose recovery * minor adjustments

comments in special notebooks. A written comment period lasting 25 days allowed those unable to attend a forum to express their views.

Information was obtained from 225 testimonials and letters received in Phase I (Table 2). More than 180 comments were expressed 875 times. These were reduced to about fifteen issues.

Using technical input on minimum viable population assessments, habitat availability, and the federal government's regional recovery goals and input from the forums, the team concluded Phase I with the preparation of an Issues Report.

Phase II centered on the Issues Report (Table 3). Copies were made available to citizens responding to news announcements and to participants on the mailing list.

The Issues Report described a variety of management options and synthesized information on how and why various techniques could be used to obtain recovery under:
1) Human management options
2) Habitat management options,
3) Wolf management, and
4) Administrative considerations (Table 3).

Each of the issues was presented as a statement and was followed by team "ideas" and supporting rationale.

Developing a State Timber Wolf Recovery Plan with Public Input: The Wisconsin Experience

Table 3. Progression of wolf recovery management strategies during the Citizen Participation process.

Issues Report	Draft Plan	Final Plan
	Goal * 60 to 100 wolves in 10 years	**Goal** * 80 wolves in 10 packs in 10 years
Human Management * Educate public * Strengthen protection * Increase patrols * Encourage landowner - DNR cooperation * Compensate for losses	**Human Management** * Education programs * Increase protective measures * Cooperative habitat management * Depredation control with compensation * Continue CP	**Human Management** * Education programs * Increase protective measures * Cooperative habitat management * Depredation control with live-stock compensation and petition USFWS to "take" wolves * Continue CP * Volunteer program
Habitat Management * Maintain adequate deer herd for hunting * Maintain access below threshold (Thiel 1985; Mech 1988b)	**Habitat Management** * Support present multiple use forest-deer management program * Promote temporary access as part of forest management	**Habitat Management** * Support present multiple use forest-deer management program
Wolf Management * Monitor wolves * Survey diseases * Take wolves causing depredations	**Wolf Management** * Continue monitoring * Disease abatement	**Wolf Management** * Continue monitoring * Disease abatement
Administrative * Determine minimum - contribution to federal recovery goals	**Administrative** * Assess progress, recommend changes	**Administrative** * Assess progress, recommend maximum changes at year 5 * Create panel to draft plan for a recovered population

The report's primary purpose was to stimulate thought and obtain practical feedback. For instance, while the team did not list a numeric population goal, they presented 60 to 100 wolves as an idea. Participants responded requesting specifics on localities, the time period, and the number of breeding packs involved in defining a "recovered" population. Some provided what they thought constituted a "recovered" population (ranging from 0 to 5,000 animals) and others suggested the team conduct minimum viable population analyses.

Meetings were organized with affected interest groups based on responses generated in Phase I. Public response to the Issues Report provided the team with insights on management options that were acceptable. This information provided the basis for preparation of a draft plan.

Phase III focused on public response to the draft plan. By this stage, previous correspondence, educational news releases, and conflict-resolution meetings provided participants with a reasonably sophisticated understanding of the problem and the various techniques that could be used to achieve recovery. Most participants accepted the team goal.

Part III – Recovery Programs   173

Issues that concerned participants included conflicts over access management, deer management and recreational hunting opportunities, livestock depredations, stocking wolves, and costs associated with wolf recovery (Tables 2 and 3). In the latter stages of Phase III, as the team prepared the final plan, participants were kept informed via personal correspondence, news releases, and dialogues with groups.

Phase IV produced a final plan that was mailed to approximately 1,500 participants after they had time to respond to the state's mandated Environmental Assessment (Table 1). This concluded the CP process, and the recovery team was dismantled. The plan established an advisory team composed of DNR officials to ensure that recovery efforts proceed as planned, and to continue gathering citizen input at certain points during the recovery period.

The CP process was useful in identifying conflicts and seeking solutions because it required working closely with affected interest groups. Major conflicts became evident from participant testimony. These included:

1) Access management
2) Deer management (would the wolves deplete the huntable surplus?)
3) Stocking versus no stocking of wolves, and
4) Livestock depredation problems.

Individuals and groups expressed conflicting views on these issues. Team members worked with groups, provided possible biological and technical solutions, and presented suggestions for solving conflicts. This strategy ultimately resolved most problems. Two examples follow.

Some groups felt the DNR should speed wolf recovery by stocking wolves from Minnesota or Ontario. Others vehemently opposed stocking wolves but expressed support for wolf recovery provided the DNR focused on working with the existing population. Proponents of stocking were apprised of the opposition. Following further negotiations, both parties accepted certain concessions and agreed that the thrust of recovery efforts would focus on the existing population unless poor response by the wolves in the fifth year of the program necessitated a limited reintroduction program. Such reintroductions would only be conducted if there was public support in the areas they would occur.

Deer hunting and access were also sources of great concern. Both generated heated debates and political pressure from the governor's office and the legislature. These two issues were viewed by the team as interrelated. Timber producers, motorized recreationist clubs (primarily snowmobile and all-terrain-vehicle groups), and hunter groups generally opposed restrictions on multiple-use management of northern forests. These parties feared wolf recovery would limit their activities because of road closures.

Groups such as local Audubon clubs and the Wisconsin Conservation Task Force (representing rare and threatened botanical communities that suffered from excessive browsing by high deer populations) believed that restricting access would benefit independent objectives (in this case, old growth forests and recovery of rare herbaceous plant life) as well as aid in wolf recovery.

Resolution of the problem involved acknowledging the importance of access for business, recreation, preservation of specific plant communities, and wolf recovery. Rare plant preservation, while an important environmental concern whose problems were associated with access, was not directly relevant to wolf recovery problems, and those participants were so informed but invited to continue in the process.

The team presented information to various groups on how deer management benefits wolves. Groups were informed that effective deer management programs rely on timber cutting to maintain the habitat types preferred by northern deer. These forestry practices rely on access systems to transport timber products.

Information on access thresholds (Thiel 1985, Mech et al. 1988b) was shared with the groups to reveal the biological limitations of the species. Participants were informed that roads do not kill wolves — people do. The causes of wolf mortality were shared with each party to identify user groups most involved in wolf deaths. Education was suggested as one manner of addressing this issue. Another mechanism was to limit access in certain areas to existing levels. Hunters were also concerned that an increase in wolves would diminish success. They were provided information on deer herd trends in areas with and without wolves to demonstrate their minimal impact on deer numbers. Hunters were also informed that their support of wolves would provide added leverage for deer habitat improvement programs. These strategies were agreeable to most parties involved in the process.

Conclusions

The CP approach replaced public hearings usually utilized by DNR and eventually minimized the distrust of citizens attending, allowing wildlife officials and state citizens a unique opportunity to cooperatively forge wildlife policy. It is our belief that this CP process was more valuable than other manners of assessing the public pulse: the resulting plan reflects the contribution of hundreds of participants whose views shaped and guided the team as it formulated a recovery program.

The plan, as approved in 1989 after a three-year CP effort, is aimed at facilitating the natural proliferation of wolves where they currently exist in scattered remote habitats in northern Wisconsin.

The goals of the final plan are to:
1) Rebuild and maintain a population of at least 80 wolves in 10 packs during three consecutive winters; at least four packs must be located in northeastern Wisconsin by the year 2000;
2) Reclassify the wolf as a state threatened animal; and
3) Contribute to federally downlisting to threatened status by providing 80 of the 100 wolves needed in a non-Min-

nesota population (U.S. Fish and Wildlife Service 1992b).

The plan outlines 12 steps directed at recovering Wisconsin's wolf population:

1) Education
2) Added protective measures
3) Cooperating with non-DNR land owners in managing for deer and wolves
4) Monitoring wolf population trends
5) Disease abatement
6) Evaluating program progress
7) Implementing livestock depredation control plans
8) Coordinating recovery actions with other agencies
9) Continuing communications with citizens
10) Establishing volunteer programs
11) Reclassifying wolves when the goal is attained and
12) Determining the efficacy of and carrying out limited translocations if the wolf population does not respond adequately in five years.

Our experience strongly suggests public acceptance of wolves continues to improve in Wisconsin. Minor areas of continuing distress are voiced largely by the Wisconsin Conservation Congress, a group representing state sportspersons, whose concern is that wolf recovery is largely funded by Pittman-Robertson revenues rather than being more fairly distributed amongst advocacy groups. Two state organizations, Timber Wolf Alliance and Timber Wolf Information Network, provide specialized educational services, and the level of public interest suggests that attitudes towards this species are changing in Wisconsin as in neighboring states (Hook and Robinson 1982, Kellert 1986, 1990).

The success of Wisconsin's recovery program depends on the DNR's commitment to recovery plan objectives, flexibility to alter management in response to both the wolf's needs and public sentiments, and the wolf's capability to colonize habitats from which it was removed decades ago.

Part Four:
Wolf-Prey Interactions

Introduction to Wolf-Prey Interactions

■ Dale R. Seip

The impact of wolf predation on prey populations depends on the number of wolves, how many prey each wolf kills, and the capacity of the prey population to sustain losses to wolves. The full spectrum of wolf-prey dynamics, ranging from little effect on the prey to complete elimination of the prey population, can result from differences in those three basic components. Wolf predation will have less impact on prey populations if: 1) the prey population has a high reproductive rate and low rate of mortality from other factors, thereby allowing the population to sustain losses to wolves; 2) the number of wolves is limited by other factors such as disease or wolf control; or 3) the prey have an effective predator avoidance strategy such as migration or use of escape terrain. In the absence of some or all of the above conditions, wolves can reduce prey to low densities and, in some cases, may even eliminate some prey species. Multiple-equilibrium wolf-prey systems are theoretically possible, but there is no compelling evidence that they commonly occur.

Introduction

The purpose of this paper is to provide a simple introduction to the papers that follow in this section. These ideas have been presented elsewhere (Seip 1992b), but wherever possible, I have used examples from papers that follow in these symposium proceedings.

Wolf-Prey Interactions

The impact of wolf (*Canis lupus*) predation on prey populations depends on the number of wolves, how many prey each wolf kills, and the capacity of the prey populations to sustain losses to wolves. The full spectrum of wolf-prey dynamics, ranging from little effect on the prey to complete elimination of some prey populations, can result from differences in those three basic components.

In the absence of wolves, prey populations would be regulated by other density-dependent limiting factors such as food competition, disease, or other predators. Density-dependent limiting factors result in a dome-shaped annual increment curve (Fig. 1). The annual increment is the difference between the number of births and the number of deaths, and indicates the annual change in the population size at different densities. At low densities, annual increment is small because, although the impact of density-dependent limiting factors is minimal, there is a small breeding population. At high population densities, annual increment is also low and eventually becomes zero because although there is a large breeding population, the growth rate is severely reduced by density-dependent limiting factors. The maximum annual increment occurs at an intermediate population density where there is a moderate-sized breeding population and the impact of density-dependent limiting factors is not yet severe.

The capacity of a prey population to sustain wolf predation depends on the magnitude of the predation losses, compared to the potential annual increment that the prey would produce in the absence of wolves. Other limiting factors including hunting, poor nutrition, and other predators will reduce the capacity of a prey population to sustain losses to wolves.

The number of prey killed by wolves depends on the number of wolves, and the number of prey killed by each wolf. Both of those factors will generally be related to the density of the prey. The change in the number of predators in response to prey density is termed the Numerical Response, and the change in the number of prey killed per predator in response to prey density is called the Functional Response (Solomon 1949).

In general, the number of wolves will increase with increasing prey density (Fig. 2, line a). Fuller (1989) summarized data from numerous studies and found a linear increase in wolf numbers with increasing prey density. The relationship is even stronger if you differentiate between vulnerable and less vulnerable prey species (Dale et al. this volume). However, the number of wolves may plateau at high prey densities if some other factor becomes important in limiting the wolf population (Fig. 2, line b). Messier (this volume) reports that wolf populations initially increase with increasing moose (*Alces alces*) populations, but level off at high moose densities. Boyce (this volume) assumes that

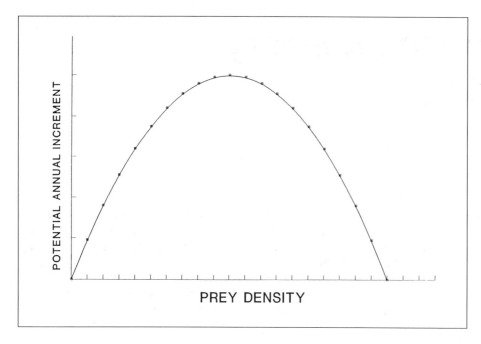

Fig. 1 *Potential annual increment or sustainable yield of a prey population.*

terrotoriality will ultimately limit the number of wolves in his computer simulation for Yellowstone.

There may be no numerical response of wolves to changes in the density of a prey species if the wolves are limited primarily by the availability of some other prey species (Fig. 2, line c). For example, Seip (1992a) found that wolves in southern British Columbia did not decline in response to declining caribou (*Rangifer tarandus*) populations because the wolves were sustained by moose.

The number of prey killed per wolf will also usually increase with increasing prey density because prey become easier to find, or reach numbers that make it profitable for wolves to search them out (Fig. 3). However, the functional response curve will level off at higher prey densities at the point where the wolves are satiated. Messier (this volume) summarized the functional response of wolves to increasing moose density and found that kill rate increased between zero and one moose/km^2 but leveled off above that density. Dale et al. (this volume) report that wolves maintained a constant kill rate over a broad range of caribou densities, although a decline in kill rate was suggested at low caribou densities.

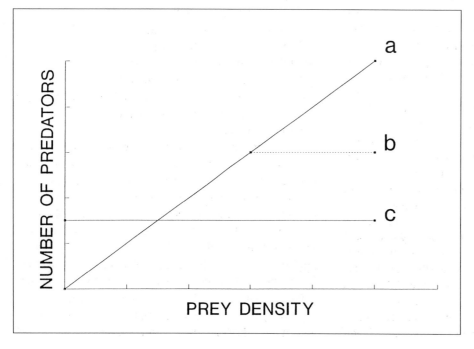

Fig. 2 *Possible numerical responses of wolf populations to increasing prey density. Line a: linear response; line b: linear response with upper plateau; line c: no numerical response.*

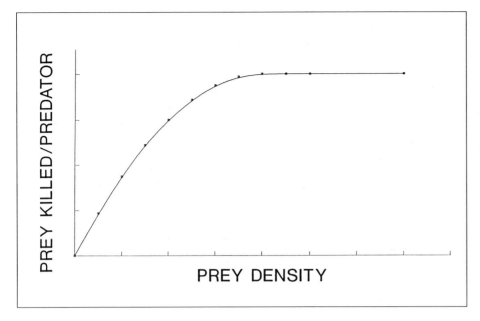

Fig. 3 *Generalized functional response of wolves to increasing prey density.*

The total number of prey killed by wolves is the product of the number of wolves, and the number of prey killed per wolf. In general, at low prey densities few prey will be killed because there will be low numbers of wolves and the wolves will have difficulty locating the sparse prey (Fig. 4). As prey increase, both the number of wolves and the number of prey killed by each wolf will generally increase. The total number of prey killed will increase exponentially due to the multiplicative effect of an increasing numerical and functional response. That exponential increase represents a density-dependent predation rate because the proportion of the population being killed is increasing. There is no requirement for a type 3 functional response (Holling 1959a) to produce density-dependent predation. Any increasing functional response will generate a density-dependent predation rate if the numerical response is also increasing (Messier this volume).

If either the functional or numerical response plateau at high prey densities, the number of prey killed will increase at a slower rate with further increases in prey density. If both the numerical and functional response level off, the number of prey killed will remain constant with further increases in prey density. Consequently, predation rate may be density-dependent at low prey densities, density-independent at

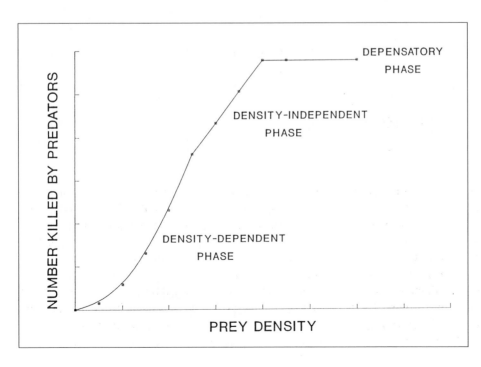

Fig. 4 *Generalized relationship between prey density and the number of prey killed by wolves.*

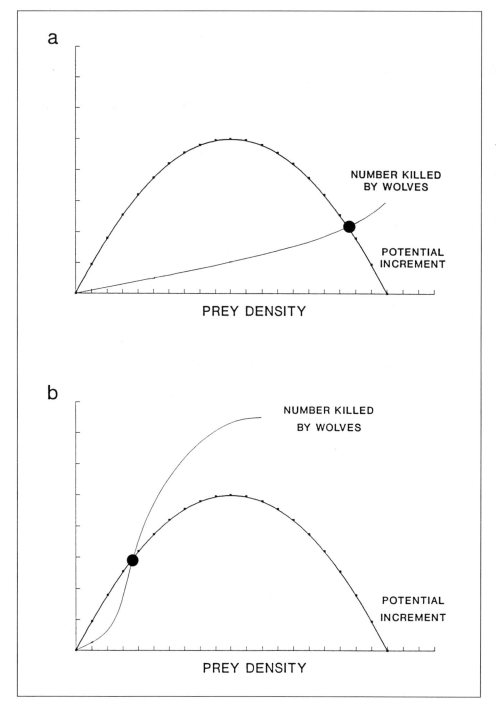

Fig. 5 *Single predator-prey equilibrium model resulting from the interaction between losses to wolves and sustainable yield of the prey population (a: equilibrium at high prey density; b: equilibrium at low prey density).*

intermediate prey densities, and inversely density-dependent (depensatory) at high prey densities.

The impact of wolf predation depends on the magnitude of predation losses compared to the potential annual increment that the prey could produce in the absence of wolves. If the number killed by wolves exceeds the potential annual increment, the prey density will decline. If the number killed by wolves is less than the potential annual increment, the prey density will increase. The wolves and prey will stabilize around a density where the number of prey killed by

wolves is equal to the potential annual increment. Actual densities may fluctuate widely around the equilibrium point from year to year in response to environmental variation (Adams et al. this volume, Mech et al. this volume). Time lags in predator responses will cause cycles around the equilibrium point.

If the number of prey killed by wolves increases slowly in response to increasing prey, relative to the potential annual increment, the wolf-prey equilibrium point will occur at a high prey density (Fig. 5a). The prey will be regulated by the combined effects of wolf predation and other density-dependent limiting factors. However, if the number of prey killed by wolves increases rapidly in response to increasing prey density, relative to the potential annual increment, the wolf-prey equilibrium will occur at a low prey density with the prey population regulated primarily by wolves (Fig. 5b). The full spectrum of wolf-prey equilibria can occur depending on the parameters for the functional and numerical response of wolves and the potential annual increment of the prey. Changes in those parameters over time, due to natural or human-caused processes, will result in changes in the wolf-prey equilibrium point (Mech et al. this volume). Boyce (this volume) provides computer simulations of wolf-prey dynamics based on relationships for the functional and numerical response of wolves, and the potential annual increment of prey populations.

Can Wolf-Prey Systems Have Multiple Equilibria?

It is theoretically possible for a predator-prey system to exhibit more than one equilibrium point. A multiple-equilibrium system will occur if the total number of prey killed by predators increases rapidly at low prey densities, but then plateaus at a number less than the maximum potential annual increment (Fig. 6). A multiple equilibrium system has two stable equilibria, one at a low prey density and one at a high prey density. At densities immediately above the low equilibrium point is a "predator pit," a range of prey densities where losses to predation exceed the potential annual increment. Prey populations within the density range of the predator pit will decline to the lower equilibrium. However,

prey populations that reach densities above the predator pit will increase to the upper equilibrium density. A prey population at either stable equilibrium point will remain at that density unless the system is perturbed. For example, temporary predator control could allow a low density prey population to increase to a density above the predator pit, at which point it would increase and stabilize at the upper equilibrium density, even if predator control was terminated.

Although multiple equilibrium systems are theoretically possible, there is no compelling evidence that they are common in wolf-prey systems. Simulation models that incorporate realistic wolf-prey relationships usually produce single wolf-prey equilibria rather than multiple equilibria (Boyce this volume). The observation that ungulate populations that have increased to high densities in response to wolf control typically decline back to pre-wolf-control densities following cessation of wolf control (Jones and Mason 1983, Gasaway et al. 1992) also suggests a single equilibrium rather than a multiple equilibrium system.

The multi-equilibrium model is an unnecessarily complex explanation requiring special conditions, when a simpler, less complex explanation is sufficient to describe most observed wolf-prey relationships. I believe that the most parsimonious model to explain wolf-prey dynamics is the single predator-prey equilibrium model, with a wide range of potential wolf and prey densities depending on the values for the component relationships.

The term "predator pit" is commonly misused. Many individuals incorrectly refer to any situation where predators regulate prey at low densities as a predator pit. Use of the term predator pit should be restricted to situations where there is evidence of a multi-equilibrium system.

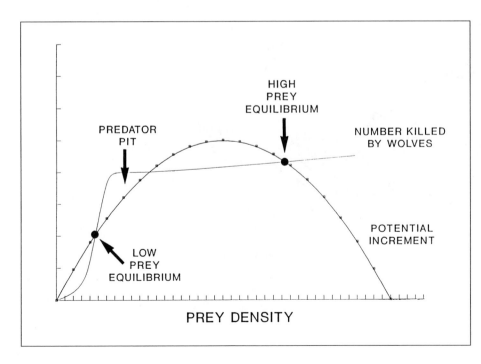

Fig. 6 A multiple-equilibrium predator-prey model with two stable equilibrium points.

Factors Affecting the Wolf-Prey Equilibrium Density

Potential Annual Increment of the Prey

Prey populations with high productivity and low levels of mortality due to other factors will be better able to sustain losses to wolves and will be able to attain higher densities. Ungulates that have high productivity (like deer) will generally coexist with wolves at a higher density than ungulates with low productivity (like caribou). Also, ungulates that experience high levels of mortality due to other limiting factors will be less able to sustain wolf predation and will be regulated at a lower density than populations without those additional limiting factors. For example, Messier (1994) suggested that wolves regulate moose at low densities when bears (*Ursus* spp.) are present as an additional mortality factor, but are unable to regulate moose at low densities when bears are absent. Similarly, hunting in combination with wolf predation reduces prey populations to lower densities (Messier and Crete 1985, Vales and Peek this volume). Consequently, even if wolves are the primary regulating factor, changes that increase the productivity of an ungulate population or reduce other mortality factors may allow the prey population to increase. For example, habitat enhancement that improves the productivity of an ungulate population may improve their ability to sustain losses to wolves (Boertje et al. this volume).

Functional Response

The functional response of wolves to increasing prey numbers is largely determined by the effectiveness of the antipredator strategies of the prey. Some large ungulates (like moose) can often fight off wolves which makes them less

vulnerable than smaller ungulates. Use of rugged, escape terrain allows species such as mountain sheep (*Ovis* spp.) and mountain goats (*Oreamnos americana*) to avoid wolves. Dale et al. (this volume) found that caribou were much more vulnerable to wolf predation than moose or Dall sheep. Klein (this volume) reported that when wolves were introduced to Coronation Island, deer (*Odocoileus hemionus*) in areas of gentle terrain were eliminated and only deer living in rugged areas survived.

Some prey species spatially separate themselves from wolves, especially during the birthing period. Some caribou avoid wolves by calving on islands (Cumming and Beange

Bison calves (left) and a mature bull (top) from Wood Buffalo National Park. Wolf predation on North American ungulates is directed at all age groups and whatever species are available in specific ecosystems. Predation is often greatest in the most vulnerable element in the population. (Photo: L.N. Carbyn)

White-tailed deer (fawn, below) and mule deer (adults, left) are the smallest ungulate prey species in wolf/prey systems. Most of the studies on the impact of wolf predation on deer populations have been carried out in Minnesota. (Photo: U.S. Fish and Wildlife Service Collection)

1987). Migrations to calving grounds are another effective strategy to become spatially separated from wolves, especially if wolves are restricted to denning areas far from the calving grounds (Bergerud and Page 1987, Adams et al. this volume). The long-distance migrations of Arctic caribou spatially separate them from most of the denning wolves (Heard and Williams 1992a). In mountainous areas, migrations to high elevation calving grounds can also reduce the contact between caribou and wolves and result in reduced wolf predation (Bergerud et al. 1984, Seip 1992a, Adams et al. this volume).

Antipredator strategies may be even more effective if there are other, more vulnerable, prey species in the area. The availability of highly vulnerable prey species will reduce the level of predation on the less vulnerable prey species. Dale et al. (this volume) found a low predation rate on mountain sheep and moose when caribou, a more vulnerable prey species, were available. However, that benefit may be only temporary if wolf numbers are able to increase in response to total prey biomass, eliminate or greatly reduce the most vulnerable prey, and then switch to the less vulnerable prey.

Changes in habitat conditions can affect the vulnerability of prey to wolf predation. Consequently, habitat management practices have the potential to alter predator-prey interactions. Reducing and fragmenting habitat may concentrate prey into a smaller area, effectively increasing their density and making it easier for wolves to locate them. Alternatively, creating new habitat allows ungulates to spread out at lower densities and reduce predator efficiency. Fires may enhance moose populations not only by improving nutrition, but also by providing more habitat for the moose to space out in to avoid wolves.

Antipredator strategies reduce the functional response of wolves. If those strategies are effective, a high prey population will be able to coexist with wolves. If prey species do not have an effective antipredator strategy, wolves can reduce prey populations to very low densities or even eliminate them (Bergerud 1992, Seip 1992b, Klein this volume).

Numerical Response

The effectiveness of antipredator strategies will also affect the numerical response of wolves. If prey are effective at fighting off, escaping or avoiding wolves, the numerical response of wolves to increasing prey densities will be limited. For example, wolves are unable to increase in response to high caribou numbers if the caribou have migrated and are unavailable to the wolves during the denning period (Bergerud and Page 1987, Heard and Williams 1992a).

The numerical response of wolves to increasing numbers of a prey will also be reduced if the wolf population is limited by other factors. Outbreaks of diseases such as rabies may prevent wolves from increasing in response to high prey numbers. Wolf control, hunting, or trapping can also reduce the numerical response of wolf populations to increasing prey densities. Gasaway et al. (1992) demonstrated that the numerical response of wolves to increasing moose densities was reduced in areas of heavy wolf harvest, resulting in higher moose densities. In areas with high road densities, human-caused mortalities reduce wolf populations, even if prey are abundant (Mech et al. 1988b). Even wolf populations in protected areas like Riding Mountain National Park, Manitoba may be limited by dispersal into surrounding areas where they experience high human-caused mortality (Carbyn 1983b). A high mortality of wolves around the park reduces the impact of wolves on prey inside the park. A similar situation may occur if wolves are reintroduced to Yellowstone Park, Wyoming. Mortality of wolves leaving the park is a critical component in predicting the likely impact of wolf recolonization (Boyce this volume).

Wolves may not decline in response to a declining prey population if they are sustained by another prey species. In that situation, wolves may be able to completely eliminate the declining prey species. For example, Seip (1992a) concluded that wolves may eliminate some caribou herds in southern British Columbia because moose sustained the wolf population when the caribou population declined.

Overall, if the numerical response of wolves to increasing prey is restricted by other limiting factors, a predator-prey equilibrium at a high prey density is more likely to occur. Alternatively, if the number of wolves increases rapidly in response to increasing prey, a low density prey population is more likely. In situations where wolf populations are sustained by several prey species, the more vulnerable species may be completely eliminated.

Summary

There is no simple answer to the question, "What effect does wolf predation have on prey populations?" The full spectrum of impacts is possible, depending on the patterns of the functional and numerical response of the wolves, and the capacity of the prey to sustain losses to predation. However, our understanding of how those component relationships interact to produce different predator-prey outcomes is greatly improving. The papers that follow in these proceedings further contribute to that understanding.

On the Functional and Numerical Responses of Wolves to Changing Prey Density

■ François Messier

The density relationship of wolf predation can be derived from two interactive processes: the functional and the numerical response of predators. It is therefore important to document predator responses to identify ranges of prey density within which wolf predation can create density dependence. Wolf functional response, i.e., the number of prey killed per predator per unit time as a function of prey density, is determined by changes in "search time" and "handling time" with prey density. Wolf numerical response, i.e., changes in predator abundance with increasing prey density, can be related to nutritional factors, spacing behavior, and aggregation of predators in high prey areas. The functional and numerical responses have a multiplicative effect on predation rate. A sigmoid, type 3 functional response is not a prerequisite for density-dependent predation rate. The shape of wolf functional response is dependent on the relative vulnerability of prey. Wolf predation is often density dependent at the lower range of prey densities. In multiprey systems, however, wolf predation may be depensatory for the most vulnerable prey as a result of a steep type 2 functional response and a numerical response that converges to a positive y-intercept. An assessment of prey selectivity with regard to age, sex, and condition, with increasing ungulate densities, would permit further refinement of ungulate population models with predation.

Introduction

Our understanding of wolf (*Canis lupus*)–ungulate systems has improved considerably in recent years. The focus has shifted from vague multifactorial hypotheses (e.g., Gasaway et al. 1983, Peek and Eastman 1983, Klein 1991) to population models with clearly identified regulatory mechanisms (Messier 1991a, 1994, Boutin 1992, Gasaway et al. 1992). This theoretical formulation has forced the distinction between density-dependent factors involved in population regulation, and other limiting factors that may influence the population rate of increase, but without any regulatory impacts. Such a distinction is central to the conceptualization of ungulate population models and the concept of maximum sustainable yield (Caughley 1976, Crête et al. 1981, Messier 1989). It has been recognized, for example, that the presence of one or more dynamic equilibria must be linked to mechanisms of density dependence, but other limiting factors can influence the manifestation, location, and stability of equilibrium points (Berryman et al. 1987, Sinclair 1989, Messier 1994).

Mortality sources cannot be categorized simply as density dependent, depensatory (i.e., inversely density dependent), or density independent. Rather, it is necessary to identify for different sources of mortality the range of densities within which negative feedback mechanisms operate. For example, food competition among large herbivores generally occurs at densities close to ecological carrying capacity (ECC) (Caughley 1976), thus restricting its regulatory impact to relatively high densities (McCullough 1992). In contrast, wolf predation may change from being density dependent at low ungulate densities, to depensatory at moderate to high ungulate densities (Messier 1991a, 1994). This dichotomous density relationship of wolf predation, however, is probably not universal as suggested by recent research on caribou (*Rangifer tarandus*) (Dale et al. this volume).

The density relationship of wolf predation can be traced to two interactive processes: the functional and the numerical response (Solomon 1949, Holling 1959b). The functional response describes how the number of prey consumed per predator varies with prey density, whereas the numerical response summarizes changes in predator numbers with prey density. The total response (the product of the functional and numerical responses), when divided by prey numbers, gives an estimate of predation rate, i.e., the proportion of the prey population subject to predation per unit of time. This theo-

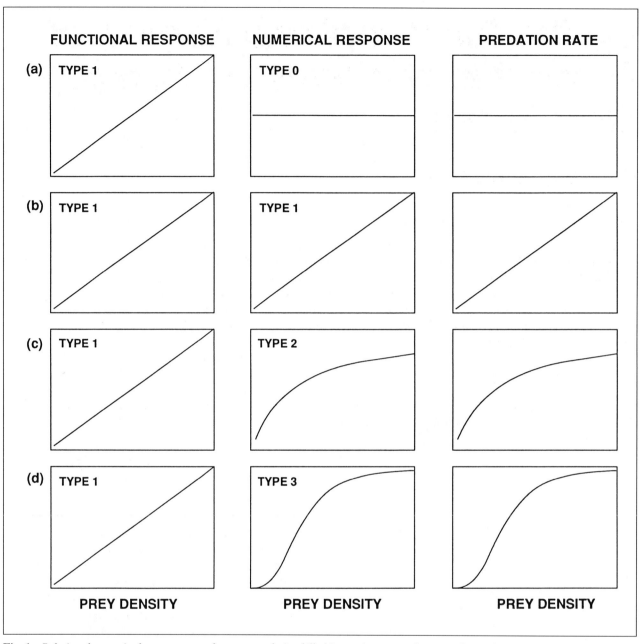

Fig. 1 *Relative changes in the percentage of a prey population killed by predators as a function of prey density for a type 1 functional response and four types of numerical responses.*

retical framework recognizes that changes in predation rate are determined by the multiplicative effect of the functional and the numerical response (Seip 1992b).

In this essay, I focus on the concepts of predator responses to changing prey density, and how they relate to mechanisms of population regulation. I believe that recognition of key patterns play an important role in designing better and more focused research. My objective is not to present an exhaustive literature review, but rather to concentrate at the conceptual level.

Concepts and Theories

The Functional Response

The relationship between per capita killing rate and population density for a given prey species is known as the predator functional response. The number of prey killed per predator per unit time is a function of "search time," the time required to locate a suitable prey, and "handling time," the time associated with capture and feeding activities. These two time components conflict, however, with handling time forc-

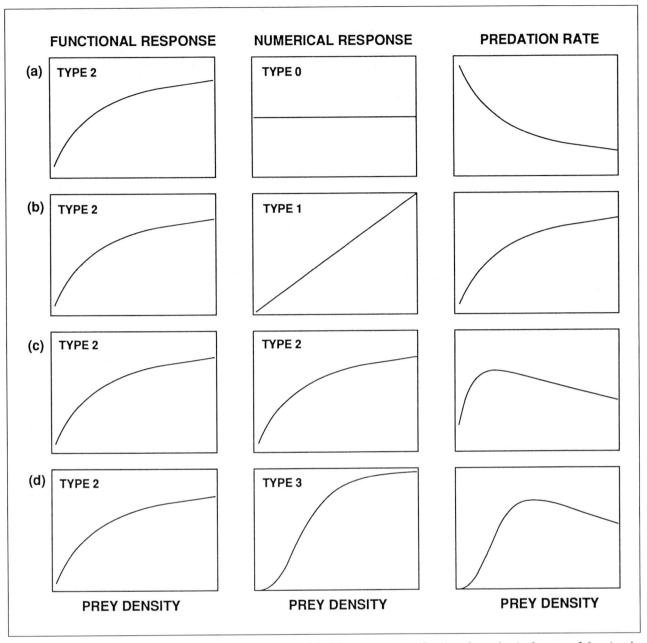

Fig. 2 *Relative changes in the percentage of a prey population killed by predators as a function of prey density for a type 2 functional response and four types of numerical responses.*

ing the functional response to plateau at high prey densities, and search time determining the rate of approach of that plateau.

Holling (1959b, 1965) described three types of functional responses. Type 1 is characterized by a linear increase in killing rate with prey density up to a plateau ultimately set by satiation. Such a response is rare in nature and only occurs when time to handle prey is trivial. The most commonly observed functional response is type 2 where killing rate increases asymptotically with prey density. In this case,

handling time takes up an increasing proportion of the predator's time as prey density increases, which eventually imposes an upper limit to killing rate. The type 3 functional response involves a sigmoid relationship between killing rate and prey density. The biological basis for the initial, accelerating portion of the type 3 functional response is complex and may involve prey switching (Murdoch 1969, Murdoch and Oaten 1975), increased predator efficiency in detecting and capturing prey (Tinbergen 1960, Holling 1965, Real 1979), presence of prey refugia (Taylor 1984),

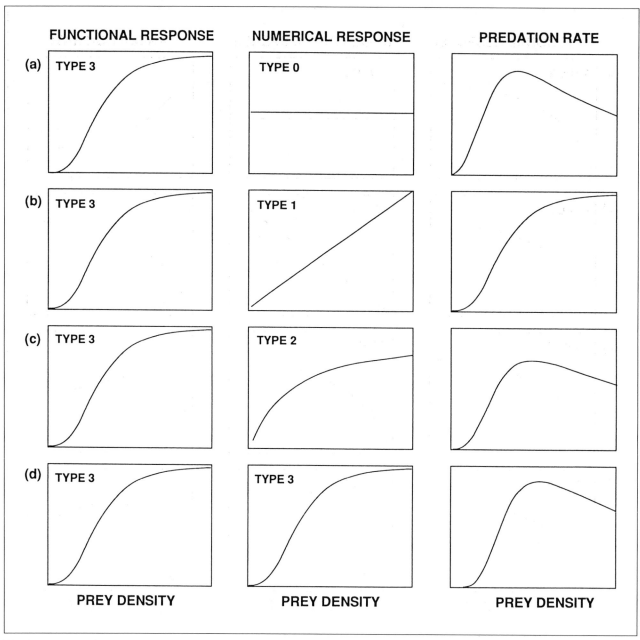

Fig. 3 *Relative changes in the percentage of a prey population killed by predators as a function of prey density for a type 3 functional response and four types of numerical responses.*

and bioenergetic maximization (Abrams 1982, Dunbrack and Giguère 1987). The upper limit of killing rate is explained by constraints associated with handling time as described above for the type 2 functional response.

The Numerical Response

Changes in predator numbers with increasing prey density (i.e., the predator numerical response) can be related to nutritional factors, spacing behavior, and aggregation of predators in high prey areas (Taylor 1984). For simplicity, I

have adopted the same types of numerical responses as for the functional response: type 1, linear response; type 2, asymptotic response; and type 3, sigmoidal response. In addition, I have considered a type 0 numerical response to represent cases where predator numbers remain constant irrespective of variation in prey density. The type 0 numerical response is particularly relevant to multiprey systems for which some prey species may be available only seasonally with little effect on predator numbers.

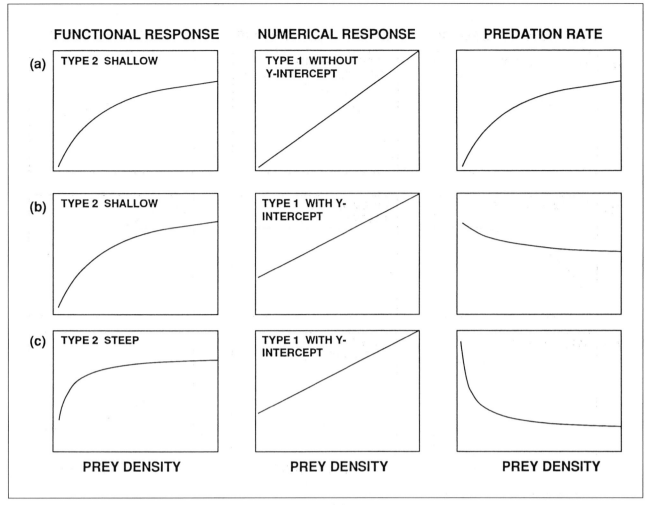

Fig. 4 *Relative changes in the percentage of a prey population killed by predators as a function of prey density for a type 2 functional response and a type 1 numerical response with a y-intercept of zero (a) or a positive y-intercept (b). The effect of the curvature of the functional response on the predation rate curve is illustrated in b and c.*

Predation Rate — One Prey System

I derived the density relationship of predation rate for each combination of functional and numerical responses (Figs. 1–3) to identify which combinations generate density-dependent predation rates. Four important conclusions emerged from this modeling exercise. First, density-dependent predation rate is associated with all three types of functional response. Second, density-dependent predation rate is common (10 out of 12 cases), not the exception. Third, density-dependent predation is often limited to the lower range of prey densities (e.g., Figs. 2c, 2d, 3a, 3c, and 3d), thus generating a dichotomous relationship. And, fourth, a fully depensatory relationship is found in only one case (Fig. 2a).

Predation Rate — Multi-Prey Systems

When more than one prey species are available, the numerical response may not converge to the origin. This situation

may occur when predators can subsist on alternate prey even if the prey species under study is driven to extinction (e.g., Bergerud and Elliot 1986, Seip 1992a). The effect of a numerical response with a positive y-intercept was investigated by computer simulations. I focused on a type 2 functional response in those simulations because of its commonness in predation studies.

A numerical response with a positive y-intercept has a profound influence on the predation rate curve (Figs. 4–6). The presence of a positive y-intercept reduces or reverts the density dependent function of predation as compared to results obtained in the previous analysis where the numerical response had a y-intercept of zero. That general pattern is found for the type 1 (Fig. 4b), type 2 (Fig. 5b), and type 3 (Fig. 6b) numerical response. However, there is also a strong interaction between a positive y-intercept in the numerical response, and the curvature of the functional response (Figs. 4c, 5c, and 6c). For example, a predator that is particularly

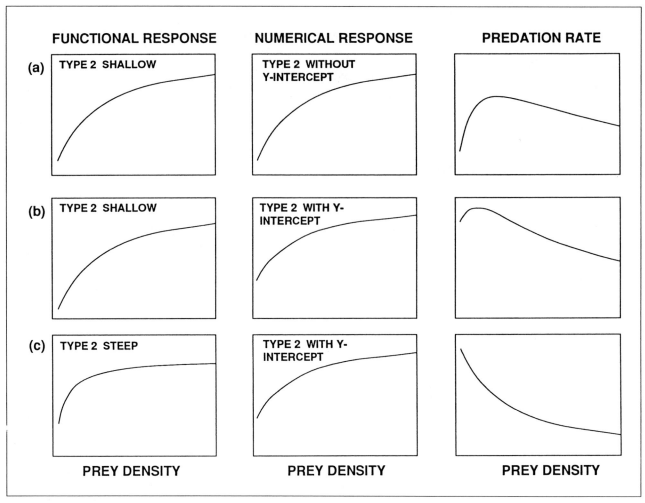

Fig. 5 *Relative changes in the percentage of a prey population killed by predators as a function of prey density for a type 2 functional response and a type 2 numerical response with a y-intercept of zero (a) or a positive y-intercept (b). The effect of the curvature of the functional response on the predation rate curve is illustrated in b and c.*

efficient in capturing prey at low densities (i.e., a type 2 functional response with a steep approach to the plateau) would force the predation rate to be strongly depensatory (Figs. 4c, 5c, and 6c).

Overall, then, predation rate is always density dependent at low prey densities when a type 2 functional response is combined with a type 1, 2, or 3 numerical response with a y-intercept of zero. But if the y-intercept of the numerical response is positive (i.e., a predator sustained by other prey) and if the predator is very efficient in killing prey at low densities (i.e., steep-sloped functional response), then depensatory predation is more likely.

Empirical Data

Wolf Functional Response

Past research on wolf feeding ecology has focused largely on mean consumption rate in winter (reviewed by Fuller 1989:28). That information, although of interest, cannot be used to evaluate the functional response of wolves because estimates of killing rate for each prey species are required. Messier (1994) recently summarized the functional response of wolves to changing moose (*Alces alces*) density. The best fit was a type 2 functional response with a maximum killing rate of 3.36 moose per wolf per 100 days during the winter period (Fig. 7). Dale et al. (this volume) also found a type 2 functional response for wolves preying on caribou. However, the two functional responses differ markedly in the rate of approach of the asymptotic killing rate, with the functional response relative to caribou being substantially steeper than the one observed for moose. This difference is likely explained by the fact that caribou tend to aggregate, which allows wolves to be more effective in killing caribou even at low densities.

Wolf Numerical Response

Packard and Mech (1980) reviewed the information on the roles of social and nutritional factors on wolf population

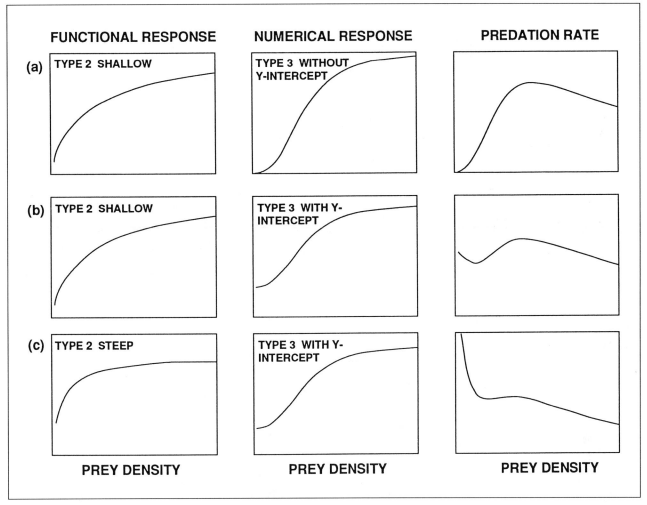

Fig. 6 *Relative changes in the percentage of a prey population killed by predators as a function of prey density for a type 2 functional response and a type 3 numerical response with a y-intercept of zero (a) or a positive y-intercept (b). The effect of the curvature of the functional response on the predation rate curve is illustrated in b and c.*

dynamics. Fuller (1989) found a linear relationship between wolf numbers and ungulate biomass ($\underline{R}^2 = 0.72$; Fig. 8), suggesting that prey base directly affects wolf density. I have shown above that a numerical response converging to a positive y-intercept has a profound effect on the density relationship of predation rate. Therefore, it is important to evaluate the statistical significance of the y-intercept in the equation published by Fuller (1989). An analysis of data presented in Appendix B of Fuller (1989) reveals that the y-intercept was not different than zero ($\underline{t} = 1.15$, $\underline{P} = 0.26$). Given that wolves are obligate predators of ungulates, one may postulate that wolves would not be present in an area totally devoid of ungulates. Thus, I calculated a new regression line that was forced to the origin (Fig. 8). The new regression line was highly significant ($\underline{P} < 0.001$) with an improved $\underline{R}^2$-value of 0.92.

The above information on wolf density relates to the sum of ungulate biomass and, therefore, does not describe the numerical response of wolves for a given prey species. Messier (1994) recently summarized the numerical response of wolves to changing moose density. Only wolf populations that were not hunted appreciably, and for which moose constituted the dominant (> 75%) prey species, were considered in my analysis. Wolf numbers were strongly related to moose density (Fig. 7), following a type 2 numerical response. A type 2 numerical response implies that spacing behavior may be setting an upper limit to wolf numbers.

Predation Rate

Information on how wolf predation rate changes with ungulate density is quite limited. Messier and Crête (1985) reported for southwestern Québec density-dependent changes of wolf predation at the lower range of moose densities. However, for Isle Royale where moose densities were substantially higher, an index of wolf predation was inversely related to moose density (Messier 1991a). Messier (1994)

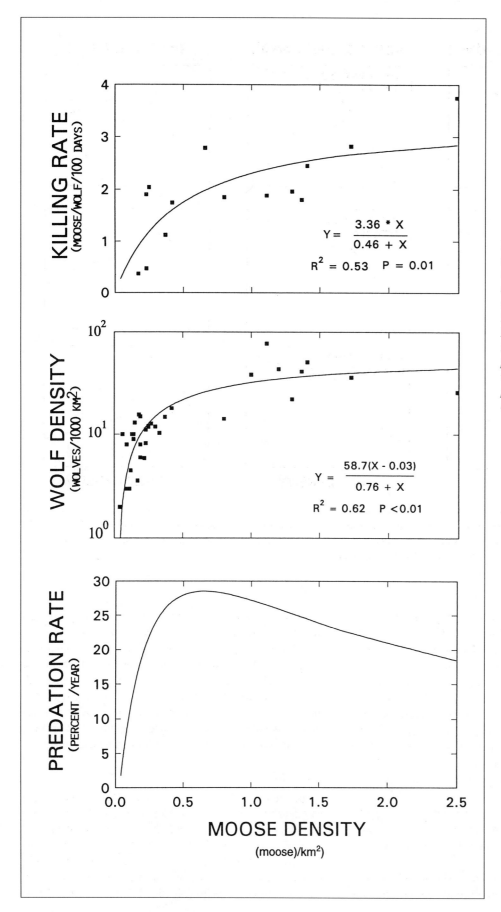

Fig. 7 *The functional and numerical responses of wolves to changing moose density as documented from 27 studies for which wolves were moderately harvested (modified after Messier 1994). Also presented in the lower panel is the predicted density relationship of wolf predation rate based on the predator total response to changing moose density.*

recently derived the density relationship of wolf predation with changing moose density based on 27 published studies. Wolf predation proved to be density dependent from 0 to 0.65 moose/km², and inversely density dependent at higher moose densities (e.g., on Isle Royale). Similar information for other northern ungulates is currently lacking, which precludes the formulation of predictive population models.

Discussion

In two classic papers, Murdoch and Oaten (1975) and Oaten and Murdoch (1975) reviewed the extent to which each type of functional response enhanced the regulation of prey populations. They concluded that only a type 3 functional response would lead to an increasing proportion of the prey population being taken by predators as prey density increases. A common misconception often found in the literature is that a type 3 functional response constitutes a prerequisite for predation rate to be density dependent. A point often missed is that the analysis of Murdoch and Oaten was based on the assumption that predators do not respond numerically to changing prey density. For wolves, however,

there is a clear indication that their density is linked to prey abundance (Packard and Mech 1980, Fuller 1989, Messier 1994). In this analysis, I have shown that all three types of functional response can be associated with density-dependent predation rate. The type of numerical response and the range of prey density under investigation represent two other important variables when assessing the density relationship of predation rate (Figs. 1–3). Most importantly, the functional and numerical responses have a multiplicative effect on the predation rate (Seip 1992b).

Determinants of the predator functional response have been investigated theoretically (Real 1979). In one-prey systems, a type 2 response is expected (Messier 1994) because predators are forced to exploit that prey irrespective of its density. However, prey vulnerability can appreciably modify the curvature of the functional response. One would expect that the functional response of wolves would vary among ungulate species, or even among seasons for a given prey species.

In multiprey systems, prey switching may cause the functional response to be sigmoid (type 3). Prey switching

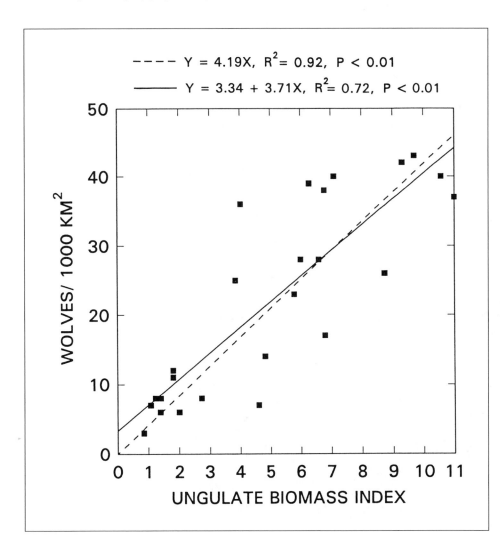

Fig. 8 *Relationship between ungulate biomass (no. deer-size ungulates/km²) and wolf density (no./1000 km²) as reported by Fuller (1989; solid line), and the new relationship based on a linear regression model without y-intercept (dashed line).*

*Moose are widely distributed over the North American continent and are among the most available prey species for wolves. Because of the more dispersed overall distribution of this species within ecosystems, its dynamic interactions with predators differs from that of clumped prey distributions such as elk (**wapiti**) herds and migratory species such as barren ground caribou. (Photo: F. Messier)*

may be particularly pronounced in areas where different prey species are spatially segregated, thus forcing the predator to adopt a search pattern targeting a single prey species at a time. The phenomenon of prey switching is highly dependent on prey profitability (Scheel 1993). Profitability, in turn, is related to the vulnerability level of each prey species *and* its density. Predators that pursue an optimal foraging strategy should ignore a prey species with low probability of capture (like moose) especially when a more vulnerable prey species (like caribou) is present (Dale et al. this volume). In such cases, a type 3 functional

response for the less vulnerable species (moose) would be expected because it would be incorporated in the predator diet only when relatively abundant. For the more vulnerable prey species (caribou), however, a type 2 functional response would be predicted because such a prey would remain part of the predator diet even when reduced at relatively low densities. In light of the fact that prey vulnerability can influence drastically the shape of the functional response, it is unfortunate that data on the relative vulnerability of northern ungulates is so limited. Chesson (1978) probably proposed the best formula to calculate

The number of prey species in different ecosystems is variable. Generally, the most complex systems (in terms of number of species) exist in the Rocky Mountains, while those of the high arctic (photo left) regions may have only one or two ungulate prey species. (Photo: L.D. Mech)

relative prey vulnerability (i.e., selectivity coefficients) when availability and use of prey are documented.

Fuller (1989) described a linear relationship between wolf numbers and ungulate biomass. That relationship should not be assumed to represent accurately the numerical response of wolves for a particular ungulate species. For example, wolf numerical response may be drastically different for migrant versus nonmigrant species, considering that wolves depend largely on the year-long prey base for successful reproduction (Messier et al. 1988). The assessment of wolf numerical response may be further complicated by seasonal aggregation of wolves in high prey areas, as it has been observed in winter yards of white-tailed deer (*Odocoileus virginianus*) (Messier 1985b, Potvin 1988), or around caribou concentrations (Parker 1973).

Wolf numbers may track changes in ungulate density with multi-year time lags (Peterson and Page 1988). Thus, time-series data of wolf numbers from a single study site may provide biased information on wolf numerical response. It would be advisable to document wolf numerical response from comparative data on wolf numbers obtained from independent study sites, but with differing prey densities (Messier and Crête 1985, Messier 1994).

Assessing the impact of wolves on ungulate populations requires the integration of various facets of predation. In this context, the functional and the numerical responses of wolves represent, without a doubt, two dominant facets, but others should be considered as well. For example, the above analyses are based on the assumption that prey individuals are all equal, irrespective of their sex, age, and nutritional condition. Changes in the composition of prey killed by wolves as a function of prey density is poorly documented. This lack of information on prey selectivity precludes, at this time, further refinement of our understanding of wolf predation on ungulates.

Acknowledgments

The Natural Sciences and Engineering Research Council of Canada supported my work through a University Research Fellowship and an operating grant for computer analyses. I appreciate the constructive comments of M. Pasitschniak-Arts, D.R. Seip, and J.A. Virgl.

Anticipating Consequences of Wolves in Yellowstone: Model Validation

■ Mark S. Boyce

Computer simulation was used to project the consequences to ungulate populations of wolf recovery in the Greater Yellowstone Ecosystem (GYE). Model structure assumes logistic functional and numerical responses, and linear substitutability among four prey: elk, bison, moose, and mule deer. Model validation considerations required that the model structure remain simple to ensure that most parameter estimates were based upon available data, while still incorporating sufficient ecological detail to capture essential dynamics. Ecological factors incorporated into stochastic simulations include over-winter mortality, density dependence in prey population growth rates, territorial limitation of the number of wolf packs, variation in summer range production, and range recovery subsequent to the 1988 fires. The outcome of wolf recovery will depend on how wolves are managed. Reduced hunter harvests of moose and elk may be advisable in certain areas. Wolves may eliminate the need for the controversial elk hunt in Grand Teton National Park.

Introduction

My purpose is to describe an expanded simulation model of wolf (*Canis lupus*)-prey dynamics for Yellowstone National Park and to discuss approaches for validation of the model. As in a previous version of the model (Boyce 1990), the user is allowed to choose among several likely management scenarios. By manipulating alternatives, the user can explore the consequences of management actions. In particular, it is essential to be able to anticipate if wolves will be culled if they leave Yellowstone or Grand Teton national parks, if poaching can be controlled within the parks, and if hunting for bison (*Bison bison*) and elk (*Cervus elaphus*) will continue in the Yellowstone River valley north of Gardiner, Montana.

The current version of the model, "Wolf5," will run on most DOS systems, and is available from the author. To obtain a free copy of the program, mail a formatted diskette (either 89 or 133 mm) and a self-addressed stamped mailer to the author at College of Natural Resources, University of Wisconsin, Stevens Point, Wisconsin, 54481 USA.

Methods

I will keep the technical description of the model to a minimum, because this is presented elsewhere (Boyce 1990, 1992, 1993, Boyce and Gaillard 1992). The core model structure is based on that developed by Boyce (1990), using stochastic difference equations to project time series of wolf and ungulate populations for 100 years into the future. As in the previous model, this version has been developed for interactive use, and provides maps showing the projected distribution of wolves. The user may select output to a graphics screen, disk, or printer.

In addition to the expanded geographic domain, the current model incorporates a new multispecies logistic functional response that I believe more realistically represents the behavior of wolves confronting alternative prey (equation 1, Appendix). The functional response governs the per capita rate at which prey are captured as a function of the number of prey available to the predators. For mammals, functional responses tend to be logistic (S-shaped), often labelled a type 3 functional response (Holling 1959a).

Justification for use of a logistic functional response is based upon the work of Garton et al. (1990) and the observation by L. D. Mech (U.S. Fish and Wildlife Service, pers. commun.) that prey switching occurs in wolf populations. An alternative is to employ a type 2 functional response, e.g., Holling's disc equation, as used in the wolf-prey model of Walters et al. (1981). Although I find the rationale for a logistic functional response to be sufficiently compelling, calculations reported in this paper have been performed using the disc equation as well.

Population and functional response parameters for each of the four species of ungulates are similar to those used by Boyce (1990), except that equation 1 has been employed (Table 1). I will not review the literature that forms the basis

Table 1. Population, functional response, and numerical response coefficients for each of four ungulate species wintering in Yellowstone National Park.

Species	r_0	b_1	W	P	A	F_{max}	R	T_h
ELK	0.28	2.7×10^{-5}	0.0233	0.00036	1.2×10^{-6}	25	0.075	0.04
BISON	0.23	9.2×10^{-5}	0.0079	0.0002	1.5×10^{-6}	10	0.13	0.1
MOOSE	0.2	2.5×10^{-4}	0.01	0.0001	1.5×10^{-6}	20	0.09	0.045
DEER	0.4	1.3×10^{-4}	0.009	0.0003	2.5×10^{-6}	110	0.015	0.009

r_0 = potential per capita population growth rate.
$b_1 = r_0/K$ = density-dependence coefficient; K = winter carrying capacity within Yellowstone.
W = coefficient scaling the response to winter severity.
P = response to green herbaceous phytomass.
A = attack constant for functional response, scaled to the relative preference by wolves (equation 1; see Boyce [1990]).
F_{max} = maximum number of prey killed per year given unlimited prey abundance — usually determined by satiation.
R = numerical response coefficient, scaled to the body mass of each prey species.
T_h = handling time.

for the functional response estimates because this is discussed in Boyce (1990) and Boyce and Gaillard (1992), and more generally by Keith (1983), Fuller (1989), Page (1989), and Huggard (1991).

The numerical response characterizes the rate at which captured prey are converted into predator offspring. Again this is usually assumed to be a logistic function for mammalian predators, simply because the numerical response is a product of the prey taken and thereby dependent upon the functional response at equation 1. The formula for numerical response is the same as in Boyce (1990). Procedures for estimating coefficients are detailed in Boyce and Gaillard (1992).

Stochastic variation enters the model through simulations of climate and hunter harvest of ungulates. Climate is modeled in detail using precipitation and temperature data from Mammoth, Cody, and Jackson, Wyoming. Regression analysis of climate data among these three areas was used to structure the stochastic projections of future climate (Boyce 1992). Carrying capacity for ungulates wintering in Yellowstone and the North Fork is determined in part by winter severity (Houston 1982, Merrill and Boyce 1991). In addition, an analysis of Landsat satellite imagery was used to adjust carrying capacity of elk and bison in Yellowstone for the green herbaceous phytomass on summer range (Merrill and Boyce 1991, Merrill et al. 1993). The effects of the 1988 fires on ungulate forage are modeled following the equations proposed by Boyce and Merrill (1991).

Relative to the northern Yellowstone elk herd, the Jackson elk herd is influenced to a greater extent by hunter harvest. Hunter harvest varies a great deal from year to year depending upon the timing of elk migration, weather, size of the elk herd, and harvest regulations (Boyce 1989). I

modeled this variation as a stochastic function based upon hunter harvest data from the Wyoming Game and Fish Department. Because most elk and bison in Jackson Hole are provisioned winter feed, winter severity does not influence herd size. Parameters for the Jackson Hole subpopulations are in Table 2.

For elk along the North Fork I have imposed three sources of stochastic variation. These include: 1) stochastic variation in hunter harvest of elk; 2) variation in winter severity; and 3) variation in summer forage. As for the Jackson elk herd, here I modeled hunter kill as a function of elk population size (Boyce 1992). Model parameters for the North Fork are summarized in Table 3.

Each of the species in the model is assumed to be governed by density dependence. For ungulates, this is assumed to be set by forage availability (both winter and summer), except for the winter-fed Jackson elk herd that may be regulated through dispersal (Sauer and Boyce 1983, Boyce 1989), and the Jackson bison herd that is culled by humans. Wolf density dependence is caused by territoriality (Walters et al. 1981, Packard and Mech 1980, 1983, Packard et al. 1983) and dispersal out of the park. Density dependence is modeled by Ricker's difference equation approximation for the logistic (Boyce 1990) or by a nonlinear variation attributable to Richards (see Appendix) modified to subtract animals killed by wolves.

The Yellowstone, Jackson Hole, and North Fork areas are modeled as separate units, but allowing for dispersal of wolves among subpopulations. This is not an unreasonable assumption because there is little dispersal of elk or other ungulates among these wintering areas (Boyce 1989).

Direction of dispersal of wolves out of Yellowstone is assumed to be random, with the number of dispersers leaving

Table 2. Population, functional response, and numerical response coefficients for each of four ungulate species in Jackson Hole.

Species	r_o	b_1	W	T	A	F_{max}	R
ELK	0.3	1.4×10^{-5}	0	3.5	1.5×10^{-6}	25	0.041
BISON	0.23	1.5×10^{-3}	0	3	4.5×10^{-6}	10	0.071
MOOSE	0.3	6.0×10^{-5}	0.01	3.5	4×10^{-6}	20	0.049
DEER	0.57	3.8×10^{-4}	0.009	3	7×10^{-6}	110	0.008

r_o = potential per capita population growth rate.
$b_1 = r_o/K$ = density-dependence coefficient; K = winter carrying capacity within Yellowstone.
W = coefficient scaling the response to winter severity.
T = exponent in Richards equation (equation 2).
A = attack constant for functional response, scaled to the relative preference by wolves (equation 1).
F_{max} = maximum number of prey killed given unlimited prey abundance — usually determined by satiation.
R = numerical response coefficient, scaled to the body mass of each prey species.
T_h = handling time — values for each species were identical to those used in Yellowstone.

Table 3. Population, functional response, and numerical response coefficients for each of the three ungulate species in the North Fork area.

Species	r_o	b_1	W	P	A	F_{max}	R
ELK	0.3	4.9×10^{-5}	0.0233	0.00036	2.5×10^{-6}	25	0.047
MOOSE	0.3	3.3×10^{-3}	0.01	0	1.5×10^{-6}	20	0.056
DEER	0.4	1.0×10^{-4}	0.009	0	2.5×10^{-6}	110	0.009

r_o = potential per capita population growth rate.
$b_1 = r_o/K$ = density-dependence coefficient; K = winter carrying capacity within Yellowstone.
W = coefficient scaling the response to winter severity.
P = response to green herbaceous phytomass.
A = attack constant for functional response, scaled to the relative preference by wolves (equation 2).
F_{max} = maximum number of prey killed given unlimited prey abundance — usually determined by satiation.
R = numerical response coefficient, scaled to the body mass of each prey species.
T_h = handling time — values for each species were identical to those used in Yellowstone and Jackson Hole.

the park proportional to the perimeter of the park that is adjacent to either the Jackson herd unit or the North Fork area. Thus, I estimated that 20% of the wolves dispersing from the core Yellowstone population will disperse into Jackson Hole, and 10% will end up in the North Fork drainage. The remaining dispersers are essentially lost to the model.

Bighorn sheep (*Ovis canadensis*) and pronghorn antelope (*Antilocapra americana*) were not included in the simulation model. Both of these prey species occur at low numbers in the area modeled and their influence on wolf population dynamics would therefore be negligible. Bighorn sheep populations are not expected to be seriously affected by

wolves because they largely avoid wolf predation by staying near escape terrain (cf. Cowan 1947, Huggard 1991). Pronghorns also are not likely to suffer heavy wolf predation because they winter near the town of Gardiner, Montana where human presence is expected to deter wolves. Yet Berger (1991) has postulated that wolves may affect coyote (*Canis latrans*) distribution such that coyote predation on pronghorns may be affected.

Program Options

Program Wolf5 projects wolf and ungulate populations, requiring input from the user on seven questions, each with

Table 4. Default responses to options in program "Wolf5."

Option	Default Alternative
CLIMATE	AVERAGE CLIMATE
MIGRATORY BEHAVIOUR	PARTIAL MIGRATIONS
ELK HUNT	CONTINUE ELK HUNT
CONFLICTS W/HUMANS	WOLVES AVOID HUMANS
LEGAL WOLF CULLS	WOLVES CULLED OUTSIDE PARK
POACHING IN PARK	LITTLE POACHING MORTALITY
INOCULUM SIZE	30 WOLVES RELEASED

options affording a total of 22 options for the future (not counting 25 possible inocula sizes). Three of these are management alternatives, and two offer the user an opportunity to anticipate wolf behavior. Because the combination of alternatives are numerous, I present a brief justification for the "default" selection for each choice for the purpose of comparing simulation results (Table 4).

Migratory behavior of wolves is assumed to increase the potential carrying capacity for wolves on their winter range. We do not know the extent to which migratory behavior is likely to develop as wolves seek prey that migrate seasonally (Shoesmith 1979, Boyce 1991a). Because seasonal movements by wolves occurred historically (Weaver 1978), the default choice here is "partial migrations," meaning that seasonal movements of wolves will occur in response to the availability of prey. But breeding wolves are expected to have restricted movements near ungulate winter ranges during the denning season.

Additional elk are added to the Yellowstone subpopulation each year if the user opts for terminating the late-season elk hunt near Gardiner, Montana. This is appropriate because the elk population model was constructed using data from the northern Yellowstone elk herd while it was being hunted, and hunting mortality has contributed to the density-dependent (compensatory) mortality observed in the population (Houston 1982, Eberhardt 1987). Further, it seems likely that the Montana Department of Fish, Wildlife and Parks will discontinue or substantially reduce hunting if elk numbers reach exceptionally low levels. Therefore, I set a lower threshold of 5,000 elk below which the hunt will be stopped even if the continued cull option is selected. Future permit quotas are set at 700 elk. Assuming 78% mean hunter success, and 10% crippling loss, the total number of elk killed by hunters during the late hunting season will average approximately 600 animals. It is unlikely that the Gardiner elk hunt will be closed, thus the most plausible default option is to continue the hunt.

If wolves are thought to incur frequent conflicts with humans, their mortality is increased by an arbitrary 15% in the model. This includes both illegal poaching mortality outside the parks as well as a higher level of damage control removals. There will certainly be occasional conflicts with humans and dispersing wolves will sometimes kill livestock (Fritts et al. 1984). Yet, because native prey are so abundant in the Yellowstone ecosystem, I set the default alternative to infrequent encounters with humans.

One of the management options discussed in the wolf recovery plan (U.S. Fish and Wildlife Service 1987) is to permit culling of wolves when they leave the recovery zone. If such legal culling is allowed, the model presumes that there will be a 15% increase in wolf mortality rate. Again, the magnitude of this value is arbitrary. For a "default" option here I assume that culling will occur when wolves leave the parks.

Will poaching on wolves occur? Here, the program allows an option where poaching may appear within the parks; the consequence will be an increase in wolf mortality rate by 20%. I am optimistic that illegal poaching can be controlled within the boundaries of the national parks, therefore, I set the default to little or no poaching within the parks.

Results

In general, the responses of ungulate populations to wolves are less pronounced in "Wolf5" than in the original "Wolf" model of Boyce (1990). This difference is a consequence of the explicit spatial structure of the model which dampens fluctuations over the three subpopulations. For example, fluctuations in Yellowstone may not be in sync with those in Jackson Hole or the North Fork, so that when the populations are totalled across areas we see less extreme fluctuations in total population size.

A major difference in predation for minor prey species occurs using equation 1 instead of the functional response used in previous versions of the model. When wolf numbers are maintained at high levels by abundant elk, we see in-

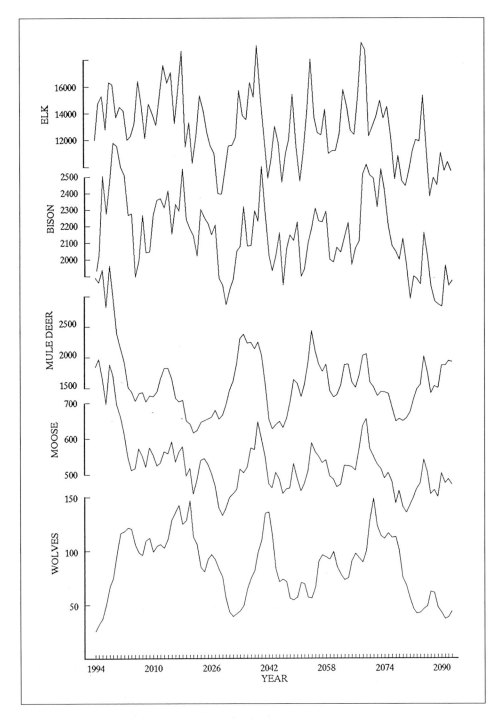

Fig. 1 *Trajectory for wolf, moose, mule deer, bison, and elk populations wintering in Yellowstone National Park for 100 years subsequent to the introduction of wolves. These population trajectories are calculated using Wolf5 under default options (see Table 4).*

creased predation rates on bison, moose (*Alces alces*), and mule deer (*Odocoileus hemionus*). The consequences are perhaps most dramatic for moose and mule deer wintering within Yellowstone National Park (Fig. 1, Tables 5–7). But because these species are relatively more abundant outside Yellowstone, the overall effects of wolf predation on ungulates in the GYE is not qualitatively different than reported by Boyce (1990).

For elk we expect to see a reduction in average population size over the next 100 years of 5–20% below that expected

without wolf recovery. Elk population response to various program options is summarized in Tables 5–7 and a sample population trajectory for Yellowstone National Park using default alternatives is given in Figure 1. Elk population response to wolf predation will be greatest in Yellowstone National Park, and least along the North Fork.

The magnitude of decline in bison numbers is higher than meets my intuition (Fig. 1, Tables 5–7), because bison are more formidable prey than elk. The extent to which bison will be taken when other prey are available is not known.

Table 5. Response to program alternatives in program "Wolf5" for wolves and ungulates in the Greater Yellowstone Ecosystem. Responses to alternatives are to be compared with the 100-year deterministic projection with wolves under the default alternatives as listed in Table 4. The first six lines present mean populations and standard deviations for each species under default conditions, and the subsequent lines contain the proportional response resulting from each alternative in the program.

Option/Alternative		N_{elk}	N_{bison}	N_{moose}	N_{deer}	N_{wolf}	Kill[1]
Stochastic Model (n = 1000)							
Default — no wolves		36726	2688	5909	10315	-	4575
Stan. deviation		4547	318	84	560	-	978
Default — with wolves		32954	2289	5565	8397	109	4400
Stan. deviation		4492	312	114	716	42	969
Deterministic Model							
Default — no wolves		37614	2685	5909	10322	-	4642
Default — with wolves		33779	2214	5527	8278	123	4496
Winter							
Climate	Severe	-0.030	-0.032	-0.001	0.024	-0.13	0.000
	Mild	0.030	0.035	0.001	0.021	0.122	-0.003
Migratory							
Behaviour	Nonmigr	0.017	0.037	0.010	0.035	-0.154	0.004
Elk Hunting	No hunt	0.029	-0.021	-0.007	-0.028	0.144	-0.136
Conflicts							
w/humans	Frequent	0.04	0.075	0.024	0.078	-0.341	0.013
Wolf Culls	None -	-0.043	-0.077	-0.026	-0.067	0.333	-0.02
Poaching	20%	0.054	0.1	0.033	0.106	-0.463	0.018

1   Hunter harvest of elk

Under no management scenarios do we see the development of a predator "pit" where low prey densities are sustained by wolf predation (see Gasaway et al. 1983, Page 1989). I attribute this to the high prey density, high prey productivity, and territorial/dispersal population limitation by wolves.

With wolves present, elk populations still undergo substantial population fluctuations, although the coefficient of variation in elk numbers decreased by approximately 10%. This observation, given the functional response at equation 1, is consistent with results reported by Boyce (1990) that were also based upon a stabilizing logistic functional response. However, substituting equation 1 with Holling's disc equation (type 2) yields increased variation occurring in prey populations under predation.

Effects of wolves on hunted populations of elk differ among areas. The Gardiner, Montana hunt is by limited quota and only a relatively small fraction of the northern herd is harvested in any particular year. Given continued quota permit regulations, we may expect no consequences of wolf recovery to the harvest of elk in Montana; rather we expect to see a reduction in herd size. In Jackson Hole and the North Fork, however, populations are harvested at higher rates, closer to the maximum sustained yield possible from these herds. Model predictions are that we can expect wolves to reduce the population size as well as reduce the average annual harvest of elk. However, the harvest reductions are relatively small: at least 5–10% for the Jackson elk herd and 1–2% for the North Fork.

Under most management scenarios, the model projects 50–170 wolves in the Yellowstone-Jackson-North Fork area

Table 6. Response to program alternatives in program "Wolf5" for Jackson Hole. The mean population size for comparison of alternative responses is from deterministic projections for 100 years with default alternatives as listed in Table 4. The first six lines present mean population size and standard deviations for each species under default conditions, and the subsequent lines include the proportional response resulting from each alternative in the program.

Option/Alternative		N_{elk}	N_{bison}	N_{moose}	N_{deer}	N_{wolf}	*Kill*[1]
Stochastic Model (n = 1000)							
Default — no wolves		15187	147	5000	1500	-	3329
Stan. deviation		1337	3	51	35	-	968
Default — with wolves		14523	135	4629	143	16	3165
Stan. deviation		1390	10	54	26	4	949
Deterministic Model							
Default — no wolves		15373	147	5002	1501	-	3392
Default — with wolves		14529	136	4924	1426	17	3246
Winter							
Climate	Severe	0.001	-0.029	0.002	0.003	0	0.001
	Mild	-0.005	0.022	-0.004	-0.006	0.118	-0.004
Migratory							
Behavior	Nonmigr	0.007	0	0.002	0.006	-0.06	0.005
Gardiner							
Elk Hunting	No hunt	-0.005	-0.007	-0.001	-0.004	0.118	-0.004
Conflicts							
w/humans	Frequent	0.023	0.007	0.006	0.02	-0.353	0.018
Wolf Culls	None	-0.036	-0.007	-0.009	-0.029	0.529	-0.028
Poaching	20%	0.033	0.007	0.009	0.029	-0.529	0.026

1   Hunter harvest of elk

during the century following reintroduction. Three of the options offered the user of program "Wolf5" involve an increase in the mortality rate for wolves, i.e., frequent conflicts with man, culling outside the park, and poaching within the park. Future wolf populations are highly sensitive to these options (Table 5).

Discussion

An overview of the Yellowstone wolf restoration program is provided by Mech (1991a). Restoring wolves to the GYE is necessary for accomplishing ecological-process management which prevails on national park and wilderness lands in the area (Boyce 1991b). Furthermore, wolf recovery could help to resolve the long-standing controversy regarding the elk hunt that occurs each fall in Grand Teton National Park (Murie 1951, Wood 1984). By affording a check on elk in Grand Teton, wolves could eliminate the perceived "need" for the hunt (Boyce 1989).

One of the mechanisms potentially driving a logistic functional response is prey switching. Because of the overwhelming abundance of elk, switching by wolves is not likely to occur among the four main ungulate prey available in Yellowstone National Park, except in a couple of situations: 1) in the Firehole area of the park, bison are sometimes at higher density than elk; and 2) in northern reaches of Jackson Hole moose densities may be higher than elk during winter. Thus we may see wolves specializing on bison in the Firehole area and on moose in northern Jackson Hole.

Table 7. Response to program alternatives in program "Wolf5" for the North Fork of the Shoshone River area. The projected population size for comparison of alternative responses is from deterministic runs for 100 years using default alternatives as listed in Table 4. The first six lines present the mean populations and standard deviations for each species under default conditions, and subsequent lines contain the proportional response resulting from each alternative in the program.

Option/Alternative		N_{elk}	N_{moose}	N_{deer}	N_{wolf}	Kill[1]
Stochastic Model (n = 1,000)						
Default — no wolves		5343	89	5512	-	637
Stan. deviation		896	2	162	-	154
Default — with wolves		5181	88	5341	7	633
Stan. deviation		967	2	157	2	162
Deterministic Model						
Default — no wolves		5745	89	5518	-	650
Default — with wolves		5623	88	5315	8	650
Winter						
Climate	Severe	-0.027	0	0.009	-0.125	0
	Mild	0.028	-0.011	-0.003	0	0
Migratory						
Behaviour	Nonmigr	0.004	0	0.006	-0.125	0
Gardiner						
Elk Hunting	No hunt	0	0	0	0	0
Conflicts						
w/humans	Frequent	0.010	0	0.018	-0.5	0
Wolf Culls	None	-0.009	-0.011	-0.016	0.5	0
Poaching	20%	0.012	0	0.02	-0.5	

1   Hunter harvest of elk

In addition to the management implications for the GYE, the behavior of program Wolf5 also gives insight into the mechanisms of population regulation in ungulates (see review by Skogland 1991). Wolf5 predicts that wolf predation will enforce a reduction in the variance in population size for ungulates, which is certainly evidence for population regulation by wolves. Despite this effect, however, there are still very substantial fluctuations in ungulate numbers, due largely to perturbations caused by severe winters of heavy snowfall and low temperatures. Indeed, a field study of an elk population undergoing fluctuations such as those simulated by program Wolf5 (Fig. 3) would be hard pressed to find evidence for regulation by wolves. Rather, one would be inclined to point to the importance of food limitation during hard winters. In fact, one would probably draw pre-

cisely the same conclusion as Skogland (1991) for reindeer (*Rangifer tarandus*), that they are "regulated in numbers by winter starvation due to density-dependent food limitation, enforced by density-independent recurrent adverse winter weather." Disentangling the effects of food limitation and predator limitation in a stochastically varying environment is a difficult problem, often only to be resolved by experimentation (Sinclair 1989, McCullough 1990).

Model Validation

How do we know if the model is good? Grant (1986) suggests four approaches for validating an ecological model. First, does the model address the problem? Second, does the model possess reasonable structure and behavior? The third approach is to conduct a sensitivity analysis of the model by

Elk populations throughout North American Rocky Mountain areas have increased to high densities in the absence of wolf predation. In the presence of wolf predation, elk numbers have decreased in the Canadian portion of the range. (Photo: U.S. Fish and Wildlife Service)

changing selected parameters in the model by an arbitrary amount and then studying system response and behavior. And the fourth is to attempt a quantitative assessment of the accuracy and precision of the model's outputs and behavior. I will address each of these components of model validation.

Does Wolf5 address the problem? I certainly believe so, insofar as the problem is anticipating the consequences of wolf recovery to wild ungulates in portions of the GYE. Yet, one might pose a different problem, e.g., what are the likely losses of domestic sheep and cattle to wolf predation in the GYE? This is certainly an interesting question that would merit further modeling, but it is explicitly beyond the scope of the present model.

Does the model possess reasonable structure and behavior? Again, I think so, but there are several points for debate here. Given the strong effects that climatic variation can have on ungulates in the GYE (Meagher 1971, Houston 1982, Merrill et al. 1988), I insist that stochastic variation must be there. I also find the evidence for a logistic functional response to be compelling (Garton et al. 1990), although the manner for dealing with multispecies interactions is inadequately understood. Density dependence is essential as is the simulation of hunter harvest.

Perhaps the point for which the structure of Wolf5 is most vulnerable to attack is the lack of age structure. In earlier versions of the model I included age structure, and found that the dynamics of the earlier model were qualitatively similar to the system without this factor. Because age structure greatly encumbered the model with serious consequences for interactive use, I eliminated age structure. This may have been a mistake, especially if age-selectivity varies with prey abundance. For wolves preying on white-tailed deer (*Odocoileus virginianus*) in Quebec, Potvin et al.

(1988) found that prime-aged deer were taken by wolves when deer were at low density, but that wolves selectively killed young and old individuals when the deer were at high density. Such an effect would be destabilizing. On the other hand, being larger prey, selectivity on elk may be more consistent at various densities, but we have no data that would suggest an appropriate magnitude for prey selectivity at various densities of the four species of ungulates included in Wolf5 . In the absence of sufficient data to justify the more complex age-structured model, I believe the simpler model structure is preferable.

Two other processes potentially affecting the dynamics of the system are not explicitly incorporated into the model: 1) variation in predation efficiency as a function of pack size (Page 1989); and 2) refugia for prey in between wolf pack territories as Mech (1977a) observed for white-tailed deer (see also Taylor and Perkins 1991). It is clear that the pack-size effect can be very important for populations of wolves comprising a small number of packs, e.g., Isle Royale (Page 1989). However, these effects will average out in a larger area so that I cannot imagine that the overall outcome will be affected.

Refugia for prey between territories may not be important in Yellowstone where the terrain is open and wolves could see and pursue ungulates occurring in areas between wolf pack territory boundaries, thereby eroding the buffer area between territories. In an earlier version of the model I attempted to incorporate such an effect by making the functional response a function of the density of wolves, imagining that interstitial spaces would decrease as wolf-pack density increased. I accomplished this using the functional response model presented at equation 4.4 in Yodzis (1989). However, my estimates of parameters for this complication

*Substantial wolf populations
have been absent from the
western United States for almost
a century. Recent efforts for the
reintroduction of wolves to this
area will require extensive
cooperation between Canada
and the United States. The
political debates on both sides
of the border will center on the
effects of wolf predation on
livestock in areas adjacent to
elk ranges, and on the ethics of
ecosystem restoration and
related subjects.
(Photo: J. Dutcher)*

were not empirically based and the behavior of the model
was not greatly affected. One might otherwise make a case
that the nature of the logistic functional response model that
I used may actually embrace a prey-refugia mechanism
(Abrams 1982). For these reasons I again opted for the
simpler version.

It would not take much to convince me of the significance
of any of these mechanisms in the future of wolf-ungulate
dynamics in Yellowstone. Yet my current assessment is that
the outcome of the model is not affected substantially, and I
am greatly concerned by the lack of data to estimate all of
the many additional parameters required to incorporate any
of these effects. To my mind, the model indeed passes the
test on reasonable structure and behavior.

The behavior of the model is reasonable, and many features of its dynamics match those described for ungulate
populations under predation (Skogland 1991). One dynami-
cal feature that can exist in a predator-prey model is the
existence of a "predator pit," i.e., in predator-prey models
possessing multiple equilibria, predation can sustain low
prey numbers, especially when alternative prey exist for the
predator. Such a pit need not exist, although with a logistic
functional response it is certainly possible, provided that
predator densities are high enough.

To evaluate the existence of a predator pit in Wolf5 , I
followed Nicholson's (1957) suggestion to reduce the prey
population whilst keeping predators at their pre-perturbation
density. This was performed for each prey species in each of
the three subpopulations, and invariably, the perturbed prey
population underwent a period of rapid growth ultimately
restoring its predisturbance population size. In no case was
there evidence of a predator pit for the parameter values
under default conditions in Wolf5 .

Whether predator pits actually occur in natural populations of wolves and ungulates is controversial. The examples
that are usually cited are confounded because of the interaction of wolf predation with hunting mortality on the prey
(e.g., Messier and Crête 1985, Skogland 1991). Although
such an interaction could not occur with the low level of
harvest imposed on elk in the northern Yellowstone herd, a
hunter-sustained "pit" or low equilibrium could be enforced
by hunting in either the Jackson or the North Fork elk herds.
I have modeled hunter harvests for these two herds based
upon the patterns of harvest as a function of numbers of elk
observed since 1950. No predator pit appears in my model
under the historical pattern of hunter harvest regulation, and
it seems unlikely that the Wyoming Game and Fish Department would entertain an alteration of hunter harvest patterns
that could enforce a predator pit.

A sensitivity analysis is the next validation stage. This has
been performed and the details are provided by Boyce and
Gaillard (1992). There is certainly nothing there that would
imply invalidation of the model. Furthermore, it is encouraging that some of the parameters for which estimates are
based upon inadequate data, for example, certain functional
response coefficients, are not highly sensitive.

The final validation approach is to see that the predictions
of the model match some real-life data. Ultimate validation
will, of course, require implementation of wolf recovery. Yet
there are data from other studies that can be investigated to
validate the numerical predictions of the model. Skogland
(1991) presents an analysis of the relationship between
predator biomass and ungulate biomass for 19 systems ranging from the arctic tundra and boreal zone through East
African savannas. Based upon the density of ungulates on
Yellowstone's winter ranges, Skogland's regression equa-

tion predicts that there should be 119 wolves in the park. Using default alternatives in Wolf5 , the model predicts an average of 114 wolves in the stochastic model and 118 in deterministic projections. The model predictions match Skogland's relationship with remarkable accuracy.

This is, of course, only a reflection of the reasonableness of the predictions of the model in terms of biomass of wolves and prey. Because empirical data from many of the same studies reviewed by Skogland were used in parameterizing my model, it may be not terribly surprising that we end up with similar results. Yet conformity between the model predictions and empirical data depend upon a large number of calculations and parameter estimates, especially the carrying capacities for prey and wolves, and the magnitude of coefficients in the functional and numerical responses. Thus the conformity between data and model predictions is reassuring.

Whether the forecasted dynamics of the predator-prey system are correct for Yellowstone remains to be seen. The predictions, nevertheless, may be viewed as useful hypotheses of how the system will behave with wolf predation.

In general, the ability of modelers to predict the behavior of complex ecological systems using simulation models has been poor (Eberhardt and Thomas 1991). One reason for this is that quantifying the interaction between species, e.g., competition and predation coefficients, requires considerable data and usually experimental situations where populations can be manipulated to document the response. Such detailed experimental data may never be available for a multispecies ungulate-wolf system, and I certainly cannot offer much confidence in my estimates of certain parameters. Likewise, we cannot place much stock in simulation projections based upon less than satisfactory parameter estimates.

On the other hand, the Yellowstone ungulate community is so overwhelmingly dominated by elk that the overall dynamics of the system will be largely driven by the interaction between elk and wolves. And our understanding of elk population biology in the GYE has a strong empirical basis (Houston 1982, Boyce 1989, Merrill and Boyce 1991). If my assumption is reasonable that wolf predation on elk is similar to that for moose, my projections for the wolf-elk system may be sound.

I regret that I cannot offer much assurance about the projections for the other ungulates, however. There is very little data on wolf predation on bison in a multispecies

system. Likewise, in general, we do not have sufficient data on wolf predation in a diverse ungulate community such as Yellowstone. My assumptions of additive predation in the original model (Boyce 1990) or linear substitutability in the present version (Wolf5) are not based upon sufficient data, but rather my intuition for what seems reasonable.

As a concluding remark, one of the fundamental principles in effective ecological modeling is finding an appropriate balance between model complexity and realism versus keeping the model simple enough so that the number of parameters is small and estimable (Grant 1986). One could certainly construct a more complex model than Wolf5 that incorporates more of the fascinating biology of wolf predation. However, I do not believe that there are sufficient data at this stage to justify such additional complexity.

Acknowledgments

I thank P. Abrams, N. Bishop, W. Brewster, S. Fritts, J.M. Gaillard, D. Gulley, M. Meagher, L. D. Mech, E. H. Merrill, R. Page, D. Seip, F. J. Singer, J. Varley, C. J. Walters, J. Weaver, and J. Yorgason for assistance, reviews, and comments.

Appendix

The multi-species disc equation has been modified to incorporate a type 3 functional response:

$$F_i = A_i N_i (\Sigma\ N_j)/(1 + T_{hi} A_i [\Sigma N_j]^2) \qquad \text{(equation 1)}$$

where N_i is the population size, $A_i \Sigma N_j$ is the attack rate, and T_{hi} is the handling time for the ith prey species, and N_j is the population size for the jth alternative prey species (see Abrams and Allison 1982). This form has been used in Wolf5 .

The Richards (1959) generalization of the difference equation approximation of the logistic is sometimes referred to as the theta-logistic:

$$N(t+1) = N(t)\exp\{r_o[1-(N[t]/K)^T]\} \qquad \text{(equation 2)}$$

where r_o is the potential per capita rate of population increase given no density dependence (N = 0), K is the asymptotic carrying capacity, and T is a term which scales the approach of the population to its K.

Projecting the Potential Effects of Wolf Predation on Elk and Mule Deer in the East Front Portion of the Northwest Montana Wolf Recovery Area

■ David J. Vales And James M. Peek

We modeled the potential effects of wolf predation on mule deer and elk populations of the Rocky Mountain East Front from Glacier National Park to and including the Dearborn River drainage in Montana. Models were used to estimate the effects of different numbers of wolves on mule deer and elk, with and without prey compensatory responses in survival and fecundity dependent upon population density. The presence of wolves would inevitably reduce the number of elk available for hunter harvest, assuming no compensatory relationships existed and population levels remained stable. Approximately 50 wolves could be sustained by elk if hunter harvest of cows and calves was reduced by half, and more could be sustained if no antlerless hunting was allowed. The mule deer population could probably support 30–45 wolves and sustain harvests of 500 animals by hunters. Hunter harvest of elk and mule deer would likely consist of fewer antlerless animals in the presence of wolves, using the assumptions in the models. The presence of wolves in this area would undoubtedly require more intensive population monitoring of the associated ungulate complex.

Introduction

We report on models that project the potential effects of wolf (*Canis lupus*) predation on elk (*Cervus elaphus*) and mule deer (*Odocoileus hemionus*) in the Rocky Mountain East Front portion of the Northwest Montana Wolf Recovery Area (U.S. Fish and Wildlife Service 1987, Fritts et al. this volume). The East Front includes that portion of the recovery area east of the Continental Divide, west of U.S. route 89, and south of Glacier National Park (Fig. 1). The East Front is approximately 5,125 km², or 32% of the total recovery area and contains about 40% of the elk in the recovery area (Montana Department of Fish, Wildlife and Parks 1988). The East Front was chosen for study because data for mule deer and particularly elk were available from Montana Department of Fish, Wildlife and Parks (MDFWP). Other prey species including bighorn sheep (*Ovis canadensis*), mountain goats (*Oreamnos americanus*), moose (*Alces alces*), and white-tailed deer (*Odocoileus virginianus*) are present, but the predominant prey base will likely be the two most abundant species, elk and mule deer.

The East Front elk population comprises five different groups (J. McCarthy, Montana Fish, Wildlife and Parks, pers. commun., 29 Sept. 1987) which winter on the Dearborn River drainage, the Sun River, the Blackleaf including Dupuyer Creek, the Badger–Two Medicine River drainages, and the St. Mary's area of Glacier National Park (Fig. 1). Fourteen elk winter ranges have been identified with a total area of 833 km² (MDFWP 1988). The winter population estimate outside Glacier Park was 4,000+ with a winter sex ratio of 33 bulls aged one year and older:100 cows one year and older, and age ratio of 40 calves:100 cows (MDFWP 1988). Martinka (1982) estimated that 300 elk wintered in the park, but we did not include this herd in the analyses because its dynamics have not been investigated. Elk summer throughout the East Front, but are patchily distributed (MDFWP 1988). We estimated elk density at 5/km² during winter (4,000 elk/833 km²) and about 1/km² in summer (5,070 elk in summer/5,125 km²).

There are seven mule deer winter ranges along the East Front, totalling about 289 km² (Anonymous 1987b). J.

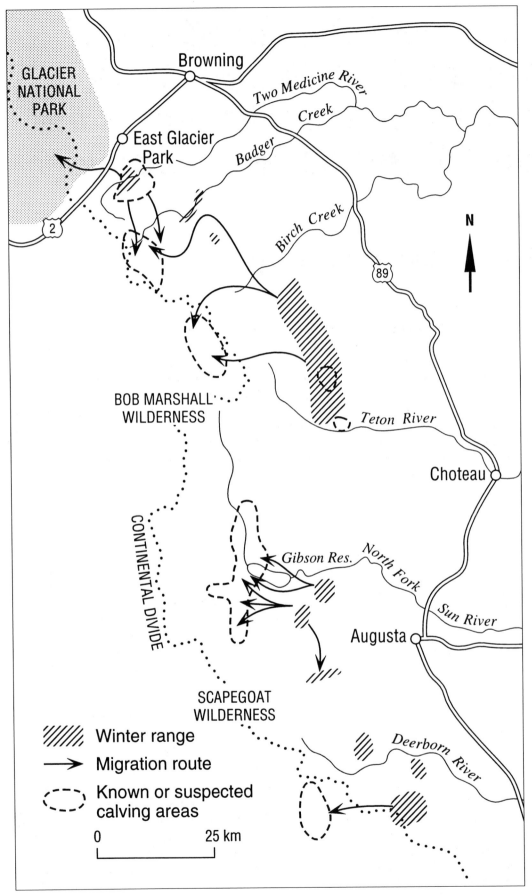

Fig. 1 *Map of the three wolf recovery areas and Rocky Mountain East Front portion of the Northwest Montana Recovery Area (from USFWS 1987, Anonymous 1987b).*

McCarthy and G. Olson (Montana Fish, Wildlife and Park, pers. commun., 28 Jan. 1988) estimated that the East Front mule deer population ranged from 6,000 to 12,000 over the 1978–1988 period. Ihsle (1982) estimated winter populations at 5,653 in 1980 and 6,014 in 1981 on the intensively studied winter ranges. We calculated an approximate winter density of 21 deer/km^2 (6,000 deer/289 km^2). Fawn:adult doe ratios ranged between 35:100 and 75:100, while the sex ratio was estimated at 30:100 from data collected by McCarthy et al. (1986).

Information on wolf-prey relationships in ecosystems where mule deer and elk were the primary prey species consists of two studies in Alberta (Carbyn 1975, Gunson 1986) and the Wolf Ecology Project in northwest Montana (Ream et al. 1986). Descriptive models of wolf-ungulate relationships were presented by Theberger and Gauthier (1985). Quantitative models of wolf-ungulate relationships have been developed by Walters et al. (1981), Keith (1983), VanBallenberghe and Dart (1983), Hastings (1984), and Fuller (1989). Recent simulations of potential wolf-ungulate interactions in and adjacent to Yellowstone National Park, Wyoming were presented by Boyce (1993), Boyce and Gaillard (1992), Garton et al. (1990, 1992), and Vales and Peek (1993). For our approach we asked two questions: will prey populations remain stable at the recent average hunter harvest across a range of wolf numbers; if not, how must hunter harvest be changed to offset losses to wolves.

Methods

We used discrete balance models (Starfield and Bleloch 1986, Walters 1986, Eberhardt 1987) with age structures truncated to young-of-the-year, yearlings, and adults. Survival rates and predation were applied seasonally (summer prehunt and winter posthunt). Harvest rates reflect the proportion of the prehunt population that was harvested by hunters.

Elk data from MDFWP (1988) and deer data from McCarthy et al. (1986) were used to obtain harvest data, and sex and age ratio estimates to calculate the proportions of young, females, and males in the populations. Because hunter harvest was the major limiting factor of elk, we assumed that hunter harvest data were the most reliable data available and built our model populations on this assumption. Wounding loss was assumed to be reflected in the observed population composition following the hunt, thus it was accounted for in the winter survival rate estimates. Harvest age structures were from 1971–1982 Sun River herd data for elk (Bucsis et al. 1985), and 1984 data for deer (hunting districts 424, 425, 427, 428, and 442 in McCarthy et al. 1985). In our initial population analysis we ran models using various combinations of survival and fecundity rates until the sex and age structure stabilized and the models gave population size, composition, and harvest that approximated observed averages for elk, or gave a population that exhib-

ited the desired response for deer (Peek and Vales 1989). For elk we used average population size of 4,000 in winter, composition of 33 bulls:100 cows:40 calves in winter, and harvest of 580 elk because we did not detect trends over a 22-year period (1964–1985) in these values. Only age structure remained stable over time for deer, and we used several models to represent observed population fluctuation between 6,000 and 12,000 deer over a 10-year period.

We modeled compensatory responses by elk and deer to wolf predation by including linear density dependent equations of fecundity and survival. Elk and mule deer hunting on the East Front selects for males, thus the posthunt sex ratio favors females. Populations exhibiting these characteristics could have a maximum sustained yield (MSY) at a population density greater than 1/2 K (Fowler 1981). East Front elk populations were managed to provide a sustained yield and prevent populations from overutilizing winter range forage (Bucsis et al. 1985). If we assume that the elk population is at MSY at 4,000, then 1/2 K might be at a size less than 4,000. We chose an arbitrary population size of 6,000 to represent K, and 3,000 for 1/2 K to help us develop density-dependent equations (Peek and Vales 1989).

One noncompensatory model (E.1) and one compensatory (density-dependent) model (E.2) was developed for elk. The E.1 model represented recent elk numbers and harvests. Three noncompensatory models (D.1, D.2, and D.3) and one compensatory model (D.4) were used for deer populations. Model D.1 used survival rates and hunter harvest rates that gave a stable mule deer population at about 6,000 with a harvest of about 1,000. Model D.2 assumed an initial population of 6,000 that grew to about 10,000 in 10 years in the absence of hunting. Model D.3 assumed an initial population of 12,000 that declined to 6,000 in 10 years in the absence of hunting. Fecundity and survival rates from population models D.2 and D.3 were combined to develop linear density-dependent functions of survival and fecundity which were used in model D.4.

For simplicity we modeled wolves as individuals with fixed predation rates rather than having the rates be a function of prey numbers (i.e., the functional response, Holling 1959b). Wolf population dynamics were not explicitly modeled, though by exploring a range of wolf numbers we accounted for potential numerical responses by wolves and their effects on prey. A range of 10–100 wolves using low and high wolf kill rates were simulated to encompass the potential range of predation anticipated on these elk and deer populations. We did not model spatial distribution of wolves; predation was assumed to occur proportionately across the entire East Front. Ungulate populations were at stable age distribution prior to application of wolf predation. The simulations with predation were run until a stable age distribution was reached before reporting model results. Predation was applied seasonally, and separate from survival rates.

Table 1. Partitioning the number and biomass of 28 animals killed/wolf/year (HIGH predation rate) among elk and deer by summer and winter. Mass is in kg by species, sex, and age. Predation rates for LOW were multiplied by 12/28.

Species, Sex and Age Class	Summer				Winter			
	n	Mass	Util.[1]	Cons.[2]	n	Mass	Util.[1]	Cons.[2]
Elk:								
Female calves	0.55	64	0.80	28	0.5	114	0.75	43
Male calves	0.55	64	0.80	28	0.5	114	0.75	43
Yearling cows	0.1	240	0.75	18	0.26	240	0.75	47
2+ cows	0.7	240	0.75	126	1.34	240	0.75	241
Spike bulls	0.1	260	0.75	19	0.3	260	0.75	58
2+ bulls	0.2	260	0.75	39	0.5	260	0.75	98
Total Elk:	**2.2**			**258**	**3.4**			**530**
Deer:								
Female fawns	1.85	19	0.80	28	1.7	35	0.75	45
Male fawns	1.85	19	0.80	28	1.7	35	0.75	45
Yearling does	0.4	60	0.75	18	0.9	60	0.75	40
2+ does	1.2	60	0.75	54	2.6	60	0.75	117
Yearling bucks	2.0	70	0.75	105	3.4	70	0.75	178
2+ bucks	1.3	70	0.75	68	3.5	70	0.75	184
Total Deer:	**8.6**			**301**	**13.8**			**609**
Total Elk + Deer	**10.8**			**559**	**17.2**			**1139**

1 Utilization is proportion of carcass consumed.
2 Consumption is kg consumed per wolf.

Hunter harvest rates were varied to explore a range of harvest strategies by using combinations of calf, cow, and bull harvest rates. For the elk models harvest rates ranged from 0.00 to 0.10 for calves, 0.00–0.09 for cows, and 0.10–0.40 for bulls, in increments of 0.01. Combinations of harvest rates examined for deer were 0.01–0.09 for fawns, 0.01–0.10 for does, 0.14–0.44 for yearling bucks, and 0.20–0.50 for 2+ bucks in increments of 0.01. All possible combinations of harvest rates in those ranges were evaluated for each level of wolf numbers and predation rates.

For comparison we used Keith's (1983) equation to estimate the number of wolves that could be supported by the East Front elk and deer populations. We also used Fuller's (1989) modification of Keith's (1983) equation to predict hunter harvest and ungulate numbers.

Relevant Aspects of Wolf Predation

The ranges in kill rates of deer and elk (13–42 days/kill/wolf) from Keith (1983), Gunson (1986), and Fuller (1989) were used to estimate the kill rates that might occur on the East Front. This would be equivalent to nine to 28 ungulates killed/wolf/year. We used two estimates of wolf annual kill rates, 12 (LOW) and 28 (HIGH) to cover the range of kill rates in the literature.

Carbyn (1975) reported that mule deer and elk were the major prey items year-long in the diet of wolves in Jasper National Park. Mule deer were the most frequent food item even though they were outnumbered by elk eight to one.

This trend was also evident in Riding Mountain National Park, where white-tailed deer comprised a proportionately greater part of the wolf diet than did elk when relative availability of the two species was considered, even though more elk were killed than deer (Carbyn 1983b). To account for the greater availability of mule deer on the East Front and their greater vulnerability to wolves, we used a ratio of four deer killed/elk killed (Table 1).

Bull elk may be more vulnerable to predation than cows (Carbyn 1975, 1983b). Carbyn (1980) reported that 39 of 57 adult elk killed by wolves were cows, a sex ratio of 46:100.

Table 2. Age structures of elk and deer in wolf-killed samples compared with proportions in the population.

Location	Species	%<1 Wolf	%<1 Pop	% Adult[1] Wolf	% Adult[1] Pop	% old[1] Wolf	% old[1] Pop	Sample Wolf	Sample Pop
NE Minnesota[2]	WT deer	17	26	68	73	15	1	127	423
NW Minnesota[3]	WT deer	34	33	35	62	31	6	29	715
E Ontario[4]	WT deer	30	35	65	63	5	2	63	444
W Ontario[5]	WT deer	17	20	61	52	22	28	331	275
Jasper N.P.[6]	Mule deer	62		31		7		13	
Jasper N.P.[6]	Elk	41		32		27		22	
Riding Mtn.[7,8]	Elk	34	19	26	41	40	40	134	132

1 Adult = 1-7; Old = > 7 years of age.
2 Mech and Frenzel 1971a. Population from hunter harvest.
3 Fritts and Mech 1981. Population from hunter harvest.
4 Kolenosky 1972. Population from hunter harvest.
5 Pimlott et al. 1969. Population from road kills.
6 Carbyn 1975. No population estimates available.
7 Carbyn 1980. Population from hunter harvest.
8 Carbyn et al. 1987. Wolf kills, 1975-1986.

No sex ratios in the harvest or the population were given, but that ratio appears high, suggesting that more bulls were being taken than what would be expected to occur in the population. We used a ratio of 46 bulls:100 cows killed by wolves in our elk models (Table 1).

Kolenosky (1972) reported a sex ratio of 250 bucks:100 does for white-tailed deer killed by wolves in Ontario. Bucks constituted 57% of the adults killed (133 bucks:100 does) by wolves in Algonquin Park (Pimlott et al. 1969) and 71% (245 bucks:100 does) in northeastern Minnesota (Mech and Frenzel 1971a). Carbyn (1975) found six adult males and two adult female mule deer killed by wolves in Jasper, a 3:1 ratio. We used a sex ratio of 2 bucks:1 doe killed by wolves in our deer models (Table 1).

Bjorge and Gunson (1989) reported that 65% of elk killed were calves, while only 35% of the population was calves. The proportions of calves killed by wolves in Jasper (Carbyn 1975) and Riding Mountain National Parks (Carbyn 1980) were similar, averaging 37.5% (Table 2). In Riding Mountain National Park, calves were taken 1.79 times greater than their estimated occurrence in the population. We estimated that 38% of the elk killed by wolves were calves (Table 1), or about 1.6 times greater than their abundance in the population.

The proportions of fawn white-tailed and mule deer killed by wolves from the five studies listed in Table 2 ranged from 17% to 62%. The average composition of 32% fawns killed by wolves was used in our models (Table 1).

Results

Model Projections of Wolf Predation on Elk

With no hunting, the E.1 elk population could support up to 76 wolves before declining, and the E.2 model could support 51–100 wolves in the absence of hunting. When varied harvest rates were applied to the E.1 model, up to 75 wolves could be supported by a stable elk population and yield a total hunter harvest of 150–600 elk (Fig. 2). Total harvest was a function of the number of wolves and percent of total harvest which was bull harvest. Harvest was greatest when bulls comprised 50–70% of the total harvest, but the sex ratio declined below 25 bulls:100 cows when harvest was maximized. At 50 wolves and low predation, cow elk harvest could not exceed 7%, while with high predation, cow harvest could not exceed 2% without causing a decline (Fig. 3). We estimated that the average cow harvest rate was 8%. Our analysis suggested that cow harvest must decline in the presence of wolves if winter elk numbers are to remain at 4,000.

By varying harvest rates in the density-dependent E.2 model, at least 80 wolves at high predation rates could be supported with total elk harvests ranging from 150 to 450 (Fig. 4). Highest harvest was obtained when between 50% and 70% of the total harvest were bulls, though winter sex ratios dropped below 30:100. A moderate harvest rate of cows (2–4%) and bulls (total harvest comprised 50% bulls) would be an optimum harvest regime for maximum herd

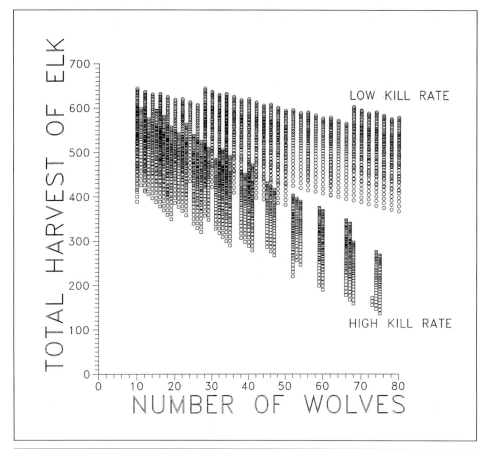

Fig. 2 *Range in total harvest of elk as a function of the number of wolves for the E.1 model elk population at LOW and HIGH kill rates. Values plotted were for finite rate of increase between 0.999 and 1.001. Late-winter initial population was 4,000. Harvest rates examined were 0–10% calves, 0–9% cows, and 10–40% bulls.*

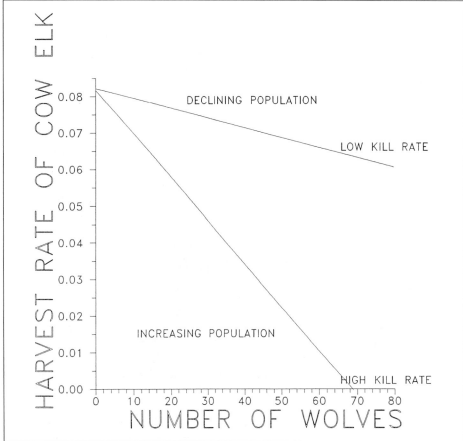

Fig. 3 *Range in cow elk harvest rate (proportion of prehunt population) as a function of the number of wolves for the E.1 model elk population at LOW and HIGH predation rates. Harvest rates above the LOW line produce a declining population; harvest rates below the HIGH line produce an increasing population. Area between the two lines is area of uncertainty where cow harvest rate depends on wolf predation rate. A cow harvest rate of 0.083 maintained a stable E.1 model population without wolves.*

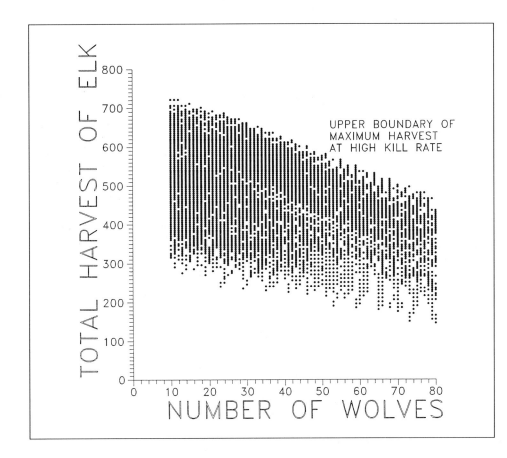

Fig. 4 *Range in total harvest of elk as a function of the number of wolves for the E.2 model elk population with compensatory responses at HIGH predation. Values plotted were for finite rate of increase between 0.9995 and 1.0005. Harvest rates examined were 0–10% calves, 0–9% cows, and 10–40% bulls.*

productivity that would also allow wolves to coexist under the E.2 density-dependent model scenario. These predictions were based upon high predation rates and would relax if predation rates were lower. High wolf numbers with the compensatory model reduced the elk population and promoted a strong compensatory response, while lower wolf numbers permitted the population to increase thereby reducing productivity.

As an alternative to reducing harvest to support wolf recovery, we explored increasing the number of elk to support wolves and maintain harvest (Fig. 5). With 50 wolves, 4,500–7,000 elk during winter, based on the E.1 model, were needed to support the average harvest of 580 animals.

Model Projections of Wolf Predation on Mule Deer

In the absence of harvest the D.1 model supported 27 (HIGH kill rates) to 57 (LOW) wolves before declining, the D.2 model supported 39–81 wolves, and the D.4 model supported 50–100 wolves. For models with hunter harvest we present results only for a harvest of 500 or more deer, at least 1% harvest of fawns and does, 14% yearling and 20% mature buck harvest, and if the population finite rate of increase was greater than 0.999. The D.1 model supported up to 20 wolves at HIGH predation while yielding a harvest of 500 to 650 deer, and up to 45 wolves at LOW predation. Model D.2 supported 36–78 wolves, depending on predation rate, and

provided at least a 500 deer harvest (Fig. 6). The D.4 density-dependent model allowed for up to 45 wolves at HIGH predation while yielding a total harvest greater that 500 deer (Fig. 7). As with elk, maximum harvest occurred when the percent of total harvest which were males were moderate (50–75%), but this was also the range that reduced the sex ratio the most.

Projections of Wolf Predation Using Keith's Equation

Assuming wolf kill rates in the range of 12–28 ungulates/wolf, wolves consuming only elk, and a rate of increase for the E.1 population in the absence of hunting of 1.0906, then 132–309 elk per wolf would be needed to maintain a stable population using Keith's (1983) equation. For the 4,000 elk on the East Front, 13–30 wolves could be supported before elk numbers declined. The D.1 model deer population at 6,000 could support 10–24 wolves without harvesting. If the D.2 model was more realistic, a deer population of 8,000 could support 22–52 wolves without harvesting, or 9–21 wolves with a harvest of 500 deer.

These analyses using Keith's (1983) equation assumed only a single species was preyed upon. If 1.2–5.6 elk and 10.8–22.4 deer are killed per wolf per year, then the E.1 elk population of 4,000 could support 65–300 wolves without harvest and the D.2 deer population at 8,000 could support

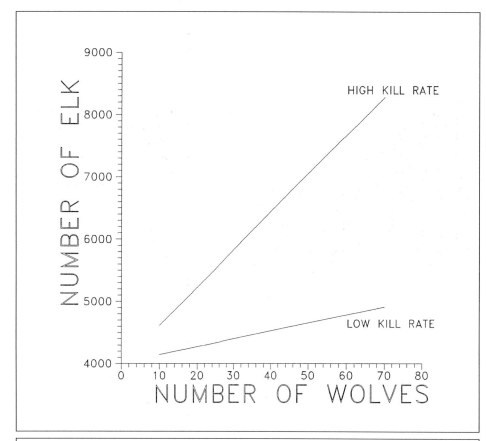

Fig. 5 *Range in number of elk needed to support a desired wolf population and maintain a stable elk population with average level of harvest (580 elk) and unchanging model E.1 life history parameters. Upper boundary for HIGH predation and lower for LOW predation rates.*

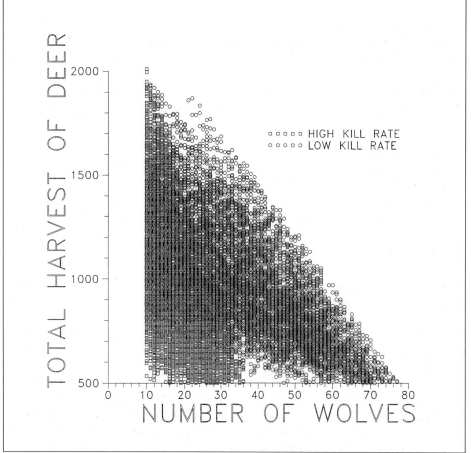

Fig. 6 *Range in total harvest of mule deer as a function of the number of wolves for the D.2 model deer population at LOW and HIGH predation rates. Values plotted were for total harvest greater than 500 and finite rate of increase greater than 0.999. Initial late-winter population was 6,000. Harvest rates examined were 1–8% fawns, 1–7% does, 24–44% yearling bucks, and 30–50% 2+ bucks.*

28–58 wolves without harvest, or 11–23 wolves with harvest.

Projections of Wolf Predation Using Fuller's Equation

There was no difference in the number of wolves predicted by Fuller's (1989) and Keith's (1983) equations. Fuller's equation predicted that with 50 wolves, total elk harvest may range from 82 at high predation (5.6 elk killed/wolf/year) to 302 at low predation (1.2 elk/wolf/year) using the E.1 model 1.0906 rate of increase. Our E.1 model predicted that harvest might range from 200 to 600 elk with 50 wolves (Fig. 2). In order for the E.1 population to support 50 wolves and the average harvest of 580 elk, Fuller's model projected that 7,100–9,500 elk would be required at the 1.0906 rate of increase. Our projections suggested that 4,500–7,000 elk would be needed for 50 wolves (Fig. 5).

Projected deer harvest using Fuller's equation with the D.1 model (6,000 deer with rate of increase 1.048) and 10 wolves ranged 64 to 180. Our projections allowed a harvest of 600–1,400 deer with 10 wolves and initial population of 6,000. With the D.2 model (rate of increase 1.0786) and 10 wolves, Fuller's equation predicted a harvest of 405 to 521 deer, while our projections were for a harvest of 500 to 1,800 deer (Fig. 6). With Fuller's equation the number of deer

needed to support 10 wolves and a harvest of 1,000 deer for the D.1 model ranged 23,000 to 25,500 deer while our models projected needing 7,000 to 8,200. Fuller's equation projected that 17,000–22,000 deer were needed for a harvest of 950 deer with 35 wolves for the D.2 model, while our model projections ranged from 6,900 to 9,700.

Discussion

Our models suggested that the East Front deer population may be more influenced by wolf predation than would elk, which would be expected because of the higher predation rates on deer. The deer projections were considered less reliable than the ones for elk because mortality factors not related to documented harvest comprised a greater share of the mortality. The degree to which other forms of nonhunting mortality would be compensated by the mortality due to wolf predation was unknown, but could be high.

The mule deer population may support 30–45 wolves, or three to four breeding pairs if pack size averaged 10, while 500 deer were harvested, but with mostly bucks harvested. That same number of wolves could also be supported by the elk population but with a reduction in cow and total harvest. In both ungulate populations, harvest of males would have to be heavy in order to achieve maximum harvest because female harvest must be reduced. Selective harvest along with

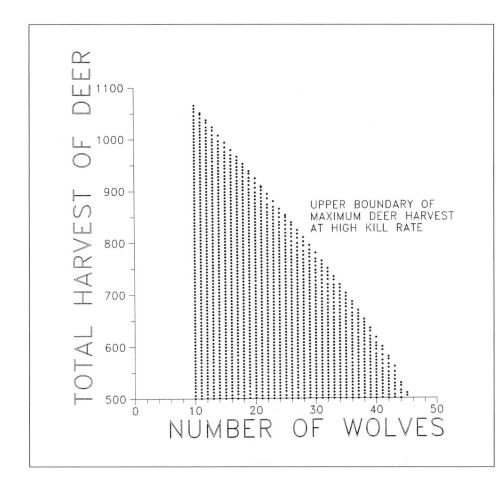

Fig. 7 *Range in total harvest of mule deer as a function of the number of wolves for the D.4 model deer population with compensatory responses at HIGH predation. Values plotted were for total harvest greater than 500 and finite rate of increase greater than 0.999. Initial late-winter population was 6,000. Harvest rates examined were 1–8% fawns, 1–7% does, 24–44% yearling bucks, and 30–50% 2+ bucks.*

selective predation on males, though, would greatly reduce the adult sex ratio.

Management other than reducing hunter harvest to support wolves might be employed. Managers might increase herd productivity by improving habitat quality in an effort to improve survival and fecundity, reduce wounding loss and illegal kill, and/or acquire more winter-spring range. More ungulates, however, would increase density and might result in increased predation if the wolf functional response was not already at an asymptote.

Differences between Fuller's (1989) equations and our model projections were likely to have been due to considering the sex-age composition of the harvest and wolf kill in our models. Fuller's equations do not consider sex- or age-specific harvest or wolf kill and thus treat males, females, and young alike. Projections using Fuller's equations would result in a very conservative estimate of harvest. Additionally, very high estimates of deer population sizes were projected to support a particular harvest and number of wolves because the sex-specific buck harvest was not considered in Fuller's equations. We strongly recommend that projections of wolf numbers, harvest, or population sizes needed to support a given level of wolves consider sex and age-specific harvest and predation in populations where hunting or predation is biased toward particular sex-age classes.

Wolves are highly opportunistic and modify kill rates and sex-age composition of kills as prey vulnerability and availability changes. Wolves exhibit a functional response in predation to prey numbers, increasing number of prey killed when prey populations are larger or more vulnerable (Messier and Crete 1985). While kill rates may be a function of prey numbers, we used static predation rates because functional response equation coefficients were unknown for elk, and we wanted to reduce model complexity. By using a range of literature-derived predation rates and composition, and a range of wolf numbers, we feel that we have bracketed the potential total response by wolves. Elk and deer density may be greater than 1/km^2 over much of the summer range, which may be high enough for kill rates to be near the asymptote of the functional response curve. Elk populations were modeled for stability, a viable management objective. Without a change in elk population size, and assuming constant distribution over time, individual wolves may not exhibit a functional response because prey numbers would not change. There could be a change in herd age or sex structure though that might alter our predictions of the proportions of each age and sex available and killed by wolves. We made projections using results of studies of prey populations which are not as heavily hunted as are the elk on the East Front, and the subset of individuals that are vulnerable to wolves in such a population may be different than what we predict from the literature.

The predation rates we used take into consideration scavenging by wolves of wounded animals and carcasses attrib-

utable to hunters because the literature-derived predation rates account for this scavenging, thus it is not considered a bias in our investigation. When our predation rates were converted to biomass, our consumption estimate of 4.7 kg/wolf/day (1700 kg/wolf/year, Table 1) at the HIGH predation rate was within those reported by Mech (1977c), Holleman et al. (1980), and Carbyn et al. (1987).

All investigations of wolf-prey relationships in North America have been done in more northerly areas where the relevant relationships may differ from what may occur on the East Front. Prey populations may exhibit more resiliency to wolf predation where growing seasons are longer and climate is generally less severe than in northern areas.

VanBallenberghe and Dart (1983), in a similar predictive exercise for moose and wolves, assumed that fecundity rates of moose were inversely related to density, and some evidence exists that this is the case for elk (Carbyn 1975, Freddy 1987, Houston 1982). The ultimate relationship would be nutritionally based, and may be related in terms of available forage per individual as that affects condition, calf production, and survival. If prey population densities decrease, their productivity could increase. Since the degree and timing of this compensatory response is largely unpredictable, models without density dependence are worth while to examine the effects of predation. However, this may bias the effects of predation on populations upward, and thus predict that lower levels of wolves can be accommodated and sustain lower levels of hunter harvest than may actually occur. It also makes the projections applicable only until compensatory responses begin to take place, with the time interval being undetermined. Nevertheless, if predation alters the overall nutritional status of a population, increased production and survival might be expected (a density-dependent compensatory response). Alternatively, a change in the age structure of females by culling older, less-productive animals thus increasing the proportion of younger females would also increase herd productivity. The magnitude, timing, and nature of the prey responses to predation may represent the largest unknown factors which influence our projections. We predict that prey populations that are lightly hunted would be more likely to demonstrate compensatory responses in production and survival when wolves are present than would populations that are more heavily hunted, as is the case with the East Front elk population.

Our predictions assume that wolf predation would be equally distributed across the entire East Front prey population south of Glacier National Park. Since wolf populations are most likely to be initially established by immigration into one or perhaps several parts of the area, this assumption will not hold, at least for the colonization period. It is also unlikely, even after a population is considered to be fully established, that wolf predation would be equally distributed across the entire prey population on the East Front. Prey population segments wintering in more severe habitats furthest from human activity may be more vulnerable to wolf predation, while those wintering out on foothills closer to human habitation may be less vulnerable. Thus, for certain population segments, our estimates of predation effects may be biased low and for others, high.

Home range size of wolves may affect the numbers of wolves that could occupy the East Front, regardless of ungulate density and composition. Wolves are territorial and packs typically occupy a certain area exclusive of other packs (Packard and Mech 1983). Wolves might have territories along the East Front that encompass both summer and wintering populations of the major prey, assumed to be mule deer and elk, as Cowan (1947) suggested for Jasper wolves. The East Front comprises approximately 5,125 km^2, of which 833 km^2 is winter range (MDFWP 1988, Lewis and Clark National Forest area including all ownerships). Recorded wolf pack territories range from 50 to 3,077 km^2 in size (Fuller and Keith 1980, Fritts and Mech 1981, Ballard et al. 1987, Carbyn et al. 1987, Fuller 1989), allowing for a range of 1.7 to 100 wolf territories on the East Front. Topography suggests home ranges would be linearly distributed along the major drainages and include summer and winter ungulate habitat. Several packs might occupy the major drainages and at least one pack could occupy each drainage. Tentatively, room for at least six packs is available on the East Front: one each in Badger–Two Medicine, Dupuyer Creek, Teton River, Dearborn, and two on the Sun River, with others probably exclusively associated with the mule deer winter ranges. Because our analyses focused only on the East Front, a portion of the entire Northwest Montana Recovery area, our estimates of number of packs and wolves might be half of what the entire recovery area could support.

If and when wolves again occupy the East Front, management must accommodate all interests that will be involved. Precise and accurate monitoring of wolves and ungulates will be necessary, based on assumptions that can be continually evaluated and updated. The presence of the wolf would require more comprehensive management of its prey base than presently exists. Management of a system which includes wolves, hunters, and big game must include management of wolf populations as well as their prey. If a natural recovery of the wolf is to occur on the East Front, provisions to manage wolf numbers and distribution must be in place, populations of predator and prey must be closely monitored, and rapid implementation of predator management will be needed to ensure that the wolf is tolerated in an area famous for its big-game hunting. There is no real reason, either technically or logistically, why the wildlife and its contemporary uses could not be adequately managed were wolves to be included in the fauna, and it is only perceptions and attitudes that would prevent this from happening.

Acknowledgments

We thank D. Harms and E. Bangs of the U.S. Fish and Wildlife Service for their support, encouragement, and reviews as we pursued this work. K. Constan, G. Erickson, G. Joslin, J. McCarthy, J. Mitchell, and J. Posewitz provided Montana Department of Fish, Wildlife, and Parks reports and other sources of information, and comments on drafts of this work. P. Paquet kindly provided information on Riding Mountain National Park wolf-prey relationships. W. Brewster, L. Carbyn, D. Mech, and V. VanBallenberghe reviewed drafts, which provided us with important direction in pursuing this work. This work was supported by U.S. Fish and Wildlife Service, McIntire-Stennis project IDAZ-MS-58 University of Idaho, and the College of Forestry, Wildlife and Range Sciences, University of Idaho. This is contribution No. 660 of the Idaho Forest, Wildlife and Range Experiment Station.

Winter Wolf Predation in a Multiple Ungulate Prey System, Gates of the Arctic National Park, Alaska

■ Bruce W. Dale, Layne G. Adams and R. Terry Bowyer

We investigated patterns of winter wolf predation, including prey selection, prey switching, kill rates, carcass utilization, and consumption rates for four wolf packs during three different study periods (March 1989, March 1990, and November 1990) in Gates of the Arctic National Park and Preserve, Alaska. Wolves killed predominately caribou (165 caribou, seven moose, and five Dall sheep) even when moose and sheep were more abundant. Prey selection varied between study periods. More moose were killed in March 1989, a particularly deep snow year, and more sheep were killed in November 1990 than during other periods. Overall kill rates ranged from 0–8 days/ungulate killed ($\bar{x}$ = 2.0, SD = 1.6) and did not vary between study periods. Pack size and species killed explained significant variation in the length of time intervals between kills. Although caribou density varied nearly 40-fold between pack territories, it had little influence on predation characteristics except at low densities, when kill rates may have declined. Caribou distribution had marked effects on wolf predation rate.

Introduction

Caribou (*Rangifer tarandus*) are an important food resource for wolves (*Canis lupus*) throughout much of their sympatric range (Murie 1944, Banfield 1954, Kelsall 1960, Kuyt 1972, Bergerud 1978a, 1983, Gauthier and Theberge 1986), and wolves are thought to have a major influence on the dynamics of caribou populations (Kuyt 1972, Miller and Broughton 1974, Bergerud 1974a, 1980, Davis et al. 1980). Despite this close association, fundamental knowledge of wolf-caribou relationships is lacking, and much must be inferred from studies of wolves and other ungulate prey, such as moose (*Alces alces*) and white-tailed deer (*Odocoileus virginianus*). Unlike other ungulate prey, barren-ground caribou are a unique resource for wolves because they are migratory, highly mobile, may occur in large groups, and their abundance and distribution may vary widely (Bergerud 1974b, Cumming 1975, Stephenson and James 1982, Valkenburg et al. 1983). Information inferred from studies of more sedentary prey may not be applicable to wolf-caribou relationships. Further, because wolves must respond behaviorally to dramatic changes in caribou availability, local abundance of caribou will affect utilization of other available ungulate prey such as Dall sheep (*Ovis dalli dalli*) and moose. In multiple prey systems, factors governing prey selection and the rate at which wolves kill various prey are largely unknown.

As part of a study of wolf ecology and demography in Gates of the Arctic National Park and Preserve, we deter-mined prey selection and kill rates in early and late winter. We predicted that deep snow conditions in late winter would result in higher kill rates due to increased vulnerability of caribou, and that wolves would switch to other ungulate prey when caribou are scarce.

We evaluated the influence of caribou abundance, snow depth, and season on wolf prey selection and kill rates. Winter 1988-1989 witnessed a near record snowfall, whereas winter 1989-1990 was near average. Therefore, characteristics of predation during March 1989 and March 1990 should reflect differences caused by variation in late-winter snow depth. The November 1990 study period represents much shallower, early-winter snow depths. Variation in predation characteristics among the November and March study periods may be due to seasonal variation in prey condition and snow depth.

Study Area

Gates of the Arctic National Park straddles the central Brooks Range in northern Alaska (68° N 153° W), and encompasses a roadless wilderness of approximately 30,000 km². The climate is largely arctic to the north of the continental divide and subarctic to the south (NPS 1987). The entire region is characterized by long, cold winters and short, warm summers. Yearly precipitation commonly ranges from 130 to 450 mm, and yearly snowfall from 89 to 203 cm. Temperatures range from -34° C to 21° C (NPS 1987).

Cumulative snowfall in late March 1989 at Bettles Field (approximately 80 km east of the study area) was 240 cm, compared to the 40-year mean of 180 cm. Cumulative snowfall in late March 1990 was also above average (218 cm), however, 79 cm fell during March. Cumulative snowfall in late November 1990 was 91 cm. We assumed that snowfall and other characteristics were similar among pack territories.

The central Brooks Range is characterized by wide river valleys and steep rugged mountains. Boreal forest (taiga) predominates along the southern border of Gates of the Arctic National Park and extends northward up south-flowing drainages to the continental divide. Shrub thickets are common above treeline. Alpine tundra occurs at higher elevations and moist tundra communities occur in the foothills and along north-flowing drainages (NPS 1987).

Wolves are distributed throughout Gates of the Arctic National Park at approximately 7.4 wolves/1000 km^2 (Adams and Stephenson 1986), a density typical of northern wolf populations (Chapman and Feldhamer 1982). Wolves in the study area are nonmigratory. Of the four packs observed in this study, only one was harvested. The Iniakuk Pack (IP) was reduced by two to three wolves each year because of trapping, however, the alpha wolves survived throughout the study period.

In addition to wolves, predators of ungulates include lynx (*Lynx canadensis*), wolverines (*Gulo gulo*), grizzly bears (*Ursus arctos*), black bears (*Ursus americanus*), coyotes (*Canis latrans*), and golden eagles (*Aquila chrysaetos*). Large prey for wolves consists of caribou, Dall sheep, and moose. Dall sheep and moose are locally abundant at about 0.5/km^2 on suitable range (Singer 1984a) and 0.12/km^2 (this study), respectively, whereas caribou are seasonally abundant. Although caribou are nearly always present, caribou use the area primarily during autumn and winter (Cameron and Whitten 1979). The Western Arctic Caribou Herd (WAH), estimated at 415,000 caribou in 1990 (P. Valkenburg, ADFG, pers. commun.) migrates southward and eastward toward the area in August–September, and a small number often winters there. WAH caribou do not show annual fidelity to winter ranges, but do not change ranges during any particular winter (Valkenburg et al. 1983). Small prey are diverse and include snowshoe hares (*Lepus americanus*) and beaver (*Castor canadensis*).

Methods

Prey Abundance and Distribution

Boundaries of wolf-pack territories were determined from observations obtained from April 1987 through March 1990, and delineated using the minimum convex polygon method (Mohr 1947). Relative abundance of moose and caribou in each pack territory was estimated during each 30-day period by aerial surveys (Gasaway et al. 1983). Relative moose densities were estimated by aerial surveys with corrections for sightability (Gasaway et al. 1986). Survey units of approximately 30 km^2 were surveyed with a search intensity of about 0.5 minutes/km^2. The sightability correction factor was determined by counting six or seven units before randomly selecting one survey unit to be recounted at a higher survey intensity (2 minutes/km^2). Density estimates for moose were calculated and statistically evaluated as described by Gasaway et al. (1986). These estimates of moose density may not be directly comparable to those from other studies because they: 1) include areas of unsuitable moose habitat; and 2) include late winter surveys (Gasaway et al. 1986).

The minimum number of caribou within each pack territory was also determined during the moose survey. It was impossible to develop a sightability correction factor because groups of caribou frequently crossed survey unit boundaries between standard and intensive surveys.

Dall sheep were not surveyed due to low sightability in winter. Although the winter distribution of sheep was not known, sheep movements from summer ranges were probably not extensive relative to wolf pack territory size (Ayres 1986). Summer sheep densities were previously estimated at about 0.5 sheep/km^2 on suitable ranges (Singer 1984a, Adams 1988).

Predation Characteristics

Prey selection, kill rate, and carcass utilization were estimated during 30-day study periods in March 1989, March 1990, and November 1990. Study packs were chosen because their territories had similar vegetation, topography, and excellent snow characteristics for tracking. Four packs with radio-collared members were located daily during each 30-day period, except for one day in March 1990, and one day in November 1990 when weather conditions prevented flying. All packs were relocated once or twice daily with Piper (PA-18) aircraft equipped with telemetry-receiving equipment (Carbyn 1983b). Upon visually locating wolves, the pelage color, number, and activity of individual wolves were recorded. The immediate area was searched for additional wolves or the presence of kills. Local vegetation, topography, and snow conditions were recorded. Whenever possible packs were backtracked to the previous location to find kills and additional pack members that would otherwise be missed.

The species and number of ungulate kills were determined from the air based on hair color, carcass size, presence of antlers or horns, and tracks at the kill site. The proportion of the carcass that had been consumed was visually estimated. All movements, activities, and kill locations were recorded on 1:63,360 or 1:250,000 scale topographic maps.

Ground investigation of 110 of 177 total kills was made three to 14 days after wolves abandoned the carcasses. At kill sites we verified species of the kill, and where sufficient evidence remained, we identified or collected specimens

Table 1. Relative moose and caribou density estimates and wolf numbers for selected wolf packs in Gates of the Arctic National Park and Preserve, Alaska.

Study Period	Pack	Caribou/km²	Moose/km²	Wolves
March 1989	Walker L.	2.34	0.12	7
	Iniakuk	0.31	0.09	5
	Unakserak	0.08	0.11	12
	Sixty Mile	0.07	0.12	11
March 1990	Walker L.	1.19	0.14	10
	Iniakuk	0.19	0.12	5
	Unakserak	0.21	0.09	8
	Pingaluk	0.50	0.08	7
November 1990	Walker L.	NA	NA	15
	Iniakuk	0.06	0.24	10[1]
	Unakserak	0.41	0.12	13
	Pingaluk	0.24	0.13	11

NA = No prey surveys were conducted.

1 Three pups are harvested early in the rate estimation period reducing pack size to 7 wolves.

(e.g., teeth, mandibles, pelvises) to determine the sex and age classes of the ungulate.

A single kill rate for each pack was estimated during each 30-day study period. Rates were estimated for a period beginning the day after location of a fresh kill and ending on the day the last kill was located. Periods of rate estimation ranged from 11–27 days. Kill rates were expressed as kills/wolf/day when assessing effects on prey populations. Wolf groups were quantitatively described as travelling pack size (Messier 1985a), because pack members are not always found together due to temporary or permanent dispersal, mortality, or fragmentation into subgroups for hunting. This measure constitutes the mean number of wolves seen in each pack during the study period. Lengths of intervals between kills (days/kill/pack) were used to analyze factors influencing kill rate.

Statistical Analyses

Analysis of covariance was used to determine differences in the mean interval between kills for different seasons and snow depths using travelling pack size, caribou density, and the numbers and species of previous kills as covariates. This statistical model was used to evaluate variation in interval length due to main effects (i.e., snow, season) while controlling for confounding variation of measurable covariates. By employing this method there was no need to adjust interval lengths for the size or number of prey killed (Ballard et al. 1987). Because of a slightly skewed distribution near zero, intervals were transformed by adding 0.5 to the interval and taking the square root of that sum (Steel and Torrie 1980).

Linear regression models were used to assess association between normal variables; log-linear models were used to assess differences in frequencies of observed behaviors; and logistic regression was employed to assess factors associated with the proportion of kills located by back-tracking wolves.

Results

Prey Availability and Prey Selection

Caribou density within pack territories ranged from 0.06–2.34 caribou/km², while moose density ranged from 0.08–0.24 moose/km² (Table 1). Wolves primarily killed caribou (93%) during the study (Table 2), but prey selection was not independent of study period (Chi square = 12.79, d.f. = 4, $\underline{P}$ = 0.012). The high numbers of moose killed in March 1989, and sheep in November 1990, constituted the major contribution to the Chi-square statistic.

There was no difference (Chi square<0.001, d.f. = 1, $\underline{P}$ = 0.98) between March 1989 and March 1990 in the proportion of calves in known-age caribou kills, so prey selection for those two study periods was pooled. The resulting age composition of known-age caribou kills was dependent on season (Chi square = 4.94, d.f. = 1, $\underline{P}$ = 0.0262) with a higher proportion of calves killed in November 1990 (35%) than during March 1989 and March 1990 (13%).

Kill Rate Estimation

Wolves spent little time on carcasses as 39% of 177 kills were located by backtracking the wolves toward their location from the previous day. There was no relationship be-

Table 2. Prey selection and kill rates for wolves in Gates of the Arctic National Park, Alaska in March 1989, March 1990 and November 1990.

Pack	Travelling Pack size	Rate Est Period (Days)	Kills			Caribou/ Wolf/Day	kg/Wolf/ Day
			Caribou	Moose	Sheep		
March 1989							
Walker L.	6.1	27	17	3	0	0.10	12.0
Iniakuk	4.8	26	12	2	0	0.10	11.1
Unakserak	7.7	24	13	1	0	0.07	5.4
Pingaluk	2.0	19	2	0	0	0.05	3.6
Sixtymile	8.5	26	14	0	0	0.06	4.4
March 1990							
Walker L.	9.8	21	19	0	0	0.09	6.3
Iniakuk	4.4	22	10	0	0	0.10	7.1
Unakserak	6.0	19	12	0	1	0.11	7.6
Pingaluk	6.1	20	10	0	0	0.08	5.6
November 1990							
Walker L.	14.3	11	15	0	0	0.10	5.7
Iniakuk	5.4	16	9	0	0	0.10	6.3
Unakserak	12.2	19	25	0	1	0.11	6.7
Pingaluk	10.6	19	7	1	3	0.03	4.1

tween kill rate and the proportion of kills located by back-tracking ($\underline{P} = 0.95$, d.f. $= 10$, n $= 12$).

Kill Rates on Caribou and Caribou Availability

Rates at which wolves killed caribou ranged from 0.37–1.36 caribou/pack/day or 0.03–0.11 caribou/wolf/day. Overall, each wolf killed 0.09 ($\underline{SD} = 0.02$, n $= 12$) caribou/day. Only at low caribou densities did caribou kill rate seem to be influenced by caribou abundance (Fig. 1). We excluded data from the Pingaluk pair of wolves for March 1989, when only two kills were documented during the rate estimation period. The Pingaluk pair killed an adult moose two days after the rate estimation period ended. Including this kill would result in doubling the daily available ungulate biomass for this pair.

Multiple Kills

Wolves frequently killed more than one animal during an attack on a group of caribou. Based on carcass locations and tracks, wolves killed 1.2 caribou per successful attack (range 1–4). The mean number of kills per successful attack was not correlated with travelling pack size ($\underline{r}^2 = 0.06$, $\underline{P} = 0.444$) or mean caribou group size within a pack territory ($\underline{r}^2 = 0.02$, $\underline{P} = 0.616$).

Effects of Snow Depth and Season on Kill Rate

Intervals between kills ranged from zero to eight days with a mean of two days ($\underline{SD} = 1.6$, n $= 118$). Interval length did not vary significantly among packs (ANCOVA, $\underline{F} = 0.25$, d.f. $= 4$, $\underline{P} = 0.908$) when travelling pack size, caribou density, and food availability (number and species of ungulates killed at each successful attack) were held as covariates.

Packs were pooled to evaluate the effects of snow and season, because kill rates among packs were not significantly different. The snow-season factor had three levels, March 1989 (late winter near record snow), March 1990 (late winter above average snow), and November 1990 (early winter conditions). Kill rates during these periods were not significantly different (Fig. 2) (ANCOVA $\underline{F} = 0.08$, d.f. $= 2$, $\underline{P} = 0.923$). The regression of covariates explained significant ($\underline{F} = 3.32$, d.f. $= 3$, $\underline{P} = 0.023$) variation in interval lengths. Travelling pack size and food availability were significant factors in the regression, however, caribou density was not.

Food Availability (Consumption Rates) and Carcass Utilization

Assuming that male, female, and calf caribou weighed 96, 76, and 36 kg, respectively (J. Davis, unpubl. data), and that

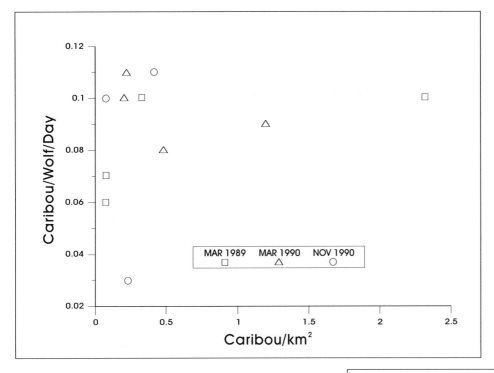

Fig. 1 *Rates at which wolves killed caribou as a function of caribou density in March 1989, March 1990, and November 1990 in Gates of the Arctic National Park.*

caribou kills were composed of 13% calves, 43.5% cows, and 43.5% bulls in March, and 35% calves, 32.5% cows, and 32.5% bulls in November (see Prey Selection), each caribou killed represented approximately 79.5 kg live weight in March, and 68.5 kg in November. We assumed adult and calf moose weighed 370 and 150 kg, respectively (Franzmann et al. 1978), and sheep kills weighed 50 kg (Bunnel and Olsen 1976), and these species were 75% and 90% consumable (Sumanik 1987). If caribou bulls, cows, and calves were 85%, 87%, and 95% consumable (Sumanik 1987), wolves had approximately 4.1–12.0 kg/wolf/day available with an overall unweighted mean of 6.9 ($\underline{SD}$ = 2.4, n = 12). Mean food availability was 8.2, 6.6, and 5.7 kg/wolf/day for March 1989, March 1990, and November 1990, respectively ($\underline{F}$ = 1.14, d.f. = 11, $\underline{P}$ = 0.36).

Wolf Activity

Travelling pack size ranged from 2–14.3 wolves (Table 2). We made 2,003 observations of individual wolves during daylight hours. Wolves were sleeping or resting in 48.8% of the observations, walking 32.1%, feeding 9.8%, engaged in social behaviors 6.8%, and running 2.5%. There was no relationship between the frequency of these behaviors and food availability.

Discussion

Prey Selection

Our data suggest that estimating prey selection patterns from systematic observation may be misleading when prey size is variable and backtracking is not feasible. In this study a high proportion of kills were located via backtracking. The

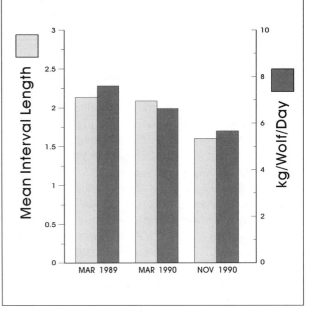

Fig. 2 *Mean length of intervals between kills and weighted mean food availability (kg/wolf/day, see text for assumptions on prey biomass) for wolves in Gates of the Arctic National Park. Cumulative snowfall was greatest in March 1989, and least in November 1990.*

amount of food available from a kill was a significant factor in explaining the length of the interval until the next kill. For example, with infrequent monitoring and without backtracking, wolves might kill and consume numerous caribou for each one detected, while every moose kill might be detected (Carbyn 1983b, Ballard et al. 1987, Fuller 1989). Prey with

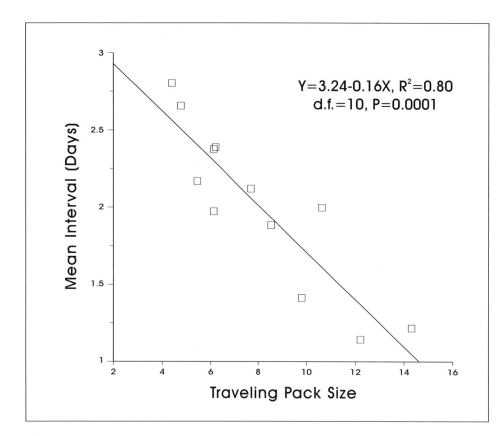

$Y=3.24-0.16X$, $R^2=0.80$
$d.f.=10$, $P=0.0001$

Fig. 3 *Relationship of kill rate to pack size. Each data point represents the mean length of intervals between kills for four packs of wolves in March 1989, March 1990, and November 1990, in Gates of the Arctic National Park.*

body mass larger than can be consumed by a pack in one feeding may be overrepresented when wolves rest near these kills between meals. Pack size, as it influences handling time, may also affect observability of kills. Wolves were most commonly observed sleeping and resting in this study (49%), and on Isle Royale, Michigan (48%) (Peterson and Page 1988). The high proportion of kills located by backtracking in this study is consistent with our conclusion that wolves frequently rested away from caribou kills.

Wolves can be highly selective predators. Carbyn (1974) reported mule deer (*Odocoileus hemionus*) were the primary prey of wolves in Jasper National Park, Alberta despite elk (*Cervus elaphus*) being three times more abundant. Carbyn (1983) also identified white-tailed deer (*Odocoileus virginianus*) as the "optimum" prey in Riding Mountain National Park, Manitoba. In that study, elk were most abundant and most consumed, but deer were consumed at a higher rate relative to available biomass. Gauthier and Theberge (1986) noted members of the Burwash caribou herd were consumed disproportionately relative to the available biomass of moose except during the calving season. However, their estimates of consumption were derived from fecal analyses employing the equations developed by Floyd et al. (1978), and relative abundance of caribou and moose was derived from censuses conducted in previous years. No data were presented on the actual distribution and availability of caribou within the home ranges of the two study packs. Burkholder (1959) believed that wolves showed no preference for either caribou

or moose in south-central Alaska, but that use was proportional to availability. Other authors have indicated caribou as highly preferred prey for wolves (Holleman and Stephenson 1981, Gasaway et al. 1983), although information regarding the relative availability of other ungulate prey was lacking.

In this study, wolves utilized caribou even when moose were numerically more abundant. We saw no evidence of prey switching because of differences in relative ungulate abundance. The trends in prey selection observed in our study may be due to less risk associated with hunting caribou (Haugen 1987), and higher profitability in killing caribou once potential prey were located. For example, adult moose in our study area occurred at low densities and may have been in excellent condition. Likewise, sheep were at low enough densities to remain in available escape terrain, resulting in low vulnerability of these species. Increased use of sheep during November 1990 may have resulted from increased vulnerability due to changes in distribution, condition, or vigilance associated with the ongoing rut. Similarly, deep snow may have increased moose vulnerability in March 1989 (Peterson 1977, Mech 1987), but the sample sizes were too small to draw firm conclusions.

Caribou, however, may have been vulnerable due to the combination of deep snow and mountainous, rough terrain. Caribou groups were generally observed on, or near, ridges that were windblown and had little or hardpacked snow cover. Tracks and locations of kill sites indicated that wolves

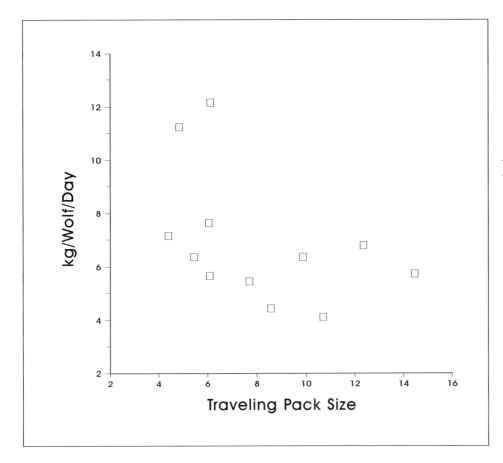

Fig. 4 *Relationship between food availability and pack size for four packs of wolves in March 1989, March 1990, and November 1990 in Gates of the Arctic National Park.*

chased caribou from these ridges into deep snow, rough terrain, and relatively dense vegetation. Because wolves often made multiple kills of caribou in single attacks, the profitability of hunting caribou increased. Further, even the lowest food availability (4.1 kg/wolf/day) indicated wolves were on a suitable plane of nutrition for reproduction (compare to 3.2 kg/wolf/day: Mech 1977c) without the risk of hunting moose (Haugen 1987) or the difficulty of hunting sheep (Sumanik 1987).

The strong preference sometimes shown by wolves for certain ungulate prey poses numerous questions for current wolf-prey theory, particularly, how widespread this phenomenon is, and how it influences wolf-prey dynamics. We analyzed data from multiple-prey systems (n = 17, excluding newly established and manipulated systems) compiled by Fuller (1989, Appendix B) to address these questions. For ungulate prey, only deer and caribou have been suggested as strongly preferred by wolves (Mech and Frenzel 1971a, Carbyn 1974, 1983a,b, Mech 1977c, Holleman and Stephenson 1981, Gauthier and Theberge 1986, Potvin et al. 1988). We assumed they were the preferred prey in systems in which they occurred and as opposed to other ungulates [i.e., moose, elk, bison (*Bison bison*), mountain goat (*Oreamnos americana*), and mountain sheep], even though those ungulates may have constituted most of the diet of wolves. We used multiple-regression analysis to detect any influence of

preferred prey (deer and caribou) on wolf density by including preferred prey and alternate prey ungulate biomass indices as separate independent variables. This expanded model explained significantly more variation in wolf density ($\underline{Y}$ = 0.006*Preferred Prey UBI+0.003* Alternate Prey UBI+4.08, full model $\underline{R}_a^2$ = 0.86, $\underline{F}$ = 17.2, $\underline{P}$<0.001) than total ungulate biomass index alone (reduced model $\underline{r}^2$ = 0.72). These results support the observed preference for deer and caribou and indicate that the abundance of preferred prey strongly influences wolf density.

Models of wolf predation behaviour should be viewed with caution when encounter rates are assumed to be the primary determinant of prey selection. Clearly, wolves did not make immediate changes in prey selection simply because of rates at which they encountered different species of ungulate prey. Relative abundance, however, may have influenced selection among sex and age classes, such as the increased use of caribou calves versus adults in November.

Kill Rates, Food Availability, and Predation Rates

Wolves may have had more food available per wolf when snow was deepest (March 1989) even though kill rate was similar to March 1990. The differences in food availability, although not significant, were due to the larger number of

Bruce W. Dale, Layne G. Adams and R. Terry Bowyer

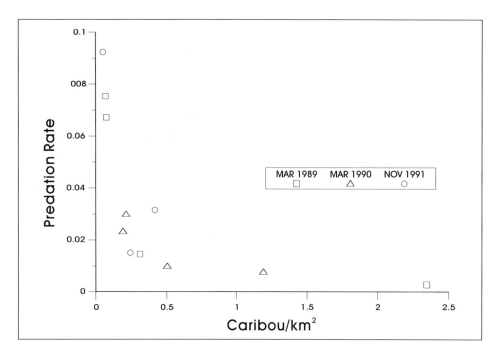

Fig. 5 *Relationship between mortality rates due to wolf predation and caribou density in four wolf pack territories in March 1989, March 1990, and November 1990 in Gates of the Arctic National Park.*

moose killed in March 1989 (Table 2), and the increased use of calves in November 1991.

The positive relationship between pack size and kill rate (Fig. 3) is similar to that reported by Messier and Crete (1985), Ballard et al. (1987), and Sumanik (1987), but contrary to Haber's (1977) conclusion that pack size had little influence on handling or search time. Hayes et al. (1991) concluded that small packs killed as often as large packs in southwest Yukon. Their data consisted of numerous pairs of wolves killing mostly moose where scavenging was high. Our data represent only larger packs killing mostly caribou, and the effects of scavengers at our study area were probably less than that reported by Hayes et al. (1991).

Snow depth, season, and prey availability were not significantly associated with kill rates suggesting: 1) these factors had little influence on the ability of wolves to kill caribou; or 2) that wolves were at or near food satiation in many cases. This latter contention is supported by the relationships between travelling pack size, kill rate, and food availability. Although big packs killed at a faster rate (P<0.0001)(Fig. 3), those packs had no more food per wolf than small packs (P> 0.05)(Fig. 4). In addition, no difference in frequency of resting or social behaviors among packs, and little correlation between caribou density and interval length suggest that, of search time and handling time, only handling time explained variation in interval length in this study. Individual wolves living in established packs in open systems may often be at or near satiation because extremes in food availability would elicit numerical responses (Zimen 1976, Mech 1975, Packard and Mech 1980, Page 1989).

For wolves in Gates of the Arctic National Park, changes in dispersal rates (Adams et al.1989a), survival, and possibly immigration (Packard and Mech 1980, Ballard et al. 1987)

could facilitate immediate numerical responses to changes in per capita food availability. In other words, the effects of functional responses on population dynamics may be short-lived. In this study, mean food availability (0.16 kg/kg wolf/day) was similar to that for wolf-moose and/or caribou systems representing a wide range of prey densities in North America (Boertje et al. 1992a).

Clearly, in the short periods of observation in Gates of the Arctic National Park, wolves killed caribou at high rates regardless of the number of caribou within a pack's territory. Spatial distribution of caribou should therefore be an important influence on predation rate (proportion killed per day) on winter ranges where wolves are territorial. Indeed, predation rate decreased markedly with increasing prey density (Fig. 5). This effect should be a strong influence on grouping behavior in caribou.

Acknowledgments

This work was funded by the National Park Service (NPS) Natural Resource Preservation Program. We would like to thank A. Lovaas (NPS–Alaska Region), and the staff at Gates of the Arctic National Park and Preserve for their support. Numerous people at the Alaska Department of Fish and Game provided advice and support, especially R. Stephenson, W. Gasaway, D. Reed, J. Davis and R. Boertje. Field work was conducted by J. Alderson, T. Burch, J. Dale, K. Faber, T. Meier, M. Masteller, and B. Shults, and pilots R. Warbelow, S. Hamilton, B. Lentsch, D. Miller, and B. Sewell. We thank P. and M. Shanahan for their hospitality and use of their cabin. A. Lovaas, E. Follmann, D. Klein, R. Stephenson and D. Mech provided useful comments on earlier drafts of this manuscipt.

Patterns of Prey Selection by Wolves in Denali National Park, Alaska

■ **L. David Mech, Thomas J. Meier, John W. Burch, and Layne G. Adams**

*The patterns of selection by wolves (**Canis lupus**) preying on moose (**Alces alces**), caribou (**Rangifer tarandus**), and Dall sheep (**Ovis dalli**) in Denali National Park and Preserve, Alaska were studied from 1986 through early 1992. Wolves and their prey were legally protected or relatively unharvested in most of the area, and wolf numbers doubled during the study. Based on remains of 294 moose, 225 caribou, and 63 sheep, wolves killed calves and old adults disproportionately, and also individuals with low marrow fat, jaw necrosis, or arthritis. Seasonal trends in proportions of various species, ages, and sex of kills were found. During the winters following winters of deep snowfalls, wolves greatly increased the proportion of caribou cows and calves taken. We conclude that in a natural system, wolves can survive on vulnerable prey even during moderate weather, and when snowfall exceeds average, they can respond by switching to newly vulnerable prey and greatly increasing their numbers.*

Introduction

Wolves tend to prey on young and older animals and those in poor condition (Murie 1944, Mech 1966a, 1970, Pimlott et al. 1969, Mech and Frenzel 1971a, Mech and Karns 1977, Haber 1977, Peterson 1977, Fritts and Mech 1981, Peterson et al. 1984, Ballard et al. 1987). However, most studies documenting these patterns were conducted where there was one primary prey species. In addition, several studies involved prey that were also subject to human harvest, and many relied on aging by tooth wear, which is less precise than counting cementum annuli (Wolfe 1969, for moose). We examine patterns of selection by wolves on three species of prey from a system in which neither wolves nor prey are harvested, and the ages of prey were based on cementum annuli.

Study area

This study was conducted from 1986 through early 1992 in Denali National Park and Preserve (Denali), Alaska (63°N, 151°W). Denali includes about 9,200 km² of "old" park (formerly Mount McKinley National Park), where wolves are legally protected, and an apron of 15,200 km² of new park and preserve where wolves can be taken under various restrictions. (During the study, four wolves were known to have been killed in this area). Denali is home to about 2,000 moose (Meier et al. 1991), 3,000-4,000 caribou, including

those adjacent to the park that are within range of park wolf packs (Adams et al. 1989a, Shults and Adams 1990), and approximately 2,000 Dall sheep. Little information exists to evaluate trends in the sheep and moose populations during the study, although moose estimates for both 1986 and 1991 were about the same (Meier 1987, Meier et al. 1991). Caribou numbers increased an average of 8% annually through 1990, then declined by 18% in 1991 (Adams et al. 1989a, this volume).

The wolf population increased an average of 27%/year from about four to eight wolves /1,000 km² in late winter 1987 to 1990 (Meier et al. this volume). Denali wolves prey on all three ungulate species as well as on various minor prey species (Murie 1944, Mech et al. 1991a).

Snowfall during the study ranged from the second lowest on record in 1985-86 to one of the highest in 1990-91 (Table 1).

Methods

We aerially located radio-tagged wolves to find their kills, and examined the remains from the ground. Wolves were captured primarily by darting from a helicopter and were fitted with radio collars. Collared wolves were located an average of three times per month with antennae-equipped PA-18 Supercub and Cessna 185 aircraft. Not all packs were located during each flight, and some packs were located

L. David Mech, Thomas J. Meier, John W. Burch, and Layne G. Adams

Table 1. Cumulative snowfall (cm) at Headquarters, Denali National Park, Alaska[1]

WINTER	CUMULATIVE SNOWFALL
1985-86	86
1986-87	104
1987-88	117
1988-89	244
1989-90	216
1990-91	391
1991-92	221

1   63-year mean is 190.5 cm.

more frequently than others. Wolves were located more often in late winter and spring than during late autumn and early winter; summer data were especially sparse.

Kill sites were examined from the ground to determine the species, cause of death, age, sex, and condition of prey. The position of the carcass, presence of blood, signs of a struggle, and manner of feeding provided clues as to whether wolves killed or merely scavenged a particular carcass. Sex was determined by the presence of antlers or antler pedicels (moose), antler size (caribou), horn shape and size (sheep), mandible, metatarsus, or metacarpus length (caribou and sheep), or pelvis shape (all species). Teeth, usually incisors, were collected for age determination by sectioning and counting cementum annuli (Matson's Laboratory, Milltown, Montana). Age of younger animals was determined by the pattern of tooth eruption. Sheep were aged by annular rings on the horns and by tooth eruption and tooth sectioning. Marrow (usually femur marrow) was collected, dried, and weighed to determine percent fat content (Neiland 1970). The reported fat percentage is probably higher than actual because some specimens were not retrieved from kills until long after the animal had died.

All bones found at kill sites were examined for abnormalities, and certain bones were collected, if available, for subsequent cleaning and examination.

Because of the disparity in sizes of the wolf's prey, intermittent sampling of wolf locations would result in a bias toward locating the largest prey, which provide more food and occupy wolves longer. Therefore, we used two approaches to analyzing the kill data for determining the proportions of moose, caribou, and sheep killed. First, we examined the observed data directly. Second, we assumed that the time wolves spent on a given age, sex, and species of prey was directly proportional to the weight of that class of prey, so the relative proportions of kill classes were adjusted accordingly. The observed number of each age, sex, and species of prey was multiplied by the reciprocal of the

assumed weight of each prey class to arrive at an adjusted proportion of each kill class. For example, assuming bull moose weighed four times as much as caribou cows, we multiplied the number of caribou cows by one and bull moose by one quarter. Sample sizes of prey remains data vary for each type because not all types of data could be collected from every kill or prey carcass found. We performed two analyses of the monthly kill proportions because of strong bias during summer against finding calf kills and disproportionate sampling of certain packs. One year-round analysis excluded calves, and one analysis for October through April included calves.

To determine if any class of prey was killed disproportionately in any given month, we used the Chi square test to compare monthly proportions of each prey class against the mean of the monthly proportions of the year-round sample. We performed this test for adults only and adult and calf samples. Significance for a given month was assumed if $P \leq 0.05$ for that month. For comparing age structures, we used the Kolmogorov-Smirnov test (Hollander and Wolfe 1973).

Results

One hundred and seven wolves were captured and radio-tagged in 25 packs distributed throughout Denali from 1986 to 1991. Some packs included up to four wolves wearing active collars concurrently because radio collars usually lasted for several years. During each year, five to 19 packs included radio-tagged members.

Remains of 294 moose, 225 caribou, and 63 sheep were found by tracking wolves. Of these, 245 moose, 221 caribou, and 60 sheep were considered wolf kills or probable wolf kills (hereafter pooled as "kills"). This is our basic sample from which various subsamples were examined for different analyses. Some 167 moose, 165 caribou, and 49 sheep were examined from the ground to determine species, age, sex, condition, abnormalities, and cause of death.

Our tallies of kills found with collared packs probably were not a representative sample of the kills made by these packs for several reasons: 1) flying efforts were not distributed evenly over the year; 2) wolves spend more time at the kills of larger animals, and 3) larger kills such as moose are more visible and identifiable from the air.

Overall, moose represented 47% of the kills found, caribou 42%, and sheep 11% (Table 2). Because of the biases (previously discussed), this sample probably exaggerates the relative numbers of moose taken and minimizes the proportion of sheep. However, the proportions may more accurately represent the relative biomass of the three prey consumed. About 15% of all moose eaten by wolves (about 40% of the bulls and 9% of cows and calves) were thought to have been scavenged. They were not included in the kill sample. Haber (1977) also found that Denali wolves scavenged considerably on bull moose.

Table 2. Composition of prey (unadjusted for weight) killed by wolves, or probably killed by wolves, in Denali National Park, Alaska, October–April 1986–1992.

	1985-86		1986-87		1987-88		Winter 1988-89		1989-90		1990-91		1991-92		TOTAL	
Species	n	%	n	%	n	%	n	%	n	%	n	%	n	%	n	%
Moose																
bulls	1	14	9	24	4	10	14	18	3	5	—	—	1	6	32	11
cows	3	43	14	37	12	30	14	18	3	5	6	14	5	28	57	20
calves	2	29	6	16	10	25	14	18	6	11	9	21	4	22	51	18
sum	6	86	29	77	26	65	42	54	12	21	15	35	10	56	140	49
Caribou																
bulls	1	14	4	11	4	10	18	23	10	18	9	21	5	28	51	18
cows	—	—	2	5	3	8	5	6	16	28	16	37	1	6	43	15
calves	—	—	—	—	—	—	—	—	10	18	2	5	1	6	13	5
sum	1	14	6	16	7	18	23	29	36	64	27	63	7	40	107	38
Sheep																
rams	—	—	—	—	5	13	6	8	6	11	—	—	—	—	17	6
ewes	—	—	3	8	1	3	6	8	3	5	1	2	—	—	14	5
lambs	—	—	—	—	1	3	1	1	—	—	—	—	1	6	3	1
sum	—	—	3	8	7	19	13	17	9	16	1	2	1	6	34	12
TOTAL	7	100	38	100	40	100	78	100	57	100	43	100	18	100	281	100

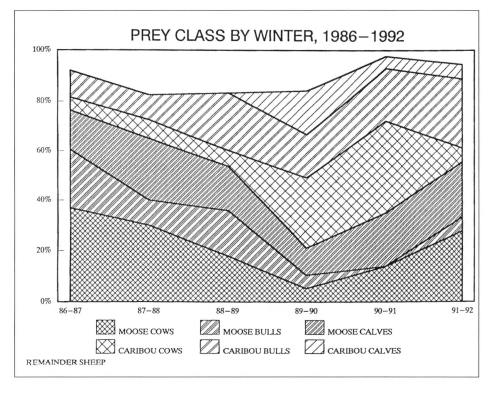

Fig. 1 *Annual proportions of each species, sex, and age of ungulates killed by wolves, or probably killed by wolves, in Denali National Park, Alaska, October through April 1986–1992.*

Table 3. Frequency of wolf kills or probable wolf kills of moose, caribou, and Dall sheep in Denali National Park, Alaska, 1986–1992[1].

Species	Adults												Total	wtd. x̄%
	Month													
	J	F	M	A	M	J	J	A	S	O	N	D		
Moose	10	23	16	11	6	3	0	1	1	10	14	5	100	36
Caribou	1	14	34	14	11	2	2	8	10	20	9	2	127	53
Sheep	1	10	7	2	0	1	0	0	1	3	4	4	33	11
p^2	0.01	0.02	0.60	0.82	0.33	0.64	0.42	0.11	0.12	0.75	0.19	0.02		

Species	Adults and Calves[1]												Total	wtd. x̄%
	J	F	M	A	M	J	J	A	S	O	N	D		
Moose	14	34	30	19	—	—	—	—	—	16	20	7	140	55
Caribou	1	16	41	17	—	—	—	—	—	21	9	2	107	32
Sheep	1	11	8	3	—	—	—	—	—	3	4	4	34	13
p^2	0.05	0.59	0.03	0.37	—	—	—	—	—	0.07	0.85	0.18		

1 data are not given for May through September for the adult and calf part of table because of the strong bias against finding kills of young animals during that period.
2 probability of no significant difference in proportion of prey species in a given month compared with year-round weighted mean proportion.

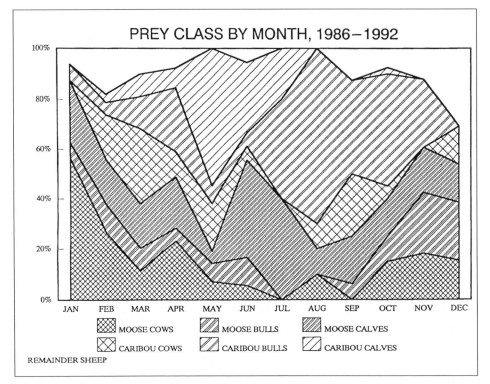

Fig. 2 *Monthly proportions of each species, sex, and age of ungulates killed by wolves, or probably killed by wolves, in Denali National Park, Alaska, October through April, 1986-1992.*

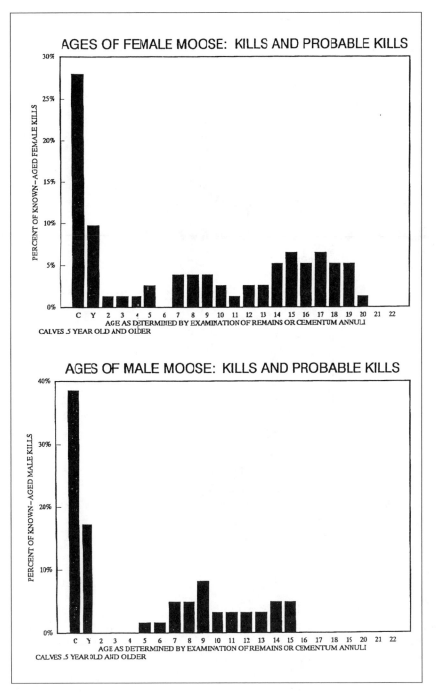

Fig. 3 *Age structure of moose killed by wolves, or probably killed by wolves, in Denali National Park, Alaska, October through April, 1986–1992.*
(Calves are ≥ 0.5-years old).

Annual and Monthly Variation in Prey Composition

The composition of wolf kills varied by both year and month. Moose formed the largest percentage of the sample during the first four years of the study, but caribou predominated in 1989–90 and 1990–91 (Table 2, Fig. 1). As caribou kills increased, both moose and sheep kills decreased. This trend held true both for the observed proportions of kills in our sample and for the proportions derived after adjustment for weight.

On a monthly basis, the total sample of kills suggested that wolves tended to kill moose calves year round, caribou calves in May, June, March, and April (1990–1992 only), caribou bulls year round, but primarily July through November, bull moose year round, but primarily in November and December, caribou cows primarily February through June, cow moose October through May, and sheep primarily September through April and especially in December (Table 3, Fig. 2). Some of these trends may have resulted from sampling error or bias. Chi square analysis indicated that significantly more moose were taken November through February,

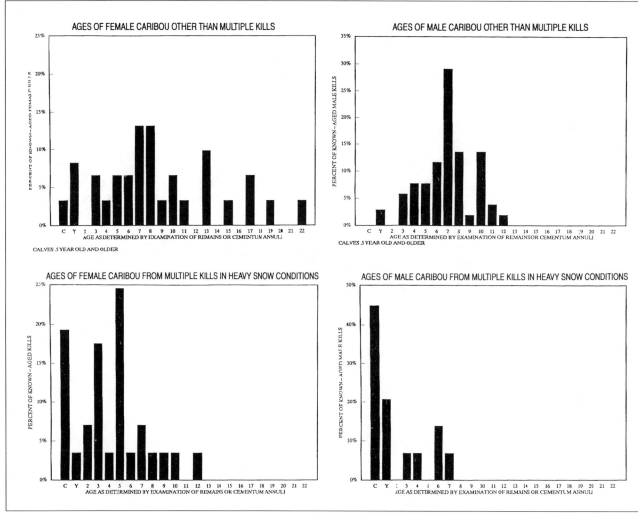

Fig. 4 *Age structure of caribou killed by wolves, or probably killed by wolves, in Denali National Park, Alaska, October through April 1986–1992.*

more caribou cows and calves in March, and more sheep in December. Although on a monthly basis the preponderance of caribou bulls taken August to October was not significantly different from its proportion of prey in other months (Table 3), bull caribou formed the single most predominant prey type for any single period of the year (Fig. 2).

Age and Sex Structure of the Kill

Denali wolves killed primarily calves and old moose and caribou of both sexes (Figs. 3 and 4), except during multiple caribou kills (see below). Although our sample of Dall sheep was small, apparently individuals aged ≥ 5 years were taken disproportionately (Fig. 5). These results parallel those of Murie (1944), Burles and Hoefs (1984), Sumanik (1987), and Hayes et al. (1991) for sheep; Mech (1966a), Peterson (1977), Haber (1977), Fuller and Keith (1980), Peterson et al. (1984), Ballard et al. (1987), Bjorge and Gunson (1989), Hayes et al. (1991), and Gasaway et al. (1992) for moose;

and Parker and Luttich (1986) for caribou. Our oldest kills of each species were estimated at ≤20 years old, ≤22 years old, and ≤13 years old for moose, caribou, and sheep, respectively.

There was no significant difference between the sex ratio of wolf-killed moose and the sex ratio of the herd (Meier et al. 1991), but wolves killed significantly more male caribou (119:100; $x^2 = 13.7$, 1 df, P<0.001) than the proportion in the population (Adams et al. 1989a). This differs from the even sex ratio found by Parker and Luttich (1986) for wolf-killed caribou in Labrador. Samples of the males of each species killed by wolves were younger than those of the females (Figs. 3–5), although only the male moose and sheep were significantly younger (P<0.05). Ballard et al. (1987) found no significant difference between the sex ratio of wolf-killed caribou and that of caribou surveyed by air in south-central Alaska.

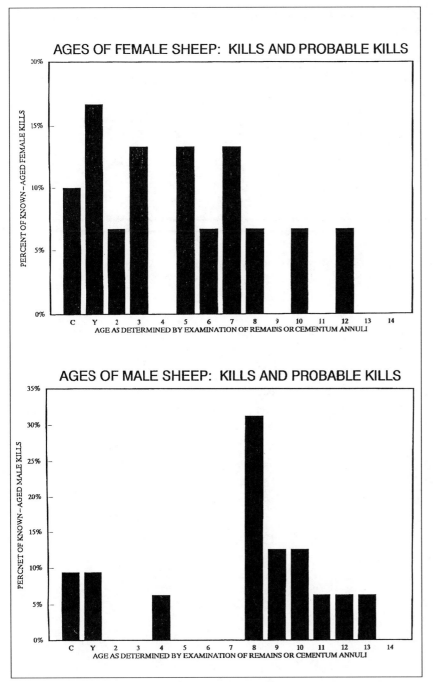

Fig. 5 *Age structure of Dall sheep killed by wolves, or probably killed by wolves, in Denali National Park, Alaska, October through April 1986–1992.*

During late winter and spring 1990 and 1991, record amounts of snow fell in the study area (Table 1), and several multiple wolf kills of caribou were found. For both males and females, the age distributions of caribou killed during these bouts of mass predation (Fig. 4) were significantly younger than those killed individually and at other times of the year (P<.01). Contrary to reports from other areas (Kelsall 1957, Eide and Ballard 1982, Miller et al. 1985, 1988b), Denali wolves returned repeatedly to feed on the frozen carcasses of the multiple kills.

Snow and Patterns of Prey Selection

The most striking change in the composition of wolf kills during our study was the major increase in the proportion and composition of caribou killed beginning the second consecutive winter (1989-1990) with above-average snowfall (Table 1, Fig.1). The proportion of adult moose we found killed in that winter greatly decreased (Fig. 1). Although winter 1988-89 was the first year of above-average snowfall during the study, the increased proportion of wolf-killed caribou cows was not found until 1989-90 and 1990-91 (Table 2), both of which also had above-average snowfall

Table 4. Percent femur marrow fat content of prey killed by wolves, or probably killed by wolves, in Denali National Park, Alaska, October–May 1986–1991.

| | WINTER | | | | | | | | | | | | | | | | |
| | 1985-1986 | | | 1986-1987 | | | 1987-1988 | | | 1988-1989 | | | 1989-1990 | | | 1990-1991 | | |
SPECIES	x̄	±SE	n	x̄	±SE	n	x̄	±SE	n	x̄	±SE	n	x̄	±SE	n	x̄	±SE	n
Moose	58	10	4	63	5	30	64	5	24	71	4	22	56	12	8	28	7	6
Caribou	79	—	1	48	13	5	40	12	6	42	7	21	59	5	11	55	5	20
Sheep	—	—	—	93	—	2	58	13	5	78	12	6	88	—	2	—	—	—

Table 5. Percent femur marrow fat content of prey killed by wolves, or probably killed by wolves, in Denali National Park, Alaska, October–April 1988–1992.

| | January | | | February | | | March | | | April | | | May | | | June | | |
SPECIES	x̄	±SE	n	x̄	±SE	n	x̄	±SE	n	x̄	±SE	n	x̄	±SE	n	x̄	±SE	n
Moose																		
bulls	58	—	1	63	12	6	60	27	5	62	—	1	73	—	2	84	—	1
cows	84	2	7	74	6	13	62	24	7	68	9	6	58	—	2	74	—	1
calves	54	9	3	67	5	7	32	8	10	37	—	2	10	—	1	38	16	3
Caribou																		
bulls	—	—	—	33	12	3	57	9	9	68	10	6	52	—	1	14	—	1
cows	—	—	—	70	7	10	62	6	22	86	—	1	62	13	5	—	—	—
calves	—	—	—	31	—	2	45	7	9	38	2	3	21	2	9	—	—	—
Sheep																		
rams	—	—	—	65	—	2	—	—	—	12	—	1	—	—	—	—	—	—
ewes	—	—	—	—	—	—	85	—	2	56	—	2	—	—	—	20	—	1
lambs	—	—	—	—	—	—												

| | July | | | August | | | September | | | October | | | November | | | December | | |
SPECIES	x̄	±SE	n	x̄	±SE	n	x̄	±SE	n	x̄	±SE	n	x̄	±SE	n	x̄	±SE	n
Moose																		
bulls	—	—	—	—	—	—	—	—	—	76	—	2	53	—	2	41	15	3
cows	—	—	—	87	—	1	—	—	—	69	6	3	80	7	4	87	—	1
calves	—	—	—	—	—	—	45	—	—	44	10	3	52	—	2	18	—	2
Caribou																		
bulls	71	—	1	84	5	3	85	2	4	39	8	12	24	9	7	—	—	—
cows	—	—	—	92	—	1	85	1	3	10	—	1	—	—	—	78	—	1
calves	—	—	—															
Sheep																		
rams	—	—	—	—	—	—	92	—	1	—	—	—	91	—	2	64	—	1
ewes	—	—	—	—	—	—	—	—	—	90	—	2	88	—	1	93	—	2

Table 6. Incidence of skeletal abnormalities in prey killed by wolves, or probably killed by wolves in Denali National Park, Alaska, October–April 1986–1992.

SPECIES	Mandibular Necrosis		Arthritis	
	n	*affected (%)*	*n*	*affected (%)*
Dall Sheep				
Female	18	8(44)	6	0(0)
Male	24	13(54)	5	0(0)
Caribou				
Female	60	0(0)	43	2(5)
Male	66	3(5)	52	7(13)
Moose				
Female	81	29(36)	41	15(37)
Age 1-13	—	——	23	0(0)
Age 14-20	—	——	18	15(83)[1]
Male	80	28(35)	52	25(48)
Age 1-4	—	——	10	0(0)
Age 5-15	—	——	42	25(60)[1]

1 Different at $\underline{P} = 0.07$

(Table 1). This may be evidence for a cumulative snow effect (Mech et al. 1987) on caribou condition. The proportion of caribou in observed wolf kills each year, including those we could not sex or age, increased with the cumulative snowfall (Table 1) for that year ($\underline{R}^2 = 0.70$; $\underline{P} = 0.02$). When a subsample of caribou kills (Table 2) that could be sexed and aged was examined relative to snowfall, it was the proportion of caribou cows in the wolf kills that varied most with snowfall ($\underline{R}^2 = 0.54$; $\underline{P} = 0.06$; bulls, $\underline{R}^2 = 0.33$; $\underline{P} = 0.17$. There was no substantial change in proportion of time spent locating various wolf packs, or in the geographic area of coverage, that might account for the switch to caribou during the study.

The occurrence of caribou calves in the sample of winter wolf kills was related to snowfall (Table 1) during the winter they were *in utero*. Caribou calves were killed by wolves during winters that followed winters of above-average snowfall, whereas after winters of below-average snowfall, no wolf-killed caribou calves were found the next winter (Table 2). This parallels the results of neonate caribou survival in the same herd. Following two winters of below-average snowfall, mortality of calves ≤30 days old averaged 39%, whereas following three winters of above-average snowfall, the average was 67% (Adams et al. this volume).

No corresponding relationship was found between winter snowfall and proportion of moose calves killed by wolves. Where moose are the primary prey of wolves, calf vulner-

ability to wolf predation is related to snowfall (Peterson 1977). In Denali, increased moose calf vulnerability based on snowfall may have been masked by the increased kill of caribou.

Nutritional Condition of Wolf-Killed Prey

The mean marrow-fat content of moose, caribou and sheep killed by wolves was low during each of the winters (October-April) of the study. Means for moose were lowest in 1990-91 (Table 4), when snow was deepest (Table 1). Marrow fat was less in moose and caribou calves than in adults, less in male caribou during October through May (no January data) than in June through September, and less in bull moose than in cows (Table 5). Percent marrow fat in 29 caribou killed in multiples during winters of deep snow averaged 66±4% compared with 47±5% for 44 caribou killed individually during all winters. The distribution of marrow fat for each species contained individuals with <20% -> 90% (Fig. 6).

Skeletal Abnormalities of Prey Killed by Wolves

More than a third of the wolf-killed moose examined showed mandibular necrosis, and a third or more had arthritis in their lumbosacral or coxofemoral joints (Table 6). Similarly, jaw necrosis and arthritis was found in wolf-killed moose on Isle Royale (Peterson 1977), on Kenai Peninsula, Alaska (Peterson et al. 1984), and earlier in Denali (Haber 1977). Arthritis

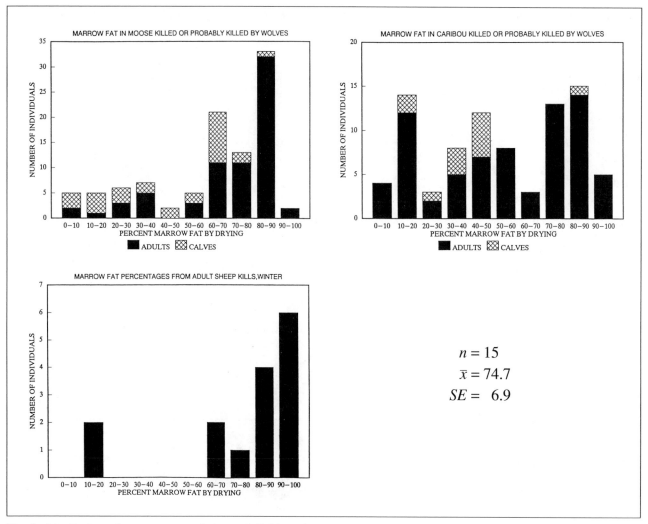

Fig. 6 *Distributions of percent marrow fat in prey killed by wolves, or probably killed by wolves, in Denali National Park, Alaska, October through April 1986–1992.*

afflicted male moose as young as five years of age, whereas no sign of it was found in cows ≤14 years old (Table 6). This contrasts with reports that arthritis afflicted moose cows as young as eight years on Isle Royale (Peterson 1977) and six years of age on Kenai Peninsula (Peterson et al. 1984). On Isle Royale, as well as in our study, the incidence of arthritis was higher in male moose (Peterson 1977).

More wolf-killed sheep than moose showed necrosis (Table 6). Murie (1944) also reported a high rate of necrosis in Denali sheep. We found no arthritis in our small sheep sample, except for a severely arthritic mandibular ramus on a 10-year-old ram.

The incidence of mandibular necrosis and arthritis in wolf-killed caribou was lower than in sheep or moose (Table 6), but the incidence of necrosis in our sample was higher than that reported by Doerr and Dietrich (1979) and several authors whose work they summarized. The incidence was higher in our male caribou than in our females, but not

significantly so ($P = 0.14$). Doerr and Dietrich (1979) found significantly more males with necrosis than females.

Discussion

The Denali wolf-prey system is, in all important respects, a natural system. Thus, our findings should represent a view of the way wolf-prey systems have functioned in the past throughout at least the northern range of the wolf. Differences with studies elsewhere could be related primarily to the fact that in most other study areas, either the wolves, the prey, or both, have been harvested or otherwise modified by humans.

In the Denali system, the number of moose, caribou, sheep, and wolves have been interacting and fluctuating naturally for many years. During our study, caribou increased (Adams et al. this volume). This finding may represent one of the exceptions implied by Seip (1991:51), when he concluded that, "Caribou generally appear unable to survive in areas where there is extensive overlap with wolves and alternate prey species."

We do not know the trend in populations of moose and sheep. No drastic decline was discernible in either, and both species remained about as widely distributed as they have been for decades (Haber 1977). Wolves consumed their prey as completely as possible, leaving only hair, rumen contents, and bones, most of them chewed. Thus, there was no indication, such as incomplete consumption of kills (Pimlott et al. 1969, Mech and Frenzel 1971a, Peterson 1977), that conditions were especially extreme for prolonged periods during most of the study.

Under these circumstances, the Denali wolves found enough prey not only to survive and reproduce, but to double in numbers (Meier et al. this volume) during a period of widely variable snowfall. They showed a high degree of selectivity in their predation patterns over different dimensions in their relationships with prey. The commonality of each dimension, however, was prey vulnerability.

Vulnerability took the form of youth, old age, poor condition, and hindrance by snow, and it varied by species, sex, time of year, and snow depth. Calves were especially important prey during summer when they are weakest, bulls before, during and after their autumn rut when they are most vulnerable, and cows in late winter when snow depth, negative energy-balance, and the drain of pregnancy reduce nutritional state. Probably the poor nutritional condition of caribou bulls during and after the rut (Table 5) explains why wolves took proportionately more bulls than cows. Although cows and calves become more vulnerable primarily during or after winters of above-average snowfall, bulls must rut every year. Rutting ungulates are generally in poor nutritional condition due to fighting and chasing females rather than feeding (Bergerud 1973, Geist 1974, Clutton-Brock et al. 1982). The reason for caribou bull vulnerability before the rut is currently under investigation (Adams et al. in preparation).

Our sample of sheep kills was small and biased. Nevertheless, it is clear that wolves kill sheep year round, apparently more during late fall, possibly a result of the vulnerability of rutting males. Murie (1944) and Haber (1977) also found that sheep were important to wolves in Denali.

Skeletal abnormalities and other possibly–debilitating factors were found among prey remains. The incidence of these conditions in the general prey population is unknown, and to what degree they contribute to prey vulnerability is open to conjecture. Jaw necrosis can result in abnormal occlusion and tooth loss, and was common in adult moose and sheep taken by wolves. Arthritis of the lumbosacral joint (between the sacrum and sixth lumbar vertebra) appears to be related to age in moose, with severe arthritis common in animals ≥15 years. Few skeletal abnormalities have been found among the remains of caribou eaten by wolves.

The mean ages of female prey animals taken were older than those of males. Because arthritis did not afflict cow moose until much older than bulls, this suggests that the arthritis may have helped predispose older individuals to predation.

Although Denali wolves were able to survive and increase during periods of below-average snowfall, above-average snowfall in Denali helped predispose prey to wolf predation. Deep snow had a direct effect on reducing prey condition and mobility and thus increasing predation by wolves (Mech and Frenzel 1971a, Mech and Karns 1977, Peterson 1977, Haber 1977, Nelson and Mech 1986b). We also found evidence of an indirect effect of snow depth on caribou calves that had been *in utero* and thus were predisposed to wolf predation during the next summer (Adams et al. this volume) and winter (Table 2), similar to findings in other wolf-prey systems (Mech and Karns 1977, Peterson 1977, Mech et al. 1987, 1991b).

The most important common denominator in predisposing Denali prey to wolves was probably nutritional condition indicated by the low marrow fat content in all of the prey species, ages, and sexes of our wolf-kill sample (Table 4). Considering that some individuals must have been predisposed by physical frailties not apparent in the bones, which were usually all that could be examined for most kills (Mech 1970), and that such animals would not necessarily show low marrow fat (Mech and DelGuidice 1985), the low average percent fat we found is striking. This is especially true given that our values are probably artificially high (see methods).

In caribou, femur fat <70% indicates that the animal's body weight has declined about to its limit (Dauphiné 1971), with total body fat <5% (Huot and Goudreault 1985). Adult caribou cows in good condition possess 11–14% body fat (Dauphiné 1971, Huot and Goudreault 1985), and bulls ≥31% (Dauphiné 1971), with marrow fat ≥70%. Starvation has been documented in adult moose at a mean marrow fat level of 52% (S.E. = 15.3) (Ballard et al. 1987).

However, several workers believe that marrow fat must reach much lower levels before indicating that an animal is near death. Stephenson and Johnson (1972), Franzmann and Arneson (1976), Peterson et al. (1984) and Hayes et al. (1991) used 20% marrow fat in adults and 10% in calves as indicators of starvation. Although there is value in being conservative, using such low levels ignores starvation physiology and risks reaching erroneous conclusions.

Ungulate marrow fat ≤70–87%, depending on species, is a direct indicator of total body fat, but by the time the marrow fat is as low as this threshold, the greater majority of body fat has already been lost (Dauphiné 1971, Huot and Goudreault 1985, Watkins et al. 1991, Holand 1992). As ungulates lose fat stores, they also lose protein, or muscle mass (Leibholz 1970, Paquay et al. 1972, Hovell et al. 1987, Torbitt et al. 1985, DelGuidice et al. 1990). In adult white-tailed deer (*Odocoileus virginianus*), for example, the $\underline{R^2}$

L. David Mech, Thomas J. Meier, John W. Burch, and Layne G. Adams

Denali National Park, formerly known as Mt. McKinley National Park, has been an important area for extensive, long-term wolf/ungulate studies dating back to 1944. Adolf Murie was the first to conduct a study. Dall sheep (top photo: L.D. Mech) are an important prey species. Current research (bottom photo) involves radio-collaring of wolves and subsidiary studies of prey species.

between weight loss and protein (muscle) loss was 0.91 (DelGuidice et al. 1990). At maximal work loads, such as when running from wolves, it is muscle glycogen that forms the major source of fuel (Froberg et al. 1971, Hultman and Nilsson 1971). Furthermore, blood glucose which also is important to a running animal, in starved individuals falls to about a third of its level in fed animals, and insulin which fosters glucose use, drops to one-tenth (Smith et al. 1983:542).

Thus, marrow-fat percentage should be viewed not so much in terms of a fat indicator, but as an indicator of fat, muscle, and energy depletion, and any level below the threshold indicates an animal in marginal condition. While it certainly is true that some animals do not actually die until their marrow fat is almost depleted, loss of vigor and vitality is a matter of degree rather than an all-or-none phenomenon. Additional stressors such as fighting, plowing through snow, or being chased by wolves probably would raise the marrow-fat threshold at which individuals in marginal condition would perish. This relationship could explain Ballard's et al. (1987) starved moose with a mean of 52% marrow fat.

Given the above considerations, we believe that most of our wolf-killed moose and caribou were in poor condition. Because such individuals would have lost considerable muscle mass as well as fat, these animals would have had little energy left to withstand chases by wolves.

The marrow fat content of Denali wolf-killed prey was consistently low despite relatively low snow depths in some years. There seemed to be no relationship between percentage marrow fat in our wolf kills and the snowfall, except that marrow fat of our moose kills was lowest during the winter of deepest snow (Tables 1 and 4).

The preponderance of low marrow fat despite low snow depth during three of the seven years of the study indicates that the unharvested Denali prey herds must include a certain proportion of individuals that are unable to secure sufficent food, even under average environmental conditions. Our data indicate that such individuals are among the oldest, youngest, and the bulls during the rut. This situation probably is typical of natural ungulate populations unharvested by humans. Wolves could depend on such vulnerable members of natural prey populations, along with the young which are generally more vulnerable, to sustain their own numbers during most years. When snowfall or other weather factors become extreme and increase prey vulnerability, wolf populations can increase (Mech 1977b, Peterson 1977) to make use of the sudden increase in resources, such as the caribou in our study.

Acknowledgments

This study was funded primarily by the U.S. National Park Service, Natural Resources Preservation Program. Denali National Park, the U.S. Fish and Wildlife Service, and the U.S.D.A. North Central Forest Experiment Station also contributed to the project. We especially thank A. Lovaas, R. Berry Jr., J. Dalle-Molle (deceased), J. Van Horn, and J. Keay for their administrative support, B. Dale, D. Shults, and A. Blakesley for field assistance, and professional pilots D. Glaser, B. Lentsch, D. Miller, S. Hamilton, and K. Butters. In addition, the help of other pilots, National Park Service staff, and volunteers is greatly appreciated. M. Nelson, R.P. Thiel, R. Peterson and W. Ballard critiqued the manuscript and offered many helpful suggestions for improvement.

L. David Mech, Thomas J. Meier, John W. Burch, and Layne G. Adams

Wolf Predation on Caribou Calves in Denali National Park, Alaska

■ Layne G. Adams, Bruce W. Dale, and L. David Mech

During 1987–1991, 29 to 45 radio-collared caribou cows were monitored daily during calving each year and their calves were radio-collared (n = 147 calves) to investigate calf production and survival. We determined characteristics of wolf predation on caribou calves and, utilizing information from a companion wolf study, evaluated the role of spacing by caribou cows in minimizing wolf predation on neonates (calves ≤ 15 days old) during a period when wolf abundance doubled. On average, 49% of the neonates died, ranging from 30% in 1987 to 71% in 1991. Overall, wolves killed 22% of the neonates produced and were the most important mortality agent. Wolves preyed on calves primarily during six days following the peak of calving and usually killed calves five to 15 days old. The mortality rate for neonates was strongly inversely correlated with average birthweight. Neonatal losses to wolves were also correlated with birthweight but not spring wolf density or mean calving elevation. Caribou concentrated on a calving ground when spring snow conditions allowed and adjusted their distribution on the calving ground depending on snow conditions and wolf distribution and abundance. Even though the wolf population doubled, the exposure of caribou calves to wolf predation did not increase, when spacing by caribou at the wolf pack territory scale was accounted for.

Introduction

Wolves (*Canis lupus*) are important predators of caribou (*Rangifer tarandus*) throughout much of northern North America and have major influences on caribou population dynamics (Bergerud 1980, Gasaway et al. 1983, Bergerud and Ballard 1988). Wolf predation on neonates is often considered a primary means by which wolves can limit the growth of caribou populations (Page 1985, Bergerud and Elliot 1986, Miller et al. 1988b), although the magnitude and characteristics of such losses to wolves are largely unknown.

Caribou use an array of temporal, spatial, and social strategies to minimize predation on newborn calves. Caribou calving is highly synchronous (Skoog 1968, Dauphiné and McClure 1974), resulting in a short annual period when young calves are abundant, thus swamping local predators (Estes 1976, Bergerud 1974b, Ims 1990). Aggregation of barren-ground caribou into large groups immediately after calving may have evolved to further reduce losses of young calves (Bergerud 1974b) through increased vigilance, dilution of predation risk, and increased confusion resulting when large groups are pursued by predators (Cumming 1975, Bertram 1978).

Bergerud and Page (1987) presented a conceptual model of spacing strategies used by caribou to minimize predation on calves. In woodland herds, caribou "space out" during calving to decrease their exposure to predation. Such herds

may be more dispersed during calving than any other time of year (Fuller and Keith 1981b, Brown et al. 1986). They select habitats, such as mountains, shorelines, and islands, that are less likely, and more difficult, for predators to search, and avoid habitats used by other ungulates (Bergerud et al. 1984, 1990; Bergerud 1985; Edmonds 1988). They also use forests and patchy snow in mountainous areas as cryptic cover and limit their movements to reduce the potential for predator encounters (Bergerud and Page 1987).

The large barren-ground herds "space away" from wolves during calving (Bergerud and Page 1987). Parturient cows migrate hundreds of kilometres from taiga winter ranges to arctic tundra calving grounds that lack other ungulate prey and support few wolves (Skoog 1968, Kuyt 1972, Stephenson and James 1982). Numbering in the tens or hundreds of thousands, calves effectively swamp the relatively few predators (Kuyt 1972, Stephenson and James 1982, Reynolds and Garner 1987, Fancy and Whitten 1991).

These spacing strategies apply to two of three caribou ecotypes (Davis and Valkenburg 1991): nonmigratory woodland caribou that live sympatrically with other ungulates; and migratory barren-ground caribou with limited overlap with other ungulates. Spacing strategies of the "Alaskan" ecotype are not adequately described, however. This ecotype accounts for 16 of 29 caribou herds in Alaska (Davis and Valkenburg 1991), and others in northwestern

Layne G. Adams, Bruce W. Dale, and L. David Mech

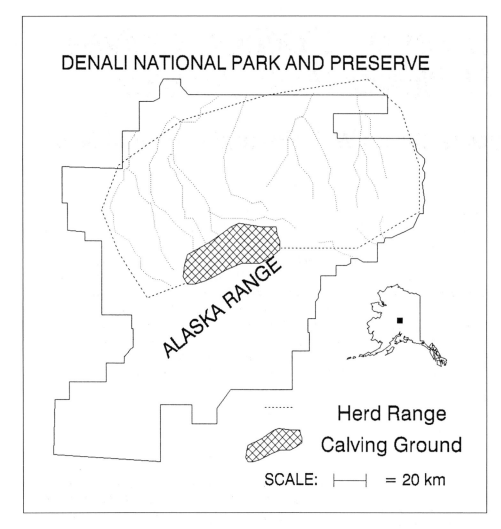

DENALI NATIONAL PARK AND PRESERVE

ALASKA RANGE

Herd Range
Calving Ground

SCALE: |———| = 20 km

Fig. 1 *Locations of the range and calving ground of the Denali Caribou Herd, Denali National Park, Alaska, 1987–1991.*

Canada. Caribou herds of this type share characteristics with the other two ecotypes, and may actually represent a continuum between them.

Similar to the woodland ecotype, Alaskan ecotype caribou share their range with other ungulates, usually moose (*Alces alces*) and Dall's sheep (*Ovis dalli*), and wolves and bears (*Ursus arctos* and *U. americanus*) are distributed throughout their range. Like barren-ground herds, herds of the Alaskan ecotype migrate en masse between seasonal ranges, live in large groups during much of the year, and often form large aggregations following calving. Since both bears and wolves occur throughout their range, Alaskan caribou cannot "space away" from predators in the same sense as the migratory barren-ground ecotype.

Our research in Denali National Park (DENA) provided an opportunity to describe wolf predation on caribou calves in a naturally-regulated predator/ungulate system and evaluate predator-evasion strategies of caribou of the Alaskan ecotype. Our objectives were to characterize wolf-caused deaths of caribou neonates ($\leq$ 15 days-old), to evaluate factors influencing the magnitude of wolf predation on calves,

and to describe the interplay between spacing of caribou and wolves during the calving season.

Study Area

The range of the Denali Caribou Herd (DCH) encompasses approximately 10,000 km^2 including most of DENA north of the crest of the Alaska Range, and areas to the south of the range and east of Mount McKinley (63°30'N, 150°30'W, Fig. 1). The Alaska Range runs northeast to southwest and is characterized by mountain peaks > 3,000 m, glaciers, and glacial valleys. In northeastern DENA, the Alaska Range is flanked by lower mountains (< 2,100 m) dissected by several major rivers flowing northward and two broad fault valleys perpendicular to the major drainages. Permanent snow and ice occur above 2,400 m, while lower mountains and foothills are covered predominantly by alpine, sedge (*Carex* spp.), and shrub (*Salix* and *Betula* spp.) tundras. Treeline occurs at about 800 m with spruce (*Picea* spp.) woodlands/forests, tussock (*Eriophorum* spp.) tundra, and riparian spruce/willow zones below. The western portion of DENA is characterized bythe tundra foothills of the Mount

McKinley/Mount Foraker massif on the south extending northward into lowland flats with spruce forests, bogs, and many north-trending watercourses.

Weather in the region is typical of the subarctic montane climate with temperatures ranging from 32° C in summer to -47° C in winter. Average annual precipitation at DENA headquarters on the eastern boundary is 38 cm, including 190 cm of snowfall. Winter snowfall was well below average during winters 1986-87 and 1987-88, and the calving ground was nearly snow-free by the onset of calving in those springs. In winter 1988-89, snow accumulation was above average throughout the region. Snow continued to fall during much of May, and was deep on the calving ground (> 1 m in many areas) during much of calving. In winter 1989-90, snowfall exceeded the long-term average, but a warmer-than-usual spring resulted in early snowmelt and greening of vegetation, and the calving ground was nearly devoid of snow by the onset of calving. Snowfall records were set during winter 1990-91, and snow on the calving ground was deep during much of that calving season.

The DCH shares its range with approximately 2,000 moose (Meier 1987) at densities ranging from 0.1 moose/km^2 in northwestern spruce lowlands to 0.5 moose/km^2 in the eastern intermountain valleys. Approximately 2,400 Dall sheep inhabit mountainous areas in the central and eastern portions of the DCH's range (Singer 1984b).

In addition to wolves, large predators in the DCH's range include grizzly and black bears. Grizzly bears occur primarily in uplands at a density of around 30 bears/1,000 km^2 (Dean 1987). Black bears occur primarily in the northwestern spruce lowlands and adjacent Kantishna Hills. Smaller predators include coyotes (*Canis latrans*), lynx (*Felis lynx*), wolverines (*Gulo gulo*), and golden eagles (*Aquila chrysaetos*).

Methods

Caribou

Thirty-four adult caribou cows were radio-collared in winter 1986-87 and 11–16 10-month-old cows were radio-collared in March of each year during 1987–91. All cows were captured by helicopter darting and were immobilized with carfentanil citrate (3.0–3.6 mg/dart) and either acepromazine maleate (5 mg/dart) or xylazine hydrochloride (25–100 mg/dart). Caribou were fitted with radio collars equipped with motion-sensitive mortality sensors. Carfentanil and xylazine effects were antagonized with naloxone hydrochloride (75–250 mg/mg carfentanil) and yohimbine hydrochloride (0.11 mg/kg body weight), respectively.

During May and early June 1987–91, all radio-collared cows ≥ 2 years old were located daily using standard telemetry techniques from fixed-wing aircraft (Piper PA-18 Supercub). Locations, group sizes, habitat characteristics, antler/udder status, and presence of calves at heel were

noted. The first location of a radioed cow with a calf was considered her calving site that year. All radioed cows were also observed from a helicopter early in the calving period to evaluate their pregnancy status, based on presence of hard antlers (Espmark 1971, Whitten 1991) and distended udders (Bergerud 1964). At about weekly intervals during May, cows that had not calved were rechecked by helicopter.

When a radio-collared cow was seen with a calf, the calf was captured and radio-collared. The helicopter capture crew landed as close to the cow-calf pair as possible, and the calf was chased on foot and caught by hand. Each calf was weighed, sexed, and its age estimated based on posture, coordination, hoof and umbilicus characteristics, and previous observations of its mother (Adams et al. 1989b). Most calves were less than one day old at capture and the remainder were three days old or less. For calves caught at two or three days of age, birthweights were estimated by subtracting 0.5 kg/day from the capture weight for each day of age over one (Robbins and Robbins 1979, L. Adams, unpubl. data). Calves were radio-collared with mortality-sensing transmitters mounted on expandable elastic collars. The handling procedure took less than two minutes per calf, and most calves immediately reunited with their dams (Adams et al. 1989a). Calves were radio-tracked daily until early June, at least weekly through June, and monthly during the rest of their first year.

In May, mortalities were investigated as soon as possible by helicopter, usually within five hours of detection. Causes of death were determined by presence of predators or evidence including tracks, scats, predator hair, wounding patterns, and disposition of calf remains. After the daily tracking period ended in early June, deaths were investigated as soon as practical and were assumed to have occurred half-way between the dates when calves were last known to be alive and deaths were first noted. Causes of death could not be determined reliably for most calves that died after the daily monitoring period.

Many characteristics of calf production and survival, including habitat selection at parturition, pregnancy rate, date of birth, birthweight, and calf survival, may be influenced by maternal age (Dauphiné 1976, Thomas 1982, Clutton-Brock et al. 1982, Ozaga and Verme 1982, Ozaga and Verme 1986, Mech and McRoberts 1990, L. Adams, unpubl. data). Therefore, a sample of radio-collared cows for evaluating calf production/survival should reflect the age structure of cows in the population. To provide such an age-justified cow subsample (AJCS), we started with the adult cows captured during winter 1986-87 and annually "recruited" 10-month-old cows randomly selected from the radio-collared cohort. The number of 10-month-olds recruited each year was determined by calculating their ratio to older cows in the herd (based on the previous fall calf:cow and calf sex ratios), and multiplying that by the number of cows in the AJCS at recruitment (May 1). We assumed overwinter calf survival was similar to that of cows, as indicated by our estimates of survival of radio-collared calves and cows (L. Adams, un-publ. data). The characteristics of spatial distribution, calf production, and calf mortality of the AJCS were assumed to be representative of all DCH cows.

We attempted three composition surveys annually. Prior to each, radio-collared cows were located to determine the survey area. Helicopter surveys were conducted within the week following the peak of calving each year, except 1989, to determine annual natality rates, based on the proportions of cows with distended udders (Bergerud 1964). Post-calving helicopter surveys were conducted between 27 May and 5 June to determine calf/cow ratios and the number of cows on the calving grounds. During the peak of the rut in late September, helicopter surveys were used to determine calf:cow, calf sex, and bull:cow ratios.

Herd size was estimated annually by one or two methods. The number of cows observed on the calving grounds during the post-calving composition survey was divided by the proportion of the AJCS in the survey area to estimate the total number of cows in the herd. The numbers of calves and bulls were determined by multiplying the cow estimate by the post-calving calf:cow ratio and fall bull:cow ratio, respectively. We also conducted photocensuses in 1987, 1990, and 1991 during late June or early July when caribou were aggregated on snowfields at high elevations (Davis et al. 1979, Valkenburg et al. 1985, Adams et al. 1989a). In the

three years that both censuses were conducted, herd estimates from the two methods were < 50 animals apart ($\bar{x}$ = 33 or 1.2%).

Wolves

A radiotelemetry study of wolves began in 1986 to determine population dynamics and wolf/prey relationships in DENA (Mech et al. 1991c, this volume; Meier et al. this volume). As of December 1991, 107 wolves had been radio-collared and five to 15 packs were monitored in any year. Results of this study included pack sizes, pup production, pack territories, and annual fall and spring wolf density estimates. Further, we attempted to locate radio-collared wolves whose territories included part of the calving ground two to three times/week in May 1987, and daily during the 1988-91 caribou calving seasons.

Results

Caribou and Wolf Population Trends

Caribou numbers increased during 1987–90 at about 8% per year and declined by 18% between fall 1990 and fall 1991 (Fig. 2). Spring wolf densities doubled during 1987-90, increasing at 28% per year (Fig. 2). However, 68% of the increase occurred between 1988 and 1989 (57% annual increase). In 1991, wolf numbers declined slightly.

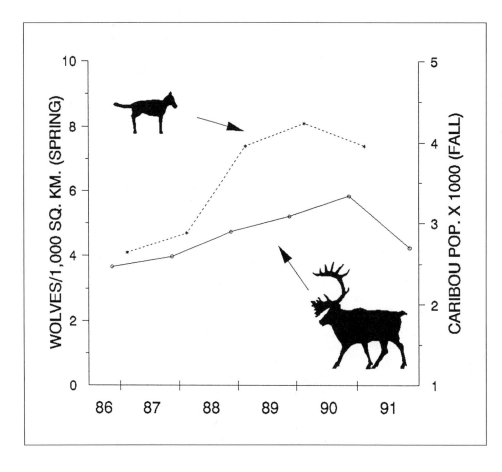

Fig. 2 *Population trends of wolves and caribou in Denali National Park, Alaska, 1986–1991.*

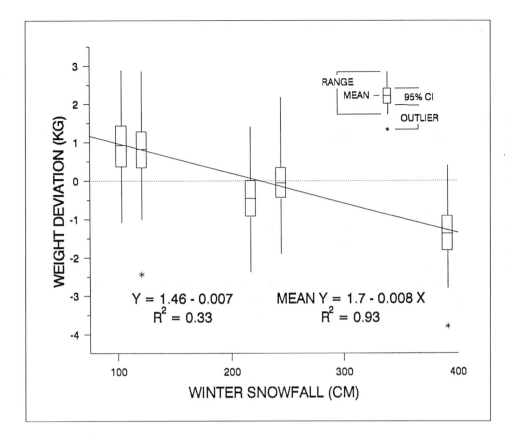

Fig. 3 *Relationships between birthweights of caribou calves from the Denali Herd, Alaska, and winter snowfall (September–May) during 1987–1991. Actual birthweights were converted to birthweight deviations in order to pool sexes. Birthweight deviation = weight of calf – grand mean for its sex.*

Calving Chronology

The onset of calving varied from 5 May in 1988 to 15 May in 1991. The peak of calving, or median calving date (Skoog 1968), for the AJCS varied between 13 and 21 May and was later following the high snowfall winters (1989-90, 1990-91). The end of calving ranged from 26 May in 1987 to 2 June in 1990.

The proportion of calves born daily for each year were aligned based on the median calving date and averaged to arrive at a pooled calving chronology for 1987–91. Overall, calves were born over a 28-day period with the peak of calving nine days after the first calf was born. The interquartile 50% of calves were born in only five days.

Caribou Birthweights

Male and female caribou calves averaged 8.3 kg (range = 4.7–10.4) and 7.5 kg (4.5–9.9) at birth, respectively. To pool birthweights of both sexes for comparisons among years, we determined the deviation for each calf from the five-year birthweight mean for its sex. The annual means of these birthweight deviations declined by 2.2 kg between 1988 and 1991 and were correlated with total winter snowfall at DENA headquarters (Fig. 3).

Caribou Dispersion and Calving Ground Characteristics

We defined the calving ground as the minimum area within the calving range of the herd where cows concentrated during calving and where, on average, 50% of the cows gave birth. Cows that did not calve on the calving ground were dispersed throughout the remainder of the herd's range. The calving ground encompassed 860 km^2 in the southwest portion of the herd's range (Fig. 1), and was predominantly open, rolling terrain with low shrub tundra at lower elevations (650-1,050 m; 530 km^2) and rugged mountains with alpine tundra, rock, scree, and permanent ice and snow at higher elevations (1,050–1,850 m; 330 km^2).

Although on average half of the AJCS cows gave birth each year on the calving ground (by definition), the proportion varied significantly depending on snow depth during calving, with fewer cows on the calving ground in deep snow springs (Table 1, $X^2 = 13.79$, 1 df, $P < 0.001$). Distribution within the calving ground also varied with snow conditions. More AJCS cows calved in the mountains above 1,050 m in years with shallow snowpacks (Table 1, $X^2 = 9.50$, 1 df, $P = 0.002$), although some cows calved at high elevations even in the years with deep snowpacks.

Cows that did not calve on the calving grounds dispersed into lowland spruce forests or mountainous areas of the Alaska Range and adjacent foothills (Table 1). In springs with deep snow, cows were more likely to use lowland forested areas ($X^2 = 5.62$, 1 df, $P = 0.02$).

The elevations at which caribou cows calved were influenced by spring snow depths (Table 1). The proportion of calves born above 900 m was significantly lower in calving

Layne G. Adams, Bruce W. Dale, and L. David Mech

Table 1. Calving distribution and habitat selection of radio-collared caribou cows, Denali National Park, Alaska, during May 1987-91.

	1987	*1988*	*1989*	*1990*	*1991*
SNOW CONDITIONS DURING CALVING SEASON	shallow	shallow	deep	shallow	deep
AJCS COWS[1]					
Monitored	29	38	45	40	40
Calves produced	23	33	35	29	28
On calving grounds	**14(61%)**	**21(64%)**	**15(43%)**	**15(52%)**	**9(32%)**
Mountains	13	18	8	11	4
Lowlands	1	3	7	4	5
Dispersed	**9(39%)**	**12(36%)**	**20(57%)**	**14(48%)**	**19(68%)**
Mountains	5	10	11	10	11
Forests	4	2	9	4	8
Calving elevation					
< 600 m	4	1	9	4	12
≥ 600 m-900 m	2	6	12	5	5
≥ 900 m-1,200 m	9	6	9	7	2
≥ 1,200 m-1,500 m	5	17	4	11	4
≥ 1,500 m	3	3	1	1	2
	23	**33**	**35**	**28**[2]	**25**[2]

1   AJCS = Age-Justified Cow Subsample or a subset of radio-collared cows select to approximate the age structure of the herd.
2   Calving elevations not determined for one and three perinatal losses in 1990 and 1991, respectively.

seasons with deep snowpacks than those with shallow snowpacks (37% versus 77%, $X^2 = 23.31$, 1 df, $P < 0.001$).

Wolf Predation on Calves

On average, 49% of calves born to AJCS cows died within 15 days of birth (Table 2). Wolves accounted for 31 of 73 deaths (42%) of radio-collared neonates over the five years of the study and were the most important cause of death. In comparison, bears, unknown large predators (i.e. bears or wolves), small predators (coyotes and golden eagles), accidents, and stillbirths/perinatal deaths (within 24 hours of birth) accounted for 33%, 4%, 4%, 1%, and 15%, respectively, of neonatal deaths. The proportion of the neonates killed by wolves was 2.5 times greater in 1990 and 1991 than in the three previous years (Table 2; 34% versus 13%, $X^2 = 8.96$, 1 df, $P = 0.003$). The 1990 and 1991 calves also experienced higher mortality between 16 and 120 days of age than did calves in other years (Table 2; $X^2 = 25.62$, 1 df, $P < 0.001$).

Birthweights, calving elevations, and spring wolf densities were evaluated as factors that may influence total and wolf-caused mortality of neonates (Fig. 4). We found a strong inverse linear relationship between the proportion of neonates that died of all causes and average birthweight. Total neonatal mortality was positively correlated with spring wolf density, but not as strongly. Also, caribou neonates survived better in years when most calving occurred at higher elevations. There was no evidence that wolves selected light birthweight calves within any year (ANOVA blocked by year, $F = 0.51$, $P = 0.48$), but the proportion of neonates killed by wolves was more strongly correlated with average birthweight than with wolf density or calving elevation.

Wolves did not begin killing calves until after the peak of calving in any year and most wolf-caused deaths occurred during six days following the calving peak (Fig. 5). Wolf-killed calves were usually five to 15 days old (Fig. 5). Deaths after 15 days of age were uncommon except in 1990 and 1991 (Table 2).

Table 2. Calf production/mortality for radio-collared cows in Denali National Park, Alaska, 1987-1991.

	1987	*1988*	*1989*	*1990*	*1991*
Radio-collared cows[1]	29	38	45	40	40
Calves produced	23	33	35	28[2]	28
Mortalities to 15 days-of-age[3]	**7(30%)**	**13(39%)**	**18(51%)**	**15(54%)**	**20(71%)**
Bear	2	6	10	3	3
Wolf	4	5	3	9	10
Stillbirth/perinatal	1	1	2	3	4
Unknown large predator	-	1	2	-	-
Coyote	-	-	-	-	1
Eagle	-	-	-	-	2
Accident	-	-	1	-	-
Mortalities 16-30 days-of-age[3]	**1(6%)**	**1(5%)**	**-**	**6(46%)**	**1(13%)**
Wolf	-	-	-	1	-
Unknown predator	1	1	-	4	1
Unknown cause	-	-	-	1	-
Mortalities 31-120 days of age[3]	**2(13%)**	**1(5%)**	**3(18%)**	**4(57%)**	**5(71%)**
Wolf	1	1	1	1	-
Unknown predator	-	-	-	3	-
Accident	-	-	1	-	1
Unknown cause	1	-	1	-	4
Calves surviving 120 days[4]	**13(57%)**	**18(55%)**	**14(40%)**	**3(11%)**	**2(7%)**

1 Cows from an age-justified subsample of radio-collared cows for each year that were ≥ 2 years-old.
2 29 calves produced but one died due to study activities.
3 Percent in parentheses is the proportion of calves alive at beginning of the period that died during the period.
4 Percent in parentheses is the proportion of calves produced that survived 120 days.

Utilizing a calving ground appeared to be an effective strategy to decrease wolf predation on calves in most years. Overall, calves born on the calving ground suffered only half the wolf predation of those born elsewhere (10/73 versus 21/74, $\underline{X}^2 = 4.76$, 1 df, $\underline{P} = 0.03$).

Wolf Abundance and Distribution on the Calving Ground

The calving ground was part of the territories of one or two wolf packs during any calving season (Table 3). The western half was in the territory of the McLeod Lake Pack in all years. McLeod Lake wolves denned adjacent to the northwest edge of the calving ground and were generally located north of the calving ground in lowland areas prior to and during the onset of calving.

Packs with access to the east half of the calving ground changed yearly. In 1987, the Clearwater Pack included the eastern half of the calving ground within their territory but

they denned 24 km to the north. Clearwater wolves were not located on or near the calving ground after early September 1987. In May 1988, we located a pair of wolves (Pirate Creek Pair) at a historic den site in the eastern half of the calving ground. They produced seven pups, and primarily used the eastern portion of the calving ground throughout May-November 1988. In November 1988, the radioed alpha female died of starvation and fate of the remaining pack members is unknown. By late winter 1988-89, the Clearwater Pack was again using the eastern half of the calving ground and denned 6 km north of it in May 1989. However, they were rarely located on the calving ground that season (one of 39 radio locations during May). The Clearwater wolves maintained a small territory during early winter 1989-90 that comprised mainly the east half of the calving ground after the adjacent Little Bear pack usurped the northern half of their previous home range. In December 1989, one radioed Clearwater wolf and two pack members were found dead, probably having

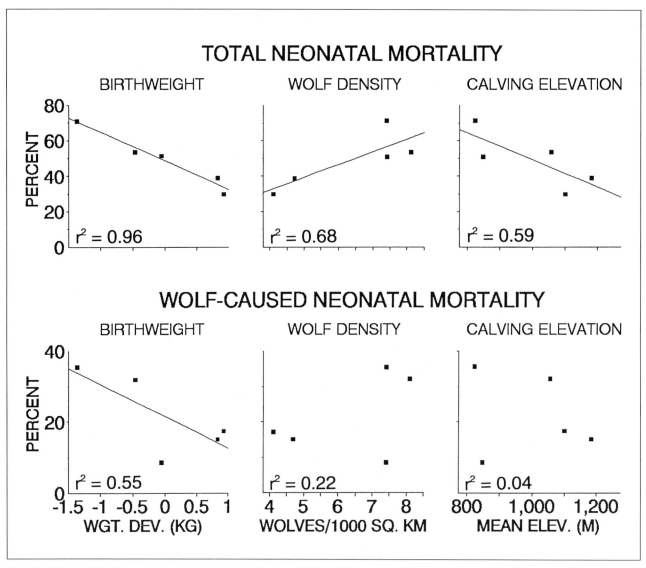

Fig. 4 *Relationships between neonatal mortality and average birthweight, spring wolf density, and mean calving elevation for the Denali Caribou Herd, Alaska, during 1987–1991. Actual birthweights were converted to birthweight deviations in order to pool sexes. Birthweight deviation = weight of calf – grand mean for its sex.*

died from starvation, and the remaining radio-collared wolf and four packmates were never observed again.

No resident wolves were known to use the eastern portion of the calving ground during May 1990 and 1991. However, two wolves were observed on 1 June 1990 on the eastern edge of the calving ground and a single wolf was radio-collared in the area on 28 May 1991, but left by 6 June. For subsequent analyses, these transient wolves were assumed to be residents during the entire calving season. It was unlikely that other undetected wolves were on the calving ground because the only radio-collared calves killed by wolves on the eastern half of the calving ground were associated with these sightings. Snow-tracking in the late winter prior to, and early winter following, the 1990-91 calving seasons also corroborated the lack of resident wolves.

In years when the snowpack was shallow during the calving season and caribou cows were able to calve in the mountainous terrain on the southern edge of the calving ground, radio-collared wolves were rarely located on the calving ground prior to the peak of calving, but were found there regularly after the peak (Table 4). During deep snow springs, when caribou calved on and adjacent to the lowland northern half of the calving ground, radioed wolves were located on the calving ground throughout calving (Table 4). Radioed wolves of calving-ground packs were found during May 1987–91 at five adult caribou and three adult moose kills prior to the peak of calving, but no adult ungulate kills were located again until early June. During May, radioed wolves were located with 22 caribou calf kills, all but one after the peak of calving.

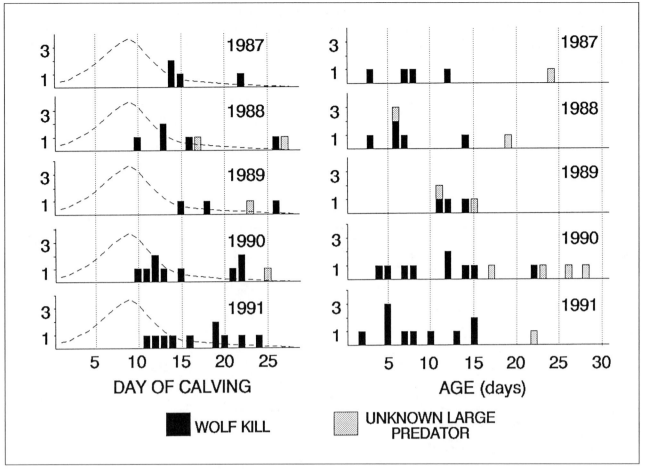

Fig. 5 *The timing and ages of wolf-killed calves in the Denali Caribou Herd, Alaska, during the calving period, 1987–1991. The dashed line represents the proportion of calves born on each day. Cross-hatched bars were calves killed by unknown large predators and are included to represent the maximum possible wolf kill.*

Numerical and spatial relationships of wolves and caribou

With a doubling of the wolf population and only a 30% increase in the caribou herd during 1987–91, increased exposure of caribou calves to wolf predation (WE) was expected and is implied by the simple ratio of wolves to calves (WE_{gross}, Table 5). These wolf:prey ratios were strongly linearly related to spring wolf density ($r^2 = 0.94$, Fig. 6). However, using WE_{gross} to measure exposure implies wolves and caribou calves were spatially distributed in the same manner; it does not account for the patchy and dissimilar distributions of both during calving. In particular, caribou calved predominantly in the eastern half of the calving ground in most years, where wolves were scarce (Fig. 7).

To account for the effects of wolf and caribou dispersion at the pack territory scale, we calculated wolf:calf ratios for each pack that had AJCS cows calving within its territory (number of adult wolves in each pack/[total calves x proportion of AJCS cows that bore calves in the territory]). The WE values for each pack were then weighted by the proportion of calves born in the territory and summed ($WE_{weighted}$).

The $WE_{weighted}$ values were 0.11–0.22 of WE_{gross} (mean = 0.16, Table 5; Fig. 8). Further, unlike WE_{gross}, $WE_{weighted}$ did not vary with wolf density (Fig. 6). Annual $WE_{weighted}$ values were highest in the two springs with deep snowpacks (1989, 1991) when snow limited the options of caribou cows selecting calving sites and the proportions on the calving ground were low (Table 1), and in 1987 when there was little snow but wolves were nearly equally distributed on the calving ground (Table 3). In the other two years (1988 and 1990) the $WE_{weighted}$ values were lower; snow depths were minimal and caribou calved primarily on the eastern half of the calving ground where wolves were particularly scarce (Table 3).

In addition to the spatial relationships described above, caribou cows also adjusted their distribution within the calving ground depending on the distribution and abundance of wolves. In 1987, the two wolf packs on the calving grounds were similar in size, and calving of AJCS cows was equally distributed between the two pack territories (Table 6). In the other four years, the pack using the western half of the calving ground was larger and AJCS cows calved dis-

Table 3. Sizes of wolf packs that had radio-collared caribou calving within their territories, May 1987–1991, Denali National Park, Alaska. Pack sizes are the largest of the spring pack estimate or the fall pack estimate minus the number of pups known to be in the pack, except where noted (dashes denote no caribou calving in pack territory that year).

Pack	Calving Ground?[1]	1987	1988	1989	1990	1991
McLeod Lake	yes	4	7	8	10	8
Pirate Creek	yes	-	2	-	2[2]	1[3]
Clearwater[4]	yes	3	-	2	-	-
"	no	-	-	-	-	-
Little Bear	no	-	-	7	-	13
McKinley River	no	5[5]	10	7[6]	10	6
East Fork	no	6	7	18	24	18
Chulitna	no	-	5[5]	-	8[5]	7[5]
Windy	no	-	6	8	-	-
Stampede	no	-	-	7	-	5
Headquarters	no	-	2	-	-	-
Foraker River	no	-	-	2	-	-

1   yes = Pack included portion of calving ground within its territory during the previous year; no = not a calving ground pack.
2   Two wolves observed late in the calving season, no known resident wolves.
3   One transient wolf observed and radio-collared in the calving season, no known resident wolves.
4   The Clearwater Pack's territory did not include the calving ground in all years.
5   No information, assumed annual median pack size.
6   Assumed from tracks seen in late winter 1989.

Table 4. Radiotelemetry results for wolves that included the calving ground of the Denali Caribou Herd within their annual territory, Denali National Park, Alaska during 1987–91.

	1987	1988	1989	1990	1991
Clearwater Pack[1]					
Adults in pack	3		2		
# radioed	3		2		
Calving ground locations[2]					
Before peak	0/4		1/16		
After	4/17		0/23		
McLeod Lake Pack					
Adults in pack	4	7	8	10	8
# radioed	2	3	3	3	1
Calving ground locations[2]					
Before peak	0/2	0/20	6/21	1/25	4/6
After	2/8	15/41	13/36	5/22	2/14

1   Clearwater Pack did not utilize the calving ground in 1989 and died out prior to the 1990 calving season.
2   Radio locations on calving ground/total radio locations.

Table 5. Abundance and numerical relationships of wolves and caribou calves during calving seasons, 1987–91, Denali National Park, Alaska.

	1987	1988	1989	1990	1991
WOLVES					
Spring density (wolves/1,000 km^2)	4.1	4.7	7.4	8.1	7.4
Wolves on caribou range					
(range = approx. 10,000 km^2)	41	47	74	81	74
CARIBOU					
Number of cows in May (≥ 1 year-old)	1,342	1,531	1,695	1,997	1,863
Natality Rate (cows with udders/cow)	0.76	0.79	0.78	0.73	0.70
Calves Born (cows x natality rate)	1,020	1,210	1,322	1,458	1,304
EXPOSURE OF CALVES TO WOLF PREDATION (WE)*					
WE$_{gross}$	0.040	0.039	0.056	0.056	0.057
WE$_{weighted}$	0.0088	0.0064	0.0083	0.0064	0.0097

* WE$_{gross}$ = range-wide wolf:calf ratio; WE$_{weighted}$ = sum of wolf:calf ratios for each pack territory weighted by proportion of calves born in that territory.

proportionately in the eastern half of the calving ground (Table 6; 1987 versus 1988–91 pooled, X^2 = 3.97, 1 df, P = 0.047). Similar patterns were noted for all AJCS cows and AJCS cows with calves at the end of the calving period (Table 6; AJCS cows 1987 versus 1988–91 pooled, X^2 = 6.34, 1 df, P = 0.01; AJCS cows with surviving calves 1987 versus 1988–91 pooled, X^2 = 3.96, 1 df, P = 0.05).

Further evidence that caribou adjusted their distribution on the calving ground in response to wolf distribution was observed in 1988, the only year wolves denned on the calving ground. From the onset of calving (6 May) to the calving peak (13 May), 10 calves were born to AJCS cows in the eastern half of the calving ground, including four within 10 km of the occupied wolf den (three of these

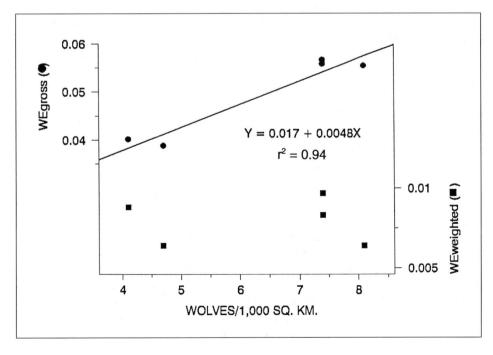

Fig. 6 *Relationships between the exposure of caribou calves in the Denali Herd, Alaska to wolf predation and spring wolf density during May 1987–1991. WE$_{gross}$ is the range-wide wolf exposure or wolf:calf ratio; WE$_{weighted}$ is the wolf exposure accounting for the distribution of calves and wolves during calving.*

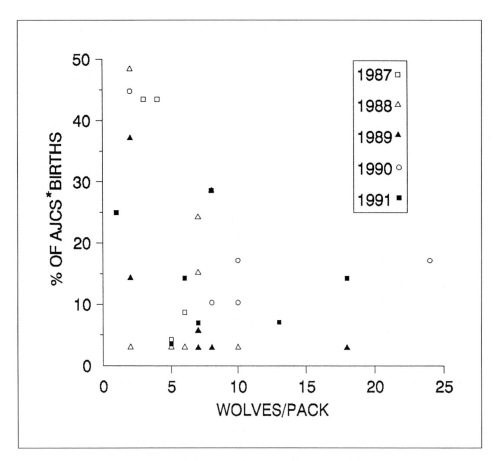

Fig. 7 *The proportion of Denali Caribou Herd cows, based on a sample of radio-collared cows that represented the age structure of the herd (AJCS), that gave birth in each wolf pack territory* **versus** *the number of adult wolves in each pack during 1987–1991. Pack sizes were based on the highest of the spring pack size estimate or the fall estimate minus the number of pups surviving to fall.*

neonates were killed by wolves). After 13 May, AJCS cows bore seven more calves in the eastern half of the calving ground, all > 10 km from the wolf den. In other years, half the calves born on the eastern half of the calving ground were born within less than 10 km of the 1988 den (1988: 4/17 < 10 km; 1987, 1989–91: 18/37 < 10 km). During the 1988 post-calving survey, we noted proportionately fewer cows with calves within 10 km of the occupied wolf den than on the remainder of the calving ground (69 cows with calves of 215 cows versus 325 cows with calves of 734 cows, respectively; $\underline{X}^2 = 10.17$, one df, $\underline{P} = 0.001$), corroborating the pattern described for AJCS cows. Most cows (716 of 949) observed during this survey were located in the center of the calving ground, more than 10 km from the Pirate Creek den on the east end and the McLeod Lake den adjacent to the west end.

Discussion

Wolves were the primary mortality agent for neonates in the DCH (Table 2) and that mortality was a major factor limiting herd growth. Overall, wolves killed 22% of the neonates produced. Wolves primarily killed calves that were five to 15 days old during six days following the peak of calving (Fig. 5). Calves less than five days old were usually alone with their dams or in small groups. They moved little and remained in habitats, including high ridges and lowland

forests, that provided cryptic cover and/or were not likely to be searched by wolves (L. Adams, unpubl. data). At about five days of age, calves entered larger nursery groups in more open habitats. In 1987–89, when calves were heavier at birth, few calves died after 15 days of age (Table 2), suggesting they may have reached a physical threshold that reduced vulnerability to wolf predation, as well as other mortality agents. The 1990 and 1991 calves, which were lighter at birth, were killed by predators throughout summer (Table 2).

Because wolves are important predators of caribou calves, caribou have developed calving strategies that should minimize wolf predation on calves. Calving DCH cows exhibited several behaviors that tended to reduce exposure of vulnerable calves to wolves. Denali caribou cows used the full suite of spacing strategies described by Bergerud and Page (1987). On average, half the cows gave birth on a calving ground that encompassed less than 9% of their year-round range, and nearly 60% calved there in years when snow did not hinder their use of the area. Cows that did not give birth on the calving ground "spaced out" throughout the year-round range of the herd, primarily in lowland spruce forests and high mountainous terrain.

Even though predators occurred throughout their range, parturient cows in effect "spaced away" from wolves by concentrating on a calving ground where wolves were comparatively scarce (Table 3). Within the calving ground, cows

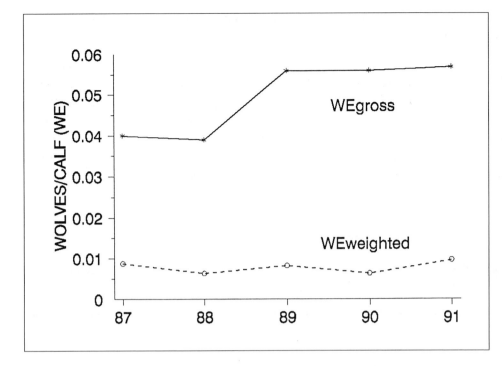

Fig. 8 *Annual patterns in the exposure of caribou calves in the Denali Herd, Alaska, to wolf predation during May 1987–1991. WE_{gross} is the range-wide wolf exposure or wolf:calf ratio; $WE_{weighted}$ accounts for the distribution of calves and wolves during calving.*

selected high ridgelines, maximizing their separation from wolves in the lowlands (Table 1). There they were far from caribou nursery herds forming at lower elevations and from the few moose in the area. Also, they blended in with the mottled snow cover, decreasing their chances of being detected by predators. Parturient cows on the calving ground avoided areas of wolf activity (Table 6), further minimizing predation risks.

Concentrating on the calving ground resulted in effective numerical swamping of wolves; losses of calves to wolves there were half those in the remainder of the herd's range. The use of a calving ground appeared to be a response primarily to wolves since grizzly bears, the other major predator of calves, were at least as abundant on the calving ground as elsewhere in the DCH range, and losses to bears were similar on and off the calving ground (L. Adams, unpubl. data).

The calving ground has unique characteristics that resulted in its use by caribou cows. First, it is at the southern extreme of wolf pack territories, and is bounded on the south by high mountainous terrain that is not habitable by wolves or their prey (Fig. 1). Second, ungulates were rare there in late winter. Caribou did not use the calving ground during November to April, except for occasional minor use of the western quarter (L. Adams, unpubl. data). The abundance of other ungulate prey on the calving ground was very low. In March 1992, moose occurred at a density of $60/1,000 \text{ km}^2$ in areas below 1050 m. Moose were particularly rare in the eastern half of the calving ground ($15/1,000 \text{ km}^2$ below 1050 m). No sheep surveys have been conducted on the calving ground but sheep were rarely observed during May field

work. Probably fewer than 20 sheep occurred throughout the calving ground ($<20/1,000 \text{ km}^2$) and they were probably not there during the winter. The lack of prey in the eastern half of the calving ground was graphically demonstrated by the extinctions of the Pirate Creek Pack in 1988 and the Clearwater Pack in 1989, when their territories were restricted to this area, and by the lack of resident wolves during 1990-91.

Cows in the DCH minimized their contact with wolves both by using a traditional calving ground where wolves were scarce, and avoiding wolf dens on or adjacent to the calving ground. The former strategy could have been based on innate selection of calving habitat or traditional knowledge of wolf distribution gained by trial and error. However, the latter strategy involved detecting and responding to wolves or wolf use of an area. If caribou merely moved away from interactions with wolves, they would tend to congregate in any areas with few wolves. In addition, prey species can detect and avoid predator odors (Muller-Schwarze 1972, Steinberg 1977, Sullivan 1986, Sullivan et al. 1990). Wolf dens, in particular, would represent areas of concentrated odors since wolves spend more time there than anywhere else in their territory.

Synchrony of calving, coupled with the use of a calving ground, also influenced predation by wolves. Wolf predation did not begin until after the calving peak (Fig. 5) which may be explained in two ways. First, at the onset of calving, wolves were preying on adult ungulates that occurred in regions of wolf territories away from the calving ground. Wolves may not have detected calving activity until nursery bands began forming in open, lowland habitats, around the peak of calving. Alternatively, killing of caribou calves may

Table 6. Wolf numbers and caribou distribution on the east and west halves of the calving grounds, May 1987–1991, Denali National Park, Alaska.

	1987		*1988*		*1989*		*1990*		*1991*	
	WEST	*EAST*	*WEST*	*EAST*	*WEST*	*EAST*	*WEST*	*EAST*	*WEST*	*EAST*
Wolves		4	3	7	2	8	2	10	2	91
AJCS caribou cows										
births	7	7	5	16	5	10	2	13	2	7
- at end of May	12	7	5	17	18	12	2	23	8	16
- with surviving calves at end of May	7	4	3	10	10	6	0	10	0	3

AJCS = Age-Justified Cow Subsample or a subset of radio-collared cows selected to approximate the age structure of cows in the herd. AJCS cows ≥ 2-years-old were monitored during the calving season.

not be profitable for wolves until there were sufficient numbers of vulnerable calves coalescing into larger groups. Compared to adult caribou and moose, individual calves would provide little food for wolves, but when grouped together, many calves can sometimes be killed easily (Miller et al. 1985, this study), thereby increasing the profitability of hunting calves.

Although the wolf population doubled during our study, the potential for increased wolf predation on caribou calves was offset by the concentration of much of the calving in a relatively small area where wolf abundance was low. The effects of wolf and caribou dispersion, at the pack territory scale, alone resulted in a six-fold decrease in the wolf exposure from that calculated on the gross range-wide basis (Table 5). Furthermore, wolf:prey ratios that accounted for spacing were not affected by changes in wolf density (Fig. 6). Spring snow conditions and the abundance and distribution of wolves with access to the calving ground contributed to the variation observed in exposure of calves to wolf predation, not range-wide wolf density.

Deaths of neonates increased during the study, and although the increased mortality was correlated with wolf density, it was more strongly correlated with average birthweight (Fig. 4), an expression of both calf and cow physical condition. Neonatal losses to wolves specifically were poorly correlated with spring wolf density but more strongly correlated with average birthweight.

Even though wolves did not select for light-born calves, when calves were born large, survival of neonates, as well as older calves, was relatively high and the proportion killed by wolves was low. This pattern occurred even in 1989 when wolf density had already achieved 91% of the overall increase observed over the five years of the study. Deep snow during the 1989 calving season should have exacerbated the

Chemical immobilization and radio-collaring has revolutionized many aspects of wildlife research. Photo shows tranquilized wolves that have been captured during predator-prey studies in Alaska. (Photo: L.D. Mech)

Modern technology has been widely applied to predator/prey studies. The picture to the left shows the use of helicopters in the capture of caribou calves. (Photo: L.D. Mech)

loss of neonates to wolves because caribou cows calved primarily at lower elevations (Table 1, Fig. 4); however, losses to wolves were the lowest for the study (Table 2).

In 1990 and 1991, when calves were smaller, they died at a higher rate throughout their first four months, and wolf predation increased significantly (Table 2). If calving elevation was a major factor in determining the amount of wolf predation, losses of neonates to wolves should have been low in 1990 since the spring snowpack was shallow and caribou calved preferentially at higher elevations (Table 1, Fig. 4). If lighter-born calves were vulnerable to wolves for a longer

time, as supported by continued losses of calves after 15 days of age in 1990 and 1991 (Table 2, Fig. 5), then preying on calves would be profitable for wolves longer in years when the entire calf cohort was lighter, resulting in greater losses of calves to wolves, even with no preferential selection for lighter calves within any year.

Mean calf birthweights declined from 1988 to 1991 as a result of nutritional stress on cows confronted with severe winter conditions (i.e. deep snow) (Bergerud 1971, Clutton-Brock et al. 1982). In addition to low birthweight, offspring produced by nutritionally stressed females may exhibit other

Calf mortality has been evaluated with the use of mortality collars. Collars on dead animals emit a distinct signal. The photo on the right was taken in Denali National Park. (Photo: L.D. Mech)

Layne G. Adams, Bruce W. Dale, and L. David Mech

effects, such as stunting, delayed emergence of motor activities and response to auditory stimulation, and marked learning deficits at maturity (Verme 1963, Zeman 1967, Stephan et al. 1971, Bresler et al. 1975, Zamenhof and Van Marthens 1977). These factors, if present in caribou calves, could contribute to prolonged vulnerability to wolf predation of calves born following severe winters.

Wolf predation on neonates is certainly a major factor limiting the growth of the DCH. However, our results indicate that interactions between wolves and the Alaskan caribou ecotype, such as the DCH, cannot be fully described through range-wide wolf:prey ratios alone and neonatal losses to wolves were not related to wolf density. The distribution of wolves, the efficacy of caribou wolf-evasion strategies, losses of neonates to mortality agents other than wolves and the effects of winter snow on caribou condition and calving dispersion have influences on wolf-caribou interactions that are masked or ignored at the gross numerical level.

Acknowledgments

This research was funded by the U.S. National Park Service Natural Resources Preservation Program, and could not have been conducted without the complete support of A. Lovaas, R. Cunningham, and R. Berry, Jr. Field assistance was provided by J. Burch, J. Dalle-Molle, L. Daniel, J. Keay, T. Meier, B. Shults, J. Van Horn and many other "calf-catchers". Safe aircraft support was provided by many helicopter and fixed-wing pilots, especially K. Butters, D. Glaser, J. Hamilton, B. Lentsch, and D. Miller. J. Bailey, F. Martin, H. Golden, K. Jenkins, A. Lovaas, D. Siniff, A. Starfield and R. Stephenson reviewed earlier versions of this manuscript and offered many helpful suggestions. We also appreciate the input provide by A. Bergerud and D. Seip. Finally, we would like thank the DENA and National Park Service–Alaska Region staffs who have facilitated the conduct of this research in many ways.

A Review of Wolf-Caribou Relationships and Conservation Implications in Canada

■ D.C. Thomas

Wolves and caribou co-evolved for thousands of years. Genetic, behavioral, environmental, ecological, and human factors can tip the balance in favor of individuals of either species. Genetics and behavior change slowly, but environmental and human factors are highly variable. Wolf reductions in the 1950's and 1960's temporarily aided many caribou populations. Some recent human developments and activities that adversely affect caribou, and favorable winters for other ungulate species, tip the balance in favor of the wolf. Caribou are the chief losers in wolf-caribou-human conflicts where wolves are protected. Caribou are constrained by their evolutionary history: low fecundity; low productivity; high vulnerability when exposed to wolves and rifle hunters; and the need for old forests, space, and isolation from wolves, other predators, other ungulate species, and human hunters. Caribou do not fit into multiple-use plans that include short-rotation forestry, recreation, and management for abundant populations of other large ungulates and wolves. Some strategies to conserve wolf and caribou populations in changing environments are discussed.

Introduction

The primary focus of this paper is caribou ecology, the role of wolves (*Canis lupus*) in caribou (*Rangifer tarandus*) dynamics, and the factors involved in wolf-caribou-human interactions. The survival of a caribou depends on balancing some key factors: food, predation, insect harassment, parasites, and weather. Behavior that reduces the risk from one factor will be compromised if another factor becomes more important for survival. For example, caribou will expose themselves to predation in order to obtain food or avoid insects.

An ecological grouping of caribou populations and the present status of caribou in Canada leads to a discussion of some genetic, morphological, behavioral, and ecological characteristics of caribou in relation to wolf predation, environmental variability, and certain human activities. Then I review interactions in wolf-caribou systems relative to changes in the environment. The rapid pace of industrial developments such as logging, mining, and tourism has overtaken ecological knowledge of species. New approaches to caribou management are needed.

We have entered a stage where existing fragmentary knowledge of wolf-caribou systems in altered landscapes must be incorporated into plans for development and the prescriptions monitored and improved. This "adaptive management" approach (Walters 1986) means that supporting every statement or management decision with scientific "proof" is unrealistic. Many of the conclusions in this review are not based on rigorous hypothesis testing in replicated studies. They are clearly speculative in nature — one biologist's interpretation of the literature combined with field observations. If they are disproved I will not be disappointed because it will mean that the necessary studies are being done.

Classification of Caribou

The conservation of caribou and wolves should be in what spatial context: country, province, region, biome, ecosystem, ecoregion, or ecodistrict? At what taxon level: species, subspecies, ecotype, population, or special gene pool? Banfield (1961) reclassified the genus *Rangifer* on morphological and phenotypic criteria: it was conspecific with four wild subspecies in North America: *caribou* (woodland = WC), *groenlandicus* and *granti* (barren-ground = BGC), and *pearyi* (polar = PC). Behavior and phenotype vary within taxa because of divergent evolution in different environments. For example, northern WC in Quebec and Labrador behave like BGC, migrating long distances between tundra and forest range. All caribou in Alaska were designated BGC (*R.t. granti*), although southern interior populations are similar (e.g., calve earlier) to WC in Yukon and northern British Columbia (B.C.). Genetic relationships among many populations, as deduced from frequencies of the transferrin allel in blood serum, generally confirm Banfield's (1961) groupings (Roed et al. 1991). In five to 10 years, caribou should be reclassified using multiple criteria: genetic (transferrin and DNA) similarities and differences, behavior, and morphology. Meanwhile, and perhaps additionally, there is need for a functional classification of *Rangifer* spp. based on ecotype (a form of caribou with a characteristic ecology).

For ecological relationships (including wolf predation), management, and conservation functions, it is useful to group caribou populations into generalized ecotypes (Bergerud 1978b; Edmonds 1988, 1991; Messier *in* Davis and Valkenburg 1991). I expand previous ecotyping to include major ecosystems used in winter and summer, migratory behavior (indicated by "-"), and predominant winter food. Thus, caribou are forest-forest (FF & F-F), forest-tundra (F-T), forest-alpine (FA & F-A), or tundra-tundra (TT & T-T) ecotypes.

Winter food divides caribou into terrestrial lichen (TL), arboreal lichen (AL), and graminoid (G) types. Most caribou occur in the major climatic zones of Humid Microthermal (HM) or Polar Tundra (Finch et al. 1957). The southern edge of the HM zone is remarkably similar to the current southern limit of caribou in Canada. An example of a detailed ecotype description would be F-A/TL. Relationships between wolves and caribou differ with each caribou ecotype. Extrapolation of results from wolf-caribou studies from one region to another are never safe, but they are safest within caribou ecotypes.

The Status of Caribou in Canada

Peary caribou (T-T/G ecotype) declined severalfold since 1961 (Miller 1990). In 1974, they were declared "threatened" by the Committee On the Status of Endangered Wildlife In Canada (COSEWIC). In 1991, populations on the Queen Elizabeth Islands and Banks Island were upgraded from "threatened" to "endangered" (Miller 1990).

Many of the major F-T/TL herds may have increased in numbers during the late 1970's and 1980's (Williams and Heard 1986, Edmonds 1991). The *groenlandicus* subspecies was estimated to number 1.2–1.6 million in the early 1980's (Williams and Heard 1986). The Porcupine herd (F-T ecotype) in the Yukon and Alaska doubled in numbers to nearly 200,000 during the late 1970's and 1980's. The F-T George River herd increased 11–14% from the 1950's to about 1984 (Messier et al. 1988).

The status of FF and F-F (collectively "forest caribou") and F-A ecotypes varies greatly. Predation, mostly by wolves, but also by lynx (*Lynx lynx*), coyote (*Canis latrans*), black and grizzly bears (*Ursus americanus* and *U. arctos*), cougars (*Felis concolor*), and wolverine (*Gulo gulo*) is an important limiting factor. Expansion of the forest industry, with associated changes in succession and the composition of predators and prey, threatens WC. In this century, the southern limit of semi-continuous caribou distribution in Canada has retracted northward. Expansion of moose popu-

lations in Ontario and B.C. (Bergerud 1974a), and perhaps elsewhere, was associated with increased predation on caribou (Darby and Duquette 1986, Darby et al. 1989, Seip 1992a). Populations in insular Newfoundland increased in numbers during the 1980's, but many of the populations in the mixed-wood boreal forest from Quebec to Alaska are stable or declining in number (Darby et al. 1989, Edmonds 1991, Rock 1992, C. Johnson, Manitoba Dep. Nat. Resources, pers. commun.) and are becoming fragmented into remnant populations.

Fires not only affect food supplies, but the ability to use other localized habitats (e.g., calving, thermal, escape) critical to caribou viability. Fires in 1989 burned a large proportion of forested lands in Manitoba. Fires from 1928 through 1970 burned 50% of an area east of Lake Winnipeg (Stardom 1977). About 39% of the winter range of a population of caribou in Alberta burned since a study by Fuller and Keith (1981b). Schaefer (1987) found that caribou made little use of forests younger than 50 years.

Another possible contributing factor to changes in numbers of forest caribou is a common parasite in eastern Canada. The meningeal worm or "brainworm" (*Parelaphostrongylus tenuis*), fatal to caribou, is carried by expanding populations of white-tailed deer (*Odocoileus virginianus*) as far west as Saskatchewan (S. Wasel, ALPAC Industries Inc., pers. commun.). Habitat differences may reduce transmission to insignificant levels.

Populations of forest caribou in Manitoba, Saskatchewan, and Alberta appear to be numerically stable (Edmonds 1991), but they face potentially serious habitat changes in future because of expanding forest industries. Caribou in B.C. are threatened by predation, forestry, and other human developments (Bergerud 1978b, 1980, 1983, 1988, Seip 1989, 1991, 1992a, 1992b). The FF/AL ecotype is most vulnerable (Stevenson 1991) with northern forms (F-A/TL ecotype) being less threatened (Edmonds 1991). Populations of WC in the Yukon are limited mainly by hunting and wolves (Farnell and McDonald 1988).

In 1984, western WC were declared "rare" ("vulnerable") by COSEWIC. Many FF and F-F populations in mixed-wood forests and those reliant on arboreal lichens in old forests obviously are endangered, others threatened. The F-A ecotype fares better; the F-T type fares the best. All the large, sustained populations of caribou are the F-T/TL ecotype. The T-T ecotype is subject to periodic and severe weather-related limitations.

Factors Affecting the Wolf-Caribou "Balance"

The predator-prey balance has three levels: individual, group, and population. The first level refers to the ability of a wolf to capture individual prey in an encounter. Usually one wolf kills one caribou in encounters. Usually several wolves combine to kill large species such as moose (*Alces*

alces) and bison (*Bison bison*). Healthy, well-nourished prey individuals (young excepted) usually can escape the predator under normal conditions. About 50% of wolf-caribou encounters in Alaska were fatal (Haber 1977).

Many genetic, morphological, physiological, behavioral, ecological, and environmental factors affect the balance between individual caribou and wolves. The importance of each factor varies temporally and spatially. Single-factor analyses produce crude approximations of complex, interdependent processes. Short-term studies of the relative importance of each factor may give misleading results. Partitioning of factors is an artificial, simplistic analysis. For example, the southern limit of the caribou distribution in Canada can only be explained by multiple, interacting factors.

The size of wolf and prey groups has a profound effect on the nature of interactions. Most research is not at this second level of the relationship, but at the third: relative numbers, densities, or mass, of predators and prey.

Genetics and Evolution

Caribou and wolves evolved together over the last 50–100K years (K = 1,000). Caribou-wolf systems are believed to predate wolf-caribou-moose-other ungulate systems in Alaska (Davis and Valkenburg 1991). Present physical forms of caribou and wolves should express characteristics such as size, conformation, and speed that reflect ecological optima of each species. Approximate equilibria of individuals in wolf-caribou systems is assumed. For example, reindeer (*R.t. platyrhynchus*) isolated from wolves on insular Svalbard (Norway) evolved relatively short legs and compact bodies (Tyler 1987). Similarly, domestic reindeer in wolf-free areas have relatively short legs (Klein et al. 1987). The wolf-caribou equilibrium in catch/escape encounters may be unbalanced by outside forces such as altered habitat, climatic change, and densities of other prey species. The size and killing efficiency of wolves may change gradually in response to different prey species, hybridization within *Canis*, and learned behavior.

Imbalances at the individual level are expressed at the population level. At the population level, the balance is dynamic (has a wide operating range) because of abrupt population changes at the birth pulse, diseases, and the uneven effect of weather variations on the fecundity and survival of wolves and caribou.

Several adaptations of caribou influence wolf-caribou relationships. Lichen feeding permits caribou to persist where other ungulates cannot. This specialization allows caribou to remain separated from other ungulate species for much of the annual cycle and thus reduce the likelihood of wolf predation and the transmission of parasites and diseases. Although caribou are lichen specialists and concentrate (high energy) feeders, they are food generalists. They eat varying proportions of graminoids, horsetails, forbs, leaves of shrubs, and lichens in a seasonal cycle.

Caribou have low fecundity. Single births begin at age two, three, or four years depending on nutritional state (Dauphine 1976). Fecundity is directly related to fat reserves and caribou cease to reproduce if fat reserves are inadequate (Thomas 1982, Thomas and Barry 1990a). The pregnancy rate in 1+ year caribou averages about 72% (range 0–100%, Thomas and Barry 1990a). Caribou cannot sustain high mortality from predators or humans because of low fecundity and productivity.

Adaptations to snow include large, rounded hooves that permit caribou to travel near the top of compacted snow and wet ground. Their hooves permit them to dig in snow for food more effectively than other species.

Adaptations to cold, including excellent insulation and relatively short appendages, permit caribou to persist in areas too cold for most other ungulate species except musk-oxen (*Ovibos moschatus*). Newborn caribou calves can maintain normal temperature at -23°C (Soppela et al. 1986). Heat stress is a greater threat to caribou (Cuyler and Øritsland 1986). The food niche and adaptations to snow and cold tend to make caribou a wilderness species.

Behavior and Ecology of Caribou Relative to Wolf Predation

Migration

Migration is an adaptive response to multiple factors that has enhanced survival under past environmental conditions. Important factors include food, predation, insects, and weather, particularly snow and thermal considerations. Most caribou populations migrate 30–800 km between summer and winter ranges. Food factors include type, phenology, quantity, quality, and availability. Furthermore, departure in summer from winter range safeguards lichens from highgrading and trampling when dry. Lichen species favored by caribou require 40 to 150 years to recover after fire (D.C. Thomas, unpubl. data.).

Migration spatially separates caribou from wolves and other predators (Bergerud and Page 1987). Calving areas of the Porcupine herd supposedly were selected primarily to reduce wolf predation (Fancy and Whitten 1991). Some large herds of BGC (F-T ecotype) make a double migration annually.

Migratory populations of caribou generally are larger and more successful than more sedentary ones. An analysis of migration length to population size would produce a strong correlation. Populations with the longest migrations and route options can reduce contact with those wolves restricted to the vicinity of dens from May to August (Kuyt 1972, Heard and Williams 1992a). The primary denning area in the forest-tundra ecotone may be only 50% of the range of a F-T population (Heard and Williams 1992a). If density limitations operate on denning wolves in summer, the wolves may never regulate a migratory caribou population.

The availability of alternate prey in summer is a key factor for wolf packs.

Delayed and relatively short spring migrations in Alberta, B.C., and Alaska were associated with low recruitment of caribou (Bergerud and Elliot 1986, Bergerud and Page 1987, Bergerud and Ballard 1988, Edmonds and Smith 1991). Predation was implicated, but not proven. Post-calving migration reduced warble (*Hypoderma tarandi*) larvae abundance compared with nonmigratory reindeer (*R.t. tarandus*) in Norway (Folstad et al. 1991).

In the absence of other limiting factors, movement of caribou to areas where food is inferior indicates avoidance of other negative factors or combinations of them. For example, F-T and F-A types migrate to calving areas where food quantity and quality is poor relative to that at lower elevations or latitudes (Kelsall 1968, Bergerud and Page 1987, Edmonds and Smith 1991). However, the calving areas are favorable in terms of predators, insects, temperature, and food during most of the postcalving period. In most years, fat reserves permit such behavior without sacrificing calf survival. Fat reserves in the F-T ecotype improve reproductive success (fitness) and secondarily provide insurance against severe snow conditions.

Movement

Movement and unpredictable movements reduce predation and other detrimental factors (insects, heat) and reduces overuse of local ranges. Thus, movements are adaptive behavioral responses to some of the same factors responsible for migrations. Caribou are constantly on the move. Distance travelled in a day varies from 25 km during migration to less than 1 km in late winter when snow makes travel energetically costly. Other stimuli such as hunting and harassment may cause caribou to move locally.

Any movement, and particularly that away from wolves, reduces the chance of encountering wolves with fixed territories or young pups. The distribution of caribou had a large effect on their predation by wolves in Alaska (Adams et al. this volume). Unpredictable movements further reduce contact. Individual groups of caribou in Jasper National Park vary wintering areas and thereby lessen contact with wolves that have territories. Recent data (P. Clarkson, Northwest Territ. Dep. of Renewable Resources, pers. commun.) indicate extensive range overlap and little strife between denning packs near treeline in Canada. Nothing is known about defense of space in winter when wolf packs follow mobile F-T caribou populations.

Group Sizes and Densities

Low and high densities and small and large group sizes can reduce wolf predation. Low caribou densities will not support wolves in the absence of alternate prey. Groups of F-T caribou unite into aggregations of thousands at certain times: the mosquito season on the tundra and at barriers such as deep snow or rivers clogged with ice. Large aggregations of caribou reduce contact with wolves restricted to denning areas. Winter concentrations of caribou concentrate wolves and results, presumably, in interpack strife. The maximum densities of wolves around caribou concentrations in winter were estimated at 56, 50, and 250 wolves/Kkm2 (Kuyt 1972, Parker 1973, Heard 1983). Parker (1973) considered 50 wolves/Kkm2 to be the density tolerance limit of wolves associated with wintering caribou. There may be safety in numbers when wolves are encountered (Cumming 1975). Nevertheless, large aggregations may be ineffective at swamping wolves because of surplus killing (Miller et al. 1985, Eide and Ballard 1982) and young calves become separated from their dams when large aggregations of caribou stampede. In summary, changes in group size and densities is a response to multiple factors: predation, insects, food, thermal, and snow. Paradoxically, low and high caribou densities reduce wolf predation.

The lowest caribou densities (1–5/Kkm^2) occur in the T-T ecotype on the polar (Queen Elizabeth) islands (Miller 1990), followed by the FF ecotype (30), the F-A ecotype (150–200), F-T forms (600–1100), and isolated, insular forms (2–8K) (Seip 1992a). Caribou on the Slate Islands in Lake Superior attained densities of 4–8K/Kkm^2. Lacking large predators, periodically they die of undernutrition (Bergerud 1980). The George River herd was temporarily at densities of 1–1.3K/Kkm^2 in 1984 before range expansion from 160 Kkm^2 to 550 Kkm^2 (Messier et al. 1988, Couturier et al. 1990). The Nelchina, Fortymile, and Western Arctic herds in Alaska/Yukon attained densities of 1.5–2K, 1K, and 1K/Kkm^2 before declining in the early 1960's. In 1989, the Western Arctic, Nelchina, and Alaska Peninsula (south) herds were at densities of 0.95, 1, and 1.1/Kkm^2 (Davis and Valkenburg 1991). The first two were increasing; the latter declining after attaining a density of 2K/Kkm^2. Calculation of range-wide densities are of questionable value for migratory caribou and wolves that seasonally occupy small proportions of the range.

Isolation

Isolation is the primary behavior of caribou to avoid wolves (Bergerud et al. 1984). Isolation is compromised if other factors such as food and insect avoidance become paramount. For example, to reduce mosquito harassment and utilize willow (*Salix* spp.) and birch (*Betula* spp.) leaves, herds of migratory F-T caribou return in midsummer to the forest-tundra ecotone, the main wolf denning area. These key-factor trade-offs are difficult to examine scientifically because of lack of controls and difficulty in measuring effects of multiple factors on fecundity and survival over many years. Isolation options decline if fire or forestry reduce and localize suitable habitat.

Some forest caribou use islands in lakes (Cumming and Beange 1985), lakeshore (Bergerud 1985), scrub or treed "islands" in bogs, and subalpine or alpine habitats (Bergerud et al. 1984, Seip 1992a), as relatively safe areas to bear and rear young calves. Water edges also provide insect relief and cooling on hot days. Caribou commonly run into lakes and rivers when pursued by wolves. Crippled caribou often remain along shorelines. When disturbed in mixed groups, females with young calves often split from them. Some F and F-F populations subject to increasing habitat loss and predation may be unable to survive unless they have escape habitat for their calves in summer.

WC persist at low densities in niches characterized by the absence or scarcity of other prey and predators including humans. As caribou numbers build, wolves may include part or all of the caribou distribution in their territories and the caribou population is reduced. This is a form of dynamic equilibrium maintained by sporadic density-dependent predation.

Mature male caribou usually isolate themselves after breeding (late October) and casting of antlers (November). Then they are vulnerable to predation (Mech et al. 1991a) because energy reserves are exhausted. In winter, most wolves are associated with the main groups of BGC that contain all elements except bulls older than three years. Adult males remain apart until about July when they are in good condition. They follow the emergence of new vegetation northward and expose themselves to predation. However, the benefits of obtaining maximum fatness and increased reproductive fitness outweighs potential death from predators.

Segregation

Segregation from other ungulates, and thereby wolves in many systems, is a strong characteristic of caribou. The degree to which separation is active or passive because of differing niches is debatable. Many F-A ecotypes use subalpine habitats where deep, soft snow impedes wolf movement. Wolves generally remain in valley bottoms in winter, where available prey are most abundant, even when a snow crust permits them to travel anywhere. Caribou descend to valley bottoms: 1) when unfavorable snow conditions occur at higher elevations; and 2) when green forage is abundant at low elevations. Caribou in Jasper National Park descend as snow thickens to 40–60 cm. They may ascend after snow compaction or a crust supports them. Nasimovich (1955 *in* Kelsall 1968) considered 40 cm of soft snow to be the tolerance limit of hunting wolves. Some F-A and F-T caribou will remain in the alpine or on the tundra if feeding conditions are suitable there. Different behavior by different components of a population increase its chances of survival. Vertical separation of wolves and caribou in mountainous terrain is influenced by other factors such as the distribution of alternative prey.

Vulnerability to Wolf Predation

Vulnerability of caribou to wolf predation is assumed, but data are few. Wolves in Alaska killed caribou, moose, and sheep at a ratio of 33.0:1.4:1.0, although all three species were abundant (Dale et al. this volume). Carbyn (1974) ranked decreasing vulnerability to wolves as: elk (*Cervus*

elaphus) calves and adult elk, deer, moose, sheep (*Ovis* spp.), caribou, and goats (*Oreamnos americanus*). Wolves at Kluane Park in Yukon ate disproportionately (by biomass) more caribou than moose except during calving (Gauthier and Theberge 1986). A direct relationship between vulnerability and body size may have some validity, even *within* large species, if other factors such as senility and physical state are ignored. For example, young and old elk and moose are vulnerable (Carbyn 1983b, Hayes et al. 1991, Mech et al. 1991a). Ungulate vulnerability is an important factor in wolf population dynamics (Keith 1983). Prey selection has opposing forces: risk to the predator and the advantage of large prey. The risk that a wolf will take in attacking large prey probably relates to degree of hunger. Vulnerability of ungulates to predation has other components (Huggard 1993).

The typical behavior of caribou when encountering wolves or humans is to maintain separation of 50–200 m and to run only when chased. Hence, their curious behavior ("prey bluffing"). Individuals may be indicating to wolves that it is fruitless to chase them. When pursued, they select the best escape route and attempt to outrun wolves. BGC flee to open or frozen lakes or open tundra. Forest caribou may learn to use elements in the forest (e.g., deep, soft snow; deadfall; shrubs) to impede wolves.

Calf caribou are vulnerable because they are followers from birth. The advantages of moving to new food sources and away from insects outweigh the increased predation. Adult caribou are vulnerable because of poor defense relative to adults of some other ungulates. Caribou do not seem to use their feet for defense against wolves. Caribou should be preferred prey because of considerable mass and low risk of injury to wolves.

Average natural mortality of caribou when predators are present typically is 50% in calves of the F-T ecotype and 50–70% in F-A and FF ecotypes (Bergerud 1980, Seip 1992a); and 7–30% in adults (Bergerud 1980, Farnell and McDonald 1988, Seip 1992a). Conversely, mortality near zero is implied to account for the irruptive growth of caribou populations where wolves are absent or rare.

Vulnerability to Hunting

Vulnerability to hunting is universally recognized. Caribou have not adapted to hunters with rifles and they cannot outdistance snowmobiles. Their susceptibility to being overhunted can bring demands for wolf management.

The Environment and Environmental Variability

Snow Conditions

Snow conditions profoundly affect caribou vulnerability. Caribou and humans when walking in compacted snow sink about the same distance and deeper than wolves. A man in winter boots has foot loads (g/cm^2) of about 175; caribou 100–125 on four feet; and wolves 45–60 on four feet (digits splayed). When running, the minimum loads are humans 350 (one foot); caribou 300–400 (one foot); and wolves 90–120 (two feet) (D.C. Thomas, unpubl. data). Foot loads of running reindeer (*R.t. tarandus*) were 379 and 442 g/cm^2 when only the front or hind foot was bearing weight as is the case at stages in the running gait (Nieminen 1990). The foot area calculated by Kelsall and Telfer (1974) and Nieminen (1990) is somewhat liberal, but applicable to crusted snow. Walking humans and caribou break through 4–6 cm crusts of hardness about 1000 g/cm2 (Thing 1977, D.C. Thomas, unpubl. data).

Deep, soft snow favors caribou, as wolves must land in soft snow in and between the small impressions made by bounding caribou. Conversely, a wolf has a distinct advantage in compacted or crusted snow that supports wolves, but not caribou. The relatively large hooves of caribou that are so important in excavating snow then become a liability. Travel in deep snow with a non-supporting surface crust is energetically costly. Snow usually is soft in the northern boreal forest. Caribou are sparse in forested habitats where nonsupporting crusting is common throughout the winter. Snow crusting throughout the winter is commonplace in maritime climates and increasingly frequent in southern continental climates. Snow crusting and icing are universal in late winter and spring. In the alpine and tundra, the snow may be sufficiently hard to support caribou with no advantage to predator or prey. Caribou may be forced to winter in areas with favorable snow conditions for foraging and provide wolves with a seasonally predictable food supply (e.g., Brown 1986).

Nutritional State
Nutritional state undoubtedly affects vulnerability of caribou to wolves. Many of the caribou killed by wolves in Jasper National Park were undernourished, based on less than 50% fat in femur marrows (D.C. Thomas, unpubl. data). Many of the caribou killed by four wolf packs in Alaska were undernourished (less than 80% fat in femoral marrow) (Mech et al. this volume). Most mortality of adult caribou in the Finlayson herd (Yukon) occurred from March to June (Farnell and McDonald 1988), when caribou could be nutritionally stressed and snow conditions unfavorable. Peary caribou in severely undernourished states were less wary of aircraft and hunters than insular caribou in good condition (D.C. Thomas, unpubl. data). Gates et al. (1986) concur for BGC. Adult elk killed by wolves in Banff National Park had lower fat reserves than controls (Huggard 1993). Wolves with abundant prey have greatest fat reserves in winter and spring when caribou may be undernourished and snow crusting is common. Wolves may be able to assess the condition of prey by their appearance, behavior, and possibly by the chemistry of urine, feces, or odor from scent glands.

Parasites and Diseases
Parasites and diseases may weaken caribou. Some caribou with multiple large cysts of *Echinococcus granulosis* in their lungs were less fat than noninfected counterparts, others not (D.C. Thomas, unpubl. data). Severely infected individuals may be vulnerable in prolonged chases by wolves. The incidence of the parasite in the Beverly herd was 4%, but multiple large cysts occurred in only 0.2%. The nasal bot, *Cephenemyia trompe*, in extreme infections, could impede air passage, or debilitate the caribou through systemic reaction to the parasite. Huot and Beaulieu (1985) found little relationship between parasite infestation levels and fat reserves in caribou. The success of a parasite that has a carnivore-ungulate cycle is enhanced if infected hosts are vulnerable to predation. Caribou debilitated by the meningeal worm ("brainworm") would be vulnerable to predation. Arthritic moose on Isle Royale were vulnerable to wolves (Peterson and Page 1988). Brucellosis (*Brucella suis*) that resulted in swollen joints would increase vulnerability. The bacteria is common in caribou on Baffin Island (E. Broughton, Agric. Canada, pers. commun.), but is rare in the large mainland herds. The moose tick (*Dermacentor albipictus*) has infected caribou in Saskatchewan (Rock 1992).

Age Structure
Age structure of a caribou population is a factor with young and old caribou being more vulnerable to wolves (Kuyt 1972, Mech et al. this volume). The age at which vulnerability lessens and then increases is not known. In one sample of radio-collared caribou, mortality of six- to 24- month caribou was similar to that of adults (Davis et al. 1988). Fecundity was highest in the more-than-11-year class in the Beverly herd (Thomas and Barry 1990a). Females in that age class must fail in a matter of months and succumb to predators. Declines in condition with age, leading to starvation, occurred as early as seven years in Svalbard reindeer (*R.t. platyrhynchus*) (Tyler 1987).

Other Predators
Other predators have the effect of increasing the incidence of parasites such as *Taenia hydatigena*, *T. krabbi*, and the giant liver fluke (*Fascioloides magna*). For example, if a canid eats any prey that harbor larvae, the adult worm may develop. They pass eggs that can infect caribou and continue the cycle. The expanding George River herd had a 50% infection incidence of flukes in a small sample obtained in 1984 (Huot and Beaulieu 1985).

Other Prey Species
Other prey species alter any balance at the population level between wolves and caribou. The wolves may be in dynamic balance with their total prey base (Fuller 1989), but incidental predation on caribou can impair their viability in multiple prey systems. Factors that increase the total prey base are beneficial to wolves and detrimental to caribou populations. Second, the other prey species harbor parasites and diseases that may be detrimental to caribou. Third, the other species may compete with caribou for limited forage. For example, moose compete with caribou for arboreal lichens in one location of Jasper National Park (Thomas 1990).

Habitat

Habitat profoundly affects wolf-caribou relationships. The quantity, quality, and availability of food is paramount to caribou. The availability of escape habitat such as rivers, lakes, islands in lakes; variable snow conditions; ungulate-poor areas; insect-poor components; size, type, and structure of forest habitat; juxtaposition of ecozones; topography, etc., are important factors in caribou survival.

Humans

Humans are direct competitors of wolves for caribou where hunting occurs legally or otherwise. In many caribou populations, hunting accounts for 3–8% of estimated numbers of caribou more than one year old. The large populations of F-T caribou should not be harvested beyond 5% to maintain constant numbers under average environmental conditions (includes wolves). Hunting more than 2–3% of F-A populations subject to wolf predation in Yukon results in declines (Farnell *in* Edmonds 1991). Southern FA, FF, and F-F ecotypes can withstand no hunting or limited harvest of mature bulls. Hunting seasons for woodland caribou were suspended in Ontario, Alberta, Saskatchewan, and Manitoba in 1929, 1980, 1987, and 1992, respectively.

Wolves are hunted and trapped legally, and poisoned illegally. Humans provide food for wolves that potentially disrupts any balance between wolves and the prey base. Food sources include wounded ungulates, viscera left at kill sites, vehicle-inflicted deaths and crippling, domestic stock, garbage dumps, etc. Intentionally providing food for wolves at one season may temporarily reduce predation (Boertje et al. this volume), but it could increase the number of wolves and predation at another season.

A major influence of human activities is to provide new access for wolves and humans. Wolves travel on highways, roads, trails, and "cutlines." They travel on any compacted trail in winter including tracks and trails of ungulates. Trappers set snares and traps on snowmobile trails. The human trails influence travel routes, the distribution of wolves, and wolf-prey contacts.

Loss of Habitat

Loss of habitat concentrates caribou in remaining habitat and may facilitate wolf predation by reducing search time, making escape of prey less likely, improving the likelihood of surprise attacks, improving access by wolves, reducing the condition of caribou, increasing the incidence of parasites and diseases, etc. For example, road and highway corridors attract moose, elk, deer, and caribou because of increased or different forage, salt, easy travel, and open space. Many road corridors are linear meadows of exotic forages with shrub borders. Potential effects are direct and indirect.

Alteration of Habitat

Alteration of habitat can affect wolf-caribou relationships by lowering the quantity, quality, and availability of food. It can also affect relationships by: providing access to previously safe places, making searches for caribou easier, making escape less likely, restricting migration and movements, increasing numbers of other ungulates, altering thermal regimes, causing direct mortality on roads and railroads, and increasing harassment of caribou.

Climatic Change

Climatic change may become a factor with a retraction northward of suitable caribou habitat mediated through slower lichen growth, more snow and crusted snow, more alternate prey species (and predators), loss of thermal habitat (e.g., snowbanks), loss of critical habitats (e.g., bogs, fens, and meadows), etc. Potential effects are highly speculative at present.

Management of Prey Species

The management of prey species to achieve high sustainable populations favors wolves (Gasaway et al. 1992). Unmanaged ungulate populations would experience boom and bust fluctuating from a combination of range overuse, severe winters, parasites and disease, overhunting, and predation. Populations depressed by wolves would recover when disease reduced or decimated the wolf population. In many parts of the boreal forest, wolf densities may be higher now than before human development and intervention.

Sociological Changes

Sociological changes will influence the degree to which predators and prey species can be managed to compensate for altered habitat that negatively affects endangered caribou populations. A major concern is increasing human density and economic structure that places jobs and development ahead of sustainable environments.

Empirical Effects of Wolf Predation on Caribou Populations

Wolves Absent

Caribou and wolves have remarkably similar distributions in Canada. Caribou are thriving in insular Newfoundland, where wolves were exterminated. The Avalon caribou population attained a density of 2K/Kkm^2 in 1979 after lynx removals (Bergerud et al. 1983b). Colonizing coyotes may become a problem. The absence of white-tailed deer and the "brainworm", fatal to caribou, may also be a factor. The Slate Islands have the highest densities of caribou (5–7K/Kkm^2) anywhere in spite of range overuse and marginal habitat (Bergerud 1980). Densities of the TT ecotype on Coats Island, limited by weather/food, fluctuate widely to about 1.1K/Kkm^2 (Gates et al. 1986). Density-dependent, food/weather factors become important in wolf-free reindeer populations in Norway (Skogland 1985, Tyler 1987). Reindeer persist in Svalbard where weather-induced mortality of adults occurs (Tyler 1987). The demography and ecology of relatively immobile caribou on wolf-free islands cannot be extrapolated to populations subject to multiple predators.

Usually the island populations have few of the stress factors (predation, hunting, human harassment, insect harassment, disease, and parasites) that most populations are subject to.

Wolves at Low-Moderate Density-Caribou Migratory and the Main Prey

In winter and spring, large numbers of migratory wolves normally are associated with the large F-T herds of caribou. On a caribou range basis, however, the wolf density is low, perhaps one to three wolves/Kkm². Wolf density may be limited in the denning area by food shortages, by interpack strife around concentrated caribou on the winter range, or by periodic disease outbreaks (e.g., rabies and distemper). Wolf predation cannot keep these migratory caribou populations at low densities. Wolves would not be able to regulate the caribou population because of high pup mortality caused by food shortages arising from the unpredictability of caribou movements in summer and by periodic disease. Trapping and hunting depressed wolf populations, but did not eliminate them even with bounties (Kuyt 1972). Severe limitation of wolf populations is now possible in tundra regions by use of snowmobiles for hunting. Increases in the Kaminuriak caribou population in the late 1970's and early 1980's coincided with caribou wintering in tundra regions. The scarcity of wolves (C. Gates, Northwest Territories Dep. of Renewable Resources, pers. commun.) can be attributed to hunters on snowmobiles although disease cannot be ruled out.

Wolves were the primary source of calf mortality on the calving grounds of two F-T herds (Miller and Broughton 1974, Miller et al. 1983). Surplus killing of calves (Miller et al. 1985), and adults (Eide and Ballard 1982) was recorded. Chipewyans viewed surplus killing by wolves of caribou in spring migration as stockpiling for later use during denning (Sharpe 1978).

Expansion of moose in the 1970's to the limit of trees (Kelsall and Telfer 1974) and population doubling between about 1948 and the early 1980's (Kelsall 1987) potentially added substantial prey to the wolf-caribou system. Most importantly, moose may provide a prey source during the critical pupping season. For example, moose was not recorded in the stomachs of 298 wolves from the taiga in the 1960's (Kuyt 1972). In contrast, moose comprised 21% and 27% of the winter diet of two samples of wolves taken near treeline by hunters from Eskimo Point (Arviat) in the 1980's (Lamothe and Parker 1989). The high rate of burning since 1969 in the boreal and transitional forests has increased the foraging habitat of moose. White-tailed deer also expanded their range northward in this century and continue to do so. They also use burned and logged areas for feeding and decline in winters of deep crusted snow.

Wolves Abundant-Caribou Migratory-Multiple Prey

Edmonds (1988) concluded that wolf predation was the primary cause of the 21% average annual mortality rate of adult, radio-collared caribou in west-central Alberta. The rate was 7% in adult females in a follow-up study (J. Edmonds, Alberta Environmental Protection, pers. commun.). The recruitment rate was 10% and the adult mortality rate was 28% in the Finlayson caribou herd (Yukon) at a wolf density of 11.3/Kkm² (one wolf:11 caribou) (Farnell and McDonald 1988).

Wolves Abundant-Caribou Relatively Stationary-Abundant Multiple Prey

Caribou survival is tenuous under such conditions. The FF ecotype in west-central Alberta barely survives with a predation rate of 21% annually (Edmonds 1988). Wolves were the known cause of the deaths of six of 12 radio-collared caribou in southern Jasper National Park (Brown et al. 1994). Wolves are only moderately abundant there (15–20 wolves — W. Bradford, Can. Parks Serv., pers. commun.), there is vertical separation in summer, some of the caribou migrate, and their use of winter habitat is highly variable.

Wolf Numbers Reduced

Recruitment of caribou increased 113% and adult mortality decreased 60% in a population where wolf numbers were reduced by 80% in Yukon (Farnell and McDonald 1988). Reduction of wolves in northeastern B.C. resulted in higher recruitment in caribou (Bergerud and Elliot 1986, Haber 1988). Mortality of calves in southern B.C. was significantly higher where wolves were present versus where they were absent or controlled (Seip 1992a).

Wolf poisoning began in the Northwest Territories in 1951, accelerated in the mid-1950's and declined in the early 1960's (Kuyt 1972). Caribou herds increased beginning in 1958 because of high recruitment rates and presumed high adult survival. Up to 2,100 wolves were taken annually (Kelsall 1968) but the response of the wolves and caribou were not adequately monitored and there was no control population. Thus, the role of predator control and weather in the caribou increase was not ascertained. In Alaska, caribou populations (e.g., Nelchina, Fortymile) rebounded from low numbers after wolf control (Gasaway et al. 1983, 1992).

Can Wolves Regulate Caribou Populations?

Theory

Regulation, as opposed to limitation (e.g., Messier 1991b), requires a density-dependent feedback process. The theory of regulation in wolf-caribou and wolf-caribou-other prey systems and reviews of limiting factors are outlined in papers by Kelsall (1968), Bergerud (1974a, 1978b, 1980, 1983, 1988), Haber and Walters (1980), Gasaway et al. (1983,1992), Skogland (1985), Tyler (1987), Messier et al. (1988), Messier (1991b), Seip (1991, 1992a, 1992b), Davis and Valkenburg (1991), and Klein (1991). There is evidence for the following: caribou do not have intrinsic (e.g., social) population limitations; predators can keep caribou populations depressed for long periods if alternate prey are abundant; caribou populations, excepting irruptive ones, are limited to varying degrees by *accessible* food; combinations of hunting, predation, and accessible food create population fluctuations precipitated or synchronized by weather/food. Continent-wide population declines occurred in the 1940's and early 1950's; increases in the late 1950's/early 1960's and 1980's.

Models are not yet available that incorporate all the variables in predator-prey systems containing caribou: social limitations in wolves; numerical, functional, and pack size responses; changing prey structures, numbers, and susceptibility to predation; habitat changes; weather; the interrelationships among variables (additive, synergistic, multiplier, depensatory, compensatory), and proximate, ultimate, lag, and other effects. All systems are exceedingly complex and dynamic. Field data are inadequate to assess the relative contribution of multiple variables. Emigration of caribou to other herds or areas, as proposed by Haber and Walters (1980), is discounted by data from marked caribou.

Progress in understanding wolf-caribou systems may benefit from modeling providing that the interaction of factors can be accommodated. The tendency to examine each limiting factor separately unduly simplifies complex ecological processes and inhibits comprehension of nature as a whole and not as a series of independent (isolated) factors. Rather than partition variables, researchers should consider ways of complexing variables to yield composite indices. Similarly, the pigeonholing of hypotheses leads to selection of the apparent best fit when elements of several hypotheses may be contributing and their relative influences no doubt vary spatially and temporally.

Semantics is a problem. Is any factor truly density independent? Or do all factors operate at varying degrees of density dependence? Compensatory and additive mortality is arbitrary partitioning of a continuous process. Dynamic equilibrium has little meaning unless the dynamic range is given. Use of means and lines of best fit obscures an appreciation of the natural variation in nature. Mean curves based on data from many predator-prey populations in different ecosystems may reveal generalized functional relationships, but they should not be accepted unconditionally as a management prescription in any one ecosystem. Less use of means and more use of variation statistics would help to illustrate the complexity and variability in nature. However, it would make modeling much more difficult.

Wolf:Caribou Ratios

Wolves may regulate caribou populations in wolf-caribou systems above a range of wolf:caribou ratios unique to each situation. In theory, about 100 caribou could sustain one wolf, assuming 50% mortality of calves averaging 5 kg of flesh and 18% mortality of adults averaging 50 kg of flesh and an intake of 2.9 kg of flesh/wolf/day. No absolute

(magic) ratio exists because wolf consumption rates are highly variable (Fuller 1989) and the size, age, and sex of prey is crucial. For example, the consumption rate of deer was 2.7 kg/wolf/day; that of moose was 5.7 kg/wolf/day (Fuller 1989).

Theberge (1990) cautioned against the use of predator-prey ratios. Pack size (Hayes et al. 1991) could be added to his list of confounding factors. However, ratios may be preferable to densities for mobile predators and clumped prey that use small proportions of the range at any one time. Empirical and theoretical ratios are one wolf per 50 (Bergerud and Elliot 1986), 100 (Bergerud 1980), and 137 (Walters et al. 1978) caribou for each sustainable wolf. Haber and Walters (1980) suggested that, in the absence of alternate prey, a ratio of 1 wolf:50 caribou and fewer than 400 caribou/Kkm^2 would place caribou in a predator pit. The Finlayson caribou population, where alternate prey were common, was declining, about stable, and increasing at wolf:caribou ratios of 1:12, 1:44, and 1:136, respectively (Farnell and McDonald 1988). The above population trends are inferred from recruitment of 10%, 15%, and 20% and adult mortality rates of 28%, 24%, and 11%, respectively for 0%, 51%, and 80% wolf reductions.

Wolf Densities versus Caribou Dynamics

Significant correlations were found between wolf density and both caribou recruitment and adult natural mortality using data from herds throughout Canada (Bergerud 1980). Growth rate was zero at about 12% recruitment and mortality corresponding to a wolf density of 6.5/Kkm^2. The reliability of many of the data points that went into the regressions are suspect because of small sample sizes and sampling methodology. The trend may be correct, but such relationships should not be used to predict unknown variables or to manage caribou.

In Yukon, caribou population decline, stability, and increase were associated with wolf densities of 11, 6, and 2/Kkm^2 (Farnell and McDonald 1988). The density of wolves over much of southern Yukon in the late 1980's was 8–10/Kkm^2 (Hayes et al. 1991). The southern limit of continuous caribou distribution in Ontario corresponds with areas where wolf densities attain 6–8/Kkm^2 compared with 2–4/Kkm^2 within the caribou distribution (Darby et al. 1989). Bergerud and Elliot (1986) and Bergerud (1988) indicated regulation at wolf densities higher than 6.5 wolves/Kkm^2. In contrast, caribou are apparently increasing in Denali Park at wolf densities of 10/Kkm^2 (Mech et al. 1991a), where caribou represented 37% of wolf kills. Area calculation is a problem in mountains and must be scrutinized in density data. For example, the winter density of wolves in Jasper National Park is four or 64/Kkm^2 depending on whether the entire park or only valley bottoms are considered. Including uninhabited range is not realistic.

Benefit of Wolf Predation to Caribou?

Present forms of wolves and caribou were shaped significantly by each other. Wolves are the primary instrument of natural selection in wolf-caribou systems. Still, the benefit of predation to prey populations is poorly understood or equivocal in the short term. Wolf predation may have prevented some caribou populations from overutilizing their range. Rifle hunting usually precludes habitat overuse by caribou except for the George River and Porcupine herds.

The value of removing less-fit prey individuals is difficult to evaluate in the short term. Such males are unlikely to breed anyway. Less fit females probably have high mortality from other factors and would not contribute many young. Fitness has genetic and learned components. Wolves may cull a disproportionate amount of prey that make poor choices about food and habitat and consequently are less fit (e.g., leaner). Isolated, wolf-free caribou on the Slate Islands are phenotypically unique (Butler and Bergerud 1978), but genetically similar to other caribou in Ontario (Roed et al. 1991). Removal of diseased and parasitized individuals that are genetically predisposed to their condition would be beneficial (e.g., arthritis). However, predation perpetuates certain parasites that require an obligate carnivore host and diseases that can be harbored by carnivores, e.g., brucellosis (Morton 1986). Predation combined with weather seasonality and vegetation phenology would tend to maintain a compressed period of breeding and births. Predators would prevent dwarfing in isolated "island" populations. Predation can increase the fecundity of prey through: 1) improved fatness of females whose young calves are killed; and, 2) improved nutrition from reduced prey densities if forage is limiting. Increased fecundity is of no consequence if predation lowers productivity/survival of female calves to one year of age or to reproductive age.

Management Options to Conserve Caribou and Wolves

Knowledge of the ecology and behavior of wolves and caribou and the effects of modification of habitats permits the manager to design programs that will improve the survival chances of both. Identification of key limiting factors and their interactions is an essential first step. Hunting and predation often are important limiting factors of caribou and may be jointly regulatory with other factors. Parasites may be important in some locations in eastern Canada. Availability of sparse winter and spring forage is a concern near the periphery of caribou distributions. Every situation is unique. Requirements of wolves are fewer: an adequate prey base and human acceptance.

Hunting

There should be no seasons on caribou unless population data indicate that a certain percentage of sex and age classes can be killed on a sustained basis. Native people must be involved in the management of caribou because they have the legal right to hunt on Crown land at any time. Without their cooperation, conservation of caribou is unlikely.

Wolf predation

Where it jeopardizes the conservation of a caribou population, wolf management should first be by indirect means such as control of alternate prey, reduce travel access, aversion techniques, etc. If direct control is necessary, it must be scientifically based, and qualified local people should be directly involved in the reduction.

Alternate prey

Alternate prey may be reduced to low densities by liberal hunting. Their distributions may be influenced by various means such as habitat manipulation; and management of food sources: management for forests with an age structure and composition suitable for caribou; reduce shrubs and sedges/grasses (e.g., along roads) by mechanical and other environmentally-safe means; abolish use of road salt or mix inhibitors with it; and remove kills and cripples along roads and railroads.

Alternate predators

Direct and indirect management of other predators can reduce the need to manage wolves. The need to take holistic approaches to management is obvious. Wolves and caribou are only two species in ecosystems. The effect of bears, lynx, wolverine, and coyotes on caribou is not known in most areas. The future of trapping and the fur industry will have a bearing on the abundance of wolves and caribou.

Habitat management

Habitat management, e.g., for medium- and old-age forests, can reduce the need for predator management. Growth of "caribou lichens" may be enhanced by thinning regenerating stands and by selective logging over compacted snow in winter. Forest reserves and special caribou conservation areas may provide secure areas. Calving areas should be protected from logging if they are lake or muskeg islands or lakeshore. Travel corridors and escape habitat should be protected; human and wolf access should be restricted or discouraged.

Forestry operations

Forestry operations must consider wildlife. Campaigns to prevent large clearcuts may be detrimental to caribou conservation in some areas designated for extensive forestry. Small clearcuts lead ultimately to small areas in mature stages. Caribou need large areas in mature or old ages unless predators are managed. Checkerboard forest-age prescriptions are incompatible with caribou conservation unless other species are intensively managed. The result may be large populations of moose, elk, deer, beaver (*Castor canadensis*), hare (*Lepus americanus*), and wolves. One strategy is managed reserves — several large (> 1,000 km^2) areas within the distribution of a population that would be managed for high proportions of mature or old ages with selective logging. The productivity of some caribou habitats can be improved concurrent with forestry.

Succession of ground lichens after logging depends on many factors. Most logging prescriptions, including extraction and seed bed preparation, are detrimental to the regeneration of lichens preferred by caribou. Seeding fragments of caribou lichens may accelerate their succession. Accelerating arboreal lichen succession is being researched in B.C. (Stevenson 1991).

Management plans

Management plans should be produced and updated for all wolf and caribou populations in each jurisdiction in Canada. Ontario has a comprehensive draft management plan for caribou — a "feature" species (Darby et al. 1989). The plan sets out management objectives (e.g., minimum of 20K caribou), ecological principles, management principles, measures to safeguard habitat, and governmental structures to ensure that the plan will be implemented (Racey et al. 1991). In 1986, Alberta drafted a recovery plan for threatened caribou (Edmonds et al. 1991). Saskatchewan and B.C. have management plans; B.C. has a Caribou Advisory Committee. Manitoba is preparing a conservation strategy (C. Johnson, Man. Dep. Nat. Resources, pers. commun.). Alberta and Quebec have forestry prescriptions that help to protect caribou (Edmonds et al. 1991, Cumming 1992).

Advisory management boards were established in 1982 and 1985, respectively, for the transboundary Beverly/Kaminuriak and Porcupine caribou herds. An international agreement was signed in 1985 to create a Porcupine Caribou Management Board. These boards or their equivalent eventually will have management authority over wildlife in land settlement areas. Management concepts and principles will have to be understood by board members and their clients. Conservation of wolves and caribou must involve native groups, industry, nongovernment organizations, and the public.

The Future of Wolf-Caribou Systems in Canada

Some FF and F-F caribou populations in the southern boreal forest soon will become threatened or endangered. Some will be lost. It is possible that populations in the northern boreal forest can be maintained if management plans can be improved over time and implemented. Caribou do not fit well in multiple-use plans.

The F-A ecotype will require intensive management in southern portions of its range. Survival is unlikely unless parks, wilderness areas, or special predator and caribou management areas are established; development is properly conducted; and wolves are managed by direct or indirect

means. The option to manage wolves and caribou directly and indirectly through hunting and trapping may be lost through public opposition to these activities. New ways of managing wolves and their distributions must be devised including aversion methods to keep wolves out of areas used by endangered caribou. Experimentation should begin on use of combinations of visual, mechanical, chemical, and auditory methods to manage the distribution of wolves. Management of wolves is repugnant to some people, but it is justified in specific circumstances because humans have altered natural ecosystems and must attempt to rectify some of the ecological imbalances.

Systems approaches are necessary to solve some of the current conservation issues. But management for endangered species is often the antithetics of ecosystem management, particularly in environments considerably modified by humans. There is increasing realization that all species cannot be conserved in all ecosystems in all places. Landscape partitioning and zonal management may be necessary.

The demand for caribou will soon outstrip supplies in all areas. The role of the wolf in caribou population dynamics will become a key issue. As hunting mortality of a F-T herd changes from five to 20%, the wolf:caribou ratio should be reduced from about 1:200 to 1:1,000 for population stability. Recruitment should increase from about 10% to 25% as the ratio of wolves:caribou decreases. There will be a need to manage many F-T and T-T populations near the optimum sustained yield. Managers must find ways to maintain large populations of caribou in the north and maintain wolves.

Conclusions

1. Wolf predation is the major direct cause of natural mortality of calf and adult caribou in most populations investigated by use of radio collars with mortality detectors. Exceptions are caribou populations where wolves are absent or rare or where bears are major predators of caribou.
2. Dense caribou populations occur only in the absence of wolves; moderately dense populations where migratory caribou can escape predation for part of the year; and low densities where migrations are short and multiple prey and predators are present in the system.
3. The main antipredator behavior of caribou is to remove themselves from wolves through migration, movements, dispersion, concentration, and use of escape habitat (e.g., water).
4. Balances between wolves and caribou at individual, group, and population levels are affected by many factors: evolution; sex and age structure, nutrition, and health of caribou and wolves; climate/weather; and ecosystem changes through time (e.g., flora, other predators, and prey).
5. Wolves can hold caribou populations at low densities at theoretical ratios below about one wolf:80-120 caribou

Mature forests are important to the conservation of woodland caribou. Habitat fragmentation and wolf predation are implicated in the current plight of the ungulate. (Photo: J. Edmonds)

in wolf-caribou systems. The caribou can be exterminated if alternate prey, such as moose, are present.

6. There is some evidence that short-migration caribou populations remain at low densities where wolf densities exceed about five to eight wolves/Kkm² and alternate prey are abundant. The relationship is obscured by human influences.

7. If released from predator depression, a caribou population can increase until a combination of factors including food limitations, weather, hunting, and predation causes the population to fluctuate over a wide range.

8. Undernutrition from various causes (habitat loss, overuse of range, forage inaccessibility because of snow) may contribute significantly to natural mortality through production of light, weak calves that are born late and by increased vulnerability of adults to predators.

9. Developments and activities of man including hunting, road and trail construction, forestry, agriculture, and management of ungulates for high sustained yield, can contribute to caribou declines, directly and indirectly through increased predation, hunting, and accidents.

Woodland Caribou face difficult challenges surviving in complex predator-prey systems where wolf densities are kept at high levels by multiply prey populations. (Photo: T. Kitchin)

10. Caribou managers must identify the role of predation in caribou population dynamics and identify the role of environmental factors on the predation rate. Proximate and ultimate causes of caribou deaths and additive versus compensatory mortality must be carefully evaluated.

11. Partitioning of limiting and regulating factors and hypotheses to explain wolf and caribou dynamics is simplistic and obscures the complex interrelatedness of factors. Cumulative effects and factor complexing is required.

12. Conservation of caribou and wolves in the same area is difficult. Research should be directed to methods of making isolated, endangered caribou less vulnerable to wolves through species aversion techniques and management of wolf distributions.

13. Management of wolves and caribou should be outlined in management plans that are incorporated into regional, provincial, and continental plans for species, species systems, and ecosystems.

14. Management options for endangered caribou populations include control of hunting, access, wolves, alternate prey, and alternate predators; habitat reserves, multiple pass forestry, zonal management, and landscape management.

15. The systematic classification of caribou should be revised with emphasis placed on genetic and behavioral differences and similarities, habitat use, and the need to protect gene pools.

16. Classification of caribou by ecotype is more useful for ecological, management, and conservation functions than are conventional taxa.

Acknowledgments

I thank H. Armbruster, W. Bradford, K. Brown, J. Edmonds, R. Edwards, D. Klein, D. Seip, and P. Panegyuk for helpful suggestions on draft copies.

The Introduction, Increase, and Demise of Wolves on Coronation Island, Alaska

■ David R. Klein

Wolves were introduced to Coronation Island in the Alexander Archipelago of southeastern Alaska in 1960. The island was previously without wolves or other large mammalian predators and supported a high density of Sitka black-tailed deer. The introduced wolves (two pair) increased to a peak population of 13 animals in four years and caused a pronounced decline in deer density. The wolves then declined to a single animal in 1968, and deer persisted only in a few areas of rough terrain and dense habitat. Wolf scats consisted primarily of deer during the first five years following their introduction, with harbor seal of secondary importance. Deer remains in the scats declined during 1966-1968 to low frequency, whereas marine invertebrates, small rodents, and birds increased markedly, and wolf remains also appeared in the scats. As deer density declined, wolves fed opportunistically on whatever was available, even resorting to cannibalism.

Introduction

Wolves (*Canis lupus ligoni*) were introduced to Coronation Island (55°53'N, 134°14'W) in the Alexander Archipelago of southeastern Alaska in 1960 (Fig. 1). This 73.3 km² island lies on the western periphery of the archipelago and, before 1960, had a high density of small black-tailed deer (*Odocoileus hemionus sitkensis*) (Klein 1965a). Neither wolves nor black bears (*Ursus americanus*) occurred there (Klein 1965b).

The terrain of Coronation Island is irregular; Karst topography is common, and cliffs rise sharply from the sea on the south and west. More than 80% of the land area is below 300 m, although Needle Peak rises to nearly 600 m. The island is under strong maritime influence, with cool summers and mild winters. Vegetation is north temperate rain forest, dominated by western hemlock (*Tsuga heterophylla*) and Sitka spruce (*Picea sitchensis*). About 80% of the island is forested, 11% muskeg, 6% subalpine, and the remaining 3% alpine, exposed rock, alder slide, and water as reported by Klein (1965a) in a detailed description of the island, its climate, and vegetation.

The Island Prior to the Introduction of Wolves

Body condition of deer and their relationship to vegetation on Coronation Island were the focus of investigations from 1959 through 1961. The studies included comparison of deer and vegetation with those of Woronkofski Island, of comparable size and 120 km to the east (Fig. 1). Woronkofski Island is under weaker maritime influence and wolves were present (Klein 1962, 1964, 1965a). Woronkofski Island deer of every age class were larger than those of Coronation Island. At one year of age, they were 17% heavier, at two years 24%, at three years 31%, and at four years or older 37%. Quantitative analysis of vegetation on the two islands showed lower plant density and species richness on Coronation Island. Sustained heavy herbivory probably caused these differences. Vegetation was less affected by deer on Woronkofski Island where occasional severe winters of heavy snow accumulation, in combination with wolf predation, resulted in wide fluctuations in deer numbers.

I suspect that nutritional constraints produced the observed differences in deer body size on the two islands. Historically, Coronation Island populations were limited primarily by availability of forage plants rather than by wolf predation, hunting pressure, or extreme snow depths. Lower nitrogen and higher fibre content in the rumen contents of Coronation Island deer verified a qualitative difference in diet (Klein 1965a).

Deer density on Coronation Island was estimated by Merriam (1967) at 3.9/km² in 1961, but he later revised this upward to 5.8–7.8/km² based on comparable frequency of deer sightings with other areas in southeastern Alaska. Subsequent deer pellet group surveys on Coronation and other

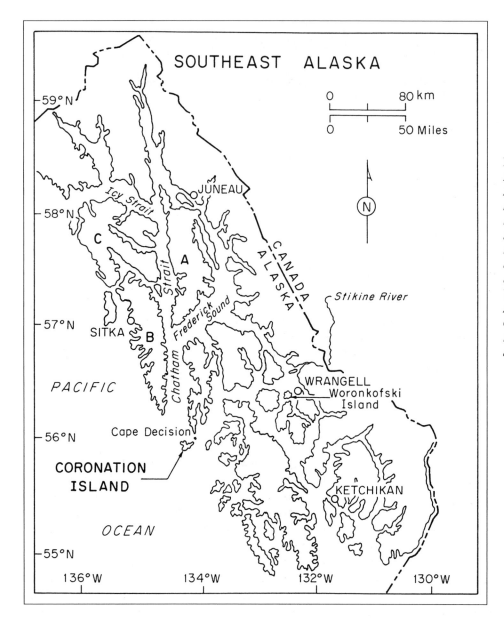

Fig. 1 *Position of Coronation Island in the Alexander Archipelago and other locations mentioned in the text. The natural distribution of wolves in southeastern Alaska includes the mainland and islands south of Frederick Sound with the exception of Coronation Island. Wolves have not established on Admiralty (A), Baranof (B), and Chichagof (C) and associated islands in the northern archipelago.*

islands in southeastern Alaska (Kirchhoff and Pitcher 1988) support this higher estimate.

The Wolf Introductions

After Klein (1964, 1965a) reported altered vegetation on Coronation Island because of foraging pressure by deer, and the associated suppressed phenotypic development of the deer, biologists of the Alaska Department of Fish and Game (ADFG) proposed introducing wolves to Coronation Island. The reason for the proposal was the belief that Coronation Island offered a unique opportunity to investigate relationships among vegetation, herbivores, and predators. These included: 1) the response of a food-limited deer population to wolf predation; 2) the growth and dynamics of a wolf population introduced to an island of limited area with a high deer density; 3) the response of vegetation following reduc-

tion of deer density; and 4) the possible changes in body condition of the deer as a consequence of their lowered density and subsequent recovery of vegetation.

Coronation Island lies within the natural distribution of deer, wolves, and black bears, in contrast to islands to the north of Frederick Sound where only deer and brown bears (*Ursus arctos*) are present (Fig. 1) (Klein 1965b). Coronation Island, however, is exposed to the Pacific Ocean; its closest proximity to a wolf-occupied island is by way of the chain of small Spanish Islands and the 2.7-km-wide Decision Passage. Strong tidal currents and rough seas that characterize the passage may account for the failure of natural wolf dispersal to the island in recorded history. Although wolves swim water channels between islands in southeastern Alaska (Klein pers. obs.), these are more protected waters with relatively calm conditions. The absence of wolves from

Table 1. Frequency of food items in wolf scats from Coronation Island, 1961-1968.

				Percent Occurrence				
YEAR	Number Scats	Deer	Harbor Seal	Wolf	Bird	Rodent	Marine Invert.	Undetermined
1961	146	78	43	0	2	0	1	2
1962	18	89	48	0				11*
1963	45	89	53	0	0	1	2	27
1964	77	95	32	0	8	0	0	14
1965	213	97	8	7	5	3	3	17
1966								
Feb	110	53	18	10	30	1	28	66
Aug	7	0	14	29				57*
1967	44	0	57	0	25	18	23	5
1968	3	33	33	0	0	33	33	0

* Not examined for bird, rodent, or marine invertebrates.

northern archipelago islands with deer provides further evidence that, unlike deer, wolves are limited in their distribution by moderately wide or rough water crossings. These islands are separated from the mainland by water channels a minimum of about 2.5 km wide. Few potential prey species for wolves other than deer live on Coronation Island (Land and Young 1984). Mink (*Mustela vison*) and river otters (*Lutra canadensis*) are primarily occupants of the beach fringe; the former is much more common than the latter. Rodents include *Microtus coronarius* and *Peromyscus sitkensis*. Birds include the blue grouse (*Dendragapus obscurus*), passerine birds, a few shore birds and waterfowl nesting in muskeg areas, and large colonies of cliff-nesting sea birds on the west and south coasts. In winter, waterfowl, mostly diving ducks, and some seabirds are present in peripheral waters. Harbor seals (*Phoca vitulina*) occasionally haul out on the rocky shores. Other marine mammals commonly present in the surrounding waters are sea lions (*Eumetopias jubata*), sea otters (*Enhydra lutris*), porpoises (primarily *Phocaena romerina* and *Phocoenoides dalli*), and whales (primarily *Balaenoptera* spp., *Megaptera nodosa*, and *Orcinus orca*). In intertidal zones, mollusks and crustaceans are common. There are no significant salmon runs into the several small streams that drain the island.

A litter of seven wolf pups obtained from a den on Kupreanof Island in 1959 and reared by ADFG biologists was a source for introduction. While in captivity the two females grew to 29 kg and the five males to more than 37 kg at approximately one year (Garceau 1960). These weights are greater than those of wolves killed in southeastern Alaska during September 1960 to June 1961 (72.4 ±4.3 (SE) lbs (27 kg) for females and 88.0 ± 3.8 lbs (33 kg) for males) (Garceau 1961).

When about 1.5 years old, two females and two males from the captive litter were individually caged and transported by boat from Petersburg to Egg Harbor at Coronation Island. They looked well when released on 27 October 1960 after four days of close confinement. Five deer were shot, three at Egg Harbor and two at Aats Bay, to provide food for the wolves.

Growth of the Wolf Population and Decline of Deer

Garceau (1961) visited the island in May 1961 and reported evidence that these wolves, although inexperienced in killing deer, had acclimated to conditions on the island. He found tracks of at least one male and one female wolf (based on track size differences) on beaches, remains of several deer showing evidence of having been killed by wolves, and wolf scats containing deer bones and hair. In July 1961, a commercial fisherman who had anchored at Egg Harbor shot the two adult female wolves. One was reported to have been lactating and both were bearing ear tags (Garceau 1962). Later in the summer howling, tracks, and fresh scats indicated that both adult males were still alive. Garceau (1962) observed tracks of wolf pups several times in August. On 11 August, he saw a wolf pup estimated to weigh 15–19 kg near an apparent rearing area.

Seventy-eight percent of wolf scats (146) collected during spring and summer of 1961 contained deer remains, whereas 43% contained harbor seal (Table 1) (Garceau

1962). Of those scats containing deer, 26% included fawn remains. Remains of 23 deer killed by wolves included 16 adults, five fawns, and two undetermined. Bone marrow was dense and fatty in 11, the fat was depleted in two, and condition of 10 could not be determined because of insufficient skeletal remains. Garceau (1962) reported wolf tracks were common throughout the island. He saw 32 live deer and abundant deer sign, suggesting that deer remained at moderate density.

In April 1963, an additional adult female wolf, trapped on Kupreanof Island, was released on Coronation Island (Merriam 1963–1968). During four days on the island, Merriam saw one wolf, tracks of two others, and heard a wolf howling. During the first two weeks of August 1963, Merriam (1963–1968) found fresh wolf tracks in all of the bays on the island. Five wolves were seen, and on the basis of wolves observed and tracks, he believed that there were at least four adults and three pups present on the island. In July 1964, during eight days on the island, Merriam (1963–1968) saw 11 adult wolves and tracks of two pups. He estimated that there were at least 13 wolves present and noted that three litters of young had been born since the introduction. Remains of 13 deer had fatty bone marrow in all but one. Before the introduction of wolves to Coronation Island bone marrow of deer dying of natural causes was predominantly without fat (Klein 1963). Fresh wolf scats (Table 1) continued to contain mostly deer, but seal and clam (*Clinocardium nuttallii*) were also present. Deer were greatly reduced and rarely seen, although tracks were present throughout the island. Pronounced regrowth from root suckering of blueberry and huckleberry (*Vaccinium* spp.) and rusty menziesia (*Menziesia furruginea*) was noted by Merriam (1963–1968), presumably as a result of the reduced foraging pressure by deer.

In July 1965, Merriam (1963–1968) spent 10 days on Coronation Island. He observed tracks of two pups and abundant adult tracks on all beaches. Deer sign, however, was absent from the north side of the island, but fresh tracks occurred on steep slopes on the south side of the island and on the higher peaks. Merriam equated these locations with escape terrain, where rough terrain and dense vegetation provided the best opportunity for deer to escape from wolves. He suggested that deer were able to survive under the high wolf density (0.18/km^2) only in such areas. He visited the Spanish Islands, separated by less than a kilometre of open water from Coronation Island, and reported no evidence of wolves. Deer sign and the overbrowsed condition of the vegetation were comparable to Coronation Island before the introduction of wolves. In 1963, vegetation transects on Coronation Island revealed that density of most deer food species had more than doubled in two years. Forbs showed the greatest increase. Merriam (1963–1968) saw one of the originally introduced male wolves close enough to recognize its ear tag, verifying its age at six years. In 201 wolf scats collected, deer continued to be the major food.

Wolf hair present in 75% of the scats was probably from grooming, but may have resulted, in part, from cannibalism. Other food items included birds, mink, mice, crabs, chitons, and clams. By August 1965, on the basis of tracks, Merriam (1963–1968) believed there were 10 wolves on Coronation Island.

In February 1966, Merriam (1963–1968) observed only three wolves, and tracks suggested they were the only individuals present. Six of 110 wolf scats collected contained wolf remains only. The percentage of scats containing deer was less than half that of the previous spring. Birds, seals, marine invertebrates, and small mammals constituted the major food items. Using leg snares, Merriam and a colleague attempted to capture the remaining wolves to evaluate their body condition. They caught and tagged one wolf immediately after their arrival on 3 February as it attempted to raid their meat cooler on the porch of the Egg Harbor cabin. This male, in poor condition, weighed 24 kg and showed little fear. The absence of tooth wear indicated it was a young animal. After recapturing it three times, they tied it to a tree for several days so that trapping for additional wolves could continue. A second male was caught on 10 February, weighing 37 kg and was in excellent condition. In August 1966, Merriam (1963–1968) observed less evidence of wolves than at any time since the introduction. Two wolves were present and the possibility of a third was suggested, but there was no evidence of pups. Trails made and previously used by wolves were becoming overgrown with vegetation. Only seven wolf scats were collected in August of 1966, in contrast to 201 in a comparable period of the previous year. Three fresh deer tracks were observed, all on the higher peaks of the island.

In a week on the island in early May 1967, Merriam (1963–1968) found tracks of only two wolves and collected 44 scats, none with deer remains present (Table 1). Seal was the predominant food item, although birds, marine invertebrates, and rodents collectively made up most of the scat contents. He found only one fresh deer track, and that was on the south side of the island. On a visit to the island in January 1968, Merriam (1963–1968) heard one wolf howling and saw one old track. He found no scats and no deer tracks on the north side of the island. In mid-July several areas had tracks of a single wolf. No fresh deer tracks were observed, but there was evidence of winter browsing on some blueberry shrubs (*Vaccinium ovalifolium*). In December, with new snow and good tracking conditions, there was evidence of only one wolf, indicated by urination marks to be a female. No deer tracks were seen. Three wolf scats collected contained deer in one, seal in another, and rodents and chitons were in the third. Merriam (1971) spent 10 days on Coronation Island during June and July 1970, visiting all beach areas. He saw fresh tracks of a single wolf but no fresh deer tracks. Evidence of winter browsing by deer was present and he found one deer pellet group.

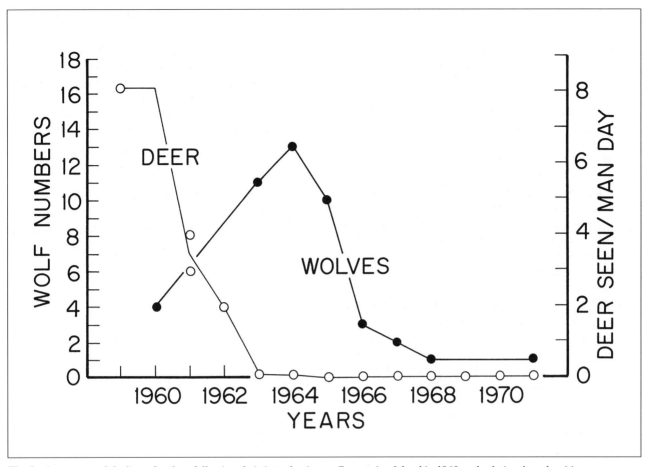

Fig. 2 *Increase and decline of wolves following their introduction to Coronation Island in 1960 and relative deer densities.*

By summer 1966, vegetation on the island showed marked response to release from foraging pressure associated with the previous high deer density. Merriam (Alaska Dept. Fish and Game, pers. commun.) established seven point-intercept, vegetation transects [100-foot (30.5-m) with points at 1-foot (.305-m) intervals] at Egg Harbor, Aats Bay, Alikula Bay, and Gish Bay in 1963. He relocated these in 1966 and reran them. From 1963 to 1966, the transects showed a 63% increase in occurrence of forest floor forbs. These included trailing bramble (*Rubus pedatus*), lace flower (*Tiarella trifoliata*), and dwarf dogwood (*Cornus canadensis*), which are forage species favored by deer. There was a 34% increase in woody shrubs and tree seedlings.

Over several weeks in 1983, Land and Young (1984) surveyed fauna on the island but saw no evidence of wolves. From 1987 and 1988, Lewis (1992) spent six months on the island in both summer and winter during a study of vegetation and deer. He found no evidence of wolves.

Discussion and Conclusions

The wolves introduced to Coronation Island increased to a density of 1/5.64 km² (0.18 wolf/km²). Deer at their peak

density in 1959 (5.8-7.8 km² = 425-572 deer), before the introduction of wolves, outnumbered wolves at their peak density in 1964 (13 wolves) by 32–43 to one. Deer density, however, was much reduced by 1964 after wolves were introduced. The potential rate of increase of wolves, assuming an even sex ratio and average litter size of six (Rausch 1967), far exceeds that of deer. There were obviously constraints on wolf reproduction that most likely included limitations in the capability of the deer population to sustain itself under the level of wolf predation that existed. Potential social inhibitions to reproduction among the wolves may also have been a factor. Although the two pair of wolves initially released were from the same litter, it is doubtful that inbreeding was a factor in limiting reproduction and survival. Shields (1983) points out that a moderate level of inbreeding is a normal consequence of wolf sociality and their disjunct distribution. At least four litters of young were produced on Coronation Island. The early removal of the two original adult females, who were litter mates, and their replacement by another wild-trapped female increased genetic diversity in the population.

Specific conclusions from this study of a wolf introduction to an island populated by deer are as follows:

1) Wolves introduced to a 73 km² island with moderately high deer density increased within four years to a peak population of about 13 animals. Wolves produced young at two years of age and at least four litters were born during this period.

2) Deer declined markedly during this same period to such low density that they were rarely seen. Deer forage species showed pronounced regrowth from the previous sustained heavy herbivory by deer.

3) Most deer killed by wolves had fatty bone marrow and were presumed to be in good condition, whereas before the introduction of wolves most deer that died were in a malnourished state without bone marrow fat.

4) As the wolf population declined over the next four years to a single animal, deer were no longer seen and their few tracks were restricted to steep slopes on the south side of the island and to the higher peaks. No young wolves were born after 1965.

5) Food consumed by wolves changed from primarily deer during their increase phase to a diversity of items apparently obtained opportunistically during the decline phase. They included harbor seal, marine invertebrates, birds, rodents, fish, mink, and river otter. Wolf hair commonly appeared in wolf scats, apparently ingested during grooming, but during the rapid decline to three wolves in 1966, six of 110 scats collected contained only wolf remains.

6) Wolves failed to cross the 900 m of water to the adjacent Spanish Islands where deer densities remained moderately high throughout the study.

7) When the wolves had declined to three individuals in 1966, of two males captured and released, one was in poor condition weighing 73% of the mean for adult males killed throughout southeastern Alaska. The other was in excellent condition weighing 14% more than the mean.

8) Recovery of deer forage species following the decline in deer density was most rapid for forbs of the forest floor. Woody shrubs responded more slowly and continued to increase throughout the study period.

9) At the low density, when deer on the island had been reduced by wolves during the eight years of the study, it was not possible for the deer to increase, even during the marked decline in wolf numbers.

10) Coronation Island with only 73.3 km², although favorable deer habitat, is too small to sustain populations of both deer and wolves.

11) Wolves in areas of strong maritime climatic influence in southeastern Alaska have the potential to suppress deer numbers below the carrying capacity of the forage resource.

Acknowledgments

H.R. Merriam was involved in the conception of the study, release of the wolves, monitoring of the wolf and deer populations, and evaluation of changes in the vegetation. He contributed materially to the interpretation of the findings from the study, but with characteristic modesty, declined shared authorship of this paper. P. Garceau assisted in the initial stages of the study. C. Land assisted in the search for original files and field notes from the study. The wolf introduction and subsequent evaluation studies were supported by Federal Aid in Wildlife Restoration funds through the Alaska Department of Fish and Game. I appreciate critical review of the manuscript by A.T. Bergerud, R.T. Bowyer, H.R. Merriam, D.R. Seip, D.C. Thomas, and an anonymous reviewer.

Part 5:
Behavior & Social Interaction

Physiological and Social Aspects of Reproduction of the Wolf and Their Implications for Contraception

■ Cheryl S. Asa

Wild canids pose special problems for contraception related to their physiological responses to various contraceptive methods and to the importance of the integrity of the social unit to their survival. The safety and efficacy of contraceptive choices must be weighed against their impact on pack integrity. A vast literature, generated from contraceptive tests using domestic dogs, can be used to predict outcomes of application to wolves. Contraceptive categories include steroid hormones, analogues of pituitary and hypothalamic hormones, immuno-contraceptives, sterilization, and castration. Potentially deleterious side effects include physiological pathology, such as uterine and mammary gland hyperstimulation and disease, and disruption of the social system, which might result in packs with no estrous females or with continuously territorial and aggressive males. Possible long-term social breakdown also might result from the failure to produce young.

Introduction

Increased interest in developing alternative methods to control wildlife populations has focused attention on contraception as a possible way to reduce or stabilize reproductive rates. Permanent sterilization is in many cases the most cost-effective approach, requiring only a single treatment, but it may limit the ability of the population to recover following crashes due, for example, to disease or starvation.

Other major factors to consider when selecting a contraceptive method include: 1) efficacy; 2) safety; 3) effects on behavior or social structure; and 4) ease of application. The wolf presents an especially difficult case for contraceptive population control because of its vulnerability to steroid hormone side effects and its complex social structure. The following review will present currently available techniques and discuss their practicality and advisability for application to free-ranging wolf populations.

Reproductive Physiology and Social Organization

The selection of the most suitable contraceptive method should be based on an understanding of its potential impact on both social and physiological systems. Several aspects of wolf reproduction could be adversely affected by currently available contraceptive approaches.

Prior to the winter breeding season, males become more territorial and urine-mark more frequently (Mech 1970, Asa et al. 1990). During the female's two- to six-week proestrous phase, characterized by elevated estrogen and sanguineous vaginal discharge (Seal et al. 1979, Asa et al. 1986), the double urine marks and increased contact probably serve to establish or maintain the bond between the pair (Rothman and Mech 1979, Asa et al. 1986).

Canids are unusual in having only one estrous and ovulation per year. Typically, only the dominant male and female breed, although the subordinate pack members are physiologically competent to reproduce (Mech 1970, Seal et al. 1979). Ovulation by a female wolf is followed either by pregnancy or hormonal pseudopregnancy. Thus, all females in a pack synchronously experience hormonal stimulation that prepares them to display maternal behavior even if they do not copulate or conceive. Prolactin, a pituitary hormone associated with parental behavior, is elevated in all adult wolves around the time of whelping (Kreeger et al. 1991) and may contribute to the acceptance of and care of the pups by the pack. The pups then stay with the pack well into adulthood, foregoing their own opportunity to reproduce until they are able to be independent (Asa, 1996).

Contraceptive alternatives include: 1) castration; 2) sterilization; 3) steroid hormones; 4) hypothalamic hormone analogues; and 5) vaccines. Because all can be applied to both sexes, but in different forms and with different results, treatment of males and females will be considered separately.

Male Contraceptive Choices

Castration

Surgical castration is contraindicated in most field situations because of the need for capture, the skill level required to perform the technique, and the chances for infection. It is permanent, which may or may not be desirable. An alternative is chemical castration, which can be performed by injection of occluding or sclerosing agents into the testes (Dixit 1979), but capture is still necessary. These methods remove the source of both sperm and testosterone production and are not reversible.

Synthetic progestins such as melengestrol acetate in implant form can be used to suppress testosterone production and spermatogenesis if given in high enough doses. Implants release hormone for two or three years, so recapture is required for continued contraception, but not for reversal.

Sterilization

Although surgical vasectomy is an option, chemical vasectomy, which involves injection of a sclerosing agent into the epididymis in much the same manner as chemical castration, is a much simpler and safer technique (Freeman and Coffey 1973, Pineda and Hepler 1981). Local scar-tissue formation blocks passage of sperm but spares testosterone production, with no resultant behavioral changes. Vas plugs, which are finding success in captive wildlife (Asa and Zaneveld, Rush Medical Center, Chicago, unpubl. data), are not practical for use in the field because of the need for microsurgery.

Reversible interruption of spermatogenesis with bisdiamine (Droebeck and Coulston 1962) is being tested in captive wolves (Zaneveld et al. 1988; Asa et al. 1995). However, the compound has to be fed daily, so unless an implantable form is developed, field application will not be feasible.

Injections of cadmium have been shown to cause permanent sterility in a variety of species (Gunn and Gould 1977) although canids have not yet been tested. Cadmium levels sufficient to cause sterility are below those that produce toxicity in other organ systems. Because temporary lesions occur at the site of injection, direct treatment of the testis might be preferable, although the option of darting without capture would not be precluded. Testosterone production declines transiently immediately following treatment but recovers to pretreatment levels.

Hormones

Because of the negative feedback that results, administration of testosterone or synthetic androgens can block production and release of endogenous hormones and result in temporary sterility. Although injections of micro-encapsulated testosterone can be delivered by dart (Turner and Kirkpatrick 1991), duration of action is still relatively short, probably less than six months. Given current technology, silastic implants deliver a more reliable dose of hormone for a longer period of time, but require capture for insertion. Uncertainty exists regarding possible long-term behavioral changes for androgen-treated males, especially with the use of the more bioactive synthetics that may heighten aggression.

Analogues of the hypothalamic hormone gonadotrophin releasing hormone (GnRH), also called luteinizing-hormone releasing-hormone (LHRH), can effectively block the cascade of hormonal events required for testosterone production and spermatogenesis (Vickery et al. 1985, 1989). Synthetic analogues occur in two forms: agonists and antagonists. Agonists work by mimicking the action of the natural hormone and succeed in suppression because they are administered in high doses that result in negative feedback. A sometimes unwanted consequence of agonist administration is the initial overstimulation which precedes the negative feedback phase. During the stimulatory period, males still are fertile and may exhibit exaggerated aggression. The present expense of agonists is prohibitive for routine contraceptive use.

Antagonists, in contrast, act to block the effect of the analogous hormone from inception of treatment. Although antagonists might be preferable for contraception, they tend to be less bioactive than agonists and so require larger doses. Additionally, they are considerably more expensive per dose, so are impractical for most applications.

If hormonal castration that results from LHRH analogue treatment is undesirable, replacement androgen can be supplied in implant form. Because the levels of androgen required for replacement are considerably lower than for suppression of spermatogenesis, overstimulation of male-type behavior need not occur.

Vaccines

Vaccines against LHRH have effects similar to those of LHRH antagonists or castration, i.e., suppression of androgens as well as sperm production. Where male-typical behavior is desired, androgen replacement can be added (Ladd et al. 1989). At present, this technique is still considered experimental due to variability in individual response and in length of effect (Gonzalez et al. 1989).

Female Contraceptive Choices

Because the reproductive organs of the female lie within the body cavity, ovariectomy and tubal ligations are not advisable in field situations where sterile surgical techniques cannot be ensured. Other options, as with males, include: 1) hormone treatment; and 2) vaccines.

Hormones

Currently, the most widely used contraceptive technique for captive wildlife is a synthetic progestin, melengestrol acetate (MGA) supplied in silicone-implant form (Porton et al.

1990). However, extensive literature from trials of various synthetic progestins with domestic dogs reports a number of serious side effects, some potentially fatal (Asa and Porton 1991). Progestin-induced hyperstimulation of uterine and mammary tissue can result in conditions ranging from pyometra to tumorigenesis (Brodey and Fidler 1966, Nelson and Kelly 1976, Goyings et al. 1977, Hansel et al. 1977, Giles et al. 1978, El Etreby 1979, Frank et al. 1979). Unfortunately, the addition of estrogen to progestin therapy, a strategy sometimes effective in reducing side effects in primates, not only does not ameliorate, but exacerbates the progestin-induced pathology in dogs (Teunissen 1952, Giles et al. 1978). For this reason in particular, progestin administration to canids should not be initiated during proestrous or estrous, periods when endogenous estrogen is high.

Various progestins are known to stimulate increased insulin production (Frank et al. 1979) and symptoms of diabetes (Nelson and Kelly 1976). Pathology of the liver and gall bladder (Nelson and Kelly 1976, Hansel et al. 1977), as well as elevated growth hormone associated with symptoms of acromegaly (Concannon et al. 1980) may result at higher doses. Depressed adrenocortical function (Fekete and Szeberenyi 1965, Concannon et al. 1980) and reduced adrenal weight (El Etreby 1979) also have been reported.

In contrast, progestins do not appear to produce deleterious effects during pregnancy. Female fetuses conceived during progestin treatment showed no signs of virilization (Duncan et al. 1964), nor did MGA delay parturition or affect survival of pups (Zimbelman et al. 1970).

Trials with yet another synthetic progestin, proligestone, showed it to be more specific in suppressing pituitary function for blocking ovulation, but less progestogenic, which may moderate side effects (Van Os et al. 1981).

Two other major classes of gonadal steroids, estrogens and androgens, have also been tested for contraceptive application in dogs. Although estrogens (e.g., diethyl-stilbestrol and estradiol cypionate) have been used to block implantation following unplanned mating, their ability to stimulate uterine disease, bone marrow suppression, aplastic anaemia, and ovarian neoplasms makes them inappropriate contraceptive compounds (Jabara 1962, Giles et al. 1978, Bowen et al. 1985).

Both testosterone (Simmons and Hamner 1973) and the synthetic androgen mibolerone (Sokolowski and Geng 1977) have proven to be effective contraceptives, but masculinizing effects include clitoral hypertrophy, vulval discharge, mounting, and increased aggression of the treated female, and virilization of fetuses.

As with males, analogues of LHRH have been tested with female dogs. The expense and requisite high doses of the antagonists have relegated them to acute treatments such as pregnancy termination (Vickery et al. 1989). In contrast, an extremely potent agonist (nafarelin) first stimulated estrous within six days of treatment, then suppressed estrous during the ensuing year of administration (Vickery et al. 1987).

Although nafarelin appears promising for use with domestic dogs, unless an implant is developed, field application will not be possible.

Vaccines

Immunization against LHRH (GnRH) shows promise for contraception, but not all trials have been successful (Gonzalez et al. 1989). Vaccines also have been developed against the zona pellucida, the glycoprotein layer coating the oocyte and pre-implantation embryo. Theoretically, immunization should block oocyte penetration by sperm without affecting ovulation and the expression of estrous behavior. However, studies with dogs have revealed additional, more generalized ovarian effects, such that long-term treatment might result in suppression of cycles and possible permanent infertility (Mahi and Yanagimachi 1979, Mahi-Brown et al. 1985, 1988).

Potential Consequences of Contraceptive Application

Methods that result in castration or its equivalent (e.g., LHRH vaccines or analogues) could be expected to have profound effects on male behavior and thus on social dynamics. Behaviors that are testosterone-dependent include urine-marking and territorial defense, as well as an interest in females. In particular, packs would be unlikely to form and existing packs might disband without the interest of the male in acquiring and protecting a female. In addition, the potential decrease in aggression in treated males might make them more vulnerable to attack by untreated males, leaving the untreated animals with no competition for access to females, reducing the impact of the technique on reproductive rates.

In contrast, sterilization by blockage of sperm or arrest of spermatogenesis, which spares testosterone production, should have no behavioral or social effects. In fact, the only negative consequence of sterilization in other mammalian social systems, i.e., protraction of the breeding season when females continue to cycle due to failure to conceive, does not apply to canids that only ovulate once a year irrespective of conception.

For females, in addition to the deleterious physiological effects of steroid hormones, the resultant suppression of ovulation and estrus would be likely to prevent pair formation and perhaps would lead to dissolution of existing packs. The LHRH vaccines and analogues would be expected to cause a similar outcome through suppression of cycles.

Although the zona pellucida vaccine theoretically should not interfere with ovarian cycles, treatment of dogs showed a more generalized affect on the ovaries that may interrupt cyclicity and result in permanent sterility. The ramifications of cycle suppression are similar to those following treatment with steroids, LHRH analogues and LHRH vaccines.

If any contraceptive method is successful, the potential social effects of the absence of pups in a pack must be considered. There should be selective pressure for a female to be able to recognize that if she does not conceive with a particular male, she has the option to select another. Although no data yet exist, it is possible to conjecture from related information how such a phenomenon might be mediated. For example, progesterone, the predominating hormone during pregnancy, is known to have mild anaesthetic effects (Merryman et al. 1954). Thus, females that are not pregnant might be more restless than pregnant females, and such restlessness might lead to social disruption. For methods that do not prevent estrus and ovulation, all adult females that ovulate would become pseudopregnant even if they do not conceive, and so are subject to the same hormonal milieu. However, it is more difficult to foresee the consequences of packs with these hormonally-primed females who never have pups with which to express their maternal drive.

In summary, the only methods that are relatively free of physiological side effect and that would not be expected to have profound effects on wolf social organization are those that block sperm passage or arrest spermatogenesis in the male. Of those, cadmium injections appear to hold the most promise for field application, but as yet have not been tested on free-ranging wildlife.

A Review of the Sensory Organs in Wolves and Their Importance to Life History

■ Cheryl S. Asa and L. David Mech

Although little research on sensory perception has been conducted on the wolf, studies of the domestic dog and other carnivores can be used as a basis for discussion. In particular, comparisons of sensory discrimination and sensitivity among canids, humans, and other carnivores can provide insight into the sensory world of the wolf. For example, the relative proportions of rods and cones in the eye are associated with visual perception of color and low light, which can be related to the visual abilities and constraints of the animal in its natural habitat. Similarly, auditory threshold and ceiling reveal the range and types of perceptible sounds, which are most interesting when related to the natural sources of those sounds. The analysis of such data allows us to hypothesize the possible perceptual world of the wolf, but also emphasizes the striking lack of information on the wolf itself, suggesting areas for further study.

Introduction

To function successfully, a carnivore must have keen senses. Anyone who has observed wolves (*Canus lupus*) can vouch for their alertness and extreme sensory sensitivity. However, quantification of these abilities in wolves has been minimal. Nevertheless, results from studies of domestic dogs (*C. familiaris*) and other carnivores can provide considerable understanding of the sensory world of the wolf. (Due to the lack of data on the canid tactile sense, this modality will not be covered.)

Vision

Wolves have two primary needs for strong visual capabilities: their social communication and their hunting lifestyle. Although they are themselves prey to both bears (*Ursus* spp.) and humans, their needs to detect other predators are generally less than those of herbivores and various smaller carnivores, which themselves might also be prey.

The importance of visual displays in communication among wolves was well illustrated by Schenkel (1947). Parts of the body used for display are made more salient by contrasting coloration. For example, eyes, ears, mouth, and tail-tips are highlighted by either darker or lighter coloration, which emphasizes the signal value of facial expressions and tail position. Likewise, the dark saddle behind the wolf's shoulders visually emphasizes the raised hackles of an aggressive individual.

Nevertheless, hunting is probably the behavior for which vision is most important. During all stages of the hunt (Mech 1970), good vision would be extremely valuable, and during the attack itself, could prevent wounding or fatality to the wolf. Even the white-tailed deer (*Odocoileus virginianus*) can kill a wolf (Frijlink 1977, Nelson and Mech 1985, Mech and Nelson 1990b).

In open areas such as the subarctic (Haber 1977), the arctic, and the high arctic, vision is probably important in helping wolves locate prey. Aerial observations of wolves chasing deer on frozen lakes in Minnesota (Mech and Frenzel 1971a) and ground observations of wolves hunting musk oxen (*Ovibus moschatus*) indicate that the vision of wolves is at least as acute as that of humans (Mech 1988b).

Nevertheless, in dogs, vision is generally considered to be the most poorly developed sense (Rosengren 1969), which means that the other senses are even more acute or keen. However, experimental conditions are difficult to manipulate so that visual acuity is not confused with recognition.

As with many other mammals, the eye of canids is lined with a *tapetum lucidum*, a reflective layer of the retina, which increases visual sensitivity in low illumination by causing light to pass more than once across the receptors in the back of the eye (Walls 1942). This would certainly be a helpful adaptation for the nocturnal hunting that wolves often do.

The proportion of rods to cones also indicates the importance of night-versus-day vision in canids. Higher proportions of rods increase low light perception, whereas cones, in addition to their role in perception of color, are adaptive for bright light. Dogs have almost 95% rods (Magrane 1977). The ability to close down pupils to reduce stimulation by bright light allows an animal that possesses a high proportion of rods to adjust to increasing light intensity, as is common in canids. This combination of features also helps account for the ability of the wolf to function visually day or night.

The power of accommodation, or ability to change the shape of the lens to alter focal length, is well developed in canids (Walls 1942). This, together with binocular vision, aids in seeing in three dimensions and better judging, for example, the distance of prey. For comparison, the degree of divergence of the eyes from the body axis, a measure of the extent of binocularity, is 4–9° in cats and 15–25° in dogs. In humans, the proportion of uncrossed optic tract fibers is about one-half, in cats one-third, and in dogs, one-fourth. Thus, humans have better binocular vision than cats or dogs. Better depth perception in cats, relative to canids, is perhaps required for capture of smaller, faster prey.

As far as color is concerned, Rosengren (1969) demonstrated that dogs could distinguish red, yellow, blue, and green, although she did not test a full range of colors nor control for brightness. In preliminary tests with red, green, blue, and yellow dye placed on the snow base of a captive enclosure, wolves more frequently found the red and yellow marks (Asa unpubl. data). This test did not control for color intensity or possible differences in odor of the dyes, but the results are consistent with the hypothesis that wolves can perceive, or may find more attractive, colors with biological relevance, i.e., red (blood) and yellow (urine mark). Mech has anecdotal evidence from close-up observation of habituated wild wolves (Mech 1988b) that they can distinguish red from other colors.

For a hunting animal it is also important to have a wide visual field. The visual field of dogs is 250°, compared with 180° for humans (Walls 1942). Certainly on arctic tundra, barren-ground, and prairies such a wide field would be of great value.

Audition

The auditory system is important to wolves primarily for communication with conspecifics including both other pack members and neighboring packs (Theberge and Falls 1967, Harrington and Mech 1979, Klinghammer and Laidlaw 1979, Field 1979, Schassburger 1987). Conceivably hearing plays some role in hunting, but if so, little if any information on such a role is available.

Many aspects of sound perception and processing have been studied in various canids. Peterson et al. (1969) reported auditory upper limits of 80 kHz for the coyote (*Canis latrans*), 65 kHz for the red fox (*Vulpes vulpes*), and 60 kHz for the dog (greyhound). Other estimates of upper limits determined for the dog are 40 kHz (Spector 1956), and 41–47 kHz for five different breeds (Heffner 1983). The different

reported levels are likely to be due to differences in experimental methods and intensities (decibels) of the sounds delivered. In terms of selective pressure, an argument could be made that the upper auditory limit for the wolf is closer to that of the coyote (80 kHz; see above) than of the dog.

For comparison, the upper auditory limits for humans and chimpanzees are 20 kHz and 33 kHz, respectively (Spector, 1956). The slightly higher upper limit for the red fox, compared to the dog, may reflect its greater dependence on rodent prey. In studies of carnivores, Peterson et al. (1969) found similarities among species within a genus but not among genera, suggesting that extrapolations beyond the genus are less reliable.

Auditory thresholds at the frequency of 100 hertz are comparable at 34 decibels for the dog, 38 for the cat and 37 for humans (Spector 1956). However, at frequencies above 5 kHz, the thresholds for dogs and cats are much lower than for humans, reflecting their superior hearing abilities in this range. The dog's ability to hear sounds at higher frequencies (i.e., above 2.5 kHz) becomes increasingly greater than man's (Fuller and DuBuis 1962).

The high-frequency limit of hearing has been correlated with the functional distance between the ears (Heffner and Masterton 1980). Thus, larger species with more widely spaced ears have a more restricted upper limit. In addition, species with larger ears are better able to hear lower sounds (Fleischer 1978). Interestingly, though, within a species, the correlation does not hold (Heffner 1983). Thus, species-specific factors other than ear placement must be associated with frequencies perceived.

According to Andreev (1925, cited in Fuller and DuBuis 1962), dogs can distinguish between pitches one tone apart on the musical scale. Such discrimination would certainly help wolves distinguish the individual howls of other wolves.

Depending on various environmental conditions, wolves apparently can hear other wolves howling at long distances. Joslin (1966) reported a maximum hearing distance of 6.4 km, and Harrington and Mech (1979) 6.4–9.6 km.

Taste

Because investigations of taste can be confounded by the influence of smell, it can be difficult to properly evaluate the significance of taste as a sensory modality. A study of dogs indicated that olfaction plays a limited role in food preferences, suggesting the independent importance of taste (Houpt et al. 1978). Nevertheless, dogs trained as flavor validators could no longer perform the tasks for which they had been trained when rendered peripherally anosmic by tracheostomy or zinc sulfate treatment (Houpt et al. 1982), emphasizing the strong association of these two senses.

Dogs possess receptors for all four major categories of taste, i.e., salt, bitter, acid, and sweet (Appelberg 1958) (Table 1). In contrast, cats do not respond to sweet tastes,

Table 1. Responses of the chimpanzee, cat, and dog to compounds representing the four major groups of taste receptors.

Category	Compound	Chimpanzee	Cat	Dog
Salty	NaCl	+	+	+
Bitter	Quinine	+	+	+
Sour	Acetic acid	+	+	+
Sweet	Saccharose	+	-	+
"	Glycerine	+	-	+
"	Saccharine	+	-	+

(Adapted from Appelberg 1958)

suggesting that, being exclusively carnivorous, cats have little need to be able to perceive sweetness. However, because canids consume berries, sweet taste receptors would be adaptive. Wolves, for example, are known to eat raspberries (*Rubus* sp.) (Van Ballenberghe et al. 1975) as well as blueberries (*Vaccinium* spp.) and strawberries (*Fragaria* spp.) (Fritts and Mech 1981). Noncontrolled experiments with captive wolves and with habituated wild wolves (Mech 1988b) indicate that wolves consume artificial food (i.e., dog food and human food) containing all four major taste categories.

Olfaction

If any one sense is more important to a carnivore for hunting than any other, it is olfaction. However, to human beings, olfaction is probably the most difficult to understand because of the limited olfactory capacity of the human. For example, hunting dogs have been reported to follow a scent trail in the right direction. Such a feat implies that hours, or sometimes days, after a trail is laid, the dog can distinguish an odor-gradient difference of only a few seconds. Wolves are likely to be at least as competent.

Olfaction, like vision, is important to wolves not only for hunting but also for social communication. Scent-marking with urine and feces plays a strong role in the life of wolves (Peters and Mech 1975, Mech and Peters 1977, Rothman and Mech 1979, Asa et al. 1985a,b, 1986, 1990, Raymer et al. 1984, 1985, 1986). Thus, wolves can be assumed to possess especially keen olfactory abilities.

The sense of smell is generally believed to be the most highly developed sense in dogs (Rosengren 1969). It has also been the most thoroughly studied, primarily because of the use of dogs in hunting and tracking and in detecting everything from illicit drugs to land mines.

In testing dogs for olfactory acuity, the dynamics of olfactory perception probably affect the results. For example, in humans and presumably other mammals, the perceived intensity of an odorant declines after prolonged exposure (Köster 1971, cited in Moulton and Marshall 1976). In addition, the speed of adaptation and of recovery from adaptation varies by odorant and increases with stimulus intensity.

Adaptation can help an animal attend to newer or more salient odors in its environment, in effect, filtering out background and older scents. Mech (unpubl. data) watched an alpha female wolf cross a pile of fresh garbage through which he had walked to a blind an hour or so earlier and saw the wolf stop when she reached his trail; the wolf would not cross Mech's trail but rather circled behind the blind to go around the trail. This observation suggests that the wolf was able to distinguish Mech's trail from all the other odors in the garbage.

Certainly a dog's ability to discriminate among odors is extremely fine. The animals can even distinguish between members of sets of twins. Although the dogs tested in such an experiment chose interchangeably when twins were presented separately, the dogs could distinguish between them when the twins were presented together (Kalmus 1955). These results suggest that the odor signature of twins is so similar that the dogs had trouble distinguishing between them unless both individuals were present for comparison.

The biological relevance of test odorants is also a factor in olfactory discrimination. For instance, dogs cannot distinguish among strong floral scents, a discrimination easily performed by humans. However, dogs can discriminate among animal odorants much better than humans can (Henning 1920, cited in Rosengren 1969, Becker et al. 1962).

Although there is some disagreement regarding olfactory thresholds of dogs as compared to humans, these differences

The auditory system is important to wolves for communication with conspecifics, both within packs and between packs. Much of howling in wolves is still not clearly understood. (Photo: L.D. Mech)

may be due to differences in experimental design and use of biologically relevant test odorants (Moulton et al. 1960, Becker et al. 1962). In any case, systematic investigations have found dogs to be 100 to 10,000 times more sensitive than humans at detecting odorants (Neuhaus 1953, Moulton and Marshall 1976, Marshall and Moulton 1981).

Dogs can detect human fingerprints on glass slides for up to six weeks. In such tests, when the slides were kept outdoors, all fingerprints were detected during the first week, with some mistakes during the second week; no fingerprint was detected after three weeks (King et al. 1964). Unfortunately, relevant information on weather during the trials was not reported. Scenting conditions are best when the ground temperature is greater than air temperature, a situation most commonly found in the evening (Budgett 1933, cited in King et al. 1964), a time favored for hunting by many animals.

Acuity studies indicate that dogs cannot detect fingerprints on completely wet slides. Detection is better on dull, rainless days than on bright, sunny days, and ambient temperature (range not given) is unimportant to detection ability. The volatile, short-chain fatty acids (compounds found, for example, in human sweat) were detected by dogs in the field for six to nine hours (Budgett 1933, cited in King et al. 1964).

Marshall and Moulton (1981) explained the superior olfactory abilities of dogs compared with humans by pointing out that, although the same proportion (1–2%) of molecules that enter the nose reach receptors in each species; 1) dogs have a much greater olfactory receptor area; 2) they probably have proportionately more active receptors, so a molecule is much more apt to reach a binding site; 3) their olfactory bulbs are much larger; 4) dogs can discriminate among different odors and can resolve complex mixtures

into components; and 5) the resulting increased reliance of dogs on olfaction may result in more efficient sniffing and attending to odors.

The relative roles of the main and accessory olfactory systems in wolf communication have not been clearly distinguished. The accessory system, which receives signals from the vomeronasal organ (VNO), is thought to mediate sexual response (Estes 1972, Scalia and Winans 1975, Wysocki 1979). In many mammals, flehmen, or lip curl, is thought to introduce relevant molecules from urine or glandular secretions into the VNO. Although wolves and other canids do not flehm, they rapidly and repeatedly press the tongue against the roof of the mouth just behind the front teeth, the site of the nasopalatine ducts which open into the nasal cavity near the VNO (Asa unpubl. data).

Pathways from the VNO via the accessory olfactory bulb reach areas of the brain associated with sexual behavior and stimulation of gonadotrophic hormones. In sexually naive male wolves, surgical transection that blocked both the main and accessory olfactory systems without removing vomeronasal organs interfered with the ability of the wolves to court and mate (Asa et al. 1986). However, removal of only the vomeronasal organs did not affect sexual behavior (Wysocki, Monell Chemical Senses Center, Philadelphia; Asa; Mech; and Seal, VA Medical Center, Minneapolis, unpubl. data). These results suggest that the main, not the accessory, olfactory system is important to sexual response in naive male wolves.

Biologists have long been puzzled by the functional significance and stimulus mechanism of the rolling response common in wolves as well as other canids. Because the behavior is best elicited by pungent odors and involves what appears to be a fixed-action-pattern response, involvement of the accessory olfactory system was suspected. However, even following VNO removal, wolves continued to respond to a fish emulsion by stereotypical rolling, whereas wolves with transmission to the main olfactory system blocked (Asa et al. 1986) did not (Asa, unpubl. data).

Of hypotheses explaining the functional significance of rolling in pungent odors, the suggestion that rolling serves to cover the wolf in a masking scent seems most likely. The more-entertaining-than-plausible interpretation provided by Gary Larson is presented by a cartoon in which a male dog arrives for a date with a female dog with bouquet in hand and exclaims when she appears at the door, "Oh Ginger you look absolutely stunning... and whatever you rolled in sure does stink."

Acknowledgments
We thank the St. Louis Zoological Park, the U.S. Fish and Wildlife Service, and the North Central Forest Experiment Station for support of this work. D. Boyd and L. Rogers reviewed an earlier draft of the manuscript and offered helpful suggestions for improvement.

Pack Structure And Genetic Relatedness Among Wolf Packs in a Naturally-Regulated Population

■ **Thomas J. Meier, John W. Burch, L. David Mech, and Layne G. Adams**

Observations of wolf pack dynamics over a six-year period in Denali National Park and Preserve, Alaska, found high rates of intraspecific strife, wolf pack dissolution and new pack formation, and the acceptance of new wolves into established packs. These observations corroborate genetic studies that found more genetic links between packs, and more genetic diversity within packs, than would be expected if most packs were composed of an unrelated breeding pair and their offspring. Longevity of packs, stability of pack territories, and the incidence of inbreeding all appear to be less than previously suggested, even in the absence of significant human disturbance. The formation of new packs by two or more local dispersers, the acceptance of unrelated wolves into existing packs, and the presence of multiple breeding females within packs would tend to blur genetic distinctions between the packs in a population.

Introduction

Wolf (*Canis lupus*) packs are generally thought to consist of a breeding pair of wolves and their offspring from several years (Mech 1970). Many of these offspring eventually disperse from their natal territory (Fritts and Mech 1981, Peterson et al. 1984, Mech 1987, Ballard et al. 1987, Fuller 1989, Gese and Mech 1991), and form new packs when they locate dispersers of the opposite sex and a vacant area to set up a territory (Rothman and Mech 1979). When a breeding pack member is lost, it may be replaced from within the pack, or by a disperser from another pack (Rothman and Mech 1979, Fritts and Mech 1981, Mech and Hertel 1983, Peterson et al. 1984, Fuller 1989). If dispersal distances were consistently long, so that few wolves who left their natal pack settled nearby, the social system could lead to a mosaic of packs in which genetic relatedness between wolves in the same pack is high (except between the two breeding wolves) and relatedness between wolves in adjacent or nearby packs is low (Woolpy and Eckstrand 1979). A pattern of genetic isolation between neighboring wolf packs has been suggested as an adaptive mechanism in the evolution of wolves (Haber 1977, Shields 1983).

By using mitochondrial DNA analysis and nuclear DNA "genetic fingerprinting," Lehman et al. (1992) found that the degree of relatedness among members of neighboring packs varies among wolf populations. In Denali National Park, Alaska, and the adjacent Preserve, wolves from different packs often showed high levels of genetic similarity, suggesting they were related at the sibling or parent/offspring level (Fig. 1). The frequency of such similarities between wolves in different packs was higher in a Minnesota wolf population, and lower in a Northwest Territories population. In all three populations, some packs contained additional wolves that were not the offspring of a single breeding pair.

Sibling or parent/offspring relatedness among wolves in neighboring packs could result from new packs being formed by wolves dispersing from a nearby pack (Rothman and Mech 1979, Fritts and Mech 1981, Peterson et al. 1984, Mech 1987, Fuller 1989, Hayes et al. 1991, Ream et al. 1991), splitting of existing packs (Jordan et al. 1967, Carbyn 1975, Haber 1977, Mech 1986), or by packs adopting wolves from neighboring packs (Rothman and Mech 1979, Fritts and Mech 1981, Van Ballenberghe 1983a, Peterson et al. 1984, Messier 1985b, Ballard et al. 1987, Fuller 1989, Hayes et al. 1991).

The presence of wolves not related to breeding animals in a pack could result from the adoption of unrelated wolves, the founding of a pack by a group of three or more wolves (Peterson et al. 1984, Messier 1985b, Fuller 1989, Mech and Nelson 1989, 1990a, Ream et al. 1991), or the presence of more than one breeding female in a pack (Murie 1944, Rausch 1967, Carbyn 1975, Haber 1977, Peterson 1977, Harrington et al. 1982, Van Ballenberghe 1983b, Peterson et al. 1984, Ballard et al. 1987, Clarkson and Liepins 1991).

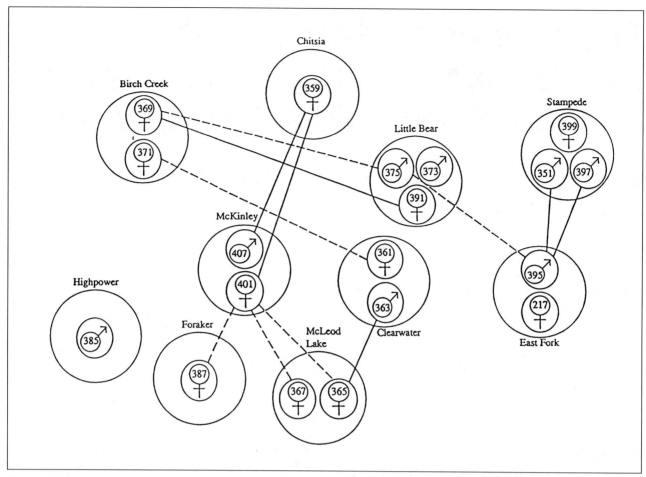

Fig. 1 *Interpack connections suggested by high VNTR ("genetic fingerprint") similarities among Denali wolves. The interpack connections are indicated by lines connecting individuals. Solid lines denote similarities greater than 2.29 standard errors above the mean value for unrelated individuals ($S_{unrelated}$) in the population. Dashed lines indicate connections between 1.52 and 2.29 standard errors above $S_{unrelated}$). Packs are in relative geographic positions, but distances are not to scale. (After Lehman et al. 1992).*

Changes in pack composition and territories resulting from intraspecific strife (Jordan et al. 1967, Wolfe and Allen 1973, Van Ballenberghe and Erickson 1973, Mech 1977b, Fuller and Keith 1980, Carbyn 1981, Fritts and Mech 1981, Ballard et al. 1987, Fuller 1989) may tend to increase new pack formation and favor other social changes that increase relatedness between packs, and decrease relatedness within packs.

Although all of these phenomena have been reported from various wolf populations, no study has documented their frequency and other details in a natural (unharvested) wolf population over a long period of time. We describe the social dynamics of an increasing wolf population in Denali National Park and Preserve (Denali), Alaska from January 1986 through May 1992, during a time when the population's genetic structure was also assessed (Lehman et al. 1992 and Fig. 1).

Study Area

Wolf packs were studied in and adjacent to Denali National Park and Preserve, north of the Alaska Range (Fig. 2). This 15,000 km² area is bounded on the south by the Alaska Range, and includes several outer ranges of hills ≤2,000 metres, partly forested glacial valleys, and a large area of forested lowlands. During the study, the area contained about 2,000 moose (*Alces alces*) (Meier 1987, Meier et al. 1991), 2,000 Dall sheep (*Ovis dalli*) (Singer et al. 1981, Taylor et al. 1988), 3,000 caribou (*Rangifer tarandus*) of the Denali Herd (Adams et al. 1989a), and part of the range of the 1,500 caribou of the Tonzona Herd (Shults and Adams 1990). Wolves are legally protected from human harvest in the wilderness area of Denali (the original Mount McKinley National Park), or 5,600 km² of the study area. They are subject to subsistence trapping by a small number of local residents in the 1980 park additions (5,800 km²), and to subsistence and sport hunting and trapping in the preserve

Table 1. Late-winter population data based on radio-collared wolf packs in Denali National Park and Preserve, Alaska, 1986–1992.

YEAR	*No. of Packs*	*No. of Wolves*	*Total[1] area (km²)*	*Wolves/ 1,000 km²*
1986	3	22	4,288	5.1
1987	7	33	8,130	4.1
1988	12	63	13,489	4.7
1989	13	101	13,686	7.4
1990	13	113	13,956	8.1
1991	12	88	11,839	7.4
1992	12	84	11,839	7.1

1   The sum of territory sizes minus any overlap between territories.

(2,800 km²) and surrounding areas. Only three wolves were known to have been killed by humans in Denali park and preserve areas north of the Alaska Range between 1986 and 1992.

Methods

Wolves were captured by aerial darting (n = 102), snaring (n = 4) and trapping (n = 1), in and around Denali. Captured wolves were fitted with radio-collars. Blood samples from 19 wolves from 10 packs, captured between December 1988 and March 1990, were tested for mitochondrial DNA and genetic fingerprinting information; another three wolves were tested only for mitochondrial DNA type (Lehman et al. 1992). Wolves were located by aerial radio-tracking an average of once every 10 days. Pack territory sizes were determined annually by calculating the area of the smallest convex polygon including all pack locations (excluding obvious, major extraterritorial forays) for the calendar year and the previous winter (e.g., October 1987–December 1988). Wolf densities were calculated by dividing the total number of wolves in the study packs for a given year by the sum of the territory sizes for those packs, minus any areas of overlap between territories.

Results

Of 107 wolves captured during this study, 55 were females and 52 were males. Based on dentition and morphology, the sample was estimated to include 44 adults, six adults or yearlings, 20 yearlings, nine yearlings or pups, and 28 pups. We often tried to capture particular adult wolves, and vulnerability to capture varies between age classes, so the sample is not representative of the population sex and age structure.

Radio-collared wolves included members of 25 different packs at the time of capture, although not all of these packs existed at the same time and six lived mostly or entirely outside the park/preserve boundary. Three wolves were dispersing or living alone when captured.

Radio-collared wolves were located 5,154 times between March 1986 and April 1992. Between three and 13 packs were monitored each year (Table 1). Estimated areas of pack territories were based on 16 to 190 ($\bar{x}$ = 60) unique pack locations per year. The size of territories defined by a low number (≤30) of locations that were inside the known pack territory mosaic was estimated by including the interstices between territory boundaries (spaces between packs in Figure 2). Late-winter density of wolves in the study area increased from 4.1 to 8.1 wolves per 1,000 km² between 1987 and 1990 (Table 1), as mean territory size decreased from 1,161 km² to 1,074 km², and mean pack size increased from 4.7 to 8.7 wolves. Densities were minimum estimates that did not include dispersing wolves or undetected new pairs. Resident lone wolves were not seen in the population.

Denali wolves inhabited relatively exclusive territories, similar to those seen in temperate, forested areas (Mech 1973, Van Ballenberghe et al. 1975, Fritts and Mech 1981, Peterson et al. 1984, Mech 1986, Fuller 1989). Nonetheless, the territory boundaries of all packs appeared to fluctuate over time, which is probably the norm for even highly territorial wolves (Mech 1977c, Potvin 1988, Ream et al. 1991).

An average of 22% of radio-collared wolves died each year, while 15% were known to disperse from the packs in which they were first captured, and 8% disappeared (either dispersed or the collar failed) per year. Of 31 radio-collared wolves that died within the study area, at least 52% (from 10 different packs) were killed by neighboring wolf packs,

Table 2. Summary of information on wolf pack dissolution: Denali National Park and Preserve, Alaska, 1986–1992.

Pack	*Longevity*	*Fate of Members*
Headquarters	≥ 1 year, probably an old pack	6 members in spring 1986 205 F killed by wolves April 1986 231 M dispersed October 1986 219 F dispersed February 1987 241 F killed by wolves March 1987 1 other died/dispersed by March 1987 251 M remained, paired in June 1987 and re-founded pack (Table 3)

Bearpaw	≥ 2 years	10 members in Fall 1987
		259 M killed by wolves January 1988
		261 F killed by wolves March 1988
		313 F killed by wolves March 1988
		6 others died or dispersed, 1 survivor
		    may have remained in area.
		Replaced by Chitsia Mountain Pack,
		    Spring 1989

Castle Rocks	9 months	8 members in Fall 1988 333 F killed by wolves November 1988 335 M killed by wolves November 1988 6 pups starved Replaced by Foraker Pack, Fall 1988.

Pirate Creek	14 months	9 members in Fall 1988
		339 F died of disease/malnutrition,
		    November 1988
		Fate of others unknown
		Area occupied by two neighboring packs
		    Winter 1988-89.

Clearwater	≥ 3.5 years	6 members in Fall 1986 223 M killed by wolves January 1989 227 F killed by wolves April 1989 363 M died of unkonwn causes December 1989 361 F dissappeared December 1989 Pups starved, Winter 1988-89 Replaced by Little Bear Pack, 1989
Stampede	2 years	9 members in Febraury 1990 349 M killed in avalanche February 1990 351 F killed in avalanche February 1990 399 F pup shot September 1990 397 M dispersed to McKinley R. Pack, May 1990 3-4 others died/dispersed; 1 or 2 may have remained in area

1   Wolves identified by number were radio-collared individuals

and another 39% died from various natural causes, some of which may also have been wolf kills. Harvest outside the park/preserve boundary accounted for the remaining 10% of mortality among radio-collared wolves that remained in the study area.

Six study packs disintegrated after the death of one or more members from natural causes (Table 2). All were replaced by newly formed packs. Many other new pairs and larger social groups formed, but did not persist (Table 3).

New Pack Formation

We knew of 16 new wolf pairs or packs that formed within Denali during the study (Table 3). These were detected when one or more of the wolves was already radio-collared (n = 9), or when a new pack was discovered by snow-tracking in a formerly vacant area (n = 7). Two new pairs died out without producing pups, five produced pups but did not successfully establish a territory, and nine succeeded in producing pups and founding packs that persisted for at least one year. The only similar information of which we are aware is for a Minnesota wolf population, where 67% of 15 adult dispersers, 31% of 26 yearling dispersers, and 25% of eight dispersing pups succeeded in settling, pairing, and denning (Gese and Mech 1991). No data on pup production were available.

At least seven of nine successful new packs were formed adjacent to or partly inside the natal territory of a founding member, a process we refer to as pack "budding." One pack, the McKinley River Pack, budded three new packs (the Chitsia Mountain, Foraker River, and Chilchukabena packs) on the edge of its territory over a three-year period, relinquishing some territory to each (Fig. 2). The Foraker River Pack in turn produced a daughter pack, the Slippery Creek Pack, three years after its formation.

In at least one case, the colonization of an adjacent area immediately followed the demise of the formerly resident pack. The Bearpaw Pack was first instrumented in April 1987 and consisted of seven black and three gray wolves. Between January and March 1988, all three radio-collared Bearpaw wolves were killed by the all-gray McKinley River Pack, which entered the Bearpaw territory and remained there for much of the winter. At least one noncollared Bearpaw wolf was wounded, and other pack members probably dispersed or were killed. Two radio-collared McKinley River wolves, joined by two other wolves of unknown origin including a black wolf that may have originated from the Bearpaw Pack, remained in the Bearpaw territory to found the Chitsia Mountain Pack. The Chitsia Mountain wolves occupied virtually the same territory, and later used the same den, as the defunct Bearpaw Pack.

Two of the new packs that arose from the McKinley River pack were founded by three or more wolves (Table 3). Both the Chitsia Mountain and Chilchukabena packs began with at least one radio-collared McKinley River wolf, one black wolf not of McKinley River origin, and one gray wolf of unknown origin. In other cases, all of the founding members of a new pack appeared to come from the same parent pack.

Pack Splitting

Two large wolf packs split into approximately equal halves, subdividing their original territories. The McLeod Lake Pack of 15 wolves split, in early May 1991, into an eastern group of eight wolves, including the alpha male, and a western group of seven wolves including two young radio-collared females. The alpha female in the original McLeod Lake Pack had died in October 1990, prior to the split. Both packs produced pups in summer 1991 and included 13 and 11 members, respectively, in fall. Although they were once observed within 1.6 kilometres of each other, the two packs occupied separate territories and apparently did not associate.

The Birch Creek Pack also split, in January 1991. This pack of 20 or more wolves split into a northern group of 11 wolves, including two radio-collared adult females, and a southern group of nine, including a radio-collared adult female and a radio-collared yearling male. Both packs were thought to have denned in summer 1991, although pup production was verified only in the southern pack. As with the McLeod Lake Pack, the territory of the original pack was split between the two groups, and no further contact between them was observed.

Adoption of Strange Wolves into Packs

Perhaps the most unusual social interactions we have observed involved strange wolves joining established packs. Eight such cases were noted, with five of the eight involving young male wolves being accepted into existing packs (Table 4). Three cases could have involved a wolf returning to his natal pack after an unsuccessful pairing attempt (Mech and Seal 1987).

Four other instances of adoption involved wolves of known origin and age, with no known history of contact with the packs they eventually settled in. In at least two of the four cases, the newcomer entered as a subordinate, rather than replacing a lost alpha wolf, which distinguishes this type of adoption from those reported by Rothman and Mech (1979) and Fritts and Mech (1981). The only female known to be adopted into another pack was captured as an adult in the Foraker Pack at a time when that pack was thought to consist only of the radio-collared alpha female, an adult male, and their six-month-old pups. On two occasions, adopted wolves entered packs near the time when similar-aged wolves born into the pack dispersed (Table 4). Most reports of the acceptance of strange wolves into packs have been from populations with high harvests, where disrupted pack structures would seem more likely to favor new social arrangements (Van Ballenberghe 1983a, Ballard et al. 1987). In Denali, however, wolves were accepted into intact, long-established packs, new packs with a single generation of pups, and

Table 3. Summary of information on wolf pair and new pack formation (Fig. 2), Denali National Park and Preserve, Alaska, 1986–1991.

Pack Name	Founded	Founders[1,2] Identity/Origin	Type	Location[2]	Longevity/Fate[1]
Sushana	< Dec. 86	235 F/unknown 237 M/unknown	new pair	vacant area	235 killed by wolves 237 to TH pack
Headquarters	Mar. 87	251 M/HQ Pack 307 F/unknown	pack reformed	HQ Pack territory	pack survived at least five years
Pirate Creek	Sept. 87	250 M/CW Pack 339 F/unknown	new pair/ budded	edge of CW territory	339 died — disease others' fate unknown
Castle Rocks	< Mar. 88	333 F/unknown 335 M/unknown	new pair	between ML and HP packs	333 and 335 killed by wolves, pups starved
Stampede	< Mar. 88	349 F/unknown 351 M/unknown	new pair	vacant area	349, 351 killed in avalanche, others died or dispersed
Little Bear	1988	gray M/unknown gray F/unknown	new pair?	replaced CW pack	pack survived at least three years
Foraker	Aug. 88	321 F/MR Pack gray M/unknown	new pair/ budded	edge of MR territory	301 died natural causes, pack survived at least four years
Swift Fork	< Oct. 88	353 M/unknown 355 F/unknown	new pair	vacant area?	355 killed by wolves 353 unknown natural death
Chitsia Mtn.	Dec. 88	359 F/unknown 315 M/MR Pack 379 M/MR Pack black M/unknown gray ?/unknown	budded	edge of MR territory	379 dispersed pack survived at least 3 years
Nenana Canyon	Apr. 90	311 M/HQ Pack gray F/unknown	new pair	between HQ and EC territories	311 dispersed others' fate unknown
Chilchu- kabena	Sept. 90	407 M/MR Pack 439 F/unknown gray ?/unknown gray ?/unknown	budded	edge of MR territory	407 killed by wolves pack survived at least 1.5 years
Myrtle Hill	Nov. 90	217 F/EF Pack gray M/unknown	budded	edge of EF territory	217 killed by wolves other' fate unknown
Stampede 2	Mar. 91	427 F/unknown 429 M/unknown 437 M/LB Pack 455 M/unknown gray ?/unknown	pack reformed	vacant area?	427 snared 437 dispersed three wolves still present 4-92
Birch Cr. N.	Jan 91	347 F/BC Pack 369 F/BC Pack 7 other wolves	pack split	half of BC territory	347 snared 369 killed by wolves
Slippery Cr.	Apr. 91	441 M/FR Pack 495 F/unknown	new pair/ budded	between MR and FR territories	pack survived at least one year
McLeod L. West	May 91	367 F/ML Pack 409 F/ML Pack +5 other wolves	pack split	half of ML territory	pack survived at least one year

1 Wolves identified by number were radio-collared individuals
2 BC = Birch Creek Pack, CW = Clearwater Pack, EC = Ewe Creek Pack; EF = East Fork Pack; FR = Foraker River Pack, HP = - Highpower Pack; HQ = Headquarters Pack; LB = Little Bear Pack; ML = McLeod Lake Pack; MR = McKinley River Pack, TH = Totek Hills Pack.

remnants of once-larger packs (Table 4). One wolf remained in the adopting pack for one year, then paired off and denned on the edge of that pack's territory.

The breeding success of other adopted wolves is not yet known, but at least two are thought to have become breeding pack members. Ten of 21 radio-collared wolves forming new pairs were alive one year after pair formation, whereas five of six wolves accepted into existing packs prior to 1992 lived for at least one year afterward. These sample sizes are too small to demonstrate a significant difference in survival (P> 0.10).

Multiple Litters in Packs

At least nine cases of multiple litters being born into the same pack in a given summer were seen, with one pack having as many as three litters in a summer and two packs raising as many as 12 pups (Table 5). Multiple litters were seen in packs occupying all habitat types used by wolves in the park and preserve.

Discussion

Lehman et al. (1992) found that 53% (10 of 19) of Denali wolves tested showed sibling- or parent/offspring-level genetic similarity to wolves in other packs in the population. An additional five (26%) showed lower (cousin-level) simi-

larity. Nine of 10 packs tested showed at least one such genetic tie to another pack, although the 19 wolves tested represented <13% of the 176 wolves in study packs during that period. Thus, many more genetic links probably existed undetected, although many of the wolves tested were breeding wolves or pack founders and the incidence of genetic ties among them could be greater than for the general population.

Our observations of new-pack formation, pack splitting, and acceptance of strange wolves into packs demonstrated a minimum of 28 close genetic connections among wolf packs in this population. Not all of these connections existed at once, because of the turnover of both individual wolves and whole packs in the population. Of 31 radio-collared wolves in the study area as of January 1992, 11 (35%) were living in a pack other than the one they were first captured from.

Most of the genetic similarities found by Lehman et al. (1992) (Fig. 1) are congruent with our behavioral observations. Clearwater wolf number 363, which was thought to have come from the McLeod Lake Pack, showed high genetic similarity to a McLeod Lake wolf. Both the Foraker and Chitsia Mountain Packs budded off from the McKinley River Pack, and the wolves in these packs that were tested resembled McKinley River wolves genetically, although those particular individuals were of unknown origin. The Little Bear and Stampede packs originated during this study, and their genetic links to more established packs (Birch

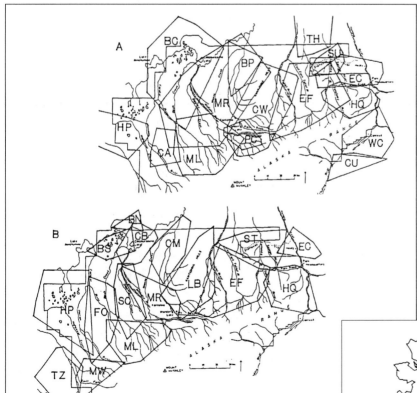

Fig. 2 *Minimum wolf pack territories, Denali National Park and Preserve: A: 1987–1988; B: 1991–1992. BC = Birch Creek Pack, BN = Birch Creek North Pack; BP = Bearpaw Pack; BS = Birch Creek South Pack; CA = Castle Rocks Pack; CB = Chilchukabena Pack; CM = Chitsia Mountain Pack; CU = Chulitna River Pack; CW = Clearwater Pack; EC = Ewe Creek Pack; EF = East Fork Pack; FO = Foraker River Pack; HP = Highpower Pack; HQ = Headquarters Pack; LB = Little Bear Pack; ML = McLeod Lake Pack; MR = McKinley River Pack; MW = McLeod Lake West Pack; PC = Pirate Creek Pack; SC = Slippery Creek Pack; ST = Stampede Pack; SU = Sushana River Pair; TH = Totek Hills Pack; TZ = Tonzona River Pack; WC = Windy Creek Pack.*

Table 4. Acceptance of wolves into established packs, Denali National Park and Preserve, Alaska.

	Adoptee				Adopting Pack				
No.	Sex	Age[1]	Origin	Date	Name	Size	Age[2]	Composition[3]	Duration/Outcome
237	M	2	Sushana	03/87	Totek Hills	15	?	Unknown	returning to natal pack? remained at least 3 years.
363	M	2	McLeod L.	03/89	Clearwater	2	3+	F adult 237 F yrl 361	became only male in pack
311	M	2	Clearwater	03/89	Headquarters	7	1	M adult 251 F adult 307 5 pups	2 pups disappeared about the same time. Remained 1 year, paired/dispersed
387	F	2	unkown	F 89	Foraker	6	1	F adult 321 M adult 4 pups	with pack 2+ years, bred in 1991
397	M	1	Stampede	09/90	McKinley R.	8	3+	F adult 401 others unkn.	remained at least 1.5 yrs 2-year-old male 407 left the pack the same month 397 joined it.
385	M	2	Highpower	05/91	Foraker R.	4	2	F adult 387 others unkn.	remained at least 1 year
429	M	3	Stampede?	02/92	Totek Hills	10+	4+	M adult 455 others unkn.	returning to natal pack?
455	M	4	Stampede?	02/92	Totek Hills	10+	4+	M adult 429 others unkn.	returning to natal pack?

1   Wolf ages based on estimated age at capture.
2   Pack age: minimum duration of pack (in years) prior to this event.
3   Wolves identified by number were radio-collared individuals

Table 5. Multiple-denning wolf packs, Denali National Park and Preserve, Alaska.

Pack	Year	Litters	Females[1]	Pups	Evidence
East Fork	1988	2	1080, ?	12	2 active dens observed
Birch Creek	1988	2	?, ?	12	large number of pups
East Fork	1989	2	1080, 217	10	2 active dens observed
East Fork	1990	3	1080, 217, ?	9	3 active dens observed
Headquarters	1990	2	307, ?	5	2 active dens observed
McLeod Lake	1990	2	309, 367, ?	11	5 pups seen earlier
Windy Creek	1990	2	377, ?	9	large number of pups
East Fork	1991	2	1080, ?	3	2 active dens observed
Little Ber	1991	2	?, ?	11	2 den areas, large number of pups.

1   Wolves identified by number were radio-collared individuals.

Creek and East Fork) are probably indicative of the source of their founding members. Relatedness among longer-established packs (Clearwater and Birch Creek, McLeod Lake and McKinley River) was less [genetic similarities were at the lower, "cousin" level of Lehman et al. (1992)], and probably dated to older colonization events.

One putative genetic link seems unrealistic: male pups, numbers 395 and 397, appeared to be related at the sibling level. However, our observations suggested that they were born into the East Fork and Stampede packs, respectively. The nature of the testing method and of genetic inheritance dictates that various pairs of individuals will show genetic similarity higher or lower than their actual pedigrees would predict (Lehman et al. 1992). Numerical values produced by this method cannot be interpreted unequivocally. Additionally, if the Stampede Pack was originally formed from an incestuous mating between two members of the adjacent East Fork Pack, wolf number 395 could have been a sibling to both, and a "double uncle" to wolf number 397, as close genetically as a sibling.

Among the within-pack genetic relationships found by Lehman et al. (1992) were two pairs of young female wolves showing low relatedness. Both packs had contained more than one breeding female in previous years, so the tested pairs could have had different mothers.

Multiple litters are probably more common than thought (Harrington et al. 1982), and appear to be a long-term pattern for wolves in at least one part of Denali (Murie 1944, Haber 1977, and Table 5). We observed or inferred the existence of multiple litters in six packs (Table 5). These multiple litters occurred during a time of increasing wolf density, an apparently adequate food supply, and often following severe winters when numerous multiple kills were seen (Mech et al., this volume). A plentiful food supply around the time of breeding might make breeding between subordinate wolves more likely, whether inhibition of breeding is mediated by behavior or physiology (Packard and Mech 1980).

The budding of a new pack on the perimeter of an established pack's range has obvious reproductive value for breeding wolves, and may even reduce interpack strife by replacing hostile, unrelated neighbors with relatives and former associates. However, observations of wolves being killed by close relatives on Isle Royale (Jordan et al. 1967, Peterson 1977) suggest that former associations or close genetic relatedness (Wayne et al. 1991) do not necessarily prevent strife when wolves meet again. We saw no cases of reassociation between packs that had separated, and the incidence of reintegration of a dispersed wolf back into its natal pack appeared no more common than the acceptance of total strangers.

The splitting of a pack, with subdivision of the territory, may ease social and nutritional stress in a large group, and may allow more efficient use of available prey (Murie 1944, Mech 1966a, Haber 1977). The McLeod Lake territory had become elongated as the pack expanded its travels farther

southwestward along the Alaska Range. The new McLeod West territory included the western part of this territory, as well as additional area outside the original McLeod Park territory. The arrangement allowed the exploitation of different moose populations and the calving grounds of two different caribou herds. Both the McLeod Lake and Birch Creek Pack splits occurred in packs with a history of multiple litters (Table 4). The McLeod Lake split was preceded by seven months by the death of the radio-collared alpha female in October 1990. Splitting in an Isle Royale wolf pack was also linked circumstantially to death of an alpha member (Jordan et al. 1967, Wolfe and Allen 1973).

It is difficult to understand the benefits of accepting an unrelated, relatively inexperienced wolf into a pack. "New blood" may allow some desirable social realignment of the pack, and certainly introduces genetic novelty if the newcomer remains to become a breeder, or pairs off with one of the pack members. Such adoptions may also be merely misplaced sociality of little adaptive significance. The occurrence of such social tolerance in a population also demonstrating widespread intraspecific strife and intolerance of strange wolves is especially puzzling.

The level of intraspecific strife seen in this study (at least 52% of all mortality of radio-collared wolves) is the highest reported in any wolf population. In most other sizeable wolf populations that have been studied, humans were the major cause of mortality. We suggest that widespread intraspecific strife and the resulting disruption of pack and population structure is a normal consequence of wolf territoriality in the absence of extensive human interference. The disintegration of six packs following the death of alpha animals provided most of the opportunities for successful new pack formation during the study (Tables 2 and 3). Mech (1977b) found that intraspecific strife resulted in the deaths of pack leaders more often than subordinate wolves, thereby maximizing disruptive effects on pack structure.

Pack budding, pack splitting, and adoption of strange wolves produce closer genetic links between members of different packs in a wolf population than would be expected if most packs originated from pairs of unrelated, distant dispersers. If adopted wolves become breeders, they could greatly decrease genetic isolation in long-established wolf packs.

Considering the limited lifespan of an individual wolf (Mech 1988a) and the potentially great lifespan of a pack, clusters of large, stable wolf packs that effectively preclude immigration could lead to inbreeding and genetic stagnation, as has been observed in a captive wolf population (Laikre and Ryman 1991) and suspected in an insular wild population (Wayne et al. 1991). However, natural mortality, the changing nutritional needs of growing or shrinking packs, and the dispersal and colonizing strategies described here seem to ensure that the characteristics of the pack-territory mosaic and the genetic makeup of packs in a thriving wolf population will not remain stable for long, contrary to earlier

Thomas J. Meier, John W. Burch, L. David Mech, and Layne G. Adams

Wolves are a highly social species and bonding among either mate begins early in life. (Photo: J. Dutcher)

claims for this same population (Haber 1977). Genetic evidence from other wolf populations also supports this view (Kennedy et al. 1991, Lehman et al. 1992).

Acknowledgments
This study was funded primarily by the U.S. National Park Service Natural Resources Preservation Program. Denali National Park, the U.S. Fish and Wildlife Service, and the USDA North Central Forest Experiment Station also contributed to the project. We especially thank A. Lovaas, J. Dalle-Molle (deceased), J. Van Horn, B. Dale, B. Shults, A. Blakesley, other employees of the National Park Service in Alaska, and pilots D. Glaser, B. Lentsch, D. Miller, S. Hamilton, and K. Butters. Sheri Forbes generously assisted with the illustrations. The assistance of numerous other volunteer technicians and professional pilots is also appreciated.

Influences of a Migratory Deer Herd on Wolf Movements and Mortality in and Near Algonquin Park, Ontario

■ Graham J. Forbes and John B. Theberge

The interaction between wolf movement, wolf mortality, and a migratory deer herd was studied over five years, from 1987 to 1991, in Algonquin Provincial Park, Ontario (7,571 km². Winter data were obtained from 38 radio-collared wolves in 22 packs for 5,405 locations. Territory size averaged 149 km², exclusive of extraterritorial movements. Mean pack size in December was 6.0 wolves and within-territory density was 4.3 wolves/100 km². Extraterritorial movements were characterized as dispersal, excursions and migrations, often related to deer migration to a wintering yard located outside of Algonquin Park. A total of 37 nondispersal movements (migrations and excursions) were recorded in two years (1990–1991, 1991–1992). Ninety-two percent of these were in groups of three or more wolves. Wolf movements were more extensive during the winters of 1990–1991 and 1991–1992 when few to no deer wintered in the park. The annual mortality rate was 30–37% and was caused mainly by humans and rabies. Mortality was often related to the deer-induced movement of park wolves out of the park; the greatest single location of wolf mortality (41%) occurred in the Round Lake deer yard. Though the population may now be stable, we discuss the potential vulnerability of the Algonquin Park wolf population in the context of protected wolves leaving park boundaries and argue for increased protection of the park population.

Introduction

In this study, we document the movement and consequences of extraterritorial activity of a protected wolf (*Canis lupus*) population in response to a deer (*Odocoileus virginanus*) migration beyond park borders. The great majority of wolf-prey studies conducted in forested environments indicate that wolves typically remain on established territories (cf. Pimlott et al. 1969, Carbyn 1981). Numerous disadvantages such as starvation and death threaten wolves traveling beyond familiar territories, so frequent long-range movement is only likely to be warranted under exceptional circumstances. Movement beyond the resident territory has been confined to dispersal or predispersal forays by sexually maturing individuals (Fritts and Mech 1981, Ballard et al. 1987, Fuller 1989, Gese and Mech 1991), whereas nondispersal movements such as extraterritorial pack or group excursions (Van Ballenberghe 1983a, Messier 1985a) have been local, short-term, and uncommonly reported. As part of an ongoing wolf-ungulate study in Algonquin Park, Ontario, we documented numerous excursions, and in some packs, the seasonal migration of wolves from Algonquin Park due to the changing availability of white-tailed deer, a

preferred prey item of Algonquin wolves (Forbes and Theberge 1992).

Mortality of animals that cross boundaries from park to private land can significantly affect park populations (Carbyn 1980, Knight and Eberhardt 1985). In the situation described here, long-range excursions by Park wolves in pursuit of migrating deer has contributed to humans being the greatest source of mortality in Algonquin Park wolves.

Study Area and Prey Base

The study was conducted from 1987 to 1992, in and near Algonquin Provincial Park, a 7,571 km² area. The park's forests are classified as a transition zone between the Boreal Forest region and the Algonquin Highlands section of the Great Lake-St. Lawrence forest region (Rowe 1972). Sugar maple (*Acer saccharum*), yellow birch (*Betula alleghaniensis*), and to a lesser extent, eastern hemlock (*Tsuga canadensis*) dominate well-drained areas, while the sandy soils on the eastern third of the park support red, white, and jack pine (*Pinus resinosa, P. banksiana, P. strobus*) and poplar species (*Populus grandidentata, P. tremuloides*). Much of the park (approximately 75%) is zoned for commercial logging using uniform shelterwood and selective harvest methods; clearcutting is a minor activity, less than 100 ha/year. The surrounding lands are either forested or support marginal agriculture. Altitude in the park varies from 180 to 380 m in the east and up to 580 m in the western uplands. Total snowfall ranges from 203 to 254 cm with greater amounts in the west. Average ambient temperature in January is -11.5°C.

Large prey of wolves in the Algonquin region include white-tailed deer, moose (*Alces alces*), and beaver (*Castor canadensis*). Deer populations have been increasing on the east side of the park, but deer typically migrate out of the park in December to a yard located 13 km southeast of the park. The yard (80km^2) supports roughly 1,500–2,500 deer, most of which originate from the park (L. Swanson, University of Waterloo, unpubl. data). Another deer yard near Black Bay, 30 km east of the Park, also attracts deer from Algonquin. The exact number of deer in this yard is not known, but is likely to be <500. Aerial deer surveys along 11, 22 km-long transects in February of 1990, 1991, 1992, and ground searches in all winters, indicated that deer were almost totally vacating the park except for two southern townships located outside our study area in the winters of 1990–1991 and 1991–1992. In 1989–1990, three small pockets of an estimated 60–100 deer remained in the park all winter. A similar situation occurred in 1988–1989 (R. Lepine, Algonquin Forestry Authority, pers. commun.). Aerial surveys for deer were not conducted in 1987–1988, but based on ground work and observations from wolf aerial work, no deer were believed to be present in the park that winter.

Average winter moose densities from 1987–1992 were estimated from aerial surveys at aerial surveys at 0.35–0.39 moose/km^2 (Ontario Ministry of Natural Resources, unpubl. data). Densities of beaver are not available, but beaver are considered common and widespread throughout the park. Some beaver are available in winter, but the numbers vary depending on the amount of open water.

We estimated 28–32 wolf packs in Algonquin Park from howling surveys and radio-tracking (Forbes and Theberge, Univ. of Waterloo, unpubl. data). Wolves and coyotes (*Canis latrans*) are present outside of Algonquin in unknown densities but coyotes have not been recorded in the park. However, coyote genes have been found in some Algonquin wolves (Lehman et al. 1991).

This study initially focused on two areas of the park: packs in the northwest section where deer were absent, and packs in the eastern third where deer were seasonally present. In 1989, the number of study packs in the northwest section was reduced by rabies, and after 1989 we were forced to focus on an intensive study area (2,380 km^2) in the eastern section (Fig. 1). The intensive study area consistently had collared packs and winter road access throughout the study period. Information on collared packs beyond the intensive study area is included as part of the extensive study area.

Commercial trapping of wolves is not allowed within the park, but outside the boundaries there are no limits or seasons. Hunting of moose and deer was not permitted in Algonquin except in 1991–1992 when local natives were granted limited hunting privileges for 3% (either sex) of the moose population and 150 deer. Tag-quotas were applied to fall-season moose and deer hunts outside of the park.

Methods

Wolves were captured in summer (May–September) along logging roads, using padded leg-hold traps (Newhouse 4, Victor 4), and immobilized with tiletamine hydrochloride and zolazepam hydrochloride (Telazol, A.H. Robins Co. Richmond, Va.). We determined sex, age, weight, and collected blood. The age of wolves was estimated from incisor wear, tooth replacement, and breeding condition. Captures were classified as pup, young (5–24 months), or adult. The young and adult wolves were radio-collared (Lotek Engineering, Aurora, Ontario) and located using fixed-wing aircraft, or from the ground. In addition to telemetry fixes, locations were derived from backtracking collared wolves, and from howls and fresh scats that could be positively attributed to a specific pack. During winter, aerial locations were made at least weekly or bi-weekly depending on weather. Telemetry efforts were also concentrated during intensive 10-day blocks of daily flights and ground checking. The block periods corresponded to early winter when deer were migrating (15 December to 5 January), mid-winter (February) and late winter (mid-March). The winter period is from 16 October to 15 April.

Each wolf location was plotted using the Universal Transverse Mercator 100m x 100m grid on 1:50,000 topographic maps, then mapped and analyzed on a rastar-based geographic information system (SPANS, Intera Tydac Inc.). Packs without collared wolves, or without a sufficient number of locations (minimum of 10) were not included in analyses. Average number of locations used in analyses was 120/year/winter. Pack size was determined for early winter (December) and late winter (mid-March) from at least three aerial or ground observations. Movements were categorized as either resident territory, or one of three types of extraterritorial activity: 1) excursions (trespassing) where wolves left resident territories for short forays (<15 km) into adjacent territories; 2) seasonal migrations (extensions) where a wolf spends an extended period (> 2 weeks) away from the resident territory then returns; and 3) dispersal, where the wolf leaves the resident territory permanently.

Wolf density was determined for within-territory and for population (intensive study area) densities. For analysis of within-territory density, the territory for each collared pack was determined using the minimum area-convex polygon technique (Mohr 1947) modified by selecting 95% of the points closest to the polygon center (Beckoff and Mech 1984, Potvin 1988). Dispersing wolves were not included in

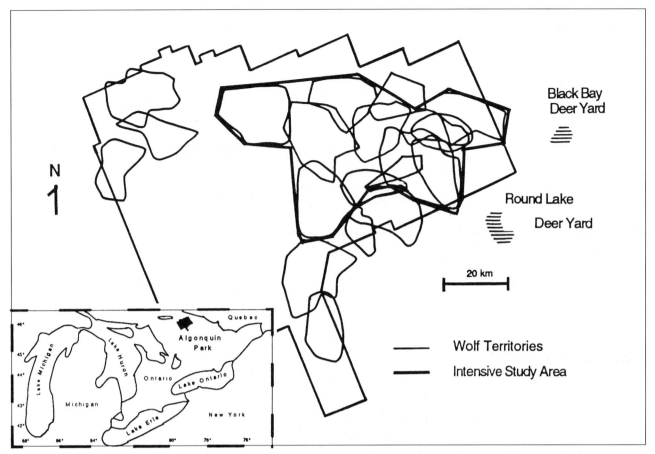

Fig. 1 *Cumulative pack data for winters 1987–1992, showing intensive study area and regional setting of Algonquin Park.*

the within-territory analysis, nor were the extraterritorial forays or seasonal extensions taken by some wolves in certain winters. Seasonal extensions by wolves to the deer yard were treated as non-territorial locations because no territories seemed to be present in, or near, the deer yard. These locations are presented as single colored dots representing different packs within the yard (Fig. 2). In winter 1991–1992, the density of wolves in the Round Lake deer yard was determined by two separate teams travelling on a small grid system of roads on 17 February and 17 March. Telemetry, howling, and track counts were used to identify minimum number and size of packs. The small area of the grid allowed us to locate the same packs from different vantage points and hence avoid duplication.

Population density also was determined from the intensive study area, including areas between individual pack territories. This analysis included extraterritorial movements and the outer 5% of the data points omitted in the minimum polygon technique. The outer boundary of the intensive study area encompasses all outer data points of collared packs that had a minimum of two years of telemetry-based data. (Several packs had limited data points for a single year and we could not confidently delineate their

territories.) Limited access to certain areas in summer, and the high incidence of mortality on collared wolves made it difficult to retain collars on all packs each year. The number of wolves in packs without collars is based on incidental observations in winter and on annual mean pack size for all packs. The data from 1987–1988 were not used for the intensive area density because the limited number of collared packs within the area precluded a reliable estimate of the other packs in the area.

Wolf mortality was analyzed using MICROMORT (Heisey and Fuller 1985) to determine cause-specific mortality probabilities and sex-class survival rates. The year was separated into two periods, winter (16 October to 15 April) and summer (16 April to 15 October), to incorporate the fall and early winter hunting and trapping, and to allow comparisons to mortality results from other studies (Potvin 1988). The number of radio-transmitter days was tallied for the summer and winter intervals until death occurred from one of four sources of mortality: human (including hunting, trapping, vehicle), rabies, other (moose injury, wolf pack), and unknown causes. In six of the eight cases, when the cause of death could not be determined, the carcass had been disturbed by scavengers, or was in an advanced state of

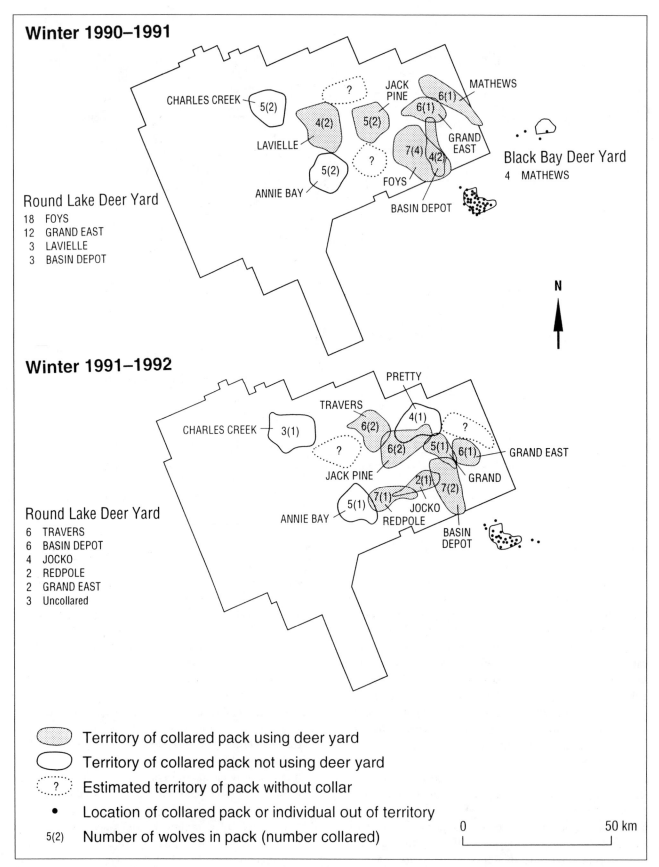

Winter 1990–1991

CHARLES CREEK — 5(2)

4(2)

LAVIELLE

5(2)

ANNIE BAY

?

JACK PINE

5(2)

6(1)

7(4) 4(2)

FOYS

BASIN DEPOT

6(1)

MATHEWS

GRAND EAST

Black Bay Deer Yard

4   MATHEWS

Round Lake Deer Yard

18   FOYS
12   GRAND EAST
 3   LAVIELLE
 3   BASIN DEPOT

N

Winter 1991–1992

CHARLES CREEK — 3(1)

TRAVERS

6(2)

?

JACK PINE

6(2)

PRETTY

4(1)

?

5(1)

6(1)

GRAND EAST

GRAND

2(1)

7(1)   7(2)

5(1)

ANNIE BAY

JOCKO

REDPOLE

BASIN DEPOT

Round Lake Deer Yard

6   TRAVERS
6   BASIN DEPOT
4   JOCKO
2   REDPOLE
2   GRAND EAST
3   Uncollared

Territory of collared pack using deer yard

Territory of collared pack not using deer yard

?   Estimated territory of pack without collar

•   Location of collared pack or individual out of territory

5(2)   Number of wolves in pack (number collared)

0   50 km

Fig. 2 *Territories of collared packs in winter 1990–91 and 1991–92.*

Wolves in a Changing World

Table 1. Territory size, wolf density and overwinter wolf losses in Algonquin Park, 1987–1992.

Winter	No. of packs	Territory size (km²)		Mean Number of wolves per pack		Change in pack size	Mean Within-territory density (wolves/100 km²)		Change in density
		Mean	Range	Early Winter	Late Winter	%	Early Winter	Late Winter	%
1987-88	5	150	98-212	6.6	4.8	-27	4.4	4.4	0
1988-89	12	137	65-187	6.8	5.1[3]	-23	5.2	3.8	-27
1989-90	9	210	130-378	6.7	5.7	-16	3.2	2.7	-16
1990-91	8	131	69-201	5.3	3.9	-26	4.0	3.0	-25
1991-92	10	119	63-191	5.1	4.1	-15	4.3	3.7	-14
Overall		149		6.0	4.7	-22	4.3	3.3	-23

1   Percent change in mean pack size from early to late winter.
2   Percent change in within-territory density of radio-collared packs from early to lake winter.
3   Based on 10 packs.

decomposition that made an accurate assessment difficult. However, the date of death could be estimated to the week, based on the last live transmission and state of decomposition.

A number of potential biases in the interpretation of MICROMORT data were addressed. Due to the number of missing collared wolves in our study (11), it was necessary to calculate both minimum and maximum survival rates. A minimum rate is based on the assumption that a missing collar indicates a dead wolf, whereas maximum rate is based on the assumption that all missing wolves are still alive. We felt this was necessary because discussions with local trappers led us to believe that some collars from missing wolves had been destroyed after the wolf had been killed. However, for missing wolves, it is likely that the only nontransmitting collars that would ever be re-located are those killed and submitted by humans. This would result in a bias increasing the amount of human-related mortality. In this study, we are confident that the assumptions regarding the use of MICRO-MORT were met, because only one wolf collar was not functioning at time of death, and we did not receive nonfunctioning collars from any human source.

Results

From 1987 to 1991, 57 wolves (33 males/24 females, 36 adults/21 young) were radio-collared from 22 packs. Three wolves were recaptured. Data on 19 radio-collared wolves were not used because the collar failed, the wolf died, or the collar was lost before the winter season began. A total of 5,405 locations were obtained from 38 wolves. Territory size

ranged from 63 km² to 378 km² with an all-year mean of 149 km² ($\pm$ 64 SE, n = 42) (Table 1). Pack territories were exclusive in all years except 1991–1992 when five packs had overlapping boundaries (Fig. 2). Summer territory location and size were similar to those in winter (Forbes and Theberge, Univ. of Waterloo, unpubl. data). Mean pack size for early winter was 6.0 ($\pm$ 1.8 SE, n = 46), ranging from two to 13 wolves. At the end of winter, mean pack size declined significantly (one-tailed t-test, P < 0.005) to 4.7 wolves ($\pm$ 1.1 SE, n = 46) (Table 1). No correlation was found between pack size and territory size (t-test, P<0.2). Within-territory mean densities for all years was 4.3 wolves/100 km² in early winter and 3.3 wolves/100 km² in late winter. The 23% decrease in mean density was significant (t-test, P<0.05). On three occasions, the premature death of the sole collared wolf in a pack precluded accurate assessment of pack size or territory in late winter. These data were excluded from analysis for late-winter density. The lowest early winter density occurred in 1989–1990, the highest was in the previous winter. The 1988–1992 average population density for the intensive study area was 2.7 wolves/100 km² ($\pm$2.7 SE, n = 4 years, 43 packs) in late winter (Table 2).

A small amount of the total extraterritorial movement was dispersing wolves. Two young wolves (5 months to 24 months) from the Grand Lake Pack left their natal territory, one in December, the other in March, and joined two adjacent packs in the north and southwest. In December 1990, the lactating female of the Grand Lake Pack left its territory and formed a new pack within the southern third of the old Grand Lake territory. Another two wolves dispersed 71 km

Table 2. Wolf population density estimate for intensive study area, Algonquin Park, 1988-1992

Winter	Early Winter Mean (wolves/100 km^2)	Late Winter Mean (wolves/100 km^2)	Change (%)[1]
1988-89	2.8	2.2	-21
1989-90	2.6	2.1	-19
1990-91	2.6	2.0	-23
1991-92	2.6	2.3	-12
Total	2.7	2.2	-19

1   Percent change in density from early to late winter

and 58 km to the Round Lake deer yard outside of the Park. Average straight-line distance of all dispersing wolves from natal territory to new territory or place of death was 31 km, with a range of 8 km to 71 km. Young wolves accounted for five of the seven dispersers; the other two were adults under three years of age. Twelve percent of the collared wolves dispersed, all during the winter period.

Short-term excursions beyond the resident territory were rare in the first three years, common in 1990–1991, and frequent in 1991–1992. Excursions in December 1991 were exceptional with seven (54%) of 13 collared wolves from six packs undertaking numerous forays coinciding with the southern seasonal migration of Algonquin deer to the Round Lake deer yard. As an example of wolf extraterritorial movement during deer migration, Figure 4 shows the extensive movements of collared wolves over a 16-day period (16–31 December 1991), while deer migrated south from the Park to the Round Lake deer yard. During this period, wolves did not appear to adhere to typical territorial distributions. On six occasions, wolves from four northerly territories trespassed into two southern pack territories and killed or scavenged three deer and one moose before returning to their resident territories within three days. In one case, a single deer carcass was visited by a minimum of five collared wolves from four packs over a nine-day period. None of the wolves were from the resident pack. All of the extraterritorial movements trespassed upon territories of known packs, an average of 2.8 packs per trespass. One excursion went in the opposite direction when both members of the Jocko Pack trespassed 13 km northwest through the territory of another pack, killed and consumed an adult deer and returned to their resident territory, within three days. On two occasions, collared wolves left their separate territories, travelled 30–35 km to the deer yard through three pack territories, and returned two days later.

Seasonal migration (excursions > 2 weeks) by packs or nondispersing individuals varied considerably during the study. In the first three winters (1987–1988 to 1989–1990), no migrations were recorded. In 1990–1991, 10 collared wolves from five collared packs, and in 1991–1992, eight collared wolves from six packs, were found in the Round Lake deer yard on 25% and 28% of their respective total winter telemetry locations (Fig. 2). Four extraterritorial movements by the Mathews Pack to the Black Bay deer yard, also outside the park, were recorded in 1990–1991, but we were not sure whether these movements represented a migration or short-term visits. Part of this yard was used by the Canadian military and aerial access was not permitted, hence we were not always able to locate this pack. In both years, several collared wolves remained in the Round Lake deer yard from late December until late winter. One of these wolves returned to its resident territory in late February. The other wolf died in early April. During both winters, wolves generally entered the Round Lake deer yard in late December, and in most cases, returned to their resident territories in March. The greatest straight-line distance travelled by a collared wolf to the yard was 62 km.

Collared wolves from half of all collared packs (n = 22), often from the center and eastern half of the park, were found within the Round Lake deer yard at some point during the study.

Though evidence indicated that deer remained unavailable outside of the deer yard until at least the end of March, the density of wolves in the yard changed considerably from early to late winter. Density in mid-February was estimated at 58 wolves/100 km^2 (46 wolves) and then declined to four wolves/100 km^2 (three wolves) in mid-March.

The majority of excursions or migrations occurred as group forays related to deer movement. A group of wolves represents a pack or a subgroup of pack members of three or more wolves observed together. Of 13 total separate movements in 1990–1991, 92% were by groups. In 1991–1992, of 24 total movements another 92% moved as groups. Most of the extraterritorial activity was related to the movement,

Table 3. Cause-specific mortality probabilities[1] for radio-collared wolves annually, and during summer (16 Apr. – 15 Oct.) and winter (16 Oct. – 15 Apr.) intervals.

	Interval Rates		
Mortality Source	*Summer*	*Winter*	*Annual*
Human	0.016 (1)[2]	0.160 (12)	0.156 (13)
Rabies	0.065 (4)	0.027 (2)	0.088 (6)
Other	0.000 (0)	0.027 (2)	0.023 (2)
Unknown	0.050 (3)	0.067 (5)	0.107 (8)

1 Probabilities were calculated using MICROMORT (Heisey and Fuller 1985).
2 Number of deaths per interval.

or the yarding, of deer; 69% of the 1990–1991 movements, and 79% of 1991–1992 movements occurred during the fall migration, or were later excursions to the deer yard. Not all group movements were by entire packs; in 1991–1992, half the wolves in each of two packs, Jack Pine and Travers, traveled over much of the eastern part of the park, while the remaining wolves stayed on territory.

Over the five-year study, 29 collared wolves were known to have died. Most of the mortality was of breeding-age animals; at the time of death, 26 were adults and three were young. Of the adults, a minimum 46% were more than four years of age. Mortality was due to: hunting (7), trapping (6), rabies (6), unknown (7), road kill (1), moose injury (1), and wolf pack (1). Human-related mortality accounted for 48% of all mortality. Cause-specific mortality probabilities indicated that human-caused mortality in winter and rabies in summer were the main sources of collared wolf mortality (Table 3).

The total percentage of collared wolves dying outside the park was 62%, of which human-related deaths accounted for 12 (75%) of the 18 deaths. Evidence exists for the death of at least two more collared wolves in the yard whose collars were smashed and the death concealed. Because these claims are unproven they are not included in the total mortality. Twelve (41%) of the 29 dead wolves died in association with the movement of deer to the Round Lake deer yard or Black Bay deer yard. Mortality in the Round Lake deer yard was human-related in seven (64%) of the 12 cases. The other deer yard-related deaths were rabies (2) and unknown (3).

Over the five-year study, the annual mortality rate was estimated to be between a minimum of 30% and a maximum of 37%, not including pups. The annual minimum survival rate was 63% ± 9 SE (n = 29) with greater chance of survival in summer (87%) than winter (72%) (Table 4). The annual maximum survival rate (assuming all missing wolves are

alive) was 70% ± 4 SE. No difference in survival rate existed between males and females (z-test, $P<0.2$).

Year-to-year mortality of radio-collared wolves varied considerably. From total number of packs in the park and mean pack size of collared packs we estimate a five-year average of 9% of the total population, or 29% of the study pack's population, were radio-collared each year. Annual mortality of collared wolves as a percentage of the total number collared at the end of each March indicated total losses from all sources as 0% in 1987–89; 54.5% in 1988–89; 17.5% in 1989–90; 61.1% in 1990–91; and 18.8% in 1991–92.

Discussion

We documented extensive winter movements by wolves beyond resident territories, even beyond adjacent packs, in response to seasonal changes in prey availability. Extraterritorial movement by wolves is generally believed to result from food shortages on the resident territory (Zimen 1976). Hoskinson and Mech (1976) and Mech (1977c) found that wolves stayed within their resident territory until deer declined. Wolves then trespassed, but only into adjacent packs.

The Algonquin wolf migration depends on the extent of deer migration from a pack's territory; in years when pockets of deer wintered in the park, wolves were not recorded in the deer yard; when deer were absent, wolves made extraterritorial movement to areas with deer (Fig. 3). Because deer are the preferred prey of Algonquin wolves, this explanation seems plausible for the Algonquin situation. Potvin (1988) believed that the lack of pack movement in Papineau-Labelle, Quebec was due to the continuous availability of small numbers of deer within territories. In a number of studies, wolves stayed on territory, but frequented areas with higher concentrations of prey (Van Ballenberghe 1983a, Messier 1985a, Ballard et al. 1987, Potvin 1988).

Table 4. Survival rates[1] for radio-collared wolves annually, and during summer (16 Apr. – 15 Oct.) and winter (16 Oct. – 15 Apr.) intervals.

	Total number of Days Surviving	No. of Deaths	Survival Rate (%)		
			Summer $\bar{x} \pm SE$	Winter $\bar{x} \pm SE$	Annual $\bar{x} \pm SE$
Male	11617 (16230)	18	85±16 (88±4)	68±25 (77±9)	58±36 (68±16)
Female	10453 (12670)	11	89±9 (91±4)	77±25 (80±16)	69±36 (73±25)
Total	22070 (28900)	29	87±4 (90±2)	72±9 (78±4)[2]	63±9 (70±4)

1   Rates were calculated using MICROMORT (Heisey and Fuller 1985).
2   Statistically significant difference between winter and summer (z-test) P<0.05.
( )   Maximum values if missing wolves are considered alive.

Carbyn (1981) and Peterson et al. (1984), however, reported extraterritorial movements when food was abundant on territory, in one case possibly related to social disruption of the pack from hunting by humans. Although extraterritorial movement is related to food availability on territory in some contexts, more work is needed on the behavioral influence on wolf movements.

Group or pack excursions by wolves have been reported in only a small number of studies. Van Ballenberghe (1983a) documented seven of 10 collared wolves from four packs undertaking numerous group forays into adjacent territories. Only two of the wolves were believed to be dispersing. The high incidence of extraterritorial movement in that study was thought to be a function of unguarded boundaries, and a concurrent decrease in the repelling of intruders. In Quebec, Messier (1985a) recorded two packs extending their territory in winter to encompass an adjacent deer yard.

Seasonal migration or movement of wolves has been recorded in tundra systems as wolves follow migrating caribou (*Rangifer tarandus*) (Kelsall 1968, Parker 1973), and in mountain systems when wolves leave high-altitude ranges to winter in valleys with lower snow depth (Seip 1990). Wolves have also been documented as shifting territories and concentrating in areas of migrating bison (*Bison bison*) in Wood Buffalo National Park (Carbyn et al. this volume). To our knowledge, the extensive degree of seasonal migration by wolves documented in this study has not been recorded for heavily forested ecosystems. At one point in mid-February 1992, almost half (48%) of the collared wolves from six of the 10 study packs had migrated to the deer yard. Only two other studies report similar, though less extensive, findings. Kolenosky (1972) reported one pack with radio-collared wolves found 8 km distant from their summer range the following winter. In the other study (Messier 1985b), four packs, and one in particular, left

resident territories on excursions to exploit deer. Both Messier's study and this study are of moose–deer systems with deer being the preferred prey. The seasonal migration of deer out of pack territory (this study) or the lack of deer year-round (Messier 1985b) leaves moose as the major available prey. In Messier's study, moose densities were lower for packs that left the territory in search of deer than for packs that stayed on territory. Moose densities in Algonquin were high throughout the study area, but moose are killed infrequently by the small Algonquin wolf subspecies (Forbes and Theberge 1992). Moose were rare outside Algonquin in the Round Lake deer yard. In either situation, it appears that deer constitute a strong impetus for movement in a multiple-prey moose-deer system.

The effect of a migrating deer herd on wolf hunting patterns and pack interaction is poorly understood. It is believed that terrotoriality in wolves provides a number of advantages, often increasing food availability, and limiting risk of death through increased familiarity with escape routes and feeding areas (Zimen 1976, Davies and Houston 1984). A wolf leaving its resident territory in response to a prey migration, however, may benefit from a higher predation rate. Nelson and Mech (1991) discovered that the fall migration period of deer, which is only 1% of the total deer year, accounted for 21% of annual wolf-caused mortality. The high mortality is attributed to the migrating deer's unfamiliarity with the terrain and escape routes, and changing snow depth conditions affecting ability to escape. The migration period also appeared to be important to Algonquin wolves; 40% of the deer carcasses (n = 20) found in winter 1991–1992, were killed during the deer migration period. The hunting patterns of extraterritorial wolves were not known, but the southern excursions of trespassing wolves documented in December 1991 appeared to be related to wolves chasing deer (Fig. 4). We speculate that as deer migrate out of a wolf territory, a long chase by that pack may take it into another territory. Though deer chases are usually under 6 km (Mech 1966b, Kolenosky 1972), one chase was documented at over 20 km (Mech and Korb 1978), and we speculate that some of the excursions we documented were the product of extended chases of migrating deer.

A number of authors have written about the antipredator advantages that yards offer deer (Nelson and Mech 1981, Messier and Barette 1985), but relatively little is known about the advantages to wolves of frequenting a yard other than the increased availability of abundant prey located in a

confined area. Intraspecific strife among nonrelated territorial wolves is cited in a number of studies as a cause of wolf mortality (Mech 1977b, Ballard et al. 1987). Wolf densities can be high in a deer yard; at one point in this study, a minimum of 46 wolves were using an 80 km^2 area on the same night, a density of 58 wolves/100 km^2. Though we found no evidence of intraspecific strife, the potential exists for injury or mortality from such crowding. Deer yards are often heavily managed for maximum deer survivorship; government-sponsored wolf control has been a common management tool in northern yards (Carbyn 1981). Conflict between wolves and local residents who feed wintering deer,

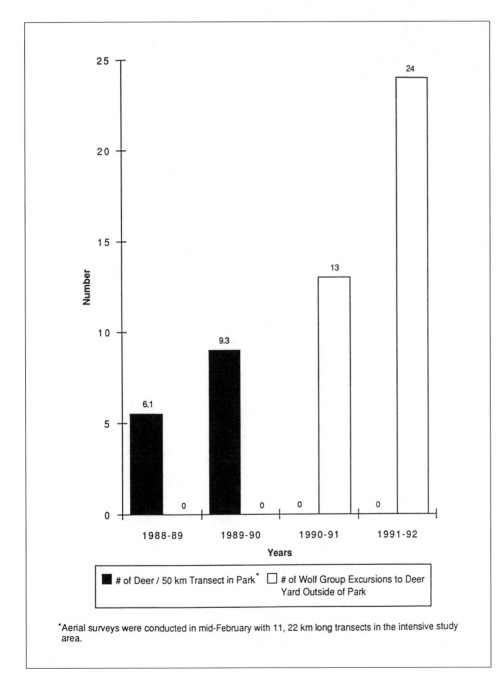

Fig. 3 *Relationship between deer over-wintering in the Park and group excursions by wolves to the Round Lake deer yard, 1988–1992. The dashed line indicates no excursions or deer were recorded for that period.*

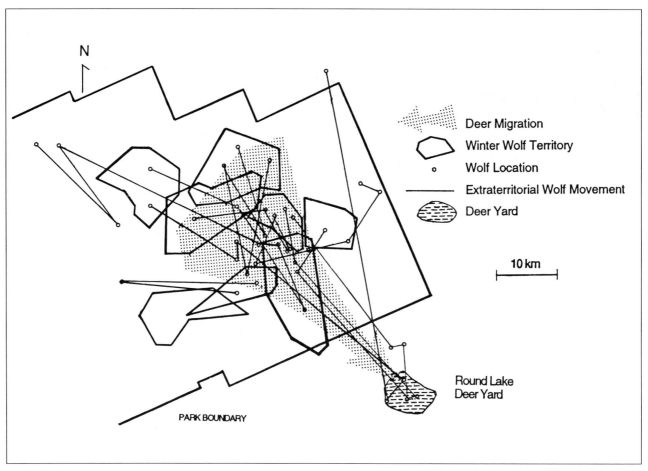

Fig. 4 *Movements by collared wolves indicating extensive extraterritorial movement southward as deer migrate south to the Round Lake deer yard, 16–31 December 1991.*

or who hunt or benefit economically from deer hunting, also contribute to wolf mortality in deer yards.

Humans are the greatest source of mortality in Algonquin Park wolves, even though the wolves are protected within the park. To what extent are the park wolves vulnerable to decline? Based on radio-collared wolves, human-caused mortality is 48% (14 of 29) of the total recorded annual mortality rate of 30–37%. At that rate, humans account, on average, for 14.4–17.7% of annual mortality. These values are comparable with another measure of seasonal mortality; overwinter declines in wolf density averaged 19%, ranging from 12–23% (Table 2). These values are considered moderate because they are below the 30–35% threshold identified as the upper limit of allowable exploitation (Keith 1983, Peterson and Page 1988, Ballard et al. 1987, Fuller 1989). Also, a decline in density was not observed over the five-year study period, nor did mortality increase when movement to the deer yard increased over the last two years and higher mortality would be expected. Mean pack size decreased during the study (Table 1), but it is not clear if this decline was due to mortality or other factors such as prey availability.

These facts could indicate that the population is stable. However, the potential for increased mortality rates, possibly beyond the 30–35% threshold, is strong because of game regulations and a desire among numerous local people to kill wolves. No policy exists for wolf conservation in the deer yard area; wolves can be legally killed in any number, in any season, by persons with small game licenses, and remain unreported (Ontario Ministry of Natural Resources 1992). In 1988–1989, mortality of collared wolves exceeded the 30–35% threshold when 41% of the total collared wolves available were killed by humans that winter. In 1992, a public snowmobile-assisted roundup in the Round Lake deer yard was cancelled only because of bad weather conditions. During past roundups in the mid-1980's, as many as 16 and 28 wolves had been killed in one day. In winter 1986–1987, 29 wolves were killed by one hunter in the Round Lake area (P. Sloan, OMNR conservation officer, pers. commun. 1991).

With park status, the Algonquin wolf population is one of few officially protected wolf populations in Canada (Theberge 1991). Studies by conservation biologists indicate that parks and refuges will be unable to preserve populations of large vertebrates over long periods from high mortality rates on animals crossing park boundaries, demographic risks in small populations, and because of genetic deterioration from population isolation (Knight and Eberhardt 1985, Shafer 1990). With increased human density and habitat loss outside Algonquin Park, the possible introgression of coyote genes (Lehman et al. 1991) due to increasing coyote populations outside the Park, and the risks to wolves associated with a history of fluctuating fur prices and periodic wolf control, it would be prudent to provide Park wolves with more adequate protection. Clearly, the present boundaries of Algonquin Park are not doing so. Because the Round Lake deer yard appears to be critical to the park wolves in certain years, efforts are needed to limit the potential for mortality in this area during certain times of the year. One possibility for managing wildlife across boundaries is to establish a Carnivore Conservation Area proposed by World Wildlife Fund Canada that facilitates predator management integrated with park purposes, the population viability of predator and prey, habitat management, sustainable harvests, and human activities (Hummel 1990).

Acknowledgments

We thank the many people who have assisted in the collaring of wolves in this study, especially C. Callaghan. In addition to their summer field work, L. Swanson and M. Theberge were invaluable in the winter monitoring program. We also thank Pem-Air, Air North Bay and Madawaska Valley Air Service, Ministry of Natural Resource staff from the Algonquin Museum, and the Algonquin District and Pembroke District, and Algonquin College. Lee Swanson and Rod Duncan were invaluable in the preparation of the manuscript. The research was funded by World Wildlife Fund Canada, Ontario Ministry of Natural Resources, Environmental Youth Corps Program, with help from Natural Sciences and Engineering Research Council, Wolf Awareness, Friends of Algonquin, Algonquin Forestry Authority, and Murray Bros. Logging Company.

Graham J. Forbes and John B. Theberge

Wolves as Interspecific Competitors in Canid Ecology

■ Rolf O. Peterson

Widespread competition has been documented between wolves and smaller canids, presumably an evolutionary outcome of competition for resources among species within the canid guild. Such interference competition is asymmetrical, with larger species such as wolves dominant over smaller-bodied species. Competitive effects are most evident between species closest in size. Wolves are able to exclude coyotes at many spatial scales, from individual pack territories to an entire region. Yet coexistence between potentially competing canids is also relatively common, and the outcome of competition may be influenced in subtle ways by topography, snow cover, season of the year, food abundance, niche overlap, population characteristics, and the overriding influence of humans. Interspecific aggression is considered an evolved behavioral response to broad-scale competition for limited food resources.

Introduction

The existence of competition between gray wolves (*Canis lupus*) and other canids was implied long ago by naturalists (e.g., Seton 1925:394), and is a persistent observation of fur trappers (Schmidt 1986). Furthermore, prominent competition between top carnivores is predicted to exist on theoretical grounds (Hairston et al. 1960).

Interspecific competition is thought to have contributed to morphological patterns among canids and other carnivores throughout evolutionary time and space (Van Valkenburgh 1991). It may also underlie the often unpopular behavior of wolves that kill domestic dogs (Fritts and Paul 1989). As wolves become reestablished in their former haunts, it is increasingly recognized that their presence or absence may have community-level consequences that extend beyond predation alone (Schmidt 1986).

This review focuses on the mechanisms of competition between wolves and other canids and the resulting effects on distribution and abundance of other canids. Pertinent here is the role of modern humans in influencing canid species prevalence.

This paper is limited to competition among North American canids, especially wolves, coyotes (*Canis latrans*) and red foxes (*Vulpes vulpes*). As coyote-fox interaction is ecologically and behaviorally similar to interactions between wolves and other canids, I have freely drawn from current understanding of competition among all three species. In addition to summarizing the literature, which already includes some important reviews (Johnson and Sargeant 1977, Schmidt 1986), I present new data on wolf-red fox interaction in 1972–1992 from Isle Royale National Park in

Michigan. Also, I report findings on canid interactions from Alaska's Kenai Peninsula (Fig. 1). Finally, I interpret canid distribution in the North American mid-continent in terms of competition overlain by strong human impacts. The latter was accomplished with data supplied by cooperators in several states and provinces. Trapper harvest of red foxes and coyotes provided indices of relative abundance for Manitoba, South Dakota, Wisconsin, and Michigan, and scentpost surveys provided similar data for Minnesota.

Mechanisms of Competition among Canids

Although ecologists have usually focused on resource competition (e.g., Diamond 1978), or exploitation competition, canid specialists have concentrated instead on interference competition. The former, indirect and difficult to demonstrate, occurs as one species removes resources from another through more efficient capture, or converts resources more efficiently into growth and reproduction. The latter, in contrast, involves direct displacement of competitively subordinate individuals, which are killed, driven away, or choose to avoid dominant competitors. Even though exploitation competition underlies the evolution of interference behavior, Connor and Bowers (1987) were unable to find any examples of spatial patterning of species arising because of exploitation competition.

The best-known mechanisms of competition among canids are direct killing and the resulting avoidance behavior in the subordinate species. Such behavior exists among conspecifics and it extends analogously toward other species. Among canid species, interference competition is strictly asymmetrical, and dominance is based on size. Wolves, then, are known to kill coyotes (Seton 1925:257, Young and Goldman 1944, Munro 1947, Stenlund 1955, Berg and Chesness 1978, Carbyn 1982a) and foxes (Stenlund 1955, Mech 1966a, Banfield 1974). Coyotes, in turn, may kill foxes (Gier 1975, Johnson and Sargeant 1977, Young 1951, Voigt and Earle 1983, Sargeant et al. 1987). Notably, aggressive behavior of large canids toward small canids is probably expressed only by territorial individuals, especially family groups (Sargeant et al. 1987; W. Berg, Minn. Dep. Natural Resources., pers. commun.).

Characteristically, the victims of interspecific aggression are not eaten, but left with fatal bites in the head and neck and frequent puncture wounds through the torso (Carbyn 1982a) (Fig. 2). In four wolf-killed coyotes, Wobeser (1992) found multiple bite wounds over the hips, back, and thorax, resulting in fractured ribs, massive hemorrhaging, and muscle lacerations.

One might expect that elimination of smaller canids at dens would be especially significant. Sargeant and Allen (1989) reported eight coyote-killed fox pups at six fox dens in North Dakota and, together with Dekker (1983), reported fox parents defensively barking near dens when approached by coyotes. I found, in 1979, one case in which a two-month-old red fox pup was killed near its den by an Isle Royale wolf.

Avoidance behavior may be of greater ecological significance than direct killing, which occurs infrequently. Survival rates of Alaskan coyotes living within wolf range were high (Thurber et al. 1992), and foxes were rarely killed by sympatric coyotes in Maine (Harrison et al. 1989) and North Dakota (Sargeant et al. 1987). Nevertheless, where canid species are regionally sympatric, they may be spatially segregated at smaller spatial scales. Local avoidance of a wolf pack by coyotes was reported in Minnesota (Berg and Chesness 1978), Alberta (Fuller and Keith 1981a), and Manitoba (Carbyn 1982a), as was fox avoidance of coyote territories in Ontario (Voigt and Earle 1983), North Dakota (Sargeant et al. 1987), Texas (Andelt 1985), and Maine (Major and Sherburne 1987, Harrison et al. 1989).

It is noteworthy that tolerance by large canids toward smaller species is also frequently reported. Paquet (1992) found that coyotes near Manitoba's Riding Mountain National Park did not avoid wolf pack territories, and he found no evidence that wolves actively sought coyotes. In fact, coyotes frequently followed wolves and scavenged their kills and even scent-marked over wolf marks (Paquet 1991b). Yet in his five-year study, Paquet found 23 wolf-killed coyotes, 11 of them near wolf-killed prey. Sargeant and Allen (1989) likewise reported occasional indifference of coyotes toward foxes, as did Mech (1966a) and Peterson (1977) for wolves towards foxes. The motivation for such tolerance is not understood, but obviously it facilitates coexistence under some situations.

Ecological Influences on Competition

The outcome of competitive interactions is contingent on many features of the environment and the local ecology of each species. Except at rearing dens, small canids invariably respond to aggression from large canids by evasion or simply running away (Mech 1966a, Dekker 1983, Sargeant and

Fig. 1 *A tranquilized coyote is radio collared in 1976 on the Kenai Peninsula, Alaska, where coyotes became established during 50 years of wolf absence. (Photo: R. Peterson)*

Fig. 2 *Victims of interspecific canid agression: (top) a wolf-killed coyote on the Kenai Peninsula, Alaska, and (bottom) a wolf-killed red fox in Isle Royale National Park, Michigan. (Photo: R. Peterson)*

Allen 1989). Fine-grained environmental features, then, are likely to be influential in direct encounters.

When running speed alone determines the outcome, larger species will invariably win the race, owing to allometric scaling of maximum speed (McMahon and Bonner 1983). This would be the case in flat tundra, grasslands with little vegetation, and on frozen lakes in winter. Seven of 11 red foxes that I have found killed by wolves in Isle Royale National Park were on frozen lakes or ponds, one was on a cleared trail, and one was in a grassy meadow. Foxes are evidently aware of their vulnerability in flat, open terrain, as on ice-covered lakes, for when they are pursued by wolves, they invariably run toward forested shorelines, where smaller canids more successfully evade pursuers.

In winter, deep, untracked snow may give large species a temporary edge when pursuing small species (Carbyn 1982a). In a four-year study in Alaska, the only direct observations of wolf-coyote interactions were on a single day in February following a heavy snowfall (Thurber et al. 1992). In chest-deep snow, two different wolf packs each chased, caught, and quickly killed a coyote. A snow crust, obviously, will quickly reverse the odds of success, for smaller canids, especially foxes, will have a lighter weight-load-on-track (Formosov 1946). Snow metamorphosis, freeze-thaw conditions in late winter and the presence of wind-crusted snow in open areas can thus affect the outcome of competitive interactions.

Degree of niche overlap (i.e., prey species in common) and food abundance can logically be expected to influence the extent of competition between species. Reliance on similar prey will increase spatial overlap and the likelihood of interspecific aggression. Theberge and Wedeles (1989) felt that flexibility in prey choice allowed foxes to coexist with coyotes in southern Yukon. Similarly, Paquet (1992) argued that both differential use of prey and abundant food allowed coyotes to coexist with wolves in Riding Mountain National Park. Abundance of food is known to affect intraspecific tolerance of wolves, both within packs (Zimen 1976) and between packs (Van Ballenberghe et al. 1975, Peterson 1977, Peterson and Page 1988), and we can surmise similar effects on interspecific interactions. Perhaps this explains coyote and wolf coexistence on the original bison-dominated prairies and plains of North America.

Communal feeding of wolves, coyotes, and foxes has been reported, especially when larger canid species are fully fed and resting (Mech 1966a, Peterson 1977, Sargeant and Allen 1989, Paquet 1992). However, this may not represent actual tolerance as much as simply the reduced ability of a large canid with a full stomach to successfully exclude a canid of a smaller but more agile species. Chases with little chance of success are unlikely to be undertaken.

Most accounts of interspecific killing are derived from winter, when direct observations and snow-tracking aid investigators. Sargeant and Allen (1989), however, provided evidence of interspecific aggression throughout the year. Voigt and Earle (1983) found that fox and coyote movements overlapped most during winter. Sargeant et al. (1987) commented on the unique vulnerability of dispersing canids to interspecific attack, from which we might infer that aggressive contacts between species are least likely during summer pup-rearing.

Actual observations of wolves killing coyotes and foxes reveal that it is frequently a group activity, possibly more common in winter when wolf packs are most cohesive. The presence of snow and ice may at times facilitate successful capture of smaller canids in winter, as discussed earlier. Finally, the greater reliance of small canids on scavenging from wolf-killed prey in winter will tend to concentrate interspecific interactions at that season.

Population characteristics may be important determinants of the outcome of interspecific competition (Sargeant et al. 1987). Relative numbers of each canid species, presence of an adjacent pool of dispersers, and rates of reproduction and mortality are all likely to influence the competitive balance among canid species, but relevant data are lacking and our understanding is very limited. Obviously, *a priori* predictions of competitive outcomes are not straightforward.

Evidence of Population Effects

Competition among wolves and other canids has been the focus of relatively few studies. Because of logistical constraints, no experimental tests of competition have been conducted. Rather, we must make inferences from spatial and temporal patterns of canid occurrence.

Accounts of interspecific aggression most commonly involve canids closest in size, i.e., wolves versus coyotes, or coyotes versus foxes. Yet wolves exhibit similar aggression toward foxes, as illustrated at Isle Royale (Mech 1966a, Peterson 1977). Nevertheless, we can postulate that if interference competition influences species distribution or abundance, it will be most evident in species pairs adjacent in size. We can also expect that spatial segregation of competing species will be evident at all spatial scales, from individual family territories and habitats to regional and continental scales (Connor and Bowers 1987).

The distribution of eight native North American canids has been greatly altered by human activities during the past 200 years, but prior to that, there was evidence of distinct spatial segregation, especially among the smaller species:

...gray wolves had a very broad distribution, probably occupying the major part of the continent except for the southeastern coastal plain. Coyotes were confined to open plains and more arid regions, mainly in the western half of the continent. Their eastern distribution seemed to follow the prairie peninsula through the midwestern states. Red foxes were present in the northern portions of the continent, while gray foxes (*Urocyon cinereoargenteus*) occupied the southern hardwood forests and coastal regions. Kit foxes (*V. velox*) occurred in the arid western states. Occupying the southeastern states were red wolves (*C. rufus*). Finally, arctic foxes (*Alopex lagopus*) occurred in the arctic biome, while the island gray fox (*V. littoralis*) occurred only on islands off the coast of southern California. (Schmidt 1986:50-52)

Human elimination of the gray wolf in most of the United States and southern portions of Canada's prairie provinces was followed by increased coyote populations on the mid-continental plains and a dramatic expansion of coyotes eastward and northward (Johnson and Sargeant 1977, Hall 1981, Nowak and Paradiso 1983).

That wolf demise actually prompted the coyote increase is best shown by the history of coyotes in Alaska. Around 1900, gold miners, armed with poison baits, provided a wolf-free corridor for coyote expansion (Gier 1975, Thurber and Peterson 1991). While coyotes are currently distributed throughout Alaska, they became common only in areas where wolves were absent or reduced, i.e., the rail belt from Anchorage to Fairbanks and adjacent portions of south-central Alaska and the Kenai Peninsula (H.T. Gier, Kansas State Univ., pers. commun.; Thurber et al. 1992).

When wolves exist in unbroken distribution through space and time, coyotes are usually excluded. Coyotes are rare within core areas of Minnesota's wolf range, but they

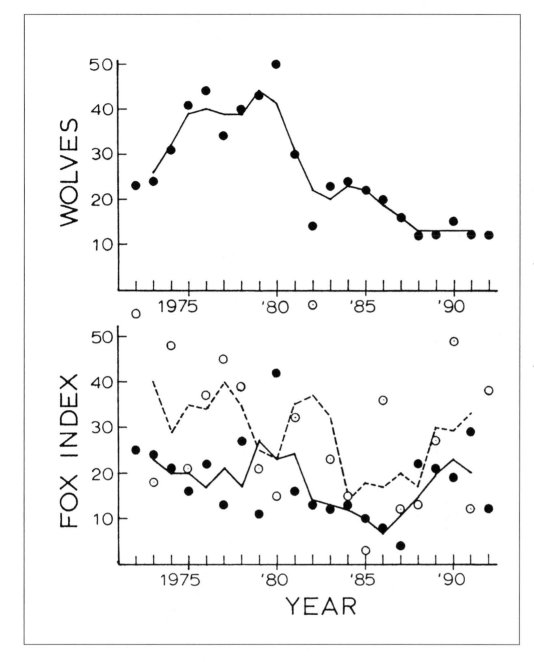

Fig. 3 *Wolf numbers (total counts) and red fox population indices in Isle Royale National Park, Michigan (three-year moving averages). Fox indices were derived from midwinter aircraft surveys and include the number of foxes more than 1 km from known moose carcasses/100 hour (solid line) and sum of maximum number of foxes observed on moose carcasses (dashed line).*

are common immediately outside (Berg and Chesness 1978; L. D. Mech, U.S. Fish and Wildlife Service, pers. commun.).

A similar inverse relationship between coyote and red fox densities has been noted in Alberta (Dekker 1990), North Dakota (Johnson and Sargeant 1977), Maine (Harrison et al. 1989), and Wyoming (Linhart and Robinson 1972). While coyotes are abundant within Riding Mountain National Park, on the fringe of wolf range, red foxes are almost absent (Paquet 1991a, Paquet 1992). The opposite is true in Wood Buffalo National Park (Carbyn et al. 1993), within contiguous wolf distribution.

Lack of dispersal from adjacent areas may facilitate complete exclusion of competitively subordinate species. On Isle Royale, competitive exclusion of coyotes by gray wolves was accomplished within a decade after the island was colonized by wolves in the late 1940's (Mech 1966a). Following the elimination of coyotes, red foxes were more commonly observed by long-time island residents (P. Edisen, U.S. National Park Service, pers. commun.).

Is wolf aggression toward foxes on Isle Royale of any population significance? Two indices of fox observations from aircraft (Fig. 3) are correlated (r = 0.49) and can serve as crude indicators of relative abundance. Actually, weak positive, not negative, associations exist between wolf numbers and fox indices ($r^2 = 0.15$, $P = 0.06$ for foxes per 100 hours, and $r^2 = 0.06$, $P = 0.17$ for foxes on kills). In any case,

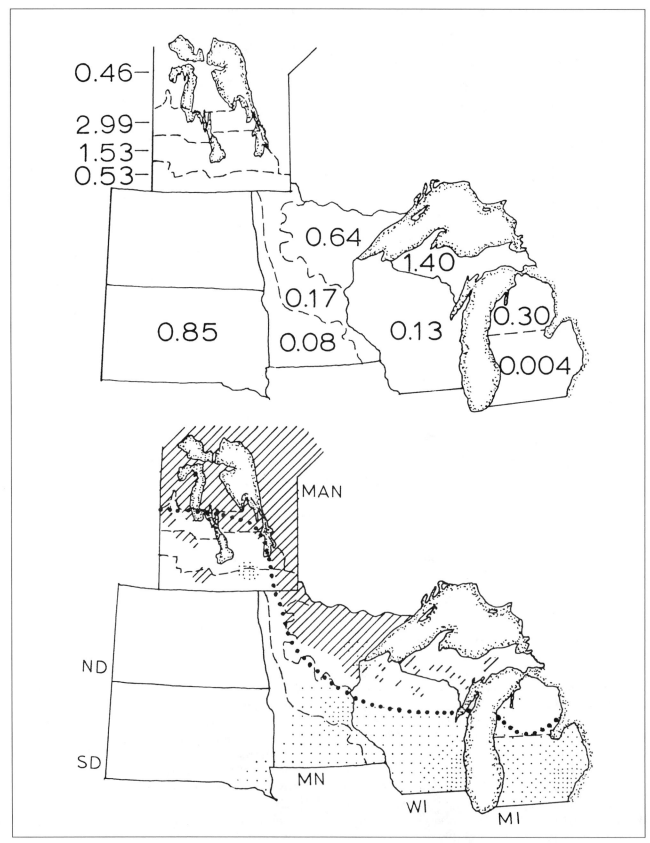

Fig. 4 *(A) Ratio of coyotes to red foxes in the midcontinent of North America, determined from harvest records (average of one to five years in 1970's and 1980's) and scent-station surveys (Minnesota only, 1985). (B) Southern limit of gray wolf distribution (hatched area) in relation to forested areas (north of dotted line) and relative human density (indicated by stippling).*

there is no evidence of wolf-induced reductions in the fox population.

More historical details of temporal canid changes are available for Alaska's Kenai Peninsula, over 25,000 km² in area, connected to the rest of Alaska by a heavily glaciated isthmus only 16 km wide. Wolves and red foxes were common furbearers there, throughout the 19th century, but both were reduced by indiscriminate harvest and poisoning at the turn of the century. Foxes persisted at low densities, but wolves were extirpated by 1915 (Peterson and Woolington 1982). Coyotes were first reported on the Kenai in 1926 (Thurber and Peterson 1991), and thereafter coyotes became so common they were a target for federal predator control in the 1940's and 1950's (Thurber et al. 1992).

Wolves recolonized the Kenai Peninsula in the 1960's, and in the 1970's they again became widespread and common (Peterson et al. 1984). Coyotes were observed killed by wolves, but overall coyote survival rate within wolf range was relatively high (Thurber et al. 1992). Capture frequency in the 1970's, however, suggested coyotes were no more numerous than wolves in remote areas on the Kenai, a fact that may be circumstantially linked to the reappearance of the wolf. Red foxes have remained rare (T. Bailey, U.S. Fish and Wildlife Service, pers. commun.), perhaps a persistent effect of exclusion by coyotes. I observed only two foxes on the Kenai in three years of intensive field work in the late 1970's. During that period, researchers ground-trapped 42 coyotes, 39 wolves, and no foxes (Thurber et al. 1992). If wolves have effectively reduced coyote density in remote regions of the Kenai, as suggested by Thurber et al. (1992), then an eventual increase in red foxes is predicted.

Sargeant et al. (1987) hypothesized that while a competitively subordinate species may be tenacious in the face of increasing competition, dispersing young may simply avoid contact with larger canid species. Thus, displacement of small species by invading larger species might be less likely than maintenance of segregation through avoidance. This might explain the persistence of coyotes and the continued low fox density on the Kenai Peninsula.

Species introductions or removals have provided the strongest empirical evidence of population-level effects of interspecific competition (Connor and Simberloff 1986). Managers contemplating control or introduction of a canid species should be alert for such opportunities. An attempt to eliminate introduced arctic foxes on an Aleutian island by introducing red foxes was proposed and debated (Schmidt 1985), yet its initiation and evaluation have not been reported (see, however, Bailey 1992).

The Role of Humans

A comprehensive understanding of canid distribution and abundance in North America must incorporate the human effects of legal harvest and illegal killing. Such effects are greater for large-bodied canids, for they present a larger target, require more space, and have a lower rate of population increase.

Humans may inadvertently provide a refuge for competitively subordinate canids. In North Dakota, most fox dens were near roads and farms, while coyotes preferred more remote areas (Sargeant et al. 1987). Likewise, wolves rarely crossed the settled edge of the Kenai National Wildlife Refuge (Thurber et al. 1994). Within wolf range on the Kenai, coyotes were more commonly captured on roads open to the public (which wolves avoided) than on closed roads (Thurber et al. 1994). Human presence will thus help perpetuate coyotes on the Kenai Peninsula.

Extending the ideas of Sargeant et al. (1987), humans may even act as keystone species, reducing or eliminating a competitively dominant canid. Across the landscape, human pressure on wild canids is proportional to both human density and canid escape cover (usually forested areas). This is best illustrated by the correlation between wolf distribution and road density (Thiel 1985, Jensen et al. 1986, Mech et al. 1988b), which in turn is related to both human density and tree cover.

In the midcontinent of North America, human activity restricts all established wolf populations to forested regions. This is illustrated by Manitoba's forested islands of wolf habitat in Duck Mountain Provincial Park and Riding Mountain National Park, and the Assiniboine River west of Winnipeg (Fig. 4). Coyotes and wolves are generally parapatric, with spatially distinct populations, along the forested edge of continuous wolf range, as in northeastern Minnesota (Berg and Chesness 1978). High dispersal enables coyotes to penetrate wolf range for tens of kilometres and explains the persistence of coyotes in Riding Mountain. Similarly, Sargeant et al. (1987) emphasized the significance of dispersal in maintaining local fox populations.

Where coyote distribution is continuous, red foxes are generally reduced, as in Riding Mountain and on the Kenai Peninsula. Complete exclusion of foxes by coyotes can be demonstrated only at small spatial scales (Dekker 1983, Sargeant et al. 1987, Harrison et al. 1989). At scales measured in tens or hundreds of square kilometres, foxes are usually sympatric with coyotes, yet their relative abundance reveals differential vulnerability to human effects, as in the Midwest.

In forested areas relatively free of wolves, such as Michigan's Upper Peninsula, coyotes are more numerous than foxes (Fig. 4). Where forests become patchy and human density is higher, red foxes tend to outnumber coyotes, as in the forest fringe crossing central Minnesota and the northern lower peninsula of Michigan. In heavily settled agricultural areas with little forest, as in southern Minnesota and southern Michigan, foxes predominate and coyotes are relatively rare. In Wisconsin, which encompasses all these conditions with relatively high human density, statewide data indicated a predominance of foxes. The relatively high coyote/fox

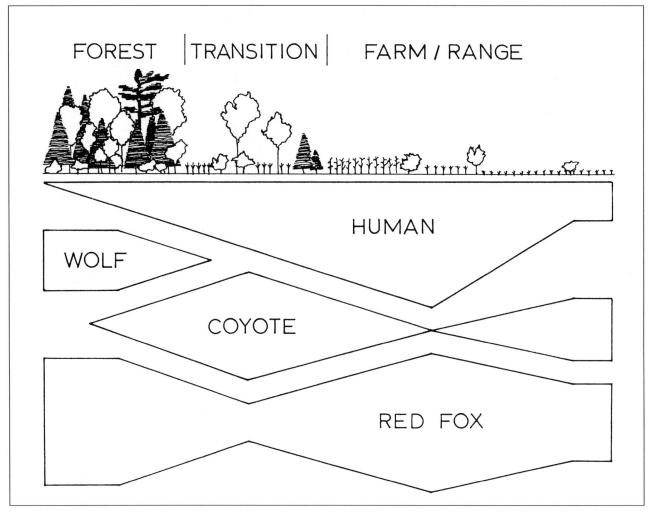

Fig. 5 *Postulated competitive relationships between humans and canids in relation to tree cover in the midcontinent of North America.*

ratio for South Dakota, where forests are generally lacking, is hypothesized to result from lower human density.

In Manitoba, foxes outnumber coyotes in the southern agricultural districts, but coyotes are more numerous farther north along the forest fringe (Fig. 4), provided wolves are absent. Still further north, within wolf habitat, coyotes are outnumbered again by foxes. Presumably, coyotes are reduced in the south by humans and in the north by wolves.

This hypothetical portrayal of interspecific relationships (Fig. 5) should be more rigorously tested and refined where detailed data are available. Harris's (1981) study of red fox and domestic dog (*Canis lupus familiaris*) distribution in the city of Bristol, England, in which children traveling to and from school reported dog and fox sightings, revealed how new approaches to data gathering may be used. As a start, more refined data on furbearer harvest would facilitate evaluation of canid abundance patterns.

Evolution of Canid Interference Behavior

The principle of competitive exclusion is based on similarity of ecological niche, an abstraction commonly related to the food economy of a species. While food habits of coyotes and red foxes overlap almost completely (Sargeant et al. 1987), wolves and coyotes exhibit more dissimilarities (Schmidt 1986). Yet there is no evidence that interspecific aggression is closely tied to the degree of niche overlap. Interference behavior (interspecific killing and avoidance behavior) ensures that competition is most prominent when two interacting species are close in size, regardless of niche overlap. If the costs of competition (e.g., risk of injury, energy expenditure) for large species were negligible, we would predict that they would attempt to exclude species with any degree of niche overlap. Alternatively, Schmidt (1986) suggested that interference behavior among canids may be an evolved response to periods of food shortage that persists even with food abundance.

Exploitative competition is commonly considered a prerequisite for the evolution of interference behavior (MacArthur 1972, Gill 1974). Persson (1985) argued that because small-bodied species with lower food requirements are generally superior in terms of exploitative competition, larger species can be competitively superior only via interference behavior.

Schmidt (1986) suggested reduction in parasite incidence as an alternate explanation for interference behavior. However, the role of disease and parasitism in population dynamics of canids is highly contingent on unique characteristics of host and disease organisms, and not of uniform significance (Brand et al. this volume). Furthermore, one might postulate serious negative effects on individual reproductive success for canids that aggressively interacted with carriers of important parasites and pathogens. In Alaska, wolves acquire rabies only in areas of overlap with arctic foxes (Brand et al., Johnson, this volume), but individual wolves that exclude rabid arctic foxes by direct interaction are likely to die (Chapman 1978).

Competition for den sites was also postulated as a possible driving force underlying interference behavior (Schmidt 1986). Although den sites are scarce in areas of permafrost, this is unlikely to be the case for canids elsewhere in North America. Furthermore, the ousting of a small canid from a den by a large canid could be readily accomplished without widespread aggression throughout the year.

I believe that the pervasive importance of food in regulating carnivore populations (e.g., for wolves, Zimen 1976, Mech 1977c, Keith 1983, Peterson and Page 1988, Fuller 1989) provides the best evolutionary perspective for understanding interference behavior among canids. While the behavior is not confined to species that show close niche overlap, the effectiveness of exclusion depends on similarity in body size.

Acknowledgments

I am grateful to L. Fredrickson, R.R.P. Stardom, W.E. Berg, C.M. Pils, and T.F. Reis, who kindly supplied unpublished data on furbearer harvest and/or abundance in their respective jurisdictions, and to A. B. Sargeant, who provided vital inspiration and encouragement.

Comparative Population Dynamics of North American Wolves and African Wild Dogs

■ Todd K. Fuller

North American wolves and African wild dogs are large, pack-hunting canids that prey mostly on medium- to large-size ungulates. Although both species are considered endangered and are legally protected in parts of their range, elsewhere they are regarded as livestock-killing pests. Many demographic characteristics of these ecological counterparts are similar (e.g., age of first reproduction, pup and adult survival rates, sources of mortality, and dispersal rates), but wolves usually have smaller litters, pack sizes, and territory/home range sizes. Although the range of densities of wild dogs and wolves are comparable and vary similarly, relative abundance of potential wild dog prey and competitors is much higher. Potential rates of increase are high for both species, and in combination with immigration from adjacent areas, have allowed some populations decimated by natural or human-related causes to recover rapidly. Wolf and wild dog populations are regulated to varying degrees by 1) prey distribution, abundance and vulnerability; 2) direct human-caused mortality; 3) disease; and, perhaps 4) competition with other large carnivores. Conservation problems and concerns for these two species are often identical.

Introduction

Wolves (*Canis lupus*) have long aroused reverence, fascination, and contempt among Holarctic humans because of their size, sociality, vocal prowess, and propensity to kill large ungulates, both wild and domestic (Lopez 1978). Wolves were perceived as competitors and potential predators of humans, thus Caucasians, in particular, persecuted them as an enemy. More recently, Europeans dispersing to Africa encountered a different-looking, taxonomically distinct (Girman et al. 1993, Wayne et al. this volume) canid, the African wild dog (*Lycaon pictus*), that possessed many of the same attributes as wolves (Mech 1975). They are sizeable, pack animals that kill large game mammals in an "unappealing" manner, and indeed are the "wolves" of Africa. As a result of their conspicuous behavior, these ecological and cultural counterparts were both deemed abominations to be exterminated, and their ensuing reduction and extirpation is remarkably parallel. As human populations expanded and cleared land for agriculture, wolves and wild dogs were shot, trapped, and poisoned to reduce competition for ungulates and eliminate the potential for livestock depredation (Young and Goldman 1944, Lopez 1978, Mech 1970, Carbyn 1987). Government representatives often carried out control campaigns on behalf of the public, even in national parks, and subsequently numbers

and distribution of both species declined precipitately in many areas (Ginsburg and Macdonald 1990).

However, this dramatic change in status, fused with increasing interest in models for human social evolution and enhanced environmental awareness, provoked a counter-perception that by the 1970's resulted in increased efforts to research ecological, behavioral, and conservation-oriented aspects of large social predators (cf. Mech 1970, van Lawick-Goodall and van Lawick-Goodall 1971). This was especially true for wolves because many reside in more economically affluent areas (i.e., North America and Europe) where research funds and technology were more readily available and, consequently, a remarkable literature has resulted (cf. summary by Carbyn 1987). A similar, limited interest was demonstrated for African wild dogs, but only in the late 1980's were scientific endeavors of comparable magnitude initiated (cf. summary by Fuller et al. 1992b).

Wolves have a charisma that stimulates human concern for the environment, including ecosystems that humans have degraded as well as those considered wilderness. Comparable value may be assigned to wild dogs, as well, because of their ecological and cultural similarity. An understanding of the parallels and differences in wolf and wild dog population ecology will not only clarify their worth in this regard, but increase our understanding of carnivore population dynam-

Table 1. Population characteristics of North American wolves and African wild dogs.

Demographic parameter	Wolves[a]	African wild dogs[b]
Pack size (includes pups > 6 mo. old)	5-12(36)[c]	10-17(50)[c]
Territory/range size (km^2)	50-1,600(13,000)[c]	400-1,500(3,800)[c]
Density (no./1,000 km^2)	3-43(92)[c]	2-35
Sex ratio (%F) of adults (> 1 year old)	11-58	25-50
Age of first female reproduction (mo.)	22	22
Breeding females/pack	1-2	1-2
Usual litter size	4-7(11)[c]	7-15(21)[c]
Annual survival rate of pups	0.35-0.70	0.14-0.73
Annual survival rate of adults	0.32-0.87	0.55-0.89
Yearling dispersal rate	0.16-0.83	0.10-0.75
Usual dispersal pattern	solitary	≥ 2 same-sex sibblings
Observed annual finite rate of change	0.40-2.40	0.83-1.77

[a]   Summarized in or reported by Mech (1970, 1974), Ballard et al (1987), Peterson and Page (1988), Fuller (1989) and Gese and Mech (1992)
[b]   Summarized by Fuller et al. (1992b).
[c]   Maximum value

---

ics and behavior in general. Despite the obvious potential for comparing certain aspects of wolf and wild dog ecology, only Mech (1975) has done so. This paper compares the demography of North American wolves and African wild dogs, and offers an assessment of conservation opportunities in the future.

Demographic Comparisons

Both wolves and wild dogs live in packs comprising unrelated mates and their offspring of one or more years (Mech 1970, Frame et al. 1979). Commonly, wild dog packs include one or more same-sex siblings of the mates (summary in Fuller et al. 1992b), but wolf packs may sometimes include an additional individual not closely related to pack members (Van Ballenberghe 1983a, Ballard et al. 1987, Lehman et al. 1992, Meier et al. this volume). Median pack size of wolves ranges from five to 12, smaller than the range of wild dogs (10–17, Table 1); in contrast to wolves, maximum size of wild dog packs observed in any one study almost always is > 20 (Fuller et al. 1992b).

The range of wolf territory size (50–1,600 km^2) encompasses that found for wild dogs, and no annual wild dog pack ranges smaller than 400 km^2 have been described (Table 1). Wild dogs are not usually described as being territorial (Kruuk 1972, Schaller 1972), but territorial tendencies for packs with larger ranges that have been observed are similar to those for wolves with similar range sizes (Fuller at al. 1992b). The reported ranges of densities of wolves and wild

dogs are similar. Nowhere, in comparison with other similar-sized mammals, are they very abundant, and they can exist at very low densities (2–5/1,000 km^2; e.g., Singer and Dalle-Molle 1985, Laurenson et al. 1990). Territory or range size appears related to density in a general way, and density for wolves and wild dogs is likely influenced most by prey density (Keith 1983, Fuller 1989, Fuller et al. 1992b). There is also some evidence to suggest that wild dog density varies with habitat type, given similar prey densities. Where habitat is more concealing and hunting is more successful, ranges may be smaller (Fuller et al. 1992b). It is unlikely that competitors influence wolf density to a large degree, but competition with spotted hyenas (Crocuta crocuta) and lions (Panthera leo) especially, may influence wild dog food acquisition and thus distribution (Fuller and Kat 1990).

Sex ratios of adult wolves and wild dogs often are skewed towards males (Table 1). There is evidence of less-skewed ratios at birth, but the mechanism by which initial or subsequent skewing occurs is unknown.

Age of first reproduction in the wild for both wolves and wild dogs is 22 months. Most commonly, only one female wolf or wild dog breeds per pack, but breeding by two females per pack is not rare where pack sizes are large (Harrington et al. 1982, Fuller et al. 1992b, Meier et al., this volume). The frequency of, and certainly the ultimate success in raising multiple litters, is likely related not only to the number of adult females present, but also to prey abundance, and the ability of the pack to provide sufficient food to pups. Certainly, specific social circumstances within the pack (e.g., total number of adults) also may influence production of multiple litters. Even a mother and daughter in the same wild dog pack have produced pups simultaneously (Fuller et al. 1992b). Parent-offspring matings apparently have not been documented for wild wolves, and only one reported case exists for wild dogs (Reich 1978).

The litter size of wolves (4–7) is about half of that of wild dogs (7–15, Table 1), and a single female wild dog has been reported by M.G.L. Mills (Fuller et al. 1992b) to produce a litter of 21 pups. This difference in mean litter size is responsible, in large part, for the difference in mean pack sizes reported for the two species.

Annual survival of pups varies greatly for both species, as well (Table 1), and is undoubtedly related to food abundance, and perhaps pack size and composition. There is evidence that pup survival is higher in packs with adult helpers (Harrington et al. 1983) that may provide additional food, and at least for wild dogs, assist in deterring predators (Fuller et al. 1992b). Wild dog pups die from a variety of causes, including predation, intraspecific strife, flooding, abandonment, and probably disease and starvation. Causes of wolf pup mortality are less known, but are probably similar (cf. Van Ballenberghe and Mech 1975).

Survival rates of adult wolves and wild dogs also vary greatly (Table 1). Rates of wild dog survival as low as those reported for wolves likely have not been observed, because no wild dogs have been studied where intensive control activities have been carried out as they have for wolves (Ballard et al. 1987). Still, human-caused mortality in the form of shooting, snaring, and vehicle collisions is common for both species, as are predation and disease (Carbyn 1987, Fuller et al. 1992b).

Although some wolf pups 10–11 months old disperse (cf. Peterson et al. 1984, Mech 1987, Fuller 1989, Gese and Mech 1991), most do so when yearlings, similar to wild dogs. Some adults of both species may also disperse, although for wild dogs it may be common for such dispersal to occur as a departure a second time from a pack formed after the first dispersal (Fuller et al. 1992b). Yearling wolf and wild dog dispersal rates both vary greatly, and likely reflect differences in food availability, and pack size and composition (Messier 1985b). Female-biased dispersal by wild dogs was recorded in Tanzania when prey abundance was quite low (Frame and Frame 1976), but often dispersal rates of both wild dogs and wolves are similar for both sexes (Gese and Mech 1991). The usual dispersal pattern of wolves is for solitary individuals to leave the pack (cf. Ballard et al. 1987, Fuller 1989, Gese and Mech 1991), but for wild dogs it is unusual if dispersers do not leave with at least one other same-sex sibling (Fuller et al. 1992b). Single wolves of the opposite sex may meet and then settle (Rothman and Mech 1979, Fritts and Mech 1981), whereas dispersing groups of wild dogs often meet similar groups of the opposite sex and settle (Fuller et al, 1992b). Maximum dispersal distance of

wolves may exceed 800 km (Fritts 1983) and for wild dogs > 250 km (Fuller et al. 1992c).

Although wild dog packs are on average larger than those of wolves, the potential rates of increase of both species are similar because observed litter sizes of wild dogs are also significantly larger than those of wolves (Table 1). Maximum actual annual rates of increase for wild dogs and wolves approaching or exceeding 2.0 have been recorded, as have annual rates of decline of > 15% (Table 1) related to excessive harvest (wolves; Ballard et al. 1987) or disease (wild dogs; Fuller et al 1992b).

Conservation Parallels

Conflicts between pack-hunting canids and humans, particularly with respect to direct competition for food, have always been present. In more recent times, this conflict reached a zenith when government personnel carried out campaigns to eliminate wolves and wild dogs in national parks in order to enhance game populations (cf. Weaver 1978, Childes 1988). Wolves and wild dogs have been systematically extirpated from many areas because of the livestock depredation they have caused (Young and Goldman 1944, Fanshawe et al. 1991).

Humans have indirectly caused most declines in wolf and wild dog numbers by eliminating habitat; that is, turning areas where prey species were abundant into agricultural lands where prey are scarce or nonexistent (Mech 1970, Fanshawe et al. 1991). In addition, some populations may become isolated, resulting in potential threats to demographic or genetic viability (Wayne et al. this volume, Fanshawe et al. 1991).

Increased contact with humans has resulted in increased disease potential because of increased contact with domestic dogs (Goyal et al. 1986, Mech et al. 1986); wild dogs and wolves have been affected by outbreaks of rabies (Alexander et al. 1992, Fuller et al. 1992b, G. Forbes, Waterloo University, pers. commun.). Canine distemper and parvovirus are pathogens that may be important in large canid conservation (Thiel 1993, Alexander et al. 1992). Increased human access into wolf and wild dog range via roads has impacted their numbers; wolves are shot, trapped, or otherwise killed more often where road densities are high (Thiel 1985, Jensen et al. 1986, Mech et al. 1988b, Mech 1989, Fuller et al. 1992a). Vehicle collisions are an important mortality source of wild dogs in the Serengeti and elsewhere (Fanshawe et al. 1991).

Currently, wild dogs number 2,000–5,000 in all of sub-Saharan Africa. Populations in West Africa will be extirpated in the immediate future if specific conservation measures are not invoked (Fanshawe et al. 1991, Ginsburg and Macdonald 1990). African wild dogs are listed as "endangered" by the U.S. Fish and Wildlife Service, but as "vulnerable" by the IUCN, although the Canid Specialist Group recommends a classification of "endangered" (Ginsberg and Madonald 1990). In North America, wolf

Todd K. Fuller

The African wild dog shows many adaptive behavioral traits similar to that of wolves. (Photo: T. Fuller)

numbers in Minnesota (1,500–1,750; Fuller et al. 1992a), Alaska (5,900–7,200; Stephenson et al., this volume), and Canada (52,000–60,000; Hayes and Gunson, this volume) are secure, but peripheral populations in other U.S. states are slowly recovering to low levels (cf. Fritts et al., Wydeven et al., this volume). Accordingly, legal protection varies by area from "endangered" to "locally vulnerable" (cf., Ginsberg and Macdonald 1990, Hayes and Gunson, Stephenson et al., Thiel and Ream this volume).

Research on both species has accelerated in recent years (Fuller et al. 1992b, this volume), and our understanding of population dynamics of large, social canids is such that some general conservation measures applicable to them, and perhaps to large carnivores in general, seem obvious. For contiguous populations of less than several hundred wolves or wild dogs, adequate areas need to be set aside specifically to ensure adequate prey densities, especially in light of competing carnivore species and humans. These areas will undoubtedly include vast tracts of private lands in some areas, as most national parks are of insufficient size (Fuller et al. 1992b). Conflicts with livestock production in these areas need to be mitigated through changes in animal husbandry practices (cf. Fritts 1982, Tompa 1983b), as well as through increased efforts to assure benefits from wildlife-based tourism (including that focused on wild carnivoves) or other commerical utilization are distributed fairly amongst landowners. It is also essential to increase monitoring of predator and prey populations, as well as of diseases that could affect them catastrophically. Wolves have received wide publicity and benefited from increased education efforts, but few people realize or care about the plight of wild dogs, so public education about this and other large carnivore species outside of North America should be a conservation priority.

These guidelines hold true for other large carnivores as well, but for many of them we do not yet have the ecological information to make intelligent comparisons and develop specific conservation strategies. As an example, another relatively large pack-hunting canid, the dhole (*Cuan alpinus*) or Asiatic wild dog has been studied little in the wild (cf. Johnsingh 1982). Its population dynamics may or may not parallel those of wolves and wild dogs, and until further research on population distribution and dynamics is carried out, the true threats to the species' continued viability remain unknown. The information we have gathered thus far on a number of large carnivore species provides important conservation insights, but we are far from claiming success in our efforts to adequately understand and manage them for future generations.

Acknowledgments

I am grateful for comments by W. Ballard, R. Peterson, and an anonymous referee, and support from the Department of Forestry and Wildlife Management, University of Massachusetts, Amherst. Page charges were defrayed by the University of Minnesota African Wild Dog Committee.

Monitoring Wolf Activity by Satellite

■ Steven G. Fancy and Warren B. Ballard

Indices of activity were monitored for 23 gray wolves in northwestern Alaska during 1987–1991 with a mercury tip switch and microprocessor in transmitters compatible with the Argos data collection and location system (Platform Transmitter Terminals [PTTs]). Wolves were more active during summer than winter. Activity indices in summer (May–September) were highest between 2200 and 0600 hours, but during winter wolves were most active between 0700 and 1600 hours. Activity indices in winter increased and became more variable as temperatures decreased. Activity sensors in PTTs can systematically monitor activity of wolves in remote areas throughout the year, but calibration studies with captive wolves are needed to determine the optimum tip switch orientation for discriminating among specific activities.

Introduction

Use of satellites to monitor movements and activities of free-ranging wildlife has expanded rapidly since 1984. The Argos Data Collection and Location System was used by the U.S. Fish and Wildlife Service and Alaska Department of Fish and Game during 1984–1990 to obtain more than 100,000 locations of caribou (*Rangifer tarandus*), polar bear (*Ursus maritimus*), muskoxen (*Ovibos moschatus*), and several other terrestrial mammals (Fancy et al. 1988, 1989, Harris et al. 1990). Recent advances in transmitter miniaturization and power supplies allow use of satellites for smaller species (e.g., wolves, geese [*Branta canadensis*]) under a wide range of study conditions.

In addition to providing animal location, sensors in the PTTs can monitor activity, ambient temperature, and other information by satellite (Fancy et al. 1988, Harris et al. 1990). We report here on the first use of satellites to monitor ambient temperature and activity of wolves. Accuracy, precision, and performance of wolf PTTs were described by Ballard et al. (this volume). Data on wolf movement patterns and comparisons of satellite telemetry with conventional VHF (very high frequency) telemetry will be presented elsewhere.

Methods

Fancy et al. (1988) presented a detailed description of the Argos system and its potential applications to wildlife research and management. Briefly, Argos instruments on two polar-orbiting satellites pass over Alaska approximately 24 times daily, receive signals from PTTs in the UHF (ultra high frequency) range, and relay data to ground stations in Alaska, Virginia, and France. Data are processed at Service Argos' computer facility in Landover, Maryland, and are received monthly on computer tapes or diskettes. Results may also be obtained three to eight hours following an overpass, using a telephone modem and computer access to the Argos computer (Fancy et al. 1988).

Beginning in April 1987, we deployed PTTs (Telonics Inc., Mesa, Arizona; mention of trade names does not constitute endorsement by the U.S. government) weighing 1.2 kg on 23 wolves weighing 28.6–51.7 kg (Table 1). Each collar was equipped with a UHF satellite transmitter and a conventional VHF radio transmitter that allowed wolves to be located from aircraft. Separate power supplies and antennas were used for each transmitter. Wolves were immobilized for collaring by darting them from a helicopter (Ballard et al. 1982, 1991c).

Each transmitter package cost approximately $3,500; annual data processing charges averaged $1,400 per PTT. To extend battery life, PTTs were programmed to transmit once each minute during the same six-hour period on alternate days. Unlike previous Telonics PTTs that used three D-size lithium batteries, prototype wolf PTTs used three C-size batteries. This smaller battery pack provided a theoretical life of six months based on six hours of operation every 48 hours at the anticipated ambient air temperatures. The electronics, antenna, and transmitted signal were similar to heavier transmitters that were tested on large mammals (Fancy et al. 1988, 1989, Harris et al. 1990).

Messages transmitted to the satellite contained both short-term (previous minute) and long-term (previous day) indices of wolf activity (Fancy et al. 1988). Six PTTs deployed in 1987 and 1988 also transmitted ambient temperature data, sensed by a thermistor in the PTT. The short-term activity index (range = 1–60) was a count of the number of seconds each minute that a mercury switch in the canister was activated. Higher counts indicated greater activity. The long-term index was the sum of short-term counts for a 24-hour period (maximum value = 86,400), and indicated total daily activity or mortality.

Table 1. Transmission dates and mercury tip-switch angles for satellite radio collars while deployed on wolves in northwest Alaska, 1987-1991.

Transmitter No.	Wolf No.	Pack	Sex	Weight (kg)	Switch Angle	Dates On/Off Wolf	No. Days on Wolf
7900	001	Rabbit Mountain	M	43.2	-4	17 Apr 87 - 29 Feb 88	319
7909	007	Jade Mountain	F	37.6	-4	25 Apr 88 - 21 Feb 89	303
7909	067	Pick River	F	39.0	+5	14 Apr 90 - 28 Jun 90	76
7910	016	Ingruksukruk	F	28.6	-4	26 Apr 88 - 13 Aug 88	110
7910	037	Pick River	F	44.9	-4	15 Apr 89 - 11 Jul 89	88
7911	012	Purcell Mountain	F	33.1	-4	13 Jun 88 - 19 Apr 89	311
7912	010	Nuna Creek	F	47.6	-4	28 Apr 88 - 6 Mar 89	313
7912	072	Upper Tag	F	39.0	+5	17 Apr 90 - 15 Jun 90	62
7913	024	Pick River	M	47.6	-4	16 Nov 88 - 18 Feb 89	95
7913	074	Ingruksukruk	M	49.4	+5	17 Apr 90 - 5 Jun 90	50
7914	014	Rabbit Mountain	F	44.9	-4	26 Apr 88 - 16 Feb 89	297
7914	032	Kiliovilik	F	36.7	+5	18 Apr 90 - 11 Jun 90	55
10908	030	Rabbit Mountain	F	37.2	-4	10 Apr 89 - 3 Jan 90	269
10909	048	Kateel River	M	51.7	-4	14 Apr 89 - 25 Jun 89	73
10910	033	Dunes	F	47.2	-4	10 Apr 89 - 1 Feb 90	298
10911	002	Purcell Mountain	F	45.4	-4	14 Apr 89 - 7 Aug 89	116
10912	040	Ingruksukruk	F	34.5	-4	14 Apr 89 - 19 Oct 89	188
10913	046	Upper Tag	F	38.1	-4	14 Apr 89 - 14 Apr 90	366
10914	033	Dunes	F	47.2	+5	18 Apr 90 - 27 Feb 91	316
10915	064	Purcell Mountain	F	39.9	+5	18 Apr 90 - 1 Dec 90	228
10916	057	Salmon River	F	50.8	+5	14 Apr 90 - 21 Jul 90	99
10917	055	Nuna Creek	F	46.7	+5	14 Apr 90 - 5 Jun 90	53
10918	050	Kiliovilik	M	40.4	+5	14 Apr 90 - 3 Jun 90	51

PTTs deployed in 1987–1989 (n = 14) had mercury tip switches oriented parallel to the wolf's spine with the anterior end angled -4° relative to the bottom of the PTT canister (Table 1). In 1990–1991, we deployed nine PTTs angled +5° to determine if activities could be better delineated.

The number of short-term activity counts received during a satellite overpass ranged from one to 13 (mean = 6.5 ± 2.0 [SD]), depending on the geometry of the overpass and the location of the wolf. We calculated a mean short-term activity index for each overpass and used it to subsequently calculate mean activity indices for each wolf and season. We compared means by two-way analysis of variance with season and switch angle as main effects (SAS 1987). To obtain hourly activity indices, we pooled data for all wolves having PTTs with the same switch angle within each season. Statistical significance was evaluated at the 95% confidence interval.

Results

Mean operation time (including days prior to deployment on the wolf and after the PTT was retrieved) for the 23 PTTs was 253 ± 79 (SE) days. This was 40% greater than their expected 180-day life. Five PTTs operated longer than one year, but five others failed within 100 days of deployment. The manufacturer cited premature battery failure as the primary reason for the short life of some PTTs.

Long-term (24-hour) activity counts were 144% (switch angle = -4°) and 820% (switch angle = +5°) higher in summer than in winter. For most wolves, activity counts were not highly correlated with movement rates. Long-term activity counts correlated with daily movement rates for only six of 22 wolves in summer and four of 12 wolves in winter. Similarly, short-term activity counts correlated with movement rates for only five of 22 wolves in summer and two of 12 wolves in winter.

Table 2. Short-term activity counts for wolves wearing PTTs (Platform Transmitter Terminals) with the anterior end of the mercury tip-switch angled -4 and +5 relative to the bottom of the PTT canister.

Switch Angle	Season	*n*	Mean	SE
-4	Summer	12	22.28	2.55
	Winter	9	12.27	1.38
+5	Summer	9	15.33	1.38
	Winter	2	1.91	0.29

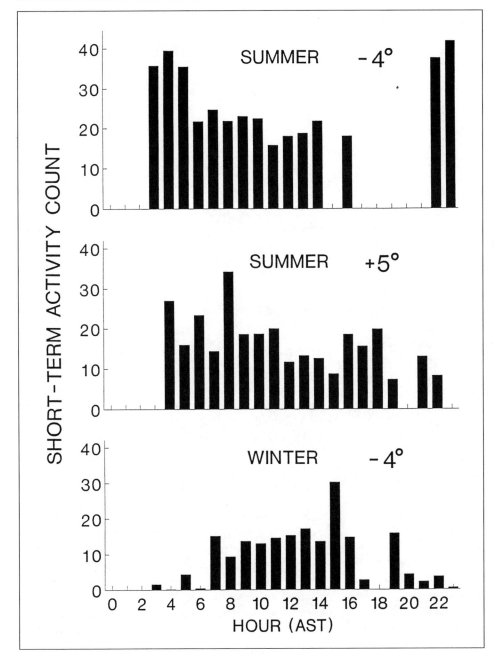

Fig. 1. *Mean hourly activity counts for 23 Gray Wolves in summer (May - September) and winter (October - April), northwestern Alaska, 1987-1991. The anterior end of mercury tip-switches in satellite transmitters were oriented -4 (n = 13, summer; n = 10, winter) or +5 (n = 9, summer) relative to the bottom of the canister.*

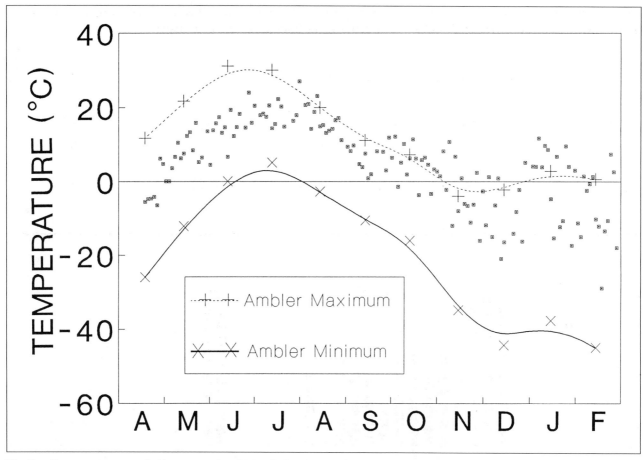

Fig. 2. *Temperatures recorded by a sensor in a PTT (Platform Transmitter Terminal) deployed on a wolf in northwestern Alaska. Monthly extreme temperatures (minimum and maximum) recorded at Ambler, Alaska, are shown.*

Mean short-term activity counts for PTTs with a -4° tip-switch angle were higher than those for PTTs with a +5° angle in both summer and winter ($F = 7.39$, $P = 0.011$). Activity counts were higher in summer than in winter for wolves wearing PTTs with either switch angle ($F = 13.54$, $P = 0.001$; Table 2). In summer, wolves appeared to be most active between 2200 and 0600 hours AST (Alaska Standard Time); in winter, activity counts were highest between 0700 and 1600 hours (Fig. 1).

Ambient temperatures transmitted by PTTs were within extremes recorded at nearby weather stations. Figure 2 shows transmitted temperatures from PTT 7900 in relation to monthly minimum and maximum temperatures recorded at Ambler, Alaska, 40 km from the wolf's territory. The wolf's winter temperatures were more variable than those in summer and frequently exceeded the maximum recorded temperature at Ambler. Behaviors such as curling the body to reduce heat loss, seeking relatively warm microenvironments, and basking on south-facing slopes probably account for the greater variation in winter temperatures.

We found significant inverse correlations between temperature and both mean short-term activity counts and stand-

ard deviation of activity counts for six of six wolves in winter, but for only one of six wolves in summer.

Discussion

Activity and temperature data for wolves were collected incidental to our primary objective of obtaining seasonal movement and home range data for determining wolf numbers (Ballard et al. 1990). Activity patterns of wolves have previously been studied at den and rendezvous sites (e.g., Mech 1970, Harrington and Mech 1982a, Ballard et al. 1991b), but this is the first study to systematically obtain activity data for wolves throughout the year.

Wolves were more active in summer than in winter, and during summer were most active between 2200 and 0600 hours. These findings agree with previous studies of wolf activity (e.g., Kolenosky and Johnston 1967, Mech 1970, Carbyn 1975, Ballard et al. 1991b). Mech (1970) and Harrington and Mech (1982a) thought the usual pattern of daytime attendance and nighttime absence of wolves from homesites was related to the wolf's inability to tolerate high summer temperatures, particularly in tundra areas where they cannot escape the heat because of lack of cover. Our finding that in winter, when temperatures were much lower, wolves were most active between 0700 and 1600 hours during the limited daylight hours, give some support to this hypothesis.

The mercury tip switches and software used to obtain activity counts may provide better discrimination among wolf activities than variable-pulse activity transmitters used by Gillingham and Bunnell (1985) and Beier and McCullough (1988), but calibration studies with captive wolves are needed (Kunkel et al. 1991). Fancy et al. (1988) found a high correlation between the short-term activity index and specific activities (e.g., lying, feeding, walking), and between the 24-hour activity index and daily movement rates for caribou, but several switch angles and counting intervals were tried with captive caribou before the best configuration for discriminating among activities was determined. Kunkel et al. (1991), using Wildlink collars (Wildlink Inc., Brooklyn Park, Minnesota 55444), were able to discriminate among three activity levels for captive wolves. Like the activity sensor used in Telonics PTTs, Wildlink collars contain a microprocessor that records the number of tip switch activations within a programmed time interval and stores the counts for later transmission.

We deployed PTTs with two switch angles on wild wolves, but lacked detailed observations needed to calibrate activity counts with specific wolf activities. The $+5°$ tip switch angle required greater movements of the wolf's neck to activate the switch and therefore produced lower counts than the $-4°$ angle, but neither angle produced counts that correlated with movement rates. Activity counts for wolves from PTTs appear to be useful as gross indices of wolf activity, but calibration studies with captive wolves are needed to determine the best switch orientation for discriminating among specific activities.

Acknowledgments

We thank L.A. Ayres, J.R. Dau, D.N. Larsen, S. Machida, K.E. Roney, T. Smith, M.A. Spindler, and T.H. Spraker for assistance with capture and radiotracking of wolves. D.J. Reed and J.C. Greslin helped with data analysis, and L.D. Mech, D.R. Klein, K.A. Keating, and A. Lovess reviewed drafts of the manuscript. Funding for this project was received from Federal Aid in Wildlife Restoration funds, Pittman-Robertson program administrative funds, and from the Alaska Department of Fish and Game, Selawik National Wildlife Refuge, and National Park Service.

Steven G. Fancy and Warren B. Ballard

Observations on the Daily Activity Patterns in the Iberian Wolf

■ Carles Vilà, Vicente Urios, and Javier Castroviejo

Four wild adult wolves (two males and two females) were radio-tracked to estimate their activity patterns (overall activity and movement) in northwestern Spain. Daily activity began one hour after dusk and ended after sunrise. Some individual variation existed. Wolves were active about 25% of the time. We found a period of lower movement at midnight. Females with pups had a different cycle (an arythmic activity pattern). After the fourth month after birth, they changed to the typical pattern described above.

Introduction

Activity patterns of animals are an adaptation for exploitation of the environment in an efficient way (Daan and Aschoff 1982). Optimum patterns evolve through hunting or searching for food when prey is more easily located or easier to catch, avoiding danger (contact with humans), the optimal use of their senses, physiological and meteorological conditioning, social behavior (solitary or pack hunters), etc. In the same way, Gittleman (1985, 1986) studied the relationship between the activity cycles and life history characteristics among carnivores.

Available papers describing activity patterns for free-ranging gray wolves are often based on only a few individuals and observations (Kolenosky and Johnston 1967, Kunkel et al. 1991, Williams and Heard 1991). Mech (1970) points out that in North America wolves are nocturnal in summer, but active as well during daytime in winter; whereas Boitani (1986) reported that in Italy, wolves are nocturnal throughout the year. Monitoring of some dens and rendezvous sites during the breeding season has yielded additional information on attendance patterns (Carbyn 1975, Harrington and Mech 1982a) and activities (Ballard et al. 1991b) in these places, but little is known about the activities outside.

The aim of this paper is to present the preliminary results of a study on the activity patterns of a population of Iberian wolves, discussing the influence of human pressure, and the changes that occur in female activity during the breeding season.

Study Area

The study was conducted in a 4,000 km^2 area in northwestern Spain, between Zamora and Len provinces (42°10'N 6°30'E) (Fig. 1). This is an unprotected area with a hunting season every year. Limited numbers of wolves can be killed with special permission when they inflict important damages upon livestock. Some illegal hunting exists. The mean altitude of the area is about 1,000 m, but reaches 2,200 m in the mountains to the north. Vegetation consists of shrubs and coniferous stands in the mountains, and large areas of mostly abandoned agricultural fields with some small forests of pyrenaic oak (*Quercus pyrenaica*) or evergreen oak (*Q. ilex*) with Cystacea in the plains. Forests cover less than 20% of the area. Small villages are widespread. People live mostly on small-scale agriculture and livestock raising. For a detailed description of the study area see Vilà (1993).

Main wild prey for wolves are roe deer (*Capreolus capreolus*), wild boar (*Sus scrofa*), hares (*Lepus europaeus*), and rabbits (*Oryctolagus cuniculus*). Domestic animals most often killed by wolves are sheep, goats, and dogs. In this area, wolves are also known to eat carrion (pigs, kitchen remains, sheep, goats, cattle, dogs), fruits, and garbage (Castroviejo et al. 1975, Reig et al. 1985, Salvador and Abad 1987, Cuesta et al. 1991).

Material and Methods

Four adult wolves (two males and two females) from different packs were trapped and radio-collared in 1988 and early 1989. During 1988 and 1989 these individuals were located daily. In addition, their activity was monitored during 24-hour periods 34 times with real-time activity sensors (tip switch sensors, Garshelis et al. 1982). During the 24-hour cycles every change in the activity level was noted, and the position of the monitored animal was estimated at half-hour intervals by ad hoc triangulation (Nams and Boutin 1991) from the nearest access. The minimum distance traveled during the 24-hour cycle was estimated by adding all the movements registered.

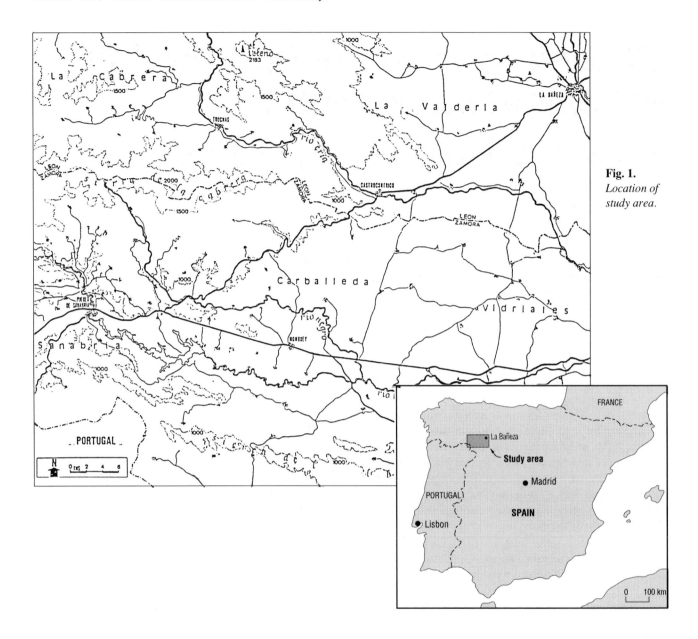

Fig. 1.
Location of study area.

For the description of the general activity patterns we considered two measures of activity: the percentage of time spent in any activity [all physical movements other than those associated with lying or standing (Ballard et al. 1991b)] detected by changes in the collar's signal, and the mean distance traveled at each hour. To compare the changes in the activity patterns during the breeding season in females, the activity levels were estimated as the percentage of time spent in activity at different periods of the day: daytime (from 0800 to 1700 h), dusk (1700 to 2000 h), night (2000 to 0500 h), and dawn (0500 to 0800 h).

Iberian wolves have their pups at the end of May or beginning of June (Grande del Brío 1984). Therefore, we considered three periods in the annual cycle of females that coincided with major changes in wolf spatial and temporal ecology: a) a "nursing period" from early June to mid-July, during which time the female stays in or near the den with

the pups younger than six weeks; b) a "post-weaning period" from mid-July to late October, by which time pups have reached five months of age and begin to move outside home sites — the mother's movements are centered around the rendezvous site (Joslin 1967), where the pups remain most of the time; and c) a "rest-of-year period" from November to May, when the female and her young move with other pack members, abandoning rendezvous sites.

We used the Kruskal-Wallis test statistic (H) to test for differences in activity among the three periods of the year. The Mann-Whitney test (U) was used to compare the activity at the same parts of the day in different periods.

Results

On average, wolves were active about 24.9% of the time (six hours per day), but showed wide variability (n = 30,

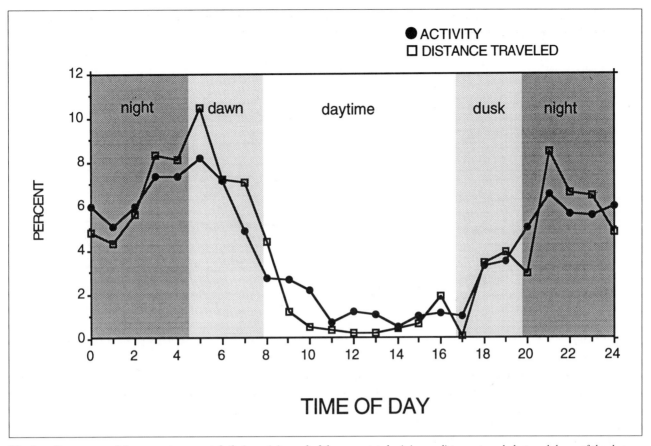

Fig. 2. *Percentage of the mean time spent daily in activity and of the mean total minimum distance traveled at each hour of the day.*

SD = 11.4, range: from 8.0 to 57.4%). During daytime wolves were active 9.7% of the time. Activity reached 16.1% at dusk. During night the total activity increased until dawn: wolves were active 38.2% of the night, and 41.7% by dawn (Fig. 2). No relevant variations of this pattern were found for the males throughout the year.

The mean minimum distance traveled was 13.0 km/day (SD = 10.7, range: 0.2 to 47.3 km/day). When we use the mean distance traveled per hour as an index of locomotor activity, the results are very similar to the overall activity described above (Fig. 2), but two peaks are clearly visible, at 2100 and 0500 h, and a low occurs in the middle of the night; thus, the global pattern is clearly bimodal. This means that the movements at the onset of night and at dawn represent a larger part of the overall activity budget than at midnight.

The activity of females with pups differed from that of wolves at other times of the year. Four 24-hour cycles were monitored during the nursing period, seven during post-weaning, and 13 during the rest-of-year period. Female wolves were active 23.8% of the time for most of the year (Table 1). Although the total activity decreased 8.7% (to 15.1%) when the pups were very young (nursing period), these differences were not significant (H = 2.66, P = 0.26).

The activity patterns of female wolves in the three periods showed wide variability (Fig. 3). During the post-weaning and rest-of-year periods females were more active during the night and at dawn. During the day, minimum activity was recorded until dusk. No significant differences were found when comparing the activity levels at each time interval in these two periods (U = 27.0 to 53.0, P = 0.14 to 0.78).

When the pups were youngest, the mother's activity pattern showed important changes (nursing period; Fig. 3, Table 1), with greater activity during the day, low levels at night and at dusk, showing a multimodal distribution. The higher values reached during the day were significantly different from those of females with older pups (post-weaning period, U = 3.0, P = 0.03) and during the rest-of-year (U = 7.0, P = 0.03). The lower values during the night were significant in comparison with those at the rest-of-year period (U = 43.0, P = 0.05) and nearly significant with the post-weaning period (U = 22.5, P = 0.11). No differences were found when comparing activity levels at dawn and at dusk in the different periods (U = 19.0 to 36.0, P = 0.18 to 0.91).

Discussion

The low mean activity levels (around 25% of the day) and high variability (Fig. 3) observed in our study could be

Table 1. Mean percentage of time breeding female wolves were active during the whole day (SD in brackets) and at each part of the day (n = number of 24-hour cycles monitored).

PERIOD	Nursing Jun-mid July (n = 4)	Post-Weaning mid July-Oct (n = 7)	Rest-of-Year Nov-May (n = 13)
Whole day	15.1 (2.2)	23.6 (10.1)	23.8 (10.4)
Daytime (8.00-17.00)	22.6	5.8	12.3
Dusk (17.00-20.00)	4.6	14.9	18.1
Night (20.00-5.00)	7.5	37.0	34.5
Dawn (5.00-8.00)	26.0	45.6	31.8

expected, if we are dealing with large predators that either feed on carrion or kill large animals, thus providing food for more than one day. This allows them to rest for longer periods [e.g., seven or more days in North America (Mech 1970, Fuller 1989)] after a successful hunt. The mean activity level in this study was much lower than that observed in most previous wolf studies. After 11,137 daytime observations of wolves during 20 winters in Minnesota [wolves are active at all times of day in winter in North America (Mech 1970)], Mech (1992) found that in 35% of the observations the animals were engaged in activities other than sleeping and resting. The same was found in 44% of winter observations in Kenai Peninsula (Peterson et al. 1984) and in 16–42% of observations in Minnesota (Mech 1977c). In the same way, data obtained by year-round radio-tracking in Italy suggest that wolves are in some kind of activity more than 65% of the time (Boitani 1986). Mech (1977c) correlates the decrease in the time spent traveling and feeding by a pack with a decline in prey numbers and lower number of kills, and suggests that this could be a strategy to diminish energy expenditure. In our study area, trophic resources do not seem to be a limitation, but the patchy environment, with fewer areas where wolves can remain during the day to avoid humans, and where prey concentrate, may contribute to lower activities and movements. Moreover, carrion is rather common and often easy to locate with minor wanderings. We could expect the same to happen in Italy, as the human pressure there is also high; however, this is not the case and the activity there remains rather high. The reason for this difference could be that in our study area wolves prey mostly on wild and domestic ungulates and feed on carrion (Castroviejo et al. 1975, Reig et al. 1985, Cuesta et al. 1991),

whereas wolves in Italy sustain themselves largely on garbage (Boitani 1986). It is likely that the wolves studied sustain themselves on resources that may require fewer hours per day to obtain.

Our results clearly show a nocturnal behavior pattern in the Iberian wolves studied, with the activity extending to the early morning hours. The information presented by Kolenosky and Johnston (1967), Mech (1970), Kunkel et al. (1991), and Williams and Heard (1991) suggests that the activity pattern for the wolves of most North America is not so clearly nocturnal. Carbyn (1975) noted that activity at rendezvous sites in Jasper National Park peaked in the early morning hours. One reason for possible differences between North America and Spain is a human population density of around 20–30 people/km[2] in our area. Here, the human population has been in competition with the wolf for millenia. Thus, the nocturnal behavior could be the result of wolves trying to minimize contact with people. In Italy, where the human pressure is also high, wolves are also nocturnal (Boitani 1986). The studies in captivity conducted on other canids by Kavanau and Ramos (1975) and Roper and Ryon (1977) suggest that the visual system of those species is best adapted for crepuscular and daytime activity. Kavanau and Ramos (1975) state that "phasing differences between adults in the laboratory and in the wild would suggest that visual-system influences in the wild were overridden by more critical factors, such as predator [and human] pressure or prey availability." This seems to be the case for Iberian wolves.

The activity pattern resulting from the movements of wolves in our study shows a tendency toward bimodality, a fact that Aschoff (1966) suggests is common to most species.

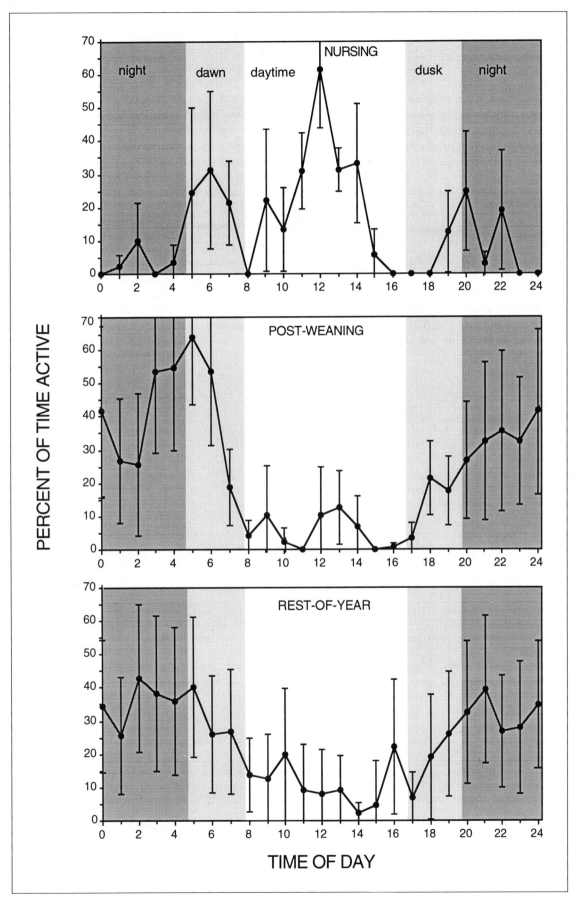

Fig. 3.
Percentage of time spent in activity by the breeding females and its variation (SD) for each period: Nursing — with cubs younger than one to two months of age (from June to mid-July), Post-Weaning — till the age of five months (from mid-July to late October), Rest-of-Year —from November to May.

Carles Vilà, Vicente Urios, and Javier Castroviejo

The comparison of the general activity patterns obtained by the different methods shows the existence of some periods when movement peaks, but in some periods, other activities (e.g., feeding, social interaction s) may have more importance. Just after dusk wolves start the search for food, but in the middle of the night they appear to have a resting period when they develop other activities not linked to movements. After that, by the end of the night and especially at dawn and early morning, movements increase, in general toward the daily resting places, usually safer and quieter than most of the areas visited during the night.

When the pups are six weeks old or younger, the mothers tend to be diurnal. During this time the females stay with the cubs almost 24 hours each day, and the activity level decreases to only 15.1%. Similarly, Harrington and Mech (1982a) and Ballard et al. (1991b) found that alpha females with young remain in the den 60 to 100% of the time, but they did not find any common activity or attendance pattern. In our study, nursing females move preferentially during daytime. In Spain, summer wolf packs (excluding pups) are usually small, in most cases including only two or three adults and yearlings (at least in one year, a radio-collared female was alone with her pups), and it seems that very often, when the female moves out from the den, the pups remain unattended (see also Harrington and Mech 1982a). The safest moment to do this is during daytime, when sunlight will help to keep the pups warm and the probability of a fox or a wild boar encountering the den is minimal, as they are also nocturnal. Both species are known to occasionally kill wolf pups. When cubs are in the post-weaning period, after their second month, female activity is similar to that of the rest of the year, but her movements are concentrated over a smaller area, centered on the rendezvous sites, where pups wait.

Acknowledgments

We acknowledge A. Kuntz, J. Reija, and J.M. Vadillo for their assistance during the field work. Three anonymous reviewers gave valuable comments to improve the manuscript. C. Keller corrected the English version. This study was carried out with the support of the Asociacin Amigos de Doñana.

Attitudes and the Perception of Wolf Social Interactions: Implications for Public Information Programs

■ Rita E. Anderson, Bonny L.C. Hill, Jenny Ryon, and John C. Fentress

Observers with little or no knowledge of wolf social interactions agree with expert classification of friendly and agonistic social interactions when attention is drawn to facial information. They also tend to rate some types of interactions as more friendly than do expert observers. To determine whether attitudes were related to these apparent biases, university students first rated several short (three- to 13- second) prosocial and agonistic interactions between pairs of wolves and then completed an extensive questionnaire. Responses to the questionnaire were analyzed to determine how the amount of experience with dogs, knowledge of, interest in, and regard for wolves, amount of outdoor activity, and attitudes towards nature and the wilderness relate to differences in the perceived friendliness of wolf social interactions. Some implications for the development of information programs are discussed.

Introduction

In this paper, we present findings on human perception of wolf (*Canis lupus*) social interactions and how attitudes affect those perceptions. We then examine some implications of these results for the development of public awareness and education programs in wolf management.

The importance of human perceptions and attitudes in the management of wolf populations has been well documented. Hook and Robinson (1982) showed that direct human persecution of wolves was responsible for the failure to reestablish wolves in Michigan during the 1970's, either through natural wolf immigration or experimental wolf reintroduction programs. The two most potent factors contributing to an antipredator attitude were fear of wolves (cf. Tucker and Pletscher 1989) and a negativistic attitude toward animals in general. Although consumptive use of wildlife was not related to a negative attitude towards predators, those most likely to kill wolves were hunters with an antipredator attitude (7% of the sampled population). Clearly, personal attitudes can influence personal behavior and, consequently, management plans.

Bath (1989, 1991b, Bath and Buchanan 1989) examined the attitudes and knowledge of the general public and specific interest groups toward the reintroduction of wolves in Yellowstone National Park. The extremes of opinions toward reintroduction were defined by the positive attitudes of members of the Defenders of Wildlife and the negative attitudes of the Wyoming Stock Growers Association. Kellert described the attitudes, knowledge, and behavior toward the timber wolf of the general public and specific interest groups in Minnesota (Kellert 1985b, 1986) and Michigan (Kellert 1991). Urban residents tended to be considerably more positive and protectionistic toward the wolf than farmers, hunters, and trappers.

Even when efforts are made to balance the impact of wolves on other animals (e.g., wild prey and predator populations, domestic animals) with the recreational value of healthy populations of wild wolves (Bath 1991b, Hill 1979, Mech et al. 1991a, Singer 1991b), the nature of wolf control and enhancement programs is certain to lead to conflict with various public groups. To minimize conflict and to maximize constructive criticism and support of wolf management programs, differences in attitudes among vari-

Rita E. Anderson, Bonny L.C. Hill, Jenny Ryon, and John C. Fentress

ous target groups need to be acknowledged and addressed when developing public awareness and education programs.

Distinguishing between Friendly and Agonistic Wolf Social Interactions

Although many have speculated that untrained (naive) observers can readily identify play in other species (Loizos 1966, Miller 1973, Fagen 1981), relevant data have been virtually nonexistent. Recently, however, Anderson, Ryon, and Fentress (1995) asked university students who had never received formal instruction about wolf social interactions to rate how friendly or agonistic a variety of common interactions between pairs of adult wolves appeared to them. The subjects consistently distinguished between playful or friendly and agonistic interactions as identified by experts when the faces of the wolves were perceptually salient (e.g., the faces were large or the action focused on the face). When the faces were not perceptually salient, subjects were less able to distinguish between the friendly and agonistic versions. Other research has similarly indicated that human facial expressions and vocalizations are often used to distinguish between rough-and-tumble play and serious fighting in children (Fry 1987, Smith and Lewis 1985).

Contrary to expectations derived from the literature (McArthur and Baron 1983), the untrained subjects in the Anderson et al. (1995) study were not more sensitive to, or prepared to see, aggression. Instead, the subjects' ratings were generally friendly. Three potential explanations were suggested for this apparent friendly bias. The first explanation focused on attitudes and beliefs. University students may view wolves in a positive light, as the "good guys" (Kellert 1985b, 1991). If "good guys" are not associated with aggression, then neither are wolves. The second explanation postulated a contrast effect: because aggression in wolves implies blood and gore, their absence may signal reduced aggression. The fact that subjects rated some of the agonistic interactions as more aggressive on a second viewing of the interactions is consistent with, but does not explain, a contrast effect. The third explanation suggested that people are generally more likely to make friendly or playful interpretations than agonistic interpretations. If true, the purported ease of identifying play (Loizos 1966, Miller 1973, Fagen 1981) may stem from a fundamental bias to perceive interactions as friendly, unless otherwise indicated by appropriate agonistic facial expressions and vocalizations or by training in the use of nonfacial visual and movement cues.

The Influence of Beliefs and Attitudes on Ratings

The present experiment was designed to examine the hypothesis that beliefs and attitudes about nature and wildlife might affect the perception of wolf social interactions. Untrained university students rated wolf social interactions as in Anderson et al. (1995) and then completed a questionnaire

designed to assess a variety of behaviors and attitudes toward nature, wildlife, and wolves. The eight attitude scales toward nature and wildlife used in the study were based on those developed by Kellert (1980c, 1989) and are briefly described in Table 1. In his study of the attitudes of the Minnesota and Michigan public toward wolves, Kellert (1985b, 1986, 1991) identified six attitude scales: naturalistic, ecologistic, moralistic, utilitarian, dominionistic, and negativistic. Except for the focus on wolves, the definitions of those scales coincide quite closely to the descriptions in Table 1. Kellert (1985a) found that a positive regard for predators was associated with higher scores on the naturalistic, ecologistic, and moralistic scales and lower scores on the negativistic and utilitarian scales.

How might attitudes towards wolves and wildlife affect the perception of wolf social interactions? We hypothesized that more friendly ratings might be associated with a strong humanistic attitude, based on "romanticized notions of animal innocence and virtue" (Kellert 1989:8) or possibly a strong moralistic attitude, based on "opposition to inflicting pain, harm, or suffering on animals" (Kellert 1989:8). More agonistic ratings might be associated with strong dominionistic or negativistic attitudes, based on "challenge, confrontation, and competition" or "little sense of kinship or affinity for animals," respectively (Kellert 1989:9). No clear predictions were made for the direction of bias (if any) associated with strong ecologistic or scientistic attitudes. We expected other variables, such as interest in and attitudes toward wolves, to affect ratings of wolf social interactions.

Method

Subjects

The subjects consisted of 91 university students from three different animal-behavior courses: 38 students at Memorial University rated the interactions on Tape 1, 21 students at Dalhousie University rated the interactions on Tape 2, and 32 students at Memorial University rated the interactions on tapes 1 and 2. Students had not received formal instruction about wolf social interactions in their course work. The total sample consisted of 63 females and 28 males. All subjects rated the interactions and then completed the questionnaire during a laboratory session.

For comparison, three experts on wolf social behavior rated the interactions in Tape 1, and two experts rated the interactions in Tape 2. All experts had studied wolf social behaviors first-hand for a minimum of two years and had hand-reared at least one wolf pup.

The Interaction Tapes

The interactions were selected from the video records of the Dalhousie Animal Behavior Field Station (Shubenacadie, Nova Scotia). All interactions were taken from tapes of ongoing social behavior where observation of the complete interactions, including vocalizations, led to almost certain

Table 1. The eight attitude scales described by Kellert (1989). The information in parentheses indicates the number of statements used to measure each attitude, the maximum sum scale value, and the actual range of scores on each scale.

Naturalistic: Interest in and affection for the outdoors and wildlife, with an emphasis on active participation and personal involvement. (5 statements, 25, 7-25)

Ecologistic: Focus on the conceptual interrelations between wildlife populations, the environment, and humans. (2 statements, 10, 3-10)

Humanistic: Affection for and attachment to individual animals, most often to pets; regarding wildlife, the focus is on animals with anthropomorphic associations, or those that are large, aesthetically pleasing, or phylogenetically close to humans. (2 statements, 10, 3-10)

Moralistic: Concern with the ethically appropriate human treatment of nonhumans, often emphasizing the equality of all animals. (4 statements, 20, 6-20)

Scientistic: Interest in nature and wildlife as objects of study and observation. (2 statements, 10, 2-10)

Utilitarian: Interest in nature and wildlife as they benefit humans, materially or practically. (6 statements, 30, 6-21)

Dominionistic: Satisfactions stemming from control and mastery of nature and wildlife. (5 statements, 25, 5-17)

Negativistic: An active dislike or fear of nature and wildlife. (6 statements, 30, 10-24)

---

identification of the tone of each event. Tape 1 consisted of: one friendly or playful and one agonistic or fighting version of facial expressions, body slams, chases, and dominance-submission interactions, plus one slightly friendly and one slightly agonistic ambiguous interaction. These interactions ranged from three to 13 seconds in length. Tape 2 consisted of 10 short duration (two- to six-second) interactions, including: one friendly or playful and one aggressive or fighting version of facial expressions, facial bites, follows, and slams, plus two ambiguous interactions. The 10 interactions on each tape were randomly ordered. Each interaction was preceded by a title indicating the interaction number. The interaction was shown at normal speed, without sound. A 20-second blank interval followed presentation of the interaction, during which subjects responded by circling a number from 1 (very playful or friendly) to 10 (very aggressive or fighting) on their response sheets. Ratings of 5 or 6 were to be used if the interaction seemed ambiguous. A rating of 5 meant that the interaction seemed slightly friendly and a rating of 6 meant that it seemed slightly aggressive. [See Anderson et al. 1995 for further details about the interactions and test procedure.]

The Questionnaire: Attitudes and Behaviors

Information on 14 attitudes and behaviors were extracted from the responses to the five-part questionnaire. **Gender** (females = 1, males = 2) and the **maximum number of dogs** owned at one time were taken directly from the questionnaire. Subjects rated their evaluative feelings about wolves on seven semantic differential scale items (like-dis-like, good-bad, interesting-boring, smart-stupid, kind-mean, pretty-ugly, and not scary-scary) on a five-point scale. The sum of the seven ratings (ranging from 7 to 35) constituted the **wolf feeling score**; the scale was inverted so that the higher number was associated with more positive feelings towards wolves. Seven other predator and prey species were also assessed on these semantic differential scales. The **wolf knowledge score** ranged from 0–13 to reflect the number correct on a 17-item true-false test derived from Kellert (1985b). [Note: Only 13 of the 17 statements were scored because four statements contained the words "all" or "only."] The **outdoor activity score** ranged from 0–6 to indicate the variety and intensity of outdoor activity. Participation in each of three types of activity (e.g., hunting and fishing, camping and hiking, bird-watching and nature photography) received a score of 2 for high frequency activity (e.g., more than 10 times per year), 1 for occasional participation, and 0 for no participation. **Interest** in observing wolves in the wild ranged from 0–3 and was assessed by the number of yes responses to a question asking whether subjects would make an effort to observe wolves in the wild and whether they would spend money or holiday time to do so.

Attitudes towards nature and wildlife were determined by responses on a five-point Likert scale (strongly agree to strongly disagree) to 52 statements which had been developed by Hill (1984) to assess attitudes of the Newfoundland public toward the environment. Some of these statements had been drawn directly from Kellert's (1980c) survey, while others had been modified or added to reflect the

Rita E. Anderson, Bonny L.C. Hill, Jenny Ryon, and John C. Fentress

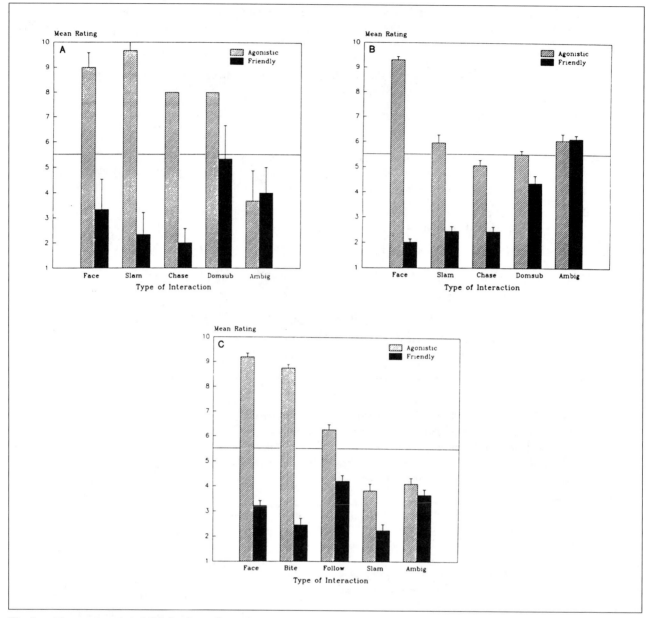

Fig. 1. *Mean ratings (+/- 1 SE) for the wolf social interactions by : (a) three wolf experts, (b) 70 naive subjects for Tape 1, and (c) 53 naive subjects for Tape 2.*

concerns of Atlantic Canada. When necessary, an inverse transformation was applied to the responses to some items in each scale so that agreement with the attitude was associated with higher scale values. The values given to each statement by each subject were then summed to yield a score for that attitude.

Results

Mean Ratings

The three experts distinguished between the agonistic and friendly versions of each type of interaction in Tape 1, except

for the ambiguous interaction (Fig. 1a). This pattern contrasts with the ratings of the 70 naive observers (Fig. 1b) who distinguished most strongly between the friendly and agonistic versions of those interactions where the faces of the wolves were perceptually salient. A similar pattern of results was observed for the two experts (not shown) and the 53 naive observers who rated the interactions in Tape 2 (Fig. 1c). When the wolf faces were not perceptually salient, untrained observers were less likely to distinguish between the friendly and agonistic versions. In some cases, the agonistic version did not even receive a mean "agonistic" rating (e.g., chases and dominance-submission in Tape 1, slams in Tape 2).

The above patterns were confirmed by the following analyses. The ratings by each subject for each type of interaction were submitted to an analysis of variance (ANOVA) where the between-subjects factor was university course (two different courses for each tape) and the within-subjects factor was the tone of the interaction (agonistic and friendly). Unless otherwise noted, all significant effects were reliable at the .01 level or beyond. University course did not interact with the tone of any interaction in any analysis. In the analysis of Tape 1 ratings, subjects rated the agonistic version of the facial expressions, slams, chases, and dominance-submission as more aggressive than the friendly versions, Fs $(1, 68) = 1341.78, 102.82, 130.99$, and 12.50, respectively (Fig. 1b). In the analysis of Tape 2 ratings, subjects rated the agonistic versions of the facial expressions, bites, follows, and slams as more aggressive than the friendly versions, Fs $(1, 51) = 478.97, 406.10, 51.21$, and 21.04, respectively (Fig. 1c). The difference between the ratings of the agonistic and friendly versions of each type of interaction by each subject was submitted to an ANOVA where university course was a between-subjects factor and type of social interaction (the five types for each tape) was a within-subjects factor. Course was not significant as a main effect or in interaction with type of interaction. Type of social interaction was significant in the analysis of the difference scores from Tape 1, $F (4, 272) = 101.90$, and Tape 2, $F (4, 204) = 79.92$. Newman-Keul's Range Tests revealed that the difference scores were larger for those interactions with a facial focus (facial expressions in Tape 1, facial expressions and facial bites in Tape 2) than for all other types of interactions.

Bias

To assess the extent of bias, ratings for the agonistic and friendly versions of each interaction were added for each subject and tested against the relevant expert mean summed rating. The lower the number, the more friendly the rating of the interactions (range 2–20). Subjects rated the facial expressions, slams, chases, and dominance-submission interactions in Tape 1 as more friendly than the experts, $ts(69) = 6.31, 9.33, 7.97$, and 9.95, respectively, and the ambiguous interactions as less friendly than the experts, $t (69) = 13.46$. Subjects rated the follows and ambiguous interactions in Tape 2 as more friendly than the experts, $t (52) = 3.78$ and 2.18, $p < .05$, respectively, and facial bites as less friendly than the experts, $t (52) = 9.03$.

Attitudes and Behaviors

The mean ratings on the seven semantic differential items for each of the eight species are shown in Figure 2. The domestic dog approached the ideal "good" animal on all scales. In addition, distinct predator and prey profiles can be seen. The profiles of predators (wolves, bears, eagles, and rattlesnakes) are similar to one another and differ from those of prey (sheep, cattle, and caribou). An ANOVA on the

attitude scores where university course was a between-subjects factor and attitude scale (the eight attitude scales) was a within-subjects factor indicated that attitudes did not differ between subjects from the three different courses, either as a main effect or in interaction with attitude scale. Consequently, no further distinction will be made between subjects in the different courses. The proportion of the maximum score for each of the attitude scales and the wolf knowledge scale for our university subjects is shown in Figure 3. This profile compares favorably to Kellert's (1980c, 1989) profiles of young adults and those with a college education, both of which also had fairly high scores on the naturalistic, ecologistic, humanistic, moralistic, and scientistic scales; fairly low scores on the utilitarian, dominionistic, and negativistic scales; and a fairly high wolf knowledge score. The pattern of intercorrelations between the attitude scales was consistent with the profile in Figure 3 and resembled the pattern reported by Kellert (1989), suggesting that these scales were valid for our sample.

The significant correlations ($ps < .05$) between scores on the naturalistic, ecologistic, humanistic, moralistic, and scientistic scales were positive (7 of 10 correlations, $rs = .22$ to $.46$), as were the significant correlations between the utilitarian, dominionistic, and negativistic scales (2 of 3 correlations, $rs = .22$ to $.46$). All but one of the significant correlations between the two groups of attitude scales were negative (7 of 15 correlations, $r = .22$; $rs = -.27$ to $-.72$). In addition, higher scores on the naturalistic ($r = .53$), humanistic ($r = .25$), moralistic ($r = .24$), and scientistic ($r = .34$) scales and lower scores on the utilitarian ($r = -.21$), dominionistic ($r = -.24$), and negativistic ($r = -.43$) scales were significantly associated with more positive feelings towards wolves as measured by the semantic differential items. A similar pattern based on a like-dislike scale was observed by Kellert (1985b) for the naturalistic, moralistic, utilitarian, and negativistic scales. A high naturalistic score was associated with more outdoor activity ($r = .25$) and an interest in observing wild wolves ($r = .27$). Individuals with stronger scientistic attitudes were also more interested in observing wild wolves ($r = .24$). Stronger negativistic attitudes were associated with lower knowledge of wolves ($r = -.27$), less interest in observing wolves in the wild ($r = -.26$), and less participation in outdoor activities ($r = -.28$).

Ratings and Attitudes

The summed ratings for each interaction used to assess the rating bias were correlated with the 14 attitudinal and behavioral measures. None of the 42 correlations involving the short-duration, facial-focus interactions were significant, 16% of the 42 correlations involving the short-duration interactions without a facial focus were significant, and 28% of the 56 correlations involving the longer-duration interactions were significant. The failure to observe any correlations between the summed ratings of any of the facial-focus interactions and the attitudinal variables is consistent with

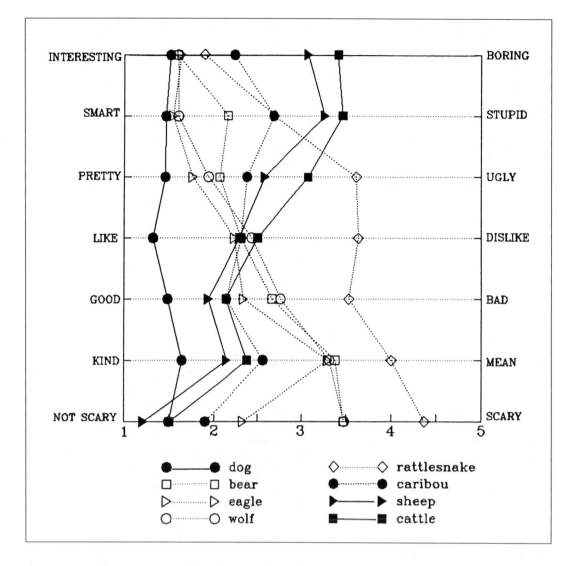

Fig. 2. *Mean ratings on the seven semantic differential items for eight different species (n = 91).*

the suggestion made by Anderson et al. (1995) that faces have a privileged position for signalling social information, even across species from wolves to humans. The fact that more correlations were significant for the longer duration than for the shorter duration interactions without a facial focus suggests that attitudes and experiences can affect the perception of social interactions, especially when the interactions are long enough to permit the observer to think about the interaction.

The pattern of simple correlations revealed that high or low scores on one scale were associated with more friendly or more aggressive ratings depending upon the type of interaction. For instance, low scores on the negativistic scale were associated with more friendly ratings of the slams ($r = .30$) and more aggressive ratings of the dominance-submission ($r = -.47$) interactions in Tape 1. To determine whether there was a higher-order relationship between the ratings and attitudes, shown in Table 2, a canonical correlation analysis was performed between the 14 behavioral and attitudinal variables and the five summed ratings for Tape 1;

a second analysis was performed using the five summed ratings for Tape 2. Subjects with missing data were deleted from the analysis, resulting in a total of 63 subjects for Tape 1 and 46 subjects for Tape 2 interactions. The first and second canonical correlations were substantially higher than the simple correlations and accounted for a significant number of relationships between the two sets of variables in the analysis of the data from Tape 1 (first canonical $r = .72$, $F(70, 214) = 1.69$, $p < .01$; second canonical $r = .68$, $F(52, 176) = 1.42$, $p < .05$). No significant canonical correlations were found in the analysis of data from Tape 2.

Results of the canonical correlation analyses were consistent with the patterns observed in the simple correlation analysis. Ratings of the facial-focus and short duration interactions were not related to any of the 14 behavioral and attitudinal variables. However, some longer-duration interactions were. A cut-off correlation of .30 between the scores and the canonical variables was used to determine which variables were relevant to interpretation of the first and second canonical variate pairs. The first canonical variate

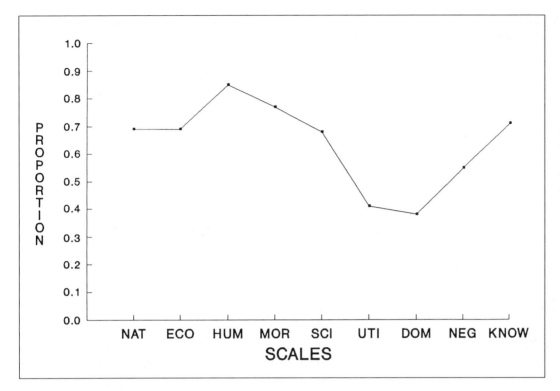

Fig. 3.
Proportion of the maximum score for each of the attitude and knowledge scales (n = 91).

Table 2. Means (maximum score) and standard deviations for the measures submitted to the canonical correlational analyses.

A: Analysis 1, Tape 1 (n = 63)			*B: Analysis 2, Tape 2 (n = 46)*		
Measure (max score)	*Mean*	*SD*		*Mean*	*SD*
FACE1 (20)	11.22	1.36	FACE2	12.39	1.56
SLAM1 (20)	8.49	3.13	BITE2	11.11	2.10
CHASE1 (20)	7.40	2.67	FOLLOW2	10.54	2.37
DOMSUB1 (20)	9.84	2.91	SLAM2	5.98	2.69
AMBIG1 (20)	12.03	2.83	AMBIG2	7.93	2.38
GENDER	1.35	0.48		1.26	0.44
MAXIMUM DOGS	1.11	1.14		1.04	0.76
WOLF FEELING (35)	24.87	4.60		25.83	3.78
WOLF KNOWLEDGE(13)	9.33	2.00		9.37	1.83
WOLF INTEREST (3)	1.98	1.25		1.89	1.23
OUTDOOR ACTIVITY (6)	3.30	1.27		3.11	1.37
NATURALISTIC (25)	17.24	3.95		18.35	3.60
ECOLOGISTIC (10)	6.84	1.45		7.07	1.58
HUMANISTIC (10)	8.29	1.88		8.59	1.57
MORALISTIC (20)	15.00	3.12		15.57	3.04
SCIENTISTIC (10)	6.83	1.99		6.70	2.16
UTILITARIAN (30)	12.60	3.06		11.91	3.02
DOMINIONISTIC (25)	9.75	2.96		9.13	2.94
NEGATIVISTIC (30)	16.25	3.67		15.46	3.50

Table 3. Correlations between the variables and their canonical variates, standardized canonical coefficients, and percent variance explained by their own canonical variables for the first and second canonical variate pairs.

Rating Variable	First Canonical Variate		Second Canonical Variate	
	Correlations	Coefficients	Correlations	Coefficients
FACE1	-.05	-.10	.14	.37
SLAM1	-.62	-.44	-.47	-.64
CHASE1	.42	.35	.35	.23
DOMSUB1	.75	.65	-.15	-.37
AMBIG1	-.26	-.32	.69	.74
% variance	24.0%		17.2%	
Personal variables				
GENDER	.45	.39	.36	.19
MAXIMUM DOGS	.35	.29	.31	.44
WOLF FEELING	.70	.43	-.37	-.58
WOLF KNOWLEDGE	.42	-.01	.00	.03
WOLF INTEREST	.31	-.00	.29	.50
OUTDOOR ACTIVITY	.18	.01	.28	.13
NATURALISTIC	.52	-.09	-.02	.22
ECOLOGISTIC	.22	.00	.29	.24
HUMANISTIC	.34	.18	-.09	.09
MORALISTIC	.02	-.15	-.34	-.19
SCIENTISTIC	.33	.04	-.40	-.39
UTILITARIAN	-.09	.07	-.07	-.36
DOMINIONISTIC	-.04	-.09	.37	.24
NEGATIVISTIC	-.73	-.55	.09	.15
% variance	15.8%		7.4%	

pair shown in Table 3 suggests that being male, having knowledge of, interest in, and positive regard for wolves, having owned more than one dog at the same time, being interested in the naturalistic, scientific, and humanistic aspects of nature and wildlife, and having little fear of nature and wildlife was associated with more aggressive ratings of chases and the dominance-submission interactions and more friendly ratings of the slams. The second canonical pair suggests that males who have owned multiple dogs, who have less positive feelings for wolves, low scores on the scientistic and moralistic scales, and high dominionistic scores were also likely to rate chases as more aggressive and slams as more friendly; however, this combination was also associated with more aggressive ratings of the ambiguous interactions.

Attitudes can affect the perception of wolf social interactions when the interactions are long enough to be interpreted.

However, attitudes do not affect the perception of these social interactions in any simple way. The type of interaction and attitude combine in fairly complex ways to create a social perception.

Conclusions and Implications

Wolf facial expressions provide a significant source of information about the tone of social interactions. Attitudes, interests, and experiences have little influence on the ratings of interactions when facial expressions are perceptually salient. Attitudes can affect the perception of wolf social interactions when wolf faces are not perceptually salient, although not necessarily in simple ways. Among these university students, the most important factors were feelings toward wolves (and to a lesser extent, knowledge of and interest in wolves), plus attitudes toward nature and wildlife on the negativistic, naturalistic, scientistic, and humanistic

Wolf behavior associated with a cooperative hunting strategy and pack cohesion makes it a subject of popular appeal to the public. This appeal translates itself to the image that the public has of the species. (Photo: J. Dutcher)

scales; gender was also important, as was multiple-dog ownership.

The attitude profile of the university students towards nature and wildlife (high naturalistic, ecologistic, humanistic, and moralistic attitudes, coupled with low utilitarian, dominionistic, and negativistic attitudes) differs substantially from the profiles of farmers, hunters, and trappers (Kellert 1980c). Our university student profile also appears to be more similar to the profile of urban residents toward the wolf than the profile of farmers (Kellert 1985b, 1986, 1991) who were more negative, hostile, and nonsupportive of wolves than any other identified group. It would be useful to examine how the attitudes and knowledge of special interest groups relate to their ratings of wolf social interactions. For example, would farmers, who tend to have stronger dominionistic and utilitarian attitudes than the general public, rate wolf social interactions differently than university students?

How attitudes affect behavior has implications for the development of educational programs on controversial issues in wolf management. The pattern of intercorrelations between the attitude scales and behaviors reveals that belief systems toward nature, wildlife, and wolves are complex and multifaceted. Furthermore, cognitive research shows that factual information is interpreted through the filter of a person's belief system. For example, children used the facts they learned from a program on whales and fishermen to reinforce their original attitudes and beliefs (Lien and Atkinson 1988).

To develop an interested and broadly informed public that can respond effectively to management plans, Lien and Atkinson (1988) suggested that educational programs must be adapted to the range of attitudes of various target groups. Because opinions on controversial issues are often based on complex belief systems, McCool and Braithwaite (1989) argued that information programs should present information about more than one content area. In addition, many have suggested that fear of wolves must be addressed in any information program (Hook and Robinson 1982, Tucker and Pletscher 1989).

One type of broad-spectrum program involving both attitudes and factual information, suggested by our research, would use videos of wolf social interaction s in an interactive fashion. People could be asked to rate (or otherwise comment on) the interactions, and then "expert" commentary could be offered. This program could be offered as part of a lecture, as an interactive display in visitor centres, as part of a wolf game modeling the value of the wolf in the ecosystem, or even as part of a short public information presentation on television.

This suggestion is based on several lines of evidence. First, video presentation is more likely to be attended to than print or lectures. In particular, short television presentations may be one way to reach groups who are resistant to other information sources (Lien and Atkinson 1988). Second, the personal involvement of rating (or commenting) engages the person more than simply reading, watching, or listening; consequently, information is more likely to be remembered (Eysenck and Keane 1990). Third, our data suggest that several aspects of the person and their belief system are involved in the rating of wolf social interactions (e.g., gender, dog ownership, feelings toward and knowledge of the

Rita E. Anderson, Bonny L.C. Hill, Jenny Ryon, and John C. Fentress

Wolf pups are usually born in dens and emerge at about three weeks of age. At birth, newborn pups are blind and deaf. The eyes open at about two weeks of age. (Photo: J. Dutcher)

wolf, negativistic, naturalistic, scientific, and humanistic attitudes). Consequently, having people view, rate, and discuss the interactions may be an effective way to activate and subsequently change critical attitudes about wolves and their actual behavior.

There is a need to promote realistic visions of wolf behavior. It is as damaging to good management for people to think about wolves as cuddly and incapable of doing harm, as it is to think about wolves as red in tooth and claw. By having people respond to wolf social interactions, one can perhaps reach those at both extremes, thereby promoting a more balanced understanding of the wolf and, hence, a greater acceptance and comprehension of the measures taken to protect and manage wolf populations.

Acknowledgments

Support from the President's NSERC Grant and a grant from the Publications Subvention Board from Memorial University and an NSERC Infrastructure Grant to the Dalhousie Animal Behavior Field Station is gratefully acknowledged.

Part Six: Taxonomy

Taxonomy and Genetics of the Gray Wolf in Western North America: A Review

■ Wayne G. Brewster and Steven H. Fritts

Early taxonomists named 24 subspecies of gray wolf in North America based on skull characteristics, body size, and color, often utilizing few specimens. Recent work using multivariate analysis, molecular genetics, and larger sample sizes suggests that this number of subspecies is unwarranted, with five North American subspecies being more reasonable. Extensive morphological overlap occurs among currently named subspecies, and names usually represent only averages or trends that supposedly occurred in an area. Highly sensitive analyses usually are needed to distinguish differences in morphology of populations. Genetic distinction among current gray wolf populations is small, at least in part due to the mobility of the species. Dispersal (implying gene flow) over long distances has been documented for wolves, including across multiple alleged subspecific ranges. Patterns of variability have not been static historically. The subspecies of wolf that was described for the central Rocky Mountains was similar to other subspecies, especially those in the western United States and southwestern Canada. Wolf populations that occurred in the northwestern United States and southwestern Canada prior to eradication may be assignable to a "supergroup" that was distinguishable from another "supergroup" occupying most of northern Canada and interior Alaska. Wolves were essentially eradicated in the Rocky Mountains south of central Canada by the 1930's, and thus any characteristics peculiar to the populations in that area of the continent were lost. Since then, wolves, most likely from Alberta and British Columbia began appearing in the northwestern United States and within the past decade established a breeding population. Indications are that wolves of current southwest Canadian stock will continue to recolonize southward within the northwestern United States; given enough time they are likely to become established in the Yellowstone area. Therefore, obtaining wolves from southern British Columbia or Alberta for reintroduction into Yellowstone and/or central Idaho would only accelerate an ongoing process and need not be viewed as compromising the "natural" or "historic" taxonomic arrangement of wolves.

Introduction

Gray wolf (*Canis lupus*) taxonomy, especially the subject of subspecies, is confusing to laymen and biologists alike (Mech 1991a). The current taxonomic classification of wolves has been questioned by a number of authors (Mech 1970, Nowak 1983, Mech 1991a). This topic has become controversial in the northern Rockies of the United States (U.S.), although current debate certainly is not limited to that area. The current controversy has prompted us to examine the history and current status of wolf systematics, especially as it relates to recovery of the wolf in the northwestern U.S. We expect wolf systematics to be an issue in most future gray wolf recovery programs.

From about 1860 to the mid-1930's, a series of events resulted in the eradication of wolves from the western U.S. and the southern Canadian provinces. These events included trapping and poisoning of wolves for their pelts, elimination of bison, drastic reduction of other native ungulates, intro-duction of domestic livestock, and finally, the assumption of predator control by the federal government with the objective of eliminating wolves from all federal land (Young and Goldman 1944, Curnow 1969, Lopez 1978, Weaver 1978). A review of the historical record and surveys indicates that a population displaying consistent reproduction has not been present in the Yellowstone area since the late 1920's (Weaver 1978). By 1925, it was unlikely that a viable population of wolves existed anywhere in Montana, and by 1940 few wolves were left in the western states (Day 1981).

A pattern of eradication similar to that in Montana, Idaho (Hansen 1986), and Wyoming also occurred in southern Alberta (Cowan 1947, Stelfox 1969, Gunson 1983a) and to a lesser extent in British Columbia (B.C.) (Tompa 1983a). During the 1970's and early 1980's wolves reoccupied southern Alberta except the prairie biome. This reoccupancy extended along the Rocky Mountain and foothills in the southwestern part of the province (Gunson 1983a). Wolf populations remained low or nonexistent in southeastern B.C. through the mid-1970's, but in recent years, have expanded into the southern parts of the province (Tompa 1983a).

The northern Rocky Mountain wolf (*C. l. irremotus*), a subspecies described by Goldman (1937:41), was listed as endangered in 1973. However, based on the likelihood of enforcement problems, the trend among wolf taxonomists to recognize fewer subspecies of wolves, and the determination that the entire species in the contiguous U.S. was in jeopardy, the entire species *Canis lupus* subsequently was listed in 1978. Therefore, the northern Rocky Mountain wolf referred to in the Northern Rocky Mountain Wolf Recovery Plan (U.S. Fish and Wildlife Service 1987) is any gray wolf in the northern Rocky Mountains, rather than a particular subspecies.

The recovery plan calls for the reestablishment of wolf populations in three areas of the northern U.S. Rocky Mountain: northwestern Montana, central Idaho, and the Yellowstone area. It was recommended that populations in the first two areas be reestablished by natural recolonization from Canadian populations and that a Yellowstone population be established by reintroduction because of the distance from robust wolf populations. This conservation action has also been recommended by Pimlott (1967b), Cole (1969b), Mech (1970, 1971, 1991a), Weaver (1978), and Peek et al. (1991) and has been discussed at numerous scientific meetings.

Since their eradication, denning of wolves was first documented in the western U.S. in 1986 (Ream et al. 1989). Subsequently, a breeding population has become established and continues to expand in western Montana (Ream et al. 1991, Fritts et al. this volume). Reports made by the public of observations of wolves and wolf sign appear to be increasing in western Montana, central and northern Idaho, Washington, and parts of northwestern Wyoming (Fritts 1991, Fritts et al. this volume). Natural recovery as far south as Yellowstone, however, is problematic.

While there is strong support for restoring wolves to Yellowstone (McNaught 1987, Bath and Buchanan 1989, Bath 1991b), many contend that wolves should not be reintroduced, and some of their reasons are based on taxonomy. Reintroduced wolves would have to come from a different part of North America, they argue, because the wolf originally inhabiting the area has been eliminated. They would of necessity be from a different subspecific area, according to the present classification. Therefore, according to this argument, it would be inappropriate to reintroduce wolves from another geographic area. Mech (1991a) observed that the layperson should not be blamed for making this argument because of the confusion surrounding wolf subspecies. Nowak (1983) also described the confusion on this subject. Our observations support the idea that there are many misconceptions about wolf taxonomy. For example, many members of the public appear to believe that single specimens should easily and confidently be assigned to subspecies on the basis of general appearance.

Another taxonomy-based argument against reintroduction is that there is now a small remnant population in the Yellowstone area (although there is no evidence for this assertion) that represents the original genetic stock. Therefore, as this argument goes, it would be inappropriate (and possibly illegal) to reintroduce wolves from another geographic area (James R. and Cat D. Urbigkit vs. Manuel Lujan, Jr. and John Turner, Civil Action No. 91CV1053B in the U.S. District Court for the District of Wyoming).

These arguments involve the interaction of the present taxonomic classification of the gray wolf and the legal provisions of the Endangered Species Act of 1973, as amended (ESA)(16 U.S.C. 1531 et seq.). The former argues that the ESA does not sanction introduction of a non-native subspecies; the latter argues against the contamination of original genetic stock, believed by some to still exist in the Yellowstone area.

Our specific objectives are to clarify the above debate by: 1) reviewing the development of the present taxonomic classification of the gray wolf in North America, with particular emphasis on the central Rocky Mountains; 2) reviewing recent genetic evaluations of wolf populations in North America; 3) briefly examining historic dynamics of wolf distribution in the area; and finally 4) assessing from a genetic standpoint the rationale of reintroducing stock from another geographic area to Yellowstone. Our conclusions also may be relevant to future wolf restoration efforts in other areas.

The Subspecies Concept

The debate cited above has much to do with the subject of subspecies designation in general. Taxonomy is the theory and practice of classifying organisms (Mayr 1970). It is an old field of science, and one that has undergone considerable evolution, with identifiable phases. Essentially, animal classification is a human attempt to identify, categorize, and describe variation in the biological world. The naming does not change the animal, but rather identifies where a taxonomist believes it would fit best into the phylogenetic array.

The distinctiveness of the gray wolf as a species is not an issue, despite the recent finding of some mitochondrial DNA (mtDNA) of apparent coyote origin in wolves from eastern North America (U.S. Fish and Wildlife Service 1990b, Lehman et al. 1991, Nowak 1991). It is the inclusion of a third latinized name (trinomial), indicating geographical race or subspecies that has led to the most controversy and confusion in taxonomy of gray wolves, as well as taxonomy in general.

Mayr (1970:12, 210) defined a species as "groups of interbreeding natural populations that are reproductively isolated from other such groups" and a subspecies as "an aggregate of local populations of a species inhabiting a geographical subdivision of the range of the species and differing taxonomically from other populations of the species." Dobzhansky (1970:310) accepted the subspecies definition and restated it candidly as "a race that a taxonomist regards as sufficiently different from other races to bestow upon it a Latin name." Note the high degree of subjectivity inherent in the subspecies definitions. It was understood that, although subspecies differ taxonomically, they belong to the same species and interbreed freely where they contact one another. Wilson and Brown (1953:105) stressed that geographical variation should be analyzed first in terms of genetically independent characters, which would then be employed synthetically to search for possible racial groupings. Avise and Ball (1990) argued that evidence for subspecific definition under the biological species concept must come from the concordant distribution of multiple, independent, genetically based traits.

O'Brien and Mayr (1991:1188) offered the following guidelines to further formalize subspecific classification: "Members of subspecies share a unique geographic range or habitat, a group of phylogenetically concordant phenotypic characters, and a unique natural history relative to other subdivisions of the species. Because they are below the species level, different subspecies are reproductively compatible. They will normally be allopatric (occupying mutually exclusive, but usually adjacent, geographic areas) and they will exhibit recognizable phylogenetic partitioning, because of the time-dependent accumulation of genetic differences in the absence of gene flow." Inherent in most recent thinking is the idea that members of a subspecies should be more closely related to one another than to individuals of another subspecies and, further, that geographic or ecological isolation (e.g., islands, mountain ranges separated by deserts, plains separated by mountain ranges, etc.) has caused gene flow between populations to be restricted and allowed differentiation of characteristics. The primary criterion in modern taxonomy is phylogenetic relatedness, i.e., organisms that share recent common ancestry are grouped together, separate from others with more distant common ancestry (Cronin 1993).

Traditionally, subspecies have been based on morphological characters and geographic distributions, with mammalian taxonomy emphasizing characteristics of the skull. Differences in morphology were assumed to reflect local adaptations or simply phenotypic expression of overall genetic differences. Many older designations are based on limited numbers of individuals and traits (Mayr 1969). Such differences are rarely discrete (e.g., coat color, size, weight). Also, it was recognized that different traits show different patterns of geographic variation (discordant geographic variation). Wilson and Brown (1953) wrote, "The tendency in this method has been to delimit races on the basis of one or several of the most obvious characters...the remainder of the geographically variable characters are then ignored, or if

they are considered at all, they are analyzed only in terms of the subspecific units previously defined."

While some subspecific designations are almost universally accepted, the lack of standardized criteria for subspecies classification has led some to question taxonomy at the subspecies level. Mayr (1954:87) stated that the subspecies is conceptually different from the species in that it is "merely a strictly utilitarian classificatory device for pigeonholing of population samples." Human judgment is heavily involved, and the subjectivity engenders disagreement among scientists. The science of taxonomy underwent a phase when the naming of great numbers of subspecies was permissible, even fashionable. By the middle of the 20th century, that practice was coming under severe criticism. Wilson and Brown (1953:108) commented, "If it is now clear that the subspecies trinomial is fast becoming an unquestioned and traditional fixture, it is equally clear, at least to us, that in its assumed function as a formal means of registering geographical variation within the species it tends to be both illusionary and superfluous." Mayr (1951:94) reviewed 12 years of study in bird speciation and observed, "Instead of expending their energy on the describing and naming of trifling subspecies, bird taxonomists might well devote more attention to the evaluation of trends in variation." Wilson and Brown (1953:108) longed for the day when "the study of geographic variation may eventually become just what the term implies, but not merely remain the subspecies mill it so largely is today." Generally, these authors protested that defining subspecies as "a genetically distinct geographical fraction of the species" was not workable and did not serve the study of variation within species.

A particular problem was that illustrations of subspecific ranges on a map leave a false impression about intrapopulation variation of characteristics. Mayr (1970:214) wrote, "As a means of simplification, the practicing taxonomist divides species taxa in a typological manner. He implies in his species catalogues that the subspecies or ecotypes into which he divides his species are well defined, more or less uniform over extensive areas, and separated from other similar units by gaps or steep and narrow zones of integradation. It is now increasingly apparent that this simplified typological picture of the species structure is the exception rather than the rule." Mayr added that, "A very different approach, based on the population structure of species, is necessary in the study of internal variation of species from the ecological and evolutionary point of view. This new approach investigates the degree of difference between neighboring populations, the presence or absence of discontinuities between populations, and the characteristics of those populations that are intermediate between phylogenetically distinct populations. It is an objective approach because it does not try to force natural populations into a preconceived framework of artificial taxonomic or ecological units and terms. A new picture of the population structure of species emerges from this new approach. It shows that all populations of a species can be classified under one (or more) of the following three structural components of species: 1) series of gradually changing contiguous populations (*clinal variation*); 2) populations that are geographically separated from the main body of the species range (*geographical isolates*); 3) rather narrow belts, often with sharply increased variability (*hybrid belts*), bordered on either side by stable and rather uniform groups of populations or subspecies." This statement about population structure should be kept in mind when reading future sections of this review.

Because of the subjective aspect of subspecies definition, most taxonomists stopped naming subspecies in the 1960's or earlier (IUCN Captive Breeding Specialists Group 1991). This movement was spurred in part because of increased recognition and acknowledgment of discordant geographic variation (Wilson and Brown 1953). Subspecies names persist in the literature, however. Some have argued that subspecies designations remain the best way of acknowledging the diversity existing within a species and that conserving subspecies is a way to preserve genetic diversity (Chambers and Bayless 1983).

The concept of subspeciation has generated several philosophical articles (see Bryant and Maser 1982:17 for references). Some of the most recent debate has focused on its usefulness in conservation efforts and issues, especially endangered taxa (Ryder 1986, O'Brien et al. 1990, Amato 1991, Geist 1991, IUCN Captive Breeding Specialists Group 1991, O'Brien and Mayr 1991). The ESA provides protection to species, subspecies, and populations. However, the policy of the U.S. Fish and Wildlife Service has been that "hybrid" endangered species, subspecies, and populations cannot be protected despite the fact that they are not uncommon in nature and in some cases warrant preserving (e.g., O'Brien et al. 1990, Geist 1991). This produced considerable confusion and conflict (O'Brien and Mayr 1991), led to a petition to delist the gray wolf (U.S. Fish and Wildlife Service 1990b), and prompted review of that policy and consideration of one that is more in keeping with preservation of biological diversity. The major point for our discussion is that interbreeding between subspecies is a common phenomenon in nature (see references in O'Brien et al. 1990). Within the past couple of years papers have appeared suggesting that for purposes of legal protection and conservation biology, wildlife managers should focus on preservation of particularly valuable or distinct populations or evolutionarily significant units (cf. Ryder 1986), and ignore the subspecies trinomial system when taxonomic status is questionable (Cronin 1993).

Increased application of molecular techniques in the past 30 years has further challenged the subspecies concept (IUCN Captive Breeding Specialist Group 1991). Sometimes the new molecular methods have shown geographic or phenotypic patterns that are consistent with old subspecies names; however, the new results frequently conflict with the old nomenclature (IUCN Captive Breeding Specialist Group 1991, Cronin 1993).

Evolution of Gray Wolf Taxonomy

The Descriptive Era

The gray wolf is thought to have originated in the Old World and immigrated into North America in the Pleistocene via the Bering Land Bridge (Kurten 1968, Nowak 1979, Kurten and Anderson 1980). The wolf's historic range was throughout North America, Europe, Asia, and Japan, with the exception of the vast deserts and high mountaintops in these regions (Goldman 1944, Mech 1970).

Many early authors (Miller 1912, Pocock 1935, Anderson 1943) noted the wide variation in characteristics of wolves including weights, measurements, and color. Color varied so much that Young (1944:59) stated, "The color of North American wolves, according to both earlier and later authorities, varies greatly, so much so that it is relatively unimportant for scientific description of the animals." Mech (1970:29) went on to say, "The wolf originally inhabited most of the Northern Hemisphere, and any animal with such a wide distribution could be expected to vary considerably from area to area. So it is with the wolf." Yet this observed variation resulted in the naming of numerous species of wolf in North America.

A number of authors have treated the phylogenetic history of other canids in North America including domestic dogs (*C. familiaris*) (Matthew 1930, Iljin 1941, Lawrence and Bossert 1975, Walker and Frison 1982) and the red wolf (*C. rufus*) (Young and Goldman 1944, McCarley 1962, Lawrence and Bossert 1967, Pimlott and Joslin 1968, Mech 1970, Nowak 1973, 1979; Wayne and Jenks 1991). Our discussion will focus on *C. lupus*.

The evolution of the taxonomy of wolves in North America occurred through identification of specimens by various early explorers and zoologists. A number of benchmark works attempted to sort out the melee. There is little doubt that these early taxonomists recognized an animal that resembled the wolf of Europe and Asia. Miller (1912:2–3; quoting Richardson 1829) presented this statement: "The American naturalists have, indeed, described some of the northern kinds of Wolf [*sic*] as distinct; but it never seems to have been doubted that a Wolf, possessing all the characters of the European Wolf, exists within the limits of the United States." However, in the early examination of specimens, the variation of individual wolves often led taxonomists to name separate species based on one or only a few specimens.

Miller (1912:1-5) attempted to provide a current synopsis of the classification and to bring standardization to the still newly evolving system. He was operating with the hypothesis that "the skulls of the American wolves of the subgenus *Canis* in the U.S. National Museum, shows that the general region lying west of the Mississippi River and Hudson Bay, and north of the Platte and Columbia rivers, is inhabited by animals of three well defined types...." He identified these as a timber-wolf type (the largest), a plains-wolf type (moderate in size), and a tundra-wolf type (similar in size to the plains-wolf type, but with different skull characteristics).

Based upon his review, he described 10 species of wolf that had been identified from North America. He listed five forms from the western U.S. and Canada as follows: *C. tundrarum* (Barren Grounds), *C. occidentalis* (Northern Interior Forests), *C. pambasileus* (Region of Mount McKinley), *C. gigas* (Region of Puget Sound), and *C. nubilus* (Interior Plains). He also listed five species that represented forms from eastern Canada, east and southeastern U.S., and Mexico. These are: *C. floridanus* (Florida), *C. frustror* (junction of Neosho and Arkansas Rivers), *C. lycaon* (eastern Canada), *C. lupus* var. *rufus* (Texas), and *C. mexicanus* (southern Mexico); *C. floridanus*, and *C. lupus* var. *rufus* and *C. frustror* to be later named subspecies of the red wolf (*C. rufus floridanus* and *C. r. rufus* respectively).

Based on the examination of 65 specimens, Nelson and Goldman (1929:165-166) redescribed the Mexican wolf. It was described as intermediate between *C. nubilus*, the wolf of the central plains, and *C. rufus*, the Texas red wolf, and assigned the name *C. nubilus baileyi*. These differences, as was the practice at the time, were measurements of various physical characteristics, particular measurements of the skull, overall size and weight, and description of color, color patterns, shades, and hues. The measurements of the type specimen were usually given, but no statistical analyses of the variation within the specimens examined were conducted. Consequently, from the published literature, it was not possible to compare the variation in new groups of specimens to the variation in already described subspecies. Remeasurement of specimens from previously described divisions would have been necessary.

None of these assigned names have been carried into present taxonomic nomenclature of the wolf in North America in their present form. However, Miller's (1912:1-5) work was influential when the next "benchmark" treatment of the taxonomic nomenclature of North American wolves was conducted.

Pocock (1935:647), in the process of assigning various specimens in the British Museum to the appropriate group, conducted a review of the classification of wolves in the world. In examining the specimens from Europe, he noted, "The rapid extermination of the Wolf [*sic*] (*Canis lupus*) in all settled areas of the northern hemisphere, where it was formerly abundant and no doubt continuously distributed, is sufficient pretext for attempting to put on record the characters and kinship of the many distinct forms that have been described, where the data are still available."

When discussing the status and stages of disappearance of wolves from sections of their European range, he (Pocock 1935:647) notes "...but nowhere is it easy to procure specimens for Museum [*sic*] purposes, partly on account of the

value of their pelts in the fur trade." Perhaps the paucity of subspecies in Europe and Asia may have been a function of wolves having been largely eliminated prior to most systematic taxonomy; perhaps there was recognition that individuals within populations varied widely in their individual characteristics.

Pocock (1935:647) noted, "This paper is based primarily upon the material in the British Museum, which so far as European wolves are concerned, is comparatively poor, consisting mainly of single skins and skulls from widely separate localities, making it impossible to estimate the range of individual and seasonal variation in any one place, and it does not seem likely that the gaps in our knowledge will now ever be filled."

However, in his discussion of the North American wolves (Pocock 1935:648) says, "The North American wolves seem to be much better known to American zoologists than are European wolves to zoologists of Europe.... About a dozen different kinds have been described, and are cited with confidence either as distinct species or as subspecies of *C. occidentalis*...." Referring to Miller (1912) and other authors he goes on to say, "As stated, the American wolves are quoted either as local races of *Canis occidentalis* or as distinct species of that genus. *I have been unable to find any characters by which these wolves can be separated specifically, as I understand that term, from the wolves of Asia and Europe* [our emphasis]." So with the stroke of a pen, Pocock in Britain changed all the names of the wolves in North America and few if any objected — taxonomists and wolves alike. Pocock (1935) converted Miller's (1912) listing from the various separate species to subspecies of *Canis lupus*. However, he often had difficulty assigning specimens that he was examining in the British Museum to the subspecies identified for the area of collection. He provided extremely detailed descriptions of his specimens and often expressed frustration in the inability to assign them to a particular category, questioning the appropriateness of some geographic differentiation, particularly when they had been described from a single specimen.

From Pocock's (1935) work, the species that had been identified by Miller (1912) from northern and western North America were considered subspecies of *Canis lupus*, as follows: **The Northern Timber Wolves:** *C. l. occidentalis*, vicinity of Mackenzie River; *C. l. pambasileus*, vicinity of Mount McKinley. **The Pacific Coast Wolves:** *C. l. gigas*, vicinity of Puget Sound; *C. l. crassodon*, Vancouver Island. **The Clouded or Plains Wolf:** *C. l. nubilus*, Central U.S. and Canada. **The Arctic Races:** *C. l. tundrarum*, The Barren Ground Wolf, Arctic tundra; *C. l. arctos*, the American arctic wolf, Melville and Ellesmere Islands; *C. l. orion*, the Greenland wolf. **The Eastern Canadian Wolf:** *Canis lycaon*.

Pocock (1935) did not resolve the taxonomic position of the eastern wolves, but apparently allowed the species *C. lycaon* to remain unchanged but not unchallenged, and continued the nomenclature of *C. l. floridanus* for the Florida wolf. However, current wolf taxonomy in North America was beginning to take shape.

A major influence on the future taxonomy was exerted by E. A. Goldman and his colleague Stanley P. Young. Goldman (1937:37) moved wolf taxonomy to its next major level. The opening paragraph of his article is worth quoting: "The wolves of North America have remained very imperfectly known until the present time, owing no doubt to the limited material for study contained in museum collections. Wolves have become extinct over vast areas, including the eastern United States, but have persisted in some of the wilder, more remote regions, especially along the backbone of the continent. The specimens that have accumulated, largely in connection with predatory animal control, now afford a fairly satisfactory basis for determining specific and subspecific relationships."

Goldman (1937) segregated six new subspecies of gray wolf as follows (number of specimens examined in parenthesis): *C. l. labradorius*, Labrador wolf (5); *C. l. ligoni*, Alexander Archipelago wolf (27); *C. l. youngi*, southern Rocky Mountain wolf (> 150); *C. l. irremotus*, northern Rocky Mountain wolf (> 30); *C. l. monstrabilis*, Texas gray wolf (25); *C. l. mogollonensis*, Mogollon Mountain wolf (120).

In addition he fixed the name of the eastern wolf as *C. l. lycaon* and updated the nomenclature of the Mexican wolf to *C. l. baileyi*. Similarly, at this time the red wolves were separated from the gray wolves as *C. rufus*, with *C. r. rufus* (the Texas type) and *C. r. floridanus* (the Florida type) being segregated. Finally, an additional subspecies of red wolf, *C. rufus gregoryi*, the Mississippi Valley wolf, was described.

Allen and Barbour (1937:230) published a description of the Newfoundland wolf based on distinctiveness of the dentition and named it *C. l. beothucus*. This subspecies was named based upon four skulls and one skin taken in the mid- to late-1800's. Because of the geographic separation of these animals from mainland populations they noted, "Here it must have been cut off from the mainland for a long period, and, finding its natural food abundant in the form of the island race of caribou, it remained and developed the local peculiarities mentioned." This race is now extinct (Goldman 1944).

The splitting of *Canis lupus* into more local geographical races in North America continued. Goldman (1941) identified what he called the giant Kenai wolf, *C. l. alces*, from five wolf skulls taken on the Kenai Peninsula, which he speculated evolved in relationship with what was called the giant Kenai moose (*Alces alces*). He also segregated *C. l. columbianus*, the B.C. wolf, from 25 specimens as those generally occupying B.C. west of the Continental Divide, but separate from the coastal variety. An additional segmentation of the arctic varieties was made at the same time. Goldman (1941:110) described the Hudson Bay wolf, *C. l. hudsonicus*, from nine specimens as representative of those wolves along the Hudson Bay, similar to *occidentalis*, but

with different characters that "seem to warrant the recognition of a regional race."

Anderson (1943) proposed the partitioning of the Saskatchewan timber wolf that had been included in *C. l. occidentalis* by previous authors (Goldman 1937) and assigning the name *C. l. griseus* based upon the examination of eight specimens. Anderson (1943) also named three new subspecies of wolves from the arctic. These included *C. l. mackenzii*, the Mackenzie tundra wolf, based upon eight specimens; *C. l. bernardi*, the Banks Island tundra wolf, based upon six skins and eight skulls; and *C. l. manningi*, the Baffin Island tundra wolf, based upon examination of 13 specimens, all taken from Baffin Island. The latter three subspecies were accepted by subsequent authors (Goldman 1944, Hall and Kelson 1959). *C. l. griseus* was not included by Goldman (1944), but was included later by Hall and Kelson (1959) and Hall (1981), but in a different form. Anderson (1943) was the first author we are aware of who attempted to portray graphically the geographical distribution of the various subspecies that had been segregated to that date (Fig 1).

Young and Goldman (1944) has remained a definitive work on the taxonomy of wolves of North America since its publication. Goldman (1944) like Anderson (1943) included a map of the geographic distribution of the subspecies so far identified (Fig. 2). As stated previously, *C. l. griseus* was not included in Goldman's (1944) work per Anderson (1943), with Goldman retaining a wider distribution of *C. l. occidentalis*. Anderson's (1943) other recommendations were included, obviously late in the publication process because Goldman (1944) stated he was not able to examine specimens.

Goldman (1944) fixed the name *C. l. fuscus* for the Cascade Mountains wolf that had been named *C. l. gigas* by earlier authors and the "large brown wolf" referenced by Lewis and Clark. This was the wolf of the Puget Sound and Columbia River area with a distribution described by Goldman (1944) as, "Formerly the forested region from the Cascade Range in Oregon and Washington west in places to the Pacific coast; south to undetermined limits along the Sierra Nevada in northeastern California, and probably northwestern Nevada, north along the coast of B.C. to undetermined limits; on the east intergrading with *columbianus* and *irremotus* can safely be assumed."

The last of the 24 currently recognized subspecies in North America was fixed by Hall and Kelson (1952). The Saskatchewan timber wolf that had been recommended by Anderson (1943) was fixed as *C.l. griseoalbus* and partitioned from *C. l. occidentalis* with the Cumberland House, Saskatchewan, specimen as the **type**; *C. l. griseoalbus* basically occurring east of the Alberta-Saskatchewan border.

Hall and Kelson (1959) included all 24 subspecies, and thus gave credibility to them. They also provided a map that depicted the geographic distribution of the subspecies (Fig. 3). The significant differences from Goldman (1944) are: 1)

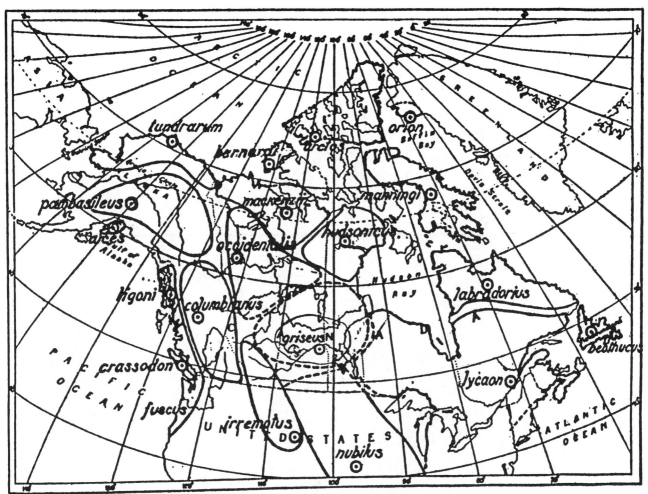

Fig. 1. *Gray wolf subspecies in North America as recognized by Anderson (1943). (Summary of the large wolves of Canada, with description of three new arctic races. J. Mammal. 24:386–393.).*

a southward shift of the area ascribed to *C. l. mackenzii*, a westward shift of *C. l. hudsonicus*, and the inclusion of *C. l. griseoalbus* joining in the vicinity of the east end of Great Slave Lake; 2) the inclusion of *C. l. griseoalbus*, which assumed the area previously ascribed to *C. l. occidentalis*, *C. l. hudsonicus*, and *C. l. nubilus*; 3) the northward description of the distribution of *C. l. fuscus* along the B.C. coast to near the southern distribution of *C. l. ligoni*, but allowing a peninsular extension of *C. l. columbianus* to the coast; 4) the extension of the distribution of *C. l. irremotus* westward to include eastern Washington and Oregon; and 5) a westward extension of the distribution of *C. l. youngi* to include northern Utah, all of Nevada, and a portion of California east of the Continental Divide.

Hall (1981) retained the same subspecies listed in Hall and Kelson (1959), even though published reports were already challenging this arrangement. He included an updated text and listing of marginal records. Changes in distribution maps reflect: 1) minor adjustment in boundary between *C. l. columbianus* and *C. l. occidentalis* in east-cen-

tral B.C.; 2) minor adjustment between *C. l. nubilus* and *C. l. youngi* in south-central Colorado; 3) a substantial reduction of the range of *C. l. labradorius* and northward extension of *C. l. lycaon* in eastern Canada; 4) a substantial shift of the range of *C. l. lycaon* northward in the southeastern U.S. because of referral of specimens in Florida and Tennessee from *C. l. lycaon* to *C. rufus*, the red wolf; and 5) the extension of the range of *C. l. baileyi* farther to the south (see Nowak this volume).

We see that the last addition of subspecific partitioning within *C. lupus* in North America was that of Hall and Kelson (1952), and that the classification has basically remained unchanged. The debate, however, has not been static.

The Multivariate Analysis Era

By the 1950's the practice of segregating species into subspecies based upon a minimal number of traits such as pelage color and pattern, minor skeletal variation, variation in size and weight, and other physical characteristics was coming

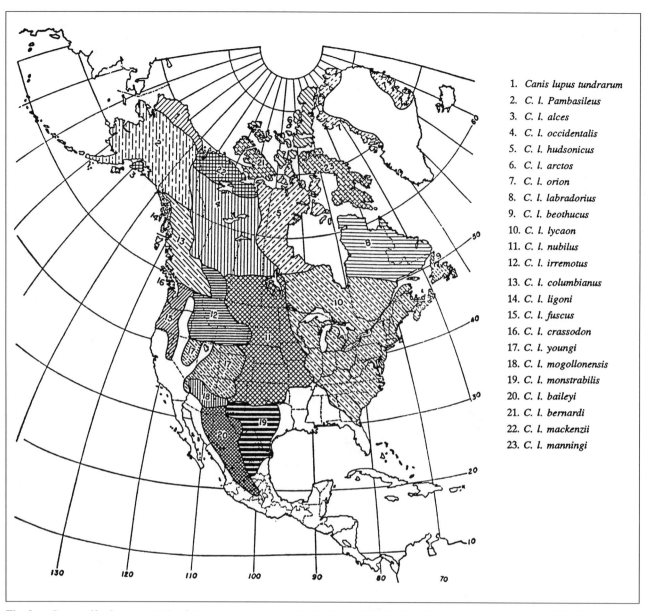

1. *Canis lupus tundrarum*
2. *C. l. Pambasileus*
3. *C. l. alces*
4. *C. l. occidentalis*
5. *C. l. hudsonicus*
6. *C. l. arctos*
7. *C. l. orion*
8. *C. l. labradorius*
9. *C. l. beothucus*
10. *C. l. lycaon*
11. *C. l. nubilus*
12. *C. l. irremotus*
13. *C. l. columbianus*
14. *C. l. ligoni*
15. *C. l. fuscus*
16. *C. l. crassodon*
17. *C. l. youngi*
18. *C. l. mogollonensis*
19. *C. l. monstrabilis*
20. *C. l. baileyi*
21. *C. l. bernardi*
22. *C. l. mackenzii*
23. *C. l. manningi*

Fig. 2.   *Gray wolf subspecies in North America as recognized by Goldman (1944). (Classification of wolves. Pages 389–636 in S. P. Young and E. A. Goldman, The wolves of North America, Amer. Wildl. Inst., Washington, D. C. 636pp).*

under scrutiny. Many species and subspecies had been identified without an analysis of the significance of the variation between individuals and between populations. This left animal taxonomy largely to the discretion of the individual taxonomists, a situation with which not everyone was comfortable. Mech (1970:30) addressed this from a wolf biologist's perspective, "When a population of wolves from one area differs substantially from populations of other areas, it is assigned to a separate *subspecies*. However, researchers in the field of animal classification, or taxonomy, have traditionally disagreed on what constitutes a significant difference. Thus some taxonomists tend to become 'splitters' — recognizing many subspecies; others become 'lumpers' — lumping several subspecies to form one and thus recog-

nizing fewer subspecies. Wolf taxonomists are no exception." Certainly, the "splitter" approach dominated during the descriptive era of wolf taxonomy.

In the late 1950's, enter multivariate analysis, a vastly more sophisticated and powerful tool for understanding geographical variation. When applied to the gray wolf the net result of the technique would be to weaken the evidence for so many subspecies. Use of multivariate analysis marked the end of the "descriptive" or "expansion" phase in naming of wolf subspecies and the beginning of an "analysis phase."

Multivariate analysis can compare multiple attributes statistically. For example, the typical display of bivariate analysis is the plotting of values based on the typical histogram with one scale on the X axis and the other on the Y axis

Fig. 3.   *Gray wolf subspecies in North America as depicted by Hall and Kelson (1959). (The mammals of North America. The Ronald Press Co., New York. 1083pp.).*

1. *C. l. alces*
2. *C. l. arctos*
3. *C. l. baileyi*
4. *C. l. beothucus*
5. *C. l. bernardi*
6. *C. l. columbianus*
7. *C. l. crassodon*
8. *C. l. fuscus*
9. *C. l. hudsonicus*
10. *C. l. griseoalbus*
11. *C. l. irremotus*
12. *C. l. labradorius*
13. *C. l. ligoni*
14. *C. l. lycaon*
15. *C. l. mackenzii*
16. *C. l. manningi*
17. *C. l. mogollonensis*
18. *C. l. monstrabilis*
19. *C. l. nubilus*
20. *C. l. occidentalis*
21. *C. l. orion*
22. *C. l. pambasileus*
23. *C. l. tundrarum*
24. *C. l. youngi*

giving a two-dimensional histogram. If a third dimension is added in the form of a third variable, the display of this trivariate analysis would be the plotting of values on an X, Y, and Z axis and can be visualized as points inside of a cube. Multivariate analysis allows the statistical comparison of variables in more than three dimensions, which is beyond the capability of most people, certainly these authors, to visualize. Jolicoeur (1959) provided an excellent discussion of the technique. More recent treatment is provided in Blackith and Reyment (1991).

Jolicoeur (1959) was the first to apply multivariate statistical analysis to North American gray wolves to evaluate geographical variation within the species. Jolicoeur examined 500 specimens from western Canada and Alaska; from Vancouver Island on the southwest, central Alaska on the

northwest, Manitoba on the east, and the arctic islands and Hudson Bay on the northeast. He statistically compared the variation among wolves across this wide geographic area, using pelage color classes and standard skull morphologic measurements used by earlier mammalogists to identify subspecies.

Some of the conclusions reached were: 1) pelage color varies, but the relative frequency of pale wolves increases in a northeastward direction from Great Slave and Great Bear Lakes toward the tundra. He proposed this may be extended southward with the frequency of darker wolves increasing southwestward along the Rocky Mountains; 2) males are about 4% larger than females; 3) wolf skulls from B.C. to the Northwest Territories become shorter and broader along a cline (gradual geographic variation) in a northeasterly direction; and 4) variation between populations appears approximately proportional to the geographical separation; that is, adjacent populations overlap considerably and the greatest differentiation is between widely separated groups such as between southwestern B.C. and the arctic.

Jolicoeur demonstrated the utility of the new analytical technique and showed that variation was not diagnostic to geographic region. That differences in means between groups with wide geographic separation were detectable was not surprising. This, from a genetic view, would result in the observed clines over large distances with species that are highly mobile. He also proposed that the difference in skull length and width may not necessarily be due to genetic differences, but rather influenced by climatic and photoperiod differences. He proposed that shorter, broader skulls in the northeastern animals are a result of more severe, earlier winters and a shorter photoperiod that occurs earlier in the juvenile development of the more northerly wolves. The observed differences may be phenotypical because of environmental factors rather than genotypic differences, or a combination of both.

Jolicoeur's (1959) concluding section includes some telling remarks that agree with contemporary thought: "Taxonomical conclusions can be based on geographical variation only inasmuch as the latter is hereditary. Even if the biometrical differences were entirely genetical, however, the overall pattern of variation between the populations sampled is more suggestive of an incompletely panmictic continuum than of distinct subspecific units. Only one population seemed sharply different from its immediate neighbors, probably as a result of insular isolation, that of Vancouver Island. An adequate analysis of variation is of course desirable for the species as a whole or at least for all its North American representatives. There are most likely far too many subspecific designations in use" (citing Miller and Kellog 1955).

Mech and Frenzel (1971b) stated that northeastern Minnesota timber wolves are assigned to *C. l. lycaon*, but that they are from an area within 150 km of the range of *C. l. nubilus* as described by Goldman (1944) and questioned whether they are an intergrade between the two subspecies. They quoted Goldman (1944:444): "Specimens from eastern Minnesota and Michigan seem more properly referable to *lycaon*, but relationship to *nubilus* is shown in somewhat intermediate characters." Goldman (1944) made no mention of black or white phases in *C. l. lycaon*; however, he noted many color variations in *C. l. nubilus* and that *C. l. nubilus* was probably extinct. Because of the observation of a small percentage of black and cream colored wolves from three counties in northeastern Minnesota and the lack of reports of wolves of other than the gray phase in the range of *C. l. lycaon*, Mech and Frenzel (1971b:62) recommended the study of the genetics of wolves in northeastern Minnesota to ascertain subspecific affiliation "while specimens are still available." More recent capture or observation of a number

of black and cream colored wolves in portions of Minnesota west of Mech and Frenzel's (1971b) study area (Fritts and Mech 1981, S. Fritts, U.S. Fish and Wildlife Service, and W. Paul, U.S.D.A., APHIS, Animal Damage Control, unpubl. data) support their idea.

Nowak (1973) compared 15 skull measurements and demonstrated, via multivariate analysis, the distinction of coyote, wolf, and dog (see also Lawrence and Bossert 1967). Nowak did not at that time attempt to deal with the subspecies of North American *C. lupus*. However, he cited Jolicoeur (1959) regarding the clines in Canada and Alaska and the distinctiveness of the Vancouver Island wolves. He also cited Rausch's (1953) conclusion that *C. l. tundrarum* and *C. l. pambasileus* could not be distinguished from each other based on criteria listed by Goldman (1944). Rausch (1953) also questioned the validity of *C. l. alces* of the Kenai Peninsula. Kelsall (1968) suggested that the subspecific boundaries depicted in north-central Canada by Hall and Kelson (1959) were meaningless. He noted that wolves from areas designated for *C. l. mackenzii* and *C. l. hudsonicus* annually invaded the areas designated for *C. l. occidentalis* and *C. l. griseoalbus*, pursuing caribou herds for hundreds of miles. Mech (1970) also suggested that improvement was needed in this taxonomic arrangement. Similarly, Fritts (1983), in reporting the record dispersal distance for a gray wolf from Minnesota to Saskatchewan, pointed out that according to accepted subspecific designations, the animal would have changed subspecies three times during its travels.

Nowak (1973) compared 14 of the continental subspecies of gray wolves described in Goldman (1944) and *C. rufus* (the red wolf; in Goldman as *C. niger*). The graphical depiction of the analysis showed an intermixture of the subspecies of *C. lupus*, with *C. rufus* relatively distinct. The tabular display of the data regarding the gray wolves showed a cline in size with an increase from south to north and from east to west. However, he noted that subspecies *C. l. alces*, *C. l. tundrarum*, *C. l. pambasileus*, and *C. l. occidentalis* of Alaska and northwestern Canada were noticeably larger in most dimensions than all other groups. Wolves of the arctic islands were smaller in overall size of skull, but had comparatively huge canine and carnassial teeth. Other than size, it was difficult to see any significant clines in characters.

Nowak's (1973) analysis indicated a smaller statistical distance between neighboring subspecies with much more overlap than between those that are separated by great geographic distance. This is evident in those represented by small series of specimens, *C. l. occidentalis* and *C. l. pambasileus* being especially close. Anderson (1943) described animals collected in 1914–1916 on Banks Island as *C. l. bernardi*. Mannning and Macpherson (1958) conducted analysis of 16 specimens collected in 1953–1955 on Banks Island and concluded that the originals had been replaced by a different kind of wolf, which they believed closest to *C. l. arctos* of Prince Patrick and Ellesmere Islands. While

Nowak (1973:36) agreed that the more recently collected skulls from Banks Island differed from the original specimens of *C. l. bernardi*, they also differed from most other skulls of *C. lupus*, and he did not agree with the assignment to *C. l. arctos* "with confidence."

A cline of geographical variation was again demonstrated by Jolicoeur (1975). He also suggested that, in addition to the previously described differentiation between arctic wolves and Rocky Mountain wolves that are widely separated, there is apparently a complex of factors operating that appear to segregate arctic wolves from those in the Northwest Territories and Manitoba and those in turn from those of the Rocky Mountains. His earlier hypothesis of environmental influences on physiology and growth determining the reduced skull characteristics in the arctic races was modified to include the possibility of hereditary influences as well as a number of other possibilities.

Using specimens of *C. l. lycaon* from Ontario, Kolenosky and Stanfield (1975) described an "Algonquin type" that is "identical" to the type described by Goldman (1944) and a "boreal type" that is larger and more massive in skull characteristics as well as total body weight. They also demonstrated sexual dimorphism within these separations. Additionally they described a "tweed type" in southern Ontario that they inferred may be due to hybridization with coyotes. They postulated that the difference may be due to evolution with the principal prey available in relative proportions; deer (*Odocoileus virginianus*) in the south with the tweed and the Algonquin types, moose in the north with *C. l. hudsonicus*, and caribou (*Rangifer tarandus*) in the central part with the boreal type of *C. l. lycaon*. They (Kolenosky and Stanfield 1975:71) stated, "The two types overlap throughout a broad band across east-central Ontario, but there is no conclusive evidence of their interbreeding." They proposed that the changes in distribution of previously distinct populations of gray wolves are due to the human-induced habitat changes and consequent range changes of ungulate prey such as moose, woodland caribou, and white-tailed deer as well as invasion by coyotes and hybridization with gray wolves.

Lawrence and Bossert (1975) investigated the relationship between dogs, coyotes, wolves, and the "New England" canids using multivariate analyses. They concluded that these animals were not "coydogs," but likely an evolving form of larger coyote with limited infusion of wolf and dog genes.

Skeel and Carbyn (1977), also using multivariate analysis of morphometric cranial characters, evaluated the morphological relationship of gray wolves in national parks of central Canada and from the central U.S. Eight separate groups of wolves were used. Locations of specimens and probable subspecies affiliation, following Goldman (1944) subspecific ranges, are: 1) Prince Albert National Park, which lies just north of *C. l. nubilus* within the southern edge of *C. l. occidentalis* and within *C. l. griseoalbus*; 2) Riding

Mountain National Park, which Goldman (1944) included within *C. l. nubilus*, whereas Hall and Kelson (1959) included it just within *C. l. griseoalbus*; 3) Wood Buffalo National Park which is within the range of *C. l. occidentalis*; and 4) Jasper National Park, which lies on the zone between *C. l. occidentalis* and *C. l. columbianus*. Other specimens of *C. l. nubilus*, *C. l. irremotus*, and *C. l. lycaon* were used for comparison. Skeel and Carbyn (1977) concluded that although the eight groups were not distinct, with considerable overlap occurring, there were meaningful geographic trends.

Using principal component analysis, five basic groups emerged. The largest wolves were geographically associated with the boreal and alpine areas, the smaller (*C. l. nubilus* and *C. l. irremotus*) with the grasslands and "southern" Rocky Mountains (obviously a Canadian perspective), and the tundra (*C. l. hudsonicus*) and Great Lakes (*C. l. lycaon*) specimens were intermediate in size. While this may appear clear cut, they went on to say (p. 742), "Overlap among the individuals was considerable; this is not surprising since the groups compared are of low taxonomic rank. Although some of the overlap is due to individuals representing the extremes, the plots demonstrated that clear separation does not exist among the groups."

Multiple discriminant analysis indicated that only two groups (*C. l. lycaon* and *C. l. hudsonicus*) were fairly distinct. When these two groups were removed and the analysis repeated, they obtained only slightly greater separation, with *C. l. nubilus* and *C. l. irremotus* overlapping most extensively and the boreal and alpine specimens ordered slightly to one side. There was, however, extensive overlap among all groups. They concluded: 1) (p. 746) "Although a combination of cranial characters can be used to separate *Canis* effectively [citing other authors] similarity of the groups was too great for differentiation at a lower taxonomic level. The tremendous overlap of individuals…illustrate [*sic*] the variability of the populations, and the poor probability of being able to identify to which population a single specimen would belong," and 2) (p. 747) "taxonomic affinities can be speculated from these results."

The largest North American wolves are from northwestern Canada and Alaska according to Goldman (1944). In examining five recent specimens, four from northwestern and one from southwestern Alberta, Gunson and Nowak (1979) found that they approximate or exceed the largest skulls previously recorded. Gunson and Nowak (1979) concluded that the wolves of the boreal-subalpine forest regions of Alberta and adjacent areas appear to be the largest of the North American gray wolves. This appears to be the general area of origin for wolves colonizing the northern Rocky Mountains of the U.S. and the Cascades of Washington. Three wolves taken in northwestern Montana in 1989–1990 had the largest skull dimensions ever recorded in the lower 48 states (R. Nowak, U.S. Fish and Wildlife Service, pers. commun.)

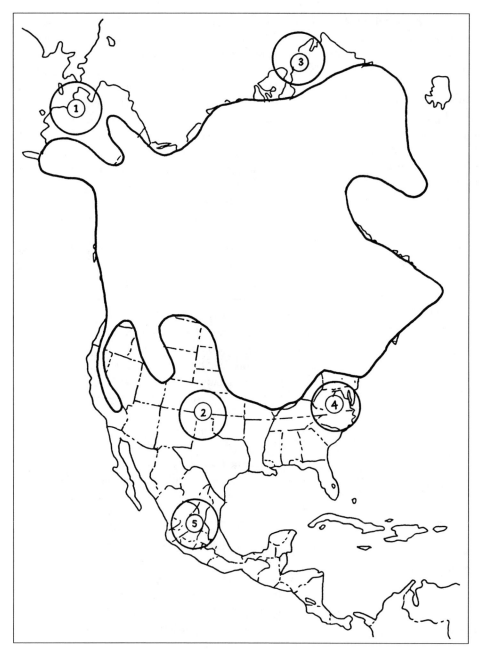

Fig. 4. *Maximum extent of Pleistocene glaciation in North America. Circles indicate hypothetical general areas of survival of wolf populations. 1 = Northern group, 2 = Southern group, 3 = **Canis lupus arctos**, 4 = Eastern **C.l. lycaon**, 5 = **C.l. baileyi**. (From: Nowak, R. M. 1983. A perspective on the taxonomy of wolves in North America. Pages 10–19 in L. N. Carbyn, ed. **Wolves in Canada and Alaska**. Can. Wildl. Serv. Rep. Ser. 45.).*

Walker and Frison (1982) used discriminant function analysis to evaluate the distinction of Wyoming canid skulls from archeological sites to determine if they were wolves or dogs. In part of their analysis they used published skull measurements of the three subspecies of Wyoming wolves as described by Goldman (1944): *C. l. youngi*, *C. l. nubilus*, and *C. l. irremotus*. They found "…complete discrimination between the groups did not occur in this analysis of Wyoming wolves. The total percent of specimens correctly placed into their original groups during the classification phase of the present analysis was 66.6%, reflecting the fact that it was hard to distinguish between the three subspecies. This lack of discrimination between the groups substantiates

the results of other investigators as to the lack of variability between geographically related subspecies of wolves…" (Walker and Frisson 1982:135).

Pedersen (1982) examined the four subspecies recognized by Goldman (1944) in Alaska (*C. l. ligoni*, *C. l. alces*, *C. l. pambasileus*, and *C. l. tundrarum*) using multivariate discriminate analysis. He recognized two phenotypically distinct subspecific groups: *C. l. ligoni* in southeast Alaska and *C. l. pambasileus* in interior and south-central Alaska. The difference between *C. l. tundrarum* and wolves in the interior occurred as a cline in which the two forms grade into each other. While the differences between interior and southeastern wolves were distinct in his analysis, insufficient

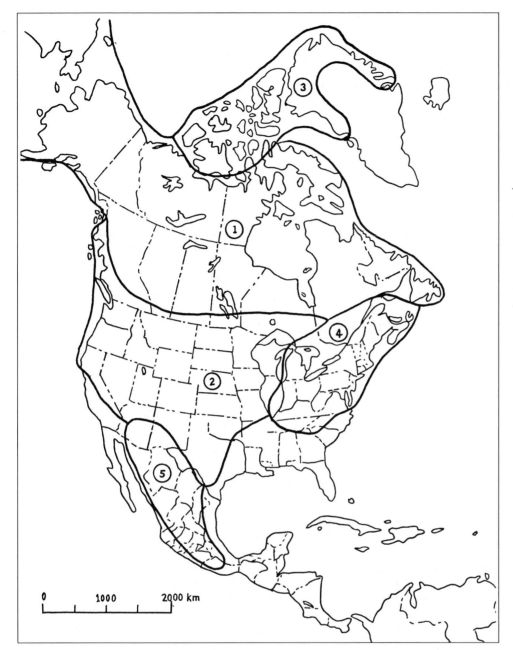

Fig. 5. *Hypothetical distribution of wolves following withdrawal of Pleistocene glaciation. 1 = Northern group, 2 = Southern group, 3 =* **Canis lupus arctos**, *4 = Eastern* **C.l. lycaon**, *5 =* **C.l. baileyi** *(From: Nowak, R. M. 1983. A perspective on the taxonomy of wolves in North America. Pages 10–19 in L.N. Carbyn, ed.* **Wolves in Canada and Alaska**. *Can. Wildl. Serv. Rep. Ser. 45.).*

samples from locations between these areas precluded evaluating if a similar cline existed.

The reevaluation of the 24 subspecies continued. Bogan and Mehlhop (1983) examined the five wolf subspecies that have been recognized in the southwestern U.S. Using both univariate and multivariate statistical procedures, they determined that of the five races, they recognized only three; *C. l. baileyi*, *C. l. youngi*, and *C. l. nubilus*, assigning the formally recognized *C. l. mogollonensis* and *C. l. monstrabilis* to *C. l. baileyi*.

A benchmark event occurred when Nowak (1983) presented his perspective on the taxonomy of the gray wolf in North America based on his review of the literature, his

previous work on wolf taxonomy, and "measurements of thousands of wolf skulls." In previous work, Nowak (1973, 1979) used multivariate stepwise discriminant analysis of 15 cranial measurements to compare 15 subspecies of *C. lupus* and the red wolf. He concluded that only specimens of red wolf stand out from the others. There was extensive overlap among the subspecies of *C. lupus*, providing little basis for simplified groupings.

Nowak (1983) commented that if he were to repeat Goldman's (1944) work he would draw fewer subspecies lines, if any. He proposed that a reassessment of gray wolf taxonomy could start with the work of Skeel and Carbyn (1977). Five groupings of wolves in North America were suggested by Nowak as one possible systematic arrangement. A cline in size from the small southern subspecies to the large subspecies of Alaska and northwestern Canada was intimated. He further suggested an affinity in characteristics among the subspecies occupying most of Alaska and inland Canada, (*C. l. tundrarum, C. l. pambasileus, C. l. occidentalis, C. l. columbianus,* and *C. l. griseoalbus*). He also suggested similarity in the grouping of wolves at and south of the U.S. and Canadian border including *C. l. irremotus, C. l. youngi, C. l. nubilus, C. l. monstrabilis,* western *C. l. lycaon* and the subspecies along the Pacific coast up to southeast Alaska. Five major groupings were presented as a hypothetical framework which may be used as a starting point for a systematic revision of *C. lupus.*

A pertinent outcome of Nowak's (1983:13) report is that Skeel and Carbyn's (1977) work suggested to him that "there may be a fairly sharp shift in characters of *C. lupus* in a zone that covers much of the U.S.-Canada border area and then swings northward in western Canada." Data from these authors were consistent with Nowak's. This zone of character shift was thought to be a possible area where a future taxonomist might draw a line dividing one subspecies covering a large part of Canada from another occupying much of the conterminous U.S., as well as the western Great Lakes region of Canada. The northern "group" would be morphologically somewhat larger.

Nowak (1983) proposed that movements of late Pleistocene ice sheets may have had much to do with current wolf taxonomy. Populations that were isolated during glaciation may have been the ancestors of wolf populations (possibly five major groupings) that reoccupied particular parts of North America after glacial retreat (Fig. 4, Fig 5). If correct, a main northern group would consist of wolves that were derived from stock isolated to the northwest of the ice sheet in Alaska and a main southern group would represent wolves that were all isolated to the south. Among potential geographic isolating mechanisms (Mayr 1970:331–334), ice sheets and large inland seas may have been the *only* effective isolating mechanisms for wolves in the history of the continent. A similar situation can be found in the relationship between the Wisconsin stage of glaciation (70,000 to 10,000 years ago) and subspeciation in North American elk (*Cervus elaphus*) (Bryant and Maser 1982).

Friis (1985) followed up on the proposals of Nowak (1983) and investigated subspecific relationships of the gray wolf in B.C. and surrounding area. Her objectives included investigation of Goldman's (1944) subspecific designations, determining whether the two "supergroups" of wolves postulated by Nowak (1983) existed in the B.C. area, determining whether B.C. coastal wolves were more closely related to the wolves of Oregon as proposed by Cowan and Guiget (1965), determining the present day affinities of wolves on Vancouver Island, and determining the present affinities of wolves in southeastern B.C. and the northwestern U.S. The approach was to use multivariate analysis to compare mu-

seum specimens (skulls) taken from the area both prior to the virtual elimination of the species from southern B.C. and the northwestern states and during recent years.

As true for other authors, Friis (1985) pointed out that wolves are quite variable animals and extensive overlap occurs in any one measurement among populations. There was no clear-cut separation of sample groups. Nonetheless, historically there was a fairly distinct separation of animals from southern and coastal groups (Vancouver Island, B.C. coast, Alaska panhandle, Oregon, Idaho-Montana) from wolves from more northern and interior areas of B.C. and Alberta (Smithers, Horseranch, Kechika, Peace, and Jasper). Oregon and Idaho samples were significantly different from all other groups and from each other. In both male and female groups, Idaho, Oregon, and Vancouver Island wolves were the smallest and the northeastern groups largest. Generally, wolves of her study area increased in size from south to north and from west to east. Northern groups appeared more closely related to one another than were the southern and coastal groups. No reason was found for distinguishing *C. l. occidentalis* from *C. l. columbianus* in the northern part of B.C. Misclassification most often occurred within "supergroups" and southern groups had higher correct classification rates than northern groups. Southern and coastal groups were judged sufficiently distinct (historically) to warrant subspecific designation. Friis' (1985) analyses supported Nowak's (1983) suggestion that in the Pacific Northwest there are two types of wolves: a large northern group, and a smaller, southern group that has expanded north along the B.C. coast and integrated with the northern wolf in the B.C. interior. Friis (1985) agreed with Nowak's (1983) postulation that these two "supergroups" could represent populations that had been isolated during the Wisconsin glaciation period and then expanded to contact and intergrade after glacial retreat.

All wolves taken in southern B.C., southern Alberta, and the northwestern U.S. since 1945 could be assigned to the northern groups (except one skull taken from Montana in 1964). In Friis' (1985) words, "…it can be stated with some confidence that the wolves occasionally reported within the historic range of *irremotus* today are far more closely related to the large northern wolves than to *irremotus*." In addition to skull characteristics and body size, color phase also supports this conclusion. More than half of the wolves being reported in the northwest U.S. in the last decade are black (Ream et al. 1991, S. Fritts, U.S. Fish and Wildlife Service, unpubl. data, R. Ream, University of Montana, pers. commun.), whereas *C. l. irremotus* was described by Goldman (1944) as light buff or varying shades of gray, with the black phase extremely rare. Dekker (1986) noted that from 1965 to 1984, 56% of 132 wolves observed in Jasper National Park were black. According to Weaver (1978) only three of 136 wolves killed within Yellowstone Park were black. Friis (1985:143–144) concluded that it is apparent that Canadian wolves have been gradually expanding their range southward into the area formally occupied by *C. l. irremotus*. She found no evidence for the continued existence of *C. l. irremotus*. According to her, "The specimens that Goldman (1944) examined for his taxonomic study were mostly collected before the wide-scale recent extirpation of the wolf in the southern portion of its range. Hence, his subspecific designations are not necessarily appropriate for wolves today reoccupying the southern portions of their range." She added, "I have found no evidence for the continued existence of either the Cascade wolf, *C. l. fuscus*, or the Northern Rocky Mountain Wolf, *C. l. irremotus*. These populations have either been eliminated or so invaded by immigrating wolves as to be no longer identifiable." It was suspected that present day wolves of Vancouver Island, the B.C. coast, and possibly the Alaska panhandle may be the only populations remaining descended from the southern wolves isolated by the Wisconsin glaciation (except of course for whatever remains of *C. l. baileyi* in Mexico).

It was with Nowak's (1983) speculations of five "supergroups" of wolves and Friis' (1985) supporting work that wolf subspecific taxonomy (at least based on morphology) was left until now. In the accompanying paper, Nowak affirmed his speculations in his 1983 paper by recognizing five original subspecies of *Canis lupus* in North America, based on multivariate analysis of measurements of about 600 skulls. An important conclusion (consistent with the earlier paper) is that individuals taken in the northwestern conterminous U.S. since 1940 represent the subspecies *occidentalis*, a large wolf of western Canada and Alaska, that generally corresponds to the northern group in his earlier paper. The only notable refinement made to the distribution of the five groups/subspecies was the extension of the southern group (*C. l. nubilus*) throughout eastern Canada (Nowak this volume).

Island and Peninsular Effects on Wolf Taxonomy

A couple of additional taxonomic situations warrant attention because they are somewhat analogous to the current situation in the northern Rockies of the U.S. Each involves a recognized subspecies becoming extinct and the area being reoccupied by wolves from another area and, allegedly, another subspecies. These examples help illustrate that, whatever pattern of geographic variation exists among wolves, it is a dynamic one. The examples involve islands or peninsulas where gene flow with mainland populations is reduced and the opportunity for differentiation of traits is greater (Mayr 1963). Islands, especially, offer a looking glass into the rate and importance of subspeciation.

The first such area is Vancouver Island, B.C. According to Cowan and Guiguet (1965) the mainland of B.C. was occupied primarily by *C. l. columbianus* and Vancouver Island by *C. l. crassodon*. The Vancouver Island wolf was first described by Hall (1932) on the basis of pelage color

and carnassial teeth characteristics. Jolicoeur (1959) thought that Vancouver Island wolves were different from neighboring subspecies, but others (cited in Nowak 1983) disagreed. Wolves were apparently never abundant on the island. They reached a low point around 1950 and by 1970 an "endangered" status was considered (Hebert et al. 1982). An increase occurred until they were observed regularly throughout the island in 1976, with hunting and trapping reinstated shortly thereafter (Archibald et al. 1991). Emigration from mainland B.C. was speculated to be the primary source of the repopulation. This conclusion was supported by Friis' (1985) taxonomic study.

Friis (1985) compared skull characteristics among pre- and post-1950 Vancouver Island and mainland wolf populations and concluded that the original island population, while not totally extirpated, could be distinguished from wolves inhabiting the coastal mainland. Friis (1985:126) commented, "The original Vancouver Island wolf population, as described by Goldman (1944) was quite distinct...but these distinctions are no longer obvious. Discriminant analysis, while clearly separating the population of original wolves, showed recent wolves to resemble mainland wolves more than the original population.... This suggests that the original population, while not extirpated, has been so invaded by wolves immigrating from the mainland as to be no longer distinguishable as a separate population." Therefore, this appears to be an example of "original" wolves with some distinguishing characteristics being "swamped" by a invasion from a neighboring mainland area.

A similar example occurred on the Kenai Peninsula, Alaska. Goldman (1944) classified Kenai Peninsula wolves as a separate subspecies (*C. l. alces*) and considered them the largest North American subspecies, based on five wolves killed there around 1904. Wolves were eradicated from the peninsula and did not recolonize it until the 1960's, whereupon they increased rapidly (Peterson and Woolington 1982). While the legitimacy of Goldman's *C. l. alces* is debatable, it is clear that the area was invaded by what was considered to be a different subspecies (Pedersen 1982). In other words, genetic stock originating in another area of Alaska now occupies the Kenai Peninsula. The current situation in the central Rockies, with a "different subspecies" colonizing vacant range to the south, is analogous to the above situations.

When the wolf became extinct on the island of Newfoundland the subspecies recognized there, *C. l. beothucus*, was lost. If wolves should ever be restored to that island, other wolves will have to be used for the reintroduction. Other areas in North America, especially within the U.S., have lost their "original" wolves and whatever distinguishing characteristics they may have had. Some areas like those above have been reoccupied; others remain unoccupied. No doubt there have been numerous instances during the past several thousands of years in which wolves were eliminated from areas of the continent by natural processes, only for that area to be recolonized by the nearest wolf population. As discussed, glaciation was probably the preeminent factor in such perturbations (see Bryant and Maser 1982).

The Influence of Molecular Taxonomy on Wolf Subspecific Classification

Use of morphological data alone has been criticized when used to infer phylogenetic relationships in animals because: 1) traits are not always discrete and overlap between populations; 2) natural selection can cause rapid divergence in morphology between closely related populations; 3) convergence can cause populations to appear similar even when they differ in phylogenetic ancestry; and 4) environmental factors (e.g., nutrition) can have striking effects on certain characteristics (Cronin 1993). Geist (1991) provided an excellent review of the inadequacy of morphometry to detect phylogenetic differences.

Recent advances in molecular genetic techniques have made it possible to directly compare phylogenetic relatedness and to characterize differences among numerous subspecies of birds and mammals. These techniques can provide a powerful tool for assessing the degree of genetic differentiation of populations (Cronin 1993). Two standard approaches that have been used extensively in comparisons of (previously identified) subspecies of animals are protein electrophoresis and mitochondrial DNA analysis. Molecular data, when available for several genes can provide a good assessment of the relationship of populations. Ryder (1986) suggested that natural history, morphology, range and distribution, and molecular genetic data *all* be considered in identifying subspecies for conservation programs. An integration of molecular and morphological characteristics is thought to be best for classification work (Ryder 1986, Avise 1989b, O'Brien and Mayr 1991, Cronin 1993).

Most genetic analyses involving canids have focused on taxonomic relationships within the family Canidae or the order Carnivora (Seal 1969, 1975, Braend and Roed 1987, Clark et al. 1975, Fisher et al. 1976, Wayne et al. 1989). Wayne and Jenks (1991) used mtDNA analyses to conclude that the red wolf is either a hybrid form between gray wolves and coyotes or a distinct taxon that hybridized with coyotes and gray wolves over much of its previous range.

Considerable discussion regarding wolf genetics has been about the frequency and effects of inbreeding in wolf packs. Because of the social nature of wolves and the presumed limited flow of genetic material between separate breeding units, several authors have implied or suggested inbreeding occurs in wolves (Mech 1970, Woolpy and Eckstrand 1979, Shields 1983, Mech 1987).

On the assumption that inbreeding is common, much colloquy has occurred about its effects. Shields (1983:91) argued that "for wolves inbreeding does not appear to be an anathema, but rather an adaptive mode of reproduction in their natural environment." One conclusion was that such a

breeding population structure is likely to increase or maintain local adaptation and species-wide genetic variability. A slightly different view was taken by Theberge (1983) who stressed the importance of gene flow and the maintenance of genetic variability locally, a view more consistent with modern conservation biology. Neither of these authors had access to much data about the degree of genetic exchange in wolf populations; both probably underestimated it (c.f. Meier et al. this volume). Nonetheless, there is now evidence that in special circumstances wolf populations can suffer from inbreeding depression.

The first such evidence is from an assessment of the causes of the reproductive failure and population decline on Isle Royale, Michigan, since 1980 (Peterson and Page 1988, Peterson and Krumenaker 1989). Wayne et al. (1991) used allozyme electrophoresis, mtDNA restriction site analysis, and genetic fingerprinting in concluding that about 50% of the heterozygosity measured had been lost, compared to mainland wolves. The wolves sampled on Isle Royale were as similar as captive populations of siblings. Recognition of potential mates as kin was suggested to have hampered breeding success. Apparently, the population that had persisted for 40 years on the island consisted entirely of offspring of a single female founder. Both the founder effect and genetic drift were thought instrumental in severely reducing genetic variability which was suspect in the population's decline. Despite development of these problems, it is important to note that the Isle Royale wolves thrived for 30 years, in 1980 reaching the highest density known for wolves. Moreover, in 1994, two new litters of four pups each were recruited into the population (Peterson 1994).

A study of inbreeding depression in a group of captive wolves in Scandinavian zoos provided strong evidence that inbreeding resulted in loss of genetic variability (Laikre and Ryman 1991). Negative impacts of intense inbreeding were blindness and reductions in juvenile weight, productivity, and longevity. This study was of wolves that were *intensively* inbred, as they represented very few founders and were not subject to natural selection. Coefficients of inbreeding were apparently higher in this captive breeding program than in any other. Nonetheless, the authors expressed the concern that the false contention that wolves do not suffer from inbreeding depression could lead to acceptance of inadequate population size in the management of wild or captive wolf populations. We should note that both of these situations documenting inbreeding were unusual in that a bottleneck effect had occurred and the opportunity for addition of new genetic material was low. In the wild, this could occur via a small founder group reaching an island (as actually happened on Isle Royale) or otherwise becoming isolated from the remainder of the wolf population.

In the absence of actual data on the amount of genetic variability within non-isolated wild wolf populations, speculation continued. For example, Woolpy and Eckstrand (1979) proposed that the social structure of wolves results in high potential for rapid evolution. Independent evolution among small units in a population depends on the amount of gene flow among units and random genetic drift within units as well as on the effective population size of each unit (Wright 1978). If gene flow between units was absent or limited and if the environment was perceived as homogeneous for all units, genetic variation within the total population would increase as the result of fixation of one allele in one unit and an alternate allele in another unit (Kennedy et al. 1991). Woolpy and Eckstrand (1979) proposed that situation for wolves. They estimated fixation time of approximately 20 years for "an average locus in the average pack" based on computer simulations using different effective population size and different levels of emigration and immigration for packs. Their conclusion was that the wolf is highly inbred, with loss of genetic variation within packs and genetic distinction between adjacent packs. If correct, then the wolf would be genetically variable as a species, but the overall level of heterozygosity for the species would be low. The findings of Woolpy and Eckstrand (1979) were questioned by Ralls et al. (1986) who pointed out that in the real world dispersal of wolves between packs would restore some of the heterozygosity that was predicted lost by their model.

Mech (1977b) suggested that selection for different genotypes within wolf populations may vary depending on prey availability. His study found that at higher wolf densities, adult pack wolves were the most secure members of the population, but as the population declined, they became the least secure because of intraspecific strife. Malnutrition affected young almost exclusively while breeding animals were preserved through reduced competition. Intraspecific strife usually affected alpha animals and would have had the opposite effect. Not only would genotypes of the losers in intraspecific conflicts be selected against, but some other genotype would be the selective agent. This process could change the gene frequency in the population, and perhaps result in an increase in a genotype more capable of coping with lowered prey densities.

New molecular techniques have been used in an increasing number of studies to actually examine genetic variability within wild wolf populations, a matter closer to the subspecies issue. In reviewing such work it is important to remember that, according to the modern definition of subspecies, low genetic differentiation (uniformity) over a broad area *generally* implies that few subspecific divisions are appropriate; high differentiation among areas implies more (or some) are appropriate (O'Brien and Mayr 1991).

Overall, the degree of genetic variability found in the Canidae has been low (Seal 1975, Kennedy et al. 1991). Mardini (1984) found no variation among electrophoretic patterns of general proteins in 20 wolves from eastern Canada. The same was true for wolves from northwestern Canada. Braend and Roed (1987) examined 146 wolves from Alaska and found a blood polymorphism through isoelectric focusing. Fisher et al. (1976) found some polymorphisms

among eight wolves from zoos and four from Minnesota. Kennedy et al. (1991) examined 188 wolves from northwestern Canada for 27 protein systems representing 37 presumptive loci. They found 13.5 and 17.9% of loci to be polymorphic, which was higher than the 11.3% found by Fisher et al. (1976). The overall level of heterozygosity found in northwestern Canada was 3%. Therefore the level of heterozygosity in natural populations of wolves is intermediate relative to that of natural populations of Carnivora and high relative to that of natural populations of other canids such as coyotes and foxes.

Kennedy et al. (1991) reported that relative to other carnivores, they found considerably less differentiation among wolves from different regions. Wolves associated with different caribou herds were genetically similar; in fact wolves were genetically similar across most of their study area. The pattern of variability found did not support the hypothesis (discussed above) that gray wolves are a highly inbred species because of their social structure. Instead, these authors stated that their findings suggested a large panmictic (randomly interbreeding) population resulting from extensive movements of individuals and packs and from natural and human impacts on pack structure and formation. In other words, no substantial evidence was found for the type of local differentiation that is necessary to support the concept of many subspecies.

The genetic relatedness of wolves in three areas of North America was examined using genetic fingerprinting (Lehman et al. 1992, Wayne et al. this volume). The authors sampled 42 wolves from 13 packs in 2,200 km^2 in northeastern Minnesota; 22 wolves from 13 packs in 17,000 km^2 in Denali Park, Alaska; 46 wolves from nine packs from 150,000 km^2 in the vicinity of Inuvik, Northwest Territories; and 36 wolves from captive colonies. Genetic fingerprinting allowed assessment of the amount of sharing of a large number of highly variable alleles in each study population. The results showed that: 1) wolf packs consist primarily of individuals that are closely related genetically, but some packs contain unrelated, nonreproducing individuals; 2) dispersal among packs within the same area is common; and 3) short-distance dispersal appears to be more common for females than for males. Generally, genetic fingerprint similarity among wolves from different packs in the three-pack clusters revealed several connections among packs that suggested exchange of individuals related as closely as parent-offspring or siblings. The evidence of a third unrelated individual within a considerable percentage of packs was not expected. Most packs are thought of as containing two essentially unrelated wolves (founding parents) and their offspring (Mech and Nelson 1990a). However, about 25% of the packs studied showed genetic evidence of a wolf from some other pack joining that pack. Observations of pack dynamics over a six-year period corroborated the results of the genetics studied (Meier et al. this volume). Again, results of this research were consistent with the idea that wolf populations are outbred unless some physical restriction to wolf movement and genetic interchange is present.

Wayne et al. (1992a) evaluated wolf population structure by analyzing mtDNA sequence variability among wolves from several areas within their New World and Old World range. Tissue samples from 350 wolves from 24 populations were analyzed. Twenty genotypes were observed, using 21 distinct restriction enzymes. Seven of the genotypes were from apparent hybridization with coyotes in eastern North America (Lehman et al. 1991) and were not included in analyses. The remaining 13 were divided among Old and New World localities. All wolf genotypes were genetically very similar. Overall, genetic differentiation among wolf populations was significant, but small in magnitude. In the New World, several genotypes occur at most localities and three of the six genotypes were nearly ubiquitous. One North American genotype was found at localities as distant as northeast Minnesota and Alaska. Geographic distributions of mtDNA haplotypes related poorly to recognized subspecific ranges.

Regarding wolf subspecies, Wayne et al. (1992a) regarded as paradoxical the small amount of genetic differentiation among New and Old World gray wolf populations and the large number of apparent subspecies defined on morphologic criteria. They believed that many of these subspecies may be defined on inadequate criteria and restated the view that most taxonomists believe the number of subspecies should be reduced (Jolicoeur 1959, Skeel and Carbyn 1977, Pedersen 1982, Nowak 1983). Moreover, they pointed out that morphology can change rapidly in small populations especially if selection is intense (citations provided but not reproduced here), and morphologic differences need not be indicative of a long history of genetic isolation. Wayne et al. (1992a) believed that genetic differentiation among historic populations of wolves was probably similar to that among extant coyotes: gene flow among localities was high and little genetic differentiation was apparent even among widely spaced populations. They also concluded that genetic distinction among gray wolf subspecies is small and may be an artifact of human-induced habitat fragmentation. Wayne et al. (1992a) did not address the possibility of five "supergroups" of wolves in North America, as postulated by Nowak (1983) and Friis (1985). However, their study produced no substantial genetic evidence to support the idea. Their finding of some genetic similarity between the Mexican wolf (*C. l. baileyi*) and Old World wolves is difficult to explain on geographic grounds. They proposed that immigration events may have occurred multiple times throughout the ice ages, and considering that many gray wolf genotypes are likely to have vanished with the extinction of wolf populations, many pieces are probably missing from the phylogenetic puzzle.

Other types of studies employing the newer techniques have been conducted or are in progress. Studies of DNA fingerprinting by Rabenhold and de Gortari (1991) have substantiated other work in showing that parentage and relatedness can be determined in gray wolves. Therefore, the relationship of individuals used in reintroduction programs could be evaluated and carefully chosen. Moreover, reintroduced wolves and their offspring could be distinguished from any "foreign" wolves (of unknown origin) that happened to show up (e.g., wolves naturally colonizing the area, wolves alleged to be members of a remnant population, wolves illegally reintroduced by members of the public). Also, wolves and coyotes can be distinguished by mtDNA fingerprinting. Research in progress may lead to the ability to compare DNA of original Yellowstone wolves (tissues preserved from control activities during the early 1900's) with currently existing wolves from other parts of North America (Vyse 1991).

An important point regarding use of molecular techniques is that only a small proportion of the wolf's genome has been examined so far. Moreover, studies of mtDNA alone cannot provide a good assessment of overall genetic differentiation (Cronin 1993). A combination of mtDNA and nuclear genes is needed for a more complete description of genetic relationships (Cronin et al. 1988, 1991a,b, Cronin 1992). Furthermore, although molecular data involving several genes can give a good assessment of phylogenetic relationships, many biologists believe that an integration of molecular and morphological data are needed for proper classification (Ryder 1986, O'Brien and Mayr 1991, Cronin 1993).

The Role of Dispersal in Subspecific Taxonomy

The findings of little genetic differentiation among wolf populations are plausible if animals disperse long distances and thus genetic exchange occurs frequently over broad areas. Gene flow is a strong inhibitor to the development of major differences in populations (Mayr 1970), and must be largely responsible for the degree of uniformity seen in the wolf throughout a broad area of the earth. During the past two decades several tagging and radio telemetry studies have shed considerable light on this aspect of wolf biology, and the findings seem consistent with a conclusion of limited genetic variability over large areas. Early taxonomists had little knowledge of how far wolves travel. The discovery of a high rate of genetic exchange *within* populations is even more recent.

Wolves that disperse frequently try to establish new packs. Most new packs are likely formed by dispersers (Rothman and Mech 1979, Fritts and Mech 1981, Fuller 1989). Pack fission is another mechanism (Mech 1966a, 1986, Meier et al. this volume). Dispersing wolves often colonize areas near the territory of their natal pack (Fritts and Mech 1981, Gese and Mech 1991), or they may travel for several hundred kilometres (Fritts and Mech 1981, Berg and Kuehn 1982, Pulliainen 1982, Stephenson and James 1982, Ballard et al. 1983, Fritts 1983, Mech 1987, Gese and Mech

A wolf in Jasper National Park. The 1995 wolf transfer from Alberta, Canada to Yellowstone Park and the central Idaho wilderness areas involved animals from this taxonomic group. Radio-tracking studies have shown that casual dispersal between central Alberta and the northern Rockies of the United States has occurred naturally. This population has a high percentage of gray and black color phases. Out of 29 wolves reintroduced, five weighed over 46 kg (100 lbs). (Photo: H. Fuhrer)

1991, Pletscher et al. 1991, Boyd et al. this volume, Stephenson et al. this volume, Wydeven et al. this volume). Wolves that disperse may even join pre-existing packs, a phenomenon once thought highly unlikely because of aggression between different packs (Lehman et al. 1992, Boyd et al. this volume, Meier et al. this volume). Maximum known distance for males is 886 km (Fritts 1983) and for females is 840 km (Ream et al. 1991). Individuals that reproduce in the new area carry their genetic material from one population to another.

Conclusions

Wolves differ in size, color, and in skull measurements and vary slightly from region to region within their vast geographic range. Except for color, none of these differences are striking, and when geographic differences in North American wolf populations have been shown, it was with the aid of extremely sensitive techniques. The natural history of the wolf is very similar throughout its range (L. D. Mech, U.S. Fish and Wildlife Service, pers. commun.). Mech (1991a:18) summed up the wolf subspecies issue as we also see it: "In reality, one race (subspecies) of wolf is pretty much the same as any other. The behavior and natural history are similar among the various races and between North American and Eurasian wolves. In fact, any real differences seem to be more related to the precise living conditions such as food type, climate, and geographic area. Physically, too, the races are similar. Only a real expert measuring many skulls can distinguish among most races. Subspecific names, like MacKenzie Valley wolf, northern Rocky Mountain wolf, Great Plains wolf, or eastern timber wolf, are more descriptors of where a given wolf comes from than of any real differences among the animals."

The 24 subspecies of gray wolves recognized in North America are based largely on the work of Goldman (1944) and other taxonomists during the first half of the 20th century. As summarized by Nowak (1983), Goldman (1944) did not employ statistical analyses or any modern taxonomic methods. He had access to very few specimens from some areas, and many of the subspecies he recognized were based on very few specimens. Goldman (1944) and others instrumental in compiling 24 subspecies worked during a period in history when it was fashionable to name many subspecies. Subsequent work including multivariate analyses of skull characteristics of many more specimens and limited genetic research suggests that too many subspecies were named.

Wolves from different areas are not distinct in any characteristic. Subspecific names usually represent only *averages* or *trends* that occur in a geographic area, but almost universally intergrade over substantial distances with neighboring designations. There is usually considerable overlap between the characteristics of neighboring subspecies. Some specimens found well within the range of one named group may be practically identical to some specimens from the ranges of other named groups (Nowak 1983, this volume). Genetic studies of wolves using molecular techniques suggest genetic differentiation among North American populations is too small to justify many subspecies (Wayne et al. 1992a, Wayne et al. this volume). Genetic mixing of all but geographically isolated wolf populations is facilitated by genetic exchange among local and distant populations through long-range dispersal and colonization of new areas. Therefore, genetic divergence among even widely separated populations is limited. No genetic exchange is now possible for the wolf in Mexico, which is completely isolated from other populations because of man's eradication of populations in the western U.S.

The taxonomy of the gray wolf in North America is in need of revision (see Nowak this volume). The most recent thinking on subspecific differentiation of North American wolves from a morphometric standpoint suggests that approximately five subspecies might be appropriate, with affinities occurring mainly in an east-west direction and a pronounced character change in the area just north of the border between Canada and the U.S. (Nowak 1983, this volume, Friis 1985). This would be consistent with the current trend in taxonomy that combines subspecies where there is no appreciable genetic difference, and no evidence of geographic or behavioral isolation. Variability within gray wolves is small, and we wonder if that which does exist warrants recognition of subspecies. Future taxonomists may consider recognizing no subspecies of the gray wolf in North America. Evidently no populations of wolves remained in the area of western North America (including Yellowstone and central Idaho) that was allegedly occupied by *C. l. irremotus* by about 1930. By 1940 wolves had been eliminated from nearly the entire western half of the U.S., and for some 700 km northward into Canadian provinces in the

lower elevation settled areas. From the 1930's to the 1950's the wolf recolonized much of southwestern Canada, but was again intensively controlled and the expansion stopped. Since that time populations in Alberta and B.C., with the exception of the prairie biome, have colonized southward, reoccupying much of the southern parts of the provinces. A wolf population has begun recolonizing northwestern Montana (cf. Fritts et al. this volume) and possibly Idaho and Washington. Increased wolf observations in the early 1950's (Singer 1979) and the mid- to late-1970's (Day 1981, Ream and Mattson 1982) corresponded to increased wolf numbers and range expansion in Alberta and B.C. (Gunson 1983a, Tompa 1983a). A pattern of sporadic yet persistent reports of wolf observations, with an occasional wolf killed, persisted throughout western Montana, northern and central Idaho. In northwestern Wyoming infrequent reports persisted, but no specimens were recorded. No persuasive evidence of reproduction was obtained from 1940 to 1986 in the western U.S. This would be consistent with low wolf numbers; probably individuals dispersing from Canada, possibly supplemented by occasional reproduction.

The skulls of wolves killed in the northwestern U.S. from 1941 to 1991 that have been examined, including a wolf from central Idaho in 1991, fall within the morphological grouping of wolves from Canada. Apparently they are somewhat larger than those that historically occurred in the area (Nowak 1983, this volume). This is a significant finding. First, it shows that wolves dispersing from packs probably several hundreds of kilometres away were getting into the northwestern U.S. Second, it strongly suggests that no "original" wolves were left in the northern Rockies of the U.S. One specimen killed in the area that resembled *C. l. irremotus* was killed a few kilometres north of Yellowstone National Park in 1988. This individual was killed suspiciously close to a captive colony of wolves, the founders of which were from central Montana, and showed some characteristics of captive rearing (R. Nowak, U.S. Fish and Wildlife Service, pers. commun.).

A much greater degree of evidence of their presence would exist, including specimens, if "original" wolves had persisted in the northern Rockies. The wolves that have colonized Montana have made their presence well known via numerous reports to agencies by members of the public and agency field personnel and by way of depredations on livestock.

From the 17th through the 19th century, wolves in North America received an ecological jolt of epic proportions, perhaps akin to that of the Pleistocene, but occurring in a mere 300 years. From about 1870 to 1930, wolves west of the Mississippi went from universally distributed robust populations to virtual extermination. Whatever the genetic relationships of those original wolves to the remainder of the species, they are gone.

Patterns of variation in wolves have not been static, but dynamic, with glaciation and human-related extirpation being major influences. Taxonomy is a "slice in time" description of an ever-changing situation, particularly at the subspecific level. There are areas of North America where in recent times a subspecies was recognized, became extinct, and the area was recolonized by wolves from the area of another recognized subspecies. Primarily, this occurred on islands and peninsulas where the probability of animal extinctions is known to be higher than in continental situations. Wolves are recolonizing northwestern Montana from west-central Canada, and their dispersal capability in the area is documented (Boyd et al. this volume). Any "original" wolves that have managed to survive in the northwestern U.S. will interbreed with those from more northerly stock. In the unlikely event that individuals of *C. l. irremotus* stock managed to survive they would probably be suffering some loss of genetic variability due to small population size (Lacy 1987). The "original stock" was a dynamic entity with long distance dispersal in and out of the area and with local extinctions and recolonizations. We need to dismiss the typological thinking of local types and recognize that local extinctions and recolonization from distant areas occurs constantly in nature. It is the rule, not the exception (Slatkin 1987).

We conclude that if *C. lupus* is to be recovered in the western U.S. it is appropriate to reintroduce wolves to the Yellowstone Park area. While original genetic stock cannot be restored to the area as it no longer exists, available evidence indicates little difference among North American wolves. If taken from southwestern Canada, reintroduced wolves would be of the same genetic stock from which natural dispersers no doubt immigrated into the original Yellowstone population. The same stock as those currently recolonizing Montana will likely get to Yellowstone without human help, as one to two individuals may have already demonstrated (Fritts et al. this volume). These wolves may average slightly larger than those that originally occupied the area, but they can be taken from areas where their habitat and prey are similar (Peek et al. 1991). Our conclusion is consistent with that of Wayne et al. (1992a:567) who stated that "conservation programs might consider behavioral or demographic factors to be more important than maintenance of the genetic purity of putative wolf subspecies when making decisions about captive breeding or reintroduction programs." In other words, because we can not bring back the northern Rocky Mountain wolf, regardless of whether it deserved to be a separate subspecies, we can do the next best thing and assist nature in restoring the wolf to the northern Rockies.

Acknowledgments

We greatly appreciate the comments of those who reviewed this and previous versions of this manuscript, including N. Bishop, L.N. Carbyn, N. Chu, M. Cronin, J. Fontaine, V. Geist, J. Gore, G. Henry. J. Malloy, L.D. Mech, S. Minta, R. Nowak, R. Refsnider, J. Varley, R. Wayne, J. Weaver, and one anonymous reviewer.

Wayne G. Brewster and Steven H. Fritts

Another Look at Wolf Taxonomy

■ Ronald M. Nowak

Multivariate analyses, using 10 measurements from each of 580 skulls of modern male wolves, indicate the presence of five subspecies of **Canis lupus** *in North America:* **arctos**, *a large-toothed arctic wolf;* **occidentalis**, *a large animal of Alaska and western Canada;* **nubilus**, *a moderate-sized wolf, originally found from Oregon to Newfoundland and from Hudson Bay to Texas;* **baileyi**, *a usually smaller wolf of the southwest; and* **lycaon**, *a small subspecies now restricted to southeastern Canada. Individuals taken in the northwestern conterminous United States since 1940 represent occidentalis. Eurasian subspecies include an arctic wolf (**albus**), a large north-central form (**communis**), and a widespread animal of moderate size (**lupus**), which resemble their North American counterparts more than they resemble one another. A small, but broad-skulled, subspecies (**cubanensis**) occurs in the Caucasus. Small, narrow-skulled wolves, showing little statistical overlap with one another or with any other populations, are present in southwestern Asia (**pallipes**) and southeastern North America (**rufus**).*

Introduction

Hall (1981), based largely on the morphological studies of Goldman (1937, 1944), recognized 24 subspecies of gray wolf (*Canis lupus*) in North America (Fig. 1). Sokolov and Rossolimo (1985) recognized nine additional subspecies of *Canis lupus* in Eurasia (Fig. 2), but reduced the accepted number in the New World to seven. Other authorities, relying mainly on morphometric techniques, also have indicated that some of the subspecies listed by Hall may be invalid (Rausch 1953, Jolicoeur 1959, Skeel and Carbyn 1977, Pedersen 1982, Walker and Frison 1982, Bogan and Mehlhop 1983, Nowak 1983, Friis 1985, Hoffmeister 1986). In contrast, there have been suggestions that the subspecies *C. l. lycaon* of the Great Lakes region, as mapped by Hall (1981), is divisible between two, three, or even four taxonomic units (Kolenosky and Standfield 1975, Schmitz and Kolenosky 1985a, Standfield 1970, Van Ballenberghe 1977). However, these suggestions might be based partly on consideration of hybrids of the gray wolf and coyote (*C. latrans*), that have appeared in the eastern Great Lakes region (Nowak 1979).

Analyses of mitochondrial DNA have indicated to some authorities that interbreeding between *C. lupus* and *C. latrans* has also taken place in the western Great Lakes region — Minnesota and adjacent parts of Ontario — and that a substantial "hybrid zone" has formed there (Lehman et al. 1991). Similar studies have suggested that the red wolf (*C. rufus*) of the southeastern United States may have resulted entirely from interbreeding of *C. lupus* and *C. latrans*, and that its historic range (Fig. 1) represents a "hybrid zone" (Wayne and Jenks 1991). Such studies have been questioned (Dowling et al. 1992). Elsewhere in this volume (Nowak et al. this volume) evidence is presented that *C. rufus* is a

primitive, distinctive kind of wolf, not a hybrid, and that interbreeding of *C. lupus* and *C. latrans*, if it has occurred at all in the western Great Lakes region, has resulted in no lasting phenotypic effects. Questions of hybridization thus are not emphasized in this paper, but the issue of whether the red wolf is a species, as regarded by most authorities, or a subspecies, as suggested by Lawrence and Bossert (1967, 1975), is of concern. In order to deal with that issue, as well as with the most meaningful systematic division of the gray wolf, this paper covers, for the first time, substantial data on morphometric variation in wolves on a worldwide basis.

Materials and Methods

This study is limited to 580 skulls of full grown male wolves taken in historical time. Previous work (Nowak 1979) showed that while the sexes are significantly different in most measurements, and preferably should not be combined in one sample, analyses using either sex produce much the same results. Skulls of animals under 12 months old, and of some large wolves under 24 months old, have not attained full size in all dimensions and thus are not usable. The number of specimens in each series, and representative of each taxon, is given in Table 1. I measured all North American and some Eurasian specimens, but most of the latter were measured by others (see "Acknowledgments") following my diagrams and descriptions. I was not selective, but used all data available from skulls known or judged to be those of full grown males and that yielded all desired measurements, though a few specimens were eliminated because of damage, incomplete collection information, or suspected influence from hybridization with domestic dogs (*C. familiaris*).

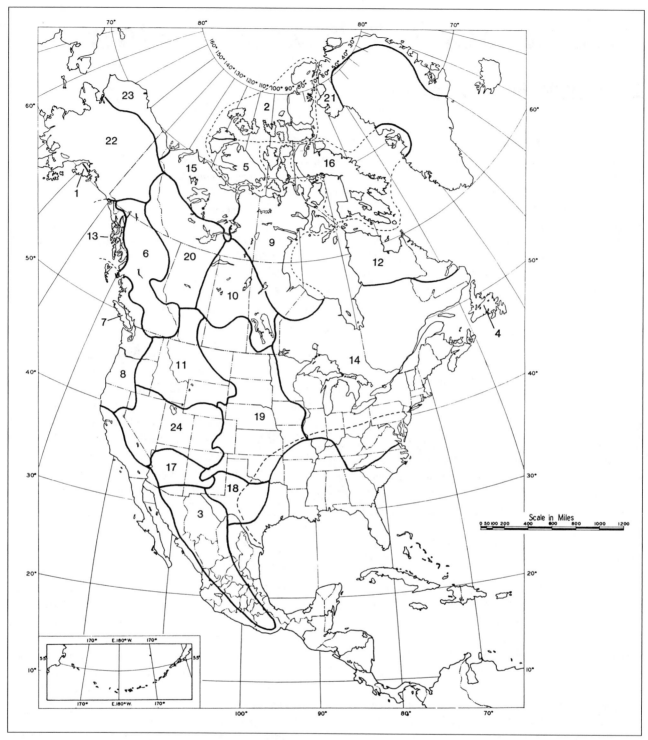

Fig. 1. *Original geographical distribution of wolves in North America. The 24 subspecies of gray wolf (**Canis lupus**) recognized by Hall (1981) are:*

1. **alces**	*7.* **crassodon**	*13.* **ligoni**	*19.* **nubilus**
2. **arctos**	*8.* **fuscus**	*14.* **lycaon**	*20.* **occidentalis**
3. **baileyi**	*9.* **griseoalbus**	*15.* **mackenzii**	*21.* **orion**
4. **beothucus**	*10.* **hudsonicus**	*16.* **manningi**	*22.* **pambasileus**
5. **bernardi**	*11.* **irremotus**	*17.* **mogollonensis**	*23.* **tundrarum**
6. **columbianus**	*12.* **labradorius**	*18.* **monstrabilis**	*24.* **youngi**

*The red wolf (**Canis rufus**) occupied the southeastern quarter of the continent, the approximate northern and western limits of its range being marked by the dashed line on the mainland.*

*The six kinds of North American wolves, as suggested by this study: a) Arctic Island wolf (**Canis lupus arctos**), photo: L.D. Mech; b) Alaskan wolf (**Canis lupus occidentalis**), photo: L.D. Mech; c) Minnesota wolf (**Canis lupus nubilus**), photo: L.D. Mech; d) Mexican wolf (**Canis lupus baileyi**), photo: D.R. Parsons; e) Algonquin park wolf (**Canis lupus lycaon**), photo: G. Forbes; f) red wolf (**Canis rufus**), photo: W. Muñoz.*

The following 10 measurements (Fig. 3) were used for analysis: 1) greatest length of skull (length from anterior tip of premaxillae to posterior point of union); 2) zygomatic width (greatest distance across zygomata); 3) alveolar length of maxillary toothrow (distance from anterior edge of alveolus of P1 to posterior edge of alveolus of M2); 4) maximum width across upper cheek teeth (greatest breadth of skull measured between outer sides of crowns of P4); 5) palatal width at first premolars (minimum width between inner margins of alveoli of P1); 6) width of frontal shield (maximum breadth across postorbital processes of frontals); 7) height from toothrow to orbit (minimum distance from outer alveolar margin of M1 to most ventral point of orbit); 8) depth of jugal (minimum depth of jugal anterior to postor-

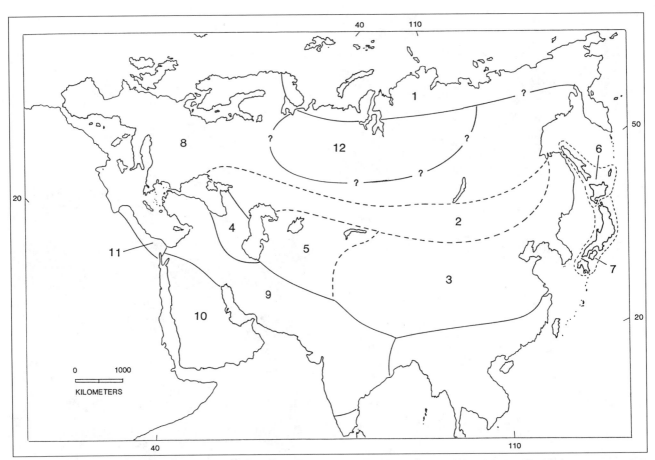

Fig. 2. *Original geographical distribution of gray wolf (**Canis lupus**) in the Old World. Sokolov and Rossolimo (1985) recognized the following subspecies: 1)* **albus**, *2)* **campestris**, *3)* **chanco**, *4)* **cubanensis**, *5)* **desertorum**, *6)* **hattai** (= **rex),** *7)* **hodophilax**, *8)* **lupus**, *9)* **pallipes**. *The subspecies 10)* **arabs**, *regarded as a synonym of* **pallipes** *by Sokolov and Rossolimo (1985), sometimes is considered valid, and the subspecies 11)* **lupaster** *sometimes is assigned to* **C. lupus** *rather than to* **C. aureus**. *This study supports combining* **campestris, chanco,** *and* **desertorum** *with the subspecies* **lupus**, *but distinguishing the subspecies 12)* **communis**. *As indicated by the question marks (?), the extent of the range of* **communis** *is problematical, and there also is uncertainty as to whether northeastern Siberia is occupied by* **communis, albus,** *or* **lupus**.

bital process, at right angle to its anteroposterior axis); 9) crown length of upper carnassial (maximum anteroposterior length of crown of P4 measured on outer side); and 10) crown width of second upper molar (maximum transverse diameter of M2 measured from outermost point to innermost point of crown). Means for all series are listed in Table 1.

These measurements are thought to express major adaptive features of the skull: overall size, grasping power, cranial protection, and cutting and crushing capacity. They are among 15 used in previous work (Nowak 1979); the others — braincase width, width of rostrum at C1, postorbital constriction, length from toothrow to bulla, and diameter of C1 — are considered redundant, less precise, and/or useful mainly to distinguish domestic dogs from wild canids, rather than to separate different kinds of wolves.

Expression of the results of this study depends entirely on computer-based, multivariate analysis of these 10 measurements. Other measurements, nonmeasurable characters of the skull, and features of the pelage and postcranial skeleton are given little or no consideration. Previous experience (Nowak 1979) indicates that such an approach is acceptable for a review of recent wolves and that evaluation of the other characters would not affect or would reinforce conclusions. However, I do recognize that utilization of a larger set of measurements or assessment of regularity in nonmeasurable characters could, in certain cases, lead some workers to distinguish additional taxonomic groupings. The measurements that I used are probably among those that best reflect what a person actually sees in a skull. Their combination and comparison through multivariate analysis is not considered a solution to classification problems, but rather a means of efficiently and objectively presenting conclusions that a person might make after examining many specimens or reviewing many individual measurements.

All measurements were subjected to canonical discriminant analysis using the Statistical Analysis System (SAS

Table 1. Means of measurements (numbered as in Fig. 3 and text) for wolf groups analyzed (listed approximately in order discussed in text).

Group	n	1	2	3	4	5	6	7	8	9	10
columbianus	8	275.8	147 .0	89.53	83.89	32.34	64.61	43.36	20.09	25.78	14.18
griseoalbus	10	271.5	144.8	89.26	84.51	34.23	66.82	44.38	20.32	27.18	14.47
occidentalis	50	276.2	148.2	90.74	85.13	33.29	68.37	43.99	21.11	26.81	14.46
pambasileus	24	275.3	148.4	91.15	85.86	33.70	68.65	44.40	20.78	27.25	14.66
tundrarum	13	273.8	146.1	90.95	84.72	32.47	68.88	43.36	20.51	27.38	15.00
main northern group (above 5 combined)	105	275.2	146.6	90.63	85.09	33.30	68.07	44.00	20.80	26.94	14.55
fuscus	10	257.4	138.7	85.82	81.71	31.33	69.29	40.67	20.72	25.52	13.47
irremotus	14	253.9	139.7	86.41	83.14	31.13	62.74	38.98	18.99	25.52	13.47
lycaon (Minnesota)	28	256.3	139.3	86.27	81.13	31.77	64.34	39.31	19.61	24.99	14.12
mogollonensis	17	253.5	140.4	84.34	81.11	31.06	66.65	39.81	19.26	25.37	13.65
monstrabilis	7	257.4	138.3	84.40	79.51	31.63	65.06	40.27	18.84	25.56	13.16
nubilus	15	256.7	137.5	84.93	80.55	31.95	65.57	39.87	19.77	25.39	13.19
youngi	28	257.5	140.0	86.25	83.18	32.79	66.55	39.45	19.89	25.65	13.81
main southern group (above 7 combined)	119	256.1	139.3	85.69	81.72	31.81	65.62	39.62	19.62	25.39	13.67
ligoni	26	263.0	144.3	86.75	82.88	33.29	67.99	41.93	20.15	25.60	14.15
crassodon	6	258.5	141.7	86.78	81.27	31.60	68.02	40.12	19.30	26.25	14.30
baileyi	21	243.9	136.3	81.78	77.40	29.98	60.62	38.95	18.79	24.49	12.59
arctos	22	256.5	142.4	86.81	84.45	32.31	65.48	41.73	19.35	27.45	13.98
hudsonicus	14	258.7	139.8	85.89	82.06	32.02	63.51	41.16	18.99	26.07	14.11
lycaon (west Ont.)	14	255.6	138.9	84.92	80.81	30.97	65.29	39.26	19.14	25.11	13.99
lycaon (Algonquin)	13	250.2	134.6	83.87	78.13	28.85	63.75	37.98	17.82	24.90	14.69
rufus	33	236.5	121.3	79.48	69.74	26.18	54.80	33.58	16.03	23.35	13.71
campestris	34	251.3	137.2	84.81	79.23	31.05	64.80	39.73	19.09	25.96	14.29
chanco	23	248.0	134.9	84.43	77.20	29.71	61.33	37.83	18.33	25.08	13.91
desertorum	20	252.3	134.1	87.57	78.25	29.58	63.04	38.73	17.99	25.72	14.00
lupus (above 3 combined)	77	250.6	135.7	85.41	78.37	30.27	63.30	38.90	18.58	25.63	14.10
albus	20	263.0	147.1	88.30	84.65	33.03	70.11	41.48	19.08	26.65	14.95
communis	20	270.2	150.9	87.70	86.08	34.19	74.48	43.01	21.40	26.83	13.89
pallipes	30	221.4	118.0	76.53	68.98	26.75	56.44	33.98	15.30	22.99	12.20
cubanensis	14	237.5	136.5	80.58	76.74	29.26	63.34	37.80	-.-	23.36	12.82

Institute 1987). This method is similar to that employed in my previous work on *Canis* (Nowak 1979) and is the same as used in various recent taxonomic studies of mammals (e.g., those by Goodyear 1991 and Jones et al. 1991). Essentially, the various measurements, weighted by their ability to best distinguish the particular groups being analyzed, assign each specimen a total numerical value referred to as the first canonical variable. The next best distinguishing combination, uncorrelated with the first, provides a second canonical variable, and so on.

Commonly, a single graphical position is plotted based on the first two canonical variables arranged as perpendicular axes. The result looks much like a bivariate scatter diagram, but the numerical positions are abstracts, and the overall mean of all the positions is standardized to zero. High positive values may actually express small size, and vice versa. Characters given greatest weight change with the set of groups being compared, and so the statistical distribution of a given group may change as it is compared to various others. The legend for each of the following graphs (Figs. 4, 6, 7, 8, 9, 10, 11, 13, 14, 15, 16, 17, 18, 19) lists the three

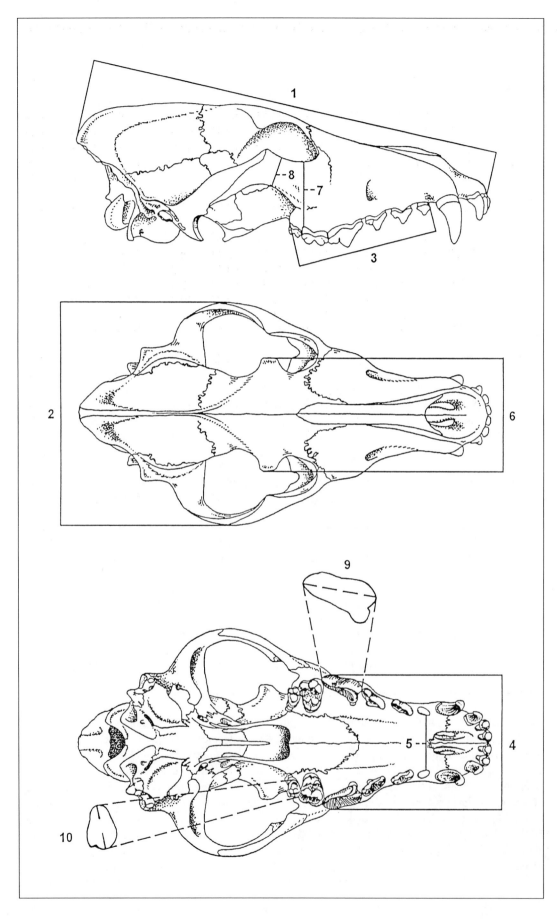

Fig. 3. *Three views of a skull of **Canis lupus**, showing the 10 characters used in statistical analyses (see text for descriptions). The drawings were made by Irene Brady, based on originals in Hall (1981).*

Table 2. Statistical distance, D^2, between nominal subspecies of *Canis lupus* in western North America.

Distance from group	tundra-rum	pamba-sileus	occiden-talis	colum-bianus	griseo-albus	fuscus	irre-motus	youngi	mogollo-nensis	nubilus	monstra-bilis	lycaon
tundrarum		1.15	1.50	5.17	2.97	12.15	12.25	9.47	10.79	11.67	10.27	10.23
pambasileus	1.15		0.68	4.18	1.58	14.34	13.09	10.75	12.68	12.81	11.07	12.15
occidentalis	1.50	0.68		2.36	.83	12.33	12.08	9.58	11.55	10.88	9.82	10.22
columbianus	5.17	4.18	2.36		6.69	15.95	12.16	12.30	13.01	12.93	10.88	11.12
griseoalbus	2.97	1.58	2.83	6.69		14.16	14.34	10.37	12.88	10.93	8.84	12.51
fuscus	12.15	14.34	12.33	15.95	14.16		5.95	2.84	2.99	1.91	4.94	3.96
irremotus	12.25	13.09	12.08	12.16	14.34	5.95		3.08	3.00	4.89	6.24	3.79
youngi	9.47	10.75	9.58	12.30	10.37	2.84	3.08		2.78	1.84	4.23	1.78
mogollonensis	10.79	12.68	11.55	13.01	12.88	2.99	3.00	2.78		2.92	3.00	2.70
nubilus	11.67	12.81	10.88	12.93	10.93	1.91	4.89	1.84	2.92		1.47	3.19
monstrabilis	10.27	11.07	9.82	10.88	8.84	4.94	6.24	4.23	3.00	1.47		5.26
lycaon	10.23	12.15	10.22	11.12	12.51	3.96	3.79	1.78	2.70	3.19	5.26	

characters that contributed most to each canonical variable. Individual specimens can be assigned positions in relation to established groups. The mean position of each group also can be plotted and the statistical distances between the means (this distance being known as the D^2 of Mahalanobis) can be calculated to assess affinity.

Results and Discussion

The North-South Division in Western North America

Past investigations (Skeel and Carbyn 1977, Nowak 1983, Friis 1985) suggested that there might be a major systematic division of North American *C. lupus* along a line extending from the Pacific to the western Great Lakes, roughly following the border between Canada and the United States. Seven named subspecies meet along this line: *columbianus*, *occidentalis*, and *griseoalbus* to the north, and *fuscus*, *irremotus*, *nubilus*, and *lycaon* to the south. I decided to compare these populations, and also several neighboring subspecies farther to the north (*tundrarum*, *pambasileus*) and south (*youngi*, *mogollonensis*, *monstrabilis*), to evaluate the idea that the statistical break along the aforementioned line might be substantially more pronounced than that separating populations falling entirely on one side of the line. The subspecies *hudsonicus*, found just to the northeast, is treated separately below. In order to allow comparison between the most geographically proximal populations of the gray wolf and red wolf in subsequent analyses, the sample of *lycaon* is

limited to Minnesota (23 specimens) and Isle Royale (five specimens) and that of *monstrabilis* is limited to Texas (seven specimens). For purposes of helping to evaluate the question of whether western Great Lakes wolves may be changing through recent hybridization with the coyote, the sample of *lycaon* is also limited to individuals taken since 1960. Otherwise, all specimens from the western conterminous United States were taken prior to 1940 (except for one skull of *monstrabilis* collected in 1942).

Plotting the means of the first two canonical variables of each named subspecies indicates a division based mainly on large size in wolves to the north and smaller size in those to the south (Fig. 4). Only the means are shown, because there was such extensive overlap between the five northern subspecies, on the one hand, and between the seven southern subspecies, on the other, that plotting all of the statistical boundaries of the groups would have made the figure too confusing. Table 2 gives the statistical distances between all subspecies, while Figure 5 maps the distances between neighboring subspecies. The statistical distance between neighbors across the Pacific-Great Lakes line is in all cases much greater than the distance between any two subspecies, whether neighbors or not, on one side of the line. Therefore, more is involved than simply a north-south cline in size. The northern series and the southern series evidently represent two main systematic groupings of *C. lupus*, which may in turn serve as standards with which other populations and individuals may be compared.

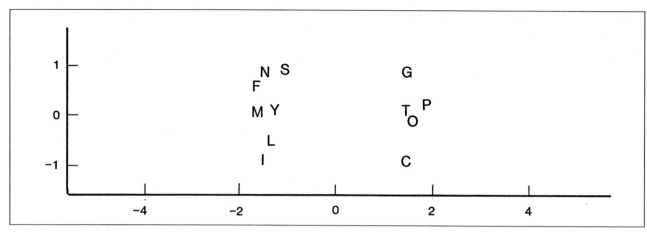

Fig. 4. *Statistical distribution of means of 12 nominal subspecies of North American **Canis lupus**, based on the first (horizontal axis) and second (vertical axis) canonical variables. Letters indicate mean positions of groups: C — **columbianus**; F — **fuscus**; G — **griseoalbus**; I — **irremotus**; L — **lycaon**; M — **mogollonensis**; N — **nubilus**; O — **occidentalis**; P — **pambasileus**; S — **monstrabilis**; T — **tundrarum**; Y — **youngi**. Characters (see Fig. 3) contributing most to high positive values are: first canonical variable, large 1, large 7, large 9; second canonical variable, small 2, small 7, large 4.*

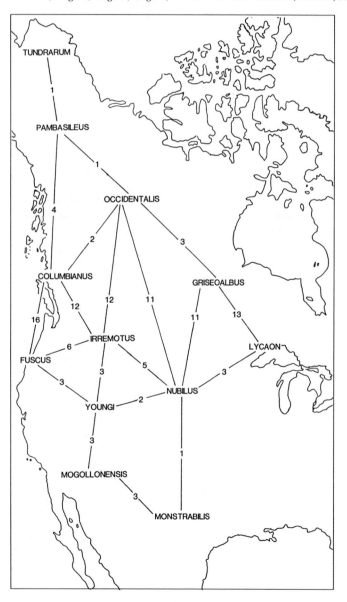

Other Subspecies of Western North America

Based on recent studies (Pedersen 1982, Bogan and Mehlhop 1983, Friis 1985) three additional nominal subspecies of western North America may be associated with the main southern group: *ligoni* of the southeastern Alaska panhandle, *crassodon* of Vancouver Island, and *baileyi* of Mexico and adjacent border parts of the southwestern United States. Friis (1985) found statistical affinity between *ligoni*, *crassodon*, and *fuscus*, but indicated that each warranted subspecific status. She also suggested that populations of coastal and south-central British Columbia were referable to *ligoni*, rather than to *fuscus*. Sokolov and Rossolimo (1985) combined *ligoni*, *crassodon*, and *fuscus* into a single subspecies. In my own analysis (Fig. 6), *fuscus* and *crassodon* are completely separable, but a series of 26 *ligoni* (as compared to 11 used by Friis) overlaps slightly with *fuscus* and substantially with *crassodon*. Moreover, when *fuscus*, *ligoni*, and *crassodon* are compared to all western populations (see below), their recognition as full subspecies becomes questionable.

Figure 7 shows an analysis in which my single main northern group, comprising the combined samples of *columbianus*, *griseoalbus*, *occidentalis*, *pambasileus*, and *tundrarum*, is compared to a single main southern group, comprising the combined samples of *fuscus*, *irremotus*, *lycaon*, *mogollonensis*, *monstrabilis*, *nubi-*

Fig. 5. *Statistical distances (rounded to whole numbers) between those 12 nominal subspecies of North American **Canis lupus** shown in Figure 4.*

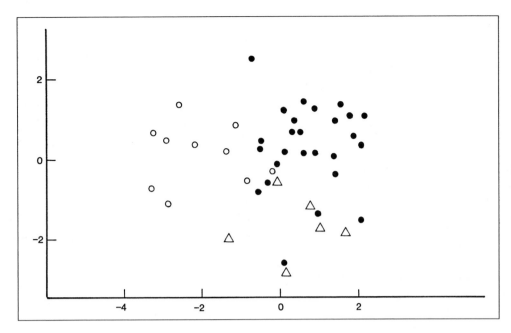

Fig. 6. *Statistical distribution of three nominal subspecies of North American* **Canis lupus**, *based on the first (horizontal axis) and second (vertical axis) canonical variables. Dots,* **ligoni***; open circles,* **fuscus***; triangles,* **crassodon***. Characters (Fig. 3) contributing most to high positive values are: first canonical variable, large 2, small 4, large 5; second canonical variable, small 9, large 1, large 4.*

lus, and *youngi.* Also considered as groups in this analysis are the nominal subspecies *ligoni, crassodon,* and *baileyi.*

The subspecies *ligoni* occurs in the same latitudinal range as the members of my main northern group, but is partly isolated by mountains, glaciers, and waterways. While in the analysis (Fig. 7) it is partly encompassed by the statistical limits of the main northern systematic group of *C. lupus*, as developed above, *ligoni* falls mostly within the limits of the main southern group. It is also statistically closer to the southern group ($D^2 = 2.7$) than to the northern group

($D^2 = 4.6$), though it probably has been influenced extensively through intergradation with the latter. Using methodology similar to mine, but somewhat larger samples, Pedersen (1982) regarded *ligoni* as subspecifically distinct from *pambasileus,* a component of my northern group.

The positions (Fig. 7) of several individuals from near the Pacific coast of British Columbia, within the range of *C. l. fuscus,* as mapped by Hall (1981), are indicative of affinity with *ligoni* and thus supportive of findings by Friis (1985). However, *crassodon* of Vancouver Island falls entirely

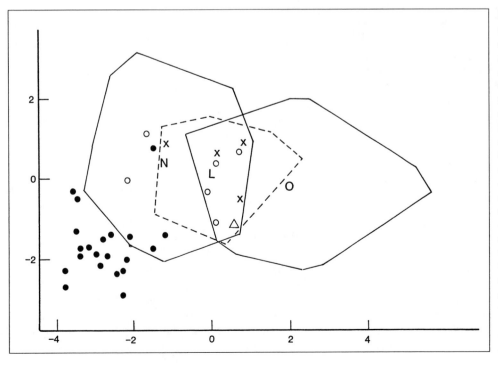

Fig. 7. *Statistical distribution of five groups and various individuals of North American* **Canis lupus***, based on the first (horizontal axis) and second (vertical axis) canonical variables. Solid lines, limits of main northern group (letter O shows mean position) and main southern group (letter N shows mean); dashed lines, limits of* **ligoni** *(letter L shows mean); dots,* **baileyi***; open circles,* **crassodon***; x's, individuals from coastal British Columbia; triangle, one individual* **labradorius***. Characters (Fig. 3) contributing most to high positive values are: first canonical variable, large 1, large 7, large 9; second canonical variable, small 2, small 7, large 1.*

within the overall statistical range of my main southern group. *Crassodon* originally was distinguished partly on the basis of nonmeasurable characters, especially in that the anterior margin of P4 is directed inward and backward. I found this feature of P4 to be pronounced in most of the 19 skulls of *crassodon* that I examined, though only in two of the six adult males used in my statistical analysis. While there is a reasonable case for giving subspecific status to *crassodon*, based on nonmeasurable characters and statistical separation from *fuscus*, its statistical position in relation to North American wolves in general, and to *ligoni* in particular, suggests inclusion within my main southern group of *C. lupus*.

Quite different is the situation of *baileyi*, which lies almost entirely outside the range of variation of the other groups. A single specimen from New Mexico, geographically well within the range of *baileyi*, is statistically close to the mean of my southern group. This individual is close to other *baileyi* in greatest length and zygomatic width, but is larger in width across upper cheek teeth, palatal width at P1, and diameter of M2. Otherwise, my findings with respect to *baileyi* correspond with those of Hoffmeister (1986), who continued to recognize *baileyi* as a subspecies with generally the same content assigned by Goldman (1944), and who placed *mogollonensis*, the nominal subspecies immediately to the north, in the synonymy of *youngi*, which in turn is here considered part of the main southern group. My findings do not correspond with those of Bogan and Mehlhop (1983), who regarded *mogollonensis* and *monstrabilis* as part of *baileyi*, with the resulting entity subspecifically distinct from *nubilus* and *youngi*.

One additional named subspecies found in western North America and south of the arctic is *alces* of the Kenai Peninsula in Alaska. The wolf evidently was eliminated from the Kenai by humans by about 1915, though a population was reestablished through migration from the north in the 1960's and 1970's (Peterson and Woolington 1982). Based on five specimens collected in 1904–1905, Goldman (1944) regarded the original population as a distinct subspecies, being perhaps the largest of North American wolves. Rausch (1953) and Pedersen (1982) questioned this designation. The original specimens consist of two adult females and three males that are not full grown and thus not suitable for inclusion in my analyses. The females are large, but are matched in this regard by several females of *occidentalis* that I have examined. All five skulls have carnassial teeth that are smaller than those of many other specimens in my main northern group. *Alces* hence appears to be a component of that group.

Adjustments to Subspecific Ranges

Most of the specimens used in my sample of *baileyi* and in the standard samples of my main northern (*columbianus*, *griseoalbus*, *occidentalis*, *pambasileus*, *tundrarum*) and southern (*fuscus*, *irremotus*, *lycaon*, *mogollonensis*, *mon-*

strabilis, *nubilus*, *youngi*) groups were assigned to nominal subspecies based on the ranges indicated by Goldman (1944) and Hall (1981). However, one individual from Duck Mountain in west-central Manitoba, classified as *nubilus* by those authorities, was included in my sample of *griseoalbus*. Several other specimens also suggest that the range of my main northern group originally extended farther to the south than usually thought, and that this range has moved still farther south in recent decades. These specimens were not included in the above standard samples, but are considered below.

Figure 8 compares my main northern and southern groups, and *baileyi*, and shows the relative positions of certain other individuals. Skulls from southern Alberta and the Little Belt Mountains of central Montana, which had been assigned by Goldman (1944) and Hall (1981) to *irremotus*, are statistically nearer to the main northern group. Admittedly, the Montana specimen could be considered part of an intergrading population, an unusually large member of the southern group (such as do occur elsewhere), or a wandering individual. Wolves are known to make extensive movements, even well across supposed subspecific lines. Fritts (1983) reported one that covered a straight-line distance of 886 km, moving from northeastern Minnesota to Saskatchewan. A specimen taken in 1925 in extreme northwestern South Dakota also falls well within the northern group and may represent a wolf that wandered southward after native populations had been extirpated.

Human persecution nearly eliminated the gray wolf from the conterminous United States. By the late 1920's the only substantive resident populations occurred in the northern Great Lakes region (Nowak 1983). The region from which wolves had disappeared corresponded largely with the range of the southern group of *C. lupus*, as designated above. Later occurrences to the west of the Great Lakes region apparently represent wandering individuals or range extensions from the north. All 11 specimens of males from the northwestern quarter of the conterminous United States, collected since 1940, fall beyond the range of variation of the southern group of *C. lupus* (Fig. 8), and probably represent a recent southward expansion of the northern group. These specimens were taken in the following states: Idaho, 1; Montana, 5; Oregon, 1; South Dakota, 2; and Washington, 2. They include three specimens collected in northwestern Montana in 1988–1989, which are the largest skulls of *C. lupus* ever taken in the conterminous United States; they approach the size of several taken in 1966–1974 in Alberta, which are the largest ever recorded for the species (Gunson and Nowak 1979). Four other specimens of males collected 1989–1991 in the Dakotas are statistically like the southern group and most likely moved westward from the existing Minnesota population.

In compiling my series of *baileyi*, I followed Hoffmeister (1986) in including a specimen from the Galiuro Mountains, Graham County, Arizona, which had been assigned to *mogollonensis* by Bogan and Mehlhop (1983), Goldman

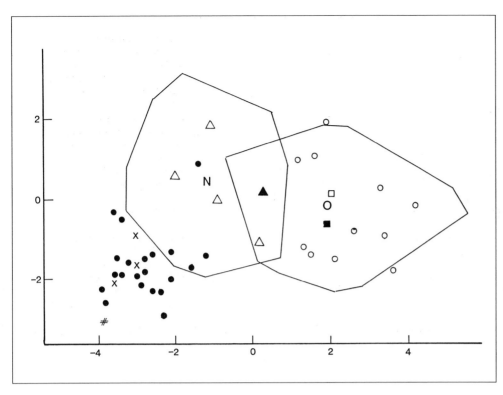

Fig. 8. *Statistical distribution of three groups and various individuals of North American* **Canis lupus**, *based on the first (horizontal axis) and second (vertical axis) canonical variables. Solid lines, limits of main northern group (letter O shows mean) and main southern group (letter N shows mean); dots,* **baileyi**; *open circles, individuals taken in the northwestern quarter of the conterminous United States since 1940; open triangles, individuals collected 1989-1991 in the Dakotas; solid triangle, individual from Alberta originally assigned to* **irremotus**; *open square, individual from Little Belt Mountains of Montana; solid square, individual taken in northwestern South Dakota in 1925; x's, individuals of* **baileyi** *collected recently in Arizona and Texas; crosshatch, individual from Gila National Forest originally assigned to* **mogollonensis**. *Characters (Fig. 3) contributing most to high positive values are: first canonical variable, large 1, large 7, large 9; second canonical variable, small 2, small 7, large 4.*

(1944), and Hall (1981). This allocation, together with others by Hoffmeister, suggests that the natural range of *baileyi* extends just to the north of the Gila River. This distribution, in turn, brings into question the status of a series of specimens taken on the Gila National Forest of New Mexico, which is bisected by the Gila River. These specimens were assigned to *mogollonensis* by Goldman. However, one seemed to me to be unusually small for that subspecies and was withheld for comparison at this point. Its position, most proximal to the statistical bounds of *baileyi*, is shown in Figure 8.

It is likely that individuals from the geographic range of *baileyi* regularly dispersed into the range of populations to the north and vice versa. After these more northerly populations were eliminated by people during the 20th century, the occurrence of wolves within their ranges would be attributable to *baileyi* dispersing from Mexico, where the subspecies evidently still survives (Ginsberg and MacDonald 1990). Such occurrence is indicated by the statistical positions (Fig. 8) of a male taken in 1957 near Concho, Apache County, Arizona, well within the original range of *mogollonensis*, and of two males collected in 1970 in Brewster County, Trans-Pecos Texas, which were reported by Scudday (1972).

Arctic Wolves

Four subspecies of *C. lupus* have been described from the arctic islands off North America, mostly on the basis of only a few specimens. A group of skulls, from the range assigned by Hall (1981) to the subspecies *arctos* and *bernardi*, is

largely distinguishable from both the main northern and main southern groups of *C. lupus* (Fig. 9). Individual skulls from the range assigned by Hall (1981) to the subspecies *mackenzii*, on the mainland nearest to the western arctic islands, are statistically encompassed by the limits of the main northern group, though are shifted in the direction of the island wolves. In contrast, the position of a specimen of *C. l. manningi* from Baffin Island is well beyond the statistical range of the other island wolves and indicative of affinity with the main southern group.

Manning and MacPherson (1958) concluded that *bernardi* of Banks Island (based on material collected in 1914–1916) had been replaced by another population (material taken in 1953–1955) that they assigned to *arctos*, but that I (Nowak 1979) thought differed both from *bernardi* and *arctos*. In reassessing this situation, it seems unlikely that the more recent specimens from Banks Island, apparently having originated from within the range of *arctos* and having been collected over a brief period, could represent anything more than a subpopulation of *arctos*, albeit one showing rather extreme characters. I also question whether the original population of *bernardi* was more than another subpopulation of *arctos* showing only modest development of the characters of the subspecies. As Jolicoeur (1959) suggested, the severe environment of the arctic might influence ontogenetic cranial development of the skull; such effect could vary from time to time, thereby increasing the impression of differences between populations.

In any event, examination of *arctos*, including the newer Banks Island material, and a review of the measurements of

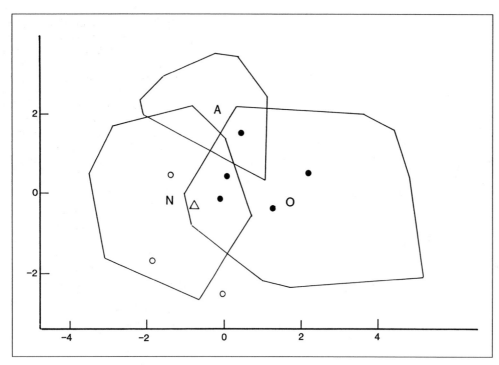

Fig. 9. *Statistical distribution of three groups and various individuals of North American **Canis lupus**, based on the first (horizontal axis) and second (vertical axis) canonical variables. Solid lines, limits of main northern group (letter O shows mean), main southern group (letter N shows mean), and **arctos** (letter A shows mean); dots, individuals of nominal subspecies **mackenzii**; open circles, individuals of **beothucus**; triangle, one individual **manningi**. Characters (Fig. 3) contributing most to high positive values are: first canonical variable, large 1, large 7, large 2; second canonical variable, small 1, large 9, large 7.*

the five known adults of original *bernardi*, as published by Goldman (1944), indicate that all of the involved populations share the most consistent distinguishing character of *arctos*, which is relatively large carnassial teeth. That condition, together with the results of canonical analysis of available material, suggest that the name *arctos* is appropriate for the subspecies occupying the region from Ellesmere to Banks and Victoria islands, and Greenland (Marquhard-Peterson this volume).

I have examined only two specimens of the Greenland wolf, *C. l. orion*, and both are probably females. I see no substantive basis for separating them from *arctos*. Goldman (1944), who saw only a single skull, also suggested affinity to *arctos*. Moreover, Dawes et al. (1986) pointed out that wolves moved freely across the ice between Ellesmere Island and Greenland, and recommended referring the animals in northern and eastern Greenland to *arctos*.

Wolves of Northeastern Canada

The nominal subspecies *C. l. hudsonicus*, which was assigned a large range to the west of Hudson Bay (Hall 1981), falls almost entirely within the range of variation of the southern group (Fig. 10). Goldman (1944) observed that the skull of *hudsonicus* is "decidedly smaller" than that of *occidentalis*, occurring just to the west, and Kolenosky and Standfield (1975) hinted at affinity between *hudsonicus*, *nubilus* (as delineated by Hall), and the western Ontario population of *lycaon*.

Skeel and Carbyn (1977) came to a different conclusion regarding *hudsonicus*. Although their preliminary multivariate analyses suggested that *hudsonicus* might be more

closely related to populations of my southern group than to those of the northern group, cluster analysis and multidimensional scaling techniques showed male *hudsonicus* to fall close to males from Wood Buffalo National Park (Alberta and Mackenzie District of Northwest Territories), within the range of *occidentalis*. A separate cluster was formed by males from Jasper (Alberta) and Prince Albert (Saskatchewan) national parks, also within the range of my northern group. This incongruity may be explainable through consideration of an unusual sex ratio in Skeel and Carbyn's sample from Wood Buffalo National Park: 24 males and five females. Although experience indicates that males frequently do outnumber females in a given series of canid specimens, a near five to one ratio is totally unexpected and is unlike that in any of the other seven samples used by Skeel and Carbyn. They reported that of the 29 specimens from Wood Buffalo Park, 20 actually were unknown as to sex and that 18 of those were classified as males by statistical probability using a stepwise discriminant analysis. I suggest that something went amiss in this operation, that females were included in the male sample, and that had these females not been used the group of males from Wood Buffalo Park would have fallen statistically nearer to the other samples of *occidentalis* than to *hudsonicus*. My own sample of *hudsonicus* consists of eight specimens known to be males and six that I judged to be males, but the latter are limited to skulls that exceed the average of the known males in greatest length.

Kelsall (1968) expressed doubt that *hudsonicus* is distinguishable from *occidentalis*, just to the west, noting that wolves from the former's range annually invade the latter's

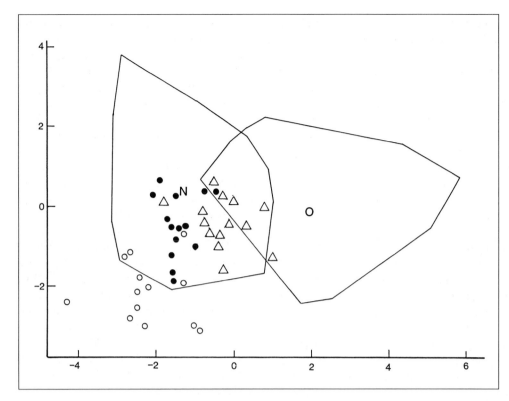

Fig. 10. *Statistical distribution of five groups of North American* **Canis lupus***, based on the first (horizontal axis) and second (vertical axis) canonical variables. Solid lines, limits of main northern group (letter O shows mean) and main southern group (letter N shows mean); dots, western Ontario* **lycaon***; open circles, Algonquin* **lycaon***; triangles,* **hudsonicus***. Characters (Fig. 3) contributing most to high positive values are: first canonical variable, large 1, large 7, large 2; second canonical variable, small 10, large 5, large 8.*

range, following caribou herds for hundreds of kilometres. However, he also stated that biologists, game officers, hunters, and trappers have long used gross morphological features to separate the wolves of the tundra, the main habitat of *hudsonicus*, from the wolves of the taiga, the main habitat of *occidentalis*. The presence of a component of the southern group of wolves in this far northern region could be associated with the failure of the main northern group of wolves to expand into a relatively unproductive habitat, in which it would have to depend almost entirely on the rather small barren-ground caribou.

Its assignment to the main southern systematic group of *C. lupus* makes *hudsonicus* a key to the classification of other northeastern populations. The statistical position of my one specimen of *manningi* (Fig. 9), being much closer to the southern group than to *arctos*, is now reasonable, because the range of *hudsonicus* extends to immediately south of Baffin Island (Fig. 1). Measurements listed by Goldman (1944) also show that *manningi* does not share the most definitive character of *arctos*, the relatively large carnassial teeth. Indeed, *manningi* originally was distinguished from *arctos* on the basis of its much smaller teeth and more slender proportions. Dawes et al. (1986) noted that wolves appearing on the west-central coast of Greenland probably originate on Baffin Island, and thus in a population here considered associated with my main southern group.

The vast range of the nominal subspecies *labradorius*, to the east of Hudson Bay, is represented only by a single specimen in my analyses. It is a large individual with closest

statistical affinity to the northern group, though it also lies just within the limits of the southern group and of *ligoni* (Fig. 7). I have seen two skulls of immature *labradorius*, unknown as to sex, and one of an adult, probably female. That examination, together with review of the measurements of three adult males listed by Goldman (1944), indicates that *labradorius* falls closest to my main southern group. Goldman suggested affinity between *labradorius* and the Newfoundland island subspecies *beothucus*, and noted that both contrast markedly with populations of *lycaon* in southeastern Canada. My own analysis of three specimens (Fig. 9) indicates that *beothucus* has affinity with my main southern group and not with *arctos*, with which it was synonymized by Sokolov and Rossolimo (1985).

Lycaon

Although Goldman (1944) considered the range of the subspecies *C. lupus lycaon* to extend westward to Minnesota, he noted that specimens from the Great Lakes region grade toward *nubilus* of the Great Plains. More recently there has been a growing consensus that the western populations of *lycaon*, at least those of Minnesota, actually are more closely related to *nubilus* than to populations of *lycaon* in Quebec and southeastern Ontario (Mech and Frenzel 1971b, Kolenosky and Standfield 1975, Skeel and Carbyn 1977, Van Ballenberghe 1977, Schmitz and Kolenosky 1985a). Evidence presented above (Figs. 4 and 5, Table 2) indicates that post-1960 Minnesota *lycaon* have affinity to pre-1940 populations of the western conterminous United States and should be combined with my main southern group of *C. lupus*. There is no suggestion that Minnesota *lycaon* has hybridized with *C. latrans* or any other species.

A series of *lycaon* from southwestern Ontario, the area north of the Minnesota border and Lake Superior, falls near the center of variation of my main southern group (Fig. 10). However, a series from southeastern Ontario is mostly beyond the range of the others. To minimize the chance of using specimens affected by hybridization between *C. lupus* and *C. latrans* (see below), I restricted my sample of southeast Ontario *lycaon* to Algonquin Provincial Park and its immediate vicinity, where there is a relatively dense and well-protected wolf population on an extensive tract of natural habitat.

My analyses support combining both Minnesota and west Ontario *lycaon* with my main southern group, but recognizing southeast Ontario *lycaon* as representative of another subspecies. The case for a remarkable division between two kinds of wolves in Ontario, a larger animal to the west and a smaller one to the southeast, was announced by Standfield (1970) and developed by Kolenosky and Standfield (1975). The latter authorities practically suggested specific separation, stating (p. 71): "the ranges of the two types overlap throughout a broad band across east-central Ontario, but there is no conclusive evidence of their interbreeding." Nonetheless, Kolenosky and Standfield's multivariate analyses of cranial measurements do show the two kinds to have about the same degree of statistical overlap that I found (Fig. 10). They also reported a third and still smaller kind of wolf, occurring in extreme southern Ontario, but suggested that it represented hybridization between *C. lupus* and *C. latrans*. My own previous work (Nowak 1979) reported the presence of such hybrids in southern Ontario and Quebec and suggested that they were contributing to the introgression of wolf genes into the coyote population now expanding through the northeastern United States.

Schmitz and Kolenosky (1985a) presented a modified interpretation of the status of *lycaon*. Based on multivariate analyses of both body and skull measurements, they concluded that the three previously identified kinds of wolves in Ontario are all clinal variants of *lycaon*, that the west Ontario population is more closely related to the southeast Ontario population than to the Minnesota population, and that the small animal of extreme southern Ontario is not a coyote-wolf hybrid, but a form of *lycaon* that arose within the last 75 years. They also recognized three morphologically distinct kinds of *C. latrans* in Ontario, noting that two of those kinds may have resulted from coyote-wolf hybridization.

In designating six distinctive kinds of wild *Canis* in Ontario (not including still others in Minnesota), Schmitz and Kolenosky may not have fully appreciated both the individual variability of the genus and the extent to which hybridization may have affected the situation. The graphical portrayals of their analyses plot only centroids and do not allow visualization of statistical approach and overlap of the different groups. Some of their results seem incongruous; for example, that wolves exhibit clinal variation, but are divisible into morphologically distinct groups, and that wolves have not been influenced by hybridization with coyotes, but that some coyote populations may be descended from coyote-wolf hybrids. Their Table 2 suggests that, for males at least, the skull of the small "wolf" of extreme southern Ontario is more like the skull of coyotes than like the skull of other wolves. Some of their cranial measurements (including five on just the mandibular and occipital condyles) may express traits that have become randomly and temporarily established in populations, rather than long-term adaptive characters. Their description of overall differences between the skulls of Minnesota and west Ontario wolves seems incorrect. The measurements for my own series of Minnesota *lycaon* and west Ontario *lycaon* are closer than those for any other two series that I examined (see Table 1).

In short, I do not accept the conclusions of Schmitz and Kolenosky (1985a), at least with respect to the relationships of west Ontario wolves and to the (nonhybrid) origin of populations in extreme southern Ontario. My analyses do strongly support the suggestions of Kolenosky and Standfield (1975) that west Ontario wolves are closely related to populations in Minnesota (and in the western conterminous United States) and that they are separated by a subspecific line from populations in southeastern Ontario.

Because the type locality of *lycaon* is Quebec City, that name would be retained, considering the above analysis, for the subspecies of wolf in southern Quebec and southeastern Ontario. Populations of western Ontario, Minnesota, and other parts of the western Great Lakes region would now be covered by the subspecific name appropriate for my entire southern group. On the basis of nomenclatural priority, that name would be *C. l. nubilus* Say, 1823. Likewise, the appropriate name for the entire northern group would be *C. l. occidentalis* Richardson, 1829. In the following discussions, however, it is sometimes more convenient to continue using the names recognized by Hall (1981).

The Red Wolf

For purposes of this study, it was decided to use only geographic/temporal samples of *C. rufus* that previous work (Nowak 1979) indicated were not affected by hybridization with *C. latrans*. One such series was taken in southern Missouri prior to 1930. Available material from that area and time shows that the red wolf and coyote were sympatric, but completely distinguishable from one another; no intermediate specimens are known. Another series comprises specimens that lived in modern time, but prior to 1940 in Florida, Alabama, Mississippi, Louisiana, and the Big Thicket area of extreme southeastern Texas. These specimens are the only usable male wild *Canis* from that region and time; no *C. latrans*, hybrids, or *C. lupus* were present. Fortuitously, these two samples are the two substantive series of *C. rufus* that are most geographically removed from one another, and

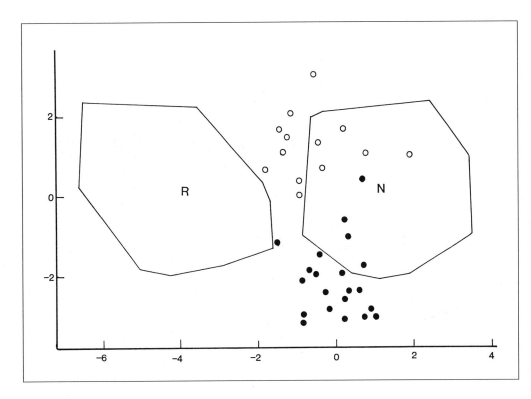

Fig. 11. *Statistical distribution of four groups of North American wolves, based on the first (horizontal axis) and second (vertical axis) canonical variables. Solid lines, limits of main southern group of* **Canis lupus** *(letter N shows mean) and of* **Canis rufus** *(letter R shows mean); dots,* **Canis lupus baileyi**; *open circles, Algonquin* **Canis lupus lycaon**. *Characters (Fig. 3) contributing most to high positive values are: first canonical variable, large 4, large 7, large 2; second canonical variable, large 1, small 2, large 10.*

so are most advantageous for assessing geographic variation. Moreover, they also represent the populations of *C. rufus* that are nearest to the most proximal populations of *C. lupus* that are represented by substantive series of specimens; as mapped by Hall (1981), those are *nubilus* and Minnesota *lycaon* in the case of Missouri *C. rufus*, and Texas *monstrabilis* in the case of the southern *C. rufus*. The two red wolf samples are thus advantageously placed with regard to assessing whether the statistical difference between *C. lupus* and *C. rufus* is greater than that separating populations within each species.

Figure 11 shows a canonical analysis comparing the combined series of *C. rufus* with the main southern group of North American *C. lupus*, and with the series of the two smallest kinds of North American gray wolf, *baileyi* and Algonquin *lycaon*. *C. rufus* does not statistically overlap any of the series of *C. lupus*, though its bounds are approached closely by a single specimen each of *lycaon* and *baileyi*. This analysis is primarily a comparison of the red wolf with the gray. Therefore, *lycaon* and *baileyi* are more extensively overlapped by other *C. lupus* than is the case in analyses comparing only groups of *C. lupus*. *Lycaon* and *baileyi* are shown to be fully distinguishable from one another, but *C. rufus* is the only North American wolf that falls completely outside the statistical range of the main northern and southern groups of *C. lupus* (the separation from the northern group is assumed based on the statistical location of *rufus* relative to the southern group).

Figure 12, based on a canonical analysis, shows the statistical distances between the two separate samples of *C.*

rufus, between those samples and the nearest neighboring nominal subspecies of *C. lupus*, and between the latter subspecies and their nearest neighboring subspecies of *C. lupus*. The statistical distances between the two red wolf samples and between the various gray wolf samples are relatively small, while the distances separating the red wolf samples from the gray wolf samples are relatively great. This distinction and indeed lack of any clinal approach, in the region where the southeastern range of *C. lupus* met the western edge of the range of *C. rufus*, is perhaps the best argument for maintaining each as a full species. Although there are no specimens to show that the gray wolf actually was sympatric with unmodified populations of the red wolf, extensive material from central Texas demonstrates that *C. lupus* occurred in the immediate vicinity of a large population of *C. rufus* x *C. latrans* and was not involved in the hybridization process (Nowak 1979, Nowak et al. this volume).

In contrast to the above, populations of *C. lupus* in southeastern Canada apparently do show a morphological approach toward *C. rufus*. Unfortunately, available specimens from the eastern United States are too scarce and too fragmentary to allow determination of whether the red and gray wolves intergraded in that region (Nowak 1979). Also, while some specimens of *C. lupus lycaon* of southeastern Ontario fall very near the statistical limits of *C. rufus* (Fig. 11), there is the possibility that those specimens have been affected by hybridization involving *C. latrans* (see above). It is tempting to speculate that Kolenosky and Standfield's (1975) finding of a trenchant division between a large wolf

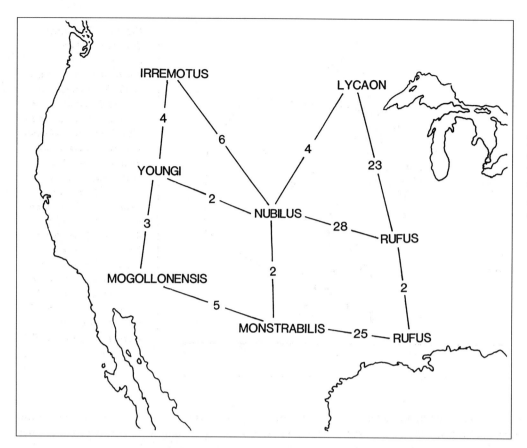

Fig. 12. *Statistical distances (rounded to whole numbers) between* **Canis rufus** *and neighboring subspecies of* **Canis lupus**.

and a small wolf in southeastern Ontario was actually the discovery of the long-sought line where the gray wolf met the red. For the moment, however, the question remains open.

Eurasian Wolves

Figure 13 shows a canonical analysis comparing series corresponding to five of the subspecies of *C. lupus* that Sokolov and Rossolimo (1985) recognized as occurring in China and the former Soviet Union. My samples are distributed as follows: *albus*, northwestern Siberia; *campestris*, southeastern European Russia and southern Siberia; *chanco*, China, the Himalayas, and extreme southeastern Siberia; *desertorum*, Kazakhstan; and *lupus* (as explained below, the involved population is reassigned to the subspecies *communis*), the Perm region in the central Urals. There is considerable overlap between the samples of *campestris*, *chanco*, and *desertorum*, but *albus* and, especially, *lupus* are more distinct. This division is reinforced when the samples of *campestris*, *chanco*, and *desertorum* are combined into a single series that is compared with the others (Fig. 14).

Few specimens and no substantial series from Europe west of Russia were available for this study. However, as shown in Figure 14, two individuals from Sweden fall well within the overall statistical limits of *campestris*, *chanco*, and *desertorum*. Sweden is the type locality of the subspecies *C. lupus lupus* Linnaeus, 1758. It therefore may be that

campestris, *chanco*, and *desertorum* are synonyms of *C. lupus lupus* and that the combined entity has a vast range extending from at least northwestern Europe to China. It then would also become necessary to apply a different name to the distinctive population of north-central Russia, which Sokolov and Rossolimo (1985) had considered part of *lupus*. According to those authorities the chronologically next available name for a Russian wolf is *C. lupus communis* Dwigubski, 1804.

Further analyses (Figs. 15 and 16) suggest that subspecies of *C. lupus* in northern Eurasia are comparable to those of North America. *C. lupus lupus*, a widely distributed wolf of moderate size, is statistically closer to the main southern group of North American *C. lupus* than to its nearest geographical neighbors. Likewise, *communis*, a large subspecies, has more affinity to the main northern group of North American *C. lupus* than to other Eurasian wolves, and *albus* shows affinity to North American arctic wolves.

The parallel situation on the two continents may extend even further. Figure 17 shows full statistical separation between *C. lupus lupus* (now comprising the combined sample of *campestris*, *chanco*, and *desertorum*) and a series of the nominal subspecies *pallipes* from Israel, including the Golan Heights, and India. This remarkable distinction of *pallipes* is comparable to the position of *rufus* of southeastern North America; both have relatively small and narrowly

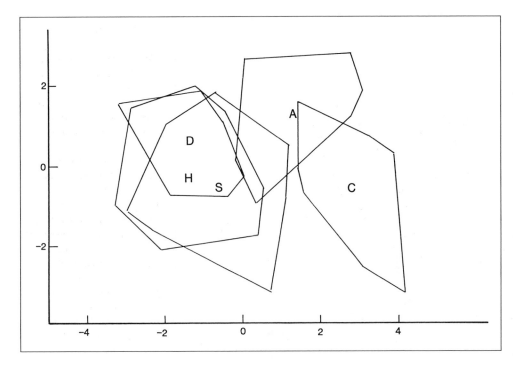

Fig. 13. *Statistical distribution of five nominal subspecies of Old World* **Canis lupus**, *based on the first (horizontal axis) and second (vertical axis) canonical variables. Solid lines, limits of* **albus** *(letter A shows mean),* **campestris** *(letter S shows mean),* **chanco** *(letter H shows mean),* **communis** *(letter C shows mean), and* **desertorum** *(letter D shows mean). Characters (Fig. 3) contributing most to high positive values are: first canonical variable, large 2, large 4, large 1; second canonical variable, small 8, large 3, large 2.*

proportioned skulls. An analysis (Fig. 18) of all three of the small southern wolves — *rufus, pallipes, baileyi* — demonstrates near total statistical separation, but very slight overlap between *rufus* and *pallipes*. That a small wolf, statistically comparable to *C. rufus*, exists far beyond the range where it could be influenced by hybridization with *C. latrans*, is further evidence against Wayne and Jenks' (1991) suggestion that the red wolf originated as a gray wolf-coyote hybrid.

Late in this study, I received measurements of a series of the sixth subspecies of *C. lupus* that Sokolov and Rossolimo (1985) recognized in the former Soviet Union, *C. l. cubanensis* of the Caucasus. Unfortunately, measurement number 8, depth of jugal, seems to have been taken incorrectly. Also received were data on a small series of wolves from eastern Uzbekistan. Because both of these series are geographically intermediate to *C. l. lupus* and *pallipes*, there was need to determine whether they might

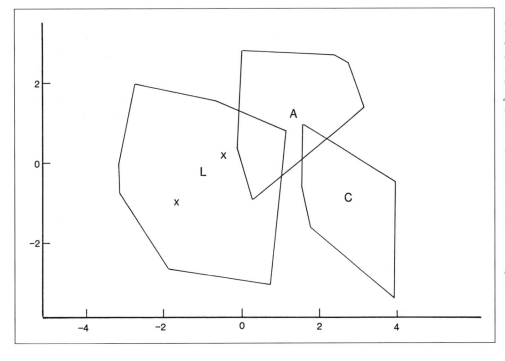

Fig. 14. *Statistical distribution of three subspecies and two individuals of Old World* **Canis lupus**, *based on the first (horizontal axis) and second (vertical axis) canonical variables. Solid lines, limits of* **albus** *(letter A shows mean),* **lupus** *(incorporating* **campestris**, **chanco**, *and* **desertorum**; *letter L shows mean), and* **communis** *(letter C shows mean); x's, two individuals of* **C. lupus lupus** *from Sweden. Characters (Fig. 3) contributing most to high positive values are: first canonical variable, large 2, large 4, large 1; second canonical variable, small 8, large 2, small 1.*

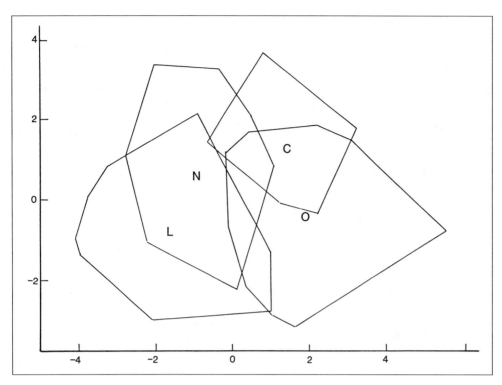

Fig. 15. *Statistical distribution of four groups of* **Canis lupus***, based on the first (horizontal axis) and second (vertical axis) canonical variables. Solid lines, limits of the Eurasian subspecies* **communis** *(letter C shows mean), the Eurasian subspecies* **lupus** *(letter L shows mean), the North American main northern group (letter O shows mean), and the North American main southern group (letter N shows mean). Characters (Fig. 3) contributing most to high positive values are: first canonical variable, large 1, large 2, large 9; second canonical variable, large 4, small 7, small 10.*

represent intergrading populations, and thus a new canonical analysis (Fig. 19) was done comparing *lupus, pallipes, cubanensis,* and the Uzbek individuals, but using only nine measurements. The Uzbek specimens fall predominantly within the statistical bounds of *lupus,* though there is a close approach to *pallipes. Cubanensis* apparently is a valid

subspecies in its own right, overlapping only slightly with *lupus* and very slightly with *pallipes.* This latter statistical connection, however, suggests that *pallipes* also be regarded as a subspecies of gray wolf. It evidently has affinity to the red wolf as well, but the geographic and temporal separation of *pallipes* and *rufus* is so great (see below), and the

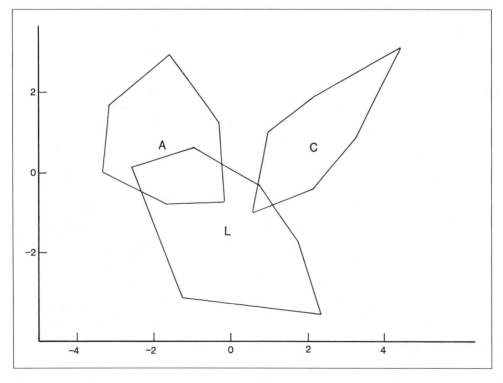

Fig. 16. *Statistical distribution of three subspecies of* **Canis lupus***, based on the first (horizontal axis) and second (vertical axis) canonical variables. Solid lines, limits of North American* **arctos** *(letter A shows mean), Eurasian* **albus** *(letter L shows mean), and Eurasian* **communis** *(letter C shows mean). Characters (see Fig. 3) contributing most to high positive values are: first canonical variable, large 1, small 7, large 8; second canonical variable, small 10, small 2, large 8.*

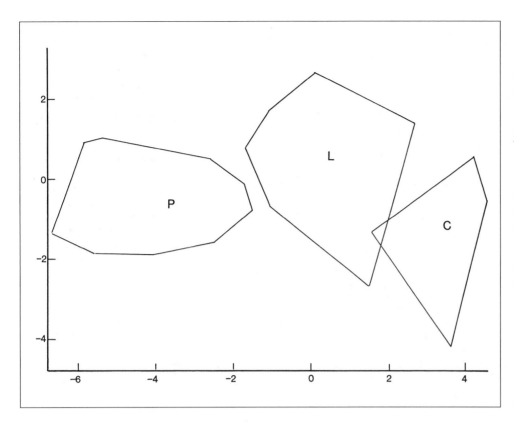

Fig. 17. *Statistical distribution of three subspecies of Old World* **Canis lupus**, *based on the first (horizontal axis) and second (vertical axis) canonical variables. Solid lines, limits of* **communis** *(letter C shows mean),* **lupus** *(letter L shows mean), and* **pallipes** *(letter P shows mean). Characters (see Fig. 3) contributing most to high positive values are: first canonical variable, large 1, large 4, large 8; second canonical variable, large 10, large 3, small 6.*

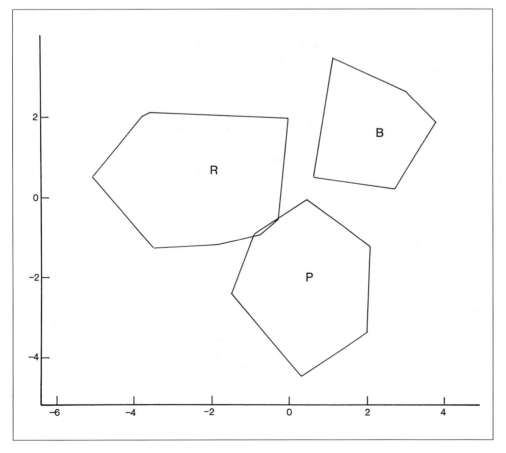

Fig. 18. *Statistical distribution of three groups of wolves, based on the first (horizontal axis) and second (vertical axis) canonical variables. Solid lines, limits of North American* **Canis rufus** *(letter R shows mean), North American* **Canis lupus baileyi** *(letter B shows mean), and Eurasian* **pallipes** *(letter P shows mean). Characters (Fig. 3) contributing most to high positive values are: first canonical variable, small 1, large 4, large 7; second canonical variable, large 1, large 2, large 8.*

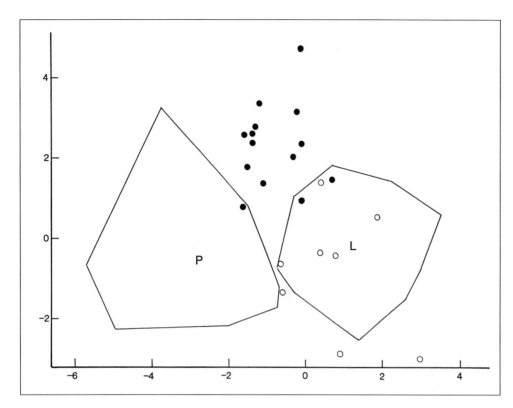

Fig. 19. *Statistical distribution of three subspecies and certain individuals of Old World* **Canis lupus**, *based on the first (horizontal axis) and second (vertical axis) canonical variables. Solid lines, limits of* **lupus** *(letter L shows mean) and* **pallipes** *(letter P shows mean); dots,* **cubanensis**; *open circles, individuals from eastern Uzbekistan. Characters (see Fig. 3) contributing most to high positive values are: first canonical variable, large 1, large 4, small 7; second canonical variable, large 2, small 1, small 9.*

morphological overlap so slight, that *rufus* is here considered to represent a full species.

Sokolov and Rossolimo (1985) recognized two other Eurasian subspecies, *hattai* (= *rex*) on Hokkaido and *hodophilax* on the other Japanese islands. Both are long extinct and are known by only a few specimens. I have measurements on one of each. Those of *hodophilax* are far below those of my other series and of little use for comparison. Those of *hattai* indicate a large animal comparable to my main northern group of North American *C. lupus*.

Sokolov and Rossolimo placed *arabs* of the Arabian Peninsula in the synonymy of *pallipes*, though Harrison (1968) and Mendelssohn (1982) had regarded *arabs* as distinct. The geographic boundary of *pallipes* and *arabs* is not well defined. Mendelssohn thought that *arabs* occurred in extreme southeastern Israel and that the rest of the country was occupied by several distinctive populations of *pallipes*. I could see no meaningful place to draw morphological lines between Israeli wolves and included all in my sample of *pallipes*. I had measurements on only two other possible specimens of *arabs* and on only a few of *lupaster* from Egypt, which Ferguson (1981) had considered a small *C. lupus* rather than a large *C. aureus* (golden jackal), as it is usually classified. These measurements are below the size limits of those of all my other series and were not subjected to comparative analysis.

Systematic Implications

Questions about species definition seem to be increasing, though complete lack of morphological intergradation, where two populations approach without physical barriers, argues for specific distinction. There is less consensus on what constitutes a subspecies. Certain characters may become established in a local, partly isolated population, and some authorities may, perhaps properly, use such characters as the basis of subspecific recognition. My investigation largely disregarded such questions and concentrated on general trends in measurable size and proportion that could be evaluated on a continent-wide or worldwide basis. Substantive statistical breaks in such trends, as discussed above, were taken as evidence of taxonomic division. A combination of my statistical analyses and other investigations (Jolicoeur 1959, Kolenosky and Standfield 1975, Skeel and Carbyn 1977, Nowak 1979, 1983, Ferguson 1981, Pedersen 1982, Friis 1985, Dawes et al. 1986, Hoffmeister 1986, Nowak et al. this volume), the nomenclatural matters discussed above, and the literature cited suggests recognition of the following species and subspecies of modern wolves, with original geographic distributions as shown (names in parentheses are additional subspecies recognized by Hall (1981) and Sokolov and Rossolimo (1985) and that would be regarded as synonyms under this classification; question marks (?) indicate subspecies that I did not subject to statistical analysis):

Canis rufus Audubon and Bachman, 1851, southeastern Kansas and central Texas to Pennsylvania and Florida (now

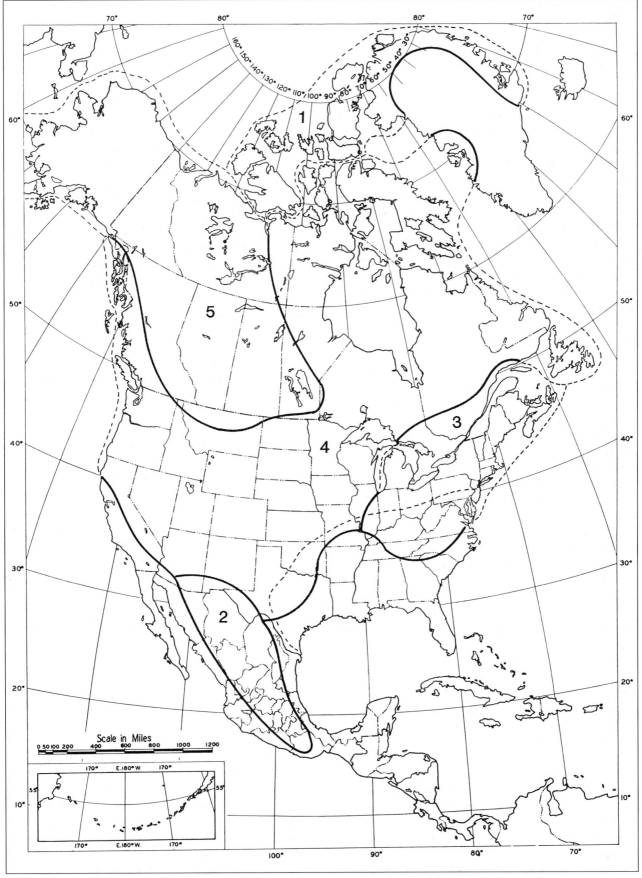

Fig. 20. *Original geographical distribution of wolves in North America, showing the five subspecies of* **Canis lupus** *recognized by this study: 1)* **arctos**, *2)* **baileyi**, *3)* **lycaon**, *4)* **nubilus**, *5)* **occidentalis**. *The red wolf (***Canis rufus***) occupied the southeastern quarter of the continent, the approximate northern and western limits of its range being marked by the dashed line on the mainland.*

evidently extirpated from the wild except for a reintroduced population in eastern North Carolina and a few individuals released at other sites);

Canis lupus pallipes Sykes, 1831, Israel to India;

(?) *Canis lupus arabs* Pocock, 1934, Arabian Peninsula;

(?) *Canis lupus lupaster* Hemprich and Ehrenberg, 1832, Egypt, Libya;

(?) *Canis lupus hodophilax* Temminck, 1839, Japan except Hokkaido (extinct);

Canis lupus lycaon Schreber, 1775, southeastern Ontario, southern Quebec, formerly south to an undetermined point in the eastern United States;

Canis lupus baileyi Nelson and Goldman, 1929, southern Arizona, southwestern New Mexico, extreme southwestern Texas, highlands of Mexico south to Oaxaca (now extirpated from the wild except for a few possible survivors in northwestern Mexico);

Canis lupus cubanensis Ognev, 1923, Caucasus and adjacent parts of Turkey and Iran;

Canis lupus lupus Linnaeus, 1758 (*campestris, chanco, desertorum*), Europe east to an undetermined point in Russia, central Asia, southern Siberia, China, Mongolia, Korea, Himalayan region (now greatly reduced in distribution, especially in western Europe);

Canis lupus nubilus Say, 1823 (*beothucus, crassodon, fuscus, hudsonicus, irremotus, labradorius, ligoni, manningi, mogollonensis, monstrabilis, youngi*), southeastern Alaska, southern British Columbia, conterminous United States from Pacific to western Great Lakes region and Texas, Ontario except southeast, northern and central Quebec, Newfoundland, northern Manitoba, Keewatin, eastern Mackenzie, Baffin Island, occasionally west-central Greenland (now evidently extirpated in the western conterminous United States);

Canis lupus arctos Pocock, 1935 (*bernardi, orion*), northern and eastern Greenland, Queen Elizabeth Islands (Ellesmere, Prince Patrick, Devon, etc.), Banks and Victoria Islands;

Canis lupus albus Kerr, 1798, extreme northern Eurasia;

Canis lupus communis Dwigubski, 1804, known with certainty only from the Ural Mountain region of north-central Russia, but probably occurring over much of eastern Europe and Siberia;

(?) *Canis lupus hattai* Kishida, 1931 (= *C. l. rex* Pocock, 1935), Sakhalin, Hokkaido (extinct);

Canis lupus occidentalis Richardson, 1829 (*alces, columbianus, griseoalbus, mackenzii, pambasileus, tundrarum*), Alaska, Yukon, Mackenzie, British Columbia, Alberta, Saskatchewan, southern Manitoba, northern Montana (now evidently expanding range into northwestern conterminous United States).

The revised historical distribution of *C. lupus* in North America is shown in Figure 20; that in Eurasia was indicated in Figure 2. The above list attempts to follow systematic order to the extent allowed by linear arrangement. Taxa considered more primitive are placed first and those considered closely related are grouped together. In this regard, the list reflects my view that the resemblance of certain North American to certain Eurasian taxa is based less on convergence than on actual phylogenetic affinity.

Fossil evidence (Nowak 1979, Kurtén and Anderson 1980) indicates that the wolf group separated from the coyote line in the early Pleistocene (perhaps about one million years ago). By the Irvingtonian, primitive small wolves, perhaps identical with modern *C. rufus*, were widespread in southern North America. A branch of this group probably entered the Old World, where it gave rise to *C. lupus*. This background, together with the above statistical analyses, suggest that *pallipes* represents a segment of the original American invading stock that underwent only modest development of the characters of *C. lupus*. Like *C. rufus* in the New World, its retention of primitive features may be associated with its relatively warm environment. Other remnants of a primitive stock of small, warmth-adapted wolves might be represented by *arabs, lupaster,* and *hodophilax,* and possibly *deitanus* of Spain (see Nowak 1979: 95), though the association of all of these taxa with *C. aureus* (golden jackal) requires investigation.

Farther north in Eurasia, *C. lupus* became larger, and apparently by the end of the Illinoian glaciation (300,000 years ago) it moved into North America (Nowak 1979). This stage in the evolution of the species is expressed today in the widespread groups of moderate-sized and generalized wolves that I have referred to *C. lupus lupus* in Eurasia and *C. lupus nubilus* in North America. Glacial movements and other environmental changes in the late Pleistocene may have resulted in splitting off of segments that gave rise to other subspecies, as suggested in previous work (Nowak 1983). *Baileyi* seems to have been isolated by desert barriers; a small gray wolf skull from San Josecito Cave, Nuevo Leon, indicates that the Mexican wolf was established by the Wisconsinan glaciation. Certain remains from Rancho La Brea (southern California) and Yukon (Nowak 1979), together with the current distribution of *arctos* and *albus,* suggest former widespread occurrence for a group of wolves represented by some of today's arctic populations.

The development of the largest gray wolves, *occidentalis* in the New World, and *communis* in the Old, may have occurred in the late Pleistocene, perhaps in connection with the disappearance of the dire wolf, lion, and several other large cursorial carnivores. During the Wisconsinan glaciation, the forebears of *occidentalis* may have been isolated in eastern Beringia, an ice-free refugium including most of Alaska. The modern distribution of *occidentalis* suggests a recent outward expansion from the northwest, perhaps involving the takeover of the range of other kinds of wolves. Remarkably, this process appears to be continuing to this day.

Conservation Implications

Reducing subspecific names to synonyms carries the danger that the affected populations will be given less attention for conservation purposes. In the case of most of the subspecies so reduced in this study, the question is largely academic, because they apparently are already extinct (*alces, beothucus, bernardi, crassodon, fuscus, irremotus, mogollonensis, monstrabilis, orion, youngi*). Of the others so reduced, none are thought to be in imminent danger of extinction (Ginsberg and Macdonald 1990), though the entire species *C. lupus* is appropriately classified as vulnerable by the World Conservation Union (IUCN). Moreover, the United States Endangered Species Act requires classification and protection, not only of endangered and threatened biological species and subspecies, but also of distinct vertebrate population segments. This provision has been interpreted broadly over the years, having been applied to morphologically or genetically distinct groups, to island populations, and frequently, to segments separated from others simply by a geopolitical line.

The conservation significance of some gray wolf subspecies is enhanced by their continued recognition as distinctive taxa, even after the above statistical analyses. *C. lupus baileyi* is represented by fewer than 10 individuals in the wild and by a small captive population (Ginsberg and Macdonald 1990). *C. l. arctos*, though widespread, occurs at low densities in a harsh, but fragile, environment (Miller this volume). *C. l. lycaon* is now known to be restricted to a small range, where it is in close proximity to human activity and is subject to genetic swamping through hybridization with *C. latrans*. *C. l. pallipes* and *C. l. arabs* have been greatly reduced in numbers and probably no longer occur in a natural ecological or behavioral context. *C. l. communis*, a newly distinguished taxon, is little known with regard to status and distribution, but could be vulnerable to consequences of political and economic upheaval.

Reintroduction of wolves to Yellowstone National Park and other areas is now under consideration, and there are questions as to the source of the animals for such projects. The above analyses indicate that the extirpated wolf population of the Yellowstone region is closely related to the living population of Minnesota, both regarded here as part of the subspecies *C. l. nubilus*. However, the subspecies *C. l. occidentalis* may have occurred originally as far south as central Montana, a short distance from Yellowstone, and may have been expanding its range southward even before human intervention. There is no reason to think that *occidentalis*, which has now reoccupied northwestern Montana, would be an inappropriate component of the Yellowstone ecosystem.

The red wolf has already been reintroduced successfully to coastal North Carolina. However, recent questions about its systematic status have led to widespread criticism of efforts being made for its conservation. My study supports recognition of the red wolf as a valid taxon and has provided further evidence against the idea that it originated as a hybrid of *C. lupus* and *C. latrans*. If the latter view were correct, we would expect the red wolf to blend morphologically into its parental species, and the striking statistical break that actually separates *C. rufus* from adjacent populations of *C. lupus* would not be possible. That a wolf population may approach *C. rufus* morphologically, without hybridization with *C. latrans*, is now demonstrated by the statistical position of the Old World *pallipes*. However, except for the slight overlap between samples of *pallipes* and *rufus*, the red wolf is statistically separate from all series of *C. lupus*, including neighboring populations. Whether *C. rufus* is considered a full species or a subspecies, it is the most distinctive kind of wolf in the world.

Acknowledgments

D. Waddington of the U.S. Fish and Wildlife Service spent many hours developing and running the computer programs for my statistical analyses. J. Baynes, L. Loges, J. Sheppard, and K. Steiffenhofer also helped with computer work. D.I. Bibikov coordinated the collection of measurements on specimens from the former Soviet Union. T. Dayan provided the data on Israeli wolves and M. Sheridan made measurements on skulls in the British Museum. I. Brady prepared the skull figure. Other assistance was given by L. Boitani, G. Henry, S. Kohl, and R. Smith.

Conservation Genetics of the Gray Wolf

■ Robert K. Wayne, Niles Lehman, and Todd K. Fuller

*We review results of molecular-genetic analyses of gray wolves and related canids that encompass multiple levels of evolutionary divergence. At the species level, our mitochondrial DNA sequence analyses show that the gray wolf is a distinct taxon closely related to the coyote and the Simien jackal (**C. simensis**). Interspecific hybridization between gray wolves and coyotes occurred in Minnesota and eastern Canada over the past hundred years reflecting habitat changes that favored the establishment and growth of coyote populations. We hypothesize that in the south-central United States, an older hybrid zone between gray wolves and coyotes developed in historic times. Conceivably, such historic or even more ancient interspecific hybridization between gray wolves and coyotes might have led to a hybrid origin of red wolves providing an alternative explanation for its intermediate form. Nuclear DNA data are needed to adequately test this hybrid origin hypothesis. At the population level, wolf packs, with some exceptions, tend to be composed of close relatives. In Minnesota, interpack dispersal of close relatives is common and may be biased toward females. We suggest that the genetic variability and distinctiveness of gray wolf populations may be strongly affected by habitat fragmentation and succession caused by human activities.*

Introduction

Conservation genetics is an emerging field that has, at its core, questions pertaining to the relatedness and variability of species and populations. The questions may be organized according to an evolutionary hierarchy from those concerning the phylogenetic relationship of species and higher taxonomic units, to genetic exchange or hybridization among closely related species, to relationships and genetic variability of populations within species and finally, to relationships of individuals within populations. Molecular-genetic techniques are available to quantify evolutionary divergence at these differing levels. Application of the results of molecular-genetic analyses to specific conservation issues is beginning to occur (e.g., Avise et al. 1989, Avise and Ball 1990, May 1990, O'Brien and Mayr 1991).

Here, we review results of our molecular-genetic studies on gray wolves (*Canis lupus*) and wolf-like canids with specific reference to four questions concerning evolution and conservation. The first question involves the phylogenetic relationship of gray wolves and other wolf-like canids. We approach this question by analyzing, with phylogenetic techniques, 2,001 base pairs (bp) of three mitochondrial protein coding genes in eight canid species. The second question addresses the issue of interspecific hybridization and is approached through analysis of mitochondrial DNA restriction-site polymorphisms and sequence data. Two hybrid zones, one between coyotes (*C. latrans*) and gray wolves and the other between these two species and red wolves (*C. rufus*) are described. The third question concerns relationships and variability of wolf populations worldwide. The pattern of genetic variability among gray wolf populations appears greatly influenced by habitat fragmentation and population size. The final question concerns relatedness of individuals within the same population. Using genetic-fingerprinting techniques, we assess relatedness of individuals within three North American wolf populations and test ideas about kinship of pack members, movement of close relatives among packs, and sex-biased dispersal.

Methods

The three molecular-genetic techniques we have used on gray wolves: allozyme electrophoresis, mitochondrial DNA (mtDNA) analysis and genetic fingerprinting, measure change in loci that differ in mutation rate and mode of inheritance. Allozyme electrophoresis, a long-standing approach used to assess the genetic variability and relatedness of taxa, involves protein-coding loci whose alleles differ in amino acid composition (Hillis and Moritz 1990). However, because the amino acid substitution rate is relatively small, it is often difficult to distinguish closely related species or populations. No fixed allelic differences have been identified among North American wolf-like canids (Ferrell et al. 1980, Wayne and O'Brien 1987) and we have not found this technique useful for systematic or population-level questions concerning gray wolves.

A technique with potentially more resolution measures mtDNA sequence change. The vertebrate mitochondrial genome is maternally inherited without recombination (clonal inheritance) and, barring mutation, all progeny of a single mating will have a mitochondrial genome identical to that of their mother (Brown 1986). Because the mitochondrial DNA sequence of mammals evolves rapidly (Brown et al. 1979), the relatedness of genetically similar populations often can be deduced (Avise et al. 1987). We indirectly assess mitochondrial DNA variation by identifying and comparing groups of individuals that share the same mitochondrial DNA restriction-fragment patterns (genotypes). Commonly, we use 15–21 restriction enzymes to deduce genotype variation within populations (Lehman et al. 1991, Lehman and Wayne 1991, Wayne et al. 1992a). We also use the polymerase chain reaction (PCR) to amplify minute quantities of DNA for direct sequencing of mitochondrial genes (Wayne and Jenks 1991).

Finally, we assess variation in a class of loci consisting of a variable number of tandem repeats (VNTR) of a specific core sequence. Alleles at VNTR loci differ in the number of repeat units they contain and thus allelic variation can be assessed at multiple loci by using a restriction enzyme that cleaves the DNA outside the repeat sequence, followed by electrophoretic separation of DNA fragments and hybridization with a probe derived from the core sequence. The result resembles a supermarket bar code and is often called a genetic fingerprint (Burke 1989). The similarity of fingerprint patterns between two individuals may reflect their genetic relatedness and can be used cautiously to infer patterns of relatedness within populations (Packer et al. 1991, Lehman et al. 1992).

Results and Discussion

Phylogenetic Relationships of the Wolf-Like Canids

Phylogenetic analysis of 2,001bp of mitochondrial DNA sequence data suggests a close relationship of North American wolf-like canids (Fig. 1). The closest relative of the gray wolf is the domestic dog, which differs by less than 2% of its cytochrome *b* sequence (Wayne and Jenks 1991). In fact, some restriction-site mtDNA genotypes in the dog cannot be distinguished from those in the gray wolf (Wayne et al. 1992a). The closest living wild canids to the gray wolf are the coyote and Simien jackal. These species differ by about 4–6% in their mtDNA sequence from each other. The four species form a monophyletic clade, that we refer to as the wolf-like canids, distinct from jackals and fox-like species.

The close relationship of wolf-like canids suggest a recent divergence from a common ancestor approximately 2–3 million years ago (assuming a sequence divergence of 2% per million years, Shields and Wilson 1987). The data are consistent with a Plio-Pleistocene appearance of the first wolf-like canids and the subsequent appearance of North

American wolf-like canids in the mid-Pleistocene (Kurtén and Anderson 1980). The close relationship of these taxa to the Simien jackal suggests the present-day form may be a relict of a past invasion into East Africa of a wolf-like canid. The Ethiopian highlands where Simien jackals presently live may have been more extensive during the colder periods of the late Pleistocene and thus they may represent a refugium for this large canid, perhaps more correctly referred to by another common name, the Ethiopian wolf (Gottelli et al. 1994).

An important conservation implication of the phylogenetic analysis is that hybridization between the four species of wolf-like canid is possible in areas where they overlap (see below). Moreover, the genetic similarity of the wolf-like canids may indicate similarity in physiological and immune responses, such that results of studies on domestic dogs may be extrapolated to other wolf-like canids. Certainly, each species will have unique physiological characteristics, but the phylogenetic analysis clearly points to the wolf-like canids as first candidates for testing the generality of results based on domestic dogs.

Hybridization Between Wolf-Like Canids

We have used mitochondrial DNA restriction-fragment analysis to characterize genetic variation in gray wolves and coyotes (Lehman et al. 1991, Lehman and Wayne 1991, Wayne et al. 1991, 1992a). In Minnesota and southeastern Canada we discovered that gray wolves often have mtDNA genotypes identical or similar to those found in coyotes. These coyote-like genotypes are classified in a mitochondrial genotype clade that otherwise contains just genotypes found in coyotes and that are about 4% divergent in DNA sequence from genotypes found in gray wolves to the west and north of Ontario (Fig. 2). We suggest that these results indicate hybridization occurs between the two species in Minnesota and southeastern Canada. Moreover, because we always found coyote-like genotypes in gray wolves and never gray-wolf-like genotypes in coyotes, the direction of successful mating is likely to be between male wolves and female coyotes. This mating asymmetry may reflect the much smaller body size of male coyotes relative to female wolves, which would make them unlikely to dominate an interspecific sexual encounter.

We hypothesized that the reason hybridization between wolves and coyotes occurs in Minnesota and eastern Canada and not elsewhere is due to both the recent arrival of coyotes there in the past 100 years and habitat changes that have favored the growth and establishment of coyotes in areas previously occupied exclusively by wolves. Coyotes can flourish in small patches of woodland and in agricultural areas where wolves have been removed or cannot now persist. We suggest that although hybridization occurs, it may not necessarily lead to phenotypic changes in gray wolf populations, particularly in large tracts of protected woodland in Minnesota where gray wolves can potentially ex-

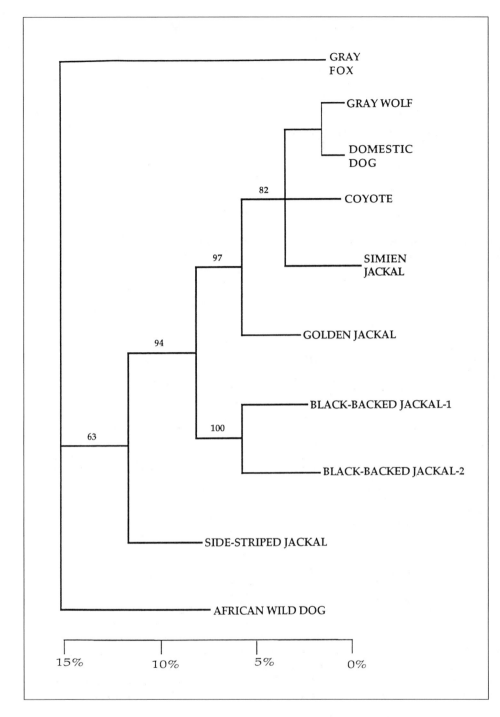

Fig. 1. *The strict consensus tree of the two most parsimonious trees, based on phylogenetic analysis of 2,001 base pairs of DNA sequence from three protein coding genes in wolf-like canids (cytochrome b, cytochrome oxidase I and II). The gray fox sequence was used to root the tree. Nodes supported in over 50% of 1,000 bootstrap replicate trees are indicated. Tree length = 868, consistency index (CI) = 0.66, CI excluding uninformative charaters = 0.51. Placement of the domestic dog is based only on 398bp of DNA sequence from cytochrome b (Wayne and Jenks 1991, Gottelli et al. 1994).*

clude coyotes. However, in some areas of southeastern Canada, canids that are intermediate in size between gray wolves and coyotes have been reported. Such forms may reflect both hybridization and adaptation to large prey or greater prey abundance (Lawrence and Bossert 1969, 1975, Richens and Hugie 1974, Kolenosky and Standfield 1975, Hilton 1978, Nowak 1979, Schmitz and Kolenosky 1985a, Thurber and Peterson 1991).

The presence of phenotypically intermediate forms and the molecular evidence for hybridization in Minnesota and

southeastern Canadian wolves suggested to us that hybridization may have also occurred in populations of red wolves in the south-central United States. The last wild populations of red wolves went extinct in east Texas and west Louisiana about 1975 (McCarley 1962, Riley and McBride 1975, Nowak 1979). In contrast to the recent arrival of the coyote in eastern Canada (Hilton 1978), coyotes have had a long history in the American south, beginning in the late Pleistocene (Kurtén 1974, Nowak 1979). Similarly, prior to the arrival of Europeans, gray wolves had existed in parts of the

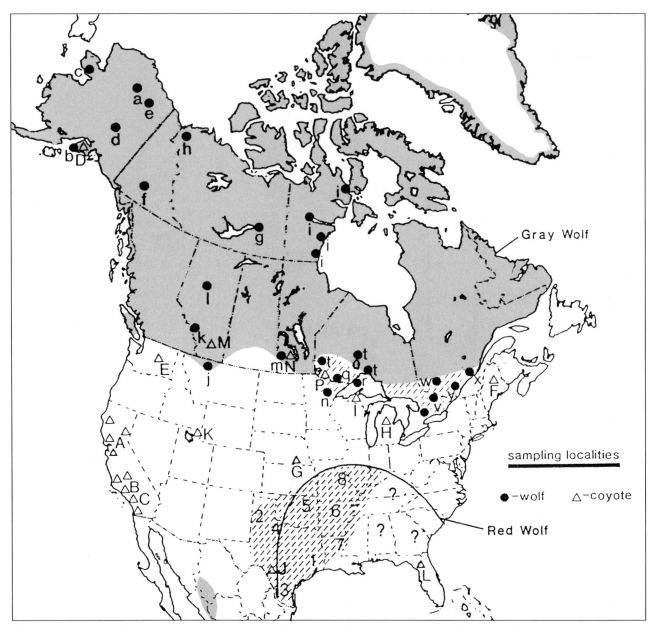

Fig. 2. *Sampling localities of gray wolves (dots), red wolves (numbers) and coyotes (triangles). For sample locality identifications see Lehman et al. (1991) and Wayne and Jenks (1991). The darkly shaded area indicates the present North American geographic range of the gray wolf. The approximate geographic range of the red wolf circa 1700 also is shown. The hatched area in eastern North America is a hybrid zone between gray wolves and coyotes and the hatched area in the south-central United States is a hybrid zone between gray and red wolves and coyotes, based on mtDNA analysis. Question marks indicate no samples have been obtained from these areas.*

eastern and south-central United States, and were likely sympatric in some areas with the red wolf (Nowak 1979, Kurtén and Anderson 1980, Jenks and Wayne 1992). Therefore, the potential existed for red wolves, gray wolves, and coyotes to hybridize over a much longer period than in southeastern Canada. Considering the habitat changes in the American south caused by European settlers, combined with red wolf extermination programs, we felt hybridization could have been more extensive and had a greater phenotypic consequence among canids of the south-central United

States than in southeastern Canada (Fig. 2, Wayne and Jenks 1991, Jenks and Wayne 1992).

To determine the extent of hybridization among canids of the south-central United States, we first analyzed samples from a red wolf breeding colony that was founded by 14 canids captured from the last remaining red wolf population and thought to be pure red wolves. Restriction-site and direct sequence analysis of 398bp of the cytochrome *b* gene from these canids revealed that they had a genotype identical to that of coyotes living in Louisiana (Wayne and Jenks 1991).

This observation suggested hybridization with coyotes had occurred in the ancestry of the captive red wolves. Theoretically, if the red wolf was a long-distinct species, pure red wolves should have a genotype phylogenetically distinct from those of coyotes and gray wolves. To assess whether a distinct red wolf genotype once existed, we examined 15-year-old samples from canids living in the areas last occupied by red wolves. We also characterized mtDNA isolated from red wolf pelts in the Smithsonian fur vault collected before 1930, a period when hybridization between coyotes and red wolves was thought, based on morphological data (Nowak 1979), to be less extensive. Our results showed that genotypes in past red wolves were phylogenetically grouped with genotypes of coyotes or gray wolves; no phylogenetically distinct red wolf genotype was uncovered. We suggested that red wolves obtained their mtDNA genotypes through hybridization with coyotes and gray wolves and, taken at face value, the data were consistent with a hybrid origin for the red wolf. For a recent analysis of nuclear genes confirming these conclusions, see Roy et al. (1994). We maintain that morphologic data are consistent with both a distinct species or hybrid origin for the red wolf (Wayne 1992, Jenks and Wayne 1992).

The conservation implications of our results are that hybridization may be an important concern in large, highly mobile species that have experienced recent habitat and range changes. Because of habitat changes, barriers may be reduced to the dispersal and to the establishment of non-native forms such that previously non-interbreeding but closely related species co-mingle and hybridize. Also, non-native forms may be intentionally introduced, such as with game fish, to supplement or restock populations, and this may lead to the hybridization and genetic assimilation of endemic forms (Waples and Teel 1990, O'Brien et al. 1990). The legal protection of hybrids is problematic because sometimes hybrids may need to be protected if they are the last repository of genes from the protected taxon (Wayne and Jenks 1991, Jenks and Wayne 1992). In other instances, such as in southeastern Canadian gray wolves, the protection of hybrids may not be desirable because it allows the continued movement of coyote genes into gray wolf populations. Potentially, habitat reconstruction and selective predator control programs could alter the relative proportions of gray wolves, hybrids, and coyotes such that hybridization may be less of a problem.

Genetic Variability and Relationships of Gray Wolf Populations

We examined variability of Old and New World populations of gray wolves using mtDNA restriction-site analysis (Lehman et al. 1991, Wayne et al. 1992a). In North America, we analyzed 310 gray wolves from 16 localities and found five genotypes that were unique to gray wolves. Six genotypes were identified in gray wolves from Minnesota and southeastern Canada that were identical or similar to geno-

types in coyotes, a finding that we interpret as reflecting hybridization (see above). The five "pure" gray wolf genotypes were, in general, widely distributed (Table 1). A unique genotype was found in Mexican (W14) and in Manitoban (W2) gray wolves, the W1 genotype was not found in Alaskan wolves, and the W3 genotype not found in wolves from eastern Canada. However, the amount of sequence divergence among wolf genotypes was small (<0.5%), and with the exception of the Mexican wolf, no fixed differences were observed among populations representing different subspecies. We concluded from this analysis that gene flow among North American gray wolf populations was high and genetic differentiation among populations was low. However, Mexican wolves showed genetic differentiation coincident with geographic isolation and Alaskan and southeastern Canadian wolves showed some differences. In the Old World, genotypic variation was larger and more structured. Seven genotypes were observed among 35 gray wolves from seven localities. These genotypes were closely related, having less than 0.3% sequence divergence, but with one exception, each locality had a unique genotype. This exception is genotype W3, which is found in Sweden and Estonia and is also widespread in northern Canada and Alaska (Table 1). We suggest that the large degree of geographic structuring in the Old relative to the New World gray wolf populations reflects the extreme degree of habitat fragmentation in the Old World. The Old World populations we sampled were, in general, small and highly isolated, thus genetic drift may have resulted in the fixation of unique genotypes in geographically isolated populations. Habitat fragmentation apparently has imposed a degree of genetic subdivision among the Old World gray wolf populations that might not have occurred historically when their distribution was more continuous.

Finally, the degree of sequence divergence among gray wolf genotypes is small, less than about 0.5%, indicating a recent divergence from a common mitochondrial DNA ancestor (Wayne et al. 1992a). Assuming this ancestor existed at the time of speciation, the origin of gray wolves may be about 250,000 years ago (assuming 2% sequence divergence per million years, Shields and Wilson 1987). This origination date is more recent than that indicated by the fossil record, which suggests a divergence time of about 500,000 years (Kurtén and Anderson 1980).

There were two important conservation implications of the results. First, gene flow was high among North American gray wolf populations and, with the exception of the Mexican gray wolf, genetic groupings corresponding with geographic or topographic subdivisions were not apparent (Young 1944). Such subdivisions, based on mtDNA restriction-site data, are common among populations of small vertebrates (Avise et al. 1987). Our gray wolf results parallel a similar survey of coyotes, which showed gene flow had stifled genetic differentiation even among widely separated populations (Lehman and Wayne 1991). Therefore, in coyo-

Table 1. Frequencies and sample sizes (in parenthesis) of gray wolf geotypes from localities in the Old and New World (see Fig. 3). Designations of genotypes are the same as in Lehman et al. (1991).

Old World	W3	W5	W6	W15	W16	W17	W18
Portugal	-	-	-	-	-	1.00 (3)	-
Sweden	1.00 (9)	-	-	-	-	-	-
Estonia	0.67(2)	-	-	-	-	-	0.33 (1)
Italy	-	-	-	1.00 (14)	-	-	-
Israel	-	-	-	-	1.00 (2)	-	-
Iran	-	1.00 (2)	-	-	-	-	-
China	-	-	1.00 (2)	-	-	-	-

New World	W1	W2	W3	W4	W14
Alaska-Denali	-	-	0.73 (16)	0.27 (6)	-
Alaska-Anaktuvik	-	-	1.00 (14)	-	-
Alaska-Nome	-	-	1.00 (8)	-	-
Alaska-Kenai			0.17 (1)		
Yukon Territory	-	-	1.00 (10)	0.83 (5)	-
Northwest Territory-Inuvik	0.75 (40)	-	0.23 (12)	-	-
Northwest Territory-Yellowknife	0.88 (7)	-	0.12 (1)	0.02 (1)	-
British Columbia Vancouver Island	-	-	1.00 (15)	-	-
Alberta	0.25 (1)	-	0.75 (3)	-	-
Montana	0.20 (1)	-	0.60 (3)	0.20 (1)	-
Manitoba	-	1.00 (4)	-	-	-
Minnesota-Northeast	0.95 (19)	-	-	0.05 (1)	-
Minnesota-North	1.00 (11)	-	-	-	-
Western Ontario	1.00 (8)	-	-	-	-
Central Ontario	0.67 (8)	-	-	0.33 (4)	-
Mexico	-	-	-	-	1.00 (4)

Coyote clade genotypes	W7*	W8*	W9*	W10*	W11*	W12*	W13*
Manitoba	1.00 (4)	-	-	-	-	-	-
Minnesota-Northeast	0.52 (24)	-	0.48 (22)	-	-	-	-
Minnesota-North	0.22 (2)	-	0.78 (7)	-	-	-	-
Michigan- Isle Royale	-	1.00 (7)	-	-	-	-	-
Western Ontario	0.53 (8)	-	0.47 (7)	-	-	-	-
Central Ontario	0.39 (5)	0.08 (1)	0.46 (6)	-	-	-	0.08 (1)
Eastern Ontario	-	-	-	0.33 (1)	0.33 (1)	0.33 (1)	-
Quebec	-	-	-	0.07 (1)	0.07 (1)	0.43 (6)	0.43 (1)

tes and gray wolves, the many subspecific designations that have been suggested do not reflect significant differentiation at the mtDNA sequence level. Many of these subspecies may have been defined with inadequately small samples and without the use of quantitative techniques (Young 1944). Some subspecies may be ecotypes that have a heterogeneous genetic basis (Kolenosky and Standfield 1975, Hilton 1978, Schmitz and Kolenosky 1985a,b, Thurber and Peterson 1991). Our results suggest that augmentation or reintroduction plans involving North American gray wolves should consider demographic or logistic factors to be more important than the genetic restoration of the native stock.

The second conservation implication concerns the effect of habitat fragmentation on levels of genetic variability and geographic substructure. In the Old World, fewer genotypes were observed at each locality and each locality, with one exception, had a unique genotype. The difference between Old and New World populations would appear to reflect the small population sizes in the Old World and extreme isolation. Such genetic subdivision provides an example of the effect of habitat fragmentation on the genetic structure of a large, rare mammal species. The presence of different but otherwise genetically similar genotypes at each locality in the Old World does not argue for separate breeding of individuals from each population because these population differences are small and a consequence of human-induced habitat changes.

Genetic Relationships within Gray Wolf Populations

Analysis of VNTR loci by utilization of core sequence probes (genetic fingerprinting) allows for a unique phenotypic profile of each individual within a population (Lehman et al. 1992). Parents, offspring, and siblings tend to show significantly higher levels of similarity in such profiles than unrelated or distantly related individuals and thus classes of relatedness can potentially be deduced (Packer et al. 1991, Lehman et al. 1992). We have characterized three populations of wolves comprising 27 wolf packs from Minnesota, Alaska (Denali National Park), and Inuvik in the Northwest Territories (Fig. 3). Classes of relatedness were determined by comparison to captive wolves for which relationships were known. Three classes of relatedness were defined according to their similarity (fraction of shared bands) on fingerprint gels. Individuals related as parent-offspring and siblings ($r = 0.5$) had fingerprint similarity coefficients of greater than about 75% shared bands, whereas values between unrelated individuals were less than about 53%. Values among individuals between these percentages were considered possible distant relatives.

Our first comparison examined variability within packs. The hypothesis based on observational data was that wolf packs were composed primarily of an unrelated mating pair and their offspring (Mech 1970, 1987). The fingerprinting data supported this hypothesis in general because similarity values within packs were significantly larger than those between individuals from different packs. However, in nine packs we found a third individual that was not closely related to other pack members.

We also examined similarity among individuals from different packs within the same area. We found that in Minnesota, comparisons between individuals from different packs showed that in seven comparisons, high values of similarity indicated relationships as parent-offspring or siblings (Fig. 4). The number of close ties between packs was fewer in Alaska (6), and in Inuvik no comparisons among packs showed high similarity values characteristic of closely related individuals. We concluded that differences among areas in the number of close relatives shared between packs reflected habitat constraints on dispersal. In Minnesota, wolf packs are restricted to areas of protected woodland and dispersal is inhibited by habitat discontinuities caused by agriculture and civilization. In Denali National Park and Inuvik, individuals may disperse out of the pack system and avoid the difficulty of integrating into neighboring established packs that normally show strong aggression to non-pack individuals. In Minnesota, interpack aggression is an important source of mortality in wolves, aside from that caused by humans.

Finally, we examined the question of sexual bias in dispersal by computing the average similarity by sex among individuals that had high values of fingerprint similarity. Females tended to have higher values of average similarity than males in all three pack systems, and in Minnesota a significantly greater number of females shared high similarity values than males. We concluded that at least in the Minnesota population, evidence existed for females dispersing a shorter distance than males. Alternatively, males may suffer greater mortality during dispersal (Lehman et al. 1992).

The conservation implications of our results are that habitat fragmentation can potentially affect the pattern of relatedness among wolves within an area. In Minnesota, young wolves may not be able to disperse as easily or may encounter greater mortality during dispersal, making the benefits of staying within their natal pack system outweigh the risk of joining an established neighboring pack. Habitat fragmentation and isolation may therefore subtly affect the genetic variability of partially isolated populations in disturbed areas.

Conclusions

1. The gray wolf is a distinct taxon phylogenetically related to coyotes and Simien jackals. The closest relative of the gray wolf is the domestic dog.
2. Interspecific hybridization may occur between coyotes, gray wolves, and red wolves. Hybridization seems widespread in southeastern Canada and Minnesota. An older hybrid zone involving gray and red wolves and

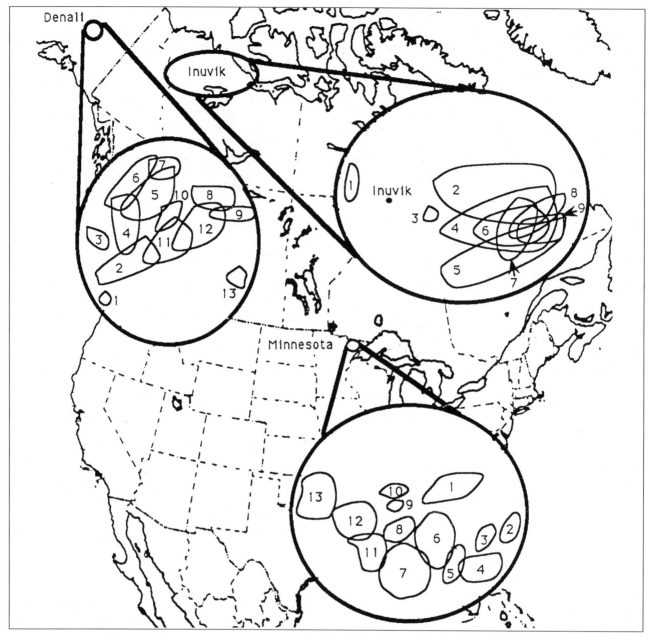

Fig. 3. *Locations and spatial relationships of gray wolf packs. Minnesota pack clusters as also shown in Fig. 4 are: 1. Emerald, 2. Kawishiwi, 3. Isabella Lake, 4. Sawbill, 5. Pike, 6. Little Gabbro, 7. Nip Creek, 8. Stampede, 9. Ely, 10. Winton, 11. Perch Lake, 12. Bear Island, 13. Tower. For other pack designations, see Lehman et al. (1992).*

coyotes may have developed in the southeastern United States after the arrival of European settlers.

3. Among gray wolf populations, little genetic differentiation is apparent. In general, among New World gray wolf populations gene flow appears to be high. The Mexican wolf, however, is genetically distinct. More genetic differences exist among Old World populations reflecting habitat fragmentation and population subdivision. The mitochondrial DNA analysis suggests there may not be a genetic basis for many past subspecific designations.

4. With some exceptions, wolf packs generally are composed of close relatives. Close relatives also may be shared among packs. A sex bias in dispersal may occur in some pack systems with males possibly dispersing farther than females. Habitat fragmentation may affect the degree of interpack dispersal and relatedness.

5. In general, our results suggest that augmentation plans need not be concerned in detail with the locality of origin of gray wolves because over large geographic areas, wolf populations are genetically similar. However, some populations, such as those in Mexico, are

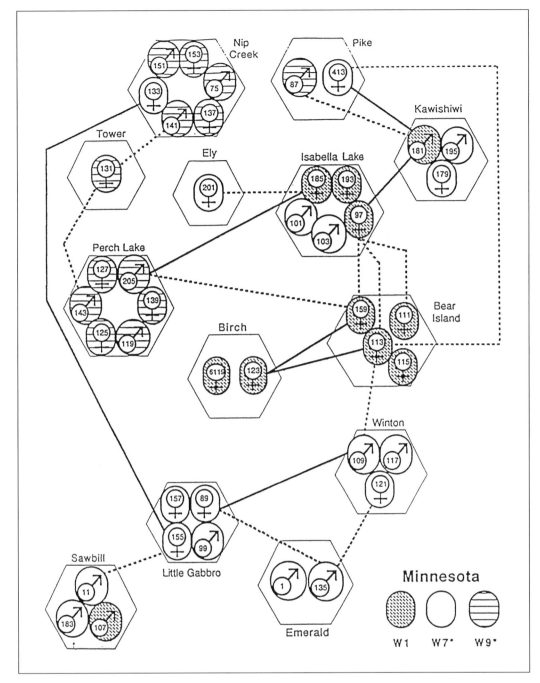

Fig. 4. *Pack membership, mtDNA genotypes (W1, W7*, W9*), and inter-pack connections suggested by high fingerprint band sharing values. Individuals are identified by numbers and have mtDNA genotypes indicated by the pattern of background shading. Gray wolf genotypes W7 and W9 highlighted by asterisks, are derived from hybridization with coyotes (Lehman et al. 1991). High similarity values among wolves from different packs are indicated by lines. Solid lines indicate similarity as high as that observed between parent-offspring or siblings. Dotted lines indicated a possible but more distant relationship. Hexagons are placed to improve interpretation of connections; for spatial relationships of packs see Figure 3.*

genetically distinct and perhaps should not be interbred with wolves from elsewhere. In contrast, other populations, such as those in many European countries, are genetically similar and because they are so small as to be affected by inbreeding depression, should be interbred with other European wolves.

Acknowledgments

We would like to thank the many collaborators who provided gray wolf and coyote tissue specimens, and in addition thank A.Eisenhawer, P. Gogan, L.D. Mech, and T. Meier. We also appreciate the helpful comments on the manuscript made by M. Bruford, D. Girman, R. Nowak, and B. Van Valkenburgh. This work was supported in part by a USPHS National Service Award GM-07104 to N.L., a U.S. National Park Service agreement with R.K.W., and a National Science Foundation grant to R.K.W. (BSR 9020282).

The Origin and Fate of the Red Wolf

■ Ronald M. Nowak, Michael K. Phillips, V. Gary Henry, William C. Hunter, and Roland Smith

The taxonomic identity of the endangered red wolf has been in question for 200 years. Some authorities consider it a species, while others think it is a subspecies of the gray wolf, or a hybrid resulting from interbreeding of gray wolf and coyote. The debate intensified recently because of mitochondrial DNA analysis and concern over the minimum viable population estimates presented in the red wolf recovery plan. The outcome of the debate will affect the vigor of the recovery program, which has been in progress since 1973. In this paper we review literature, carry out a new analysis of fossil and modern specimens, and conclude that the red wolf is a valid species or, at the very least, a subspecies of the gray wolf. We recommend that the United States Fish and Wildlife Service continue to aggressively pursue recovery of the red wolf.

Introduction

The taxonomic identity of the red wolf (*Canis rufus*) has been in question ever since the animal was first discovered 200 years ago. The issue took on particular interest about 30 years ago when there was recognition that the red wolf was nearly extinct. Since then, most authorities have regarded the red wolf as a full biological species (McCarley 1962, 1978, Paradiso 1968, Paradiso and Nowak 1971, 1973, Atkins and Dillon 1971, Riley and McBride 1972, Gipson et al. 1974, Shaw 1975, Freeman 1976, Elder and Hayden 1977, Atkins 1978, Nowak 1979, Ferrel et al. 1980). However, Lawrence and Bossert (1967, 1975) argued that it is a subspecies of the gray wolf (*Canis lupus*) and Mech (1970:22–25) suggested that it may be a fertile hybrid population resulting from interbreeding of the gray wolf and coyote (*Canis latrans*).

Despite the taxonomic debate, the red wolf was listed as endangered in 1967 and began receiving priority treatment with passage of the U.S. Endangered Species Act (ESA) of 1973 (Public Law No. 93-205). Recovery efforts took a major step in 1986 with the initiation of a reintroduction project in the Alligator River National Wildlife Refuge (ARNWR), northeastern North Carolina (Phillips and Parker 1988, Parker and Phillips 1991, Phillips et al., this volume). The project has been successful, and we now think that it is possible to restore populations of red wolves to other areas in the southeastern United States (Phillips et al. this volume). Additionally, it has become clear that the red wolf recovery program generates benefits that extend beyond the immediate preservation of the species, to positively affect local citizens and communities, larger conservation efforts, and other imperiled species (Phillips 1990b).

The taxonomic debate recently intensified because of genetic analysis (Wayne and Jenks 1991) and concern over the minimum viable population (MVP) estimates presented in the Red Wolf Recovery Plan (U.S. Fish and Wildlife Service 1989:21–53). The MVP estimates call for maintaining 325 red wolves in captivity and 225 in the wild. Such populations should ensure for 150+ years the persistence of 80% to 85% of the genetic diversity found in the original red wolf founding stock. However, it has been suggested that the expense and spatial requirements of maintaining such populations would be excessive if the red wolf is determined to be less than a full species (L.D. Mech, U.S. Fish and Wildlife Service, pers. commun.).

Obviously, the outcome of the taxonomic debate will greatly influence the vigor of the red wolf recovery program. Indeed, the debate prompted the American Sheep Industry Association to present a petition to the Secretary of the Interior requesting that the red wolf be removed from the List of Endangered and Threatened Wildlife, thus stopping recovery actions. To help resolve the issue, the U.S. Fish and Wildlife Service (USFWS) has reviewed pertinent literature and other available information, carried out some new analyses of fossil and modern specimens, and prepared this paper. In addition, the Service has published a finding (Henry 1992) that the petition has not presented substantial information indicating that delisting is warranted.

Morphological Studies

The red wolf is intermediate to the coyote and gray wolf in most physical characteristics (Paradiso and Nowak 1972, Mech 1974b, Bekoff 1977). The disproportionately long legs and large ears of the red wolf are the two most obvious external features separating that species from both the coy-

Ronald M. Nowak, Michael K. Phillips, V. Gary Henry, William C. Hunter, and Roland Smith

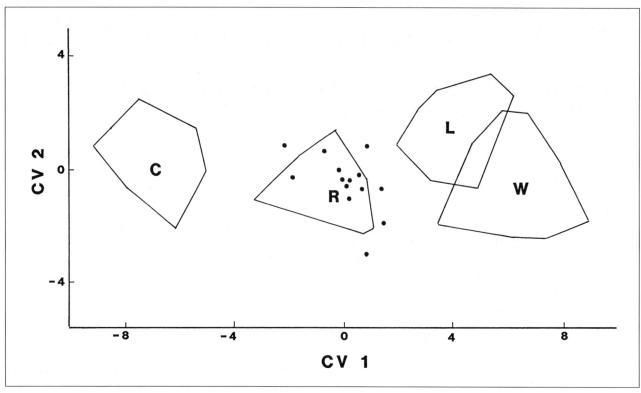

Fig. 1. *Plot of first and second cononical variables (CV1 and CV2) of a canonical discriminant analysis of skulls of **Canis**. Letters indicate mean positions of known groups: coyote (C), red wolf (R), Minnesota and Isle Royale wolf (L), Alaska gray wolf (W). Solid lines show boundaries of distributions of known groups. Dots indicate positions of nine individuals used to found (ie., establish) existing captive and reintroduced population of red wolf, and five individuals that had been released in North Carolina.*

ote and gray wolf. Experienced observers can usually distinguish adults of the three species on the basis of these external features (Riley and McBride 1972). Also, Atkins (1978) and Atkins and Dillon (1971) studied brain morphology in six species of the genus *Canis* and concluded that *C. rufus* is a valid taxon.

Various studies of skull morphology, some of them employing discriminant analysis of measurements, indicate that the red wolf is a distinct species (McCarley 1962, Paradiso 1968, Paradiso and Nowak 1971, 1973, Gipson et al. 1974, Freeman 1976, Elder and Hayden 1977, Nowak 1979). Such techniques are commonly used to define taxonomic units (Dragoo et al. 1991, Jones et al. 1991, Wilson et al. 1991). Lawrence and Bossert (1967, 1975) also studied canid skull morphology, but concluded that the red wolf is not more than subspecifically distinct from the gray wolf.

Nowak (1992) conducted a new canonical discriminant analysis of 10 measurements of skulls of three known groups: 50 coyotes from Idaho, 38 gray wolves from Alaska, and 28 gray wolves from Minnesota and Isle Royale in the 1960's and 1970's. In addition, 22 red wolves from before 1940 in Florida, Alabama, Mississippi, Louisiana, and the Big Thicket area of southeastern Texas were compared as individuals to the known groups. Also compared as individu-

als were nine founders of the red wolf captive population (see additional discussion below) and five of their descendants from the ongoing ARNWR reintroduction project. All groups were composed only of complete skulls thought to represent full-grown males, and each group comprised every specimen available from the indicated time and/or location. The pre-1940 red wolf sample was from a geographic and temporal range in the southeastern U.S. that previous work (Nowak 1979) suggested was not affected by hybridization with the coyote; no other appropriate specimens of wild *Canis* of any kind were available from this range. Nowak (1992) found complete separation between the coyote, gray wolf, and red wolf samples.

For purposes of this paper, another analysis was done, using the same specimens and methodology (SAS Institute 1987), but treating the pre-1940 red wolf sample as a known group. Graphical results (Fig. 1) show the three species (i.e., *C. latrans*, *C. rufus*, and *C. lupus*) to be distinct from one another. The red wolf falls roughly between the coyote and gray wolf, but does not merge with either. Minnesota and Isle Royale gray wolf populations have affinity to those of Alaska and are not indicative of hybridization with the coyote, as has been suggested by some recent genetic study (see below). The captive and reintroduced red wolf popula-

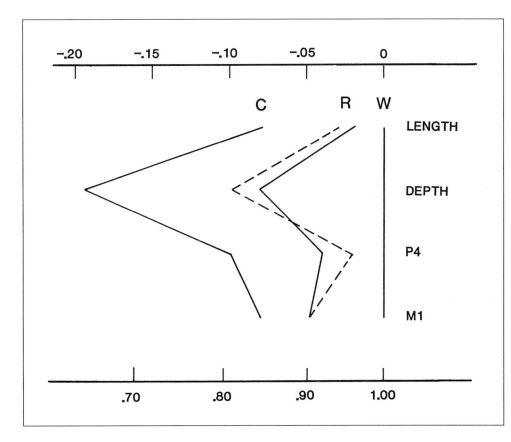

Fig. 2. *Ratio diagram comparing means of four measurements of lower jaw of 109 modern* **C. lupus** *from the western United States (W), 198 modern* **C. latrans** *from the western United States (C), 125 modern* **C. rufus** *collected prior to 1930 (R), and 4 Irvingtonian* **C. rufus** *from Florida (dashed line). Measurements are: length, distance from anterior edge of alveolus of first lower premolar to posterior edge of alveolus of third lower molar; depth, minimum depth from dorsal surface of mandible between third and fourth lower premolars to ventral surface of mandible; p4, crown length of fourth lower premolar; ml, crown length of first lower molar. A log difference scale is provided above, and a ratio scale below, the diagram.*

tions are statistically near original *C. rufus*. Their apparent partial displacement in the direction of *C. lupus* possibly expresses a relative increase in certain cranial dimensions associated with advanced age and/or captive rearing of most of the involved animals. Study of this and other questions is continuing.

Fossil and Historical Evidence

As indicated below, mitochondrial DNA analysis can be used to support the contention that the red wolf originated entirely from hybridization between coyote and gray wolf. However, this suggestion is not supported by studies of the fossil record and large series of specimens collected in historical time (Gipson 1978, Nowak 1979). The red wolf, in much the same form as now, was present in North America through the Irvingtonian and Rancholabrean periods (middle to late Pleistocene). Figure 2 shows that specimens from the Irvingtonian of Florida are approximately the same, in size and proportion, as specimens of modern *C. rufus*. This species seems to represent an intermediate, surviving stage in the course of wolf evolution from a small coyote-like ancestor to the modern gray wolf (Kurtén and Anderson 1980:169, Nowak 1979:118–120).

Both *C. lupus* and *C. latrans* originally occurred throughout western North America, as far east as central Texas and Missouri, and *C. lupus* also occupied the northeastern United States. Until *C. latrans* began moving into Arkansas, Lou-

isiana, and east Texas in the mid twentieth century, there were no records of either species in southeastern North America in historical time (Lawrence and Bossert 1967, Nowak 1979). Nonetheless, Wayne and Jenks (1991) seemed to suggest that at some indefinite time in the past *C. lupus* and *C. latrans* did move into the southeast, where they interbred and formed a vast hybrid zone, the resulting population being called the red wolf.

Had the red wolf originated entirely from hybridization between coyote and gray wolf, as suggested by Wayne and Jenks, one would expect a complete blend of all three species throughout the designated range of the red wolf. However, specimens from about 1890–1930 suggest that hybridization was then just getting under way in the region where the western portion of the red wolf's range met the southeastern portion of the coyote's range (Nowak 1979:34–44). In most of the region the two species were sympatric or in close proximity, with hybrid individuals having appeared at but a few restricted localities. Only in central Texas was there a substantial hybrid zone, where *C. latrans* and *C. rufus* blended into one another. As shown in Figure 3, *C. lupus* was also present in central and western Texas, but specimens of it are statistically far removed from *C. rufus*, *C. latrans*, and the hybrid population (Nowak 1979:41–43). This situation argues against both the view that the red wolf is conspecific with the gray and the view that the gray wolf hybridized with the coyote to form the red wolf.

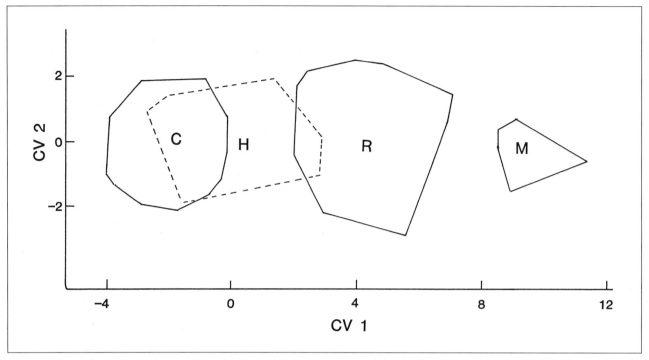

Fig. 3. *Plot of first and second canonical variables (CV1 and CV2) of a canonical discriminant analysis of skulls of male* **Canis** *(adapted from Nowak 1979:42). Solid lines with centrally located letters indicate statistical distributions of known groups: 165* **C. latrans** *from western United States (C); 70* **C. rufus** *collected before 1930 in south-central United States (R); 7* **C. lupus** *from central and western Texas (M). Dashed lines around the letter H indicate the statistical distribution of 43 specimens taken before 1930 in central Texas and thought to represent a hybrid population of* **C. latrans** *x* **C. rufus***.*

Later material shows the spread of a true hybridization process, and the steady reduction of unmodified red wolf populations. By the 1960's, such groups had largely disappeared, although available skulls from 1963–1970 in extreme southeastern Texas indicate that the population there was still predominately like original *C. rufus* (Nowak 1979:44–51). A number of animals were subsequently live-captured in that area and adjacent southwestern Louisiana, and used to form a breeding pool for eventual reintroduction (Carley 1975).

According to Henry (1992), the existing red wolf populations are descended from animals selected on the basis of the best morphological and taxonomic information available at the time. From fall 1973 to July 1980, more than 400 wild canids from southeastern Texas and southwestern Louisiana were examined in the course of the red wolf recovery program. Of those, 43 were admitted to the breeding/certification program as probable red wolves. Final proof of genetic integrity was determined through captive breeding and examination of offspring. That process, plus some inadvertent mortality, resulted in only 14 animals becoming the founding stock of the red wolf populations now in existence.

Behavioral and Ecological Studies

McCarley (1978) found consistent differences between the vocalizations of red wolf and coyote. Riley and McBride

(1972) and Shaw (1975) noted behavioral and ecological differences between free-ranging populations of red wolf and coyote in Texas and Louisiana and concluded that *C. rufus* is a valid taxon.

Preliminary results from the ARNWR reintroduction shed additional light on red wolf behavior and ecology (Henry 1992, Phillips et al. this volume). Reintroduced red wolves are very social; most of the animals belong to packs that occupy territories. It is not unusual for yearling and two-year-old red wolves to associate with their parents, assist with pup-rearing, and restrict movements to their natal home range. Reintroduced red wolves are relatively intolerant of strange conspecifics, and intraspecific aggression led to the death of seven wolves. A similar social structure was observed for red wolves in Texas and Louisiana (Riley and McBride 1972). Thus, in terms of sociality red wolves are similar to gray wolves (Mech 1970:38–146). In contrast, coyotes are often more asocial, with animals belonging to breeding pairs or small family groups. Pups often disperse before their second summer. Home ranges of the groups sometimes overlap, and intraspecific aggression is not thought to be an important source of mortality (Gier 1975, Andrews and Boggess 1978, Danner and Smith 1980, Althoff and Gipson 1981, Bekoff and Wells 1982, Roy and Dorrance 1985, Windberg et al. 1985, Harrison 1986:1–55, Gese et al. 1989, Person and Hirth 1991).

Analysis of 1,300 scats indicates that white-tailed deer (*Odocoileus virginianus*) and raccoons (*Procyon lotor*) are the primary year-round food items for reintroduced red wolves. Although some of the deer are probably eaten as carrion, we have documented wolf predation of apparently healthy adult deer. Most raccoons are probably taken as live prey. Gray wolves also rely heavily on ungulates (Mech 1970:168-192, Peterson 1977:49–66). Deer and raccoons are of tertiary or lesser importance to coyotes in the southern States, use of deer tends to be seasonal (greatest during fawning period and hunting season), and adult deer are often eaten as carrion (Korschgen 1957, Fooks 1961, Wilson 1967, Gipson 1974, Meinzer et al. 1975, Michaelson and Goertz 1977, Smith and Kennedy 1983, Wooding et al. 1984, Lee and Kennedy 1986, Leopold and Krausman 1986, Blanton and Hill 1989, Windberg and Mitchell 1991).

Genetic Analyses

A karyological study showed that all members of North American *Canis* have a diploid chromosome number of 78, and that the chromosomes appear identical in each species (Chiarelli 1975). One serological study found no distinction between North American members of the genus *Canis* (Seal 1975). A second found that wild canids sampled from the last naturally occurring red wolf population possessed an allele absent in coyotes and domestic dogs (*Canis familiaris*) from the same area; this allele was suggestive of the survival of a gene originating in the red wolf population (Ferrell et al. 1980).

Analysis of mtDNA indicated that red wolves from the current and historical populations possessed either a gray wolf or a coyote mtDNA genotype (Wayne and Jenks 1991). The investigators offered three explanations for the results. Firstly, the red wolf could have been a distinct species with unique mtDNA that either was missed in their survey or had become extinct through genetic drift. Either way, the species was then subjected to hybridization with coyotes and gray wolves. Secondly, the red wolf could have been a subspecies of the gray wolf that was morphologically, but not genetically, distinct from other gray wolves. This subspecies then hybridized with coyotes. Thirdly, the red wolf phenotype could have been derived solely from gray wolf and coyote interbreeding.

As suggested by the fact that Wayne and Jenks (1991) presented three explanations for their results, mtDNA analysis is not a panacea for solving complicated taxonomic problems. Accordingly, use of mtDNA relationships to infer species relationships must proceed with caution (Cronin 1991). Vertebrate mtDNA is inherited matrilineally and clonally without recombination and can be considered one locus from a phylogenetic standpoint. However, a single-locus (gene) phylogeny may not be the same as the species phylogeny (Pamilo and Nei 1988, Dowling and Brown 1989). An example of discordant mtDNA and species rela-

tionships was reported in deer (Carr et al. 1986, Cronin et al. 1988). Processes of population genetics must be considered to explain phylogenetic relationships of closely related taxa (Avise 1989a, Dowling and Brown 1989), and assessment of many loci are needed for derivation of correct species trees (Pamilo and Nei 1988).

The relationship between mtDNA analysis and systematics is further confused by the fact that mtDNA only affects the function of mitochondria. Nuclear DNA codes for phenotypic characteristics that define species. Because of its mode of inheritance and because it is largely unaffected by natural selection, a foreign type of mtDNA can persist in a population despite the total elimination of phenotypes derived from nuclear DNA that came from the same foreign source. Once foreign mtDNA is introduced into a population, it (or possibly a mutated version) will persist as long as the foreign matriline exists. Although the presence of coyote or gray wolf mtDNA genotypes in red wolves would indicate that hybridization, however limited, did take place at one time, it does not show that red wolves possess significant amounts of coyote-derived or gray-wolf-derived nuclear DNA.

Wayne and Jenks' (1991) interpretation of genetic data was challenged by Dowling et al. (1992). The latter authorities stated that failure to find diagnostic molecular characteristics among morphologically distinctive forms does not imply conspecificity and that levels of genetic divergence are not valid measures of specific status. They indicated that mtDNA analysis, among other evidence, supports the position that the red wolf is closely related to the gray and that it has hybridized with the coyote, but not that it actually originated as a hybrid.

We are not yet convinced that the current techniques of mtDNA analysis are fully reliable for purposes of hybridization study. The application of such methods to the red wolf situation follows closely on similar work done with material from the Great Lakes region (Lehman et al. 1991). The latter study reported the formation of a "hybrid zone," said to involve the spread of coyote mtDNA to 62% of gray wolves in Minnesota and to 100% of those on Isle Royale. However, observations by field personnel in those areas indicate no change in the morphological, behavioral, or ecological characters of the wolves (L.D. Mech, U.S. Fish and Wildlife Service, pers. commun., R.O Peterson, Michigan Tech. Univ., pers. commun.). While it would theoretically be possible for coyote mtDNA to spread to the extent reported, it would be unlikely to do so without otherwise affecting the wolf population. However, even if the mtDNA situation has been interpreted correctly for both the Great Lakes region and the current red wolf population, the latter, like the Isle Royale and Minnesota gray wolf, still could retain all other characters of the original species, and thus not represent a hybrid zone in the usual sense. As reported above, the red wolf is wolf-like in all characteristics, except perhaps its disproportionately large ears and long legs, and probably

Ronald M. Nowak, Michael K. Phillips, V. Gary Henry, William C. Hunter, and Roland Smith

The origin and nature of the red wolf has been extensively debated. Some consider it a species, others a subspecies, while a third school of thought considers it a hybrid between the gray wolf and coyote. (Photo: D. Bryan)

possesses wolf-derived nuclear DNA. Indeed, both O'Brien and Mayr (1991) and Wayne and Jenks (1991) recognized the uniqueness of the red wolf and argued for continued protection.

In assessing the work of Wayne and Jenks (1991), Henry (1992) observed that this study used recently developed techniques and was the first to examine mtDNA in the red wolf. Thus the study may be subject to further review and should not now be regarded as conclusive. He noted that while additional study of mtDNA is needed, a current interpretation that is compatible with other evidence would be that limited interbreeding has occurred, leading to the incorporation of coyote-type mtDNA in the red wolf population. However, any coyote nuclear DNA that was subject to selection appears to have been bred out. He added that mtDNA samples cannot be taken in more than half of the historical range of the red wolf, including the region most removed from the ranges of the coyote and gray wolf; thus there is no way to determine the original genetic composition of the species.

Hybridization is common among closely related vertebrate species, and hundreds of "hybrid zones" have been identified (Barton and Hewitt 1985, 1989). Such cases sometimes involve endangered species, for example the blue and

fin whales (Spilliaert et al. 1991). Recent advances in genetic analyses make it difficult to interpret hybridization relative to the Biological Species Concept (BSC), which emphasizes reproductive isolation between taxa (Mayr 1940, O'Brien and Mayr 1991). However, many views on speciation, including the BSC, provide for limited genetic interchange between taxa so long as hybridization is not so pervasive as to cause the disintegration of the integrity of the species involved (Mayr 1940, Amato 1991, O'Brien and Mayr 1991).

Unfortunately, genetic assessments of the red wolf have been taken out of context, been used as grounds to challenge the integrity of the entire red wolf conservation effort, and received much publicity in the popular media (*New York Times*, 12 March 1991; *Newsweek*, 12 August 1991; *Scientific American*, October 1991; *Washington Post*, 24 June 1991). In an otherwise effective discussion of the hybridization issue, O'Brien and Mayr (1991) accepted unpublished reports that the red wolf is nothing more than a hybrid of gray wolf and coyote. No supporting evidence was provided either by themselves or by the sources they cited, but their paper was widely quoted. Later, Gittleman and Pimm (1991) evidently seized upon the work of Wayne and Jenks (1991), before it was even published, and added a background of their own to criticize efforts being made to reestablish the red wolf.

We realize that the taxonomic identity of the red wolf cannot be unequivocally defined from available data. Accordingly, we support the Red Wolf Recovery Program's decision to sponsor an analysis of the species' nuclear DNA and further investigations of wolf and coyote skull morphology. Additionally, because young *Canis* show distinct and significant differences in behavioral ontogeny (Bekoff and Jamieson 1975, Bekoff 1978), the Recovery Program should consider initiating a study to analyze the development of agonistic behavior and social play in red wolves. Linear discriminant function analysis would permit direct comparison to other studies of canid behavioral development and skull morphology. Bekoff (1978) and Bekoff et al. (1975) demonstrated the utility of using behavioral phenotypes to assess taxonomic relationships.

Legal questions will persist concerning the continued protection and recovery of an endangered species that has been subjected to introgression from other species. Fortunately, the USFWS is in the process of developing a policy concerning protection of such species under the ESA. This policy will rescind all previous solicitors' opinions regarding protection of such species, and will require each situation to be managed on a case-by-case basis.

The Red Wolf Recovery Team proposed that the USFWS organize a symposium dedicated to discussions of the "species concept" and the ESA, in order to address questions concerning protection of threatened and endangered species that have been subjected to introgression. It is hoped that the symposium's conclusions would serve as guidelines for interpreting complex data sets, such as those generated from genetic analyses, and may well result in changes to the definition of species as recognized by the ESA.

Conclusions

We think that evidence best supports the contention that *Canis rufus* is a valid taxon, probably a full species. At the very least, *C. rufus* is a subspecies of *Canis lupus*. Thus, we recommend that the USFWS continue to aggressively pursue recovery of the red wolf, as mandated by the ESA.

Acknowledgments

We are grateful to C. Carley, L. Loges, L.D. Mech, R. Peterson, and D. Waddington.

Ronald M. Nowak, Michael K. Phillips, V. Gary Henry, William C. Hunter, and Roland Smith

Part Seven:
Infectious and Parasitic Diseases

Infectious and Parasitic Diseases of the Gray Wolf and Their Potential Effects on Wolf Populations in North America

■ Christopher J. Brand, Margo J. Pybus, Warren B. Ballard, and Rolf O. Peterson

Numerous infectious and parasitic diseases have been reported for the gray wolf, including more than 10 viral, bacterial, and mycotic diseases and more than 70 species of helminths and ectoparasites. However, few studies have documented the role of diseases in population dynamics. Disease can affect wolf populations directly by causing mortality or indirectly by affecting physiological and homeostatic processes, thriftiness, reproduction, behavior, or social structure. In addition, wolves are hosts to diseases that can affect prey species, thus affecting wolf populations indirectly by reducing prey abundance or increasing vulnerability to predation. Diseases such as canine distemper and infectious canine hepatitis are enzootic in wolf populations, whereas rabies occurs in wolves primarily as a result of transmission from other species such as arctic and red foxes. Contact between wolves and domestic pets and livestock may affect the composition of diseases in wolves and their effects on wolf populations. Dogs were suspected of introducing lice and canine parvovirus to several wolf populations. The latter disease appears to have had initial demographic effects and is now enzootic in several wolf populations. The potential for diseases to affect wolf populations and other wild and domestic animals should be considered in wolf management plans, particularly in plans for reintroduction of wolves to areas within their former range.

Introduction

Published information on infectious and parasitic diseases of the gray wolf (*Canis lupus*) is largely composed of case reports, parasite surveys, and serological surveys of viral and bacterial pathogens. The effects of diseases on wolf population dynamics are largely unstudied, with the exception of scattered descriptive accounts of epizootics (Rausch 1958, Chapman 1978, Todd et al. 1981, Carbyn 1982b). Knowledge of the actual and potential influence of diseases on wolf populations can be important to wolf management programs, particularly for endangered populations and in areas where wolves are reintroduced. We review current literature on infectious and parasitic diseases in wolves, summarize information on the role of diseases in wolf population dynamics, and discuss considerations of disease in management of wolves.

Methods

We searched data bases for publications about parasites and diseases of wolves in *Current Contents, Wildlife Abstracts,*

Wildlife Review, Biosis, and *Biological Abstracts.* Additional information was obtained from personal communication with researchers of diseases of wolves and other canids. We review these sources of information to provide an overview of the occurrence and significance of diseases of gray wolves in North America. Reference is made to diseases in other canid species when little or no information was available for the wolf, but when the disease is of potential significance to wolves.

Viral Diseases

Rabies

Rabies has probably occurred sporadically in nearly all, if not all, areas wolves have occupied (e.g., Cowan 1949, Mech 1970, Rausch 1973, Tabel et al. 1974, Custer and Pence 1981a, Sidorov et al. 1983, Butzeck 1987, Zarnke and Ballard 1987, Theberge et al. 1994). Mech (1970) identified rabies as one of the most important diseases of wild wolves, and Murie (1944) and Cowan (1949) speculated that rabies might limit wolf numbers. Since the early 1970's, several accounts have suggested that rabies may be an important periodic or local cause of mortality. However, documented accounts of rabies in North American wolves are few, and the role of rabies in population regulation is unknown.

Ironically, as widespread as rabies is, relatively little information exists beyond the effects on individual wolves. Rausch (1973) reported that wolves without rabies appear to avoid individuals with the disease, but supporting evidence was not provided. Infected wolves may attack other wolves. Chapman (1978) reported the occurrence of rabies in one wolf pack on the Brooks Mountain Range in Alaska during 1977. He observed one wolf, which was later diagnosed with rabies, actively attacking other pack members. Subsequently, at least seven of 10 pack members died within five days, and rabies was confirmed in three wolves tested. At least five of the wolves died at two rendezvous sites, causing Chapman (1978) to speculate that rabid wolves tend to seek or remain in familiar areas, and therefore are not likely to transmit the disease to other wolf packs.

Rabies was one of several factors suspected to have contributed to a major decline of wolves in northwest Alaska after 1976 (Davis et al. 1980). However, only one wolf from the area was actually confirmed with rabies (Ritter 1981). Theberge et al. (1994) reported that rabies accounted for 21% of mortality among 29 radio-collared wolves that died in Algonquin Provincial Park, Ontario, during 1987-1992. Mortality from rabies occurred in three different packs within a nine-month period.

Wolves are not considered the primary vector of rabies, except in several countries in the eastern Mediterranean (Sikes 1970) and Asia (MacDonald and Voigt 1985). Wolves usually contract the disease from other vector species such as arctic foxes (*Alopex lagopus*) and red foxes (*Vulpes vulpes*) (Mech 1970, Rausch 1973, Ritter 1981, Theberge et al. 1994). A rabies epizootic among arctic and red foxes occurred in northwest Alaska (D. Ritter, Alaska Public Health Laboratory, Univ. of Alaska, pers. commun.). During February and late April 1990, three radio-collared wolves from two packs were found dead, and were diagnosed as having died from rabies (W.B. Ballard, Cooperative Wildlife Research Unit, Faculty of Forestry, University of New Brunswick, unpubl. data). During the ensuing three months, an additional five radio-collared wolves were found dead. Decomposition of the carcasses precluded testing for rabies, but this disease was suspected because no physical injuries were evident (Ballard et al. 1990). By 1 August 1990, eight radio-collared wolves in four packs had died from rabies (five of 21, one of seven, one of two, and one of one) (W.B. Ballard, unpubl. data). For rabies to have been transmitted between packs, infected wolves either had contact with adjacent pack members along territory edges, or dispersed into other pack areas. All known wolf deaths occurred within the known territory of each pack. Wolves in this area are generally not migratory, although packs may follow migrating caribou to their wintering grounds in some years (Ballard et al. 1990). Although dispersal could account for transmission of the disease in some cases, it is most likely that arctic and red foxes spread the disease to wolves. The rabies epizootic apparently did not spread beyond the four packs. Thus, rabies can eliminate single wolf packs and at times be a significant cause of mortality in a wolf population.

Canine distemper

Canine distemper has been reported in captive wolves since 1904 (Budd 1981), but Choquette and Kuyt (1974) were apparently the first to demonstrate serological evidence of infection in wild wolves in northern Canada (two of 86 seropositive). Because the wolf population had been substantially reduced prior to their study, they suggested that the low prevalence of distemper in the Northwest Territories may have been due to lowered opportunity for exposure in the reduced population. They suggested, based on the work of Trainer and Knowlton (1968) on coyotes (*Canis latrans*), that distemper was enzootic in wolves and only became an important mortality factor when compounded by other factors; e.g., crowding and malnutrition.

Stephenson et al. (1982) reported that wolves in three areas of Alaska (Nelchina Basin, Tanana Flats, and Yakutat) were seropositive for distemper. The relatively low seroprevalence (6–12%) suggested that exposure was either rare or perhaps fatal. Zarnke and Ballard (1987) further examined the wolf population in the Nelchina Basin for exposure to distemper during 1975 through 1982 (12% seroprevalence). Seropositive wolves were present during six of eight years, suggesting that distemper was enzootic in this population. Zarnke and Ballard (1987) also compared frequency of exposure to distemper in the wolf population to the frequency of the disease in dogs (*Canis familiaris*) from the area and concluded that dogs were not a direct source of infection for wolves. No deaths were attributed to distemper in any of 150 radio-collared wolves. In north-central Minnesota, 48% of 71 wolves sampled from 1977 to 1984 were seropositive for distemper (T.K. Fuller, Univ. of Massachusetts, pers. commun.).

Carbyn (1982b) was the first to provide evidence that distemper caused mortality in free-ranging wolves. Three of five known deaths from disease in Riding Mountain National Park, Manitoba, were caused by distemper, and he suggested that the number discovered was far less than the actual number. All known deaths occurred in five- to eight-month-old pups. Carbyn (1982b) concluded that diseases contributed to the 50% decline in the wolf population in the park. Distemper was the second largest known mortality factor. Peterson et al. (1984) also reported deaths of two yearling wolves from distemper in 1978 and 1980 on the Kenai Peninsula, Alaska.

Other than the accounts provided by Carbyn (1982b) and Peterson et al. (1984), there is no evidence that distemper is a significant mortality factor in wolves. Distemper usually infects dog pups at three to nine weeks of age (Gillespie and

Carmichael 1968), so mortality from distemper in wolves could easily occur undetected. However, most wolf populations in North America exhibit good recruitment, therefore distemper is not likely an important source of mortality.

Infectious canine hepatitis

Choquette and Kuyt (1974) were the first to report the serological evidence for infectious canine hepatitis (ICH) in free-ranging wolves in northern Canada: 11 (13%) of 86 wolves tested were seropositive. Stephenson et al. (1982) reported 100% exposure to ICH in three wolf populations in the Tanana Flats and Nelchina Basins, Alaska, during 1976-1979, but only a 40% exposure in northwest Alaska. Zarnke and Ballard (1987) reported an overall antibody prevalence of 81% in the Nelchina wolf population during 1975 through 1982. Annual prevalence varied from 72 to 100%. Both studies concluded that exposure to ICH was much higher in Alaska than in northern Canada. Forty-two percent of the exposed wolves were pups, suggesting early exposure. Zarnke and Ballard (1987) concluded that ICH was enzootic in Alaskan wolves. There was no relation between the occurrence of the disease in domestic dogs and seroprevalence in free-ranging wolves. Mortality in wolves from ICH has not been reported.

Canine parvovirus

Canine parvovirus (properly designated CPV-2) is a relatively new infectious organism that appeared in 1976 or 1977 in Europe and was first recognized as a disease agent in dogs in 1978 (Pollock 1984). CPV-2 subsequently spread rapidly, and was common in dogs worldwide by 1980. Although its origin remains uncertain, it is similar to mink enteritis virus and feline panleukopenia virus (FPV), and possibly arose from a mutation of FPV or a third closely related virus (Pollock 1984).

The first evidence of exposure to CPV-2 among wolves and coyotes in North America was apparently in 1978–1979, based on retrospective serological studies (Barker et al. 1983, Thomas et al. 1984, Mech et al. 1986), although Goyal et al. (1986) provided evidence of CPV exposure in wolves in Minnesota as early as 1975. During 1978–1983, Mech et al. (1986) reported an increased seroprevalence in wolves in Minnesota that paralleled results from surveys in coyotes in Texas, Utah, and Idaho (Thomas et al. 1984). Among coyotes, seroprevalence increased rapidly from 0% in 1979 to ≥ 50% in 1980. Positive hemagglutination-inhibition (HI) titers predominated through 1983, when data were last reported, suggesting the disease was enzootic in coyotes (Thomas et al. 1984). The prevalence of positive HI titers among wolves in Minnesota reached 65% in 1980, and ranged between 36% and 44% during 1981–1983 (Mech et al. 1986). In a separate study in north-central Minnesota, CPV-2 antibody was not found in 11 wolves sampled in 1977; but during 1981–84, 15 (26%) of 57 wolves were seropositive (T.K. Fuller, Univ. of Massachusetts, pers. commun.).

In south-central Alaska, the first positive serum neutralizing titer in wolves was reported in 1980, and during the next two years 50% of 18 wolves sampled had positive titers to CPV-2 (Zarnke and Ballard 1987). Similarly, initial CPV-2 titers among wolves on the Kenai Peninsula in south-central Alaska were recorded in 1979 (Bailey et al. this volume). R.P. Thiel (Wisconsin Dept. of Natural Resources, pers. commun.) found positive HA titers to CPV-2 in 67% of 24 wolves from Wisconsin. He also recovered the remains of four wolves from Wisconsin that appeared to have died from disease and parasitism; two of these wolves were previously seropositive to CPV-2, although CPV-2 was not considered a primary cause of death.

There are no published reports of mortality or clinical illness from CPV-2 among free-ranging wolves, although losses of captive wolves have been high, as in other canids. In 1983, CPV-2 claimed 11 of 12 pups and yearlings in a captive wolf colony in Minnesota (Mech and Fritts 1987). J. Zuba (Univ. of Wisconsin College of Veterinary Medicine, pers. commun.) conducted the only experimental study of the effects of CPV-2 on wolves. Results of this study were similar to those conducted on dogs. Wolves that were challenged with the virus seroconverted and thereafter had positive titers to CPV-2; about 30% of these animals showed clinical signs of disease, and about 10% of the animals would probably have died without supportive care.

CPV-2 became the focal point of concern in the late 1980's as the wolf population in Isle Royale National Park (Michigan) declined to an all-time low level (R.O. Peterson, unpubl. data). A spectacular crash occurred in 1980–1982 when this island population dropped from a maximum of 50 to 14 wolves, cumulatively including the deaths of more than 52 individuals. All nine wolf pups known to be alive in 1981 died before midwinter surveys began, coincident with an outbreak of CPV-2 among dogs in Houghton, Michigan, the mainland departure point for visitors to the island. While the presence of CPV-2 on Isle Royale was confirmed by the presence of positive titers in several wolves in the late 1980's (N.J. Thomas, Natl. Wildl. Health Res. Center, pers. commun.), the link between high mortality in the early 1980's and CPV remains circumstantial.

Oral papillomatosis

Oral papillomatosis was reported in two wolves (and 10 coyotes) from Alberta during 1971–1976 (Samuel et al. 1978). These two wolf pups were found dead together near a poisoned bait center. This viral disease resulted in mild infection of the lips with multiple (<20) tumors in the wolf pups, although lesions in the coyotes ranged from mild to severe (Fig. 1).

Debilitation or mortality from oral papillomatosis has not been reported in free-ranging canids. The disease probably does not cause direct mortality, but may alter behavior or feeding, as suggested for coyotes (Trainer et al. 1968), result in secondary infections, or be associated with other debili-

Christopher J. Brand, Margo J. Pybus, Warren B. Ballard, and Rolf O. Peterson

Fig. 1. *Canine oral papillomatosis in a coyote from Alberta. Photo: M.J. Pybus.*

tating diseases such as mange. Spontaneous recovery with long-lasting immunity has been suggested in coyotes (Trainer et al. 1968).

Bacterial and Fungal Diseases

Brucellosis

Brucellosis is a contagious disease caused by the bacterium *Brucella* spp., including up to five recognized strains. The disease primarily affects ruminants, often resulting in abortion, orchitis, or other reproductive disorders.

In Alaska, Neiland (1975) reported on seroprevalence to *Brucella* spp. in wolves and other carnivores that were associated with infected caribou (*Rangifer tarandus*) in the Arctic herd. A 45% (10/22) prevalence of agglutinating titers among adult wolves contrasted to the 9% (1/11) prevalence among red foxes and 7% among sled dogs, presumably a result of transmission from consumption of caribou infected with *B. suis* biovar 4. Neiland (1975) found no serologic reactors among 98 wolves tested from the Porcupine caribou herd range and on St. Lawrence Island. Zarnke and Ballard (1987) reported 1% (1/67) antibody prevalence among wolves in south-central Alaska. They attributed this low rate

to the relatively low infection rate in caribou of the Nelchina herd (less than 5% seropositive) and the increased use of moose (*Alces alces*), a species rarely infected with brucellosis. Pinigan and Zabrodin (1970) found 11% (12/110) of wolves exposed to brucellosis, presumably *B. suis* biovar 4, in Siberian reindeer (*Rangifer tarandus*) ranges. In Alberta, 31% (4/13) of wolves examined in Wood Buffalo National Park were infected with *Brucella abortus* biotype 1 (S.V. Tessaro, Agriculture Canada, pers. commun.); however, titers were not detected in three wolves collected 80 km south of the park (Zarnke and Yuill 1981).

The effects of *Brucella* infection in wolves under natural conditions is unknown. Neiland and Miller (1981) experimentally infected two gravid wolves with *B. suis* biovar 4; although clinical disease was not observed in these wolves, four of six pups in one litter were born dead. The surviving pups were killed by the bitch within 24 hours of birth. Although brucellosis was not diagnosed as the cause of death among the pups, *B. suis* biovar 4 was isolated from the liver of each of the seven pups and from the spleen of five. *Brucella suis* biovar 4 was also isolated from a wide variety of organs of both bitches, including the liver, spleen, mammary glands, and lymph nodes; the uterine horns were infected in one. Whether these deaths could be attributed indirectly to brucellosis is not known, however, consumption of aborted fetuses and placentae by infected dogs is common (Carmichael and Kenney 1970). Neiland and Miller (1981) concluded that reproductive failure was a "probable, but essentially unproven, consequence of ill-timed infections" in wolves.

Leptospirosis

Leptospirosis is a bacterial infection caused by the genus *Leptospira*, and includes 170 known species, or serovarieties. Evidence for infection in wolves is limited. Zarnke and Ballard (1987) found detectable antibodies in only 1/82 (1%) wolves sampled in south-central Alaska. However, Khan et al. (1991) found serologic evidence of infection in 52 (11.4%) of 457 wolves tested from northern Minnesota. They identified nine species: *L. grippotyphosa* (5.3%), *L. bratislava* (3.9%), *L. autumnalis* (3.3%), *L. canicola* (2.8%), *L. pomona* (1.5%), *L. pyrogenes* (1.5%), *L. ballum* (0.7%), *L. copenhageni* (0.7%), and *L. hardjo* (0.4%).

Sources of infection in wild mammals are from infective urine, and among carnivores, through the food chain (Reilly et al. 1970). Interspecies transmission to wolves is possible through predation and scavenging or intraspecies by contact with urine, such as through scent marking. In northern Minnesota, seroprevalence to one or more species was 2.6 times greater in wolves near farming areas (20.1%) than in wolves from nonfarming areas (7.7%) (Khan et al. 1991). This difference is possibly due to increased contact with infected livestock and contaminated livestock waste. Leptospirosis is endemic in bovine, porcine, and equine populations in Minnesota (Khan et al. 1991). However, *L. grippotyphosa*, the most prevalent species in wolves (5.3%), was also found in 89 (27.1%) of 328 moose (Diesch et al. 1972), yet was the least common species in domestic livestock in Minnesota (Khan et al. 1991).

Leptospirosis ranges from an inapparent to fatal disease, depending on host and serovariety. Clinical disease or population effects of leptospirosis in wild canids have not been reported. In domestic dogs, disease conditions from mild unapparent to severe are caused primarily by *L. icterohaemorrhagiae* and *L. canicola* (Alston et al. 1958).

Limited information does not suggest that leptospirosis is important in wolves; however, this disease may warrant concern where desired wolf reintroduction or recolonization sites include areas of enzootic leptospirosis among prey or other carnivore species and where wolves may act as a reservoir and source of infection for wild and domestic animals.

Lyme disease

Lyme disease (borreliosis), caused by the bacterium *Borrelia burgdorferi*, affects humans, horses, and dogs. The disease was first recognized in New England in 1975, and possibly as early as 1969 in Wisconsin, and has since been reported with increasing frequency in at least 43 states and in eastern Canada. Infection usually results from the bite of infected ticks, primarily *Ixodes dammini*. White-tailed deer (*Odocoileus virginianus*) serve as hosts for adult *I. dammini* ticks while small mammals, primarily white-footed mice (*Peromyscus leucopus*) and eastern chipmunks (*Tamias striatus*), are hosts for immature ticks. Although these hosts become infected with *B. burgdorferi*, they do not appear to show clinical signs of disease. Burgess and Windberg (1989) provided evidence of transplacental transmission of *B. burgdorferi* infection in free-ranging coyotes, and J.M. Gustafson (Univ. of Wisconsin College of Veterinary Medicine, pers. commun.) reported transplacental transmission in natural- and laboratory-infected ranch-raised foxes. Contact transmission has also been reported in dogs and ranch-raised foxes (Burgess 1986; J.M. Gustafson, pers. commun.).

Evidence that wild wolves become infected with Lyme disease is limited to a serosurvey of trapped wolves in Wisconsin and Minnesota (Kazmierczak et al. 1988). Two of 78 wolves were positive with the indirect fluorescent antibody test; one had a titer indicative of active infection, whereas a low titer in the other wolf suggested either an early or late stage of infection or transient exposure without actual infection.

Although clinical Lyme disease has not been found in wild wolves, Kazmierczak et al. (1988) demonstrated potential susceptibility through intravenous inoculation of one wolf with *B. burgdorferi* in the laboratory. Lymphadenopathy (disease of the lymph nodes) was observed, but other manifestations of disease were not present. Subcutaneous inoculation of a different wolf and ingestion of suckling white-footed mice inoculated with the bacterium by two others did not result in infection. However, in dogs, Lyme disease is characterized by arthritis, arthralgia, fever, and lymphadenitis (Lissman et al. 1984, Kornblatt et al. 1985). Abortion and fetal mortality have been reported in infected humans and horses (Schlesinger et al. 1985, Burgess et al. 1989). Effects on reproduction in infected wolves are not known.

Tularemia

Tularemia, caused by the bacterium *Francisella tularensis*, has not been reported in wolves, although coyotes and red, gray, and kit (*Vulpes macrotis*) foxes are susceptible (summarized in Bell and Reilly 1981). Signs of tularemia in red foxes include anorexia, diarrhea, and noisy, labored breathing. Pathologic changes in red and gray foxes include enlargement of lymph nodes, liver, and spleen; necrosis in the liver and spleen; and congested tubercle-like areas or diffuse consolidation in the lungs.

Zarnke and Ballard (1987) reported a seroprevalence to tularemia of 25% in wolves from Alaska and speculated that most healthy adults probably recover from the disease. Transmission of tularemia to carnivores is most likely from infected lagomorph or rodent prey.

Bovine tuberculosis

Bovine tuberculosis, caused by the bacterium *Mycobacterium bovis,* is primarily a disease of cattle and other ungulates (Thoen and Hines 1981, Tessaro 1986). Other species, including carnivores, may become infected, but infections are probably limited to individual or small local populations closely associated with ungulates.

Carbyn (1982b) reported the occurrence of bovine tuberculosis in wolves from Riding Mountain National Park, Manitoba; this is the only published account of the disease in wild wolves. Among 21 wolves radio-collared during 1975–1979, two of 14 known deaths were attributed to tuberculosis, one isolate being identified as *M. bovis.* Both deaths occurred in pups, presumably litter mates, in an emaciated condition. The source of infection was not identified. Transmission to these siblings could have been from infected prey or carrion, an infected bitch, or contaminated soil. *Mycobacterium bovis* can survive in the environment a few weeks, although some species of mycobacteriae can remain viable in soil for four years or more (Thoen and Hines 1981). Lesions observed were characteristic of tuberculosis in domestic animals and included nodules in the lung and liver and enlargement of intestinal lymph nodes. Carbyn (1982b) attributed the decline in the wolf population (from 120 in 1975 to 63 in 1978) partly to disease, including tuberculosis.

In Wood Buffalo National Park, where bovine tuberculosis is enzootic in bison (*Bison bison*), there was no evidence of infection in 13 wolves examined as part of an epidemiological study of tuberculosis (S.V. Tessaro, Agriculture Canada, pers. commun.).

Blastomycosis

Thiel et al. (1987) reported a fatal case of the fungal disease blastomycosis (*Blastomyces dermatitidis*) in a wolf in Minnesota. Blastomycosis is enzootic in Minnesota (Schlosser 1980) and Wisconsin (Sarosi et al. 1979, McDonough and Kuzma 1980) and is a problem in dogs in these states (Archer 1985). The fungus is probably transmitted from point sources in the environment; the disease is not contagious. The limited distribution of blastomycosis suggests that its potential effects are limited to wolf populations in Wisconsin and Minnesota.

Helminths

At least 24 species of nematodes (roundworms), 21 species of cestodes (tapeworms), nine species of trematodes (flukes), and three species of acanthocephala (spiny-headed worms) have been reported from gray wolves (Mech 1970). In addition to general survey reports and individual species reports, there have been rigorous community analyses of the helminth fauna of wolves throughout North America. Custer and Pence (1981a) used similarity indices and multivariate analyses to compare seven parasite surveys conducted from northern Alaska and Canada to the southern United States.

Wolves have a characteristic helminth fauna and high index of similarity throughout much of their range (Holmes and Podesta 1968, Custer and Pence 1981a). Cestode species provide the most predictable element of parasite communities in wolves; in particular, taeniid cestodes (Freeman et al. 1961, Holmes and Podesta 1968, Custer and Pence 1981b), many of which use vertebrate intermediate hosts to complete the life cycle.

Custer and Pence (1981a) defined two regional clusters of helminth communities in gray wolves: northern regions (Alaska, Yukon, and Northwest Territories), and southern regions (Minnesota, Manitoba, and Alberta). Regional differences in species composition largely reflect differences in wolf diets and associated parasites of prey species. Wolf populations in the far north (characterized by a common occurrence of *Taenia krabbei* and, less frequent, *T. hydatigena* and *Echinococcus granulosus*) feed almost exclusively on cervids, particularly moose and caribou (Mech 1970, Choquette et al. 1973). Southern populations (characterized by common *T. hydatigena*, moderate *E. granulosus*, and low *T. krabbei* occurrence) rely more heavily on white-tailed deer (Thompson 1952, Stenlund 1955, Pimlott et al. 1969, Mech 1970) and beaver (*Castor canadensis*) (Pimlott et al. 1969, Peterson 1977, Shelton and Peterson 1983).

Helminth parasites of wolves often have limited pathogenicity and thus have minimal effect in regulating wolf populations. This likely reflects the predominance of tapeworm infections since the worms feed on nutrients absorbed from the gut contents rather than from the host itself. Tapeworms attach to the intestinal wall simply as a holdfast (to avoid being swept away) and not as a means of damaging the gut wall to feed on blood or tissues. In contrast, there is potential for damage to individual wolves from some species of nematodes and trematodes.

Dog heartworm

The dog heartworm, *Dirofilaria immitis,* is found in the heart and pulmonary arteries of a variety of hosts (Fig. 2), particularly domestic dogs. Mosquitoes are the main vectors of transmission. Pathologic changes and death from dog heartworm have been reported in gray wolves held in zoos in enzootic areas (Hartley 1938, Coffin 1944, Pratt et al. 1981). Clinical pathology in wolves includes detectable heart murmurs and pulse deficits; gross pathology includes cardiac enlargement and chronic passive congestion (Pratt et al. 1981). Preventive medication is recommended when captive wolves are maintained in heartworm enzootic areas. Canine heartworm may have been a significant factor in the decline of red wolves (*Canis rufus*) in the southeastern U.S. (McCarley and Carley 1979). Mech and Fritts (1987) reported *D. immitis* in free-ranging wolves in Minnesota and expressed concern over the possible effects on wolf populations in Minnesota and Wisconsin.

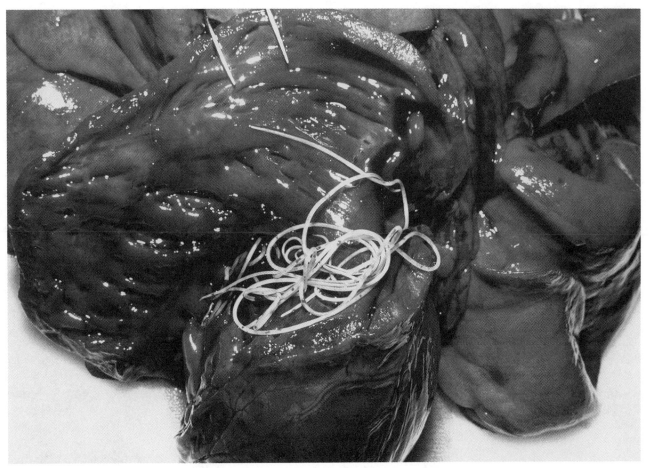

Fig. 2. *Heartworms* (**Dirofilaria immitis**) *in a red wolf from Alligator National Wildlife Refuge, North Carolina. Photo by N.J. Thomas.*

Dog Hookworm

The dog hookworm, *Ancylostoma caninum*, is a large blood-feeding nematode which attaches to and abrades the intestinal wall. Infections in dogs have been associated with anaemia, emaciation, diarrhea, and death. In free-ranging canids, mortality of infected red wolves (McCarley and Carley 1979, Custer and Pence 1981a) and coyotes (Mitchell and Beasom 1974) is suspected. Although this parasite has not been reported in gray wolves, it may be a threat where it is enzootic in other canids. A different species of hookworm, *Uncinaria stenocephala*, has been reported in gray wolves but its pathogenicity has not been assessed.

Liver fluke

Metorchis conjunctus, a trematode found in the gall bladder and bile duct of a variety of fish-eating mammals, has been implicated as a potential pathogen of wolves. It was found in one of 98 wolves from Alberta (Holmes and Podesta 1968) and seven of 211 wolves from Saskatchewan (Wobeser et al. 1983). In Saskatchewan, five of seven cases were from a population of wolves known to consume fish. No pathologic change was seen in the wolf from Alberta; how-

ever, thickened nodules or cord-like swellings (greatly dilated bile ducts) were seen throughout the liver of infected wolves from Saskatchewan; and in two cases, infections also were associated with extensive damage to the pancreas. Wobeser et al. (1983) concluded that damage to the pancreas could affect endocrine or exocrine function but could not determine whether health of infected wolves was impaired. Population regulatory effects of this fluke are not known, but, if they occur, would be restricted to local populations that consume fish.

Hydatid tapeworm

Although the hydatid tapeworm, *Echinococcus granulosus*, does not directly cause mortality in wolf populations, Messier et al. (1989) considered it an integral part of the moose-wolf population dynamics in southwestern Quebec. These authors documented a direct relation between prevalence of hydatid cysts in moose, density of wolves, and rate of wolf predation on moose. They proposed the following regulatory mechanism: as density of wolves increases, sites used extensively by wolves are contaminated with large numbers of *E. granulosus* eggs in wolf feces. The prevalence and intensity

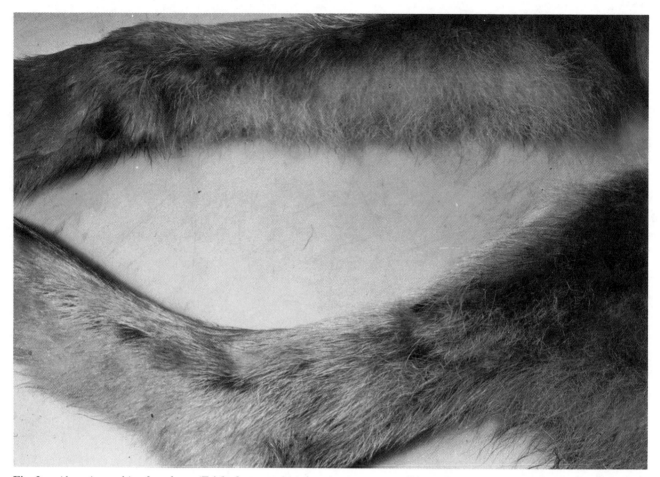

Fig. 3. *Alopecia resulting from louse (**Trichodectes canis**) infestation in a gray wolf from Minnesota. Photo by J. Runningen.*

of hydatid cysts increase in moose populations using these areas. Since most cysts occur in pulmonary tissue (Sweatman 1952, Addison et al. 1979), moose with large numbers of cysts are to likely suffer decreased stamina (Cowan 1951, Mech 1966a, Rau and Caron 1979) and increased physical impairment (Messier et al. 1989). Heavily infected moose may display behavioral changes detected by wolves (Mech 1970) and be selected as prey. Thus, the parasite enhances the regulatory effect of wolf predation on moose (Messier and Crete 1985) and affects wolf population dynamics through increased prey susceptibility.

Ectoparasites

There are few reports of ectoparasites on gray wolves. Fleas (*Pulex simulans, Ctenocephalides canis*) (Skuratowicz 1981, Hristovski and Beliceska 1982), ticks (*Amblyomma americanum, A. maculatum, Dermacentor albipictus, D. variabilis, Ixodes* spp.) (Pence and Custer 1981, Archer et al. 1986), and deer fly (*Lipoptena cervi*) (Itamies 1979) occur, but infestations appear rare. The major ectoparasites on wolves are lice and mites.

Lice

The dog louse (*Trichodectes canis*) has been reported recently on free-ranging gray wolves throughout most of their range in North America. Infestations on dogs in North America are common and likely are the source of initial infestations in wild canids. Lice are transmitted by direct contact between infested and uninfested individuals. They transfer readily from females to pups.

Louse infestations on wolves involve varying degrees of alopecia (hair loss) (Fig. 3). Guard hairs often are missing or broken and underfur is matted (Schwartz et al. 1983, Mech et al. 1985). The matting of the fur tends to distinguish louse infestations from sarcoptic mange (see below). Damage to the hair is self-inflicted and reflects attempts to remove the lice by biting, chewing, and scratching. Damage is most often seen on the shoulders and groin; but, in severely affected wolves, only the head, legs, and tail remain undamaged. In addition, a "mousy" smell often is associated with infested wolves. Pups appear to be affected more frequently and severely than adults.

There is little evidence that *T. canis* directly affects the dynamics of wolf populations (Schwartz et al. 1983, Mech et al. 1985). Adult wolves with severe alopecia and secon-

Fig. 4.   *Sarcoptic mange in a gray wolf from Alberta. Photo by J.R. Gunson.*

dary inflammation and bacterial infections were reportedly in good body condition. Severe infestations may contribute to reduced survival of individual pups (Schwartz et al. 1983), but this has not been confirmed (Mech et al. 1985).

In 1981 and 1982, *T. canis* was reported in five of 20 wolf packs on the Kenai Peninsula, Alaska. Wildlife managers were concerned that lice would spread to other packs in Alaska and northern Canada. Thus, federal and state officials treated infested wolves with ivermectin administered by intramuscular injection or in treated baits (Taylor and Spraker 1983). The intensive treatment program continued for two to three years. Currently, the dog louse occurs on wolves throughout the Kenai Peninsula, but has not been reported elsewhere in Alaska (R.L. Zarnke and T. Spraker, Alaska Dept. of Fish and Game, pers. commun.).

Mites (mange)

Sarcoptic mange is the most conspicuous and probably most significant ectoparasite of wolves. The mite, *Sarcoptes scabei*, is distributed worldwide, exhibits little host specificity, and transfers readily among a variety of host species (Sweatman 1971). In North America, it is common on red foxes but also occurs on coyotes and wolves throughout their range.

There is a long history of mange or "mange-like" conditions in free-ranging canids in North America. Pike (1892:53) concluded that a disease resembling mange was responsible for the death of numerous hairless wolves throughout northern regions. As early as 1909, sarcoptic mange was introduced into Montana on large numbers of experimentally infested coyotes and wolves in an attempt to control free-ranging canids (Knowles 1909:130, 1914:229-230). This experiment may have been the source of mange on wild canids in western Canada (Green 1951). Currently, mange is enzootic in western Canada, and its effects on pup survival may be significant in cyclic population fluctuations in wolves throughout the region (Todd et al. 1981).

Sarcoptic mites cause extensive irritation and damage as they burrow into skin and tunnel within the epidermis. The life cycle is short and new generations of mites can appear every 14 days (Sweatman 1971). Mites are transferred to new hosts by direct contact with infested animals or by using rubbing posts contaminated with mites.

Wolves with mange usually have severe hair loss with relatively little exudate or crusting (Fig. 4). Severe infestations often involve extensive alopecia, crusted lesions, and thickened, slate-gray skin over much of the body. Heavily infested wolves can have lower weight and fat deposits than uninfested animals (Todd et al. 1981). Loss of condition is more marked in pups than in adults. Behavioral changes relating to food habits have been documented in infested coyotes (Todd et al. 1981). Similar behavior of infested wolves was suspected but not verified.

Based largely on circumstantial evidence, several researchers believe mange is an important regulating factor in wild canid populations (Pike 1892:53, Murie 1944, Cowan 1951, Green 1951, Todd et al. 1981). During a 10-year period in Alberta, mange was present each year, but the prevalence differed annually and locally. The number of cases increased when wolf densities increased, and the number of surviving pups decreased as the prevalence of mange increased (Todd et al. 1981).

Discussion

Diseases and parasites must affect reproduction, mortality, immigration, or emigration (dispersal) to be important in population dynamics of wolves. Effects need not result in death, but can include sublethal effects on physiological and homeostatic processes, thriftiness, reproduction, and behavior, which in turn can affect wolf population dynamics.

Assessing direct and indirect influences of diseases on wolf populations is difficult for a variety of reasons:

1) Wolves may die directly from disease or parasites, but the probability of locating carcasses is remote unless individual survival is monitored intensively (e.g., by radiotelemetry). Scavenging, decomposition, and freezing can render carcasses and tissues unsuitable for necropsy, histopathology, and supporting diagnostic tests.

2) Important population processes such as fetal and neonatal survival are difficult or impossible to monitor in free-ranging wolves.

3) Sublethal effects of disease are extremely difficult to diagnose and document in wild populations. Clinical or pathological evidence that a disease is contributing or predisposing to another cause of death is rarely available and, if available, is usually speculative.

4) Multiple infectious and parasitic agents are frequently found at necropsy. Evaluating the significance of multiple agents and their additive and synergistic effects is difficult and often speculative. For example, Appel (1988) reported that dogs suffered high mortality from dual infections of CPV-2 and canine corona virus even though neither virus by itself was highly virulent.

5) Contributing factors, such as food shortage leading to nutritional stress, may combine with disease factors to increase the significance of otherwise innocuous or sublethal infections.

6) Interpretation of disease prevalence in a population based on serological data can be misleading because seropositive animals represent only survivors of exposure rather than incidence or prevalence of disease.

7) Experimental studies of diseases in captive and free-ranging wolves employing adequate controls are lacking.

8) Long-term studies of wolf populations are few, yet these will probably provide the most important data by which population processes are elucidated.

9) Where population density alone is estimated on an annual basis, increased reproductive success may compensate for high mortality rates, hiding important demographic responses to disease. For instance, annual mortality rates of > 35% were required to measurably reduce wolf density (Gasaway et al. 1983, Keith 1983, Peterson et al. 1984, Ballard et al. 1987, Fuller 1989). Otherwise, increased reproduction or reduced dispersal may compensate for increased mortality.

Direct and circumstantial field evidence and extrapolation from studies in captive wolves and other canids suggest that diseases and parasites affect population dynamics through direct and indirect means. Mortality of wolves in the wild has been documented for rabies, canine distemper, parvovirus, blastomycosis, tuberculosis, and mange; in some instances, epizootics were associated with population declines (Davis et al. 1980, Carbyn 1982b, W.B. Ballard, unpubl. data, R.O. Peterson, unpubl. data). Other parasites and diseases such as canine heartworm, hookworm, and infectious canine hepatitis that can be fatal to other canids are also present in wild wolf populations, but there is little or no evidence that these diseases directly cause mortality or affect gray wolf populations.

Circumstantial evidence further suggests that sublethal infections of some parasites and diseases also affect wolf populations. Infections that can debilitate or alter behavior in other canids (Lyme disease, oral papillomatosis, sarcoptic mange) may have similar effects in wolves, but extrapolation between species and between captive and wild conditions should be made with caution. Likewise, inferences from other canids on potential effects on reproduction from diseases such as brucellosis and Lyme disease also require caution.

Despite the evidence of parasites and diseases affecting some wolf populations, the role of disease in limiting wolf populations remains unknown. In other canid populations, relations between population density and some diseases such as sarcoptic mange (Todd et al. 1981), rabies (Debbie 1991, Fekadu 1991), and canine distemper (Trainer and Knowlton 1968) have been suggested.

Management Considerations

Management of the wolf in North America has relied traditionally on information from research and monitoring of population size and structure, predation and diets, social organization and structure, home ranges and movements, recruitment, and mortality rates. The influence of diseases on these population characteristics has not been fully recognized by some agencies, yet limited information summarized here suggests that disease may be an important factor in some cases. Knowledge of diseases in a population and how they influence wolf populations may be important to management, whether they are enzootic (e.g., canine distemper virus, infectious canine hepatitis) or sporadically introduced from other sources (dog louse, rabies, CPV-2). The role of the wolf as reservoir or host of some diseases may also have important implications for public health and the health of domestic animals and other wildlife.

Man's impact on the environment may play a role in the composition of diseases in wolves and their effects on wolf populations. For example, increased contact between domestic pets and livestock may result in the establishment of diseases not present or not important in historic times, such as CPV-2. Fragmentation of wolf habitat may result in more isolated wolf populations that may be more severely affected by new or existing diseases, particularly in areas of reintroduction into former wolf range.

Current efforts to reintroduce the wolf to its former range will be successful only if individuals survive and reproduce. Disease potential in areas of reintroduction should be one of the many considerations in planning such programs (Johnson this volume). The presence and risk of diseases that can be transmitted to wolves at relocation sites, particularly from other wild canids and domestic and feral dogs should be evaluated; special attention should be paid to diseases that are not present in the originating wolf population. Prophylaxis (prevention) for certain diseases has been recom-

mended for individual relocated wolves, including vaccination for rabies, canine distemper, CPV-2, leptospirosis, and ICH, and those diseases of which we know little in wolves (influenza, parainfluenza, and corona virus [Albert et al. 1987]). However, there are little data on the efficacy or safety of domestic animal vaccines in wildlife (Fowler 1978). Although some vaccinations may provide at least some degree of protection, little is known about the duration of protection for standard canine vaccines in wolves, and progeny would not be protected beyond the duration of maternal antibody. Modified live vaccines (MLV) have been generally proven to be more effective than killed vaccines. Although captive wolves are frequently vaccinated with MLVs, these vaccines can produce active disease, particularly in species for which the vaccine was not developed (Fowler 1978).

Diseases should also be considered in selecting areas for wolves to be captured for relocation. Introduction of diseases from originating populations to the release site could jeopardize other wildlife and domestic animals and the success of the reintroduction. Health assessment for wolves to be reintroduced should include testing for specific parasites and diseases, and appropriate treatment and prophylaxis (Albert et al. 1987).

Acknowledgments

We thank P.R. Krausman, T.K. Fuller, and J.C. Franson for critical review of this manuscript.

Christopher J. Brand, Margo J. Pybus, Warren B. Ballard, and Rolf O. Peterson

Rabies In Wolves and Its Potential Role In a Yellowstone Wolf Population

■ Mark R. Johnson

Worldwide, rabies vectors are predominantly dogs and foxes. The wolf is a vector in regions of the Mediterranean and Soviet republics. In the United States (U.S.) and Canada, primary vectors are skunk, fox, or raccoon, while other species receive infection as "spillover." Distinct strains of terrestrial rabies have developed for each primary host. The spread of rabies is influenced by ecological factors such as host biology and distribution, and species susceptibility. Wolves in North America are not primary vectors, infected wolves are relatively rare, and no confirmed cases in wild wolves have occurred in the lower 48 states. Rabies has not been reported in Yellowstone National Park. In states surrounding the Greater Yellowstone Area, skunks are the principal vector and a skunk rabies outbreak is unlikely to extend into Yellowstone National Park, where skunks are rare. Geographic distribution, distribution among species, and ecological factors influencing rabies spread, suggest the addition of the wolf to the greater Yellowstone area is unlikely to contribute additional risks associated with rabies to humans, domestic animals, or wildlife.

Introduction

Wolves (*Canis lupus*) and rabies are often discussed together — at times, due to the fact that rabid wolves have threatened or killed humans (Baltazard and Bahmanyar 1955) and at other times due to man's imagination and misconceptions. With the possibility of having wolves either reintroduced into Yellowstone National Park and its surrounding area or naturally established by immigration from Montana or Idaho, there is a need to: 1) examine the potential for wolves to carry and transmit rabies; 2) assess potential risks to people, domestic animals, and wildlife; and 3) evaluate rabies as a potential mortality factor in a recolonizing Yellowstone wolf population. To assess these potential roles, I have reviewed rabies epizootiology, distribution among species, geographic distribution, and influence on wolf populations.

History

Rabies in wolves was of significant concern in early Europe (Sikes 1970, Lopez 1978, Lawrence 1986), although it is difficult to assess the actual prevalence of rabid wolves and the degree of impact on European man and domestic livestock. In the 18th century, some accounts report more than 100 human deaths in a single year (Rutter and Pimlott 1968, Mech 1970). Other accounts describe far fewer occurrences (Lopez 1978). Historians and researchers generally agree

that rabid wolves were the primary cause for wolf attacks on humans in Europe in the 17th and 18th centuries. These historians and researchers also agree that rabid wolves have been significantly more abundant in Europe than in North America (Rutter and Pimlott 1968, Mech 1970, Sikes 1970, Lopez 1978, Beran 1981, Lawrence 1986).

In the U.S., rabies was predominantly a disease of domestic animals prior to the late 1950's, with dogs as the primary carriers. Since the late 1950's, when laws were established requiring canine vaccinations and control of stray dogs (*Canis familiaris*), the number of reported rabies cases has decreased in domestic dogs, cats, horses, cattle, and humans, while the number of reported rabies cases in wildlife has increased (Fig. 1) (Centers for Disease Control (CDC) 1985, Reid-Sanden et al. 1990). This increase in wildlife rabies reports might be due the public's increased attention to wildlife rabies rather than an increase in the actual number of infected wild animals (McLean 1970a).

An example of what rabies distribution among species in the U.S. might have been prior to control is provided by recent trends in Mexico. In 1984, domestic animals comprised 95%, and wild animals 4%, of positive rabies cases (Fig. 2); of the domestic animals with rabies, 94% were dogs (Fig. 3) (CDC 1985). Dogs also comprised 94% of Mexican domestic animals with rabies in 1989 (Reid-Sanden et al. 1990) and 1990 (Uhaa et al. 1992). Recent trends in Canada are similar to those in the U.S. with decreasing occurrence

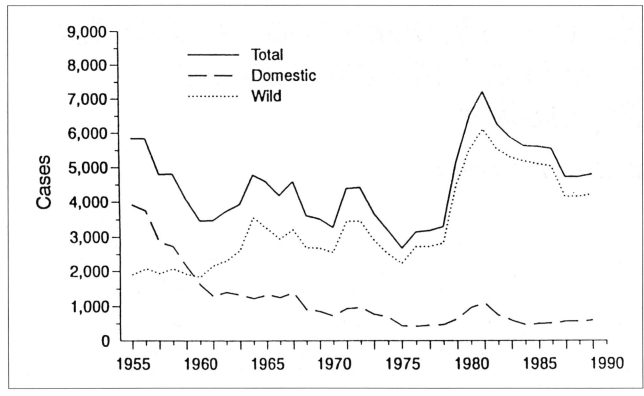

Fig. 1. *Rabies cases diagnosed in animals in the United States from 1955 to 1989 (Reid-Sanden et at. 1990).*

in domestic animals and humans, and increasing occurrence in wildlife (CDC 1985). Canada also maintains rabies control programs utilizing animal vaccinations, stray dog control programs, and population control of rabies carriers, such as skunks (*Mephitis mephitis*) (Pybus 1988).

The Virus and Infection

Rabies is a viral disease caused by a member of the group Rhabdoviridae that infects all warm-blooded animals (Ettinger 1983). Rabies virus is highly specialized to infect, migrate, and multiply within nerve cells of peripheral nerves, the spinal cord, and brain. Transmission usually occurs through bite wounds from infected animals. Virus must be present in the saliva for transmission to occur by biting. Human exposure also has occurred through contact with saliva from handLing of rabid animals by veterinary students, professionals, and owners of domestic animals (Smith and Baer 1988), and by trappers (MacInnes 1987, Ritter 1991). On rare occasions, rabies has been passed to humans by aerosol transmission in bat caves or by corneal transplant from an infected human donor (Baer 1991).

Once entering the body, viral particles multiply within local muscle tissue (Beran 1981) and then develop an affinity for nerve cells. Virus multiplication may then progress slowly along peripheral nerves to the spinal cord, brain, and into salivary glands. At times, rabies infections that have

progressed to the brain and spinal cord may cause death before the virus is present in the salivary glands. Incubation periods average from two to 12 weeks, but may be as short as 10 days and as long as six months or more (Sikes 1970). These periods vary dramatically due to factors including individual and species variation, number of virus particles received, and location of wound. Due to the variability of signs that may be exhibited by rabid animals, rabies can be easily mistaken for other diseases such as distemper, choke, encephalitis, and toxicosis.

For accurate diagnosis, most laboratories use fluorescent antibody tests of brain tissues and inoculation of fresh brain extracts into test animals or tissue cultures. Some labs use more recently developed immunocytochemical assays, which can test formalin-fixed tissues. Histological examination for Negri bodies may also support a diagnosis of rabies.

Disease Ecology

Worldwide, the domestic dog is the most important vector or primary host of rabies. The arctic fox (*Alopex lagopus*) is a circumpolar primary host. The red fox (*Vulpes vulpes*) and domestic dog are the primary hosts in central and western Europe. Although the wolf is considered a major rabies vector in eastern Mediterranean regions and in some republics of the former Soviet Union (Cherkasskiy, 1988, World Health

United States

The United States and its territories reported 5,630 cases of rabies to the CDC in 1984, down 4% from the 5,881 cases reported for the previous year. This includes rabies in wild animals, domestic and farm animals, and humans.

Reported Cases

Wild Animals	5,174
Domestic & Farm Animals	453
Humans	3
TOTAL	5,630

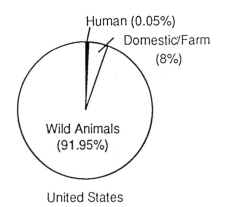

Canada

Canada reported 1,699 cases of rabies in 1984, down 25% from the 2,252 reported cases in 1983. As in the United States, wild animals accounted for the majority of all cases. The only human who died from rabies was a Canadian priest who was bitten by a rabid dog while in the Dominican Republic.

Reported Cases

Wild Animals	1,365
Domestic and Farm Animals	333
Humans	1
TOTAL	1,699

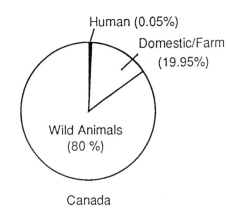

Mexico

Mexico reported 10,346 cases of rabies in 1984, a marked increase over the 3,487 cases reported in 1983. Unlike the United States and Canada, where wild animals were the principal hosts of the disease, the greatest number of reported cases were in domestic and farm animals.

Reported Cases

Wild Animals	431
Domestic and Farm Animals	9,857
Humans	58
TOTAL	10,346

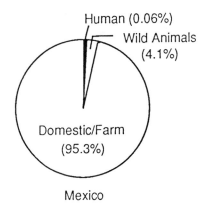

Fig. 2.   *Rabies in North America in 1984, CDC 1985.*

United States

In the United States, there was a 22% decrease in rabies in domestic and farm animals, from 584 reported in 1983 to 453 in 1984. Cattle continued to be the predominant animal infected, followed by cats, which in turn, outnumbered dogs for the fourth consecutive year.

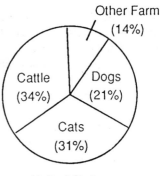

Canada

Canada reported 333 cases of rabid domestic and farm animals in 1984 compared with 559 in 1983, a 40% reduction. As in the United States, cattle accounted for the majority of cases, with cats the second most frequently diagnosed rabid domestic animal. The province of Ontario accounted for 89% of all reported rabid domestic and farm animals in Canada in 1984.

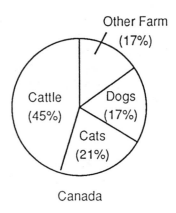

Mexico

Mexico reported a marked increase in the number of reported rabid dogs in 1984 (9,274) compared with 1983 (3,176). This large increase accounted for most of the overall increase in reported rabies for all types of animals in Mexico in 1984.

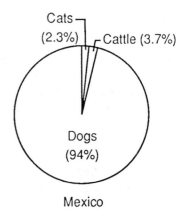

Fig. 3. *Rabies in domestic animals in North America in 1984, CDC 1985.*

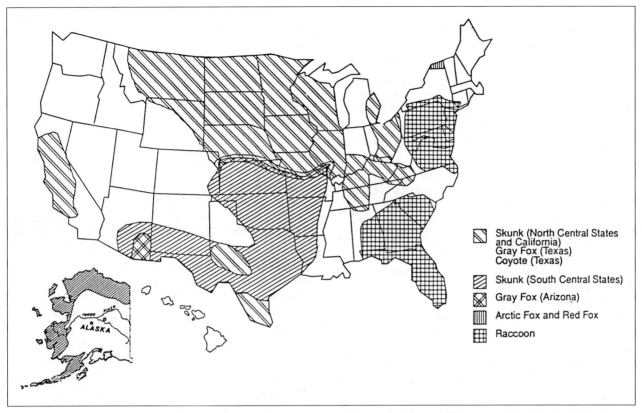

Fig. 4. *Distribution of five antigenically distinct rabies virus strains and the predominant wildlife species affected in the United States during 1991. (Krebs et al. 1992).*

Organization 1990), the Mediterranean wolf is becoming less significant as a rabies vector as wolves are extirpated. In the former Soviet Union, the red fox and domestic dogs are primary hosts. In some former republics, the wolf and raccoon dog (*Nyctereutes procyonoides*) are considered vectors of less significance than the fox and domestic dog (World Health Organization 1990). A 1988 rabies outbreak in Finland possibly originated from wolves migrating from the former Soviet Union (Nyberg et al. 1992).

Rabies occurs in two basic forms, based on epizootiology: bat rabies and terrestrial rabies. The relationship between bat rabies and terrestrial rabies is unknown. Bat rabies has been identified in most Canadian provinces and in every state except Alaska and Hawaii (Reid-Sanden et al. 1990). Although bat rabies can produce occasional exposure to humans and animals, terrestrial rabies poses the greater risk of exposure to humans, domestic animals, and wildlife (Smith and Baer 1988).

In North America, there are at least five distinct strains of terrestrial rabies. Each strain is specialized for a particular host, such as skunk, fox, or raccoon (*Procyon lotor*). Each strain can be distinguished from the others with laboratory techniques using monoclonal antibodies (multiple copies of a specific protein) (Smith et al. 1984, 1986, Smith 1988, Smith and Baer 1988).

Associated with each of these five strains are five outbreaks of rabies currently occurring in the U.S. and Canada (Fig. 4). Two outbreaks involving skunks, and distinguishable using monoclonal antibodies, occur in north-central states, south-central Canada and California, and in south-central states, respectively. Raccoon rabies is occurring in northeastern and southeastern states. Arctic fox rabies is present in Alaska, Northwest Territories, and southeastern Canada where it has spread into red fox. Gray fox (*Urocyon cinereoargenteus*) rabies is located in a small area of Arizona (Fig. 4) (Reid-Sanden et al. 1990, Krebs et al. 1992). Each outbreak is limited geographically (Fig. 4) and has one principal host accounting for 50–90% of the rabies cases. All other infected animals (with the exception of bats) within the outbreak receive the disease as "spillover" or incidental exposure from infections spreading among the principal host, as is verified with monoclonal antibodies. In 1991, skunks, raccoons, bats, and foxes collectively comprised 97% of wildlife rabies and 88% of all animal rabies in the U.S. (Krebs et al. 1992), which demonstrates how primary hosts comprise the majority of rabies cases. The biology and habits of the primary host influence the spread of rabies. Skunks are sedentary animals with small home ranges and minimal migration or dispersal. Such behavior produces slow movement of the disease (Pybus 1988). Geological features such as cliffs, mountains, and wide summer streams appear to be significant barriers to skunks and thus affect the directions of movement in an outbreak (Pybus 1988). Where skunks are the primary host, rabies infections predominantly pass from skunk to skunk and outbreaks progress among areas of high skunk densities. This suggests that rabies is limited to the habitat of the primary host. In Wyoming, a skunk rabies epizootic is currently occurring in the state and partially extends into Montana. The path of this outbreak is progressing along the lower, drier elevations (such as Big-horn County) where skunk densities are high and it appears to be circumventing the Greater Yellowstone Area (K. Mills, Wyoming State Veterinary Laboratory, Laramie, Wyoming, pers. commun.) where skunk densities are low (Park Wild-life Observation File, Yellowstone National Park, unpubl. data). This rabies outbreak is not likely to extend into Yel-lowstone National Park or the surrounding national forests where skunks are rare.

The distribution of rabies in Alaska also demonstrates how rabies can be limited to the habitat of the primary host. In that state, rabies is limited to western and northern areas and is rare in the interior, relating to the distribution of red and arctic foxes (Fig. 4). Even though wolves are present throughout most of Alaska, they become infected with rabies primarily from foxes and therefore rabies in Alaskan wolves is limited to areas cohabitated by red and arctic foxes (Alaska State Rabies Certification Program, Fairbanks, Alaska, un-publ. data).

Another major factor significantly affecting the spread and natural control of rabies in wildlife is the difference in susceptibility among species. In experiments with skunks and foxes, foxes were 100 times more susceptible than skunks to infection from virus isolated from a fox salivary gland (Sikes 1962, Parker and Wilsnack 1966). These re-searchers also demonstrated that foxes given lethal doses of virus were less likely to have virus in saliva before death than foxes infected with smaller amounts of virus. Skunks in-fected with rabies virus were more likely than foxes to have infectious saliva and generally excreted more virus in their saliva than foxes. Although rabid foxes can excrete enough virus in saliva to infect other foxes, only a small percentage of infected foxes could excrete enough virus to infect skunks. Conversely, in areas of skunk rabies, foxes may occasionally be infected with rabies, but the large amounts of virus excreted by skunks are likely to kill an infected fox before virus is excreted in the saliva (Smith and Baer 1988). These differences in susceptibility to rabies between skunks and foxes appear to limit outbreaks in foxes in areas of skunk rabies and limit outbreaks in skunks in areas of fox rabies.

In addition to differences in susceptibility, varying clini-cal signs of infected foxes and skunks may be due to differ-ences in the pathogenicity (the ability to produce disease) among virus strains (Baer 1991); disease produced by strains in their respective primary host species may be most "suit-able" to spreading rabies, while the disease produced in other

species may be either too mild or lethal to allow these "unsuitable" host species to be carriers of the strain (Baer 1991).

Comparison among Several States

Table 1 demonstrates the distribution of reported rabies cases among domestic and wild animals from diagnostic laboratories representing states within the Greater Yellow-stone Area (Idaho, Montana, Wyoming) and in states with substantial wolf populations (Alaska and Minnesota). Cases reported from diagnostic laboratories are limited to animals that people have encountered and therefore may not repre-sent the actual prevalence of rabies in wild populations. These encounters are not necessarily aggressive acts upon humans, but involve trappers, biologists, and recreationists finding sick or dead animals. Nonetheless, the annual rabies reports from each state demonstrate consistent trends in distribution of rabies among wildlife species and provide an accurate means of comparing the epizootiology of rabies among various states. Idaho essentially has no terrestrial rabies. All wildlife cases have been in bats. The only domestic animal having rabies was a domestic cat that was infected with a bat strain of rabies in 1990. In Montana, Wyoming, and Minnesota, the skunk strain of rabies is enzootic, with skunks comprising over 50% of rabies cases (Table 1); few foxes or raccoons have been infected. In Alaska, where the fox strain of rabies is enzootic, red and arctic foxes are the most common species infected with rabies, comprising 92% of reported rabies cases (Table 1).

Rabies has never been reported in Yellowstone National Park. In 39 years of nature notes (1920-58), there are no references to rabies (N. Bishop, Yellowstone National Park, Wyoming, pers. commun.). Also, in the past 30 years, any animals (except for rodents and birds) that have bitten people in the park have been tested for rabies; all tests have been negative (M. Meagher, Yellowstone National Park, Wyo-ming, pers. commun.).

Influences on Wolf Populations

In the U.S. and Canada, few wolves are reported with rabies. Of 61,036 laboratory-confirmed cases in wildlife in the U.S. from 1981 to 1991, only 16 (0.03%) were wolves: three captive wolves in North Dakota in 1981, one captive wolf in Minnesota in 1987 (see Table 1), and 12 wild wolves from Alaska over this 10-year period (CDC 1983, CDC 1984, CDC 1985, CDC 1986, CDC 1987, CDC 1988, CDC 1989, Reid-Sanden et al. 1990, Krebs et al. 1992, Uhaa et al. 1992). In Canada, 70 (4%) wolves of 18,308 wildlife cases were confirmed with rabies from 1982 to 92 (Animal Health Division, Agriculture Canada, Ottawa, unpubl. data).

One reason that wolves are rarely reported with rabies may be that diagnostic reports are limited to animals encoun-tered by humans. In remote areas of Alaska and Canada, rabies in wolves may be reported sporadically because of

Table 1. Confirmed rabies cases reported in Alaska, Minnesota, Montana, Wyoming, and Idaho from 1986 to 1990. (Sources: R. Moulton, Idaho Department of Health and Welfare, Boise, Idaho, pers. commun.; James 1990; Minnesota Veterinary Diagnostic Laboratory Annual Reports 1986-90; D. Ritter, Alaska Division of Public Health, Fairbanks, Alaska, unpubl.; Wyoming State Veterinary Laboratory Annual Reports 1986-90.)

Species	Alaska (fox)[1]	Minnesota (skunk)	Montana (skunk)	Wyoming (skunk)	Idaho (bat)	Total
Badger			2			2
Bat		28	67	90	27	212
Bobcat		1				1
Cat		57	19	7	1	84
Cattle		91	65	9		165
Coyote				1		1
Dog	9	48	6	6		69
Fox (arctic)	65					65
Fox (red)	87	5	1			93
Goat		2				2
Horse		15	13	4		32
Pig			3			3
Prairie Dog				1		1
Raccoon		2	8			10
Sheep			1			1
Skunk		287	864	438		1,589
Wolf	3	1[2]				1
Total	164	536	1,050	556	28	2,331

1 Predominant rabies strain within each state.
2 Captive wolf.

---

low human densities, except where wolf radiotelemetry studies are conducted.

Another reason wolves are rarely reported with rabies is that wolves are not primary hosts of this disease (Stephenson et al. 1982). Since wolves are infected as "spillover" from primary hosts, such as the red and arctic fox, relatively low numbers of infected wolves can be expected.

In Minnesota, where the skunk strain of rabies is enzootic, no free-ranging wolves from an estimated population of 1,700 wolves (Fuller et al. 1992a) have been reported with rabies. However, it appears that Minnesota wolves are rarely exposed, since only six skunks (3%) of 190 confirmed with rabies in 1988 and 1989 (Minnesota Department of Health, 1988 and 1989, rabies surveillance data, unpublished) were from counties within the 1988–89 estimated wolf range in Minnesota (Fuller et al. 1992a).

The influence of rabies on wolf populations is not fully understood. Murie (1944) and Cowan (1949) suggested that rabies might be a limiting factor in wolf populations. Chapman (1978a) observed a wolf pack fighting among themselves and three to four weeks later located six dead pack members. Two dead wolves were intact enough to be examined and were diagnosed positive for rabies. Most reported infections in wolves in Alaska and Canada occur during epizootics in arctic and red foxes (Chapman 1978a, Baer 1991).

In 1984, the U.S. Fish and Wildlife Service initiated a study of wolves in the Arctic National Wildlife Refuge in Alaska. The following year, nine radio-collared wolves were found dead. Five wolves were diagnosed with rabies, and four were too decomposed to be tested (Ritter 1991). In Algonquin Provincial Park, Ontario, wolves have been found dead and either diagnosed with rabies or identified with sticks lodged in their mouths suggesting that rabies was the cause of death (Forbes and Theberge this volume).

The clinical signs of wolves infected with rabies appear to vary considerably. In Europe and Asia, rabid wolves have demonstrated aggressive behavior. In Iran, a rabid wolf reportedly attacked 29 people, three cows, and a horse before it was killed (Baltazard and Bahmanyar 1955). In North America, the clinical signs of rabies in wolves have not been adequately documented. Infected wolves may attack wolves or other animals (Ballantyne and O'Donoghue 1954, Chapman 1978a, Mech 1970, Rausch 1958, Tabel et al. 1974) or humans (Ritter 1991).

In North Dakota, where the skunk strain is enzootic, one of a group of five captive wolves stopped eating, became weak and wobbly, had seizures, and was euthanized four days after illness began. Postmortem laboratory results revealed rabies infection. The remaining wolves were euthanized and two additional wolves were diagnosed with rabies (Univ. North Dakota, Veterinary Diagnostic Laboratory, unpubl. data). In Minnesota, two captive wolves were apparently exposed by a rabid skunk entering their pen. One wolf had been previously vaccinated for rabies. The owners suspected the skunk was rabid and subsequently observed the two wolves. Six to eight weeks later, the unvaccinated wolf began showing signs of listlessness, drooling, and weakness and eventually stopped eating and drinking and died. The vaccinated wolf survived and did not develop clinical signs (wolf owner, Cannon Falls, Minnesota, pers. commun.). In Algonquin Provincial Park, Ontario, wolves found dead with sticks lodged in their mouths and confirmed with rabies (Forbes and Theberge this volume) suggest that infected wolves may attack trees, shrubs, or other inanimate objects. All rabies strains identified from Ontario have been fox strain. Although the few incidents where wolves were likely to have been infected with a skunk strain of rabies have demonstrated nonaggressive forms of this disease, it is not known if clinical signs of rabid wolves infected with a skunk strain of rabies are typically different from those infected with a fox strain.

In North America, reports of human exposure to rabies from wolves are rare. In 1833, a white wolf suspected of being rabid was reported to attack people in two separate camps, four miles apart, on the upper Green River in western Wyoming. Most of those bitten (mountain men, traders, and Indians) died (DeVoto 1947). Alaska has had three confirmed human deaths from rabies, two by rabid wolves. One human in Alaska died from a rabid sled dog. In 1942, an Eskimo hunter was severely bitten by a wolf near Noorvik, Alaska, and died from rabies (Ritter 1991). In 1943, an Eskimo boy died from rabies after being mauled by a wolf while collecting ice for drinking water near Wainwright, Alaska (Ritter 1991). In Canada, nine wild wolves were tested for potentially exposing humans to rabies from 1978–84. These exposures were not necessarily aggressive attacks.

Two of the nine wolves were diagnosed positive for rabies. No human deaths occurred from these exposures (Prins and Yates 1986).

In the lower 48 states, the only confirmed human rabies exposure from wolves occurred from a captive wolf, which died of rabies in central Minnesota (Table 1). In this incident, the owner was exposed by cutting himself while skinning the dead wolf. Post-exposure treatment was given to the owner with no sickness occurring (wolf owner, Cannon Falls, Minnesota, pers. commun.).

Discussion and Recommendations

Literature review, data from rabies surveillance programs, and personal communications with contributors demonstrate that currently, in North America, wolves infrequently become infected with rabies and do not play a significant role in the spread of this disease. In addition, the patterns of terrestrial rabies epizootiology demonstrate that the spread of this disease is limited by the biology and habitat of its primary host. Therefore, it is unlikely that a skunk rabies outbreak would extend into Yellowstone Park; and the addition of the wolf to the Greater Yellowstone Area is unlikely to contribute additional risks associated with rabies to humans, domestic animals, or wildlife.

The clinical signs of rabies in gray wolves have not been adequately described. Because a single rabies strain can potentially produce different clinical signs in different species (Baer 1991), it is important for biologists and veterinarians to identify strains infecting wolves, especially if they are from areas where multiple strains are suspected. Identification of these strains also will contribute to our understanding of rabies epizootiology and its relationship to wolves and other wildlife.

Regardless of whether wolves are reestablished, it is prudent to remain attentive to any potential rabies cases in Yellowstone National Park. The following recommendations are for monitoring rabies prevalence in and around the Greater Yellowstone Area and to maximize efforts for rabies prevention:

1) Continue testing any animals involved in a biting animal/human encounter.
2) Identify strain using monoclonal antibodies for any positive rabies cases.
3) Monitor Montana, Wyoming, and Idaho state diagnostic laboratory annual reports for positive rabies cases, identifying species infected, county, location, and rabies strain, if tested.
4) Continue to require all park personnel keeping dogs and cats within the park to maintain current rabies vaccinations for their pets and follow all "leash law" policies.
5) Continue policy requiring all pets owned by visitors to be restrained and prohibited from backcountry trails.
6) Address the issue of rabies in possible wolf reintroduction by:

a. Determining if rabies is enzootic in the region where wolves will be collected for reintroduction and by identifying rabies strain and prevalence.

b. Evaluating the safety and efficacy of rabies vaccines in gray wolves and vaccinate reintroduced wolves if a safe and effective rabies vaccine is deemed available.

Acknowledgments

Livestock and public health agencies from Alaska, Idaho, Minnesota, Montana, Wyoming, and Ontario generously provided rabies reports. G. Baer and staff members of the rabies laboratory for CDC were extremely helpful with national reports, figures, and perspectives. Wildlife perspectives in the spread of rabies were generously provided by E. Follmann, University of Alaska; C. MacInnes, Ontario Ministry of Natural Resources; K. Mills, Wyoming Veterinary Diagnostic Laboratory; M. Pybus, Alberta Fish and Wildlife Division; and J. Theberge and G. Forbes, University of Waterloo. D. Ritter, Alaska Division of Public Health and R. Zarnke, Alaska Fish and Game Department were especially helpful in their critical reviews of this paper.

Exposure of Wolves to Canine Parvovirus and Distemper on the Kenai National Wildlife Refuge, Kenai Peninsula, Alaska, 1976–1988

■ **Theodore N. Bailey, Edward E. Bangs, and Rolf O. Peterson**

We tested 55 serum samples from 50 wolves and four from coyotes, live-captured on the Kenai National Wildlife Refuge, Kenai Peninsula, Alaska, between 1976 and 1988, for exposure to canine parvovirus (CPV) and canine distemper virus (CDV). Exposure to CPV was first detected in wolves in December 1979 and increased to a high of 67% of wolves sampled between 1983 and 1984. Exposure to CDV was first detected in wolves in June 1979 and varied from 0% to 67% throughout the testing period. Twelve percent of the sampled wolves had been exposed to both viruses. More males than females had been exposed to CPV; more adults/yearlings than pups had been exposed to CDV. Wolves that had been exposed to both CPV and CDV had significantly lower hemoglobin levels. The effects of CPV on wolf pup survival were unknown. Only one of four tested coyotes had been exposed to CPV and none to CDV. Numerous domestic dogs adjacent to the refuge are a continual source of both diseases.

Introduction

Canine parvovirus (CPV) was first recognized and became an important disease among domestic dogs (*Canis familiaris*) in 1978 (Parrish et al. 1985); there was a worldwide epizootic in 1981 (Yang 1987). Serum antibodies to CPV were first reported in wolves (*C. lupus*) in Alaska in 1980 (Zarnke and Ballard 1987). Prevalence of CPV exposure in wolves from the Nelchina Basin in mainland Alaska was 31% (n = 32) between 1975 and 1982, but no mortality among adult wolves was attributed to the disease (Zarnke and Ballard 1987).

The first wolf mortality attributed to canine distemper virus (CDV) in Alaska was a yearling male from the Kenai National Wildlife Refuge (KNWR) found dead on 13 September 1978 (Peterson et al. 1984). An adult female wolf from the same pack was found dead on 15 January 1980 and also diagnosed with CDV. Exposure to CDV among 57 wolves tested throughout mainland Alaska was 7% (Stephenson et al. 1982) and 12% among 12 wolves tested from the Nelchina Basin in mainland Alaska between 1975 and 1982 (Zarnke and Ballard 1987).

Because there was no information on the prevalence of CPV and CDV exposure among wolves and coyotes (*C. l.*

latrans) on the Kenai Peninsula, which is almost detached from mainland Alaska, we tested blood samples taken from 50 wolves and four coyotes captured between 1976 and 1988.

Study Area

Wolves and coyotes were live-captured on the KNWR, an area of 7,970 km^2 on the western Kenai Peninsula (KP) in south-central Alaska (Fig. 1). Topography, climate, and vegetation on the KNWR have been previously described (Peterson et al. 1984). Most (85%) serum samples from wolves and all sera from coyotes were collected on the KNWR north of the Kenai River. Eight serum samples were from wolves from the central portion of the KNWR south of the Kenai River and north of the Kasilof River. Most wolf packs, with some exceptions during the latter part of the study period, used territories previously named and described by Peterson et al. (1984); pack names, in parenthesis, are used here for reference.

Size of wolf packs averaged 15.3 during 1976–1977, but declined to 8.0–8.6 by 1981–82 due to increasing human harvest (Peterson et al. 1984). Population density ranged from 11.4–19.5 wolves/1,000 km^2. In the early 1980's,

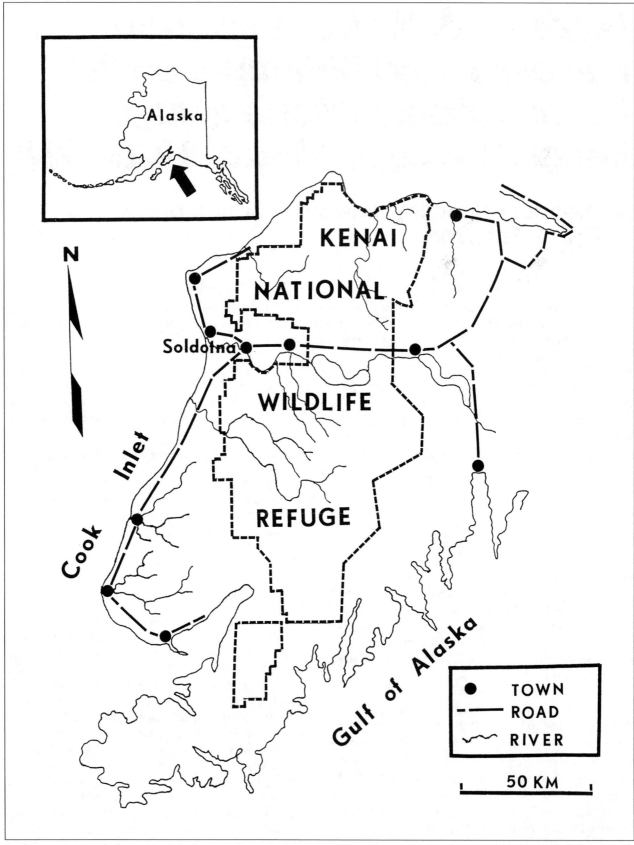

Fig. 1. *Kenai Peninsula and location of the Kenai National Wildlife Refuge.*
Upper left inset shows location of Kenai Peninsula in Alaska.

wolves on the KNWR became infested with biting dog lice (*Trichodectes canis*) (Schwartz et al. 1983).

Methods

Wolves were live-trapped from May through October with leg-hold traps, and captured from November through April by means of tranquilizer darts fired from helicopters (Peterson et al. 1984). Coyotes were incidentally captured while trapping for wolves. Both species were weighed and a 1–3 cc sample of whole blood was taken. Packed-cell volume (PCV) values were obtained by centrifuging heparinized whole blood samples in capillary tubes 75 mm long by 0.56 mm in a Clay Adams Readacrit centrifuge. Hemoglobin values were recorded with a Clay Adams Hemoglobinometer.

Fifty-five blood serum samples from 50 individual wolves were tested for exposure to CPV and CDV from 1976 to 1988. Tested wolves were associated with at least nine recognized packs that used the KNWR in 1981 (Peterson et al. 1984). Five wolves were tested twice at approximately seven-, eight-, 12-, 15- and 36-month intervals and four coyotes once between 1976 and 1988.

Sera were aspirated from centrifuged whole blood samples and frozen. Serological tests for evidence of antibodies to CPV using the technique described by Carmichael et al. (1980) were performed at the National Wildlife Health Research Center, Madison, Wisconsin. Sera with titers greater than or equal to 1:320 were considered to be positive evidence of exposure to CPV (or a virus which cross reacts with it).

To test for CDV, sera were diluted 1:5 in Hank's balanced salt solution (BSS) and heat inactivated at 56°C for 30 minutes. Serial twofold dilutions of each serum (1:5 to 1:640) were prepared using Hank's BSS in 96 well plates at 0.05 ml/well. A 0.05 ml solution of reference CDV diluted in Hank's BSS containing 50 infectious units/0.05 ml was added to each serum dilution and incubated 30 minutes at 37°C. African green monkey (*Cercopithecus aethiops*) kidney cells (0.15 ml) were added to each well and the well incubated at 37°C in 2% carbon dioxide for a total of seven days. Test wells were read for vial cytopathic effect every other day for seven days. The titer of each serum was expressed as the last dilution that completely neutralizes the cytopathic effect of CDV. Any titers greater than or equal to 1:5 were considered to be evidence of exposure to CDV. The tests included the following controls: 1) a tissue culture infectious dosage ($TCID_{50}$) of the reference virus stock; 2) a serum control for each serum tested; 3) a cell culture control; and 4) a positive and negative serum control. Sex, age, weight, and blood condition parameters (hemoglobin and packed-cell-volume) from unexposed and exposed wolves were tested for statistical significance (p<0.050) using Yates corrected-for-continuity, 2X2 contingency table G-tests and t-tests, respectively (Zar 1984).

Results

Exposure to CPV was not detected among seven wolves that were tested from five separate packs (one pack sampled twice) between 1976 and 1978, or among 12 wolves that were tested from six packs in 1979 (Table 1). The first detection was in an adult female captured 12 December 1979; another adult female and a male pup captured the same day in the same pack (Killey River Pack) tested negative. By 1987, CPV exposure was detected in sera of wolves in six of nine known packs. However, only one wolf per pack was sampled from two of the three packs that tested negative. Wolves from the Skilak Lake Pack were the only wolves to consistently test negative to CPV exposure between 1976 and 1988. With the exception of wolves from the Killey River Pack, once CPV exposure was detected in a wolf in a pack, wolves captured subsequently from the same pack usually tested positive for CPV exposure.

Once detected, exposure of wolves to CPV rapidly increased from 22% during the early period of the study (1979 to 1981) to 67% during the later period (1986 to 1988) (Table 1). Forty-four percent of all wolves sampled between 1979 and 1988 (n = 48) tested positive to CPV exposure. Only one of the four coyotes tested had been exposed to CPV, an adult male captured 1 October 1980 near the Swanson River Oilfield. It had a high CPV titer (1:1,280), but appeared to be in good physical condition. Exposure of wolves to CDV between 1976 and 1988 was first detected in an adult female captured 6 June 1979 (Big Indian Creek Pack). No wolves tested prior to 1979 were positive, but in 1979, six of 15 wolves (40%) tested positive (Table 1). Annual prevalence of exposure to CDV among wolves varied considerably between 1976 and 1988. In 1980, three of six wolves tested positive, but in 1984, all tested wolves (n = 11) were negative. In 1988, only two wolves were tested but from the same pack (Point Possession Pack); both tested negative. Exposure to CDV was detected among wolves from three of seven wolf packs tested in 1979, but in only one of three packs tested in 1980. All three lone wolves tested between 1976 and 1988 tested positive to CDV exposure (one also tested positive to CPV exposure). All four coyotes tested negative to CDV exposure.

Sex and age differences were detected among wolves testing positive or negative for exposure to CPV and CDV (Table 2). Exposure of wolves to CPV was significantly (P<0.050) related to sex; a greater percentage of males (42%) than females (34%) tested positive. Exposure of wolves to CDV was significantly (P<0.050) related to age; more adults and yearlings (65%) tested positive than pups (5%).

There was no significant differences in mean PCV values or body weight among wolves that tested positive and negative to exposure to CPV and CDV. However, significantly (P<0.050) higher hemoglobin values were found among wolves that tested negative to exposure to

Table 1. Wolf sera and wolf packs tested for canine parvovirus (CPV) and canine distemper virus (CDV) (positive tests/total tested), Kenai National WildLife Refuge, Alaska, 1976-1988.

YEAR	WOLF SERA			WOLF PACKS	
	CPV	*CDV*	*CPV & CDV*	*CPV*	*CDV*
1976	0/1	0/1	0/1	0/1	0/1
1977	0/4	0/4	0/4	0/3	0/3
1978	0/2	0/2	0/2	0/2	0/2
1979	1/15	6/15	0/15	1/7	4/7
1980	1/6	2/6	1/6	2/3	2/3
1981	1/2	0/2	1/2	1/1	1/1
1983	0/1	0/1	0/1	0/1	0/1
1984	8/11	0/11	0/11	3/4	0/4
1986	1/5	1/5	1/5	2/3	1/3
1987	1/6	1/6	3/6	3/4	3/4
1988	2/2	0/2	0/2	1/1	0/1
Total	**15/55**	**10/55**	**6/55**	-	-

both viruses compared to wolves that tested positive to exposure to both viruses.

Four wolves were retested at seven- to 36-month intervals. Only one wolf, an adult female (Killey River Pack), tested negative for exposure to both viruses each time. Another adult female wolf from the same pack that tested negative to CPV and CDV exposure 11 December 1979 tested positive to exposure to both viruses 2 March 1981. A yearling female (Bear Lake Pack) and a yearling male (Elephant Lake Pack) that had been exposed to CPV when first captured also tested positive to CPV eight and 36 months later, respectively. The yearling male also tested positive to CDV exposure when retested.

An adult male wolf (Elephant Lake Pack) captured 22 June 1986 had the highest measured CPV titer (1:1,280), the lowest recorded PCV value (25.4), and hemoglobin value (11.2). He was blind in the right eye and his pelage had changed from the typical brownish-gray color to almost white compared to his condition on 8 February 1983. At that time, the CPV and hemoglobin values were higher (37 and 17, respectively). He was eventually shot by a hunter at relatively close range near a moose carcass 29 April 1987 despite the fact that most wolves on the KNWR generally avoid humans and are difficult to approach on the ground.

Discussion and Management Implications

We suspect that CPV and a parasite (biting dog lice) were transmitted by domestic dogs into the wolf and coyote population on the KNWR. There was an outbreak of CPV in 1980 among domestic dogs in and near the town of Soldotna, less than 1 km from the KNWR boundary (B. Richards, Richard's Veterinary Clinic, Soldotna, pers. commun.). This followed a similar CPV outbreak among dogs in the Anchorage area. Free-roaming dogs are abundant along the western KNWR boundary. Trappers on and off the refuge report periodically capturing dogs in snares or traps set for wolves and coyotes. Some trappers use dog teams on the refuge to run their traplines,. Between 1989 and 1991, about 500–600 dogs were impounded and approximately 300 were destroyed annually in Soldotna (D. Baxter, Animal Control Officer, Soldotna, pers. commun.). Some years during the early- to mid-1980's, up to 1,000 dogs were impounded annually in Soldotna. We received periodic reports from the public during this period of lone wolves observed near domestic dogs. Radio-collared lone wolves have also been located in or near developed areas inhabited by dogs adjacent to the KNWR. Once CPV or CDV was established among wolf packs, dispersing wolves could have spread both viruses to other packs. All three lone wolves tested had been exposed to CDV and one had been exposed to CPV. The CPV virus has been known to persist in dog feces at room

Table 2. Sexes and ages of wolves testing positive for exposure to canine parvovirus (CPV) and canine distemper virus (CDV) (positive tests/total tested) on the Kenai National WildLife Refuge, Alaska, 1976-1988.

		Serological test results — Exposed to:		
SEX	AGE	CPV	CDV	CPV & CDV
Male	adult	2/9	0/9	0/9
	yearling	1/5	1/5	3/5
	pup	5/11	1/11	0/11
	unknown	0/1	0/1	0/1
Female	adult	1/11	4/11	2/11
	yearling	1/8	4/8	1/8
	pup	5/7	0/7	0/7
	unknown	0/3	0/3	0/3
Total		**15/55**	**10/55**	**6/55**

temperature for at least six months and perhaps longer (Pollock 1982, Komolafe 1985).

As did the wolves we sampled, male dogs also appear to have a higher prevalence of exposure to CPV than females (Zupancik et al. 1987). Continual or periodic exposure to CPV was documented among individual wolves for periods of five to 38 months. Because the virus may persist in scats of dogs for up to six months at room temperature (Pollack 1982, Komolafe 1985), investigation by scent-marking wolves of wolf scats containing the virus may periodically expose them to the CPV.

Adult wolves on the KNWR appeared more susceptible to CDV exposure than juveniles. Two wolves, sequentially tested, developed antibodies to CDV after they were at least one year old. Blood serum from an adult wolf later found dead on 15 January 1980 and diagnosed with CDV (Peterson et al. 1984), tested negative for the antibody when captured 68 days earlier.

The effects of CPV and CDV on wolf pup survival on the KNWR was unknown because young pups were not tested. Morbidity and mortality from CPV in dogs were highest in three- to four-month-old pups (Hirasawa et al. 1987). Because the same pattern might be expected to occur among wolf pups (Carbyn 1982b), close monitoring of pups would be necessary to document direct CPV-induced mortality. All wolves tested in this study were at least six months old when tested, and thus were survivors of any early litter mortality.

Carbyn (1982b) believed that diseases, particularly CDV, may have played an important role in reducing the population density of wolves in Riding Mountain National Park,

Manitoba, Canada. The KNWR and Riding Mountain National Park wolf populations have some common characteristics. Both are located in areas that are relatively small, isolated from other wolf habitat, and have boundaries where contact between wolves and dogs is common. Immigration and emigration are limited, and human harvest has been a major cause of mortality.

The prevalence of CPV exposure among wolves tested on the KNWR was greater than that previously reported among wolves elsewhere in Alaska (Zarnke and Ballard 1987) or in Minnesota (Mech et al. 1986). Prevalence of CDV exposure was also higher among wolves on the KNWR compared to wolves tested elsewhere in Alaska. Exposure of a wolf to CPV was first detected on the KNWR slightly earlier than reported for wolves elsewhere in Alaska (Zarnke and Ballard 1987).

Immigration of wolves cannot be relied upon to help balance any population losses or genetic susceptibility to disease on the KP because it is nearly isolated from mainland Alaska. At least four radio-collared wolves dispersed from the KP to mainland Alaska over the past 14 years. None of several hundred wolves radio-collared outside the KP by various agencies over the same period have been reported on the KP.

As human development expands into areas adjacent to the KNWR once used by wolves and coyotes, and as human and dog use of the refuge increases, opportunities for the transmission of disease and parasites from dogs to wolves and coyotes on the refuge will continue.

Theodore N. Bailey, Edward E. Bangs, and Rolf O. Peterson

Acknowledgments

We thank T.J. Roffe, J.C. Franson, and D. Doherty of the U.S. Fish and Wildlife Service, National Wildlife Health Research Center, Madison, Wisconsin for supporting and conducting the serology studies. We acknowledge the support of all KNWR managers and other staff members from 1976 to 1988 and the many KNWR and Student Conservation Association volunteers who helped capture wolves. J.D. Woolington collected serum samples between 1976 and 1980 and Alaska Department of Fish and Game personnel, especially T.H. Spraker and C.C. Schwartz, helped in many winter wolf captures. Kenai Air helicopter pilots V.L. and C.R. Lofstedt provided excellent and safe flying support during winter capture operations. Veterinarian B.L. Richards provided technical assistance and advice throughout the latter part of the study period.

Serum Chemistry Values for Captive Mexican Wolves

■ Marlene D. Drag

Although serum chemistry values for the gray wolf have been determined, there is no published information for serum chemistry values for the rare Mexican wolf subspecies. I determined mean serum chemistry values from blood samples collected from captive juvenile and adult Mexican wolves restrained with nets. Mean serum glucose (120 mg/dL) for 10 adult females was greater than the reference interval for domestic dogs. Mean serum urea nitrogen (26 mg/dL) for 10 males was slightly greater than for dogs. All other mean values were within reference intervals for domestic dogs, although values from individuals did fall above or below the range of normality. Wolf pups between ages seven and 24 weeks had age-related increases in serum urea nitrogen, total protein, albumin, and globulin, and decreases in alkaline phosphatase, phosphorus, and lactic dehydrogenase. Mean glucose ranged from 120 mg/dL to 134 mg/dL. Similar changes have been reported in domestic dog pups. The data indicate that reference intervals established for domestic dogs may be used to evaluate serum values from Mexican wolves. However, laboratory results and knowledge of how the sample was collected must be correlated with clinical signs to determine the physiologic state of the animal.

Introduction

Northern Mexico, Arizona, and New Mexico were once the range of a subspecies of gray wolf (*Canis lupus*) now known as the Mexican wolf (*C. l. baileyi*) (Nelson and Goldman 1929). In 1982, fewer than 30 wolves were estimated to live wild in Mexico and a Mexican wolf has not been sighted in the United States in more than 20 years (U. S. Fish and Wildlife Service 1982). The 50 Mexican wolves in captivity are on the United States endangered species list. The Wild Canid Survival and Research Center, Tyson Research Center, Eureka, Missouri houses 13 individuals. Captive propagation of the species is expected to result in an increase in the number of wolves so that reintroduction into the wild will be possible (Parsons and Nicholopoulos this volume). The future of the Mexican wolf is strictly dependent on the wellbeing of the captive population.

Although serum chemistry values of the gray wolf have been determined (Seal et al. 1975, Seal and Mech 1983), there is no published information of the serum chemistry values of the Mexican subspecies. Reference values are important to evaluate disease and nutritional states of the animal as well as its overall health. The objectives of this study were to determine mean serum reference values for captive adult Mexican wolves and document changes that occur as the animals mature. These standard values could then serve as a guide when evaluating the disease and nutritional states of other wolves of the Mexican subspecies.

Materials and Methods

Housing consisted of 0.20 to 0.65 hectare outdoor enclosures surrounded by chain link fencing. Dry dog food[1], pretreated with heartworm preventive medication[2], and water were provided *ad libitum*.

Blood samples were obtained between 1985 and 1991 during any procedures prescribed by the Mexican Wolf Captive Management Committee that required handling of an animal. Thirty-eight samples were obtained from 10 male wolves and 23 samples from 10 females, all more than 24 weeks of age. The sera for determination of values at age seven, 11, and 16 weeks were obtained from two pups from the same litter. A third sample from an 11-week-old pup of a different litter was also acquired. Reference values obtained at 24 weeks were from nine pups from four litters. Wolves (> 24 weeks of age) were captured with nets and restrained with v-shaped poles; blood was obtained by cephalic or saphenous venipuncture. Wolves (age seven, 11, 16, and 24 weeks) were captured with nets and restrained by hand for blood collection from a jugular vein. Blood was

Table 1. Reference serum values of Mexican wolves more than 24 weeks of age.

| | Females Wolves (10)[1] | | Males Wolves (10) | | Dog[2] |
	Mean	Range	Mean	Range	Range
Glucose (mg/dL)	120	55-193	111	41-255	70-115
Serum urea nitrogen (mg/dL)	21	10-36	26	11-60	10-25
Creatinine (mg/dL)	1.0	0.4-1.8	1.1	0.5-24	1.0-2.0
Cholestrol (mg/dL)	113	77-160	106	55-145	90-280
Total bilirubin (mg/dL)	0.3	0.1-1.2	0.3	0.1-0.8	0.0-0.8
Total protein (g/dL)	6.6	4.5-7.8	7.0	5.7-8.6	5.2-7.9
Albumin (g/dL)	3.2	2.3-4.1	3.5	2.8-4.6	2.3-3.8
Globulin (g/dL)	3.3	1.9-4.6	3.3	1.0-4.7	1.8-5.2
Alkaline phosphatase (U/L)	35	10-113	32	14-57	10-400
Aspartate aminotransferase (U/L)	58	29-124	68	24-436	5-100
Alanine aminotransferase (U/L)	45	20-129	53	23-282	1-150
Lactic dehydrogenase (U/L)	220	55-524	244	103-708	10-400
Creatine phosphokinase (U/L)	324	100-691	298	69-770	10-400
Amylase (U/dL)	311	116-473	282	119-683	0-3000
Lipase (U/L)	132	80-424	178	75-996	0-1000
Calcium (mg/dL)	9.4	8.1-11.0	9.6	7.4-10.5	7.1-12.5
Phosphorus (mg/dL)	3.4	1.7-10.1	3.9	1.0-7.3	3.0-6.0
Sodium (mEq/L)	152	144-169	152	146-165	140-155
Potassium (mEq/L)	4.8	4.1-6.6	5.1	4.0-6.4	4.3-5.5
Chloride (mEq/L)	116	110-129	115	107-126	104-116

1 = sample size
2 = Southwest Veterinary Diagnostics, Inc.

collected using 20-gauge, 1-inch needles and 12-ml plastic syringes. Blood was placed into evacuated tubes (SST, 4-ml)[3] and allowed to clot for 30 minutes. Samples were centrifuged for five minutes at 4,750 rpm and the sera removed and refrigerated. Commercial laboratory analyses[4] of the samples were obtained within 24 hours of collection.

Serum samples were analyzed for glucose, urea nitrogen, creatinine, cholesterol, total bilirubin, total protein, albumin, globulin, alkaline phosphatase, aspartate aminotransferase, alanine aminotransferase, lactic dehydrogenase, creatine phosphokinase, amylase, lipase, calcium, phosphorus, sodium, potassium, and chloride. Mean serum values were calculated for each parameter and compared to reference intervals established by the laboratory for normal domestic dogs. The reference intervals established by the

laboratory are reflective of values that have been previously published (Duncan and Prasse 1977, Hoskins 1990:206–209, Lane and Robinson 1970, Lawler 1989) and encompass all breeds and ages of dogs.

Results

All serum values for wolves more than 24 weeks of age, with the exception of glucose and urea nitrogen, were within established adult canine reference intervals (Table 1). The mean glucose of 120 milligram/deciliter (mg/dL) for female wolves and the mean serum urea nitrogen of 26 mg/dL for male wolves were slightly greater than the established reference intervals. Individual values for total serum protein, albumin, globulin, urea nitrogen, total bilirubin, glucose,

Table 2. Reference serum values of Mexican wolf pups.

	Weeks of Age			
	7 (2)[1]	*11 (3)*	*16 (2)*	*24 (9)*
Glucose (mg/dL)	120	134	133	128
Serum urea nitrogen (mg/dL)	12	8.0	16	20
Creatinine (mg/dL)	0.6	0.6	0.6	0.8
Cholestrol (mg/dL)	149	119	127	170
Total bilirubin (mg/dL)	0.2	0.1	0.2	0.2
Total protein (g/dL)	4.0	4.5	4.6	5.6
Albumin (g/dL)	2.4	2.7	2.5	3.2
Globulin (g/dL)	1.7	1.8	2.1	2.4
Alkaline phosphatase (U/L)	329	295	160	164
Aspartate aminotransferase (U/L)	59	45	31	47
Alanine aminotransferase (U/L)	27	38	18	46
Lactic dehydrogenase (U/L)	568	391	216	206
Creatine phosphokinase (U/L)	380	345	—	388
Amylase (U/dL)	343	263	—	212
Lipase (U/L)	305	309	—	198
Calcium (mg/dL)	10.5	10.9	9.8	10.2
Phosphorus (mg/dL)	9.9	8.4	6.6	6.5
Sodium (mEq/L)	143	149	148	151
Potassium (mEq/L)	6.7	5.9	4.9	5.6
Chloride (mEq/L)	111	109	109	112

1   = sample size
2   = Southwest Veterinary Diagnostics, Inc.

creatinine, cholesterol, aspartate aminotransferase, alanine aminotransferase, creatine phosphokinase, lactic dehydrogenase, sodium, phosphorus, potassium, and chloride were measured outside of reference intervals.

Mean total serum protein increased from 4.0 gram/deciliter (g/dL) in seven-week-old pups to 6.6 g/dL in females and 7.0 g/dL in males (more than 24 weeks of age) (Table 2). The increase in total protein was due to increased albumin and globulin levels.

Mean serum urea nitrogen increased with age and was higher for males than females (> 24 weeks of age). Mean serum alkaline phosphatase and serum phosphorus decreased with age. Mean serum phosphorus was highest in seven-week-old wolf pups (9.9 mg/dL) and declined with

age. Mean serum glucose was higher in all ages of pups than in animals more than 24 weeks of age. Mean serum lactic dehydrogenase was highest in wolf pups at seven weeks of age, decreased at 24 weeks, and increased slightly in older animals. The remaining serum chemistry levels did not show age-related changes.

Discussion

Mean serum total protein of Mexican wolf pups (age 24 weeks) was similar to the value of 5.5 g/dL reported by Seal et al. (1975) in wild-caught gray wolf pups. Serum total protein in 24-week-old domestic dogs (*C. familiaris*) ranged from a mean of 6.4 g/dL in beagles (Bulgin et al. 1970), to

5.8 g/dL in other breeds (Lawler 1989). Serum total protein can be lowered by malnutrition, parasitism, hemorrhage, renal disease, liver disease, or immune dysfunction. Serum total protein can be increased by dehydration, chronic infection, and inflammation.

Although mean serum total protein of Mexican wolf pups was slightly lower than reference values in dog pups, they did show the expected age-related increase. The protein increase was due to increasing albumin and globulin levels, similar to changes reported in domestic dog pups (Lawler 1989). Serum albumin increased with growth, probably as a result of increased protein intake. The increase in globulin values was associated with increased gamma globulin production, likely due to antigenic exposure (Hoskins 1990: 206–209).

Increased protein intake was also reflected by increased serum urea nitrogen in maturing Mexican wolf pups. Serum urea nitrogen (20 mg/dL) in captive Mexican wolves at 24 weeks of age was comparable to values from wild-caught Minnesota wolves at the same age (21 mg/dL) (Seal et al. 1975). Bulgin et al. (1970) and Lawler (1989) reported reference values of 14 mg/dL and 15 mg/dL, respectively, for dog pups of the same age. Seal et al. (1975) hypothesized that a diet of animal flesh contributed to the higher serum urea nitrogen in the wild pups; however, this would not account for a similar trend in the captive population of Mexican wolf pups fed a commercial dog food. In addition to the amount of protein in the diet, time of food consumption in relation to time of sample collection influences serum urea nitrogen. Serum urea nitrogen can remain elevated for five to six hours after a meal (Bressani and Braham 1977).

The serum urea nitrogen values were higher in male Mexican wolves more than 24 weeks of age than in females. A similar finding was reported in dogs (Lane and Robinson 1970). In captive wolves (Seal and Mech 1983), males had higher serum urea nitrogen concentrations than females only during the winter. The writers attributed the difference also to a higher average food intake by males. Although increased serum urea nitrogen could suggest dietary differences in all ages of Mexican wolves, other physiologic changes must also be considered. Hydration status and primary renal or postrenal disease can also increase serum urea nitrogen (Duncan and Prasse 1977). Renal failure usually elevates serum urea nitrogen and creatinine; however, this was not believed to be a factor in this study. It seems, therefore, that serum urea nitrogen values in male wolves may run higher in clinically normal animals.

Young domestic dogs have serum alkaline phosphatase levels two to three times greater than those of adult dogs (Hoskins 1990:206–209), which reflects osteoblast activity in growing animals. Smith and Rongstad (1980) documented a similar response in wild coyotes (C. latrans); alkaline phosphatase decreased progressively up to eight months of age. Alkaline phosphatase in Mexican wolf pups was higher than in dog pups (Lawler 1989), but the values

from wolves more than 24 weeks of age were similar to those from adult dogs. One must realize, however, that normal bone growth in larger breed dogs and wolves may not be completed before two years of age. Therefore, a slightly higher alkaline phosphatase value in a wolf before the age of two years is strongly suggestive of continuing bone growth.

Alkaline phosphatase isoenzymes are also released from the placenta, kidney, intestines, and liver (Duncan and Prasse 1977). Increased alkaline phosphatase, especially in older animals, has been shown to reflect liver disease, stress, neoplasia, or pregnancy.

Higher mean serum phosphorus in Mexican wolf pups was similar to dog pups (Lawler, 1989). Higher phosphorus levels occur in young animals because of metabolic processes involved in bone formation (Duncan and Prasse 1977). Phosphorus levels in wild Minnesota wolf pups (6.5 mg/dL) (Seal et al. 1975) and captive Mexican wolf pups were the same. Similar values in the captive and wild populations indicate that, although wild gray wolves have a higher intake of animal flesh (calcium to phosphorus ratio of 1:20 in muscle meat), the higher serum phosphorus level is not solely related to dietary factors. The elevated phosphorus values in young animals are probably due to normal physiologic mechanisms of bone development. Lower values measured in adults may result from physiologic maturity, decreased dietary phosphorus, renal disease, heavy exercise, or hypothermia. No animal in this study exhibited clinical signs of disease.

Serum glucose in Mexican wolves may elevate as a result of capture, and is illustrated by the wide range of individual values found in all groups of wolves. Exercise, fright, and stress cause epinephrine release and an increase in blood glucose levels (Duncan and Prasse 1977). Similar elevations of glucose have also been reported in wild-caught Minnesota pups (Seal et al. 1975). Wild-caught adult coyotes had higher glucose levels than pen-raised coyotes (Smith and Rongstad 1980). The elevation in mean glucose in young and adult female wolves reflects the excited state and not disease. Lower glucose levels can result from severe exertion, as well as malnutrition or hepatic disease. The details of blood collection, therefore, must be known in order to accurately interpret results.

An isoenzyme of lactic dehydrogenase is found in skeletal muscle (Duncan and Prasse 1977). Lactic dehydrogenase in Mexican wolf pups was higher at all ages than reported for dog pups (Lawler 1989). An increase in lactic dehydrogenase can occur due to muscle stimulation induced during capture. Mean levels of lactic dehydrogenase in adult Mexican wolves were within the reference intervals for domestic dogs, however, some individual values were higher. As with glucose values, the method of capture should be known in order to evaluate lactic dehydrogenase values that fall outside the expected range of normality.

A variety of diseases and nondisease states influence serum biochemistry values (Lawler 1989, Duncan and Prasse 1977). However, it is not unusual for values from a single blood sample to fall outside of reference intervals in normal subjects. My results suggest that mean reference values for adult Mexican wolves fall within reference intervals established for adult domestic dogs. Growing Mexican wolf pups have values and patterns of change similar to those published for domestic dog pups, although an increase in sample size would help establish normal ranges. Reference intervals for domestic dogs can reasonably be used for interpretation of serum values from Mexican wolves, provided that knowledge of how and when the sample was collected is available.

Endnotes

1. Purina Hi Pro, Ralston Purina Co, St. Louis, Missouri.
2. Caricide Liquid, Shering-Plough Animal Health, Kenilworth, New Jersey.
3. Becton, Dickinson and Co, Rutherford, New Jersey.
4. Southwest Veterinary Diagnostics Inc., Phoenix, Arizona.

Part Eight:
Research Techniques

Comparison of Two Methods to Age Gray Wolf Teeth

■ **Warren B. Ballard, Gary M. Matson, and Paul R. Krausman**

We compared the Harris' Modified Hematoxylin stain (HMH) with the Giemsa Stain (GS) for aging wolf canine and first premolar teeth. Ages derived from canine teeth for the two stains were not significantly different ($\underline{P} = 1.00$). Premolar teeth stained with the HMH could not be accurately aged, but those stained with the GS provided ages that were not significantly different ($\underline{P} = 0.43$) from those provided by canines with the HMH. Based on our results, wolf premolars stained by the GS method and canine teeth stained with the HMH method appear to provide similar ages, suggesting that premolar teeth extracted from live wolves can be used to estimate age by the less expensive GS method. However, further evaluation with known-age specimens is needed.

Introduction

Obtaining accurate and precise age estimates of gray wolves (*Canis lupus*) has been difficult. Gray wolves have been aged by tooth wear and replacement (Van Ballenberghe et al. 1975, Fuller and Keith 1980, Fritts and Mech 1981, Ballard et al. 1987), examination of epiphyseal cartilage of long bones (Rausch 1967), counts of cementum annuli (Goodwin and Ballard 1985), and dentine width and root closure (Parker and Maxwell 1986). Tooth wear and replacement can be unreliable, particularly beyond the pup and yearling age classes, because factors other than age may cause wear variation. Also, aging by tooth wear is subjective and depends on the experience of the estimator. Examination of long bones allows wolves to be placed into pup or adult age classes, but with unknown accuracy and precision. Similarly, root closure and dentine width only allows identification of pup and yearling age classes.

Counts of cementum annuli from teeth that have been sectioned and stained provide the most accurate and precise estimates of ages for most wildlife species (Grue and Jensen 1979, Fancy 1980). This method was reported useful with wolves, based on known-age specimens, by Goodwin and Ballard (1985). They used the Harris' modified hematoxylin stain (Cable 1958) with hot bath (HMH). Although the method provided relatively accurate age estimates, it was only useful on canine teeth and thus was not practical for live wolves. E.A. Goodwin (Alaska Dept. Fish and Game, Anchorage) and W.B. Ballard (unpubl. data) attempted to stain first premolar teeth using the same method but could not

consistently identify cementum annuli. They concluded that further research was needed on the suitability of using incisors and premolars for aging wolves.

Since the late 1970's, biologists from Alaska, Northwest Territories, and Yukon Territory (G. Matson, Matson's Laboratory, Milltown, Mont., pers. commun.) have extracted premolar teeth from live wolves for determining age. The Giemsa stain (GS) (Schneider 1973, Stone et al. 1975) has been widely used (n = 2,481 wolves from Alaska and Canada [unpubl. data]) because teeth can be commercially processed at relatively low cost. However, the GS aging method has not been adequately evaluated with known-age specimens, nor has it been compared with other methods. Ideally the method should be tested with known-age specimens, but these are difficult to obtain. Goodwin and Ballard (1985) used known-age specimens for validation of the HMH method. We wanted to examine the GS staining method but lacked known-age specimens for adequate evaluation. Consequently, we compared the two staining and aging methods using many of the specimens aged by Goodwin and Ballard (1985). Because their method was developed based on known-age material, we assumed that the HMH ages using canine teeth were accurate and used them as baseline values.

Our objectives in this study were to: 1) compare estimated ages obtained from counting cementum annuli in wolf canine teeth using the HMH with hot bath to those obtained by staining with GS (Schneider 1973, Stone et al. 1975) using a standardized aging model (G.M. Matson, unpubl.

Warren B. Ballard, Gary M. Matson, and Paul R. Krausman

Table 1. Deviation of ages of wolf canine teeth using the Giemsa Stain method from those using the Harris' Modified Hematoxylin with hot bath (HMH).

	Deviation from HMH canine ages (years)		
HMH Ag	*-1*	*0*	*+1*
1		2	
2	1	2	1
3	2	4	1
4		1	3
5		1	
6	2		
7			
8	1		
9			
10			1
Totals	**6**	**10**	**6**

data); 2) test GS on premolar teeth from wolves aged by Goodwin and Ballard (1985) using HMH; 3) compare ages obtained between canine and premolar teeth using the GS method; and 4) provide a model for aging wolf canine and premolar teeth to standardize methods for aging gray wolves.

Methods

Procedures for cutting, staining, and estimating the age of wolf canine and premolar teeth using the HMH method were described by Goodwin and Ballard (1985); procedures used for the GS method were described by Schneider (1973), Stone et al. (1975), and Matson (1981). All specimens were obtained from wolves harvested in south-central Alaska. A wolf birthdate of 1 May (Ballard et al. 1991b) was used for aging purposes. Goodwin and Ballard (1985) determined canine cementum age by identifying the first well-developed dark annulus as the age indicator for two-year-olds. Their model was similar to that described by Linhart and Knowlton (1967) for aging coyote canines (*Canis latrans*). Matson (1981) determined both canine and premolar cementum ages based on a poorly defined but often present first annulus in one-year-old wolves. The latter model was similar to that described for coyote canines by Allen and Kohn (1976). Evidence from both wolf canine and first premolar tooth sections indicates the dark cementum annulus first becomes visible at the extreme periphery of canine and premolar teeth collected in March and April. The addition of one year to the

dark annulus count in teeth collected during late winter provides the age to the nearest full year.

Cementum ages of canine teeth previously aged by Goodwin and Ballard (1985) were compared with ages obtained with the GS method based on canines extracted from the same wolves. One or two first premolars were extracted from each wolf skull, stained and aged by the GS method, and then ages were compared with those obtained from the canines using the HMH and GS methods. Teeth that were severely altered in histology because of resorption, heat exposure, or breakage were excluded from analyses. Ages for different teeth from the same wolf were assigned without knowledge of prior results. Comparisons among tooth-stain methods were compared by Wilcox on matched pairs tests (Ott 1988).

Results and Discussion

Wolf ages estimated from canine teeth (n = 22) using the HMH and GS method were not significantly different ($\underline{Z}$ = 0.0, $\underline{P}$ = 1.00). All of the GS ages were within one year of the estimates provided by the HMH method (Table 1). Both methods of staining and annulus counting provided similar age estimates for canine teeth.

There were no significant differences ($\underline{Z}$ = 0.79, $\underline{P}$ = 0.43) between HMH canine ages and premolars stained by the GS method. Forty-eight percent of the GS ages (n = 67) were identical to the ages provided by the HMH method and 87% within ± 1 year of the HMH age (Table 2). There was a slight tendency for older animals (> 6 years) to

A

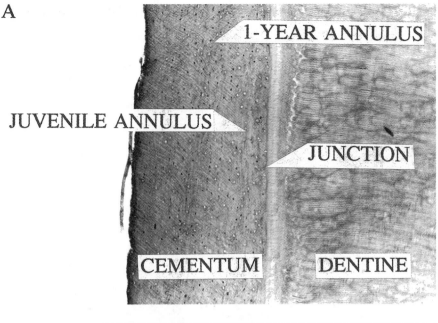

B

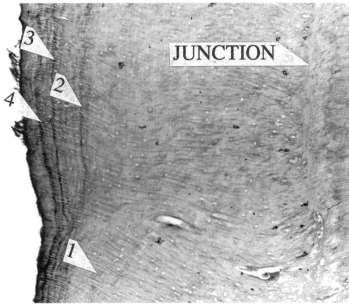

Fig. 1. *Wolf canine midsagittal sections. 60X. A. Wolf No. 122062. 5 mm above root tip. Known age = 22 months. Tooth collected on 21 March. B. Wolf No. 122179. 2 mm above root tip. 60X. Not known age. Cementum age = four years. Tooth collected on 31 December. A "juvenile annulus" (JA) may be formed before the age of one year. It is differentiated from the 1-year annulus by two characteristics: 1) it is present at the root tip, as the first identifiable annulus distal to the dentine, but is absent above the root tip; and 2) it is simple with only a single component and stains indistinctly. The one-year annulus is present both at the root tip and above it, and stains less distinctly than the two-year annulus. The first prominent annulus is the two-year annulus. Annuli formed during subsequent years are similar to the two-year annulus in staining intensity and characteristics. All annuli may be complex to varying degrees, having more than a single component. Light cementum is produced in successively narrower bands, with the greatest width occurring during the first summer and autumn of life. The dark annuli appears to be formed during winter, and first becomes visible in late March or April just before the assumed 1 May birthday. To determine the age of summer-autumn-winter-collected teeth each dark annulus is counted as one year. To determine the age of spring-collected teeth the last formed annulus is not counted as a year of age until after the assumed birthday of 1 May. Fractions of the year may be added to the annulus count according to the month of tooth collection.*

be underaged by 1–2 years with premolars. Age estimates from premolars using the GS method were significantly lower ($\underline{Z} = 1.98$, $\underline{P} = 0.048$) than GS canine ages (Table 3).

These differences suggest there are unidentified sources of error in the aging models of one or both tooth types. Canine teeth sections have thicker cementum layers than premolars, and greater separation between annuli permits the complex repeated annual patterns to be more easily identified. The illustrated description of the aging method for canines (Fig. 1) and premolars (Fig. 2) provides reference that helps insure consistency of annulus interpretation. The complete reference standard or "model" defines the criteria for annulus identification and identifies the season during which the annulus was formed.

Goodwin and Ballard's (1985) known-aged sample was largely composed of pup and yearling age classes (86% of 63 samples). Consequently both the HMH and the GS methods are in need of validation with a larger sample size of older wolf age classes. Based on our results, wolf premolars stained by the GS method and canine teeth stained with the HMH method appear to provide similar ages. Perhaps more importantly, premolar teeth can be extracted from live wolves and aged by the GS method.

Use of the GS method for aging canine and premolar wolf teeth has two distinct advantages over the HMH method described by Goodwin and Ballard (1985): 1) the GS method has been successfully used on premolar teeth; and 2) the GS method is considerably cheaper to use. The HMH method

Warren B. Ballard, Gary M. Matson, and Paul R. Krausman

Table 2. Deviation of wolf premolar teeth ages using Giemsa stain method from ages obtained from canine teeth using Harris' modified hematoxylin stain with hotbath (HMH).

HMH Age	Deviation from HMH canine ages (years)						
	-4	-3	-2	-1	0	+1	+2
1					4	3	
2				3	7	3	2
3			3	5	8	2	
4				1	8	4	1
5					4	1	
6			1	4	1		
7							
8	1		1				
Totals	**1**	**0**	**5**	**13**	**32**	**13**	**3**

Table 3. Deviations of wolf premolar teeth ages from canine teeth ages using Giesma Stain (GS) method.

GS Canine Age	Deviation from GS canine ages (years)						
	-3	-2	-1	0	+1	+2	+3
1				1			
2			1	3	1	1	
3			2	7			
4		1		2			
5		1	2	6	1		
6							
7	2		2				
Totals	**2**	**2**	**7**	**19**	**2**	**1**	**0**

was labor intensive (25 teeth processed per day) and currently cost approximately $10.55/tooth (E.A. Goodwin, unpubl. data). Because of the high costs and intensive labor, large numbers of teeth could not be processed on a routine basis. In contrast, the GS method currently costs about $2.85/tooth and commercial processing is available.

The tooth cementum method, though useful, is in need of more evaluation and refinement. The development of an accurate and precise method of cutting, staining, counting cementum annuli, and estimating ages of wolf teeth has been inadequately evaluated because of lack of standardization and an insufficient number of known-age samples from several age classes. There is a strong need for wolf biologists to pool their known-age specimens so that aging methods can be appropriately tested and refined. A number of questions remain concerning the deposition of annuli and their interpretation. Goodwin and Ballard (1985) estimated that the first annulus was deposited between 18 and 22 months of age in canine teeth, but the assessment was based on only four wolves. Using different criteria a "juvenile" annulus, formed before one year of age, and a one-year annulus can be identified in known-age teeth (Figs. 1 and 2). We need to

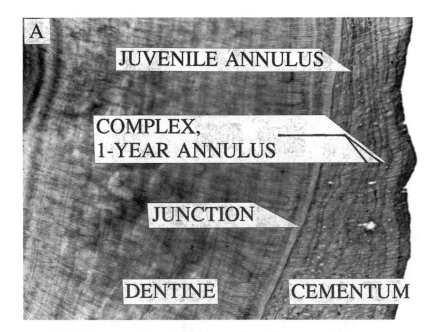

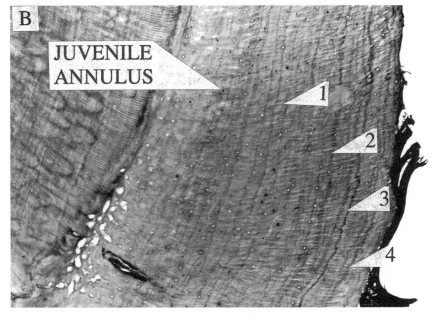

Fig. 2. *Wolf PM1 midsagittal sections. 60X. A. Wolf No. 122062. 2 mm above root tip. Known age = 22 months. Tooth collected on 21 March. B. Wolf No. 122179. 2 mm above root tip. 60X. Not known aged. Cementum age = 4 years. Tooth collected on 31 December. This aging model is similar to that for the canine tooth but the smaller size of the premolar compresses annuli closely together, making identification of annuli different. Complex annuli are sources of cementum aging error in canine and premolar teeth. There are two criteria for differentiating the complex annulus from its nonannual components: 1) the major annulus component is uniformly present at most points of the tooth section; and 2) complex annuli are uniformly spaced at regular but diminishing distances during successive years.*

determine if there are differences in the timing and extent of annulus deposition in different teeth and in wolves from different regions.

Use of the GS method for processing wolf premolar teeth has potential for estimating ages of free-ranging wolves but requires further testing with known-age specimens. Accuracy can be further improved by using only experienced personnel and a combination of root closure, examination of long bones, and tooth eruption and wear, along with the estimates provided by cementum annuli.

Acknowledgments

This study was funded by several Federal Aid in Wildlife Restoration Projects, the Alaska Department of Fish and Game, U.S. National Park Service, and University of Arizona. L. Aumiller, R. Forrest, C. Gardner, E. Goodwin, K. Klug, L. Metz, and J. Whitman assisted with processing specimens. S.A. Arnett, L.N. Carbyn, A.F. Cunning, S.H. Fritts, C. Shanks, R.O. Stephenson, and D. Thomas provided constructive criticism of early drafts.

Warren B. Ballard, Gary M. Matson, and Paul R. Krausman

Accuracy, Precision, and Performance of Satellite Telemetry for Monitoring Wolf Movements

■ Warren B. Ballard, Daniel J. Reed, Steven G. Fancy, and Paul R. Krausman

We placed 23 satellite platform transmitter terminals (1.08–1.22 kg) on wolves in northwest Alaska during 1987 through 1991. Male and female wolves aged 10 months to eight years were monitored with no apparent adverse effects on them. We obtained 3,801 relocations from the 23 transmitters, an average of 29 relocations/month from each. Transmitters were programmed to operate four to six hours every two days and had a mean life span (including days before and after use on a wolf) of 253 days (range = 67–482 days). Average life span while attached to wolves was 181 days (range = 50–366 days). Accuracy of 1,885 relocations at seven known sites varied among transmitters and averaged 336 and 728 m for best and low quality relocations, respectively. The estimated locations from several transmitters were biased toward south and west directions. Costs (1992) per satellite relocation averaged about $44 U.S., in comparison to about $166 with conventional telemetry methods using fixed-wing aircraft. Satellite telemetry has great potential for providing improved data sets for evaluation of wolf territory sizes and movements, but currently lacks accuracy and precision for detailed habitat or landscape use assessments.

Introduction

Satellite telemetry has become a widely accepted tool for studying movements of large mammals and birds (Fancy et al. 1988, 1989, Harris et al. 1990), particularly where logistics or movement patterns make conventional telemetry methods costly or impractical. The U.S. Fish and Wildlife Service and the Alaska Department of Fish and Game have cooperated since 1984 to develop, test, and refine the use of satellite telemetry for studying large ungulates and predators. Advances in transmitter miniaturization and power supplies have made satellite transmitters feasible for studies of smaller species such as wolves (*Canis lupus*). In early 1987, Telonics Inc. (Mesa, Arizona) developed a satellite transmitter that used three C-cell batteries. The 1,200 g transmitter package (includes satellite transmitter, its power supply, a very high frequency (VHF) tracking beacon and its power supply, packaging, and the attachment collar) were the smallest available and appeared light enough to be used safely on wolves. Service Argos refers to a satellite transmitter as a platform transmitter terminal (PTT).

Several investigators have examined the accuracy and precision of PTTs (Mate et al. 1986, Craighead and Craighead 1987, Fancy et al. 1988, Stewart et al. 1989, Harris et al. 1990, Keating et al. 1991), but only the latter

three reports provided evaluations of the systems after 1987 when Service Argos made improvements in calculating locations and quality indices (Keating et al. 1991). Of the latter three studies, only Keating et al. (1991) evaluated the system using PTTs as small as ours. We report on the accuracy and precision of the Argos system, and evaluate the performance of PTTs used on free-ranging gray wolves in northwest Alaska during 1987–1991. We define accuracy as the closeness of an estimated relocation to the true location, whereas precision refers to the repeatability of the measurement.

Study Area and Methods

We placed PTTs on free-ranging wolves in northwest Alaska (65° 15', 67° 30' N; 156° 30', 160° 00' W). The area encompassed Kobuk Valley National Park, Selawik National Wildlife Refuge, portions of Noatak National Preserve, and Koyukuk National Wildlife Refuge. The study area has been described by Ballard et al. (1990) and Ballard (1993).

Fancy et al. (1988) and Harris et al. (1990) provided detailed accounts of the history, use, and applications of the Argos Data Collection and Location System (DCLS). Argos instruments on two polar-orbiting satellites pass over Alaska approximately 24 times each day. The satellites receive signals from the PTTs in the ultrahigh frequency (UHF) range and relay data to ground stations located in Alaska, Virginia, and France. Data are provided to users monthly on computer tapes but can be accessed approximately three to eight hours following a satellite overpass using a telephone modem and computer links (Fancy et al. 1988). Each satellite relocation is given a location quality index (NQ) by Argos reflecting its expected accuracy; NQ 3, 68% of locations reportedly accurate within 150 m; NQ 2, 68% of locations reportedly accurate within 350 m; NQ 1, 68% of locations reportedly accurate within 1,000 m; and NQ 0, quality of relocations determined by user (Service Argos 1989). The quality of each relocation depends on the number and quality of messages received during an overpass, stability of the PTT's oscillator, geometry of the overpass, and other factors (Fancy et al. 1988, Harris et al. 1990, Keating et al. 1991). Standard processing by Argos includes only high quality relocations (i.e., NQs 1–3). Other processing options include nonguaranteed (NQ 0), which provides additional relocations, but the error associated with the relocation is not specified by Argos and must be determined by the user. The NQ 0 processing costs an additional $1.25/day/PTT and provides the greatest number of relocations, but many are inaccurate with no objective methods for separating accurate from inaccurate relocations. Keating et al. (1991) reported errors ranging from 128 to 396 170 m for NQ 0 relocations. We performed a preliminary analysis of our NQ 0 relocations and also found errors up to several km. Consequently, we excluded the 3,573 NQ 0 relocations (48% of all locations) from our accuracy and precision analyses and focused only on NQs 1–3.

A PTT can be programmed to transmit to the satellite with a variety of on/off time periods. The 13 units deployed in 1988 and 1989 transmitted for six hours daily through the first 30 days and then six hours every two days (six hours on/42 hours off) until battery exhaustion, while the 10 units deployed in 1987 and 1990 transmitted for six hours every two days until battery exhaustion. Units deployed in 1987 and 1990 had a life expectancy of 181 days whereas those deployed in 1988 and 1989 had an expected life span of 157 days. Two of the PTTs deployed in 1988 had a four-hour transmission schedule after the initial 30-day period and their life expectancy was 185 days. There was no significant difference ($t = -2.4$, $P < 0.05$) in the number of locations provided by four- or six-hour transmissions, so the data were pooled.

We exposed 1–1.5 cm of the UHF antenna on each unit prior to activating each PTT because a partially exposed antenna may increase location accuracy (S.G. Fancy and W.B. Ballard, unpubl. data). The latter relationship is most directly related to signal strength (W.P. Burger, Telonics Inc., Mesa, Arizona, pers. commun.). Each collar was cut and the antenna was pulled out so it remained flush up against the collar.

Each PTT contained a mercury tip switch to monitor short and long-term activity, a temperature sensor that provided the internal temperature of each canister, a low voltage indicator to indicate when batteries were becoming depleted, and a conventional VHF transmitter to allow each animal to be relocated by conventional radiotelemetry. The UHF and VHF transmitters had separate power supplies and antennas. Descriptions of temperature and activity sensors and wolf activity patterns as determined by satellite telemetry are described by Fancy and Ballard (this volume).

Four generations of PTT collar design were used during the study. The initial prototype PTT used in 1987–1988 weighed 1.22 kg, was rather bulky, and could only be deployed on adult wolves. The design was modified to reduce the size and weight of the units. The first modification involved eliminating the urethane shock buffer from the front and rear of the canister housing the transmitter. The sides of this second generation PTT (1.16 kg) were encased in urethane to protect the antenna as it exited the canister before entering the collar. On several collars the urethane was separating from the canister. If glass to metal feedthroughs for the antennas were broken as this urethane separated from the canister, water could potentially enter the canister. For the third generation (1.08 kg), the urethane caps were eliminated and the antenna exited the top of the canister directly into the collar. The fourth generation (1.10 kg) involved narrowing the depth of the canister and the collar.

Wolves were immobilized for deployment of PTTs by darting from helicopters using methods described by Ballard et al. (1982, 1991b). Conventional VHF transmitters were deployed on one to three other members of a pack to aid in locating the pack and the individual with the PTT. Prior to deployment, when wolves died and after the PTTs had been retrieved, they were allowed to continue transmitting from fixed known locations. All PTTs were unobstructed, transmitted from the ground, and were not on a wolf. Service Argos requires that an average elevation of transmission be designated prior to deployment. The designated elevation for this study was sea level, while the elevation of known locations averaged 29.4 m (range = 0–91 m). Known locations were determined from 1:63,360 scale U.S. Geological Survey maps. Satellite and known locations were converted to Universal Transverse Mercator (UTM) coordinates and differences between them were calculated using LOTUS spreadsheets.

Statistical Tests

We analyzed locations with NQs 1–3 separately because all previous studies have found significant differences in location errors among each NQ category. For each NQ category, we used each combination of PTT, year, and known location as a treatment. Homogeneity of variances was tested within each NQ category with Bartlett-Box F test (Snedecor and Cochran 1973). Unequal variances were found ($P < 0.001$)

within each category. Differences among treatments by NQ category were then analyzed using the Kruskal-Wallis test (Ott 1988). If significant differences (P < 0.05) were detected, we performed multiple comparison of treatment means using Mann-Whitney U tests (Ott 1988).

Location errors were compared among locations for each PTT within the same year using Mann-Whitney tests (Ott 1988). Results of these analyses were pooled, and we report differences using Fisher's combined probability tests of significance (Sokal and Rohlf 1969). Location error was also evaluated by year using the same statistical procedures described above by comparing errors for each PTT positioned at the same site between years. Proportional distributions were analyzed using log-linear models and Chi-square analyses of log-transformed odds ratios. Directional error and bias were measured with Hotelling's one-sample test (Batschelet 1981:144). Because of differences in location errors among transmitters and locations, differences in location quality, and whether the PTTs were transmitting on or off a wolf, different subsets of data were tested for each analysis.

Results

Performance

During spring 1987, we used two prototype PTTs on gray wolves in northern Alaska (Ballard and Fancy 1988). One PTT failed after one month (not included), but the other performed flawlessly for 13 months (Ballard and Fancy 1988). During 1988–1990, an additional 22 PTTs were used on wolves of various sizes in northwest Alaska, and on both sexes, ranging in age from 10 months to eight years and weighing 28.6 to 51.7 kg. None of the females equipped with PTTs denned during the study. Subsequent visual observations from fixed-wing aircraft and physical examinations during re-collaring suggested none of the wolves were adversely affected by the size or weight of the PTTs. However, the collars (50.0–68.3 mm in width) caused excessive rubbing of guard hairs and underfur and would probably significantly reduce the value of the hides of animals shot or trapped and commercially sold.

During April 1987 through May 1991, signals from the 23 wolf PTTs were received by satellite during 14,669 overpasses and 7,374 relocations (NQs 0–3) were calculated. An additional 7,295 sets of sensor data without relocations were obtained. Satellites received an average of 1.5 signals/overpass in which at least one signal was received. Fewer relocations/month were obtained for each PTT when deployed on a wolf than when free-standing (X^2 = 1,473, P < 0.001). An average of 29 ± 18 relocations (n = 106 months) with sensor data was provided per month of transmission while attached to the wolf compared to 51 ± 29 relocations/month (n = 31 months) when not attached. We obtained 3,801 relocations ranging in quality from NQ 1–3 from the 23 PTTs used on free-ranging wolves; NQ

1 = 2,869, NQ 2 = 879, and NQ 3 = 53. Each PTT transmitted (in contrast to life span that includes both transmission and nontransmission days) an average of 72 days ± 46 (range = 9–148 days) and provided an average of 2.2 ± 0.7 relocations/day of transmission (range = 1.2–3.9 relocations).

Average total life span (includes periods on and off wolves) for the 23 wolf PTTs used during 1987 through 1991 was 253 ± 128 (SD) days (range = 67–482 days). Average life span while actually on a wolf, including wolves that died prior to PTT failure, was 181 ± 112.7 days (range = 50–366 days, n = 23). The latter value did not differ from an average life span of 187 ± 109 days (range = 50–366 days, n = 14) for PTTs that expired while attached to a wolf. The latter two values were similar to the theoretical life span predicted by Telonics based on battery life with a duty cycle of six hours on and 42 hours off. Longer life spans for PTTs not attached to animals have been reported previously by Fancy et al. (1988) and Harris et al. (1990). Variance in life spans of PTTs depend primarily on variability among individual battery packs, specific current drains of electronics, repetition periods, duty cycles, operating temperatures, and standing voltage wave ratios. The latter term refers to the proximity of the antenna to the animal that causes the antenna to become detuned. Power output of the PTT automatically adjusts to overcome antenna detuning and, consequently, can increase battery drain by up to approximately 20% (S.M. Tomkiewicz, Telonics Inc., Mesa, Arizona, pers. commun.).

Average life spans for PTTs that ceased operation while attached to wolves differed significantly by year of deployment (H = 5.4, P = 0.067). Excluding the 1987 prototype PTT (n = 1,319-day actual life span), which functioned for 175% of the expected battery life, average life span for this subset of PTTs declined each year; 1988 = 259 ± 86 days (n = 4), 1989 = 211 ± 106 days (n = 5), and 1990 = 104 ± 65 days (n = 5). PTTs deployed during 1988 through 1990 achieved 165, 134, and 57% of their expected battery life, respectively. Premature battery failure or failure of sockets which connect microprocessors to the main board could have been responsible for the poor performance of the PTTs during 1990 (W.P. Burger, Telonics Inc., pers. commun.).

After one wolf died in 1990 and remained motionless for several days, the PTT ceased transmitting to the satellite. When the PTT was retrieved, successful transmission was resumed. Telonics examined the PTT and was unable to duplicate the failure, and could not detect any problems. It was possible that the antenna radiation pattern on the dead wolf prevented signal reception at the satellite (W.P. Burger, Telonics Inc., pers. commun). Also, faulty microprocessor plugs and variation in batteries were suspected reasons for premature failure of PTTs deployed on grizzly bears (*Ursus arctos*) in northwest Alaska during the same time period as this study (Ballard et al. 1991d). J. Weaver (Univ. of Montana, Missoula, pers. commun.) and P. Paquet (Jasper Natl. Park, Jasper, Alberta, pers. commun.) also had shorter life spans for PTTs manufactured in 1990 (n = 2) compared with those manufactured in 1989 (n = 2).

Very high frequency transmitters in the PTT canister were inferior to conventional VHF transmitters in terms of signal strength. J. Weaver (Univ. of Montana, pers. commun.) reached a similar conclusion for similar PTTs. Initially, most VHF signals from PTTs could be received from an aircraft at a distance of 10–20 km, but reception distance declined with time. When the UHF units expired, the VHF transmission distance was < 1 km, and in several cases the units could not be heard until the aircraft flew directly overhead.

Accuracy and Precision

Average location error for NQs 1–3 for all PTTs (n = 16) at seven known locations during three years of deployment was 577 ± 610 m (n = 1885). Mean errors for locations with NQs 1, 2, and 3 were 728 ± 757, 551 ± 528, and 336 ± 220 m, respectively. We found significant differences ($\underline{P} < 0.05$) for location errors among PTTs (Table 1). However, there were no significant differences in location errors by NQ for location (NQ 1 $\underline{P} = 0.53$, NQ 2 $\underline{P} = 0.84$, and NQ 3 $\underline{P} = 0.42$) or year of deployment (NQ 1 $\underline{P} = 0.23$, NQ 2 $\underline{P} = 0.73$, and NQ 3 $\underline{P} = 0.95$) when each PTT was analyzed separately. Average error by location ranged from an average of 259 m for NQ 3 at Kateel River to 1,049 m for NQ 2 at Kotzebue, Alaska (Table 2). Sixty-eight percent of the relocations were < 734, < 556, and < 360 m from the known location for NQs 1 through 3, respectively.

We compared the frequency of relocations by NQ for PTTs on and off the wolf. A three-way log-linear model (PTT X NQ class X on or off animal) was fitted to examine whether the distribution of relocations between NQ codes was independent of the PTT and/or whether the PTT was on or off a wolf (Agresti 1984). The full model could not be rejected ($\underline{P} < 0.001$) indicating the distribution of NQ codes was not independent of PTT nor whether it was deployed on or off a wolf. Location quality code distributions differed among PTTs when the collar was on or off a wolf. As an exploratory measure, a two-way log-linear model (PTT X NQ class) was fitted to NQ code distributions for when PTTs were deployed on wolves, and a separate model for when PTTs were not on wolves. Neither full two-way model was rejected ($\underline{P} < 0.001$ and $\underline{P} < 0.001$, respectively), indicating that the distribution of NQ codes was dependent on the individual PTT and whether it was on or off the wolf.

There were significant directional error biases in locations reported for different PTTs and locations ($\underline{P} < 0.05$). Generally, locations provided by the Argos system were biased toward the south and west (Table 3). All NQ 2 and 3 relocations with the exception of those from Shungnak had significant directional biases ($\underline{P} < 0.05$), 71% of which were toward southerly and westerly directions. Surprisingly, NQ

1 relocations for both Selawik and Kotzebue were not significantly ($\underline{P} > 0.05$) biased.

Lastly, we tested the hypothesis that the accuracy of relocations could be improved by exposing the UHF antenna slightly outside the collar material. We placed one PTT on a domestic dog at a known location (termed Experiment 1), and after several days of transmission, we exposed the UHF antenna and the PTT was again allowed to transmit (Experiment 2). We then removed the PTT from the dog and allowed the PTT to transmit from the same location (Experiment 3). Significant differences in location error were found between Experiment 1 ($\bar{x} = 3,695 \pm 1,829$ m, n = 30) and experiments 2 ($\bar{x} = 2,624 \pm 774$ m, n = 23) and 3 ($\bar{x} = 2,268 \pm 450$ m, n = 20)(Mann-Whitney U test, $\underline{P} < 0.002$). No differences were detected between experiments 2 and 3 ($\underline{P} = 0.64$). These analyses suggest exposing the UHF antenna can improve the quality of relocations.

Discussion

Numerous factors influence the accuracy of relocations obtained with satellite telemetry. Harris et al. (1990) reported that PTT oscillator instability, changes in PTT elevation, animal movement, insufficient number of transmissions reaching the satellite, errors in satellite orbital data, computational algorithms, and mapping methods affected location accuracy. Fancy et al. (1988) and Harris et al. (1990) also found that changes in ambient air temperature, antenna size, deployment on animals versus transmission from inanimate positions, and maximum satellite elevation during an overpass affected accuracy of satellite relocations. Harris et al. (1990) reported that there may be an interaction among PTT, satellite overpass, and whether the PTT was on or off an animal with regard to reductions in precision of relocations. Keating et al. (1991) also had similar results. Our findings agree with those of Fancy et al. (1988), Harris et al. (1990), and Keating et al. (1991).

Directional bias in satellite locations has been reported in all studies that have evaluated accuracy and precision (Fancy et al. 1988, Harris et al. 1990, and Keating et al. 1991). Fancy et al. (1988) reported west and northwest biases while Keating et al. (1991) reported longitudinal biases primarily in a southeasterly direction. Fancy et al. (1988) suggested that part of the bias could be the result of using U.S. Geological Survey topographic maps, which use the NAD27 projection of the earth whereas Argos uses the WGS84 system. However, Harris et al. (1990) reported that even after adjusting the data to account for the differences in the two projections, significant biases remained, but errors were small (i.e., <150 m) in relation to total variation. Keating et al. (1991) also adjusted for type of map projection and concluded that directional errors were largely caused by distance from satellite and differences in estimated and actual PTT elevation. P.Y. Letraon (Service Argos, Landover, Maryland, unpubl. data) estimated that errors in cal-

Table 1. Summary of average location error of 16 wolf PTTs transmitting from known fixed locations in northwest Alaska, 1988–1991.

	Quality of Relocation[1]											
	NQ1			*NQ2*			*NQ3*			*ALL*		
Radio No.	*Mean*	*SD*	n	*Mean*	*SD*	n	*Mean*	*SD*	n	*Mean*	*SD*	n
1	930	1169	65	722	498	56	457	309	28	763	855	149
2	818	621	34	595	581	83	341	198	74	536	508	191
3	1009	1176	17	1100	910	14	280	190	6	925	1001	37
4	1049	992	29	586	410	45	409	220	21	688	667	95
5	815	570	102	656	553	53	422	204	26	712	544	181
6	421	329	114	370	196	37	477	384	15	415	310	166
7	550	836	8	556	609	8	452	151	4	533	632	20
8	704	623	13	592	429	14	452	252	4	621	498	31
9	1283	1140	10				256	40	2	1112	1106	12
10	497	270	7	456	179	9	342	86	4	448	202	20
11	589	586	282	368	267	202	263	139	191	431	435	675
12	811	823	24	619	700	33	407	197	12	657	703	69
13	1188	853	29	557	679	36	384	164	7	794	791	72
14	1026	984	19	808	992	38	384	318	6	834	952	63
15	1405	1560	14	754	567	15	316	131	10	875	1071	39
16	905	672	11	561	342	48	757	609	6	637	451	65
All	728	757	778	551	528	691	336	220	416	577	610	1885

1   NQ = location quality index

Table 2. Summary of average location error by location of transmission for 16 wolf PTTs in northwest Alaska, 1988–1991.

	Quality of Relocations											
	NQ1			*NQ2*			*NQ3*			*All*		
Location[1]	*Mean*	*SD*	n	*Mean*	*SD*	n	*Mean*	*SD*	n	*Mean*	*SD*	n
Selawik Cabin	967	962	290	618	584	408	414	258	188	689	719	886
Pick River	642	582	16	576	419	26	327	213	26	496	421	68
Kotzebue	907	1102	21	1049	899	15	372	303	8	858	949	44
Shungnak	333	163	5	683	382	9	267	123	2	522	349	16
Rabbit Mtn.	373	272	94	288	139	22	269	140	5	353	250	121
Kateel River	576	538	268	359	242	198	259	137	187	420	400	653
Kiliovilik	781	580	84	1097	749	13				824	611	97
All	728	757	778	551	528	691	336	220	416	577	610	1885

1   Latitude-Longitude (decimal degrees) and elevations of known sites was as follows: Selawik Cabin = 66.6065N — 159.0918 W, 1 m;
Pick River = 66.5219 N — 156.4340 W, 34 m; Kotzebue = 66.8987 N — 162.5970 W, 0 m; Shungnak = 66.8880 N — 157.1359 W, 45 m;
Rabbit Mtn. = 66.6361; N — 158.8071 W, 36 m; Kateel River = 65.3315 N — 158.5909 W, 91 m; and Kiliovilik = 66.4641
N — 158.6720 W, 19 m.

Table 3. Summary of average directional bias of wolf PTTs by location and NQ category as determined from known locations in northwest Alaska, 1988–1991.

Location	NQ1 Mean Angle	NQ1 n	NQ2 Mean Angle	NQ2 n	NQ3 Mean Angle	NQ3 n
Pick River	334*	16	328*	26	330*	26
Shungnak	277	5	222	9		
Kateel River	237*	268	224*	198	237*	187
Kiliovilik River	240*	84	225*	13		
Rabbit Mt.	237*	94	202*	22	223*	5
Selawik	195	290	211*	408	195*	188
Kotzebue	103	21	135*	15	94*	8

* Significant directional bias ($P < 0.05$).

culated locations could be 0.5–3.5 the error in actual versus assumed altitude of the PTT. Because our baseline altitude was at sea level and most of the PTTs were tested at Selawik cabin this source of error should have been minimal in this study.

Keating et al. (1991) reported 68 percentile errors of 1,188 m, 903 m, and 361 m for NQs 1 through 3, respectively, in comparison to expected precision (Service Argos 1984, Clark 1989) of 1,510 m, 528 m, and 226 m, respectively. Our errors of 551 m and 336 m for NQs 2 and 3 were similar to those reported by Service Argos (1984) and Keating et al. (1991), but our mean error of 728 m for NQ 1 was considerably lower than those reported previously. Some of the reported differences were due to a less rigorous study design than that of Clark (1989) or Keating et al. (1991) and because Argos estimates are based on independent distributions of x and y coordinates whereas our estimates were based on joint distributions. Also, relatively small sample sizes may have influenced our results. Additionally, our collars were configured differently than those used in previous studies, and our study was conducted farther north. Therefore, system performance should have benefited from a higher number of total overpasses and overpasses with good pass geometry than at lower latitudes. We should have had more locations with more overpasses and a higher probability for getting more NQ 3 locations.

Potentially large variation in location errors among wolf PTTs could complicate data interpretation depending on study objectives. Users of wolf PTTs cannot afford the time or funds to conduct accuracy and precision checks for each study area and individual PTT. At the least, however, users should allow each PTT to transmit for several days prior to deployment so that gross differences in PTT accuracy can be assessed.

Keating et al. (1991) stated that use of satellite telemetry for assessing "localized movements and habitat use" is an alluring alternative to conventional telemetry, but substantial improvements in data quality are necessary before such studies can be conducted. We add that it is also a method that has become "in vogue" and prestigious to use even though some study objectives might be more efficiently accomplished with conventional telemetry or other methods. Even assuming average location errors of 300–700 m, such data have limited use, particularly when examining habitat utilization, unless an investigator is only interested in broad associations. However, assessing localized movements and habitat use is a matter of scale that is dependent on the species being studied and its landscape. If patches of prey or habitat are distributed coarsely (i.e. > 2 km) across a landscape and the study animal moves great distances each day (e.g. 10–20 km) then satellite telemetry may provide data of sufficient precision to allow assessment of habitat use.

Investigators must carefully consider study objectives before deciding to use satellite telemetry. In our case, use of satellite telemetry appeared justified because weather, short daylight, and winter logistics precluded location of wolves frequently enough with conventional telemetry to accurately determine movements. In northern latitudes, wolves either occupy large territories (i.e., 1,000 to 2,000 km²) or they travel long distances (hundreds or thousands of km) following migratory caribou (*Rangifer tarandus*). Maintaining radio contact would be difficult and perhaps impossible. The location errors we discovered are probably acceptable for estimating wolf territory sizes or tracking animal movements under those circumstances. Territory sizes and movement characteristics are probably more accurately described with satellite telemetry than with conventional radiotelemetry, particularly in northern latitudes where territories are larger, because of the continuous uniform monitoring. A preliminary analysis for one wolf pack indicated the annual territory size determined by satellite data (n = 415) was approximately 75% larger than that found through conventional radiotelemetry (n = 38) (Ballard and Fancy 1988). Relocations obtained with conventional telemetry are often clumped, auto-correlated, and too infrequent to accurately assess territory or home range sizes.

Unless PTT-equipped wolves were accompanied by other wolves equipped with conventional VHF transmitters, relocation of animals by the PTT VHF transmitter was nearly impossible. Because VHF and UHF units are contained within the same collar, the length of the VHF antenna is reduced from 457 mm to 229 mm, resulting in a reduction in transmission range of approximately 75%. Keating et al. (1991) suggested that signals from each unit might interfere with each other and result in both poorer quality satellite relocations and reduced range from the VHF unit. However, there appears to be no basis for this hypothesis, and the relatively short antenna explains the lack of range of the VHF transmitter (S.M. Tomkiewicz, Telonics Inc., pers. commun.). Unless the range on the VHF transmitter can be significantly improved, future investigators might consider removing them from the unit to lighten the PTT. Elimination of the VHF unit would lighten the PTT by approximately 75 g. The C-cell batteries could be replaced by D-cell batteries which theoretically should increase the life span of the PTT, but would result in an increase in weight of approximately 100 g (W.P. Burger, Telonics Inc., pers. commun.).

PTTs in 1992 cost $3,500 (U.S.)/unit and can be refurbished for approximately $800/unit. Data processing costs from Service Argos are based on the equivalent of a PTT transmitting one to six times each day for one year (PTT-year). Each PTT-year (1992) costs $4,000 and the fee for special animal process costs an additional $1.50/day/PTT. Each conventional VHF radio collar costs $330/unit and has a life span of approximately three years. We assumed each wolf pack would contain a minimum of three collars; one PTT and two VHF collars for the PTT-equipped pack and three conventional collars for the VHF-equipped pack. We assumed each PTT-equipped pack would be visually observed six times/year to collect data on productivity, den site locations, mortality; only standard normal processing would

be used (requires 0.5 PTT-year of data processing); and each PTT would transmit six hours every two days for six months or longer (requires one recapture per year). We also assumed a study duration of three years, capture costs of $1,000/individual, and one hour of fixed-wing aircraft charter ($140/hour) per relocation for VHF equipped packs (W.B. Ballard, unpubl. data). Using the above assumptions, the average annual cost to maintain a PTT and two VHF transmitters in a wolf pack over a three-year period was $7,327. Assuming the PTT transmitted an average of six months and provided an average of 28 relocations/month (168 locations), the average cost/relocation was $44. To attain the same number of relocations with conventional VHF telemetry each relocation would cost about $148. Assuming a more realistic monitoring intensity of once/week, the average annual cost/relocation was $166.

Cost per relocation was cheaper for both methods when a greater number of relocations were obtained per year. For an average wolf study lasting three years and requiring 50 relocations per year, costs per relocation were $147 and $172 for PTT and VHF transmitter equipped packs, respectively. Differences between the two methods increased as the total numbers of relocations/year increased. At 200 relocations/year average cost/relocation was $37 and $147, respectively, whereas for 400 locations average cost was $22 and $144, respectively. Reasons for these large differences include high initial costs for wolf PTTs but subsequently low monitoring costs in comparison to low initial costs for conventional VHF transmitters, but relatively high fixed monitoring costs (one hour charter aircraft/relocation). Clearly, use of satellite telemetry is cost-effective for obtaining large quantities of movement and relocation data, and may also provide indications of activity patterns once additional effort has been made to calibrate and categorize such data (Fancy and Ballard this volume).

Acknowledgments

Funding for this study was provided by the U.S. National Park Service, the U.S. Fish and Wildlife Service, the Alaska Department of Fish and Game, the University of Arizona, and several Alaska Federal Aid to Wildlife Restoration Projects. Constructive criticism on early drafts was provided by S. Abbott, L. Adams, L.A. Ayres, W.P. Burger, A.F. Cunning, S.H. Fritts, G.W. Garner, A. Lovaas, F.L. Miller, S.R. Peterson, C.A. Shanks, S.M. Tomkiewicz, J. Weaver, and one anonymous referee.

Warren B. Ballard, Daniel J. Reed, Steven G. Fancy, and Paul R. Krausman

Use of Line-Intercept Track Sampling for Estimating Wolf Densities

■ Warren B. Ballard, Mark E. McNay, Craig L. Gardner, and Daniel J. Reed

During spring 1990 and spring 1991 we tested the use of line-intercept sampling of tracks for estimating wolf densities for a known wolf population occupying a 6,464 km² study area in northwest Alaska, and for a population estimated by traditional aerial reconnaissance in a 5,011 km² survey area in interior Alaska. In each study area we used seven randomly chosen samples, each consisting of five systematically spaced transects. Based upon telemetry studies, the minimum number of wolves known to occupy the northwest Alaska study area was 48. The population estimated based upon line-intercept sampling was 50.7 (80% ci = 33.4 to 67.9). The biological confidence interval was 43 to 68. The estimated numbers of wolves occupying the interior survey area, based upon aerial reconnaissance surveys, was 41. The population estimate based upon line-intercept sampling was 33.4 (80% ci = 23.2 to 43.6). The biological confidence interval was 25 to 44. Advantages of the line-intercept procedure over other survey methods include objectivity, repeatability, speed, reduced cost, reasonable accuracy, and measurable precision.

Introduction

Obtaining accurate and precise estimates of wolf (*Canis lupus*) population density is costly and time consuming because of relatively low density and secretive behavior of the species. Since the early 1970's a number of state, provincial, and federal governments have attempted to monitor the status of wolf populations regularly. Methods included harvest statistics (Rausch 1967), howling surveys (Harrington and Mech 1982b), hunter observations to assess trend (Crete and Messier 1987), a variety of aerial reconnaissance surveys (Stephenson 1978, Gasaway et al. 1983, Crete and Messier 1987), and radiotelemetry studies (cf. Ballard et al. 1987, Fuller and Snow 1988). A number of problems exist with each method.

Howling surveys are time consuming, expensive, require road access, are limited to relatively small areas, and are imprecise (Crete and Messier 1987, Fuller and Sampson 1988b). Estimates obtained from hunter observations are also relatively imprecise and require a large sample of hunters (Crete and Messier 1987), which is not practical for many areas of North America. Aerial track counts using transects were evaluated and found unsatisfactory by Crete and Messier (1987).

Aerial reconnaissance surveys (Stephenson 1978, Gasaway et al. 1983) are widely used in western Canada and

Alaska for assessing wolf densities. This method differs considerably from the aerial track counts evaluated by Crete and Messier (1987); smaller and slower aircraft are used, pilots and observers are experienced wolf trackers, and transects are flown only in homogeneous habitats. Varying intensity searches are conducted of habitats frequented by wolves (e.g., ridges, shorelines, and streams). When wolf tracks are encountered they are followed until wolves are observed and the number and color composition of the pack are determined. Pack size is estimated from tracks if wolves are not observed. Tracks, wolves observed, and prior knowledge of wolf pack locations are used to form a mosaic of wolf pack areas. Numbers of wolves in each area are estimated from the survey data resulting in best, low, and high estimates that are not estimates of precision. This method appears to work well in Alaska with resident wolf packs, but may not in areas where part or all of the wolf population is migratory and/or wolves exist in relatively low densities. The method was evaluated on a cursory basis by Stephenson (1978), who determined that in one area the method provided a good estimation (within 80–96%) of wolf density in relation to what was estimated from radiotelemetry studies. W.B. Ballard (Alaska Dept. Fish and Game, unpubl. data) had similar results with a test of a pilot-observer team that was "current" (fewer than five years since last wolf survey) at wolf tracking. However, results were 50% lower with a pilot-observer team that was experienced but not current (more than five years since last wolf survey).

To date, the best method for estimating wolf population density involves use of radiotelemetry to estimate pack territories and-sizes, and the numbers of wolves in each pack. While the resulting density estimates are accurate and repeatable (Fuller and Snow 1988), they are also expensive and time consuming to obtain, and do not contain measures of precision. High cost makes this method impractical for routine management.

A cost-effective and practical method of surveying wolves over large geographic areas would ideally be accurate and have a high degree of precision. Becker (1991) reported a method for estimating lynx (*Felis lynx*) and wolverine (*Gulo gulo*) densities in Alaska using a line-intercept track sampling method that we have termed the track intercept probability estimator (TIP survey). The greatest potential advantage for use on wolves is that it provides a measure of precision not previously available. The TIP survey method has been used for surveying wolves (Becker and Gardner 1990, Gardner and Becker 1991), but its accuracy and precision within a known population of wolves has not been assessed, nor have the results been compared with those from traditional aerial reconnaissance surveys. This study compares TIP survey (Becker 1991) estimates to a radiotelemetry-based estimate (Kobuk study area) and to an estimate based upon aerial reconnaissance surveys (Minto study area). We discuss advantages and disadvantages in relation to other available survey methods.

Study Area and Methods

The Kobuk study area included the winter range of the western Arctic caribou (*Rangifer tarandus*) herd and portions of Kobuk Valley National Park, Selawik National Wildlife Refuge, and Koyukuk National Wildlife Refuge in northwest Alaska. Within the 12,279 km² wolf study area (Ballard et al. 1990), we selected a 6,464 km² TIP survey area (Fig. 1) where radio contact had been maintained with three wolf packs during the previous three years. Two additional packs without collared members (uncollared packs) were observed within the TIP survey area before the survey, and their numbers were determined by direct count prior to the survey. Territory boundaries of instrumented packs were estimated using outermost radio-relocations (Mohr 1947). Territories of uncollared packs were estimated based upon their spatial relationship to collared packs, wolf sightings, and mapped travel routes observed during capture and monitoring flights.

During spring 1991, we conducted aerial reconnaissance surveys (Stephenson 1978) in the Minto study area to determine wolf densities (Fig. 2). Surveys were conducted during clear weather, one to five days following fresh snowfalls ≥ 75 mm. One to three aircraft (Piper Supercub or

Bellanca Scout) searched 1,000–2,500 km² search blocks on each of five survey days. We resurveyed search blocks on different days and concentrated search efforts on probable wolf travel routes. Once encountered, wolf tracks were followed until wolves were sighted or pack size could be estimated from tracks. We backtracked wolves until tracks appeared old and plotted all track segments on 1:250,000 scale U.S. Geological Survey maps.

The aerial reconnaissance estimate of wolf numbers included wolves observed plus track estimates. Individual packs were identified by size and color composition. Relative timing of track observations, hunter and trapper sightings, and repetitive surveys of search blocks helped differentiate between observed packs and those estimated from tracks. No correction factor was applied for single wolves because we had no basis for estimating single wolves. Before completing the aerial reconnaissance survey we conducted a TIP survey within a 5,011 km² portion of the Minto study area to provide an alternate estimate of wolf numbers and to compare the TIP survey estimate with that obtained from the aerial reconnaissance survey.

For both study sites, the TIP survey areas were designed as rectangles and positioned on a 1:250,000 scale map so that randomly selected transects would have a high probability of crossing wolf travel routes (e.g., ridges and streams). Locations of surveyed transects were selected using a randomly repeated systematic sample design (Becker 1991). Each sample unit consisted of five systematically spaced transects that were 38.6 km long in the Kobuk study area and 25.2 km long in the Minto study area. A random sample of seven of these sample units was selected by randomly choosing the starting point on the x-axis for the first transect in each systematic sample. The randomization was restricted by forcing a minimum spacing of 1.6 km between any two adjacent transects. Other combinations of numbers of samples and transects can be used, but previous experience indicated that seven samples composed of five transects was a desirable sampling scheme (Gardner and Becker 1991). We calculated 80% confidence intervals (CI) for each estimate. We chose 80% CIs to prevent making a Type II error of falsely concluding that there was no change in the population.

General procedures for conducting the survey were described by Becker (1991), Becker and Gardner (1990), and Gardner and Becker (1991). The mathematical equations, sampling theory, and model assumptions are detailed in Becker (1991). Becker (1991) outlined four assumptions necessary when line-intercept track surveys are conducted from fixed-wing aircraft: 1) all wolves in the study area move and deposit tracks prior to the survey; 2) all wolf tracks that cross a transect are detectable and identifiable; 3) tracks encountered can be followed to the wolf's present location and backtracked to where it had bedded down during the snowstorm or where the tracks can be classified as "old"; and 4) the distance wolves traveled parallel to the x-axis since the last snowstorm can be determined by tracking. Field

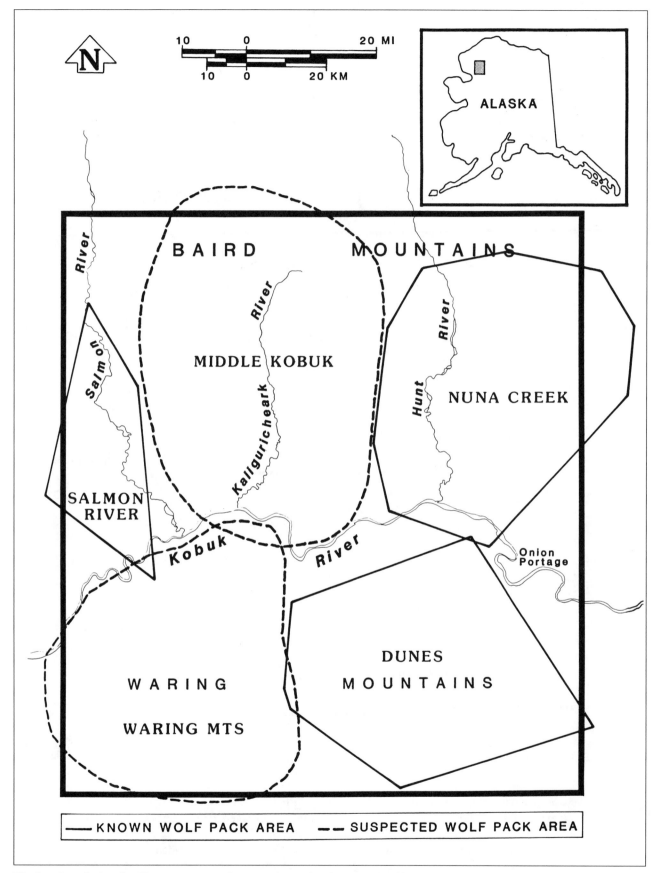

Fig. 1. *Boundaries of wolf survey area in relation to observed and suspected wolf pack territory boundaries in northwest Alaska.*

Warren B. Ballard, Mark E. McNay, Craig L. Gardner, and Daniel J. Reed

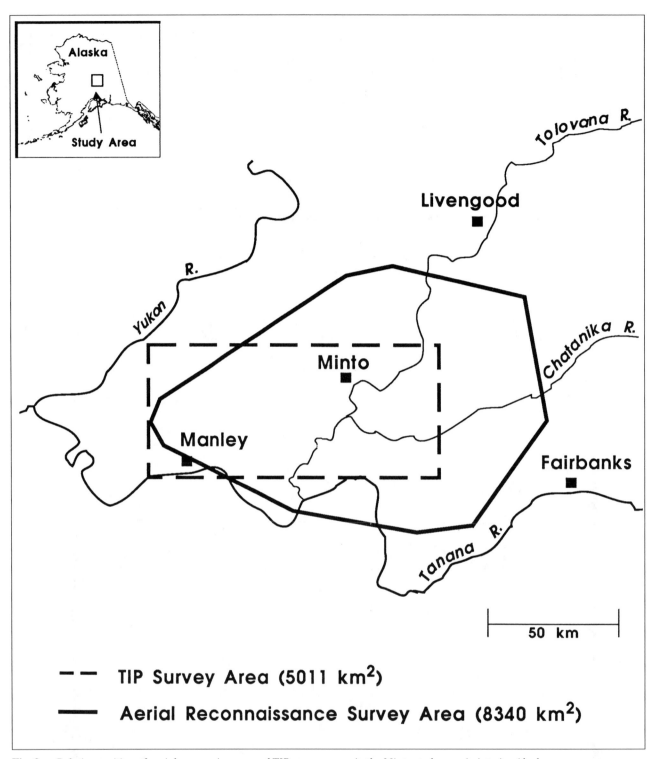

Fig. 2. *Relative position of aerial reconnaissance and TIP survey areas in the Minto study area in interior Alaska.*

procedures were designed to ensure compliance with these assumptions and to verify their validity.

Each survey aircraft (Piper Supercubs and Bellanca Scout) was assigned seven transects. Transects were initiated from the western boundary of both study areas. Following completion of all assigned transects, each air-

craft flew irregular searches (herein referred to as renegade searches) between transect lines to check if any wolf tracks had been missed. Survey aircraft maintained airspeeds of approximately 90–130 km/hour at altitudes of 60–160 m.

Before and after the survey in the Kobuk study, a separate aircraft (Piper Supercub) that did not participate in the survey used radiotelemetry to locate and backtrack all radio-collared wolves associated with the study. This allowed us to determine if all radio-collared wolves were in the study area and were available for counting. It also provided an opportunity to determine if the survey aircraft could locate, backtrack, and estimate pack sizes for packs of known numbers.

Topography of the survey area ranged from flat (30 m) along the Kobuk River and along the southern boundary of the area to the gently sloping north- or south-facing slopes from the crest (536 m) of the Waring Mountains. North of the Kobuk River, which runs through the area from east to west, several steep ridges (1,100 m) run from north to south.

Vegetation of the area ranged from thick black (*Picea mariana*) and white (*P. glauca*) spruce forests along the Kobuk River and its major tributaries, grading into sparser stands of spruce and mixed shrub consisting of willow (*Salix* spp.), alder (*Alnus* spp.), and birch (*Betula glandulosa*, *B. nana*, and *B. papyrifera*). Higher elevations were dominated by mat-cushion and upland tundra and bare rock.

The area has a maritime climate during snow-free periods. Winter and summer temperatures average -11.5° and 9.4°C, respectively. The area is often snow-covered from October through May. Annual precipitation averages 680 mm, half of which occurs during July and August.

The Minto study area ranges in elevation from 90 to 1,400 m. The southern portion of the study area is characterized by flat terrain with numerous lowland lakes interspersed with mixed birch, both black and white spruce, and wet marshlands. North of Minto Flats, the terrain rises through rolling, forest-covered hills to a prominent east-west alpine tundra ridge along the northern boundary of the area. Drainages flow south into the Tanana River.

Climate of the area is continental. Annual precipitation averages 310 mm, half of which occurs during June, July, and August. Accumulated snow depths average 480 mm on 1 March and average daily temperatures range from 15.3 °C in July to -21.8 °C in January.

Results

Kobuk Study Area

A snowstorm from 26–28 April 1990 brought 48 mm of fresh snow to the study area, adding to 64 cm already on the ground. An earlier storm from 21–23 April resulted in 310 mm of fresh snow, so survey conditions were excellent on 1 May. On 1 May 1990, approximately three days after the storm, five fixed-wing aircraft flew seven systematic samples consisting of five, 38.6 km long transects (Fig. 3). We expended 36.6 hours flying transects and renegade searches. During the approximate 5–7.5 hours of renegade searches four of five aircraft found no additional wolf sign. One aircraft missed a pack of three wolves (Waring Mountain pack) that had crossed the southernmost transect on two occasions.

Forty-eight wolves were accounted for during the survey (Table 1): 43 wolves observed and tracks of five others. All five packs known to occur within the study area were located.

All wolves encountered were successfully tracked and backtracked. However, there were discrepancies between pack size estimates during the survey and those obtained before and after the survey. For example, the radio-tracking aircraft could only account for 10 wolves in packs from the Salmon River and middle Kobuk River, but the survey crew counted 11 in each. The Dunes pack contained five individuals that had been observed daily during the preceding two-week period, while the survey crew (based upon track counts) estimated six to seven wolves. The Nuna Creek pack numbered 18 wolves the morning before the survey, but during and after the survey only 16 wolves were counted in the pack. Some time during the survey two radio-collared wolves split away from their pack and died and were missed during the survey. Subsequent observations revealed that a rabies enzootic was in progress (Brand et al. this volume). Although no lone wolves were radio-collared, losses from some instrumented packs over the previous three-week period (Nuna Creek pack originally had numbered 21 individuals) suggested some lone wolves were either in the area, had been killed by local hunters, or died of rabies.

Wolves were encountered on several of the systematic samples (Table 1). Average group size was 8 ± 5.6 (SD) and average distance moved perpendicular to the transects since the last snowstorm was 18.9 ± 9.3 (SD) km per wolf group. The resulting wolf population estimate based upon the transects was 50.7 with an 80% confidence interval (CI) of 33.4–67.9 (Table 1). The density estimate was 7.8 wolves/1,000 km^2 (80% CI = 5.2-10.5 wolves/1,000 km^2).

Minto Study Area

We flew 50.5 hours on aerial reconnaissance surveys in the Minto study area between 12 March and 2 April 1991. The best estimate was 61 wolves (7.3 wolves/1,000 km^2) composed of 12 packs within the 8,340 km^2 study area (Table 2). We calculated low and high estimates of 55 and 71 wolves, respectively, by excluding or including packs whose separate identities could not be clearly established. Among the 12 packs included in the best estimate, pack sizes ranged from two to 12 wolves and averaged 5.1 wolves per pack.

Deriving estimates from aerial reconnaissance surveys requires subjective decisions because complete home ranges are not known and estimates are often based upon tracks rather than observed wolves. Searching the survey area repeatedly after consecutive snowfall events helped us differentiate between adjacent packs because we gained additional wolf movement information after each fresh snowfall. For example, during aerial reconnaissance searches on 21 March, three days following a 75 mm snowfall, we encountered wolf tracks in the northeastern corner of the study area

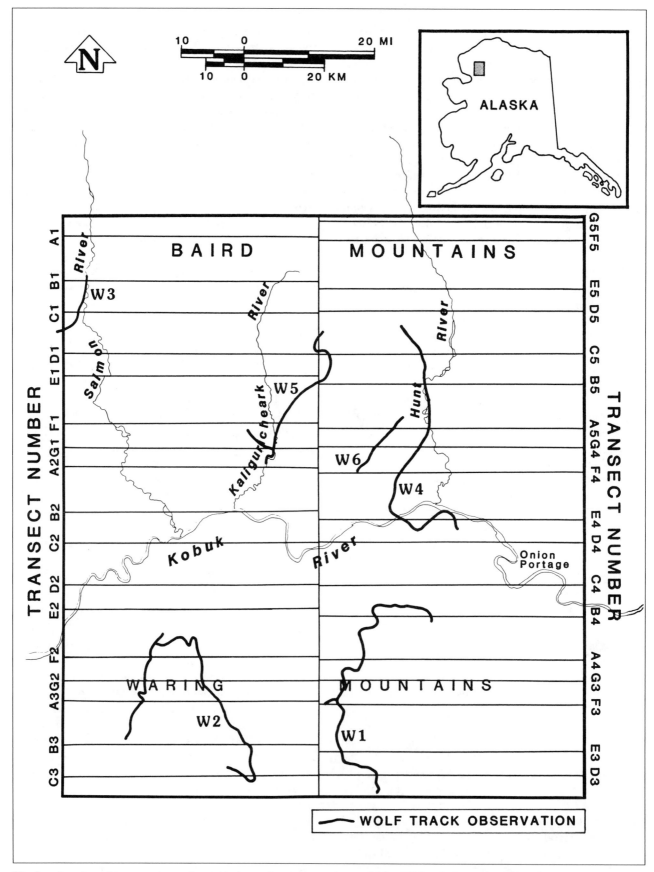

Fig. 3. *Location of transects in northwest Alaska used to survey wolves on 1 May 1990 and observed wolf travel routes.*

Table 1. Wolf survey data obtained on 1 May 1990 and calculations used to estimate population size within a 6,464 km^2 study area, northwestern Alaska.

Wolf group	Pack Name	Est. no. wolves (no.obs.)	Known no. wolves	Dist. move (km)	P[1]	T[2]
W1	Dunes	6(2)	5	27.3	0.8258	7.27
W2	Waring	3(2)	3	21.8	0.6591	4.55
W3	Salmon	11(11)	11[3]	8.0	0.2424	45.38
W4	Nuna	16(16)	18	29.3	0.8864	18.05
W5	Kobuk	11(11)	11[3]	19.1	0.5758	19.10
W6	single	1(1)		7.8	0.2348	4.26

Samp. ID	Wolf groups	Pop. est. based on ith sample = sum T for each group
A	W1, W2, W4, W6	34.13
B	W1, W2, W3, W4, W5	94.35
C	W2, W3, W4, W5	87.08
D	W1	7.27
E	W1, W4	25.32
F	W1, W2, W4, W5, W6	53.23
G	W1, W2, W4, W5, W6	53.23
	Total	354.61[a]

a   Total Population Estimate = 354.61/7 = 50.66; 80% Confidence Interval = 33.38 to 67.94
1   Probability observed (P) = distance moved perpendicular to transect/x-axis X no. of transects.
2   T = pack size/P.
3   Ten wolves were observed in each pack prior to survey.

---

that led us 90 km along an open ridge to the northwestern corner of the study area. Two aircraft encountered the track segment and although only six wolves were sighted, each search team independently estimated 10–14 wolves from tracks. Later, on 1 and 2 April, after fresh snowfall covered the tracks observed on 21 March, we saw three packs totalling 19 observed wolves in the vicinity of the track segment observed on 21 March.

Although resurveying the study area following consecutive snowfalls enhanced our aerial reconnaissance survey estimate, at some time during aerial reconnaissance surveys money or weather preclude further efforts and subjective decisions enter into the final estimate. In this case, of the 55 wolves estimated in the low estimate, only 39 wolves were actually observed and, hence, the minimum estimate could be construed as 39 wolves (4.7 wolves/1,000 km^2).

On 31 March, two days after a large storm deposited 580 mm of snow, we flew a TIP survey within a 5,011 km^2 rectangle within the Minto study area (Fig. 4). Three aircraft (two Supercubs and one Bellanca Scout) flew seven systematic samples consisting of five, 25.2-km transects. We flew 19.5 hours to complete transects and to conduct renegade searches between transects. The entire TIP survey area had been searched by aerial reconnaissance surveys on 20 and 21 March, but all tracks observed during those surveys had been covered by snow between 24 and 29 March.

During the TIP survey, we encountered tracks of four wolf packs totalling 25 wolves that crossed transects. We successfully tracked three packs until wolves were sighted, the fourth pack (two wolves) was tracked to where the wolves were concealed by thick spruce. A fifth pack (Baker pack) was found between transects during the renegade search, but that pack had moved only a short perpendicular distance and failed to cross survey transects. The following day, during aerial reconnaissance surveys, a sixth pack (Hut-

Warren B. Ballard, Mark E. McNay, Craig L. Gardner, and Daniel J. Reed

Table 2. Estimated-size and color composition of wolf packs identified within the 8,340 km² Minto study area on aerial reconnaissance surveys, 12 March–2 April 1991.

Pack ID#	Pack name	Estimated number of wolves (no. observed)	Color composition
M1	C.O.D.[1]	2(0)	Tracks only
M2	Tolovana[1]	6(6)	1 black, 5 gray
M3	Swanneck[1]	12(12)	11 black, 1 gray
M4	Dugan[1]	5(3)	1 black, 2 gray
M5	Baker[1]	7(7)	5 black, 2 gray
M6	Hutlinana[1]	6(6)	4 black, 2 gray
M7	Globe	3(0)	Tracks only
M8	Tatalina	8(0)	Tracks only
M9	Chatanika	3(3)	3 black
M10	Minto Lakes	2(2)	1 black, 1 gray
M11	Manley[1]	3(0)	Tracks only
M12	Standard	4(0)	Tracks only
M13	Wolverine Mountain	2(0)	Tracks only
M14	Uncle Sam[1]	2(1)	1 black
M15	Deadman	2(1)	1 black
M16	Dunbar	4(0)	Tracks only

Best estimate[2]	61 (39) = 7.3 wolves/1000 km²
Low estimate[3]	55 (39) = 6.6 wolves/1000 km²
High estimate[4]	71 (41) = 8.5 wolves/1000 km²

1 Denotes packs observed within the TIP survey area.
2 Best estimate included packs M1-M12.
3 Low estimate excluded packs M7, M11, M13-M16.
4 High estimate included all packs M1-M16.

linana pack) was successfully tracked within the TIP survey area. Again, the entire track segment lay within the TIP survey area, but had not crossed any of the survey transects. Therefore, we did not detect two wolf packs totalling 13 wolves during the TIP survey. Because those packs did not cross survey transects, they did not enter into calculations of the TIP wolf population estimate. We continued aerial reconnaissance surveys through 2 April, but found no additional packs.

Wolves were encountered on all seven systematic samples within the Minto TIP survey area (Table 3). Average group size was 6.3 ± 4.2(SD) and average distance moved perpendicular to the transects since last snowfall averaged 13.1 ± 5.7 (SD) km per group. The TIP wolf population estimate within the 5,011 km² survey area was 33.4 with an 80% confidence interval (CI) of 23.2 to 43.6 (Table 3). The density estimate was 6.7 wolves/1,000 km² (80% CI = 4.6 - 8.7 wolves/1,000 km²). In comparison, the best estimate from the aerial reconnaissance survey for the TIP survey area (5,011 km²) was 41 wolves, and the density estimate for the entire Minto study area (8,340 km²) from aerial reconnaissance surveys was 7.3 wolves/1,000 km². Therefore, similar wolf population and density estimates were obtained from the aerial reconnaissance and TIP surveys.

Discussion

The TIP survey method is objective and repeatable, and appears to alleviate the problem of dealing with the proportion of lone wolves in the population estimate (Fuller and Snow 1988). Other methods rely on estimates from the

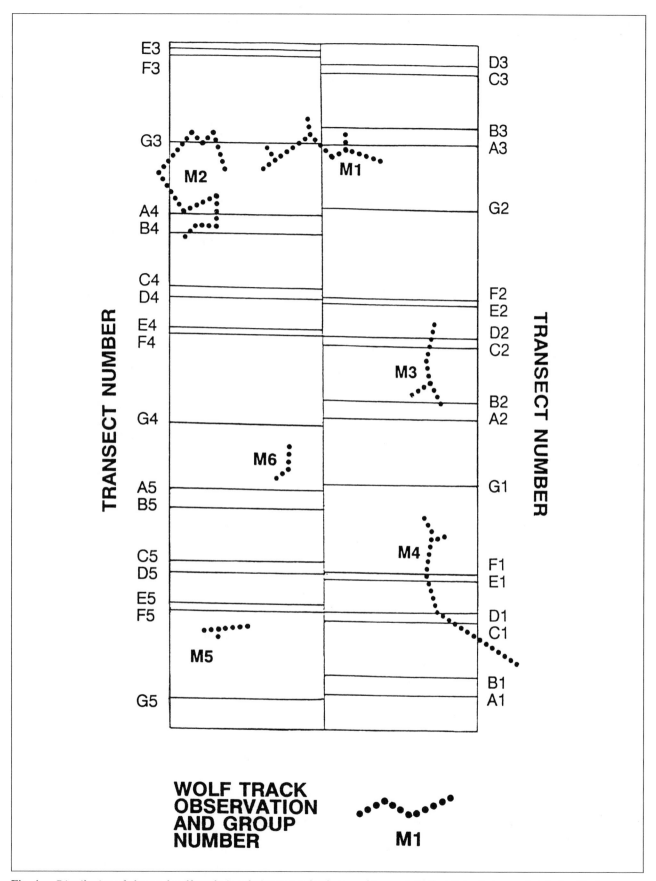

Fig. 4. *Distribution of observed wolf tracks in relation to randomly spaced transects in the Minto study area in interior Alaska.*

Table 3. Summary of wolf survey conducted on 31 March 1991 and calculations used to estimate population size within the 5,011 km² Minto study area, interior Alaska.

Wolf group	*Pack name*	*Estimated number of wolves (no. observed)*	*Distance moved (km)*	*P*[1]	*T*[2]
M1	C.O.D.	2(0)	6.45	0.162	12.35
M2	Tolovana	6(6)	12.98	0.326	18.40
M3	Swanneck	12(12)	12.50	0.314	38.22
M4	Dugan	5(3)	20.32	0.511	9.78

Sampling ID	*Wolf groups encountered*	*Population estimate based on i[th] Sample = sum T for each group*
A	M1, M2	30.75
B	M2, M3	56.62
C	M3, M4	48.00
D	M3, M4	48.00
E	M4	9.78
F	M4	9.78
G	M1, M2	30.75
TOTAL		233.6

Total population estimate = 233.68/7 = 33.38

80% confidence interval = 23.21 - 43.55

1   Probability observed ($\underline{P}$) = distance moved perpendicular to transect/x-axis X number of transects.
2   T = pack size / $\underline{P}$.

---

literature or costly radiotelemetry studies. With the line-intercept method, the proportion of lone wolves included within the estimate is determined by actual survey data.

The maximum size of a survey area for application of the TIP survey method is limited primarily by the number of aircraft and available flight time per aircraft. Factors that affect how aircraft are utilized include: 1) numbers and lengths of transects to be surveyed; 2) target animal densities and movement rates and patterns since last snowfall, which influence time necessary for forward- and backtracking; and 3) commute times between aircraft facilities and the study area, ferry times between transects, and the availability of cached fuel in or near the study area. Because the survey method is dependent upon the distance moved by target animals perpendicular to the transects, surveying the entire area quickly is important. While all tracks of target animals intercepting a transect must be detected and tracked, all

target animals in the survey area need not be detected by having their tracks intercept a transect.

The size of our study areas (6,464 km² and 5,011 km²) was limited by available aircraft, logistics, and in the Kobuk study by the desire to evaluate the assumption of track detectability, which required a high probability that tracks made by instrumented packs would be intercepted by more than one transect. The aircraft were assigned 270 km and 294 km of transects to search and averaged 7.3 hours and 6.5 hours of survey effort (not including ferry time) in the Kobuk and Minto study areas, respectively. Each aircraft's time budget was allocated approximately two hours of commute time, about 6–6.5 hours to fly the transects and follow intercepted tracks, and about 0.5–1 hour for renegade searches. Because of the potential for pilot fatigue, maximum flight time per survey day should not exceed 8.0 hours. Study areas ranging from 4,556 to 10,343 km² have been surveyed with this method (Becker and Gardner 1990; Gardner and Becker 1991; G. Carroll, Alaska Dep. of Fish and Game, unpubl. data; this study). The study areas could have been doubled in size with modest increases in commute time. However, doubling would have required less intensive sampling (fewer transects or fewer samples), less time per aircraft for renegade searches, and probably would have resulted in decreased precision. The sampling intensity we used provided increased precision because most packs crossed several transects; therefore, data from most packs were included in more than one systematic sample.

The survey method has a number of potential problems, most of which are common to all aerial survey techniques. Spotting wolf tracks in the snow from aircraft and then tracking and backtracking requires a higher level of pilot expertise than for most other wildlife surveys. Use of inexperienced pilots would undoubtedly result in underestimates of wolf population sizes. Although experienced observers are helpful, most of the spotting and tracking depends on the pilot.

Based upon computer simulations, Gardner and Becker (1991) recommended conducting TIP surveys four to five days following a snowstorm. That recommendation assumed a snowfall of more than 70 mm and relatively low caribou densities. Our surveys were conducted on the second or third days following a snowstorm and accurately estimated the numbers of wolves relative to known or estimated numbers inhabiting the area. More research is necessary to determine the optimum period for conducting TIP surveys on wolves.

Lack of population closure (i.e., failure of all wolves whose home ranges overlap the study area to be within the study area during the survey) may also affect density estimates derived from aerial reconnaissance or general line-intercept surveys, because survey area boundaries often cut through portions of several wolf pack territories. The aerial reconnaissance survey method can greatly overestimate wolf densities when wolves are observed in the area, but only a small portion of their home range occurs there. In one instance, a wolf population was overestimated by the aerial reconnaissance method by 16% in a 8,671 km^2 area. One wolf pack that had less than 10% of its territory within the count area was included in the estimate (W.B. Ballard and J.S. Whitman, Alaska Dept. of Fish and Game, unpubl. data).

Becker (1991) suggested that during TIP surveys intercepted tracks be completely tracked forward and backward, so the distance wolves traveled parallel to the x-axis could be accurately mapped. Then, if ≥ 50% of that distance was traveled within the study area, the data for that pack would be included in wolf estimate calculations. An alternative method would include only data from wolves that were in the study area during the aerial survey. If wolves made tracks in the study area but then left prior to the survey, data from those packs would not be considered. The latter method would provide a better estimate of wolves in the study area

on the day the survey was flown, but it could yield extreme, imprecise estimates when a wolf pack was found shortly after it had entered the study area. We recommend using Becker's closure rule because it would tend to provide a better-behaved precision estimate and a better overall seasonal estimate of wolf density. During our surveys, we used Becker's (1991) recommendations in those instances when wolves were tracked outside the study area (Figs. 3 and 4). Closure rules are necessary to prevent biased wolf density estimates.

Gardner and Becker (1991) reported that an ongoing wolf-hunting season affected use of the method in their study area. Apparently wolf packs had been hunted (aircraft assisted) immediately before the counts were initiated, and packs and individual pack members were scattered over large areas. Hunting regulations over most of Alaska until recently allowed hunters to use aircraft to spot wolves and then land to shoot. This practice became illegal in many areas of the state beginning 1 July 1992; consequently, this factor should be less important in future surveys.

Tracking wolves through dense forest from fixed-wing aircraft is difficult, time consuming, and requires good snow conditions. Becker and Gardner (1990) suggested accurate counts would not be expected in large areas with low sightability, such as those with dense forests. If sightability was low, the assumption that all tracks could be detected and followed would probably be violated. The Kobuk study area contained thick stands of spruce along riparian areas, yet survey conditions were near ideal because dense vegetation only occurred in relatively narrow strips surrounded by open habitat types. In contrast, the Minto study area contained large forested areas. We did not fail to detect wolf tracks in the forested habitats, based on renegade searches and on subsequent aerial reconnaissance surveys. But more testing, using radio-collared wolves, is needed to evaluate sightability in closed habitats under varying conditions of light, snow, and wolf densities.

Wolf packs stay close to ungulate kills for two- to five-day periods (Ballard et al. 1987) and for as long as eight to 15 days (Messier 1985a, Ballard et al. 1987). Consequently, some packs may not move between the last snowstorm and the time the survey is conducted. The point estimate of population size if these packs are encountered may be unreasonably high and could have low precision. For example, if the Baker Creek pack of seven wolves (Minto survey area) had crossed a transect with its perpendicular distance of only 1.0 km, the estimate would have been 72.8 wolves rather than 33.4, and the 80% Confidence Interval would have been ± 64% of the estimate rather than ± 30% of the estimate. Lengthening the period between end of snowfall and initiation of the survey will decrease the chance that such packs occur, as apparently was the case for Becker and Gardner (1990).

Our original intent was to develop a wolf census method for use on the wintering grounds of the western Arctic

Warren B. Ballard, Mark E. McNay, Craig L. Gardner, and Daniel J. Reed

caribou herd. Because the TIP method is highly dependent on good wolf tracking conditions, it cannot be used in areas of high ungulate density, particularly on caribou winter range. No accurate and precise methods currently exist for surveying wolves on caribou winter range, other than radio-telemetry. Although no caribou were present in our Minto study area and only small, scattered groups were encountered in our Kobuk study area, large numbers would greatly complicate survey attempts.

In spite of the above potential problems, the TIP method contains a measure of precision not obtained with other aerial survey methods. Equally important, the method is objective, repeatable, fast, and appears to provide reasonably accurate population estimates. Unlike aerial reconnaissance surveys, investigators are not required to distinguish between different wolf packs, or to detect all wolf packs within the survey area. Currently, statistical precision obtained with the TIP method is low. The biological precision (number observed and the upper 80% limit), however, is a large improvement over other wolf-survey methods. We hope to further improve precision by experimenting with different transect orientation designs and by more closely defining optimum survey periods following snowfall.

The TIP method is less expensive than telemetry studies. Total costs for such surveys ($135/hour/aircraft) exclusive of manpower ranged from $1,900–$2,600 (U.S. dollars) in south-central Alaska (Gardner and Becker 1991) to $3,250 in the Minto study area and $11,100 in the Kobuk study area. The Kobuk study costs represented an extreme because of difficult logistics that required aircraft and personnel from outside areas. The actual Kobuk survey cost was $4,758, the remainder being transportation costs. Gardner and Becker's (1991) costs represent the low end because experienced

pilots and observers were located close to the study areas and commute times were minimal.

Accurate and precise density estimates may allow extrapolation of survey results to larger areas of management significance. Simple extrapolations to obtain population estimates may be appropriate if study area boundaries contain representative proportions of habitat for the larger area of interest. Extrapolation may otherwise have to be based upon habitat types, prey densities, or other criteria. Survey areas can also serve as trend count areas to monitor long-term population status.

This study demonstrated that the track intercept probability estimator can provide useful, relatively accurate, and precise wolf population estimates. Further refinement of the technique is needed to improve precision, but useful estimates are now attainable if proper conditions exist and experienced personnel are used.

Acknowledgments

We express our sincere thanks to the following skilled pilots and biologists who participated in one or more aspects of this study: L.A. Ayres, R. Brubaker, R. Boertje, C. Conkle, E. Crain, J. Dau, R. Delong, R. Eagan, A. Greenblatt, R. Hunter, J. Knudson, D.N. Larson, J. Lee, H. McMahan, D. Miller, M. Robus, J. Rood, D. Witmer, and P. Valkenburg. The study was funded by the U.S. National Park Service, Alaska Department of Fish and Game, U.S. Fish and Wildlife Service, the University of Arizona, and several Alaska Federal Aid in Wildlife Restoration Projects. S. Arnett, A.F. Cunning, W. Fuller, P.R. Krausman, A. Lovaas, F.L. Miller, and S.R. Peterson provided constructive criticism on early drafts of the manuscript. C. Hepler and E. Lenart helped prepare the figures.

Citizen Participation in Developing a Wolf Management Plan for Alaska: An Attempt to Resolve Conflicting Human Values and Perceptions

■ **Dale A. Haggstrom, Anne K. Ruggles, Catherine M. Harms, and Robert O. Stephenson**

The subject of wolves and their management evokes diverse and polarized opinions, making this issue one of the more difficult for wildlife managers to resolve. We review the history and results of Alaska's recent attempt to develop a wolf management plan acceptable to most of the state's residents. A citizen participation process including a citizen planning team, forums, open houses, and discussions with civic groups was used to attempt to reach consensus. Despite early success, the Alaska Department of Fish and Game was unable to maintain a process that was widely perceived as fair. The public and media were not kept sufficiently informed about the planning effort or wolf biology and management, and the public was not kept adequately involved. Combined with an unwillingness on the part of some interests to compromise, this prevented the department from developing a wolf management plan acceptable to most Alaskans. We discuss problems encountered and make recommendations for others wishing to attempt such a public process. Despite the outcome, we believe this public process provides a promising vehicle for agencies seeking acceptable solutions to complex and controversial issues.

Introduction

Alaska has so far accommodated moderate human impact on the land without, for the most part, jeopardizing its wildlife, including large carnivores. Alaska's wildlife managers are striving to maintain this careful approach to wildlife use and management, while recognizing the need to accommodate different personal, cultural, and economic values within the context of biological and ecological realities. However, predator management, especially wolf (*Canis lupus*), remains contentious and continues to be one of the most difficult challenges facing wildlife biologists.

Alaska is home to an estimated 6,000–7,000 wolves. They are neither threatened nor endangered, and in most of the state are as plentiful as their food supplies allow. Alaska encompasses approximately 145 million hectares of which ownership is about 60% federal, about 20% state, and about 10% private (Alaska Dept. of Nat. Resourc. 1992). There are approximately 600,000 people, of whom about 10% live in rural areas (U.S. Dept. of Commerce 1990).

Lifestyles and cultures in Alaska range from those who depend on wild resources to those who obtain food from supermarkets. Alaska resource values reflect the diversity found in the lower 48 states, ranging from preservation to management and use to benefit human needs and desires. A Yale University study (Kellert 1985a) showed that Alaskans as a group were more knowledgeable about wolves and more committed to coexisting with wolves than any other group. However, Kellert also found that Alaskans possess a more utilitarian attitude toward wolves, as opposed to more preservationist attitudes elsewhere in the United States.

Due to the large amount of federally managed land in Alaska and its expanse of wilderness, there is a strong interest in resource management by those living outside Alaska. Resource management debates in Alaska include not only Alaskan rural, urban, hunting, nonhunting, commercial, resource exploitation, conservation, and preservation voices, but also non-Alaskan voices.

The last 20 years of wolf management actions and public reactions in Alaska (Harbo and Dean 1983, Stephenson et al. this volume) caused groups that should have been united in ensuring the future of wildlife habitat to work against one another to influence management decisions involving less critical issues. This history of confrontation eroded public trust in the Department of Fish and Game (department) and/or some individuals within it.

Historically, the department has communicated more with the hunting than the nonhunting public. Staff have struggled to understand and accommodate diverse, and sometimes conflicting, wildlife values among the public. This dilemma is not unique to Alaska (Wagner 1991). The personal values of some people are so deeply held that it is difficult, if not impossible, for them to recognize and fairly accommodate other interests.

History of the Planning Effort

During spring 1986, the last wolf control program conducted by the state was halted by concerned citizens who used political sensitivities to their advantage. Some staff, who had seen many apparently sound management programs stopped for nonbiological reasons, realized that department programs, and the system for involving the public in management decisions, had not kept pace with changes in societal values. It appeared that new approaches would be needed if the department were to retain the latitude to enhance some wildlife systems for benefits to people. An open planning process that fairly addressed the values and concerns of all Alaskans seemed to be the best means for meeting the legal mandate of providing a wide array of uses of wildlife.

In August 1987, the director of the Division of Wildlife Conservation endorsed the concept of broad public participation in planning the management of predator-prey systems, with a focus on wolves and wolf management. However, progress was slow. Frustrated by the controversy and its impact on other programs, some staff were hesitant to address the wolf management issue, or did not feel a solution was possible. Others sought to develop a management plan that most of the people in Alaska could accept. Nearly two years were required to build staff support for this idea.

In November 1989, the department requested support from the Board of Game (board), the seven-member public body responsible for enacting wildlife regulations in Alaska, for a public planning process. The problem was stated as follows:

> The wide range of public desires for wolves and their prey is not adequately satisfied by Alaska's current management practices and policies. This has caused a continual series of conflicts as opposing groups attempt to unilaterally influence management decisions.

After gaining the board's support, the department consulted with its traditional constituency as well as other individuals and organizations in an effort to better understand what people wanted for wildlife in Alaska. The depart-

ment invited people to help find areas where compromise might be possible. Support from some of the public was slow to develop. Many of those contacted were hesitant to embark on a long public process. Some feared the process would either further delay management actions, or lead to hasty decisions. Others seemed reluctant to engage in a dialogue that would entail mutual respect or foster compromise.

A needs assessment (Bleiker and Bleiker 1981) was conducted to identify effective ways to find out how people wanted wildlife managed and to involve them in the process. Four methods seemed most promising: a citizen planning team, forums, open houses, and presentations to civic groups. We describe the planning team approach in some detail, as it proved particularly effective and was well received by the public. The other methods were not as fully implemented and a fair comparison is not possible.

Wolf Management Planning Team

The Alaska Wolf Management Planning Team (team) represented many of the diverse values held by Alaskans regarding wolves and wolf management. It consisted of 12 members selected from a list of 60 people recommended by the public, a representative of the department, and a representative of the board. The department tried to create a team that included all major interests. Individuals were selected based on their ability to both represent their personal values and work effectively with people whose values were different.

The men and women comprising the public members were a diverse group not only in values, but also in lifestyle, residence, age, and ethnicity. Members represented rural and urban hunting, nonhunting, guiding, and trapping interests. There were members of local and national environmental and hunting organizations, members of Fish and Game Advisory committees, and educators. All shared the goal of ensuring viable wolf populations throughout Alaska in the future. The team was charged with making recommendations to the department and the Board on how wolves should be managed.

At the team's first meeting on 14 and 15 November 1990, the framework and ground rules for the group were established. The department hired the Keystone Center, a nonprofit organization specializing in mediation of difficult issues, to facilitate and chair all meetings. The team used a process in which members strove for consensus, while allowing each individual to maintain their basic values. To promote the open exchange of ideas necessary to reach consensus, the group adhered to these basic rules:

- Each person was to articulate their own interests and concerns.
- Each was to try to understand the interests and concerns of others, listening and keeping an open mind throughout the process.

- Each was to try to fashion solutions that satisfied all interests (not solely their own).
- Each was to understand that not every recommendation eventually made by the Team would be their first choice.

To further ensure that an open discussion ensued and that no one compromised their values, the group agreed to more specific rules:

- Team members did not serve as formal representatives of organizations or agencies to which they belonged, but rather as individuals.
- All values were respected and considered valid.
- All comments were depersonalized.
- All disagreements were discussed on a professional level.
- Everyone had equal access to the floor.

A key component of the process was public participation. The team recognized that public participation in its deliberations was desirable, but realized that public dialogue during each meeting would be cumbersome. The public were invited to attend team meetings, but not participate in the discussions. Written testimony was solicited from the public and the team held two public meetings, one in Anchorage and one in Fairbanks, at which the public were invited to share their thoughts on wolf management in Alaska. The team announced the date, time, and location of all meetings through the news media, distributed meeting summaries to all interested parties, and prepared news releases following each meeting.

The team held six, two- to three-day meetings during which they discussed definitions of terms; the history of wolf management in Alaska; basic wolf biology; predator-prey dynamics; pack dynamics; population censusing techniques; state and federal regulations, laws, and enforcement capabilities; the use of aircraft in hunting and trapping wolves; long-term population goals; management goals; predator control; ethics; assessment of user groups and needs, attitudes and values of the public; methods and means; interagency coordination; information and education needs; and the role of politics and biology in wolf management decisions.

In June 1991, the team offered its recommendations (Alaska Wolf Management Planning Team 1991) to the department, describing areas of consensus reached by the members. The team recognized in its report that public participation and the consideration of the values of all Alaskans were necessary if the history of adversarial management of wolves was to give way to a constructive dialogue.

Strategic Wolf Management Plan

During summer 1991, the department drafted a Strategic Wolf Management Plan (Alaska Department of Fish and Game 1992a) based primarily on the team's final report, but which also included information offered by other members of the public and wildlife scientists. The draft strategic plan

was released for public review in September 1991 and public comments were incorporated.

The team and its facilitator met with the board during October 1991 to brief them on the process, rules, and results of the team's effort. The department expected to offer a status report to the board and complete the process on its own schedule. However, the board took possession of the draft plan and chose to work with the public and the department to finalize and adopt the strategic plan during the meeting.

To allow increased flexibility to include the public in its deliberations, the board chairman recessed the official meeting and convened the board as a "committee of the whole." This committee asked department personnel, three members of the team, and three members of the public to help conduct a word-by-word review of the draft strategic plan. After three days of revision, the board reconvened its official meeting and unanimously approved the plan.

The strategic plan provided guidelines to address wolf management (and therefore system management) in Alaska. The goal of the plan was to ensure the long-term conservation of wolves throughout Alaska, while providing for diverse human values and uses of wildlife, as well as increasing public awareness of wolves and their uses (Alaska Department of Fish and Game 1992a). It recognized that no single type of wildlife management can provide for a wide variety of uses, and described seven zones, where management strategies would range from complete protection of wolves to manipulation of wolf numbers to maintain or enhance human uses of ungulate species. The board's intent was to identify more areas where wolves could be protected and more areas where wolves could be intensively managed to provide opportunities for people to hunt ungulates (Alaska Board of Game 1991).

The strategic plan did not actually apply the zone concept anywhere within the state. It provided the framework for the public process needed to develop area-specific management plans, in which management objectives and strategies would be incorporated through the zone system. It also provided a public process for the development of implementation plans for those areas where wolf control would be needed.

Area-Specific and Implementation Plans

In its final report, the planning team recommended development of operational plans for high priority game management units within one year. In following that recommendation, the department focused initially on portions of south-central and interior Alaska. In November 1991, it asked the public to consider the primary uses of wildlife in specific areas, and suggest appropriate management zones.

These two areas contained most of the state's human population, road system, and lands that were important and accessible to most of the state's hunting and nonhunting public. Included were areas where wolf control had been used in the past in an effort to maintain harvest levels of ungulates, and most of the areas where wolf control was likely to be proposed in the future. For these reasons, the department expected management of wolves and their prey in these two areas to be more controversial than elsewhere and, therefore, a good test of the public process.

Over the next four months, department staff conducted public workshops in six communities, attended meetings with interest groups, and spent hundreds of hours talking with concerned people. More than 200 written responses were collected and reviewed prior to drafting area-specific plans.

As efforts progressed, it became obvious that most of the area under consideration was being zoned for moderate to intensive management. Some argued this was appropriate, because active management is precluded by federal ownership over much of the remainder of the state (this information was not effectively presented to the public), and that much of the area contained in the initial area-specific plans is accessible to the majority of Alaskans and has a long history of management for harvest. Others viewed these accessible areas as equally important to the nonhunting public.

The department revised the area-specific plans twice before presenting them to the board in March 1992. The board again convened as a "committee of the whole," involving members of the public and department in a review of the draft plans. The board tentatively approved the zone designations and management objectives in the draft plans. It also directed the department to combine the two area-specific plans into one document, revise the plan to reflect tentatively approved zone changes, review the management objectives with the public, and prepare draft implementation plans for wolf control in those areas tentatively approved for intensive management.

Department staff attempted to comply with these board directives during summer 1992. For example, in one portion of the planning area (east-central Alaska), staff developed and distributed a questionnaire to assess local attitudes toward wildlife management, while developing their portion of the draft area-specific plan. This questionnaire also solicited opinions from tourism-related small businesses. However, similar efforts were not undertaken elsewhere and department staff did not actively seek participation by major tourism agencies or businesses in the planning effort.

Instead, area-specific and implementation plans (Alaska Department of Fish and Game 1992b) were generally prepared by the department with little opportunity for the public to help or learn about their content prior to release for public comment in September. This approach left the public with no option but to react to documents they had not helped prepare.

When the drafts were released for public review, the department tried to focus public attention on the area-specific plans in order to confirm the management objectives for the areas identified for intensive management and to

discuss strategies for meeting them, as directed by the board. However, many in the public wanted to discuss the implementation options, because these would govern proposed wolf control programs.

Some hunters were displeased that the draft implementation plans did not include the full range of biologically feasible options. They wanted the board to review options that would yield larger prey populations and, in some cases, wolf populations, and harvest rates higher than those proposed by the department. Subsequently, department staff produced additional, more intensive management options for the board's consideration. However, these were not available to the public prior to the November 1992 meeting.

Public Reaction

By the November 1992 Board meeting, most Alaskans interested in wolf management were aware of the planning process. The two days of public testimony were different from those experienced prior to the planning effort. Many who testified suggested ways to fairly accommodate interests different from their own.

Some environmentalists who had previously opposed any wolf control testified that they could now accept it under some circumstances. The Northern Alaska Environmental Center testified in support of a management program that included temporary wolf population reduction to reverse the decline of the Delta caribou (*Rangifer tarandus*) herd and restore harvests. The Alaska Wildlife Alliance, which had consistently challenged state wolf management programs in the past, also seemed willing to compromise.

Likewise, some sportsmen recognized the volatility of the issue and expressed a willingness to accept fewer programs and programs of a smaller scope. The obvious effort by many people to fairly consider the values and needs of others was encouraging. It appeared that achieving consensus among the major interests in the state was possible. However, there was substantial pressure from some interests to maximize management in traditional hunting areas and from others to minimize management or eliminate it altogether.

During a one-day recess following public testimony, department staff met to formulate the official department recommendations to the board. Based on their knowledge of public concerns expressed before and during the board meeting, staff attempted to balance areas where wolves would be protected and areas where wolf numbers could be controlled to more intensively manage prey to benefit people.

Subsequently, the board, without benefit of a "committee of the whole," revised and adopted the area-specific plan for south-central and interior Alaska according to the department's recommendations. It also adopted implementation plans for three wolf control programs. The area-specific plans increased the area in the state where wolves would be completely protected from hunting and trapping to about

3%, and created areas where wolf numbers would be controlled in about 3.5 % of the state.

The board believed their decisions represented a fair compromise resulting from a fair planning process. Many in the public also felt this balance between protected and intensively managed areas was reasonable. However, environmentalists who participated in the planning process and agreed to limited wolf control felt betrayed. They felt the board did not appreciate the magnitude of their concessions, and had assumed that environmentalists would support more extensive programs if the board provided additional protection for wolves on some state lands. Uncertainty over zoning prospects for the rest of the state also caused some concern. Following the board's actions, the spirit of compromise among Alaskans diminished as rhetoric escalated and public opinion re-polarized.

In retrospect, the temporary departure from an open process during the November 1992 Board meeting and the lack of any public involvement in board deliberations marked a turning point. Concessions made during the public process prior to the board meeting had led many people to support a more conservative approach than that passed by the board. After the meeting, some environmentalists and hunters expressed concern that critical questions had not been asked, alternatives had not been adequately explored, and more extensive programs had been approved than were either biologically necessary or socially acceptable.

Concessions made to various interest groups (i.e., areas closed to hunting and trapping wolves near Fairbanks, Anchorage, and Denali National Park) were not negotiated with group representatives or those living in affected areas, and were presented to the board without public review. Thus, these recommendations were widely viewed as unfair, unnecessary, or inadequate by many in the public.

During subsequent board deliberations, the issue of potential caribou viewing opportunities was raised and the large migrations of caribou in Alaska were compared to ungulate migrations in east Africa. These comments, taken out of context, resulted in news articles suggesting tourism was the primary reason for wolf control in Alaska when, in reality, the department had never viewed tourism as adequate justification for active management.

Neither the department nor the board adequately recognized, informed, or involved the interests of the public outside Alaska. Some of these concerned people were knowledgeable and well informed. Others were not or held pre-existing misconceptions about wolves and wolf ecology, and were easily influenced by inaccurate or misleading information promoted by some extreme interest groups and disseminated in the national media.

This oversight created difficulties when a national animal rights group used the media's focus on tourism to enlist support for their opposition to the control programs by calling for a tourism boycott of Alaska. The potential rami-

fications of people canceling visits to Alaska were apparent to both the state's tourism industry and administration.

On 4 December 1992, the governor announced that he would not implement regulations establishing new wolf protection areas and control programs until further review. He invited concerned people from around the country to a "wolf summit" in Fairbanks in January 1993. On 22 December, the Fish and Game commissioner announced that department staff would not conduct aerial wolf control in 1993. These announcements prompted many Alaskans to voice dissatisfaction with the governor and commissioner for bowing to outside interests.

More than 125 people were invited to participate in the wolf summit held 16–18 January 1993. Politicians, Alaskan natives, representatives of environmental groups, animal rights groups, hunting and trapping organizations, the tourism industry, members of the media, members of the fish and game advisory committees, and professional wildlife biologists from Alaska and elsewhere attended. The summit was open to the public and, at times, up to 1,500 people attended. Professional facilitators were hired to conduct the meetings.

Speakers reviewed wolf natural history, predator-prey dynamics, the planning process, effects on tourism, and Alaskan, national, and international perspectives on wolf management. Participants then met in nine smaller groups facilitated by representatives of the Office of the Ombudsman to discuss the planning process and management decisions about wolves. After about eight hours of discussion, each group compiled a list of consensus points. Facilitators then identified the following areas of agreement:

1. The planning process used, especially the Alaska Wolf Management Planning Team, was good and the department need not start over.
2. The department should begin proactive education and information efforts about wolves.
3. The International Union for Conservation of Nature and Natural Resources (IUCN) Wolf Specialist Group guidelines (IUCN 1983) regarding wolf control and some elements of the Yukon Territory's wolf management plan (Yukon Wolf Management Planning Team 1992) should be incorporated into Alaska's wolf management plan.
4. The state needed to take steps to make its Board of Game and Advisory Committee process more broadly representative of the public's diverse interests.
5. More time was required for a fair and open public process to be successful.

Each group concluded that wolf control could be considered, but none were able, in the brief time available, to reach consensus on the circumstances under which control was justified.

On 27–28 January 1993, the board met to reconsider the area-specific plans, implementation plans, and regulations adopted in November, based on concerns that emerged following those decisions. At the department's recommendation, the Board rescinded the area-specific and implementation plans to allow reevaluation, and deleted parts of the strategic plan detailing the process for determining zones, and area-specific and implementation plans. It then directed the department to prepare proposals for wolf control and scheduled a meeting for June 1993 to discuss these proposals and other aspects of the wolf management issue.

The political climate and public sentiments surrounding wolf management continue to be contentious. There seems to be heightened mistrust both of the agency and among various public interests. At the board's request, the department has focused on when, where, and how wolf control might be conducted, rather than a more comprehensive planning effort. With this approach, the outcome will be determined largely by the board and department with less extensive public involvement, and is likely to be perceived as unfair. Thus, we believe it unlikely that the wolf management controversy will be fully resolved in the near future.

Recommendations

1. *There must be agreement on the goal of the planning process.*

   An agency cannot be perceived as using a public planning process to achieve a predetermined result. This is worse than taking action without benefit of public involvement. Members of the public expect their participation to influence a program. If they perceive that it does not, they feel angry, betrayed, and disillusioned. Further, it severely damages the credibility of the agency, jeopardizing future support and public involvement. Internal damage can occur if staff believe there is a commitment to a public process different from that supported by the agency's leadership. As others have learned, it is easy for an agency or individuals to lose credibility and hard to regain it; trust and candor arise from positive experiences (Bartolome 1989).

   In the Alaska situation, the emphasis of staff who initiated the planning effort in 1986 was on maintaining a fair process, with the department accepting the results within ecological, fiscal, and statutory constraints, regardless of the outcome. However, following the gubernatorial election of 1990, the focus of the planning effort shifted toward providing an outcome that the administration considered a fair balance between use and protection.

2. *The agency's planning authority and responsibility must be maintained throughout the planning effort.*

   The agency conducting the planning effort must be perceived as the proper institution to address the problem.

   In Alaska, the division of responsibility between the board and the department is not clear for matters involving planning. However, the board has neither the resources nor time to complete such a process. The department should have retained full responsibility for the wolf planning process, working with the public to develop management plans, documenting public participation, and obtaining substantial consensus before proposing regulatory changes to the board.

3. *Adequate time must be allocated to the planning process.*

   A planning process must proceed at the rate necessary to achieve consent rather than meet administrative deadlines or political pressures. In Alaska, the urgency created by public and political pressure to resolve this issue and the attempt to meet the board's administrative schedule had some negative effects:

   a. Public contact was minimized, jeopardizing the perception of fairness.

   b. Topics were not revisited to correct errors. For example, two major shortcomings in the department's approach were identified early in the planning effort, but insufficient time was provided to address them. First, the plans focused too narrowly on the management of wolves and their major prey species. Astute observers pointed out that it was illogical for wolf management to dictate wildlife use priorities in an area; they felt the process should be reversed so that human use priorities would determine wolf management needs. Second, the zoning system was confusing and inadequate for many situations. It unsuccessfully attempted to blend human use and wolf management into a single classification.

   c. The department dealt concurrently with planning steps that should have been sequential. For example, when it became apparent that population and harvest objectives used in the area-specific plans had not been adequately reviewed by the public, staff were not given time to obtain such a review and revise accordingly.

4. *Teamwork and coordination must be encouraged.*

   Public communication and conflict resolution on a major public issue cannot be done by a few interested employees. An agency must provide leadership and resources for a coordinated, effective effort.

   In Alaska, the department slowed the planning process on several occasions to provide additional time to attempt consensus among the interested public, but a coordinated, effective effort was sometimes lacking. Thus, additional time did not significantly improve the public process, and in some cases, exacerbated existing frustration among segments of the public who felt too little progress was being made. We recommend a team approach to maintain a coordinated, effective effort in which agency leadership, other staff, and potentially affected interests outside the agency are informed and involved.

5. *Staff must make public communication a priority, acquire the skills necessary to do the job, and involve the public in all phases of the process.*

   This will prevent an agency from generating plans based largely on its own perception of public desires. When a plan is developed based on public reaction rather than ongoing involvement, agency credibility can be compromised.

6. *All potentially affected interests must be identified and involved in the planning process.*

   Inadvertently ignoring an interest will alienate those involved and can slow or halt progress in resolving an issue. The department did not adequately involve either the Alaska tourism industry or interest groups outside Alaska in the planning process, leading these interests to react to the planning effort with negative press coverage and political interference late in the process.

   Attempts to reconcile extreme views often dominated each phase of the process, reducing the influence of those with more moderate views and furthering the tendency for those involved to frame issues and regard interests in terms of stereotypes. Efforts to inform and involve less extreme groups were inadequate, leading them to "choose sides" when disagreements among more extreme interests led to a stalemate.

7. *The public and media must be kept informed.*

   A proactive public information effort before and during the planning process can reduce misperceptions, foster consensus among those with opposing views, and result in a better plan. An informed public is less influenced by extreme views. An ongoing effort to work with the media will also reduce inaccurate, biased reporting that can needlessly aggravate public distrust.

   In the Alaska situation, the department often did not keep the public and media adequately informed. For example, the needs assessment indicated presentations to civic groups would be effective, but few were actually done.

Conclusions

The department did not succeed in its recent attempt to develop a statewide compromise wolf management plan that most Alaskans could accept. The citizen participation effort fell short in part because the department did not maintain a process that was perceived as fair, was unable to fully incorporate public comments and concerns into the plan, and did not adequately inform the public and media.

Although early efforts seemed promising, three events significantly affected the outcome. The 1990 gubernatorial election shifted the focus from process to outcome. The October 1991 board meeting transferred control and timing of the planning process from the department to the board. The November 1992 board meeting discontinued the previous practice of including the public in deliberations. We believe these events undermined the trust of those who had made a good-faith effort to participate, and resulted in board actions that did not have sufficient public acceptance within Alaska.

The department and board are now pursuing a more focused approach to identify areas where wolf management, including control, is considered urgent. Their goal is to reach some middle ground between the extremes on where and how wolves will be managed in these areas. The department will propose what it considers moderate management approaches to the board for its consideration and public review.

Despite the outcome, the planning effort has yielded some benefits for the department. Some staff have learned how to communicate more effectively and involve people in decision making. Lines of communication with new interests have been established, and rapport with existing interests has, in some instances, been enhanced. We feel the department has taken an important step toward learning how to better work with the public to resolve controversial issues. The experience and knowledge gained should serve the department well in the years to come, and serve as a catalyst for further introspection and constructive change.

Society's values toward wildlife and expectations for management have become more diverse, and in some instances, are incompatible. Wildlife professionals are struggling to manage for increasingly diverse human interests. However, these changes are difficult to accept for some members of the public and wildlife professionals accustomed to wildlife management's traditional role.

Alaska attempted to address an inherently difficult issue. The antagonism and mistrust surrounding wolf management in Alaska has existed for decades. It was probably optimistic to expect the department to resolve this controversy in just a few years. Nonetheless, this experience has reaffirmed our belief that active citizen participation can help overcome distrust and lead to constructive dialogue. Despite the outcome, we believe that when properly conducted, a program of public involvement can resolve controversial issues, even one as contentious as wolf management.

Acknowledgments

We are grateful to many people who helped us prepare this paper. In particular, we wish to acknowledge M.A. Matthews, C.A. Smith, Dr. S. Todd, and D.G. Kelleyhouse, whose reviews of the many drafts of this paper were extremely helpful in clarifying information, documenting history, and making the final draft more readable.

Dale A. Haggstrom, Anne K. Ruggles, Catherine M. Harms, and Robert O. Stephenson

Part Nine:
Management Techniques

Review of Wolf Control Methods in North America

■ H. Dean Cluff and Dennis L. Murray

*Wolves have been controlled for centuries in North America. During early European settlement, pitfalls and deadfalls were widely used until less laborious methods were introduced. Snares, stomach piercers, and set guns were easily prepared and commonly used. Steel leg-hold traps were available by the 1630's, and were likely the most common method of controlling wolves. Although still used today, leg-hold traps have been modified to render them more humane. Bounties and incentives, once common across the continent, have now been abandoned due to inefficiency and expense. Poisons were an effective and economical method to control wolves, but their use is rapidly declining because of public opposition. Shooting from the air is effective, but the practice is highly controversial and is also declining. Today, lethal control usually targets specific animals rather than entire populations. Wildlife managers are implementing nonlethal techniques because of growing public disfavor for killing wolves. The use of guard dogs (**Canis familiaris**) to protect livestock is gaining in popularity. Other techniques include light, sound, and chemical repellents, aversive conditioning, fences, and relocation of problem individuals. These methods have met with moderate success, but require further testing. Diversionary feeding during ungulate calving periods and reproductive suppression via sterilization are intended specifically to reduce wolf predation on wild ungulates; neither method has yet demonstrated its large-scale utility or applicability. Nonlethal control will remain favorable to the public during the foreseeable future and will likely supersede lethal control in all but the most extreme cases.*

Introduction

The current distribution and abundance of wolves (*Canis lupus*) in North America are the result of habitat change and eradication efforts over the past 350 years. People have intentionally killed wolves for fur (Carbyn 1987), protection of livestock and game (Young and Goldman 1944), disease control (Ballantyne and O'Donoghue 1954), and out of fear (e.g., Lopez 1978). Although wolf control occurs less often now than in the past, several government agencies have recently killed wolves to reduce predation on wild ungulates (e.g., Bergerud and Elliot 1986, Atkinson and Janz 1991) or livestock (e.g., Gunson 1983b, Tompa 1983b, Fritts et al. 1992). Currently, only in Yukon do they continue to kill wolves for the benefit of ungulates, but Alaska intends to do the same in the near future. Elsewhere, governments intervene on an *ad hoc*, site-specific basis to alleviate livestock depredation by wolves.

The present status of wolves differs among jurisdictions, and this influences the policies by which they are managed. Wolves are not abundant in the contiguous United States (U.S.) except in Minnesota (Fuller et al. 1992a), and only federal agents can control wolves there (Fritts et al. 1992, Bangs et al. this volume). The few wild wolves that remain in Mexico receive full legal protection (Ginsberg and Macdonald 1990). Presently, wolves are harvested in Alaska,

Northwest Territories (N.W.T.), Yukon, and six Canadian provinces (Carbyn 1987, Hayes and Gunson this volume). Where wolves are killed by the public, the harvest is subject to limits on the number taken, harvest seasons, and control methods.

A variety of techniques have been used to kill wolves in North America; these have ranged widely in effectiveness, selectivity, and humaneness. Many of the nonselective and inhumane methods used in the past have been modified or replaced by techniques that reverse these characteristics (Andelt 1987). Public sensitivity to the killing of predators has made wolf control a delicate issue, of which wildlife biologists and legislators are well aware when deciding on its application (Archibald et al. 1991, Gasaway et al. 1992, Fritts 1993a). Indeed, killing predators indiscriminately is no longer seen as an acceptable solution to predator-prey problems (Gasaway et al. 1992), and that approach has generally yielded to the limited removal of individuals or packs (Connolly 1978a). Therefore, wolf harvest and control must be implemented through humane, cost-effective, yet efficient, methods and be acceptable to the public (Pimlott 1961a, Kellert 1985a, Thompson and Gasson 1991). In this paper, we update previously published reviews of wolf control methods and discuss lethal versus nonlethal methods in the context of public acceptability.

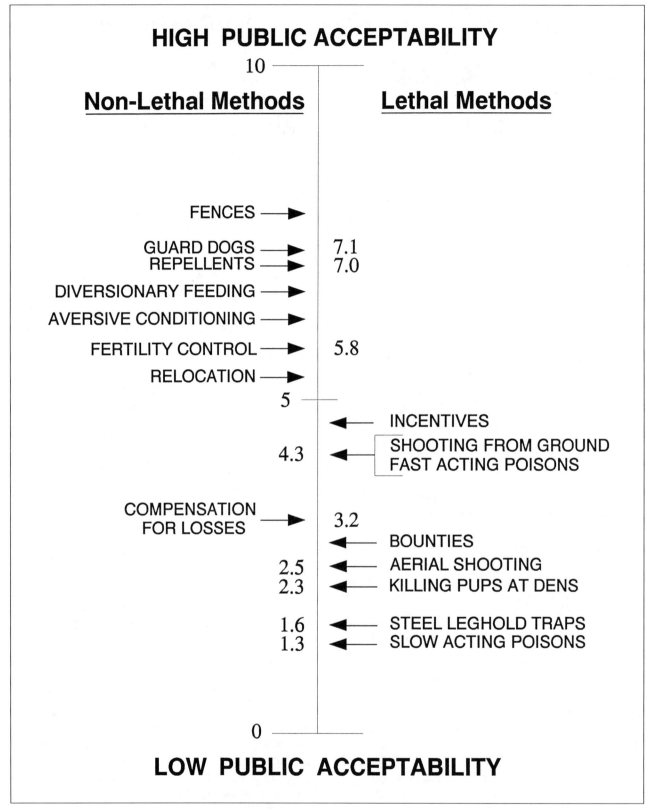

Fig. 1. *Public acceptability of predator control techniques. Although first reported with respect to coyote control, the public acceptability rankings of these methods are likely applicable to wolf control. Numbers opposite a control technique quantify public acceptability on a scale of 1–10 based on U.S. Fish and Wildlife Service (1978), Arthur (1981), and Andelt (1987). We ranked other wolf control methods that were not listed for coyotes (no numbers opposite technique) based on the literature and speculation. We assumed public acceptability tends to be influenced more by humaneness than other considerations such as cost-effectiveness.*

Lethal Methods

Trapping Devices

1. Pitfalls and Deadfalls.

The pitfall is indeed an ancient method of capture, having been referenced in the Old Testament (Young and Goldman 1944). Pitfalls in North America were used primarily by native Americans (Mason 1902:467) and European settlers (Young and Goldman 1944). The pitfall trap simply consisted of a deep hole in the ground that animals were attracted to, fell in, but could not escape. Standard pits in Mexico were modified by the early Spaniards by tapering the trench to a "V" at the bottom and lining the trench walls with smooth-faced rock or split logs (Young and Goldman 1944, Bateman 1971). Other pitfalls were surrounded with leg-hold traps or bedded with sharpened stakes to impale prey (Andersch 1906:322). Other modifications included pits filled with water to drown victims or rotating lids for multiple captures (Bateman 1971). Pitfalls were used in most eastern colonies and were considered successful at reducing depredations by wolves (Young and Goldman 1944) as were the snowpits used by native Americans in northern areas (Mason 1902:467, Novak 1987). The elaborate design and time invested in preparing these traps probably contributed to their demise when alternative methods became available.

Although deadfalls have been used to kill wolves and bears (*Ursus* spp.), their construction was elaborate to ensure proper functioning. Deadfalls for large mammals were constructed by raising one log above another at one end by means of an upright stick. Additional logs were usually added to increase the weight of the falling log. When triggered, the log would crush its victim. Lewis and Clark (1904–05, cited in Young and Goldman 1944) reported the use of deadfalls by native North Americans for wolves and other wildlife in the early 1800's. A variation on the deadfall was the ice boxtrap used in the Arctic against wolves (Young and Goldman 1944). Although construction of deadfalls is still taught in instructional books and videos in some trapper education programs, these traps are seldom used.

2. Snares

Snares capture an animal by the neck or foot. The first snares were made from twisted bark, rawhide, or hair, and were simply a noose with a slip knot (Bateman 1971, Boddicker 1982). Recent snare materials include wire, cable, and synthetic cords (Bateman 1971, Guthery and Beasom 1978). Present-day snares for wolves are made with double-twisted aircraft control cable and a variety of locks and swivels.

The use of snares to capture wolves is poorly documented, although they were widely used by native American and European trappers for centuries (Young and Goldman 1944). Today, snares are also used with other capture methods to extend the trapping period when weather renders leg-hold traps ineffective (Boddicker 1982). Injuries to wolves caught in foot snares set for bears may cause fewer injuries to captured wolves than leg-hold traps. Furthermore, foot snares tend to be difficult to conceal and usually capture only the least wary wolves.

Recent snare developments include coiled steel power snares and stop-lock neck snares (e.g., Nellis 1968). Stop-lock neck snares, used more for live-captures than trapping for fur, prevent the loop from tightening beyond the circumference of the wolf's neck. These snares have the potential for reducing injuries by not restricting air or blood flow and may also allow smaller, nontarget animals to escape. However, wolf researchers at Isle Royale National Park (R. Peterson, Michigan Tech. Univ., pers. commun.) and Banff National Park (P. Paquet, John/Paul and Associates, pers. commun.) have expressed concern over the use of these snares because of an expected 3-10% mortality rate. These mortalities usually occur from improper snare action or entanglement of a live-snared wolf in the surrounding vegetation.

3. Steel Traps

A variety of primitive traps were available in North America soon after the first colonies were settled (Gerstell 1985). The modern steel leg-hold trap reflects the basic design of traps made more than 2,000 years ago from animal sinews or plant fibers and the more recent wooden torsion traps (Gerstell 1985). European treadle and torsion traps gradually had their wooden parts replaced by metal and eventually evolved into the Newhouse brand (WoodStream Corp., Lititz, Pennsylvania) of leg-hold traps used in recent decades (Thomas 1984, Novak 1987).

Steel traps are classified as either killer or leg-hold traps (Gerstell 1985). Killer traps grab or pierce the head, neck, or body of the victim by using claws, spears, or pinchers (e.g., see Gerstell 1985, Novak 1987). Before the mid 1700's, iron traps were large, handmade killing devices for striking wolves on the head or body (Mason 1902:473, Young and Goldman 1944, Gerstell 1985). These large traps were impractical for field use and seldom used. The smaller leg-hold traps were transportable and had paired jaws that held an animal's leg or foot when closed. The leg-hold trap became a popular means of wolf control, especially where bounties were offered. Steel traps were favored over snares and deadfalls because of their relative ease in setting and reliability of capture (Harding 1978).

Steel traps were first used to remove wolves in the early 1630's in present-day Massachusetts (Schorger 1950, Gerstell 1985). Steel traps were locally made until the mid 1800's, but by 1875, mass-produced traps were common (Gerstell 1985). In the 1860's, the No. 4 and No. 14 Newhouse traps were available for capturing wolves. The No. 4½ Newhouse wolf trap was added in 1895 in response to the demand from western ranchers for a stronger trap (Gerstell 1985). In the early 1920's, the No. 114 Newhouse trap was manufactured specifically for the larger Alaskan wolves

(Young and Goldman 1944). The Manning wolf trap was designed in 1980 for similar purposes (Gerstell 1985).

Wolves had been practically extirpated in the eastern U.S. by the time leg-hold traps were in widespread use. The leg-hold trap's notoriety led to its ban in some American states (Clark 1980) except for use by personnel conducting research or depredation control. However, trapping wolves commercially or for control continued in the western U.S. and northward, but now only occurs in Alaska, Canada, Minnesota, and Montana. Wolves were also trapped in many western national parks during the early 1900's (Singer 1987, Wright 1992). During the 1960's–1990's, most wolf researchers minimized injuries by live-capturing wolves with modified steel leg-hold traps. Actual accounts of wolf control in Mexico from 1925 to 1950 are lacking (Brown 1983), however, Mexican ranchers in the 1950's purchased traps from the U.S. to protect cattle in Durango and Zacatecas states (McBride 1980).

Opposition to the Leg-hold Trap
Concern about animal injury resulting from steel traps surfaced in North America by 1900 (Gerstell 1985). The public's disfavor with the steel trap grew during the 1920's and influenced trap use and development. Furthermore, traps considered inhumane were prohibited in some states in the 1930's (Herscovici 1985, Gentile 1987). Additional bans followed, but antitrapping efforts gradually declined and all statewide bans were lifted by 1948 (Gentile 1987). Legislation against leg-hold trap use has been introduced repeatedly since the 1960's on the behalf of many antitrapping organizations (Herscovici 1985, Gentile 1987, Boggess et al. 1990). This resulted in the restriction of leg-hold traps in several states by the 1970's (Gerstell 1985).

Opposition to the leg-hold trap is related to injuries sustained during capture. Although trap research, trapper education, and legislation have reduced injuries considerably (Baker and Dwyer 1987, Novak 1987), public acceptance of leg-hold traps remains low (Kellert 1981). Padded jaws on leg-hold traps are considered more humane for coyotes (*C. latrans*) than unpadded jaws (Linhart et al. 1986, Todd and Skinner 1990). The padded jaw Braun wolf trap (Wayne's Tool Innovations Inc., Campbell River, British Columbia) is available commercially for wolves, however, it is unacceptable to some American [S.H. Fritts, U.S. Fish and Wildlife Service (USFWS), pers. commun.] and Canadian (P. Paquet, John/Paul Associates, pers. commun.) researchers because of injuries it can inflict on wolves. Toothed-jawed traps (e.g., No. 14 Newhouse, No. 7 McBride) with a wide offset (1.8 cm) can cause less damage than smooth-jawed traps (Kuehn et al. 1986).

Wolf trappers have historically preferred leg-hold traps having jaws with teeth, likely as assurance against escapes. However, in some cases, the offset on toothed-jawed traps has facilitated escape (W.J. Paul, Anim. Damage Control, pers. commun.). Teeth on traps have been outlawed in some

jurisdictions in Canada and the U.S., and since the early 1970's their use is no longer permitted when trapping for fur (Bateman 1971, Novak 1987). Wolf researchers and control personnel also used traps with offset, toothed-jaws because of reduced foot damage compared to smooth-jawed traps (Kuehn et al. 1986, R.T. McBride, Rancher's Supply Inc., pers. commun.). However, Animal Damage Control (ADC) personnel in Minnesota have not seen reduced injuries in wolves captured with traps having the toothed, but offset jaws (W.J. Paul, ADC, pers. commun.). Steel trap exchange programs now exist to accelerate leg-hold trap replacement (e.g., in N.W.T. and Yukon) although toothed traps remain in circulation primarily for research and removal of problem wolves (e.g., Van Ballenberghe 1984).

Tranquillizer tabs that mildly sedate a captured animal when the tab is bitten may reduce injuries and thereby increase public acceptance of leg-hold traps (Balser 1965, Andelt 1985); apparently these have not been tried with wolves. Other alternative trap designs include under-pan springs or shear pin modifications that reduce capture of non-target species based on weight. Wolf traps modified with under-pan springs have reduced captures of nontarget species by 50–75% during depredation control trapping in Minnesota (W.J. Paul, ADC, pers. commun.).

Bounties
Bounties are probably the oldest predator management tool, having been used to control wolves for at least 2,700 years. Bounties were usually a financial award, but sometimes livestock or goods were offered (Young and Goldman 1944). Originating in Greece and once common throughout Europe, wolf bounties were implemented in North America following European settlement in the 1600's (Young and Goldman 1944, Young 1970). Soon, almost every eastern colony had a wolf bounty and these were to remain in almost continuous effect for more than two centuries. For example, Virginia had wolf bounties until 1940, although wolves had essentially been exterminated from the eastern U.S. by 1900 (Young and Goldman 1944). Imposition of bounties continued as human settlement and exploration moved westward, until virtually every American state or territory offered bounties at various times during the 1700's to 1900's (Young and Goldman 1944, Hubert 1982).

Bounties were the mainstay for professional wolfers who killed wolves throughout the western U.S. in the late 1800's (Mech 1970). Bounties continued in some western states into the 1940's, although wolves were rare in the west by the 1930's (Young and Goldman 1944, Brown 1983). Despite an absence of wolves in almost all areas of the contiguous U.S., five states still had wolf bounties on the legislative records as late as 1971 (Cain et al. 1972). Undoubtedly, some wolf bounties were paid for coyotes because few jurisdictions always distinguished between the two species.

As in the American colonies, bounties in Canada were initially solicited by the public because they perceived wolves as responsible for extensive depredation on livestock (e.g., Banville 1981). Consequently, wolf bounties in Canada may have occurred in the early 1700's (Omand 1950), although the first documented bounty was in Upper Canada (Ontario) in 1793 (Pimlott 1961b, Kolenosky 1983). Bounties were soon established elsewhere and by 1900, all Canadian provinces with wolves also had bounties.

Newfoundland had implemented its wolf bounty in 1839, and wolves became extinct 90 years later (Dodds 1983). Wolves were already nearly extinct in Nova Scotia and New Brunswick by 1870 (Cameron 1958) and bounties were not necessary. Quebec officially imposed legislation against wolves in 1861 (Banville 1978). On matters of wolf control, Québec and Ontario seemingly spared no expense. Between 1905 and 1961, more than $1 million was paid for 8,542 wolves killed for bounty in Québec (Banville 1981), while in Ontario, more than $2 million in bounties were paid for wolves and coyotes claimed between 1925 and 1972 (Pimlott 1961b, 1963, Kolenosky 1983). A supplementary bounty was also offered in some counties in Québec and Ontario (Pimlott 1961a). Québec repealed its public bounty in 1961 and abolished other forms of remuneration in 1971 (Banville 1981). Ontario's provincial bounty ended in 1972 after public protests (Theberge 1973a), although some counties offered bounties for several more years (Kolenosky 1983, Theberge 1991).

In the western provinces, conflicts between ranchers and wolves arose as domestic animals grazed on lands adjacent to forested areas. Bounties were invoked in Manitoba in 1878 (Stardom 1983), in 1899 for Saskatchewan and Alberta (Pimlott 1961a), and in 1900 in British Columbia (B.C.) (Pimlott 1961a). As in the U.S., bounties offered by western governments could be supplemented by stockgrowers' associations (B. Lawton 1907, unpubl. Annu. Rep., Dept. of Agric., Edmonton, Alberta). In B.C., 9,205 wolves were taken between 1909 and 1955 (Tompa 1983a). Between 1922 and 1956, the B.C. government paid approximately $1 million for claims and administration (Pimlott 1961a). Although the number of wolves removed by bounties was significant, the system was not the main reason for the decline in wolf numbers seen at that time (Tompa 1983a).

Closure of bounties in most of western Canada resulted after the Predator Control Conference in Calgary in 1954 (Pimlott 1961a). Alberta and B.C. terminated their provincial wolf bounty that same year (Gunson 1983a, Tompa 1983a); Saskatchewan had already done so in 1949 (Slough et al. 1987). Manitoba did not end its bounty system until 1965 (Stardom 1983).

Most wolf bounties in the western provinces were intended to protect livestock. However, those imposed in the N.W.T. (Heard 1983), and Yukon (Smith 1983), were primarily for game management purposes. Bounties in both territories were passed and repealed over many years. Approximately 10,100 wolves were bountied from 1924 to 1943 in the N.W.T. (Heard 1983). In Yukon, 2,796 bounty

claims were made between 1929 and 1971 (Smith 1983). Bounties ended in 1971 in Yukon (Smith 1983) and in 1975 in the N.W.T. (Heard 1983).

By 1960, Alaska and Minnesota were the only states with viable wolf populations. Meanwhile, Alaska still maintained wolf (and coyote) bounties, which had been introduced in 1915 and cost $1.5 million to 1958 (Lensink 1958). Bounties were discontinued in 1968 for most areas in the state (Harbo and Dean 1983), but were not completely repealed until 1972 (Melchoir et al. 1987). An average of 1,200 wolves were bountied in Alaska each year prior to the limits imposed for wolf control in 1969 (Harper 1970, McKnight 1973). Minnesota repealed its wolf bounty in 1965 and the wolf received federal protection there in 1974 (Van Ballenberghe 1974).

Inadequacies of the Bounty System

The bounty's importance in reducing wolf populations in North America is doubtful, despite the many thousands of wolves that were killed (Criddle 1925, Jacobsen 1945, Pimlott 1961a,b, Cain et al. 1972, Kolenosky 1983). Government-sponsored wolf bounties are no longer offered in North America and given the current distribution of wolves, public opposition to the method, and fiscal restraint of many governments, there appears little chance that bounties will ever regain widespread use (Theberge 1973b, Melchoir et al. 1987). Wildlife biologists consider bounties as rural welfare rather than an acceptable management tool (e.g., Theberge 1973b), although some segments of society still consider bounties a viable control technique (Novak 1987).

Bounties may have controlled wolves at the edge of their range where numbers were low, bounty payments high, and capture techniques efficient (Mech 1970). Bounties initiated higher rates of wolf cull in some cases (e.g., Lensink 1958, Banville 1981, Heard 1983); however, these increases may have reflected only temporary changes in wolf numbers rather than permanent reductions. In parts of Canada and Alaska, wolves have persisted even where wolf bounties have occurred for extended periods. In Québec (Banville 1981), Ontario (Pimlott 1961a,b), and Alaska (Lensink 1959), similar numbers of wolves were bountied at the beginning and end of the bounty period. Furthermore, large tracts of land in these areas remained relatively undisturbed from human activity and surely provided reservoirs for wolves. A large proportion of animals bountied were killed incidentally and not as a result of the bounty system (Latham 1953, Keefe 1958), which added little to population reduction. Sometimes, adult female wolves in traps were released to maintain future reproduction, whereas trapped juveniles were occasionally held captive only to be killed later for adult bounty (Young and Goldman 1944). Other incidences of fraud included use of domestic dog, coyote, or counterfeit ears submitted as proof of wolves killed (Young and Goldman 1944, Banville 1981). Claims were also made for wolves taken outside the paying jurisdiction (Young and Goldman 1944, Fritts 1982, Brown 1983).

Incentives

Several governments have introduced incentives intended to stimulate wolf harvests. Incentives differ from bounties by not offering a financial reward for each wolf that is killed, restricting those who can qualify, and targeting specific areas or populations for control. An incentive can take on the allure of a competition or a contest, which may be more acceptable to the public than a bounty (Fig. 1). Governments have awarded monetary prizes to the best wolf trappers in Québec (Banville 1981) and the Yukon (Smith 1983). In Québec, hunters could have the lower jaw of wolves they killed engraved and encased in acrylic. However, few wolves were claimed and the program was abandoned due to public pressure (Theberge 1973a, Banville 1981).

Some incentives seem no different than supplemental bounties. In 1983, the Yukon territorial government gave incentive payments of $200 for each wolf trapped in the territory. This strategy did not significantly increase the wolf harvest and was discontinued after three years (R.D. Hayes, Yukon Fish and Wildl. Br., pers. commun.). Alberta is considering reimbursing trappers above market value for wolf pelts and, in the past, has provided complimentary trapping supplies (Alberta Fish and Wildl. Div. 1991). A similar technique used in B.C. was largely unsuccessful because few trappers took the time and effort required to trap wolves (Janz 1987).

In 1989, the Alberta Fish and Game Association (AFGA), a nongovernment organization, attempted to reduce wolf predation on game by offering a $150 incentive to registered trappers to trap wolves (AFGA, Predator management plan, suppl. to Western Canada Outdoors, January/February 1989, 4pp.). Only 20 claims were received and the program was dropped after one year because of public opposition (G. Page, AFGA, pers. commun.). Apparently, a $150 incentive was also insufficient for trappers to expend the extra effort to trap wolves. Incentives, like bounties, will likely be abandoned as a management technique.

Poisons

The use of poisons or toxicants has been the most efficient way of reducing predators over large areas (Connolly 1978a), and consequently poisons have been used extensively against wolves. Poisons interfere with the body's metabolism by impeding essential metabolic pathways. The use of poisons is controversial because of their relative non-selectivity and reputation for inhumaneness. Wolves have been controlled primarily with strychnine, sodium monofluoroacetate (Compound 1080), cyanide, and thallium sulphate. Other poisons such as arsenic (e.g., Brown 1983), radiator antifreeze (ethylene glycol), and extracts from boiled spruce (*Picea* spp.) needles were less common. We describe the four main poisons and their historical use

against wolves. Generally, the extent of each poison used has reflected its supply, government policy, and public opposition.

1. Strychnine

Strychnine is an alkaloid extracted from the seeds of the *Strychnos nux vomica* tree and occurs as odorless, colorless crystals or white powder (Riggs and Kulig 1990). Strychnine was introduced in Germany in the 16th century as a rodenticide (Linsella et al. 1971), but was not widely used on carnivores in the U.S. until after it was domestically manufactured in 1834 (Young and Goldman 1944). Once ingested, strychnine affects the central nervous system, causing convulsions (Brookes 1975). Action of the diaphragm is inhibited, resulting in death by respiratory failure and cardiac arrest (Riggs and Kulig 1990). Acquired tolerance to strychnine has been reported in pigs (*Sus scrofa*), dogs, and several species of rodents (Lee et al. 1990), but not in wolves or coyotes.

Strychnine has been widely used for wolf control in western North America (Carney 1902:84, Dunlap 1988). Typically, the poison was placed in a bait such as lard or carrion. Only 0.13–0.26 grams (2–4 grains) of powder were needed to kill a wolf (Bailey 1907:4, Young and Goldman 1944). Strychnine crystals were partly dissolved in water to form a paste and applied between the hide and flesh of a carcass, creating a particularly effective technique to remove most scavengers feeding on the carrion. Strychnine use was short-lived in the eastern U.S. because wolf numbers were low by the time it was widely available (Young and Goldman 1944, Dunlap 1988). The poison was more prevalent in the midwest, and its use peaked between 1860 and 1885, notwithstanding prohibition in some areas (Young and Goldman 1944).

Ungulate carcasses were poisoned with strychnine to kill wolves inside Yellowstone National Park in 1877, which nearly led to their extirpation there (Weaver 1978). Predator control continued inside the U.S. national parks despite the newly established National Park Service in 1916. However, public sentiment toward predators was changing and the use of poison, primarily strychnine, was last reported in Rocky Mountain National Park, Colorado, in 1922 and banned from all national parks in 1930 (Cahalane 1939:232, Wright 1992). Strychnine was also used by professional wolfers during the mid- to late-1800's when wolves on the plains were apparently numerous (Young and Goldman 1944), but then its use declined when wolves were extirpated in 1926, partly because of strychnine use (Jorgensen 1970). Strychnine is now illegal in the U.S. for all above-ground purposes (Fritts 1993a).

In Canada in the late 1850's, the Hudson's Bay Company used strychnine to prevent wolves from killing horses in the eastern slopes region of Alberta (Spry 1963). Carcasses laced with strychnine (wolfing) was a popular and lucrative method of taking wolves during the 1860's and 1870's throughout western Canada (Rodney 1969). Wolves were poisoned for their pelts, to protect livestock, and in retaliation for scavenging on meat caches left by hunters (Young and Goldman 1944, Gunson 1983a). Consequently, the number of wolves on the Canadian prairie had been drastically reduced by 1890.

In 1952, strychnine was used to control rabies in western Canada (Ballantyne and O'Donoghue 1954, Ballantyne 1958, Gunson 1983a, b). However, such depopulation schemes would likely generate much public opposition if used today (Winkler and Bögel 1992). The rabies prevention program in western Canada ended in 1956, but poison was still used afterward to enhance ungulate numbers in the northern areas of the prairie provinces (Gunson 1983b, Heard 1983). Reducing wolves for game management ended in Alberta in 1966, but strychnine was still used in northwestern areas of the province because livestock depredation continued to be a problem there (Gunson 1983a, Bjorge and Gunson 1985).

Strychnine was used in Manitoba from 1950 to 1965 (Stardom 1983) and from the mid-1930's to 1976 in Saskatchewan (Wiltse 1983). Its use in Saskatchewan as a preventative measure against livestock depredations ended between 1976 and 1980 (Seguin 1991). However, strychnine is still used in both provinces to remove wolves that kill livestock (Hayes and Gunson this volume). The B.C. government does not use strychnine for wolf control; however, its illegal use occurred in 1991 when individuals killed wolves in the southeast corner of the province. That particular campaign caused international concern because it hampered U.S. wolf recovery efforts in northwestern Montana (D. Pletscher, Univ. Mont., pers. commun.).

In Ontario, poisons were used for several years to control wolves (Pimlott 1961b, Pimlott et al. 1969) but they were eventually banned in the 1970's (Kolenosky 1983). In 1965–1966, Québec initiated control with poisons, although this program was revised in 1971 to include only the wintering yards of white-tailed deer (*Odocoileus virginianus*) (Banville 1983). The poisoning effort, announced in 1972, was criticized throughout North America and the government later withdrew its proposal (Theberge 1973a).

Strychnine poisoning was used inconsistently from 1921 to 1972 in the Yukon Territory (Smith 1983). Renewed public demand for wolf control in the Whitehorse area prompted a brief campaign with strychnine baits in 1982 and 1983 (Hayes et al. 1991). In the N.W.T., strychnine use began in 1951 on caribou (*Rangifer tarandus groenlandicus*) winter ranges, but declined until 1964 (Heard 1983). In one instance in May 1956, 68 wolves were killed with a single carcass poisoned near Lady Gray Lake, N.W.T. (W.A. Fuller, Athabasca, Alta., pers. commun.). Wolves were also poisoned on Banks Island in the N.W.T. during 1955–1959 to reduce wolf predation on trapped arctic foxes (*Alopex lagopus*); many foxes were also killed (Usher 1971, Heard 1983).

There was no fixed policy for the management of predators within Canadian park boundaries before 1959, but local park authorities generally encouraged wolf control (Cowan 1947, Carbyn 1974). Strychnine was used in Wood Buffalo National Park to reduce wolf predation on bison from 1935 to 1940 (Mitchell 1976), the 1940's and 1950's (Fuller and Novakowski 1955), and the 1960's (Carbyn et al. 1993). In Jasper National Park (JNP), a declining bighorn sheep (*Ovis canadensis*) population led to a four-year wolf control program in 1950, just prior to poison use being discontinued in the park (Carbyn 1974). Although national park policy banned wolf control in 1959, kills from strychnine poisoning still occurred thereafter in JNP and WBNP, but went unrecorded (Carbyn et al. 1993, E. Kuyt, Can. Wildl. Serv., pers. commun.).

Market hunting of ungulates was extensive in Alaska at the turn of the century, and much wolf control occurred via strychnine (Harbo and Dean 1983). However, poison stations in southeast Alaska were restricted by law to late fall and winter, to reduce the incidental killing of bears. Wolf removal continued intermittently in the southeast until Alaska became a state in 1959, after which the state assumed wolf management authority and abolished poisoning (Harbo and Dean 1983).

In Mexico, wolves were not extensively controlled until the 1930's and 1940's when strychnine became available from American ranchers (McBride 1980). At first many wolves were killed, but by the late 1950's so few remained in the desert states of Chihuahua and Sonora that survivors often bore individual names (McBride 1980, USFWS 1982).

2. Sodium Monofluoroacetate (Compound 1080)

Sodium monofluoroacetate is a colorless, odorless, and tasteless water-soluble salt, also known as compound 1080 or Fratol (Brookes 1975). Sodium monofluoroacetate was first synthesized in Europe in the 1890's but its extreme toxicity to mammals was not recognized until the 1940's (King 1990). (Reference to the poison as compound 1080 began in 1944 after the laboratory serial number assigned to it at the time). Compound 1080 poisoning results from the blocking of a major metabolic pathway for releasing energy from food (Metts 1990). However, this view has been challenged based on enzyme kinetics (Kun 1982).

The effects of 1080 poisoning are delayed 30 minutes to three hours while the poison is metabolized (Atzert 1971, Metts 1990). Vomiting usually results, followed by convulsions, a period of apprehension, auditory hallucinations, and abnormal facial sensations (Metts 1990). [It is this sequence of events prior to death that have horrified the public and contributed to the U.S. Presidential Ban on these poisons in 1972 (Lynch and Nass 1981, Sibbison 1984)]. Death usually occurs within 24 hours (King 1990). Repeated sublethal doses may be lethal by causing damage to kidneys (Polenick 1982) and testes (King 1990). Mammals, particularly canids and felids, are sensitive to 1080 poisoning, although native fauna in Australia have developed some tolerance to it (King et al. 1978, 1989, King 1990).

Approved use of 1080 at bait stations was delayed by the USFWS until 1947 because of concern for nontarget wildlife (Dunlap 1988). Once approved, 1080 was strictly regulated so that it could not be used in aerially-dropped baits. Also, its use was restricted to west of the 100th meridian because the land was less settled there, predation was still a major problem, and other methods were not effective (Dunlap 1988). This poison was primarily directed at coyotes because wolves were already rare in the contiguous U.S. by the 1940's. Even though Mexico's wolf population was declining rapidly in the 1950's (Leopold 1959), 1080 was introduced to control the spread of rabies (McBride 1980, USFWS 1982) which hastened the demise of the Mexican wolf (McBride 1980). Compound 1080 is now banned in the U.S. (Dunlap 1988), but the poison is still used in B.C. (Hayes and Gunson this volume).

In Canada, the B.C. government favored 1080 for wolf control instead of strychnine or cyanide because of its high toxicity (Hatler 1981, Tompa 1983a). The provincial government began using 1080 in 1949 (B.C. Ministry of Environment 1979) and throughout the 1950's, 1080 was distributed over much of central and northern B.C. as part of a long-term, indiscriminate wolf reduction program. Baits were dropped by aircraft onto frozen lakes and rivers and were not checked because of the high cost of flying (Hoffos 1987). Aerially dropped poison baits are the epitome of nonselective poisoning and since the 1970's, such abuses helped initiate antipoisoning campaigns in North America.

Widespread poisoning in B.C. ceased in 1961, but localized wolf removal continued in grazing and heavily hunted areas (Tompa 1983a). In December 1978, a moratorium on poisons was declared, but it was not effective at reducing poisoning by guides and outfitters. Additional restrictions followed in 1980 for controlling livestock depredations (B.C. Ministry of Environment 1979). Legislation restricted an annual maximum of 250 individual wolf baits, and no more than 12 individual baits could be placed at the site where livestock depredation was confirmed (Tompa 1983a,b). Baits had to be covered with soil or snow to reduce nontarget mortalities (Tompa 1983a). Baits not taken after two weeks were to be removed. Currently, B.C. is the only province to use 1080 for wolf control, although its use in other provinces may increase as 1080 replaces strychnine supplies (C. Brown, Alberta Agric., pers. commun.).

3. Cyanide

Cyanide occurs naturally in some plants and microbes or can be manufactured (Hall and Rumack 1990, Syracuse Res. Corp. 1991). Cyanide has been used for wolf control because of its extreme toxicity and availability. The M-44 (meaning mechanical with a 0.44 calibre case) or modified "coyote-getter," has been the primary delivery mechanism for cyanide poisoning. Sodium cyanide is the most widely used

form in coyote-getters, M-44s, and the larger M-50 (specifically for wolves). The M-44 and M-50 consist of a metal stake, ejector, and capsule holder or top, inside which is a plastic capsule containing the sodium cyanide mixture.

Because cyanide is a highly toxic, fast-acting poison, ingestion of a lethal dose causes a reaction within seconds and death within minutes (Eisler 1991). The LD_{50} (lethal dosage that would kill 50% of the individuals in a population) for dogs is 1.0–2.0 mg/kg (Matheny 1976). Acute cyanide poisoning marks a rapid progression to coma, convulsions, shock, respiratory failure, and death (Vogel et al. 1981, Hall and Rumack 1990). Although cyanide poisoning is potentially reversible, the amount of cyanide normally administered overwhelms the body's defenses and poisoning occurs (Hall and Rumack 1990).

Between 1944 and 1948, cyanide bait guns ("getters") were promoted by the USFWS to kill coyotes and wolves (see Landon 1952, USFWS 1982, Doughty 1983), despite few wolves remaining in the western U.S. (see Brown 1983). Cyanide bait guns were also used for government wolf control programs in Yukon in the 1950's (Smith 1983). In 1953, the Predator Control Branch in Alaska modified the "coyote-getter" for use on wolves (M-50) and it became the standard method of control in summer. In several jurisdictions, "getters" were also commonly used in winter, especially on frozen lakes where baits could be secured in the ice and poisoned carcasses easily found.

The M-44 replaced the primer-powered, 0.38 calibre cyanide ejector of the coyote-getter in the mid-1960's (Matheny 1976, Connolly 1988). Its use declined in the late 1960's and early 1970's because of human risk and suspected tolerance in target species (Cain et al. 1972, Matheny 1976). Sodium cyanide capsules for predator control were prohibited by the U.S. Environmental Protection Agency (EPA) in 1972 in association with the Presidential Ban on predacides. However, the agency permitted M-44s after February 1976 if an antidote kit for cyanide poisoning was carried by control personnel (Eisler 1991).

Following reregistration, the M-44 was widely used to control damage by coyotes in the contiguous U.S. (Connolly 1978a). This increase in use may have been because it was more selective than the leg-hold trap (Robinson 1943, Eisler 1991). Cyanide guns (M-44s) have not been approved by the EPA for use on wolves (Fritts 1993a). Furthermore, relatively high lethal doses are required for large target animals, and cyanide's nonspecificity to wildlife has hampered widespread use. This poison is more suitable for small-scale control situations such as local depredations on livestock. Cyanide inserted in livestock collars has been effective protection against coyote predation (Eisler 1991), although some coyotes have been wary about attacking collared animals (e.g., Savarie and Sterner 1979). Toxic collars have not been used to reduce depredation by wolves, and likely would not be legal in the contiguous U.S. given current legislation regarding cyanide use.

4. Thallium.

Thallium sulfate is a colorless, odorless, and tasteless powder introduced in the U.S. in the 1930's (Metts 1990). Initial symptoms of thallium toxicity include fever, gastrointestinal difficulties, delirium, convulsions, and coma (Saddique and Peterson 1983). Small doses of thallium may result in the death of victims two to five days after ingestion; large doses may be fatal within 24 hours (Robinson 1948).

The greatest use of thallium to kill wolves occurred in Mexico from 1950 to the late 1960's (Brown 1983). This substance had limited use in predator control programs in the U.S., partly because of its slow killing action and nonselectivity (Robinson 1948, Cain et al. 1972). Consequently, thallium was used infrequently during the 1940's to 1950's (Dunlap 1988). Thallium was replaced by compound 1080 in the 1950's, restricted in the U.S. in 1957, and finally prohibited in 1965 (Saddique and Peterson 1983). To our knowledge, thallium was not widely used to control wolves in Canada.

Aerial Shooting

Shooting wolves from either fixed-wing aircraft or helicopter has been a particularly effective control technique because it can eliminate large numbers of wolves in a region within a few weeks (Mech 1970). Aerial shooting occurs in open areas during winter when snow on the ground facilitates tracking and wolves are easily sighted. Occasionally, individual wolves are chased and harassed to the point of exhaustion before being shot (Mech 1970). The use of aircraft to control predators began by 1923 when ranchers in the western U.S. sought to protect livestock from coyotes (Wade 1976). Aerial hunting for wolves occurred later in 1943 when federal game agents in Alaska began additional control of wolves to offset a decline in caribou numbers (Leopold and Darling 1953). During 1948 to 1959, private operators and government personnel used light aircraft to shoot wolves (Rausch and Hinman 1977). In the late 1940's, Minnesota allowed aerial hunting by private individuals in its northern wilderness areas, with up to 38 wolves being killed in one flight (Mech 1970). Wolves that escaped from aerial attacks quickly learned to avoid aircraft (e.g., Stenlund 1955).

Following the designation of wolves as big game animals in 1963, the Alaskan government restricted aerial hunting by private operators. In arctic Alaska, wolves were more vulnerable to aerial shooting than in forested areas, and a yearly bag limit of two wolves was imposed for each aircraft (Rausch 1965). Public criticism in 1972 forced the Alaska Department of Fish and Game (ADFG) commissioner to suspend aerial shooting (Rausch and Hinman 1977). However, the Alaska Board of Game circumvented the federal law by allowing airplanes to transport wolves, wolverines (*Gulo gulo*), and foxes if they had not been not harassed or shot from the air (Laycock 1990). Thus, the concept of "land-and-shoot" hunting began. Therefore, from 1972 to

1989, aircraft pursuit and harvesting of wolves was allowed, provided that hunters landed before shooting, and used a rifle instead of a shotgun (Van Ballenberghe 1991). The method encouraged illegal aerial hunting (Ballard et al. 1987), and was interpreted in lawsuits as *de facto* wolf control (Stephenson et al. this volume). Public opposition continued (Van Ballenberghe 1991), and in 1992, land-and-shoot hunting was banned altogether (R.O. Stephenson, ADFG, pers. commun.). Thereafter, aerial shooting was only permitted by ADFG personnel on state-approved wolf management programs (ADFG 1992c). Recent changes have led to ground-based control only, by Department personnel and those under the Department's direct supervision (R.O. Stephenson, ADFG, pers. commun.). Same-day-airborne hunting is also permitted, which allows the use of aircraft for transportation, but not land-and-shoot. The distinction is that the hunter can only legally shoot wolves (or other furbearers) from at least 91.5 m (100 yards) beyond the landed aircraft (R.O. Stephenson, ADFG, pers. commun.).

Shooting wolves from the air has been common in experimental wolf reductions. Such programs occurred in parts of Québec (Potvin et al. 1992b), B.C. (Seip 1989), and Alaska (Rausch and Hinman 1977, Gasaway et al. 1983, 1992). Radio-collared wolves were used to locate other pack members in Alaska (Ballard and Stephenson 1982), the Yukon (Hayes et al. 1991), and Québec (Potvin et al. 1992b), a technique sometimes referred to as the "Judas principle." Ballard and Stephenson (1982) reported that the expense of locating and shooting wolves was lower if at least one member of a pack was radio-collared. However, the authors discouraged complete removal of a pack, arguing that members left alive would maintain the territory by not dispersing. In February 1985, Alaska temporarily halted its aerial shooting because the U.S. Federal Communications Commission ruled that the state's use of radio-collars to kill wolves was illegal (Smith 1985).

Aerial shooting was the primary method of killing wolves in B.C.'s controversial Kechika and Muskwa wolf control areas (Elliot 1985a, 1985b, Bergerud and Elliot 1986). As in other jurisdictions, public opposition to aerial shooting in B.C. was strong. Extensive media coverage contributed to the opposition, and these programs were abandoned in 1987 after almost 1,000 wolves were killed (Haber 1988). Operational costs of the Kechika-Muskwa wolf control calculated from aircraft fuel, equipment, and travel were estimated at $140/wolf (Elliot 1985a, b). However, costs were more than $2,000/wolf in a Québec study once "Judas" wolves were radio-collared (Potvin et al. 1992b). Yukon's Finlayson Lake wolf control program (1983 to 1989) averaged $600/wolf shot, while the initial year of Aishihik's control program (1992/93) averaged $2,500/wolf taken (A.M. Baer, Yukon Fish and Wildl. Br., pers. commun.). Operational costs for the two Yukon programs differ because of unexpected reconnaissance efforts in the Aishihik area and its associated start-up costs. Average costs/wolf shot would be

$100 to $400 less if wolf carcasses were not salvaged (A.M. Baer, Yukon Fish and Wildl. Br., pers. commun.).

Recent efforts to enhance ungulate numbers in Alaska and the Yukon by shooting wolves from the air has generated massive public opposition. Wolves were to be shot in some areas of Alaska during winter 1992/93, but the plan was quickly aborted when public interest groups threatened a tourist boycott of the state. This boycott could have removed $85 million from the state's economy (Anonymous 1993). Alaska's Board of Game has now authorized a ground-based wolf control program in a small area south of Fairbanks, primarily to increase caribou numbers in the Delta herd (R.O. Stephenson, ADFG, pers. commun.). The Yukon recently resumed its aerial shooting program in the Aishihik area during winter 1992/93 to assist caribou recovery. Similar plans had been aborted in February 1992. Despite conservation groups launching a campaign to pressure the Yukon government to abandon its control program (B.T. Aniśkowicz, Canadian Nature Federation, pers. commun.), aerial shooting continued.

Mech (1970) noted that shooting animals from an aircraft is considered a sport by some people, while others see it as the lowest form of recreation imaginable. Public opposition exists for all forms of aerial hunting for sport, and shooting wolves by government personnel is not considered more acceptable than by private operators. Consequently, this method has been ranked low on the public acceptability scale (Fig. 1). One exception may be in Montana, where occasional aerial shooting of problem wolves is reluctantly accepted by the public, because minimizing livestock depredation is instrumental to wolf recovery in that state (Bangs et al. this volume).

Other Lethal Methods

1. Set Guns
European settlers to North America in the 1650's used the "wolf-" or "set gun" to kill wolves. Set guns consisted of a firearm anchored to a tree near a wolf trail and a string tied to the trigger that lead across the trail or to a bait (Young and Goldman 1944). The use of set guns was restricted to outside the townsite and could only be activated during the night because of potential danger to humans. It is unlikely that this method ever received widespread use because of its high risk factor (Young and Goldman 1944).

2. Fish Hooks and Stomach Piercers
European settlers also killed wolves by suspending baited fish hooks (Young and Goldman 1944). The Inuit and Inuvialuit peoples used a moistened piece of baleen (whalebone) and fashioned it into an "S" or "U" shape. Sinew was wrapped around the baleen and covered with fat. The sinew was cut when baits were deployed. A wolf that swallowed a frozen bait ball had its stomach pierced when the tallow or fat softened and released the baleen spring (Young and Goldman 1944). Variations in the technique substituted ba-

leen with a sharp blade, wing of a bird, or broken glass. A similar technique in the New England states used hooks and thread in tallow (Young and Goldman 1944). Dehydrated sponges, left at carcasses or in baits, also killed wolves. When sponges were swallowed, they expanded inside the stomach, but were not digested, causing the animal to starve (Banville 1981).

3. Hunting Drives and Corrals
Ring-hunts or circular hunts were organized in many states during the early to mid-1800's to control wolves (Young and Goldman 1944). Residents from several counties would gather, encircle an area, and drive wolves out. Two to 10 wolves could be killed in a single drive. Early settlers also drove wolves by foot, horseback, or with fire to waiting hunters (Young and Goldman 1944).

Corral traps were used by the Blackfoot Indians to capture wolves. A circular trench about 4 m in diameter was dug to accommodate posts tied together to form an enclosure and then baited (Young and Goldman 1944). Posts were angled inward and resembled a truncated cone. One trapper dubiously claimed he caught 83 wolves and coyotes in a corral trap in a single night (Young and Goldman 1944:296).

4. Denning
Den hunting was a laborious but effective method of reducing wolves. Individuals would dig out the den and kill the pups. Forked sticks, or wire twisted into the fur were used to remove pups from a den (Young and Goldman 1944). Explosives, poison, smoke, and exhaust fumes were also used to kill den inhabitants. Denning was used to control wolves from Mexico and the southern U.S. (USFWS 1982) to the far north in Canada (Loughrey 1958). Denning is unpopular with the public probably because of its inhumaneness and killing of pups, which are deemed innocent victims (Fig. 1).

5. Hunting and Trapping
In addition to bounties, governments controlled wolves by hiring their own wolf hunters. These individuals differed from professional wolfers in that they were employed by government and could work on a fixed salary or commission. Government hunters were often preferred over wolfers because hunters devoted their entire effort to wolf control and were considered less likely to be fraudulent. Hunters were sent to specific areas where wolves were particularly troublesome, or where bounty hunters were not effective. Wolf hunters were common in Europe (Boitani this volume) and were eventually employed in North America. The first record of government hunters occurred in Pennsylvania in 1705, when a bounty system failed to solve problems with wolves (Young and Goldman 1944). Similarly, other jurisdictions, such as Québec, employed government wolf trappers in the 1960's and 1970's to replace an ineffective bounty system (Banville 1981).

Government personnel are still involved in wolf control for livestock protection, but kill wolves only when necessary

(Fritts et al. 1992, Gunson 1992, Bangs et al. this volume, Hayes and Gunson this volume). Government trapping has been more favorable in the U.S. than other lethal control methods because it targets specific wolves involved in depredations, and allows continued protection to other individuals in the endangered wolf population (Bangs et al. this volume).

Wolves in Canada are sometimes shot incidentally or are intentionally pursued by hunters where allowed (Hayes and Gunson this volume). Dogs such as the Irish wolfhound were once used to hunt, chase and combat wolves, although more for entertainment than as an effective method of control (Young and Goldman 1944). Wolves continue to be trapped by the public in most of Canada (Carbyn 1987, Hayes and Gunson this volume) and Alaska (Stephenson et al. this volume). The significance of classifying wolves as fur-bearers or big game animals allows some measure of protection for the species, although in many jurisdictions, liberal hunting and trapping seasons and bag limits exist (Van Ballenberghe 1992). However, legal status is irrelevant when not enforced (e.g., McBride 1980).

Nonlethal and Indirect Methods

Some methods were cheap, indirect, but effective ways to control wolves early, thereby reducing or eliminating greater efforts later. Historically, these methods included fences, guard dogs, and burning dense, wooded areas to drive out wolves near cattle pastures (Young and Goldman 1944, Rutter and Pimlott 1968). Although preventive methods of wolf control could include antecedent control with lethal techniques, prevention tends to be synonymous with nonlethal methods. Because public opposition to lethal wolf control is high, killing wolves is often the last resort. Guard dogs, fences, repellents, diversionary feeding, and fertility control are examples of nonlethal methods used today to prevent wolves from conflicting with humans and livestock. Unlike other nonlethal methods, relocation of problem animals (e.g., Fritts et al. 1984) and compensation to ranchers for depredation losses (e.g., Bjorge and Gunson 1983) act solely to mitigate, rather than prevent, damage.

Nonlethal methods originated for protecting livestock in agricultural settings, but some methods are being examined for wolf control in wilderness areas. We only briefly discuss nonlethal methods that directly affect wolves because most techniques are still experimental and some are discussed elsewhere in these proceedings. Indirect methods such as proper husbandry of livestock or habitat enhancement techniques for ungulates are also discussed elsewhere (Fritts 1982, Bjorge and Gunson 1985, Andelt 1987, Boertje et al. this volume).

Guard Dogs

Several dog breeds including the Hungarian Komondor and Great Pyrenees have been used for centuries by Old World shepherds to protect livestock from wolf predation (Bordaux 1974, Linhart et al. 1979, Green and Woodruff 1980). These and other dog breeds were brought to the New World by 16th century Spanish conquistadors (Pfeifer and Goos 1982). The use of dogs by livestock owners remained infrequent until the 1970's when use of many poisons was discontinued (Green and Woodruff 1980, McGrew and Blakesley 1982). Many livestock producers still consider guard dogs as a complementary method while relying on other techniques for control (Andelt 1992).

Guard dogs work by being attentive to livestock and driving away intruders (McGrew and Blakesley 1982). Guard dogs are not an immediate solution to a predator control problem because they must be socialized to the animals they protect (Coppinger and Coppinger this volume). Two years are usually required for a guard dog program to be in place once the need has been identified (R. Coppinger, Hampshire College, pers. commun.).

The use of guard dogs in North America has focused on reducing depredations by coyotes (e.g., Pfeifer and Goos 1982), and is among the most publicly acceptable methods of predator control (Fig. 1). However, guard dogs and wolves could potentially behave as conspecifics which would negate any guarding behavior. Guard dogs have been used successfully in Eurasia against wolves, but wolves are also known to attack and kill domestic dogs (Fritts and Paul 1989). Research has been conducted in Minnesota to determine the effectiveness of dogs against livestock depredation by wolves (Coppinger and Coppinger this volume). While guard dogs should be viewed as a technique available to ranchers, initial trials in Minnesota have shown they were not effective in preventing livestock depredations in wooded pastures (W. J. Paul, ADC, pers. commun.).

Guard dogs have recently been introduced on an experimental basis to protect domestic sheep (*Ovis aries*) on forestry clear-cuts on Vancouver Island, B.C. The sheep assist in brush control on clear-cuts while dogs protect sheep from depredation by bears, cougars (*Felis concolor*), and wolves (DogLog 1(1):2–4 1990, Livestock Guard Dog Assoc., Hampshire College, Amherst, Massachusetts).

Fences

Fences were used to protect domestic sheep from wolf predation in early Europe (Wade 1978). Potentially, fences are the least controversial technique for controlling livestock losses from wolf predation (Fig. 1). Most landowners in the early American colonies are likely to have had fences to retain livestock and some probably constructed antiwolf fences. The first record of a fence for controlling wolves was in 1717, when a wooden fence to encircle several towns in the Cape Cod area of Massachusetts was proposed (Young and Goldman 1944). Although it was never built, the proposal testifies to the paranoia toward wolves and livestock depredations in colonial times.

Early in the 20th century, ranchers used woven wire fences to protect small numbers of livestock from wolves, but larger ranges were not usually enclosed (B. Lawton 1907, unpubl. Annu. Rep., Dept. of Agric., Edmonton, Alberta, Young and Goldman 1944). Some ranchers in the southwestern U.S. advocated a wolf-proof fence along the U.S.-Mexico border in the 1920's (Brown 1983). The U.S. government experimented with several types of wolf- and coyote-proof fences to reduce depredations on livestock; none were found practical (Young and Goldman 1944, Wade 1982). Except for some concern that fences helped eliminate red wolves (*C. rufus*) in parts of Texas (Caroline 1973), widespread use of fencing as a nonlethal control technique for wolves has not occurred.

Modern electric fences have successfully excluded coyotes (Gates et al. 1978, Dorrance and Bourne 1980, Linhart et al. 1982, deCalesta 1983), but tests on wolves have not been reported. Most wolf problems occur in marginal areas, where livestock often range freely. Because cattle pastures are usually large and often in rugged country, the assembly and successful operation of an electric fence is difficult and expensive.

Light and Sound Repellents

Strobe lights, propane exploders, sirens, and recorded sounds have all been used against coyote depredations on livestock (Wade 1978, Andelt 1987). Each method has demonstrated moderate repellent effects for coyotes, but little testing on wolves has occurred. Flashing highway lights were used to scare wolves in pastures in Minnesota with ambiguous results (Fritts 1982). However, lights were later shown to be useful where lethal control was not possible (Fritts et al. 1992). Fritts (1982) reported attaching flags to fences and trees to scare wolves in Minnesota, a technique similar to "fladre" used in drives to control wolves in parts of Europe and Russia (Carbyn 1977). Smaller pastures are more conducive to use of flashing lights and flagging than large ones (Fritts 1982).

Coyotes readily adapt to most repellent devices (Wade 1978), and the response of wolves is probably similar. Irregularity of stimulus appears to be the common ingredient for success in repellency, and using repellents in concert with other deterrents or husbandry practices may increase their effectiveness. In many cases, wolf depredation on livestock may not be regular enough to warrant continual use of these repellents or conduct a valid test of their effectiveness.

Chemical Repellents

Chemical irritants and olfactory repellents are designed to reduce predation on livestock. These chemicals are manufactured in the form of repellent body sprays, collars, and eartags for livestock, as well as actual odor stations (Wade 1978). Some effective repellents are either too irritating to be applied on livestock, or too short-lived to be practical (Lehner et al. 1976). For example, an eartag to prevent

predatory neck bites on livestock is commercially available (Sterner and Shumake 1978), but tests of this device (Linhart et al. 1977) and of repellent collars (Jankovsky et al. 1974 cited in Sterner and Shumake 1978) have not indicated reduced depredations by coyotes. These devices may be particularly ineffective if neck bites are not always used in the kill. Although we have not found any records of chemical repellents tested on wolves, their results may be similar to those for coyotes. Habituation often results from prolonged usage (Linhart et al. 1977, Sterner and Shumake 1978), therefore we expect repellents have limited potential in reducing depredations by wolves.

Aversive Conditioning

Aversive conditioning is a behavioral modification technique intended to reduce attacks on livestock through the use of chemical emetics or electric shock (e.g., Linhart et al. 1976). The former method consists of injecting a carcass with a noxious substance such as lithium chloride (LiCl), and allowing predators to feed on the bait. Predators become ill and, theoretically, associate the illness with the bait species, thereby avoiding those animals in the future (Gustavson et al. 1974). This technique is undoubtedly more acceptable to the public than lethal control by poisons (Fig. 1), but it is still seen as invasive. Furthermore, its effectiveness has not been adequately tested.

Early experiments with lithium chloride on captive coyotes (e.g., Gustavson 1979, Ellins and Catalano 1980, Gustavson et al. 1982), and wolves (Gustavson et al. 1976) have demonstrated suppression of attacks on prey via aversive conditioning. Gustavson (1982) experimentally tested taste aversion on wild wolves in Minnesota. However, his evidence that aversion to baits by wolves reduces depredation on livestock was confounded by the availability of bait, its actual consumption by wolves, and the concomitant control by other methods. Thus, taste aversion could not be unequivocally credited with a decrease in livestock losses.

Relocation of Problem Animals

Relocating individuals from areas of conflict with humans or livestock has been successful for bears (Brannon 1987, Ballard and Miller 1990), but may be less so for wolves. Wolves can move long distances (Van Camp and Gluckie 1979, Fritts 1983) and may also return to their point of capture (Henshaw and Stephenson 1974, Fritts et al. 1984). More than 100 wolves have been captured where conflicts with livestock have occurred in Minnesota, and translocated into nonagricultural forests inhabited by other wolves. Indeed, translocated wolves have not remained at the release site and, depending on the relocation distance, some have returned to the capture area (Henshaw and Stephenson 1974, Fritts et al. 1984, 1985, Fritts 1993b). Relocation is expensive, and its application is further restricted when the costs and time necessary for live capture are included. However, capture costs may be reduced if aerial capture is possible.

Predator control programs were important measures taken to reduce human/wolf competition for game populations and to reduce wolf depredations on livestock. Poisoning programs were an effective means of eliminating entire wolf packs. These wolves were poisoned by provincial agencies on a lake adjacent to Prince Albert National Park, Saskatchewan. (Photo: L.N. Carbyn)

Hoffos (1987) thought that the territorial nature of resident wolf packs could preclude survival of some relocated wolves, making relocation essentially no different than lethal control. However, survival of wolves translocated in Michigan (Weise et al. 1975) and problem wolves in Minnesota (Fritts et al. 1984, 1985) was comparable to that of other wolves.

In Montana, wolves have been recolonizing their former range. Those that prey on livestock have been subsequently live-trapped and relocated (Bangs et al. this volume). Marked individuals that continued to depredate livestock were destroyed. Because the wolf is classified as endangered in Montana, costs of relocations have been less important than in other areas where established wolf populations exist.

Diversionary Feeding

Diversionary feeding of predators during ungulate calving periods has been suggested as a viable alternative to lethal wolf control for game management (Gasaway et al. 1992). This technique is socially acceptable, but costly, because carcasses must usually be flown to remote sites and must be available for consumption for several weeks (Boertje et al. this volume). Diversionary feeding of wolves and grizzly bears (*Ursus arctos*) has not increased survival of neonate caribou (Boertje et al. 1990), but moderate success has been achieved for moose (*Alces alces*) calves (Boertje et al. 1991). However, large amounts of carrion must be provided before predation is successfully diverted. The technique may not work if predator survival or physical condition is enhanced, or if supplemental food causes predator immigration into the area (Boertje et al. this volume). Also, successful diversionary feeding of predators asserted with improved postcalving survival, which may not always occur in cases where wolf predation is strictly compensatory to other mortality factors.

Fertility Control

In the last 30 years, research into fertility control of predators via chemosterilants has accelerated because of public rejection of lethal control techniques (Kirkpatrick and Turner 1985). Apart from reducing predator reproduction and population size, this technique could reduce livestock losses by lowering the nutritional demands of animals that would otherwise breed and raise young (Connolly 1978b, Andelt

1987, Seal 1991). This result might be especially effective if sterilized wolves living near livestock held their territories and excluded other wolves (S.H. Fritts, USFWS, pers. commun.). Antifertility agents include chemicals, antigens, or synthetic hormones that cause sterility to males and females (Asa this volume). Field tests have been attempted on foxes (*Vulpes*) and coyotes (e.g., Balser 1964, Oleyar and McGinnes 1974, Stellflug et al. 1978, 1984), but sterilization has only met with moderate success thus far. Problems have arisen with the effectiveness of the sterilant (Linhart and Enders 1964), its delivery to a significant proportion of the population, and the short duration of sterility (Linhart et al. 1968). Only recently has fertility control been attempted on wild wolves. Preliminary results with vasectomized wolves in Minnesota showed that they do not necessarily lose pair bonds or territories (S.H. Fritts, USFWS, pers. commun.).

Sterilization of wild wolf populations may never prove to be an effective means of control (Boertje et al. this volume). While many other nonlethal techniques target individual animals, fertility control normally is predicated on the successful treatment of a high proportion (70–95%) of the population (Connolly and Longhurst 1975), a level that may not be attainable in the wild. Wolf populations are not usually closed, and immigration of nonsterile individuals would decrease the proportion of nonbreeders. Furthermore, the secondary effects of sterilization on wolf social behavior and pack structure would have to be thoroughly studied before the technique could be widely used (Kirkpatrick and Turner 1985, Caughley et al. 1992).

Conclusions

Public opinion, either by itself or through the mechanism of legislation, has shaped the evolution of wolf control in North America. Wolf control has seen several phases, from intentional destruction of populations to selective removal of individuals. Currently, lethal methods have either been modified to be more humane, or replaced altogether by nonlethal techniques. Lethal control still occurs, but nonlethal methods usually must be shown to be ineffective before wolves are killed. However, current lethal control programs do not attempt to, nor are they likely to, extirpate the wolf from its present range. Today, opposition to lethal control is based more on ethical considerations than on preservation of endangered populations. Wolf control is an inherently sensitive topic and will remain so to a growing, urbanized society increasingly opposed to killing any wildlife. Consequently, nonlethal methods will continue to be favored, regardless of whether they are the most practical and cost-effective options.

Acknowledgments
We thank the many people who provided us with information for this review. S.H. Fritts was particularly helpful with recent literature and initiated communications with other researchers. L.N. Carbyn, Canadian Wildlife Service (Edmonton), S. Boutin, Department of Zoology, University of Alberta (Edmonton), and L.B. Keith, Department of Wildlife Ecology, University of Wisconsin (Madison), provided logistical support while we researched the manuscript. Earlier versions benefited from the comments of L.N. Carbyn, S.H. Fritts, J.R Gunson, R.D. Hayes, W.J. Paul, and C. Shanks. We thank W.A. Fuller for contributing information and M.L. Poulle for assisting with our presentation at the symposium.

Methods for Reducing Natural Predation on Moose in Alaska and Yukon: An Evaluation

■ **Rodney D. Boertje, David G. Kelleyhouse, and Robert D. Hayes**

We compared several proposed and current methods of reducing natural predation on moose. These included: 1) artificial or "diversionary" feeding of grizzly bears and black bears during the moose calving period; 2) enhancing moose habitat; 3) promoting increases in alternate prey; 4) reducing predator birth rates; 5) conventional public hunting and trapping of predators; and 6) aircraft-assisted wolf harvest. We ranked each method as low, moderate, or high in terms of biological effectiveness, social acceptability, cost-effectiveness, and ease of implementation. Diversionary feeding of bears ranked moderate to high in all categories, except cost-effectiveness. Enhancing moose habitat ranked high in terms of social acceptability and moderate in terms of biological effectiveness, but cost-effective tools are needed. Promoting increases in alternative prey (i.e., caribou) and reducing wolf birth rates ranked low to moderate in terms of biological effectiveness and ease of implementation. Before reducing wolf birth rates, cost-effective, safe, species-specific, and socially acceptable tools need to be developed. Conventional public hunting of bears received high ratings in all categories. Aircraft-assisted wolf harvest also received high ratings, except in terms of social acceptability. A management strategy for reducing predation is outlined.

Introduction

Controlling numbers of wolves (*Canis lupus*), black bears (*Ursus americanus*), and/or grizzly bears (*U. arctos*) to enhance moose (*Alces alces*) populations is an effective strategy when predation is a major limiting factor and moose are below food-limited densities (Gasaway et al. 1983, 1992, Ballard and Larsen 1987, Crête 1987, Van Ballenberghe 1987, Bergerud and Snider 1988). Subarctic wolf-bear-moose systems have higher densities of moose after effective predator control. Also, these systems can support higher hunter harvests than similar systems without predator control (Gasaway et al. 1992). We believe that the long-term viability of wolf and bear populations can be safely protected while practicing localized predator control.

To reduce controversy over predator control, Gasaway et al. (1992) listed five alternatives to predator control by government agencies, and recommended that they be evaluated. We attempt this task with the goal of directing future predator-control research and management. We evaluated six methods of controlling wolf and/or bear predation: 1) artificial or "diversionary" feeding of bears during calving; 2) enhancing moose habitat; 3) promoting increases in alternate prey; 4) reducing predator birth rates; 5) conventional public harvest of predators; and 6) aircraft-assisted wolf harvest. Details are provided where these techniques are specific to bears or wolves.

Methods

Evaluations were based on four criteria:

1) How biologically effective will the technique be in elevating low-density, predator-limited moose populations or reversing predator-driven declines in moose (Gasaway et al. 1983, 1992)? Substantial population control is needed in these cases (e.g., keeping the spring wolf numbers at 15–40% of the precontrol autumn number for six springs [Gasaway et al. 1983, Farnell and Hayes, in prep.] or an equivalent impact on predation rates). Less intensive predator control may be sufficient to maintain moose at high densities (Gasaway et al. 1992), but is more difficult to implement because no immediate problem is apparent.

2) Are the methods socially acceptable? Social acceptance was evaluated in terms of the likelihood of gaining the political and public support necessary to implement a specific method (Archibald et al. 1991).

3) What is the cost-effectiveness of the technique in terms of operating costs? Other associated costs were not considered.

4) Disregarding social acceptability, can the technique be easily implemented as the demand arises? Managers must have means for achieving population-management objectives. Without accessible tools, managers will fail to meet time-specific objectives.

Evaluation of Techniques

Artificial or "Diversionary" Feeding of Bears during Calving

Feeding bears can potentially increase moose numbers where moose calves are major prey of bears. High bear predation rates (40–58%) have been documented in all Alaska and Yukon studies of radio-collared moose calves (Boertje et al. 1987, Larsen et al. 1989, Schwartz and Franzmann 1989, Ballard et al. 1991a, Osborne et al. 1991). This predation occurs even when moose are well nourished (Gasaway et al. 1992). Baits can be used to attract bears because bears are efficient scavengers. Artificial feeding (hereafter "diversionary" feeding) of bears during moose calving diverts bears from killing calves and enhances calf survival through spring. Bears kill relatively few moose calves after spring (Boertje et al. 1988).

There are three studies in which bears and wolves were artificially fed during moose calving and subsequent moose calf survival was monitored. During May and June 1985, Boertje et al. (1987) air-dropped 12 metric tons of moose carcasses and scrap meat in a 1,000-km^2 area to attract bears for collaring in and around a concentrated moose calving area in east-central Alaska. They observed evidence of grizzly bears, black bears, and wolves feeding at carcass sites. The early winter 1985 calf:cow ratio increased to 53:100 (n = 17 cows) compared with 11–15:100 (n = 26-39, P < 0.005; Chi Square Test of Independence) during the preceding three years and 26–36:100 (n = 25-27, P < 0.10) during the following two years when baits were not available to predators. The 1985 response was not evident in three untreated adjacent areas (10–19:100, n = 25-70, P < 0.005). Although these results suggest that diversionary feeding resulted in increased calf:cow ratios, some increase could have resulted from the slow recovery of bears (four to five days) immobilized with drugs.

In 1990, Boertje et al. (1993b) tested whether diversionary feeding of bears and wolves could improve moose calf:cow ratios in a different 1,650-km^2 study area in east-central Alaska. Twenty-six metric tons of moose carcasses (n = 87 baits at 61 sites, x̄ = 300 kg) were distributed in three equal proportions 14–15 May, 21–22 May, and 30 May. Median calving date was 21 May. Bears (mostly grizzly bears) and wolves consumed 79% of the baits by 14 June. This was evidenced by disarticulated skeletons and incidental observations of both bears and wolves consuming baits.

Moose calf:cow ratios were higher (P < 0.005) during early winter 1990 (42 calves:100 cows ≥29 months, n = 86 cows) compared with eight prior years (x̄ = 25, range = 12–38:100, n = 51–75) and 1990 untreated sites (11–27:100, n = 85–204).

In 1991, the experiment was repeated in the same 1,650-km^2 study area with only 16 metric tons of moose carcasses (Boertje et al. 1993b). During early winter 1991, moose ratios were 32 calves:100 cows ≥29 months (n = 100) in the treated area, compared with 16–37:100 (n = 58–225) in untreated adjacent areas. The smaller amount of bait may have been insufficient to significantly enhance calf survival, considering the size of the area and number of bears present.

Biologists in the state of Washington have six years of experience with diversionary feeding of black bears to protect forest plantations (Ziegltrum 1990). A commercial bear ration was developed and field-tested. Feeding has partially replaced lethal control of bears. Bears were fed a complete, sugar-based pelleted ration *ad libitum* from mid-March through June to divert them from stripping bark and feeding on exposed sapwood. Feeding proved more cost-effective and more socially acceptable than lethal control of bears. The program has been expanded each year.

Despite success with diversionary feeding, this technique ranked moderately effective as a predator-management tool (Table 1) for two reasons. First, diversionary feeding could increase predator numbers by enhancing predator physical condition, productivity, and juvenile survival, and by temporarily attracting predators from adjacent areas. This would confound predator-prey management problems. Feeding could occur for only two to four weeks to minimize effects on predators and maximize benefits to moose. Also, feeding levels could be adjusted to merely supplant the nutrition naturally obtained from killing neonates, if studies experimented with different levels of preferred food.

Second, although feeding can be successful in reducing early bear predation on moose calves, wolves may compensate with increased predation later in the year. For example, Hayes et al. (1991) found that wolves removed 64% of the moose calves in a low-density population during each of two winters in southern Yukon. However, most studies have documented that most moose mortality occurs during the first three weeks of life (Boertje et al. 1987, 1988; Larsen et al. 1989; Ballard et al. 1991a).

Diversionary feeding ranked high in social acceptability (Table 1) because no killing of predators was involved (Arthur et al. 1977). Public attitudes have been favorable in Alaska when predators were fed moose carcasses. Disfavor may arise if costly commercial food sources are used. Disfavor may also arise if bears are perceived as conditioned or dependent on the feeding program, therefore feeding time should be minimal (three to four weeks).

Diversionary feeding was ranked low in cost-effectiveness and moderate in terms of ease of implementation (Ta-

Table 1. Relative evaluation of six methods of increasing predation-limited moose populations in areas suited to the particular methods, based on four criteria.

	Diversionary feeding of bears during calving	Enhancing moose habitat	Allowing increases in alternate prey	Reducing wolf birth rates	Conventional public hunting of bears	Aircraft-assisted wolf harvest
Biological effectiveness	Moderate	Moderate	Low	Low to moderate	Moderate to high	High
Social acceptability	High	High	Moderate to high	Moderate	High	Low
Cost-effectiveness	Low	Low to high	High	Low to Moderate	High	Moderate to high
Ease of implementation	Moderate	Low	Low	Low to Moderate	High	High

ble 1). It is expensive and difficult to acquire, store, and distribute bait that is environmentally safe, socially acceptable, inexpensive, and effective. Local availability of suitable bait may determine the choice of foods. Commercial bear food (e.g., from Washington at $2/kg) may be too expensive unless manufactured close to delivery sites. Twenty metric tons of bait were needed to divert grizzly bears (16 bears/1,000 km^2, [Boertje et al. 1987]) from moose calves in a 1,650-km^2 area in east-central Alaska. Using commercial food sources, annual bait costs may total $40,000, and transportation costs would escalate if off-road areas were selected for feeding programs.

In the 1985 (Boertje et al. 1987) and 1990 (Boertje et al. 1993b) programs, train-killed moose were collected during winter at the railroad's expense. These moose were stored under sawdust and distributed at the U.S. military's expense during helicopter training missions. In 1991, starved moose and those killed by traffic were collected by volunteer groups in Fairbanks, Alaska (Boertje et al. 1993b). Moose were distributed using Alaska Department of Fish and Game (ADF&G) vehicles, a DeHavilland Beaver aircraft, and a riverboat. These subsidized operations were affordable ($4,000–$9,000 /year), but large numbers of moose carcasses are seldom available. Alternative foods need to be tested. Development of chemical attractants for coyotes (*C. latrans*) (Green 1987, Scrivner et al. 1987) may be useful in researching techniques to attract and detain bears.

Enhancing Moose Habitat

Three mechanisms are listed that could decrease the impact of predation, but further research is needed to test the widespread existence of these mechanisms. First, burning has

been associated with improved moose nutritional status (Schwartz and Franzmann 1989), which may decrease the vulnerability of individual moose to predation. However, Gasaway et al. (1992) concluded that moose nutrition is a minor factor affecting low-density moose populations in most of Alaska and Yukon. Second, the killing or hunting efficiency of predators may decline in burns or commercially logged areas. Predators may be disadvantaged by the fallen timber in burns. Also, moose are often scattered randomly throughout large burns in interior Alaska and Yukon. In contrast, in unburned habitat, moose density is highest in narrow zones of shrubs, e.g., riparian or subalpine areas, where predators can travel easily and predictably find moose. Third, increased moose density following burning has been related to increased productivity (Schwartz and Franzmann 1989), and to increased time moose spend in burns (Peek 1974, Gasaway et al. 1989). These factors could indirectly reduce the impact of predation on a moose population by increasing local moose:predator ratios (Gasaway et al. 1983, Schwartz and Franzmann 1989).

Evidence that moose density may increase substantially as a result of burning is indicated by a moose density of 417 moose/1,000 km^2 in the large 26-year-old Teslin burn in southern Yukon (2,515-km^2 survey area [Gasaway et al. 1992]). This density is three times higher than the average density in 20 areas (> 2,000 km^2 each) where wolves and bears were similarly lightly harvested and moose were the primary prey (Gasaway et al. 1992). Moose densities in these other areas ranged from 45 to 269 moose/1,000 km^2. No other area had the uniformly extensive, ideal habitat of the Teslin burn.

Fig. 1. *Moose carcasses being distributed by Alaska Department of Fish and Game personnel to feed bears. Moose killed by trains or traffic in winter were collected and stored under sawdust. The carcasses were distributed during moose and caribou calving seasons. Studies concluded that, by feeding bears, one can successfully divert bears from killing newborn moose calves (Photo: R. D. Boertje).*

Social acceptability of habitat enhancement ranked high (Table 1) relative to other techniques, although decreased air quality from burning has been unfavorable. Cost-effectiveness of this method would be variable depending on the methods of habitat enhancement. Prescribed burns have huge costs associated with containment ($500/km² in Alaska). Funds from commercial logging could help pay for ways to encourage browse species favored by moose.

Habitat enhancement of large areas (> 2,000 km²) is not currently available as a wildlife management tool. The ADF&G has statutory mandates to manage wildlife, but no statutory authority to enhance habitat for wildlife. Wildfires are usually contained by land managers, regardless of opportunities for enhancing moose habitat. Prescribed burning and extensive logging of moose habitat are in their infancy in Alaska and Yukon, but may increase in the near future.

Managers and researchers need to be capable of implementing coordinated, long-term studies of predator-moose-habitat relationships, pre- and posthabitat enhancement, before habitat enhancement can be evaluated as a tool to decrease predation on moose.

Promoting Increases in Alternative Prey
Gasaway et al. (1992) proposed allowing caribou (*Rangifer tarandus*) to increase as a method for increasing moose

numbers. Caribou have escaped predation regulation without strong human intervention (Skoog 1968). Moose, in contrast, require substantial human intervention to escape predation limitation by both wolves and bears in Alaska and Yukon (Coady 1980, Yesner 1989, Gasaway et al. 1992). Decreased predation on moose may follow large increases in caribou (Holleman and Stephenson 1981, Ballard et al. 1987:38, Boertje et al. 1993b), but exceptions occur when caribou change movement patterns (Boertje et al. 1993b). Wolf numbers correlate with ungulate biomass (Keith 1983, Fuller 1989, Gasaway et al. 1992). Therefore, it may be difficult to reduce total predation on moose when caribou increase, unless measures to prevent increases in wolf populations are implemented.

This method is viewed as a waiting process, not a tool, and therefore ranked low in terms of ease of implementation (Table 1). Hunters may have to forego some opportunity to hunt caribou, while waiting for moose to increase. This lowers the potential social acceptability of this method (Table 1).

Reducing Predator Birth Rates
Surgery, implants, inoculations, and oral administration of drugs have been used to reduce predator birth rates (Stellflug and Gates 1987, Orford et al. 1988). However, wolf preda-

Fig. 2. *Moose in a 24-year-old burn on the Kenai Peninsula, Alaska. Ideal moose habitat can occur 10 to 30 years after wildfire in Alaska, and moose density is often relatively high in these habitats. (Photo: J.L. Davis)*

tion and movement studies indicate that birth control may have low to moderate effectiveness in reducing predation for several reasons. First, the maintenance of wolf pairs in an exploited population can result in significantly higher per capita wolf kill rates (Hayes et al. 1991). Second, ingress of subadult wolves into wolf control areas may offset the results of birth control. For example, in a highly exploited wolf population in south central Alaska, 28% of 135 wolves dispersed, and 22% of dispersers were accepted into existing packs (Ballard et al. 1987). Immigrating wolves may be accepted at a greater rate in an area where birth control is practiced. Also, lightly harvested adjacent populations may have a greater percentage of dispersing wolves than observed in the highly exploited wolf population in south-central Alaska. Ingress would be less significant if treated wolf populations were insular or peninsular. Translocation of young wolves combined with sterilization of adult pairs may significantly reduce predation.

Birth control for grizzly bears is not recommended because of inherently low reproductive rates. Female bears have lower immigration rates than wolves (Ballard et al. 1987, Reynolds 1990), therefore bear populations would be slow to recover from birth control. Reducing birth rates of

black bears may have some application in specific circumstances, because black bear densities and productivity are higher than those of grizzly bears (Reynolds 1990, Schwartz and Franzmann 1991).

Social acceptability of predator birth control was ranked moderate (Table 1). This evaluation was based on responses received following a press release that mentioned birth control as a potential predator-control technique in Alaska. The cost-effectiveness of birth control was ranked low to moderate, because of high implementation costs (Table 1). Implementation of the most common birth control techniques (surgery, implants, or inoculation) requires immobilization of individual predators, which is extremely difficult and expensive in remote areas of Alaska and the Yukon. For example, recent costs to collar a wolf pack or a grizzly bear averaged $2,000 in a remote, largely forested study area in east-central Alaska.

Distributing baits containing chemosterilants is an alternative to immobilizing individual predators. The use of chemicals, however, requires registration by the Environmental Protection Agency, and preregistration research costs may total millions of dollars. Chemosterilants would not be approved if found to impair nontarget species, such

Fig. 3. *Caribou are secondary prey of wolves in most of central Alaska; moose are the primary prey. Waiting for caribou numbers to increase in hopes that predation on moose will decline is not a viable strategy for attaining management objectives. When caribou increase in numbers, they often move beyond the range of resident wolf packs and leave the resident moose with relatively high predation rates. (Photo: J.L. Davis)*

as wolverines (*Gulo gulo*). Species-specific delivery systems will be required, thereby necessitating further development costs.

Conventional Public Hunting and Trapping

"Conventional public harvest" of wolves and bears is defined as hunting and trapping exclusive of aircraft-assisted or snowmachine-assisted hunting. As a predator-control technique, conventional harvest received high ratings in social acceptability, cost-effectiveness, and ease of implementation, in part because of minimal agency involvement (Table 1). Conventional harvest of wolves has effectively reduced or stabilized wolf numbers below food-limited levels near populated areas (e.g., on the Kenai Peninsula [Peterson et al. 1984] and north of Anchorage [Gasaway et al. 1992:42]). Harvest of black bears using bait likewise has reduced black bear densities near Fairbanks (Hechtel 1991). Attempts have been made in limited remote areas in Alaska to encourage public harvest of wolves and grizzly bears to stimulate increases in ungulates.

The ADF&G promoted trapper-education programs in two remote areas to stimulate interest in wolf trapping and

snaring and to increase success rates. This promotion included trapper workshops and the production and distribution of a video on canid trapping techniques. A nonprofit native organization provided wolf snares to trappers in select villages. Total numbers of wolves trapped did not increase in these areas (Pegau 1987, Nowlin 1988). The inherent wariness of wolves, poor access, and a lack of economic incentives for trapping wolves contributed to the failure of this program to increase wolf harvest.

In contrast, hunters have increased grizzly bear harvest sufficiently to reduce grizzly bear densities in two remote Alaska study areas. Reported annual harvests averaged about 8–9% in an east-central Alaska (Boertje et al. 1987, Gasaway et al. 1992) and a central Alaska study site (Reynolds 1990). These harvest rates can cause long-term, slow declines averaging about 2% annually (Reynolds 1990). Methods used to encourage grizzly bear harvest in east-central Alaska included: liberalizing hunting regulations on grizzly bears, increasing the number of hunters by increasing opportunity to hunt male ungulates, and encouraging hunters to harvest grizzly bears through information

Fig. 4. *Conventional public harvest of bears can be used as a management tool to reduce predation on moose calves. At the same time, managers can protect the viability of bear populations. (Photo: R.L. Zarnke)*

and education. Liberalized hunting regulations included: lengthening the hunting season, deleting a resident grizzly bear tag (fee) requirement, and increasing the bag limit to one bear/year, as opposed to the usual bag limit of one bear/four years. The harvest of sows accompanied by cubs and yearlings was not authorized.

In the east-central Alaska study site, moose were below food-limited densities, and grizzly predation was a major factor limiting the moose population (Boertje et al. 1987, Gasaway et al. 1992). Moose calves per 100 cows during fall increased in this area, coincidental to potential declines in grizzly numbers. Grizzly harvests averaged 8% annually during 1982–88 (Boertje et al. 1987, Gasaway et al. 1992). Assuming this harvest rate equates to a 2% annual decline (Reynolds 1990), the grizzly population declined 14% by 1989. Moose calves per 100 cows $\geq$ 2 years old increased from a range of 19–27 ($\bar{x} = 23$) during 1982–1988 to 32–48 ($\bar{x} = 38$; $\underline{P} < 0.05$, Mann-Whitney two-sided test) during 1989–1991. Other factors did not favor increased moose calf survival. For example, wolf densities were higher ($\underline{P} = 0.026$, Student's t-test) during fall 1989–1991 ($\bar{x} = 7.3$ wolves/1,000 km^2) than fall 1982–1988 ($\bar{x} = 5.9$ wolves/1,000 km^2), alternative prey (caribou) declined, and

snow depths were greater during late winter 1990 and 1991 (Boertje et al. 1993a).

Field studies on the effects of bear harvest on moose calf survival are needed where: 1) moose are below food-limited densities; 2) bear predation is a major factor limiting moose; and 3) bear reductions are publicly sanctioned. Managers need to know the degree to which reductions in bears affect moose calf survival in different ecosystems. Managers also need to know whether decreasing trends in numbers of bears harvested per unit effort will provide sufficient information to manage bears (e.g., without expensive bear population estimates). Increased bear harvests are not recommended: 1) where bear predation accounts for a small fraction of total predation; 2) where moose are near food-limited densities, unless additional moose harvest is desired; or 3) in coastal areas where bears are the primary species of management concern.

Aircraft-Assisted Wolf Harvest

Public and agency wolf harvests using aircraft have proven effective at reducing annual fall wolf numbers and stabilizing populations below food-limited levels (Gasaway et al. 1983, 1992, Ballard et al. 1987, Farnell and Hayes, in prep.

Rodney D. Boertje, David G. Kelleyhouse, and Robert D. Hayes

Fig. 5. *Wolf hides collected during agency wolf control programs have been auctioned to the public. (Photo: ADF&G)*

Boertje et al. 1996). The public has reduced wolf numbers using light, fixed-wing aircraft in areas with high proportions of unforested, open terrain and suitable snow conditions for tracking and landing. Large portions of interior Alaska north of the Alaska Range are ill-suited to this method. The use of aircraft was discontinued where wolves were extremely vulnerable (e.g., portions of northern and northwestern Alaska). In these areas, snowmachines replaced aircraft as a tool to effectively reduce or regulate wolf numbers.

During the 1980's, wolves were regularly held below food-limited densities by public, aircraft-assisted wolf harvest in only a portion of south-central Alaska (Ballard et al. 1987). Wary wolves are able to avoid aircraft-assisted harvest in more forested areas of Alaska. The primary method has been land-and-shoot harvest in which the hunter lands near the wolf before shooting. Shooting from the air was discontinued in 1972 in Alaska, except under state permit in specific areas (Harbo and Dean 1983, Stephenson et al. this volume). In November 1992, Alaska's Board of Game passed regulations allowing the use of aircraft only for wolf "control" not wolf "harvest." Agency wolf control programs have involved aerial shooting from light, fixed-wing aircraft and helicopters. Radiotelemetry has occasionally been used

in these programs to help locate packs, especially where tracking conditions were poor. Only one ADF&G aerial wolf control program survived legal proceedings and reviews for four years of effective wolf control (> 60% reduction of pre-control wolf numbers). The ADF&G shot 18–67 wolves annually during four years in this area (Gasaway et al. 1983). The program was followed by a 5-6 fold increase in moose numbers (Boertje et al. 1996). A similar, seven-year agency wolf control program in east-central Yukon (1983-1989) also resulted in elevated moose numbers (Farnell and Hayes, in prep.).

Aircraft-assisted wolf harvest is viewed as having the lowest social acceptability of the six methods evaluated in Table 1. Harbo and Dean (1983) and Stephenson et al. (this volume) trace the history of court cases reflecting this low social acceptability. Indeed, the major motivation for investigating alternative techniques is the low social acceptability of this method (Gasaway et al. 1992).

Cost-effectiveness of this method is relatively high. For example, the public can effectively reduce wolves to low densities without agency assistance in portions of south-central and western Alaska. In interior Alaska and southern Yukon, operating costs of agency-sponsored aerial wolf reductions have ranged from about $500 to $1,000 per wolf,

Wolves in a Changing World

yet returns have been high in terms of additional ungulate harvest (Boertje et al. 1996, R. Farnell, Yukon Fish and Wildl. Br., pers. commun.). Administrative and educational costs associated with aircraft-assisted wolf harvest are high, in part because of low social and political acceptability. Social and political factors also affect how easily managers can implement this tool.

Management Strategy

Several recommendations are given for circumstances where the local public has sanctioned predator control to meet management objectives for moose. These are: 1) rank areas based on suitable habitat, overall demand, management and research capabilities, and social and economic costs; 2) evaluate the suitability of several combined tech-

niques for a specific area; 3) educate and inform the general public, as well as public advisory groups; and 4) adopt a formal process for approving area-specific wildlife management plans in areas with and without anticipated predator control. It is essential that the public be informed about trade-offs between social- and biological-based management decisions.

Acknowledgments
We appreciate reviews of this manuscript by W.L. Regelin, D.J. Reed, A.K. Ruggles, C.A. Smith, W.B. Ballard, S.D. Miller, J.W. Schoen, and anonymous reviewers. Funding was provided by Federal Aid in Wildlife Restoration and the Alaska Department of Fish and Game.

Rodney D. Boertje, David G. Kelleyhouse, and Robert D. Hayes

Economic Evaluation of Vancouver Island Wolf Control

■ Roger Reid and Doug Janz

We discuss the meaning of economic values and how economic evaluations can be used as one criterion in judging wildlife enhancement projects. Benefit cost analyses of two wolf control programs on Vancouver Island are presented. Benefits of the programs are estimated by comparing the actual number of deer hunter days with wolf control to hunter days that would be expected in the absence of the program. The increased numbers of hunter days with wolf control are measures of the benefits of the control programs to hunters. The values of these benefits are found by applying average daily deer hunting values for the area to the increased hunter effort. The present values of the benefits were compared to the present values of the operational and manpower costs to give benefit-cost ratios for the two wolf control programs. The paper concludes with a discussion of the uses and limitations of the evaluations.

Introduction

Society is often unaware of the economic values of environmental resources that typically do not involve commercial transactions. While the measures of these values are usually simulated, and as such, are not as robust as market values, they do provide an indication of the economic significance of these resources. As a consequence, decisions that diminish or enhance these resources carry economic benefits and costs that should be taken into account when decisions are made.

Wolves (*Canis lupus*) and wolf control are highly emotional issues that usually produce a polarization of views. For example, in British Columbia (B.C.), one control program between 1984 and 1988 led to more public calls and correspondence than any other single wildlife management issue. One neglected aspect has been the economic consequences of wolves and their control. Any limiting factor that reduces wildlife population size, be it logging or wolf predation, will adversely affect those who enjoy wildlife and benefit from its existence. Similarly, actions to increase wildlife populations will benefit wildlife users although it will harm those opposed to control. These social costs and benefits should be taken into account in assessing the effects of wolves and wolf control.

The purpose of this paper is to describe how economic analysis can be used to evaluate wolf control based on an actual program on Vancouver Island in B.C. The first section of the paper is an introduction to economic values and how they are measured. The following section evaluates an ex-

perimental control project carried out on Vancouver Island. The final section presents an economic evaluation of a full control program for Vancouver Island.

Meaning and Measurement of Economic Value

Economists measure the value of goods and services by how much better off consumers are as a result of their provision. Individuals set values they place on goods and services by the maximum amount they would pay for each unit purchased. The price actually paid is typically less than the maximum amount that individual would be willing to pay. The difference between the maximum amount and the actual amount paid represents the net value to the consumer of the commodity. Economists call this measure consumer surplus.

Most wildlife in Canada are common property resources. No individual or legal entity has ownership rights to these resources. Wildlife are owned equally, or in common, by the citizens living in the jurisdiction in which they are contained. In the case of privately-owned goods and services, it is possible to determine their values by observing their sale in organized markets. However, because no private property rights are attached to common property resources, they are not usually exchanged in markets. As a result, there is no market price that signals the value users place on these resources. In order to estimate the value of common property resources, economists either simulate markets for these resources or observe actual behavior that suggests the value associated with these resources.

Table 1. Resident deer hunters, hunter days, and harvest on Vancouver Island.

YEAR	Hunter	Hunter Days	Harvest
1976	25,276	149,920	10,228
1977	23,206	130,553	11,439
1978	25,998	163,592	13,053
1979	25,382	170,938	11,015
1980	25,619	179,386	13,171
1981	25,242	187,584	11,807
1982	24,140	191,451	10,317
1983	18,271	139,019	8,079
1984	17,572	135,169	8,779
1985	16,011	124,138	7,125
1986	15,689	121,766	6,402
1987	11,328	78,634	6,454
1988	9,319	65,482	5,784
1989	11,716	78,074	7,449
1990	12,266	89,798	7,995
1991	11,312	96,513	8,190

Source: Annual Hunter Sample, Wildlife Branch, B.C. Ministry of the Environment, Lands and Parks.

The most commonly used method to value wildlife resources is called the Contingent Valuation Method (CVM). Detailed descriptions of this method can be found in Hanley (1989) and Carson and Mitchell (1989). The CVM involves replicating a market situation that treats the common property resource as if it were a private property resource and then determines the price people would pay for it. The CVM is a survey technique that first describes a hypothetical market for an environmental resource and then asks the respondent how much he would be willing to pay for the amount he is presently using or changes in this amount. Responses are contingent on the hypothetical market described. While the CVM can be used to determine values of a specific site, it is frequently used to determine values for large areas. For example, Filion et al. (1989) used the CVM to determine values associated with different types of wildlife activities in the Canadian provinces. In B.C., the CVM was used to determine the values of resident hunting (Reid 1985) and to estimate the values of nonhunting wildlife-related activities (Reid et al. 1986).

An economic evaluation compares the economic benefits to society of a proposed project to its costs. That is, a comparison is made between the situation "with" the project and what would happen "without" the project. The benefits and costs of a project, no matter when they occur, should all be valued in the "constant" dollars of a particular year. A constant dollar refers to a dollar that provides the same purchasing power or command over goods and services from year to year.

Different types of benefits may result from a wildlife project including recreational, nonuser values, genetic preservation and scientific knowledge. While each of these types of benefits can be valued conceptually, in practice, only recreational benefits can be fully valued by economists.

Background to Vancouver Island Wolf Control

The number of resident deer hunters on Vancouver Island and the number of hunter days and harvest illustrate two general patterns over the period 1976 to 1991 (Table 1). Between 1976 and 1982, the number of hunters ranged between 23,000 and 26,000 while the harvest varied between 10,000 and 13,000. However, over this period, the number of hunter days rose steadily, indicating an increasing effort per deer harvested. The substantial drop in hunter numbers and effort in 1983 was precipitated by a doubling of all hunting license fees in that year and was compounded by the state of the economy and demographic and other factors. This result was common across the province.

Fig. 1. *Wildlife Management Units — Vancouver Island Region.*

From 1983 through 1988, the number of deer hunters, hunter days, and harvest on Vancouver Island fell steadily. Over this period, the number of hunters fell by 65%, hunter days by 72%, and harvest by 33%. While deer hunting in the rest of the province also fell in the first couple of years after the 1983 fee increase, it had largely stabilized by 1985 and has remained steady since then. Over the same period, deer hunter numbers and effort have almost doubled in the East Kootenays. The decrease in deer populations on Vancouver Island has been cited by a number of sportsmen as the primary reason for the fall in hunter numbers. One of the main factors contributing to the declining deer populations has been the increase in wolf populations during the 1970's and 1980's.

During the 1950's and 1960's, wolves were rarely seen on Vancouver Island and concern over their populations led to a ban on hunting and trapping. By 1970, an "endangered species" designation was considered for the Vancouver Island wolf. However, wolf sign and sightings began to increase in the early 1970's and, by 1976, wolves were regularly observed throughout Vancouver Island. Numbers increased sufficiently to reinstate a hunting season in 1977 and a trapping season in 1979.

A few studies have examined the relationship between wolf and deer populations on Vancouver Island. Hebert et al. (1982) found that the largest declines in deer populations occurred within the 90% home range of wolf packs and the largest increases occurred in the buffer zones between pack

Table 2. Estimated resident deer hunter days.

YEAR	M.U.'s 12 & 13	M.U. 11
1976	17,557	12,350
1977	15,085	10,448
1978	18,310	11,660
1979	14,659	8,597
1980	17,584	9,142
1981	14,860	6,715
1982	12,758	6,359
1983	8,288	4,117
1984	6,471	5,574
1985	4,809	3,844
1986	4,729	4,584
1987	3,164	4,494
1988	2,500	2,697
1989	2,573	4,437
1990	2,486	4,192
1991	3,618	4,357

home ranges. However, Hatter (1984) found that by 1981, the buffer zone between packs was eliminated by expansion and overlap of wolf pack ranges in response to declining availability of prey. Hatter determined that wolf predation was the primary factor limiting deer population growth on northern Vancouver Island. Detailed discussion of these issues can be found in Janz (1989) and Archibald et al. (1991).

(a) Experimental Control Program

In order to better understand the impact of wolves on deer populations, the B.C. Wildlife Branch initiated an experimental wolf control program on northern Vancouver Island in 1982. The program was conducted in the Nimpkish Valley, which covers an area of about 2,000 km². At one time, the Nimpkish provided about 10% of the provincial deer harvest. The experiment was designed to permit comparisons of wolf densities and deer trends between the wolf removal zone (RZ) made up of Management Unit (MU) 1–11 and a nonremoval zone composed of part of MU 1–10 (Fig. 1). Over the four-year study period, 64 wolves were killed in the RZ. Wolf densities in RZ were reduced from 44 wolves/1,000 km² to 4–5 wolves/1,000 km² in the winter of 1984–1985. Over the study period, survival of deer fawns improved significantly in the removal zone, while there was little change in the nonremoval area (Atkinson and Janz 1991).

One benefit of wolf control to resident hunters is the value of the increase in hunter days made possible by the program. This requires forecasting what would have happened to hunting in the RZ in the absence of the control program. A number of studies have used different models to predict rates of participation and number of days in different types of recreation. Among these studies are Cicchetti (1973), Hay and McConnell (1979), Milon and Clemmons (1991), and Rockel and Kealy (1991). However, most of these models require large amounts of data that are typically unavailable for specific sites. Further, these models tend to explain relatively small amounts of variation in levels of recreation.

An advantage of the present study is that it is an ex-post evaluation of a project. Hunting effort in adjacent MUs that did not receive reductions in wolves could be expected to provide a reliable prediction of how hunting effort in the RZ would have behaved in the absence of control. Because the experimental nonremoval zone comprised only about 10% of MU 1-10 and wolves were removed (legally and illegally) from parts of the MU, it was felt to be unrepresentative of what would happen to hunter effort in the absence of wolf control.

Management Units 1-12 and 1-13 provide a better indication of what would have happened to hunter effort without control in the RZ. These MUs displayed similar hunting trends to those in MU 1-11 (RZ) prior to control, but did not receive any wolf removal. Between 1976 and 1982, hunting

Table 3. Estimated benefits of experimental control.

YEAR	Column (1) Hunter Days (RZ) No Control	Column (2) Change in Hunter Days	Column (3) Annual Value ($1991)	Column (4) Present Value
1983	4,117	0	$ 0	$ 0
1984	3,228	2,346	$ 87,500	$ 81,030
1985	2,402	1,442	$ 53,790	$ 46,100
1986	2,364	2,220	$ 82,800	$ 65,740
1987	1,584	2,910	$108,540	$ 79,780
1988	1,253	1,444	$ 53,860	$ 36,680
1989	1,289	3,148	$117,420	$ 73,970
1990	1,240	2,952	$110,110	$ 64,190
1991	1,699	2,658	$ 99,140	$ 53,530
				$501,020

effort in both areas was declining, but the decrease was proportionately greater in the RZ (Table 2). Beginning in 1983, hunting effort in the RZ stabilized, while effort in MUs 12 and 13 continued to fall.

Forecasting what hunting effort in the RZ might have been without the experimental control program is shown in Column 1 of Table 3. The expected change in hunter days due to control is found as the difference in the number of hunter days with and without the program, shown in Column 2. The change in hunter days were then valued at the average value for a resident deer hunter day for Vancouver Island. Deer hunter days for Vancouver Island are estimated to be worth $37.30 for resident hunters. The annual values of deer hunting benefits are shown in Column 3 of Table 3.

Because the benefits of the control program accrue to resident hunters in different years, it is necessary to discount the annual values to a common present value. This was done by applying the discount rate of 8%, used in evaluating projects in B.C., to give the present values of the annual benefits shown in Column 4.

The primary costs associated with the experimental control program were for staff salaries, vehicle operation, and traps and supplies. The operational budget of the project was $60,000 to $70,000 annually, in 1991 dollars (Table 4).

The present values of the expected benefits and costs of the experimental control program can be compared in a couple of ways. First, the ratio of benefits to costs for the program is about 1.8. This indicates that for every dollar spent on the program, we could expect about $1.80 worth of resident hunter benefits. A second method of comparing benefits and costs is the difference between the values. This

gives a net benefit from the experimental control program of $222,210. The value of the expected benefits to resident hunters exceeded the costs by this amount.

It should be noted that the experimental wolf control program on northern Vancouver Island was designed primarily for scientific purposes and not with the intention of producing benefits for resident hunters. As a consequence, it may not be appropriate to judge this project according to economic benefit cost criteria that only considers user benefits. It is difficult to quantify and value scientific knowledge in a form that can be incorporated into an economic evaluation. Nevertheless, the analysis does suggest that wolf control on Vancouver Island provides positive benefits to resident hunters.

(b) Vancouver Island Wolf Control

In the spring of 1986, ministerial approval was given for an operational wolf control program on Vancouver Island. The program was implemented that summer. The purposes of the program were to restore important deer herds and ensure the maintenance of viable populations of predators and ungulates. Wolf control on the northern part of Vancouver Island was concentrated in areas where old-growth logging deferrals had been agreed to for the protection of important deer habitat. On southern Vancouver Island, wolf control centered on watersheds with declining deer populations.

Registered trappers were trained and equipped to trap wolves. All wolves killed were submitted for inspection. Prior to control, the wolf population on the Island was estimated at 430–590. An estimated 255 wolves were killed between the summer of 1986 and the spring of 1989. Approximately 81% were removed by trapping and the remain-

Table 4. Experimental wolf control program costs.

YEAR	($1991)	Present Value
1982	$70,950	$ 70,950
1983	$67,240	$ 62,260
1984	$64,630	$ 51,320
1985	$62,620	$ 49,720
1986	$60,630	$ 44,560
		$278,810

Table 5. Benefits of Vancouver Island wolf control.

YEAR	(1) Hunter Days no control	(2) Hunter Days (Control)	(3) Change in Hunter Days	(4) Value of Hunter Days	(5) Present Value Hunter Days
1986	121,766	121,766	— -	— -	— -
1987	75,469	78,815	3,346	$124,880	$ 115,560
1988	61,131	65,627	4,496	$167,700	$ 143,720
1989	68,895	78,443	9,548	$356,140	$ 282,780
1990	65,244	90,909	25,665	$957,300	$ 703,610
1991	93,526	95,727	2,201	$ 82,100	$ 55,910
					$1,301,580

der by hunting. The post-control average wolf density for Vancouver Island was 8–12 wolves/1,000 km². Deer populations in monitored watersheds generally increased during the control program (Archibald et al. 1991).

Wolf control was conducted on a watershed basis over most of the accessible portions of Vancouver Island. However, there were a few large areas that received little or no control. These areas included MUs 8, 12, and 13 on the northern tip (Fig. 1). In order to evaluate a control program that covered the entire island, these three management units were used to represent what might be expected to happen to hunting effort in the absence of any control program. The annual percentage change in hunting effort in these three units was used to forecast and compare to actual hunting effort in the remaining 10 management units beginning in 1987, when the effects of wolf control would first be felt (Column 1, Table 5).

The forecast of the expected number of hunter days with the control program also used the previous method. However, in this case, the annual percentage change in hunter effort in areas with wolf control was used to predict hunting effort in MUs 8, 12, and 13 for the control period. Adding this forecast to the estimated hunter days in the 10 management units with control gives a forecast of hunting effort if wolf control was practised over all of Vancouver Island (Column 2 of Table 5).

The difference between the expected number of hunter days with and without control provides an estimate of the annual change in hunter days made possible by wolf control (Column 3, Table 5). The annual values of the change in days

Table 6. Annual cost Vancouver Island Wolf Control

YEAR	Contrac-tors	Traps (Purchase and Repair)	Staff	Other	Total Annual Costs	Present Value
1986	25,220	25,300	43,610	— -	$94,130	$ 94,130
1987	49,400	6,350	27,260	5,880	88,890	82,310
1988	28,400	1,990	19,750	— -	50,140	42,970
1989	— -	— -	3,920	— -	3,920	3,100
					$237,000	$222,520

are found by applying the daily value of $37.30. The present values of the annual values of the change in hunter days were found using a discount rate of 8%. This gives a present value of expected benefits for resident deer hunters due to wolf control of $1,301,580.

The costs of a wolf control program for Vancouver Island were estimated as the sum of the costs of the operational wolf control program and the amount it would cost to control wolves in the three MUs (8, 12, and 13) not included in the operational program. The main costs associated with wolf control would be for the hiring of contractors to trap wolves, staff time in planning, supervising, and monitoring the program and the purchase and repair of traps (Table 6). In the case of the operational program, auxiliary staff spent close to two years working on the project, while one regular staff member spent 80% of a year on the project and a second spent 50% of a year on the project.

The annual costs were discounted to their present values using a discount rate of 8%. This gave a present value of costs for the program of $222,520. The present value of the net benefits of the program are estimated to be $1,079,060. The program has a benefit cost ratio of 5.9 or produces $5.90 of resident deer hunter benefits for every dollar of costs incurred on the program. These results suggest that a wolf control program on Vancouver Island would be quite efficient in producing benefits for resident deer hunters. This is not surprising given that historically, deer hunting on Van-

couver Island has been popular and wolf control can have a relatively rapid impact on deer populations.

Conclusions

This paper has presented an economic evaluation of a wolf control program for Vancouver Island. The evaluation was limited to considering the benefits to resident deer hunters and did not try to take account of benefits from wildlife viewing, nonuse values or changes in scientific knowledge. In addition, the analysis did not make allowance for the costs incurred by those opposed to wolf control. Given these limitations, the results suggest that, based on the criterion of economic efficiency, a wolf control program for Vancouver Island is desirable. This is largely due to depressed deer populations and high hunter potential.

The type of analysis presented in the paper can be applied to a range of situations affecting wildlife populations. Economic evaluations can be performed on most types of wildlife enhancement projects that lead to increased populations. Similarly, economic values can be used to measure the loss of wildlife values due to competing land uses such as logging. These provide measures of the amount of compensation required when wildlife opportunities are lost or whether mitigation is worthwhile. Perhaps the most important use of these values is to inform the public and politicians of the value of wildlife.

Interactions Between Livestock Guarding Dogs and Wolves

■ Raymond Coppinger and Lorna Coppinger

The success of Old World guarding dogs in causing coyotes to avoid flocks of sheep and goats on ranches in the United States (U.S.) indicated that they might also work here against wolves. Results showed that individual guarding dogs stationed in wolf territories (a large pasture with captive wolves and a Minnesota forest with wild wolves) prevented or reduced access to supplies of meat for limited periods. "Protection" of this simulated prey occurred because 1) wolves tended to avoid areas occupied by dogs; and 2) dogs disrupted depredatory sequences by wolves. Neither dogs nor wolves were injured. The dogs showed a strong potential for success. These findings suggest that guarding dogs are particularly fitting when the predator is a threatened or endangered species.

Introduction

Nonlethal protection of livestock from wolves (*Canis lupus*) with guarding dogs (*C. familiaris*) is a tradition among shepherds in Europe and Asia (Coppinger and Coppinger 1993, Fig. 1). Boitani (1987) noted that sheep in Italy are "well protected" against wolves by guarding dogs, although damage does occur. Schmitt (1989) reviewed descriptive literature from France and Italy, relying on work of Coppinger et al. (1983) and Green and Woodruff (1984) in the U.S. for technical information. None of these reviews reported any directed research on the use of dogs against wolves.

Livestock-guarding dogs on U.S. farms and ranches provided substantial reduction or elimination of predation against coyotes (*C. latrans*) and domestic dogs (Coppinger et al. 1988, Green and Woodruff 1990a, Andelt 1992). In all but a few cases, dogs prevented depredation not by killing the predator but by "warning it away" (McGrew and Blakesley 1982), which they do because they are an integral part of the flock (Coppinger et al. 1987).

Wolves, however, also cause damage to livestock in the U.S. (Fritts et al. 1992, Bangs et al. this volume), and are seen as a serious threat especially by producers adjacent to areas proposed for reintroduction of wolves (Fischer 1987, Bath and Buchanan 1989, Fritts 1993a). Unregulated lethal methods of control are incompatible with the wolf's status as threatened or endangered. Nonlethal control, e.g., live-trapping and relocation of offending wolves (Fritts 1993b) or taste aversion conditioning (Gustavson and Nicolaus 1987), can be effective but needs consistent human implementation.

Even though guarding dogs are used in Europe and Asia to protect against wolves, ranchers and wildlife damage control personnel have expressed reservations about guarding dog effectiveness against North American wolves. Systems of livestock management are different here compared with abroad, where human shepherds and night confinement are common. Reports of wolves killing dogs in Alaska (Lopez 1978), Minnesota (Fritts and Paul 1989), and Europe (cf. Brtek and Voskr 1987) and the pack-hunting behavior of wolves, lead to questions about a guarding dog's safety.

Protection of Carcasses at a Wolf-Frequented Bait Station by Introduction of a Guarding Dog

Methods

The purpose of this trial was to learn if a guarding dog could prevent a pack of wolves from feeding at a pile of meat they were accustomed to visiting. In July 1987, three bait stations 1 km apart (Fig. 2) were established in a forest in northern Minnesota wolf range, set back 10 m from a north-south dirt road (County Road 344) near Bigfork, Minnesota. Station 3 served as a control site.

Road-killed deer (*Odocoileus virginianus*), farm-culled cows, calves or pigs, and butcher scraps were used as bait to attract wolves, with each site containing a minimum of 10 kg of meat. The 0.5 ha sites were delineated with radio-controlled fencing (Invisible Fencing Inc., 4300 Evergreen Lane, Annandale, Virginia 22003), which kept a guarding

Fig. 1. *One of about five shar planinetz dogs that protects a migrating flock of about 2,000 sheep in southwestern Yugoslavia (near Tetovo). The main predators are wolves. (Photo: R. Coppinger)*

dog inside the perimeter, but had no effect on wolves. Two experienced livestock guarding dogs (male, 45 kg, maremma x shar planinetz, and female, 45 kg, Anatolian shepherd) were trained to stay within fenced areas.

The sites were inspected morning and evening. Wolf activity was noted from tracks along the dirt road. Tracks were erased after each observation period. During a lead-in period (7 July to 4 August), wolves fed regularly at all three stations. On 4 and 5 August, dogs were placed at stations 1 and 2. During the test period (4–31 August) dogs were removed for a four-day hiatus (18–21 August) to determine if wolves would still feed at the now unprotected sites.

Results

After 29 July, when wolves first used all three bait stations, wolf visits were high at the control (Station 3) site (97%; 33 of 34 nights) and at test sites when no dog was present (78%; 25 of 32), but low (19%; 7 of 36) at sites when the dog was present. A Chi-square test on these numbers yielded a significant *P* value (Table 1).

Once the dogs were present on the test sites there was a period of avoidance by wolves, followed by increasing ap-

proach-threat behavior and finally overt aggression, driving the dog from the area. Neither dog nor wolf were injured. Wolves visited both stations during the hiatus.

The wolves were active around Station 1, but not until 29 August was the first altercation noted. At least three wolves were involved. Tufts of wolf and dog hair implied an active fight, which continued along the road for a distance of 2 km to an abandoned cabin. There, the dog backed himself into a corner where he was found bedded down the next morning. The wolf tracks returned along the road to the bait station and the bait was gone.

Both dogs were placed at Station 1 on 30 and 31 August. Bait was taken from the two unattended sites and no further aggression was directed toward the dogs, even though wolves were still active in the area. The trial was stopped after the two days because the bear-hunting season began.

Two black bears (*Ursus americanus*) visited Station 1 every day during most of the lead-in period (7–25 July), but returned only once (the first day) after the dog arrived. Ravens (*Corvis* sp.) plundered all three sites, but limited their visits to the control site once the dogs were in place. Both species have been known to prey on sheep.

Table 1. Number of nights that wolves fed at bait stations in Minnesota, July–August, 1987.

	Dog present	*Dog absent*	*Total*
Wolf takes bait	7	58	65
Wolf does not take bait	29	8	37
Total	36	66	102

$\underline{P} < 10^{-5}$

Introduction of a Dog into Large, Fenced, Captive Wolf Enclosures

Methods

Trials were held at Wolf Park (Battle Ground, Indiana) with captive North American wolves. Behaviors were noted according to ethograms of wolf and canine behavior (Goodman and Klinghammer, Wolf Park, unpubl. data 1984). The guarding dog was a crossbred Anatolian shepherd x shar planinetz male weighing 45 kg. It had been a subject in a bait station trial against wolves the previous year.

Trial A

On 9 July, a dead calf was placed in the center of a 20 ha fenced wheat field. The dog's travel trailer with the door open was positioned 15 m away from the carcass. The dog wore a radio-collar (Invisible Fencing Inc.), and a 0.25 ha perimeter wire was placed around the trailer, carcass, and dog to prevent the dog from leaving. Three female wolves were then released into the pasture.

Trial B

From 15–30 August this same dog was housed in a 123 m by 54 m pen with a flock of 20 sheep. Two adjacent pens contained three wolves (two males and one female) and two wolves (one male and one female). Observations were made daily for 15 days, for two or three one-hour periods, for a total of 43 hours.

Trial C

On 3 September, another encounter was arranged between the same dog and a single male wolf, which also weighed 45 kg. These two animals had interacted frequently

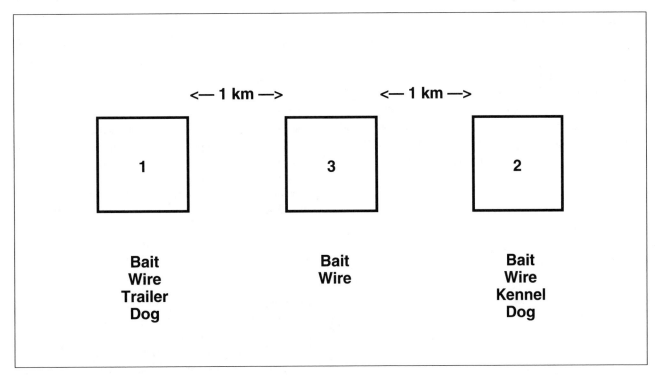

Fig. 2. *Configuration of the three bait stations.*

Table 2. Responses of male dog in pen with sheep, to approaches by captive wolves in adjacent pens.

Wolf ID	Wolf approach	Dog response	THH	THL	FF	Other
Male	50	28	9*	17*	2	3
Female	29	13	0*	4*	0	8
Group	26	19	4	8	2	7
Total	105	60	13	29	4	18

THH = High Level Threat; THL = Low Level Threat; FF = Fence Fight; Other = leg raise, urination, etc.

Note: Total behaviors do not equal total responses because the dog did not always give a recordable behavior, or gave more than one behavior per response.

*THH plus THL responses are different to male and female wolves ($\underline{P} < 0.05$).

and agonistically through a wire fence. The dog and then the wolf were released into the same field, with no trailer, carcass or wire.

Results

Trial A

Within five minutes the three wolves approached the carcass, were attacked by the dog, were chased by the dog to the limits of its radio-controlled boundary, cooperatively attacked the dog as it retreated from the boundary, and claimed the carcass as the dog retreated into its trailer. The dog bit at one wolf's hind leg during the chase, but no cuts were found on any animals in spite of frequent losses of footing during the skirmish.

Trial B

Enumeration of the interactions through the fence between dog and wolves is given in Table 2. The (male) dog reacted to male and female wolves approaching the fence about 50% of the time. However, approaches by male wolves elicited threatening behavior 93% of the time as compared with 31% for females (a Chi-square test yielded $\underline{P} < 0.05$). Similarly, the dog displayed high level threat only to male wolves.

Trial C

The dog avoided eye contact with the wolf and turned its head away, but then attacked when the wolf was < 1 m away. The wolf was knocked down and over, and the dog held its cheek and neck fur and skin with its teeth. The dog was in balance, but the wolf showed more aggression. We terminated the encounter; no wounds were found.

Discussion

Because wolves sometimes kill and eat dogs, it has been suggested that they regard dogs as a prey species. In each of

the trials, however, guarding dogs and wolves appeared to treat each other as conspecifics.

In the forest bait station trials, even though isolated from all social attachments and in a strange place, two separated livestock-guarding dogs survived encounters with wolves with no damage. When observed, wolves and dogs displayed behaviors to each other that were typically intraspecific. In trials with penned animals, dogs treated male and female wolves differently, but in the same way they would treat male and female dogs.

Similar behaviors between wolf and dog have also been described by Lorenz and Pinardi (Hampshire College, pers. commun.), Boitani (1987), O'Gara (Montana Coop. Wildl. Res. Unit, pers. commun.), Carnio (Metro Toronto Zoo, unpubl. data), and Brown (1983, citing Musgrave 1921). Even though the trials were set up to the disadvantage of the dogs, and even though "battles" took place, no observable injury to any of the participants occurred.

Conclusions

Intraspecific-like social displays altered wolf feeding behavior when a dog was present by delaying the onset of or interrupting depredatory routines by the wolf. Such delays reduce the efficiency of the wild predator. "Protection" was also achieved because the wolf avoided the dog. Two dogs worked better than one, and also reduced separation anxieties in isolated areas. These studies point out facets of dog/wolf behavior useful for wolf recovery programs, and for protecting livestock in areas where wolves are present.

Acknowledgments

Our thanks for help on this study go to U.S. Department of Agriculture Animal Damage Control for funding, B. Paul for advice, R. Danielson for field work in Minnesota, M. Forman and E. Klinghammer for field work at Wolf Park, T. Fuller and S. Fritts for manuscript review, and B. Schultz for statistics.

Recommendations for More Effective Wolf Management

■ Peter L. Clarkson

Throughout history there has been real and perceived competition between people and wolves for prey species. New attitudes about wolves developed in the late 1960's and wolf management became a complex and controversial public issue. The controversies in Alaska, Yukon, and northern British Columbia (B.C.) show how complex and emotional wolf management has become. Recommendations presented are based on common problems encountered in these three areas. The recommendations focus on wolf management policy and plan formation and include: 1) developing a comprehensive wolf management policy and plan; 2) including a public involvement program; 3) considering all factors that influence wolf management; 4) consideration of wolf management strategies; 5) evaluating wolf management techniques; and 6) setting up land use zones for multiple strategy wolf management.

Introduction

Wolf (*Canis lupus*) management is the most controversial issue in recent wildlife management (Carbyn 1983c). The public's polarized love/hate relationship with wolves has placed wildlife managers in the center of the controversy (Clarkson 1990). Finding an acceptable solution to the controversy should be a priority with wildlife agencies involved in active wolf management.

This paper focuses on the management of nonendangered wolf populations (Carbyn 1983a). However, some recommendations may apply to the management of endangered wolves.

Definition of Wolf Management

Wolf management is the way a government agency allows people to influence a wolf population in their jurisdiction. This management ranges from active wolf control, research, or population reintroduction, to more passive management where wolves exist undisturbed by people. Depending on the area and the public demand, wolf management can be for consumptive or nonconsumptive use. Pimlott (1961b) defined wolf management as a "complex of things that might be undertaken to control or protect wolves depending on the status of the wolf population and on the effect that they are having on game or livestock." Within a jurisdiction there may be several wolf management strategies to meet the needs of different public uses. Deciding what management strategies meet the needs of the public while ensuring long-term wolf survival is the challenge in wolf management (Pimlott 1961a, Carbyn 1983a).

Wolf Management History

Wolf management in North America has ranged from complete eradication to total protection (Allen 1954, Trefethen 1975). People have perceived the wolf to be everything from the devil to a romantic symbol of wilderness (Lopez 1978). The indigenous peoples of North America generally held the wolf in high regard and admired its special hunting skills (Nelson 1983). As North America was settled, wolves were eliminated in agricultural and ranching areas (Allen 1954). In back country and wilderness areas wolves were killed to increase desirable game species (Lopez 1978). The first formal wildlife management activities in North America involved wolf control and bounty programs (Trefethen 1975).

As the discipline of wildlife management evolved and matured, biologists and wildlife managers began to question the role wolves played in natural ecosystems (Leopold 1933:230). By the mid 1900's government agencies had begun to study wolf-prey relationships and set guidelines for wolf management (Murie 1944, Errington 1946, Cowan 1947). Public attitudes toward wolves also changed in the 1960's and 1970's as people became more environmentally informed and concerned about wildlife management. In the 1960's and 1970's, the growing positive public sentiment for wolves began to conflict with existing negative feeling. The public became polarized on the issue of wolf management. Most of the sentiment for wolf preservation came from southern, urban areas, and support for wolf control came from northern, rural areas (Clarkson 1990). Wildlife managers faced the task of describing the ecological parameters in a wolf-prey system and had to respond to changing societal uses and values regarding wildlife (Wagner 1989, 1991).

Public	Economics	Politicians
—local, national international	—cost of programs	—local
—supporters	—money available	—provincial
—opposers	—secondary economic	—state
—federal	influences	—territorial - others

Education and Training	WILDLIFE MANAGER	Media

Wildlife Professionals	Wildlife	
—other agency biologists	—wolves	
—university biologists	—ungulates	
—independent biologists		

Fig. 1. *Wildlife managers position and influences.*

Wolf Management Controversies

The decision by wildlife agencies to begin wolf control programs in Alaska, Yukon, and B.C. in the mid 1970's and early 1980's escalated the wolf management controversy (Harbo and Dean 1983, Hoffos 1983, Haber 1988, Clarkson 1990). The issue quickly became socially complex and was no longer a biological-ecological problem solved by determining existing wolf-prey relationships (Clarkson 1990). Evaluation of the controversies in Alaska, Yukon, and B.C. identified common problems that included:

1) No comprehensive and acceptable wolf management policy and plan.

2) Inadequate public information and education programs before initiating wolf management.

3) Questioning of the agencies' biological justification for wolf management.

4) Consideration focused primarily on biological aspects before management decisions were made.

5) A common responsibility for management that placed agencies between public groups with conflicting interests (Fig. 1).

6) A poor working relationship with the media before and during the wolf management controversies.

Recommendations

Six recommendations are made to help wildlife managers in making wolf management more acceptable and effective. The recommendations do not provide easy solutions for acceptable and effective wolf management. However, they do provide a working framework and help identify the different aspects to consider when developing wolf management policy and plans.

Develop a comprehensive wolf management policy and plan before any wolf management action is initiated.

A comprehensive wolf management policy and plan are necessary before any wolf managementaction begins. Hardin (1977), Hardin and Baden (1977), Kalymon (1981), and Nemetz (1980) have all addressed the problems of public resource management and conclude resources are better managed with well-developed policies and plans. This development sets the mandate for wolf management and helps resolve conflicts within a jurisdiction (Ministry of Environment 1982). Without such development, management problems are often piecemeal, and may be unduly influenced by the most vocal and politically orientated special interest groups (Dorrance 1983).

Comprehensive policies and plans should provide a means for the public to participate and have their concerns addressed. This should also occur at a time when issues can

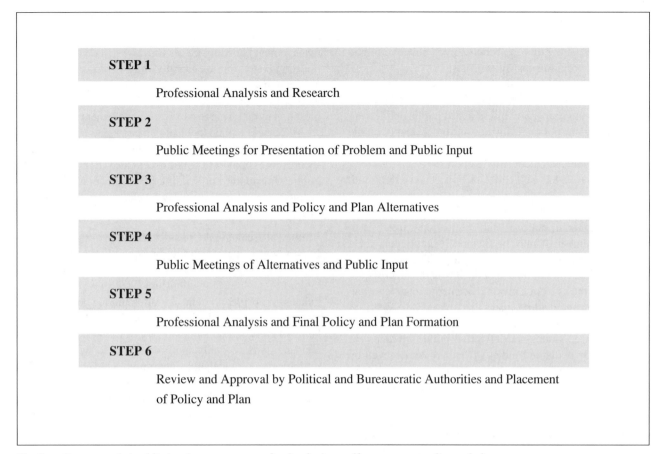

STEP 1

Professional Analysis and Research

STEP 2

Public Meetings for Presentation of Problem and Public Input

STEP 3

Professional Analysis and Policy and Plan Alternatives

STEP 4

Public Meetings of Alternatives and Public Input

STEP 5

Professional Analysis and Final Policy and Plan Formation

STEP 6

Review and Approval by Political and Bureaucratic Authorities and Placement of Policy and Plan

Fig. 2.   *Recommended public involvement program for developing wolf management policy and plans.*

be rationally discussed, not in the middle of controversial management actions. A comprehensive wolf management policy and plan are necessary to address all public concerns and allow the public and wildlife managers to understand how wolves are managed in all situations.

The recent wolf management controversies in Alaska, Yukon, and B.C. have shown wildlife agencies in those jurisdictions the importance of a comprehensive wolf management policy and plan. All three jurisdictions have or are drafting wolf management policies and plans.

Ensure that a public involvement program is included when developing a wolf management policy and plan.

Public involvement programs are often used to help form policy. However, public involvement is especially crucial when the management direction and decisions will be controversial. The high level of public interest in wolf management suggests that a public involvement program is essential for establishing a wolf management policy and plan. Because wolves are a public resource and managed with public funds, it is important that all concerned groups have an opportunity to have input. An effective public involvement

program should incorporate professional analysis and public participation (Fig. 2).

Wolf management controversies in Alaska, Yukon, and B.C. could have been reduced by using effective public involvement programs before any management action began. Special interest groups from Alaska and Yukon that opposed the wolf management programs were concerned that they did not have an opportunity to comment on wolf management decisions. As a result they felt, their interests were ignored (Hall, Alaska Wildlife Alliance, pers. commun.; Munson, Yukon Conservation Society, pers. commun.).

Without an effective public involvement program, special interest groups or individuals feel their only recourse is to protest and affect the political, legal, or economic influences of wolf and wildlife management. Public involvement programs should be conducted before considering any management action. They should not be information sessions to inform the public of predetermined management strategies.

Conducting an effective public involvement program can be expensive and time consuming. Wildlife agencies must be sure the benefits of the program outweigh the consequences and costs of not including such a program. Evaluation of the wolf management controversies in Alaska, Yukon, and B.C. show that the benefits from effective public involvement programs justify the costs.

Before starting an extensive public involvement program it is helpful to assess existing public opinion and identify special interest groups. Surveys to assess public opinion are used to determine political direction and other areas of public debate and are developing in the wildlife managementWildlife management field (Kellert 1976, 1985a, Hook and Robinson 1982, Self 1982, Filion et al. 1983, Bath 1987).

The wolf management controversies have shown there are local, regional, national, and international interests in wolf management. It may be financially impossible for a provincial, territorial, or state agency to conduct a meaningful national or international public involvement program. However, protests from a national or international level can affect the management programs.

An agency responsible for wolf management has the challenge of conducting an effective public involvement program with available funding. This may be achieved by conducting a program within the affected jurisdiction and inviting national or international interest groups to participate.

An effective public involvement program may not satisfy all interest groups. Opposing interests cannot be both satisfied for all management areas.

Consider all influencing factors when developing a wolf management policy and plan.

Wolf management has undergone considerable change since European settlement. Today these influences represent the increased public concern and awareness of natural resource management (Hendee 1974, Wagner 1989, 1991). Dansereau (1957 as cited in Berryman 1972) realized that many factors influenced natural resource management:

> Resource management has moved from an ecological to a sociological period, so that the application of what we know is limited by the accepted socio-political, economic framework or climate.

The recent wolf management controversies in Alaska, Yukon, and B.C. show the importance of considering other influences. Management controversies developed in part because wildlife agencies focused on the biological-ecological considerations and did not carefully consider all social, economic, and political factors influencing wolf management.

The factors that influence wolf management fit into four categories: 1) philosophical; 2) biological-ecological; 3) socio-political; and 4) economic (Fig. 3).

Philosophical Considerations
Philosophical considerations are the underlying influences on wolf management. These considerations include our per-

ceptions of wolves and nature, how and why we manage natural resources, and who benefits from management. Wolf management philosophies are formed by: 1) human perception of nature, and specifically that of wolves; 2) human association and contact with wolves; 3) the potential impact wolves have on a given human lifestyle; and 4) past and present natural resource and wolf management strategies.

An objective philosophical perspective concerning wolf management is needed to make objective decisions and to secure professional and public acceptance (Berryman 1972). Public philosophies on wildlife managementWildlife management and specifically on wolves have an influence on management decisions.

Biological-Ecological Considerations
In past wolf management programs, wildlife agencies have put most of their time and effort into assessing the existing biological-ecological relationships between wolves and ungulates. Wolf-prey systems are often unique because of the many influencing variables on the natural system. Research helps identify the dynamics of a specific system. Wildlife managers are generally more comfortable with assessing biological-ecological considerations. The education and training of most wildlife professionals have focused on this area. Information collected on wolf-ungulate relationships reveals what is biologically and ecologically possible so that what is socially desirable can be chosen in relation to what it will cost.

When assessing the biological-ecological factors that influence wolf management the following points should be considered:
1) Present knowledge about wolf-prey relationships and how much of this information is transferable from one area to another;
2) Information on the existing wolf-ungulate relationships in the area;
3) Impact of other predators on the ungulate population;
4) Impact of people on the ungulate population;
5) Present condition of the ungulate habitat;
6) Effect of weather and climate on the ungulate population;
7) Wolf and prey numbers and their existing population trends;
8) Length of control program needed to achieve the expected results of an increase in the ungulate population; and
9) Whether an increase in the ungulate population will allow it to maintain higher population levels, or whether wolves will increase and again reduce the ungulate population.

Social-Political Considerations
The opinions and views held by different sectors of the public (local, regional, national, international) were powerful influences in the past wolf management controversies (Clarkson 1990). Depending on the direction of the wolf

Philosophical Factors

—philosophy of management

—public perception of wolves

—human association and contact
   with wolves

—public resource management

—opposing philosophies

Ecological-Biological Factors

—wolf-prey densities

—habitat carrying capacit

—climate

—wolf-prey relationships

**WOLF MANAGEMENT
POLICY AND PLANS**

Social-Political Factors

—public supporting management

—public opposing management

—politicians

—media

Economic Factors

—costs of wolf management

—costs of not managing wolves

—indirect costs and benefits

—benefits of wolf management

—effectiveness of programs

Fig. 3. *Factors that influence wolf management policy and plans.*

management program (protect or control) the different public groups attempt to influence the management direction by: 1) expressing their opinions directly to the wildlife agency or management board; 2) lobbying politicians to inform them of their concerns so the politicians may influence the direction of wolf management; or 3) protesting to the public to increase public pressure. Wolf management is mostly a social-political problem as described by Hardin (1983):

> The dispute (game management decision) is inescapably political because the animals are on public land; it is controversial because the answer depends not only on the facts that can be scientifically determined, but also on conflicting human value systems, which is an area for policy decisions.

Understanding and addressing social-political considerations results in a more acceptable policy and plan (Hendee 1974, Wagner 1989).

Economic Considerations

Economics have an influence on wolf management because wolf management is a government responsibility and public tax dollars are spent on it. As the public and government become more economically aware, future wolf management programs will need to be economically justified. Connolly

(1978a) recognized the role of economics and stated the following on predator control for big game management:

> Because of conflicting public attitudes over ungulate and predator management objectives, as well as the increasing costs of predator control, careful biologic and economic justification is required for the exercise of predator control. In general predator control is justified in big game management only when it will produce substantial ungulate increases at reasonable cost without undue damage to other environmental values and when the increased production will be used.

Economic influences and concerns are assessed with cost-benefit and cost-effectiveness analyses (Gross 1975, Quade 1975, Bish 1977, Andrews 1982, Yates 1985). Cost-benefit analysis compares the value of resources consumed in an endeavor with the outcomes produced by the endeavor (Yates 1985). Cost-benefit analysis is a powerful tool for decision making as it can be used to help choose among programs that have different objectives (Quade 1975). Programs with different objectives are easily compared by measuring the costs and benefits in monetary units (dollars) and then comparing the cost:benefit ratio of each program.

Table 1. Comparison of wolf management techniques.

Management Techniques	Selection of Target Species	Cost/Wolf	Short Term Effect	Long Term Effect	Public Opposition
Poison	p - m[1]	1 - h[2] $3-400(1) $320 (2)	m - h	m - h *	h
Aerial Shooting Government	h	h $1000(3) $2500(4)	m - h	m - h *	m
Aerial Shooting Public	m	l	p	p	m - h
Ground Shooting	h	l - m	p	p	l
Trapping or Snaring	p - m	m	p - m	p - m *	l
Bounty	p - h	m $200 (5)	p	p	m - h
Total protection	N/A	l	N/A	N/A	l - h
Interpretive	h	N/A	N/A	N/A	l
Research	h	l - h	N/A	N/A	l

p - poor, l - low, m - moderate, h - high
N/A - Not Applicable
1 - dependent on size of control area
2 - dependent on access to control area
(1) Kowal and Runge (1981); (2) Bjorge and Gunson (1983); (3) Kellyhouse (1982);
(4) Alaska Wildlife Alliance Newsletter July-August (1983); (5) YTG News Release December 22, 1983

Cost-benefit analysis can help managers decide whether spending money on wolf control or other wildlife managementWildlife management programs is justified. Liroff (1982) lists the strengths, limits, and lessons of cost-benefit analysis and recommends that it not be used to make decisions, but help in the decision-making process.

Cost-effectiveness analysis is a form of system analysis that compares the dollar or resource costs of alternative programs with the effectiveness of the programs (Quade 1975). Program effectiveness depends on reaching the desired objective (Quade 1975). Cost-effectiveness analysis is appropriate in wolf management for comparing the costs and effectiveness of various management programs that have the same objective.

Consider all wolf management strategies when developing a policy and plan.

Wildlife managementWildlife management agencies have a range of management strategies from maintaining viable wolf populations in wilderness areas to controlling wolves for the purpose of increasing ungulate populations (B.C. Ministry of Environment 1979; Manitoba Dept. of Mines, Natl. Res. and Env. 1984; Alaska Board of Game 1980; Yukon Wolf Man. Team 1992). However, public interest groups will feel their concerns for wolf management are not addressed if they are only briefly mentioned in a policy statement, but not in a management plan, or as part of an active management program.

Evaluate all wolf management techniques before they are included in a wolf management policy and plan.

Wolf management programs may involve various techniques such as trapping, snaring, poisoning, aerial shooting, ground hunting, bounties, total protection, and interpretation. An evaluation of all the techniques is necessary to determine their effectiveness, costs and benefits, and public acceptance. It will not benefit a wildlife agency to have an

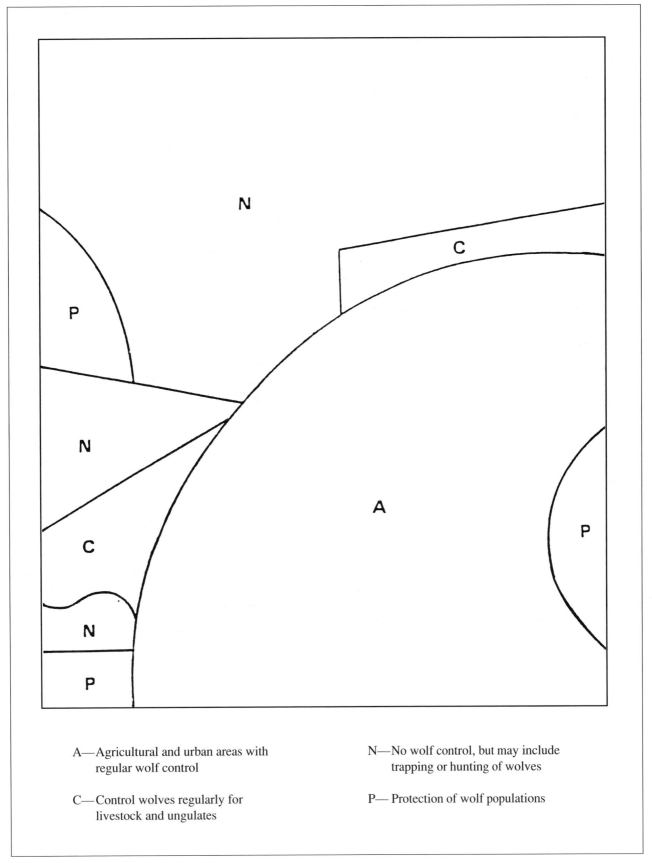

Fig. 4. *Land use zoning strategy for wolf management.*

A—Agricultural and urban areas with regular wolf control

C—Control wolves regularly for livestock and ungulates

N—No wolf control, but may include trapping or hunting of wolves

P— Protection of wolf populations

Peter L. Clarkson

acceptable wolf management strategy and then make the program controversial by using an unacceptable technique.

The wolf management controversies in Alaska, Yukon, and B.C. proved that some management techniques were controversial (Clarkson 1990). Table 1 summarizes the effectiveness and public opposition to different management techniques. The ratings (poor, low, moderate, high) given for each technique are generalized and there may be exceptions. Ratings are subjective, as they are based on my analysis of the controversies and other wolf management.

Formally apply land use zoning for multiple strategy wolf management.

Land use zoning can help solve management problems in jurisdictions that have to consider multiple strategy wolf management. Most wildlife agencies use a zoning strategy for wildlife managementWildlife management. Wildlife managementWildlife management units or big game zones divide jurisdictions and different management strategies apply in different zones. In jurisdictions where wolves are managed for both consumptive and nonconsumptive uses, zoning is a tool for achieving different management objectives. Zoning involves dividing a jurisdiction into separate areas and deciding the priority use for each area. Zoning is currently being developed for wolf management in several jurisdictions in Canada and Alaska. Figure 4 is an oversimplification of land use zoning, but it shows how the idea works.

Setting the boundaries of management zones will be easy for some areas and difficult for others. Private agricultural lands with livestock fall into Zone A classification (control when needed). Other areas such as parks or sanctuaries may already provide protection for wolves (Zone P). Areas that are more difficult to zone include public land that is subject to a variety of uses. Determining which areas will have wolf control or total wolf protection requires careful professional assessment and public participation. Agencies will need to decide what zones are appropriate for their areas based on the existing wolf population, wolf-human competition, and public sentiment.

Zoning may present problems because zones that protect wolves may supply wolves to zones managed for no wolves. Fritts et al. (1992) found that as wolves in the forested areas of northern Minnesota increased they were constantly creating problems in livestock areas. Miner (1967) protested that Algonquin Park, Ontario, was a "wolf factory" that raised wolves that left the park to prey on livestock and deer.

Zones should be as large as possible because wolves are highly mobile and immigration and emigration may reduce the effectiveness of zones. It is not possible to satisfy all special interests in a given area. Someone's favorite hunting area may be zoned "total protection of wolves," which may result in lower ungulate populations; or someone else's hiking area may be zoned "wolf control," and that will reduce wolf viewing opportunities.

Acknowledgments

Many people have taken the time to discuss wolf management with me and I am indebted and grateful for all of the time, information, and opinions received. I would especially like to thank S. Herrero, V. Geist, M. Bayer, and J.B. Cragg. B. Hayes (Yukon Fish and Wildlife) and B. Stephenson (Alaska Fish and Game) always had the time to discuss wolves, wolf management, and management problems. Their ideas, comments, and information were always appreciated. J. Gunson and K. Schmidt (Alberta Fish and Wildlife) provided an opportunity for me to work on the Nordegg wolf-elk project and both were always keen to discuss wolf management. Thanks to the staff and members of the following organizations for their time and consideration: Alaska Department of Fish and Game, U.S. Fish and Wildlife Service, National Park Service, Denali National Park, Yukon Fish and Wildlife, Parks Canada, Kluane National Park, Renewable Resources GNWT, Alaska Wildlife Alliance, Yukon Conservation Society, Interior Alaska Wildlife Federation, Whitehorse Fish and Game, Council for Yukon Indians, and the University of Alaska.

Part Ten:
Looking Ahead
Into the 21st Cenutry

What Do We Know About Wolves and What More Do We Need to Learn?

■ L. David Mech

*The wolf (**Canis lupus**) has been one of the most studied of all wild species. The first scientific study of the wolf was published in 1938, and since then several books and monographs and thousands of articles have been published about the animal. Nevertheless, much still remains to be learned. This paper examines some of those subjects such as certain aspects of scent marking, howling, reproduction, dispersal, effect of predation, activity patterns, diseases, genetics, taxonomy, management, and recovery. The most important subjects requiring additional study include wolf-prey relations, reproduction, determinants of wolf population change, and genetic influences on dispersal. In some cases, answers must be sought in long-term studies, continued naturalistic observation, and controlled experiments. Improved technology, such as molecular genetics and computerized radio-tracking equipment, can help solve the remaining mysteries in other cases.*

Introduction

Ever since Sigurd Olson (1938) published the results of one of the first scientific field studies of wolves, the species has been one of the most studied of all wildlife. At least three bibliographies of wolf literature have recently been published, the largest containing some 420 pages (Tucker 1988, Klinghammer and Sloan 1989, Minta 1990). The United States National Park Service has published four monographs on the wolf (Murie 1944, Mech 1966a, Peterson 1977, Cook 1993), and the Wildlife Monograph Series includes seven wolf monographs, the most for any single species except white-tailed deer (*Odocoileus virginianus*). Several technical books on wolves and many popular ones have been published, and there has even been one book printed about the wolf's soul (Fox 1980).

The two longest studies of predator-prey systems both involve wolves: the continuing Isle Royale wolf/moose study started in 1959 (Mech 1966a, Jordan et al. 1967, Peterson 1977, Allen 1979, Peterson and Page 1988) and the wolf/deer study in the Superior National Forest of northeastern Minnesota, now in its 23nd year (Mech and Frenzel 1971a, Mech and Karns 1977, Nelson and Mech 1981, Mech 1986, Nelson and Mech 1986a, Mech et al. 1987, L.D. Mech and M.E. Nelson, U.S. Fish and Wildlife Service, unpubl. data). In Alaska, some 100 wolf packs have been radio-tagged and monitored (Stephenson et al. this volume) and in Minnesota more than 600 individual wolves have been radio-tracked, more than 500 in the Superior National Forest alone.

Clearly, science knows something about the wolf. Nevertheless, at present we are still collecting new information about the animal. Many areas of wolf biology bear significant gaps, several of which are discussed below.

Movements

Great amounts of snow-tracking and radio-location data are available for wolves, and much is known about wolf terrotoriality, movements, dispersal, colonization, pack formation, and other aspects of wolf spatial ecology (Mech 1973, 1987, Fritts and Mech 1981, Peterson et al. 1984). However, few telemetry or snow-tracking data are available for nighttime, except when wolves are backtracked between consecutive daily locations (Mech 1966a, Kolenosky 1972, Dale et al. 1994), an expensive and time-consuming technique that requires long stretches of suitable weather.

Here, improved satellite and Global Positions System (GPS) tracking should soon solve the problem. Satellite collars need to be lighter and more efficient so they can be placed on any wolf and transmit for at least a year. Alternatively, GPS technology combined with Wildlink data acquisition technology (Mech 1991b, Kunkel et al. 1991) also holds great promise. Some day, we should be able to send a signal to a radioed wolf and download many days' worth of 15-minute location data, or remotely anesthetize the wolf (Mech et al. 1990, Mech and Gese 1992) and merely plug the collar into a computer to download weeks of such data.

Dispersal

Wolves disperse at several times of the year and in many distances and directions (Mech and Frenzel 1971a, Van Ballenberghe et al. 1975, Fritts and Mech 1981, Peterson et al. 1984, Mech 1987, Fuller 1989, Gese and Mech 1991). But why do some disperse at less than one year of age, while others wait until nearly five, and what triggers dispersal? Do wolves leave voluntarily from the pack, or are they coerced?

What determines a wolf's decision about which direction and distance to disperse? Two of my radioed wolves from the Superior National Forest, originally caught only 5 km apart and thus probably related, ended up being killed 272 km northwest of their capture points 10 years, but only 11 km, apart. Was this coincidence, or are there genes that influence the distance and direction of dispersal? Dispersal data from earlier studies provided some evidence that wolves from the same pack may disperse in similar directions (Mech 1987), but analyses of additional data were ambiguous about this issue (Gese and Mech 1991),

Why do at least some dispersing wolves in colonizing populations such as that in northwestern Montana (Ream et al. 1991) and Wisconsin (R.P. Thiel, Wisconsin Dept. of Natl. Res., pers. commun.) disperse back toward the source population rather than attempting to expand the colonizing population range as might be expected? Further radio-tracking studies of colonizing wolf populations would help answer some of these questions, as well as shed more light on the entire process of colonization.

Manipulation and experimentation in the wild would also contribute considerably to answering many of the above questions. When a wolf starts to disperse and a definite direction is established, the animal could be: 1) recaptured by capture collar (Mech et al. 1990, Mech and Gese 1992), returned to its natal territory and followed again; or 2) it could be displaced 90° relative to its territory and released to see whether it would follow a parallel bearing, or head for a point along its original bearing. What would it do if taken 180° from its original bearing, but behind its territory, and released?

Besides these basic biological questions about dispersal, there are also several practical functions that need addressing. What constitutes effective dispersal barriers? What proportion of dispersing wolves is stopped by various kinds of barriers? Conversely, what are the characteristics of good wolf dispersal corridors? To what extent will wolf populations adapt to dispersal barriers and corridors?

Effects of Wolf Predation on Prey Populations

Are wolves a major limiting factor on their prey populations? Almost 25 years ago, I addressed this question in my book *The Wolf* (Mech 1970). At that time, there was evidence from some studies that wolves were controlling their prey populations and from other studies that they were not. The results of two of the longest running predator-prey studies, the Isle Royale wolf-moose investigation (Mech 1966a, Peterson 1977, Allen 1979, Peterson and Page 1988) and the Superior National Forest wolf-deer study (Mech 1986, Nelson and Mech 1986a) are available, yet we still argue about the meaning of the data (Mech et al. 1987, McRoberts et al. 1995, Peterson and Page 1988 *versus* Messier 1991a, 1995).

Similarly, examiners of other wolf-prey systems have disagreed about their findings (Bergerud et al. 1983a, Bergerud and Snider 1988 *versus* Thompson and Peterson 1988, Van Ballenberghe 1985, 1989, Eberhardt and Pitcher 1992 *versus* Bergerud and Ballard 1988, 1989, Keith 1983 *versus* Theberge 1990). Elaborate wolf control studies have been conducted (Gasaway et al. 1983, 1992, Bergerud and Elliot 1986, Ballard et al. 1987, Crete and Jolicoeur 1987, Larsen et al. 1989), but Boutin (1992:125) argued cogently that "evidence for predation acting as a major limiting factor in most moose populations is less than convincing." Disagreement also pervades even the most fundamental understanding of wolf-prey dynamics (Haber 1977 *versus* Seip this volume, Dale et al. 1994 *versus* Seip this volume, Messier this volume).

That wolf predation can limit prey populations has always been obvious (Mech 1966a, 1970, Pimlott 1967a, Mech and Karns 1977, Gasaway et al. 1983, Carbyn et al. 1993). That is, wolf predation is at least partly additive to other mortality factors, depending on circumstances. Subtract the wolf from a wolf-prey system, and generally prey numbers increase (reviews in Bergerud and Elliot 1986, Theberge and Gauthier 1985).

What has long been in question and still not settled is: 1) the extent to which wolf predation is additive; 2) the degree to which wolves regulate (Murray 1982) their prey populations; and 3) the precise role of other factors in predisposing prey to different degrees of limitation by wolves. Prey populations in natural wolf-prey systems (little interference by humans) often increase markedly despite wolf populations uncontrolled by humans (Peterson 1977, Nelson and Mech 1986a, Peterson and Page 1988, Mech et al. this volume). Thus it is clear that factors other than wolf predation play a critical role in modulating wolf influence on prey numbers.

Moose and other prey are subject to mortality and adversity from several factors other than predation: weather, parasitism, disease, and starvation. Many obvious and subtle factors that predispose prey to wolf predation have been documented. Extreme youth and old age have been known predisposing factors ever since Murie (1944) published his study of wolves and Dall sheep (*Ovis dalli*), and it has been documented repeatedly (Mech 1966a, 1970, Peterson 1977, Fritts and Mech 1981, Peterson et al. 1984, Ballard et al. 1987, Mech et al. this volume).

However, more subtle and profound factors have also been uncovered that predispose prey to wolf predation, such as snow depth (Mech and Karns 1977, Nelson and Mech 1986b), maternal undernutrition resulting from severe winters (Peterson 1977, Mech and Karns 1977, Mech et al. 1987, Mech et al. 1991b), maternal age (Ozoga and Verme 1986, Mech and McRoberts 1990, Kunkel and Mech 1994), location relative to wolf pack territories (Mech 1977a, Fritts and Mech 1981, Nelson and Mech 1981, Kunkel and Mech 1994), fall migration (Hoskinson and Mech 1976, Nelson and Mech 1991), and undernutrition of grandmother (Mech et al. 1991b). Nevertheless, the wolf is often credited for being the major cause of prey declines, and interpretations of wolf-prey dynamics rest heavily on simple measures of wolf density or on wolf:prey ratios (Gasaway et al. 1983, 1992, Bergerud et al. 1983a, Messier and Crete 1985, Bergerud and Ballard 1988, 1989, Bergerud and Snider 1988, Messier 1991a, but cf. Theberge 1990).

How will we determine to what extent and under what conditions wolf predation is compensatory or additive? How will we learn how much human hunting a wolf-prey system can tolerate without causing a serious prey decline? Wolf-prey population modeling (Walters et al. 1981, Keith 1983, Theberge and Gauthier 1985, Fuller 1989, Boyce this volume, Peek and Vales this volume) has given some insight into these questions. Its contributions should not be overrated because we are only beginning to understand some of the more subtle factors predisposing ungulates to predation (see above), and because system models are simplified versions of complexities we hardly yet appreciate. Clearly, data required to test competing theoretical views is sparse (Van Ballenberghe 1987, Boutin 1992).

To a great extent, conclusions about the precise role of the wolf in limiting or regulating prey numbers are, I believe, a function of personal emphasis. While some authors tend to view the wolf as the major factor limiting prey in a wolf-prey system, others emphasize predisposing circumstances as indirect factors affecting prey numbers, with wolves being the direct factors. This disparity of views is healthy, for each viewpoint tends to act as a check on the other. Certainly Boutin's (1992) suggested experiments, and other predator-removal tests, should be conducted. However, I am not certain that even those tests will settle the disagreement. Differences in basic outlook between the schools of thought may cause proponents of each to interpret the results differently.

Wolf Population Regulation

What factors regulate wolf populations? Certainly food is important (Mech 1977c, Packard and Mech 1980, Peterson and Page 1988). However, the relationships documented so far between wolf density and some index to food, such as biomass, while strong, have shown great variability (Keith 1983, Fuller 1989). This supports the general importance of food to wolf numbers but leaves unanswered the critical question of just how prey biomass influences wolf population change. Packard and Mech (1980) contended that the important regulating factor is "vulnerable prey biomass,"

but no one has yet determined for any wolf-prey system specifically what constitutes "vulnerable prey biomass." This is still one of the greatest needs to understanding wolf populations.

Genetics

Ten years ago, the question of the extent and effect of inbreeding in wolves was debated (Theberge 1983, Shields 1983). Since then, molecular genetics techniques have shed considerable light on the subject, confirming telemetry studies that wolves in adjacent packs are often closely related (Wayne et al. 1991, Lehman et al. 1992). This implies that breeding between closely related individuals may be taking place, yet enough distant dispersal is occurring so that the chances for outbreeding are substantial (Fritts and Mech 1981, Mech 1987, Fuller 1989, Gese and Mech 1991).

Furthermore, 10 years ago, incest had only been documented for captive wolf packs. It has also been occurring on Isle Royale (Wayne et al. 1991) because of the restricted gene pool. However, the effect on a wolf population of breeding between closely related individuals is still not clear. The most inbred wild wolf population anywhere, the Isle Royale population, thrived from about 1949 through 1980, when it reached 50 members (Peterson and Page 1988). Since then, it declined drastically and languished at about 12 animals, but in 1994 began increasing (Peterson 1994).

That inbreeding can cause deleterious effects in a population was documented in a captive pack in Scandinavia (Laikre and Ryman 1991). The prevalence of such effects in captivity and the relevance of this information to populations subject to natural selection, however, is not clear. For example, the inbred captive population showed a decline in weight of eight-month-old animals over the generations, although weight data were not included in the report. Generally, eight-month-old animals reach almost adult weight (Van Ballenberghe and Mech 1975, L.D. Mech, National Biological Survey, unpubl. data), yet the weights of adult wolves on Isle Royale are not significantly lower than those of mainland wolves from which their population rose some 40 years before (R.O. Peterson, Michigan Technological University, pers. commun.). Certainly, it has been demonstrated on Isle Royale that ≥ 35 years of inbreeding did not restrain the population (Peterson and Page 1988). Much more insight into the genetic structure of populations can be expected as the newly-available biochemical tools are applied to various problems.

Scent Marking

Of all the senses, probably olfaction is the most used and least understood (Asa and Mech this volume), and a better knowledge of olfaction, as well as of the other senses, would have great value in understanding both how wolves hunt and how best to live-capture wolves for study and management.

Wolves pursuing a moose in the winter landscape on Isle Royale. Wolf-moose studies on the 538 km2 island represent the longest ongoing study of a wolf/prey system anywhere. These studies have revealed much about the relationship of wolves, moose, vegetation, and climate that would not have been possible with short-term studies. (Photo: R. Peterson)

That wolves are truly olfactory animals is easily seen in what little we know about scent marking.

Wolves scent mark for at least two reasons: territorial defense and advertisement (Peters and Mech 1975), and courtship and pair bonding (Rothman and Mech 1979). Many of the circumstances and factors involved in scent marking are known, yet there are some important gaps. For example, what factors cause raised-leg urination (RLU) in males or flexed-leg urination (FLU) in females? In the wild, I have observed both during all seasons. However, in captive wolves, FLU frequency is much reduced except close to and during the breeding season (Asa et al. 1990). Although some degree of sexual maturity appears to be necessary for RLUs and FLUs, this physiological state is not sufficient for them. What other factors are involved?

In a saturated wolf population, lone wolves usually do not mark until they encounter a potential mate (Rothman and Mech 1979). However, in two regions almost devoid of wolves, northwestern Montana in 1979 and 1980 (Boyd 1982) and Wisconsin in the 1980's (R.P. Thiel, Wisconsin Dept. of Natl. Res., pers. commun.), lone wolves were found to be scent marking. Was this difference because lone wolves

in saturated populations need to maintain low profiles to prevent being killed by territorial wolf packs? Moreover, in areas almost devoid of other wolves, do lone wolves scent mark to advertise their presence and increase chances of meeting potential mates? A parallel question is whether lone wolves use scent trails to find each other. Presumably they do, but documentation is lacking.

Specifically, what role do secretory chemicals play in wolf courtship and reproduction? Given the well-established odor effects in rodents, such as estrus synchronization (Whitten 1956), facilitation of reproductive maturation (Vandenbergh 1967, 1969) and pregnancy blockage (Bruce 1960), might not body chemicals play similar roles in an animal that so blatantly scent marks and investigates marks? Numerous interesting chemicals exist in wolf urine and anal gland secretions, at least some of which tend to peak seasonally (Raymer et al. 1984, 1985, 1986). But why? And what of an estrus pheromone? Widely known from common experience in dogs, and highly suspected in wolves, this pheromone has yet to be isolated.

Precisely what are the roles of scats and anal glands in wolf scent marking? Our captive alpha and beta males deposited scats significantly more toward the end of their enclosure closest to human approach and where they were fed and drugged, and under some circumstances anal gland secretions were deposited on the scats (Asa et al. 1985a). Do scats and anal gland secretions then merely back up urine marking as territorial advertisement and defense, or is other information conveyed?

How will these questions be answered? Obviously, it will take a concerted effort involving captive animals, behavioral studies, and laboratory analyses, plus continued field observations. One of the techniques most needed to help unravel the mystery will be the development of a biological assay system involving a behavioral response by the wolf to a given chemical. Our attempts at such testing were unsuccessful (C.A. Asa et al., St. Louis Zoological Park, unpubl. data).

Howling

In two of the main circumstances in which wolves howl, reasonable explanations have been proposed. Individuals sometimes use howling as a means of reassembling the pack (Murie 1944, Mech 1966a). When around pups or kills, packs tend to chorus howl in response to vocalizations of neighboring packs, thus indicating a territorial defense function (Harrington and Mech 1979).

However, anyone who has watched wild wolf packs up close knows that there is a special social function of howling that so far defies cogent, detailed explanation. Crisler (1958: 151) described it this way: "Like a community sing, a howl is…a happy social occasion. Wolves love a howl. When it is started, they instantly seek contact with one another, panting and bright-eyed, to join in, uttering, as they near, fervent little wows, jaws wide, hardly able to wait to sing."

What is the function of this social howling? My impression from watching the Ellesmere wolves is that it has strong bonding and motivating elements (Mech 1991c). However, I still do not fully understand chorus howling. Hopefully, close naturalistic observation coupled with experimentation and manipulation will bring us closer to a more complete understanding. No doubt studies of captive wolves could contribute considerably.

Most of the studies of wolf howling have centered around packs. Most lone wolves in a saturated population respond significantly less often to human howls than do pack wolves, but some tend to move closer to the howler (Harrington and Mech 1979). Does howling serve to attract loners to each other? Possibly lone wolves in a sparse wolf population might tend to howl more often than loners in saturated populations. L.N. Carbyn (Canadian Wildl. Serv., pers. commun.) watched a single wolf in Jasper National Park for 40 minutes walking some 3 km and constantly howling in what appeared to be an attempt to connect with either a single wolf or a pack. Whether it was a lone wolf or a separated pack member is unknown. The subject of lone wolf howling

bears much exploration not just to answer the question, but also because it may bear on use of howling surveys to locate wolves in colonizing areas.

Reproduction

Although much is known about wolf reproduction (Seal et al. 1979, Packard et al., 1983, 1985), several intriguing questions remain. What is the role of scent marking in reproduction? The frequency of double-urine marking before and during estrus and its role in pair bonding (Rothman and Mech 1979) strongly suggest that important chemical communication is occurring between male and female. The possibility of male urine facilitation for female estrus seems strong, and all the various types of effects shown for rodents (see above) may also operate in wolves. It will take carefully controlled experiments with captive wolves to determine this.

Chemical communication also may play a role in determining age of first sexual maturity. We know that some 10-month-old wolves in captivity in the absence of adults, can mate and produce pups (Medjo and Mech 1976, Zimen 1976), but that other wolves in the presence of adults do not breed until almost two years old under some conditions (Peterson et al. 1984, Fuller 1989) and ≥ three years old under others (Mech and Seal 1987).

A third mystery about wolf reproduction is the function of pseudopregnancy, the phenomenon in which ovulatory but nonpregnant wolves show the same endocrine profiles as pregnant animals (Seal et al. 1979) and pseudo-pseudopregnancy, in which wolves appear to be pseudopregnant but have not even ovulated, and thus have no corpora lutea to produce progesterone (Mech and Seal 1987).

Pseudopregnancy and pseudo-pseudopregnancy may be two stages of the same behavioral phenomenon, but physiologically how do they work? They appear to allow wolves to practice many of the important correlates of reproduction without actually reproducing (Mech and Seal 1987). Determining why wolves undergo these states, and whether all wolves do, will probably take additional captive studies involving both behavioral and laboratory investigations, as well as the use of the capture collar to allow serial recapture of wild wolves during the breeding season (Mech et al. 1990, Mech and Gese 1992).

Activity

Despite all the radio-tracking and aerial observation that has been done of wolves, little information is available about wolf activity patterns, because aerial tracking is expensive and cannot be conducted at night and because standard activity collars have too short a range to be monitored continuously. Therefore, activity information is limited to the results of a few piecemeal studies (Mech 1966a,1977c, 1992, Kolenosky and Johnston 1967, Harrington and Mech 1982a, Peterson et al. 1984, Vila et al. this volume). This

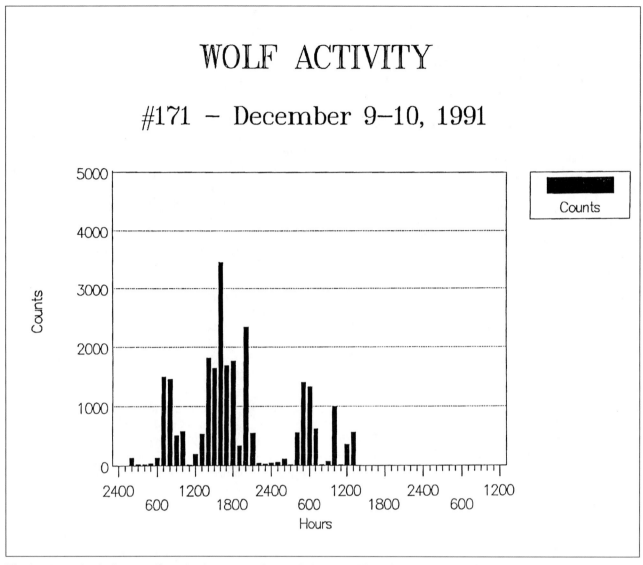

Fig. 1. *Example of relative wolf activity data retrieved remotely from a Wildlink activity collar (Kunkel et al. 1991) on a wolf in Minnesota. "Counts" represent number of tilts per hour of a mercury tilt switch in the collar.*

problem may now be solved with new technology. Both satellite tracking (Keating et al. 1991, Ballard et al. this volume), and the Wildlink activity system (Kunkel et al. 1991) yield profuse amounts of 24-hour-per-day activity data. Satellite tracking provides activity data with each of several locations per day, and the Wildlink system stores hourly indexes to activity for the most recent 36-hour intervals (Fig. 1). Widespread application of these two technologies should greatly improve our knowledge of wolf activity patterns year around.

Taxonomy

In 1983, Nowak suggested that a revision of wolf subspecies in North America might lead to lumping the 24 currently recognized races into perhaps five (Nowak 1983). His recent analysis of skull measurements supports this finding (Nowak this volume). Meanwhile, the techniques of molecular genetics have provided insight into the relatedness of wolves in various parts of the world (Lehman et al. 1992, Wayne et al. 1992a). These latter studies indicated that from the standpoint of ancestral matrilines, there appear to be at least 13 mitochondrial DNA (mtDNA) haplotypes (not races) of North American wolves.

However, the geographical distribution of mtDNA haplotypes relates poorly to subspecific ranges. In fact, some areas contain wolves of as many as four of the haplotypes, and many packs contain members with at least two (Lehman et al. 1992). The major exception is the Mexican wolf (*C.l. baileyi*), which so far seems to have its own unique mtDNA haplotype (Wayne et al. 1992b, Wayne et al. this volume).

Can additional biochemical techniques help taxonomists better sort out the various wolf subspecies? Certainly that should be a quest. On the other hand, strong argument can be made for better description of geographic variation in wolves (Brewster and Fritts this volume), and detecting biochemical correlates of such variation would be of great value.

Another area of wolf taxonomy on which molecular techniques have shed additional light, but which needs considerably more, involves the red wolf (*Canis rufus*). With present specimens having the appearance of a wolf x coyote (*Canis latrans*) hybrid (i.e., large ears, medium-sized feet), these creatures historically have been a taxonomic enigma. Various authors have explained the red wolf's unusual appearance and limited distribution (southeastern United States) by proposing that it is everything from an ancient ancestral wolf (Nowak 1979, Nowak et al. this volume) to a wolf x coyote hybrid (Mech 1970, Jenks and Wayne 1992).

Over 400 *Canis* spp. were live-trapped in red wolf range from 1973 through 1980, and of those the largest 43 were selected as probable red wolves and held captive (Parker et al. 1989). Through captive breeding and further artificial selection, any individual showing signs of hybridization with coyotes was removed from the program. Fifteen individuals then became the progenitors of a current captive population of red wolves with four matrilinies.

All four captive red wolf matrilines, 77 *Canis* spp. taken from 1974 to 1976 from the larger sample, and six museum specimens from 1905 to 1930 have possessed mtDNA indistinguishable from that of coyotes (mostly) or of gray wolves (Wayne and Jenks 1991). The authors of the study offered two possible explanations for their results: 1) they could have missed some red wolves in their sampling; or 2) the red wolf could be a cross between the gray wolf and the coyote. Nowak et al. (this volume) added a third possibility — that the red wolf could be a subspecies of gray wolf that is morphologically, but not genetically, distinct. Presumably, they mean not genetically distinct by the methods currently used to conduct biochemical assays.

It is hoped that, through examination of nuclear DNA of present living specimens, some of the hypotheses about the red wolf can be supported or refuted. Such studies are currently under way (R.K. Wayne, University of California, pers. commun.). Captive studies involving planned interbreeding between red wolves and coyotes, red wolves and gray wolves, and coyotes and gray wolves are sorely needed to provide known hybrids that can be compared morphologically and biochemically with red wolves.

The development of more refined molecular techniques is required to answer these and many other genetic and taxonomic questions. For example, the need is strong for genetic tests to distinguish wolves from domestic dogs and hybrids. Some day we may find genetic material that encodes gross morphological differences among wolves.

Diseases

The role of disease in adversely affecting wolf populations has been documented by Choquette and Kuyt (1974), Riley and McBride (1972) and Carbyn (1982b). From this, we can probably conclude that generally disease is not important to most wolf populations. However, the advent of three diseases new to wolves in northern areas has changed the picture: canine parvovirus (CPV), first found in dogs in 1977 (Eugster and Nairn 1977); heartworm (*Dirofilaria immitis*), which probably spread northward when southern dogs were brought northward for field trials, and Lyme disease. Wolves have not had time to evolve strong defenses against these three afflictions, so the possibility exists that they will reduce wolf numbers.

The lack of increase of Isle Royale wolves (Peterson and Krumenaker 1989), as well as the lack of a vigorous wolf increase in Wisconsin (Wydeven et al. this volume), may be the result of CPV. However, documentation of the effect of CPV on wild wolf populations was indirect (Brand et al. this volume) until an inverse relationship was found between the percentage of wolves in northeastern Minnesota showing positive titers in a given year and the number of pups surviving, as well as with the percent change in the population (Mech and Goyal 1993).

Heartworm was found in one Minnesota wolf in 1986 and in another in 1988 (L.D. Mech, National Biological Service, unpubl. data). The spread of this parasite seems to have been slow. However, because of the physical blockage of the heart chambers and aorta that this worm can cause, it probably could cut years off a wolf's life.

Lyme disease antibodies were found in 2.5% of the 528 wolves examined in Minnesota and Wisconsin, and they tended to cluster mostly around the southwest end of Lake Superior (Thieking et al. 1992). Although ill effects of Lyme disease on wild wolves has not been documented, it is known to be detrimental to dogs.

We are only beginning to learn about the possible effects of these three new diseases on wolves. It behooves all workers who handle wild wolves to test them for these diseases and to look for effects on individuals in the population. Through this means and controlled studies of captive wolves, we can best determine the influence new diseases may have on wolf populations.

Wolf Management and Recovery

Although great strides have been made in learning about many aspects of wolf biology, there has been relatively little progress in refining wolf management methods. Most wolf management involves controlling wolf populations or individuals, and the primary techniques used have long been steel-trapping, poisoning, snaring, or aerial shooting, depending on goals and circumstances (Cluff and Murray this volume). These methods are distasteful to much of the public, so alternative nonlethal techniques are greatly needed. Furthermore, innovative ways of educating the public about the needs for wolf management in some areas and for wolf recovery in others would be most welcome.

Livestock Depredation Control

In addition to lethal control to minimize livestock depredations, translocation (Fritts et al. 1984, 1985, Bangs et al. this volume), aversive conditioning (Fritts 1982), and use of livestock-guarding dogs (Green and Woodruff 1990b, Andelt 1992, Coppinger and Coppinger this volume) have been attempted. Although none of these techniques has proven useful in general application, each may be valuable under specific circumstances. All need further research.

One new technique that may have value in alleviating livestock depredation in recovering or reintroduced wolf populations is the use of the capture collar (Mech and Gese 1992). If wolves cannot be killed but must be removed, the capture collar at least ensures that the individual could be recaptured if it returns to the depredation area, or if it preys on livestock elsewhere. Currently, batteries in the collar must now be changed every four months, but improved technology promises to increase that period.

Investigation into why some wolves sometimes kill livestock and others do not might be revealing because most wolves do not kill livestock even when in or near their territories (Fritts and Mech 1981). Precisely how important are poor animal husbandry practices (Fritts 1982) in encouraging livestock depredation? Are wolf prey search patterns traditional? Does the availability and vulnerability of natural prey significantly affect livestock depredation rate, as Mech et al. (1988a) and Fritts et al. (1992) have suggested?

Wolf Management to Increase Prey

While wolf control to increase prey remains controversial among wildlife biologists (Gasaway et al. 1983, Mech 1985, Boutin 1992), refinements have been proposed in defining conditions under which control may work (Theberge and Gauthier 1985).

Poisoning and aerial shooting are the main techniques used for managing wolves to increase prey. Attempts have also been made to artificially saturate food supply for wolves during prey calving season to reduce wolves' motivation to kill calves (Boertje et al. this volume). Although the results have been equivocal so far, additional research on this technique and alternative methods of wolf management and livestock protection should be tried.

One other alternative method of managing wolf populations that needs further research is sterilization. Conceivably, sterilization could be useful in special situations where lethal wolf control would be politically difficult. S.H. Fritts and L.D. Mech (U.S. Fish and Wildlife Service, unpubl. data) have vasectomized wild wolves and found that at least under some conditions, such a wolf can remain pair-bonded and territorial for $\geq$ 2 breeding seasons. However, much work is required to devise broad-scale sterilization techniques that could be applied practically, effectively, and economically.

Wolf recovery

Wolves will live anywhere there is suitable prey regardless of habitat (Young and Goldman 1944, Mech 1970). For wolf recovery programs, however, human interaction with wolves must also be considered in determining suitable habitat. The primary consideration is proximity to livestock and pets, which can cause political resistance to wolf recovery and severe animosity toward wolves and considerable difficulty in controlling wolves (Mech 1979, Fritts 1993a). Therefore, candidate areas for wolf recovery should be extensive wilderness areas with, or near, minimal areas of livestock grazing or human residence. Wolves tend to follow prey migrations, so seasonal and diurnal prey movements must be considered in choosing recovery areas.

Research needs related to wolf recovery involve primarily an examination of the amount of various types of human activity compatible with wolf recovery or survival. For example, although some consensus has been reached on the threshold of road density above which wolf survival is jeopardized in Wisconsin, Michigan, and Minnesota (Thiel 1985, Jensen et al. 1986, Mech et al. 1988b), there are exceptions (Fuller 1989, Mech 1989) and more research is needed. What is the road-density threshold for other areas? What differences do road-user frequency and road-user motivation make, or topography, visibility, vegetation type, and density? There is no reason to believe that there will be one road density applicable to all areas and times.

Other recovery-oriented research needs relate to actual methods of reintroduction. Translocated wolves usually roam far from their release area (Weise et al. 1979, Henshaw et al. 1979, Fritts et al. 1984, Fritts 1993b, Bangs et al. this volume), unless held there for long periods (Phillips and Parker 1988, Phillips et al. this volume). Consequently, investigation of how long holding periods must be to break the wandering or homing tendency would be valuable.

Once wolves are reestablished, how can their success be monitored? There is widespread agreement on the need for monitoring reintroduced individuals via telemetry. However, how long is population monitoring via telemetry necessary? How can wolves be censused accurately without telemetry?

Reestablishment of wolves (Phillips and Parker 1988, Phillips et al. this volume), and natural recolonization (Ream et al. 1991), if well monitored, provide excellent opportunities to learn much about wolf populations and their social spacing, movements, dispersal, and hunting patterns. We should be ever alert to make the most of these unique opportunities. The first and most important step in that direction is simple description of every aspect of population establishment, and use of radio-tracking to do so is essential.

From a scientific standpoint, the live-capture, examination, and radio-tracking of as many individuals as possible in the first several generations of the colonization is optimal.

Conclusion

The wolf is a long-lived species occurring in low densities over large areas, and its prey are also long-lived. Thus, wolf-prey systems are especially subject to spatial and temporal variations. In addition, wolves are elusive and tend to inhabit less accessible areas, so it is difficult, expensive, and time consuming to study them, and data are accumulated slowly.

Wolf pack members can change packs over the years (Van Ballenberghe 1983a, Fuller 1989, Mech 1991c, Boyd et al. this volume, Meier et al. this volume); pack territories can be usurped by other packs (cf. Meier et al. this volume); packs can split (Mech 1966a, 1986, Carbyn 1975, Ream et al. 1991, Meier et al. this volume); and individual wolves can take different mates over time (Mech 1991c). Environmental effects on the wolf-prey system can be cumulative (Mech et al. 1987), and nutritional effects can span genera-

tions (Mech et al. 1991b). Therefore, in many cases, short-term studies provide incomplete information at best and misleading information at worst.

The pieces of information missing from the puzzle we call the wolf are many and varied (i.e., information about diseases, genetics, movements, spacing, relations with prey, recovery, and management). Consequently, the techniques necessary to find those pieces must also be many and varied. Nevertheless, the best approach to obtaining the remaining needed information is the conduct of long-term studies involving a combination of field, captivity, and laboratory work and using the latest advances in technology.

Acknowledgments

This study was supported by the U.S. Fish and Wildlife Service and the North Central Forest Experiment Station. L.N. Carbyn, S.H. Fritts and M.L. Phillips critiqued early drafts of the manuscript, and other authors checked various sections. All offered helpful suggestions for improvement, and I thank them.

Epilogue

A Personal View on Wolf Conservation and Threatened Carnivores in North America

■ Monte Hummel — World Wildlife Fund Canada

When large areas of big-game range are no longer inaccessible, when the annual hunting kill has finally approached the production of the herds, what will our attitude be then? Will we be willing to share deer, moose and caribou with the wolves?

Douglas Pimlott, founding Chairman of the IUCN Wolf Specialist Group, speculated about the future for wolves in the latter part of this century (Pimlott 1961a). From a vantage point now closer to the end of the century, and looking beyond, I'd like to speculate on possible scenarios going into the 21st century.

In many respects, Pimlott was a man ahead of his time. It is important to remember that he lived during an era when there were still wide-spread wolf control programs in North America. These controls were largely set out to increase ungulate production for sport hunting or to control predation on livestock. In the United States, excluding Alaska, over the preceding decades such programs had exterminated the wolf except for Minnesota. Pimlott was deeply concerned about Canada repeating this mistake. He worked tirelessly to get rid of laws and measures that reflected indiscriminate persecution which he regarded as an out-dated attitude toward wolves. I have revisited these questions under the headings_food, space, and attitudes.

Food

When Pimlott drafted the original IUCN *Wolf Manifesto*, in September 1973, eleven of the twelve clauses emphasized a protectionist viewpoint, recognizing the wolf as a predator with a right to exist entirely unrelated to its known value or disbenefit to people. Only one clause dealt with what should be done under circumstances where people were not prepared to share with the wolf.

> Where wolf control measures are necessary, they should be imposed under strict scientific management, and the methods must be selective, highly discriminatory, of limited time duration and have minimum side effects on other animals in the eco-system.

I have argued elsewhere (Hummel 1988) that since the original drafting of this Manifesto, virtually all the changes (in 1982 and 1984) have focused on this clause, loosening it up, to make the overall document more accepting of wolf control, consequently focusing less on the obligation to share. Do these changes in the Manifesto reflect a more general shift in social attitudes from more to less acceptance of the wolf?

In my view, the 1982 and 1984 changes in the *Manifesto* run against the general grain of public opinion which has moved steadily in the other direction. I believe the majority of people already believe, and I predict even more will believe, that it is not ethically justifiable to manipulate wild populations to ensure that human predation can be maximized, whether for recreational or subsistence purposes. Humans are now being asked by other humans to live within natural fluctuations and carrying capacities of ecosystems, rather than constancy seeking to push back our God-given limits.

So, although there are a few last remaining wolf control programs in North America as I write this, I submit they are just that — the last remaining few. I predict that within the first quarter of the next century, no such programs will be sanctioned by governments anywhere in North America, and we will be looking back wondering why we ever undertook them, from both a biological and ethical standpoint. To this extent, the majority of society has cast its vote to "share deer, moose, and caribou with the wolves". It is only a matter of how long it will take for the majority to prevail.

Space

Whether or not we are prepared to share wild *space* with the wolf is a much more challenging question.

For those of us who have studied them, I believe that wolves and other large carnivores provide us with a deep sense of place. That place in North America is usually roadless big wilderness, although as we have seen in this symposium, in other parts of the world this is often less so. Wolves living in Italy is a case in point.

Wilderness and natural areas are among the most endangered spaces everywhere. I believe that protecting the world's top predators, and the natural spaces which they require, poses the most fundamental challenge I can imagine to the present drift of human society.

I am repeatedly struck by how clearly we can feel we've been in wolf-country, or bear or cougar-country, with bush sign all around us, without ever actually seeing a wolf, a bear, or a cougar. I would go so far as to say that it literally doesn't matter whether or not we've contacted the animal itself. We've experienced it anyway, through tracks, scats, howling, scent-marks, dens and carcasses. More important, we've co-experienced its living space. To be sure, we don't sense the environment in the same way a wolf does, but it's the same environment we both sense.

When you think of all the scientific papers written, where do they inevitably start? With aspects of the place, aspects of the "study area" such as vegetation and watersheds. More fundamentally, they outline the natural history, including glaciation, geology, soils, landforms, climate and seasonal change, in other words, the evolutionary forces that have shaped and continue to shape a particular piece of wolf-country.

In reflecting on this, Aldo Leopold (1949) said: "Only those able to see the pageant of evolution can be expected to value its theatre, the wilderness, or its outstanding achievements." In Leopold's terms, top predators are among the most outstanding achievements of wilderness, evolving as they have over centuries to preside at the top of the food chain. And what a wonderful phrase to describe the place where wolf researchers work: "the theatre of evolution"! According to Leopold, we're not just conserving wolves. We're insisting that the world respect the natural caldrons where biological change takes place.

While it's true that all the habitat in the world is no good if we continue to persecute wolves, it's also true that we can change our attitudes 'till we're blue in the face, but without habitat, there will be nothing out there to love or to hate.

So, wolves and other top predators have become flagship species for both attitudes and space. In particular, the *space* required to maintain at least minimum viable populations of large carnivores has become a "back-of-the-envelope" way of assessing whether or not the size and configuration of wilderness reserves are adequate. This family of animals not only conveys a sense of place, but whether or not we are seriously committed to protecting that place.

If saving species really means saving spaces, how are we doing? To answer this, I'll review some information from World Wildlife Fund Canada's Fourth Annual Endangered Spaces Progress Report (1993).

The goal of WWF Canada's Endangered Spaces campaign is to complete a network of protected areas representing all of Canada's natural regions by the year 2000. So far, of the 434 natural regions in this country, only 32 or 7% are represented by protected areas. A further 164 natural

regions or 38% are either moderately or partially represented, and a final 226 or 52% are not represented at all. Already in Canada, we have lost the opportunity to establish a protected area of 50,000 hectares or more in over 100 of our 434 natural regions. This is the factual track record of a country which is generally regarded as being a leader in the field of protected areas.

In the U.S., where a wilderness philosophy dates further back, only 50 of Bailey and Kuchler's 261 ecosystem types, that's just 19%, are represented in designated wilderness units of 100,000 acres or more. All but three of these 50 are in the western USA or Alaska. 107 ecosystem types, or 41% are represented by wilderness areas smaller than 100,000 acres, and 104 ecosystem types, that's 40%, are not represented at all (Noss 1991).

In summary, less than 10% of our natural regions are represented by protected areas in Canada, while about 40% are partially represented, and over half are not represented at all. In the U.S., about 20% are represented, 40% are partially represented, and the remaining 40% are not represented at all.

These numbers offer an important way of measuring how well we are doing at conserving biodiversity on this continent. The story they tell is pretty grim. It is no accident that these numbers mirror the fate of large carnivores in significant parts of North America. There is a direct relationship between remaining protected areas, and remaining populations of top predators in the U.S. and increasingly so in Canada. It would be interesting to see a similar analysis for Europe and the former Soviet Union.

Attitudes

Having argued that the fate of our megafauna is closely tied to our willingness to share food with them, and the fate of endangered spaces, let me conclude by coming back to Pimlott's question about human attitudes.

I believe there is a tremendous pent-up demand for change building in North America. People have a real sense of personal loss associated with natural places we experienced in childhood or at other times, but now those places have been degraded or wrecked. Canadians, in particular, do not elect politicians to watch our natural heritage go "down the drain". This can equally well be said for Americans. Instead, voters want to know wildlife and wilderness is still out there, and that something is being done to conserve it. This feeling extends right across regional and cultural differences.

In the last few years, through concepts such as integrated resource management, environmental assessment and sustainable development, governments and industry have come to accept that we must at least minimize negative impacts on the environment. But the view that significant areas of our lands and waters shouldn't be developed at all is still heresy.

We still have great difficulty in simply letting things change at the hands of nature.

These are the deep-rooted forces which are challenged when we try to carve out a future for wolves and other large carnivores. This family of animals, which demands relatively undisturbed natural space, and plenty of it, serves to test the real depth of our commitment to conservation. They have a way of calling our bluff. And so far, our response has been to let them disappear on a tragic scale.

I believe people today are stuck in what John Livingston (1981) calls the "dominant techno-industrial paradigm". But that same worldview is generating widespread anxiety about where it is taking us. What we have is akin to Toffler's Third Wave analogy (1989). The old dominant wave of super-consumption and growth is being set into a "chop" by a newer counter-wave of concern for the environment and quality. Sometimes, there's calm on the surface, but a struggle below, as one current fights the other for control. Other times, there is an out-and-out clash, as one wave smashes head on into the other. In 1968, Doug Pimlott said, "I dare to think that in this battle we could be witnessing the birth of a new conservation ethic. An ethic which has as a basic tenet that the fate of other animals of the world must not be judged simply on the basis of the materialistic aims and aspirations of one species."

Literature Cited

Literature Cited

A

Aastrup, P., C. Bay, and B. Christensen. 1986. Biologiske miljoundersogelser i Nordgronland, 1984-85. Greenland Fish. and Environ. Res. Inst., Copenhagen, Denmark. 113 pp.

Abrams, P.A. 1982. Functional responses of optimal foragers. Am. Nat. **120**: 382-390.

Abrams, P.A., and T.D. Allison. 1982. Complexity, stability, and functional response. Am. Nat. **119**: 240-249.

Achuff, P.L., and R. Petocz. 1988. Preliminary resource inventory of the Arjin Mountains Nature Reserve, Xinjiang, People's Republic of China. World Wide Fund for Nat., Gland, Switzerland. 78 pp.

Adams, L.G. 1988. Dall sheep survey, Gates of the Arctic National Park and Preserve 1987. U.S. Natl. Park Serv. Nat. Resour. Rep. No. AR-88/15. 46 pp.

Adams, L.G., and R.O. Stephenson. 1986. Wolf survey, Gates of the Arctic National Park and Preserve 1986. U.S. Natl. Park Serv. Nat. Resour. Rep. No. AR-86/04. 14 pp.

Adams, L.G., B.W. Dale, and B. Shults. 1989a. Population status and calf mortality of the Denali caribou herd, Denali National Park and Preserve, Alaska, 1984-1988. U.S. Natl. Park Serv. Nat. Resour. Rep. No. AR-89/13. 131 pp.

Adams, L.G., F.J. Singer, and B.W. Dale. 1995. Caribou and calf mortality in Denali National Park, Alaska. J. Wildl. Manage. 59(3): 584-594.

Adams, L.G., R.O. Stephenson, B.W. Dale, and B. Shults. 1989b. Population ecology of wolves in Gates of the Arctic National Park and Preserve, Alaska 1988 Progress Report. U.S. Natl. Park Serv. Nat. Resour. Rep. No. AR-89/15. 42 pp.

Addison, E.M., A. Fyvie, and F.J. Johnson. 1979. Metacestodes of moose, *Alces alces,* of the Chapleau Crown Game Reserve, Ontario. Can. J. Zool. **57**: 1619-1623.

Agresti, A. 1984. Analysis of ordinal categorical data. John Wiley and Sons, New York, N.Y. 287 pp.

Alaska Board of Game. 1980. Alaska Board of Game policies and resolutions. Unpubl. 80-25-806. Juneau. (unpaginated).

Alaska Board of Game. 1991. Board report on the strategic wolf management plan for Alaska. Juneau. November. 8 pp.

Alaska Department of Fish and Game. 1991. A strategy for managing Alaska's wolves. Fairbanks. 11 pp. (draft).

Alaska Department of Fish and Game. 1992a. Strategic wolf management plan for Alaska. pp. S7-S14 *in* Alaska's wolves. How to manage for the 90s. Alaska's Wildl. (Jan./Feb.; Suppl.).

Alaska Department of Fish and Game. 1992b. Area-specific wolf management plan for southcentral/interior Alaska. 76 pp.

Alaska Department of Fish and Game. 1992c. Alaska's wolves. How to manage for the 90s. Alaska's Wildlife (Jan./Feb.; Suppl.). 15 pp.

Alaska Department of Natural Resources. 1992. A strategic plan: into the 21st century. October. 16 pp.

Alaska Wolf Management Planning Team. 1991. Unpubl. Final Rep., Alaska Dep. Fish and Game, Juneau. June. 16 pp.

Albert, C., P.A. Goodmann, and E. Klinghammer. 1987. Health care of wolves in captivity. pp. 61-82 *in* H. Frank, ed. Man and wolf: advances, issues, and problems in captive wolf research. Dr. W. Junk, Dordrecht, The Netherlands.

Alberta Fish and Wildlife Division. 1991. Management plan for wolves in Alberta. Wildl. Manage. Plann. Ser., No. 4. 90 pp.

Alexander, K.A., J.D. Richardson, and P.W. Akt. 1992. Disease and conservation of African wild dogs. Swara **15**: 13-14.

Allen, D.L. 1954. Our wildlife legacy. Funk and Wagnalls, New York, N.Y. 422 pp.

Allen, D.L. 1979. The wolves of Minong: their vital role in a wild community. Houghton Mifflin, Boston, Mass. 499 pp.

Allen, G.M., and T. Barbour. 1937. The Newfoundland wolf. J. Mammal. **18**: 229-234.

Allen, J.A. 1989. Searching for search image. Trends Ecol. Evol. **4**: 361.

Allen, S.H., and S.C. Kohn. 1976. Assignment of age-classes in coyotes from canine cementum annuli. J. Wildl. Manage. **40**: 796-797.

Alston, J.M., J.C. Brown, and C.J.A. Doughty. 1958. Leptospirosis in man and animals. E. and S. Livingstone, Edinburgh and London, U.K. 367 pp.

Althoff, D.P., and P.S. Gipson. 1981. Coyote family spatial relationships with reference to poultry losses. J. Wildl. Manage. **45**: 641-649.

Amato, G.D. 1991. Species hybridization and protection of endangered animals. Science (Washington, D.C.) **253**: 250.

Andelt, W.F. 1985. Behavioral ecology of coyotes in south Texas. Wildl. Monogr. **94**: 45 pp.

Andelt, W.F. 1987. Coyote predation. pp. 128-140 *in* M. Novak, J.A. Baker, M.E. Obbard, and B. Malloch, eds. Wild furbearer management and conservation in North America. Ontario Trappers Assoc., North Bay, Ont.

Andelt, W.F. 1992. Effectiveness of livestock guarding dogs for reducing predation on domestic sheep. Wildl. Soc. Bull. **20**: 55-62.

Andersch, L. 1906. Hunters and trappers guide. 2nd ed. Andersch Brothers, Minneapolis, Minn. 431 pp.

Anderson, R.M. 1943. Summary of the large wolves of Canada, with description of three new arctic races. J. Mammal. **24**: 386-393.

Anderson, R.M. 1946. Catalogue of Canadian Recent mammals. Natl. Mus. Can. Bull. **102**: 238 pp.

Andreev, A.A. 1925. The resonance theory of Helmholz in the light of new observations upon the function of the peripheral and of the acoustic analyzer in the dog. pp. 339-363 *in* Pavlov Jubilee Volume, Leningrad.

Andrews, R.D., and E.K. Boggess. 1978. Ecology of coyotes in Iowa. pp. 249-265 *in* M. Bekoff, ed. Coyotes: biology, behavior, and management. Academic Press, New York, N.Y.

Andrews, R.N.L. 1982. Cost-benefit analysis as regulatory reform. pp. 107-135 *in* D. Swartzman, R.A. Liroff, and K.G. Croke, eds. Cost-benefit analysis and environmental regulations: politics, ethics, and methods. Conserv. Found., Washington, D.C.

Anonymous. 1972. Wildlife (Protection) Act. Government of India, New Delhi.

Anonymous. 1986. Report of the AVMA Panel on Euthanasia. J. Am. Vet. Med. Assoc. 188-252-28.

Anonymous. 1987a. Gray wolves may again howl in Yellowstone. Logan Herald Journal, Logan, Ut. Feb. 11, p. B1.

Anonymous. 1987b. Interagency Rocky Mountain Front Wildlife Monitoring/Evaluation Program: management guidelines. Montana Dep. Fish Wildl. and Parks, Helena. 71 pp.

Anonymous. 1990. Animal Damage Control Program. Draft Environmental Impact Statement. U.S. Dep. Agric. APHIS, DEIS. 90-001. Washington, D.C.

Anonymous. 1991. United Conservation Alliance News. 1: 1-3.

Anonymous. 1993. Alaska wolf plan defeated by communication failures. Int. Wolf **3**(1): 10-15.

Appel, M.J.G. 1988. Does canine coronavirus augment the effects of subsequent parvovirus infection? Vet. Med. **83**: 360-366.

Appelberg, B. 1958. Species differences in the taste qualities mediated through the glossopharyngeal nerve. Acta Physiol. Scand. **44**: 129-137.

Archer, J.R. 1985. Epidemiology of canine blastomycosis in Wisconsin. M.S. Thesis, Univ. Wisconsin, Stevens Point. 47 pp.

Archer, J.R., S.J. Taft, and R.P. Thiel. 1986. Parasites of wolves, *Canis lupus*, in Wisconsin, as determined from fecal examinations. Proc. Helminthol. Soc. Wash. **53**: 290-291.

Archibald, W.R., D. Janz, and K. Atkinson. 1991. Wolf control: a management dilemma. Trans. North Am. Wildl. and Nat. Resour. Conf. **56**: 497-511.

Arizona Game and Fish Department. 1990. Preliminary results of a public opinion survey of Arizona residents and interest groups about the Mexican wolf. Phoenix, Ariz. 58 pp.

Arthur, L.M. 1981. Coyote control: the public response. J. Range Manage. **34**: 14-15.

Arthur, L.M., R.L. Gum, E.H. Carpenter, and W.W. Shaw. 1977. Predator control: the public viewpoint. Trans. North Am. Wildl. and Nat. Resour. Conf. **42**: 137-145.

Asa, C.S. 1996. Hormonal and experiential factors in the expression of social and parenting behavior in canids. *In* J.A. French and N.G. Solomon, eds. Cooperative breeding in mammals. Cambridge Univ. Press, New York, N.Y.

Asa, C.S., and I. Porton. 1991. Concerns and prospects for contraception in carnivores. Annu. Proc. Am. Assoc. Zoo Vet. 1991: 298-303.

Asa, C.S., L.D. Mech, and U.S. Seal. 1985a. The use of urine, faeces, and anal-gland secretions in scent-marking by a captive wolf (*Canis lupus*) pack. Anim. Behav. **33**: 1034-1036.

Asa, C.S., L.D. Mech, U.S. Seal, and E.D. Plotka. 1990. The influence of social and endocrine factors on urine-marking by captive wolves (*Canis lupus*). Horm. Behav. **24**: 497-509.

Asa, C.S., E.K. Peterson, U.S. Seal, and L.D. Mech. 1985b. Deposition of anal-sac secretions by captive wolves (*Canis lupus*). J. Mammal. **66**: 89-93.

Asa, C.S., U.S. Seal, E.D. Plotka, M.A. Letellier, and L.D. Mech. 1986. Effect of anosmia on reproduction in male and female wolves (*Canis lupus*). Behav. Neur. Biol. **46**: 272-284.

Asa, C.S., L.J.D. Zaneveld, L. Munson, M. Callahan, and A.P. Byers. 1995. Efficacy, safety and reversibility of a bisdiamine as a male-directed contraceptive in gray wolves (*Canis lupus*). Annu. Proc. Am. Assoc. Zoo Vet. 1995: 396-397.

Aschoff, J. 1966. Circadian activity pattern with two peaks. Ecology **47**: 657-662.

Atkins, D.L. 1978. Evolution and morphology of the coyote brain. pp. 17-35 *in* M. Bekoff, ed. Coyotes: biology, behavior, and management. Academic Press, New York, N.Y.

Atkins, D.L., and L.S. Dillon. 1971. Evolution of the cerebellum in the genus *Canis*. J. Mammal. **52**: 96-107.

Atkinson, K.T., and D.W. Janz. 1991. Effect of wolf control on black-tailed deer in the Nimpkish Valley on Vancouver Island. British Columbia Min. Environ. Wildl. Bull. No. B-65. 35 pp.

Atzert, S.P. 1971. A review of sodium monofluoroacetate (compound 1080), its properties, toxicity and use in predator and rodent control. U.S. Fish and Wildl. Serv. Spec. Rep. No. 146.

Avant Courier [Bozeman]. 1883a. Killing game in the Park. Feb. 15.

Avant Courier [Bozeman]. 1883b. Game in the Park. Feb. 22.

Avise, J.C. 1989a. Gene trees and organismal histories: a phylogenetic approach to population biology. Evolution **43**: 1192-1208.

Avise, J.C. 1989b. A role for molecular genetics in the recognition and conservation of endangered species. Trends Ecol. Evol. **4**: 279-281.

Avise, J.C., and R.M. Ball. 1990. Principles of geneaological concordance in species concepts and biological taxonomy. pp. 45-67 *in* D. Futuyma and J. Antonovich, eds. Oxford surveys in evolutionary biology. Vol. 7. Oxford Univ. Press, Oxford, U.K.

Avise, J.C., C.D. Ankney, and W.S. Nelson. 1989. Mitochondrial gene trees and the evolutionary relationships of mallard and black ducks. Evolution **44**: 1109-1119.

Avise, J.C., J. Arnold, R.M. Ball, E. Bermingham, T. Lamb, J.E. Neigel, C.A. Reeb, and N.C. Saunders. 1987. Intraspecific phylogeography: the mitochondrial DNA bridge between population genetics and systematics. Annu. Rev. Ecol. Syst. **18**: 489-522.

Ayres, L.A. 1986. The movement patterns and foraging ecology of Dall sheep in the Noatak National Preserve, Alaska. M.S. Thesis, Univ. of California, Berkeley. 84 pp.

B

Bader, H.R. 1989. Wolf conservation: the importance of following endangered species recovery plans. Harvard Environ. Law Rev. **13**: 517-533.

Baer, G.M. (ed.) 1991. The natural history of rabies. CRC Press, Boca Raton, Fla. 620 pp.

Bailey, E.P. 1992. Red foxes, *Vulpes vulpes*, as biological control agents for introduced Arctic foxes, *Alopex lagopus*, on Alaskan islands. Can. Field-Nat. **106**: 200-205.

Bailey, V. 1907. Directions for the destruction of wolves and coyotes. U.S. Dep. Agric. Bur. Biol. Surv. Circ. No. 55. 6 pp.

Bailey, V. 1930. Animal life of Yellowstone National Park. Charles C. Thomas, Baltimore, Md. 241 pp.

Baker, J.A., and P.M. Dwyer. 1987. Techniques for commercially harvesting furbearers. pp. 970-995 *in* M. Novak, J.A. Baker, M.E. Obbard, and B. Malloch, eds. Wild furbearer management and conservation in North America. Ontario Trappers Assoc., North Bay, Ont.

Ballantyne, E.E. 1956. Rabies control programme in Alberta. Can. J. Comp. Med. Vet. Sci. **20**: 21-30.

Ballantyne, E.E. 1958. Rabies control in Alberta. J. Am. Vet. Assoc. 125: 316-326.

Ballantyne, E.E., and J.G. O'Donoghue. 1954. Rabies control in Alberta. J. Am. Vet. Med. Assoc. **125**: 316-326.

Ballard, W.B. 1982. Gray wolf-brown bear relationships in the Nelchina Basin of south-central Alaska. pp. 71-80 *in* F.H. Harrington and P.C. Paquet, eds. Wolves of the world: perspectives of behavior, ecology, and conservation. Noyes, Park Ridge, N.J.

Ballard, W.B. 1992. Bear predation on moose: a review of recent North American studies and their management implications. Alces **28** (Suppl.): 162-176.

Ballard, W.B. 1993. Demographics, movements, and predation rates of wolves in northwest Alaska. Ph.D. Thesis, Univ. Arizona, Tucson. 358 pp.

Ballard, W.B., and J.R. Dau. 1983. Characteristics of gray wolf, *Canis lupus*, den and rendezvous sites in south-central Alaska. Can. Field-Nat. **97**: 299-302.

Ballard, W.B., and S.G. Fancy. 1988. Satellite radio-tracking of wolves. Int. Union Conserv. Nature Nat. Resour./Spec. Surviv. Comm. Wolf Specialist Group, Univ. Alaska, Fairbanks. 17 pp.

Ballard, W.B., and D.G. Larsen. 1987. Implications of predator-prey relationships to moose management. Swed. Wildl. Res. **1** (Suppl.): 581-602.

Ballard, W.B., and S.L. Miller. 1990. Effects of reducing brown bear density on moose calf survival in southcentral Alaska. Alces **26**: 9-13.

Ballard, W.B., and R.O. Stephenson. 1982. Wolf control — take some and leave some. Alces **18**: 276-300.

Ballard, W.B., R. Farnell, and R.O. Stephenson. 1983. Long distance movement by gray wolves, *Canis lupus*. Can. Field-Nat. **97**: 333.

Ballard, W.B., A.W. Franzmann, and C.L. Gardner. 1982. Comparison and assessment of drugs used to immobilize Alaskan gray wolves (*Canis lupus*) and wolverines (*Gulo gulo*) from a helicopter. J. Wildl. Dis. **18**: 339-342.

Ballard, W.B., S.M. Miller, and J.S. Whitman. 1986. Modeling a south-central Alaskan moose population. Alces **22**: 201-244.

Ballard, W.B., T.H. Spraker, and K.P. Taylor. 1981a. Causes of neonatal moose calf mortality in south central Alaska. J. Wildl. Manage. **45**: 335-342.

Ballard, W.B., R.O. Stephenson, and T.H. Spraker. 1981b. Nelchina Basin wolf studies. Alaska Dep. Fish and Game Fed. Aid in Wildl. Restoration. Final Rep., Projs. W-17-9 through W-17-11. 201 pp.

Ballard, W.B., J.S. Whitman, and C.L. Gardner. 1987. Ecology of an exploited wolf population in south-central Alaska. Wildl. Monogr. **98**: 54 pp.

Ballard, W.B., J.S. Whitman, and D.J. Reed. 1991a. Population dynamics of moose in south-central Alaska. Wildl. Monogr. **114**: 49 pp.

Ballard, W.B., L.A. Ayres, C.L. Gardner, and J.W. Foster. 1991b. Den site activity patterns of gray wolves, *Canis lupus*, in southcentral Alaska. Can. Field-Nat. **105**: 497-504.

Ballard, W.B., L.A. Ayres, K.E. Roney, and T.H. Spraker. 1991c. Immobilization of gray wolves with a mixture of tiletamine hydrochloride and zolazepam hydrochloride. J. Wildl. Manage. **55**: 71-74.

Ballard, W.B., L.A. Ayres, K.E. Roney, D.J. Reed, and S.G. Fancy. 1991d. Demography of Noatak grizzly bears in relation to human exploitation and mining development. Alaska Dep. Fish and Game Fed. Aid in Wildl. Restoration. Final Prog. Rep., Proj. W-23-2. 227 pp.

Ballard, W.B., L.A. Ayres, S.G. Fancy, D.J. Reed, K.E. Roney, and M.A. Spindler. 1990. Demography and movements of wolves in relation to the Western Arctic caribou herd of northwest Alaska. Alaska Dep. Fish and Game Spec. Rep. Nome. 150 pp.

Balser, D.S. 1964. Management of predator populations with antifertility agents. J. Wildl. Manage. **28**: 352-358.

Balser, D.S. 1965. Tranquilizer tabs for capturing wild carnivores. J. Wildl. Manage. **29**: 438-442.

Baltazard, M., and M. Bahmanyar. 1955. Essai pratique du serum antirabique chez les mordus par loups enragés. (Practical trial of antirabies serum in those bitten by rabid wolves). Bull. World Hlth. Org. **13**: 747-772.

Banfield, A.W.F. 1954. Preliminary investigation of the barren-ground caribou. Part 1. Former and present distribution, migrations and status. Part 2. Life history, ecology and utilization. Can. Wildl. Serv. Wildl. Manage. Bull. Ser., Nos. 10A (79 pp.) and 10B (112 pp.). Ottawa, Ont.

Banfield, A.W.F. 1961. A revision of the reindeer and caribou, genus *Rangifer*. Natl. Mus. Can. Bull. **177**: 137 pp.

Banfield, A.W.F. 1974. The mammals of Canada. Univ. Toronto Press, Toronto, Ontario. 438 pp.

Bangs, E.E. 1991. Return of a predator: wolf recovery in Montana. West. Wildlands **17**(1): 7-13.

Banks, V. 1988. The red wolf gets a second chance to live by its wits. Smithson. **18**: 100-107.

Banville, D. 1978. Compte rendu du colloque sur le contrôle des prédateurs tenu Québec le 17 Février 1978. Ministère de Tourisme, de la Chasse et de la Pêche, P.Q. 36 pp.

Banville, D. 1981. Bilan du contrle des prédateurs du gros gibier au Québec de 1905 1980. Ministère du Loisir, de la Chasse et de la Pêche, P.Q. 54 pp.

Banville, D. 1983. Status and management of wolves in Quebec. pp. 41-43 *in* L.N. Carbyn, ed. Wolves in Canada and Alaska: their status, biology, and management. Can. Wildl. Serv. Rep. Ser., No. 45.

Barichello, N., J. Carey, R. Sumanik, R.D. Hayes, and A.M. Bayer. 1989. The effects of wolf predation on Dall sheep populations in southwest Yukon. Yukon Fish and Wildl. Br. Rep., Whitehorse. 24 pp.

Barker, I.K., R.C. Povey, and D.R. Voigt. 1983. Response of mink, skunk, red fox and raccoon to inoculation with mink virus enteritis, feline panleukopenia and canine parvovirus and prevalence of antibody to parvovirus in wild carnivores in Ontario. Can. J. Comp. Med. **47**: 188-197.

Barlow, J.W., and D.P. Heap. 1872. Report of a reconnaissance of the basin of the upper Yellowstone in 1871. Senate Exec. Doc. 66, 42nd Congress, 2nd Session. 43 pp.

Barmore, W.J. 1987. The distribution and abundance of ungulates in the northern Yellowstone ecosystem in pristine times and today. Paper presented at the Greater Yellowstone Coalition's Scientific Congress on The Northern Yellowstone: issues and alternatives of ecosystem management. 12 ms. pp.

Bartolome, F. 1989. Nobody trusts the boss completely — now what? Harvard Bus. Rev. 1989 (Mar./Apr.): 135-142.

Barton, N.H., and G.M. Hewitt. 1985. Analysis of hybrid zones. Annu. Rev. Ecol. Syst. **16**: 113-148.

Barton, N.H., and G.M. Hewitt. 1989. Adaptation, speciation, and hybrid zones. Nature (Lond.) **141**: 497-503.

Bateman, J. 1971. Animal traps and trapping. Stackpole Books, Harrisburg, Pa. 286 pp.

Bath, A.J. 1987. Attitudes of various interest groups in Wyoming toward wolf reintroduction in Yellowstone National Park. Report submitted to the U.S. Natl. Park Serv., Washington, D.C. 116 pp.

Bath, A.J. 1989. The public and wolf reintroduction in Yellowstone National Park. Soc. and Nat. Resour. **2**: 297-306.

Bath, A.J. 1991a. Public attitudes about wolf restoration in Yellowstone National Park. pp. 367-378 *in* R.B. Keiter and M.S. Boyce, eds. The Greater Yellowstone ecosystem: redefining America's wilderness heritage. Yale Univ. Press, New Haven, Conn.

Bath, A.J. 1991b. Public attitudes in Wyoming, Montana, and Idaho toward wolf restoration in Yellowstone National Park. Trans. North Am. Wildl. and Nat. Resour. Conf. **56**: 91-95.

Bath, A.J. 1992. Identification and documentation of public attitudes toward wolf reintroduction in Yellowstone National Park. pp. 2-3 to 2-30 *in* J.D. Varley and W.G. Brewster, eds. Wolves for Yellowstone? A report to the United States Congress. Vol. IV. Research and analysis. U.S. Natl. Park Serv., Yellowstone National Park, Mammoth, Wyo.

Bath, A.J., and T. Buchanan. 1989. Attitudes of interest groups in Wyoming toward wolf restoration in Yellowstone National Park. Wildl. Soc. Bull. **17**: 519-525.

Bath, A.J., and C. Phillips. 1990. Statewide surveys of Montana and Idaho resident attitudes toward wolf reintroduction in Yellowstone National Park. Report submitted to Friends for Animals, Natl. Wildl. Fed., U.S. Fish and Wildl. Serv., and U.S. Natl. Park Serv. 38 pp.

Batschelet, E. 1981. Circular statistics in biology. Academic Press, New York, N.Y. 371 pp.

Bay, C., and D. Boertmann. 1988. Biologisk-arkoeologisk kortloegning af Gronlands ostkyst mellem 75°N of 79°30'N. Greenland Botanical Surv., Bot. Mus., Copenhagen. 63 pp.

Beaufort, F.G. de. 1987. Ecologie historique du loup en France. Thèse de Doctorate, Université de Rennes I, Rennes, France. 4 vol. 1104 pp.

Becker, E.F. 1991. A terrestrial furbearer estimator based on probability sampling. J. Wildl. Manage. **55**: 730-737.

Becker, E.F., and C.L. Gardner. 1990. Wolf and wolverine density estimation techniques. Alaska Dep. Fish and Game Fed. Aid in Wildl. Restor. Prog. Rep., Proj. W-23-3, Study 7.15. 17 pp.

Becker, R.F., J.E. King, and J.E. Markee. 1962. Studies on olfactory acuity in dogs. II. Discriminatory behaviour in a free environment. J. Comp. Physiol. Psychol. **55**: 773-780.

Bednarz, J.A. 1988. The Mexican wolf: biology, history and prospects for reestablishment in New Mexico. U.S. Fish and Wildl. Serv. Endang. Spec. Rep. No. 18. 70 pp.

Beier, P., and D.R. McCullough. 1988. Motion-sensitive radio collars for estimating white-tailed deer activity. J. Wildl. Manage. **52**: 11-13.

Bekoff, M. 1977. *Canis latrans*. Mammalian species No. 79. Am. Soc. Mammal.

Bekoff, M. 1978. Behavioral development in coyotes and eastern coyotes. pp. 97-126 *in* M. Bekoff, ed. Coyotes: biology, behavior, and management. Academic Press, New York, N.Y.

Bekoff, M., and R. Jamieson. 1975. Physical development in coyotes (*Canis latrans*) with a comparison to other canids. J. Mammal. **56**: 685-692.

Bekoff, M., and L.D. Mech. 1984. Simulation analyses of space use: home range estimates, variability, and sample size. Behav. Res. Meth. Instrumentation Comput. **16**: 32-37.

Bekoff, M., and M.C. Wells. 1982. Behavioral ecology of coyotes: social organization, rearing patterns, space use, and resource defense. Z. Tierpsychol. **60**: 281-305.

Bekoff, M., H.L. Hill, and J.B. Mitton. 1975. Behavioral taxonomy in canids by discriminant function analysis. Science (Washington, D.C.) **190**: 1223-1225.

Bell, J.F., and J.R. Reilly. 1981. Tularemia. pp. 213-231 *in* J.W. Davis, L.H. Karstad, and D.O. Trainer, eds. Infectious diseases of wild mammals. 2nd ed. Iowa State Univ. Press, Ames.

Bennett, L.E. 1994. Colorado gray wolf recovery: a biological feasibility study final report. U.S. Fish and Wildl. Serv. Denver, Colo. 318 pp.

Bennike, O., A.K. Higgins, and M. Kelly. 1989. Mammals of central North Greenland. Polar Rec. **25**: 43-49.

Beran, G.W. 1981. Rabies and infections by rabies-related viruses. pp. 57-87 *in* J.H. Steele, ed. CRC handbook series in zoonoses. Section B. Viral zoonoses. Vol. II. CRC Press, Boca Raton, Fla.

Berg, W.E., and R.A. Chesness. 1978. Ecology of coyotes in northern Minnesota. pp. 229-247 *in* M. Bekoff, ed. Coyotes: biology, behavior, and management. Academic Press, New York, N.Y.

Berg, W.E., and D.W. Kuehn. 1982. Ecology of wolves in north-central Minnesota. pp. 4-11 *in* F.H. Harrington and P.C. Paquet, eds. Wolves of the world: perspectives of behavior, ecology, and conservation. Noyes, Park Ridge, N.J.

Berger, J. 1991. Greater Yellowstone's native ungulates: myths and realities. Conserv. Biol. **5**: 353-363.

Bergerud, A.T. 1964. A field method to determine annual parturition rates for Newfoundland caribou. J. Wildl. Manage. **28**: 477-480.

Bergerud, A.T. 1971. The population dynamics of Newfoundland caribou. Wildl. Monogr. **25**: 55 pp.

Bergerud, A.T. 1973. Movements and rutting behaviour of caribou (*Rangifer tarandus*) at Mount Alberta, Quebec. Can. Field-Nat. **87**: 357-369.

Bergerud, A.T. 1974a. Decline of caribou in North America following settlement. J. Wildl. Manage. **38**: 757-770.

Bergerud, A.T. 1974b. The role of the environment in the aggregation, movement and disturbance behaviour of caribou. pp. 552-584 *in* V.S. Geist and F. Walther, eds. The behaviour of ungulates and its relation to management. Vol. 2. Int. Union Conserv. Nature Nat. Resour. Publ., New Ser., No. 24.

Bergerud, A.T. 1978a. Caribou. pp. 83-101 *in* J.L. Schmidt and D.L. Gilbert, eds. Big game of North America: ecology and management. Stackpole Books, Harrisburg, Pa.

Bergerud, A.T. 1978b. The status and management of caribou in British Columbia. Report to the Minister of Recreation and Conservation, Victoria, B.C. 150 pp.

Bergerud, A.T. 1980. A review of the population dynamics of caribou and wild reindeer in North America. Proc. Int. Reindeer/Caribou Symp. **2**: 556-581.

Bergerud, A.T. 1983. The natural population control of caribou. pp. 14-61 *in* F.L. Bunnell, D.S. Eastman, and J.M. Peek, eds. Symposium on natural regulation of wildlife populations. Proc. No. 14, For. Wildl. and Range Exp. Stn., Univ. Idaho, Moscow.

Bergerud, A.T. 1985. Antipredator strategies of caribou: dispersion along shorelines. Can. J. Zool. **63**: 1324-1329.

Bergerud, A.T. 1988. Caribou, wolves and man. Trends Ecol. Evol. **3**: 68-72.

Bergerud, A.T. 1992. Rareness as an antipredator strategy to reduce risk for moose and caribou. pp. 1008-1021 *in* D.R. McCullough and R.H. Barrett, eds. Wildlife 2001: populations. Elsevier Appl. Sci., New York, N.Y.

Bergerud, A.T., and W.B. Ballard. 1988. Wolf predation on caribou: the Nelchina herd case history, a different interpretation. J. Wildl. Manage. **52**: 344-357.

Bergerud, A.T., and W.B. Ballard. 1989. Wolf predation on Nelchina caribou: a reply. J. Wildl. Manage. **53**: 251-259.

Bergerud, A.T., and J.P. Elliot. 1986. Dynamics of caribou and wolves in northern British Columbia. Can. J. Zool. **64**: 1515-1529.

Bergerud, A.T., and R.E. Page. 1987. Displacement and dispersion of parturient caribou at calving as an antipredator tactic. Can. J. Zool. **65**: 1597-1606.

Bergerud, A.T., and J.B. Snider. 1988. Predation in the dynamics of moose populations: a reply. J. Wildl. Manage. **52**: 559-564.

Bergerud, A.T., H.E. Butler, and D.R. Miller. 1984. Antipredator tactics of calving caribou: dispersion in mountains. Can. J. Zool. **62**: 1566-1575.

Bergerud, A.T., R. Ferguson, and H.E. Butler. 1990. Spring migration and dispersion of woodland caribou at calving. Anim. Behav. **39**: 360-368.

Bergerud, A.T., W. Wyett, and J.B. Snider. 1983a. The role of wolf predation in limiting a moose population. J. Wildl. Manage. **47**: 977-988.

Bergerud, A.T., M.J. Nolan, K. Curnew, and W.E. Mercer. 1983b. Growth of the Avalon Peninsula, Newfoundland caribou herd. J. Wildl. Manage. **47**: 989-998.

Berryman, A.A., N.C. Stenseth, and A.D. Isaev. 1987. Natural regulation of herbivorous forest insect populations. Oecologia (Berlin) **71**: 174-184.

Berryman, J.H. 1972. The principles of predator control. J. Wildl. Manage. **36**: 395-400.

Bertram, B.C.R. 1978. Living in groups: predators and prey. pp. 64-96 *in* J.R. Krebs and N.B. Davies, eds. Behavioural ecology: an evolutionary approach. Blackwell Sci. Publ., Oxford, U.K.

Biggs, J.R. 1988. Reintroduction of the Mexican wolf into New Mexico: an attitude survey. M.Sc. Thesis, New Mexico State Univ., Las Cruces. 66 pp.

Bird, G. 1972. The Cheyenne: their history and way of life. Univ. Nebraska Press, Lincoln. 213 pp.

Bish, R.L. 1977. Environmental resource management: public or private? pp. 217-228 *in* G. Hardin and J. Baden, eds. Managing the commons. W.H. Freeman, San Francisco, Calif.

Bjarvall, A. 1983. Scandinavia's response to a natural repopulation of wolves. Acta Zool. Fenn. **174**: 273-275.

Bjorge, R.R., and J.R. Gunson. 1983. Wolf predation of cattle on the Simonette River pastures in northwestern Alberta. pp. 106-111 *in* L.N. Carbyn, ed. Wolves in Canada and Alaska: their status, biology, and management. Can. Wildl. Serv. Rep. Ser., No. 45.

Bjorge, R.R., and J.R. Gunson. 1985. Evaluation of wolf control to reduce cattle predation in Alberta. J. Range Manage. **38**: 483-487.

Bjorge, R.R., and J.R. Gunson. 1989. Wolf, *Canis lupus*, population characteristics and prey relationships near Simonette River, Alberta. Can. Field-Nat. **103**: 327-334.

Black, R.F. 1964. The physical geography of Wisconsin. pp. 171-177 *in* Wisconsin Legislative Reference Bureau, The Wisconsin Blue Book 1964. Madison, Wis.

Blackith, R.E., and R.A. Reyment. 1991. Multivariate morphometrics. 2nd ed. Academic Press, New York, N.Y. 233 pp.

Blackmore, W. 1872. Personal Diaries #6 and #7. Unpubl. Rep. on file, Yellowstone National Park Research Library, Mammoth, Wyo. Original diary held by Western History Dep., Denver Public Library, Denver, Colo. Diary 6: 114 pp.; Diary 7: 74 pp.

Blanco, J.C., L. Cuesta, and S. Reig. (eds.) 1990. El lobo (*Canis lupus*) en Espana: situacion, problematica y apuntes sobre su ecologia. Ministerio de Agricultura Pesca y Alimentacio; ICONA; publicationes del Instituto nacional para la conservacion del la naturaleza. Madrid, Spain 118 pp.

Blanton, K.M., and E.P. Hill. 1989. Coyote use of white-tailed deer fawns in relation to deer density. Proc. Annu. Conf. Southeast. Assoc. Fish and Wildl. Agencies **43**: 470-478.

Bleiker, A., and H. Bleiker. 1981. Citizen participation handbook for public officials and other professionals serving the public. 4th ed. Institute for Participatory Planning, Laramie, Wyo. 156 pp.

Boddicker, M.L. 1982. Snares for predator control. Proc. Vertebr. Pest Conf. **10**: 50-54.

Boertje, R.D. and R.O. Stephenson. 1992. Effects of ungulate availability on wolf reproductive potential in Alaska. Can. J. Zool. 70: 2441-2443.

Boertje, R.D., C.L. Gardner, and P. Valkenburg. 1993a. Interrelationships involved in achieving population objectives for caribou, moose, wolves, and grizzly bears in Subunit 20E. Unpubl. Prog. Rep., Alaska Dep. Fish and Game, Fairbanks. 18 pp.

Boertje, R.D., P. Valkenburg, and M.E. McNay. 1996. Increases in moose, caribou, and wolves following wolf control in Alaska. J. Wildl. Manage. 60(3): in press

Boertje, R.D., W.C. Gasaway, D.V. Grangaard, and D.G. Kelleyhouse. 1988. Predation on moose and caribou by radio-collared grizzly bears in eastcentral Alaska. Can. J. Zool. 66: 2492-2499.

Boertje, R.D., D.V. Grangaard, P. Valkenburg, and S.D. Dubois. 1993b. Testing socially-acceptable methods of managing predationreducing predation on caribou and moose neonates by diversionary feeding of predators, Macomb Plateau 1990-1993. Alaska Dep. Fish and Game Fed. Aid in Wildl. Restoration. Final Rep., Projs. W-23-3 through W-23-5, and W-24-1. 31 pp.

Boertje, R.D., W.C. Gasaway, D.V. Grangaard, D.G. Kelleyhouse, and R.O. Stephenson. 1987. Factors limiting moose population growth in Game Unit Subunit 20E. Alaska Dep. Fish and Game Fed. Aid in Wildl. Restoration Prog. Rep., Proj. W-22-5. 86 pp.

Boertje, R.D., W.C. Gasaway, P. Valkenburg, S.D. DuBois, and D. Grangaard. 1990. Testing socially-acceptable methods of managing predation: reducing predation on caribou and moose neonates by diversionary feeding of predators on the Macomb Plateau, Alaska. Dep. Fish and Game, Fed. Aid in Wildl. Restoration Prog. Rep. Juneau. 11pp.

Bogan, M.A., and P. Mehlhop. 1983. Systematic relationships of gray wolves (*Canis lupus*) in southwestern North America. Univ. New Mexico Mus. Southwest. Biol. Occas. Pap. 1: 21 pp.

Boggess, E.K., G.R. Batcheller, R.G. Linscombe, J.W. Greer, M. Novak, S.B. Linhart, D.W. Erickson, A.W. Todd, D.C. Juve, and D.A. Wade. 1990. Traps, trapping and furbearer management. Wildl. Soc. Tech. Rev. 90-1: 31 pp.

Boitani, L. 1982. Wolf management in intensively used areas of Italy. pp. 158-172 *in* F.H. Harrington and P.C. Paquet, eds. Wolves of the world: perspectives of behavior, ecology, and conservation. Noyes, Park Ridge, N.J.

Boitani, L. 1986. Dalla parte del lupo. L'airone di G. Mondadore Associati Spa, Milano. 268 pp.

Boitani, L. 1987. The wolf in Eurasia. pp. 6-9 *in* Proc. Int. Wolf Symp., Washington, D.C., 22 May 1987.

Boitani, L. 1992. Wolf research and conservation in Italy. Biol. Conserv. 61: 125-132.

Boitani, L., and M.L. Fabbri. 1983. Strategia nazionale di conservazione del lupo. Richerche di Biologia della Selvaggina No. 72: 31 pp.

Boitani, L., and E. Zimen. 1979. The role of public opinion in wolf management. pp. 471-477 *in* E. Klinghammer, ed. The behavior and ecology of wolves. Garland STPM Press, New York, N.Y.

Bordaux, E.S. 1974. Messengers from ancient civilizations. Academy Books, San Diego, Calif. 43 pp.

Boutin, S. 1992. Predation and moose population dynamics: a critique. J. Wildl. Manage. 56: 116-127.

Bowen, R.A., P.N. Olson, M.D. Behrendt, S.L. Wheeler, P.W. Husted, and T.M. Nett. 1985. Efficacy and toxicity of estrogens commonly used to terminate canine pregnancy. J. Am. Vet. Med. Assoc. 186: 783-788.

Boyce, M.S. 1989. The Jackson elk herd: intensive wildlife management in North America. Cambridge Univ. Press, New York, N.Y. 306 pp.

Boyce, M.S. 1990. Wolf recovery for Yellowstone National Park: a simulation model. pp. 3-3 to 3-58 *in* Yellowstone National Park, U.S. Fish and Wildlife Service, University of Wyoming, University of Idaho, Interagency Grizzly Bear Study Team, and the University of Minnesota Cooperative Park Studies Unit, eds. Wolves for Yellowstone? A report to the United States Congress. Vol. II. Research and analysis. U.S. Natl. Park Serv., Yellowstone National Park, Mammoth, Wyo.

Boyce, M.S. 1991a. Migratory behaviour and management of elk (*Cervus elaphus*). Appl. Anim. Behav. Sci. 29: 239-250.

Boyce, M.S. 1991b. Natural regulation or the control of nature? pp. 183-208 *in* R.B. Keiter and M.S. Boyce, eds. The Greater Yellowstone ecosystem: redefining America's wilderness heritage. Yale Univ. Press, New Haven, Conn.

Boyce, M.S. 1992. Wolf recovery for Yellowstone National Park: a simulation model. pp. 123-138 *in* D.R. McCullough and R.H. Barrett, eds. Wildlife 2001: populations. Elsevier Appl. Sci., New York, N.Y.

Boyce, M.S. 1993. Predicting the consequences of wolf recovery to ungulates in Yellowstone National Park. pp. 234-269 *in* R.S. Cook, ed. Ecological issues on reintroducing wolves into Yellowstone National Park. U.S. Natl. Park Serv. Sci. Monogr. NPS/NRYELL/NRSM-93/22.

Boyce, M.S., and J. Gaillard. 1992. Wolves in Yellowstone, Jackson Hole, and the North Fork of the Shoshone River: simulating ungulate consequences of wolf recovery. pp. 4-73 to 4-115 *in* J.D. Varley and W.G. Brewster, eds. Wolves for Yellowstone? A report to the United States Congress. Vol. IV. Research and analysis. U.S. Natl. Park Serv., Yellowstone National Park, Mammoth, Wyo.

Boyce, M.S., and E.H. Merrill. 1991. Effects of the 1988 fires on ungulates in Yellowstone National Park. Proc. Tall Timbers Fire Ecol. Conf. **17**: 121-132.

Boyd, D.K. 1982. Food habits and spatial relations of coyotes and a lone wolf in the Rocky Mountains. M.S. Thesis, Univ. Montana, Missoula. 109 pp.

Boyd, D.K., and M.D. Jimenez. 1994. Successful rearing of young by wild wolves without mates. J. Mammal. **75**: 14-17.

Boyd, D.K., L.B. Secrest, and D.H. Pletscher. 1992. A wolf, *Canis lupus*, killed in an avalanche in southwestern Alberta. Can. Field-Nat. **106**: 526.

Bradier, P. 1985. Representation populaire du loup, sa rehabilitation, son avenir. Thèse de Doctorate, Ecole Vétérinaire, Alfort, France. 185 pp.

Bradley, F.H. 1873. Geological report. pp. 190-270 *in* F.W. Hayden, ed. Sixth annual report of the United States Geological Survey of the territories for the year 1872. U.S. Gov. Print. Off., Washington, DC.

Braend, M., and K.H. Roed. 1987. Polymorphism of transferrin and esterase in Alaskan wolves: evidence of close molecular homology with the dog. Anim. Genet. **18**: 143-148.

Brandenburg, J. 1991. White wolf: living with an arctic legend. NorthWord Press, Minocqua, Wisc. 160 pp.

Brannon, R.D. 1987. Nuisance grizzly bear, *Ursus arctos,* translocations in the Greater Yellowstone area. Can. Field-Nat. **101**: 569-575.

Brayer, H.O. (ed.) 1942. Exploring the Yellowstone with Hayden, 1872: diary of Sidford Hamp. Ann. Wyoming **14**: 253-298.

Bresler, D.E., G. Ellison, and S. Zamenhof. 1975. Learning deficits in rats with malnourished grandmothers. Develop. Psychobiol. **8**: 315-323.

Bressani, R., and J.E. Braham. 1977. Effect of frequency of feeding on blood serum urea changes in dogs. Nutr. Rep. Int. **16**: 305-316.

Brezzi, P. 1978. Le civilite del Medioevo europeo. 4 vol. Eurodes, Roma. 2240 pp.

British Columbia Ministry of the Environment. 1979. Preliminary wolf management plan for British Columbia. Fish and Wildl. Br., Victoria, B.C. 30 pp.

Brittan, M.R. 1953. A note concerning wolves in Glacier National Park, Montana. J. Mammal. **34**: 127-129.

Brodey, R.S., and I.J. Fidler. 1966. Clinical and pathological findings in bitches treated with progestational compounds. J. Am. Vet. Med. Assoc. **149**: 1406-1415.

Brookes, V.J. 1975. Poisons: properties, chemical identification, symptoms, and emergency treatment. 3rd ed. R.E. Krieger, Huntington, N.Y. 304 pp.

Brown, D.E. (ed.) 1983. The wolf in the southwest: the making of an endangered species. Univ. Arizona Press, Tucson. 195 pp.

Brown, W.K. 1986. The ecology of a woodland caribou herd in central Labrador. M.Sc. Thesis, Univ. Waterloo, Ont. 332 pp.

Brown, W.K., J.L. Kansas, and D.C. Thomas. 1994. The Greater Jasper Ecosystem Caribou Research Project, final report. Rep. to Parks Canada and World Wildlife Fund, Canada, by TAEM and Sentor Consultants, Calgary.

Brown, W.K., J. Huot, P. Lamoth, S. Luttich, M. Pare, B. St.-Martin, and J.B. Theberge. 1986. The distribution and movement patterns of four woodland caribou herds in Quebec. Proc. Int. Reindeer/Caribou Symp. **4**: 43-49.

Brown, W.M. 1986. The mitochondrial genome of animals. pp. 95-128 *in* R. MacIntyre, ed. Molecular evolutionary biology. Cornell Univ. Press, Ithaca, N.Y.

Brown, W.M., M. George, and A.C. Wilson. 1979. Rapid evolution of animal mitochondrial DNA. Proc. Natl. Acad. Sci. U.S.A. **76**: 1967-1971.

Brtek, L., and J. Voskar. 1987. Food biology of the wolf in Slovak Carpathians. Biologia (Bratislava) **42**: 985-990.

Bruce, H.M. 1960. Further observations on pregnancy block in mice caused by proximity of strange males. J. Reprod. Fertil. **1**: 311-312.

Bryan, T.S. 1979. The geysers of Yellowstone. Colorado Associated Univ. Press, Boulder. 225 pp.

Bryant, L.D., and C. Maser. 1982. Classification and distribution. pp. 1-59 *in* J.W. Thomas and D.E. Toweill, eds. Elk of North America: ecology and management. Stackpole Books, Harrisburg, Pa.

Bubenik, A.B. 1972. North American moose management in light of European experiences. North Am. Moose Conf. 8: 276-295.

Bucsis, R.A., C.R. Watts, F.G. Feist, G.R. Olson, and J.J. McCarthy. 1985. Big game survey and inventory — Region Four. Montana Dep. Fish Wildl. and Parks Proj. W-130-R-16. 61 pp.

Budd, J. 1981. Distemper. pp. 31-44 *in* J.W. Davis, L.H. Karstad, and D.O. Trainer, eds. Infectious diseases of wild mammals. 2nd ed. Iowa State Univ. Press, Ames.

Budgett, H.M. 1933. Hunting by scent. Eure and Spottiswoode, London.

Bulgin, M.S., S.L. Munn, and W. Gee. 1970. Hematologic changes to 4.5 years of age in clinically normal beagles. J. Am. Vet. Med. Assoc. **157**: 1064-1070.

Bunnell, F.L., and N.A. Olsen. 1976. Weights and growth of Dall sheep in Kluane Park and Preserve, Yukon Territory. Can. Field-Nat. **90**: 157-162.

Burbank, J.C. 1990. Vanishing lobo: the Mexican wolf and the southwest. Johnson, Boulder, Colo. 208 pp.

Bureau, M.J. 1992. Mortality and seasonal distribution of elk in an area recently recolonized by wolves. M.S. Thesis, Univ. Montana, Missoula. 109 pp.

Burgess, E.C. 1986. Experimental inoculation of dogs with *Borrelia burgdorferi*. Zbl. Bkt. Hyg. A **263**: 49-54.

Burgess, E.C., and L.A. Windberg. 1989. *Borrelia* sp. infection in coyotes, black-tailed jack rabbits and desert cottontails in southern Texas. J. Wildl. Dis. **25**: 47-51.

Burgess, E.C., A. Gendron-Fitzpatrick, and M. Mattison. 1989. Foal mortality associated with natural infection of pregnant mares with *Borrelia burgdorferi*. Proc. Int. Conf. Equine Infect. Dis. **5**: 217-220.

Burke, T. 1989. DNA fingerprinting and RFLP analysis. Trends Ecol. Evol. **4**: 136-139.

Burkholder, B.L. 1959. Movements and behavior of a wolf pack in Alaska. J. Wildl. Manage. **23**: 1-11.

Burles, D., and M. Hoefs. 1984. Winter mortality of Dall sheep in Kluane National Park. Can. Field-Nat. **98**: 479-484.

Burpee, L.J. (ed.) 1907. The journal of Anthony Hendry, 1754-55. V. York Factory to the Blackfeet country. Royal Soc. Can. pp. 307-354.

Burton, R. 1990. Wolves breeding in northeast Greenland. Polar Rec. **26**: 334.

Burton, R.W. 1940. The Indian wild dog. J. Bombay Nat. Hist. Soc. **41**: 691-715.

Butler, H.E., and A.T. Bergerud. 1978. The unusual story of the Slate Islands caribou. Naturalist Can. (Ottawa) **7**: 37-40.

Butzeck, S. 1987. The *Canis lupus* wolf being a vector of rabies to German population in the 16th and 17th century. Z. Gesamte Hyggrenzgeb. **33**: 666-669.

Buys, C. 1975. Predator control and ranchers' attitudes. Environ. Behav. **7**: 81-89.

C

Cable, R.M. 1958. An illustrated laboratory manual of parasitology. 4th ed. Burgess, Minneapolis, Minn. 165 pp.

Cagnolaro, L., D. Rosso, M. Spagnesi, and B. Venturi. 1974. Inchiesta sulla distribuzione del lupo in Italia e nei Cantoni Ticino e Grigioni. Richerche di Biologia della Selvaggina No. 61: 91 pp.

Cahalane, V.H. 1939. The evolution of predator control policy in the national parks. J. Wildl. Manage. **3**: 229-237.

Cahalane, V.H. 1941. Wildlife surpluses in the national parks. Trans. N. Am. Wildl. Conf. **6**: 355-361.

Cain, S.A., J.A. Kadlec, D.L. Allen, R.A. Cooley, M.G. Hornocker, A.S. Leopold, and F.H. Wagner. 1972. Predator control 1971. Report by the Advisory Committee on Predator Control to the Council on Environmental Quality and U.S. Dep. Inter. 207 pp.

Cameron, A.W. 1958. Mammals of the islands in the Gulf of St. Lawrence. Natl. Mus. Can. Bull. **154**: 165 pp.

Cameron, R.D., and K.R. Whitten. 1979. Seasonal movements and sexual segregation of caribou determined by aerial survey. J. Wildl. Manage. **43**: 626-633.

Cannon, K.P. 1992. A review of archaeological and paleontological evidence for the prehistoric presence of wolf and related prey species in the northern and central Rockies' physiographic province. pp. 1-175 to 1-265 *in* J.D. Varley and W.G. Brewster, eds. Wolves for Yellowstone? A report to the United States Congress. Vol. IV. Research and analysis. U.S. Natl. Park Serv., Yellowstone National Park, Mammoth, Wyo.

Capogrossi Colognesi, L. 1982. L'agricoltura romana: guida storica e critica. Laterza, Roma. 183 pp.

Carbyn, L.N. 1974. Wolf population fluctuations in Jasper National Park, Alberta, Canada. Biol. Conserv. **6**: 94-101.

Carbyn, L.N. 1975. Wolf predation and behavioural interactions with elk and other ungulates in an area of high prey diversity. Ph.D. Thesis, Univ. Toronto, Ont. 234 pp.

Carbyn, L.N. 1977. Report on the Canadian Wildlife Service involvement in IUCN-WWF wolf project (1240) in Poland. Report submitted to the International Union for Conservation of Nature and Natural Resources/Species Survival Commission Wolf Specialist Group. 44 pp.

Carbyn, L.N. 1980. Ecology and management of wolves in Riding Mountain National Park, Manitoba. Can. Wildl. Serv. for Parks Can. Larger Mammal Systems Stud. Rep. No. 10. 184 pp.

Carbyn, L.N. 1981. Territory displacement in a wolf population with abundant prey. J. Mammal. **62**: 193-195.

Carbyn, L.N. 1982a. Coyote population fluctuations and spatial distribution in relation to wolf territories in Riding Mountain National Park, Manitoba. Can. Field-Nat. **96**: 176-183.

Carbyn, L.N. 1982b. Incidence of disease and its potential role in the population dynamics of wolves in Riding Mountain National Park, Manitoba. pp. 106-116 *in* F.H. Harrington and P.C. Paquet, eds. Wolves of the world: perspectives of behavior, ecology, and conservation. Noyes, Park Ridge, N.J.

Carbyn, L.N. 1983a. Management of non-endangered wolf populations in Canada. Acta Zool. Fenn. **174**: 239-243.

Carbyn, L.N. 1983b. Wolf predation on elk in Riding Mountain National Park, Manitoba. J. Wildl. Manage. **47**: 963-976.

Carbyn, L.N. (ed.) 1983c. Wolves in Canada and Alaska: their status, biology, and management. Can. Wildl. Serv. Rep. Ser., No. 45. Ottawa, Ont. 135 pp.

Carbyn, L.N. 1987. Gray wolf and red wolf. pp. 378-393 *in* M. Novak, J.A. Baker, M.E. Obbard, and B. Malloch, eds. Wild furbearer management and conservation in North America. Ontario Trappers Assoc., Toronto, Ont.

Carbyn, L.N., and T. Trottier. 1987. Responses of bison on their calving grounds to predation by wolves in Wood Buffalo National Park. Can. J. Zool. **65**: 2072-2078.

Carbyn, L.N., and T. Trottier. 1988. Descriptions of wolf attacks on bison calves in Wood Buffalo National Park. Arctic **41**: 297-302.

Carbyn, L.N., S. Oosenbrug, and D. Anions. 1993. Wolves, bison...and the dynamics related to the Peace-Athabasca Delta in Canada's Wood Buffalo National Park. Circumpolar Res. Ser., No. 4, Canadian Circumpolar Institute, Univ. Alberta, Edmonton. 270 pp.

Carbyn, L.N., P. Paquet, and D. Meleshko. 1987. Long-term ecological studies on wolves, coyotes, and ungulates in Riding Mountain National Park. Draft Rep. on file, Can. Wildl. Serv., Edmonton, Alta. pp.

Carley, C.J. 1975. Activities and findings of the Red Wolf Recovery Program from late 1973 to July 1, 1975. U.S. Fish and Wildl. Serv. 215 pp.

Carmichael, L.E., and R.M. Kenney. 1970. Canine brucellosis: the clinical disease, pathogenesis, and immune response. J. Am. Vet. Med. Assoc. **156**: 1726-1734.

Carmichael, L.E., J.C. Joubert, and R.V.H. Pollock. 1980. Hemagglutination by canine parvovirus: serologic studies and diagnostic applications. Am. J. Vet. Res. **41**: 784-791.

Carney, E. 1902. The gray wolf. For. Stream **58**: 84.

Caro, T.M. 1989. Missing links in predator and antipredator behaviour. Trends Ecol. Evol. **4**: 333-334.

Caroline, M. 1973. A brief account of wild animal predation problems in Texas. pp. 57-59 *in* Management practices to evade predatory losses. Texas A. and M. Univ. Agric. Res. Ext. Cent., San Angelo.

Carr, S.M., S.W. Ballinger, J.N. Derr, L.H. Blankenship, and J.W. Bickham. 1986. Mitochondrial DNA analysis of hybridization between sympatric white-tailed deer and mule deer in west Texas. Proc. Natl. Acad. Sci. U.S.A. **83**: 9576-9580.

Carson, R.T., and R.C. Mitchell. 1989. Using surveys to value public goods: the contingent valuation method. Resources for the Future, Washington, D.C. 463 pp.

Castroviejo, J., F. Palacios, J. Garzon, and L. Cuesta. 1975. Sobre la alimentacion de los canidos Ibericos. Proc. Congr. Int. Union Game Biol. **12**: 39-46.

Caughley, G. 1976. Wildlife management and the dynamics of ungulate populations. Appl. Biol. **1**: 183-246.

Caughley, G., R. Pech, and D. Grice. 1992. Effect of fertility control on a population's productivity. Wildl. Res. **19**: 623-627.

Centers for Disease Control. 1983. Rabies surveillance annual summary, 1980-1982. U.S. Dep. Hlth. Hum. Serv., Atlanta, Ga. 29 pp.

Centers for Disease Control. 1985. Rabies surveillance annual summary, 1983. U.S. Dep. Hlth. Hum. Serv., Atlanta, Ga. 24 pp.

Centers for Disease Control. 1985. Rabies surveillance annual summary, 1984. U.S. Dep. Hlth. Hum. Serv., Atlanta, Ga. 32 pp.

Centers for Disease Control. 1986. Rabies surveillance annual summary, 1985. U.S. Dep. Hlth. Hum. Serv., Atlanta, Ga. 24 pp.

Centers for Disease Control. 1987. Rabies surveillance summary, 1986. U.S. Dep. Hlth. Hum. Serv., Atlanta, Ga. MMWR 36: 27 pp.

Centers for Disease Control. 1988. Rabies surveillance summary, 1987. U.S. Dep. Hlth. Hum. Serv., Atlanta, Ga. MMWR 37: 19 pp.

Centers for Disease Control. 1989. Rabies surveillance summary, 1988. U.S. Dep. Hlth. Hum. Serv., Atlanta, Ga. MMWR 38: 21 pp.

Central Idaho Wolf Recovery Steering Committee. 1990. Central Idaho wolf recovery: a management report 1990. U.S. Dep. Agric. For. Serv. Publ. No. R1-90-49. 15 pp.

Chadde, S.W., and C.E. Kay. 1991. Tall-willow communities on Yellowstone's northern range: a test of the "natural-regulation" paradigm. pp. 231-262 *in* R.B. Keiter and M.S. Boyce, eds. The Greater Yellowstone ecosystem: redefining America's wilderness heritage. Yale Univ. Press, New Haven, Conn.

Chambers, S.M., and J.W. Bayless. 1983. Systematics, conservation and the measurement of genetic diversity. pp. 349-363 *in* C.M. Schonewald-Cox, S.M. Chambers, B. MacBryde, and L. Thomas, eds. Genetics and conservation: a reference for managing wild animal and plant populations. Benjamin-Cummings Publ., Menlo Park, Calif.

Chapman, J.A., and G.A. Feldhamer (eds.) 1982. Wild mammals of North America: biology, management, and economics. Johns Hopkins Univ. Press, Baltimore, Md. 1147 pp.

Chapman, R.C. 1978. Rabies: decimation of a wolf pack in arctic Alaska. Science (Washington, D.C.) **201**: 365-367.

Cherkasskiy, B.L. 1988. Roles of the wolf and raccoon dog in the ecology and epidemiology of rabies in the USSR. Rev. Infect. Dis. **10**: 634-636.

Chesson, J. 1978. Measuring preference in selective predation. Ecology **59**: 211-215.

Chiarelli, A.B. 1975. The chromosomes of the Canidae. pp. 40-53 *in* M.W. Fox, ed. The wild canids: their systematics, behavioral ecology, and evolution. Van Nostrand Reinhold, New York, N.Y.

Childes, S.L. 1988. The past history, present status and distribution of the hunting dog *Lycaon pictus* in Zimbabwe. Biol. Conserv. **44**: 301-316.

Choquette, L.P.E., and E. Kuyt. 1974. Serological indication of canine distemper and of infectious canine hepatitis in wolves (*Canis lupus* L.) in northern Canada. J. Wildl. Dis. **10**: 321-324.

Choquette, L.P.E., G.G. Gibson, E. Kuyt, and A.M. Pearson. 1973. Helminths of wolves, *Canis lupus*, in the Yukon and Northwest Territories. Can. J. Zool. **51**: 1087-1091.

Cicchetti, C.J. 1973. Forecasting recreation in the United States. D.C. Health, Lexington, Mass. 200 pp.

Clark, B. 1980. Leg-hold trapping. Defenders **55**: 388-391.

Clark, D.D. 1989. Use of Argos for animal tracking in the Rocky Mountain Region of North America. pp. 129-176 *in* Proceedings of the North American Argos Users' Conference and Exhibit. Service Argos, Inc., Landover, Md.

Clark, P., G.E. Ryan, and A.B. Czuppon. 1975. Biochemical genetic markers in the family Canidae. Austral. J. Zool. **23**: 411-417.

Clark, T.W., and D. Zaunbrecher. 1987. The Greater Yellowstone ecosystem: the ecosystem concept in natural resource policy and management. Renew. Resour. J. **5**: 8-16.

Clark, T.W., R. Crete, and J. Cada. 1989. Designing and managing successful endangered species recovery programs. Environ. Manage. **13**: 159-170.

Clarkson, P.L. 1990. Wolf management. An evaluation and recommendations. M.Environ.Des., Univ. Calgary, Alta. 144 pp.

Clarkson, P.L., and I.S. Liepins. 1991. Inuvialuit wildlife studies: western Arctic wolf research project progress reports, April 1989-January 1991. Govt. Northwest Territ. Dep. Renewable Resour. 31 pp.

Clawson, C.C. 1871. Notes on the way to Wonderland, or, A ride to the infernal regions. New North-West, Deer Lodge, MT. Sept. 9, 16, 23, 30 (1871); Oct. 14 (1871); Nov. 4, 11, 18, 25 (1871); Dec. 2, 16 (1871).

Clawson, C.C. 1872. The region of the wonderful lake Yellowstone. New North-West, Deer Lodge, MT. Dec. 2, 16 (1871); Jan 13, 27 (1872a); Feb. 10, 24 (1872b); May 18 (1872c); June 1 (1872d).

Clutton-Brock, T.H., F.E. Guiness, and S.D. Albon. 1982. Red deer: behavior and ecology of two sexes. Univ. Chicago Press, Chicago, Ill. 378 pp.

Coady, J.W. 1980. History of moose in northern Alaska and adjacent regions. Can. Field-Nat. **94**: 61-68.

Coffin, D.L. 1944. A case of *Dirofilaria immitis* infection in a captive-bred timber wolf (*Canis occidentalis* Richardson). North Am. Vet. **25**: 611.

Cohen, M.N. 1977. The food crisis in prehistory: overpopulation and the origins of agriculture. Yale Univ. Press, New Haven, Conn. 341 pp.

Cohn, J. 1990. Endangered wolf population increases. BioScience **40**: 628-632.

Cole, G.F. 1969a. The elk of Grand Teton and southern Yellowstone National Parks. Yellowstone Library and Mus. Assoc. 80 pp.

Cole, G.F. 1969b. Mission-oriented research in the natural areas of the National Park Service. Res. Note No. 5, Yellowstone National Park, Mammoth, Wyo. 6 pp.

Cole, G.F. 1971. Yellowstone wolves (*Canis lupus irremotus*). Res. Note No. 4, Yellowstone National Park, Mammoth, Wyo. 6 pp.

Cole, G.F. 1983. A naturally regulated elk population. pp. 62-81 *in* F.L. Bunnell, D.S. Eastman, and J.M. Peek, eds. Symposium on natural regulation of wildlife populations. Proc. No. 14, For. Wildl. and Range Exp. Stn., Univ. Idaho, Moscow.

Committee on Energy and Natural Resources, United States Senate. 1990. Hearing before the Subcommittee on Public Lands, National Parks and Forests on S-2674, to provide for the reestablishment of the gray wolf in Yellowstone National Park and in central Idaho wilderness areas (September 19, 1990). U.S. Gov. Print. Off., Washington, D.C. 193 pp.

Comstock, T. 1875. Geological report. pp. 85-95 *in* W.A. Jones, report upon the reconnaissance of northwestern Wyoming including Yellowstone National Park, made in the summer of 1873. U.S. Gov. Print. Off., Washington, D.C.

Concannon, P., N. Altszuler, J. Hampshire, W.R. Butler, and W. Hansel. 1980. Growth hormone, prolactin, and cortisol in dogs developing mammary nodules and an acromegaly-like appearance during treatment with medroxyprogesterone acetate. Endocrinology **106**: 1173-1177.

Connolly, G.E. 1978a. Predators and predator control. pp. 369-394 *in* J.L. Schmidt and D.L. Gilbert, eds. Big game of North America: ecology and management. Stackpole Books, Harrisburg, Pa.

Connolly, G.E. 1978b. Predator control and coyote populations: a review of simulation models. pp. 327-345 *in* M. Bekoff, ed. Coyotes: biology, behavior, and management. Academic Press, New York, N.Y.

Connolly, G.E. 1988. M-44 sodium cyanide ejectors in the Animal Damage Control Program, 1976-1986. Proc. Vertebr. Pest Conf. **13**: 220-225.

Connolly, G.E., and W.M. Longhurst. 1975. The effects of control on coyote populations: a simulation model. Univ. California, Berkeley, Coop. Ext. Serv. Bull. 1872: 37 pp.

Connor, E.F., and M.A. Bowers. 1987. The spatial consequences of interspecific competition. Ann. Zool. Fenn. **24**: 213-226.

Connor, E.F., and D. Simberloff. 1986. Competition, scientific method, and null models in ecology. Am. Scient. **74**: 155-162.

Cook, C.W., D.E. Folsom, and W. Peterson. 1965. The valley of the Upper Yellowstone; an exploration of the headwaters of the Yellowstone River in the year 1869. A.L. Haines, ed. Univ. Oklahoma Press, Norman. 79 pp.

Cook, R.S. 1993. (ed.) Ecological issues on reintroducing wolves into Yellowstone National Park. U.S. Natl. Park Serv. Sci. Monogr. NPS/NRYELL/NRSM-93/22. 328 pp.

Coppinger, L., and R. Coppinger. 1993. Two different jobs, two different dogs: dogs for herding and for guarding livestock. Ch. 13 *in* T. Grandin, ed. Livestock handling and transport. CAB International, Oxon, U.K.

Coppinger, R., J. Lorenz, J. Glendinning, and P. Pinardi. 1983. Attentiveness of guarding dogs for reducing predation on domestic sheep. J. Range Manage. **36**: 275-279.

Coppinger, R., L. Coppinger, G. Langeloh, L. Gettler, and J. Lorenz. 1988. A decade of use of livestock guarding dogs. Proc. Vertebr. Pest Conf. **13**: 209-214.

Coppinger, R., J. Glendinning, E. Torop, C. Matthay, M. Sutherland, and C. Smith. 1987. Degree of behavioral neoteny differentiates canid polymorphs. Ethology **75**: 89-108.

Couturier, S., K. Brunelle, D. Vandal, and G. St.-Martin. 1990. Changes in the population dynamics of the George River caribou herd, 1976-1987. Arctic **43**: 9-20.

Cowan, I.McT. 1947. The timber wolf in the Rocky Mountain national parks of Canada. Can. J. Res. **25**: 139-174.

Cowan, I.McT. 1949. Rabies as a possible population control of arctic Canidae. J. Mammal. **30**: 396-398.

Cowan, I.McT. 1951. The diseases and parasites of big game mammals of western Canada. Proc. Annu. Game Conv. **5**: 37-64.

Cowan, I.McT., and C.J. Guiguet. 1965. The mammals of British Columbia. British Columbia Prov. Mus. Handbook No. 11: 414 pp.

Crabtree, R.L., F.G. Burton, T.R. Garland, D.A. Cataldo, and W.H. Rickard. 1989. Slow-release radioisotope implants as individual markers for carnivores. J. Wildl. Manage. **53**: 949-954.

Craighead, D.J., and J.J. Craighead. 1987. Tracking caribou using satellite telemetry. Natl. Geogr. Res. **3**: 462-479.

Craighead, J.J., G. Atwell, and B.W. O'Gara. 1972. Elk migrations in and near Yellowstone National Park. Wildl. Monogr. **29**: 48 pp.

Creed, W.A., F. Haberland, B.E. Kohn, and K.R. McCaffery. 1984. Harvest management: the Wisconsin experience. pp. 243-260 *in* L.K. Halls, ed. The white-tailed deer: ecology and management. Stackpole Books, Harrisburg, Pa.

Crete, M. 1987. The impact of sport hunting on North American moose. Swed. Wildl. Res. **1** (Suppl.): 553-563.

Crete, M., and H. Jolicoeur. 1987. Impact of wolf and black bear removal on cow:calf ratio and moose density in southwestern Quebec. Alces **23**: 61-87.

Crete, M., and F. Messier. 1987. Evaluation of indices of gray wolf, *Canis lupus,* density in hardwood-conifer forests of southwestern Quebec. Can. Field-Nat. **101**: 147-152.

Crete, M., R.J. Taylor, and P.A. Jordan. 1981. Optimization of moose harvest in southwestern Quebec. J. Wildl. Manage. **45**: 598-611.

Criddle, N. 1925. The habits and economic importance of wolves in Canada. Dominion of Canada Dep. Agric. Bull. No. 13 (New Ser.). 24 pp.

Crisler, L. 1958. Arctic wild. Harper Brothers, New York, N.Y. 301 pp.

Cronin, M.A. 1991. Mitochondrial-DNA phylogeny of deer (Cervidae). J. Mammal. **72**: 553-566.

Cronin, M.A. 1992. Intraspecific variation in mitochondrial DNA of North American cervids. J. Mammal. **73**: 70-82.

Cronin, M.A. 1993. Mitochondrial DNA in wildlife taxonomy and conservation biology: cautionary notes. Wildl. Soc. Bull. **21**: 339-348.

Cronin, M.A., M.E. Nelson, and D.F. Pac. 1991a. Spatial heterogeneity of mitochondrial DNA and allozymes among populations of white-tailed deer and mule deer. J. Hered. **82**: 118-127.

Cronin, M.A., E.R. Vyse, and D.G. Cameron. 1988. Genetic relationships between mule deer and white-tailed deer in Montana. J. Wildl. Manage. **52**: 320-328.

Cronin, M.A., S.C. Amstrup, G.W. Garner, and E.R. Vyse. 1991b. Interspecific and intraspecific mitochondrial DNA variation in North American bears (*Ursus*). Can. J. Zool. **69**: 2985-2992.

Cuesta, L., F. Barcena, F. Palacios, and S. Reig. 1991. The trophic ecology of the Iberian wolf (*Canis lupus signatus* Cabrera, 1907). A new analysis of stomach's data. Mammalia **55**: 239-254.

Cumming, H.G. 1975. Clumping behavior and predation with special reference to caribou. Proc. Int. Reindeer/Caribou Symp. **1**: 474-497.

Cumming, H.G. 1992. Woodland caribou: facts for forest managers. For. Chron. **68**: 481-491.

Cumming, H.G., and D.B. Beange. 1985. Dispersion and movements of woodland caribou near Lake Nipigon in Ontario. J. Wildl. Manage. **51**(1): 69-79.

Cumming, H.G., and D.B. Beange. 1987. Dispersion and movements of woodland caribou near Lake Nipigon, Ontario. J. Wildl. Manage. **51**: 69-79.

Curnow, E. 1969. The history of the eradication of the wolf in Montana. M.S. Thesis, Univ. Montana, Missoula. 99 pp.

Curotto, E. 1958. Dizionario mitologia universale. SEI, Torino. 756 pp.

Curry-Lindahl, K. 1965. The plight of Scandinavia's large carnivores. Animals **4**: 92-97.

Curtis, J.T. 1959. The vegetation of Wisconsin: an ordination of plant communities. Univ. Wisconsin Press, Madison. 657 pp.

Custer, J.W., and D.B. Pence. 1981a. Host-parasite relationships in wild Canidae of North America I. Ecology of helminth infections in the genus *Canis*. Proc. Worldwide Furbearer Conf. **1**: 730-759.

Custer, J.W., and D.B. Pence. 1981b. Ecological analyses of helminth populations of wild canids from the Gulf coastal prairies of Texas and Louisiana. J. Parasitol. **67**: 289-307.

Cuyler, L.C., and N.A. ritsland. 1986. Seasonal variations and responses to normal activity of the deep body temperature in the Svalbard reindeer (*Rangifer tarandus platyrhynchus*). Proc. Int. Reindeer/Caribou Symp. **4**: 81-86.

D

Daan, S., and J. Aschoff. 1982. Circadian contributions to survival. pp. 305-321 *in* J. Aschoff, S. Daan, and G.A. Groos, eds. Vertebrate circadian systems: structure and physiology. Springer-Verlag, Berlin.

Dale, B.W., L.G. Adams, and R.T. Bowyer. 1994. Functional response of wolves preying on barren-ground caribou in a multiple-prey ecosystem. J. Anim. Ecol. **63**: 644-652.

Danner, D.A., and N.S. Smith. 1980. Coyote home range, movement, and relative abundance near a cattle feedyard. J. Wildl. Manage. **44**: 484-487.

Dar, M., and R. Gaur. 1983. Ladakh. pp. 25-39 *in* Editor anon. The Wildlife of Jammu and Kashmir. A Sanctuary Publication for the Department of Wildlife Protection, Jammu and Kashmir Government, Srinagar, India.

Darby, W.R., and L.S. Duquette. 1986. Woodland caribou and forestry in Ontario. Proc. Int. Reindeer/Caribou Symp. **4**: 87-94.

Darby, W.R., H.R. Timmermann, J.B. Snyder, K.F. Abraham, R.A. Stefanski, and C.A. Johnson. 1989. Woodland caribou in Ontario: background to a policy. Ontario Min. Nat. Resour., Toronto. 38 pp.

Darokhan, M.D. 1986. Animal husbandry in Ladakh: an ecological perspective. pp. 71-74 *in* Editor anon. Ecology and principles for sustainable development. Proceedings of a conference co-hosted by the Ladakh Project and the Ladakh Ecological Development Group in Leh, Ladakh, September 2-4, 1986. Ladakh Project, Bristol, U.K.

Dauphiné, T.C., Jr. 1971. Physical variables as an index to condition in barren-ground caribou. Trans. Northeast Fish and Wildl. Conf. **28**: 91-108.

Dauphiné, T.C., Jr. 1976. Biology of the Kaminuriak population of barren-ground caribou. Part 4. Growth, reproduction and energy reserves. Can. Wildl. Serv. Rep. Ser., No. 38. 69 pp.

Dauphiné, T.C., Jr., and R.L. McClure. 1974. Synchronous mating in barren-ground caribou. J. Wildl. Manage. **38**: 54-66.

Davies, N.B., and A.I. Houston. 1984. Territory economics. pp. 146-169 *in* J.R. Krebs and N.B. Davies, eds. Behavioural ecology: an evolutionary approach. Blackwell Sci. Publ., Oxford, U.K.

Davis, J.L., and P. Valkenburg. 1991. A review of caribou population dynamics in Alaska emphasizing limiting factors, theory and management implication. Proc. North Am. Caribou Workshop **4**: 184-207.

Davis, J.L., P. Valkenburg, and S.J. Harbo. 1979. Refinement of the aerial photo-direct count-extrapolation caribou census technique. Alaska Dep. Fish and Game Fed. Aid Wildl. Restoration. Final Rep., Proj. W-17-11. 23 pp.

Davis, J.L., P. Valkenburg, and D.J. Reed. 1988. Mortality of Delta herd caribou to 24 months of age. Proc. North Am. Caribou Workshop **3**: 38-51.

Davis, J.L., P. Valkenburg, and H.V. Reynolds. 1980. Population dynamics of Alaska's western arctic caribou herd. Proc. Int. Reindeer/Caribou Symp. **2**: 595-604.

Dawes, P.R. 1978. Ulve i Nordgronland. Tidsskriftet Gronland **10**: 289-303.

Dawes, P.R., M. Elander, and M. Ericson. 1986. The wolf (*Canis lupus*) in Greenland: a historical review and present status. Arctic **39**: 119-132.

Day, G.L. 1981. The status and distribution of wolves in the northern Rocky Mountains of the United States. M.S. Thesis, Univ. Montana, Missoula. 130 pp.

Dean, F.C. 1987. Brown bear density, Denali National Park, and sighting efficiency adjustment. Int. Conf. Bear Res. and Manage. **7**: 3743.

Debbie, J.G. 1991. Rabies control of terrestrial wildlife by population reduction. pp. 477-484 *in* G.M. Baer, ed. The natural history of rabies. 2nd ed. CRC Press, Boca Raton, Fla.

deCalesta, D.S. 1983. Building an electric anti-predator fence. Pac. Northwest Coop. Ext. Bull. **225**: 11 pp.

Dekker, D.W. 1983. Denning and foraging habits of red foxes, *Vulpes vulpes*, and their interaction with coyotes, *Canis latrans*, in central Alberta, 1972-1981. Can. Field-Nat. **97**: 303-306.

Dekker, D.W. 1985a. Responses of wolves, *Canis lupus*, to simulated howling on a homesite during fall and winter in Jasper National Park, Alberta. Can. Field-Nat. **99**: 90-93.

Dekker, D.W. 1985b. Elk population fluctuations and their probable causes in the Snake Indian Valley of Jasper National Park: 1970-1985. Alberta Nat. **15**: 49-54.

Dekker, D.W. 1986. Wolf, *Canis lupus*, numbers and colour phases in Jasper National Park, Alberta: 1965-1984. Can. Field-Nat. **100**: 550-553.

Dekker, D.W. 1987. The not-so-natural history of Jasper National Park. Park News **23**(4): 26-29.

Dekker, D.W. 1989. Population fluctuations and spatial relationships among wolves, coyotes, and red foxes in Jasper National Park, Alberta. Can. Field-Nat. **103**: 261-264.

Dekker, D.W. 1990. Population fluctuations and spatical relationships among wolves, coyotes, and red foxes in Jasper National Park, Alberta. Alberta Nat. 20: 15-20.

Delacy, W.W. 1876. A trip up the south Snake River in 1863. Contrib. Hist. Soc. Montana **1**: 100-127.

DelGiudice, G.D., L.D. Mech, and U.S. Seal. 1990. Effects of winter undernutrition on body composition and physiological profiles of white-tailed deer. J. Wildl. Manage. **54**: 539-550.

Delibes, M. 1990. Status and conservation needs of the wolf in the Council of Europe member States. Counc. Europe Nat. Environ. Ser., No. 47: 47 pp.

Despain, D.G. 1990. Yellowstone vegetation: consequences of environment and history in a natural setting. Roberts Rinehart, Boulder, Colo. 239 pp.

Despain, D., D. Houston, M. Meagher, and P. Schullery. 1986. Wildlife in transition: man and nature on Yellowstone's northern range. Roberts Rinehart, Boulder, Colo. 142 pp.

DeVoto, B. 1947. Across the wide Missouri. Houghton Mifflin Company, Boston, Mass. 483 pp.

Diamond, J.M. 1978. Niche shifts and the rediscovery of interspecific competition. Am. Scient. **66**: 322-331.

Diesch, S.L., D.E. Hasz, and P.D. Karns. 1972. Survey of Minnesota moose for leptospirosis and brucellosis. Proc. U.S. Anim. Hlth. Assoc. **76**: 645-657.

Dixit, V.P. 1979. Chemical sterilization of male dogs (*Canis familiaris*) after single intratesticular administration of methalibure (ICI-33828), dexamethasone, metopiron (SU-4885, Ciba), niridazole (33644-Ba, Ciba), a-chlorohydrin (U-5897) and danazol. Indian J. Exp. Biol. **17**: 937-940.

Doane, G.C. 1870. Battle drums and geysers. O. Bonney and L. Bonney, eds. Swallow Press, Chicago, Ill. 622 pp.

Doane, G.C. 1875. Yellowstone expedition of 1879. Senate Exec. Doc. 51, 41st Congress, 3rd Session. 40 pp.

Doane, G.C. 1876. Expedition of 1876-1877. Unpubl. Rep. on file, Yellowstone National Park Library, Mammoth, Wyo. 44 pp.

Dobyns, H.F. 1983. Their numbers become thinned: Native American population dynamics in eastern North America. Univ. Tennessee Press, Knoxville. 378 pp.

Dobzhansky, T. 1970. Genetics of the evolutionary process. Columbia Univ. Press, New York, N.Y. 505 pp.

Dodds, D.G. 1983. Terrestrial mammals. pp. 509-550 *in* G.R. South, ed. Biogeography and ecology of the Island of Newfoundland. Dr. W. Junk, The Hague, The Netherlands.

Dorrance, M.J. 1982. Predation losses of cattle in Alberta. J. Range Manage. **35**: 690-692.

Dorrance, M.J. 1983. A philosophy of problem wildlife management. Wildl. Soc. Bull. **11**: 319-324.

Dorrance, M.J., and J. Bourne. 1980. An evaluation of anti-coyote electric fencing. J. Range Manage. **33**: 385-387.

Doerr, J.G., and R.A. Dieterich. 1979. Mandibular lesions in the western arctic caribou herd of Alaska. J. Wildl. Dis. **15**: 309-318.

Doughty, R.W. 1983. Wildlife and man in Texas. Environmental change and conservation. Texas A. and M. Univ. Press, College Station. 246 pp.

Dowling, T.E., and W.M. Brown. 1989. Allozymes, mitochondrial DNA, and levels of phylogenetic resolution among four minnow species (*Notropis*: Cyprinidae). Syst. Zool. **38**: 126-143.

Dowling, T.E., B.D. DeMarais, W.L. Minckley, M.E. Douglas, and P.C. Marsh. 1992. Use of genetic characters in conservation biology. Conserv. Biol. **6**: 7-8.

Dragoo, J.W., J.R. Choate, T.L. Yates, and T.P. O'Farrell. 1991. Evolutionary and taxonomic relationships among North American arid-land foxes. J. Mammal. **71**: 318-332.

Drobeck, H.P., and F. Coulston. 1962. Inhibition and recovery of spermatogenesis in rats, monkeys, and dogs medicated with bis(dichloroacetyl)diamines. Exp. Molec. Pathol. **1**: 251-274.

Duby, G. 1974. The early growth of the European economy: warriors and peasants from the seventh to the twelfth century. Weidenfeld and Nicholson, London, U.K. 292 pp.

Duffield, J.W. 1992. An economic analysis of wolf recovery in Yellowstone: park visitor attitudes and values. pp. 2-31 to 2-87 *in* J.D. Varley and W.G. Brewster, eds. Wolves for Yellowstone? A report to the United States Congress. Vol. IV. Research and analysis. U.S. Natl. Park Serv., Yellowstone National Park, Mammoth, Wyo.

Dunbrack, R.L., and L.A. Giguere. 1987. Adaptive responses to accelerating costs of movement: a bioenergetic basis for the type-III functional response. Am. Nat. **130**: 147-160.

Duncan, G.W., S.C. Lyster, J.W. Hendrix, J.J. Clark, and H.D. Webster. 1964. Biologic effects of melengestrol acetate. Fertil. Steril. **15**: 419-432.

Duncan, J.R., and K.W. Prasse. 1977. Veterinary laboratory medicine: clinical pathology. Iowa State Univ. Press, Ames. 243 pp.

Dunlap, T. 1988. Saving America's wildlife. Princeton Univ. Press, Princeton, N.J. 222 pp.

Dunlop, T.R. 1983. Values for varmints: predator control and environmental ideas 1920-1939. Pac. Hist. Rev. 33 pp.

Dunraven, W.T. 1967. The Great Divide: travels in the upper Yellowstone in the summer of 1874. Univ. Nebraska Press, Lincoln. 377 pp.

E

Eberhardt, L.L. 1987. Population projections from simple models. J. Appl. Ecol. **24**: 103-118.

Eberhardt, L.L., and K.W. Pitcher. 1992. A further analysis of the Nelchina caribou and wolf data. Wildl. Soc. Bull. **20**: 385-395.

Eberhardt, L.L., and J.M. Thomas. 1991. Designing environmental field studies. Ecol. Monogr. **61**: 53-73.

Edmonds, E.J. 1986. Draft restoration plan for woodland caribou in Alberta. Alberta Fish Wildl. Rep. 74 pp.

Edmonds, E.J. 1988. Population status, distribution, and movements of woodland caribou in west central Alberta. Can. J. Zool. **66**: 817-826.

Edmonds, E.J. 1991. The status of woodland caribou in western Canada. Proc. North Am. Caribou Workshop **5**: 91-107.

Edmonds, E.J., and K. Smith. 1991. Calf production and survival, and calving and summer habitat use of mountain caribou in west central Alberta. Alberta Fish and Wildl. Div. Rep. 28 pp.

Edmonds, E.J., K. Smith, R. Wynes, and R.A. Quinlan. 1991. A management program to restore caribou populations in west-central Alberta. Proc. North Am. Caribou Workshop **4**: 210-217.

Eide, S., and W.B. Ballard. 1982. Apparent case of surplus killing of caribou by gray wolves. Can. Field-Nat. **96**: 87-88.

Eisler, R. 1991. Cyanide hazards to fish, wildlife and invertebrates: a synoptic review. U.S. Fish and Wildl. Serv. Biol. Rep. No. 85. 55 pp.

Elder, W.H., and C.M. Hayden. 1977. Use of discriminant function in taxonomic determination of canids from Missouri. J. Mammal. **58**: 17-24.

El Etreby, M.F. 1979. Effect of cyproterone acetate, levonorgestrel and progesterone on adrenal glands and reproductive organs in the beagle bitch. Cell Tiss. Res. **200**: 229-243.

Ellins, S.R., and S.M. Catalano. 1980. Field application of the conditioned taste aversion paradigm to the control of coyote predation on sheep and turkeys. Behav. Neur. Biol. **29**: 532-536.

Elliott, J.P. 1985a. Kechika Enhancement Project of northeastern B.C.: wolf/ungulate management. 1984-85 annual report. British Columbia Min. Environ. Wildl. Working Rep. No. WR-13. Fort St. John. 28 pp.

Elliott, J.P. 1985b. Muskwa Wolf Management Project of northeastern B.C. 1984-85 annual report. British Columbia Min. Environ. Wildl. Working Rep. No. WR-14. Fort St. John. 44 pp.

Elliott, J.P. 1989. Wolves and ungulates in British Columbia's northeast. pp. 97-123 *in* D. Seip, S. Pettigrew, and R. Archibald, eds. Wolf-prey dynamics and management. British Columbia Min. Environ. Wildl. Working Rep. No. WR-40.

Engstrom, D.R., C. Whitlock, S.C. Fritz, and H.E. Wright, Jr. 1991. Recent environmental changes inferred from the sediments of small lakes in Yellowstone's northern range. J. Paleolimnol. **5**: 139-174.

Errington, P.L. 1946. Predation and vertebrate populations. Q. Rev. Biol. **21**: 144-177, 221-245.

Espmark, Y. 1971. Antler shedding in relation to parturition in female reindeer. J. Wildl. Manage. **35**: 175-177.

Estes, R.D. 1972. The role of the vomeronasal organ in mammalian reproduction. Mammalia **36**: 315-341.

Estes, R.D. 1976. The significance of breeding synchrony in the wildebeest. E. Afr. Wildl. J. **14**: 135-152.

Ettinger, J.E. 1983. Textbook of veterinary internal medicine, diseases of the dog and cat. Vol. 1. W.B. Saunders, Philadelphia, Pa. 1124 pp.

Eugster, A.K., and C. Nairn. 1977. Diarrhea in puppies: parvovirus-like particles demonstrated in the feces. Southwest Vet. **30**: 59.

Everts, T.C. 1871. Thirty-seven days of peril. Scribner's Monthly **3**: 1-17.

Eysenck, M.W., and M.T. Keane. 1990. Cognitive psychology: a student's handbook. Erlbaum Press, Hillsdale, N.J. 557 pp.

F

Fagen, R.M. 1981. Animal play behavior. Oxford Univ. Press, New York, N.Y. 684 pp.

Fancy, S.G. 1980. Preparation of mammalian teeth for age determination by cementum layers: a review. Wildl. Soc. Bull. **8**: 242-248.

Fancy, S.G., and K.R. Whitten. 1991. Selection of calving sites by Porcupine herd caribou. Can. J. Zool. **69**: 1736-1743.

Fancy, S.G., L.F. Pank, K.R. Whitten, and W.L. Regelin. 1989. Seasonal movements of caribou in arctic Alaska as determined by satellite. Can. J. Zool. **67**: 644-650.

Fancy, S.G., L.F. Pank, D.C. Douglas, C.H. Curby, G.W. Garner, S.C. Amstrup, and W.L. Regelin. 1988. Satellite telemetry: a new tool for wildlife research and management. U.S. Fish and Wildl. Serv. Resour. Publ. No. 172. 54 pp.

Fanshawe, J., L.H. Frame, and J.R. Ginsberg. 1991. The wild dog: Africa's vanishing carnivore. Oryx **3**: 1-10.

Farnell, R., and R.D. Hayes. The impacts of wolf control on wolves and woodland caribou in the Finlayson area, Yukon. Yukon Fish and Wildl. Br., Whitehorse. 43 pp. (in prep.).

Farnell, R., and J. McDonald. 1988. The influence of wolf predation on caribou mortality in Yukon's Finlayson caribou herd. Proc. N. Am. Caribou Workshop **3**: 52-70.

Fekadu, M. 1991. Canine rabies. pp. 367-378 *in* G.M. Baer, ed. The natural history of rabies. 2nd ed. CRC Press, Boca Raton, Fla.

Fekete, G., and Sz. Szeberényi. 1965. Data on mechanism of adrenal suppression by medroxyprogesterone acetate. Steroids **6**: 159-166.

Ferguson, W.W. 1981. The systematic position of *Canis aureus lupaster* (Carnivora: Canidae) and the occurrence of *Canis lupus* in North Africa, Egypt and Sinai. Mammalia **45**: 459-465.

Ferrell, R.E., D.C. Morizot, J. Horn, and C.J. Carley. 1980. Biochemical markers in a species endangered by introgression: the red wolf. Biochem. Genet. **18**: 39-49.

Field, R. 1979. A perspective on syntactics of wolf vocalizations. pp. 182-205 *in* E. Klinghammer, ed. The behavior and ecology of wolves. Garland STPM Press, New York, N.Y.

Fiennes, R. 1976. The order of wolves. Hamish-Hamilton, London. 206 pp.

Filion, F.L., A. Jacquemot, P. Boxall, R. Reid, P. Bouchard, E. Duwors, and P. Gray. 1989. The importance of wildlife to Canadians: the economic significance of wildlife related recreational activities. Supply and Services Canada, Ottawa, Ont. 40 pp.

Filion, F.L., S.W. James, J.L. Ducharme, W. Pepper, R. Reid, P. Boxall, and D. Teillet. 1983. The importance of wildlife to Canadians. Supply and Services Canada, Ottawa, Ont. 40 pp.

Finch, V.C., G.T. Trewartha, A.H. Robinson, and E.H. Hammond. 1957. Elements of geography, physical and cultural. McGraw-Hill Book, Toronto, Ont. 693 pp.

Findley, J.S., A.H. Harris, D.E. Wilson, and C. Jones. 1975. Mammals of New Mexico. Univ. New Mexico Press, Albuquerque. 360 pp.

Fischer, H. 1987. Reintroduction of wolves to Yellowstone Park: implementing the proposed recovery. pp. 62-63 *in* Proc. Int. Wolf Symp., Washington, D.C., 22 May 1987.

Fischer, H. 1989. Restoring the wolf: Defenders launches a compensation fund. Defenders **64**(1): 9, 36.

Fischer, H. 1991. Discord over wolves. Defenders **66**(4): 35-39.

Fisher, R.A., W. Putt, and E. Hackel. 1976. An investigation of the products of 53 gene loci in three species of wild Canidae: *Canis lupus*, *Canis latrans*, and *Canis familiaris*. Biochem. Genet. **14**: 963-974.

Flath, D.L. 1979. The nature and extent of reported wolf activity in Montana. Joint meeting including the Montana Chapter of the Wildlife Society, Feb. 1, 1979. Missoula, Mont. 17 pp.

Fleischer, G. 1978. Evolutionary principles of the mammalian middle ear. Adv. Anat. Embryol. Cell Biol. **55**: 70 pp.

Flook, D.R. 1963. Range relationships of some ungulates native to Banff and Jasper National Parks, Alberta. pp. 119-128 *in* D.J. Crisp, ed. Grazing in terrestrial and marine environments. Br. Ecol. Soc. Symp. Publ. No. 4.

Floyd, T.J., L.D. Mech, and P.D. Jordan. 1978. Relating wolf scat content to prey consumed. J. Wildl. Manage. **42**: 528-532.

Fogleman, V.M. 1989. American attitudes toward wolves: a history of misperception. Environ. Ethics **10**: 63-94.

Folstad, I., A.C. Nilssen, O. Halvorsen, and J. Anderson. 1991. Parasite avoidance: the cause of post-calving migrations in *Rangifer*? Can. J. Zool. **69**: 2423-2429.

Fooks, L.G. 1961. Food habits of indigenous Canidae and Felidae in Arkansas based on complete and sample analysis of stomach contents. M.S. Thesis, Univ. Arkansas, Fayetteville. 55 pp.

Forbes, G.J., and J.B. Theberge. 1992. Importance of scavenging on moose by wolves in Algonquin Provincial Park, Ontario. Alces **28**: 235-241.

Forman, R.T., and E.W. Russell. 1983. Evaluation of historical data. Ecol. Soc. Bull. **64**: 5-7.

Formosov, A.N. 1946. Snow cover as an integral factor of the environment and its importance in the ecology of mammals and birds. Univ. Alberta Can. Circumpolar Inst. (formerly Boreal Inst. North. Stud.) Occas. Pap. No. **1**. Edmonton. 141 pp. (Translation of Russian original by W. Prychodko and W.O. Pruitt, Jr.)

Fowler, C.W. 1981. Comparative population dynamics in large mammals. pp. 437-455 *in* C.W. Fowler and T.D. Smith, eds. Dynamics of large mammal populations. John Wiley and Sons, New York, N.Y.

Fowler, M.E. 1978. Zoo and wild animal medicine. W.B. Saunders Company, Philadelphia, Pa. 1127 pp.

Fox, J.L., and A.J.T. Johnsingh. India country report. *In* D. Shackleton, ed. IUCN Caprinae Action Plan. Int. Union Conserv. Nature Nat. Resour., Gland, Switzerland. (in press).

Fox, J.L., and C. Nurbu. 1990. Hemis, a national park for snow leopard in India's Trans-Himalaya. Int. Ped. Book Snow Leopards **6**: 71-84.

Fox, J.L., C. Nurbu, and R.S. Chundawat. 1991a. The mountain ungulates of Ladakh, India. Biol. Conserv. **58**: 167-190.

Fox, J.L., C. Nurbu, S. Bhatt, and A. Chandola. 1994. Wildlife conservation and land use changes in the Transhimalayan region of Ladakh, India. Mount. Res. Devel. **14**: 39-60.

Fox, J.L., S.P. Sinha, R.S. Chundawat, and P.K. Das. 1991b. Status of the snow leopard, *Panthera uncia*, in northwest India. Biol. Conserv. **55**: 283-298.

Fox, M.W. 1980. The soul of the wolf. Little, Brown, Boston, Mass. 131 pp.

Frame, L.H., and G.W. Frame. 1976. Female African wild dogs emigrate. Nature (London, U.K.) **263**: 227-229.

Frame, L.H., J.R. Malcolm, G.W. Frame, and H. van Lawick. 1979. Social organization of the African wild dogs (*Lycaon pictus*) on the Serengeti Plains, Tanzania. Z. Tierpsychol. **50**: 225-249.

Frank, D.A. 1990. Interactive ecology of plants, large mammalian herbivores, and drought in Yellowstone National Park. Ph.D. Thesis, Syracuse Univ., N.Y. 126 pp.

Frank, D.W., K.T. Kirton, T.E. Murchison, W.J. Quinlan, T.J. Coleman, E.S. Gilbertson, E.S. Feenstra, and F.A. Kimbell. 1979. Mammary tumors and serum hormones in the bitch treated with medroxyprogesterone acetate or progesterone for four years. Fertil. Steril. **31**: 340-346.

Franz, D.N. 1975. Central nervous system stimulants. pp. 359-366 *in* L.S. Goodman and Gilman (eds). The pharmacological basis of therapeutics. 5th ed., Macmillan, New York, N.Y.

Franzmann, A.W., and P.D. Arneson. 1976. Marrow fat in Alaskan moose femurs in relation to mortality factors. J. Wildl. Manage. **40**: 336-339.

Franzmann, A.W., and C.C. Schwartz. 1986. Black bear predation on moose calves in highly productive versus marginal moose habitats on the Kenai Peninsula, Alaska. Alces **22**: 139-154.

Franzmann, A.W., R.E. LeResche, R.A. Rausch, and J.L. Oldemeyer. 1978. Alaskan moose measurements and weights and measurement-weight relationships. Can. J. Zool. **56**: 298-306.

Freddy, D.J. 1987. The White River elk herd: a perspective, 1960-1985. Colorado Div. Wildl. Tech. Publ. No. 37. 64 pp.

Freeman, C., and D.S. Coffey. 1973. Sterility in male animals induced by injection of chemical agents into the vas deferens. Fertil. Steril. **24**: 884-890.

Freeman, R.C. 1976. Coyote x dog hybridization and red wolf influence in the wild *Canis* of Oklahoma. M.A. Thesis, Northeastern Oklahoma State Univ., Tahlequah, Okla. 62 pp.

Freeman, R.S., A. Adorjan, and D.H. Pimlott. 1961. Cestodes of wolves, coyotes, and coyote-dog hybrids in Ontario. Can. J. Zool. **39**: 527-532.

Freemuth, J. 1992. Idaho public survey No. 3. Survey Research Center, College of Social Sciences and Public Affairs, Boise State Univ., Boise, Id. 3 pp.

Friis, L.K. 1985. An investigation of subspecific relationships of the grey wolf, *Canis lupus*, in British Columbia. M.Sc. Thesis, Univ. Victoria, B.C. 162 pp.

Frijlink, J.H. 1977. Patterns of wolf pack movements prior to kills as read from tracks in Algonquin Provincial Park, Ontario, Canada. Bijfragen Tot De Dierkunde **47**: 131-137.

Fritts, S.H. 1982. Wolf depredation on livestock in Minnesota. U.S. Fish and Wildl. Serv. Resour. Publ. No. 145. 11 pp.

Fritts, S.H. 1983. Record dispersal by a wolf from Minnesota. J. Mammal. **64**: 166-167.

Fritts, S.H. 1990. Management of wolves inside and outside Yellowstone National Park and possibilities for wolf management zones in the Greater Yellowstone area. pp. 1-5 to 1-58 *in* Yellowstone National Park, U.S. Fish and Wildlife Service, University of Wyoming, University of Idaho, Interagency Grizzly Bear Study Team, and the University of Minnesota Cooperative Park Studies Unit, eds. Wolves for Yellowstone? A report to Congress. Vol. II. Research and analysis. U.S. Natl. Park Serv., Yellowstone National Park, Mammoth, Wyo.

Fritts, S.H. 1991. Wolves and wolf recovery efforts in the northwestern United States. West. Wildlands **17**: 2-6.

Fritts, S.H. 1993a. Controlling wolves in the Greater Yellowstone area. pp. 173-233 *in* R.S. Cook, ed. Ecological issues on reintroducing wolves into Yellowstone National Park. U.S. Natl. Park Serv. Sci. Monogr. NPS/NRYELL/NRSM-93/22.

Fritts, S.H. 1993b. Reintroductions and translocations of wolves in North America. pp. 1-27 *in* R.S. Cook, ed. Ecological issues on reintroducing wolves into Yellowstone National Park. U.S. Natl. Park Serv. Sci. Monogr. NPS/NRYELL/NRSM-93/22.

Fritts, S.H., and L.D. Mech. 1981. Dynamics, movements, and feeding ecology of a newly protected wolf population in northwestern Minnesota. Wildl. Monogr. **80**: 79 pp.

Fritts, S.H., and W.J. Paul. 1989. Interactions of wolves and dogs in Minnesota. Wildl. Soc. Bull. **17**: 121-123.

Fritts, S.H., E.E. Bangs, and J.F. Gore. 1994. The relationship of wolf recovery to habitat conservation and biodiversity in the northwestern United States. Landsc. Urb. Plann. **28**: 23-32.

Fritts, S.H., W.J. Paul, and L.D. Mech. 1984. Movements of translocated wolves in Minnesota. J. Wildl. Manage. **48**: 709-721.

Fritts, S.H., W.J. Paul, and L.D. Mech. 1985. Can relocated wolves survive? Wildl. Soc. Bull. **13**: 459-463.

Fritts, S.H., W.J. Paul, L.D. Mech, and D.P. Scott. 1992. Trends and management of wolf-livestock conflicts in Minnesota. U.S. Fish and Wildl. Serv. Resour. Publ. No. 181. 27 pp.

Froberg, S.O., L.A. Carlson, and L.G. Ekelund. 1971. Local lipid stores and exercise. Adv. Exp. Med. Biol. **11**: 307-313.

Fry, D.P. 1987. Differences between playfighting and serious fighting among Zapotec children. Ethol. Sociobiol. **8**: 285-306.

Fuller, J.L., and E.M. DuBuis. 1962. The behaviour of dogs. pp. 415-452 *in* E.S. Hafez, ed. The behaviour of domestic animals. Bailliere, Tindall and Cox, London, U.K.

Fuller, T.K. 1989. Population dynamics of wolves in north-central Minnesota. Wildl. Monogr. **105**: 41 pp.

Fuller, T.K. 1990. Dynamics of a declining white-tailed deer population in north-central Minnesota. Wildl. Monogr. **110**: 37 pp.

Fuller, T.K., and P.W. Kat. 1990. Movements, activity, and prey relationships of African wild dogs (*Lycaon pictus*) near Aitong, southwestern Kenya. Afr. J. Ecol. **28**: 330-350.

Fuller, T.K., and L.B. Keith. 1980. Wolf population dynamics and prey relationships in northeastern Alberta. J. Wildl. Manage. **44**: 583-602.

Fuller, T.K., and L.B. Keith. 1981a. Non-overlapping ranges of coyotes and wolves in northeastern Alberta. J. Mammal. **62**: 403-405.

Fuller, T.K., and L.B. Keith. 1981b. Woodland caribou population dynamics in northeastern Alberta. J. Wildl. Manage. **45**: 197-213.

Fuller, T.K., and D.W. Kuehn. 1983. Immobilization of wolves using ketamine in combination with xylazine or promazine. J. Wildl. Dis. **19**: 69-72.

Fuller, T.K., and B.A. Sampson. 1988. Evaluation of a simulated howling survey for wolves. J. Wildl. Manage. **53**: 60-63.

Fuller, T.K., and W.J. Snow. 1988. Estimating wolf densities from radiotelemetry data. Wildl. Soc. Bull. **16**: 367-370.

Fuller, T.K., W.E. Berg, G.L. Radde, M.S. Lenarz, and G.B. Joselyn. 1992a. A history and current estimate of wolf distribution and numbers in Minnesota. Wildl. Soc. Bull. **20**: 42-55.

Fuller, T.K., P.W. Kat, J.B. Bulger, A.H. Maddock, J.R. Ginsberg, R. Burrows, J.W. McNutt, and M.G.L. Mills. 1992b. Population dynamics of African wild dogs. pp. 1125-1139 *in* D.R. McCullough and R.H. Barrett, eds. Wildlife 2001: populations. Elsevier Appl. Sci., New York, N.Y.

Fuller, T.K., M.G.L. Mills, M. Borner, M.K. Laurenson, and P.W. Kat. 1992c. Long distance dispersal by African wild dogs in East and South Africa. J. Afr. Zool. **106**: 535-537.

Fuller, W.A., and N.S. Novakowski. 1955. Wolf control operations, Wood Buffalo National Park, 1951-52. Can. Wildl. Serv. Wildl. Manage. Bull. Ser. 1, No. 11. 23 pp.

Fumagalli, V. 1992. L'uomo e l'ambiente nel Medioevo. Ed. Laterza, Roma. 118 pp.

Fur Institute of Canada. 1991. Annual report of the Fur Institute of Canada. 10 Lower Spadina Ave., Toronto, Ont.

G

Galloway, P. 1991. The archaeology of ethnohistorical narrative. pp. 453-469 *in* D.H. Thomas, ed. Columbian consequences. Vol. 3. The Spanish borderlands in Pan-American perspective. Smithson. Inst. Press, Washington, D.C.

Ganhar, J. 1979. The wildlife of Ladakh. Haramukh Publications, Srinagar, India. 91 pp.

Garceau, P. 1960. Reproduction, growth and mortality of wolves. Alaska Dep. Fish Game Annu. Rep. Prog., Invest. Proj., Vol. 1: 458-483.

Garceau, P. 1961. Wolf management investigations. Alaska Dep. Fish and Game, 1960-61 Pittman-Robertson Proj. Rep., Vol. 2(10). 30 pp.

Garceau, P. 1962. Wolf predation on Sitka black-tailed deer. Alaska Dep. Fish and Game Fed. Aid in Wildl. Restoration. Rep. W-6-R-3, K-1: 3-16.

Gardner, C.L., and E.F. Becker. 1991. Wolf and wolverine density estimation techniques. Alaska Dep. Fish and Game Fed. Aid in Wildl. Restoration Prog. Rep., Proj. W-23-3, Study 7.15. 8 pp.

Garshelis, D.L., H.B. Quigley, C.R. Villarrubia, and M.R. Pelton. 1982. Assessment of telemetric motion sensors for studies of activity. Can. J. Zool. **60**: 1800-1805.

Garton, E.O., R.L. Crabtree, B.B. Ackerman, and G. Wright. 1990. The potential impact of a reintroduced wolf population on the northern Yellowstone elk herd. pp. 3-59 to 3-91 *in* Yellowstone National Park, U.S. Fish and Wildlife Service, University of Wyoming, University of Idaho, Interagency Grizzly Bear Study Team, and the University of Minnesota Cooperative Park Studies Unit, eds. Wolves for Yellowstone? A report to the United States Congress. Vol. II. Research and analysis. U.S. Natl. Park Serv., Yellowstone National Park, Mammoth, Wyo.

Garton, E.O., R.L. Crabtree, B.B. Ackerman, and G. Wright. 1992. Potential impacts of Yellowstone wolves on Clarks Fork elk herd. pp. 4-131 to 4-146 *in* J.D. Varley and W.G. Brewster, eds. Wolves for Yellowstone? A report to the United States Congress. Vol. IV. Research and analysis. U.S. Natl. Park Serv., Yellowstone National Park, Mammoth, Wyo.

Gasaway, W.C., S.D. Dubois, D.J. Reed, and S.J. Harbo. 1986. Estimating moose population parameters from aerial surveys. Univ. Alaska Biol. Pap. No. 22: 108 pp.

Gasaway, W.C., S.D. Dubois, R.D. Boertje, D.J. Reed, and D.T. Simpson. 1989. Response of radio-collared moose to a large burn in central Alaska. Can. J. Zool. **67**: 325-329.

Gasaway, W.C., R.O. Stephenson, J.L. Davis, P.E.K. Shepherd, and O.E. Burris. 1983. Interrelationships of wolves, prey, and man in interior Alaska. Wildl. Monogr. **84**: 50 pp.

Gasaway, W.C., R.D. Boertje, D.V. Grangaard, D.G. Kelleyhouse, R.O. Stephenson, and D.G. Larsen. 1992. The role of predation in limiting moose at low densities in Alaska and Yukon and implications for conservation. Wildl. Monogr. **120**: 59 pp.

Gasaway, W.C., R.D. Boertje, D.J. Reed, J.L. Davis, D.F. Holleman, R.O. Stephenson, and W.B. Ballard. 1990. Testing socially acceptable methods of managing predators: reducing wolf predation on moose through increased caribou abundance. Alaska Dep. Fish and Game Fed. Aid in Wildl. Restoration Prog. Rep., Proj. W-23-3. 8 pp.

Gates, C.C., J.Z. Adamczewski, and R. Mulders. 1986. Population dynamics, winter ecology, and social organization of Coats Island caribou. Arctic **39**: 216-222.

Gates, N.L., J.E. Rich, D.D. Godtel, and C.V. Hulet. 1978. Development and evaluation of anti-coyote fencing. J. Range Manage. **31**: 151-153.

Gauthier, D.A., and J.B. Theberge. 1986. Wolf predation in the Burwash caribou herd, southwest Yukon. Proc. Int. Reindeer/Caribou Symp. **4**: 137-144.

Geikie, A. 1882. Geological sketches at home and abroad. Macmillan, London, U.K. 382 pp.

Geist, V. 1974. On the relationship of social evolution and ecology in ungulates. Am. Zool. **14**: 205-220.

Geist, V. 1991. Phantom subspecies: the wood bison *Bison bison "athabascae"* Rhoads 1897 is not a valid taxon, but an ecotype. Arctic **44**: 283-300.

Gentile, J.R. 1987. The evolution of antitrapping sentiment in the United States: a review and commentary. Wildl. Soc. Bull. **15**: 490-503.

Gerstell, R. 1985. The steel trap in North America. Stackpole Books, Harrisburg, Pa. 352 pp.

Gese, E.M., and L.D. Mech. 1991. Dispersal of wolves (*Canis lupus*) in northeastern Minnesota, 1969-1989. Can. J. Zool. **69**: 2946-2955.

Gese, E.M., O.J. Rongstad, and W.R. Mytton. 1989. Population dynamics of coyotes in southeastern Colorado. J. Wildl. Manage. **53**: 174-181.

Gibbon, J. 1874. The wonders of Yellowstone. J. Am. Geol. Soc. N.Y. **5**: 112-137.

Gier, H.T. 1975. Ecology and behavior of the coyote (*Canis latrans*). pp. 247-262 *in* M.W. Fox, ed. The wild canids: their systematics, behavioral ecology, and evolution. Van Nostrand Reinhold, New York, N.Y.

Gilbert, F.F. 1991. Trapping — an animal rights issue or a legitimate wildlife management technique — The move to international standards. Trans. North Am. Wildl. Nat. Resour. Conf. 56: 400-408.

Giles, R.C., R.P. Kwapien, R.G. Geil, and H.W. Casey. 1978. Mammary nodules in beagle dogs administered investigational oral contraceptive steroids. J. Not. Cancer Inst. **60**: 1351-1364.

Gill, D.E. 1974. Intrinsic rate of increase, saturation density, and competitive ability. II. The evolution of competitive ability. Am. Nat. **108**: 103-116.

Gillespie, J.H., and L.E. Carmichael. 1968. Distemper and infectious hepatitis. pp. 11-130 *in* E.J. Catcott, ed. Canine medicine. Am. Vet. Publ., Wheaton, Ill.

Gillette, W.C. 1870. Personal diary of 1870 expedition to Yellowstone Park area. Unpubl. Rep. on file, Yellowstone National Park Library, Mammoth, Wyo. 18 pp.

Gillingham, M.P., and F.L. Bunnell. 1985. Reliability of motion-sensitive radio collars for estimating activity of black-tailed deer. J. Wildl. Manage. **49**: 951-958.

Ginsberg, J.R., and D.W. Macdonald. 1990. Foxes, wolves, jackals, and dogs: an action plan for the conservation of canids. Int. Union Conserv. Nat. Natural Resour., Gland, Switzerland. 116 pp.

Gipson, P.S. 1974. Food habits of coyotes in Arkansas. J. Wildl. Manage. **38**: 848-853.

Gipson, P.S. 1978. Coyotes and related *Canis* in the southeastern United States with a comment on Mexican and Central American *Canis*. pp. 191-208 *in* M. Bekoff, ed. Coyotes: biology, behavior, and management. Academic Press, New York, N.Y.

Gipson, P.S., J.A. Sealander, and J.E. Dunn. 1974. The taxonomic status of wild *Canis* in Arkansas. Syst. Zool. **23**: 1-11.

Girman, D.J., P.W. Kat, M.G.L. Mills, J. Ginsberg, J. Fanshawe, C. Fitzgibbon, M. Borner, V. Wilson, K. Laurenson, and R.K. Wayne. 1993. Molecular genetic and morphologic analyses of the African wild dog (*Lycaon pictus*). J. Hered. **84**: 450-459.

Gittleman, J.L. 1985. Carnivore body size: ecological and taxonomical correlates. Oecologia (Berlin) **67**: 540-554.

Gittleman, J.L. 1986. Carnivore life history patterns: allometric, phylogenetic, and ecological associations. Am. Nat. **127**: 744-771.

Gittleman, J.L., and S.L. Pimm. 1991. Crying wolf in North America. Nature (Lond.) **351**: 524-525.

Glick, D., M. Carr, and B. Harting. 1991. An environmental profile of the Greater Yellowstone ecosystem. Greater Yellowstone Coalition, Bozeman, Mont. 132 pp.

Glover, R. (ed.) 1962. David Thompson's narrative of his explorations in western America, 1784-1812. The Champlain Soc., Toronto, Ont. 410 pp.

Goble, D.D. 1992. Of wolves and welfare ranching. Harvard Environ. Law Rev. **16**: 101-127.

Goldman, E.A. 1937. The wolves of North America. J. Mammal. **18**: 37-45.

Goldman, E.A. 1941. Three new wolves from North America. Proc. Biol. Soc. Wash. **54**: 109-114.

Goldman, E.A. 1944. The wolves of North America. Part 2. Classification of wolves. pp. 389-636 *in* S.P. Young and E.A. Goldman, eds. The wolves of North America. Dover, New York/American Wildl. Inst., Washington, D.C.

Gomez-Pompa, A., and A. Kaus. 1992. Taming the wilderness myth. BioScience **42**: 271-279.

Gonzalez, A., A.F. Allen, K. Post, R.J. Mapletoft, and B.D. Murphy. 1989. Immunological approaches to contraception in dogs. J. Reprod. Fertil. **39** (Suppl.): 189-198.

Goodwin, E.A., and W.B. Ballard. 1985. Use of tooth cementum for age determination of gray wolves. J. Wildl. Manage. **49**: 313-316.

Goodyear, N.C. 1991. Taxonomic status of the silver rice rat, *Oryzomys argentatus*. J. Mammal. **72**: 723-730.

Gourley, J. 1929. Expedition into the Yellowstone country 1870, or, A reminiscence of James A. Gourley. Yellowstone National Park Research Library, Mammoth, Wyo. 4 pp. (typescript).

Goyal, S.M., L.D. Mech, R.A. Rademacher, M.A. Khan, and U.S. Seal. 1986. Antibodies against canine parvovirus in wolves of Minnesota: a serologic study from 1975 through 1985. J. Am. Vet. Med. Assoc. **189**: 1092-1094.

Goyings, L.S., J.H. Sokolowski, R.G. Zimbelman, and S. Geng. 1977. Clinical, morphological, and clinico-pathologic findings in beagles treated for two years with melengestrol acetate. Am. J. Vet. Res. **38**: 1923-1931.

Grace, E.S. 1976. Interactions between men and wolves at an arctic outpost on Ellesmere Island. Can. Field-Nat. **90**: 149-156.

Grande del Brio, R. 1984. El lobo iberico, biologia y mitologia. Hermann Blume, Madrid. 175 pp.

Grant, W.E. 1986. Systems analysis and simulation in wildlife and fisheries science. John Wiley and Sons, New York, N.Y. 338 pp.

Graves, H.S., and E.W. Nelson. 1919. Our national elk herds: a program for conserving the elk on national forests about the Yellowstone National Park. U.S. Dep. Agric. Circ. No. 51. 34 pp.

Green, H.U. 1951. The wolves of Banff National Park. Can. Dep. Resour. and Devel., Natl. Parks Br., Ottawa, Ont. 47 pp.

Green, J.S. 1987. Biological control, field-lure tests and sheep/cattle bonding. pp. 76-85 *in* J.S. Green, ed. Protecting livestock from coyotes. U.S. Sheep Exp. Stn., Univ. Idaho, Dubois.

Green, J.S., and R.A. Woodruff. 1980. Is predator control going to the dogs? Rangelands **2**: 187-189.

Green, J.S., and R.A. Woodruff. 1984. The use of three breeds of dog to protect rangeland sheep from predators. Appl. Anim. Ethol. **11**: 141-161.

Green, J.S., and R.A. Woodruff. 1990a. ADC guarding dog program update: a focus on managing dogs. Proc. Vertebr. Pest Conf. **14**: 233-236.

Green, J.S., and R.A. Woodruff. 1990b. Livestock guarding dogs: protecting sheep from predators. U.S. Dep. Agric. Info. Bull. 588. 31 pp.

Grimm, R.L. 1939. Northern Yellowstone winter range studies. J. Wildl. Manage. **3**: 295-306.

Grinnell, G.B. 1876. Zoological report. pp. 68-89 *in* W. Ludlow, ed. Report of a reconnaissance from Carroll, Montana Territory on the Upper Missouri to the Yellowstone National Park and return, made in the summer of 1875. U.S. Gov. Print. Off., Washington, D.C.

Gross, A.M. 1975. Is cost-benefit analysis beneficial? Is cost-effectiveness analysis effective? Levinson Policy Institute, 46 pp.

Grue, H., and B. Jensen. 1979. Review of the formation of incremental lines in tooth cementum of terrestrial mammals. Dan. Rev. Game Biol. **11**: 48 pp.

Gruell, G.E. 1973. An ecological evaluation of Big Game Ridge. U.S. Dep. Agric. For. Serv., Intermountain Region, Ogden, UT. 62 pp.

Gunn, A., C. Shank, and B. McLean. 1991. The history, status and management of muskoxen on Banks Island. Arctic **44**: 188-195.

Gunn, S.A., and T.C. Gould. 1977. Cadmium and other mineral elements. pp. 377-474 *in* A.D. Johnson, W.R. Gomes, and N.L. Vandemark, eds. The testis. Vol. III. Influencing factors. Academic Press, New York, N.Y.

Gunnison, J.W. 1852. The Mormons, or, Latter-Day Saints. Lippincott, Grambo, Philadelphia, Pa. 168 pp.

Gunson, J.R. 1983a. Status and management of wolves in Alberta. pp. 25-29 *in* L.N. Carbyn, ed. Wolves in Canada and Alaska: their status, biology, and management. Can. Wildl. Serv. Rep. Ser., No. 45.

Gunson, J.R. 1983b. Wolf predation of livestock in western Canada. pp. 102-105 *in* L.N. Carbyn, ed. Wolves in Canada and Alaska: their status, biology, and management. Can. Wildl. Serv. Rep. Ser., No. 45.

Gunson, J.R. 1986. Wolves and elk in Alberta's Brazeau country. Bugle **4**: 29-33.

Gunson, J.R. 1992. Historical and present management of wolves in Alberta. Wildl. Soc. Bull. **20**: 330-339.

Gunson, J.R., and R.M. Nowak. 1979. Largest gray wolf skulls found in Alberta. Can. Field-Nat. **93**: 308-309.

Gustavson, C.R. 1979. An experimental evaluation of aversive conditioning for controlling coyote predation: a critique. J. Wildl. Manage. **43**: 208-209.

Gustavson, C.R. 1982. An evaluation of taste aversion control of wolf (*Canis lupus*) predation in northern Minnesota. Appl. Anim. Ethol. **9**: 63-71.

Gustavson, C.R., and L.K. Nicolaus. 1987. Taste aversion conditioning in wolves, coyotes and other canids: retrospect and prospect. pp. 169-200 *in* H. Frank, ed. Man and wolf: advances, issues, and problems in captive wolf research. Dr. W. Junk, Dordrecht, The Netherlands.

Gustavson, C.R., J.R. Jowsey, and D.N. Milligan. 1982. A 3-year evaluation of taste aversion coyote control in Saskatchewan. J. Range Manage. **35**: 57-59.

Gustavson, C.R., J. Garcia, W.G. Hankins, and K.W. Rusiniak. 1974. Coyote predation control by aversive conditioning. Science (Washington, D.C.) **184**: 581-583.

Gustavson, C.R., D.J. Kelly, M. Sweeney, and J. Garcia. 1976. Prey-lithium aversions. I. Coyotes and wolves. Behav. Biol. **17**: 61-72.

Guthery, F.S., and B.L. Beasom. 1978. Effectiveness and selectivity of neck snares in predator control. J. Wildl. Manage. **42**: 457-459.

H

Habeck, J.R. 1970. The vegetation of Glacier National Park. U.S. National Park Service and the Univ. Montana, Missoula. 123 pp.

Haber, G.C. 1977. Socio-ecological dynamics of wolves and prey in a subarctic ecosystem. Ph.D. Thesis, Univ. British Columbia, Vancouver, B.C. 786 pp.

Haber, G.C. 1988. Wildlife management in northern British Columbia: Kechika-Muskwa wolf control and related issues. Wolf Haven America, Tenino, Wash. 194 pp.

Haber, G.C., and C.J. Walters. 1980. Dynamics of the Alaska-Yukon caribou herds and management implications. Proc. Int. Reindeer/Caribou Symp. **2**: 645-663.

Hadly, E. 1990. Late Holocene mammalian fauna of Lamar Cave and its implications for ecosystem dynamics in Yellowstone National Park, Wyoming. M.S. Thesis, Northern Arizona Univ., Flagstaff. 128 pp.

Hainard, R. 1961. Les mammiferes sauvages d'Europe. I. Delachaux et Niestle, Neuchatel, Switzerland. 350 pp.

Haines, A.L. (ed.) 1965. The valley of the Upper Yellowstone; an exploration of the headwaters of the Yellowstone River in the year 1869. Univ. Oklahoma Press, Norman. 79 pp.

Haines, A.L. (ed.) 1977. The Yellowstone storya history of our first national park. Vol. 1. Yellowstone Library and Museum Association and Colorado Associated Univ. Press, Yellowstone National Park, Mammoth, Wyo. 385 pp.

Hairston, N.G., F.E. Smith, and L.B. Slobodkin. 1960. Community structure, population control, and competition. Am. Nat. **94**: 421-425.

Hall, A.H., and B.H. Rumack. 1990. Cyanide. pp. 1103-1111 in L.M. Haddad and J.F. Winchester, eds. Clinical management of poisoning and drug overdose. 2nd ed. W.B. Saunders, Philadelphia, Pa.

Hall, E.R. 1932. Remarks on the affinities of the mammalian fauna of Vancouver Island, British Columbia, with descriptions of a new subspecies. Univ. California Publ. Zool. 38: 415-423.

Hall, E.R. 1981. The mammals of North America. 2nd ed. 2 vols. John Wiley and Sons, New York, N.Y. 1181 pp.

Hall, E.R., and K.R. Kelson. 1952. Comments on the taxonomy and geographic distribution of some North American marsupials, insectivores, and carnivores. Univ. Kansas Publ. Mus. Nat. Hist. 5: 319-341.

Hall, E.R., and K.R. Kelson. 1959. The mammals of North America. Vol. 2. The Ronald Press, New York, N.Y. 536 pp.

Hammill, J. 1992. Wolf reproduction confirmed on mainland Michigan! Int. Wolf **2**(1): 14-15.

Hampton, H.D. 1971. How the U.S. Cavalry saved our national parks. Indiana Univ. Press, Bloomington. 246 pp.

Hanley, N.D. 1989. Valuing non-market goods using contingent valuation. J. Econ. Surv. **3**: 235-252.

Hansel, W., P.W. Concannon, and K. McEntee. 1977. Plasma hormone profiles and pathological observations in medroxyprogesterone acetate-treated beagle bitches. pp. 145-161 in S. Garattini and H.W. Berendes, eds. Pharmacology of steroid contraceptive drugs. Raven Press, New York, N.Y.

Hansen, J. 1986. Wolves of northern Idaho and northeastern Washington. Unpubl. Rep., Montana Coop. Wildl. Res. Unit, Missoula. 88 pp.

Harbo, S.J., and F.C. Dean, Jr. 1983. Historical and current perspectives on wolf management in Alaska. pp. 51-64 in L.N. Carbyn, ed. Wolves in Canada and Alaska: their status, biology, and management. Can. Wildl. Serv. Rep. Ser., No. 45.

Hardin, G. 1983. Sentiment, guilt and reason in the management of wild herds. Co-evol. Q. 1983 (Winter): 22-28.

Hardin, G. 1977. The tragedy of the commons. pp. 16-30 in G. Hardin and J. Baden, eds. Managing the commons. W.H. Freeman, San Francisco, Calif.

Hardin, G., and J. Baden. (eds.) 1977. Managing the commons. W.H. Freeman, San Francisco, Calif. 294 pp.

Harding, A.R. 1978. Wolf and coyote trapping. A.R. Harding, Columbus, Oh. 252 pp.

Harmer, S.F., and A.E. Shipley. (eds.) 1902. The Cambridge natural history: Mammalia (F.E. Beddard). Macmillan, London, U.K. 805 pp.

Harper, F. 1942. The name of the Florida wolf. J. Mammal. **23**: 339.

Harper, J. 1970. Wolf management in Alaska. pp. 24-27 in S.E. Jorgensen, C.E. Faulkner, and L.D. Mech, eds. Proceedings of a symposium on wolf management in selected areas of North America. U.S. Fish and Wildl. Serv. Bur. Sport Fish. and Wildl., Region 3, Twin Cities, Minn.

Harper, J.R. (ed.) 1971. Paul Kane's frontier, including wanderings of an artist among the Indians of North America. Univ. Texas Press, Austin. 350 pp.

Harrington, F.H., and L.D. Mech. 1978. Howling at two Minnesota wolf pack summer homesites. Can. J. Zool. **56**: 2024-2028.

Harrington, F.H., and L.D. Mech. 1979. Wolf howling and its role in territory maintenance. Behaviour **68**: 207-249.

Harrington, F.H., and L.D. Mech. 1982a. Patterns of homesite attendance in two Minnesota wolf packs. pp. 81-105 in F.H. Harrington and P.C. Paquet, eds. Wolves of the world: perspectives of behavior, ecology, and conservation. Noyes, Park Ridge, N.J.

Harrington, F.H., and L.D. Mech. 1982b. An analysis of howling response parameters useful for wolf pack censusing. J. Wildl. Manage. **46**: 686-693.

Harrington, F.H., and P.C. Paquet. (eds.) 1982. Wolves of the world: perspectives of behavior, ecology, and conservation. Noyes, Park Ridge, N.J. 474 pp.

Harrington, F.H., L.D. Mech, and S.H. Fritts. 1983. Pack size and wolf pup survival: their relationship under varying ecological conditions. Behav. Ecol. Sociobiol. **13**: 19-26.

Harrington, F.H., P.C. Paquet, J. Ryon, and J.C. Fentress. 1982. Monogamy in wolves: a review of the evidence. pp. 209-222 *in* F.H. Harrington and P.C. Paquet, eds. Wolves of the world: perspectives of behavior, ecology, and conservation. Noyes, Park Ridge, N.J.

Harris, M. 1887. Annual report to the superintendent, Yellowstone National Park. U.S. Gov. Print. Off., Washington, D.C. 28 pp.

Harris, R.B., S.G. Fancy, D.C. Douglas, G.W. Garner, T.R. McCabe, and L.F. Pank. 1990. Tracking wildlife by satellite: current systems and performance. U.S. Fish and Wildl. Serv. Tech. Rep. No. 30. 52 pp.

Harris, S. 1981. An estimation of the number of foxes in the city of Bristol, and some possible factors affecting their distribution. J. Appl. Ecol. **18**: 455-465.

Harrison, D.J. 1986. Coyote dispersal, mortality, and spatial relationships with red foxes in Maine. Ph.D. Thesis, Univ. Maine, Orono. 142 pp.

Harrison, D.J., J.A. Bissonette, and J.A. Sherburne. 1989. Spatial relationships between coyotes and red foxes in eastern Maine. J. Wildl. Manage. **53**: 181-185.

Harrison, D.L. 1968. The mammals of Arabia. Vol. 2. Ernest Benn, Ltd., London, U.K. 381 pp.

Hartley, J. 1938. Pathology of *Dirofilaria* infestation. Zoologica (New York, N.Y.) **23**: 235-251.

Hartmann, H. 1983. Pflanzengesellschaften entlang du Kashmirroute in Ladakh. Johrbuch Vereinzum Schutz der Bergwelt 1983: 131-173.

Hartmann, H. 1990. Pflanzengesellschaften aus der alpinen Stuge des westlichen, Sudlichen und Ostlichen Ladakh mit besonderer Berucksichtigung der rasenbildenden Gesellschaften. Candolla **45**: 525-574.

Hastings, A. 1984. Age-dependent predation is not a simple process. II. Wolves, ungulates, and a discrete time model for predation on juveniles with a stabilizing tail. Theor. Popul. Biol. **26**: 271-282.

Hatler, D.F. 1981. An analysis of livestock predation and predator control effectiveness in northwest British Columbia. Report prepared for the Minister of the Environment, Fish and Wildlife Branch, Victoria, B.C. 98 pp.

Hatter, I.W. 1984. Effects of wolf predation on recruitment of black-tailed deer on northeastern Vancouver Island. M.S. Thesis, Univ. Idaho, Moscow. 156 pp.

Hatter, I.W. 1988. Effects of wolf predation on recruitment of black-tailed deer on northeastern Vancouver Island. British Columbia Min. Environ. Wildl. Rep. R-23. 82 pp.

Hawkes, D., and J.F. O'Connell. 1981. Affluent hunters? Some comments in light of the Alyawara case. Am. Anthropol. **83**: 622-626.

Haugen, H.S. 1987. Den-site behavior, summer diet, and skull injuries of wolves in Alaska. M.S. Thesis, Univ. Alaska, Fairbanks. 205 pp.

Hay, M.J., and K.E. McConnell. 1979. An analysis of participation in nonconsumptive wildlife recreation. Land Econ. **55**: 460-471.

Hayden, F.V. 1872. Preliminary report of the United States geological survey of Montana and portions of adjacent territories; being a fifth annual report of progress. House Exec. Doc. 326, 42nd Congress, 2nd Session.

Hayes, R.D., A. Baer, and D.L. Larsen. 1991. Population dynamics and prey relationships of an exploited and recovering wolf population in the southern Yukon. Yukon Fish and Wildl. Br. Final Rep. TR-91-1. Whitehorse. 67 pp.

Heard, D.C. 1983. Historical and present status of wolves in the Northwest Territories. pp. 44-47 *in* L.N. Carbyn, ed. Wolves in Canada and Alaska: their status, biology, and management. Can. Wildl. Serv. Rep. Ser., No. 45.

Heard, D.C., and T.M. Williams. 1992a. Distribution of wolf dens on migratory caribou ranges in the Northwest Territories, Canada. Can. J. Zool. **70**: 1504-1510.

Heard, D.C., and T.M. Williams. 1992b. Wolf den distribution on migratory barren-ground caribou ranges in the Northwest Territories. Proc. N. Am. Caribou Workshop **4**: 249-250. (abstract).

Hebert, D.M., J. Youds, R. Davies, H. Langin, D. Janz, and G.W. Smith. 1982. Preliminary investigations of the Vancouver Island wolf (*Canis lupus crassodon*) prey relationships. pp. 54-70 *in* F.H. Harrington and P.C. Paquet, eds. Wolves of the world: perspectives of behavior, ecology, and conservation. Noyes, Park Ridge, N.J.

Hechtel, J.L. 1991. Population dynamics of black bear populations, Fort Wainwright, Alaska. Final report to the U.S. Army, Nat. Resour. Rep. 91-2, Fairbanks, Alas. 62 pp.

Heffner, H. 1983. Hearing in large and small dogs: absolute thresholds and size of tympanic membrane. Behav. Neurosci. **97**: 310-318.

Heffner, H., and R.B. Masterton. 1980. Hearing in Glires: domestic rabbit, cotton rat, feral house mouse, and kangaroo rat. J. Acoust. Soc. Am. **68**: 1584-1599.

Heisey, D.M., and T.K. Fuller. 1985. Evaluation of survival and cause-specific mortality rates using telemetry data. J. Wildl. Manage. **49**: 668-674.

Hendee, J.C. 1974. A multiple satisfaction approach to game management. Wildl. Soc. Bull. **2**: 104-113.

Henderson, A.B. 1867. A narrative of a prospecting trip in the summer of 1867. pp. 38-47 *in* Unpubl. Rep. on file, Yellowstone National Park Research Library, Mammoth, Wyo.

Henderson, A.B. 1870. Narrative of a prospecting expedition to the East Fork and Clark's Fork of Yellowstone...1870. pp. 48-458 *in* Unpubl. Rep. on file, Yellowstone National Park Research Library, Mammoth, Wyo.

Henderson, A.B. 1894. Journal of the Yellowstone Expedition of 1866 under Captain Jeff Standifer...Also the diaries kept by Henderson during his prospecting journeys in the Snake, Wind River and Yellowstone Country during the years 1866-72. Ms. No. 452, Coe Collection, Beinecke Library, Yale Univ., New Haven, Conn. Typescript at Yellowstone National Park Library, Mammoth, Wyo. 68 pp.

Henning, H. 1920. Geruchsversuche am Hund. Z. Biol. **70**: 1-8.

Henry, V.G. 1991a. Great Smoky Mountains National Park: a red wolf reintroduction proposal. U.S. Fish and Wildl. Serv. Final Environ. Assess. 24 pp.

Henry, V.G. 1991b. Endangered and threatened wildlife and plants; determination of experimental population status for an introduced population of red wolves in North Carolina and Tennessee. Fed. Regist. 56: 56325-56334.

Henry, V.G. 1992. Finding on a petition to delist the red wolf (*Canis rufus*). Fed. Regist. 57: 1246-1250.

Henshaw, R.E. 1982. Can the wolf be returned to New York? pp. 395-422 *in* F.H. Harrington and P.C. Paquet, eds. Wolves of the world: perspectives of behavior, ecology, and conservation. Noyes, Park Ridge, N.J.

Henshaw, R.E., and R.O. Stephenson. 1974. Homing in the gray wolf (*Canis lupus*). J. Mammal. 55: 234-237.

Henshaw, R.E., R. Lockwood, R. Shideler, and R.O. Stephenson. 1979. Experimental release of captive wolves. pp. 319-345 *in* E. Klinghammer, ed. The behavior and ecology of wolves. Garland STPM Press, New York, N.Y.

Heptner, V.G., N.P. Naumov, P.B. Jurgenson, A.A. Sludski, A.F. Cirkova and A.G. Bannikov. 1974. Die Saugetiere der Sowjetunion. Bd. II. Gustav Fischer Verlag, Jena. 1006 pp.

Herscovici, A. 1985. Second nature. The animal rights controversy. CBC Enterprises, Can. Broadcasting Corp., Toronto, Ont. 254 pp.

Hickerson, H. 1965. The Virginia deer and intertribal buffer zones in the upper Mississippi Valley. pp. 43-65 *in* A. Leeds and A.P. Vayda, eds. Man, culture and animals: the role of animals in human ecological adjustments. American Assoc. for the Advancement of Science, Publ. No. 78, Washington, D.C.

Higgins, A.K. 1990. Breeding of the polar wolf in Greenland. Polar Rec. 26: 55-56.

Hill, B.L.C. 1984. Relationships between Newfoundland and Labrador residents' environmental/wildlife attitudes, demographic characteristics and experiences in wildlife related outdoor activity. M.Sc. Thesis, Memorial Univ. Newfoundland, St. John's. 125 pp.

Hill, E.L. 1979. The ecology of the timber wolf (*Canis lupus* Linn.) in southern Manitobawilderness, recreational and agricultural aspects. M.Sc. Thesis, Univ. Manitoba, Winnipeg. 147 pp.

Hillis, D.M., and C. Moritz. 1990. Molecular systematics. Sinauer Press, Sunderland, Mass. 588 pp.

Hilton, H.H. 1978. Systematics and ecology of the eastern coyote. pp. 209-228 *in* M. Bekoff, ed. Coyotes: biology, behavior, and management. Academic Press, New York, N.Y.

Hirasawa, T., S. Iwake, K. Watanabe, K. Mikazuki, S. Makino, and Y. Hayashi. 1987. Outbreak of canine parvovirus infection and its elimination in a closed beagle colony. J. Vet. Med. B **34**: 598-606.

Hoare, W.H.B. 1927. Report on investigations (affecting Eskimos and wildlife District of Mackenzie) 1925-1926 together with general recommendations. Dep. Inter., Northwest Territ. and Yukon Br., Ottawa, Ont. 44 pp.

Hofer, E. 1887. Winter in wonderland. For. Stream **28**(1): 222-223; (2): 246-247; (3): 270-271; (4): 294-295; (5): 318-319 editions of April 7, 14, 21, 28, and May 5.

Hoffman-Krayer, E. 1942. Handworterbuch des deutschen Aberglaubens. Bd. IX. W. de Gruyter, Berlin. 860 pp.

Hoffmeister, D.F. 1986. Mammals of Arizona. University of Arizona Press, Tucson. 602 pp.

Hoffos, R. 1983. Wolf management in British Columbia: the public controversy. M.Sc. Thesis, Simon Fraser Univ. 95 pp.

Hoffos, R. 1987. Wolf management in British Columbia: the public controversy. British Columbia Min. Environ. and Parks Wildl. Br. Bull. No. B-52. 75 pp.

Holand, O. 1992. Fat indices versus ingesta-free body fat in European roe deer. J. Wildl. Manage. 56: 241-245.

Hollander, M., and D.A. Wolfe. 1973. Nonparametric statistical methods. John Wiley and Sons, New York, N.Y.

Holleman, D.F., and R.O. Stephenson. 1981. Prey selection and consumption by Alaskan wolves in winter. J. Wildl. Manage. 45: 620-628.

Holleman, D.F., R.G. White, J.R. Luick, and R.O. Stephenson. 1980. Energy flow through the lichen-caribou-wolf food chain during winter in northern Alaska. Proc. Int. Reindeer/Caribou Symp. **2**: 202-206.

Holling, C.S. 1959a. Some characteristics of simple types of predation and parasitism. Can. Entomol. **91**: 385-398.

Holling, C.S. 1959b. The components of predation as revealed by a study of small-mammal predation of the European pine sawfly. Can. Entomol. **91**: 293-320.

Holling, C.S. 1965. The functional response of predators to prey density and its role in mimicry and population regulation. Mem. Entomol. Soc. Can. **45**: 60 pp.

Holmes, J.C., and R. Podesta. 1968. The helminths of wolves and coyotes from the forested regions of Alberta. Can. J. Zool. **46**: 1193-1204.

Holmes, R., B. O'Neill, R. Duncan, and K. Proescholdt. 1991. The debate about delisting the wolf in Minnesota. Point: counterpoint. Int. Wolf **1**(1): 9-13.

Holroyd, G.L., and K.J. Van Tighem. 1983. The ecological (biophysical) land classification of Banff and Jasper National Parks. Vol. 3. Part A. The wildlife inventory. Can. Wildl. Serv. for Parks Canada. 444 pp.

Hook, R.A., and W.L. Robinson. 1982. Attitudes of Michigan citizens toward predators. pp. 382-394 *in* F.H. Harrington and P.C. Paquet, eds. Wolves of the world: perspectives of behavior, ecology, and conservation. Noyes, Park Ridge, N.J.

Hornaday, W.T. 1906. Camp-fires in the Canadian Rockies. Charles Scribner's Sons, New York, N.Y. 353 pp.

Horr, H.R. 1873. Letter to Secretary of the Interior, November 14. File microcopies of records in the National Archives: No. 62, Roll 1records of the Office of the Secretary of the Interior relating to the Yellowstone National Park, 1872-1886 and 1872-1882 (letters received). Yellowstone National Park Research Library, Mammoth, Wyo.

Horr, H.R. 1874. Letter to the Secretary of the Interior, May 25. File microcopies of records in the National Archives: No. 62, Roll 1records of the Office of the Secretary of the Interior relating to the Yellowstone National Park, 1872-1886 and 1872-1882 (letters received). Yellowstone National Park Research Library, Mammoth, Wyo.

Hoskins, J.D. 1990. Veterinary pediatrics. W.B. Saunders Company, Philadelphia, Pa. 556 pp.

Hoskinson, R.L., and L.D. Mech. 1976. White-tailed deer migration and its role in wolf predation. J. Wildl. Manage. **40**: 429-441.

Houpt, K.A., P.P. Davis, and H.F. Hintz. 1982. Effect of peripheral anosmia on dogs trained as flavor validators. Am. J. Vet. Res. **43**: 841-843.

Houpt, K.A., H.F. Hintz, and P. Shepherd. 1978. The role of olfaction in canine food preferences. Chem. Senses Flav. **3**: 281-290.

Houston, D.B. 1968. The Shiras moose in Jackson Hole, Wyoming. U.S. Natl. Park Serv. Tech. Bull. No. 1. 110 pp.

Houston, D.B. 1982. The northern Yellowstone elk: ecology and management. Macmillan, New York, N.Y. 474 pp.

Hovell, F.D. DeB., E.R. Orskov, D.J. Kyle, and N.A. MacLeod. 1987. Undernutrition in sheep. Nitrogen repletion by N-depleted sheep. Br. J. Nutr. **57**: 77-88.

H.R. Exec. Doc. 241, 42nd Congress, 3rd Session. 1873. Letter from Montana citizens, December 9.

Hristovski, N., and M. Beliceska. 1982. Some species of arthropods in wild and domestic members of the family Canidae in the Bitola District, Macedonia, Yugoslavia. Wiad. Parazytol. **28**: 167-168.

Hubert, G.F. 1982. History of midwestern furbearer management and a look to the future. Proc. Midwest Fish and Wildl. Conf. **43**: 175-191.

Huggard, D.J. 1991. Prey selectivity of wolves in Banff National Park. M.Sc. Thesis, Univ. British Columbia, Vancouver. 119 pp.

Huggard, D.J. 1993. Prey selectivity of wolves in Banff National Park. II. Age, sex and condition of elk. Can. J. Zool. **71**: 140-147.

Hultkrantz, A. 1965. Type of religion in the arctic hunting cultures: a religion-ecological approach. Lulea, Stockholm, Sweden. 160 pp.

Hultman, E., and L.H. Nilsson. 1971. Liver glycogen in man, effect of different diets and muscular exercise. Adv. Exp. Med. Biol. **11**: 143-151.

Hummel, M. 1988. The IUCN/WWF perspective on wolf conservation. pp. 136-142 *in* D. Seip, S. Pettigrew, and R. Archibald, eds. Wolf-prey dynamics and management. British Columbia Min. Environ. Wildl. Working Rep. No. WR-40.

Hummel, M. 1990. A conservation strategy for large carnivores in Canada. World Wildlife Fund Report, Toronto, Ont. 98 pp.

Huot, J., and M. Beaulieu. 1985. Relationship between parasite infection levels and body fat reserves in George River caribou in spring and fall. Proc. North Am. Caribou Workshop **2**: 317-327.

Huot, J., and F. Goudreault. 1985. Evaluation of several indices for predicting total body fat of caribou. Proc. North Am. Caribou Workshop **2**: 157-175.

I

Ihsle, H.B. 1982. Population ecology of mule deer with emphasis on potential impacts of gas and oil development along the east slope of the Rocky Mountains, north-central Montana. M.S. Thesis, Montana State Univ., Bozeman. 85 pp.

Iljin, N.A. 1941. Wolf-dog genetics. J. Genet. **42**: 359-414.

Ims, R.A. 1990. The ecology and evolution of reproductive synchrony. Trends Ecol. Evol. **5**: 135-140.

International Union for Conservation of Nature and Natural Resources. 1983. Manifesto on wolf conservation. I.U.C.N. Bull. **5**(5): 2 pp.

Itamies, J. 1979. Deer-fly, *Lipoptena cervi*, on the wolf. Luonnon Tutkija **83**: 19.

IUCN Captive Breeding Specialist Group. 1991. Subspecies, populations, hybridization and conservation of threatened species. CBSG Working Group, Int. Union for the Conserv. of Nature. CBSG Working Group Meeting, Washington, D.C., 29-30 May 1991.

J

Jabara, A.G. 1962. Induction of canine ovarian tumors by diethylstilbestrol and progesterone. Austral. J. Exp. Biol. Med. Sci. **40**: 139-152.

Jackson, H.H.T. 1961. Mammals of Wisconsin. Univ. Wisconsin Press, Madison. 504 pp.

Jackson, R. 1991. A wildlife survey of the Qomolangma Nature Preserve, Tibet Autonomous Region, People's Republic of China. Trip Report. Woodlands Mountain Institute, Franklin, W.Va. 61 pp.

Jackson, W.H. 1875. pp. 1-48 *in* Descriptive catalogue of the photographs of the United States Geological Survey of the territories for the years 1869 to 1875, inclusive. U.S. Geol. Surv., Washington, D.C.

Jacobsen, W.C. 1945. The bounty system and predator control. California Fish and Game **31**: 53-63.

James, D.D. 1983. Seasonal movements, summer food habits, and summer predation rates of wolves in northwest Alaska. M.S. Thesis, Univ. Alaska, Fairbanks. 105 pp.

James, D.O. 1990. Montana rabies statistics for fiscal years 1986 to 1990. Montana Dep. Livestock, Helena.

Janz, D.W. 1987. Vancouver Island wolf control program. Progress report, April 1, 1986, to April 30, 1987. British Columbia Min. Environ. and Parks Wildl. Working Rep. No. WR28. 11 pp.

Janz, D.W. 1989. Wolf-deer interactions on Vancouver Islanda review. pp. 26-42 *in* D. Seip, S. Pettigrew, and R. Archibald, eds. Wolf-prey dynamics and management. British Columbia Min. Environ. Wildl. Working Rep. No. WR-40.

Janz, D., and I. Hatter. 1986. A rationale for wolf control in the management of the Vancouver Island predator-ungulate system, B.C. Wildl. Bull. B-45, 35 pp.

Jenks, S.M., and R.K. Wayne. 1992. Problems and policy for species threatened by hybridization: the red wolf as a case study. pp. 237-251 *in* D.R. McCullough and R.H. Barrett, eds. Wildlife 2001: populations. Elsevier Appl. Sci., New York, N.Y.

Jensen, W.R., T.K. Fuller, and W.L. Robinson. 1986. Wolf, *Canis lupus*, distribution on the Ontario-Michigan border near Sault Ste. Marie, Ontario. Can. Field-Nat. **100**: 363-366.

Jobes, P.C. 1991. The Greater Yellowstone social system. Conserv. Biol. **5**: 387-394.

Johnson, D.H., and A.B. Sargeant. 1977. Impact of red fox predation on the sex ratio of prairie mallards. U.S. Fish and Wildl. Serv. Wildl. Res. Rep. No. 6. 56 pp.

Johnson, R. 1974. On the spoor of the Big Bad Wolf. J. Environ. Ed. **6**: 37-39.

Johnston, J., and J. Erickson. 1990. Public survey of central Idaho wolf occurrence. Unpubl. Rep., U.S. Dep. Agric. For. Serv., Boise National Forest, Boise, Id. 9 pp.

Johnsingh, A.J.T. 1982. Reproductive and social behaviour of the dhole, *Cuon alpinus* (Canidae). J. Zool. (Lond.) **198**: 443-463.

Jolicoeur, P. 1959. Multivariate geographical variation in the wolf *Canis lupus* L. Evolution **13**: 283-299.

Jolicoeur, P. 1975. Sexual dimorphism and geographical distance as factors of skull variation in the wolf *Canis lupus* L. pp. 54-61 *in* M.W. Fox, ed. The wild canids: their systematics, behavioral ecology and evolution. Van Nostrand Reinhold, New York, N.Y.

Jones, C.A., S.R. Humphrey, T.M. Padgett, R.K. Rose, and J.F. Pagels. 1991. Geographic variation and taxonomy of the southeastern shrew (*Sorex longirostris*). J. Mammal. **72**: 263-272.

Jones, G.W., and B. Mason. 1983. Relationships among wolves, hunting, and population trends of black-tailed deer in the Nimpkish Valley on Vancouver Island. British Columbia Min. Environ. Fish and Wildl. Rep. No. R-7. 26 pp.

Jones, W.A. 1875. Report upon the reconnaissance of northwest Wyoming including Yellowstone National Park, made in the summer of 1873. War Dep., U.S. Gov. Print. Off., Washington, D.C. 331 pp.

Jordan, P.A., P.C. Shelton, and D.L. Allen. 1967. Numbers, turnover, and social structure of the Isle Royale wolf population. Am. Zool. **7**: 233-252.

Jorgensen, S.E. 1970. The wolf as an endangered animal in the conterminous United States. pp. 1-2 *in* S.E. Jorgensen, C.E. Faulkner, and L.D. Mech, eds. Proceedings of a symposium on wolf management in selected areas of North America. U.S. Fish and Wildl. Serv. Bur. Sport Fish. and Wildl., Reg. 3, Twin Cities, Minn.

Joslin, P.W.B. 1966. Summer activities of two timber wolf (*Canis lupus*) packs in Algonquin Park. M.A. Thesis. Univ. Toronto, Toronto, Ont. 98 pp.

Joslin, P.W.B. 1967. Movements and home sites of timber wolves in Algonquin Park. Am. Zool. **7**: 279-288.

K

Kachroo, P., B.L. Sapru, and U. Dhar. 1977. Flora of Ladakh, an ecological and taxonomical appraisal. Bisen Sign and Mahendra Pal Singh, New Delhi. 169 pp.

Kalmus, H. 1955. The discrimination by the nose of the dog of individual human odours and in particular of the odours of twins. Br. J. Anim. Behav. **3**: 25-31.

Kalymon, B.A. 1981. The management of Canadian resources: concepts and cases. McGraw-Hill Ryerson, Toronto, Ont. 245 pp.

Kaminski, T., and A. Boss. 1981. The gray wolf: history, present status and management recommendations. Unpubl. Rep., U.S. Dep. Agric. For. Serv., Boise National Forest, Boise, Id. 111 pp.

Kaminski, T., and J. Hansen. 1984. Wolves of central Idaho. Unpubl. Rep., Montana Coop. Wildl. Res. Unit, Missoula. 197 pp.

Kansas, J.L. 1981. A wolf-elk predator-prey interaction in Jasper National Park. Alberta Nat. **11**: 78-80.

Kavanau, J.L., and J. Ramos. 1975. Influences of light on activity and phasing of carnivores. Am. Nat. **109**: 391-418.

Kay, C.E. 1990. Yellowstone's northern elk herd: a critical evaluation of the "natural regulation" paradigm. Ph.D. Thesis, Utah State Univ., Logan. 490 pp.

Kay, C.E. 1994. Aboriginal overkill: the role of Native Americans in structuring western ecosystems. Human Nature **5**: 359-398.

Kay, C.E., and F.H. Wagner. 1994. Historic condition of woody vegetation on Yellowstone's northern range: a critical test of the "natural regulation" paradigm. pp. 159-169 *in* D. Despain, ed. Plants and their environments. Proc. First Bienn. Conf. Greater Yellowstone ecosystem. U.S. Natl. Park Serv. Tech. Rep. NPS/NRYELL/NRTR-93/xx.

Kay, J. 1985a. Native Americans in the fur trade and wildlife depletion. Environ. Rev. **9**: 118-130.

Kay, J. 1985b. Preconditions of natural resource conservation. Agric. Hist. **59**: 124-135.

Kay, J., and C.J. Brown. 1985. Mormon beliefs about land and natural resources, 1847-1877. J. Hist. Geol. **11**: 253-267.

Kaye, R.G., and J.M. Roulet. 1983. The distribution and status of wolves. Can. Parks Serv., Four Mountain Parks Plann. Prog. Background Pap. 17 pp.

Kazmierczak, J.J., E.C. Burgess, and T.E. Amundson. 1988. Susceptibility of the gray wolf (*Canis lupus*) to infection with the Lyme disease agent, *Borrelia burgdorferi*. J. Wildl. Dis. **24**: 522-527.

Keating, K.A., W.G. Brewster, and C.H. Key. 1991. Satellite telemetry: performance of animal-tracking systems. J. Wildl. Manage. **55**: 160-171.

Keefe, C.E. 1958. The bounty system in Oregon. Oregon State Game Comm. Bull. **13**: 3-4, 7.

Keener, J.M. 1970. History of the wolf in Wisconsin. pp. 4-5 *in* S.E. Jorgensen, C.E. Faulkner, and L.D. Mech, eds. Proceedings of a symposium on wolf management in selected areas of North America. U.S. Fish and Wildl. Serv. Bur. Sport Fish. and Wildl., Reg. 3, Twin Cities, Minn.

Keiter, R.B., and P.K. Holscher. 1990. Wolf recovery under the Endangered Species Act: a study in contemporary federalism. Public Land Law Rev. **11**: 19-52.

Keith, L.B. 1983. Population dynamics of wolves. pp. 66-77 *in* L.N. Carbyn, ed. Wolves in Canada and Alaska: their status, biology, and management. Can. Wildl. Serv. Rep. Ser., No. 45.

Kellert, S.R. 1976. Perceptions of animals in American society. Trans. North Am. Wildl. and Nat. Resour. Conf. **41**: 533-546.

Kellert, S.R. 1980a. Attitudes of the American public relating to animals. U.S. Gov. Print. Off., Washington, D.C.

Kellert, S.R. 1980b. Contemporary values of wildlife in American society. pp. 31-60 *in* W. Shaw and I. Zube, eds. Wildlife values. U.S. Dep. Agric. For. Serv. Rocky Mount. For. and Range Exp. Stn. Inst. Ser., No. 1.

Kellert, S.R. 1980c. American attitudes toward and knowledge of animals. Int. J. Stud. Anim. Prob. **1**: 87-119.

Kellert, S.R. 1981. Trappers and trapping in American society. Proc. Worldwide Furbearer Conf. **1**: 1971-2003.

Kellert, S.R. 1985a. Public perceptions of predators, particularly the wolf and the coyote. Biol. Conserv. **31**: 167-189.

Kellert, S.R. 1985b. The public and the timber wolf in Minnesota. Unpubl. Rep., Yale Univ. School For. and Environ. Stud., New Haven, Conn. 175 pp.

Kellert, S.R. 1986. The public and the timber wolf in Minnesota. Trans. North Am. Wildl. and Nat. Resour. Conf. **51**: 193-200.

Kellert, S.R. 1989. Perceptions of animals in America. pp. 5-24 *in* R.J. Hoage, ed. Perceptions of animals in American culture. Smithson. Inst. Press, Washington, D.C.

Kellert, S.R. 1990a. Public attitudes and beliefs about the wolf and its restoration in Michigan. Unpubl. Rep., Yale Univ. School For. and Environ. Stud., New Haven, Conn. 126 pp.

Kellert, S.R. 1990b. Human dimensions of wolf introduction: A report prepared for the Wildlife Society's Committee on Reintroduction of wild canids. Yale Univ. Sch. For. Environ. Studies, 17 pp. (unpubl.)

Kellert, S.R. 1991. Public views of wolf restoration in Michigan. Trans. North Am. Wildl. and Nat. Resour. Conf. **56**: 152-161.

Kellert, S.R., and M.O. Westervelt. 1981. Trends in animal use and perception in 20th century America. U.S. Fish and Wildl. Serv. 166 pp.

Kelly, L.S. 1926. "Yellowstone Kelly". The memoirs of Luther S. Kelly. M.M. Quaife (ed). Yale Univ. Press, New Haven, Conn. 268 pp.

Kelleyhouse, D.G. 1982. Increased efficiency of department wolf management efforts. Memorandum, Alaska Dep. Fish and Game, Tok.

Kelsall, J.P. 1957. Continued barren-ground caribou studies. Can. Wildl. Serv. Manage. Bull. Ser. 1, No. 12. 148 pp.

Kelsall, J.P. 1960. Cooperative studies of barren-ground caribou. Can. Wildl. Serv. Wildl. Manage. Bull. Ser. 1, No. 15. 148 pp.

Kelsall, J.P. 1968. The migratory barren-ground caribou of Canada. Can. Wildl. Serv. Monogr. Ser., No. 3. 340 pp.

Kelsall, J.P. 1987. The distribution and status of moose (*Alces alces*) in North America. Swed. Wildl. Res. **1** (Suppl.): 1-10.

Kelsall, J.P., and E.S. Telfer. 1974. Biogeography of moose with particular reference to western North America. Naturaliste Can. (Que.) **101**: 117-130.

Kennedy, P.K., M.L. Kennedy, P.L. Clarkson, and I.S. Liepins. 1991. Genetic variability in natural populations of the gray wolf, *Canis lupus*. Can. J. Zool. **69**: 1183-1188.

Khan, M.A., S.M. Goyal, S.L. Diesch, L.D. Mech, and S.H. Fritts. 1991. Seroepidemiology of leptospirosis in Minnesota wolves. J. Wildl. Dis. **27**: 248-253.

King, D.R. 1990. 1080 and Australian fauna. Agric. Prot. Bd. Tech. Ser., No. 8. 27 pp.

King, D.R., A.J. Oliver, and R.J. Mead. 1978. The adaptation of some Western Australian mammals to food plants containing fluoroacetate. Austral. J. Zool. **26**: 699-712.

King, D.R., L.E. Twigg, and J.L. Gardner. 1989. Tolerance to sodium monofluoroacetate in dasyurids from Western Australia. Austral. Wildl. Res. **16**: 131-140.

King, J.E., R.F. Becker, and J.E. Markee. 1964. Studies on olfactory discrimination in dogs. 3. Ability to detect human odour trace. Anim. Behav. **12**: 311-315.

Kinloch, A. 1885. Large game shooting in Tibet, the Himalayas, and northern India. W. Thacker, London, U.K. 147 pp.

Kirchnoff, M.D., and K.W. Pitcher. 1988. Deer pellet group surveys in southeast Alaska 1981-1987. Alaska Dep. Fish and Game Fed. Aid in Wildl. Restoration Prog. Rep., Proj. W-22-6, 2.9. 113 pp.

Kirkpatrick, J.F., and J.W. Turner, Jr. 1985. Chemical fertility control and wildlife management. BioScience **35**: 485-491.

Kirwan, C.J. 1992. Wolves and recovery plans: the difficult road to wolf preservation in the Greater Yellowstone area. UMKC Law Rev. **60**: 517-540.

Klein, D.R. 1962. Rumen contents analysis as an index to range quality. Trans. North Am. Wildl. and Nat. Resour. Conf. **27**: 150-164.

Klein, D.R. 1963. Physiological response of deer on ranges of varying quality. Ph.D. Thesis, Univ. of British Columbia, Vancouver. 167 pp.

Klein, D.R. 1964. Range-related differences in growth of deer reflected in skeletal ratios. J. Mammal. **45**: 226-235.

Klein, D.R. 1965a. Ecology of deer range in Alaska. Ecol. Monogr. **35**: 259-284.

Klein, D.R. 1965b. Postglacial distribution patterns of mammals in the southern coastal regions of Alaska. Arctic **18**: 7-20.

Klein, D.R. 1991. Limiting factors in caribou population ecology. Proc. North Am. Caribou Workshop **5**: 30-35.

Klein, D.R., M. Meldgaard, and S.G. Fancy. 1987. Factors determining leg length in *Rangifer tarandus*. J. Mammal. **68**: 642-655.

Klinghammer, E., and L. Laidlaw. 1979. Analysis of 23 months of daily howl records in a captive grey wolf pack (*Canis lupus*). pp. 153-181 *in* E. Klinghammer, ed. The behavior and ecology of wolves. Garland STPM Press, New York, N.Y.

Klinghammer, E., and M. Sloan. 1989. Wolf literature references. Ethology Series No. 4, Institute of Ethology, North American Wildlife Park Foundation, Inc., Battle Ground, Ind.

Knight, R.R., and L.L. Eberhardt. 1985. Population dynamics of Yellowstone grizzly bears. Ecology **66**: 323-334.

Knowles, M.E. 1909. Mange in coyotes. Breeder's Gaz. **55**: 130.

Knowles, M.E. 1914. Fighting coyotes with mange inoculation. Breeder's Gaz. **66**: 229-230.

Kolenosky, G.B. 1972. Wolf predation on wintering deer in east-central Ontario. J. Wildl. Manage. **36**: 357-369.

Kolenosky, G.B. 1983. Status and management of wolves in Ontario. pp. 35-40 *in* L.N. Carbyn, ed. Wolves in Canada and Alaska: their status, biology, and management. Can. Wildl. Serv. Rep. Ser., No. 45.

Kolenosky, G.B., and D.H. Johnston. 1967. Radio-tracking timber wolves in Ontario. Am. Zool. **7**: 289-303.

Kolenosky, G.B., and R.O. Standfield. 1975. Morphological and ecological variation among gray wolves (*Canis lupus*) of Ontario, Canada. pp. 62-72 *in* M.W. Fox, ed. The wild canids: their systematics, behavioral ecology and evolution. Van Nostrand Reinhold, New York, N.Y.

Komolafe, O.O. 1985. The possible existence of an immune-carrier state in canine parvovirus infections. Microbiol. Lett. **30**: 119-120.

Kornblatt, A.N., P.H. Urband, and A.C. Steere. 1985. Arthritis caused by *Borrelia burgdorferi* in dogs. J. Am. Vet. Med. Assoc. **186**: 960-964.

Korschgen, L.J. 1957. Food habits of the coyote in Missouri. J. Wildl. Manage. **21**: 424-43.

Koster, E.P. 1971. Adaptation and cross-adaptation in olfaction. Ph.D. Thesis, State Univ. Utrecht, The Netherlands. 212 pp.

Koterba, W.D., and J.R. Habeck. 1971. Grasslands of the North Fork Valley, Glacier National Park, Montana. Can. J. Bot. **49**: 1627-1636.

Koth, B., D.W. Lime, and J. Vlaming. 1990. Effects of restoring wolves on Yellowstone area big game and grizzly bears: opinions of fifteen North American experts. pp. 4-51 to 4-81 *in* Yellowstone National Park, U.S. Fish and Wildlife Service, University of Wyoming, University of Idaho, Interagency Grizzly Bear Study Team, and the University of Minnesota Cooperative Park Studies Unit, eds. Wolves for Yellowstone? A report to the United States Congress. Vol. II. Research and analysis. U.S. Natl. Park Serv., Yellowstone National Park, Mammoth, Wyo.

Kowal, E.H., and W. Runge. 1981. An evaluation of the 1976-1977 Wolf Control Program. Unpubl. Rep., Dept. North. Saskatchewan Resour. Br., Wildl. Div., Regina, Sask. 17 pp.

Krebs, J.R. 1971. Territory and breeding density in the great tit, *Parus major* L. Ecology **52**: 2-22.

Krebs, J.W., R.C. Holman, U. Hines, T.W. Strine, E.J. Mandel, and J.E. Childs. 1992. Rabies surveillance in the United States during 1991. J. Am. Vet. Med. Assoc. **201**: 1836-1848.

Kreeger, T.J., U.S. Seal, M. Callahan, and M. Beckel. 1990. Physiological and behavioral responses of gray wolves (*Canis lupus*) to immobilization with tiletamine and zolazepam. J. Wildl. Dis. **26**: 90-94.

Kreeger, T.J., U.S. Seal, Y. Cohen, E.D. Plotka, and C.S. Asa. 1991. Characterization of prolactin secretion in gray wolves (*Canis lupus*). Can. J. Zool. **69**: 1366-1374.

Krefting, L.W. 1974. Moose distribution and habitat selection in north central North America. Naturaliste Can. (Que.) **101**: 81-100.

Kruuk, H. 1972. The spotted hyena: a study of predation and social behavior. Univ. Chicago Press, Chicago, Ill. 335 pp.

Kuehn, D.W., T.K. Fuller, L.D. Mech, W.J. Paul, S.H. Fritts, and W.E. Berg. 1986. Trap-related injuries to gray wolves in Minnesota. J. Wildl. Manage. **50**: 90-91.

Kun, E. 1982. Monofluoroacetic acid (compound 1080), its pharmacology and toxicology. Proc. Vertebr. Pest Conf. **10**: 34-41.

Kunkel, K.E., and L.D. Mech. 1994. Wolf and bear predation on white-tailed deer fawns in northeastern Minnesota. Can. J. Zool. **72**: 1557-1565.

Kunkel, K.E., R.C. Chapman, L.D. Mech, and E.M. Gese. 1991. Testing the Wildlink activity-detection system on wolves and white-tailed deer. Can. J. Zool. **69**: 2466-2469.

Kurtén, B. 1968. Pleistocene mammals of Europe. Aldine Publishing Company, Chicago, Ill. 317 pp.

Kurtén, B. 1974. A history of coyote-like dogs (Canidae, Mammalia). Acta Zool. Fenn. **140**: 1-38.

Kurtén, B., and E. Anderson. 1980. Pleistocene mammals of North America. Columbia Univ. Press, New York, N.Y. 442 pp.

Kuyt, E. 1962. Movements of young wolves in the Northwest Territories of Canada. J. Mammal. **43**: 270-271.

Kuyt, E. 1972. Food habits and ecology of wolves on barren-ground caribou range in the Northwest Territories. Can. Wildl. Serv. Rep. Ser., No. 21. 36 pp.

L

Lacy, R.C. 1987. Loss of genetic diversity from managed populations: interacting effects of drift, mutation, immigration, selection, and population subdivision. Conserv. Biol. **1**: 143-158.

Ladd, A., Y.Y. Tsong, G. Prabhu, and R. Thau. 1989. Effects of long-term immunization against LHRH and androgen treatment on gonadal function. J. Reprod. Immunol. **15**: 85-101.

Laikre, L., and N. Ryman. 1991. Inbreeding depression in a captive wolf (*Canis lupus*) population. Conserv. Biol. **5**: 33-40.

Lamoth, A.R., and G.H. Parker. 1989. Winter feeding habits of wolves in the Keewatin District, Northwest Territories. Musk-ox **37**: 144-149.

Land, C.R., and E.L. Young, Jr. 1984. Occurrence of wildlife on the Coronation and Spanish Islands, Alaska. Alaska Dep. Fish and Game. 28 pp.

Lande, R., and G.F. Barrowclough. 1987. Effective population size, genetic variation, and their use in population management. pp. 87-123 *in* M.E. Soulé, ed. Viable populations for conservation. Cambridge Univ. Press, New York, N.Y.

Landon, C.R. 1952. Predator control in Texas. pp. 11-15 *in* Sheep and Goat Raiser Newsletter. (August).

Lane, D.R., and R. Robinson. 1970. The utility of biochemical screening in dogs. I. Normal ranges. Br. Vet. J. **126**: 230-237.

Langford, N.P. 1972. The discovery of Yellowstone Park 1870. Univ. Nebraska Press, Lincoln. 188 pp.

Larsen, D.G., D.A. Gauthier, and R.L. Markel. 1989. Causes and rate of moose mortality in the southwest Yukon. J. Wildl. Manage. **53**: 548-557.

Latham, R.M. 1953. An analysis of the Pennsylvania bounty system. Trans. North Am. Wildl. Conf. **18**: 158-167.

Laurenson, K., M. Borner, S. Lelo, and R. Burrows. 1990. Conservation status of the wild dog (*Lycaon pictus*) in the Serengeti ecosystem. Serengeti Res. Inst., Tanzania. 6 pp. (typewritten progress report).

Lawler, D. 1989. Canine reference intervals for blood values. Ralston Purina, St. Louis, Mo.

Lawrence, B., and W.H. Bossert. 1967. Multiple character analysis of *Canis lupus*, *latrans*, and *familiaris*, with a discussion of the relationships of *Canis niger*. Am. Zool. **7**: 223-232.

Lawrence, B., and W.H. Bossert. 1969. The cranial evidence for hybridization in New England *Canis*. Breviora **330**: 1-13.

Lawrence, B., and W.H. Bossert. 1975. Relationships of North American *Canis* shown by a multiple character analysis of selected populations. pp. 73-86 *in* M.W. Fox, ed. The wild canids: their systematics, behavioral ecology and evolution. Van Nostrand Reinhold, New York, N.Y.

Lawrence, R.D. 1986. In praise of wolves. Henry Holt, New York, N.Y. 245 pp.

Laycock, G. 1990. How to kill a wolf. Audubon (Nov.): 44-48.

Lecker, H.B. 1884. A camping trip to the Yellowstone National Park. Am. Field **2**: 41-42, 71-72, 93-94, 117, 141-142 (1884); 166, 190-191, 214 (1884); 236-237 (1884); 261-262 (1884); 286, 310-311 (1884a); 335-336 (1884); 359-360 (1884); 382-383 (1884b); 407-408, 430-431, 455-456 (1884) editions of Jan. 12, 19, 26; Feb., 2, 9, 16, 23; March 1, 8, 15, 22, 29; April 5, 12, 19, 26; May 3, 10.

Lee, D.S., M.K. Clark, and J.B. Funderburg, Jr. 1982. A preliminary survey of the mammals of mainland Dare County, North Carolina. pp. 20-61 *in* E.F. Potter, ed. A survey of the vertebrate fauna of mainland Dare County, North Carolina. Unpubl. Rep., U.S. Fish and Wildl. Serv., Raleigh, N.C.

Lee, L.L., W.E. Howard, and R.E. Marsh. 1990. Acquired strychnine tolerance by pocket gophers. Proc. Vertebr. Pest Conf. **14**: 87-90.

Lee, R.B., and I. Devore. (eds.) 1968. Man the hunter. Aldine Publishing, Chicago, Ill. 415 pp.

Lee, R.M., and M.L. Kennedy. 1986. Food habits of the coyote in Tennessee. Proc. Annu. Conf. Southeast. Assoc. Fish and Wildl. Agencies **40**: 364-372.

Lehman, N., and R.K. Wayne. 1991. Analysis of coyote mitochondrial DNA genotype frequencies: estimation of effective number of alleles. Genetics **128**: 405-416.

Lehman, N., P. Clarkson, L.D. Mech, T.J. Meier, and R.K. Wayne. 1992. A study of the genetic relationships within and among wolf packs using DNA fingerprinting and mitochondrial DNA. Behav. Ecol. Sociobiol. **30**: 83-94.

Lehman, N., A. Eisenhawer, K. Hansen, L.D. Mech, R.O. Peterson, P.J.P. Gogan, and R.K. Wayne. 1991. Introgression of coyote mitochondrial DNA into sympatric North American gray wolf populations. Evolution **45**: 104-119.

Lehner, P.N., R. Krumm, and T. Cringan. 1976. Tests for olfactory repellents for coyotes and dogs. J. Wildl. Manage. **40**: 145-150.

Leibholz, J. 1970. The effect of starvation and low nitrogen intakes on the concentration of free amino acids in the blood plasma and on the nitrogen metabolism in sheep. Austral. J. Agric. Res. **21**: 723-734.

Leighton, T., M. Ferguson, A. Gunn, E. Henderson, and G. Stenhouse. 1988. Canine distemper in sled dogs. Can. Vet. J. **29**: 299.

Lenihan, M.L. 1987. Montanans ambivalent on wolves. The Montana Poll. Unpubl. Rep., Univ. Montana Bur. Bus. Econ. Res. (cosponsored by the Great Falls Tribune, Great Falls, Mont.) 6 pp.

Lensink, C.J. 1959. Predator control with bounties in Alaska. Alaska Dep. Fish and Game Rep. No. 10. 12 pp.

Leopold, A.S. 1933. Game management. Charles Scribner's Sons, New York, N.Y. 481 pp.

Leopold, A.S. 1949. A Sand County Almanac: and sketches here and there. Oxford Univ. Press, New York, N.Y. 295 pp.

Leopold, A.S. 1959. Wildlife of Mexico. Univ. California Press, Berkeley. 568 pp.

Leopold, A.S., and F.F. Darling. 1953. Wildlife in Alaska. An ecological reconnaissance. The Ronald Press, New York, N.Y. 129 pp.

Leopold, B.D., and P.R. Krausman. 1986. Diets of 3 predators in Big Bend National Park, Texas. J. Wildl. Manage. **50**: 290-295.

Leopold, A.S., S.A. Cain, C.M. Cottam, I.N. Gabrielson and T.L. Kimball. 1964. Predator and rodent control in the United States. Trans. North Am. Wildl. Nat. Resour. Conf. 29: 27-49.

Lewis, M., and W. Clark. 1893. The history of the Lewis and Clark Expedition. E. Coues, ed. Originally published by Francis P. Harper, New York, N.Y.; republished by Dover, New York, N.Y. Vol. **1**: 1-352; Vol. **2**: 353-820; Vol. **3**: 821-1364.

Lewis, S.W. 1992. Relationships between deer and vegetation on Coronation Island, southeastern Alaska. M.S. Thesis, Univ. Alaska, Fairbanks. 93 pp.

Licht, D.S., and S.H. Fritts. 1994. Gray wolf (*Canis lupus*) occurrences in the Dakotas. Am. Midl. Nat. **132**: 74-81.

Lien, J., and J. Atkinson. 1988. Education programs about whales. pp. 160-169 *in* Selected papers from the Third Biennial Conference and Symposium of the Am. Cetacean Soc., Monterey, Calif.

Lindsay, E.H., and N.T. Tessman. 1974. Cenozoic vertebrate localities and faunas in Arizona. J. Arizona Acad. Sci. **9**: 3-24.

Linhart, S.B., and R.K. Enders. 1964. Some effects of diethylstilbestrol on reproduction in captive red foxes. J. Wildl. Manage. **28**: 358-363.

Linhart, S.B., and F.F. Knowlton. 1967. Determining age of coyotes by tooth cementum layers. J. Wildl. Manage. **31**: 362-365.

Linhart, S.B., and W.B. Robinson. 1972. Some relative carnivore densities in areas under sustained coyote control. J. Mammal. **53**: 880-884.

Linhart, S.B., H.H. Brusman, and D.S. Balser. 1968. Field evaluation of an antifertility agent, stilbestrol, for inhibiting coyote reproduction. Trans. North Am. Wildl. and Nat. Resour. Conf. **33**: 316-327.

Linhart, S.B., J.D. Roberts, and G.J. Dasch. 1982. Electric fencing reduces coyote predation on pastured sheep. J. Range Manage. **35**: 276-281.

Linhart, S.B., G.J. Dasch, C.B. Male, and R.M. Engeman. 1986. Efficiency of unpadded and padded steel foothold traps for capturing coyotes. Wildl. Soc. Bull. **14**: 212-218.

Linhart, S.B., G.J. Dasch, J.D. Roberts, and P.J. Savarie. 1977. Test methods for determining the efficacy of coyote attractants and repellents. pp. 114-122 *in* W.B. Jackson and R.E. Marsh, eds. Symposium on test methods for vertebrate pest control and management materials. Am. Soc. Testing and Materials Spec. Tech. Publ. 625. Philadelphia, Pa.

Linhart, S.B., J.D. Roberts, S.A. Shumake, and R. Johnson. 1976. Avoidance of prey by captive coyotes punished with electric shock. Proc. Vertebr. Pest Conf. **7**: 302-306.

Linhart, S.B., R.T. Sterner, R. Carrigan, and D. Henne. 1979. Komondor guard dogs reduce sheep losses to coyotes: a preliminary evaluation. J. Range Manage. **32**: 238-241.

Linsella, F.S., K.R. Long, and H.G. Scott. 1971. Toxicology of rodenticides and their relation to human health. J. Environ. Hlth. **33**: 231-237, 361-365.

Liroff, R.A. 1982. Cost-benefit analysis in environmental regulation: will it clear the air or muddy the water? pp. 1-11 *in* D. Swartzman, R.A. Liroff, and K.G. Croke, eds. Cost-benefit analysis and environmental regulations: politics, ethics, and methods. Conserv. Found., Washington, D.C.

Lissman, B.A., E.M. Bosler, H. Camay, B.G. Ormiston, and J.L. Benach. 1984. Spirochete-associated arthritis (Lyme disease) in a dog. J. Am. Vet. Med. Assoc. **185**: 219-220.

Livingston, J. 1981. The fallacy of wildlife conservation. McClelland and Stewart, Toronto, Ont. 117 pp.

Llewellyn, L. 1978. Who speaks for the timber wolf? Trans. N. Am. Wildl. and Nat. Res. Conf. **43**: 442-452.

Lloyd, H. 1927. Transfers of elk for re-stocking. Can. Field-Nat. **41**: 126-127.

Loizos, C. 1966. Play in mammals. Symp. Zool. Soc. London **18**: 1-9.

Lopez, B.H. 1978. Of wolves and men. Charles Scribner's Sons, New York, N.Y. 309 pp.

Lopez, R.S. 1962. Naissance de l'Europe. A. Colin, Paris. 457 pp.

Lopez, R.S. 1971. The commercial revolution of the Middle Ages, 950-1350. Prentice-Hall, London, U.K. 224 pp.

Loughrey, A.G. 1958. Predator control in northern Canada 1957-58. Unpubl. Rep., Can. Wildl. Serv., Dep. North. Affairs and Nat. Resour., Ottawa, Ont. 52 pp.

Lovaas, A.L. 1970. People and the Gallatin elk herd. Montana Fish and Game Dep., Helena. 44 pp.

Ludlow, W. 1876. Report of a reconnaissance from Carroll, Montana Territory on the Upper Missouri to the Yellowstone National Park and return, made in the summer of 1875 by William Ludlow. U.S. Gov. Print. Off., Washington, D.C. 141 pp.

Lynch, G.W., and R.D. Nass. 1981. Sodium monofluoroacetate (1080): relation of its use to predation on livestock in western national forests, 1960-78. J. Range Manage. **34**: 421-423.

M

MacArthur, R.H. 1972. Geographical ecology: patterns in the distribution of species. Harper and Row, New York, N.Y. 269 pp.

MacDonald, D.W., and D.R. Voigt. 1985. The biological basis of rabies models. pp. 71-108 *in* P.J. Bacon, ed. Population dynamics of rabies in wildlife. Academic Press, London, U.K.

MacGregor, J.G. 1974. Overland by the Yellowhead. Western Producer Book Service, Saskatoon, Sask. 270 pp.

MacInnes, C.D. 1987. Rabies. pp. 910-929 *in* M. Novak, J.A. Baker, M.E. Obbard, and B. Malloch, eds. Wild furbearer management and conservation in North America. Ontario Trappers Assoc., North Bay, Ont.

Mack, J.A., W.G. Brewster, and S.H. Fritts. 1992. A review of wolf depredation on livestock and implications for the Yellowstone area. pp. 5-21 to 5-44 *in* J.D. Varley and W.G. Brewster, eds. Wolves for Yellowstone? A report to the United States Congress. Volume IV. Research and analysis. U.S. Natl. Park Serv., Yellowstone National Park, Mammoth, Wyo.

Mack, J.A., F.J. Singer, and M.E. Messaros. 1990. The ungulate prey base for wolves in Yellowstone National Park II: elk, mule deer, white-tailed deer, moose, big-horned sheep, and mountain goats in the areas adjacent to the park. pp. 2-39 to 2-218 *in* Yellowstone National Park, U.S. Fish and Wildlife Service, University of Wyoming, University of Idaho, Interagency Grizzly Bear Study Team, and the University of Minnesota Cooperative Park Studies Unit, eds. Wolves for Yellowstone? A report to the United States Congress. Volume II. Research and analysis. U.S. Natl. Park Serv., Yellowstone National Park, Mammoth, Wyo.

Mågård, L. 1988. Ynglefund af polarulv (*Canis lupus arctos*) ved Danmarkshavn, Nordøstgrønland. Flora og Fauna **94**: 89-92.

Magrane, W.G. 1977. Canine ophthalmology. 3rd ed. Lea and Febiger, Philadelphia, Pa. 258 pp.

Mahi, C.A., and R. Yanagimachi. 1979. Prevention of *in vitro* fertilization of canine oocytes by anti-ovary antisera: a potential approach to fertility control in the bitch. J. Exp. Zool. **210**: 129-135.

Mahi-Brown, C.A., R. Yanagimachi, J.C. Hoffman, and T.T.F. Huang, Jr. 1985. Fertility control in the bitch by active immunization with porcine zonae pellucidae: use of different adjuvants and patterns of estradiol and progesterone levels in estrous cycles. Biol. Reprod. **32**: 761-772.

Mahi-Brown, C.A., R. Yanagimachi, M.L. Nelson, H. Yanagimachi, and N. Palumbo. 1988. Ovarian histopathology of bitches immunized with porcine zonae pellucidae. Am. J. Reprod. Immunol. Microbiol. **18**: 94-103.

Mails, T. 1972. The mystic warriors of the plains. Doubleday, Garden City, N.Y. 280 pp.

Major, J.T., and J.A. Sherburne. 1987. Interspecific relationships of coyotes, bobcats, and red foxes in western Maine. J. Wildl. Manage. **51**: 606-616.

Mallinson, J. 1978. The shadow of extinction: Europe's threatened wild mammals. Macmillan, London, U.K. 224 pp.

Mandernack, B.A. 1983. Food habits of Wisconsin timber wolves. M.S. Thesis, Univ. Wisconsin, Eau Claire. 52 pp.

Manning, T.H. 1960. The relationship of the Peary caribou and barren-ground caribou. Arct. Inst. North Am. Tech. Pap. No. 4: 52 pp.

Manning, T.H., and A.H. Macpherson. 1958. The mammals of Banks Island. Arct. Inst. North Am. Tech. Pap No. 2: 74 pp.

Manitoba Department of Mines, Natural Resources and Environment. 1984. Policy directive, timber wolf control: procedural directive, timber wolf control for human safety and the protection of property: procedural directive, timber wolf control for wildlife management. Man. Dep. Mines Nat. Resour. and Environ., Winnipeg, Man.

Mardini, A. 1984. Species identification of tissues of selected mammals by agarose gel electrophoresis. Wildl. Soc. Bull. **12**: 249-251.

Marquard-Petersen, U. 1994. Dens and summer pack size of arctic wolves in Hold with Hope, East Greenland. Polar Rec. **30**(172): 46-49.

Marshall, D.A., and D.G. Moulton. 1981. Olfactory sensitivity to alpha-ionone in humans and dogs. Chem. Senses **6**: 53-61.

Martinka, C.J. 1982. Wildlife management in Glacier National Park: a regional perspective. pp. 48-56 *in* R.C. Scace and C.J. Martinka, eds. Towards the biosphere reserve: exploring relationships between parks and adjacent lands. U.S. Natl. Park Serv., Washington, D.C.

Mason, O.T. 1902. Traps of the American Indiansa study in psychology and invention. pp. 461-472 *in* 1901 Annu. Rep. of the Board of Regents of the Smithsonian Institution. U.S. Gov. Print. Off., Washington, D.C.

Mate, B., G. Rathburn, and J. Reed. 1986. An Argos-monitored radio tag for tracking manatees. Argos Newslett. **26**: 2-7.

Matheny, R.W. 1976. Review and results of sodium cyanide spring loaded ejector mechanism (SCSLEM) experimental programs. Proc. Vertebr. Pest Conf. **7**: 161-177.

Matson, G.M. 1981. Workbook for cementum analysis. Matson's Laboratory, P.O. Box 308, Milltown, Mont. 30 pp.

Matthew, W.D. 1930. The phylogeny of dogs. J. Mammal. **11**: 117-138.

Matthiessen, P. 1959. Wildlife in America. Viking Press, New York, N.Y. 304 pp.

May, R. 1990. Taxonomy as destiny. Nature (Lond.) **347**: 129-130.

Mayr, E. 1940. Speciation phenomena in birds. Am. Nat. **74**: 249-278.

Mayr, E. 1951. Speciation in birds. Progress report in the years 1938-1950. Proc. Int. Ornithol. Congr. **10**: 91-131.

Mayr, E. 1954. Notes on nomenclature and classification. Syst. Zool. **3**: 86-89.

Mayr, E. 1963. Animal species and evolution. The Belknap Press of Harvard Univ. Press, Cambridge, Mass. 797 pp.

Mayr, E. 1969. Principles of systematic zoology. McGraw-Hill Book, New York, N.Y. 428 pp.

Mayr, E. 1970. Populations, species and evolution: an abridgement of animal species and evolution. The Belknap Press of Harvard University Press, Cambridge, Mass. 453 pp.

McArthur, L.Z., and R. Baron. 1983. Toward an ecological theory of social perception. Psychol. Rev. **90**: 215-238.

McBride, R.T. 1980. The Mexican wolf (*Canis lupus baileyi*): a historical review and observations on its status and distribution. U.S. Fish and Wildl. Serv. Endang. Spec. Rep. No. 8. 38 pp.

McCarley, H. 1962. The taxonomic status of wild *Canis* (Canidae) in the south central United States. Southwest. Nat. **7**: 227-235.

McCarley, H. 1978. Vocalizations of red wolves (*Canis rufus*). J. Mammal. **59**: 27-35.

McCarley, H., and C.J. Carley. 1979. Recent changes in distribution and status of wild red wolves (*Canis rufus*). U.S. Fish and Wildl. Serv. Endang. Spec. Rep. No. 4. 38 pp.

McCarthy, J.J., C.R. Watts, F.G. Feist, C.R. Olson, and R.A. Buesis. 1985. Big Game Survey and InventoryRegion Four. Montana Dept. Fish Wildl. and Parks Job Prog. Rep., Proj. No. W-130-R-16. 34 pp.

McCarthy, J.J., C.R. Watts, F.G. Feist, C.R. Olson, and R.A. Buesis. 1986. Big Game Survey and InventoryRegion Four. Montana Fish Wildl. and Parks Job Prog. Rep., Proj. No. W-130-R-17. 25 pp.

McCool, S.F., and A.M. Braithwaite. 1989. Beliefs and behaviors of backcountry campers in Montana toward grizzly bears. Wildl. Soc. Bull. 17: 514-519.

McCullagh, C.B. 1987. The truth of historical narratives. History and Theory 26: 30-45.

McCullough, D.R. 1990. Detecting density dependence: filtering the baby from the bathwater. Trans. North Am. Wildl. and Nat. Resour. Conf. 55: 534-543.

McCullough, D.R. 1992. Concepts of large herbivore population dynamics. pp. 967-984 *in* D.R. McCullough and R.H. Barrett, eds. Wildlife 2001: populations. Elsevier Appl. Sci., New York, N.Y.

McDonough, E.S., and J.F. Kuzma. 1980. Epidemiological studies on blastomycosis in the state of Wisconsin. Sabouraudia 18: 173-183.

McEwen, E.H. 1955. A biological survey of the west coast of Banks Island1955. Unpubl. Rep. CWSC-26, Can. Wildl. Serv. East. Reg. Ottawa, Ont., 55 pp.

McGrew, J.C., and C.S. Blakesley. 1982. How Komondor dogs reduce sheep losses to coyotes. J. Range Manage. 35: 693-696.

McKnight, D.E. 1973. The history of predator control in Alaska. Unpubl. Rep., Alaska Dep. Fish and Game, Juneau. 9 pp. (mimeograph).

McLean, R.G. 1970. Wildlife rabies in the United States: recent history and current concepts. J. Wildl. Dis. 6: 229-235.

McMahon, T.A., and J.T. Bonner. 1983. On size and life. Scientific American Books, New York, N.Y. 255 pp.

McNaught, D.A. 1987. Wolves in Yellowstone National Park? Park visitors respond. Wildl. Soc. Bull. 15: 518-521.

McNay, M.E. 1992. Unit 20A moose management report. pp. 200-243 *in* S. Abbott, ed. Moose management report. Alaska Dep. Fish and Game Fed. Aid in Wildl. Restoration Rep., Projs. W-23-3 and W-23-4.

McRoberts, R.E., L.D. Mech, and R.O. Peterson. 1995. The cumulative effect of consecutive winters' snow depth on moose and deer populations: a defense. J. Anim. Ecol. 64: 131-135.

Meagher, M.M. 1971. Winter weather as a population regulating influence on free-ranging bison in Yellowstone National Park. American Association for the Advancement of Science. Symposium on Research in National Parks, Philadelphia, Pa. (mimeograph).

Meagher, M.M. 1973. The bison of Yellowstone National Park. U.S. Natl. Park Serv. Sci. Monogr. Ser., No. 1. 161 pp.

Meagher, M. 1986. Summary of possible wolf observations, 1977-1986. Yellowstone National Park, Mammoth, Wyo. 2 pp. (mimeograph).

Mech, L.D. 1966a. The wolves of Isle Royale. Fauna of the National Parks of the U.S., Fauna Ser., No. 7. U.S. Gov. Print. Off., Washington, D.C. 210 pp.

Mech, L.D. 1966b. Hunting behavior of timber wolves in Minnesota. J. Mammal. 47: 347-348.

Mech, L.D. 1970. The wolf: the ecology and behavior of an endangered species. Doubleday/Natural History Press, Garden City, N.Y. 384 pp.

Mech, L.D. 1971. Where wolves are and how they stand. Nat. Hist. 80: 26-29.

Mech, L.D. 1973. Wolf numbers in the Superior National Forest of Minnesota. U.S. Dep. Agric. For. Serv. Res. Pap. No. NC-97. 10 pp.

Mech, L.D. 1974a. Current techniques in the study of elusive wilderness carnivores. Proc. Int. Congr. Game Biol. 11: 315-322.

Mech, L.D. 1974b. *Canis lupus*. Mammalian spec. No. 37. Am. Soc. Mammal. 6 pp.

Mech, L.D. 1975. Hunting behavior in two similar species of social canids. pp. 363-368 *in* M.W. Fox, ed. The wild canids: their systematics, behavioral ecology and evolution. Van Nostrand Reinhold, New York, N.Y.

Mech, L.D. 1977a. Wolf-pack buffer zones as prey reservoirs. Science (Washington, D.C.) 198: 320-321.

Mech, L.D. 1977b. Productivity, mortality, and population trends of wolves in northeastern Minnesota. J. Mammal. 58: 559-574.

Mech, L.D. 1977c. Population trend and winter deer consumption in a Minnesota wolf pack. pp. 55-83 *in* R.L. Phillips and C. Jonkel, eds. Proceedings of the 1975 predator symposium. Bull. For. Conserv. Exp. Stn., Univ. Montana, Missoula. 268 pp.

Mech, L.D. 1979. Some considerations in re-establishing wolves in the wild. pp. 445-457 *in* E. Klinghammer, ed. The behavior and ecology of wolves. Garland STPM Press, New York, N.Y.

Mech, L.D. 1985. How delicate is the balance of nature? Natl. Wildl. (Feb.-Mar.): 54-58.

Mech, L.D. 1986. Wolf numbers and population trend in the central Superior National Forest, 1967-1985. U.S. Dep. Agric. For. Serv. Res. Pap. No. NC-270. 6 pp.

Mech, L.D. 1987. Age, season, distance, direction, and social aspects of wolf dispersal from a Minnesota pack. pp. 55-74 *in* B.D. Chepko-Sade and Z.T. Halpin, eds. Mammalian dispersal patterns. Univ. Chicago Press, Chicago, Ill.

Mech, L.D. 1988a. Longevity in wild wolves. J. Mammal. 69: 197-198.

Mech, L.D. 1988b. The arctic wolf: living with the pack. Key Porter Books, Toronto, Ont. 128 pp.

Mech, L.D. 1989. Wolf population survival in an area of high road density. Am. Midl. Nat. 121: 387-389.

Mech, L.D. 1991a. Returning the wolf to Yellowstone. pp. 309-322 *in* R.B. Keiter and M.S. Boyce, eds. The Greater Yellowstone ecosystem: redefining America's wilderness heritage. Yale Univ. Press, New Haven, Conn.

Mech, L.D. 1991b. Field testing a new generation of radio-telemetry equipment. Trans. Congr. Int. Union Game Biol. **13**: 593-597.

Mech, L.D. 1991c. The way of the wolf. Voyageur Press, Stillwater, Minn. 120 pp.

Mech, L.D. 1992. Daytime activity of wolves during winter in northeastern Minnesota. J. Mammal. **73**: 570-571.

Mech, L.D. 1995. The challenge and opportunity of recovering wolf populations. Conserv. Biol. **9**: 1-9.

Mech, L.D., and L.D. Frenzel, Jr. (eds.) 1971a. Ecological studies of the timber wolf in northeastern Minnesota. U.S. Dep. Agric. For. Serv. Res. Pap. NC-52. 62 pp.

Mech, L.D., and L.D. Frenzel, Jr. 1971b. The possible occurrence of the Great Plains wolf in northeastern Minnesota. pp. 60-62 *in* L.D. Mech and L.D. Frenzel, Jr., eds. Ecological studies of the timber wolf in northeastern Minnesota. U. S. Dep. Agric. For. Serv. Res. Pap. NC-52. 62 pp.

Mech, L.D., and S.H. Fritts. 1987. Parvovirus and heartworm found in Minnesota wolves. Endang. Spec. Tech. Bull. **12**: 5-6.

Mech, L.D., and G.D. DelGiudice. 1985. Limitations of the marrow-fat technique as an indicator of condition. Wildl. Soc. Bull. **13**: 204-206.

Mech, L.D., and E.M. Gese. 1992. Field testing the Wildlink capture collar on wild wolves. Wildl. Soc. Bull. **20**: 221-223.

Mech, L.D., and S.M. Goyal. 1993. Canine parvovirus effect on wolf population change and pup survival. J. Wildl. Dis. **29**: 330-333.

Mech, L.D., and H.H. Hertel. 1983. An eight-year demography of a Minnesota wolf pack. Acta Zool. Fenn. **174**: 249-250.

Mech, L.D., and P.D. Karns. 1977. Role of the wolf in a deer decline in the Superior National Forest. U.S. Dep. Agric. For. Serv. Res. Pap. NC-148. 23 pp.

Mech, L.D., and M. Korb. 1978. An unusually long pursuit of a deer by a wolf. J. Mammal. **59**: 860-861.

Mech, L.D., and R.E. McRoberts. 1990. Survival of white-tailed deer fawns in relation to maternal age. J. Mammal. **71**: 465-467.

Mech, L.D., and M.E. Nelson. 1989. Polygyny in a wild wolf pack. J. Mammal. **70**: 675-676.

Mech, L.D., and M.E. Nelson. 1990a. Non-family wolf, *Canis lupus*, packs. Can. Field-Nat. **104**: 482-483.

Mech, L.D., and M.E. Nelson. 1990b. Evidence of prey-caused mortality in three wolves. Am. Midl. Nat. **123**: 207-208.

Mech, L.D., and R.M. Nowak. 1981. Return of the gray wolf to Wisconsin. Am. Midl. Nat. **105**: 408-409.

Mech, L.D., and R.P. Peters. 1977. The study of chemical communication in free-ranging mammals. pp. 321-332 *in* S.D. Muller-Schwarze and M.M. Mozell, eds. Proceedings of the symposium on chemical signals in vertebrates. Plenum, New York, N.Y.

Mech, L.D., and R.A. Rausch. 1975. The status of the wolf in the United States, 1973. pp. 83-88 *in* D.H. Pimlott, ed. Proceedings of the First Working Meeting of Wolf Specialists and of the First International Conference on the Conservation of the Wolf. Int. Union Conserv. Nature Nat. Resour. Suppl. Pap. No. 43.

Mech, L.D., and U.S. Seal. 1987. Premature reproductive activity in wild wolves. J. Mammal. **68**: 871-873.

Mech, L.D., S.H. Fritts, and W.J. Paul. 1988a. Relationship between winter severity and wolf depredations on domestic animals in Minnesota. Wildl. Soc. Bull. **16**: 269-272.

Mech, L.D., T.J. Meier, and J.W. Burch. 1989. Demography and distribution of wolves, Denali National Park and Preserve, Alaska. U.S. Natl. Park Serv. Nat. Resour. Prog. Rep. No. AR-89/11. 36 pp.

Mech, L.D., T.J. Meier, and J.W. Burch. 1991a. Denali Park wolf studies: implications for Yellowstone. Trans. North Am. Wildl. and Nat. Resour. Conf. **56**: 86-90.

Mech, L.D., M.E. Nelson, and R.E. McRoberts. 1991b. Effects of maternal and grandmaternal nutrition on deer mass and vulnerability to wolf predation. J. Mammal. **72**: 146-151.

Mech, L.D., S.H. Fritts, G.L. Radde, and W.J. Paul. 1988b. Wolf distribution and road density in Minnesota. Wildl. Soc. Bull. **16**: 85-87.

Mech, L.D., S.M. Goyal, C.N. Bota, and U.S. Seal. 1986. Canine parvovirus infection in wolves (*Canis lupus*) from Minnesota. J. Wildl. Dis. **22**: 104-106.

Mech, L.D., K.E. Kunkel, R.C. Chapman, and T.J. Kreeger. 1990. Field testing of commercially manufactured capture collars on white-tailed deer. J. Wildl. Manage. **54**: 297-299.

Mech, L.D., R.E. McRoberts, R.O. Peterson, and R.E. Page. 1987. Relationship of deer and moose populations to previous winters' snow. J. Anim. Ecol. **56**: 615-627.

Mech, L.D., T.J. Meier, J.W. Burch, and L.G. Adams. 1991c. Demography and distribution of wolves, Denali National Park and Preserve, Alaska. U.S. Natl. Park Serv. Nat. Resour. Rep. No. AR-91/01. 32 pp.

Mech, L.D., R.P. Thiel, S.H. Fritts, and W.E. Berg. 1985. Presence and effects of the dog louse *Trichodectes canis* (Mallophaga, Trichodectidae) on wolves and coyotes from Minnesota and Wisconsin. Am. Midl. Nat. **114**: 404-405.

Medjo, D., and L.D. Mech. 1976. Reproductive activity in nine- and ten-month-old wolves. J. Mammal. **57**: 406-408.

Meier, T.J. 1987. 1986 aerial moose censusDenali National Park and Preserve. U.S. Natl. Park Serv. Nat. Resour. Rep. No. AR-87/10. 15 pp.

Meier, T.J., J.A. Keay, J.C. Van Horn, and J.W. Burch. 1991. 1991 aerial moose survey, Denali National Park and Preserve. U.S. Natl. Park Serv. Nat. Resour. Rep. No. AR-91/06. 20 pp.

Meinzer, W.P., D.N. Ueckert, and J.T. Flinders. 1975. Food niche of coyotes in the rolling plains of Texas. J. Range Manage. **28**: 22-27.

Melchoir, H.R., N.F. Johnson, and J.S. Phelps. 1987. Wild furbearer management in the western United States and Alaska. pp. 1115-1128 *in* M. Novak, J.A. Baker, M.E. Obbard, and B. Malloch, eds. Wild furbearer management and conservation in North America. Ontario Trappers Assoc., North Bay, Ont.

Mendelssohn, H. 1982. Wolves in Israel. pp. 173-195 *in* F.H. Harrington and P.C. Paquet, eds. Wolves of the world: perspectives of behavior, ecology, and conservation. Noyes, Park Ridge, N.J.

Merriam, H.R. 1963-1968. Monthly reports. Alaska Dep. Fish and Game Div. Game, Juneau.

Merriam, H.R. 1967. Deer report. Alaska Dep. Fish and Game, Juneau. Vol. 8: 7-12.

Merriam, H.R. 1971. Deer report. Alaska Dep. Fish and Game, Juneau. Vol. 11: 5-6.

Merrill, E.H., and M.S. Boyce. 1991. Summer range and elk population dynamics in Yellowstone National Park. pp. 263-274 *in* R.B. Keiter and M.S. Boyce, eds. The Greater Yellowstone ecosystem: redefining America's wilderness heritage. Yale Univ. Press, New Haven, Conn.

Merrill, E.H., M.S. Boyce, R.W. Marrs, and M.K. Bramble-Brodahl. 1988. Relationships among climatic variation, grassland phytomass and ungulate population dynamics on the northern range of Yellowstone National Park. Unpubl. Final Rep., U.W. Natl. Park Serv. Res. Cent., Univ. Wyoming, Laramie. 64 pp.

Merrill, E.H., M.K. Bramble-Brodahl, R.W. Marrs, and M.S. Boyce. 1993. Estimation of green herbaceous phytomass from Landsat MSS data in Yellowstone National Park. J. Range Manage. **46**: 151-156.

Merryman, W., R. Boiman, L. Barnes, and I. Rothchild. 1954. Progesterone "anesthesia" in human subjects. J. Clin. Endocrinol. **14**: 1567-1569.

Messier, F. 1984. Moose-wolf dynamics and the natural regulation of moose populations. Ph.D. Thesis, Univ. British Columbia, Vancouver, B.C. 143 pp.

Messier, F. 1985a. Social organization, spatial distribution, and population density of wolves in relation to moose density. Can. J. Zool. **63**: 1068-1077.

Messier, F. 1985b. Solitary living and extraterritorial movements of wolves in relation to social status and prey abundance. Can. J. Zool. **63**: 239-245.

Messier, F. 1989. Towards understanding the relationship between wolf predation and moose density in southwestern Quebec. pp. 13-25 *in* D. Seip, S. Pettigrew, and R. Archibald, eds. Wolf-prey dynamics and management. British Columbia Min. Environ. Wildl. Working Rep. No. WR-40.

Messier, F. 1991a. The significance of limiting and regulating factors on the demography of moose and white-tailed deer. J. Anim. Ecol. **60**: 377-393.

Messier, F. 1991b. On the concepts of population limitation and population regulation as applied to caribou demography. Proc. North Am. Caribou Workshop **4**: 260-277.

Messier, F. 1994. Ungulate population models with predation: a case study with the North American moose. Ecology **75**: 478-488.

Messier, F. 1995. Is there evidence for a cumulative effect of snow on moose and deer populations? J. Anim. Ecol. **64**: 136-140.

Messier, F., and C. Barrette. 1985. The efficiency of yarding behaviour by white-tailed deer as an antipredator strategy. Can. J. Zool. **63**: 785-789.

Messier, F., and M. Crête. 1985. Moose-wolf dynamics and the natural regulation of moose populations. Oecologia (Berlin) **65**: 503-512.

Messier, F., M.E. Rau, and M.A. McNeill. 1989. *Echinococcus granulosus* (Cestoda: Taeniidae) infections and moose-wolf population dynamics in southwestern Quebec. Can. J. Zool. **67**: 216-219.

Messier, F., J. Huot, D. Le Henaff, and S. Luttich. 1988. Demography of the George River caribou herd: evidence of population regulation by forage exploitation and range expansion. Arctic **41**: 279-287.

Metts, B.C. 1990. Other rodenticides. pp. 1123-1130 *in* L.M. Haddad and J.F. Winchester, eds. Clinical management of poisoning and drug overdose. Ch. 72. Phosphorus, strychnine, and other rodenticides. 2nd ed. W.B. Saunders, Philadelphia, Pa.

Michaelson, K.A., and J.W. Goertz. 1977. Food habits of coyotes in northwest Louisiana. Louisiana Acad. Sci. **40**: 77-81.

Millar, W.N. 1915. Game preservation in the Rocky Mountains Forest Reserve. Dep. Inter. For. Br. Bull. No. 51. 69 pp.

Miller, F.L. 1978. Interactions between men, dogs and wolves on western Queen Elizabeth Islands, Northwest Territories, Canada. Musk-ox **22**: 70-72.

Miller, F.L. 1990. Peary caribou status report. Can. Wildl. Serv. West and North. Reg. Rep. 64 pp.

Miller, F.L. 1993. Status of wolves in the Canadian Arctic Archipelago. Can. Wildl. Serv. West. and North. Reg., Edmonton, Alta., Tech. Rep. Ser., No. 173. 63 pp.

Miller, F.L., and E. Broughton. 1974. Calf mortality on the calving grounds of the Kaminuriak caribou. Can. Wildl. Serv. Rep. Ser., No. 26. 26 pp.

Miller, F.L., E. Broughton, and A. Gunn. 1983. Mortality of newborn migratory barren-ground caribou calves, Northwest Territories, Canada. Acta Zool. Fenn. **175**: 155-156.

Miller, F.L., E. Broughton, and A. Gunn. 1988a. Mortality of migratory barren-ground caribou on the calving grounds of the Beverly herd, Northwest Territories, 1981-1983. Can. Wildl. Serv. Occas. Pap. No. 66. 26 pp.

Miller, F.L., A. Gunn, and E. Broughton. 1985. Surplus killing as exemplified by wolf predation on newborn caribou. Can. J. Zool. **63**: 295-300.

Miller, F.L., A. Gunn, and E. Broughton. 1988b. Utilisation of carcasses of newborn caribou killed by wolves. Proc. North Am. Caribou Workshop **3**: 73-87.

Miller, F.L., R.H. Russell, and A. Gunn. 1977. Distribution, movements and numbers of Peary caribou and musk-oxen on western Queen Elizabeth Islands, Northwest Territories, 1972-1974. Can. Wildl. Serv. Rep. Ser., No. 40. 55 pp.

Miller, G.S. 1912. The names of the large wolves of northern and western North America. Smithson. Misc. Coll. **59**: 5 pp.

Miller, G.S., and R. Kellogg. 1955. List of North American Recent mammals. U.S. Natl. Mus. Bull. **205**: 954.

Miller, S. 1973. Ends, means and Galumphing: some leit-motifs of play. Am. Anthropol. **75**: 87-98.

Milon, J.W., and R. Clemmons. 1991. Hunters' demand for species variety. Land Econ. **67**: 401-412.

Miner, M. 1967. More about deer and wolves. An open letter to Ontario's MPPs. 2 pp.

Ministry of the Environment. 1982. Guidelines for wildlife policy in Canada. Supply and Services Canada, Ottawa, Ont. 14 pp.

Minnesota Veterinary Diagnostic Laboratory. 1986-1990. Annual Reports. Univ. Minnesota, St. Paul.

Minta, S. 1990. Annotated wolf bibliography for the northern Rockies. U.S. Forest Service and Northern Rockies Conservation Cooperative, Kalispell, Mont. 465 pp.

Minta, S.C. 1992. Tests of spatial and temporal interaction among animals. Ecol. Applic. **2**: 178-188.

Mitchell, R.B. 1976. A review of bison management, Wood Buffalo National Park, 1972-1976. pp. B1-B43 *in* J.G. Stelfox, ed. Wood Buffalo National Park: bison research 1972-1976. Can. Wildl. Serv./Parks Canada 1976 Annu. Rep.

Mitchell, R.L., and S.L. Beasom. 1974. Hookworms in south Texas coyotes and bobcats. J. Wildl. Manage. **38**: 455-458.

Moberly, H.J., and W.R. Cameron. 1929. When fur was king. Dutton, New York, N.Y. 237 pp.

Mohr, C.O. 1947. Table of equivalent animal populations of North American small mammals. Am. Midl. Nat. **37**: 233-249.

Montana Agriculture Statistics. 1991. Montana Agric. Stats. Vol. XXVII. Helena. 81 pp.

Montana Agriculture Statistics. 1992. A summary of results. Montana Crop and Livestock Reporter, Helena. May 14, 1992. 4 pp.

Montana citizens. 1878. Petition to Secretary of the Interior, April. File microcopies of records in the National Archives: interior relating to the Yellowstone National Park, 1872-1886 and 1872-1886 (letters received). Yellowstone National Park Research Library, Mammoth, Wyo.

Montana Department of Fish, Wildlife, and Parks. 1988. Fish and wildlife of the Bob Marshall Wilderness Complex and surrounding area. 161 pp.

More, T. 1978. Wildlife in children's stories: the empirical Mother Goose. U.S. Dept. Agric. For. Serv. Northeast. For. and Exp. Stn., Amherst, Mass. 24 pp.

Morgan, S.O. (ed.) 1990a. Wolf. Annual report survey-inventory activities. Vol. XX. Part XV. Alaska Dep. Fish and Game Fed. Aid in Wildl. Restoration Rep., Proj. W-23-3. 158 pp.

Morgan, S.O. (ed.) 1990b. Deer. Annual report survey-inventory activities. Vol. XX. Part VI. Alaska Dep. Fish and Game Fed. Aid in Wildl. Restoration Rep., Proj. W-23-2. 60 pp.

Morrison, B. 1978. Peary caribou: a study of natural mortality. Unpubl. Rep., Northwest Territ. Wildl. Serv., Yellowknife, N.W.T. 15 pp.

Morton, J.K. 1986. Role of predators in reindeer brucellosis in Alaska. Proc. Int. Reindeer/Caribou Symp. **4**: 368. (abstract).

Moulton, D.G., and D.A. Marshall. 1976. The performance of dogs in detecting alpha-ionone in the vapor phase. J. Comp. Physiol. **110**: 287-306.

Moulton, D.G., E.H. Ashton, and J.I. Eayrs. 1960. Studies in olfactory acuity. 4. Relative detectability of n-aliphatic acids by the dog. Anim. Behav. **8**: 117-128.

Mowat, F. 1963. Never cry wolf. Dell, New York, N.Y. 175 pp.

Muller-Schwarze, D. 1972. Responses of young black-tailed deer to predator odors. J. Mammal. **53**: 393-394.

Munro, J.A. 1947. Observations of birds and mammals in central British Columbia. British Columbia Prov. Mus. Occas. Pap. No. 6: 165 pp.

Murdoch, W.W. 1969. Switching in general predators: experiments on predator specificity and stability of prey populations. Ecol. Monogr. **39**: 335-354.

Murdoch, W.W., and A. Oaten. 1975. Predation and population stability. Adv. Ecol. Res. **9**: 131 pp.

Murie, A. 1940. Ecology of the coyote in the Yellowstone. Fauna of the National Parks of the United States, Fauna Ser., No. 4. U.S. Gov. Print. Off., Washington, D.C. 206 pp.

Murie, A. 1944. The wolves of Mount McKinley. Fauna of the National Parks of the U.S., Fauna Ser., No. 5. U.S. Gov. Print. Off., Washington, D.C. 238 pp.

Murie, O.J. 1951. Do you want hunting in our National parks? Nat. Hist. **60**: 464-467.

Murray, B.G. 1982. On the meaning of density dependence. Oecologia (Berlin) **53**: 370-373.

Myrberget, S. 1990. Wildlife management in Europe outside the USSR. N.I.N.A. Utredning Trondheim. 100 pp.

N

Nams, V.O., and S. Boutin. 1991. What is wrong with error polygons? J. Wildl. Manage. **55**: 172-176.

Nash, R. 1967. Wilderness and the American mind. Yale Univ. Press, New Haven, Conn. 256 pp.

Nath, A. 1982. Some observations on wildlife in the upper Suru/northern Zanskar/Markha valley of Ladakh. Int. Ped. Book Snow Leopards **3**: 11-24.

National Park Service. 1987. Gates of the Arctic National Park and Preserve, Alaska general management plan/land protection plan/wilderness suitability review. 299 pp.

National Park Service and Fish and Wildlife Service. (eds.) 1990a. Wolves for Yellowstone? A report to the United States Congress. Vol. I. Executive summary. Yellowstone National Park, Mammoth, Wyo. 38 pp.

National Park Service and Fish and Wildlife Service. (eds.) 1990b. Wolves for Yellowstone? A report to the United States Congress. Vol. II. Research and analysis. Yellowstone National Park, Mammoth, Wyo. 575 pp.

National Agricultural Statistics Board, U.S. Department of Agriculture. 1992. Cattle and calves death loss. Report, May 1, 1992, Washington, D.C. 24 pp.

Nee, J.A., and G. Oakley. 1986. Wolf management. pp. 49-54 *in* WOLF! A modern look. Wolves in American Culture Committee, Boise, Id., and Northward, Ashland, Wis.

Neiland, K.A. 1970. Weight of dried marrow as indicator of fat in caribou femurs. J. Wildl. Manage. **34**: 904-907.

Neiland, K.A. 1975. Further observations on rangiferine brucellosis in Alaskan carnivores. J. Wildl. Dis. **11**: 45-53.

Neiland, K.A., and L.G. Miller. 1981. Experimental *Brucella suis* type 4 infections in domestic and wild Alaskan carnivores. J. Wildl. Dis. **17**: 183-189.

Nellis, C.H. 1968. Some methods for capturing coyotes alive. J. Wildl. Manage. **32**: 402-405.

Nelson, E.W., and E.A. Goldman. 1929. A new wolf from Mexico. J. Mammal. **10**: 165-166.

Nelson, L.W., and W.A. Kelly. 1976. Progestogen-related gross and microscopic changes in female beagles. Vet. Pathol. **13**: 143-156.

Nelson, M.E., and L.D. Mech. 1981. Deer social organization and wolf predation in northwestern Minnesota. Wildl. Monogr. **77**: 53 pp.

Nelson, M.E., and L.D. Mech. 1985. Observation of a wolf killed by a deer. J. Mammal. **66**: 187-188.

Nelson, M.E., and L.D. Mech. 1986a. White-tailed deer numbers and population trend in the central Superior National Forest, 1967-1985. U.S. Dep. Agric. For. Serv. Res. Pap. NC-271. 8 pp.

Nelson, M.E., and L.D. Mech. 1986b. Relationship between snow depth and gray wolf predation on white-tailed deer. J. Wildl. Manage. **50**: 471-474.

Nelson, M.E., and L.D. Mech. 1991. Wolf predation risk associated with white-tailed deer movements. Can. J. Zool. **69**: 2696-2699.

Nelson, R.K. 1983. Make prayers to the raven. Univ. Chicago Press, Chicago, Ill. 292 pp.

Nemetz, P.N. (ed.) 1980. Resource policy: international perspectives. Institute for Research on Public Policy, Montréal, P.Q. 371 pp.

Neuhaus, W. 1953. Uber die Riechscharfe des Hundes fur Fettsauren. Z. Vergl. Physiol. **35**: 527-552.

Nicholson, J. 1957. Comments on the paper of T.B. Reynoldson. Cold Springs Harbor Symp. Quant. Biol. **22**: 326.

Nieminen, M. 1990. Hoof and foot loads for reindeer. Proc. Int. Reindeer/Caribou Symp. **5**: 249-254.

Noffsinger, R.E., R.W. Laneu, A.M. Nichols, D.L. Stewart, and D.W. Steffeck. 1984. Prulean Farms Wildlife Coordination Act Report. Unpubl. Rep., U.S. Fish and Wildl. Serv., Raleigh, N.C. 200 pp.

Norris, P.W. 1880. Report upon the Yellowstone National Park to the Secretary of the Interior by P.W. Norris, Superintendent, for the year 1879. U.S. Gov. Print. Off., Washington, D.C. 31 pp.

Norris, P.W. 1881. Annual report of the Superintendent of the Yellowstone National Park to the Secretary of the Interior for the year 1880. U.S. Gov. Print. Off., Washington, D.C. 64 pp.

Norris, P.W. No date. Meanderings of a mountaineer, or, The journals and musings (or storys) of a rambler over prairie (or mountain) and plain. Ms. prepared from newspaper clippings (1870-75) and handwritten addition, annotated about 1885. Huntington Library, San Marino, Calif.

Norton, H.J. 1873. Wonderland illustrated, or, Horseback rides through the Yellowstone National Park. Harry J. Norton, Virginia City, Mont. 132 pp.

Noss, R. 1991. What can wilderness do for biodiversity? pp. 51-56 *in* Wild Earth, Canton, N.Y.

Novak, M. 1987. Traps and trap research. pp. 941-969 *in* M. Novak, J.A. Baker, M.E. Obbard, and B. Malloch, eds. Wild furbearer management and conservation in North America. Ontario Trappers Assoc., North Bay, Ont.

Nowak, R.M. 1972. The mysterious wolf of the south. Nat. Hist. **81**: 51-53, 74-77.

Nowak, R.M. 1973. North American Quaternary *Canis*. Ph.D. Thesis, Univ. Kansas, Lawrence. 424 pp.

Nowak, R.M. 1979. North American Quaternary *Canis*. Univ. Kansas Mus. Nat. Hist. Monogr. No. 6: 154 pp.

Nowak, R.M. 1983. A perspective on the taxonomy of wolves in North America. pp. 10-19 *in* L.N. Carbyn, ed. Wolves in Canada and Alaska: their status, biology, and management. Can. Wildl. Serv. Rep. Ser., No. 45.

Nowak, R.M. 1991. A response to O'Brien and Mayr. Science (Washington, D.C.) **251**: 1187-1188.

Nowak, R.M. 1992. The red wolf is not a hybrid. Conserv. Biol. **6**: 593-595.

Nowak, R.M., and J.L. Paradiso. 1983. Walker's mammals of the world. 4th ed. 2 vols. Johns Hopkins Univ. Press, Baltimore, Md. 1362 pp.

Nowlin, R.A. 1988. Unit 25 Wolf Survey-Inventory Report. pp. 55-59 *in* S.O. Morgan, ed. Annual Report of Survey-Inventory Activities. Vol. XVIII. Part XV. Alaska Dep. Fish and Game Fed. Aid in Wildl. Restoration Prog. Rep., Proj. W-22-6.

Nyberg, M., K. Kulonen, E. Neuvonen, C. Ek-Kommonen, M. Nuorgam, and B. Westerling. 1992. An epidemic of sylvatic rabies in Finlanddescriptive epidemiology and results of oral vaccination. Acta Vet. Scand. **33**: 43-75.

O

Oakley, G. 1986. Historic review. pp. 1-7 *in* WOLF! A modern look. Wolves in American Culture Committee, Boise, Id., and Northward Inc., Ashland, Wis.

Oaten, A., and W.W. Murdoch. 1975. Functional response and stability in predator-prey systems. Am. Nat. **109**: 289-298.

O'Brien, S.J. 1991. Species hybridization and protection of endangered animals. Science (Washington, D.C.) **253**: 251-252.

O'Brien, S.J., and E. Mayr. 1991. Bureaucratic mischief: recognizing endangered species and subspecies. Science (Washington, D.C.) **251**: 1187-1188.

O'Brien, S.J., M.E. Roelke, N. Yuhki, K.W. Richards, W.E. Johnson, W.L. Franklin, A.E. Anderson, O.L. Bass, Jr., R.C. Belton, and J.S. Martenson. 1990. Genetic introgression within the Florida panther, *Felis concolor coryi*. Natl. Geogr. Res. **6**: 485-494.

Oleyar, C.M., and B.S. McGinnes. 1974. Field evaluation of diethylstilbestrol for suppressing reproduction in foxes. J. Wildl. Manage. **38**: 101-106.

Olson, S.F. 1938. Organization and range of the pack. Ecology **19**: 168-170.

Omand, D.N. 1950. The bounty system in Ontario. J. Wildl. Manage. **14**: 425-434.

O'Neill, B.B. 1988. The law of wolves. Environ. Law **18**: 227-240.

Ontario Ministry of Natural Resources. 1992. Hunting regulations summary: fall '91-spring '92. Queen's Printer, Toronto, Ont.

Oosenbrug, S.M., and L.N. Carbyn. 1985. Wolf predation on bison in Wood Buffalo National Park. Can. Wildl. Serv. Rep., Edmonton, Alta., 264pp. (unpublished).

Orford, H.J.L., M.R. Perrin, and H.H. Berry. 1988. Contraception, reproduction and demography of free-ranging Etosha lions (*Panthera leo*). J. Zool. (Lond.) **216**: 717-733.

Ortalli, G. 1973. Natura, storia e mitografia del lupo nel Medioevo. La Cultura **9**: 257-311.

Ott, L. 1988. An introduction to statistical methods and data analysis. PWS-Kent, Boston, Mass. 855 pp.

Ozaga, J.J., and L.J. Verme. 1982. Physical and reproductive characteristics of a supplementally-fed white-tailed deer herd. J. Wildl. Manage. 46(2): 281-301.

Ozaga, J.J., and L.J. Verme. 1986. Relation of maternal age to fawn-rearing success in white-tailed deer. J. Wildl. Manage. **50**: 480-486.

P

Packard, J.M., and L.D. Mech. 1980. Population regulation in wolves. pp. 135-150 *in* M.N. Cohen, R.S. Malpass, and H.G. Klein, eds. Biosocial mechanisms of population regulation. Yale Univ. Press, New Haven, Conn.

Packard, J.M., and L.D. Mech. 1983. Population regulation in wolves. pp. 151-174 *in* F.L. Bunnell, D.S. Eastman, and J.M. Peek, eds. Symposium on natural regulation of wildlife populations. Proc. No. 14, For. Wildl. and Range Exp. Stn., Univ. Idaho, Moscow.

Packard, J.M., L.D. Mech, and U.S. Seal. 1983. Social influences on reproduction in wolves. pp. 78-85 *in* L.N. Carbyn, ed. Wolves in Canada and Alaska: their status, biology, and management. Can. Wildl. Serv. Rep. Ser., No. 45.

Packard, J.M., U.S. Seal, L.D. Mech, and E.D. Plotka. 1985. Causes of reproductive failure in two family groups of wolves (*Canis lupus*). Z. Tierpsychol. **68**: 24-40.

Packer, C., D.A. Gilbert, A.E. Pussey, and S.J. O'Brien. 1991. A molecular genetic analysis of kinship and cooperation in African lions. Nature (Lond.) **351**: 562-565.

Page, R.E. 1985. Early caribou calf mortality in northwestern British Columbia. M.Sc. Thesis, Univ. Victoria, B.C. 129 pp.

Page, R.E. 1989. The inverted pyramid: ecosystem dynamics of wolves and moose on Isle Royale. Ph.D. Thesis, Michigan Tech. Univ., Houghton. 62 pp.

Pamilo, P., and M. Nei. 1988. Relationships between gene trees and species trees. Molec. Biol. Evol. **5**: 568-583.

Paquay, R., R. De Baere, and A. Lousse. 1972. The capacity of the mature cow to lose and recover nitrogen and the significance of protein reserves. Br. J. Nutr. **27**: 27-37.

Paquet, P.C. 1991a. Winter spatial relationships of wolves and coyotes in Riding Mountain National Park, Manitoba. J. Mammal. **72**: 397-401.

Paquet, P.C. 1991b. Scent-marking behavior of sympatric wolves (*Canis lupus*) and coyotes (*C. latrans*) in Riding Mountain National Park. Can. J. Zool. **69**: 1721-1727.

Paquet, P.C. 1992. Prey use strategies of sympatric wolves and coyotes in Riding Mountain National Park, Manitoba. J. Mammal. **73**: 337-343.

Paradiso, J.L. 1968. Canids recently collected in east Texas, with comments on the taxonomy of the red wolf. Am. Midl. Nat. **80**: 529-534.

Paradiso, J.L., and R.M. Nowak. 1971. A report on the taxonomic status and distribution of the red wolf. U.S. Fish and Wildl. Serv. Spec. Wildl. Rep. No. 145. 36 pp.

Paradiso, J.L., and R.M. Nowak. 1972. *Canis rufus*. Mammalian species No. 22. Am. Soc. Mammal. 4 pp.

Paradiso, J.L., and R.M. Nowak. 1973. New data on the red wolf in Alabama. J. Mammal. **54**: 506-509.

Parker, G.R. 1973. Distribution and densities of wolves within barren-ground caribou range in northern mainland Canada. J. Mammal. **54**: 341-348.

Parker, G.R., and S. Luttich. 1986. Characteristics of the wolf (*Canis lupus labradorius* Goldman) in northern Quebec and Labrador. Arctic **39**: 145-149.

Parker, G.R., and J.W. Maxwell. 1986. Identification of pups and yearling wolves by dentine width in the canine. Arctic **39**: 180-181.

Parker, G.R., D.C. Thomas, E. Broughton, and D.R. Gray. 1975. Crashes of muskox and Peary caribou populations in 1973-74 in the Parry Islands, Arctic Canada. Can. Wildl. Serv. Prog. Note, No. 56. 10 pp.

Parker, R.L., and R.E. Wilsnack. 1966. Pathogenesis of skunk rabies virus: quantitation in skunks and foxes. Am. J. Vet. Res. **27**: 33-38.

Parker, W.T. 1986. A technical proposal to reestablish the red wolf in the Alligator River National Wildlife Refuge, North Carolina. U.S. Fish and Wildl. Serv. 20 pp.

Parker, W.T. 1987. A strategy for establishing and utilizing red wolf populations on islands. U.S. Fish and Wildl. Serv. Red Wolf Manage. Ser., Tech. Rep. No. 2. 9 pp.

Parker, W.T. 1990. A proposal to reintroduce the red wolf into the Great Smoky Mountains National Park. U.S. Fish and Wildl. Serv. Red Wolf Manage. Ser., Tech. Rep. No. 7. 33 pp.

Parker, W.T., and M.K. Phillips. 1991. Application of the experimental population designation to the recovery of endangered red wolves. Wildl. Soc. Bull. **19**: 73-79.

Parker, W.T., M.P. Jones, and P.G. Poulos. 1986. Determination of experimental population status for an introduced population of red wolves in North Carolina final rule. Fed. Regist. **51**: 41790-41796.

Parker, W.T., R. Smith, T. Foose, and U.S. Seal. 1989. Agency review draft red wolf recovery plan. U.S. Fish and Wildl. Serv., Atlanta, Ga.

Parrish, C.R., P.H. O'Connell, J.F. Evermann, and L.E. Carmichael. 1985. Natural variation of canine parvovirus. Science (Washington, D.C.) **230**: 1046-1048.

Paseneaux, C., and P. Tucker. 1991. Wolf reintroduction in Yellowstone: the debate continues. Point: counterpoint. Int. Wolf **1**(3): 7-10.

Paul, W.J., and P.S. Gipson. 1994. Wolves. pp. 123-129 *In* Prevention and control of wildlife damage. Univ. Nebraska Press Coop. Ext. Serv., Lincoln.

Paulson, I. 1970. La religion des peuples arctic. pp. 335-399 *in* H.C. Puech, ed. Histoire des religions. Libraire Gallimard, Paris.

Pedersen, S. 1982. Geographical variation in Alaskan wolves. pp. 345-361 *in* F.H. Harrington and P.C. Paquet, eds. Wolves of the world: perspectives of behavior, ecology, and conservation. Noyes, Park Ridge, N.J.

Peek, J.M. 1974. Initial response of moose to a forest fire in northeastern Minnesota. Am. Midl. Nat. **91**: 435-438.

Peek, J.M., and D.S. Eastman. 1983. Factors which naturally control moose populations. pp. 175-193 *in* F.L. Bunnell, D.S. Eastman, and J.M. Peek, eds. Symposium on natural regulation of wildlife populations. Proc. No. 14, For. Wildl. and Range Exp. Stn., Univ. Idaho, Moscow.

Peek, J.M., and D.J. Vales. 1989. Projecting the effects of wolf predation on elk and mule deer in the East Front portion of the Northwest Montana Wolf Recovery Area. Unpubl. Rep., U.S. Fish and Wildl. Serv., Helena, Mont. 89 pp.

Peek, J.M., E.E. Brown, S.R. Kellert, L.D. Mech, J.H. Shaw, and V. Van Ballenberghe. 1991. Restoration of wolves in North America. Wildl. Soc. Tech. Rev. **91-1**: 21 pp.

Pegau, R.E. 1987. Unit 19 Wolf Survey-Inventory Report. pp. 36-37 *in* B. Townsend, ed. Annual report of survey-inventory activities. Vol. XVII. Part XV. Alaska Dep. Fish and Game Fed. Aid in Wildl. Restoration Prog. Rep., Proj. W-22-5.

Pence, D.B., and J.W. Custer. 1981. Host-parasite relationships in the wild Canidae of North America II. Pathology of infectious diseases in the genus *Canis*. Proc. Worldwide Furbearer Conf. **1**: 760-845.

Person, D.K., and H. Hirth. 1991. Home range and habitat use of coyotes in a farm region of Vermont. J. Wildl. Manage. **55**: 433-441.

Persson, L. 1985. Asymmetrical competition: are larger animals competitively superior? Am. Nat. **126**: 261-266.

Peters, R.P., and L.D. Mech. 1975. Scent-marking in wolves: a field study. Am. Scient. **63**: 628-637.

Peterson, F.A., W.C. Heaton, and S.D. Wruble. 1969. Levels of auditory response in fissiped carnivores. J. Mammal. **50**: 566-578.

Peterson, R.O. 1977. Wolf ecology and prey relationships on Isle Royale. U.S. Natl. Park Serv. Sci. Monogr. Ser., No. 11. 210 pp.

Peterson, R.O. 1994. Out of the doldrums for Isle Royale wolves? Int. Wolf 4(2): 19.

Peterson, R.O., and R.J. Krumenaker. 1989. Wolves approach extinction on Isle Royale: a biological and policy conundrum. George Wright Forum **6**: 10-15.

Peterson, R.O., and R.E. Page. 1988. The rise and fall of Isle Royale wolves, 1975-1986. J. Mammal. **69**: 89-99.

Peterson, R.O., and J.D. Woolington. 1982. The apparent extirpation and reappearance of wolves on the Kenai Peninsula, Alaska. pp. 334-344 *in* F.H. Harrington and P.C. Paquet, eds. Wolves of the world: perspectives on behavior, ecology, and conservation. Noyes, Park Ridge, N.J.

Peterson, R.O., J.D. Woolington, and T.N. Bailey. 1984. Wolves of the Kenai Peninsula, Alaska. Wildl. Monogr. **88**: 52 pp.

Pfeifer, W.K., and M.W. Goos. 1982. Guard dogs and gas exploders as coyote depredation control tools in North Dakota. Proc. Vertebr. Pest Conf. **10**: 55-61.

Phillips, M.K. 1990a. Media and public involvement in red wolf restoration. pp. 85-98 *in* B. Holaday, ed. Proc. Arizona wolf symposium '90, Tempe, Ariz., 23-24 March 1990.

Phillips, M.K. 1990b. Measures of the value and success of a reintroduction project: red wolf reintroduction in Alligator River National Wildlife Refuge. Endang Spec. Update **8**: 24-26.

Phillips, M.K., and W.T. Parker. 1988. Red wolf recovery: a progress report. Conserv. Biol. **2**: 139-141.

Pickard, R. 1987. Archaeological resource description of the Canadian National Railway Corridor, Jasper National Park. Micro. Rep. Ser. 337, Environ. Can., Ottawa, Ont. 137 pp.

Pike, W.M. 1892. The barren ground caribou of northern Canada. Macmillan, London. 300 pp.

Pimlott, D.H. 1961a. Wolf control in Canada. Can. Aud. **23**: 145-152.

Pimlott, D.H. 1961b. Wolf control in Ontariopast, present and future. Federal-Provincial Wildl. Conf. **25**: 54-74.

Pimlott, D.H. 1963. Wolf control and management in Ontario. Ontario Fish and Wildl. Rev. **2**: 20-28.

Pimlott, D.H. 1967a. Wolf predation and ungulate populations. Am. Zool. **7**: 267-278.

Pimlott, D.H. 1967b. Wolves and men in North America. Study No. 5. Defenders of Wildlife News **42**: 36-53.

Pimlott, D.H., and P.W. Joslin. 1968. The status and distribution of the red wolf. Trans. North Am. Wildl. and Nat. Resour. Conf. **33**: 373-389.

Pimlott, D.H., J.A. Shannon, and G.B. Kolenosky. 1969. The ecology of the timber wolf in Algonquin Provincial Park. Ont. Dep. Lands and For. Res. Rep. (Wildl.) No. 87. 92 pp.

Pineda, M.H., and D.I. Hepler. 1981. Chemical vasectomy in dogs. Long-term study. Theriogenology **16**: 1-11.

Pinigan, A.F., and V.A. Zabrodin. 1970. On the natural nidality of brucellosis. Vest. Sel'skokhoz Nauki (Moscow) **7**: 96-99.

Pletscher, D.H., R.R. Ream, R. DeMarchi, W.G. Brewster, and E.E. Bangs. 1991. Managing wolf and ungulate populations in an international ecosystem. Trans. North Am. Wildl. and Nat. Resour. Conf. **56**: 539-549.

Pocock, R.I. 1935. The races of *Canis lupus*. Proc. Zool. Soc. (Lond.), Pt. 3: 617-686.

Polenick, S. 1982. The case against 1080. Defenders **57**(4): 28-35.

Pollock, R.V.H. 1982. Experimental canine parvovirus infection in dogs. Cornell Vet. **72**: 113-119.

Pollock, R.V.H. 1984. The parvoviruses. Part II. Canine parvovirus. Compend. Cont. Ed. **6**: 653-664.

Pomerantz, G.A., and K.A. Blanchard. 1992. Successful communication and education strategies for wildlife conservation. Trans. North Am. Wildl. and Nat. Resour. Conf. **57**: 156-163.

Porton, I., C.S. Asa, and A. Baker. 1990. Survey results on the use of birth control methods in primates and carnivores in North American zoos. Proc. Am. Assoc. Zool. Parks and Aquar. 1990: 489-497.

Potvin, F. 1988. Wolf movements and population dynamics in Papineau-Labelle reserve, Quebec. Can. J. Zool. **66**: 1266-1273.

Potvin, F., H. Jolicoeur, and J. Huot. 1988. Wolf diet and prey selectivity during two periods for deer in Quebec: decline versus expansion. Can. J. Zool. **66**: 1274-1279.

Potvin, F., L. Breton, C. Pilon, and M. Macquart. 1992a. Impact of an experimental wolf reduction on beaver in Papineau-Labelle Reserve, Quebec. Can. J. Zool. **70**: 180-183.

Potvin, F., H. Jolicoeur, L. Breton, and R. Lemieux. 1992b. Evaluation of an experimental wolf reduction and its impact on deer in Papineau-Labelle Reserve, Quebec. Can. J. Zool. **70**: 1595-1603.

Pratt, S.E., J.J. Mall, J.D. Rhoades, R.E. Hertzog, and R.M. Corwin. 1981. Dirofilariasis in a captive wolf pack. Vet. Med. and Small Anim. Clinician **76**: 698-699.

Prins, L., and W.D.G. Yates. 1986. Rabies in western Canada, 1978-1984. Can. Vet. J. **27**: 164-169.

Puech, H.C. (ed.) 1970. Histoire des religions. Libraire Gallimard, Paris. 441 pp.

Pulliainen, E. 1982. Behavior and structure of an expanding wolf population in Karelia, northern Europe. pp. 134-145 *in* F.H. Harrington and P.C. Paquet, eds. Wolves of the world: perspectives of behavior, ecology, and conservation. Noyes, Park Ridge, N.J.

Pybus, M.J. 1988. Rabies and rabies control in striped skunks (*Mephitis mephitis*) in three prairie regions of western North America. J. Wildl. Dis. **24**: 434-449.

Q

Quade, E.S. 1975. Analysis for public decisions. American Elsevier, New York, N.Y. 322 pp.

R

Rabenhold, P.P., and M. de Gortari. 1991. DNA fingerprinting of gray wolves. Final Report to the Univ. of Wyoming, U.S. National Park Service, Res. Cent., Dep. of Biol. Sci., Purdue Univ., West Lafayette, Ind. 38 pp.

Racey, G.D., K. Abraham, W.R. Darby, H.R. Timmermann, and Q. Day. 1991. Can caribou and the forest industry coexist: the Ontario scene. Proc. North Am. Caribou Workshop **5**: 108-115.

Rachael, J.S. 1992. Mortality and seasonal distribution of white-tailed deer in an area recently colonized by wolves. M.S. Thesis, Univ. Montana, Missoula. 115 pp.

Ralls, K., P.H. Harvey, and A.M. Lyles. 1986. Inbreeding in natural populations of birds and mammals. pp. 35-56 *in* M.E. Soulé, ed. Conservation biology: the science of scarcity and diversity. Sinauer Associates, Sunderland, Mass.

Ramenofsky, A.F. 1987. Vectors of death: the archaeology of European contact. Univ. New Mexico Press, Albuquerque. 300 pp.

Randall, D. 1980. Wolves for Yellowstone: experts say 'yes', though cautiously, to re-introduction. Defenders **55**: 188-190.

Rau, M.E., and F.R. Caron. 1979. Parasite-induced susceptibility of moose to hunting. Can. J. Zool. **57**: 2466-2468.

Rausch, R. 1958. Some observations on rabies in Alaska, with special reference to wild Canidae. J. Wildl. Manage. **22**: 246-260.

Rausch, R.A. 1964. Progress in management of the Alaskan wolf population. Proc. Alaskan Sci. Conf. **15**: 43 (abstract).

Rausch, R.A. 1967. Some aspects of the population ecology of wolves, Alaska. Am. Zool. **7**: 253-265.

Rausch, R.A. 1973. Rabies in Alaska: prevention and control. U.S. Dep. Hlth. Ed. Welfare Arct. Hlth. Res. Cent. Rep. No. 111. 20 pp.

Rausch, R.A., and R.A. Hinman. 1977. Wolf management in Alaska—an exercise in futility? pp. 147-156 *in* R.L. Phillips and C. Jonkel, eds. Proceedings of the 1975 predator symposium. Bull. For. and Conserv. Exp. Stn., Univ. Montana, Missoula.

Rausch, R.L. 1953. On the status of some Arctic mammals. Arctic **6**: 91-148.

Rausch, R.L., and F.S.L. Williamson. 1959. Studies on the helminth fauna of Alaska. XXXIV. The parasites of wolves, *Canis lupus* L. J. Parasitol. **45**: 395-403.

Raymer, J., D. Wiesler, M. Novotny, C.S. Asa, U.S. Seal, and L.D. Mech. 1984. Volatile constituents of wolf (*Canis lupus*) urine as related to gender and season. Experientia **40**: 707-709.

Raymer, J., D. Wiesler, M. Novotny, C.S. Asa, U.S. Seal, and L.D. Mech. 1985. Chemical investigation of wolf (*Canis lupus*) anal-sac secretion in relation to breeding season. J. Chem. Ecol. **11**: 593-608.

Raymer, J., D. Wiesler, M. Novotny, C.S. Asa, U.S. Seal, and L.D. Mech. 1986. Chemical scent constituents in urine of wolf (*Canis lupus*) and their dependence on reproductive hormones. J. Chem. Ecol. **12**: 297-314.

Raymond, R.W. 1873. The heart of the continent: the hot springs and geysers. Harper's Weekly **17** (Apr. 5): 272-274.

Raynolds, W.F. 1868. The report of Brevet Brigadier General W.F. Raynolds on the exploration of the Yellowstone and the county drained by that river, 1834-1843. Sen. Exec. Doc. 77, 40th Congr., 1st Sess. U.S. Gov. Print. Off., Washington, D.C. 174 pp.

Real, L.A. 1979. Ecological determinants of functional response. Ecology **60**: 481-485.

Ream, R.R. 1984. The wolf is at our door: population recovery in the northern Rockies. West. Wildlands **10**: 2-7.

Ream, R.R., and U.I. Mattson. 1982. Wolf status in the northern Rockies. pp. 362-381 *in* F.H. Harrington and P.C. Paquet, eds. Wolves of the world: perspectives of behavior, ecology, and conservation. Noyes, Park Ridge, N.J.

Ream, R.R., M.W. Fairchild, and D.K. Boyd. 1986. Wolf Ecology Project Progress Report, July 1985 through June 1986. Univ. Montana Sch. For. Montana Coop. Wildl. Res. Unit, Missoula. 26 pp.

Ream, R.R., M.W. Fairchild, D.K. Boyd, and A. Blakesley. 1989. First wolf den in western United States in recent history. Northwest. Nat. **70**: 39-40.

Ream, R.R., M.W. Fairchild, D.K. Boyd, and D.H. Pletscher. 1991. Population dynamics and home range changes in a colonizing wolf population. pp. 349-366 *in* R.B. Keiter and M.S. Boyce, eds. The Greater Yellowstone ecosystem: redefining America's wilderness heritage. Yale Univ. Press, New Haven, Conn.

Ream, R.R., R. Harris, J. Smith, and D. Boyd. 1985. Movement patterns of a lone wolf, *Canis lupus*, in unoccupied wolf range, southeastern British Columbia. Can. Field-Nat. **99**: 234-239.

Reich, A. 1978. A case of inbreeding in the African wild dog, *Lycaon pictus*, in the Kruger National Park. Koedoe **21**: 119-123.

Reid, R.T. 1985. The value and characteristics of resident hunting (results of the 1981 survey). British Columbia Min. Environ. Wildl. Br. 153 pp.

Reid, R.T., M. Stone, and F. Rothman. 1986. Report on the British Columbia Survey of non-hunting and other wildlife activities for 1983. British Columbia Min. Environ. Wildl. Br. 182 pp.

Reid-Sanden, F.L., J.G. Dobbins, J.S. Smith, and D.B. Fishbein. 1990. Rabies surveillance in the United States during 1989. J. Am. Vet. Med. Assoc. **197**: 1571-1583.

Reig, S., L. De la Cuesta, and F. Palacios. 1985. The impact of human activities on the food habits of red fox and wolf in Old Castille, Spain. Rev. Ecol. (Terre Vie) **40**: 151-155.

Reilly, J.R., L.E. Hanson, and D.H. Ferris. 1970. Experimentally induced predator chain transmission of *Leptospira grippotyphosa* from rodents to wild Marsupialia and Carnivora. Am. J. Vet. Res. **31**: 1443-1448.

Reynolds, H.V. 1990. Population dynamics of a hunted grizzly bear population in the northcentral Alaska Range. Alaska Dep. Fish and Game Fed. Aid in Wildl. Restoration Prog. Rep., Proj. W-23-2. 63 pp.

Reynolds, H.V., and G.W. Garner. 1987. Patterns of grizzly bear predation on caribou in northern Alaska. Int. Conf. Bear Res. and Manage. **7**: 59-68.

Richards, F.J. 1959. A flexible growth function for empirical use. J. Exp. Bot. **10**: 290-300.

Richardson, J. 1829. Fauna Boreali-Americana. John Murray: London xvi + 300 pp.

Richens, V.B., and R.D. Hugie. 1974. Distribution, taxonomic status, and characteristics of coyotes in Maine. J. Wildl. Manage. **38**: 447-454.

Riggs, B.S., and K. Kulig. 1990. Strychnine. pp. 1119-1123 *in* L.M. Haddad and J.F. Winchester, eds. Clinical management of poisoning and drug overdose. 2nd ed. W.B. Saunders, Philadelphia, Pa.

Riley, G.A., and R.T. McBride. 1972. A survey of the red wolf (*Canis rufus*). U.S. Fish and Wildl. Serv. Sci. Rep. (Wildl.) No. 162. 15 pp.

Riley, G.A., and R.T. McBride. 1975. A survey of the red wolf (*Canis rufus*). pp. 263-277 *in* M.W. Fox, ed. The wild canids: their systematics, behavioral ecology and evolution. Van Nostrand Reinhold, New York, N.Y.

Ritter, D.G. 1981. Rabies. pp. 6-12 *in* R.A. Dieterich, ed. Alaska wildlife diseases. Univ. Alaska, Fairbanks.

Ritter, D.G. 1991. Rabies in Alaskan furbearers: a review. Presented at the Sixth North. Furbearer Conf., Fairbanks, Alas., 10-11 April 1991.

Robbins, C.T., and B.L. Robbins. 1979. Fetal and neonatal growth patterns and maternal reproductive effort in ungulates and subungulates. Am. Nat. **114**: 101-116.

Robinson, W.B. 1943. The "humane coyote-getter" vs. the steel trap in control of predatory animals. J. Wildl. Manage. **7**: 179-189.

Robinson, W.B. 1948. Thallium and compound 1080 impregnated stations in coyote control. J. Wildl. Manage. **12**: 279-295.

Rock, T.W. 1992. A proposal for the management of woodland caribou in Saskatchewan. Saskatchewan Dep. Nat. Resour. Wildl. Tech. Rep. No. 92-3. 28 pp.

Rockel, M.L., and M.J. Kealy. 1991. The value of nonconsumptive wildlife recreation in the United States. Land Econ. **67**: 422-434.

Rodney, W. 1969. Kootenai Brown: his life and times, 1839-1916. Gray's, Sidney, B.C. 251 pp.

Roed, K.H., M.A.D. Fergeson, M. Crete, and T.A. Bergerud. 1991. Genetic variation in transferrin as a predictor for differentiation and evolution of caribou from eastern Canada. Rangifer **11**: 65-74.

Roper, T.J., and J. Ryon. 1977. Mutual synchronization of diurnal activity rhythms in groups of red wolf/coyote hybrids. J. Zool. (Lond.) **182**: 177-185.

Rosengren, A. 1969. Experiments in color discrimination in dogs. Acta Zool. Fenn. **121**: 1-19.

Rothman, R.J., and L.D. Mech. 1979. Scent-marking in lone wolves and newly-formed pairs. Anim. Behav. **27**: 750-760.

Rowe, J.S. 1972. Forest regions of Canada. Can. For. Serv. Publ. No. 1300. 172 pp.

Rowell, G. 1983. China's wildlife lament. Int. Wildl. **13**(6): 4-11.

Roy, L.D., and M.J. Dorrance. 1976. Methods of investigating predation of domestic livestock: a manual for investigating officers. Alberta Agr., Edmonton, 54 pp.

Roy, L.D., and M.J. Dorrance. 1985. Coyote movements, habitat use, and vulnerability in central Alberta. J. Wildl. Manage. **49**: 307-313.

Roy, M.S., E. Geffen, D. Smith, E.A. Ostrander, and R.K. Wayne. 1994. Patterns of differentiation and hybridization in North American wolf-like canids. MOI Biol. Evol. II: 553-570.

Rush, W.M. 1932. Northern Yellowstone elk study. Montana Fish and Game Comm. 131 pp.

Russell, O. 1965. Osborne Russell's journal of a trapper, 1834-1843. A.L. Haines, ed. Univ. Nebraska Press, Lincoln. 191 pp.

Rutter, R.J., and D.H. Pimlott. 1968. The world of the wolf. J.B. Lippincott, Philadelphia, Pa. 202 pp.

Ryder, O.A. 1986. Species conservation and systematics: the dilemma of subspecies. Trends Ecol. Evol. **1**: 9-10.

S

Saddique, A., and C.D. Peterson. 1983. Thallium poisoning: a review. Vet. Hum. Toxicol. **25**: 16-22.

Sahlins, M.D. 1972. Stone age economics. Aldine-Atherton Press, Chicago, Ill. 348 pp.

Salvador, A., and P.L. Abad. 1987. Food habits of a wolf population (*Canis lupus*) in Léon province, Spain. Mammalia **51**: 45-52.

Salwasser, H.A., C. Schonewald-Cox, and R. Baker. 1987. The role of interagency cooperation in managing for viable populations. pp. 159-173 *in* M.E. Soulé, ed. Viable populations for conservation. Cambridge Univ. Press, New York, N.Y.

Samuel, W.M., G.A. Chalmers, and J.R. Gunson. 1978. Oral papillomatosis in coyotes (*Canis latrans*) and wolves (*Canis lupus*) of Alberta. J. Wildl. Dis. **14**: 165-169.

Sargeant, A.B., and S.H. Allen. 1989. Observed interactions between coyotes and red foxes. J. Mammal. **70**: 631-633.

Sargeant, A.B., S.H. Allen, and J.O. Hastings. 1987. Spatial relations between sympatric coyotes and red foxes in North Dakota. J. Wildl. Manage. **51**: 285-293.

Sarosi, G.A., M.R. Eckman, S.F. Davies, and W.K. Laskey. 1979. Canine blastomycosis as a harbinger of human disease. Ann. Int. Med. **91**: 733-735.

SAS Institute, Inc. 1987. SAS/STAT guide for personal computers, version 6. 1028 pp.

Sauer, J.R., and M.S. Boyce. 1983. Density dependence and survival of elk in northwestern Wyoming. J. Wildl. Manage. **47**: 31-37.

Savarie, P., and R. Sterner. 1979. Evaluation of toxic collars for selective control of coyotes that attack sheep. J. Wildl. Manage. **43**: 780-783.

Scalia, F., and S.S. Winans. 1975. The differential projections of the olfactory bulb and accessory olfactory bulb in mammals. J. Comp. Neurol. **161**: 31-55.

Schaefer, J.A. 1987. Fire and woodland caribou (*Rangifer tarandus caribou*): an evaluation of range in southeastern Manitoba. M.Sc. Thesis, Univ. Manitoba, Winnipeg. 144 pp.

Schaefer, J.A., and W.O. Pruitt, Jr. 1991. Fire and woodland caribou in southeastern Manitoba. Wildl. Monogr. **116**: 39 pp.

Schaller, G.B. 1972. The Serengeti lion: a study in predator-prey relations. Univ. Chicago Press, Chicago, Ill. 480 pp.

Schaller, G.B. 1977. Mountain monarchs: wild sheep and goats of the Himalaya. Univ. Chicago Press, Chicago, Ill. 425 pp.

Schaller, G.B. 1990. Saving China's Wildlife. International Wildlife Vol. 28(1): 30-41.

Schaller, G.B., Ren Junrang, and Qiu Mingjiang. 1988a. Status of the snow leopard *Panthera uncia* in Qinghai and Gansu Provinces, China. Biol. Conserv. **45**: 179-194.

Schaller, G.B., Li Hong, Talipu, Ren Junrang, and Qiu Mingjiang. 1988b. The snow leopard in Xinjiang, China. Oryx **22**: 197-204.

Schaller, G.B., Li Hong, Talipu, Lu Hua, Ren Junrang, Qiu Mingjiang, and Wang Haibin. 1987. Status of large mammals in the Taxkorgan Reserve, Xinjiang, China. Biol. Conserv. **42**: 53-71.

Schassburger, R.M. 1987. Wolf vocalization: an integrated model of structure, motivation and ontogeny. pp. 313-347 *in* H. Frank, ed. Man and wolf: advances, issues, and problems in captive wolf research. Dr. W. Junk, Dordrecht, The Netherlands.

Scheel, D. 1993. Profitability, encounter rates, and prey choice of African lions. Behav. Ecol. **4**: 90-97.

Schenkel, R. 1947. Expression studies of wolves. Behaviour **1**: 81-129.

Schlesinger, P.A., P.H. Duray, and S.A. Burke. 1985. Maternal fetal transmission of the Lyme disease spirochete. Am. J. Trop. Med. Hyg. **34**: 355-360.

Schlosser, W.D. 1980. Canine blastomycosis in Minnesota. M.S. Thesis, Univ. Minnesota, Minneapolis. 54 pp.

Schmidt, K.P., and J.R. Gunson. 1985. Evaluation of wolf-ungulate predation near Nordegg, Alberta: Second Year Progress Report, 1984-85. Alberta Fish and Wildl. Div. Rep. 53 pp.

Schmidt, R.H. 1985. Controlling arctic fox populations with introduced red foxes. Wildl. Soc. Bull. **13**: 592-594.

Schmidt, R.H. 1986. Community-level effects of coyote population reduction: a symposium. pp. 49-65 *in* J. Cairns, Jr., ed. Community toxicity testing. Am. Soc. for Testing and Materials Spec. Tech. Publ. 920, Philadelphia, Pa.

Schmidt, R.H. 1989. Animal welfare and wildlife management. Trans. North Am. Wildl. and Nat. Resour. Conf. **54**: 468-575.

Schmitt, R. 1989. Chiens de protection des troupeaux. Ethnozootechnie **43**: 51-58.

Schmitz, O.J., and G.B. Kolenosky. 1985a. Wolves and coyotes in Ontario: morphological relationships and origins. Can. J. Zool. **63**: 1130-1137.

Schmitz, O.J., and G.B. Kolenosky. 1985b. Hybridization between wolf and coyote in captivity. J. Mammal. **66**: 402-405.

Schneider, K.B. 1973. Age determination of sea otter. Alaska Dep. Fish and Game Fed. Aid in Wildl. Restoration Prog Rep., Projs. W-17-4 and W-17-5. 25 pp.

Schorger, A.W. 1950. A brief history of the steel trap and its use in North America. Trans. Wisconsin Acad. Sci. Arts and Lett. **40**: 171-199.

Schullery, P., and L. Whittlesey. 1992. The documentary record of wolves and related wildlife species in the Yellowstone National Park area prior to 1882. pp. 1-3 to 1-73 *in* J.D. Varley and W.G. Brewster, eds. Wolves for Yellowstone? A report to the United States Congress. Vol. IV. Research and analysis. U.S. Natl. Park Serv., Yellowstone National Park, Mammoth, Wyo.

Schwartz, C.C., and A.W. Franzmann. 1989. Bears, wolves, moose, and forest succession, some management considerations on the Kenai Peninsula, Alaska. Alces **25**: 1-10.

Schwartz, C.C., and A.W. Franzmann. 1991. Interrelationship of black bears to moose and forest succession in the northern coniferous forest. Wildl. Monogr. **113**: 58 pp.

Schwartz, C.C., R. Stephenson, and N. Wilson. 1983. *Trichodectes canis* on the gray wolf and coyote on Kenai Peninsula, Alaska. J. Wildl. Dis. **19**: 372-373.

Scrivner, J.H., R. Teranishi, W.E. Howard, D.B. Fagre, and R.E. Marsh. 1987. Coyote attractants and a bait delivery system. pp. 38-55 *in* J.S. Green, ed. Protecting livestock from coyotes. U.S. Sheep Exp. Stn., Univ. Idaho, Dubois.

Scudday, J.F. 1972. Two recent records of gray wolves in west Texas. J. Mammal. **53**: 598.

Seal, U.S. 1969. Carnivora systematics: a study of hemoglobins. Comp. Biochem. Physiol. **31**: 799-811.

Seal, U.S. 1975. Molecular approaches to taxonomic problems in the Canidae. pp. 27-39 *in* M.W. Fox, ed. The wild canids: their systematics, behavioral ecology and evolution. Van Nostrand Reinhold, New York, N.Y.

Seal, U.S. 1991. Fertility control as a tool regulating captive and free-ranging wildlife populations. J. Zoo and Wildl. Med. **22**: 1-5.

Seal, U.S., and L.D. Mech. 1983. Blood indicators of seasonal metabolic patterns in captive adult gray wolves. J. Wildl. Manage. **47**: 704-715.

Seal, U.S., L.D. Mech, and V. Van Ballenberghe. 1975. Blood analyses of wolf pups and their ecological and metabolic interpretation. J. Mammal. **56**: 64-75.

Seal, U.S., E.D. Plotka, J.M. Packard, and L.D. Mech. 1979. Endocrine correlates of reproduction in the wolf. I. Serum progesterone, estradiol and LH during the estrous cycle. Biol. Reprod. **21**: 1057-1066.

Seguin, R. 1991. A wolf management strategy for Saskatchewan. Unpubl. info. base, Saskatchewan Parks and Renewable Resour. 14 pp.

Seip, D.R. 1989. Caribou-moose-wolf interaction in central British Columbia. pp. 57-69 *in* D. Seip, S. Pettigrew, and R. Archibald. Wolf-prey dynamics and management. British Columbia Min. Envir. Wildl. Working Rep. No. WR-40.

Seip, D.R. 1990. Ecology of woodland caribou in Wells Gray Provincial Park. British Columbia Min. Environ. Wildl. Bull. No. B-68. 43 pp.

Seip, D.R. 1991. Predation and caribou populations. Proc. North Am. Caribou Workshop **5**: 46-52.

Seip, D.R. 1992a. Factors limiting woodland caribou populations and their interrelationships with wolves and moose in southeastern British Columbia. Can. J. Zool. **70**: 1494-1503.

Seip, D.R. 1992b. Wolf predation, wolf control and the management of ungulate populations. pp. 331-340 *in* D.R. McCullough and R.H. Barrett, eds. Wildlife 2001: populations. Elsevier Appl. Sci., New York, N.Y.

Self, B.E., Jr. 1982. Public attitudes regarding selected wildlife issues in British Columbia. British Columbia Min. Environ. Fish and Wildl. Bull. No. B-14. 55 pp.

Server, F.E. 1876-77. Diary of a trip through Yellowstone Park and down the Snake River to Fort Hall. Unpubl. Rep., File No. 507, Montana State Univ. Arch., Bozeman, Mont.

Service Argos. 1984. Location and data collection satellite system: user's guide. Service Argos, Inc., Landover, Md. 36 pp.

Service Argos. 1989. Location and data collection satellite system: user's guide. Insert 01. Tables. Service Argos, Landover, Md.

Seton, E.T. 1925. Lives of game animals. Vol. 1. Parts 1 and 2. Doubleday/ Doran, Garden City, N.Y. 640 pp.

Shafer, C.L. 1990. Nature reserves: island theory and conservation practice. Smithson. Inst. Press, Washington, D.C. 189 pp.

Sharpe, H.S. 1978. Comparative ethnology of the wolf and the Chipewyan. pp. 55-79 *in* R.L. Hall and H.S. Sharpe, eds. Wolf and man: evolution in parallel. Academic Press, New York, N.Y.

Shaw, J.H. 1975. Ecology, behavior and systematics of the red wolf (*Canis rufus*). Ph.D. Thesis, Yale Univ., New Haven, Conn. 99 pp.

Shelton, P.C., and R.O. Peterson. 1983. Beaver, wolf and moose interactions in Isle Royale National Park, USA. Acta Zool. Fenn. **174**: 265-266.

Shields, G.F., and A.C. Wilson. 1987. Calibration of mitochondrial DNA evolution in geese. J. Molec. Evol. **24**: 212-217.

Shields, W.M. 1983. Genetic considerations in the management of the wolf and other large vertebrates: an alternative view. pp. 90-92 *in* L.N. Carbyn, ed. Wolves in Canada and Alaska: their status, biology, and management. Can. Wildl. Serv. Rep. Ser., No. 45.

Shoesmith, M.W. 1979. Seasonal movements and social behavior of elk on Mirror Plateau, Yellowstone National Park. pp. 166-176 *in* M.S. Boyce and L. Hayden-Wing, eds. North American elk: ecology, behavior and management. Univ. Wyoming, Laramie.

Shults, B., and L.G. Adams. 1990. Status and distribution of the Tonzona caribou herd 1989 progress report. U.S. Natl. Park Serv. Prog. Rep. No. AR-89/02. 13 pp.

Sibbison, J. 1984. EPA and the politics of poison: the 1080 story. Defenders **59**(1): 4-15.

Siddall, P. 1989. Public survey of central Idaho wolf occurrence. Unpubl. Rep., Boise National Forest, Boise, Id. 20 pp.

Sidorov, G.N., V.P. Savitsky, and A.D. Botvinken. 1983. The landscape distribution of predatory mammals of the family Canidae as a factor of formation of the rabies virus range in the south-east of the USSR. Zool. Zh. **62**: 761-770.

Sikes, R.K. 1962. Pathogenesis of rabies in wildlife. I. Comparative effect of varying doses of rabies virus inoculated into foxes and skunks. Am. J. Vet. Res. **23**: 1041-1047.

Sikes, R.K., Sr. 1970. Rabies. pp. 3-19 *in* J.W. Davis, L.H. Karstad, and D.O. Trainer, eds. Infectious diseases of wild mammals. Iowa State Univ. Press, Ames.

Siminski, D.P. 1990. International studbook for the Mexican gray wolf (*Canis lupus baileyi*). Arizona-Sonora Desert Mus., Tucson, Ariz. 14 pp.

Simms, S.R. 1984. Aboriginal Great Basin foraging strategies: an evolutionary analysis. Ph.D. Thesis, Univ. Utah, Salt Lake City. 286 pp.

Simms, S.R. 1992. Wilderness as a human landscape. pp. 183-201 *in* S.I. Zeveloff, L.M. Vause, and V.H. McVaugh, eds. Wilderness tapestry. Univ. Nevada Press, Reno. 306 pp.

Simmons, J.G., and C.E. Hamner. 1973. Inhibition of estrus in the dog with testosterone implants. Am. J. Vet. Res. **34**: 1409-1419.

Sinclair, A.R.E. 1989. Population regulation in animals. pp. 197-241 *in* J.M. Cherrett, ed. Ecological concepts: the contribution of ecology to an understanding of the natural world. Blackwell Sci. Publ., Oxford, U.K.

Singer, F.J. 1979. Status and history of timber wolves in Glacier National Park, Montana. pp. 19-42 *in* E. Klinghammer, ed. The behavior and ecology of wolves. Garland STPM Press, New York, N.Y.

Singer, F.J. 1984a. Aerial Dall sheep count, 1982, 1983 and 1984, Gates of the Arctic National Park and Preserve. U.S. Natl. Park Serv. Nat. Resour. Rep. No. AR-84/2. 21 pp.

Singer, F.J. 1984b. Some population characteristics of Dall sheep in six Alaska National Parks and Preserves. Proc. Biennial Symp. North. Wild Sheep and Goat Counc. **4**: 1-10.

Singer, F.J. 1987. Dynamics of caribou and wolves in Denali National Park, 1898-1985. pp. 117-157 *in* Toward the year 2000. Proceedings of the conference on science in the National Parks 1986, Fort Collins, Colo. George Wright Soc. and U.S. Natl. Park Serv.

Singer, F.J. 1990. The ungulate prey base for wolves in Yellowstone National Park I. Five species of ungulates on the northern Yellowstone elk winter range, elk park-wide. pp. 2-3 to 2-37 *in* Yellowstone National Park, U.S. Fish and Wildlife Service, University of Wyoming, University of Idaho, Interagency Grizzly Bear Study Team, and the University of Minnesota Cooperative Park Studies Unit, eds. Wolves for Yellowstone? A report to the United States Congress. Vol. II. Research and analysis. U.S. Natl. Park Serv., Yellowstone National Park, Mammoth, Wyo.

Singer, F.J. 1991a. The ungulate prey base for wolves in Yellowstone National Park. pp. 323-348 *in* R.B. Keiter and M.S. Boyce, eds. The Greater Yellowstone ecosystem: redefining America's wilderness heritage. Yale Univ. Press, New Haven, Conn.

Singer, F.J. 1991b. Some predictions concerning a wolf recovery into Yellowstone National Park: how wolf recovery may affect park visitors, ungulates and other predators. Trans. North Am. Wildl. and Nat. Resour. Conf. **56**: 567-583.

Singer, F.J., and J. Dalle-Molle. 1985. The Denali ungulate-predator system. Alces **21**: 339-358.

Singer, F.J., J. Dalle-Molle, and J. Van Horn. 1981. Dall sheep count, 1981. Unpubl. Rep., U.S. Natl. Park Serv., Anchorage, Alas. 11 pp.

Singer, P. 1975. Animal liberation: a new ethics for our treatment of animals. New York Review. New York, N.Y. 301pp.

Skeel, M.A., and L.N. Carbyn. 1977. The morphological relationship of gray wolves (*Canis lupus*) in national parks of central Canada. Can. J. Zool. **55**: 737-747.

Skinner, M.P. 1924. The Yellowstone nature book. A.C. McClurg, Chicago, Ill. 221 pp.

Skinner, M.P. 1927. The predatory and fur-bearing animals of the Yellowstone National Park. Roosevelt Wild Life Bull. **4**: 163-281.

Skinner, M.P. 1928. The elk situation. J. Mammal. **9**: 309-317.

Skogland, T. 1985. The effects of density-dependent resource limitations on the demography of wild reindeer. J. Anim. Ecol. **54**: 359-374.

Skogland, T. 1991. What are the effects of predators on large ungulate populations? Oikos **61**: 401-411.

Skoog, R.O. 1968. Ecology of the caribou (*Rangifer tarandus granti*) in Alaska. Ph.D. Thesis, Univ. California, Berkeley. 699 pp.

Skoog, R.O. 1983. Results of Alaska's attempts to increase prey by controlling wolves. Acta Zool. Fenn. **174**: 245-247.

Skuratowicz, W. 1981. Siphonaptera occurring on Carnivora in Poland. Gmenta Faunistica **25**: 369-410.

Slatkin, M. 1987. Gene flow and the geographic structure of populations. Science (Washington, D.C.) **236**: 787-792.

Slatter, D. 1981. Fundamentals of veterinary ophthalmology. W.B. Saunders, Philadelphia, Pa.

Slough, B.G., R.H. Jessup, D.I. McKay, and A.B. Stephenson. 1987. Wild furbearer management in western and northern Canada. pp. 1062-1076 *in* M. Novak, J.A. Baker, M.E. Obbard, and B. Malloch, eds. Wild furbearer management and conservation in North America. Ontario Trappers Assoc., North Bay, Ont.

Smith, A.E. 1985. Victories for wolves. Defenders **60**(2): 46.

Smith, B.L. 1983. Historical and present status of wolves in the Yukon Territory. pp. 48-50 *in* L.N. Carbyn, ed. Wolves in Canada and Alaska: their status, biology, and management. Can. Wildl. Serv. Rep. Ser., No. 45.

Smith, E.L., R.L. Hill, I.R. Lehman, R.J. Lefkowitz, P. Handler, and A. White. 1983. Principles of biochemistry. Part 2. General aspects. 7th ed. McGraw-Hill, New York, N.Y.

Smith, G.A. 1901. The life of Henry Drummond. McClure, Phillips, New York, N.Y. 503 pp.

Smith, G.J., and O.J. Rongstad. 1980. Serologic and hematologic values of wild coyotes in Wisconsin. J. Wildl. Dis. **16**: 491-497.

Smith, J.S. 1988. Monoclonal antibody studies of rabies in insectivorous bats of the United States. Rev. Infect. Dis. **10**(S4): 637-643.

Smith, J.S., and G.M. Baer. 1988. Epizootiology of rabies: the Americas. pp. 267-299 *in* J.B. Campbell and K.M. Charlton, eds. Rabies. Kluwer Acad. Publ., Boston, Mass.

Smith, J.S., J.W. Sumner, L.F. Roumillat, G.M. Baer, and W.G. Winkler. 1984. Antigenic characteristics of isolates associated with a new epizootic of raccoon rabies in the United States. J. Infect. Dis. **149**: 769-774.

Smith, J.S., F.L. Reid-Sanden, L.F. Roumillat, C. Trimarchi, K. Clark, G.M. Baer, and W.G. Winkler. 1986. Demonstration of antigenic variation among rabies virus isolates by using monoclonal antibodies to nucleocapsid proteins. J. Clin. Microbiol. **24**: 573-580.

Smith, P.K., and K. Lewis. 1985. Rough-and-tumble play, fighting, and chasing in nursery school children. Ethol. Sociobiol. **6**: 175-181.

Smith, R.A., and M.L. Kennedy. 1983. Food habits of the coyote (*Canis latrans*) in western Tennessee. J. Tennessee Acad. Sci. **58**: 27-28.

Snedecor, G.W., and W.G. Cochran. 1973. Statistical methods. Iowa State Univ. Press, Ames. 593 pp.

Sokal, R.R., and F.J. Rohlf. 1969. Biometry. W.H. Freeman, San Francisco, Calif. 776 pp.

Sokolov, V.E., and O.L. Rossolimo. 1985. Taxonomy and variability. pp. 21-50 *in* D.I. Bibikov, ed. The wolf: history, systematics, morphology, ecology. USSR Acad. Sci., Nauka, Moscow.

Sokolowski, J.H., and S. Geng. 1977. Biological evaluation of mibolerone in the female beagle. Am. J. Vet. Res. **38**: 1371-1376.

Solomon, M.E. 1949. The natural control of animal populations. J. Anim. Ecol. **18**: 1-35.

Soper, J.D. 1970. The mammals of Jasper National Park, Alberta. Can. Wildl. Serv. Rep. Ser., No. 10. 80 pp.

Soppella, P.M., M. Nieminen, and J. Timisjarvi. 1986. Thermoregulation in reindeer. Proc. Int. Reindeer/Caribou Symp. **4**: 273-278.

Soulé, M.E. (ed.) 1987. Viable populations for conservation. Cambridge Univ. Press, New York, N.Y. 189 pp.

Spector, W.S. (ed.) 1956. Handbook of biological data. W.B. Saunders, Philadelphia, Pa. 325 pp.

Spencer, J.S., Jr., W.B. Smith, J.T. Hahn, and G.K. Raile. 1988. Wisconsin's Fourth Forest Inventory, 1983. U.S. Dep. Agric. For. Serv. North Carolina Exp. Stn. Resour. Bull. NC-107. 158 pp.

Spilliaert, R., G. Vikingsson, U. Arnason, A. Palsdottir, J. Sigurjonsson, and A. Arnason. 1991. Species hybridization between a female blue whale (*Balaenoptera musculus*) and a male fin whale (*B. physalus*): molecular and morphological documentation. J. Hered. **82**: 269-274.

Spry, I.M. 1963. The Palliser Expedition: an account of John Palliser's British North American Expedition, 1857-1860. Macmillan, Toronto, Ont. 310 pp.

Standfield, R.O. 1970. Some considerations on the taxonomy of wolves in Ontario. pp. 32-38 *in* S.E. Jorgensen, C.E. Faulkner, and L.D. Mech, eds. Proceedings of a symposium on wolf management in selected areas of North America. U.S. Fish and Wildl. Serv. Bur. Sport Fish. and Wildl., Region 3, Twin Cities, Minn.

Stardom, R.R.P. 1977. Winter ecology of woodland caribou, *Rangifer tarandus caribou*, and some aspects of the winter ecology of moose, *Alces alces andersoni*, and white-tailed deer, *Odocoileus virginianus dacotensis* (Mammalia: Cervidae), in southern Manitoba. M.Sc. Thesis, Univ. Manitoba, Winnipeg. 157 pp.

Stardom, R.R.P. 1983. Status and management of wolves in Manitoba. pp. 30-34 *in* L.N. Carbyn, ed. Wolves in Canada and Alaska: their status, biology, and management. Can. Wildl. Serv. Rep. Ser., No. 45.

Starfield, A.M., and A.L. Bleloch. 1986. Building models for conservation and wildlife management. Macmillan, New York, N.Y. 253 pp.

Statistics Canada. Annual reports: fur production. Agric. Div. Cat. No. 23-207. Ottawa, Ont.

Steel, R.G.D., and J.H. Torrie. 1980. Principles and procedures of statistics: a biometrical approach. 2nd ed. McGraw-Hill, New York, N.Y. 633 pp.

Steinberg, H. 1977. Behavioral responses of the white-tailed deer to olfactory stimulation using predator scents. M.S. Thesis, Pennsylvania State Univ., University Park.

Stelfox, J.G. 1969. Wolves in Alberta: a history 1800-1969. Alberta — Lands For. Parks Wildl. Mag. **12**(4): 18-27.

Stelfox, J.G. 1971. Bighorn sheep in the Canadian Rockies: a history 1800-1970. Can. Field-Nat. **85**: 101-122.

Stelfox, J.G. et al. (Warden Service). 1974. The abundance and distribution of caribou and elk in Jasper National Park, 1971-1973. Can. Wildl. Serv. Warden Serv. Rep. 84 pp.

Stellflug, J.N., and N.L. Gates. 1987. Antifertility research. pp. 5-9 *in* J.S. Green, ed. Protecting livestock from coyotes. U.S. Sheep Exp. Stn., Univ. of Idaho, Dubois.

Stellflug, J.N., N.L. Gates, and R.G. Sasser. 1978. Reproductive inhibitors for coyote population control: developments and current status. Proc. Vertebr. Pest Conf. **8**: 185-189.

Stellflug, J.N., C.W. Leathers, and J.S. Green. 1984. Antifertility effect of busulfan and DL-6-(N-2-pipecolinomethyl)-5-hydroxy-indane maleate (PMHI) in coyotes (*Canis latrans*). Theriogenology **22**: 533-543.

Stenlund, M.H. 1955. A field study of the timber wolf (*Canis lupus*) on the Superior National Forest, Minnesota. Minn. Dep. Conserv. Tech. Bull. No. 4. 55 pp.

Stephan, J.K., B. Chow, L.A. Frohman, and B.F. Chow. 1971. Relationship of growth hormone to the growth retardation associated with maternal dietary restriction. J. Nutr. **101**: 1453-1458.

Stephens, P.W., and R.O. Peterson. 1984. Wolf-avoidance strategies of moose. Holarct. Ecol. **7**: 239-244.

Stephenson, B. 1991. An Alaskan perspective on wolves: a response to G. Laycock's "How to kill a wolf". Int. Wolf **1**(3): 3-6.

Stephenson, R.O. 1978. Characteristics of exploited wolf populations. Alaska Dep. Fish and Game Fed. Aid in Wildl. Restoration Prog. Rep., Projs. W-17-4 and W-17-5. 52 pp.

Stephenson, R.O. 1982. Nunamiut Eskimos, wildlife biologists and wolves. pp. 434-440 *in* F.H. Harrington and P.C. Paquet, eds. Wolves of the world: perspectives of behavior, ecology, and conservation. Noyes, Park Ridge, N.J.

Stephenson, R.O., and D.D. James. 1982. Wolf movements and food habits in northwest Alaska. pp. 26-42 *in* F.H. Harrington and P.C. Paquet, eds. Wolves of the world: perspectives of behavior, ecology, and conservation. Noyes, Park Ridge, N.J.

Stephenson, R.O., and L.J. Johnson. 1972. Wolf report. Alaska Dep. Fish and Game Fed. Aid in Wildl. Restoration Prog. Rep., Proj. W-17-3. Vol. X. 51 pp. (mimeograph).

Stephenson, R.O., D.G. Ritter, and C.A. Nielsen. 1982. Serologic survey for canine distemper and infectious canine hepatitis in wolves in Alaska. J. Wildl. Dis. **18**: 419-424.

Sterner, R.T., and S.A. Shumake. 1978. Coyote damage-control research: a review and analysis. pp. 297-325 *in* M. Bekoff, ed. Coyotes: biology, behavior, and management. Academic Press, New York, N.Y.

Stevenson, S. 1991. Forestry and caribou in British Columbia. Proc. North Am. Caribou Workshop **5**: 124-129.

Stewart, B.S., S. Leatherwood, P.K. Yochem, and M.P. Heide-Jorgensen. 1989. Harbor seal tracking and telemetry by satellite. Mar. Mammal Sci. **5**: 361-375.

Stirling, I.G., and W.R. Archibald. 1977. Aspects of predation of seals by polar bears. J. Fish. Res. Board Can. **34**: 1126-1129.

Stone, W.B., A.S. Clawson, D.E. Slingerlands, and B.L. Weber. 1975. Use of Romanowsky stains to prepare tooth sections for aging mammals. N.Y. Fish and Game J. **22**: 156-158.

Strauch, T.B. 1992. Holding the wolf by the ears: the conservation of the northern Rocky Mountain wolf in Yellowstone National Park. Univ. Wyoming Coll. Law Land Wat. Rev. **27**: 33-81.

Strickland, D. 1983. Wolf howling in parksthe Algonquin experience in interpretation. pp. 93-95 *in* L.N. Carbyn, ed. Wolves in Canada and Alaska: their status, biology, and management. Can. Wildl. Serv. Rep. Ser., No. 45.

Strong, W.E. 1968. A trip to the Yellowstone National Park in July, August, and September, 1875. R.A. Bartlett, ed. Univ. Oklahoma Press, Norman. 176 pp.

Stuart, J. 1876. The Yellowstone Expedition of 1863. Contrib. Hist. Soc. Montana **1**: 149-233.

Sullivan, T.P. 1986. Influence of wolverine (*Gulo gulo*) odor on feeding behavior of snowshoe hares (*Lepus americanus*). J. Mammal. **67**: 385-388.

Sullivan, T.P., D.R. Crump, H. Wieser, and E.A. Dixon. 1990. Response of pocket gophers (*Thomomys talpoides*) to an operational application of synthetic semiochemicals of stoat (*Mustela erminea*). J. Chem. Ecol. **16**: 941-949.

Sumanik, R.S. 1987. Wolf ecology in the Kluane Region, Yukon Territory. M.S. Thesis, Michigan Tech. Univ., Houghton. 102 pp.

Sweatman, G.K. 1952. Distribution and incidence of *Echinococcus granulosus* in man and other animals with special reference to Canada. Can. J. Publ. Hlth. **43**: 480-486.

Sweatman, G.K. 1971. Mites and pentastomes. pp. 3-64 *in* J.W. Davis and R.C. Anderson, eds. Parasitic diseases of wild mammals. Iowa State Univ. Press, Ames.

Swofford, D.L. 1990. PAUP: Phylogenetic analysis using parsimony (version 3.0). Illinois Natural Hist. Surv., Champaign.

Syracuse Research Corporation. 1991. Toxicological profile for cyanide. Prepared for the U.S. Department of Health and Human Services, Public Hlth. Serv., Atlanta, Ga. 132 pp. (draft).

Tabel, H., A.H. Corner, W.A. Webster, and C.A. Casey. 1974. History and epizootiology of rabies in Canada. Can. Vet. J. **15**: 271-281.

Taylor, D.L., J. Dalle-Molle, and J. Van Horn. 1988. Survey of Dall sheep, Denali National Park and Preserve1987. U.S. Natl. Park Serv. Nat. Resour. Rep. No. AR-88/13. 22 pp.

Taylor, R.J. 1984. Predation. Chapman and Hall, New York, N.Y. 166 pp.

Taylor, R.J., and P.J. Perkins. 1991. Territory boundary avoidance as a stabilizing factor in wolf-deer interactions. Theor. Popul. Biol. **39**: 115-128.

Taylor, W.P., and T.H. Spraker. 1983. Management of a biting louse infestation in a free-ranging wolf population. Annu. Proc. Am. Assoc. Zoo Vet. 1983: 40-41.

Tessaro, S.V. 1986. The existing and potential importance of brucellosis and tuberculosis in Canadian wildlife: a review. Can. Vet. J. **27**: 119-124.

Teunissen, G.H.B. 1952. The development of endometritis in the dog and the effect of oestradiol and progesterone on the uterus. Acta Endocrinol. **9**: 407-420.

Theberge, J.B. 1973a. Wolf management in Canada through a decade of change. Naturaliste Can. (Ottawa) **2**: 3-10.

Theberge, J.B. 1973b. Death of a legislative fossil: Ontario's wolf and coyote bounty. Ontario Nat. **13**(3): 32-37.

Theberge, J.B. 1983. Considerations in wolf management related to genetic variability and adaptive change. pp. 86-89 *in* L.N. Carbyn, ed. Wolves in Canada and Alaska: their status, biology, and management. Can. Wildl. Serv. Rep. Ser., No. 45.

Theberge, J.B. 1989. When is wolf control to increase ungulate numbers justified? *in* Wolf. Prey dynamics and management. British Columbia Min. Environ., Wildl. Branch, Wildl. Working Rep. No. WR-40, 161-161.

Theberge, J.B. 1990. Potentials for misinterpreting impacts of wolf predation through prey:predator ratios. Wildl. Soc. Bull. 18: 188-192.

Theberge, J.B. 1991. Ecological classification, status, and management of the gray wolf, *Canis lupus*, in Canada. Can. Field-Nat. **105**: 459-463.

Theberge, J.B. 1992. Wolves, Algonquin Park and the hierarchy of ecology. *in* Islands of Hope. L. Labatt and B.C. Heluke (eds). Forestry Books.

Theberge, J.B., and J.B. Falls. 1967. Howling as a means of communication in timber wolves. Am. Zool. **7**: 331-338.

Theberge, J.B., and D.A. Gauthier. 1985. Models for wolf-ungulate relationships: when is wolf control justified? Wildl. Soc. Bull. **13**: 449-458.

Theberge, J.B., and C.H.R. Wedeles. 1989. Prey selection and habitat partitioning in sympatric coyote and red fox populations, southwest Yukon. Can. J. Zool. **67**: 1285-1290.

Theberge, J.B., G.J. Forbes, and T. Bollinger. 1994. Rabies in wolves of the Great Lakes region. J. Wildl. Dis. **30**: 563-566.

Thieking, A., S.M. Goyal, R.F. Berg, K.I. Loken, L.D. Mech, and R.P. Thiel. 1992. Seroprevalence of Lyme disease in Minnesota and Wisconsin wolves. J. Wildl. Dis. **28**: 177-182.

Thiel, R.P. 1978. The status of the timber wolf in Wisconsin, 1975. Trans. Wisconsin Acad. Sci. Arts and Lett. **66**: 186-194.

Thiel, R.P. 1985. Relationship between road densities and wolf habitat suitability in Wisconsin. Am. Midl. Nat. **113**: 404-407.

Thiel, R.P. 1988. Dispersal of a Wisconsin wolf into upper Michigan. Jack-Pine Warbler **66**: 143-147.

Thiel, R.P. 1989. Wisconsin timber wolf recovery plan. Wisconsin Endang. Resour. Rep. **50**: 37 pp.

Thiel, R.P. 1993. The timber wolf in Wisconsin: the death and life of a magnificent predator. Univ. Wisconsin Press, Madison. 253 pp.

Thiel, R.P., and J. Hammill. 1988. Wolf specimen records in upper Michigan, 1960-1986. Jack-Pine Warbler **66**: 149-153.

Thiel, R.P., and R.J. Welch. 1981. Evidence of recent breeding activity in Wisconsin wolves. Am. Midl. Nat. **106**: 401-402.

Thiel, R.P., L.D. Mech, G.R. Ruth, J.R. Archer, and L. Kaufman. 1987. Blastomycosis in wild wolves. J. Wildl. Dis. **23**: 321-323.

Thieszen, A.W. 1992. An examination of the decision-making process of the Wolf Management Committee negotiations: a case study. M.S. Thesis, Univ. Montana, Missoula. 198 pp.

Thing, H. 1977. Behavior, mechanics and energetics associated with winter cratering by caribou in northwestern Alaska. Univ. Alaska Biol. Pap. No. 18: 41 pp.

Thoen, C.O., and E.M. Hines. 1981. Tuberculosis. pp. 263-274 *in* J.W. Davis, L.H. Karstad, and D.O. Trainer, eds. Infectious diseases of wild mammals. 2nd ed. Iowa State Univ. Press, Ames.

Thomas, D.C. 1982. The relationship between fertility and fat reserves of Peary caribou. Can. J. Zool. **60**: 597-602.

Thomas, D.C. 1990. Moose diet and use of successional forests in the Canadian taiga. Alces **26**: 24-29.

Thomas, D.C., and S.J. Barry. 1990a. Age-specific fecundity of the Beverly herd of barren-ground caribou. Proc. Int. Reindeer/Caribou Symp. **5**: 257-263.

Thomas, D.C., and S.J. Barry. 1990b. A life table for female barren-ground caribou in north-central Canada. Proc. Int. Reindeer/Caribou Symp. **5**: 177-186.

Thomas, G. 1984. Live holding device research. pp. 150-152 *in* Proc. Western Assoc. Fish and Wildl. Agencies and the Western Div., Am. Fish. Soc., Victoria, B.C., 16-19 July 1984.

Thomas, N.J., W.J.K. Foreyt, J.F. Evermann, L.A. Windberg, and F.F. Knowlton. 1984. Seroprevalence of canine parvovirus in wild coyotes from Texas, Utah, and Idaho (1972-1983). J. Am. Vet. Med. Assoc. **185**: 1283-1287.

Thompson, D.Q. 1952. Travel, range, and food habits of timber wolves in Wisconsin. J. Mammal. **33**: 429-442.

Thompson, I.D., and R.O. Peterson. 1988. Does wolf predation alone limit the moose population in Pukaskwa Park?: a comment. J. Wildl. Manage. **52**: 556-559.

Thompson, T., and W. Gasson. 1991. Attitudes of Wyoming residents on wolf reintroduction and related issues. Wyoming Game and Fish Dep., Cheyenne. 43 pp.

Thurber, J.M., and R.O. Peterson. 1991. Changes in body size associated with range expansion in the coyote (*Canis latrans*). J. Mammal. **72**: 750-755.

Thurber, J.M., R.O. Peterson, T.D. Drummer, and S.A. Thomasma. 1994. Gray wolf response to refuge boundaries and roads in Alaska. Wildl. Soc. Bull. **22**: 61-68.

Thurber, J.M., R.O. Peterson, J.D. Woolington, and J.A. Vucetich. 1992. Coyote coexistence with wolves on the Kenai Peninsula, Alaska. Can. J. Zool. **70**: 2494-2498.

Thwaites, R.G. 1905. Original journals of the Lewis and Clark Expedition. Vol. 5. Dodd, Mead, New York, N.Y. 395 pp.

Tilt, W., R. Norris, and A.S. Eno. 1987. Wolf recovery in the northern Rocky Mountains. National Audubon Soc. and Nat. Fish and Wildl. Found., Washington, D.C. 31 pp.

Tinbergen, L. 1960. The natural control of insects in pinewoods. 1. Factors influencing the intensity of predation by songbirds. Arch. Néerl. Zool. **13**: 266-336.

Tobey, R.W., and W.B. Ballard. 1985. Increased mortality in gray wolves captured with acepromazine and etorphine hydrochloride in combination. J. Wildl. Dis. **21**: 188-190.

Todd, A.W., and D.L. Skinner. 1990. Evaluating efficiency of footholding devices for coyote capture. Wildl. Soc. Bull. **18**: 166-175.

Todd, A.W., J.R. Gunson, and W.M. Samuel. 1981. Sarcoptic mange: an important disease of coyotes and wolves of Alberta, Canada. Proc. Worldwide Furbearer Conf. **1**: 706-729.

Toffler, A. 1989. The third wave. Bantam Books, New York, N.Y. 537 pp.

Tompa, F.S. 1983a. Status and management of wolves in British Columbia. pp. 20-24 *in* L.N. Carbyn, ed. Wolves in Canada and Alaska: their status, biology, and management. Can. Wildl. Serv. Rep. Ser., No. 45.

Tompa, F.S. 1983b. Problem wolf management in British Columbia: conflict and program evaluation. pp. 112-119 *in* L.N. Carbyn, ed. Wolves in Canada and Alaska: their status, biology, and management. Can. Wildl. Serv. Rep. Ser., No. 45.

Torbit, S.C., L.H. Carpenter, D.M. Swift, and A.W. Alldredge. 1985. Differential loss of fat and protein by mule deer during winter. J. Wildl. Manage. **49**: 80-85.

Trainer, D.O., and F.F. Knowlton. 1968. Serologic evidence of diseases in Texas coyotes. J. Wildl. Manage. **32**: 981-983.

Trainer, D.O., F.F. Knowlton, and L. Karstad. 1968. Oral papillomatosis in the coyote. Bull. Wildl. Dis. Assoc. **4**: 52-54.

Trefethen, J.B. 1975. An American crusade for wildlife. Winchester Press, New York. 409 pp.

Trenholm, V.C., and M. Carley. 1964. The Shoshonis: sentinels of the Rockies. Univ. Oklahoma Press, Norman. 363 pp.

Tuan, Y. 1970. Treatment of the environment in ideal and actuality. Am. Scient. **58**: 244-249.

Tuck, L.M. 1952. The Newfoundland Wolf. Nfdl. Q. 75: 21-56.

Tucker, P. 1988. Annotated gray wolf bibliography. U.S. Fish and Wildl. Serv. 117 pp.

Tucker, P., and D.H. Pletscher. 1989. Attitudes of hunters and residents toward wolves in northwestern Montana. Wildl. Soc. Bull. **17**: 509-514.

Tucker, P.A., D.L. Davis, and R.R. Ream. 1990. Wolves: identification, documentation, population monitoring and conservation considerations. Natl. Wildl. Fed. North. Rockies Nat. Resour. Cent., Missoula, Mont. 27 pp.

Turi, J.O. 1931. Turi's book of Lapland. Jonathan Cape, London. 376 pp.

Turner, J.V.N., and R.H. Dennis. 1989. Confirmed breeding of polar wolf in northeast Greenland in 1988. Polar Rec. **25**: 353.

Turner, J.W., Jr., and J.F. Kirkpatrick. 1991. New developments in feral horse contraception and their potential application to wildlife. Wildl. Soc. Bull. **19**: 350-359.

Tyler, N.J.C. 1987. Natural limitation of the abundance of the High Arctic reindeer. Ph.D. Thesis, Cambridge Univ., New York, N.Y.

U

Uhaa, I.J., E.J. Mandel, R. Whiteway, and D.B. Fishbein. 1992. Rabies surveillance in the United States during 1990. J. Am. Vet. Med. Assoc. **200**: 920-929.

Urbigkit *vs.* Lujan. 1991. CIV No. 91-CV-1053-B (D. Wyo. Nov. 15, 1991).

U.S. Department of Commerce. 1990. Characteristics of the population — Alaska/1990 census of population. U.S. Gov. Print. Off., Washington, D.C. 281 pp.

U.S. Fish and Wildlife Service. 1978. Predator damage in the west: a study of coyote management alternatives. Washington, D.C. 168 pp.

U.S. Fish and Wildlife Service. 1980. Northern Rocky Mountain Wolf Recovery Plan. Denver, Colo. 67 pp.

U.S. Fish and Wildlife Service. 1982. Mexican Wolf Recovery Plan. Albuquerque, New Mex. 103 pp.

U.S. Fish and Wildlife Service. 1987. Northern Rocky Mountain Wolf Recovery Plan. Denver, Colo. 119 pp.

U.S. Fish and Wildlife Service. 1988a. Interim Wolf Control Plan: northern Rocky Mountains of Montana and Wyoming. Denver, Colo. 29 pp.

U.S. Fish and Wildlife Service. 1988b. Black-footed Ferret Recovery Plan. Denver, Colo. 154 pp.

U.S. Fish and Wildlife Service. 1989. Wolf recovery in Montana: First Annual Report. Helena, Mont. 26 pp.

U.S. Fish and Wildlife Service. 1989. Red Wolf Recovery/Species Survival Plan. Atlanta, Ga. 110 pp.

U.S. Fish and Wildlife Service. 1990a. Amendment No. 1 for including Idaho and northeast Washington to the Interim Wolf Control Plan for the northern Rocky Mountains of Montana and Wyoming. Portland, Or. 21 pp.

U.S. Fish and Wildlife Service. 1990b. Endangered and threatened wildlife and plants: notice of finding on a petition to delist the gray wolf (*Canis lupus*). Fed. Regist. **55**: 49657-49659.

U.S. Fish and Wildlife Service. 1992a. Analysis of public comments on reintroduction of the gray wolf to Yellowstone National Park and central Idaho. Helena, Mont. 15 pp.

U.S. Fish and Wildlife Service. 1992b. Recovery Plan for the Eastern Timber Wolf. Twin Cities, Minn. 73 pp.

U.S. National Park Service. 1988. Management policies. Washington, D.C. 156 pp.

Usher, P.J. 1971. The Banks islanders: economy and ecology of a frontier trapping community. Vol. 2. Economy and ecology. Dep. Indian Affairs and North. Devel. North. Sci. Res. Group Publ. No. NSRG 71-4. 180 pp.

V

Vales, D.J., and J.M. Peek. 1990. Estimates of the potential interactions between hunter harvest and wolf predation on the Sand Creek, Idaho, and Gallatin, Montana, elk populations. pp. 3-93 to 3-167 *in* Yellowstone National Park, U.S. Fish and Wildlife Service, University of Wyoming, University of Idaho, Interagency Grizzly Bear Study Team, and the University of Minnesota Cooperative Park Studies Unit, eds. Wolves for Yellowstone? A report to the United States Congress. Vol. II. Research and analysis. U.S. Natl. Park Serv., Yellowstone National Park, Mammoth, Wyo.

Vales, D.J. and J.M. Peek. 1993. Estimating the relations between hunter harvest and gray wolf predation on the Gallatin, Montana, and Sand Creek, Idaho, elk populations. pp. 118-172 *in* R.S. Cook, ed. Ecological issues on reintroducing wolves into Yellowstone National Park. U.S. Natl. Park Serv. Sci. Monogr. NPS/NRYELL/NRSM-93/22.

Valkenburg, P., J.L. Davis, and R.D. Boertje. 1983. Social organization and seasonal range fidelity of Alaska's western arctic caribou preliminary findings. Acta Zool. Fenn. **175**: 125-126.

Valkenburg, P., D.A. Anderson, J.L. Davis, and D.J. Reed. 1985. Evaluation of an aerial photocensus technique for caribou based on radio-telemetry. Proc. North Am. Caribou Workshop **2**: 287-299.

Valkenburg, P., D.G. Kelleyhouse, J.L. Davis, and J.M. VerHoef. 1994. Case history of the forty mile caribou herd. Rangifer 14(1): 11-22.

Van Ballenberghe, V. 1974. Wolf management in Minnesota: an endangered species case history. Trans. North Am. Wildl. and Nat. Resour. Conf. **39**: 313-322.

Van Ballenberghe, V. 1977. Physical characteristics of timber wolves in Minnesota. pp. 213-219 *in* R.L. Phillips and C.J. Jonkel, eds. Proceedings of the 1975 predator symposium. Bull. For. and Conserv. Exp. Stn., Univ. Montana, Missoula.

Van Ballenberghe, V. 1981. Population dynamics of wolves in the Nelchina Basin, southcentral Alaska. Proc. Worldwide Furbearer Conf. **1**: 1246-1258.

Van Ballenberghe, V. 1983a. Extraterritorial movements and dispersal of wolves in southcentral Alaska. J. Mammal. **64**: 168-171.

Van Ballenberghe, V. 1983b. Two litters raised in one year by a wolf pack. J. Mammal. **64**: 171-172.

Van Ballenberghe, V. 1984. Injuries to wolves sustained during live capture. J. Wildl. Manage. **48**: 1425-1429.

Van Ballenberghe, V. 1985. Wolf predation on caribou: the Nelchina herd case history. J. Wildl. Manage. **49**: 711-720.

Van Ballenberghe, V. 1987. Effects of predation on moose numbers: a review of recent North American studies. Swed. Wildl. Res. **1** (Suppl.): 431-460.

Van Ballenberghe, V. 1989. Wolf predation on the Nelchina caribou herd: a comment. J. Wildl. Manage. **53**: 243-250.

Van Ballenberghe, V. 1991. Forty years of wolf management in the Nelchina Basin, southcentral Alaska: a critical review. Trans. North Am. Wildl. and Nat. Resour. Conf. **56**: 561-566.

Van Ballenberghe, V. 1992. Conservation and management of gray wolves in the USA: status, trends and future directions. pp. 1140-1149 *in* D.R. McCullough and R.H. Barrett, eds. Wildlife 2001: populations. Elsevier Appl. Sci., New York, N.Y.

Van Ballenberghe, V., and W.B. Ballard. 1994. Limitation and regulation of moose populations: the role of predation. Can. J. Zool. 72: 2071-2077.

Van Ballenberghe, V., and J. Dart. 1983. Harvest yields from moose populations subject to wolf and bear predation. Alces **18**: 258-275.

Van Ballenberghe, V., and A.W. Erickson. 1973. A wolf pack kills another wolf. Am. Midl. Nat. **90**: 490-493.

Van Ballenberghe, V., and L.D. Mech. 1975. Weights, growth, and survival of timber wolf pups in Minnesota. J. Mammal. **56**: 44-63.

Van Ballenberghe, V., A.W. Erickson, and D. Byman. 1975. Ecology of the timber wolf in northeastern Minnesota. Wildl. Monogr. **43**: 43 pp.

Van Camp, J., and R. Gluckie. 1979. A record long-distance move by a wolf (*Canis lupus*). J. Mammal. **60**: 236-237.

Vandenbergh, J.G. 1967. Effect of the presence of a male on the sexual maturation of female mice. Endocrinology **81**: 345-349.

Vandenbergh, J.G. 1969. Male odor accelerates female sexual maturation in mice. Endocrinology **84**: 658-660.

van Lawick-Goodall, H., and J. van Lawick-Goodall. (eds.) 1971. Innocent killers. Houghton Mifflin, Boston, Mass. 222 pp.

Van Os, J.L., P.H. Van Laar, E.P. Oldenkamp, and J.S.C. Verschoor. 1981. Oestrus control and the incidence of mammary nodules in bitches, a clinical study with two progestogens. Vet. Q. **3**: 46-56.

Van Tighem, K.J., J.L. Kansas, B. Jesperson, and D. Allison. 1980. An incident of wolf predation on sheep and elk in Jasper National ParkAlberta. Alberta Nat. **10**: 61-62.

Van Valkenburgh, B. 1991. Iterative evolution of hypercarnivory in canids (Mammalia: Carnivora): evolutionary interactions among sympatric predators. Paleobiology 17: 340-362.

Varley, J.D., and W.G. Brewster. (eds.) 1992. Wolves for Yellowstone? A report to the United States Congress. Vol. IV. Research and analysis. U.S. National Park Serv., Yellowstone National Park, Mammoth, Wyo. 750pp

Verme, L.J. 1963. Effect of nutrition on growth of white-tailed deer fawns. Trans. North Am. Wildl. and Nat. Resour. Conf. **28**: 431-443.

Vest, J.H.C. 1988. The medicine wolf returns: traditional Blackfeet concepts of *Canis lupus*. West. Wildlands **14**: 28-33.

Vickery, B.H., G.I. McRae, and J.C. Goodpasture. 1987. Clinical uses of LHRH analogs in dogs. pp. 517-543 *in* B.H. Vickery and J.J. Nestor, Jr., eds. LHRH and its analogs: contraceptive and therapeutic applications. Part 2. MTP Press, Lancaster, U.K.

Vickery, B.H., G.I. McRae, J.C. Goodpasture, and L.M. Sanders. 1989. Use of potent LHRH analogues for chronic contraception and pregnancy termination in dogs. J. Reprod. Fertil. **39** (Suppl.): 175-187.

Vickery, B.H., G.I. McRae, W.V. Briones, B.B. Roberts, A.C. Worden, B.D. Schanbacher, and R.E. Falvo. 1985. Dose response studies on male reproductive parameters in dogs with nafarelin acetate, a potent LHRH agonist. J. Androl. **6**: 53-60.

Victor, P.-E., and J. Larivire 1980. Les loups. F. Nathan, Paris. 191 pp.

Vila, C. 1993. Aspectos morfologicos y ecologicos del lobo iberico *Canis lupus* L. Ph.D. Thesis, Univ. Barcelona, Spain. 299 pp.

Vogel, S.N., T.R. Sultan, and R.P. Ten Eyck. 1981. Cyanide poisoning. Clin. Toxicol. **18**: 367-383.

Voigt, D.R., and B.D. Earle. 1983. Avoidance of coyotes by red fox families. J. Wildl. Manage. **47**: 852-857.

Vyse, E. 1991. Comparison of mitochondrial DNA in wolves and coyotes in the Northern Rockies using the polymerase chain reaction technique. pp. 183-186 *in* U.S. Natl. Park Serv., Rocky Mountain Reg., Denver, Colo.

W

Wade, D.A. 1976. The use of aircraft in predator control. Proc. Vertebr. Pest Conf. **7**: 154-160.

Wade, D.A. 1978. Coyote damage: a survey of its nature and scope, control measures and their application. pp. 347-368 *in* M. Bekoff, ed. Coyotes: biology, behavior, and management. Academic Press, New York, N.Y.

Wade, D.A. 1982. The use of fences for predator damage control. Proc. Vertebr. Pest Conf. **10**: 24-33.

Wagner, F.H. 1989. American wildlife management at the crossroads. Wildl. Soc. Bull. **17**: 354-360.

Wagner, F.H. 1991. Changing institutional arrangements for setting natural resources policy. *In* Proceedings of the symposium on the ecological implications of livestock herbivory in the west. Proc. 42nd Annu. Meeting Am. Inst. Biol. Sci., San Antonio, Tex. 10 pp.

Walker, D.N., and G.C. Frison. 1982. Studies on Amerindian dogs, 3: Prehistoric wolf dog hybrids from the northwestern plains. J. Archaeol. Sci. **9**: 125-172.

Walls, G.L. 1942. The vertebrate eye and its adaptive radiation. Harper, New York, N.Y. 785 pp.

Walters, C.J. 1986. Adaptive management of renewable resources. Macmillan, New York, N.Y. 374 pp.

Walters, C.J., M. Stocker, and G.C. Haber. 1981. Simulation and optimization models for a wolf-ungulate system. pp. 317-337 *in* C.W. Fowler and T.D. Smith. Dynamics of large mammal populations. John Wiley and Sons, New York, N.Y.

Walters, C.J., R. Hilborn, R. Peterman, M. Jones, and B. Everitt. 1978. Porcupine caribou workshop. Draft report on submodels and scenarios. Unpubl. Rep., Univ. British Columbia Inst. Anim. Res. Ecol., Vancouver. 41 pp.

Waples, R.S., and D.J. Teel. 1990. Conservation genetics of Pacific salmon. I. Temporal changes in allele frequency. Conserv. Biol. **4**: 144-156.

Watkins, B.E., J.H. Witham, D.E. Ullrey, D.J. Watkins, and J.M. Jones. 1991. Body composition and condition evaluation of white-tailed deer fawns. J. Wildl. Manage. **55**: 39-51.

Wayne, R.K. 1992. On the use of molecular genetic characters to investigate species status. Conserv. Biol. **6**:559-569.

Wayne, R.K., and S.M. Jenks. 1991. Mitochondrial DNA analysis implying extensive hybridization of the endangered red wolf *Canis rufus*. Nature (Lond.) **351**: 565-568.

Wayne, R.K., and S.J. O'Brien. 1987. Allozyme divergence within the Canidae. Syst. Zool. **36**: 339-355.

Wayne, R.K., N. Lehman, and S.M. Jenks. 1992b. The use of morphologic and molecular techniques to estimate genetic variability and relationships of small endangered populations. pp. 217-236 *in* D.R. McCullough and R.H. Barrett, eds. Wildlife 2001: populations. Elsevier Appl. Sci., New York, N.Y.

Wayne, R.K., N. Lehman, M.W. Allard, and R.L. Honeycutt. 1992a. Mitochondrial DNA variability of the gray wolf: genetic consequences of population decline and habitat fragmentation. Conserv. Biol. **6**: 559-569.

Wayne, R.K., B. Van Valkenburgh, P.W. Kat, T.K. Fuller, W.E. Johnson, and S.J. O'Brien. 1989. Genetic and morphological divergence among sympatric canids. J. Hered. **80**: 447-454.

Wayne, R.K., D.A. Gilbert, N. Lehman, K. Hansen, A. Eisenhawer, D. Girman, R.O. Peterson, L.D. Mech, P.J. Gogan, U.S. Seal, and R.J. Krumenaker. 1991. Conservation genetics of the endangered Isle Royale gray wolf. Conserv. Biol. **5**: 41-51.

Weaver, J.L. 1978. The wolves of Yellowstone. U.S. Natl. Park Serv. Nat. Resour. Rep. No. 14. 37 pp.

Weaver, J.L. 1993. Refining the equation for interpreting prey occurrence in gray wolf scats. J. Wildl. Manage. **57**: 534-538.

Weiler, G.J., and G.W. Garner. 1987. Wolves of the Arctic National Wildlife Refuge: their seasonal movements and prey relationships. pp. 691-742 *in* G.W. Garner and P.E. Reynolds, eds. Baseline study of the fish, wildlife, and their habitats. U.S. Fish and Wildl. Serv., 1985 Update Rep.

Weise, T.F., W.L. Robinson, R.A. Hook, and L.D. Mech. 1975. An experimental translocation of the eastern timber wolf. Audubon Conserv. Rep. 5. 28pp.

Weise, T.F., W.L. Robinson, R.A. Hook, and L.D. Mech. 1979. An experimental translocation of the eastern timber wolf. pp. 346-419 *in* E. Klinghammer, ed. The behavior and ecology of wolves. Garland STPM Press, New York, N.Y.

White, R. 1991. It's your misfortune and none of my own: a history of the American West. Univ. Oklahoma Press, Norman. 644 pp.

Whitlock, C.W.B., S.C. Fritz, and D.R. Engstrom. 1991. A prehistoric perspective on the northern range. pp. 289-308 *in* R.B. Keiter and M.S. Boyce, eds. The Greater Yellowstone ecosystem: redefining America's wilderness heritage. Yale Univ. Press, New Haven, Conn.

Whitten, K.R. 1991. Antler retention and udder distension as indicators of parturition in free-ranging caribou. Proc. North Am. Caribou Workshop **4**: 170-173.

Whitten, W.K. 1956. The effect of removal of the olfactory bulbs on the gonads of mice. J. Endocrinol. **14**: 160-163.

Williams, T.M. 1990. Summer diet and behaviour of wolves denning on barren-ground caribou range in the Northwest Territories, Canada. M.Sc. Thesis, Univ. Alberta, Edmonton. 75 pp.

Williams, T.M., and D.C. Heard. 1986. World status of wild *Rangifer tarandus* populations. Proc. Int. Reindeer/Caribou Symp. **4**: 19-28.

Williams, T.M., and D.C. Heard. 1991. Predation rates, movement and activity patterns, pup survival and diet of wolves associated with dens on the range of the Bathurst caribou herd, June-August 1991. Northwest Territ. Dep. Renewable Resour. Wildl. Manage. Div. Prog. Rep. 25 pp.

Wilson, D.E., M.A. Bogan, R.L. Brownell, Jr., A.M. Burdin, and M.K. Maminov. 1991. Geographic variation in sea otters, *Enhydra lutris*. J. Mammal. **72**: 22-36.

Wilson, E.O., and W.L. Brown. 1953. The subspecies concept and its taxonomic application. Syst. Zool. **2**: 97-111.

Wilson, W.C. 1967. Food habits of the coyote, *Canis latrans*, in Louisiana. M.S. Thesis, Louisiana State Univ., Baton Rouge. 49 pp.

Wiltse, E. 1983. Summary of the status of wolves in Saskatchewan. p. 125 *in* L.N. Carbyn, ed. Wolves in Canada and Alaska: their status, biology, and management. Can. Wildl. Serv. Rep. Ser., No. 45.

Windberg, L.A., and C.D. Mitchell. 1991. Winter diets of coyotes in relation to prey abundance in southern Texas. J. Mammal. **71**: 439-447.

Windberg, L.A., H.L. Anderson, and R.M. Engeman. 1985. Survival of coyotes in southern Texas. J. Wildl. Manage. **49**: 301-306.

Winkler, W.G., and K. Bogel. 1992. Control of rabies in wildlife. Sci. Am. **226**: 86-92.

Wobeser, G. 1992. Traumatic, degenerative, and developmental lesions in wolves and coyotes from Saskatchewan. J. Wildl. Dis. **28**: 268-275.

Wobeser, G., W. Runge, and R.R. Stewart. 1983. *Metorchis conjunctus* (Cobbold, 1860) infection in wolves (*Canis lupus*), with pancreatic involvement in two animals. J. Wildl. Dis. **19**: 353-356.

Wolf Management Committee. 1991. Reintroduction of wolves in Yellowstone National Park and the central Idaho wilderness area: a report to the U.S. Congress. Unpubl. Rep., U.S. Fish and Wildl. Serv., Denver, Colo. 31 pp.

Wolfe, M.L. 1969. Age determination in moose from cementum layers of molar teeth. J. Wildl. Manage. **33**: 428-431.

Wolfe, M.L., and D.L. Allen. 1973. Continued studies of the status, socialization, and relationships of Isle Royale wolves, 1967 to 1970. J. Mammal. **54**: 611-635.

Wood, P. 1984. The elk hunt goes on at Grand Teton. Natl. Parks **58**: 29-31.

Wooding, J.B., E.P. Hill, and P.W. Sumner. 1984. Coyote food habits in Mississippi and Alabama. Proc. Annu. Conf. Southeast. Assoc. Fish and Wildl. Agencies **38**: 182-188.

Woolpy, J.H., and I. Eckstrand. 1979. Wolf pack genetics, a computer simulation with theory. pp. 206-224 *in* E. Klinghammer, ed. The behavior and ecology of wolves. Garland STPM Press, New York, N.Y.

World Health Organization. 1990. Report of a WHO/NVI workshop on arctic rabies. WHO/Rabies Res. 90.35. 22 pp.

World Wildlife Fund Canada. 1993. Endangered spaces. Prog. Rep. No. 4. 48 pp.

Wright, G.A. 1984. People of the high country: Jackson Hole before the settlers. Peter Lang, New York, N.Y. 181 pp.

Wright, R. 1990. Are animals people too? New Republic 202 (11): 20-27.

Wright, R.G. 1992. Wildlife research and management in the national parks. Univ. Illinois Press, Urbana. 224 pp.

Wright, S. 1978. Evolution and the genetics of populations. Vol. 4. Variability within and among natural populations. Univ. Chicago Press, Chicago, Ill. 580 pp.

Wydeven, A.P. 1993. Wolves in Wisconsin: recolonization underway. Int. Wolf **3**(1): 18-19.

Wyoming State Veterinary Laboratory. 1986-1990. Annual reports. Univ. Wyoming, Laramie.

Wysocki, C.J. 1979. Neurobehavioral evidence for the involvement of the vomeronasal system in mammalian reproduction. Neurosci. Biobehav. Rev. **3**: 301-341.

Y

Yang, T.J. 1987. Parvovirus-induced regression of canine transmissible venereal sarcoma. Am. J. Vet. Res. **48**: 799-800.

Yates, B.T. 1985. Cost-effectiveness analysis and cost-benefit analysis: an introduction. Eval. Stud. Rev. Annu. **11**: 315-342.

Yellowstone National Park, U.S. Fish and Wildlife Service, University of Wyoming, University of Idaho, Interagency Grizzly Bear Study Team, and the University of Minnesota Cooperative Park Studies Unit. (eds.) 1990. Wolves for Yellowstone? A report to the United States Congress. Volume II. Research and analysis. U.S. Natl. Park Serv., Mammoth, Yellowstone National Park, Wyo. 750 pp.

Yesner, D.R. 1989. Moose hunters of the boreal forest? A re-examination of subsistence patterns in the western subarctic. Arctic **42**: 97-108.

Yodzis, P. 1989. Introduction to theoretical ecology. Harper and Row, New York, N.Y. 384 pp.

Young, S.P. 1944. The wolves of North America. Part I. Their history, life habits, economic status, and control. pp. 1-385 *in* S.P. Young and E.A. Goldman. The wolves of North America. Dover, New York, N.Y./Am. Wildl. Inst., Washington, D.C.

Young, S.P. 1951. The clever coyote. Part I. Its history, life habits, economic status and control. pp. 3-226 *in* S.P. Young and H.H.T. Jackson, eds. The clever coyote. Univ. Nebraska Press, Lincoln, and the Wildl. Manage. Inst., Washington, D.C.

Young, S.P. 1970. The last of the loners. Macmillan, New York, N.Y. 316 pp.

Young, S.P., and E.A. Goldman. 1944. The wolves of North America. Dover, New York, N.Y./Am. Wildl. Inst., Washington, D.C. 636 pp.

Young, S.P., and H.H.T. Jackson. (eds.) 1951. The clever coyote. Univ. Nebraska Press, Lincoln, and the Wildl. Manage. Inst., Washington, D.C. 411 pp.

Yount, H. 1881. Report of the gamekeeper. pp. 62-63 *in* P.W. Norris. Fifth annual report of the superintendent of Yellowstone National Park. U.S. Gov. Print. Off., Washington, D.C.

Yukon Wolf Management Planning Team. 1992. The Yukon Wolf Conservation and Management Plan. Yukon Dep. Renewable Resour., Whitehorse. 18 pp.

Z

Zamenhof, S., and E. Van Marthens. 1977. The effects of chronic undernutrition over generations on rat brain development. Fed. Proc. **36**: 1108. (abstract).

Zaneveld, L.J.D., J.W. Burns, S. Beyler, W.A. Depel, and S.W. Shapiro. 1988. Development of a potentially reversible vas deferens occlusion device and evaluation in primates. Fertil. Steril. **49**: 527-533.

Zar, J.H. 1984. Biostatistical analysis. 2nd ed. Prentice-Hall, Englewood Cliffs, N.J. 718 pp.

Zarnke, R.L., and W.B. Ballard. 1987. Serologic survey for selected microbial pathogens of wolves in Alaska, 1975-1982. J. Wildl. Dis. **23**: 77-85.

Zarnke, R.L., and T.M. Yuill. 1981. Serologic survey for selected microbial agents in mammals from Alberta, 1976. J. Wildl. Dis. **17**: 453-461.

Zeman, F.J. 1967. Effect on the young rat of maternal protein restriction. J. Nutr. **93**: 167-173.

Ziegltrum, G. 1990. Animal damage control. 1990 annual report. Washington Protection Assoc., Olympia, Wash. 29 pp.

Zimbelman, R.G., J.W. Lauderdale, J.H. Sokolowski, and T.G. Schalk. 1970. Safety and pharmacologic evaluations of melengestrol acetate in cattle and other animals: a review. J. Am. Vet. Med. Assoc. **157**: 1528-1536.

Zimen, E. 1976. On the regulation of pack size in wolves. Z. Tierpsychol. **40**: 300-341.

Zimen, E. 1978. Der Wolf: Mythos und Verhalten. Meyster Verlag GmbH, Munchen. 373 pp.

Zimen, E., and L. Boitani. 1979. Status of the wolf in Europe and the possibilities of conservation and reintroduction. pp. 43-83 *in* E. Klinghammer, ed. The behavior and ecology of wolves. Garland STPM Press, New York, N.Y.

Zupancic, Z., R. Ramadan, and J. Madic. 1987. Serological studies of canine parvovirus infection in Zagreb, Yugoslavia. Vet. Arh. **57**: 53-61.

Index

A

Aboriginal peoples   83, 84
Adams, Layne G.   44, 48, 182, 185,
    223, 224, 230, 231, 236, 239,
    240, 241, 245, 247, 248, 256,
    257, 264, 293, 294, 467
Adaptation   8, 263, 287, 289, 335,
    355, 368, 401
Aerial shooting   50, 51, 52, 499,
    500, 512, 532, 543, 544
African wild dog   325, 326, 327
Age classes   37, 220, 225, 229,
    270, 295, 455, 457, 458
Aging techniques   49
Aggression   317
Agriculture   8, 9, 111, 112, 122,
    127, 128, 129, 158, 272, 304,
    325, 335, 405, 526
Agriculture Canada   422, 424, 436
Aircraft-assisted   505, 510, 512, 513
Alaska   3, 11, 14, 15, 30, 32, 43,
    44, 45, 46, 47, 48, 49, 50, 51,
    52, 53, 54, 57, 77, 91, 135,
    138, 141, 154, 223, 225, 226,
    228, 230, 231, 232, 233, 234,
    235, 236, 237, 238, 239, 240,
    245, 246, 248, 249, 250, 251,
    252, 253, 254, 255, 257, 258,
    260, 261, 262, 263, 264, 265,
    266, 268, 275, 276, 277, 279,
    280, 293, 294, 295, 296, 298,
    300, 301, 302, 315, 316, 317,
    318, 321, 323, 328, 329, 332,
    333, 353, 361, 362, 363, 364,
    365, 366, 367, 369, 370, 375,
    377, 382, 384, 396, 403, 405,
    410, 420, 421, 422, 423, 424,
    427, 435, 436, 437, 438, 439,
    441, 442, 445, 446, 455, 456,
    459, 461, 462, 463, 464, 465,
    466, 467, 469, 470, 471, 472,
    474, 475, 477, 478, 479, 480,
    481, 482, 483, 484, 485, 486,
    487, 491, 493, 494, 495, 497,
    498, 499, 500, 501, 505, 506,
    507, 508, 509, 510, 511, 512,
    513, 523, 527, 528, 529, 530,
    532, 534, 537
Alberta   21, 22, 23, 25, 26, 27, 28,
    29, 30, 31, 32, 85, 86, 87, 88,
    90, 91, 92, 93, 94, 107, 108,
    110, 118, 120, 124, 135, 137,
    138, 140, 213, 228, 262, 264,
    267, 268, 271, 316, 319, 353,

358, 363, 366, 371, 372, 384,
    385, 386, 396, 421, 422, 424,
    425, 427, 428, 464, 495, 496,
    497, 498, 502, 504, 534
Alces alces   37, 45, 64, 78, 87, 117,
    136, 148, 179, 192, 203, 211,
    223, 231, 246, 263, 294, 304,
    358, 422, 503, 505
Anderson, Rita E.   35, 36, 341, 342,
    343, 346, 356, 358, 359, 362,
    396, 400, 402, 403, 411
Animal damage control   127
Animal rights   13, 15, 124, 485
Asa, Cheryl S.   283, 284, 285, 287,
    288, 289, 290, 291, 503, 539,
    540, 541
Aversive condition   502, 544
Aversive conditioning   491, 502

B

Bailey, Theodore N.   64, 260, 321,
    396, 421, 441, 496
Ballard, Warren B.   43, 44, 45, 46,
    47, 48, 49, 135, 138, 139, 154,
    156, 221, 225, 227, 230, 231,
    236, 237, 241, 242, 243, 245,
    264, 268, 293, 294, 297, 303,
    309, 311, 312, 326, 327, 328,
    329, 332, 335, 336, 340, 370,
    419, 420, 421, 422, 423, 428,
    441, 445, 455, 456, 457, 458,
    461, 462, 463, 467, 469, 470,
    479, 499, 502, 505, 506, 508,
    509, 512, 513, 538, 539, 542
Banff National Park   28, 29, 91,
    120, 135, 136, 137, 266, 493
Bangs, Edward E.   61, 107, 114,
    118, 119, 127, 129, 134, 139,
    221, 441, 491, 500, 501, 503,
    523, 544
Biomass   37, 49, 102, 155, 162,
    163, 185, 193, 195, 197, 208,
    209, 214, 220, 226, 227, 228,
    229, 232, 265, 508, 539
Body size   265, 275, 323, 353, 366,
    400
Boertje, Rodney D.   48, 49, 184,
    185, 230, 267, 480, 501, 503,
    504, 505, 506, 507, 508, 510,
    511, 544
Boitani, Luigi   3, 5, 7, 8, 10, 11, 14,
    335, 338, 397, 500, 523, 526

Bounties   5, 6, 13, 26, 110, 143,
    169, 268, 491, 493, 494, 495,
    496, 500, 532
Bowyer, Terry R.   223, 280
Boyce, Mark S.   78, 122, 179, 183,
    186, 199, 200, 202, 203, 204,
    205, 208, 209, 213, 539
Boyd, Diane K.   117, 119, 120,
    123, 125, 132, 135, 139, 140,
    154, 291, 371, 373, 540, 545
Bradford, Wesley   85, 268, 273
Brain   36, 262, 266, 267, 290, 378,
    410, 432
Brand, Christopher J.   116, 323,
    419, 473, 543
Breeding   60, 143, 157, 326, 356
    multiple litters   299, 301, 326, 327
Breeding season   162, 283, 285,
    335, 336, 540, 541, 544
Brewster, Wayne G.   76, 107, 122,
    127, 139, 141, 209, 221, 353,
    385, 543
British Columbia   14, 21, 22, 23,
    25, 26, 27, 29, 30, 31, 33, 107,
    117, 119, 135, 180, 186, 261,
    353, 382, 383, 396, 494, 495,
    515, 527
Brucellosis   48, 266, 270, 422, 423,
    428
Burch, John W.   156, 231, 260, 293

C

Canine distemper   39, 40, 42, 47,
    93, 327, 419, 420, 428, 429,
    441, 444, 445
Canine parvovirus   48, 147, 151,
    155, 156, 419, 421, 441, 444,
    445, 543
Captive propagation   141, 447
Carbyn, Ludwig N.   11, 15, 16, 17,
    21, 28, 30, 31, 32, 76, 88, 89,
    90, 91, 93, 124, 125, 186, 213,
    214, 215, 220, 221, 224, 227,
    228, 229, 265, 293, 294, 303,
    310, 311, 316, 317, 319, 325,
    327, 332, 335, 338, 363, 364,
    365, 366, 370, 373, 375, 381,
    386, 387, 394, 419, 420, 424,
    428, 445, 459, 491, 497, 501,
    502, 503, 504, 527, 538, 541,
    543, 545

Carrying capacity   30, 35, 38, 39, 40, 41, 48, 111, 122, 187, 200, 201, 202, 209, 280
  harvesting   217, 499
Castroviejo, J.   335, 338
Cementum annuli   231, 232, 455, 458, 459
Censusing   483
Cervus elaphus   37, 63, 78, 85, 117, 135, 199, 211, 228, 265, 366
Chemical repellent   491, 502
Chundawat, Raghunandan S.   95, 100, 101, 102
Citizen participation   52, 481, 487
Clarkson, Peter L.   23, 28, 29, 30, 33, 39, 42, 264, 293, 527, 528, 530, 534
Cluff, H. Dean   5, 124, 491, 543
Competition   13, 101, 103, 179, 187, 209, 285, 315, 316, 318, 321, 322, 323, 325, 326, 327, 338, 342, 369, 496, 503, 527, 534
Computer simulation   180, 183, 191, 199, 369, 479
Condition   9, 14, 16, 39, 42, 48, 49, 50, 53, 63, 65, 73, 83, 84, 87, 92, 94, 107, 124, 132, 148, 159, 161, 179, 183, 185, 187, 197, 204, 205, 206, 208, 220, 223, 224, 226, 228, 231, 232, 239, 241, 242, 243, 245, 249, 258, 259, 260, 263, 264, 265, 266, 267, 268, 269, 270, 275, 276, 277, 278, 280, 285, 287, 288, 290, 304, 310, 312, 317, 321, 329, 335, 371, 386, 422, 423, 424, 427, 428, 443, 444, 473, 479, 480, 491, 502, 503, 506, 512, 523, 530, 539, 541, 544
Congress   53, 61, 75, 80, 82, 107, 109, 111, 114, 120, 121, 122, 123, 130, 158, 165, 175
Consensus   13, 14, 43, 52, 387, 394, 401, 481, 482, 483, 484, 485, 486, 487, 544
Conservation   3, 10, 15, 30, 31, 32, 37, 41, 43, 50, 53, 54, 62, 83, 84, 101, 102, 103, 108, 111, 114, 116, 117, 118, 121, 122, 124, 128, 134, 140, 143, 146, 156, 159, 165, 166, 174, 175, 261, 262, 270, 271, 272, 273, 312, 313, 325, 326, 327, 328,

354, 356, 368, 373, 397, 399, 400, 403, 405, 409, 414, 446, 481, 482, 483, 485, 500, 529, 534
Control methods   13, 491, 492, 501
Control policy   127
Coppinger, Lorna   523
Coppinger, Raymond   523
Cuon alpinus   97, 328
Cyanide   26, 27, 143, 496, 498

D

Dale, Bruce D.   127, 179, 180, 184, 185, 187, 192, 196, 223, 243, 245, 265, 302, 481, 537, 538
Defence   8, 30, 73
Defenders of Wildlife   50, 51, 52, 109, 113, 118, 122, 129, 131, 146, 341
Dekker, Dick   85, 86, 87, 89, 92, 94, 123, 316, 319, 321, 366
Denali   48, 231, 232, 233, 234, 235, 236, 237, 238, 239, 240, 241, 242, 243, 245, 246, 248, 249, 250, 251, 252, 253, 254, 255, 256, 257, 258, 259, 269, 293, 294, 295, 296, 297, 298, 299, 300, 301, 302, 369, 405, 485, 534
Denning   500
Density   4, 21, 22, 23, 29, 30, 31, 32, 37, 39, 41, 44, 45, 47, 48, 49, 55, 57, 64, 70, 91, 95, 101, 102, 128, 135, 138, 139, 140, 147, 151, 152, 153, 155, 179, 180, 181, 182, 183, 184, 185, 186, 187, 188, 189, 190, 191, 192, 193, 194, 195, 196, 197, 199, 200, 201, 202, 204, 205, 206, 207, 208, 209, 211, 213, 215, 217, 220, 221, 223, 224, 225, 226, 227, 229, 230, 245, 247, 248, 250, 252, 253, 255, 257, 258, 260, 263, 264, 265, 267, 268, 269, 275, 276, 278, 279, 280, 295, 301, 303, 304, 305, 307, 308, 311, 312, 313, 320, 321, 322, 326, 338, 368, 425, 428, 441, 445, 469, 470, 473, 476, 479, 480, 505, 506, 507, 509, 520, 539, 544
  competition   5, 13, 101, 103, 179, 187, 209, 285, 315, 318, 321,

322, 323, 325, 326, 327, 338, 342, 369, 496, 503, 527, 534
  extinction   5, 83, 146, 191, 257, 370, 373, 397
Depredation   11, 23, 27, 29, 62, 102, 109, 118, 119, 120, 121, 122, 123, 124, 127, 128, 130, 131, 132, 133, 134, 139, 146, 159, 165, 168, 172, 173, 174, 175, 325, 327, 372, 491, 493, 494, 495, 497, 498, 500, 501, 502, 503, 523, 544
Disease   40, 41, 42, 48, 83, 84, 93, 116, 119, 122, 147, 148, 151, 156, 172, 173, 175, 179, 186, 263, 266, 267, 268, 270, 283, 285, 296, 298, 323, 325, 327, 328, 417, 419, 420, 421, 422, 423, 424, 427, 428, 429, 431, 432, 435, 436, 437, 438, 441, 445, 447, 449, 450, 491, 537, 538, 543, 545
Dispersal   5, 57, 117, 133, 135, 136, 137, 138, 139, 140, 147, 148, 149, 150, 152, 154, 162, 186, 200, 204, 225, 230, 276, 293, 301, 303, 304, 319, 321, 325, 326, 327, 353, 362, 369, 370, 371, 372, 373, 399, 403, 405, 406, 420, 428, 435, 537, 538, 539, 544
Distemper   39, 40, 42, 47, 93, 268, 327, 419, 420, 421, 428, 429, 432, 441, 444, 445
Diurnal   340, 544
Divergent evolution   261
Diversionary feeding   491, 501, 503, 505, 506
Diversity, species   17, 41, 53, 85, 111, 118, 157, 279, 280, 293, 356, 409, 481
DNA   40, 41, 120, 141, 145, 262, 293, 295, 354, 368, 370, 375, 399, 400, 401, 402, 403, 405, 406, 407, 409, 411, 413, 414, 415, 542, 543
Donelon, Steve   135
Drag, Marlene D.   410, 447
Drugs   289, 506, 508
Duck Mountain   321, 384

E

Ecology   3, 6, 8, 21, 29, 30, 43, 44,
45, 47, 48, 95, 108, 109, 116,
117, 125, 145, 169, 192, 213,
223, 261, 262, 263, 267, 270,
315, 316, 325, 326, 336, 349,
412, 432, 485, 504, 537

Ecosystem   14, 16, 17, 41, 48, 63,
65, 75, 77, 78, 79, 80, 81, 83,
84, 119, 120, 122, 123, 139,
140, 168, 196, 199, 202, 204,
213, 261, 262, 269, 270, 271,
273, 310, 325, 349, 397, 511,
527

Ecotypes   245, 246, 262, 265, 267,
355, 405

Effective population size   369

Endangered species   14, 17, 60, 77,
103, 107, 111, 112, 114, 124,
128, 141, 143, 147, 168, 169,
271, 356, 414, 415, 447, 517,
523

Endangered Species Act   9, 59, 60,
77, 107, 108, 109, 112, 127,
143, 157, 169, 354, 397, 409

Energy expenditure   322, 338

Environmental Impact Statement
61, 107, 109, 111, 123, 141,
145

Evolution   3, 13, 44, 261, 263, 271,
293, 315, 323, 325, 354, 355,
356, 363, 369, 396, 399, 411,
504

Experimental population   11, 60,
62, 111, 121, 122, 123

Extinction   5, 83, 146, 191, 257,
370, 373, 397

F

Fancy, Steven G.   245, 263, 329,
333, 455, 461, 462, 463, 464,
467

Fat   232, 238, 239, 240, 241, 242,
243, 263, 264, 266, 278, 428,
500

Fences   491, 501, 502

Fentress, John C.   341, 342

Fighting   185, 241, 242, 342, 343,
437

Fish   56, 83, 84, 111, 112, 114,
117, 121, 129, 145, 146, 163,
200, 202, 208, 211, 213, 221,

280, 291, 343, 349, 403, 425,
437, 439, 446, 485, 500

Fitness   45, 83, 139, 264, 265, 270

Fontaine, Joseph A.   107, 127, 373

Food
chain   423
niche   263

Foraging   83, 84, 87, 196, 266, 268,
276, 278, 279

Forbes, Graham J.   302, 303, 304,
307, 310, 327, 377, 438, 439

Fox, Joseph L.   95, 96, 97, 98, 102,
103, 319

Fritts, Steven H.   11, 59, 61, 62,
107, 111, 113, 114, 119, 121,
122, 123, 124, 127, 128, 129,
130, 132, 133, 134, 135, 138,
139, 140, 141, 152, 154, 155,
156, 202, 209, 211, 215, 221,
231, 289, 293, 294, 295, 297,
303, 315, 327, 328, 353, 354,
362, 366, 370, 371, 372, 373,
384, 421, 424, 455, 459, 467,
491, 494, 496, 498, 501, 502,
503, 504, 523, 526, 534, 537,
538, 539, 543, 544, 545

Fuller, Todd K.   16, 29, 32, 59,
102, 114, 128, 138, 139, 148,
150, 152, 154, 155, 156, 179,
192, 193, 195, 200, 213, 214,
219, 220, 221, 227, 229, 236,
262, 288, 293, 294, 295, 303,
305, 309, 310, 312, 323, 325,
326, 327, 328, 338, 370, 399,
420, 421, 428, 429, 455, 469,
480, 497, 504, 508, 526, 538,
539, 541, 545

Functional response   27, 49, 180,
181, 184, 185, 187, 188, 189,
190, 191, 192, 193, 195, 196,
199, 200, 201, 202, 204, 205,
207, 208, 209, 213, 220, 230

Fur   15, 21, 23, 25, 31, 33, 38, 43,
78, 85, 87, 270, 313, 315, 357,
403, 426, 491, 494, 500, 526

G

Garbage dumps   267

Gardner, Craig L.   49, 459, 469,
470, 479, 480

Gene flow   143, 353, 355, 367,
368, 369, 370, 403, 406

Genetic diversity   157, 279, 293,
356, 409

Genetics   41, 116, 145, 159, 261,
263, 353, 362, 368, 369, 399,
413, 537, 539, 542, 545

Genotype   141, 369, 370, 400, 402,
403, 405, 407, 413

Gestation   143

Gilbert, F.   13, 15, 124

Gore, James F.   107, 373

Greenland   41, 42, 55, 56, 57, 357,
386, 387, 396

Guard dogs   491, 501

Gunson, John R.   16, 17, 21, 26,
27, 28, 32, 59, 62, 85, 89, 90,
91, 94, 110, 125, 128, 132,
134, 135, 140, 213, 214, 215,
236, 328, 353, 363, 372, 384,
427, 491, 495, 497, 498, 501,
504, 532, 534

H

Habitat   3, 14, 17, 21, 22, 32, 45,
47, 48, 49, 53, 55, 56, 57, 60,
62, 64, 67, 68, 75, 77, 85, 86,
87, 90, 91, 94, 95, 96, 97, 98,
99, 100, 101, 102, 111, 113,
114, 117, 119, 128, 129, 138,
140, 141, 143, 145, 147, 152,
156, 157, 161, 165, 167, 168,
169, 170, 172, 173, 174, 175,
184, 185, 220, 221, 224, 245,
247, 250, 256, 257, 262, 263,
264, 265, 266, 267, 268, 269,
270, 271, 272, 273, 275, 280,
287, 299, 313, 318, 321, 322,
326, 327, 355, 363, 370, 373,
387, 388, 399, 400, 402, 403,
405, 406, 429, 436, 438, 445,
461, 466, 469, 479, 480, 482,
491, 501, 505, 507, 508, 509,
513, 519, 530, 531, 544

Haggstrom, Dale H.   52, 53, 481

Hair   36, 51, 93, 224, 241, 247,
277, 278, 280, 315, 426, 427,
463, 482, 493, 524

Harms, Catherine M.   481

Harvesting   217, 499

Hayes, Roberts D.   21, 27, 28, 31,
44, 53, 230, 236, 241, 265,
269, 293, 328, 491, 496, 497,
498, 499, 501, 504, 505, 506,
509, 512, 534

Heartworm 165, 424, 425, 428, 447, 543
Henry, V. Gary 157
Herbivores 5, 8, 187, 276, 287
Hill, Bonnie L.C. 247, 298, 299, 300, 341, 343, 413
Hormones 283, 284, 285, 290, 503
Hosts 266, 419, 423, 424, 427, 432, 435, 437
Howling 31, 69, 78, 79, 80, 87, 118, 138, 147, 148, 277, 278, 288, 290, 302, 304, 305, 469, 537, 541
Human 3, 5, 6, 7, 8, 9, 10, 11, 13, 14, 15, 16, 17, 21, 22, 23, 29, 30, 32, 36, 37, 42, 44, 47, 49, 50, 54, 56, 60, 64, 65, 68, 70, 74, 83, 84, 85, 91, 94, 95, 96, 98, 100, 102, 108, 111, 113, 114, 119, 120, 122, 124, 128, 130, 132, 134, 138, 140, 142, 143, 147, 150, 151, 154, 155, 156, 159, 165, 168, 172, 173, 183, 186, 200, 201, 202, 204, 205, 206, 220, 221, 231, 240, 243, 261, 262, 263, 265, 266, 267, 268, 270, 271, 272, 287, 288, 289, 290, 293, 294, 295, 301, 303, 305, 307, 309, 310, 312, 313, 315, 318, 320, 321, 322, 325, 327, 328, 335, 338, 341, 342, 343, 345, 346, 348, 349, 350, 354, 355, 363, 369, 370, 372, 373, 384, 397, 399, 405, 423, 431, 432, 435, 436, 437, 438, 441, 444, 445, 481, 483, 486, 487, 491, 492, 494, 495, 496, 498, 500, 501, 502, 503, 504, 508, 523, 530, 531, 534, 538, 539, 541, 544
  demography 223, 267, 326
  disturbance 79, 114, 208, 293
Hunter, William C. 39, 113, 174, 200, 204, 205, 206, 211, 409, 480, 500, 516
Hunting 5, 6, 8, 9, 15, 16, 17, 21, 22, 23, 24, 27, 31, 32, 37, 42, 43, 45, 47, 48, 50, 51, 52, 53, 55, 62, 63, 64, 65, 67, 68, 71, 74, 75, 78, 83, 84, 85, 87, 92, 93, 95, 96, 98, 101, 102, 110, 119, 120, 121, 159, 167, 170, 172, 173, 174, 179, 184, 186, 199, 202, 204, 205, 206, 208, 211, 213, 215, 217, 219, 220,

221, 225, 228, 229, 258, 262, 264, 265, 267, 268, 269, 270, 271, 272, 273, 275, 287, 288, 289, 290, 294, 304, 305, 309, 310, 312, 325, 326, 327, 328, 335, 343, 349, 367, 413, 479, 481, 482, 483, 484, 485, 497, 499, 500, 501, 505, 507, 510, 511, 515, 516, 517, 518, 519, 520, 521, 523, 524, 527, 532, 533, 534, 539, 544

I

Ice ages 370
Idaho 22, 59, 60, 61, 62, 73, 77, 78, 107, 108, 109, 110, 111, 112, 113, 114, 115, 116, 117, 118, 119, 120, 121, 122, 123, 124, 135, 136, 138, 140, 221, 353, 354, 366, 371, 372, 384, 410, 421, 431, 436, 437, 438, 439
  Idaho Wolf Recovery Steering Committee 109, 114, 115, 118
Immunity,disease 422
Inbreeding 32, 139, 279, 293, 301, 368, 407, 539
Incentives 491, 496, 510
Interbreeding 102, 354, 356, 363, 369, 375, 388, 403, 409, 413, 414, 543

Interspecific competition 315, 318, 321
  predation 5, 10, 11, 21, 23, 27, 29, 30, 31, 32, 41, 43, 45, 47, 48, 49, 50, 51, 52, 53, 54, 62, 73, 83, 84, 85, 88, 91, 92, 94, 100, 102, 114, 117, 127, 132, 179, 181, 182, 183, 184, 185, 186, 187, 188, 191, 192, 193, 194, 195, 197, 201, 202, 203, 204, 206, 207, 208, 209, 211, 213, 214, 215, 216, 217, 218, 219, 220, 221, 223, 224, 229, 230, 237, 239, 241, 245, 246, 250, 251, 253, 255, 256, 257, 258, 259, 260, 261, 262, 263, 264, 265, 266, 267, 268, 269, 270, 271, 272, 273, 275, 276, 279, 310, 315, 325, 327, 372,

413, 419, 423, 425, 426, 428, 491, 493, 494, 495, 496, 497, 498, 500, 501, 502, 503, 505, 506, 507, 508, 509, 510, 511, 515, 518, 523, 537, 538, 539, 544
Interspecific interaction 318
  bear and wolf 49
Islands 21, 30, 35, 36, 37, 38, 39, 40, 41, 42, 44, 55, 85, 90, 152, 157, 166, 184, 245, 262, 264, 267, 270, 275, 276, 277, 278, 280, 318, 321, 355, 357, 361, 362, 363, 367, 373, 385, 386, 394, 396
Isle Royale 59, 91, 94, 155, 193, 195, 207, 228, 239, 240, 266, 301, 315, 316, 317, 318, 319, 368, 381, 410, 413, 421, 493, 537, 538, 539, 540, 543
Isolation 94, 111, 261, 264, 313, 355, 362, 372, 403, 405, 414
  genetic 293, 301, 370

J

Janz, Doug 27, 491, 515, 518
Jasper National Park 28, 29, 85, 86, 88, 89, 90, 92, 93, 118, 135, 214, 228, 264, 266, 338, 363, 366, 371, 497, 541
Jimenez, Michael D. 125, 127, 132, 140
Johnson, Mark R. 9, 51, 76, 168, 241, 262, 271, 316, 323, 431

K

Kananaskis 90, 135, 136, 138, 140
Kay, Charles E. 64, 73, 74, 75, 77, 78, 80, 81, 82, 83
Kelleyhouse, David R. 487, 505
Klein, David R. 184, 185, 187, 268, 273, 275, 276, 333
Krausman, Paul R. 413, 429, 455, 461, 480

L

Lehman, Niles 293, 294, 299, 301, 302, 326, 354, 399, 400, 402, 405, 406, 539
Life history/cycles 29, 49, 50, 218, 335

Livestock   3, 4, 6, 8, 9, 10, 11, 15, 23, 26, 27, 29, 30, 31, 59, 62, 77, 95, 98, 100, 101, 102, 103, 107, 109, 111, 112, 113, 114, 118, 120, 121, 122, 123, 124, 127, 128, 129, 130, 131, 132, 133, 134, 139, 142, 146, 158, 159, 165, 166, 172, 173, 174, 175, 202, 325, 327, 328, 335, 353, 372, 419, 423, 429, 431, 439, 491, 494, 495, 497, 498, 499, 500, 501, 502, 503, 523, 524, 526, 527, 533, 534, 544

Longevity
  of packs   293
Lucash, Chris   157
Lycaon pictus   325
Lyme disease   423, 428, 543

M

Maine   62, 316, 319
Malnutrition   296, 369, 420, 449, 450
Mammals   14, 322, 356, 497
  evolution   3, 13, 14, 44, 261, 263, 271, 293, 315, 322, 323, 325, 354, 355, 356, 363, 369, 396, 399, 411, 504
  productivity   39, 45, 48, 54, 94, 103, 147, 184, 204, 217, 220, 261, 263, 270, 271, 368, 467, 506, 507, 509
Management programs   14, 17, 43, 53, 174, 341, 419, 482, 484, 499, 529, 530, 531, 532
Manitoba   22, 23, 25, 26, 27, 28, 29, 30, 32, 33, 59, 90, 91, 186, 228, 262, 267, 271, 315, 316, 321, 322, 361, 363, 384, 396, 403, 420, 424, 445, 495, 497, 532
Marquard-Petersen, Ulf   55, 57
Matson, Gary M.   232, 455, 456
McNay, Mark E.   512
Mech, L. David   5, 16, 36, 44, 45, 59, 83, 108, 111, 114, 122, 135, 136, 138, 139, 140, 148, 152, 154, 155, 169, 174, 182, 192, 195, 199, 200, 205, 207, 215, 220, 221, 228, 229, 230, 231, 236, 241, 245, 247, 265, 266, 283, 287, 288, 289, 293, 294, 295, 297, 301, 303, 304,

309, 310, 311, 316, 321, 323, 325, 326, 327, 332, 335, 338, 340, 341, 353, 354, 356, 360, 362, 368, 370, 371, 409, 419, 421, 424, 426, 431, 438, 447, 450, 455, 469, 537, 538, 539, 540, 541, 544, 545
Meier, J.   371
Meier, Thomas   231, 248, 293, 294, 326, 368, 370, 545
Messier, François   28, 29, 91, 135, 136, 138, 154, 155, 179, 180, 181, 184, 187, 192, 193, 194, 195, 196, 197, 208, 220, 225, 230, 262, 264, 268, 293, 303, 309, 310, 311, 327, 425, 426, 469, 479, 538, 539
Mexico   60, 61, 62, 141, 142, 143, 144, 145, 146, 357, 367, 372, 382, 385, 396, 406, 431, 447, 491, 493, 494, 497, 498, 499, 500, 502
Michigan   14, 59, 60, 62, 144, 149, 152, 169, 228, 315, 317, 319, 321, 341, 342, 362, 368, 413, 421, 493, 502, 539, 544
Migration   39, 40, 44, 47, 56, 67, 73, 100, 117, 140, 179, 185, 200, 202, 220, 230, 263, 264, 267, 268, 269, 271, 272, 301, 303, 304, 308, 309, 310, 325, 341, 367, 369, 370, 384, 428, 431, 435, 445, 485, 503, 504, 509, 534, 539, 544

Miller, Frank L.   30, 35, 36, 37, 38, 40, 69, 223, 237, 243, 245, 260, 268, 302, 342, 356, 357, 362, 422, 423, 467, 480, 502, 513
Minnesota   3, 6, 9, 11, 59, 60, 61, 62, 77, 94, 110, 127, 132, 133, 135, 138, 139, 144, 147, 148, 149, 150, 151, 152, 154, 155, 156, 169, 174, 215, 287, 293, 297, 315, 316, 318, 320, 321, 328, 333, 338, 341, 342, 362, 369, 370, 375, 377, 379, 381, 384, 387, 388, 389, 397, 399, 400, 401, 403, 405, 406, 410, 413, 420, 421, 423, 424, 426, 436, 437, 438, 439, 445, 450, 491, 494, 495, 499, 501, 502,

504, 523, 525, 526, 534, 537, 542, 543, 544
Modeling   49, 117, 191, 207, 209, 269, 349, 539
Montana   22, 28, 59, 60, 62, 67, 70, 74, 75, 76, 77, 78, 84, 107, 108, 109, 110, 111, 112, 113, 114, 115, 116, 117, 118, 119, 120, 121, 123, 124, 125, 127, 128, 129, 130, 131, 132, 133, 134, 135, 136, 137, 138, 140, 199, 201, 202, 204, 211, 212, 213, 221, 232, 353, 354, 363, 366, 372, 373, 384, 385, 396, 397, 427, 431, 436, 437, 438, 439, 464, 494, 497, 500, 502, 503, 526, 538, 540
Moose   5, 21, 28, 29, 30, 32, 37, 43, 45, 46, 47, 48, 49, 50, 52, 63, 64, 65, 66, 70, 71, 74, 78, 80, 87, 88, 91, 94, 117, 135, 140, 148, 179, 180, 184, 185, 186, 192, 193, 194, 195, 196, 199, 203, 204, 205, 206, 209, 211, 220, 223, 224, 225, 226, 227, 228, 229, 230, 231, 232, 233, 234, 235, 236, 237, 238, 239, 240, 241, 242, 246, 247, 252, 257, 258, 262, 263, 265, 266, 267, 268, 269, 270, 272, 294, 301, 304, 305, 308, 309, 310, 319, 358, 363, 422, 423, 424, 425, 426, 444, 503, 505, 506, 507, 508, 509, 510, 511, 512, 513, 537, 538, 540
Mortality   11, 14, 22, 29, 37, 43, 46, 47, 48, 49, 50, 92, 94, 114, 117, 119, 128, 134, 140, 143, 147, 148, 150, 151, 154, 161, 179, 184, 186, 187, 199, 202, 205, 208, 219, 225, 230, 239, 245, 247, 248, 250, 251, 252, 256, 258, 259, 260, 263, 265, 266, 267, 268, 269, 270, 271, 272, 273, 297, 301, 303, 305, 307, 309, 310, 311, 312, 313, 318, 325, 327, 329, 405, 412, 419, 420, 421, 423, 425, 428, 431, 441, 445, 467, 493, 503, 506, 538
  of wolves   21, 45, 47, 93, 119, 130, 174, 186, 202, 303, 305, 309, 311, 312, 428, 441

Murray, Dennis L.   5, 124, 313, 491, 538, 543

N

National Parks   14, 22, 28, 29, 30, 32, 45, 48, 54, 55, 59, 63, 64, 65, 67, 70, 72, 74, 75, 76, 77, 82, 85, 86, 87, 88, 89, 90, 91, 92, 93, 97, 99, 100, 101, 102, 103, 107, 108, 109, 110, 111, 114, 116, 117, 118, 119, 120, 121, 122, 123, 124, 127, 128, 130, 131, 132, 135, 136, 137, 138, 140, 157, 165, 186, 199, 200, 202, 203, 205, 211, 213, 214, 215, 220, 221, 223, 224, 225, 226, 227, 228, 229, 230, 231, 232, 233, 234, 235, 236, 237, 238, 239, 240, 242, 243, 245, 246, 248, 250, 251, 254, 255, 258, 259, 260, 264, 266, 293, 294, 295, 296, 298, 299, 300, 302, 310, 315, 316, 317, 318, 319, 321, 325, 327, 328, 333, 338, 341, 363, 366, 371, 372, 386, 397, 405, 407, 420, 421, 422, 424, 431, 436, 438, 445, 459, 461, 467, 470, 480, 485, 493, 494, 496, 497, 503, 534, 537, 541
New Mexico   9, 60, 61, 62, 141, 143, 144, 145, 146, 384, 385, 396, 447
Niche   112, 263, 265, 315, 318, 322, 323
Nicholopoulos, Joy E.   60, 62, 141, 447
Niemeyer, Carter C.   127
North Dakota   62, 316, 319, 321, 436, 438
Northern Rocky Mountain   77, 107, 108, 109, 110, 140, 354, 363
Nowak, Ronald M.   21, 35, 36, 41, 59, 107, 108, 139, 141, 147, 157, 169, 318, 353, 354, 356, 359, 362, 363, 364, 365, 366, 367, 370, 372, 373, 375, 378, 379, 381, 384, 385, 388, 389, 394, 396, 401, 402, 403, 407, 409, 410, 411, 412, 542, 543
Nursing   336, 337, 338, 339, 340
Nutrition   39, 49, 179, 185, 187, 190, 192, 197, 220, 229, 239,

241, 259, 263, 264, 266, 270, 271, 272, 275, 301, 368, 369, 420, 428, 447, 449, 450, 503, 506, 507, 538, 539, 545

O

Olfactory   289, 290, 291, 502, 540
Ovulation   283, 285, 286

P

Packs   44, 45, 46, 47, 48, 56, 57, 59, 77, 80, 83, 84, 86, 87, 88, 89, 93, 94, 113, 115, 116, 117, 118, 120, 121, 122, 123, 124, 130, 133, 135, 137, 139, 142, 147, 148, 149, 150, 151, 152, 155, 156, 162, 169, 172, 173, 174, 199, 207, 221, 223, 224, 225, 226, 228, 229, 230, 231, 232, 239, 248, 249, 250, 251, 252, 253, 254, 264, 266, 283, 285, 286, 288, 290, 293, 294, 295, 296, 297, 298, 299, 300, 301, 302, 303, 304, 305, 306, 307, 308, 309, 310, 317, 318, 326, 327, 335, 340, 368, 369, 370, 371, 372, 399, 405, 406, 407, 412, 420, 427, 441, 443, 444, 463, 467, 469, 470, 473, 475, 476, 478, 479, 480, 491, 502, 503, 509, 510, 512, 517, 518, 537, 539, 540, 541, 542, 545
   formation   22, 43, 45, 47, 50, 63, 65, 70, 72, 73, 84, 85, 87, 94, 95, 97, 98, 103, 112, 113, 114, 116, 117, 118, 122, 123, 124, 125, 127, 133, 134, 142, 145, 162, 169, 170, 171, 172, 173, 174, 175, 192, 193, 195, 197, 221, 223, 228, 231, 245, 254, 263, 284, 285, 293, 294, 297, 298, 299, 301, 369, 413, 450, 527, 529, 537
   splitting   293, 297, 299, 301, 358, 396
Paquet, Paul C.   3, 28, 76, 135, 221, 316, 318, 319, 464, 493, 494
Parsons, David R.   60, 62, 125, 141, 377, 447
Pathogens   323, 327, 419
Pathology   283, 285, 424, 428

Peek, James M.   111, 122, 184, 187, 211, 213, 354, 539
Peterson, Rolf O.   44, 47, 71, 78, 81, 91, 94, 135, 138, 140, 154, 155, 197, 228, 231, 236, 239, 240, 241, 243, 266, 288, 293, 295, 301, 310, 312, 315, 316, 317, 318, 321, 323, 326, 327, 328, 338, 367, 368, 384, 386, 401, 405, 413, 415, 419, 420, 421, 424, 428, 441, 443, 445, 467, 480, 493, 499, 510, 537, 538, 539, 540, 541, 543
Phillips, Michael K.   111, 112, 113, 127, 129, 157, 158, 162, 166, 168, 409, 412, 544, 545
Pletscher, Daniel H.   10, 14, 59, 62, 110, 113, 114, 116, 117, 118, 119, 125, 127, 130, 134, 135, 139, 341, 349, 371, 497
Poisons   69, 491, 496, 497, 498, 501
Prairie   6, 21, 69, 70, 80, 288, 318, 353, 372, 437, 497
Predation   5, 10, 11, 21, 23, 27, 29, 30, 31, 32, 41, 43, 45, 47, 48, 49, 50, 51, 52, 53, 54, 62, 73, 83, 84, 85, 88, 91, 92, 94, 100, 102, 114, 117, 132, 179, 181, 182, 183, 184, 185, 186, 187, 188, 191, 192, 193, 194, 195, 197, 201, 202, 203, 204, 206, 207, 208, 209, 211, 213, 214, 215, 216, 217, 218, 219, 220, 221, 223, 224, 229, 230, 237, 239, 241, 245, 246, 250, 251, 253, 255, 256, 257, 258, 259, 260, 261, 262, 263, 264, 265, 266, 267, 268, 269, 270, 271, 272, 273, 275, 276, 279, 310, 315, 325, 327, 372, 413, 419, 423, 425, 426, 428, 491, 493, 494, 495, 496, 497, 498, 500, 501, 502, 503, 505, 506, 507, 508, 509, 510, 511, 515, 518, 523, 537, 538, 539, 544
Predator control   14, 15, 16, 32, 49, 51, 77, 78, 95, 103, 107, 183, 268, 321, 353, 403, 483, 492, 496, 498, 499, 501, 503, 505, 513, 531
Predator pit   183, 208, 269
Predator-prey systems   47, 76, 269, 482, 537

Prey
    availability   45, 48, 141, 196,
        230, 265, 301, 309, 310, 312,
        338, 369
    selection   46, 48, 223, 224, 225,
        226, 227, 228, 229, 265
    switching   30, 189, 195, 196, 199,
        205, 223, 228
Protection   6, 17, 30, 38, 41, 45, 57,
        62, 72, 100, 101, 102, 103,
        110, 111, 112, 114, 121, 122,
        124, 130, 140, 147, 156, 173,
        268, 303, 313, 328, 341, 356,
        378, 397, 403, 414, 415, 429,
        483, 485, 486, 491, 495, 498,
        501, 509, 519, 523, 526, 527,
        532, 533, 534, 544
Public involvement   43, 53, 170,
        485, 486, 487, 527, 529, 530
Public opinion survey   113, 145,
        170
Pybus, Margo J.   419, 422, 432,
        435, 436, 439

Q

Quotas   202, 304

R

Rabies   13, 39, 40, 48, 88, 135,
        186, 268, 303, 304, 305, 309,
        323, 327, 419, 420, 428, 429,
        431, 432, 433, 434, 435, 436,
        437, 438, 439, 473, 497, 498
Radio-tracking
    techniques   22
Radiotelemetry   22, 29, 44, 51, 52,
        115, 116, 129, 133, 148, 248,
        254, 428, 437, 462, 467, 469,
        470, 473, 478, 480, 512
Range expansion   22, 264, 372
Rangifer tarandus   15, 27, 30, 35,
        45, 87, 136, 180, 187, 206,
        223, 231, 245, 261, 294, 310,
        329, 363, 422, 466, 470, 484,
        497, 508
Ream, Robert R.   28, 59, 107, 115,
        116, 117, 118, 119, 123, 124,
        125, 135, 139, 293, 295, 328,
        366, 372, 545
Recolonization   11, 61, 121, 124,
        128, 135, 147, 169, 186, 354,
        373, 423, 544

Recovery   3, 23, 27, 29, 31, 32, 41,
        43, 53, 59, 60, 61, 62, 77, 105,
        107, 109, 110, 111, 112, 113,
        114, 115, 116, 117, 118, 119,
        120, 121, 122, 123, 124, 125,
        127, 128, 129, 133, 134, 140,
        141, 143, 144, 145, 146, 154,
        156, 157, 167, 168, 169, 170,
        171, 172, 173, 174, 175, 199,
        202, 203, 204, 205, 207, 208,
        211, 212, 217, 221, 276, 280,
        289, 353, 354, 409, 412, 415,
        422, 497, 500, 506, 526, 537,
        543, 544, 545
Recovery plan   59, 60, 62, 77, 109,
        111, 122, 158, 169, 170, 171,
        175, 202, 271, 354, 409
Reed, Daniel J.   230, 333, 461, 469,
        513
Regression analysis   200, 229
Reid, Roger   431, 436, 515
Reintroduction   3, 10, 11, 14, 60,
        61, 62, 85, 107, 109, 111, 112,
        113, 114, 120, 121, 122, 123,
        124, 141, 142, 143, 145, 146,
        157, 158, 159, 160, 162, 164,
        165, 166, 167, 168, 172, 174,
        205, 341, 353, 354, 367, 370,
        373, 397, 405, 409, 410, 412,
        419, 423, 429, 438, 439, 447,
        523, 527, 544
Relatedness   135, 140, 145, 273,
        293, 294, 301, 355, 368, 369,
        370, 399, 400, 405, 406, 542
Relocation   136, 429, 461, 462,
        463, 464, 465, 467, 470, 491,
        501, 502, 503, 523
Rendezvous sites   50, 87, 114, 332,
        336, 338, 340, 420
Repellent   491, 501, 502
Reproduction   47, 55, 57, 107, 118,
        119, 165, 197, 229, 279, 283,
        315, 318, 325, 326, 353, 368,
        372, 419, 423, 428, 495, 503,
        537, 540, 541
Reproductive rate   179, 283, 285,
        509
Richardson, Katherine   43, 356,
        388, 396
Riding Mountain   22, 28, 29, 90,
        91, 186, 214, 215, 221, 228,
        316, 318, 319, 321, 363, 420,
        424, 445

Rocky Mountains   21, 22, 29, 77,
        107, 108, 109, 110, 135, 140,
        196, 353, 354, 361, 363
Ruggles, Anne K.   481, 513
Rumen   241, 270, 275, 297, 329,
        368, 372, 461, 473, 543
Ryon, Jenny   338, 341, 342

S

Saskatchewan   22, 23, 25, 26, 27,
        30, 33, 152, 262, 266, 267,
        271, 358, 362, 384, 386, 396,
        425, 495, 497, 503
Satellite tracking   542
Scavenging   56, 95, 100, 220, 230,
        318, 423, 428, 497
Scent-marking   289, 445
Schullery, Paul   63, 65, 123
Schultz, Ronald N.   147, 156, 526
Seal   37, 39, 40, 148, 168, 275,
        277, 278, 283, 290, 297, 368,
        369, 413, 447, 449, 450, 503,
        541
Seip, Dale R.   11, 28, 124, 179,
        180, 185, 186, 191, 197, 209,
        240, 260, 262, 264, 265, 268,
        273, 280, 538
Sexual dimorphism   363
Sheep   7, 9, 28, 45, 48, 63, 64, 66,
        70, 71, 74, 77, 78, 84, 87, 94,
        96, 98, 99, 100, 101, 118, 127,
        128, 129, 130, 132, 136, 138,
        184, 185, 201, 207, 211, 223,
        224, 225, 226, 227, 228, 229,
        231, 232, 233, 234, 235, 236,
        237, 238, 239, 240, 241, 242,
        246, 247, 257, 265, 294, 335,
        409, 437, 497, 501, 523, 524,
        525, 526, 538
Smell   288, 289, 426
Smith, Christian A.   43
Smith, Roland   157, 409
Snares   15, 23, 143, 267, 278, 444,
        491, 493, 510
Snow   16, 22, 38, 39, 42, 73, 85,
        92, 93, 94, 95, 97, 98, 99, 100,
        101, 103, 148, 165, 174, 206,
        223, 224, 225, 226, 227, 228,
        229, 230, 231, 232, 237, 239,
        241, 242, 243, 245, 246, 247,
        248, 249, 250, 252, 253, 256,
        257, 258, 259, 260, 263, 264,
        265, 266, 267, 268, 270, 272,

275, 278, 288, 297, 304, 310, 312, 315, 317, 318, 469, 470, 473, 475, 476, 478, 479, 480, 493, 498, 499, 510, 511, 512, 537, 538

Social organization 286, 428

South Dakota 62, 315, 322, 384, 385

Steel traps 15, 493, 494

Stephenson, Robert O. 43, 44, 46, 47, 49, 57, 124, 223, 224, 228, 229, 230, 241, 245, 260, 328, 370, 371, 420, 421, 437, 441, 459, 469, 470, 481, 499, 500, 501, 502, 508, 512, 534, 537

Subsistence hunting 53, 74

Succession 48, 73, 92, 161, 162, 262, 271, 399

Survival 25, 31, 47, 49, 60, 85, 92, 94, 95, 101, 102, 103, 111, 113, 114, 118, 122, 128, 132, 133, 138, 140, 143, 144, 148, 150, 151, 154, 155, 157, 162, 166, 211, 213, 220, 230, 239, 245, 247, 248, 258, 261, 263, 264, 265, 267, 268, 270, 271, 279, 283, 285, 299, 305, 307, 309, 310, 316, 321, 325, 326, 327, 364, 413, 427, 428, 441, 445, 447, 502, 503, 506, 511, 518, 527, 544
    competition 5, 13, 103, 179, 187, 209, 285, 315, 316, 318, 321, 322, 323, 325, 326, 327, 338, 342, 369, 534

Switching 30, 189, 195, 196, 199, 205, 223, 228, 231

T

Teeth 15, 130, 225, 232, 290, 362, 367, 377, 384, 386, 387, 455, 456, 457, 458, 459, 494, 526

Telemetry 22, 29, 44, 45, 48, 51, 52, 115, 116, 117, 129, 133, 148, 150, 224, 247, 248, 254, 304, 305, 308, 329, 370, 428, 437, 461, 462, 464, 466, 467, 469, 470, 473, 478, 480, 512, 537, 539, 544

Territorial behavior 8

Territoriality 148, 180, 200, 301, 310, 537

Texas 59, 62, 76, 84, 141, 143, 144, 146, 157, 316, 357, 358, 375, 381, 385, 388, 389, 394, 396, 401, 410, 411, 412, 421, 502

Theberge, John B. 14, 16, 17, 21, 27, 28, 29, 30, 31, 213, 223, 228, 229, 265, 269, 288, 303, 304, 307, 310, 312, 313, 318, 368, 419, 420, 438, 439, 495, 496, 497, 538, 539, 544

Thiel, Richard P. 59, 147, 148, 169, 243, 328, 421, 538, 540

Thomas, Donald C. 156, 209, 231, 247, 261, 263, 266, 280, 293, 421, 425, 459, 493

Toxicants 15, 16, 27, 496

Translocation 109, 118, 122, 130, 132, 133, 134, 160, 175, 544

Transmitter 48, 51, 159, 165, 166, 247, 305, 329, 333, 461, 462, 463, 464, 467

Trapping 15, 21, 22, 23, 24, 25, 26, 27, 30, 31, 43, 45, 48, 51, 52, 53, 55, 74, 95, 101, 102, 107, 110, 131, 143, 148, 150, 159, 161, 162, 167, 172, 186, 224, 268, 270, 271, 278, 294, 295, 304, 305, 309, 353, 367, 443, 482, 483, 484, 485, 493, 494, 496, 498, 500, 501, 505, 510, 517, 519, 521, 523, 532, 533, 543
    in predator control 14, 15, 16, 32, 49, 51, 77, 78, 95, 103, 107, 183, 268, 321, 353, 403, 483, 492, 496, 498, 499, 501, 503, 505, 513, 531

Treaty Indians 93

Tundra 23, 35, 38, 40, 47, 208, 224, 245, 246, 249, 261, 262, 263, 264, 265, 266, 268, 288, 310, 317, 332, 357, 358, 361, 362, 363, 364, 366, 379, 381, 382, 384, 387, 396, 473

U

Urios, Vincente 335

Ursus spp. 30, 35, 46, 74, 80, 85, 97, 114, 184, 224, 246, 262, 275, 276, 287, 329, 463, 493, 503, 505, 524

V

Vaccination 429, 431, 432, 438

Valen, Terry 169

Values 25, 50, 54, 107, 124, 132, 162, 183, 201, 208, 213, 216, 217, 218, 219, 241, 253, 301, 310, 312, 337, 344, 360, 361, 379, 382, 383, 385, 386, 387, 389, 391, 392, 393, 394, 405, 407, 443, 444, 447, 448, 449, 450, 451, 455, 463, 481, 482, 483, 484, 487, 515, 516, 519, 520, 521, 528, 531

Vectors 424, 431, 435

Viable population 60, 96, 102, 103, 124, 135, 172, 173, 353, 409, 519

Vulpes spp. 40, 74, 288, 315, 420, 423, 432, 503

W

Wayne, Robert K. 145, 399

White, Cliff C. 135

Whittlesey, Lee 63, 65, 123

Wildlife conservation 102, 103

Wildlife management 31, 53, 78, 112, 124, 146, 170

Wolf
    activity patterns 332, 335, 336, 337, 338, 340, 462, 467, 537, 541, 542
    age determination 148, 231, 232, 278, 304, 455, 458
    behavior 5, 6, 15, 17, 21, 22, 23, 24, 27, 29, 30, 31, 32, 37, 42, 43, 45, 47, 48, 49, 50, 51, 52, 53, 62, 63, 64, 65, 67, 68, 71, 74, 75, 78, 83, 84, 85, 86, 87, 88, 89, 90, 91, 92, 93, 94, 95, 96, 98, 100, 101, 102, 109, 110, 117, 119, 120, 121, 132, 139, 142, 154, 159, 165, 166, 167, 170, 172, 173, 174, 179, 184, 185, 186, 188, 192, 199, 202, 208, 211, 213, 215, 217, 219, 220, 221, 225, 227, 228, 229, 232, 241, 258, 262, 263, 264, 265, 267, 268, 269, 270, 271, 272, 273, 275, 287, 288, 289, 290, 297, 300, 304, 305, 309, 310, 312, 318, 325, 326, 327, 328, 333, 335, 338, 340, 341, 342, 343, 344, 345, 346,

348, 349, 350, 354, 367, 413, 421, 425, 445, 479, 481, 482, 483, 484, 485, 491, 496, 497, 499, 500, 501, 503, 505, 506, 507, 508, 510, 511, 515, 516, 517, 518, 519, 520, 521, 523, 524, 526, 527, 532, 533, 534, 539, 544

bounty   5, 51, 110, 147, 494, 495, 496, 500, 527

breeding season   162, 283, 285, 335, 336, 540, 541, 544

canine distemper   39, 40, 42, 47, 93, 419, 428, 429, 441, 444, 445

captive breeding   61, 143, 144, 157, 168, 368, 373, 412, 543

dens   50, 90, 101, 114, 142, 257, 263, 300, 316, 350

density   4, 21, 22, 23, 29, 30, 31, 32, 37, 39, 41, 44, 45, 47, 48, 49, 55, 57, 64, 70, 91, 95, 101, 102, 128, 135, 138, 139, 140, 147, 151, 152, 155, 179, 180, 181, 182, 183, 184, 185, 186, 187, 188, 189, 190, 191, 192, 193, 194, 195, 196, 197, 199, 200, 201, 202, 204, 205, 206, 207, 208, 209, 211, 213, 215, 217, 220, 221, 223, 224, 225, 226, 227, 229, 230, 245, 247, 248, 250, 252, 253, 255, 257, 258, 260, 263, 264, 265, 267, 268, 269, 275, 276, 278, 279, 280, 295, 301, 303, 304, 305, 307, 308, 311, 312, 313, 321, 326, 338, 368, 425, 428, 441, 445, 469, 470, 473, 476, 479, 480, 505, 506, 507, 509, 520, 539, 544

depredation   11, 23, 27, 29, 62, 102, 109, 118, 119, 120, 121, 122, 123, 124, 127, 128, 130, 131, 132, 133, 134, 139, 146, 159, 165, 168, 172, 173, 174, 175, 325, 327, 372, 491, 493, 494, 495, 497, 498, 500, 501, 502, 503, 523, 544

dispersal   135, 140, 276, 538

distribution   4, 148, 152, 153, 154, 245, 255, 257, 273, 319, 320, 321, 354

ecology   6, 21, 29, 30, 43, 44, 45, 47, 48, 95, 117, 145, 169, 192, 223, 261, 262, 267, 270, 316,

325, 326, 336, 349, 412, 485, 537

economic importance   16, 25, 294

estrous   143, 283, 285

extirpation   14, 21, 31, 127, 143, 325, 367, 372, 496

fecundity   7, 94, 211, 213, 220, 261, 263, 264, 270

flukes in   266

food consumption   450

food habits   30, 48, 49, 50, 95, 100, 322, 428

habitat   3, 14, 17, 21, 22, 32, 45, 47, 48, 49, 53, 55, 56, 60, 62, 64, 67, 68, 75, 77, 85, 86, 87, 90, 91, 94, 95, 96, 97, 98, 99, 100, 101, 102, 111, 113, 114, 117, 119, 128, 129, 138, 140, 141, 143, 145, 147, 152, 156, 157, 161, 165, 167, 168, 169, 170, 172, 173, 174, 175, 184, 185, 220, 221, 224, 245, 247, 250, 256, 257, 262, 263, 264, 265, 266, 267, 268, 269, 270, 271, 272, 273, 275, 280, 287, 299, 313, 318, 321, 322, 326, 327, 355, 363, 370, 373, 387, 388, 399, 400, 402, 403, 405, 406, 429, 436, 438, 445, 461, 466, 469, 479, 480, 482, 491, 501, 505, 507, 508, 509, 513, 519, 530, 531, 544

harvest   21, 25, 31, 200, 208, 320, 491

harvest strategies   214

home range   132, 136, 137, 138, 139, 148, 149, 157, 161, 162, 221, 228, 251, 325, 332, 412, 428, 435, 467, 473, 479, 517, 518

hybridization   32, 143, 263, 363, 370, 375, 381, 388, 389, 391, 397, 399, 400, 401, 402, 403, 405, 407, 410, 411, 412, 413, 414, 543

infectious canine hepatitis   47, 419, 421, 428, 429

interbreeding   102, 354, 356, 363, 369, 375, 388, 403, 409, 413, 414, 543

legal classification   61, 62

lethal capture methods   15, 16, 51, 69, 70, 74, 88, 101, 102, 107, 143, 268, 321, 353, 491, 493, 497, 498, 532, 543

life history   29, 49, 50, 218, 335

litter size   48, 142, 279, 326, 327

live capture methods   160, 462, 493

management plan   30, 53, 59, 62, 121, 122, 128, 271, 273, 341, 349, 419, 481, 482, 483, 485, 486, 487, 496, 532

mange in   427, 428

maturation   540

Mexican   59, 60, 61, 62, 141, 142, 143, 145, 146, 158, 357, 358, 370, 377, 396, 403, 406, 447, 449, 450, 498, 542

mortality   11, 14, 21, 29, 37, 43, 45, 46, 47, 48, 49, 50, 92, 93, 94, 114, 117, 119, 128, 130, 134, 140, 143, 147, 148, 150, 151, 154, 161, 174, 179, 184, 186, 187, 199, 202, 205, 208, 219, 225, 230, 239, 245, 247, 248, 250, 251, 252, 256, 258, 259, 260, 263, 265, 266, 267, 268, 269, 270, 271, 272, 273, 297, 301, 303, 305, 307, 309, 310, 311, 312, 313, 318, 325, 327, 329, 405, 412, 419, 420, 421, 423, 425, 428, 431, 441, 445, 467, 493, 503, 506, 538

movement   13, 30, 31, 43, 44, 48, 69, 73, 101, 117, 124, 128, 132, 136, 138, 139, 140, 148, 152, 157, 161, 166, 202, 224, 245, 264, 265, 267, 268, 271, 303, 305, 307, 308, 309, 310, 312, 318, 329, 330, 332, 333, 335, 336, 337, 338, 340, 342, 356, 366, 369, 370, 384, 396, 399, 403, 412, 428, 435, 436, 461, 464, 466, 467, 473, 478, 508, 509, 537, 544, 545

nematodes   424

overexploitation   15

pack size   56, 88, 142, 147, 151, 155, 207, 219, 225, 226, 227, 228, 229, 230, 248, 254, 256, 269, 295, 303, 305, 307, 309, 312, 325, 326, 327, 470, 473, 475, 478

pelage   86, 142, 224, 359, 361, 367, 378, 444

pelt   23, 25

population   21, 29, 43, 45, 49, 91, 147, 193, 201, 213, 230, 245,

248, 265, 271, 273, 323, 326, 328, 419, 425, 426, 428, 480

prey switching 30, 189, 195, 196, 199, 205, 223, 228

public information 22, 107, 113, 114, 117, 118, 170, 349, 487, 528

public involvement 43, 53, 170, 485, 486, 487, 527, 529, 530

rabies in 13, 39, 40, 88, 135, 186, 268, 303, 304, 305, 309, 323, 327, 419, 420, 428, 429, 431, 432, 435, 436, 437, 438, 439, 473, 497, 498

radio-tracking 148, 295, 304, 338, 473, 537, 538, 541, 544, 545

reintroduction 3, 10, 11, 14, 60, 61, 85, 107, 109, 111, 112, 113, 114, 120, 121, 122, 123, 124, 141, 142, 143, 145, 146, 157, 158, 159, 160, 162, 164, 165, 166, 167, 168, 172, 174, 205, 341, 353, 354, 367, 370, 373, 405, 409, 410, 412, 419, 423, 429, 438, 439, 447, 523, 527, 544

senses 69, 287

serum chemistry values 447

sex ratios 215, 247

simulation 180, 183, 191, 199, 200, 201, 202, 207, 209, 213, 369, 479

size 355, 356, 362, 367, 389, 543

skinning 438

strychnine 5, 15, 16, 26, 27, 69, 70, 143, 496, 497, 498

subspecies 35, 39, 41, 47, 61, 102, 107, 110, 120, 139, 141, 143, 145, 261, 262, 310, 353, 354, 355, 356, 357, 358, 359, 360, 361, 362, 363, 364, 365, 366, 367, 368, 369, 370, 371, 372, 373, 375, 376, 378, 381, 382, 383, 384, 385, 386, 387, 388, 389, 390, 391, 392, 393, 394, 395, 396, 397, 403, 405, 409, 413, 414, 415, 447, 542, 543

surplus killing 264, 268

survival 25, 31, 47, 49, 60, 85, 92, 94, 95, 102, 103, 111, 113, 114, 118, 122, 128, 132, 133, 138, 140, 143, 148, 150, 151, 154, 155, 166, 211, 213, 220, 230, 239, 245, 247, 248, 258, 261, 263, 264, 265, 267, 268, 270, 279, 283, 285, 299, 305, 307, 309, 321, 325, 326, 327, 364, 413, 427, 428, 441, 445, 502, 503, 506, 511, 518, 527, 544

tapeworms 424

taxonomy 42, 141, 353, 354, 355, 356, 357, 358, 360, 364, 365, 366, 367, 372, 537, 543

territories 30, 31, 32, 47, 48, 83, 89, 139, 140, 148, 149, 151, 152, 207, 221, 223, 224, 225, 230, 248, 251, 253, 254, 257, 264, 265, 293, 294, 295, 297,

298, 299, 303, 304, 305, 307, 308, 309, 310, 315, 316, 318, 412, 441, 466, 467, 470, 479, 495, 503, 504, 523, 539, 544, 545

thallium 496, 499

trapping 15, 21, 22, 23, 24, 25, 26, 27, 31, 43, 45, 48, 51, 52, 53, 55, 74, 95, 107, 110, 131, 143, 150, 159, 167, 172, 186, 224, 270, 271, 278, 294, 295, 304, 305, 309, 353, 367, 443, 482, 483, 484, 485, 493, 494, 496, 501, 505, 510, 517, 519, 523, 532, 533, 543

Wolf Management Committee 109, 111, 121

Wood Buffalo 28, 29, 30, 32, 310, 319, 363, 386, 422, 424, 497

Wydeven, Adrian P. 59, 114, 124, 147, 169, 328, 371, 543

Wyoming 14, 59, 62, 67, 75, 77, 78, 84, 107, 109, 110, 111, 112, 113, 114, 115, 116, 117, 118, 121, 124, 170, 186, 200, 208, 213, 319, 341, 353, 354, 364, 372, 436, 437, 438, 439

Y

Yellowstone National Park 14, 55, 63, 64, 65, 67, 70, 72, 74, 75, 76, 77, 82, 85, 87, 107, 108, 109, 120, 121, 123, 199, 200, 203, 205, 213, 341, 372, 397, 431, 436, 438, 496